What's What

What's What

A Visual Glossary of the Physical World

Reginald Bragonier Jr.

and

David Fisher

HAMMOND®

INCORPORATED

MAPLEWOOD, NEW JERSEY

Printed in the United States of America

Library of Congress Cataloging in Publication Data

Bragonier, Reginald.
  What's what, a visual glossary of the physical world.

  Includes index.
  Summary: Pictures of common objects and the parts of which they are composed, classed under general categories such as living things, transportation, and personal items, are identified by name.
    1. Picture dictionaries, English. [1. Picture dictionaries. 2. Vocabulary. 3. English language—Terms and phrases] I. Fisher, David, 1946-   . II. Title.
AG250.B7   031'.02   81-7149
ISBN 0-8437-3329-2   AACR2

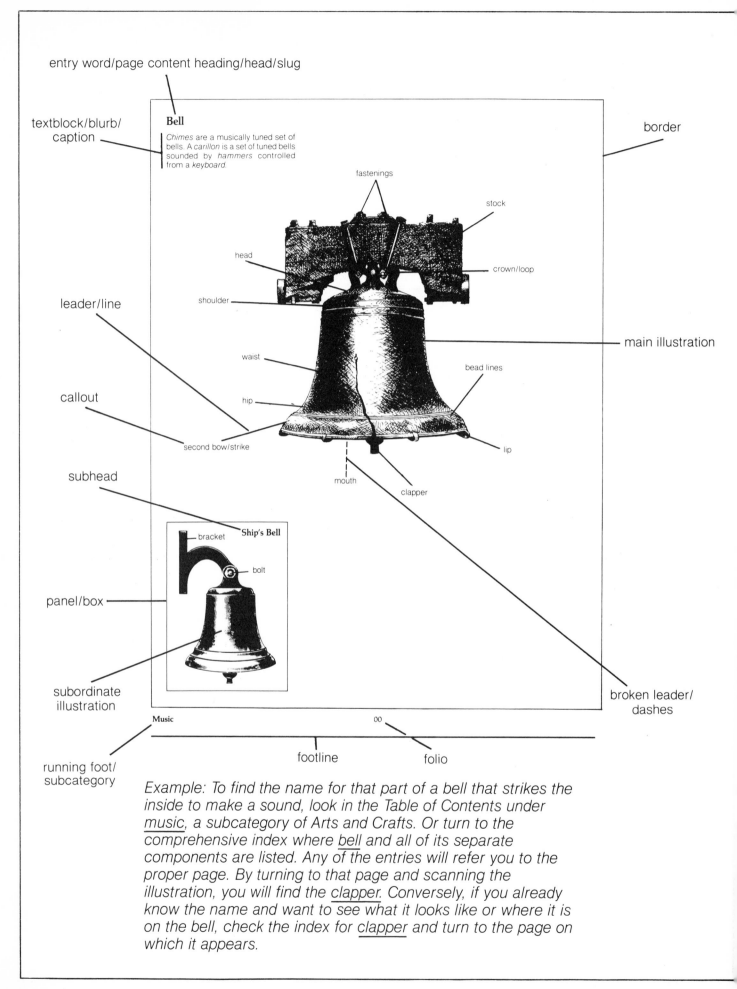

entry word/page content heading/head/slug

textblock/blurb/caption

border

Bell

Chimes are a musically tuned set of bells. A *carillon* is a set of tuned bells sounded by *hammers* controlled from a *keyboard*.

fastenings

stock

head

crown/loop

shoulder

leader/line

main illustration

waist

bead lines

callout

hip

second bow/strike

lip

subhead

mouth

clapper

panel/box

Ship's Bell

bracket

bolt

subordinate illustration

broken leader/dashes

running foot/subcategory

Music

00

footline

folio

Example: To find the name for that part of a bell that strikes the inside to make a sound, look in the Table of Contents under music, *a subcategory of Arts and Crafts. Or turn to the comprehensive index where* bell *and all of its separate components are listed. Any of the entries will refer you to the proper page. By turning to that page and scanning the illustration, you will find the* clapper. *Conversely, if you already know the name and want to* see *what it looks like or where it is on the bell, check the index for* clapper *and turn to the page on which it appears.*

What It Is

Until now, it has been all but impossible to find words you've forgotten or never knew to begin with. The reason for this is obvious: to use a dictionary you need to know the word in order to find it. WHAT'S WHAT provides access to words in an entirely new way—*visually.* Readers can now find words they are seeking by turning to detailed illustrations in which all the visible parts are identified and labeled. This system of visual classification puts within verbal reach of everyone, for the first time, the words used to describe the myriad objects in our everyday world.

The objects chosen for inclusion in WHAT'S WHAT have been selected on the basis of their usefulness to contemporary readers; and although no single volume of this kind can be encyclopedic in its coverage, WHAT'S WHAT is both comprehensive in its scope and practical in its treatment of individual items. Thus, illustrations generally include only the visible parts of objects. However, when it is necessary or desirable to identify part of an item not actually shown, its location is indicated by a broken line. Variations and styles of objects have been presented only when the object's parts make it so distinctive that the item itself has a unique name—lorgnette, for example, which appears on the eyeglasses page. In addition, considerable use has been made of composite illustrations—nonliteral representations combining diverse elements found among similar objects.

How It Works

The book's system of classification is simple and straightforward. Since every object in the physical world is part of a larger whole, the reader can find any detail by locating the larger item. All objects fall naturally into one of the following twelve categories: *The Earth; Living Things; Shelters and Structures; Transportation; Communications; Personal Items; The Home; Sports and Recreation; Arts and Crafts; Machinery, Tools and Weapons; Uniforms, Costumes and Ceremonial Attire;* and *Signs and Symbols.*

To locate an item, turn first to the Table of Contents, where each entry is arranged by category and subcategory according to the object's nature and use. There you will readily determine in what part of the book the item is located. An automobile, for example, is listed under Transportation. An object, or the name of a part, can also be found by consulting the all-inclusive index at the back of the book. A collar stay, for example, can be located by looking under "shirt," "collar," or any other part of a shirt known to the reader, since all these entries will refer to the page on which a shirt is illustrated and all its parts are identified. Rigorous cross-referencing makes the task of finding any item or detail in the book even simpler.

And Why

WHAT'S WHAT is far more than an ordinary reference book. Aided by well-known artists and experts in the visual-arts fields, the editors have made every effort to produce a book that is as engaging as it is informative. Its use, it is hoped, will entertain as well as enlighten.

TABLE OF CONTENTS

THE EARTH – 1

The Planetary System (2–3): the universe
The Earth (4–6): inner world, cartographer's world, wind and ocean currents
Terrains (7–12): land features, mountains, volcano, cave, glacier
Water Systems (13–15): river, wave, shoreline and continental margin
Weather (16–19): clouds, storm systems, weather monitoring equipment, weather map
Maps (20–22): geographic, political, thematic, nautical chart, topographic map

LIVING THINGS – 23

Man (24–29): the human body, literary anatomy, skeletal and muscular systems, internal organs, sense organs, the extremities
Edible Animals (30–33): cow, lamb, pig, poultry
Domestic Animals (34–36): dog, cat, horse
Wild Animals (37–47): bird, spider, insects, reptiles, amphibians, fish, marine life, shellfish, ultimate beast
Plants (48–56): tree, root system, leaf, flower, vegetables, fruit, succulents, special plants, grass

SHELTERS AND STRUCTURES – 57

House (58–67): foundation, frame, exterior, door, window, staircase, fence, building materials, brick wall
Architectural Designs from Other Lands (68–71): international architecture, arch, column
Special Purpose Buildings (72–94): Capitol, White House, prison, skyscraper, elevator, escalator, castle, fortifications, teepee, domed structures, church, temple, courtroom, circus, amusement park, airport, railroad yard
Other Structures (95–100): bridge, tunnel, canal lock, dam, offshore oil rig, barn and silo

TRANSPORTATION– 101

Automobile (102–110): exterior, cutaway, interior, engine, gasoline pump, traffic control devices, highway
Public Transportation (111–115): railroad crossing, railroad, bus, subway
Carriers (116–117): truck, trailer
Emergency Vehicles (118–121): police car, ambulance, fire engine
Public Service Vehicles (122–123): tow truck, street cleaner, garbage truck
Cycles (124–125): bicycle, motorcycle
Recreational Vehicles (126): camper, snowmobile
Carriages (127): stagecoach, hansom cab
Boats and Ships (128–145): nautical terminology, rowboat, sailboat, sail, outboard engine, powerboat, tanker, passenger ship, surface fighting ship, aircraft carrier, submarine, tugboat and fireboat, hovercraft and hydrofoil
Aircraft (146–153): helicopter, private aircraft, glider, civil aircraft, cockpit, combat fighter, pilot's instrument panel, blimp
Spacecraft (154–158): space shuttle, launch pad, flight deck, lunar lander, lunar buggy, flight suit

COMMUNICATIONS – 159

Print Communications (160–169): pen and pencil, correspondence, typewriter, typography, printing, book, newspaper, magazine cover, contents page and feature
Visual Communications (170–174): still cameras and film, movie camera, projectors, accessories
Aural Communications (175–179): tape recorder, phonographic equipment, telephone, transceiver
Audiovisual Communications (180–182): video recorder, television, satellite

TABLE OF CONTENTS *(Continued)*

PERSONAL ITEMS – 183

Men's Apparel (184–190): jacket and vest, shirt, belt and suspenders, pants, neckwear, underwear

Women's Apparel (191–194): foundation garments, jacket and pants, blouse and skirt, dress

Unisex Clothing (195–197): sweater, outerwear

Headwear (198–199): men's hats, women's hats

Footwear (200–203): man's shoe, woman's shoe, boot and sandal, shoe accessories

Fasteners (204–205): pin, zipper, buttons

Hairstyles and Facial Hair (206–210): shavers, men's hair, hair grooming implements, women's hairstyles, hairstyling implements

Cosmetics (211–213): toothbrush, makeup, beauty products

Jewelry (214–215): gemstone, ring, pendant

Timepieces (216): wristwatch, pocket watch

Eyeglasses (217): lens shapes, lorgnette and monocle

Bags (218): handbag

Wallet and Currency (219–223): paper money, coin, check, credit card, traveler's check, money order

Smoking Materials (224–225): cigar, cigarette, pipe

Umbrella (226)

THE HOME – 227

Living Room (228–237): fireplace, clock, chair, lounger, sofa, candelabrum, lamps and lighting, window coverings

Dining Room (238–242): table, sidepieces, place setting, dessert setting, carpet

Kitchen (243–265): sink and compactor, stove, refrigerator, dishwasher, openers, coffee makers, toaster, blenders, juicers, knives, pots and pans, mixing and measuring tools, preparation utensils, strainers and drainers, grinders and graters, food ingredients, prepared foods, desserts, snack food, containers, labeling and packaging

Bedroom (266–268): bed and bedding, dressers

Bathroom (269–271): faucet and sink, bathtub and shower, toilet

Playroom/Utility Room (272–281): desk, desktop equipment, sewing machine, iron, washer and dryer, broom and mop, vacuum cleaner, fire extinguisher, luggage

Yard (282–284): children's gear and playground equipment, barbecue and hammock

SPORTS AND RECREATION – 285

Team Sports (286–293): baseball, football, ice hockey, basketball, soccer and lacrosse

Competitive Sports (294–313): track and field, running shoe, field events equipment, hurdle, pole vault, gymnastics, trampoline, boxing, golf, tennis, handball and squash, jai alai, fencing, swimming and diving, bowling, shuffleboard and croquet, volleyball and badminton

Table Games (314–315): pool and billiards, ping-pong

Individual Sports (316–328): darts, kites, roller skating and skateboarding, ice skates, skiing, sledding and tobogganing, water skiing, wind-surfing and surfing, scuba diving, hot air ballooning, parachuting and hang-gliding, mountain climbing

Equestrian Sports (329–331): riding equipment, flat and harness racing

Automobile Racing (332–333): Grand Prix, drag racing

Outdoor Sports (334–337): fishing, camping and backpacking

Bodybuilding (338)

Board Games (339): chess and checkers, backgammon and mahjong

Casino Games (340–342): slot machine, roulette wheel, craps table, dice, cards

ARTS AND CRAFTS – 343

Performing Arts (344–345): stage, theater

Music (346–361): bell (see page iv), sheet music, orchestra, violin, woodwinds, brasses, organ, piano, guitar, electric guitar, drums, bagpipe, accordion and folk instruments, musical accessories

Fine Arts (362–373): elements of composition, painting equipment, sculpting tools, potting, woodcut printing, silk screen and scrimshaw, lithography, intaglio and etching, stained glass, framing

Cartooning (374–375)

Crafts (376–380): sewing, decorative stitching, knitting, weaving, sewing pattern

TABLE OF CONTENTS *(Continued)*

MACHINERY, TOOLS AND WEAPONS – 381

Power Systems (382–389): wind systems, solar power system, nuclear power reactor, power line, vacuum tube and transistor, battery, receptacle and plug, meter and fuse box

Climate Control Units (390–394): furnace, hot water heater, air conditioner, heat exchanger, wood-burning stove

Engines (395–397): steam engine, internal combustion engine, jet engines

Household Tools (398–416): workbench, vise, nails and screws, nuts and bolts, hammer, screwdriver, pliers, wrench, handsaw, power saw, drills, planing and shaping tools, sander, plumbing tools, electrician's tools, measuring tools, painting tools, Swiss Army knife

Gardening Tools (417–421): hoe and rake, shovel and shears, sprinkler and nozzles, lawn mower, wheelbarrow and seeder, chainsaw

Rancher's Equipment (422): lariat, branding iron, barbed wire

Trapping Devices (423): mousetrap, bear trap, lobster trap

Agricultural Tools (424): tractor, hitch and harrow

Construction Equipment (425–426): bulldozer, transit and jackhammer

Computing Tools (427–431): voting booth, key punch, computer, cash register, calculators

Scientific Tools (432–433): microscope, telescope and binoculars

Sensing Devices (434–437): radar and sonar, detectors, laboratory equipment

Medical Tools (438–446): examination equipment, medical tables, treatment aids, supportive devices, dental corrective devices, dental unit, dental equipment, tooth chart

Security Devices (447–450): safe, door locks, key and padlock, hinge and hasp

Chain and Pulley (451)

Execution Devices (452): electric chair, gallows, guillotine

Weapons (453–466): cutting and thrusting weapons, medieval arms, armor, bow and arrow, cannon and catapult, shotgun and rifle, handguns, automatic rifle and machine gun, mortar and bazooka, grenade and land mine, tank, missile and torpedo

UNIFORMS, COSTUMES AND CEREMONIAL ATTIRE – 467

Royal Vestments (468–469): attire, crown, orb and scepter

Religious Attire (470–471): vestments and ritual items

Wedding Attire (472): bride and groom

Servants' Attire (473): maid and butler

Native Attire (474–475): cowboy and Indian, Arab and Chinese dress

Historical Costumes (476): general, pirate, miser and wizard

Performers' Costumes (477–479): clown, ballet dancer, drum major

Military Attire (480–481): dress and combat

Municipal Uniforms (482–484): policemen, firemen

SIGNS AND SYMBOLS – 485

Flags (486)

Heraldry (487)

Road Signs (488–489)

Public Signs (490–491)

Religious Symbols (492)

Signs of the Zodiac (493)

Symbols of Science, Business and Commerce (494–495)

Sign Alphabet and Braille (496)

Grammatical Symbols (497)

Proofreader's Marks (498)

Graffiti (499)

TOMBSTONE AND COFFIN – 500

The Earth

This section offers various ways of looking at the earth, ranging from showing the earth as a small planet in the larger space it shares with other heavenly bodies to physical features and symbolic depictions illustrating aspects and details of the earth's surface.

Nonliteral renditions, such as the illustration of the universe, condense information visually by pulling together disparate elements for labeling. Cutaway illustrations like the one of the earth's inner layers are used only when elements considered essential to show and identify are not readily visible. The cave illustration, on the other hand, is rendered in cross section in order to show parts and details which might not be apparent in a traditional illustration.

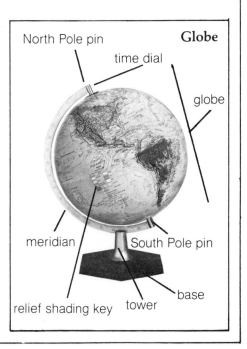

Globe

North Pole pin
time dial
globe
meridian
South Pole pin
relief shading key
tower
base

The Universe

This whimsical creation of the universe includes such bits and pieces of the entire *cosmic mass* as the *solar system, local galaxies* and *external galaxies*. Observable *planets* are illuminated by the light of our sun. *Meteors*, or *shooting stars*, are seen as streaks of light in the *sky* as they are vaporized on entering earth's atmosphere.

spiral galaxy

red supergiant star

side

elliptical galaxies

full face

common spiral ga

black hole

irregular galaxie

asteroids/planetoids

barrel spiral ga

Pluto

nebula/interstellar cloud

Neptune

stars

Ura

doppler shift

constellation

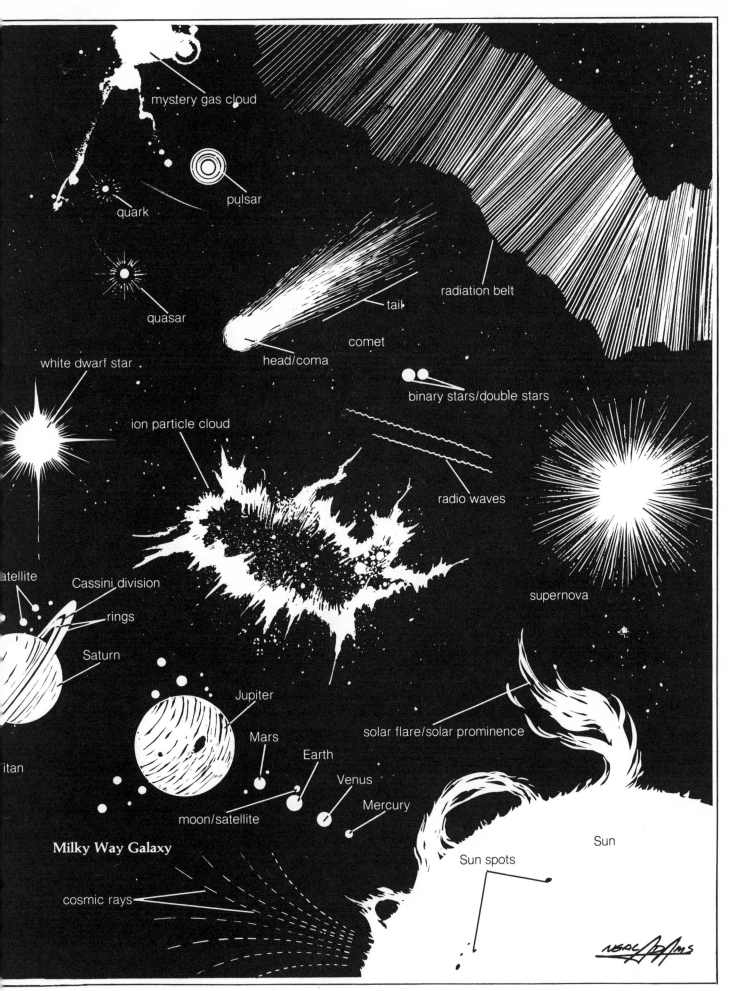

mystery gas cloud

quark

pulsar

quasar

radiation belt

tail

comet

head/coma

binary stars/double stars

white dwarf star

ion particle cloud

radio waves

supernova

satellite

Cassini division

rings

Saturn

Jupiter

Mars

Earth

solar flare/solar prominence

Venus

Mercury

moon/satellite

Titan

Milky Way Galaxy

Sun

Sun spots

cosmic rays

The Planetary System

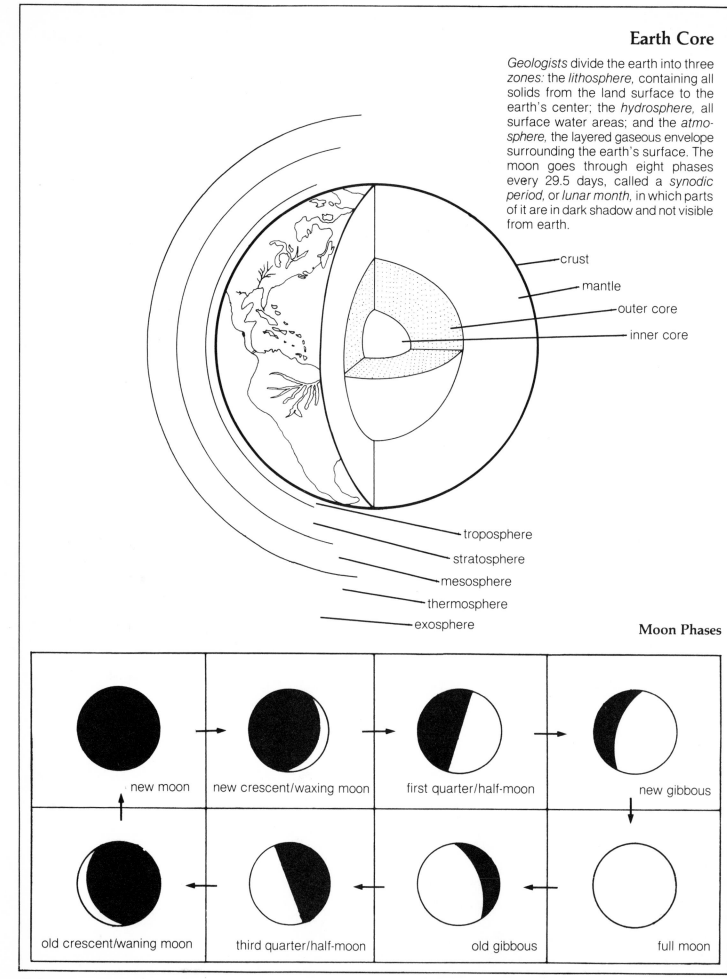

Earth Core

Geologists divide the earth into three *zones:* the *lithosphere,* containing all solids from the land surface to the earth's center; the *hydrosphere,* all surface water areas; and the *atmosphere,* the layered gaseous envelope surrounding the earth's surface. The moon goes through eight phases every 29.5 days, called a *synodic period,* or *lunar month,* in which parts of it are in dark shadow and not visible from earth.

crust

mantle

outer core

inner core

troposphere

stratosphere

mesosphere

thermosphere

exosphere

Moon Phases

new moon

new crescent/waxing moon

first quarter/half-moon

new gibbous

old crescent/waning moon

third quarter/half-moon

old gibbous

full moon

Cartographer's World

Position on the earth's *grid* can be determined by finding exact *latitude*, *north* or *south* of the equator, and *longitude*, *east* or *west* of the prime meridian. As the earth makes its daily rotation, the sun crosses every meridian once each day. When this occurs, all points on the meridian experience *noon* at the same instant. At the same time on the opposite side of the earth it is *midnight* and a new *calendar day* is beginning. There is a difference of one hour in *solar time* every 15 *degrees*. The world time zone map shows how the theoretical division of the world into 24 equal *time belts* has been modified to follow *political* or *geographical boundaries*.

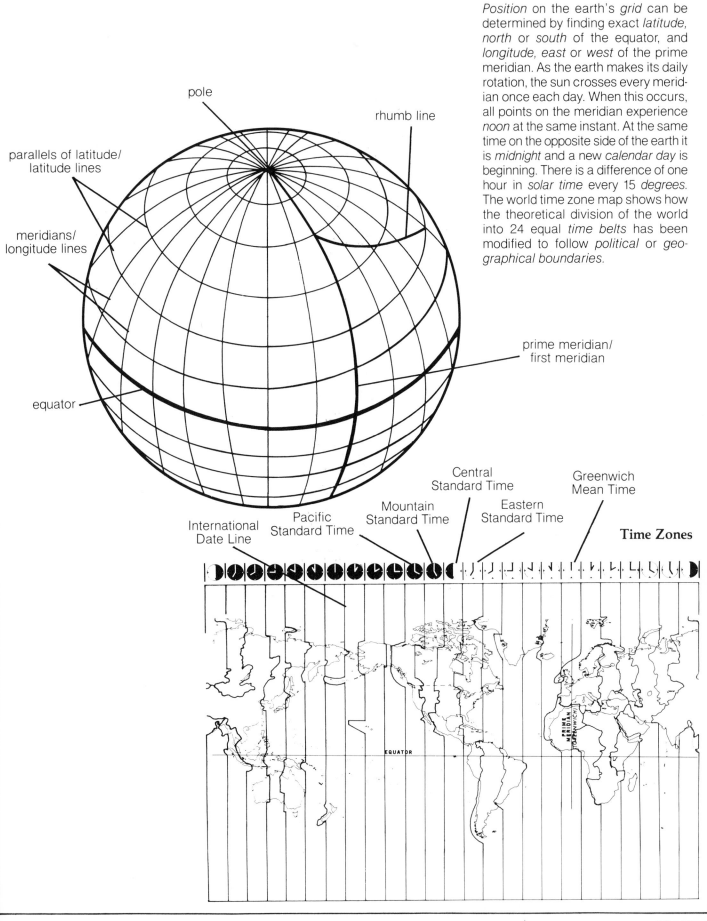

pole

rhumb line

parallels of latitude/
latitude lines

meridians/
longitude lines

equator

prime meridian/
first meridian

Time Zones

International
Date Line

Pacific
Standard Time

Mountain
Standard Time

Central
Standard Time

Eastern
Standard Time

Greenwich
Mean Time

EQUATOR

PRIME MERIDIAN (GREENWICH)

The Earth

Wind and Ocean Currents

The *zonal patterns* of wind are displaced northward and southward seasonally. Those shown here prevail in winter. *Seasonal currents* change speed and direction due to seasonal winds, whereas *permanent currents* experience relatively little change.

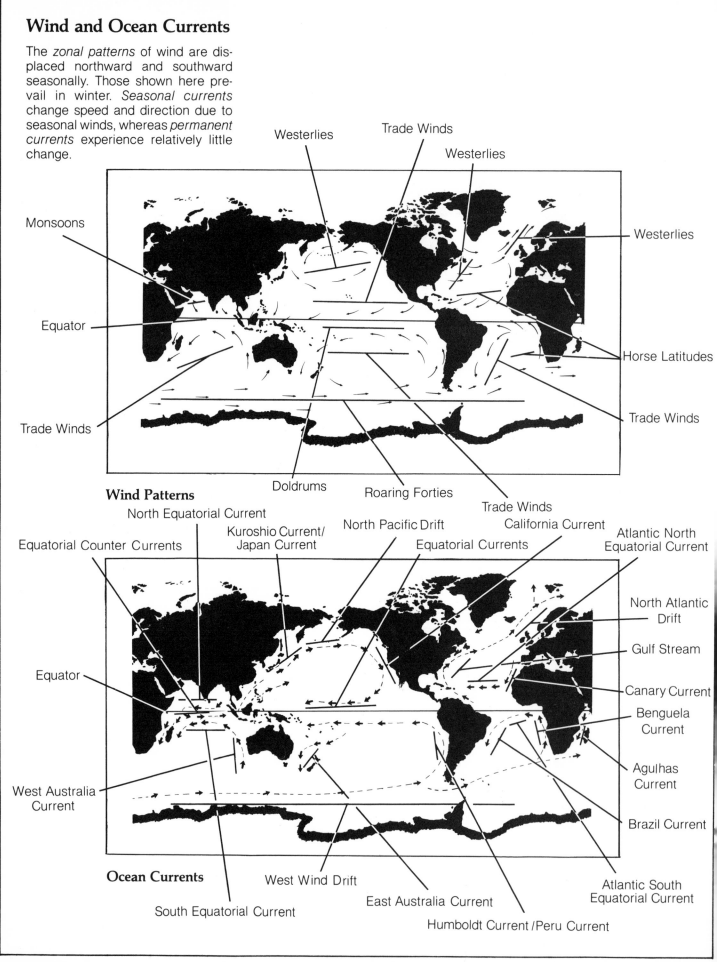

Westerlies

Trade Winds

Westerlies

Monsoons

Westerlies

Equator

Horse Latitudes

Trade Winds

Trade Winds

Wind Patterns

Doldrums

Roaring Forties

Trade Winds

North Equatorial Current

North Pacific Drift

California Current

Kuroshio Current/Japan Current

Equatorial Currents

Atlantic North Equatorial Current

Equatorial Counter Currents

North Atlantic Drift

Gulf Stream

Equator

Canary Current

Benguela Current

West Australia Current

Agulhas Current

Brazil Current

Ocean Currents

West Wind Drift

South Equatorial Current

East Australia Current

Atlantic South Equatorial Current

Humboldt Current / Peru Current

Land Features

A part of an *ocean* or *sea* extending into the land is a *gulf*. A narrow finger of land extending into the water is a *spit*. A sand or gravel bar connecting an island with the *mainland* or another island is a *tombolo*.

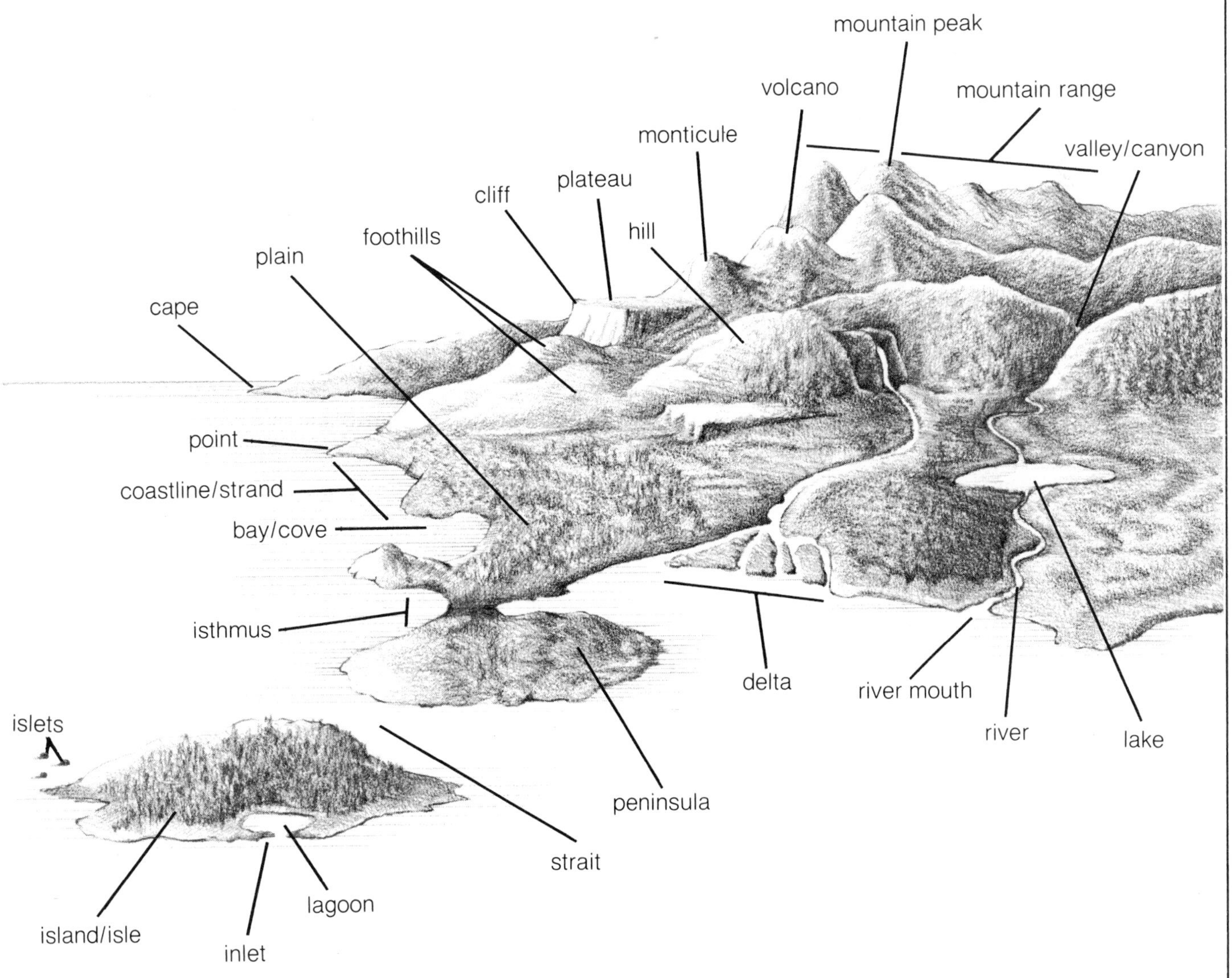

mountain peak

volcano

mountain range

monticule

valley/canyon

plateau

cliff

hill

foothills

plain

cape

point

coastline/strand

bay/cove

isthmus

delta

river mouth

river

lake

islets

peninsula

strait

island/isle

inlet

lagoon

Terrains

Mountains

A series of mountains, such as the Alpine mountains shown here, is a *range.* A circular space in mountains is a *cirque,* or *cwm.* A *kame* is a ridge or material left by a retreating *ice sheet.* An isolated hill or mountain rising abruptly from the surrounding land is a *butte.*

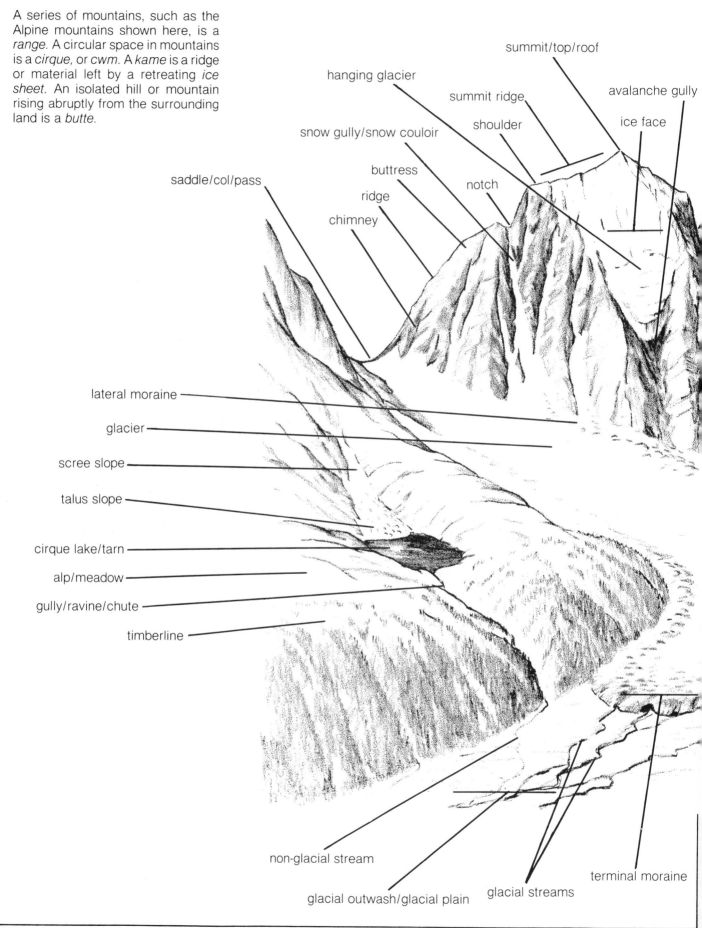

summit/top/roof

hanging glacier

summit ridge

avalanche gully

shoulder

ice face

snow gully/snow couloir

saddle/col/pass

buttress

notch

ridge

chimney

lateral moraine

glacier

scree slope

talus slope

cirque lake/tarn

alp/meadow

gully/ravine/chute

timberline

non-glacial stream

glacial outwash/glacial plain

glacial streams

terminal moraine

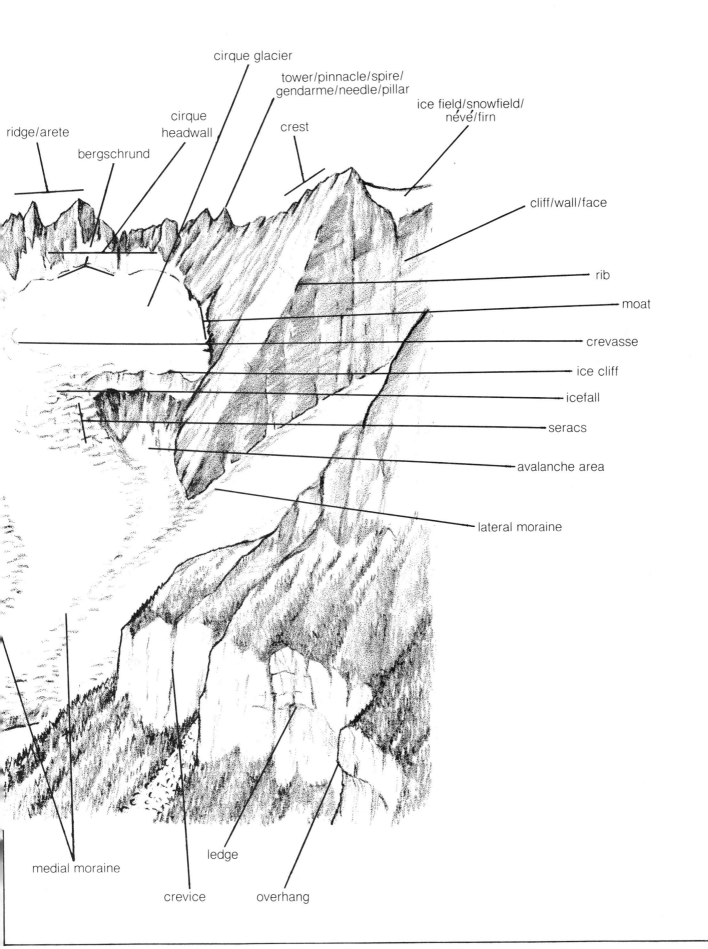

ridge/arete

bergschrund

cirque glacier

cirque headwall

tower/pinnacle/spire/ gendarme/needle/pillar

crest

ice field/snowfield/ névé/firn

cliff/wall/face

rib

moat

crevasse

ice cliff

icefall

seracs

avalanche area

lateral moraine

medial moraine

crevice

ledge

overhang

Terrains

Volcano

In *central-vent volcanoes,* such as the one shown here, material erupts from a single pipe. *Fissure volcanoes* extrude material along extensive *fractures.*

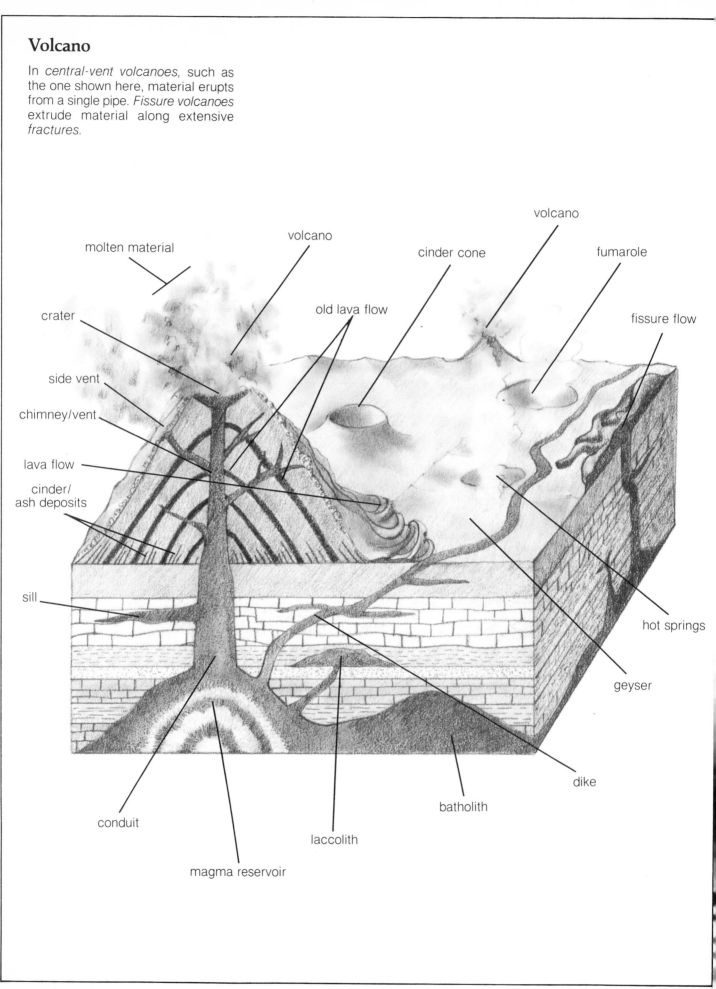

molten material

volcano

crater

side vent

chimney/vent

lava flow

cinder/ ash deposits

sill

old lava flow

cinder cone

volcano

fumarole

fissure flow

hot springs

geyser

dike

batholith

laccolith

magma reservoir

conduit

Cave Cross Section

The exploration of caves, or *caverns*, is called *spelunking* or *caving*. The area lighted by daylight just inside a cave entrance is the *twilight zone*. An underground structure containing many *galleries, chambers* or *rooms* is a *cave system*. Anything formed inside a cave, *cavern* or *grotto*, by dripping water is *dripstone*. Knobby calcite growths often found on *walls* and *floors* of once-submerged caves are called *cave coral* or *cave popcorn*.

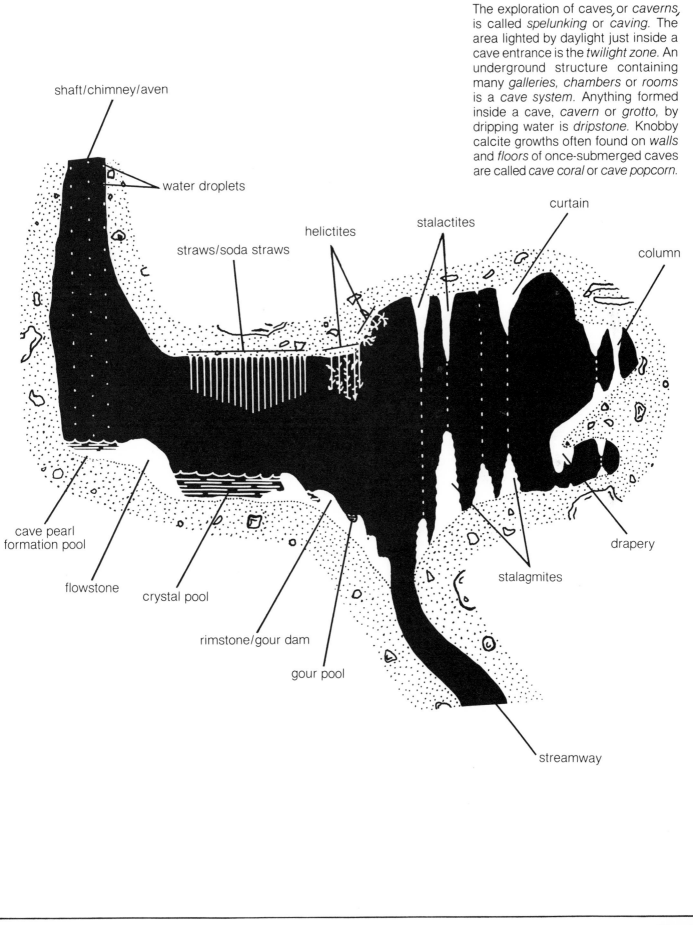

shaft/chimney/aven

water droplets

straws/soda straws

helictites

stalactites

curtain

column

cave pearl
formation pool

flowstone

crystal pool

rimstone/gour dam

gour pool

stalagmites

drapery

streamway

Terrains

Glacier

When a glacier terminates at the water's edge, sections break off, or *calve,* to form icebergs. Icebergs often break apart to form smaller, separate *bergs, bergy bits* or *bitty bergs.* Even smaller sections are called *growlers. Ice packs,* formed when the water surface between floating ice freezes, are called *floes.* Sections that break off are called *floebergs.*

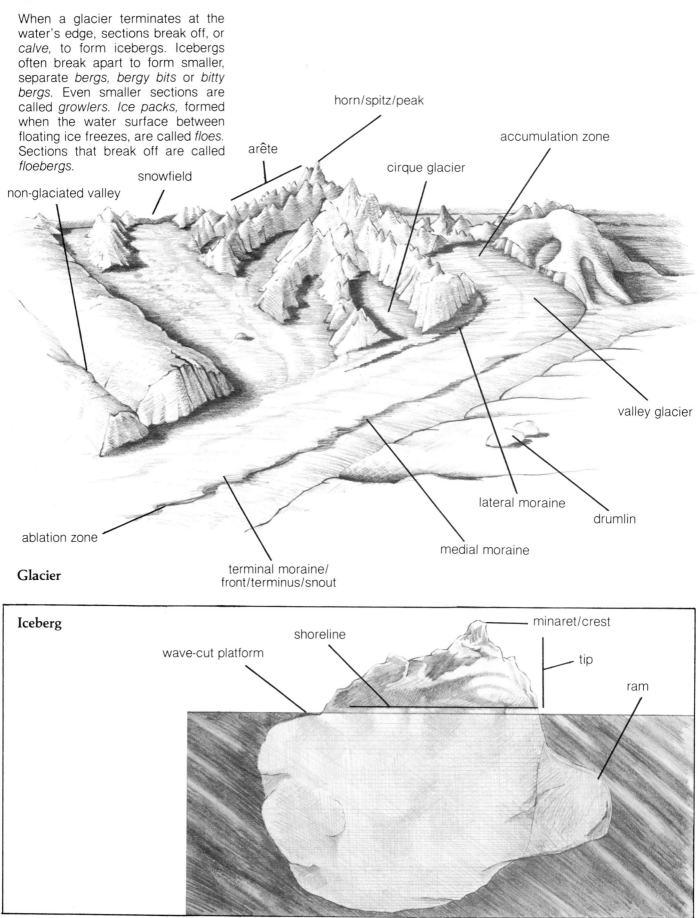

horn/spitz/peak

accumulation zone

arête

cirque glacier

snowfield

non-glaciated valley

valley glacier

lateral moraine

drumlin

medial moraine

ablation zone

terminal moraine/
front/terminus/snout

Glacier

Iceberg

shoreline

minaret/crest

wave-cut platform

tip

ram

River

A *river system* consists of the main river and its tributaries or branches. It drains from a *river basin*, and flows along a *course*, or *watercourse*, cutting a *channel* through the land. A *flood* occurs when it overflows its banks.

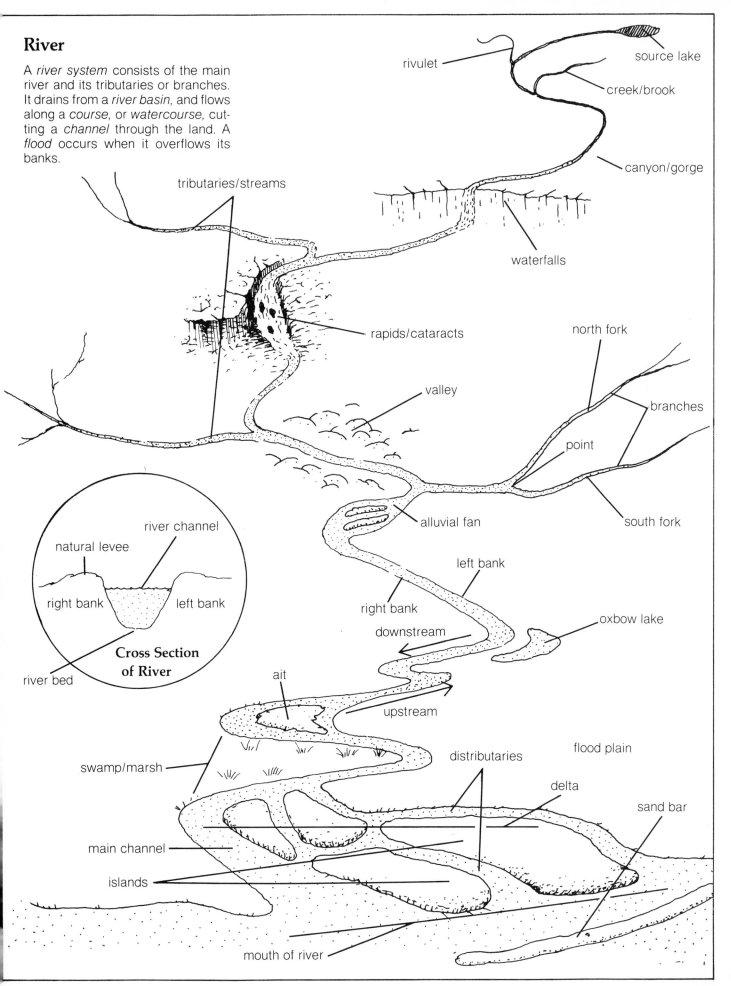

rivulet

source lake

creek/brook

canyon/gorge

tributaries/streams

waterfalls

rapids/cataracts

north fork

branches

valley

point

alluvial fan

south fork

left bank

Cross Section of River

river channel

natural levee

right bank

left bank

right bank

downstream

river bed

oxbow lake

ait

upstream

flood plain

swamp/marsh

distributaries

delta

sand bar

main channel

islands

mouth of river

Water Systems

Wave and Shoreline

Wavelength is the linear distance between two wave crests, *period* is the time it takes two crests to pass a given point, and *wave height* is the vertical distance measured from the trough to the crest of a wave. There are *surface waves, tidal waves, internal waves, tsunamis, storm surges* and *seiches.* Long, crestless waves are *swells.* The rapid flow of water up onto the *beach face* following the breaking of *surf* is the *uprush* or *swash.*

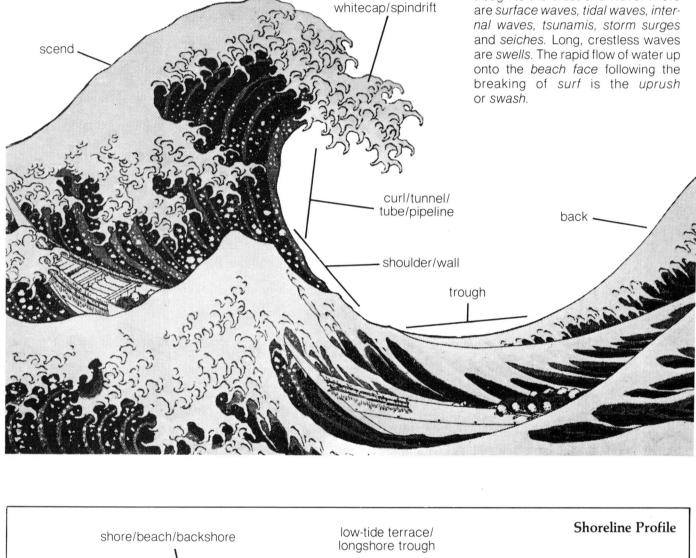

crest

whitecap/spindrift

scend

curl/tunnel/ tube/pipeline

back

shoulder/wall

trough

Shoreline Profile

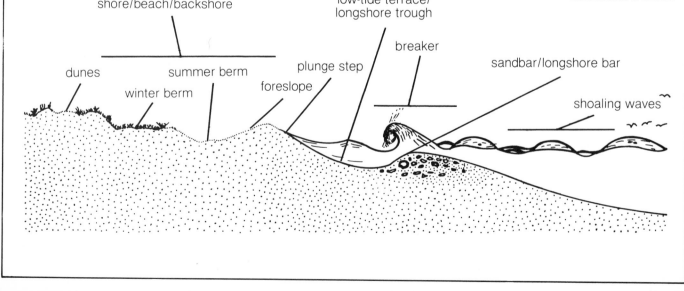

shore/beach/backshore

low-tide terrace/ longshore trough

breaker

dunes

summer berm

plunge step

sandbar/longshore bar

winter berm

foreslope

shoaling waves

Coastline and Continental Margin

The *littoral zone* is that part of the shoreline that lies between *high* and *low tides.* The continental shelf is the submerged border of *landmasses* extending into the *ocean basin.* The *100-fathom curve* has long been used as the outer limit of the continental shelf.

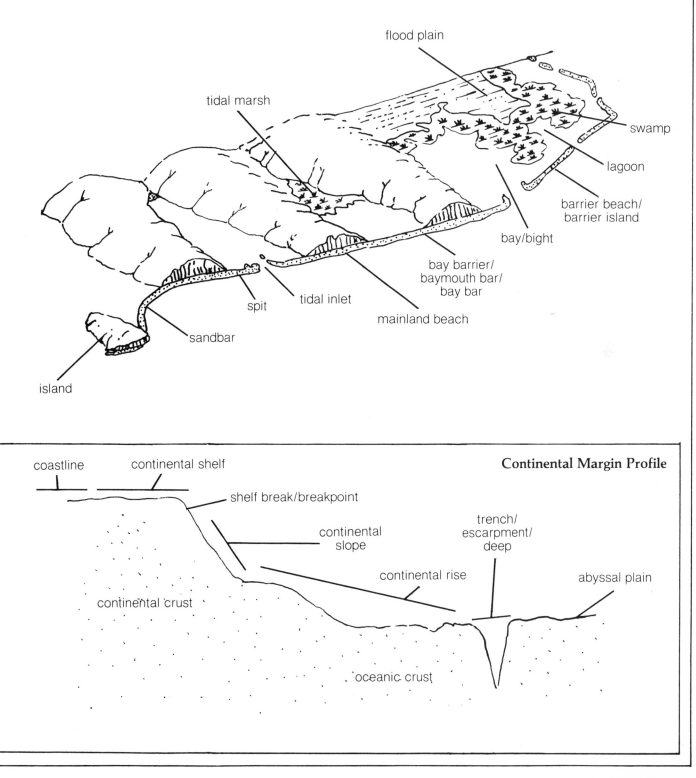

flood plain

tidal marsh

swamp

lagoon

barrier beach/ barrier island

bay/bight

bay barrier/ baymouth bar/ bay bar

mainland beach

spit

tidal inlet

sandbar

island

Continental Margin Profile

coastline

continental shelf

shelf break/breakpoint

continental slope

trench/ escarpment/ deep

continental rise

abyssal plain

continental crust

oceanic crust

Water Systems

Clouds

The name of a cloud describes both its appearance and its height above the ground. Clouds are formed from tiny droplets of water or *ice crystals* and continually change shape due to evaporation, wind and *air movements*.

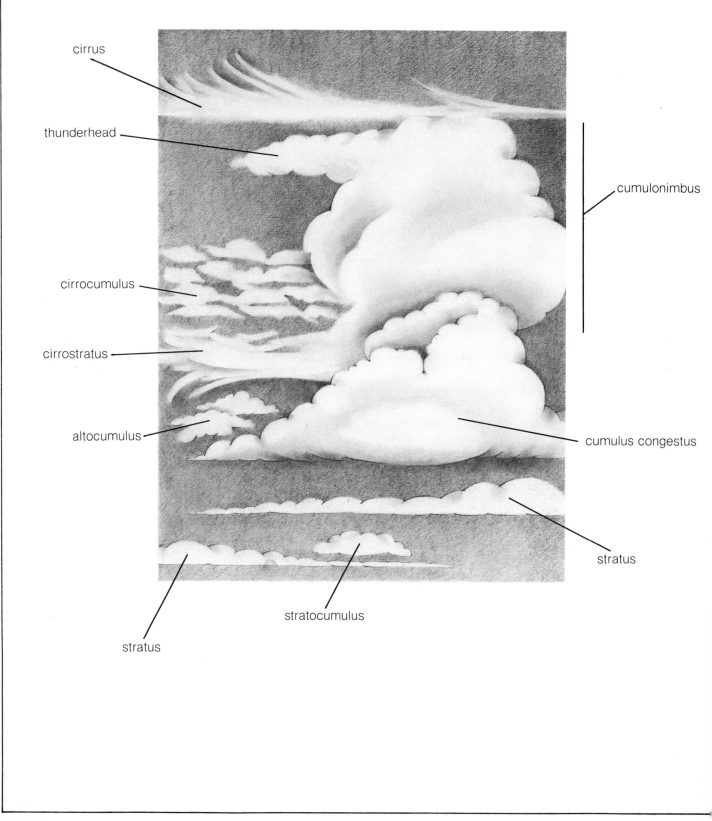

cirrus

thunderhead

cirrocumulus

cirrostratus

altocumulus

cumulonimbus

cumulus congestus

stratus

stratocumulus

stratus

Storm Systems

Thunderstorms carry the same general features: lightning, *thunder*, strong gusts of *wind*, heavy *showers*, and occasionally *hailstones.* When hurricanes occur in the Pacific, they are called *typhoons.* Tornados are also known as *twisters.*

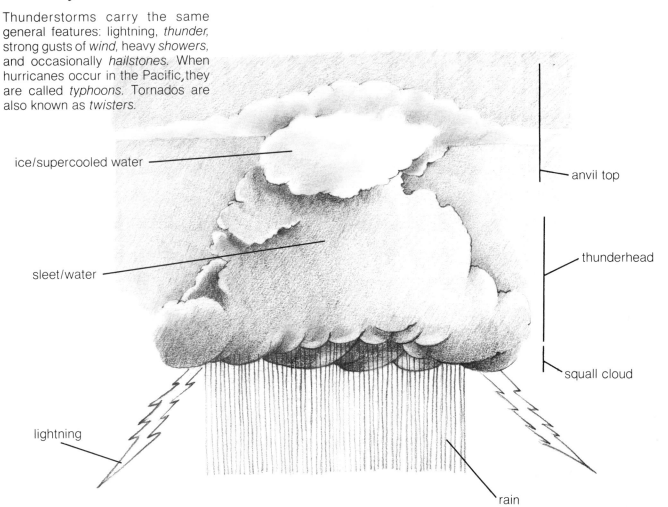

ice/supercooled water

sleet/water

lightning

anvil top

thunderhead

squall cloud

rain

Thunderstorm

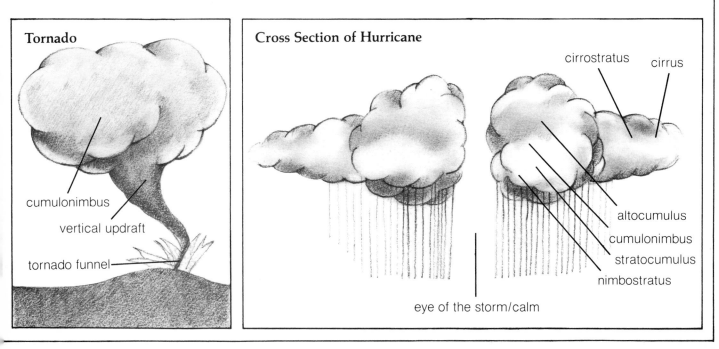

Tornado

cumulonimbus

vertical updraft

tornado funnel

Cross Section of Hurricane

cirrostratus

cirrus

altocumulus

cumulonimbus

stratocumulus

nimbostratus

eye of the storm/calm

Weather Monitoring Equipment

Equipment, such as that shown here, helps a *meteorologist* predict weather and make *weather forecasts*.

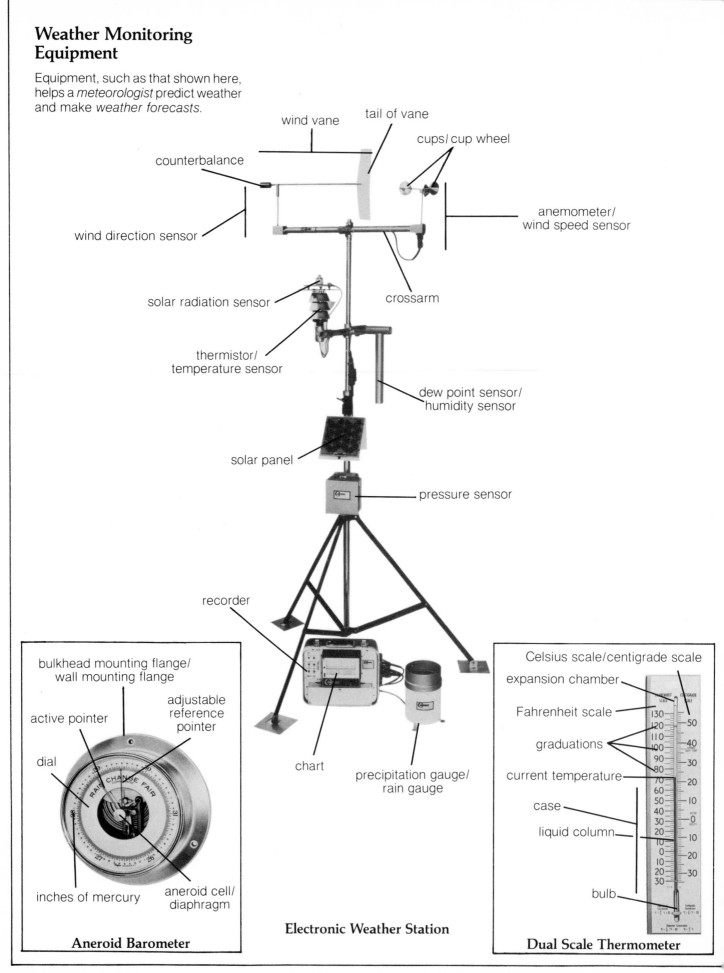

wind vane

tail of vane

cups/cup wheel

counterbalance

anemometer/ wind speed sensor

wind direction sensor

crossarm

solar radiation sensor

thermistor/ temperature sensor

dew point sensor/ humidity sensor

solar panel

pressure sensor

recorder

bulkhead mounting flange/ wall mounting flange

adjustable reference pointer

active pointer

dial

chart

precipitation gauge/ rain gauge

inches of mercury

aneroid cell/ diaphragm

Aneroid Barometer

Electronic Weather Station

Celsius scale/centigrade scale

expansion chamber

Fahrenheit scale

graduations

current temperature

case

liquid column

bulb

Dual Scale Thermometer

Weather Map

This composite weather map, or *synoptic chart,* displays conditions over a broad area. The numbers around the station model indicate *temperature,* *barometric pressure* and *pressure change.*

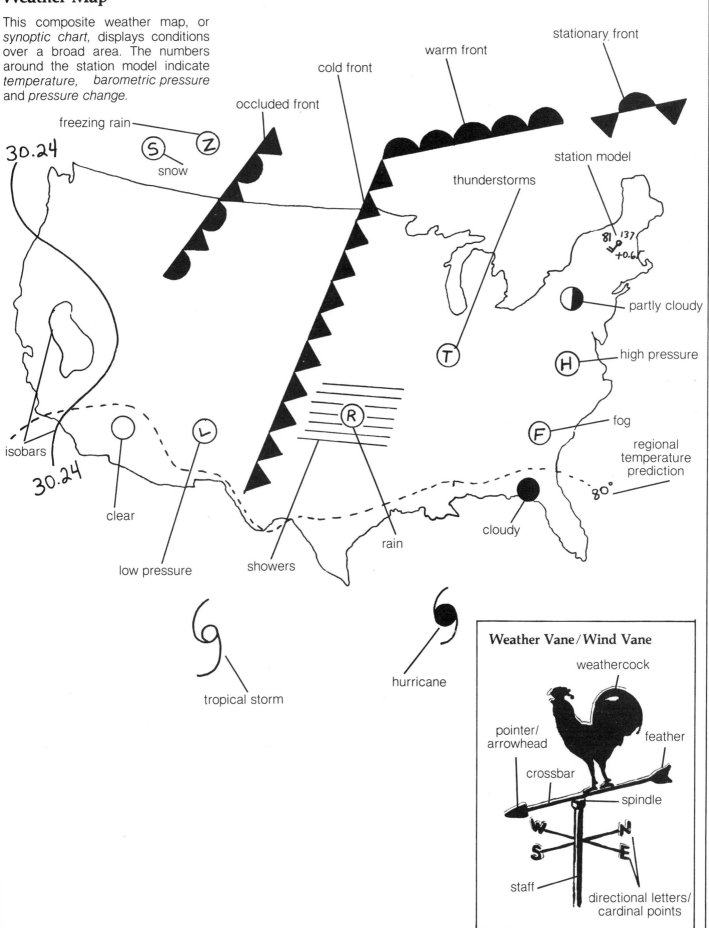

stationary front

warm front

cold front

occluded front

freezing rain

snow

S Z

30.24

station model

thunderstorms

81 137
+0.6

partly cloudy

high pressure

H

fog

F

T

regional temperature prediction

80°

isobars

30.24

clear

L

R

rain

cloudy

low pressure

showers

tropical storm

hurricane

Weather Vane/Wind Vane

weathercock

pointer/ arrowhead

feather

crossbar

spindle

staff

directional letters/ cardinal points

Map

The science of *mapmaking* is also known as *cartography*. The *projection* of a map is the framework on which its main components, *linework*, point or area symbols and type are placed.

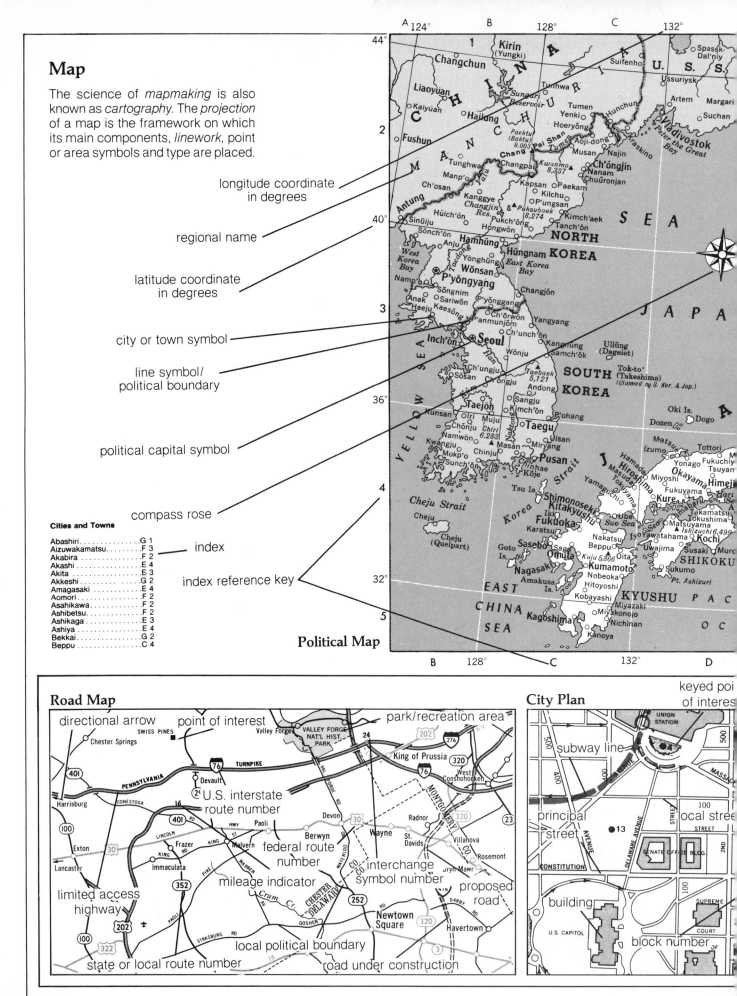

longitude coordinate in degrees

regional name

latitude coordinate in degrees

city or town symbol

line symbol/ political boundary

political capital symbol

compass rose

index

index reference key

Cities and Towns

Abashiri	G 1
Aizuwakamatsu	F 3
Akabira	F 2
Akashi	E 4
Akita	E 3
Akkeshi	G 2
Amagasaki	E 4
Aomori	F 2
Asahikawa	F 2
Ashibetsu	F 2
Ashikaga	E 3
Ashiya	E 4
Bekkai	G 2
Beppu	C 4

Political Map

Road Map

directional arrow

point of interest

park/recreation area

U.S. interstate route number

federal route number

interchange symbol number

mileage indicator

limited access highway

local political boundary

road under construction

state or local route number

proposed road

City Plan

keyed point of interest

subway line

principal street

local street

building

block number

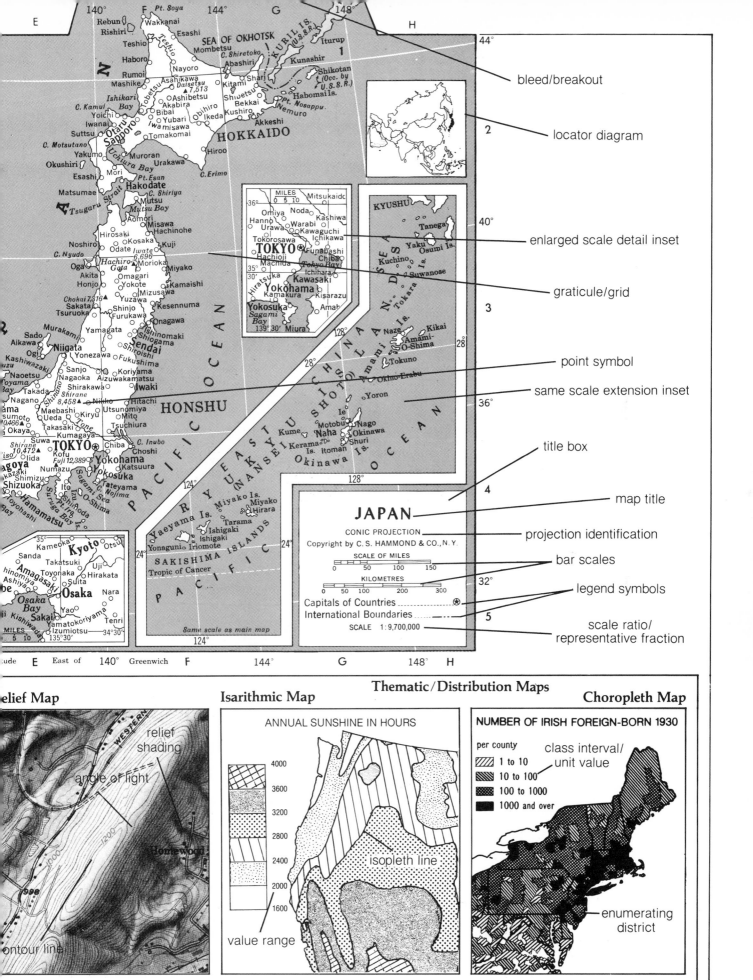

bleed/breakout

locator diagram

enlarged scale detail inset

graticule/grid

point symbol

same scale extension inset

title box

map title

projection identification

bar scales

legend symbols

scale ratio/
representative fraction

JAPAN

CONIC PROJECTION
Copyright by C. S. HAMMOND & CO., N.Y.

SCALE OF MILES

0   50   100   150

KILOMETRES

0   50   100   200   300

Capitals of Countries .... ⊛
International Boundaries .... —··—··—

SCALE 1:9,700,000

Thematic/Distribution Maps

Relief Map

relief shading

angle of light

contour line

Isarithmic Map

ANNUAL SUNSHINE IN HOURS

4000
3600
3200
2800
2400
2000
1600

isopleth line

value range

Choropleth Map

NUMBER OF IRISH FOREIGN-BORN 1930

per county
1 to 10
10 to 100
100 to 1000
1000 and over

class interval/
unit value

enumerating
district

Nautical Chart and Topographic Map

On nautical charts, *sounding datum reference* is stated in the *chart title*. *Depth conversion scales* are provided to enable the mariner to work in *meters, fathoms,* or *feet*. The space outside a chart or map, used to identify and explain the map, is the *map margin*.

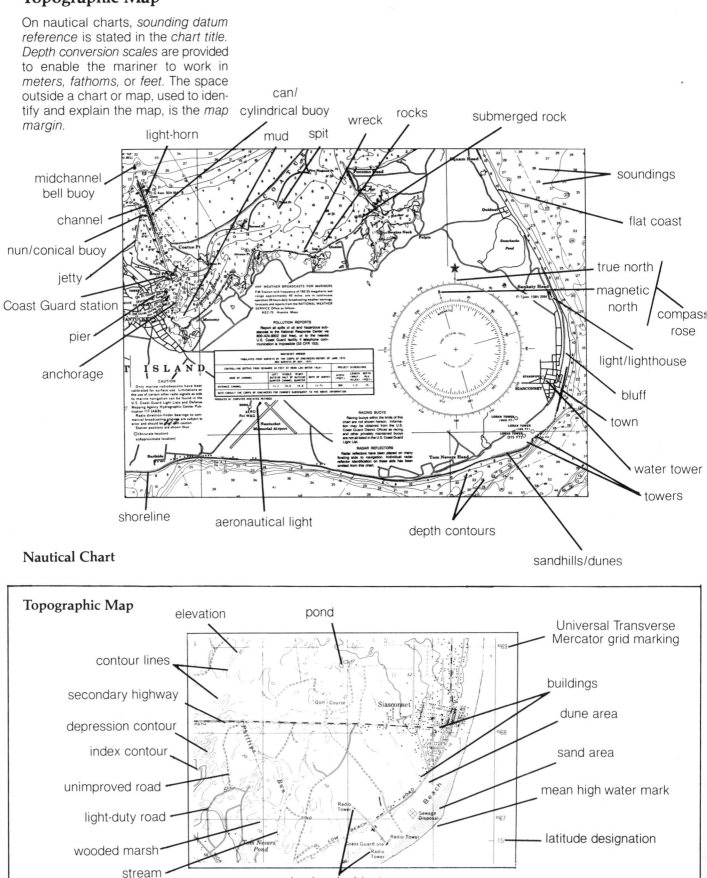

Nautical Chart

Topographic Map

Living Things

For ease of reference, this section has been divided into five subcategories: man, edible animals, domestic animals, wild animals, and plants. The animals and plants selected for inclusion within each subsection contain most of the parts common to all members of the major families they represent.

With the exception of man, examined more closely than any other subject in this section because of his obvious importance to us, only the external parts of living things have been identified. However, edible animals have been illustrated in such a way as to show those parts which supply our daily food. Domestic and wild animals, some of them grouped by habitat, are represented by single members of a species. But because there are parts which are unique to certain animals, a composite "beast" has been created to illustrate some of them.

The plant kingdom is represented from the roots up, literally, including coverage of parts of a flower, special plants, and edible portions called fruits and vegetables.

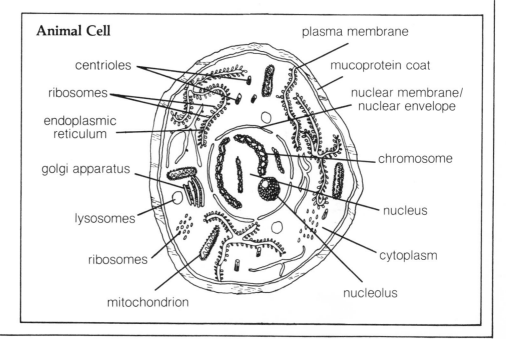

Animal Cell

centrioles

ribosomes

endoplasmic reticulum

golgi apparatus

lysosomes

ribosomes

mitochondrion

plasma membrane

mucoprotein coat

nuclear membrane/ nuclear envelope

chromosome

nucleus

cytoplasm

nucleolus

The Human Body

The body, less the *head* and *limbs,* is referred to as the *trunk* or *torso.*

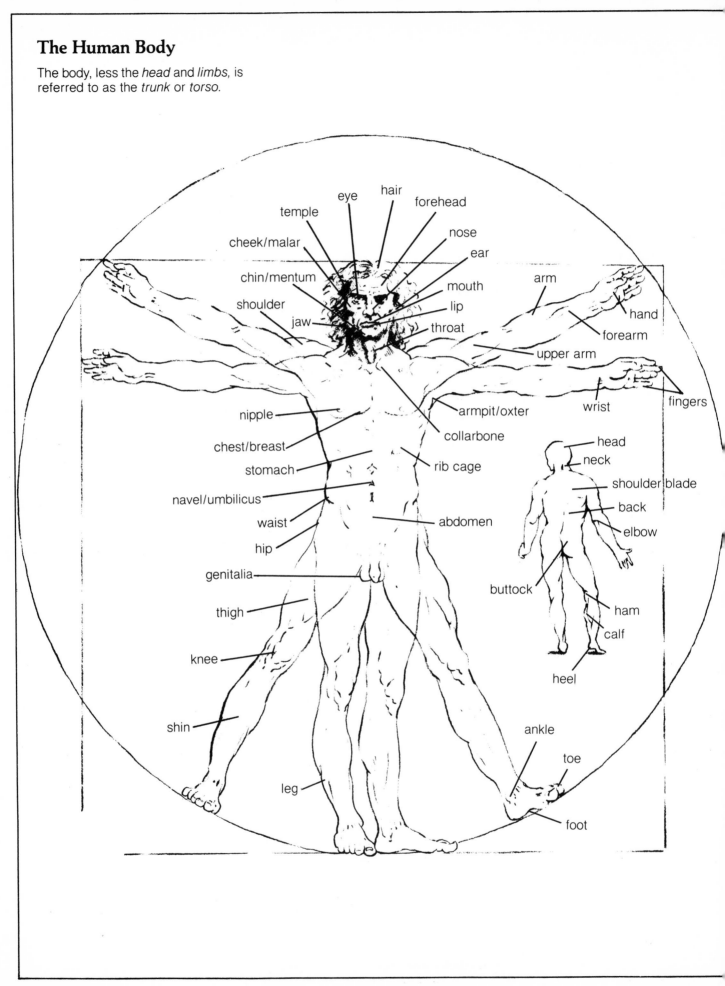

temple
eye
hair
forehead
cheek/malar
nose
ear
chin/mentum
mouth
shoulder
lip
jaw
throat
arm
hand
forearm
upper arm
armpit/oxter
wrist
fingers
nipple
collarbone
chest/breast
stomach
rib cage
navel/umbilicus
waist
abdomen
hip
genitalia
thigh
knee
shin
leg

head
neck
shoulder blade
back
elbow
buttock
ham
calf
heel
ankle
toe
foot

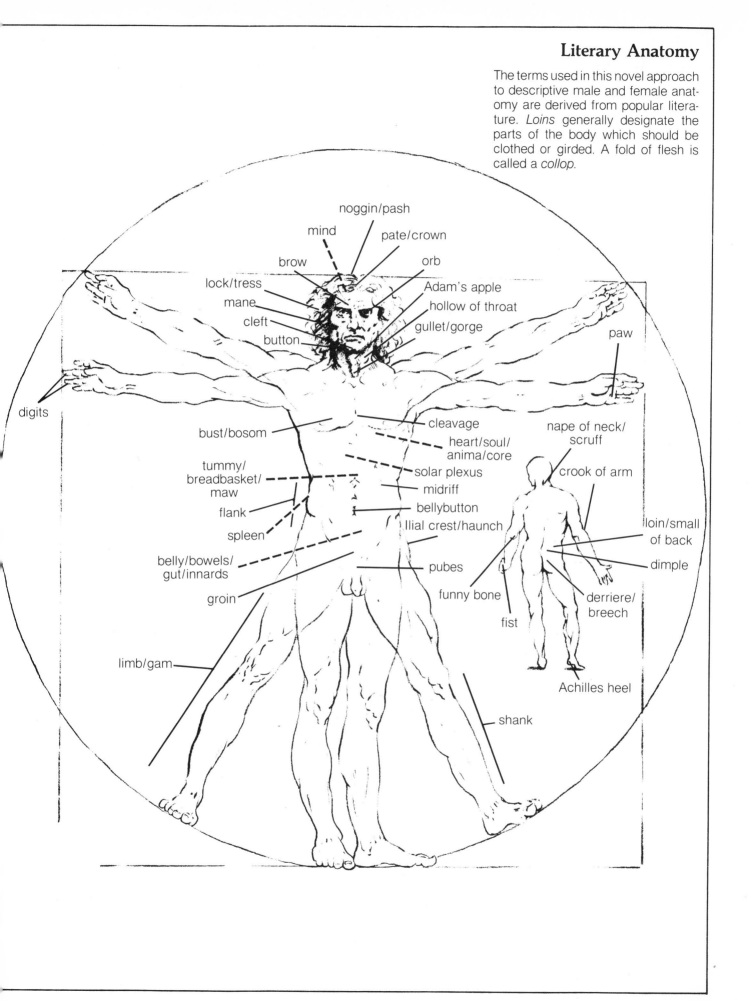

Literary Anatomy

The terms used in this novel approach to descriptive male and female anatomy are derived from popular literature. *Loins* generally designate the parts of the body which should be clothed or girded. A fold of flesh is called a *collop*.

noggin/pash

mind

pate/crown

brow

orb

lock/tress

Adam's apple

mane

hollow of throat

cleft

gullet/gorge

button

paw

digits

cleavage

bust/bosom

nape of neck/ scruff

heart/soul/ anima/core

tummy/ breadbasket/ maw

solar plexus

crook of arm

midriff

flank

bellybutton

loin/small of back

spleen

Ilial crest/haunch

belly/bowels/ gut/innards

dimple

pubes

groin

derriere/ breech

funny bone

limb/gam

fist

shank

Achilles heel

Man

Skeletal and Muscular System

Voluntary muscles are subject to or controlled by will, pulling on *bones* of the *skeleton* to produce movement. *Involuntary muscles,* like the heart, act independently of volition. Where one bone meets another is a *joint.* *Cartilage,* or *gristle,* is a flexible type of connective tissue. The bony structure in which the brain is housed is the *cranium.*

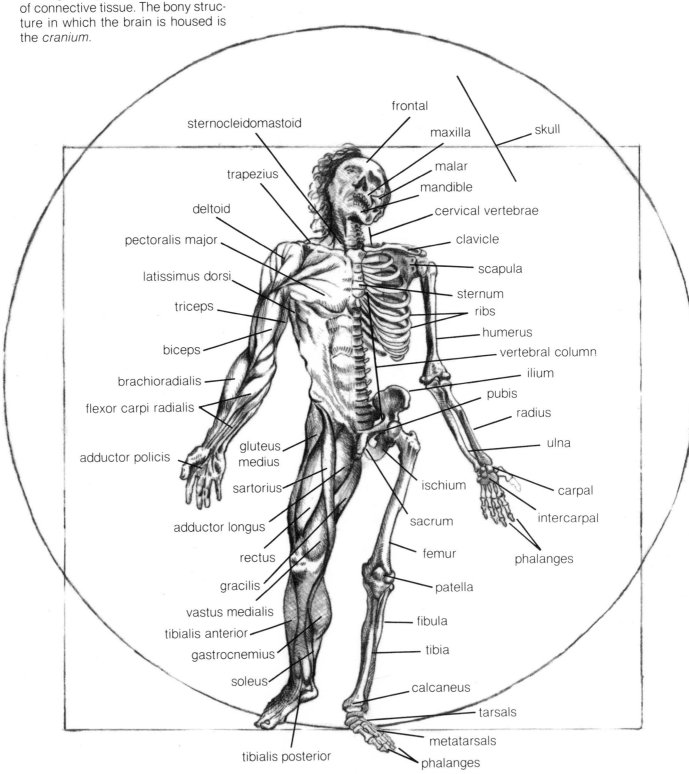

frontal

sternocleidomastoid

maxilla

skull

trapezius

malar

mandible

deltoid

cervical vertebrae

pectoralis major

clavicle

scapula

latissimus dorsi

sternum

triceps

ribs

humerus

biceps

vertebral column

brachioradialis

ilium

flexor carpi radialis

pubis

radius

ulna

adductor policis

gluteus medius

sartorius

ischium

carpal

adductor longus

sacrum

intercarpal

rectus

femur

phalanges

gracilis

patella

vastus medialis

fibula

tibialis anterior

tibia

gastrocnemius

soleus

calcaneus

tarsals

metatarsals

tibialis posterior

phalanges

Internal Organs

The stomach and intestines are the principal organs of the *digestive system*, or *alimentary canal*, and the *pancreas*, liver and *gall bladder* all aid in the nutrition process and the elimination of wastes. The heart is the pump of the *circulatory system*, sending blood through *arteries*, *veins* and *capillaries*. The lungs are the center of the *respiratory system*.

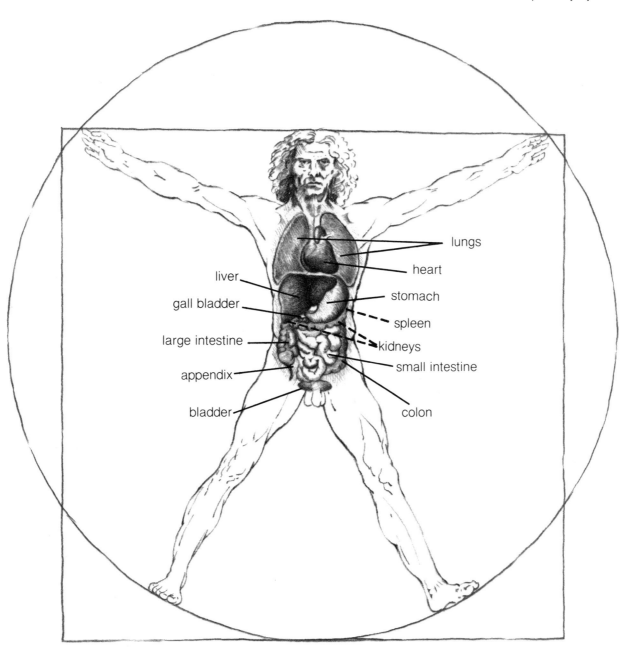

lungs

heart

liver

stomach

gall bladder

spleen

large intestine

kidneys

appendix

small intestine

bladder

colon

Man

Sense Organs

The eye, which is located in an *eye socket*, or *orbit*, is covered with a transparent layer called the *cornea*. The angle formed where upper and lower eyelids come together is called the *cantus*. The junction nearest the nose is the *inner cantus*, the other is the *outer cantus*. The tongue rubs against the *palate* at the top of the mouth. The *pharynx* is the beginning of the *throat*, or *gullet*.

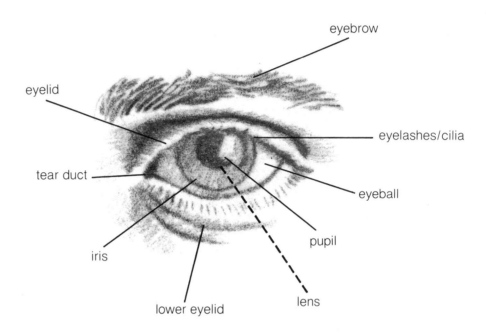

eyebrow

eyelid

eyelashes/cilia

tear duct

eyeball

pupil

iris

lower eyelid

lens

Eye

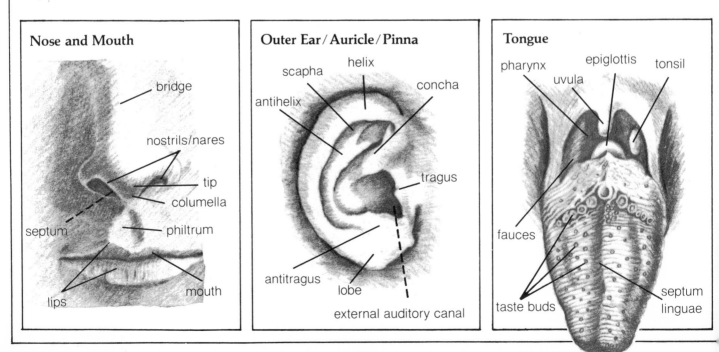

Nose and Mouth

bridge

nostrils/nares

tip

columella

septum

philtrum

lips

mouth

Outer Ear / Auricle / Pinna

scapha

helix

antihelix

concha

tragus

antitragus

lobe

external auditory canal

Tongue

pharynx

uvula

epiglottis

tonsil

fauces

taste buds

septum linguae

The Extremities

The space between the thumb and extended forefinger is the *purlicue*. A *fingerprint* is an ink impression of the *arches, loops* and *whorls* created by ridges of skin in the finger pad. The *back of the hand* is called the *opisthenar*.

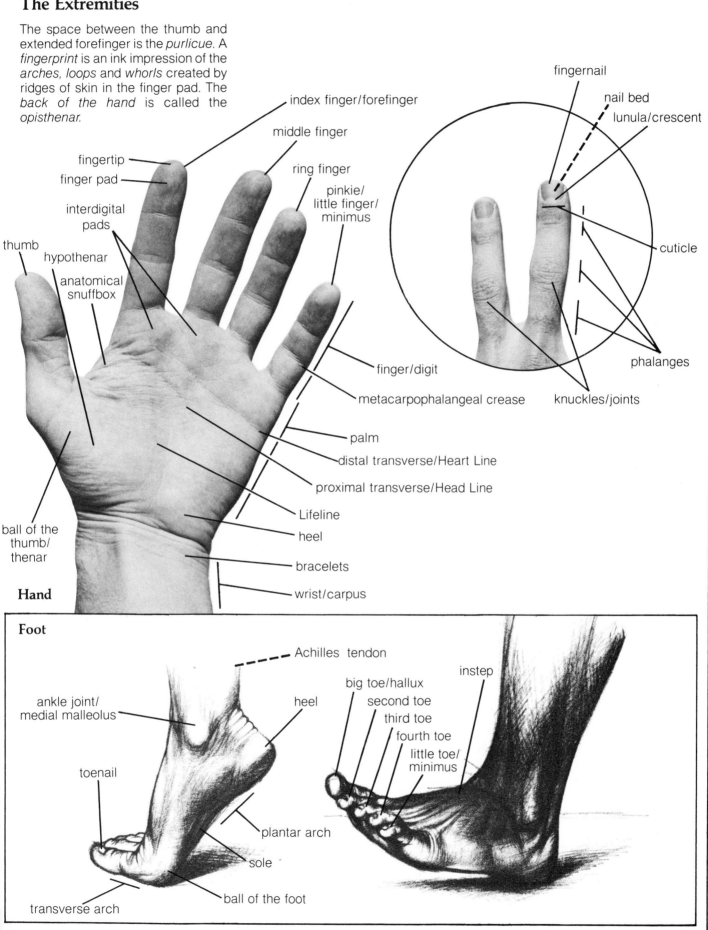

fingernail

nail bed

lunula/crescent

index finger/forefinger

middle finger

ring finger

pinkie/ little finger/ minimus

fingertip

finger pad

interdigital pads

cuticle

thumb

hypothenar

anatomical snuffbox

phalanges

finger/digit

knuckles/joints

metacarpophalangeal crease

palm

distal transverse/Heart Line

proximal transverse/Head Line

Lifeline

ball of the thumb/ thenar

heel

bracelets

wrist/carpus

Hand

Foot

Achilles tendon

instep

ankle joint/ medial malleolus

heel

big toe/hallux

second toe

third toe

fourth toe

little toe/ minimus

toenail

plantar arch

sole

transverse arch

ball of the foot

Cow

Young *cattle* are *calves;* females are *heifers* until they give birth and are then cows; males are *bulls.* Castrated males, raised for *beef,* are *steers.* Castrated males, raised as draft animals, are *oxen.* The body, or *torso,* of a cow is known as the *barrel.*

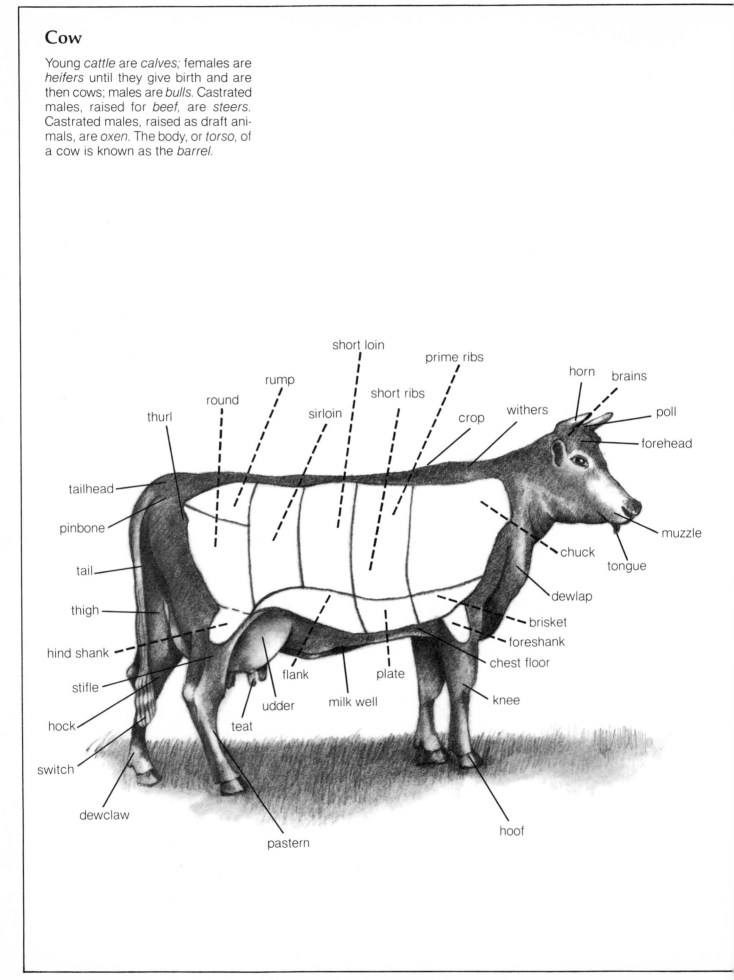

short loin

rump

round

thurl

short ribs

sirloin

prime ribs

crop

withers

horn

brains

poll

forehead

tailhead

pinbone

tail

thigh

hind shank

stifle

hock

switch

dewclaw

pastern

teat

udder

flank

milk well

plate

muzzle

tongue

chuck

dewlap

brisket

foreshank

chest floor

knee

hoof

Sheep

A young sheep is called a *lamb*. An adult male is a *ram;* an adult female is a *ewe*. The meat of a young sheep is called *lamb*, while that of an animal over eighteen months old is called *mutton*.

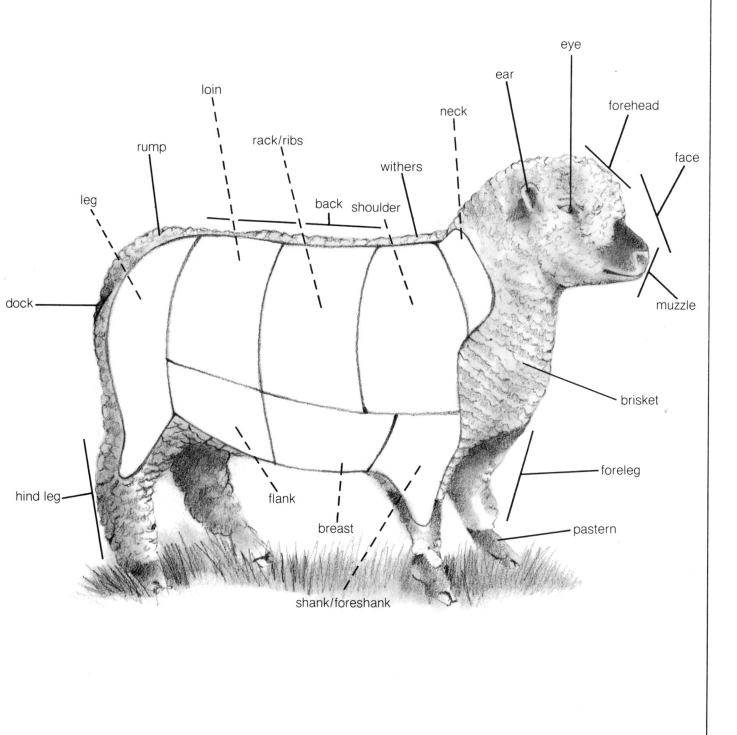

loin

rack/ribs

rump

leg

back   shoulder

withers

neck

ear

eye

forehead

face

dock

muzzle

brisket

foreleg

hind leg

flank

breast

pastern

shank/foreshank

31

Edible Animals

Pig

Young pigs are called *shoats*. Small or sub-adult domestic animals are *pigs* or *gruntlings*. If they weigh over 120 pounds, they are called *hogs*. Adult males are *boars*. Adult females are *sows*. Pigs, hogs, boars and sows are referred to as *swine*. Pig meat is called *pork*.

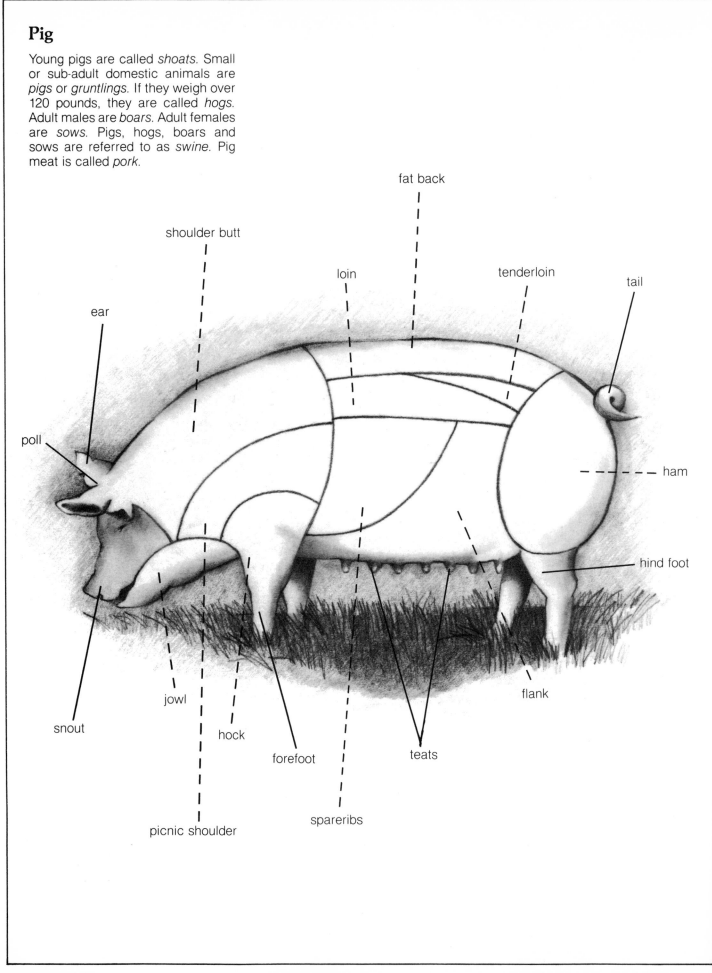

fat back

shoulder butt

loin

tenderloin

tail

ear

poll

ham

hind foot

flank

jowl

snout

hock

forefoot

teats

picnic shoulder

spareribs

Poultry

Chickens, turkeys, *ducks, geese* and *pheasants* are known collectively as *fowl* in the wild, as *poultry* if domesticated. A male chicken is a *rooster;* a female is a *hen.* A male turkey is a *tom.* Young chickens are *chicks;* young turkeys are *poults.* A *capon* is a male chicken that has been castrated before sexual maturity. Unlike other poultry, ducks have *webbed feet* and broad, flat *bills* with small *teeth.* Among the *entrails* of a fowl, the most edible are the *giblets,* the *heart,* the *liver* and the *gizzard.*

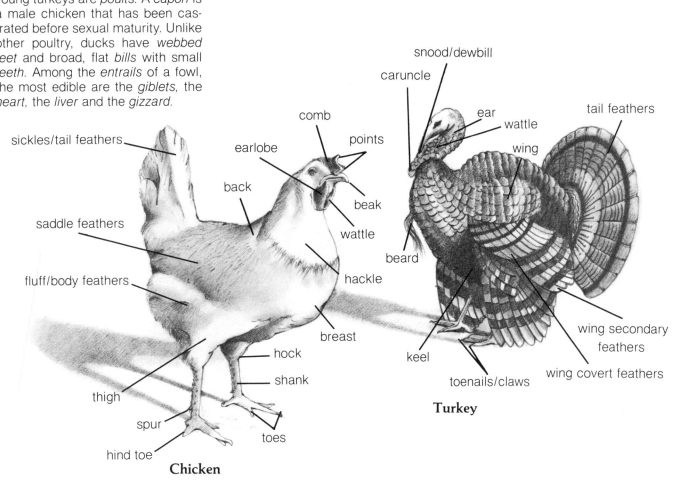

sickles/tail feathers

comb

earlobe

points

back

beak

saddle feathers

wattle

fluff/body feathers

hackle

breast

hock

shank

thigh

spur

toes

hind toe

Chicken

snood/dewbill

caruncle

ear

wattle

wing

tail feathers

beard

keel

toenails/claws

wing secondary feathers

wing covert feathers

Turkey

Poultry Parts

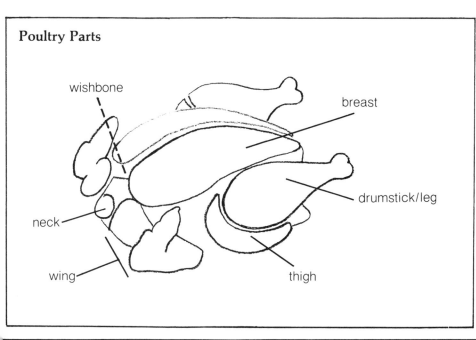

wishbone

breast

drumstick/leg

neck

wing

thigh

Edible Animals

Dog

Dogs are digitigrade animals; they walk on what are anatomically their four *fingertips,* or pads. The fifth finger, or *thumb,* a functionless inner claw, is known as a *dewclaw,* and does not reach the ground. The bushy tail of a rough-coated dog is called a *brush.* A smooth-coated dog's tail is a *stern.*

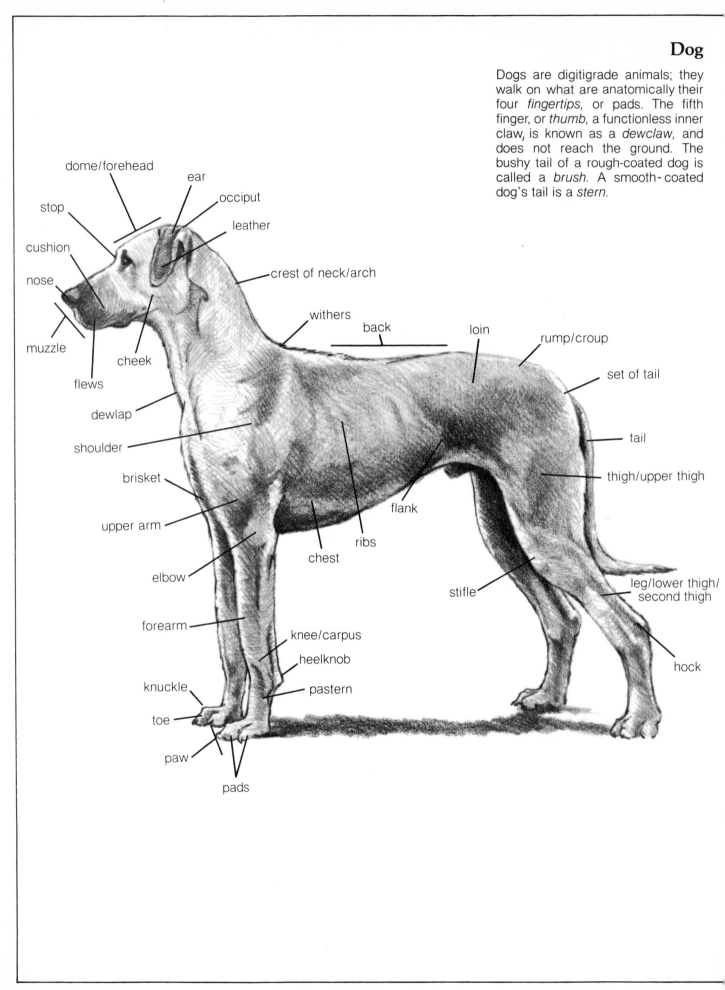

dome/forehead
ear
occiput
stop
leather
cushion
crest of neck/arch
nose
withers
back
loin
rump/croup
muzzle
set of tail
cheek
flews
tail
dewlap
thigh/upper thigh
shoulder
brisket
flank
upper arm
ribs
elbow
chest
stifle
leg/lower thigh/
second thigh
forearm
knee/carpus
heelknob
hock
knuckle
pastern
toe
paw
pads

Cat

Newborn cats are called *kittens*, adult males are *tomcats*, and adult females are *cattas*. Cats are capable of drawing their *toenails*, or *claws*, into *sheaths* located above the *pads* of their feet. A cat's *muzzle* consists of the *nose* and *jaw* sections of its face.

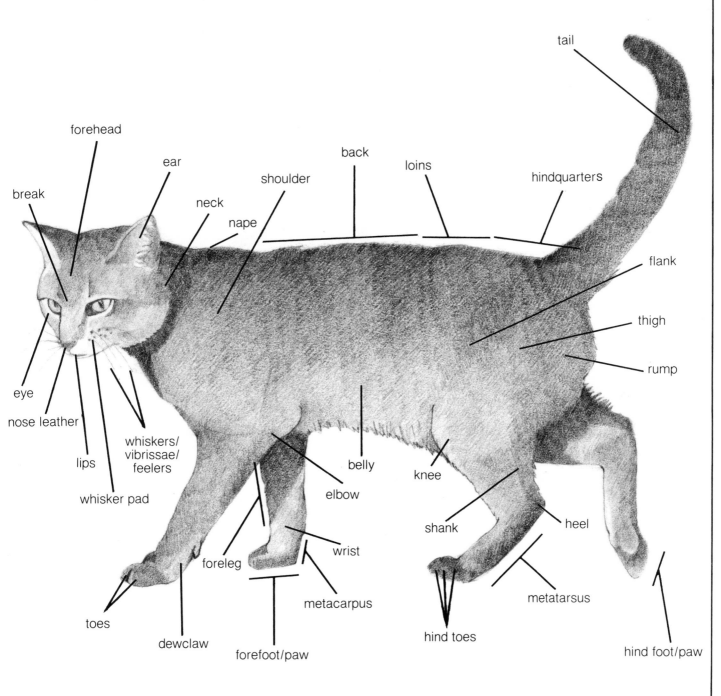

forehead

ear

break

neck

shoulder

nape

back

loins

hindquarters

tail

flank

thigh

rump

eye

nose leather

lips

whiskers/
vibrissae/
feelers

whisker pad

toes

dewclaw

foreleg

forefoot/paw

belly

elbow

wrist

metacarpus

knee

shank

hind toes

heel

metatarsus

hind foot/paw

Domestic Animals

Horse

A horse less than a year old is a *foal*. Male foals are *colts*, females are *fillies*. A mature male is a *stallion*, a female is a *mare*. In breeding, the male parent is a *sire*, the female is a *dam*. A castrated male is called a *gelding*.

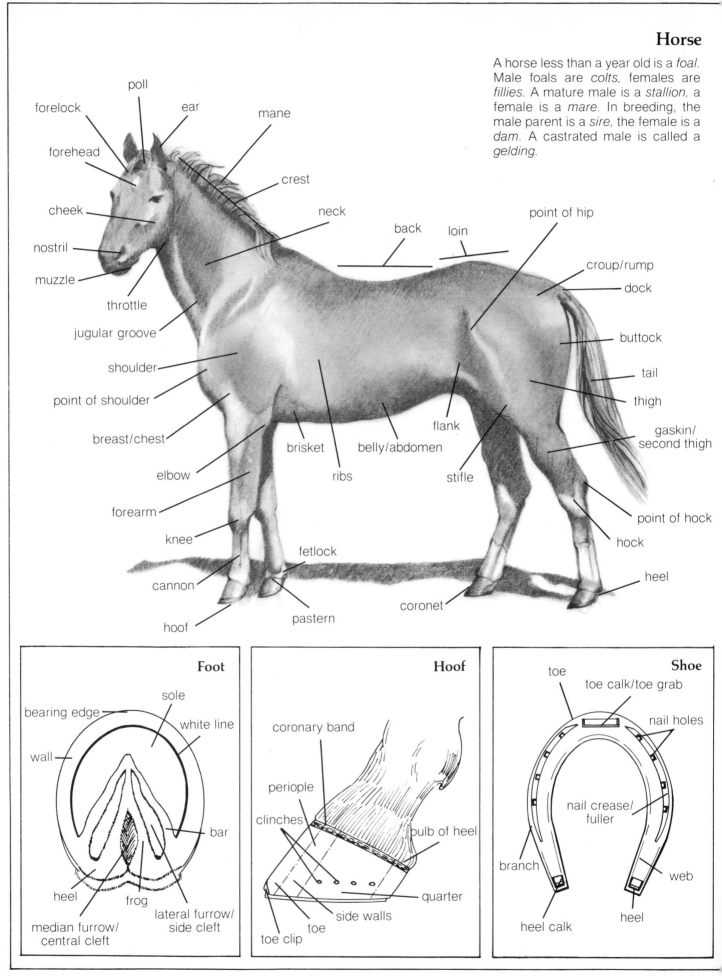

poll
forelock
ear
mane
forehead
crest
cheek
neck
nostril
muzzle
throttle
jugular groove
shoulder
point of shoulder
breast/chest
elbow
forearm
knee
cannon
hoof
pastern
fetlock
brisket
ribs
belly/abdomen
flank
stifle
coronet
back
loin
point of hip
croup/rump
dock
buttock
tail
thigh
gaskin/second thigh
point of hock
hock
heel

Foot

sole
bearing edge
white line
wall
bar
heel
frog
lateral furrow/side cleft
median furrow/central cleft

Hoof

coronary band
periople
clinches
bulb of heel
quarter
side walls
toe
toe clip

Shoe

toe
toe calk/toe grab
nail holes
nail crease/fuller
branch
web
heel
heel calk

Bird

A *flight feather* consists of tightly meshed *barbs* along the vane. *Contour feathers* and an *undercoat* of fine *down* cover the bird's body. A featherless portion of a bird's skin is called an *apterium*.

beak/bill/neb/nib

forehead

crown

lore

ear coverts/auricular

nostril

upper mandible

nape

lower mandible

chin

back

throat

scapulars

wing

wing coverts

secondaries

rump

thigh

foot

tail feathers

primaries

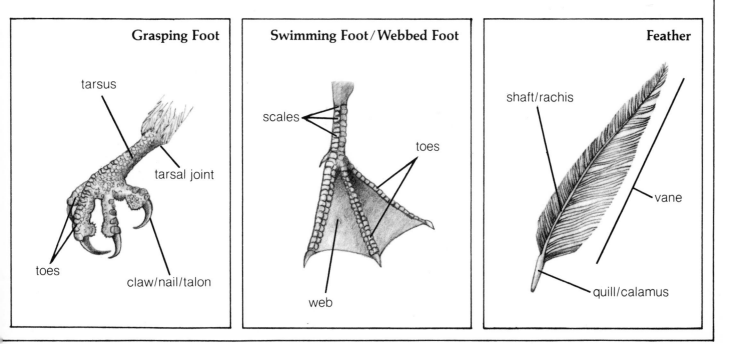

Grasping Foot

tarsus

tarsal joint

toes

claw/nail/talon

Swimming Foot/Webbed Foot

scales

toes

web

Feather

shaft/rachis

vane

quill/calamus

Wild Animals

Spider

Spiders produce *silk threads* which they use to make webs, *nests* or *parachutes* that allow the wind to carry them from one location to another. When a spider spins a web, it first constructs a *bridge* between two supports and fashions an *orb* beneath. A *scaffolding web* of dry thread is then used to lay down a *viscid spiral* of sticky thread.

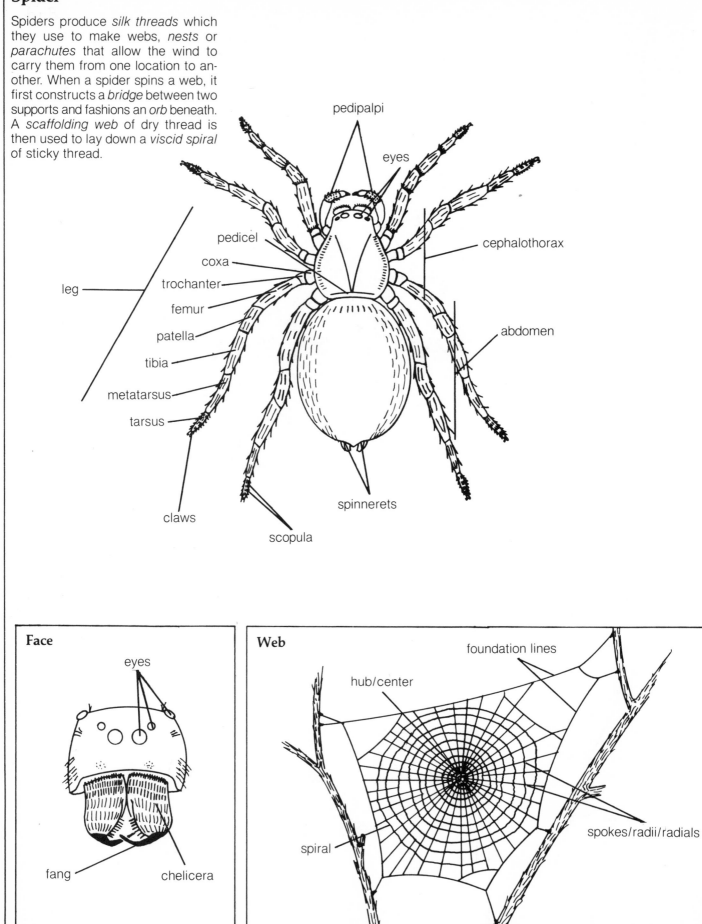

pedipalpi

eyes

pedicel

coxa

trochanter

femur

patella

tibia

metatarsus

tarsus

leg

claws

scopula

spinnerets

cephalothorax

abdomen

Face

eyes

fang

chelicera

Web

foundation lines

hub/center

spiral

spokes/radii/radials

Insects

Insects have shell-like outer coverings called *exoskeletons*. Most undergo four stages during *metamorphosis:* the *egg*, the *larva*, the *pupa*, and the *adult*.

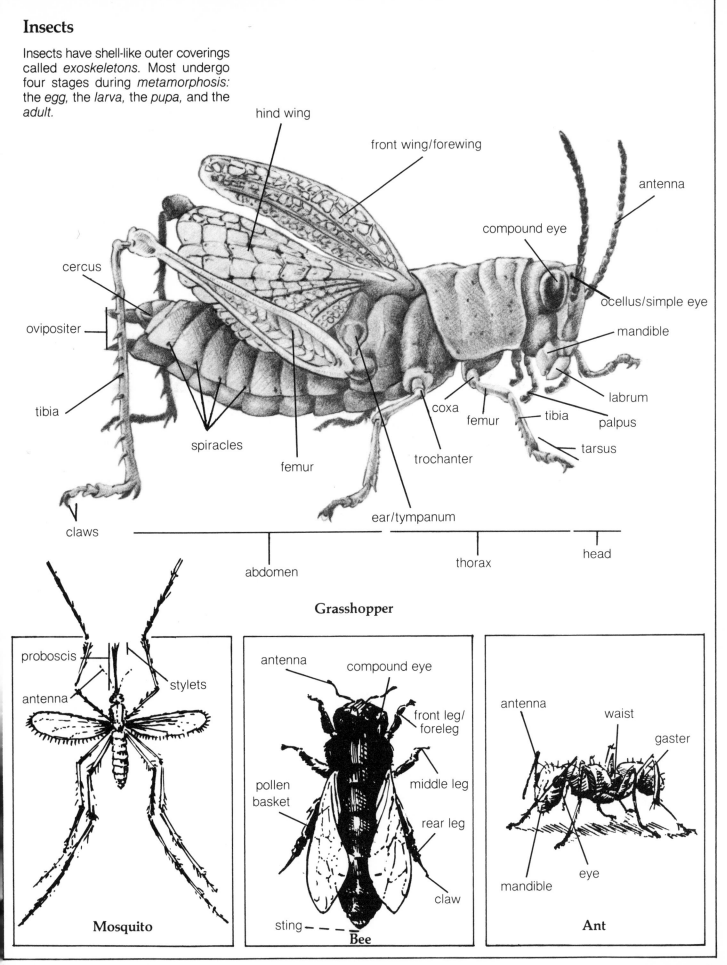

hind wing

front wing/forewing

antenna

compound eye

ocellus/simple eye

cercus

mandible

ovipositer

labrum

tibia

femur

tibia

palpus

spiracles

tarsus

femur

coxa

trochanter

claws

ear/tympanum

abdomen

thorax

head

Grasshopper

proboscis

stylets

antenna

antenna

compound eye

antenna

waist

gaster

front leg/
foreleg

pollen
basket

middle leg

rear leg

mandible

eye

claw

sting

Mosquito

Bee

Ant

Reptiles

In addition to the reptile families represented here, there is the lizard-like *tuatara,* a leftover from the days of the *dinosaurs,* with a vestigial *third eye* on the top of its head. All *poisonous snakes* inject their prey with *venom* through fangs, but not all venomous snakes have *"hypodermic fangs,"* like the rattler shown here. The flattened swelling below a cobra's head is called the *hood.* Most land-living turtles are called *tortoises.* Turtles that live in the sea have *flippers.* Many *skinks,* which are lizards, have no legs or eyelids.

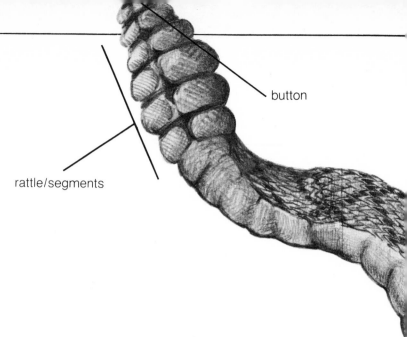

button

rattle/segments

Snake

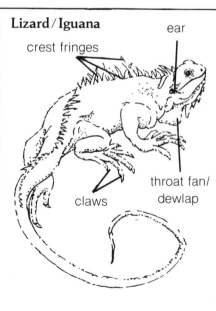

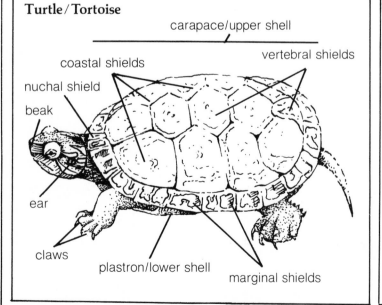

Turtle / Tortoise

carapace/upper shell

coastal shields

vertebral shields

nuchal shield

beak

ear

claws

plastron/lower shell

marginal shields

Lizard / Iguana

ear

crest fringes

claws

throat fan/ dewlap

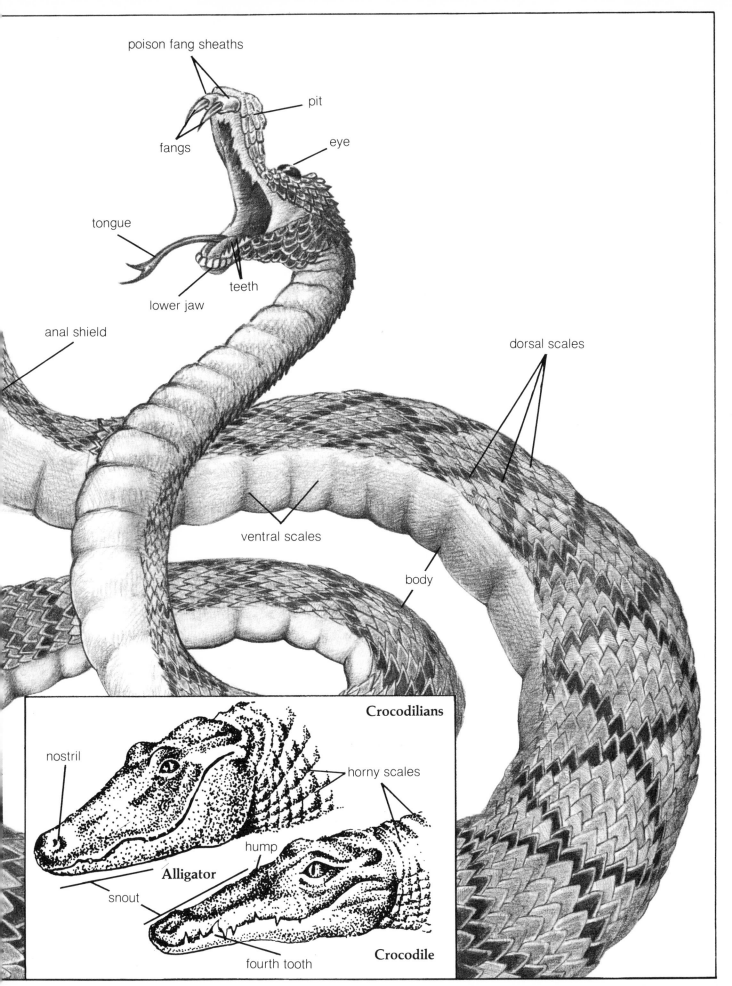

poison fang sheaths

fangs

pit

eye

tongue

lower jaw

teeth

anal shield

dorsal scales

ventral scales

body

Crocodilians

nostril

horny scales

hump

Alligator

snout

fourth tooth

Crocodile

Wild Animals

Amphibians

Frogs and toads resemble one another closely, but toads are characteristically more terrestrial and have rougher, drier skin.

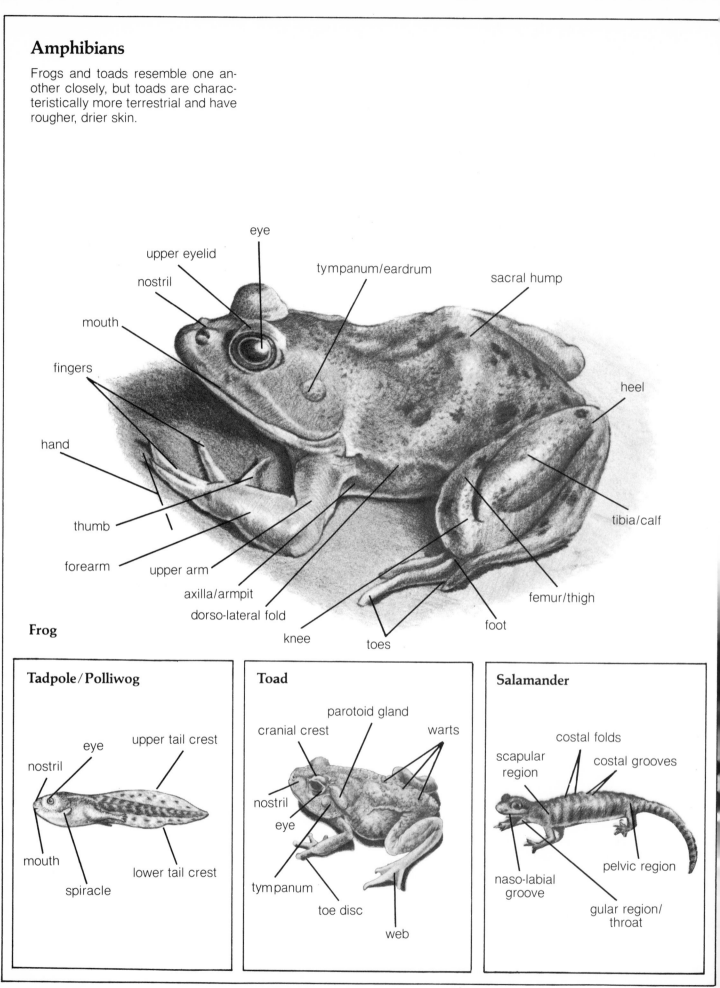

eye

upper eyelid

nostril

tympanum/eardrum

sacral hump

mouth

fingers

heel

hand

thumb

forearm

upper arm

tibia/calf

axilla/armpit

dorso-lateral fold

femur/thigh

Frog

knee

toes

foot

Tadpole/Polliwog

eye

upper tail crest

nostril

mouth

lower tail crest

spiracle

Toad

parotoid gland

cranial crest

warts

nostril

eye

tympanum

toe disc

web

Salamander

costal folds

scapular region

costal grooves

naso-labial groove

pelvic region

gular region/throat

Marine Life

Fish often swim in groups, called *schools,* and reproduce by depositing eggs, or *spawning.* Recently hatched or small adult fish are called *fry.*

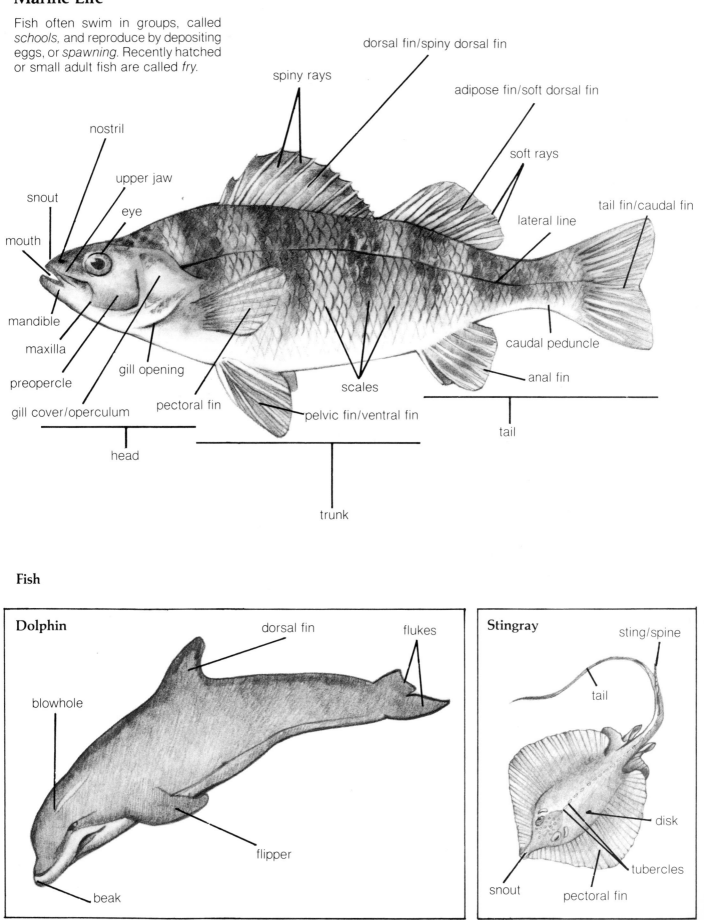

spiny rays

dorsal fin/spiny dorsal fin

adipose fin/soft dorsal fin

soft rays

tail fin/caudal fin

lateral line

nostril

upper jaw

snout

eye

mouth

mandible

maxilla

preopercle

gill opening

gill cover/operculum

pectoral fin

scales

pelvic fin/ventral fin

caudal peduncle

anal fin

tail

head

trunk

Fish

Dolphin

dorsal fin

flukes

blowhole

flipper

beak

Stingray

sting/spine

tail

disk

tubercles

snout

pectoral fin

Wild Animals

Marine Life

The *mantle* of an octopus is the tough protective wrapper that covers the body and gives it shape. Octopuses and squid have *chromatophores,* or *pigment cells,* which enable them to change color, as well as *ink glands,* or *sacs,* that secrete protective *"ink."* Starfish have *mouths* on their *oral surfaces.* Coral polyps live within limestone *skeletons,* which form the basis for *coral reefs.*

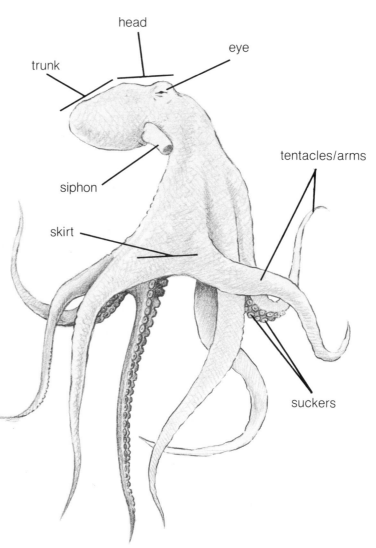

head
eye
trunk
tentacles/arms
siphon
skirt
suckers

Octopus / Devilfish

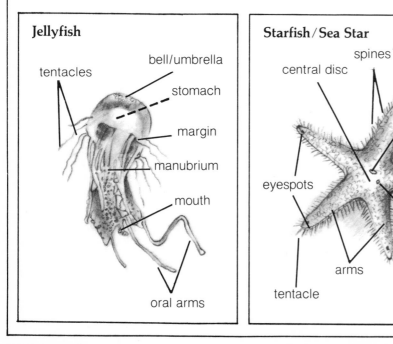

Jellyfish

tentacles
bell/umbrella
stomach
margin
manubrium
mouth
oral arms

Starfish / Sea Star

spines
central disc
madreporite
eyespots
anus
arms
tentacle

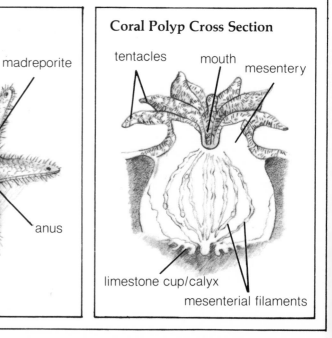

Coral Polyp Cross Section

tentacles
mouth
mesentery
limestone cup/calyx
mesenterial filaments

Shellfish

Lobsters with only one claw are called *culls,* and lobsters that have lost both claws are known as *pistols. Crustaceans,* such as lobsters, *crabs, shrimp, crayfish* and *barnacles,* are covered with a coating of *chitin,* which varies in hardness according to *lime* content. Scallops, clams, *snails, oysters* and *mussels* are *mollusks.* The study of mollusks is *malacology.* The study of shells only is *conchology.*

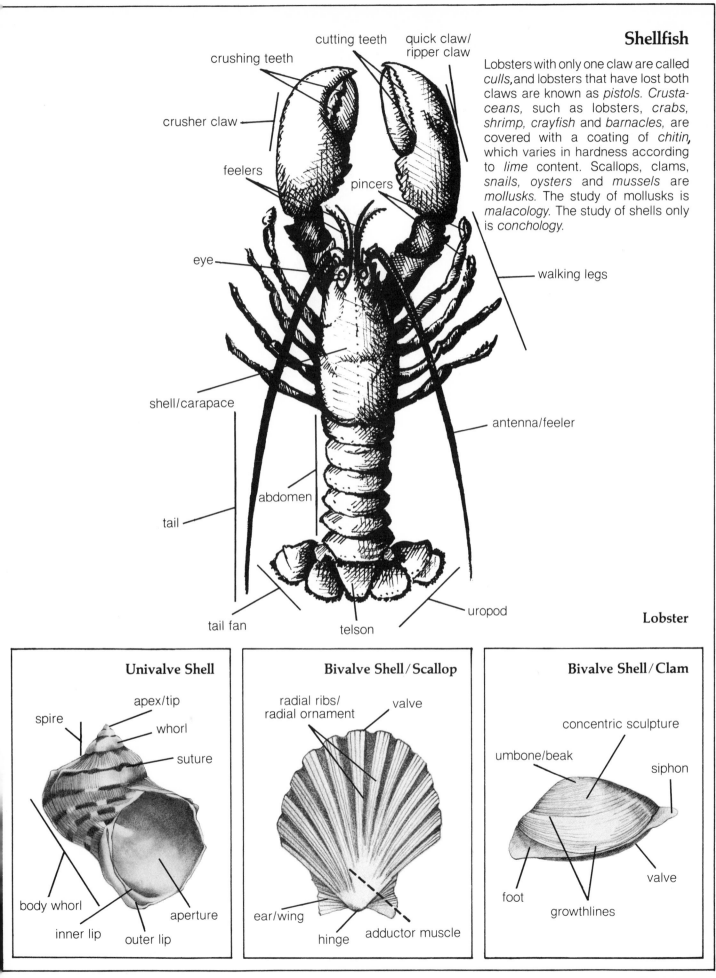

crushing teeth

cutting teeth

quick claw/ ripper claw

crusher claw

feelers

pincers

eye

walking legs

shell/carapace

antenna/feeler

tail

abdomen

tail fan

telson

uropod

Lobster

Univalve Shell

spire

apex/tip

whorl

suture

body whorl

inner lip

outer lip

aperture

Bivalve Shell/Scallop

radial ribs/ radial ornament

valve

ear/wing

hinge

adductor muscle

Bivalve Shell/Clam

concentric sculpture

umbone/beak

siphon

foot

growthlines

valve

Wild Animals

Ultimate Beast

This remarkable *creature* calls attention to those parts of animals which are distinctive to particular species. Missing are posterior extensions, or *tails,* which vary from long, thin tails that end in a *brush* and have a horny appendage called a *thorn* in the middle, such as a lion's, to brushy fox tails and stubby boar tails. Another composite animal is the legendary *manticore,* which combined the head of a man, the body of a lion, and the tail of a *dragon* or *scorpion.*

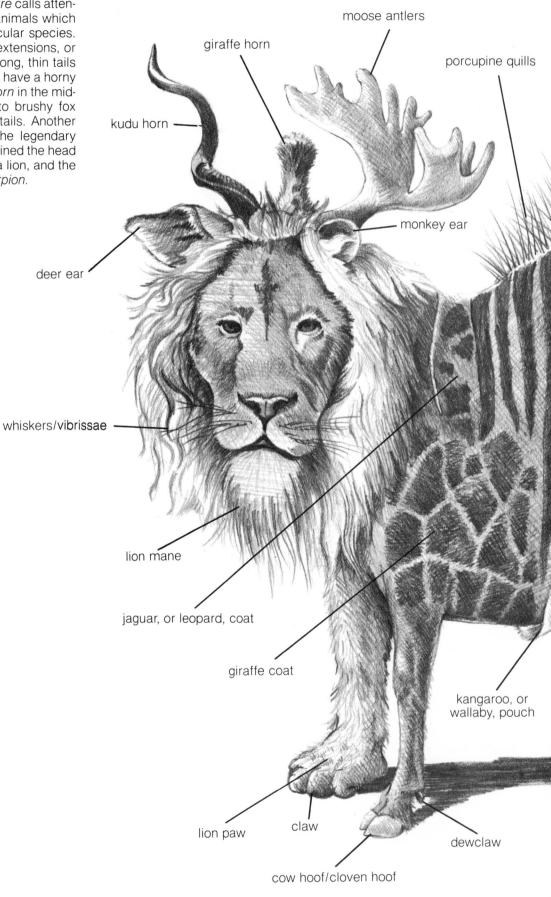

moose antlers

giraffe horn

porcupine quills

kudu horn

monkey ear

deer ear

whiskers/vibrissae

lion mane

jaguar, or leopard, coat

giraffe coat

kangaroo, or wallaby, pouch

lion paw

claw

dewclaw

cow hoof/cloven hoof

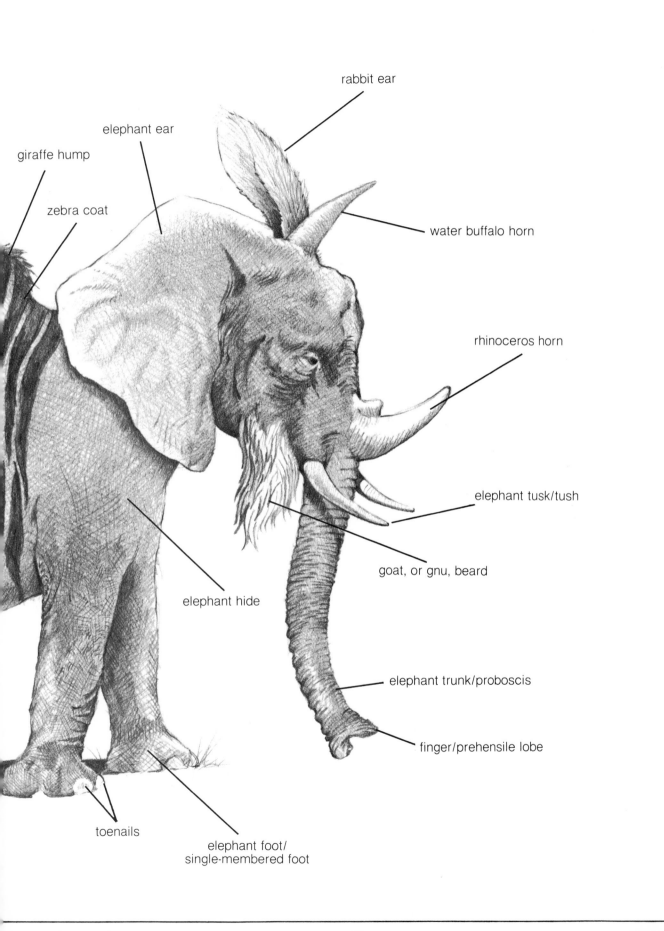

rabbit ear

elephant ear

giraffe hump

zebra coat

water buffalo horn

rhinoceros horn

elephant tusk/tush

goat, or gnu, beard

elephant hide

elephant trunk/proboscis

finger/prehensile lobe

toenails

elephant foot/
single-membered foot

Wild Animals

Tree

When a tree is cut down, what remains attached to the *root* is called a *stump*.

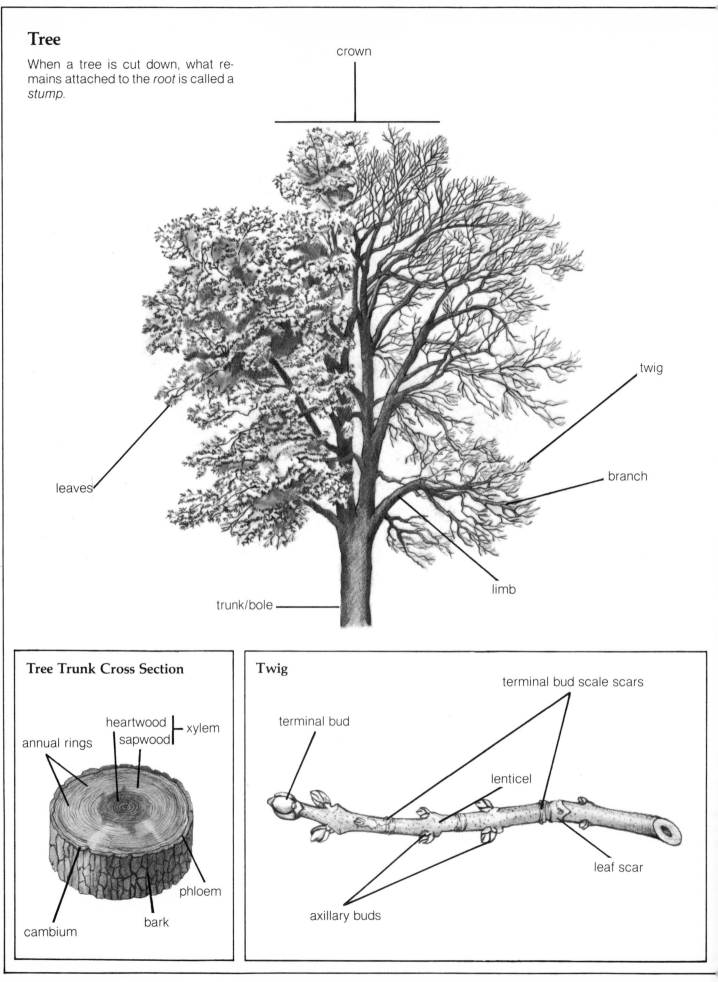

crown

twig

branch

leaves

limb

trunk/bole

Tree Trunk Cross Section

heartwood
sapwood
xylem

annual rings

phloem

cambium

bark

Twig

terminal bud scale scars

terminal bud

lenticel

leaf scar

axillary buds

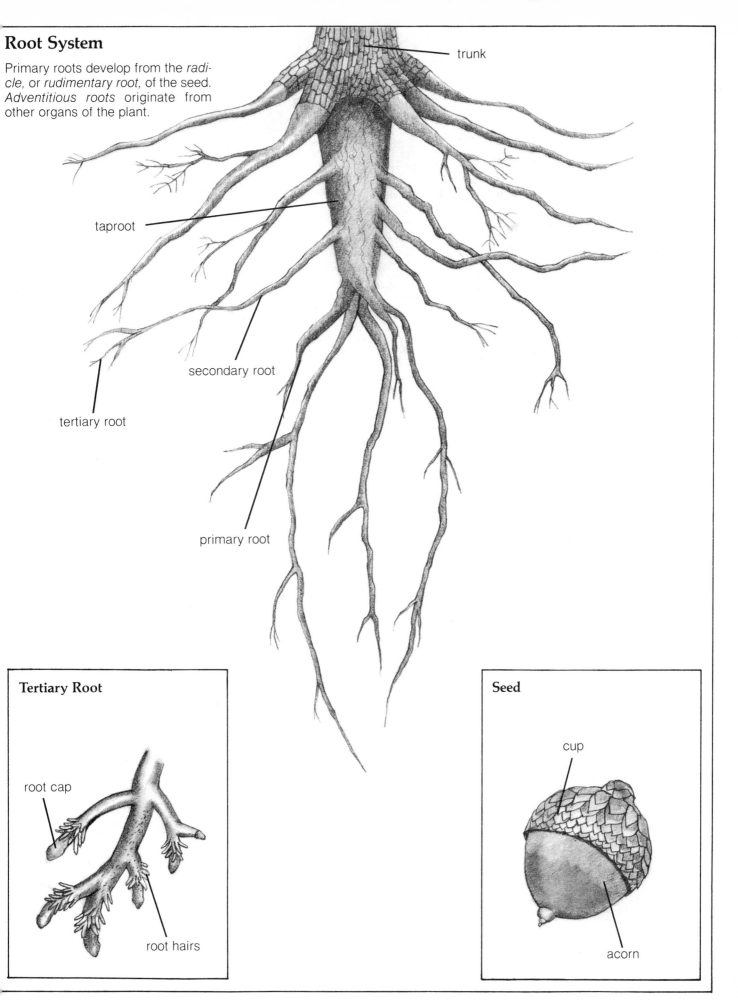

Root System

Primary roots develop from the *radicle*, or *rudimentary root*, of the seed. *Adventitious roots* originate from other organs of the plant.

trunk

taproot

secondary root

tertiary root

primary root

Tertiary Root

root cap

root hairs

Seed

cup

acorn

Plants

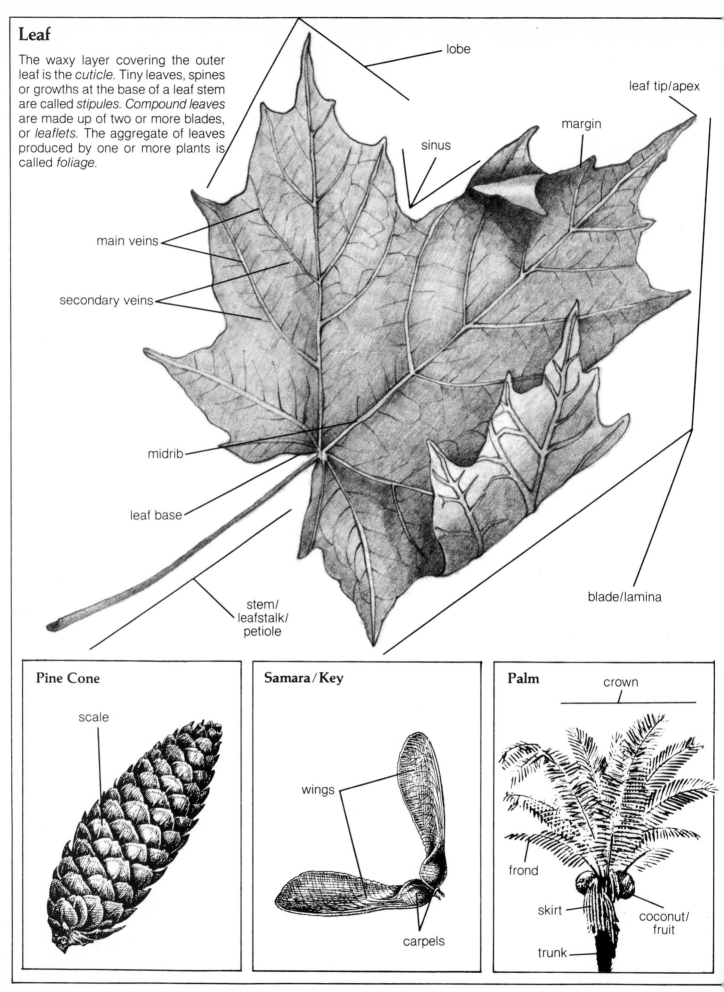

Leaf

The waxy layer covering the outer leaf is the *cuticle*. Tiny leaves, spines or growths at the base of a leaf stem are called *stipules*. *Compound leaves* are made up of two or more blades, or *leaflets*. The aggregate of leaves produced by one or more plants is called *foliage*.

lobe

leaf tip/apex

margin

sinus

main veins

secondary veins

midrib

leaf base

stem/ leafstalk/ petiole

blade/lamina

Pine Cone

scale

Samara/Key

wings

carpels

Palm

crown

frond

skirt

coconut/ fruit

trunk

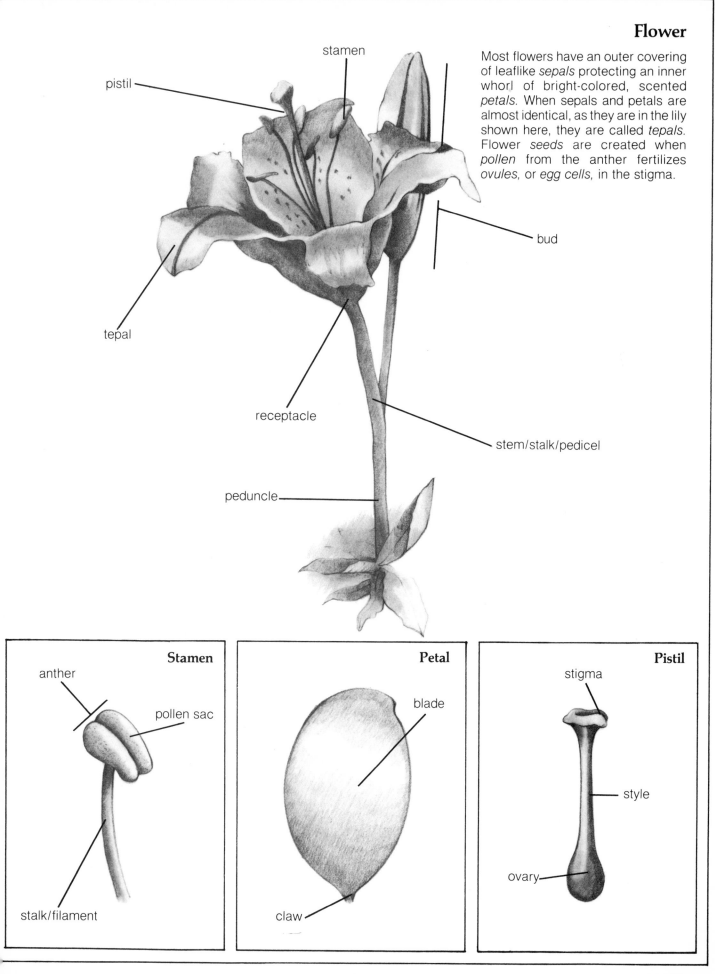

Flower

stamen

pistil

Most flowers have an outer covering of leaflike *sepals* protecting an inner whorl of bright-colored, scented *petals.* When sepals and petals are almost identical, as they are in the lily shown here, they are called *tepals.* Flower *seeds* are created when *pollen* from the anther fertilizes *ovules,* or *egg cells,* in the stigma.

bud

tepal

receptacle

stem/stalk/pedicel

peduncle

Stamen

anther

pollen sac

stalk/filament

Petal

blade

claw

Pistil

stigma

style

ovary

Plants

Vegetables

A vegetable is that part of a plant that can be eaten. The roots of carrots, beets and turnips are edible, as are asparagus stems, potato tubers, leek and onion leaf bases, cabbage, lettuce and spinach leaves, the *immature fruit,* or *ovary,* of cucumbers, peas and summer squash, and the *mature fruit* of tomatoes and winter squash.

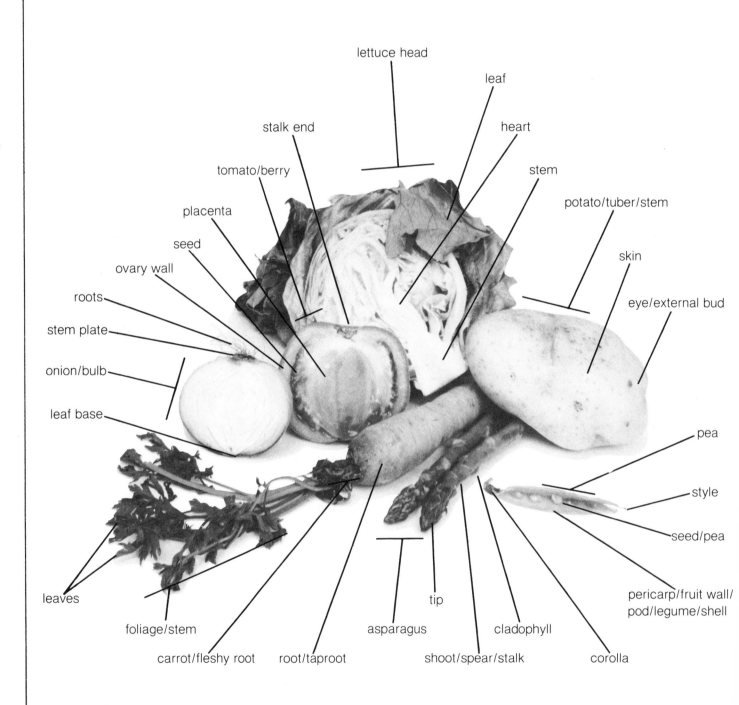

lettuce head

leaf

stalk end

heart

tomato/berry

stem

placenta

potato/tuber/stem

seed

skin

ovary wall

eye/external bud

roots

stem plate

onion/bulb

leaf base

pea

style

seed/pea

leaves

pericarp/fruit wall/
pod/legume/shell

foliage/stem

tip

asparagus

cladophyll

corolla

carrot/fleshy root

root/taproot

shoot/spear/stalk

Fruits

Nuts and crops commonly referred to as vegetables, such as tomatoes and melons, are actually *vegetable fruits*. Fruits are classed according to the number of ovaries they have: They range from simple fruits, such as peaches, to aggregate fruits, such as strawberries. Each segment of *multiple fruits,* such as pineapples and figs, is edible.

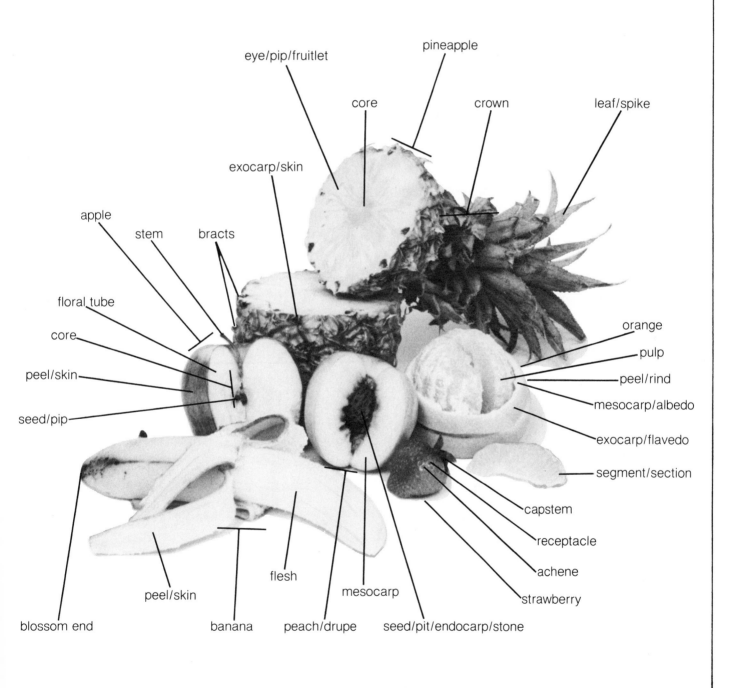

eye/pip/fruitlet

pineapple

core

crown

leaf/spike

exocarp/skin

apple

stem

bracts

floral tube

core

peel/skin

seed/pip

orange

pulp

peel/rind

mesocarp/albedo

exocarp/flavedo

segment/section

capstem

receptacle

achene

strawberry

blossom end

peel/skin

banana

flesh

mesocarp

peach/drupe

seed/pit/endocarp/stone

Plants

Succulents

Succulents are plants with *fleshy tissue* that have the ability to store moisture for long periods of time in their stem. Some cacti have protective *glochidia*, razor-sharp hairlike bristles, in addition to spines and flowers.

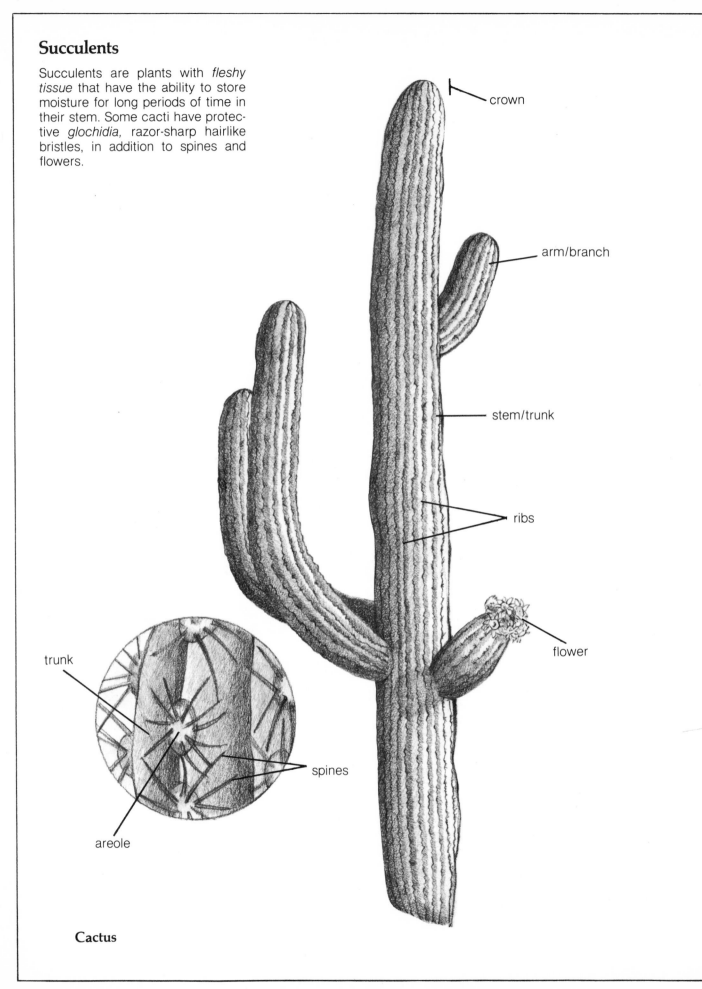

crown

arm/branch

stem/trunk

ribs

flower

trunk

spines

areole

Cactus

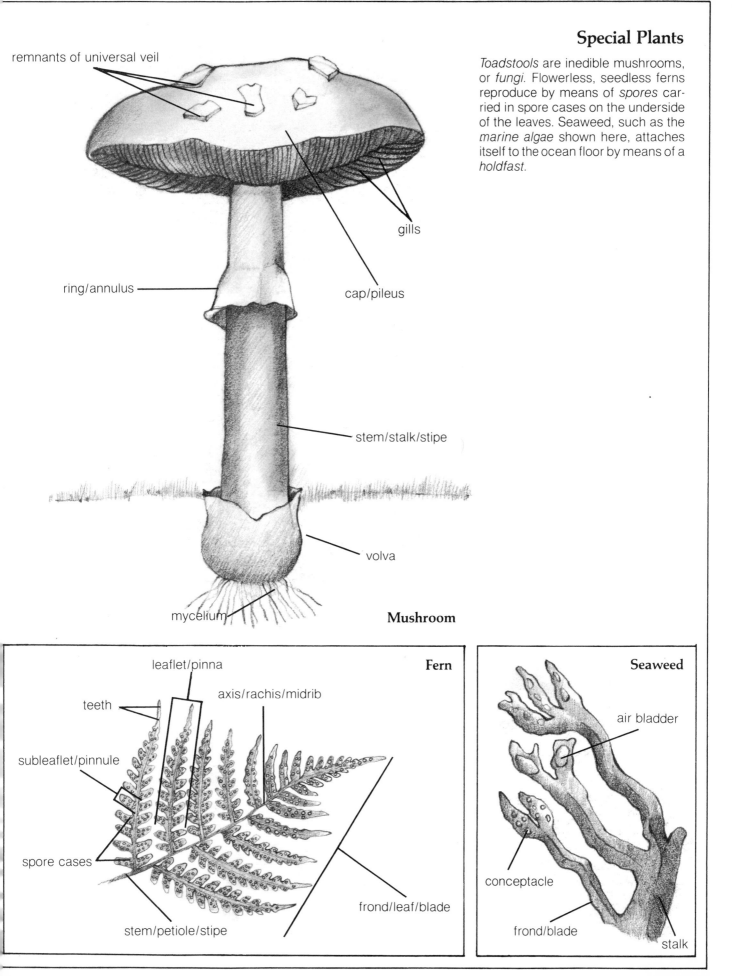

remnants of universal veil

Special Plants

Toadstools are inedible mushrooms, or *fungi*. Flowerless, seedless ferns reproduce by means of *spores* carried in spore cases on the underside of the leaves. Seaweed, such as the *marine algae* shown here, attaches itself to the ocean floor by means of a *holdfast*.

gills

ring/annulus

cap/pileus

stem/stalk/stipe

volva

mycelium

Mushroom

Fern

leaflet/pinna

teeth

axis/rachis/midrib

subleaflet/pinnule

spore cases

stem/petiole/stipe

frond/leaf/blade

Seaweed

air bladder

conceptacle

frond/blade

stalk

Plants

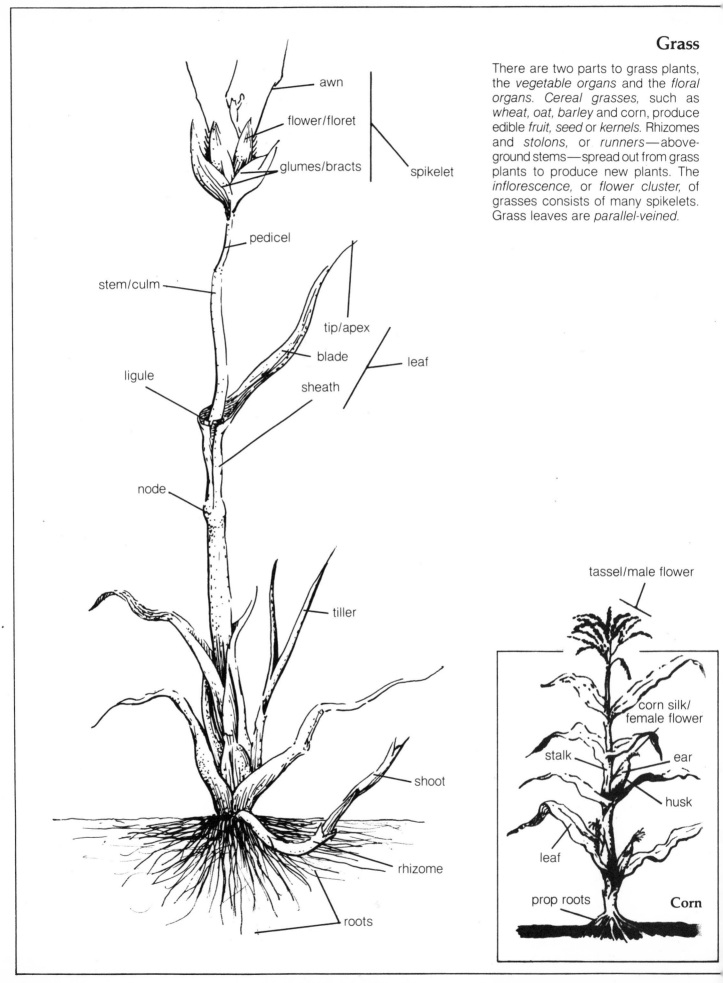

Grass

There are two parts to grass plants, the *vegetable organs* and the *floral organs*. *Cereal grasses*, such as *wheat, oat, barley* and corn, produce edible *fruit, seed* or *kernels.* Rhizomes and *stolons*, or *runners*—above-ground stems—spread out from grass plants to produce new plants. The *inflorescence*, or *flower cluster*, of grasses consists of many spikelets. Grass leaves are *parallel-veined.*

awn

flower/floret

glumes/bracts

spikelet

pedicel

stem/culm

tip/apex

blade

leaf

ligule

sheath

node

tiller

shoot

rhizome

roots

tassel/male flower

corn silk/ female flower

stalk

ear

husk

leaf

prop roots

Corn

Shelters and Structures

Since man's most basic shelter is a house, it is illustrated in a variety of ways, from foundation and frame to windows and walls.

The shelters and structures in the rest of the section are grouped in three subcategories: designs from other lands, which range from pagodas to pyramids; special-purpose buildings such as the Capitol and the White House, skyscrapers and prisons, amusement parks and airports; and other structures which bear on our everyday lives—bridges, tunnels, canals and dams.

The terms for the parts of objects found in most shelter interiors are the same as those found in a house, all of which have been illustrated. But those of a courtroom are sufficiently different to merit coverage, as are the parts of a skyscraper's elevator and escalator. In some cases floor plans and cross-section illustrations have been used to facilitate the reader's access to terms which are unique to a particular structure.

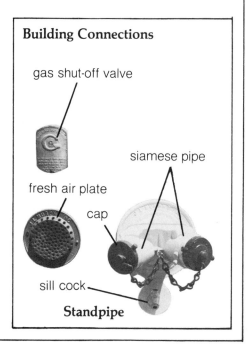

Building Connections

gas shut-off valve

siamese pipe

fresh air plate

cap

sill cock

Standpipe

Foundation

Some houses are built on sunken *posts,* or *piers.* Others are built on concrete floors, or *slabs.* The area of a house built below ground level is the *basement.* Houses without basements usually have an area between the floor joists and the ground called a *crawl space,* through which access is gained to inspect pipes.

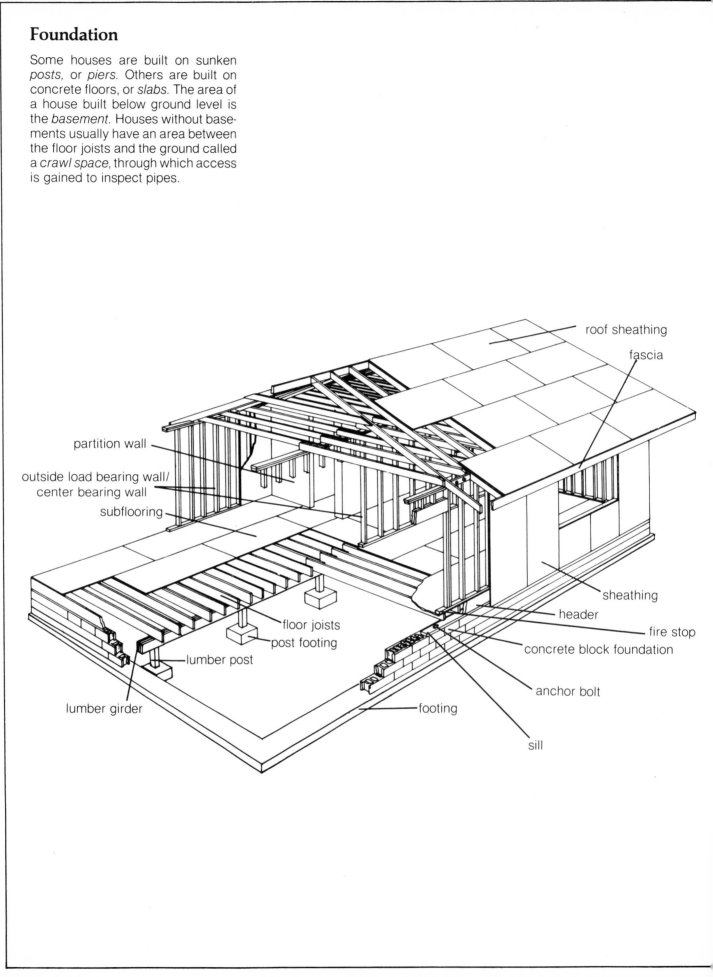

roof sheathing

fascia

partition wall

outside load bearing wall/ center bearing wall

subflooring

sheathing

header

fire stop

floor joists

post footing

concrete block foundation

lumber post

anchor bolt

lumber girder

footing

sill

Frame

Any diagonally placed piece of timber in a frame is a *brace.* A *cat* is a small piece of lumber nailed between studs for reinforcement. *Beams* are squared off pieces of timber, such as *joists,* used to support *floor* or *ceiling,* or *lintels,* horizontal *members* designed to carry loads above openings such as doors and windows.

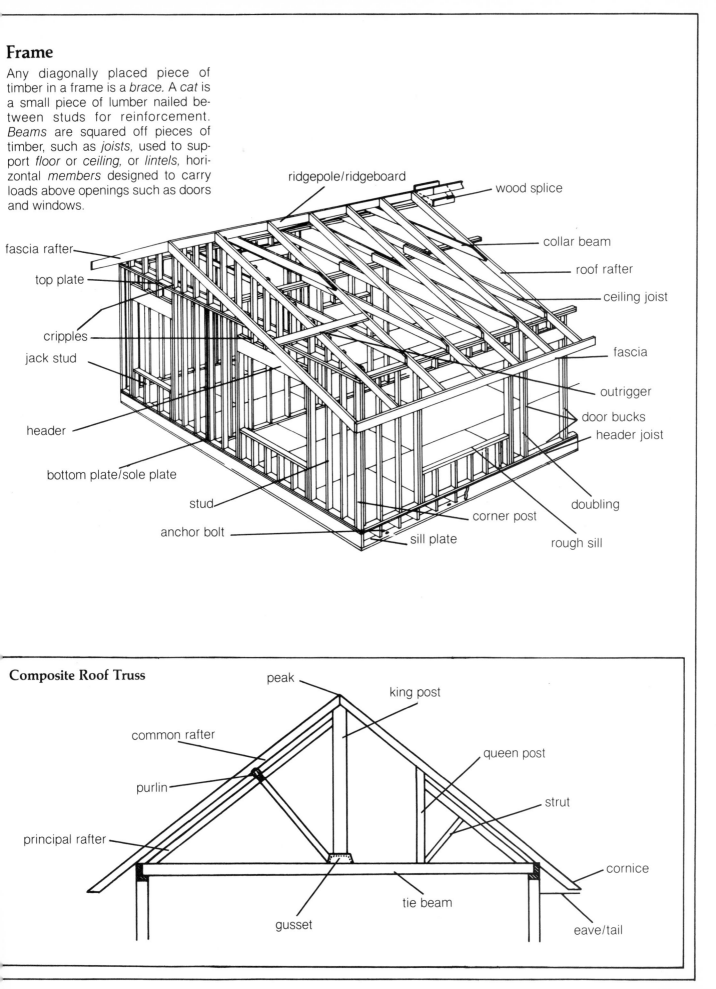

ridgepole/ridgeboard

wood splice

collar beam

fascia rafter

roof rafter

top plate

ceiling joist

cripples

fascia

jack stud

outrigger

door bucks

header

header joist

bottom plate/sole plate

stud

doubling

anchor bolt

corner post

sill plate

rough sill

Composite Roof Truss

peak

king post

common rafter

queen post

purlin

strut

principal rafter

cornice

gusset

tie beam

eave/tail

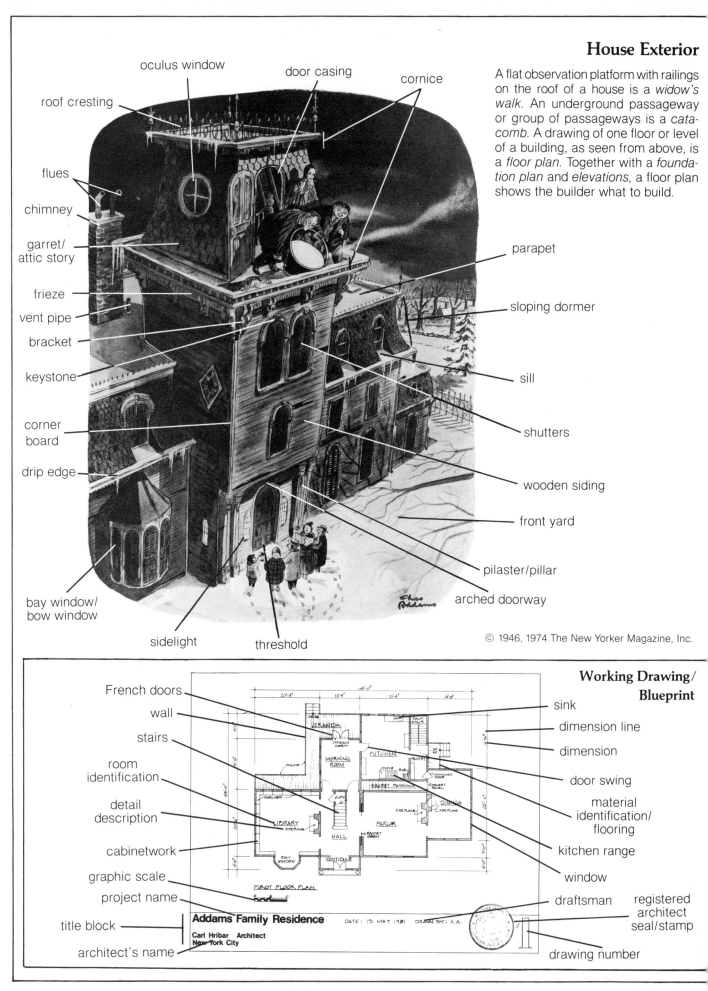

House Exterior

oculus window

door casing

roof cresting

cornice

flues

chimney

garret/attic story

frieze

vent pipe

bracket

keystone

corner board

drip edge

bay window/bow window

sidelight

threshold

parapet

sloping dormer

sill

shutters

wooden siding

front yard

pilaster/pillar

arched doorway

A flat observation platform with railings on the roof of a house is a *widow's walk*. An underground passageway or group of passageways is a *catacomb*. A drawing of one floor or level of a building, as seen from above, is a *floor plan*. Together with a *foundation plan* and *elevations*, a floor plan shows the builder what to build.

Working Drawing/Blueprint

French doors

wall

stairs

room identification

detail description

cabinetwork

graphic scale

project name

title block

architect's name

sink

dimension line

dimension

door swing

material identification/flooring

kitchen range

window

draftsman

registered architect seal/stamp

drawing number

Addams Family Residence

DATE: 15 MAY 1981 DRAWN BY: K.A.

Carl Hribar Architect
New York City

FIRST FLOOR PLAN

VERANDA

MORNING ROOM

KITCHEN

PANTRY

SECRET PASSAGE

LIBRARY

HALL

PARLOR

DINING

BAY WINDOW

VESTIBULE

House Exterior

The room or space under the roof is the *attic*. The lowest story of a house is called the *basement* if it is at least partly below ground or street level. A part of a house projecting on one side or subordinate to the main structure is called a *wing*. *Patios, terraces, decks* and *porches* adjoin a house and are used for play or relaxation. An open *gallery* alongside a house with its own roof is a *veranda*. The trees, shrubs, paths and gardens around a house are called *landscaping*.

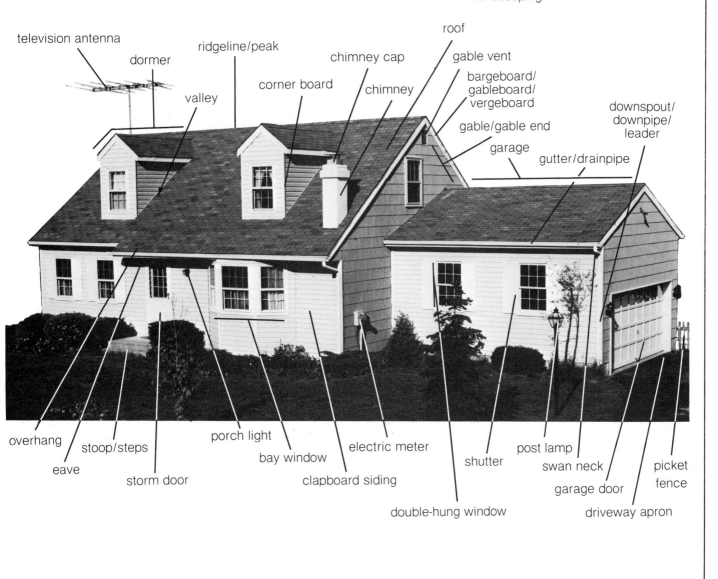

television antenna

dormer

ridgeline/peak

valley

corner board

chimney cap

chimney

roof

gable vent

bargeboard/
gableboard/
vergeboard

gable/gable end

garage

downspout/
downpipe/
leader

gutter/drainpipe

overhang

eave

stoop/steps

storm door

porch light

bay window

clapboard siding

electric meter

double-hung window

shutter

post lamp

swan neck

garage door

picket
fence

driveway apron

Door

The *sill*, *threshold*, or *saddle* is that part directly beneath the door. Entrance doors are often covered by *screendoors*. A door cut in half horizontally whose two parts can be used independently is called a *Dutch door*. A door having glass panes throughout or nearly throughout its length is a *French door*. The rubber-tipped projection attached to the wall behind an opening door to protect it from the impact is a *doorstop*.

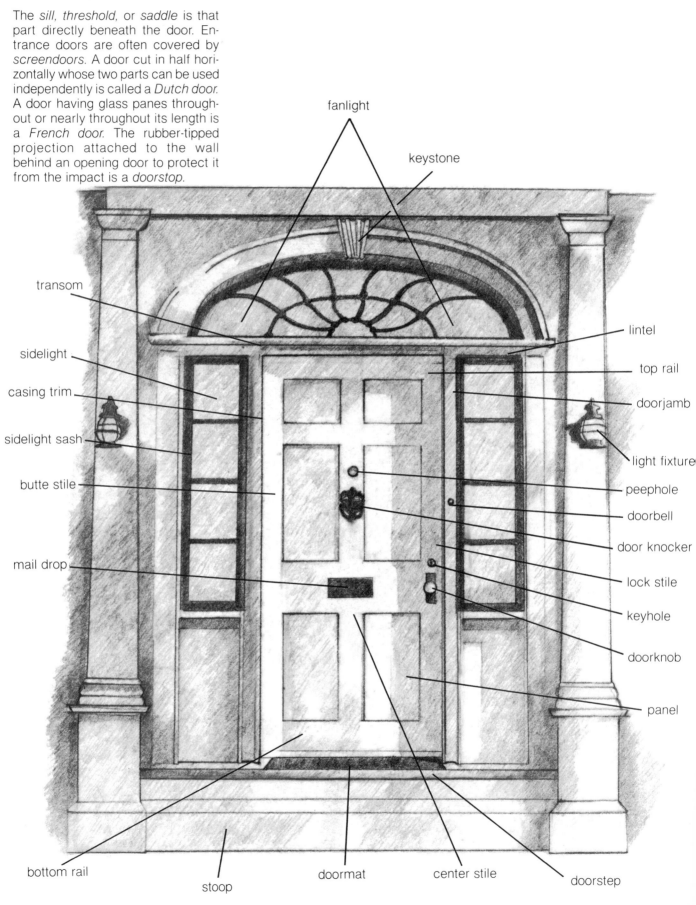

fanlight

keystone

transom

sidelight

casing trim

sidelight sash

butte stile

mail drop

lintel

top rail

doorjamb

light fixture

peephole

doorbell

door knocker

lock stile

keyhole

doorknob

panel

bottom rail

stoop

doormat

center stile

doorstep

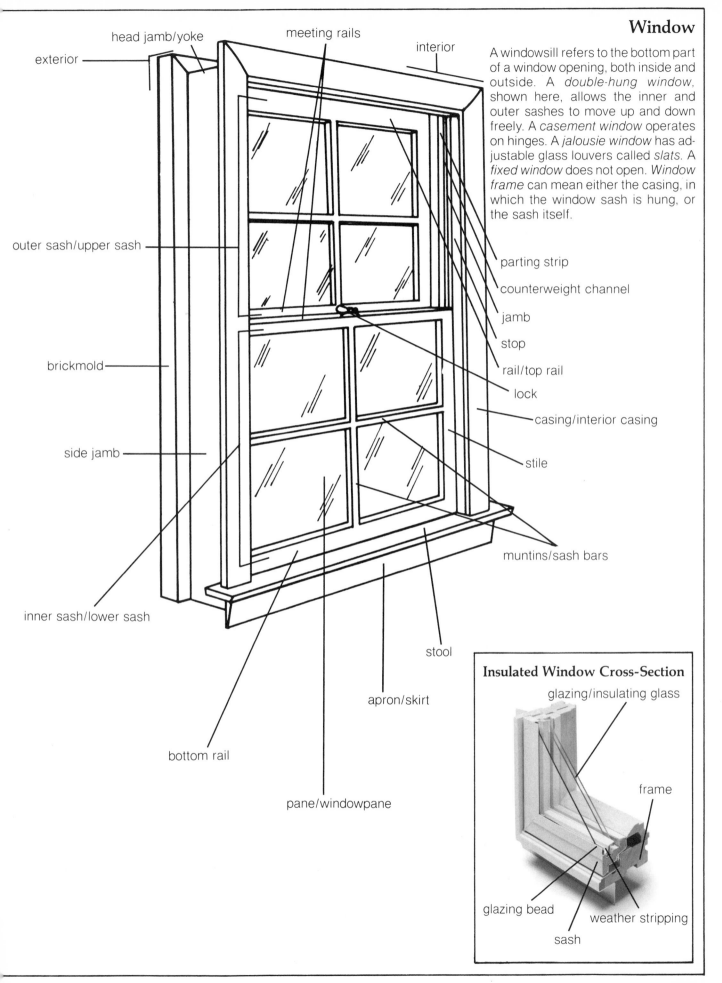

Window

head jamb/yoke

exterior

meeting rails

interior

A windowsill refers to the bottom part of a window opening, both inside and outside. A *double-hung window*, shown here, allows the inner and outer sashes to move up and down freely. A *casement window* operates on hinges. A *jalousie window* has adjustable glass louvers called *slats*. A *fixed window* does not open. *Window frame* can mean either the casing, in which the window sash is hung, or the sash itself.

parting strip

counterweight channel

jamb

stop

rail/top rail

lock

casing/interior casing

stile

outer sash/upper sash

brickmold

side jamb

inner sash/lower sash

muntins/sash bars

stool

bottom rail

apron/skirt

pane/windowpane

Insulated Window Cross-Section

glazing/insulating glass

frame

glazing bead

weather stripping

sash

House

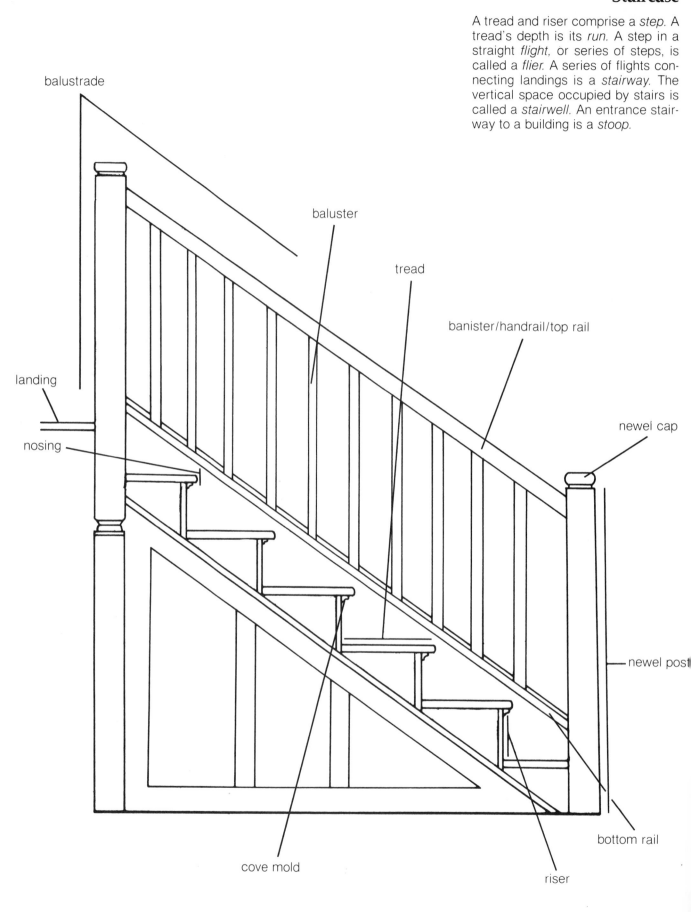

Staircase

A tread and riser comprise a *step*. A tread's depth is its *run*. A step in a straight *flight*, or series of steps, is called a *flier*. A series of flights connecting landings is a *stairway*. The vertical space occupied by stairs is called a *stairwell*. An entrance stairway to a building is a *stoop*.

balustrade

baluster

tread

banister/handrail/top rail

landing

newel cap

nosing

newel post

cove mold

bottom rail

riser

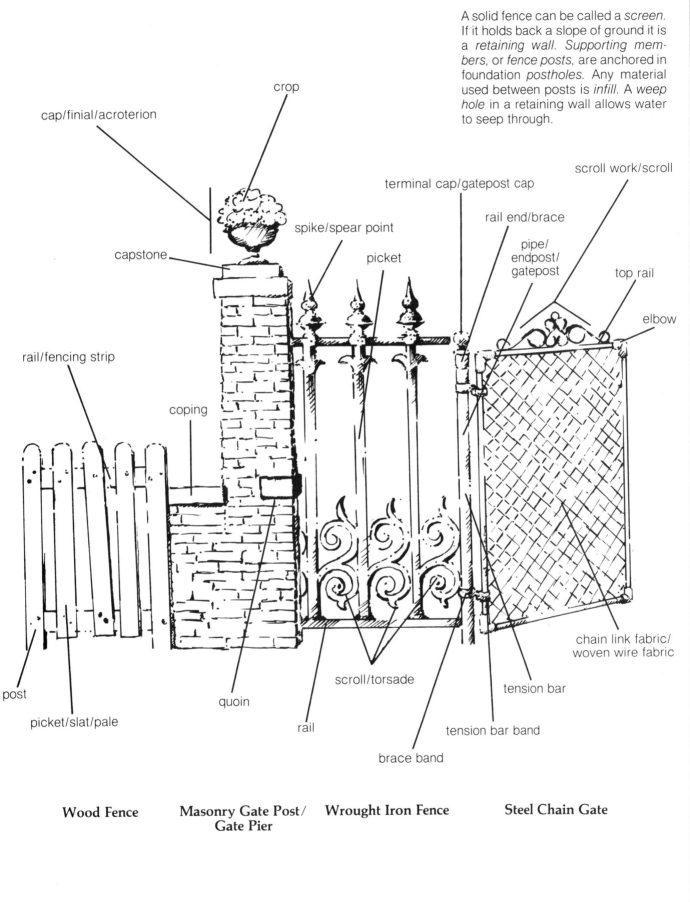

Fence

A solid fence can be called a *screen*. If it holds back a slope of ground it is a *retaining wall*. *Supporting members*, or *fence posts*, are anchored in foundation *postholes*. Any material used between posts is *infill*. A *weep hole* in a retaining wall allows water to seep through.

crop

cap/finial/acroterion

capstone

scroll work/scroll

terminal cap/gatepost cap

rail end/brace

spike/spear point

pipe/ endpost/ gatepost

picket

top rail

elbow

rail/fencing strip

coping

post

picket/slat/pale

quoin

rail

scroll/torsade

brace band

tension bar band

tension bar

chain link fabric/ woven wire fabric

Wood Fence   **Masonry Gate Post/ Gate Pier**   **Wrought Iron Fence**   **Steel Chain Gate**

Building Materials

Boards are *timber,* or lumber, cut in long, flat *slabs.* When used in construction, boards are referred to as *beams,* or *balks.* When they are used to support a pitched roof, they are called *rafters.* A *plank* is thicker than a board. *Shakes* are *wooden shingles,* but cracks in wood caused by wind or frost are also called shakes. A *spall* is a chip or flaking of brick.

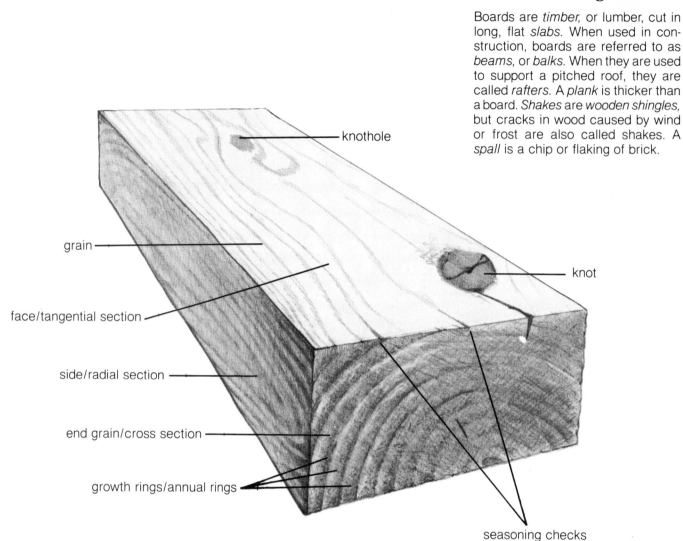

knothole

grain

knot

face/tangential section

side/radial section

end grain/cross section

growth rings/annual rings

seasoning checks

Lumber

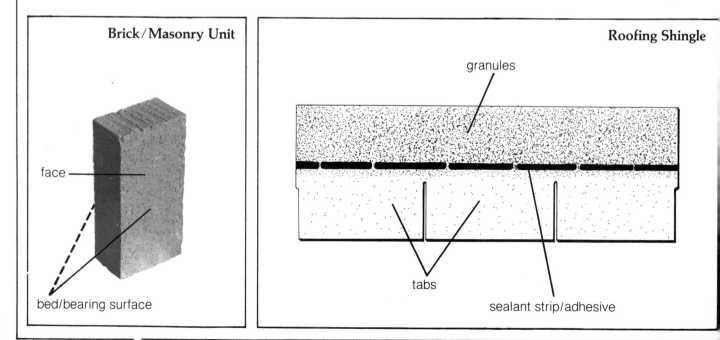

Brick/Masonry Unit

face

bed/bearing surface

Roofing Shingle

granules

tabs

sealant strip/adhesive

Brick Wall

Bricks and brick faces take on different names, depending on where and how they are used or exposed. Structures built of *stone* or brick are called *masonry.* The pattern in which a wall is laid is its *bond.* The exposed surface is the *face.* A piece of iron or steel used to brace a wall is a *cramp,* while a recess left within for pipes or ducts is a *chase.* A *tie* is any material that holds masonry together.

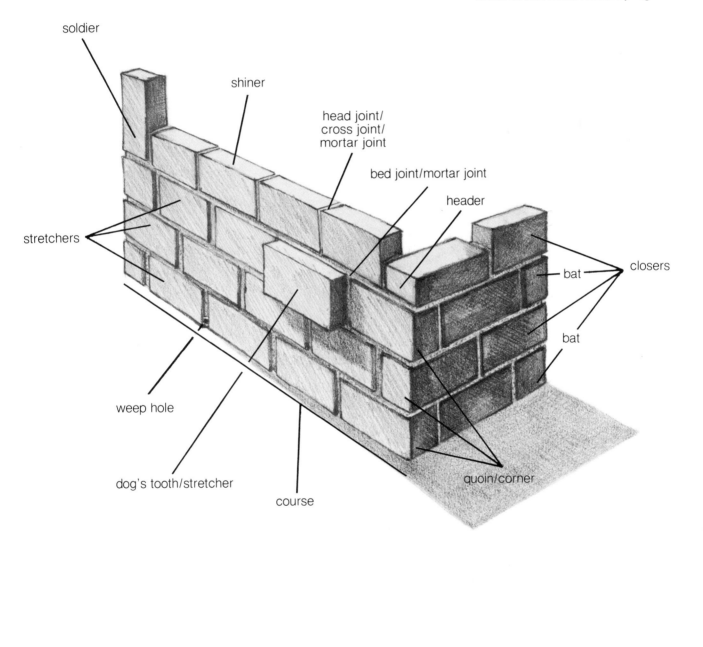

soldier

shiner

head joint/
cross joint/
mortar joint

bed joint/mortar joint

header

stretchers

closers

bat

bat

weep hole

dog's tooth/stretcher

course

quoin/corner

International Architecture

The Japanese developed the *whole-timbered building,* with *interlocking timbered joints.* Minarets, from which *criers,* or *muezzins,* call people to prayer, are normally attached or annexed to a mosque. Obelisks were often surrounded by *pillars,* or stelae, erected in honor of gods. Pyramids, *quadrilateral structures,* were used as tombs or temples. Flat-topped pyramids called *mastabas* were strictly *funerary structures,* while *zig-gurats,* stepped pyramids supporting a *shrine,* were used for worship.

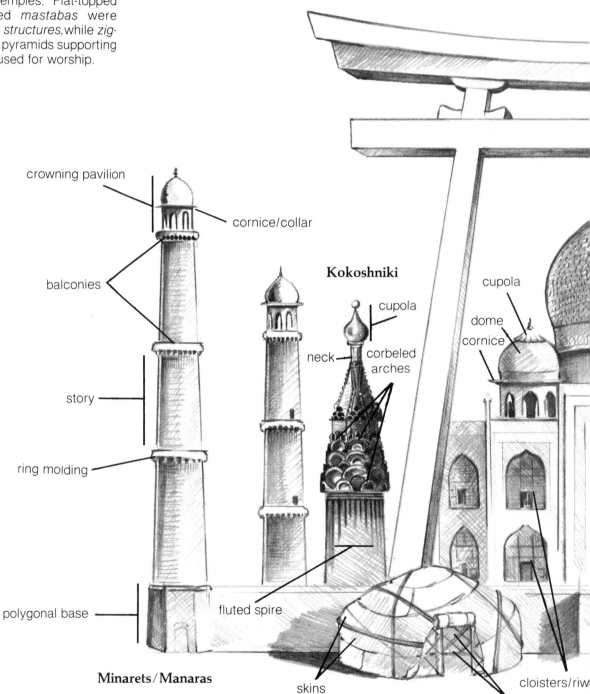

Torii/Shinto Temple Gateway

crowning pavilion

cornice/collar

balconies

Kokoshniki

cupola

neck

corbeled arches

cupola

dome

cornice

story

ring molding

fluted spire

polygonal base

skins

framework

cloisters/riw

Minarets/Manaras

Yurt

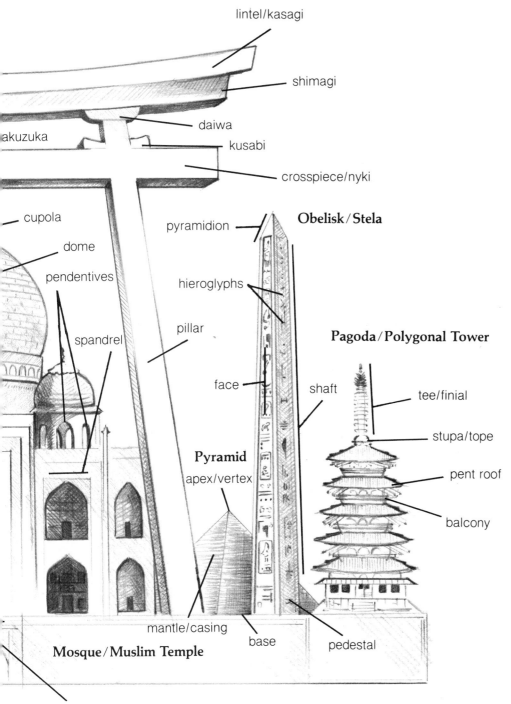

lintel/kasagi

shimagi

daiwa

akuzuka

kusabi

crosspiece/nyki

cupola

dome

pendentives

spandrel

pillar

pyramidion

Obelisk / Stela

hieroglyphs

Pagoda / Polygonal Tower

face

shaft

tee/finial

stupa/tope

pent roof

balcony

Pyramid

apex/vertex

mantle/casing

base

pedestal

Mosque / Muslim Temple

prayer hall/liwan/
main sanctuary

Arch

The distance between the imposts is called the *span*. The *rise* is the distance between the top of the imposts and the highest point of the intrados. The *crown* is the highest point of the extrados. The area of an arch extending from the crown to the impost is the *haunch*, or *hance*.

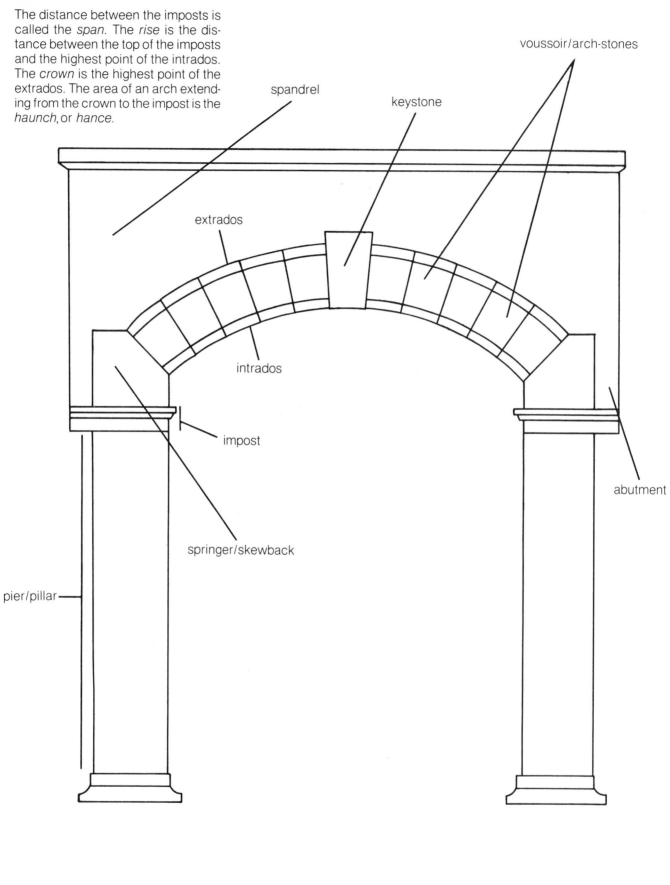

spandrel

keystone

voussoir/arch-stones

extrados

intrados

impost

abutment

springer/skewback

pier/pillar

Column

The clear space between two columns is *intercolumniation*.

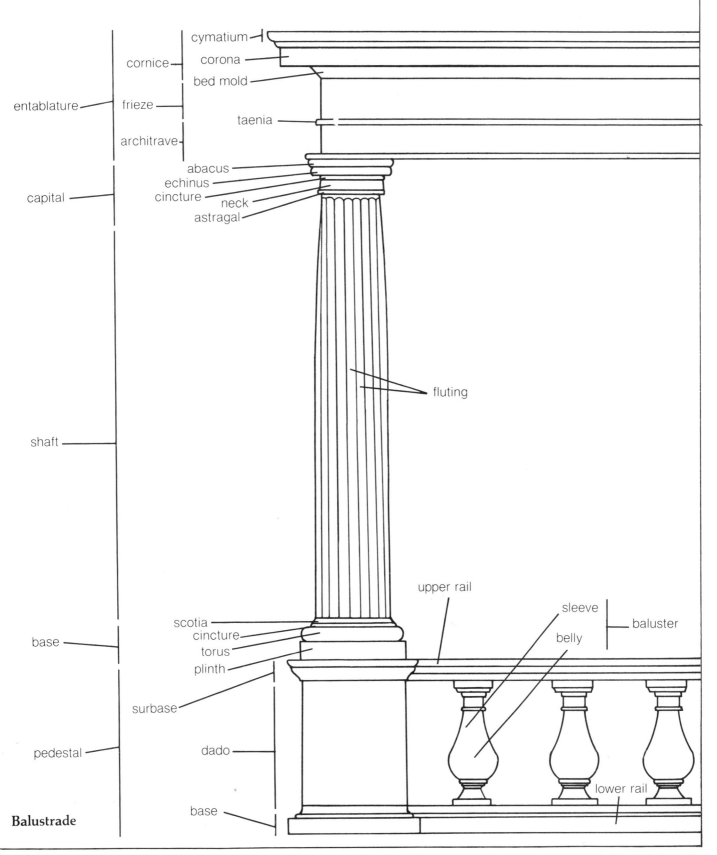

cymatium

cornice

corona

bed mold

entablature

frieze

taenia

architrave

abacus

echinus

capital

cincture

neck

astragal

fluting

shaft

upper rail

sleeve

scotia

baluster

cincture

base

torus

belly

plinth

surbase

pedestal

dado

base

lower rail

Balustrade

Architectural Designs from Other Lands

Capitol

The first floor of the Capitol contains the *Hall of Columns, House* and *Senate corridors, committee rooms, restaurants, transportation offices* and a *post office.* When the House is called to order, the *Mace of the House of Representatives* is placed on a cylindrical *pedestal* to the right of the Speaker's desk. On the Senate side is a *chandelier* with two bulbs below it. The red one indicates an executive session; the white, a regular session. Visitors to the chambers of Congress sit in *galleries.*

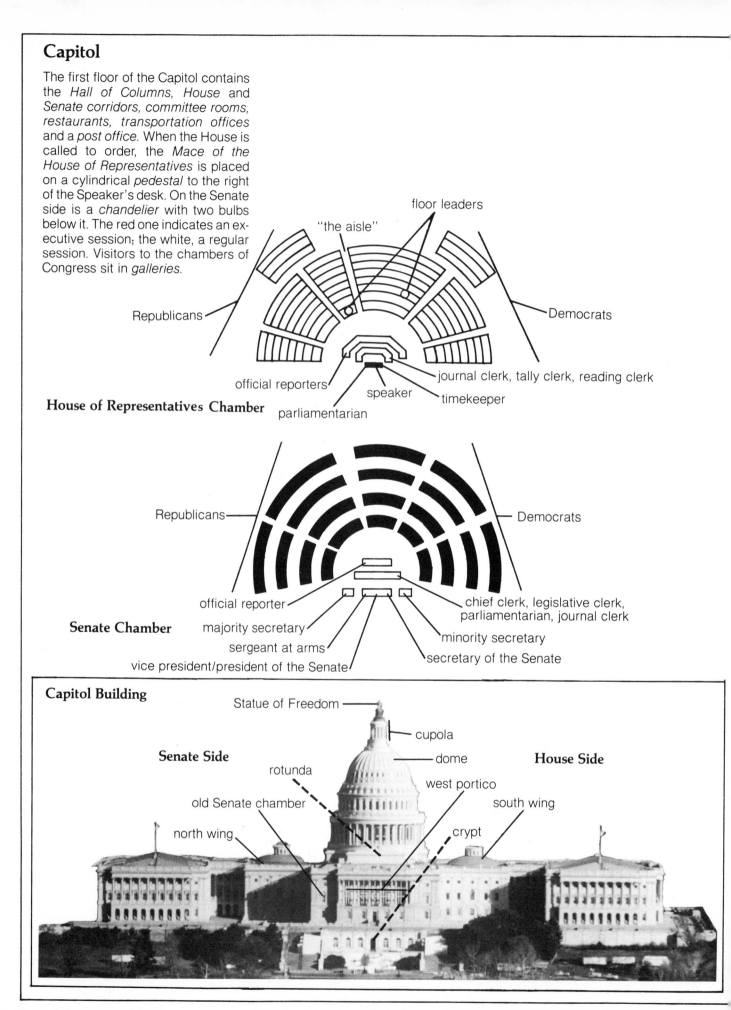

"the aisle"

floor leaders

Republicans

Democrats

official reporters

speaker

journal clerk, tally clerk, reading clerk

timekeeper

parliamentarian

House of Representatives Chamber

Republicans

Democrats

official reporter

majority secretary

sergeant at arms

vice president/president of the Senate

chief clerk, legislative clerk, parliamentarian, journal clerk

minority secretary

secretary of the Senate

Senate Chamber

Capitol Building

Statue of Freedom

cupola

dome

Senate Side

House Side

rotunda

west portico

old Senate chamber

south wing

north wing

crypt

White House

The White House, a historic *mansion* that serves as the President's *home* and *office,* contains *portraits, antiques* and *memorabilia.* In addition to the rooms and offices shown here, there is a bombproof *command post* in the cellar and a *helipad* on the south lawn.

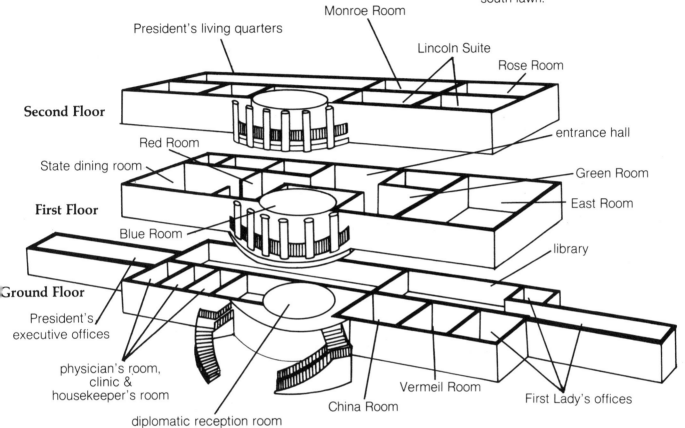

Second Floor

President's living quarters
Monroe Room
Lincoln Suite
Rose Room
entrance hall

First Floor

Red Room
State dining room
Green Room
East Room
Blue Room
library

Ground Floor

President's executive offices
physician's room, clinic & housekeeper's room
diplomatic reception room
China Room
Vermeil Room
First Lady's offices

House Plan

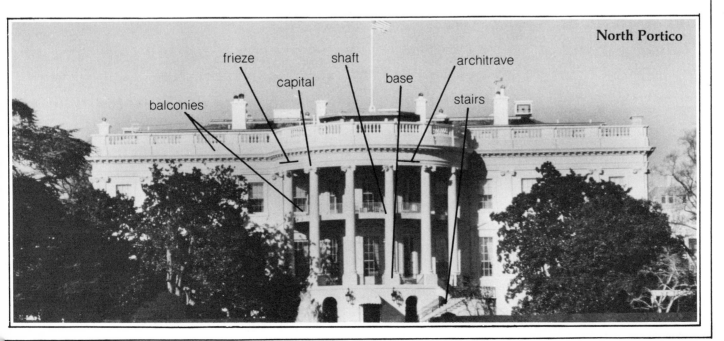

balconies
frieze
capital
shaft
base
architrave
stairs

Special Purpose Buildings

Prison

Maximum security prisons, such as the one seen here, are characterized by high *walls, armed guards* and *security checkpoints. Minimum security prisons* may be surrounded by *chainlink fences* and have *security systems* that are largely electronic, with *doors, alarms, TV monitors* and *intercoms* monitored by *central computers. Prisoners,* or *inmates,* in all *correctional facilities,* including *jails,* live in *cells* with *barred doors.*

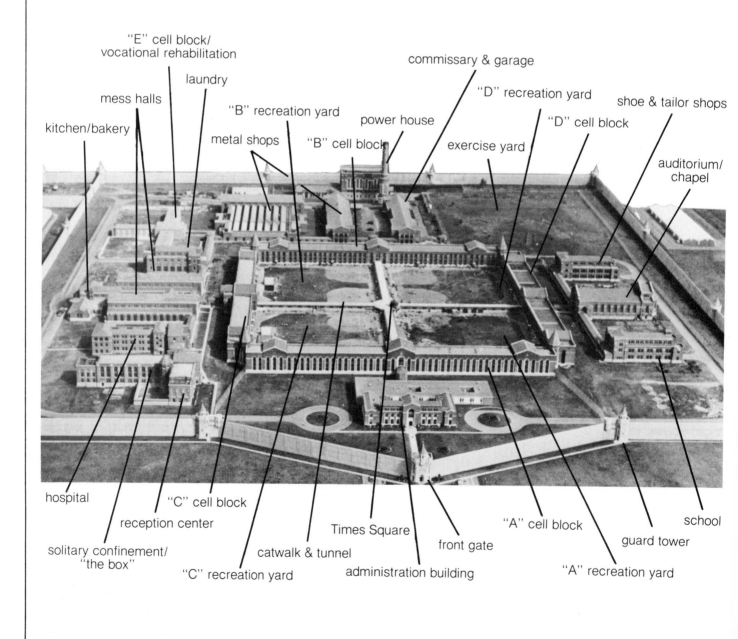

"E" cell block/ vocational rehabilitation

laundry

commissary & garage

"D" recreation yard

mess halls

"B" recreation yard

shoe & tailor shops

kitchen/bakery

metal shops

power house

"D" cell block

"B" cell block

exercise yard

auditorium/ chapel

hospital

"C" cell block

Times Square

"A" cell block

school

reception center

front gate

guard tower

solitary confinement/ "the box"

catwalk & tunnel

administration building

"A" recreation yard

"C" recreation yard

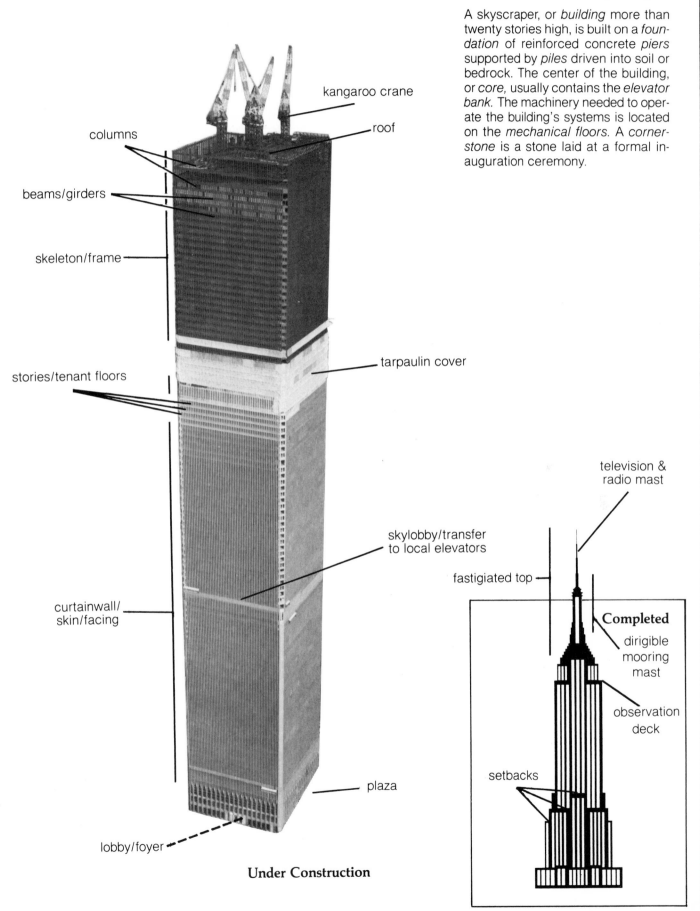

Skyscraper

A skyscraper, or *building* more than twenty stories high, is built on a *foundation* of reinforced concrete *piers* supported by *piles* driven into soil or bedrock. The center of the building, or *core,* usually contains the *elevator bank.* The machinery needed to operate the building's systems is located on the *mechanical floors.* A *cornerstone* is a stone laid at a formal inauguration ceremony.

kangaroo crane

columns

roof

beams/girders

skeleton/frame

tarpaulin cover

stories/tenant floors

television & radio mast

fastigiated top

Completed

skylobby/transfer to local elevators

dirigible mooring mast

observation deck

curtainwall/ skin/facing

setbacks

plaza

lobby/foyer

Under Construction

Special Purpose Buildings

Elevator

There is padding which makes up the *safety edges* on the *shafts,* or inner-most sides, of elevator doors. Most elevator cars have *emergency top exits* in the *canopy* or real ceiling as well as *service cabinets* which contain *fan switches, light* and *start switches.* An individual who directs people to the next available car in a *bank* of elevators is called a *starter.*

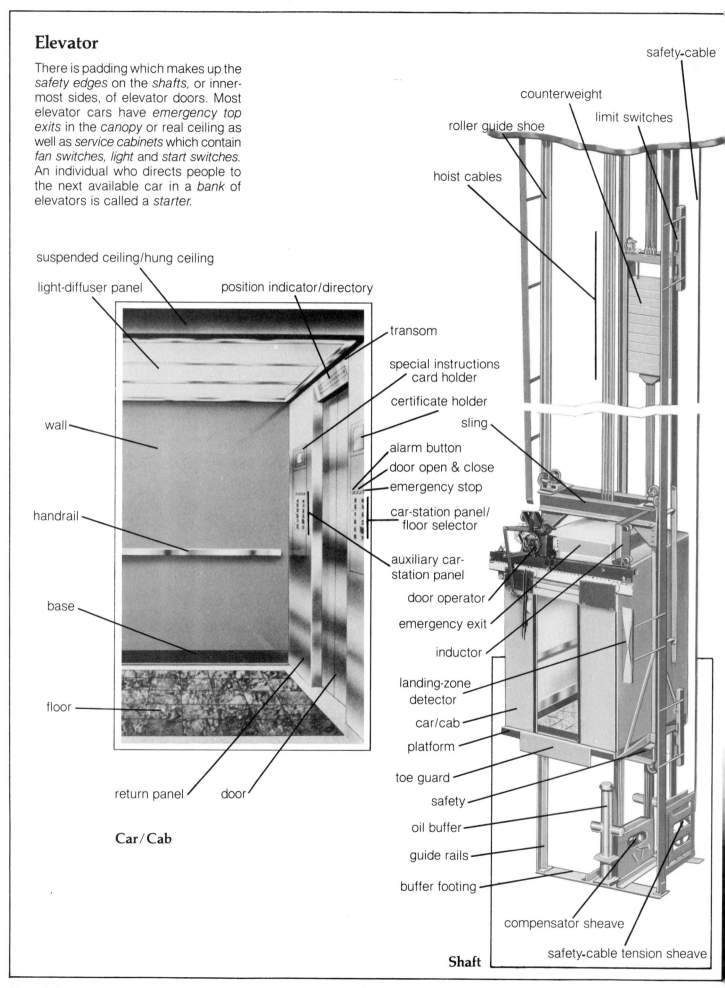

suspended ceiling/hung ceiling

light-diffuser panel

position indicator/directory

transom

special instructions card holder

certificate holder

wall

alarm button

door open & close

emergency stop

car-station panel/floor selector

handrail

auxiliary car-station panel

base

door operator

emergency exit

inductor

landing-zone detector

car/cab

platform

toe guard

safety

oil buffer

floor

guide rails

buffer footing

return panel

door

Car/Cab

safety-cable

counterweight

limit switches

roller guide shoe

hoist cables

sling

compensator sheave

safety-cable tension sheave

Shaft

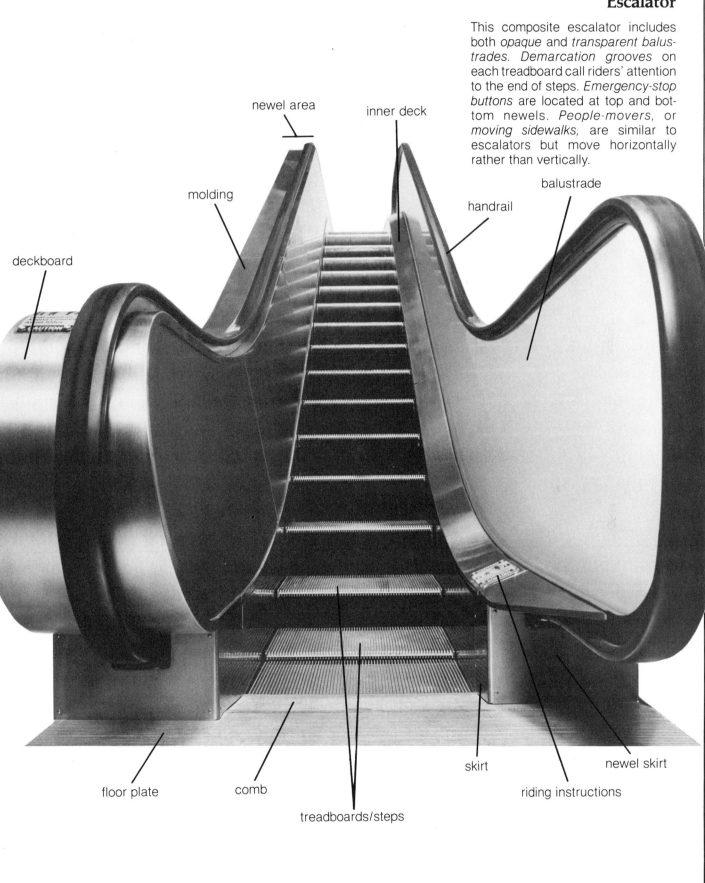

Escalator

This composite escalator includes both *opaque* and *transparent balustrades*. *Demarcation grooves* on each treadboard call riders' attention to the end of steps. *Emergency-stop buttons* are located at top and bottom newels. *People-movers*, or *moving sidewalks*, are similar to escalators but move horizontally rather than vertically.

newel area

inner deck

molding

balustrade

handrail

deckboard

skirt

newel skirt

floor plate

comb

riding instructions

treadboards/steps

Special Purpose Buildings

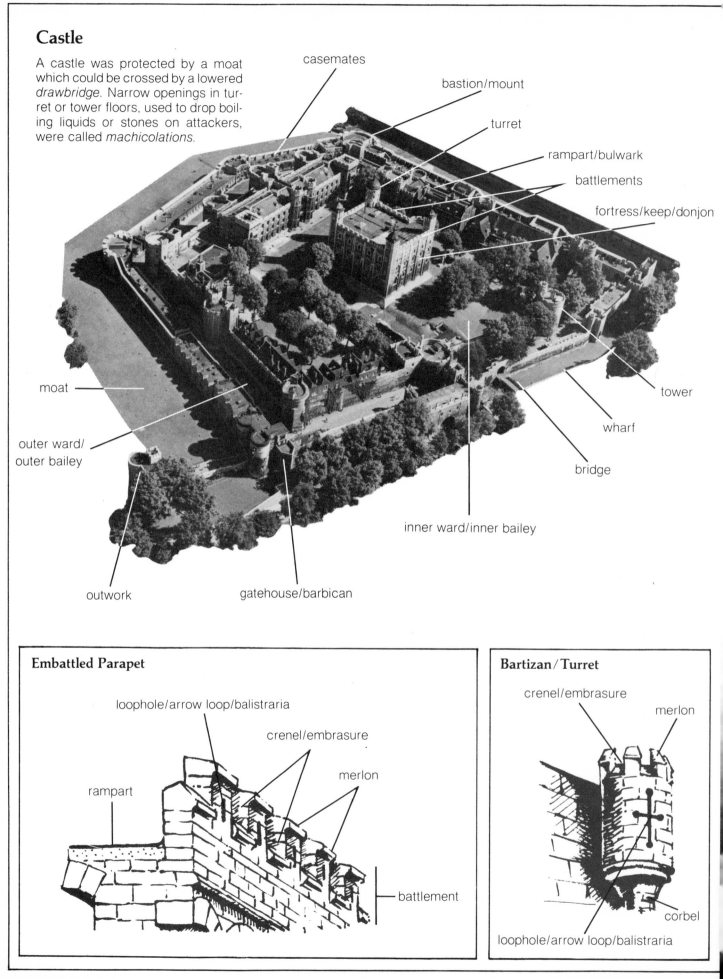

Castle

A castle was protected by a moat which could be crossed by a lowered *drawbridge*. Narrow openings in turret or tower floors, used to drop boiling liquids or stones on attackers, were called *machicolations*.

casemates

bastion/mount

turret

rampart/bulwark

battlements

fortress/keep/donjon

tower

wharf

bridge

inner ward/inner bailey

moat

outer ward/
outer bailey

outwork

gatehouse/barbican

Embattled Parapet

loophole/arrow loop/balistraria

crenel/embrasure

merlon

rampart

battlement

Bartizan/Turret

crenel/embrasure

merlon

corbel

loophole/arrow loop/balistraria

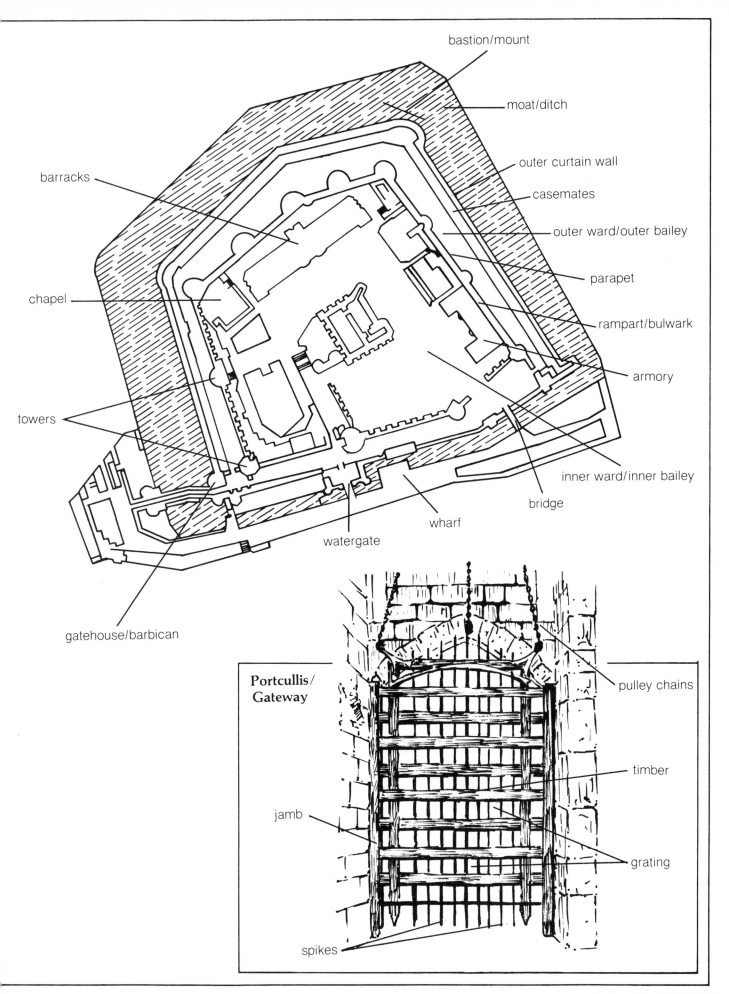

bastion/mount

moat/ditch

outer curtain wall

casemates

outer ward/outer bailey

parapet

rampart/bulwark

armory

barracks

chapel

towers

inner ward/inner bailey

bridge

wharf

watergate

gatehouse/barbican

Portcullis/ Gateway

pulley chains

timber

jamb

grating

spikes

Special Purpose Buildings

Fortifications

This *field fortification* or *trading post* was protected by wooden walls from behind which soldiers could fire on attackers from raised *parapets*. *Powder* and *ammunition* were stored in a building called a *magazine*.

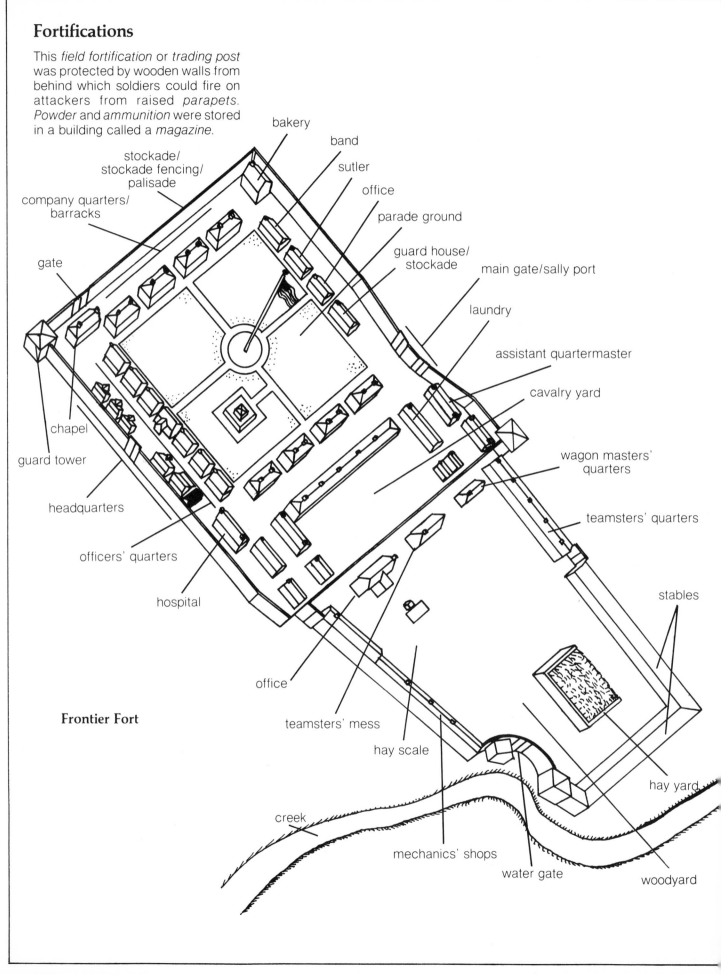

bakery

band

sutler

office

parade ground

guard house/ stockade

stockade/ stockade fencing/ palisade

company quarters/ barracks

gate

chapel

guard tower

headquarters

officers' quarters

hospital

office

Frontier Fort

main gate/sally port

laundry

assistant quartermaster

cavalry yard

wagon masters' quarters

teamsters' quarters

stables

hay yard

woodyard

water gate

mechanics' shops

creek

hay scale

teamsters' mess

Fortifications

Permanent fortifications, such as the *point* of the star fort illustrated here, had *walls* and *slopes* made of *masonry* and earth. They often had *casemates; bombproofs,* walls impervious to explosives; *drawbridges* and *earthen breastworks,* breast-high protection for soldiers.

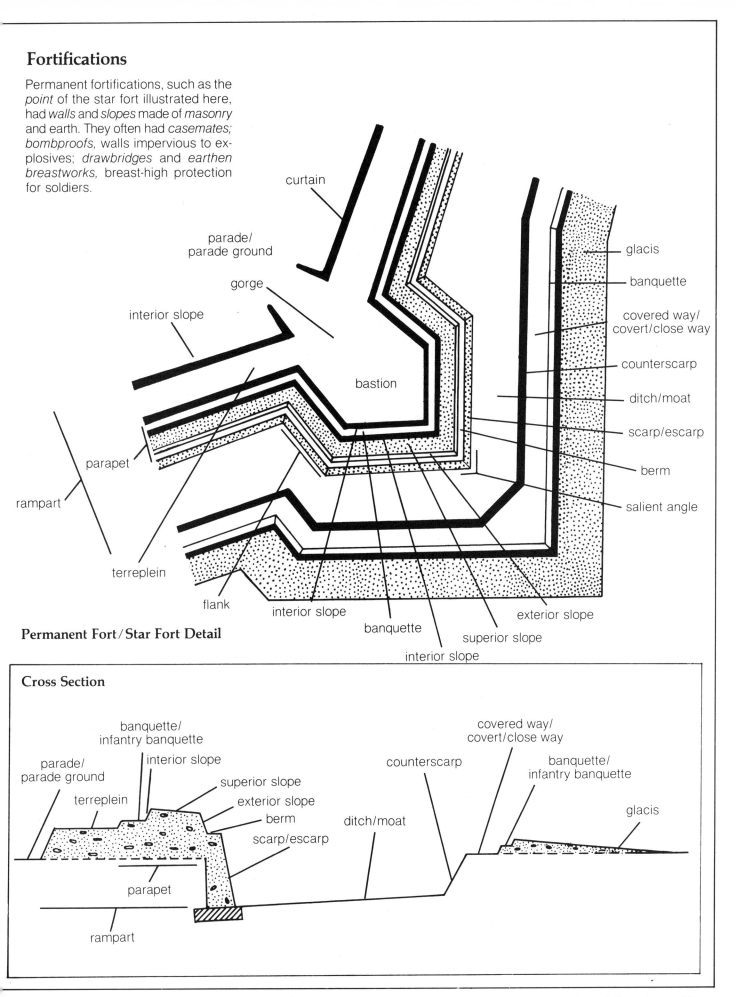

curtain

parade/ parade ground

gorge

interior slope

bastion

glacis

banquette

covered way/ covert/close way

counterscarp

ditch/moat

scarp/escarp

berm

salient angle

parapet

rampart

terreplein

flank

interior slope

banquette

interior slope

superior slope

exterior slope

Permanent Fort/Star Fort Detail

Cross Section

banquette/ infantry banquette

interior slope

parade/ parade ground

superior slope

exterior slope

berm

scarp/escarp

terreplein

covered way/ covert/close way

counterscarp

banquette/ infantry banquette

glacis

ditch/moat

parapet

rampart

Special Purpose Buildings

Tepee/Teepee/Tipi

The *pole frame* of an Indian tepee was held together at the top by a *hide rope*. It was covered with dressed buffalo *skins* and had a *fire pit* on the floor within. Other Indian dwellings included *wigwams*, rounded or oval-shaped lodges formed by poles over-laid with *bark*, *mats* or skins; *wickiups*, huts made of *brushwood* or covered with mats; and *hogans*, dwellings constructed of *earth* and *branches* and covered with *mud* or *sod*.

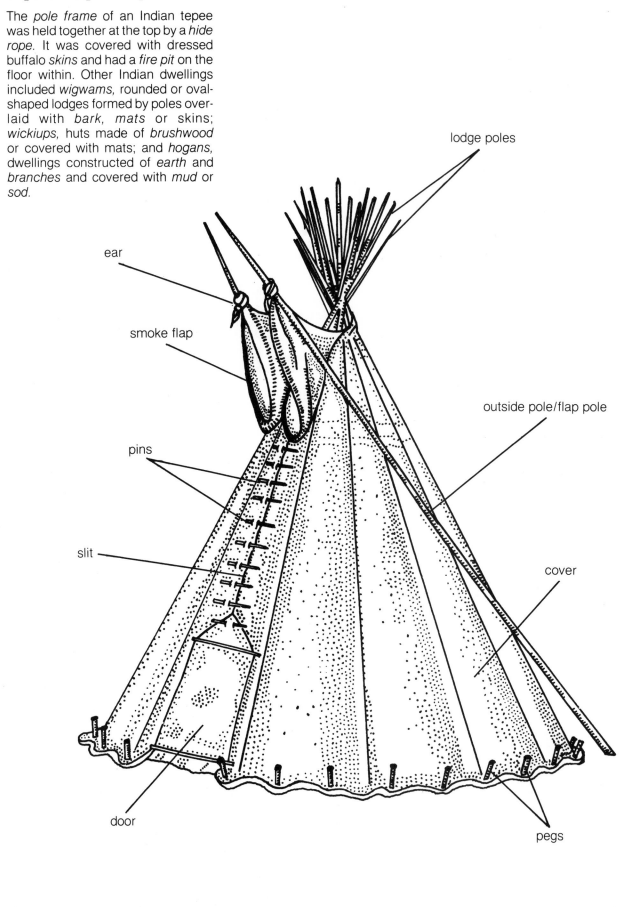

lodge poles

ear

smoke flap

pins

slit

outside pole/flap pole

cover

door

pegs

Domed Structures

Traditionally, a dome is a circular *vault* whose walls exert equal thrust in all directions, resisted by a *tension ring.* The geodesic dome consists of a *grid* of *compression* or *tension members* lying upon *great circles* running in three directions in any given area.

Igloo/Iglu

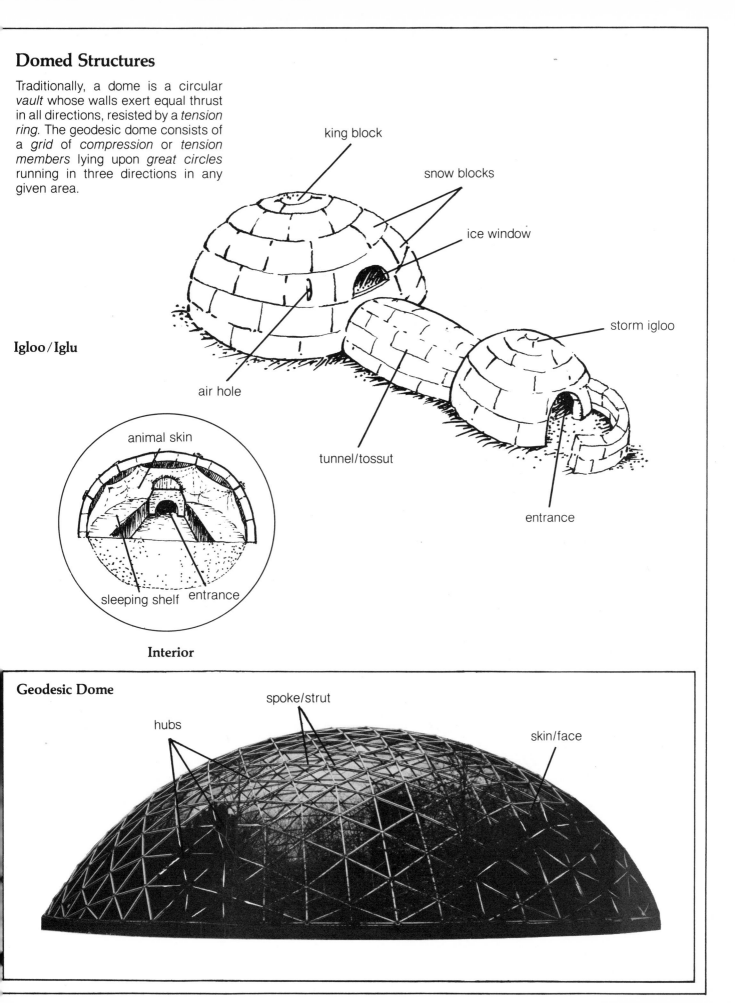

king block

snow blocks

ice window

storm igloo

air hole

tunnel/tossut

entrance

animal skin

sleeping shelf   entrance

Interior

Geodesic Dome

spoke/strut

hubs

skin/face

Special Purpose Buildings

Church/Cathedral

A small building used for worship is called a *chapel*. Living quarters used by church clergy are the *rectory*. The office in which church business is conducted is the *chancellery*.

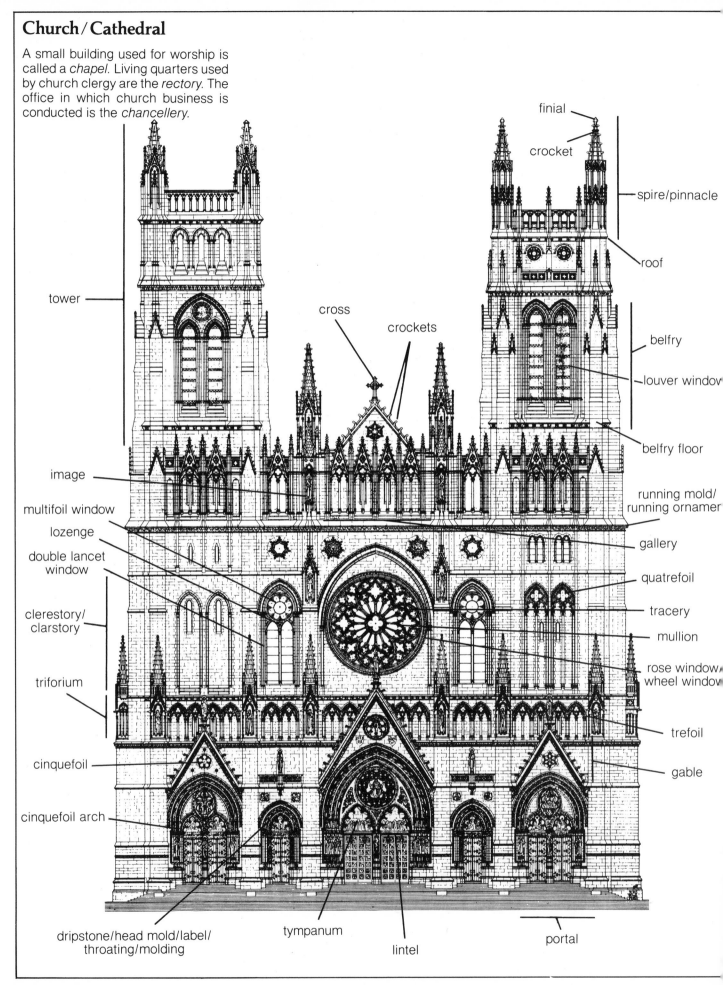

finial

crocket

spire/pinnacle

roof

cross

crockets

belfry

louver window

belfry floor

tower

image

multifoil window

lozenge

double lancet window

running mold/running ornament

gallery

quatrefoil

tracery

mullion

rose window/wheel window

trefoil

gable

clerestory/clarstory

triforium

cinquefoil

cinquefoil arch

dripstone/head mold/label/throating/molding

tympanum

lintel

portal

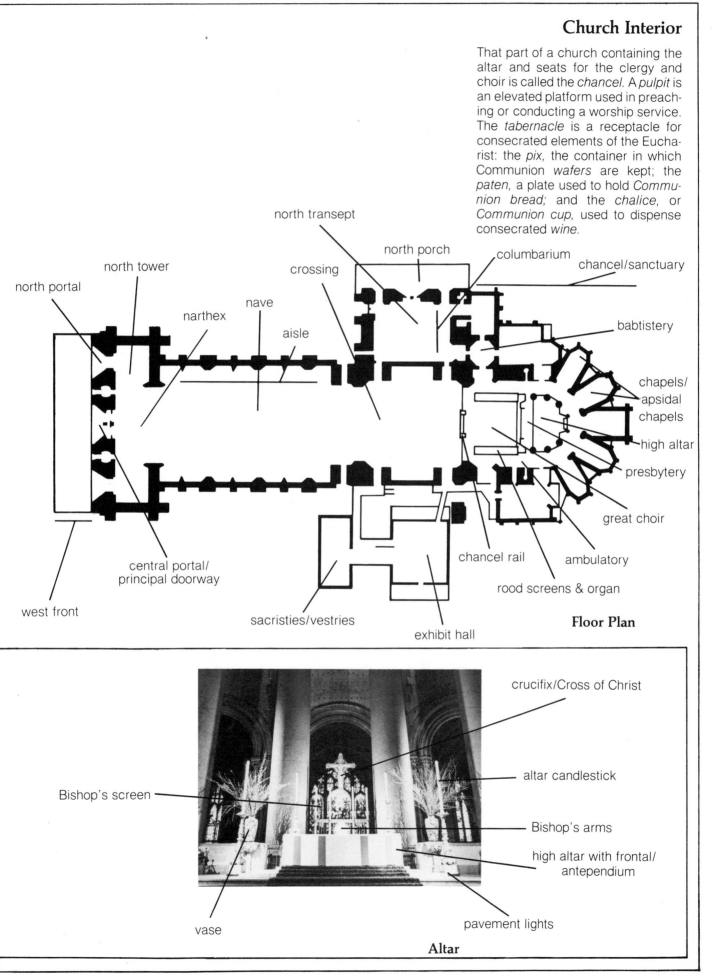

Church Interior

That part of a church containing the altar and seats for the clergy and choir is called the *chancel*. A *pulpit* is an elevated platform used in preaching or conducting a worship service. The *tabernacle* is a receptacle for consecrated elements of the Eucharist: the *pix*, the container in which Communion *wafers* are kept; the *paten*, a plate used to hold *Communion bread*; and the *chalice*, or *Communion cup*, used to dispense consecrated *wine*.

north transept

north porch

crossing

columbarium

chancel/sanctuary

north tower

north portal

narthex

nave

aisle

babtistery

chapels/
apsidal
chapels

high altar

presbytery

great choir

central portal/
principal doorway

chancel rail

ambulatory

rood screens & organ

west front

sacristies/vestries

exhibit hall

Floor Plan

crucifix/Cross of Christ

altar candlestick

Bishop's screen

Bishop's arms

high altar with frontal/
antependium

pavement lights

vase

Altar

Special Purpose Buildings

Synagogue/Temple

The Torah is a parchment or leather *scroll* containing the first five books of the *Scriptures,* or *Pentateuch,* written in Hebrew. It is tied closed with a beltlike *wrapper.*

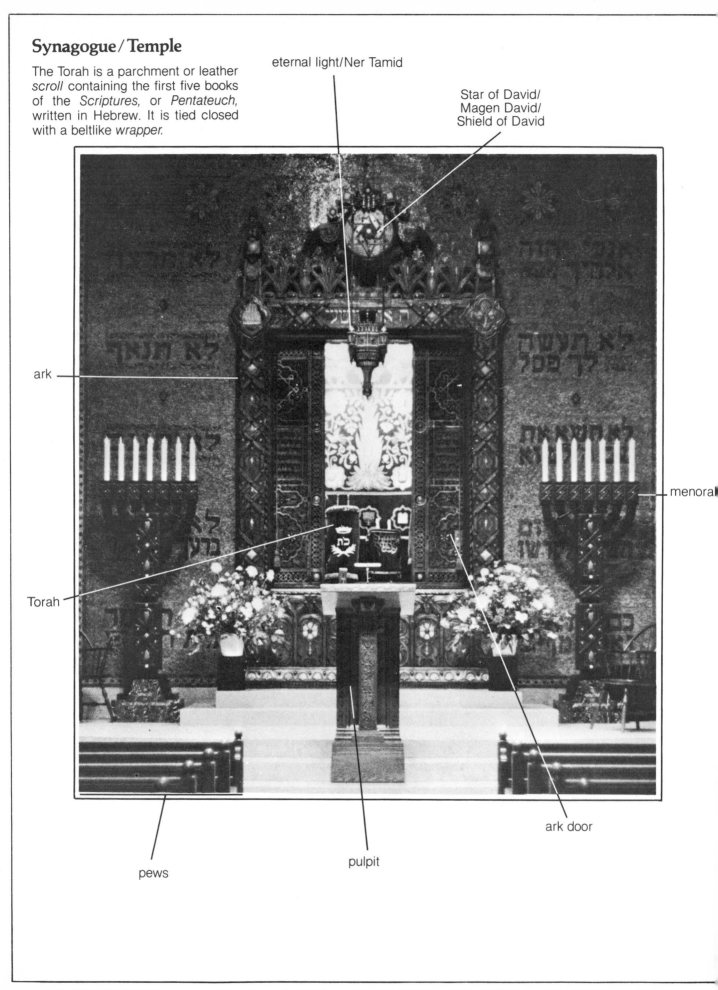

eternal light/Ner Tamid

Star of David/ Magen David/ Shield of David

ark

menora

Torah

ark door

pews

pulpit

Courtroom

The small anteroom off the courtroom in which the *judge* changes into his *robes* and holds conferences is called the *judge's chambers*. After a *jury* has heard a case, it deliberates in a *jury room*. A judge may sometimes use a malletlike *gavel* during proceedings.

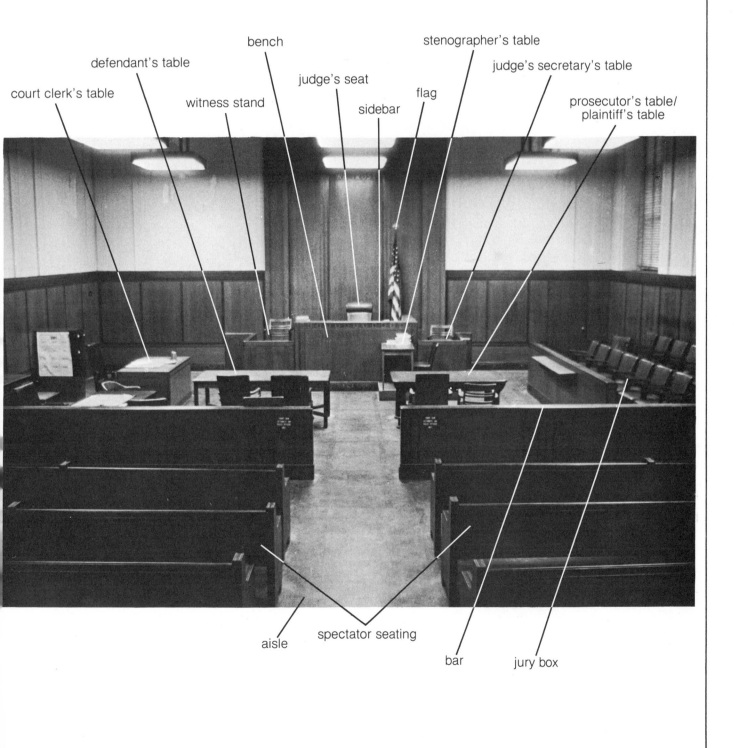

court clerk's table

defendant's table

witness stand

bench

judge's seat

sidebar

flag

stenographer's table

judge's secretary's table

prosecutor's table/ plaintiff's table

aisle

spectator seating

bar

jury box

Special Purpose Buildings

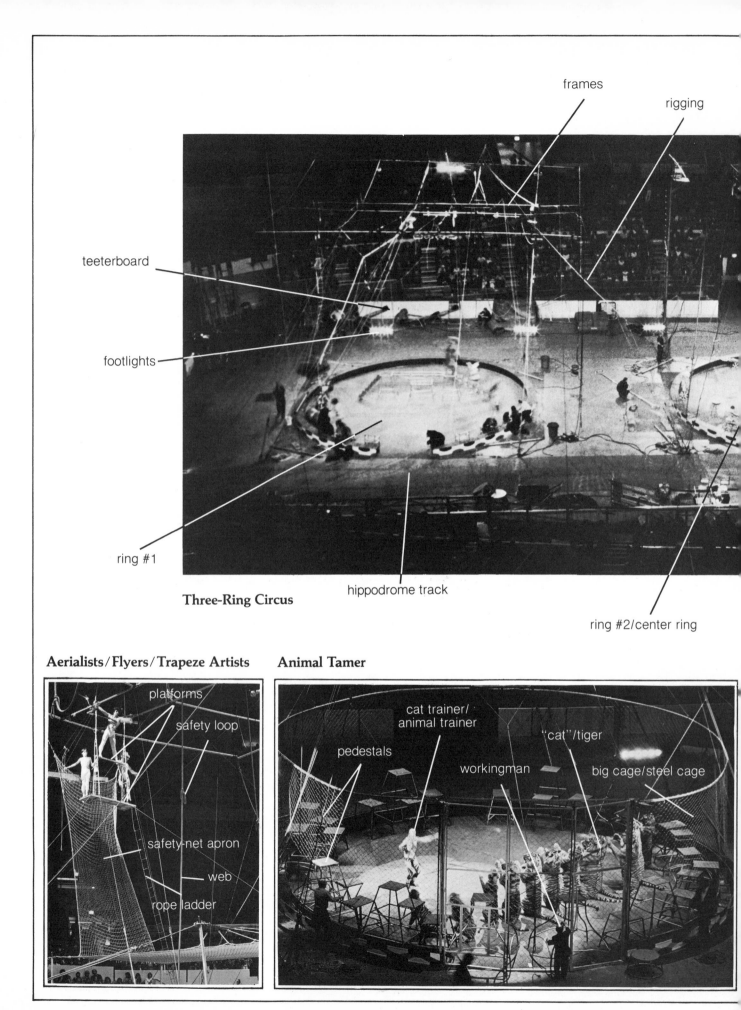

frames

rigging

teeterboard

footlights

ring #1

Three-Ring Circus

hippodrome track

ring #2/center ring

Aerialists/Flyers/Trapeze Artists

platforms

safety loop

safety-net apron

web

rope ladder

Animal Tamer

cat trainer/
animal trainer

"cat"/tiger

pedestals

workingman

big cage/steel cage

Circus

Circuses traditionally take place in tents erected by *roustabouts* and begin with a *parade* in which all the performers enter the *arena*. A *ringmaster*, usually clad in *top hat* and *tails*, announces acts, including *animal* and *clown acts; tightrope*, or *high-wire acts;* and *jugglers*. In the past, *sideshows*, which took place in an adjoining tent, featured *tattooed ladies*, *giants*, *midgets*, *sword-swallowers* and *fire-eaters*.

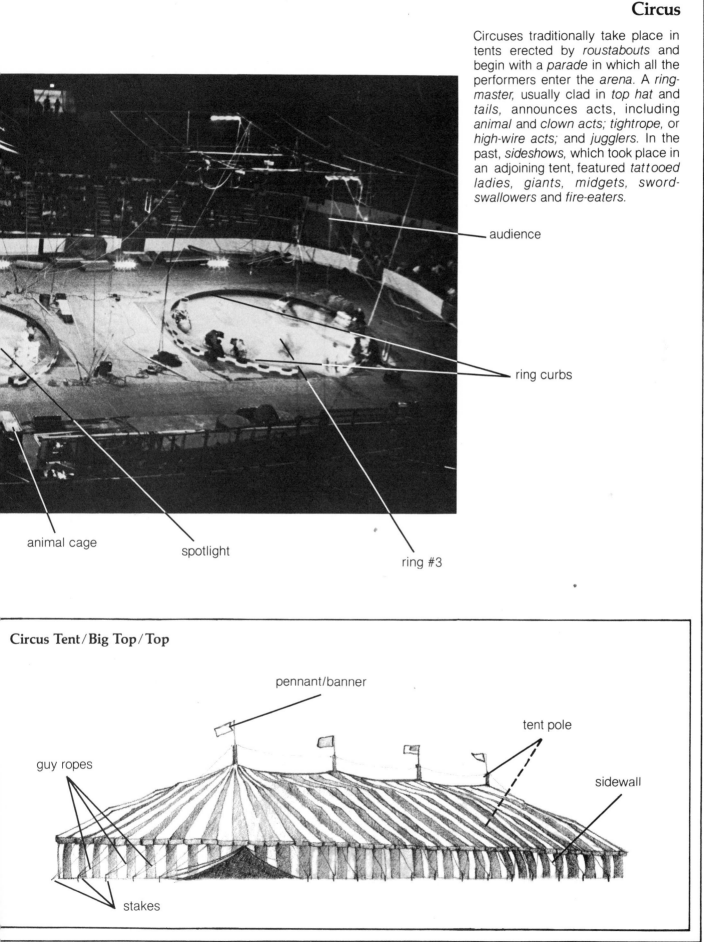

audience

ring curbs

animal cage

spotlight

ring #3

Circus Tent / Big Top / Top

pennant/banner

tent pole

guy ropes

sidewall

stakes

Special Purpose Buildings

Amusement Park

A roller coaster consists of *hills, straightaways* and *loops. Upstop wheels* lock roller-coaster cars to the track, *guide wheels* are used for turns and tractor wheels are used for gliding.

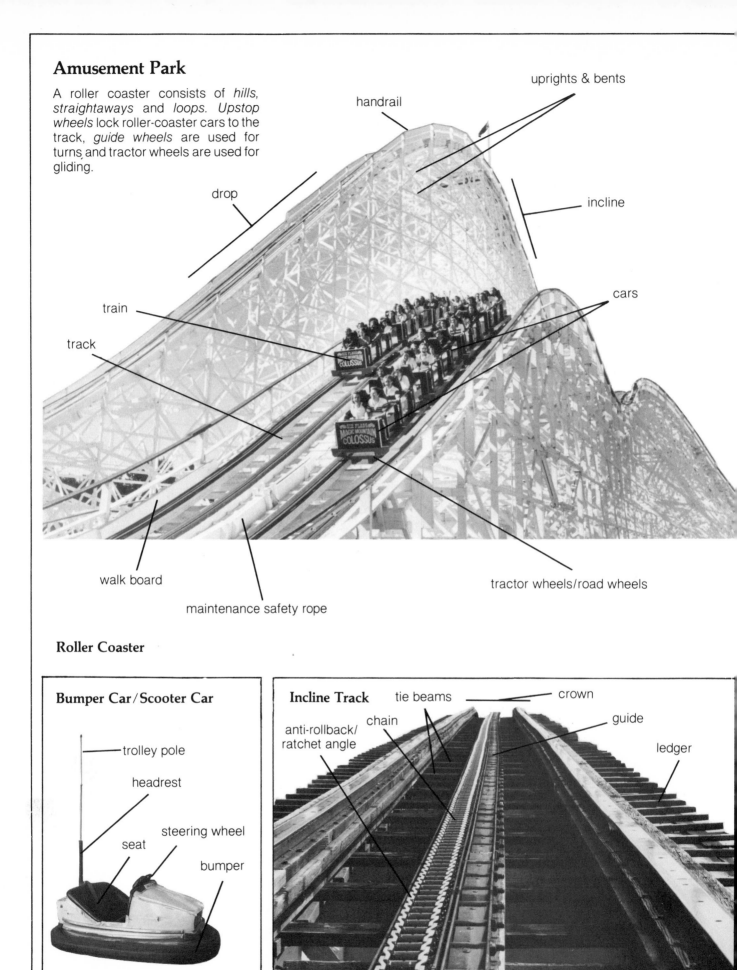

uprights & bents

handrail

drop

incline

train

cars

track

walk board

maintenance safety rope

tractor wheels/road wheels

Roller Coaster

Bumper Car/Scooter Car

trolley pole

headrest

steering wheel

seat

bumper

Incline Track

tie beams

crown

anti-rollback/ ratchet angle

chain

guide

ledger

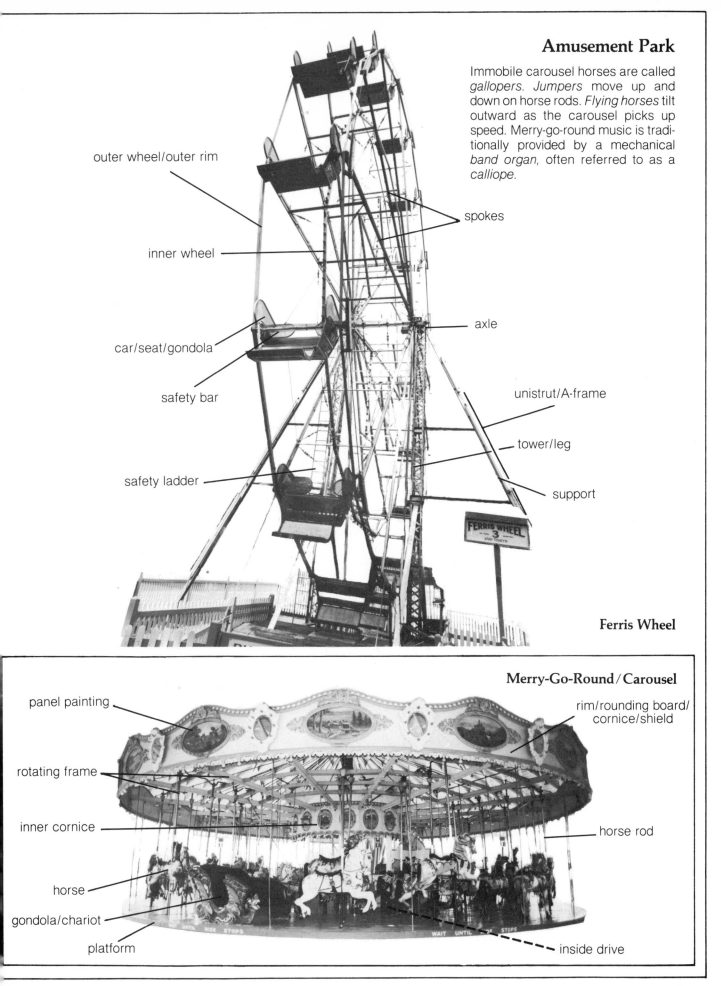

Amusement Park

Immobile carousel horses are called *gallopers*. *Jumpers* move up and down on horse rods. *Flying horses* tilt outward as the carousel picks up speed. Merry-go-round music is traditionally provided by a mechanical *band organ*, often referred to as a *calliope*.

outer wheel/outer rim

spokes

inner wheel

axle

car/seat/gondola

safety bar

unistrut/A-frame

tower/leg

safety ladder

support

Ferris Wheel

Merry-Go-Round / Carousel

panel painting

rim/rounding board/ cornice/shield

rotating frame

inner cornice

horse rod

horse

gondola/chariot

platform

inside drive

91

Special Purpose Buildings

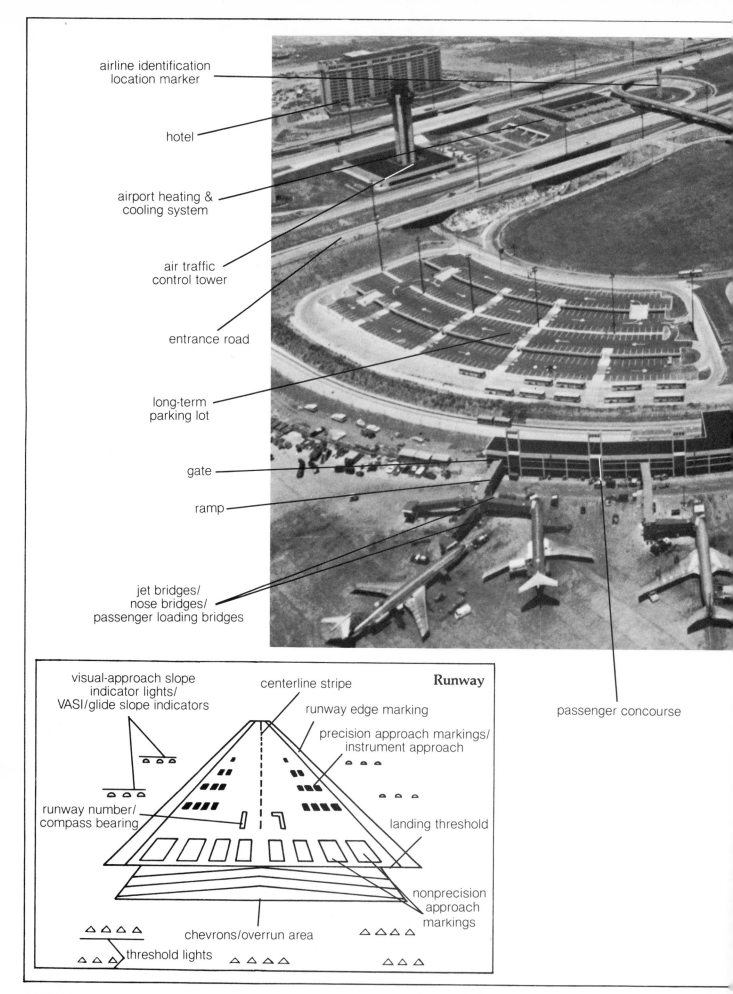

airline identification location marker

hotel

airport heating & cooling system

air traffic control tower

entrance road

long-term parking lot

gate

ramp

jet bridges/ nose bridges/ passenger loading bridges

passenger concourse

Runway

visual-approach slope indicator lights/ VASI/glide slope indicators

centerline stripe

runway edge marking

precision approach markings/ instrument approach

runway number/ compass bearing

landing threshold

nonprecision approach markings

chevrons/overrun area

threshold lights

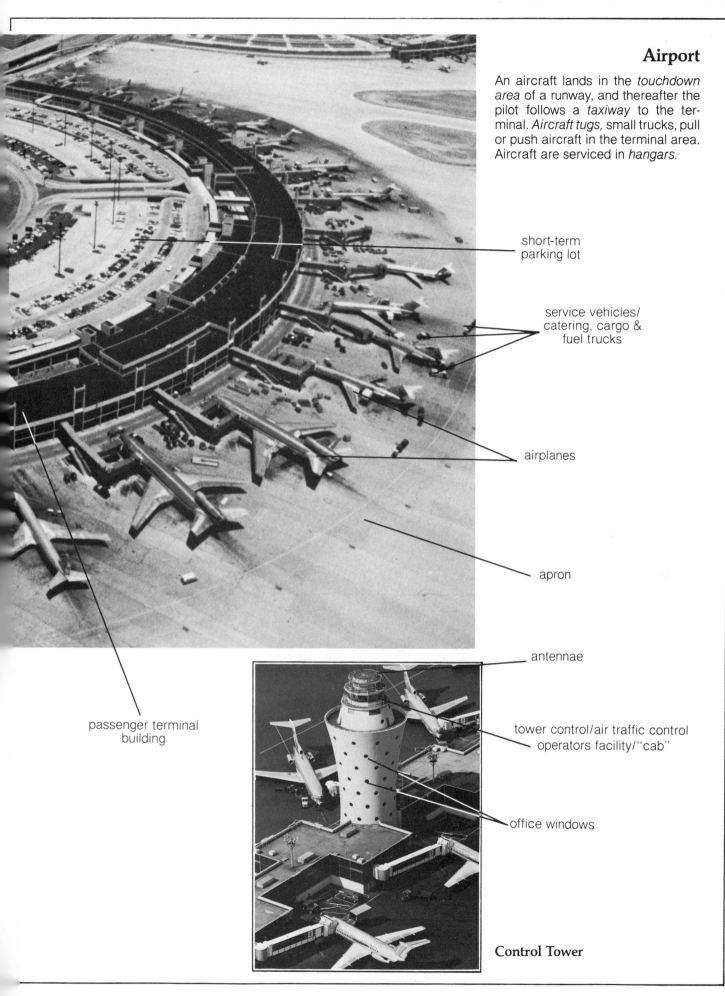

Airport

An aircraft lands in the *touchdown area* of a runway, and thereafter the pilot follows a *taxiway* to the terminal. *Aircraft tugs,* small trucks, pull or push aircraft in the terminal area. Aircraft are serviced in *hangars.*

short-term parking lot

service vehicles/ catering, cargo & fuel trucks

airplanes

apron

passenger terminal building

antennae

tower control/air traffic control operators facility/"cab"

office windows

Control Tower

Special Purpose Buildings

Railroad Yard

A railroad yard, or *marshalling yard*, consists of a system of *parallel tracks*, *crossovers* and *switches* where *cars* are formed into *trains* and where cars, *locomotives* and other *rolling stock* are kept when not in use or awaiting repair. In *hump yards*, freight cars are pushed down a *hump* onto a *siding*, determined by a *yardmaster*, to be coupled to a forming train. *Electropneumatic retarders* control the speed of the cars as they move along the tracks.

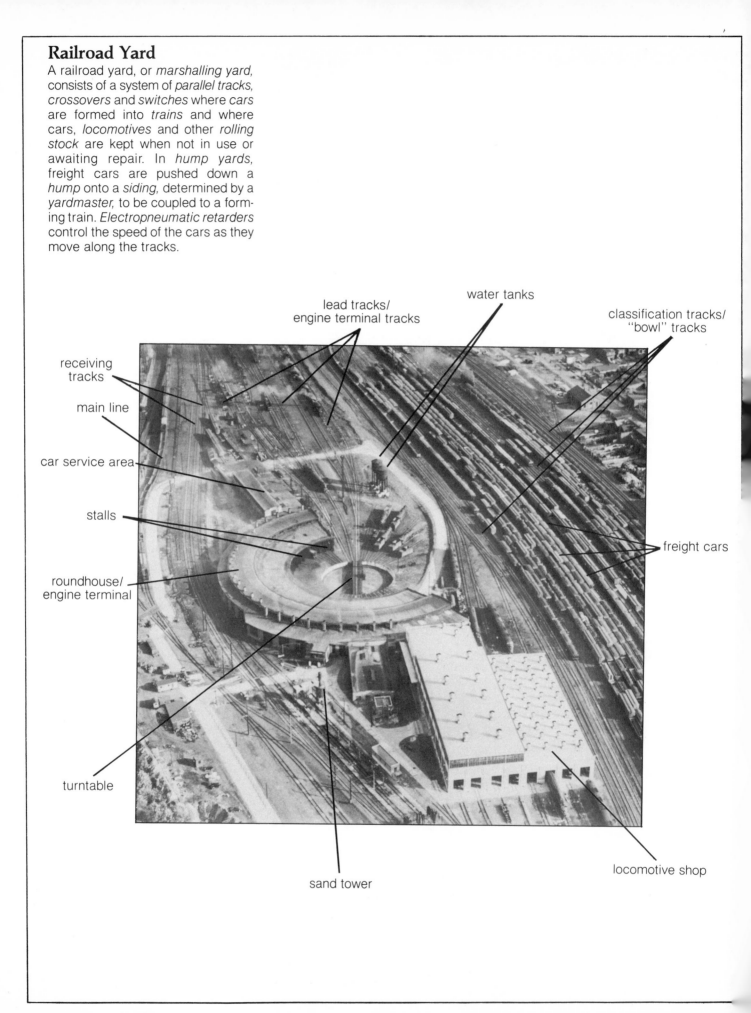

lead tracks/
engine terminal tracks

water tanks

classification tracks/
"bowl" tracks

receiving
tracks

main line

car service area

stalls

roundhouse/
engine terminal

freight cars

turntable

sand tower

locomotive shop

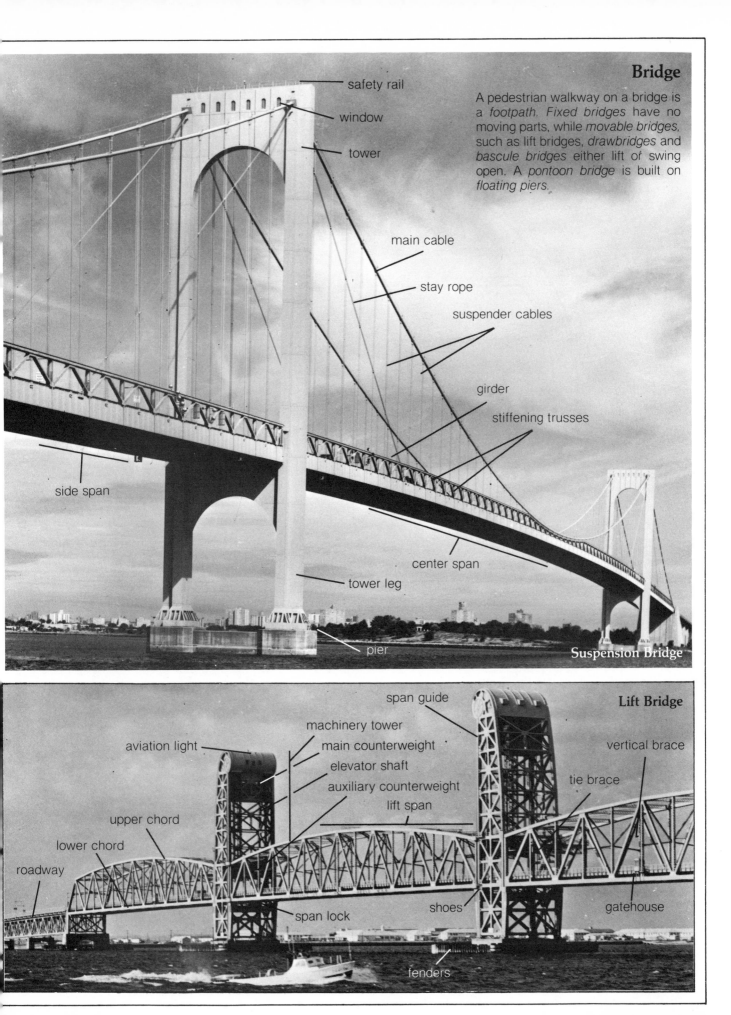

Bridge

A pedestrian walkway on a bridge is a *footpath*. *Fixed bridges* have no moving parts, while *movable bridges*, such as lift bridges, *drawbridges* and *bascule bridges* either lift or swing open. A *pontoon bridge* is built on *floating piers*.

safety rail

window

tower

main cable

stay rope

suspender cables

girder

stiffening trusses

side span

center span

tower leg

pier

Suspension Bridge

Lift Bridge

span guide

machinery tower

aviation light

main counterweight

elevator shaft

auxiliary counterweight

lift span

vertical brace

tie brace

upper chord

lower chord

roadway

span lock

shoes

gatehouse

fenders

Other Structures

Tunnel

Tunnels that take water to hydroelectric plants or to municipal waterworks and those that remove storm water and sewage are called *conduits*. Tunnels cut through rock frequently require no *lining*. Underwater tunnels can be ventilated by *shafts* leading to the surface or by *exhaust* or *booster fans* at the ends.

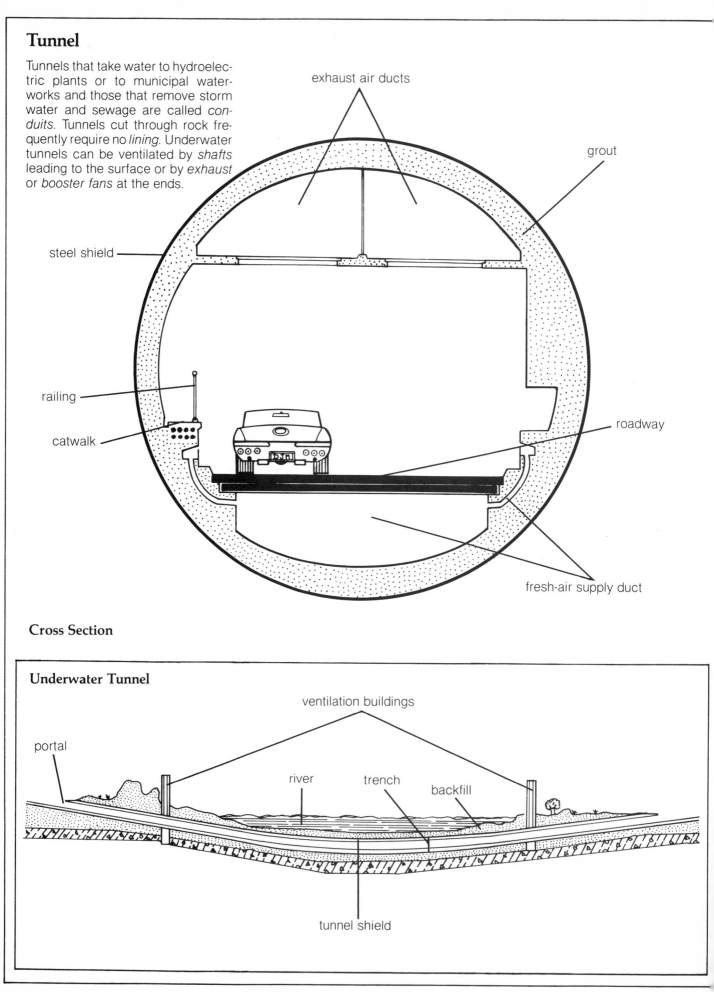

exhaust air ducts

grout

steel shield

railing

catwalk

roadway

fresh-air supply duct

Cross Section

Underwater Tunnel

ventilation buildings

portal

river

trench

backfill

tunnel shield

Canal Lock

The water level in a canal lock is raised or lowered through *sluice gates* in the lock wall or *floor.* *Shipboard lines* or *hawsers* secured to *bollards* along the lockside hold the vessel steady while the lock is in operation. Before *electric locomotives* were used, animals would haul boats through locks following a *towpath.*

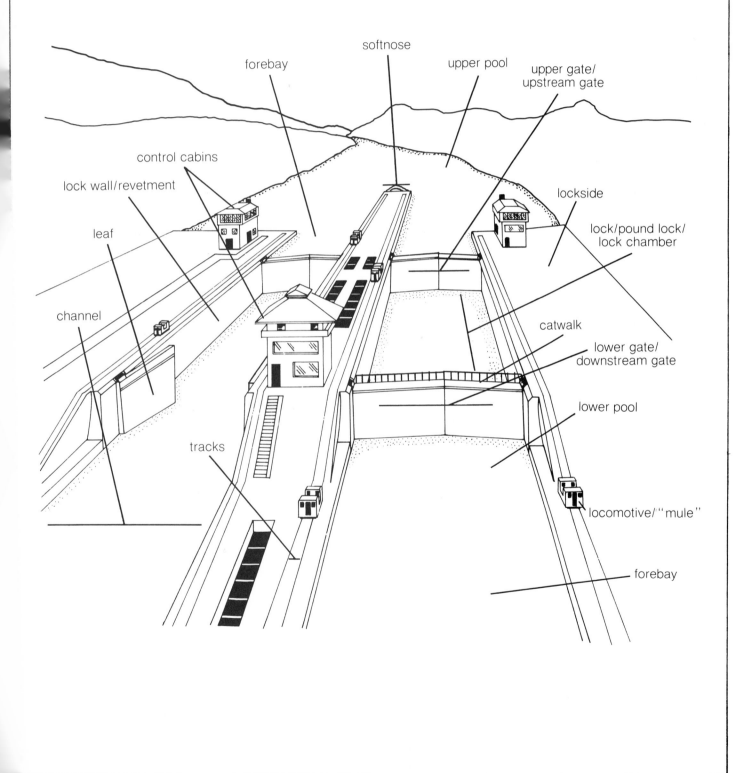

softnose

forebay

upper pool

upper gate/ upstream gate

control cabins

lock wall/revetment

lockside

leaf

lock/pound lock/ lock chamber

channel

catwalk

lower gate/ downstream gate

lower pool

tracks

locomotive/"mule"

forebay

Other Structures

Dam

Many dams have steep channels divided by partitions into pools, called *fishways* or *fish ladders,* that enable fish to swim upriver. Other dams have *log chutes* designed to allow logs to pass through. A *dike,* or *levee,* is an earthwork construction built to block water rather than to regulate its flow.

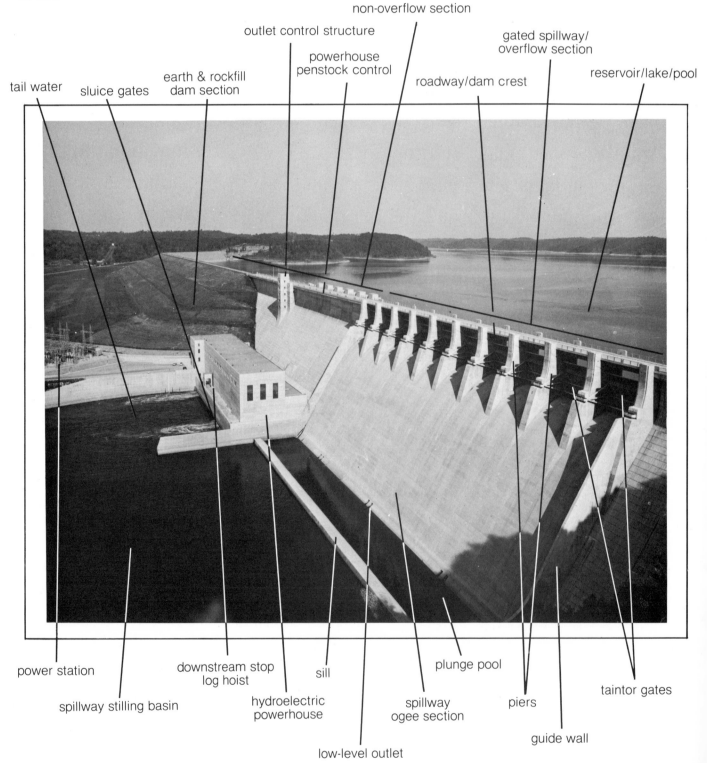

non-overflow section

outlet control structure

powerhouse penstock control

gated spillway/ overflow section

roadway/dam crest

reservoir/lake/pool

tail water

sluice gates

earth & rockfill dam section

power station

downstream stop log hoist

sill

plunge pool

piers

taintor gates

spillway stilling basin

hydroelectric powerhouse

spillway ogee section

guide wall

low-level outlet

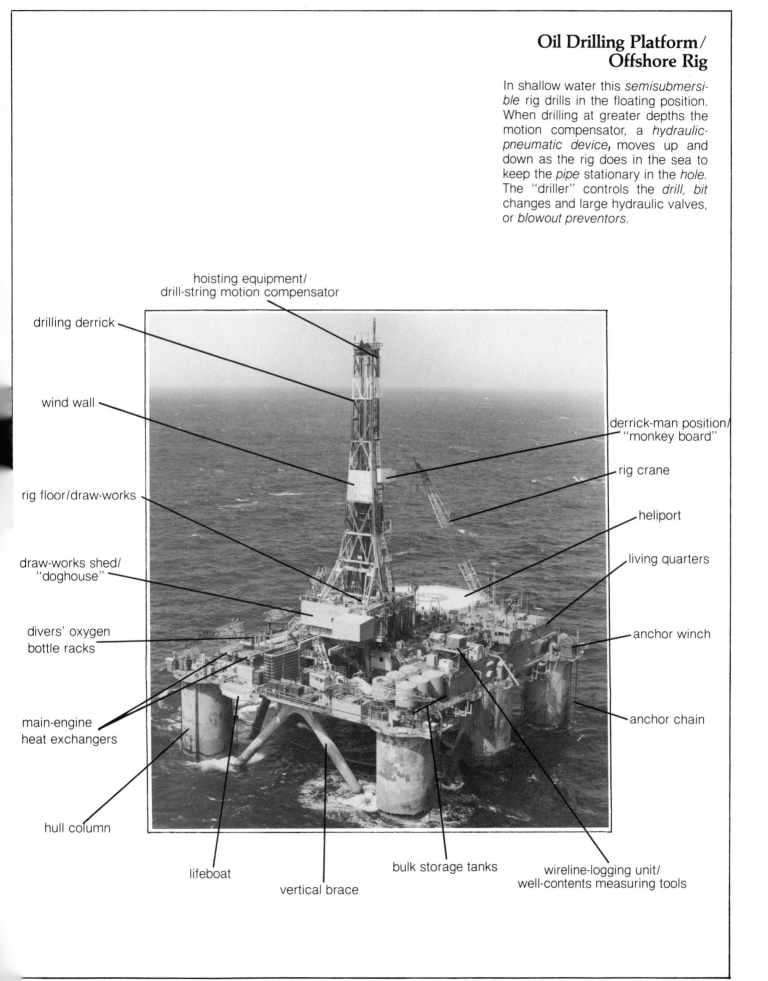

Oil Drilling Platform/ Offshore Rig

In shallow water this *semisubmersible* rig drills in the floating position. When drilling at greater depths the motion compensator, a *hydraulic-pneumatic device,* moves up and down as the rig does in the sea to keep the *pipe* stationary in the *hole.* The "driller" controls the *drill, bit* changes and large hydraulic valves, or *blowout preventors.*

hoisting equipment/
drill-string motion compensator

drilling derrick

wind wall

derrick-man position/
"monkey board"

rig crane

rig floor/draw-works

heliport

draw-works shed/
"doghouse"

living quarters

divers' oxygen
bottle racks

anchor winch

main-engine
heat exchangers

anchor chain

hull column

lifeboat

bulk storage tanks

wireline-logging unit/
well-contents measuring tools

vertical brace

Other Structures

Barn and Silo

A barn *floor* is divided in the center by a *feed passage* that may be lined with *stanchions* to hold cows. On either side are *manure gutters,* and on each side of these are *mangers, boxes* or *troughs,* from which horses or cattle eat. Hay is stored in a *loft,* a storage room next to the roof. Surrounding a barn is a *yard* with a *manure pit* large enough to back a wagon into. Other barnyard structures, adjoining the main barn or built nearby, include *grain pits,* or *bins; springhouses; smokehouses,* and *pigpens.*

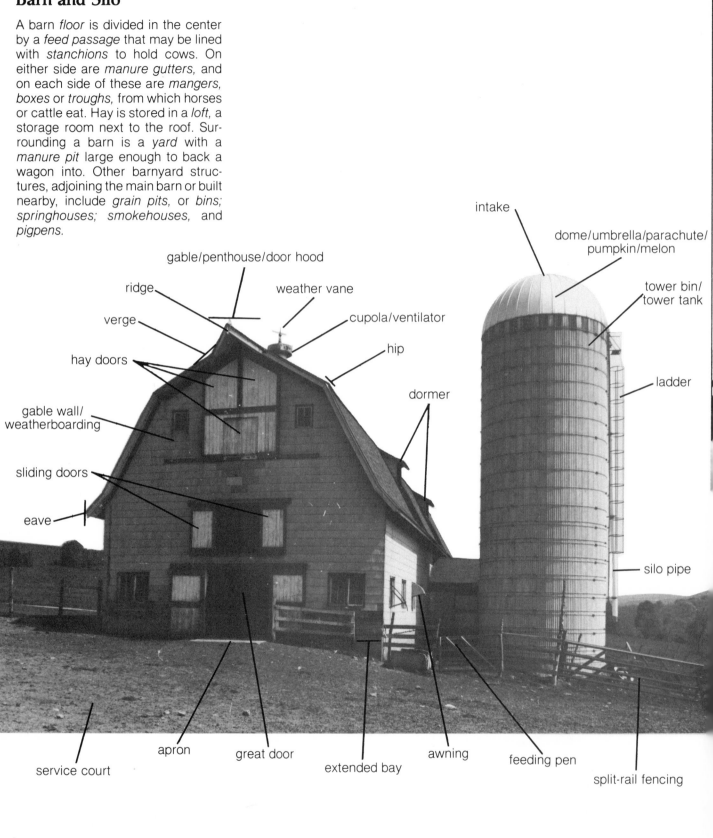

intake

dome/umbrella/parachute/
pumpkin/melon

gable/penthouse/door hood

ridge

verge

weather vane

tower bin/
tower tank

cupola/ventilator

hay doors

hip

ladder

dormer

gable wall/
weatherboarding

sliding doors

eave

silo pipe

apron

great door

awning

feeding pen

service court

extended bay

split-rail fencing

Barn

Silo

Transportation

All the major forms of transportation are incorporated in this section, beginning with the most ubiquitous mode of everyday travel—the automobile. Coverage of the car begins with an illustration of a specially built model displaying all the exterior parts that appear or have appeared on recent designs. Also included is a cutaway drawing that shows the major but often unseen interior components of a car as well as illustrations of a car engine, interior dash and traffic control devices.

The other major subcategories cover public conveyances; emergency, public service and recreational vehicles; boats and ships; aircraft and spacecraft. Vehicles used for military purposes, such as fighting ships and aircraft, are included in this section as well.

Cutaway illustrations have been used to show the reader the interior parts of an ocean liner and the cockpits of a jumbo jet, military fighter and space shuttle.

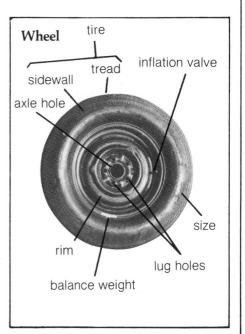

Wheel tire
inflation valve
tread
sidewall
axle hole
size
rim
lug holes
balance weight

Automobile/Car Exterior

The *body* of this specially designed car, or *customized automobile*, rests on a *chassis* consisting of a *frame* and wheels. Older cars often had *rumble seats* instead of trunks. On *convertibles,* the entire top folds into a compartment called the *boot.* Many contemporary cars have sliding *sun roofs* or *moon roofs.* A *sedan* usually has four doors and full-width front and rear seats. A *coupe* is a smaller version of a sedan, having only two doors. A *station wagon* is a boxlike car with storage space behind the rear seat, which may have *fold-down seats* for additional passenger seating. A high-performance car with a low-slung body is a *sports car.*

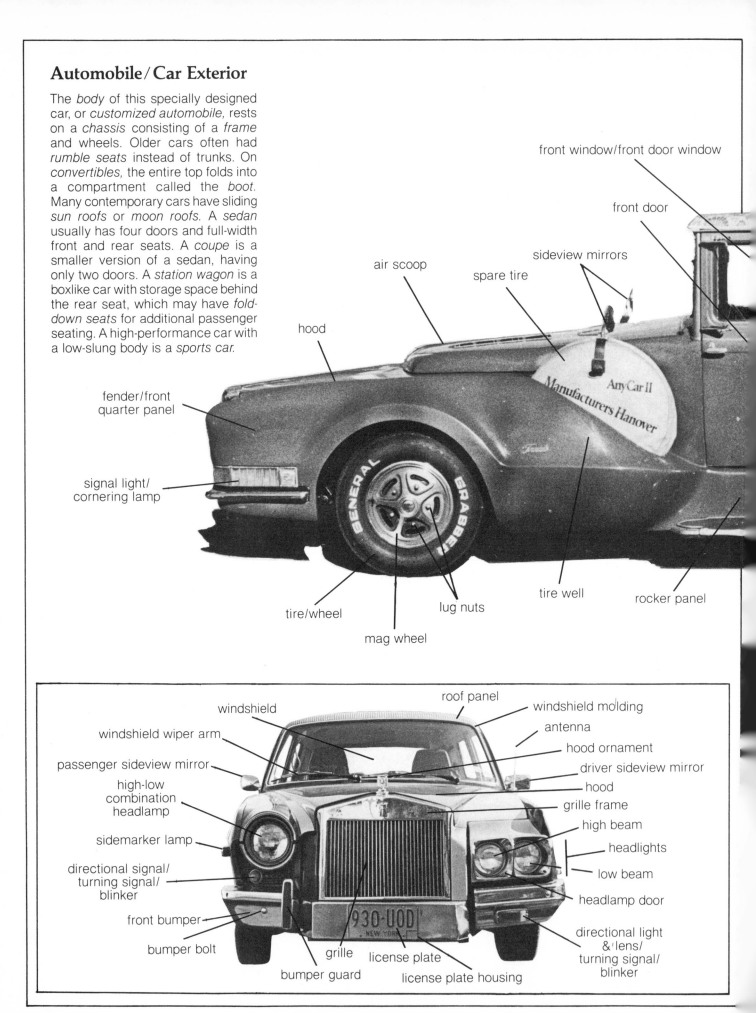

front window/front door window

front door

sideview mirrors

air scoop

spare tire

hood

AnyCar II
Manufacturers Hanover

fender/front quarter panel

signal light/cornering lamp

tire well

rocker panel

tire/wheel

lug nuts

mag wheel

windshield

roof panel

windshield molding

windshield wiper arm

antenna

passenger sideview mirror

hood ornament

high-low combination headlamp

driver sideview mirror

hood

sidemarker lamp

grille frame

high beam

directional signal/turning signal/blinker

headlights

low beam

front bumper

headlamp door

bumper bolt

930-UOD
NEW YORK

grille

license plate

directional light & lens/turning signal/blinker

bumper guard

license plate housing

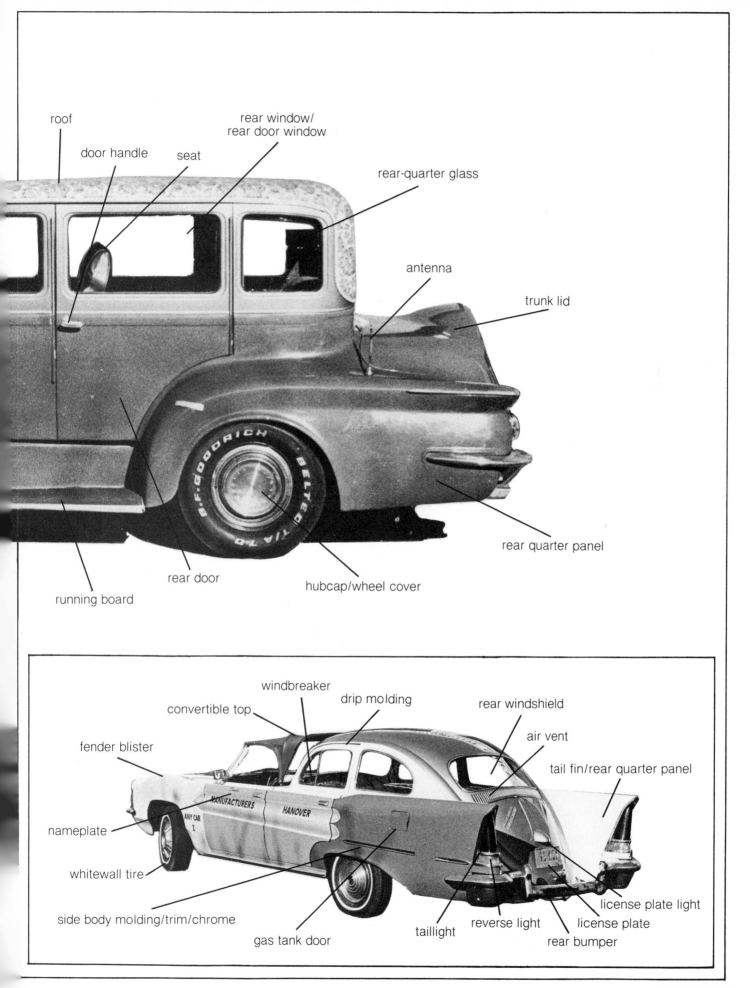

roof

rear window/
rear door window

door handle   seat

rear-quarter glass

antenna

trunk lid

rear quarter panel

running board

rear door

hubcap/wheel cover

windbreaker

convertible top

drip molding

rear windshield

fender blister

air vent

tail fin/rear quarter panel

nameplate

whitewall tire

side body molding/trim/chrome

gas tank door

taillight

reverse light

rear bumper

license plate light

license plate

Automobile Cutaway

Various systems are incorporated in a car: a *power train,* which consists of *clutch,* transmission, driveshaft and rear axle; a *cooling system* designed to control engine temperature; an *electrical system* to power the engine *starter motor,* accessories and lights; a *suspension system* to provide a smooth ride; and a *braking system.*

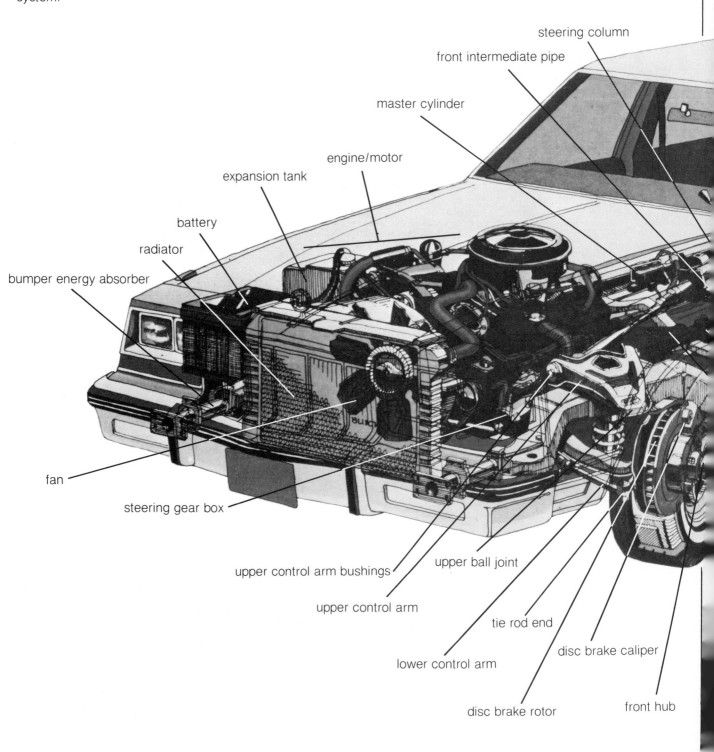

steering column

front intermediate pipe

master cylinder

engine/motor

expansion tank

battery

radiator

bumper energy absorber

fan

steering gear box

upper control arm bushings

upper control arm

upper ball joint

tie rod end

lower control arm

disc brake caliper

disc brake rotor

front hub

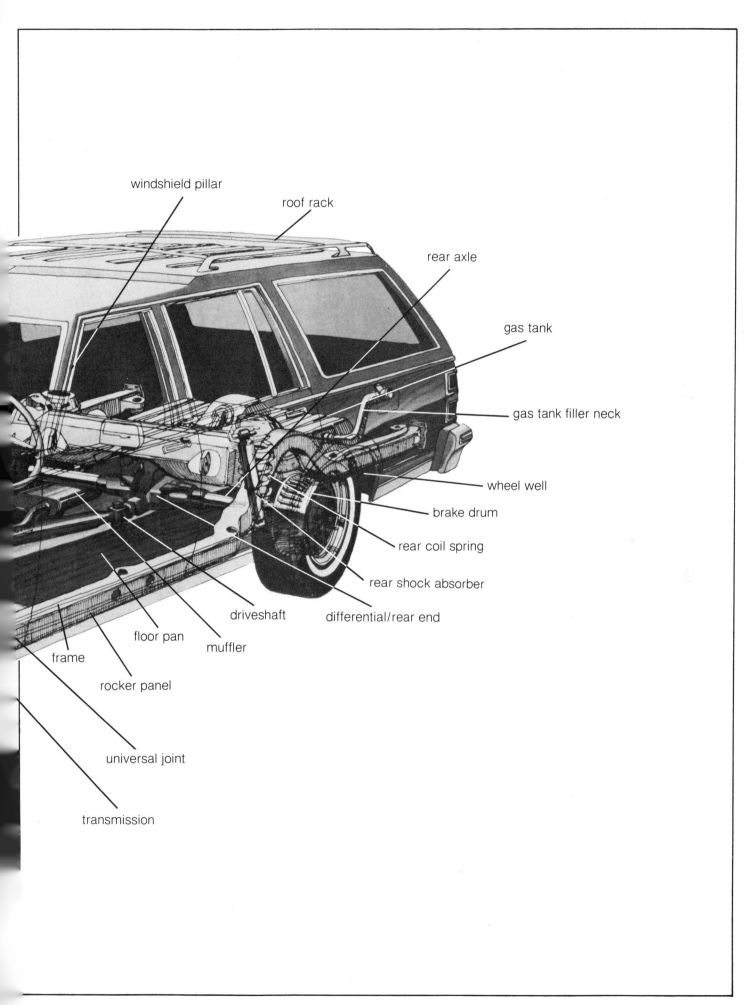

windshield pillar

roof rack

rear axle

gas tank

gas tank filler neck

wheel well

brake drum

rear coil spring

rear shock absorber

differential/rear end

driveshaft

floor pan

muffler

frame

rocker panel

universal joint

transmission

Car Interior

In addition to parts shown on this *dash*, or *dashboard*, are *headlight* and *warning light controls, hood release, engine choke* and *hand throttle, windshield wiper speed control* and *directional signal switch*. Above the dash, there is usually a *rearview mirror*. Flip-down *sun visors* are located above the windshield. Car seats are equipped with *seat belts* or *safety belts*.

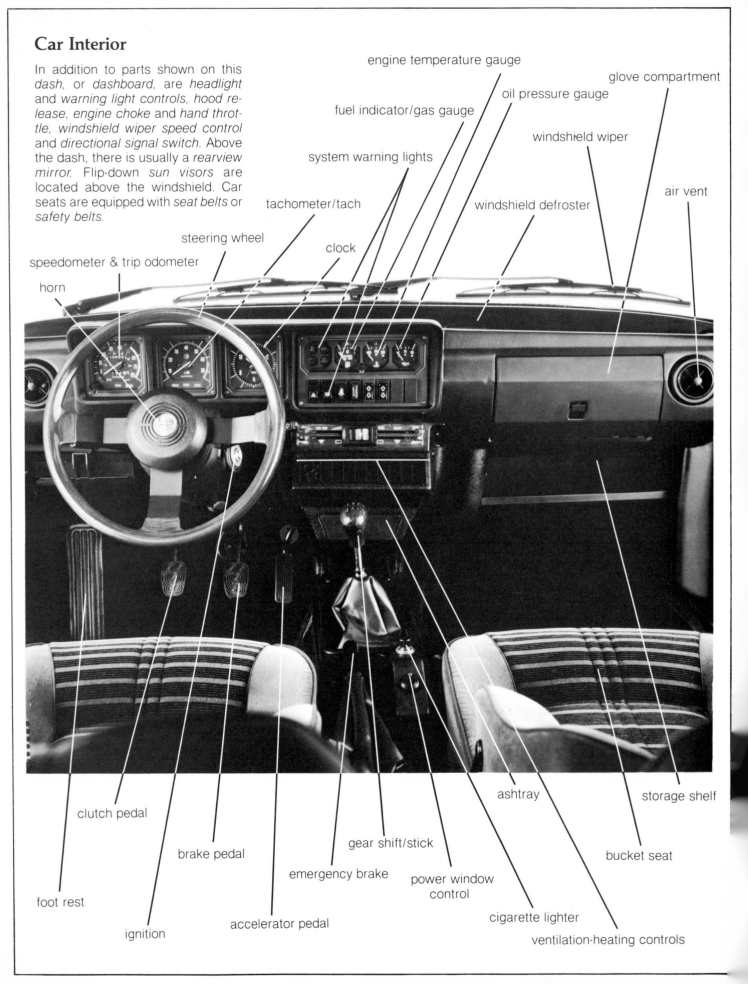

engine temperature gauge

glove compartment

oil pressure gauge

fuel indicator/gas gauge

windshield wiper

system warning lights

air vent

windshield defroster

tachometer/tach

clock

steering wheel

speedometer & trip odometer

horn

clutch pedal

brake pedal

foot rest

ignition

accelerator pedal

emergency brake

gear shift/stick

power window control

ashtray

storage shelf

bucket seat

cigarette lighter

ventilation-heating controls

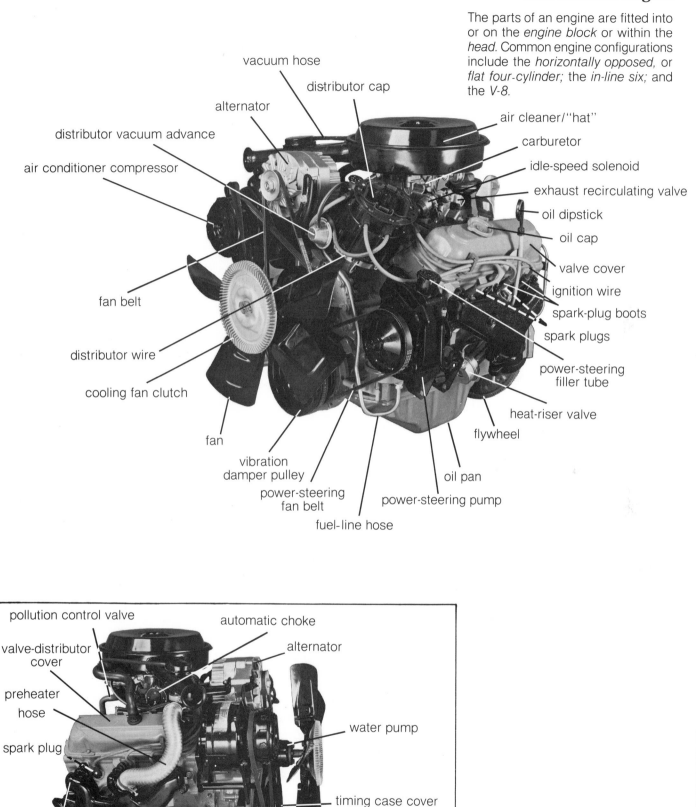

Automobile Engine

The parts of an engine are fitted into or on the *engine block* or within the *head*. Common engine configurations include the *horizontally opposed,* or *flat four-cylinder;* the *in-line six;* and the *V-8.*

vacuum hose

distributor cap

alternator

distributor vacuum advance

air conditioner compressor

air cleaner/"hat"

carburetor

idle-speed solenoid

exhaust recirculating valve

oil dipstick

oil cap

valve cover

ignition wire

spark-plug boots

spark plugs

power-steering filler tube

heat-riser valve

flywheel

fan belt

distributor wire

cooling fan clutch

fan

vibration damper pulley

power-steering fan belt

fuel-line hose

power-steering pump

oil pan

pollution control valve

automatic choke

valve-distributor cover

alternator

preheater hose

water pump

spark plug

timing case cover

oil filter

motor mount

exhaust manifold

oil pan

starter motor

Gasoline Pump

Service station islands can be *self-service* or *full-service*. Gas pumps draw supplies from underground *storage tanks*. Gasoline is purchased in different *grades* determined by *octane number*.

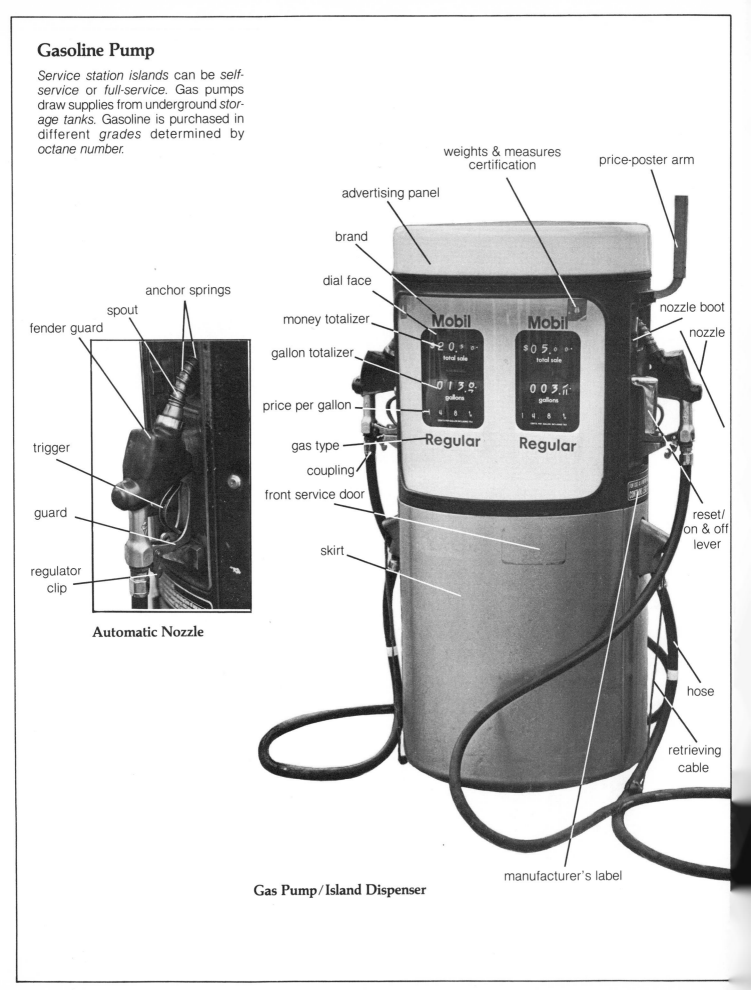

anchor springs

spout

fender guard

trigger

guard

regulator clip

Automatic Nozzle

weights & measures certification

price-poster arm

advertising panel

brand

dial face

money totalizer

gallon totalizer

price per gallon

gas type

coupling

front service door

skirt

nozzle boot

nozzle

reset/ on & off lever

hose

retrieving cable

manufacturer's label

Gas Pump/Island Dispenser

Traffic Control Devices

Four-face traffic signals, or lights, are operated manually by a traffic-control official or run automatically by an electric *timer.* Parking meters, set atop *pipe standards,* contain *self-starting timers.* Jammed meters activate a *slot closer* so that additional coins cannot be inserted in the *slot block.* Some meters have a *washer detector* that allows *washers* and *slugs* to pass through without registering time on the *dial.*

span wire

upper arm

span-wire hanger assembly

universal cross connection

rosette cap

tunnel visor

lens/red light/ stop signal

yellow light/ caution signal

face

green light/ proceed signal

body

Traffic Light

Parking Meter

time & rate plate

dial window

violation flag

coin slot

coin viewing window receptacle

handle

instruction plate

lock

coin box/vault

Highway

Energy absorbing barriers, or *impact attentuation devices,* are positioned in gore areas to reduce accidents. Some roads are lined with *guard-rails,* or *railings. Milestones,* or *mile markers,* provide distance information between specific points. Many *expressways, freeways* and *thruways* have *rest areas, scenic overlooks* and *service areas.*

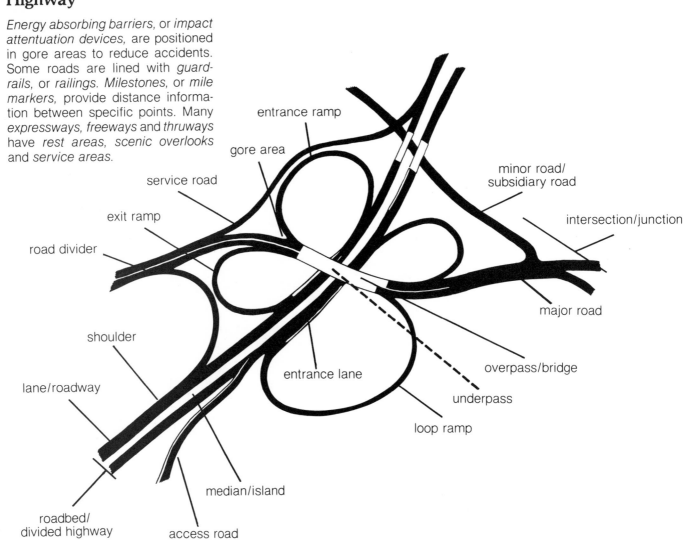

entrance ramp
gore area
service road
exit ramp
road divider
shoulder
lane/roadway
roadbed/
divided highway
access road
median/island
entrance lane
loop ramp
underpass
overpass/bridge
major road
intersection/junction
minor road/
subsidiary road

Cloverleaf / Interchange

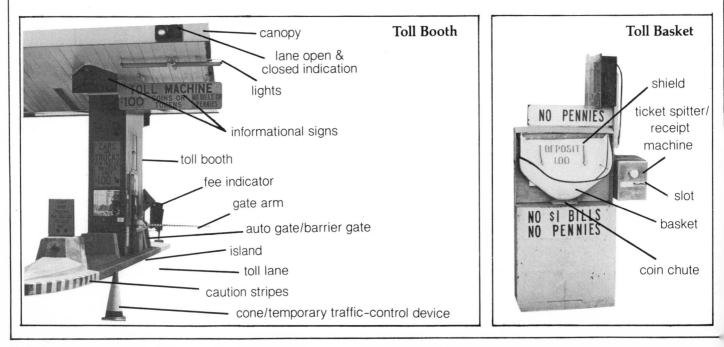

Toll Booth

canopy
lane open & closed indication
lights
informational signs
toll booth
fee indicator
gate arm
auto gate/barrier gate
island
toll lane
caution stripes
cone/temporary traffic-control device

Toll Basket

shield
ticket spitter/ receipt machine
slot
basket
coin chute

NO PENNIES
DEPOSIT 1.00
NO $1 BILLS NO PENNIES

Railroad Crossing

A railroad *roadway* consists of two rails, or tracks, and all their supporting elements, including *railroad bridges, tunnels* and *embankments.* The roadway follows the *right of way.* The distance between rails is the *gauge,* while the degree of rise or fall in a *roadbed* is the *grade.* The top of a rail is the *railhead.* The bottom is the *rail foot.*

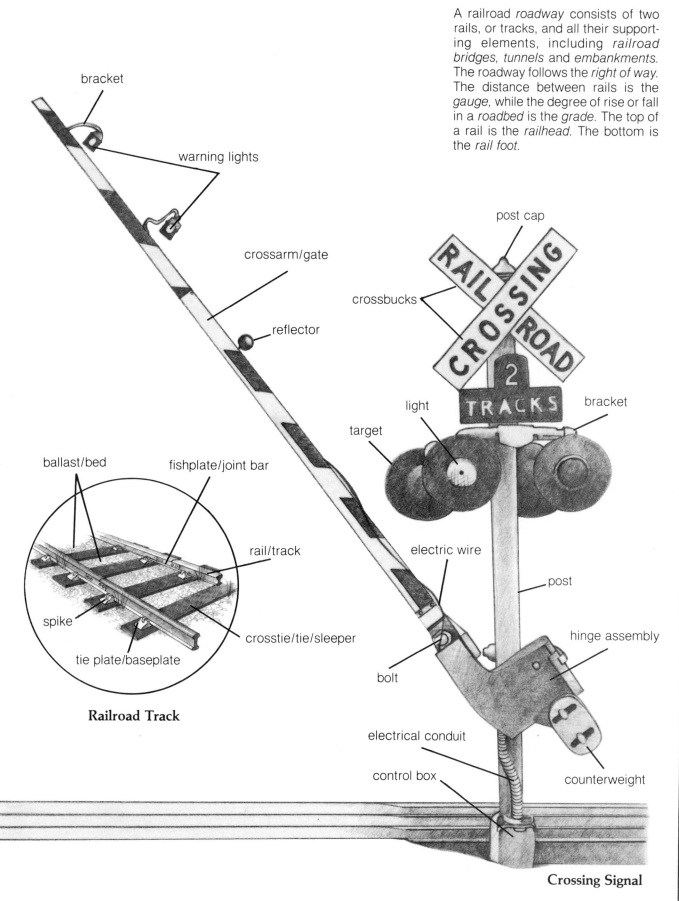

bracket

warning lights

crossarm/gate

reflector

post cap

crossbucks

RAIL

CROSSING

ROAD

2 TRACKS

light

target

bracket

electric wire

post

hinge assembly

bolt

counterweight

electrical conduit

control box

ballast/bed

fishplate/joint bar

rail/track

spike

crosstie/tie/sleeper

tie plate/baseplate

Railroad Track

Crossing Signal

Railroad

In addition to the locomotives shown here, there are *diesel* and *electric locomotives. Open-top cars,* boxcars and flatcars are the main types of *freight cars,* while *passenger trains* consist of *dining cars, sleeping cars, lounge* or *observation cars* and *baggage cars.*

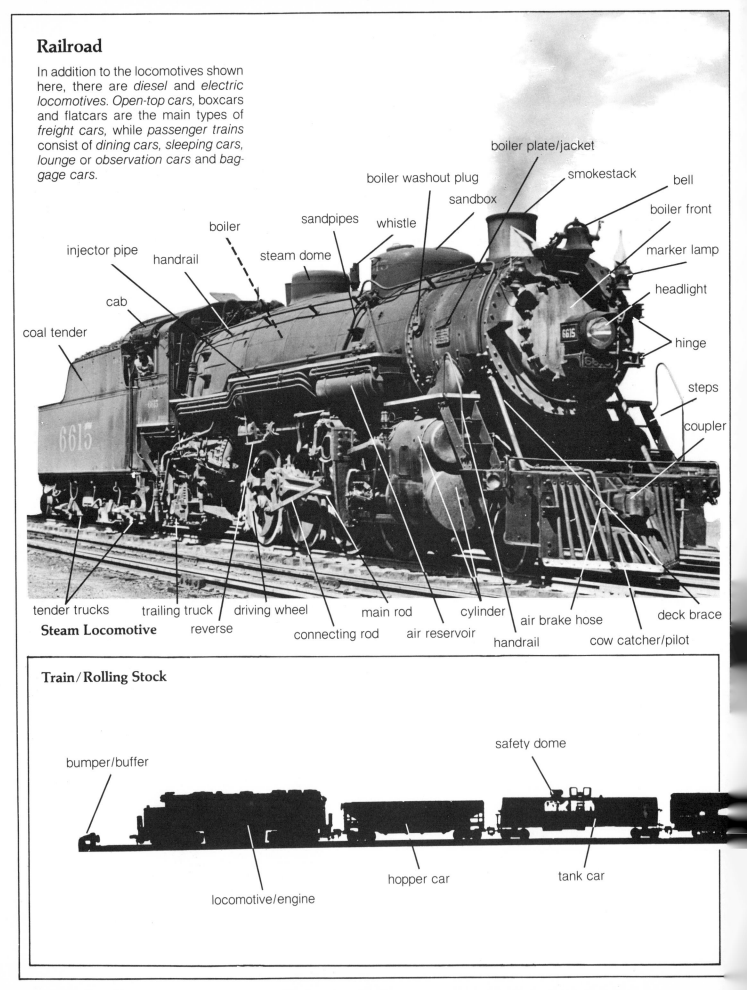

boiler plate/jacket

boiler washout plug

smokestack

bell

sandbox

boiler front

marker lamp

sandpipes

whistle

boiler

headlight

injector pipe

steam dome

handrail

hinge

cab

steps

coal tender

coupler

6615

tender trucks

trailing truck

driving wheel

main rod

cylinder

air brake hose

deck brace

reverse

connecting rod

air reservoir

cow catcher/pilot

Steam Locomotive

handrail

Train/Rolling Stock

safety dome

bumper/buffer

hopper car

tank car

locomotive/engine

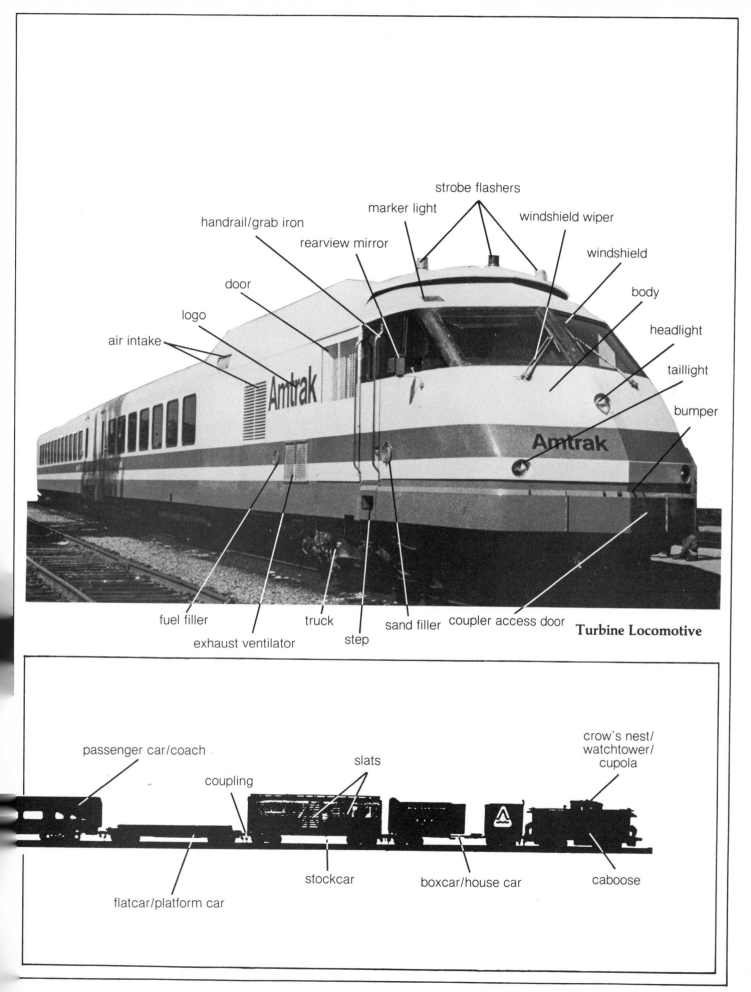

strobe flashers

marker light

windshield wiper

handrail/grab iron

windshield

rearview mirror

body

door

headlight

logo

taillight

air intake

bumper

Amtrak

Amtrak

fuel filler

truck

sand filler

coupler access door

Turbine Locomotive

exhaust ventilator

step

crow's nest/
watchtower/
cupola

passenger car/coach

slats

coupling

stockcar

boxcar/house car

caboose

flatcar/platform car

Bus

Long-distance coaches have airplanelike *reclining seats* with *overhead baggage racks* and *reading lights.* They may also have *lavatories* and *roof ventilation hatches.* *Sightseeing buses* have *transparent roofs,* at least in part, to increase the viewing area.

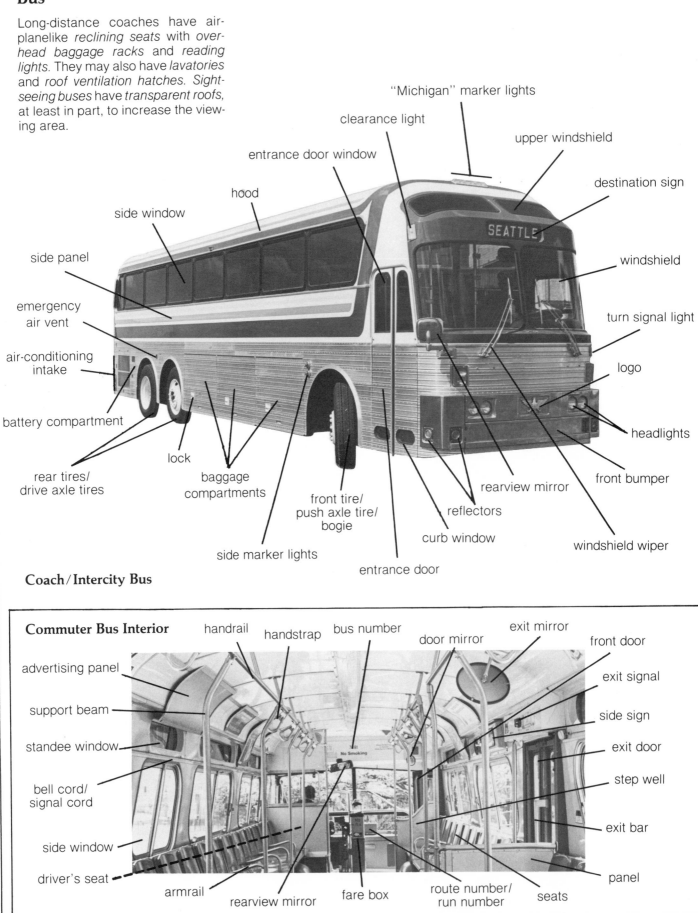

"Michigan" marker lights

clearance light

upper windshield

entrance door window

destination sign

hood

side window

SEATTLE

windshield

side panel

turn signal light

emergency air vent

logo

air-conditioning intake

headlights

battery compartment

front bumper

lock

rear tires/ drive axle tires

baggage compartments

rearview mirror

reflectors

front tire/ push axle tire/ bogie

curb window

windshield wiper

side marker lights

entrance door

Coach/Intercity Bus

Commuter Bus Interior

handrail

handstrap

bus number

exit mirror

door mirror

front door

advertising panel

exit signal

support beam

side sign

standee window

exit door

bell cord/ signal cord

step well

exit bar

side window

driver's seat

panel

armrail

rearview mirror

fare box

route number/ run number

seats

Subway

A subway, or *rapid transit system*, usually consists of a *train* which derives its power from a *third rail*; subterranean *tunnels*, or *tubes; elevated tracks;* and *subway stations*, or *stops*, along each *route*.

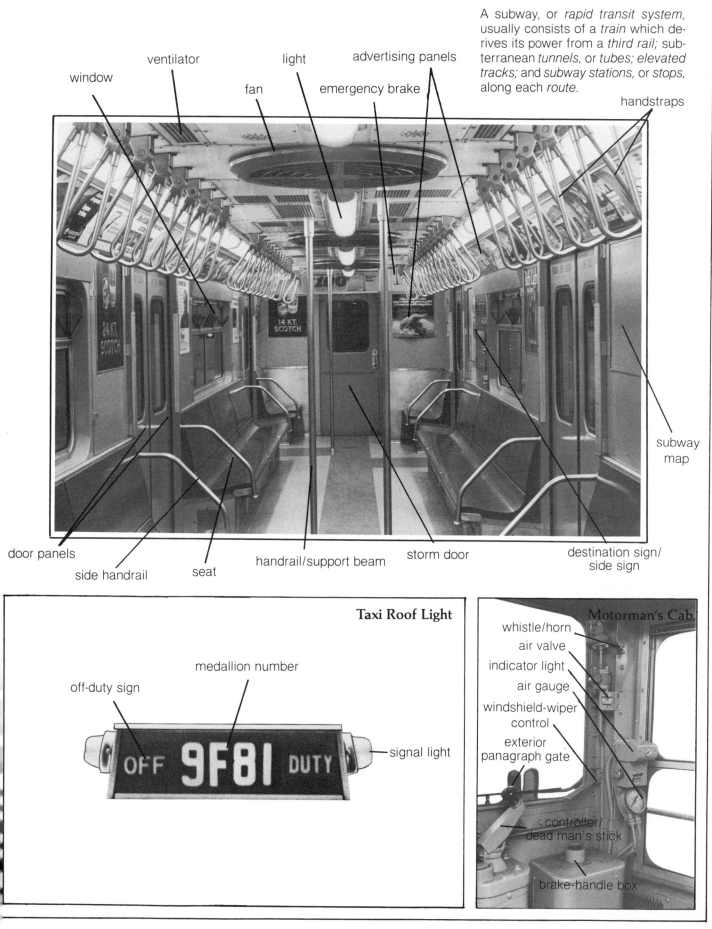

window
ventilator
light
fan
emergency brake
advertising panels
handstraps
door panels
side handrail
seat
handrail/support beam
storm door
destination sign/ side sign
subway map

Taxi Roof Light

off-duty sign
medallion number
signal light

OFF **9F8I** DUTY

Motorman's Cab

whistle/horn
air valve
indicator light
air gauge
windshield-wiper control
exterior panagraph gate
controller/ dead man's stick
brake-handle box

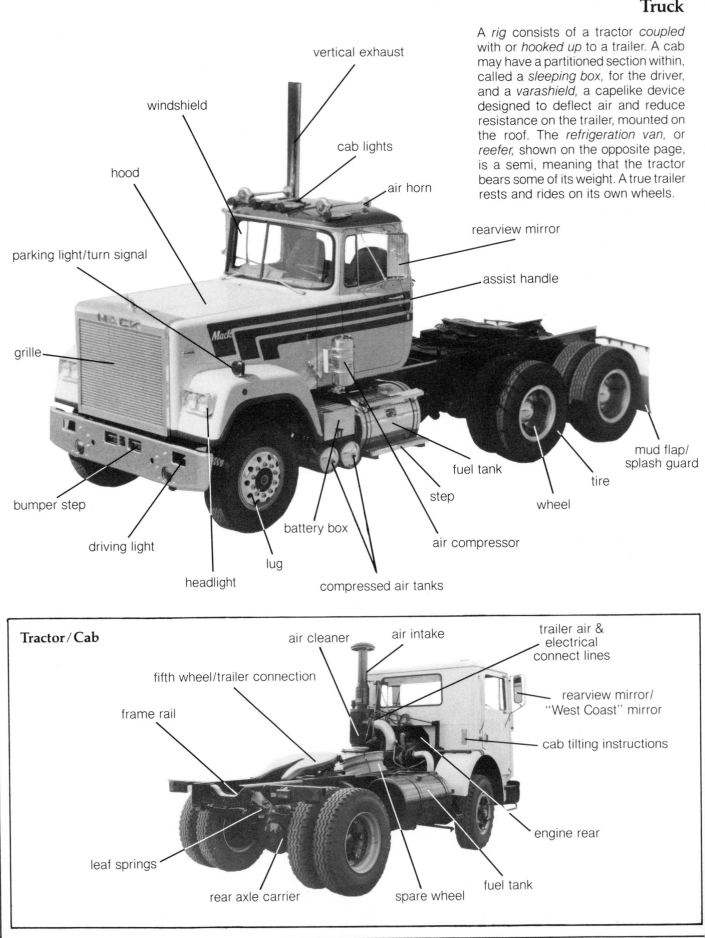

Truck

A *rig* consists of a tractor *coupled* with or *hooked up* to a trailer. A cab may have a partitioned section within, called a *sleeping box,* for the driver, and a *varashield,* a capelike device designed to deflect air and reduce resistance on the trailer, mounted on the roof. The *refrigeration van,* or *reefer,* shown on the opposite page, is a semi, meaning that the tractor bears some of its weight. A true trailer rests and rides on its own wheels.

vertical exhaust

windshield

cab lights

air horn

hood

rearview mirror

parking light/turn signal

assist handle

grille

mud flap/splash guard

tire

fuel tank

bumper step

step

wheel

battery box

air compressor

driving light

lug

headlight

compressed air tanks

Tractor/Cab

air cleaner

air intake

trailer air & electrical connect lines

fifth wheel/trailer connection

frame rail

rearview mirror/ "West Coast" mirror

cab tilting instructions

leaf springs

engine rear

rear axle carrier

spare wheel

fuel tank

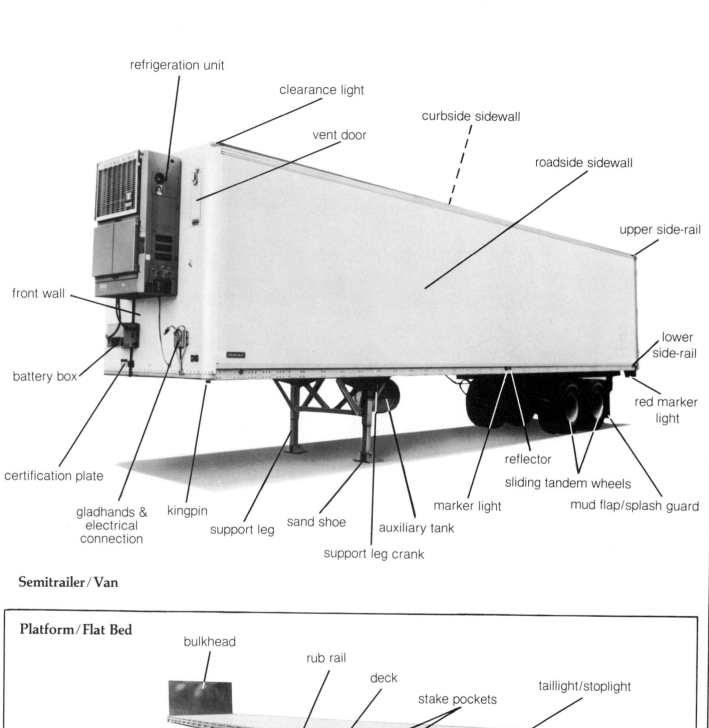

refrigeration unit

clearance light

curbside sidewall

vent door

roadside sidewall

upper side-rail

front wall

lower side-rail

battery box

red marker light

certification plate

reflector

sliding tandem wheels

mud flap/splash guard

gladhands & electrical connection

kingpin

support leg

sand shoe

marker light

auxiliary tank

support leg crank

Semitrailer/Van

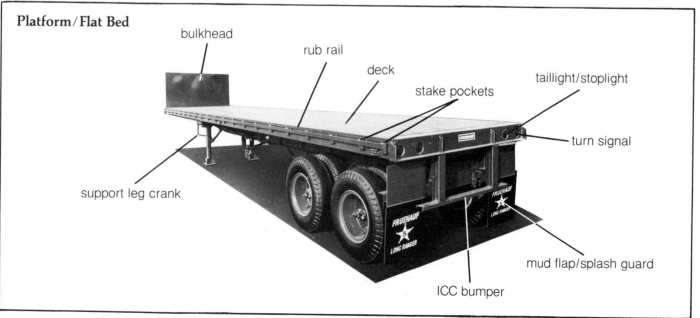

Platform/Flat Bed

bulkhead

rub rail

deck

stake pockets

taillight/stoplight

turn signal

support leg crank

mud flap/splash guard

ICC bumper

Carriers

Police Car

Many police cars have *alley lights*, strong floodlights at either end of the light bar on the roof. A wire screen between the driver's seat and the back seat of the car is called the *cage*. Contained in the trunk of many police cars are a *hurst tool*, or *jaws of life*, a *haligan tool*, an *oxygen unit*, *flares*, a *fire extinguisher*, a *riot gun*, a *first-aid kit*, *blankets* and a *pillow*.

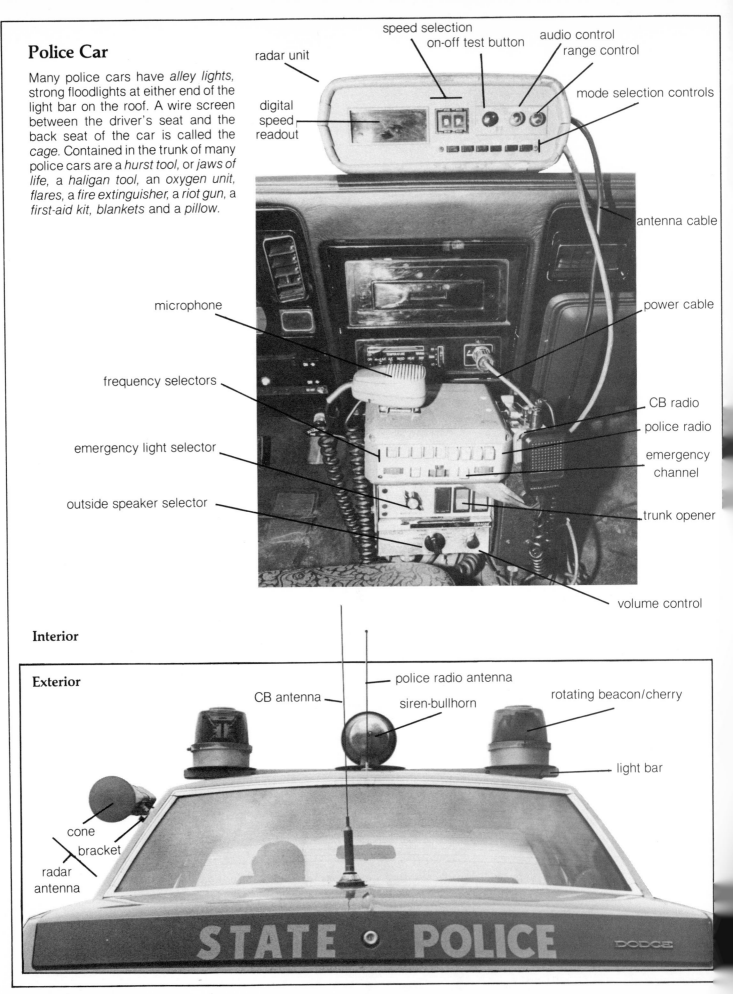

speed selection
on-off test button
radar unit
audio control
range control
digital speed readout
mode selection controls
antenna cable
microphone
power cable
frequency selectors
CB radio
police radio
emergency light selector
emergency channel
outside speaker selector
trunk opener
volume control

Interior

Exterior

CB antenna
police radio antenna
siren-bullhorn
rotating beacon/cherry
light bar
cone
bracket
radar antenna

STATE ● POLICE

DODGE

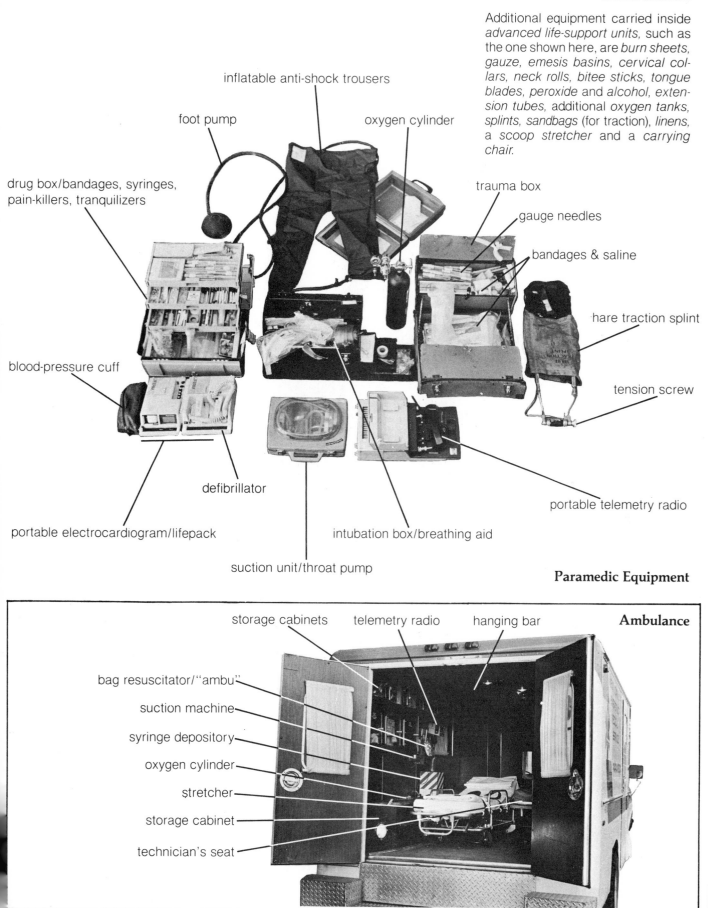

Ambulance

Additional equipment carried inside *advanced life-support units,* such as the one shown here, are *burn sheets, gauze, emesis basins, cervical collars, neck rolls, bitee sticks, tongue blades, peroxide* and *alcohol, extension tubes,* additional *oxygen tanks, splints, sandbags* (for traction), *linens,* a *scoop stretcher* and a *carrying chair.*

inflatable anti-shock trousers

foot pump

oxygen cylinder

trauma box

gauge needles

drug box/bandages, syringes, pain-killers, tranquilizers

bandages & saline

hare traction splint

blood-pressure cuff

tension screw

defibrillator

portable telemetry radio

portable electrocardiogram/lifepack

intubation box/breathing aid

suction unit/throat pump

Paramedic Equipment

storage cabinets   telemetry radio   hanging bar   **Ambulance**

bag resuscitator/"ambu"

suction machine

syringe depository

oxygen cylinder

stretcher

storage cabinet

technician's seat

Emergency Vehicles

Fire Engine

On a fire truck, the entire tower ladder and control platform revolve on a *turntable*. Contained within a pumper is a water *booster tank* for fighting small fires, a *booster hose-reel*, for letting out hose line, and an *extension ladder*. Most fire fighting *apparatus* also carry *air tanks, lift-nets, EMT,* or *first aid boxes,* and *smoke ejectors*.

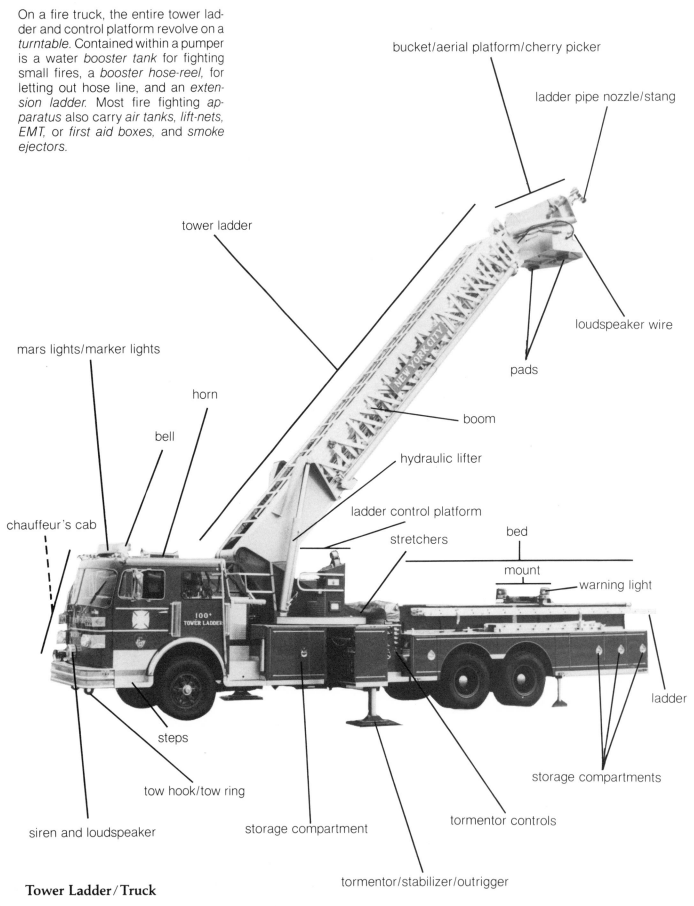

bucket/aerial platform/cherry picker

ladder pipe nozzle/stang

tower ladder

loudspeaker wire

mars lights/marker lights

pads

horn

boom

bell

hydraulic lifter

ladder control platform

chauffeur's cab

stretchers

bed

mount

warning light

ladder

steps

storage compartments

tow hook/tow ring

storage compartment

tormentor controls

siren and loudspeaker

tormentor/stabilizer/outrigger

Tower Ladder/Truck

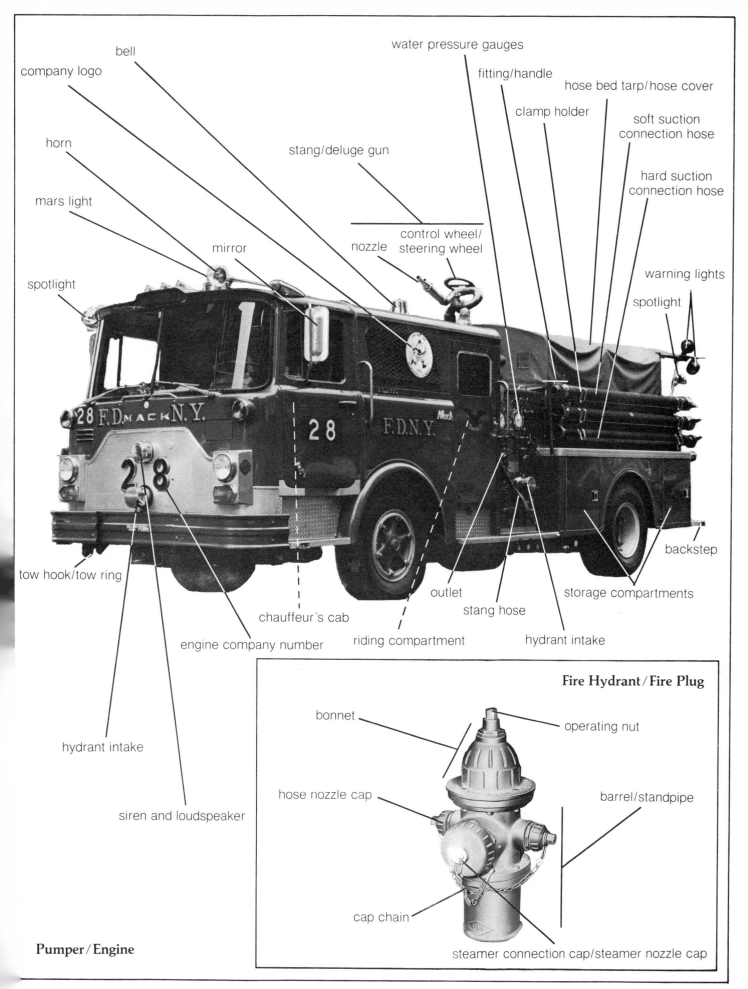

bell

company logo

water pressure gauges

fitting/handle

hose bed tarp/hose cover

horn

clamp holder

soft suction
connection hose

mars light

stang/deluge gun

hard suction
connection hose

mirror

spotlight

control wheel/
steering wheel

nozzle

warning lights

spotlight

tow hook/tow ring

chauffeur's cab

engine company number

outlet

stang hose

storage compartments

backstep

riding compartment

hydrant intake

hydrant intake

siren and loudspeaker

Fire Hydrant / Fire Plug

bonnet

operating nut

hose nozzle cap

barrel/standpipe

cap chain

steamer connection cap/steamer nozzle cap

Pumper / Engine

Emergency Vehicles

Tow Truck/Wrecker

Tow trucks, or *rigs*, that respond to accident reports are called "chasers." A fully-equipped tow truck carries *fire extinguishers*, *battery charger*, *battery jumper cables*, and a two-pronged *lockout tool* which enables the operator to open locked car doors.

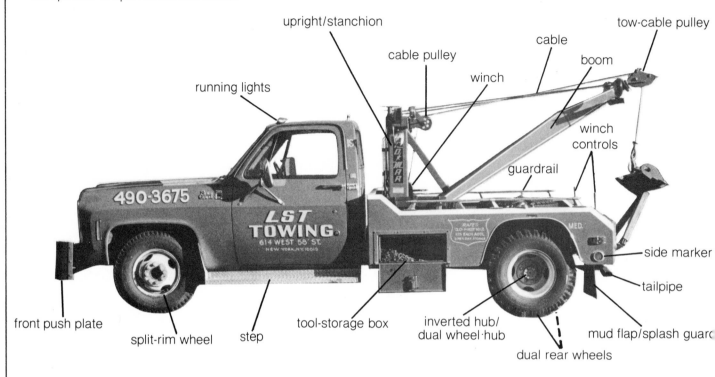

upright/stanchion

cable pulley

winch

cable

boom

tow-cable pulley

running lights

winch controls

guardrail

side marker

tailpipe

front push plate

split-rim wheel

step

tool-storage box

inverted hub/ dual wheel·hub

dual rear wheels

mud flap/splash guard

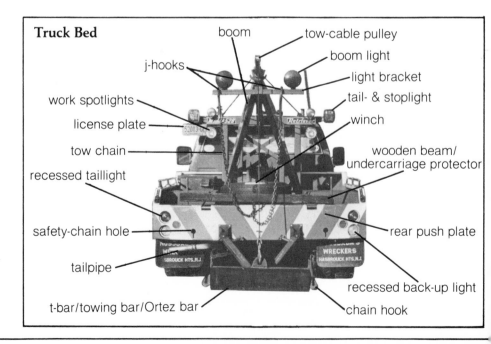

Truck Bed

boom

tow-cable pulley

boom light

j-hooks

light bracket

tail- & stoplight

work spotlights

winch

license plate

wooden beam/ undercarriage protector

tow chain

recessed taillight

safety-chain hole

rear push plate

tailpipe

recessed back-up light

t-bar/towing bar/Ortez bar

chain hook

Sanitation Vehicles

Garbage collectors, sanitation men,
or *"sanmen,"* also use a large, water-
carrying truck called a *flusher* to wet
down and clean streets.

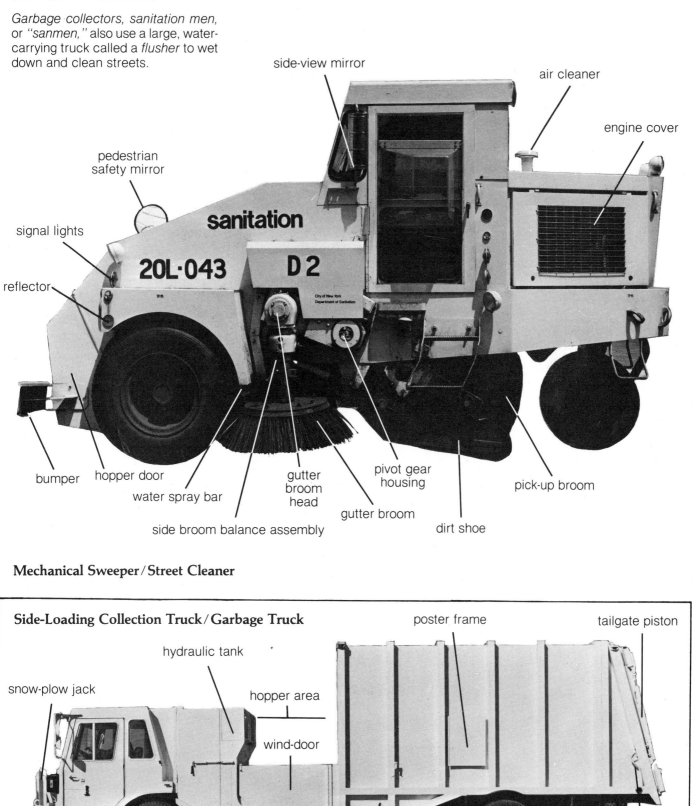

side-view mirror

air cleaner

engine cover

pedestrian
safety mirror

signal lights

sanitation

20L·043

D 2

City of New York
Department of Sanitation

reflector

bumper

hopper door

water spray bar

gutter
broom
head

side broom balance assembly

gutter broom

pivot gear
housing

dirt shoe

pick-up broom

Mechanical Sweeper/Street Cleaner

Side-Loading Collection Truck/Garbage Truck

poster frame

tailgate piston

hydraulic tank

snow-plow jack

hopper area

wind-door

snow-plow frame

packer controls/
ram controls

body lock handle

fuel tank

body

hydraulic line

Public Service Vehicles

Bicycle

This illustration combines elements from the most popular bicycle styles. The *frame* is the skeleton to which the *wheels* and all other components are attached. A one-wheel cycle is called a *unicycle*. A three-wheeler is a *tricycle*.

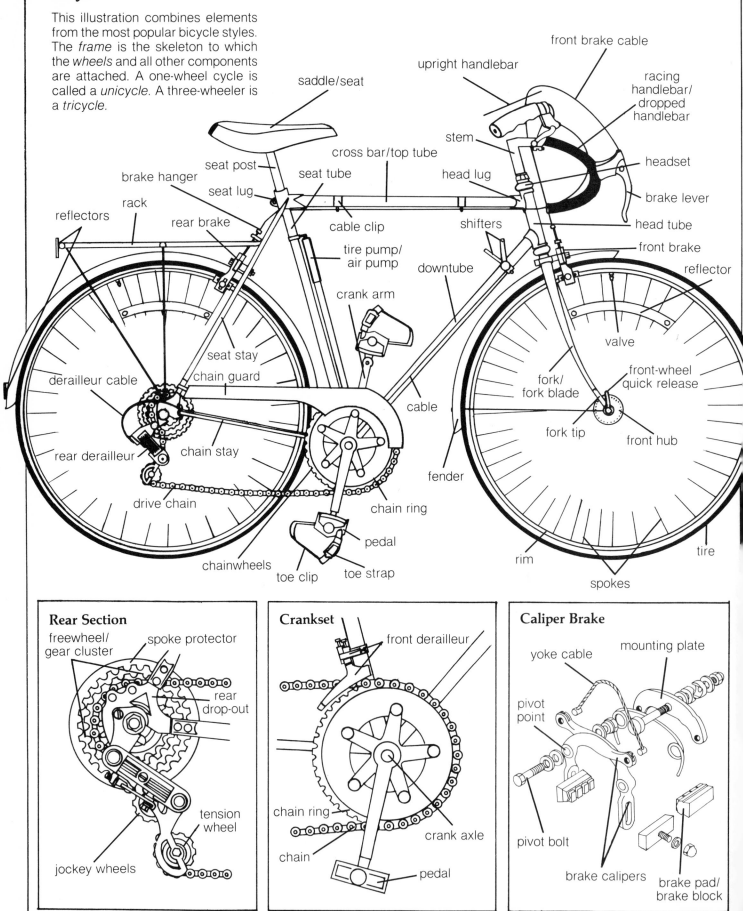

saddle/seat

front brake cable

upright handlebar

racing handlebar/ dropped handlebar

stem

seat post

brake hanger

seat tube

cross bar/top tube

head lug

headset

rack

seat lug

brake lever

reflectors

rear brake

cable clip

shifters

head tube

tire pump/ air pump

downtube

front brake

reflector

crank arm

valve

seat stay

fork/ fork blade

front-wheel quick release

derailleur cable

chain guard

cable

rear derailleur

chain stay

fork tip

front hub

drive chain

fender

chain ring

rim

pedal

tire

chainwheels

toe clip

toe strap

spokes

Rear Section

freewheel/ gear cluster

spoke protector

rear drop-out

tension wheel

jockey wheels

Crankset

front derailleur

chain ring

crank axle

chain

pedal

Caliper Brake

yoke cable

mounting plate

pivot point

pivot bolt

brake calipers

brake pad/ brake block

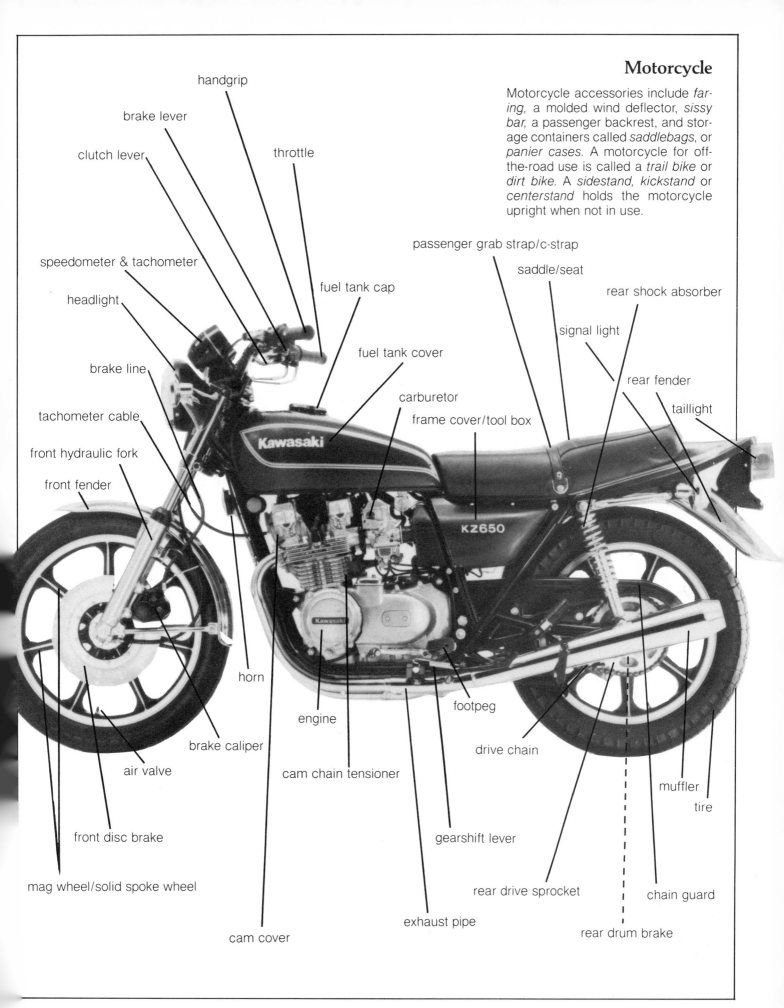

Motorcycle

Motorcycle accessories include *faring,* a molded wind deflector, *sissy bar,* a passenger backrest, and storage containers called *saddlebags,* or *panier cases.* A motorcycle for off-the-road use is called a *trail bike* or *dirt bike.* A *sidestand, kickstand* or *centerstand* holds the motorcycle upright when not in use.

handgrip

brake lever

clutch lever

throttle

speedometer & tachometer

fuel tank cap

headlight

fuel tank cover

brake line

carburetor

tachometer cable

frame cover/tool box

front hydraulic fork

front fender

passenger grab strap/c-strap

saddle/seat

rear shock absorber

signal light

rear fender

taillight

Kawasaki

KZ650

horn

brake caliper

air valve

front disc brake

mag wheel/solid spoke wheel

cam cover

engine

cam chain tensioner

footpeg

gearshift lever

drive chain

muffler

tire

exhaust pipe

rear drive sprocket

chain guard

rear drum brake

Recreational Vehicles

The *heating* and *cooking units* in the rear *coach* of a camper run on *propane gas*. Unlike campers, which run under their own power, *trailers* are hitched behind a vehicle and towed. Other *off-the-road vehicles* include *four-wheel drive jeeps* and *dune buggies*.

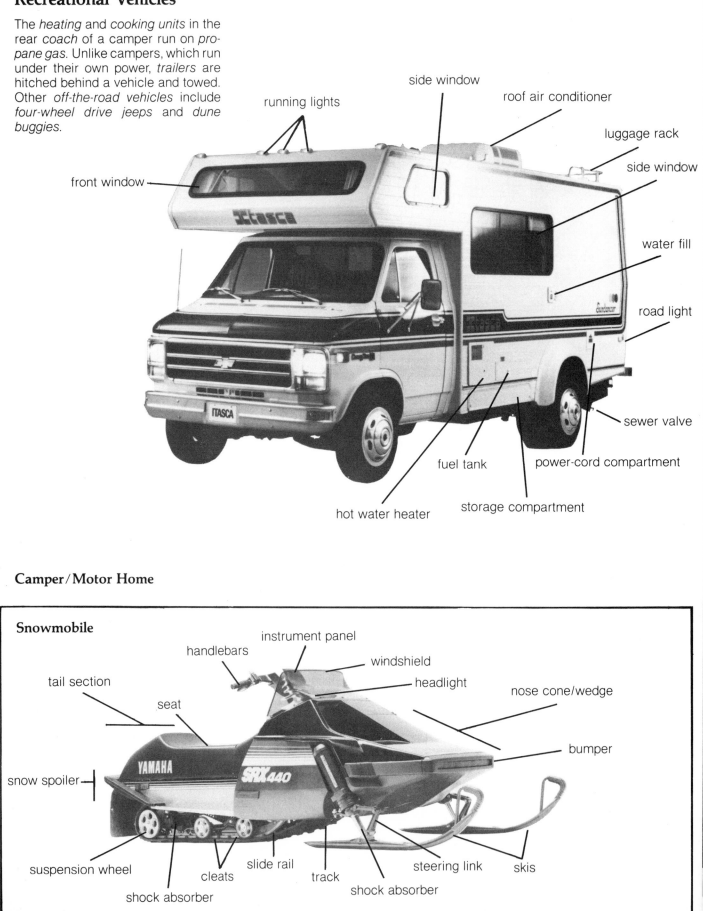

running lights

side window

roof air conditioner

luggage rack

front window

side window

water fill

road light

sewer valve

power-cord compartment

fuel tank

storage compartment

hot water heater

Camper/Motor Home

Snowmobile

instrument panel

handlebars

windshield

headlight

tail section

nose cone/wedge

seat

bumper

snow spoiler

suspension wheel

cleats

slide rail

track

steering link

skis

shock absorber

shock absorber

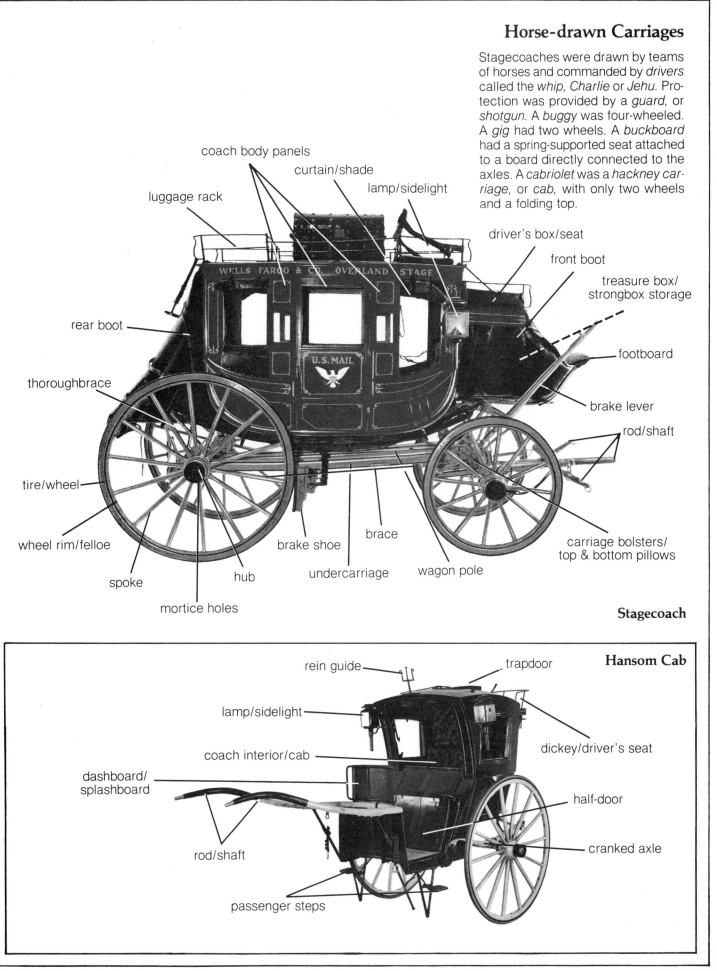

Horse-drawn Carriages

Stagecoaches were drawn by teams of horses and commanded by *drivers* called the *whip, Charlie* or *Jehu*. Protection was provided by a *guard*, or *shotgun*. A *buggy* was four-wheeled. A *gig* had two wheels. A *buckboard* had a spring-supported seat attached to a board directly connected to the axles. A *cabriolet* was a *hackney carriage*, or *cab*, with only two wheels and a folding top.

coach body panels

curtain/shade

lamp/sidelight

luggage rack

driver's box/seat

front boot

treasure box/ strongbox storage

rear boot

footboard

thoroughbrace

brake lever

rod/shaft

tire/wheel

wheel rim/felloe

brake shoe

brace

carriage bolsters/ top & bottom pillows

spoke

hub

undercarriage

wagon pole

mortice holes

WELLS FARGO & CO. OVERLAND STAGE

U.S. MAIL

Stagecoach

Hansom Cab

rein guide

trapdoor

lamp/sidelight

coach interior/cab

dickey/driver's seat

dashboard/ splashboard

half-door

rod/shaft

cranked axle

passenger steps

Nautical Terminology

The outer shell of a boat is the *hull*. A hull's greatest width is the *beam*. Any line running from one side of a boat to the other is said to run *athwartships*. That part of a boat facing the direction from which the wind is blowing is called the *windward* side. The opposite side is called the *leeward* side.

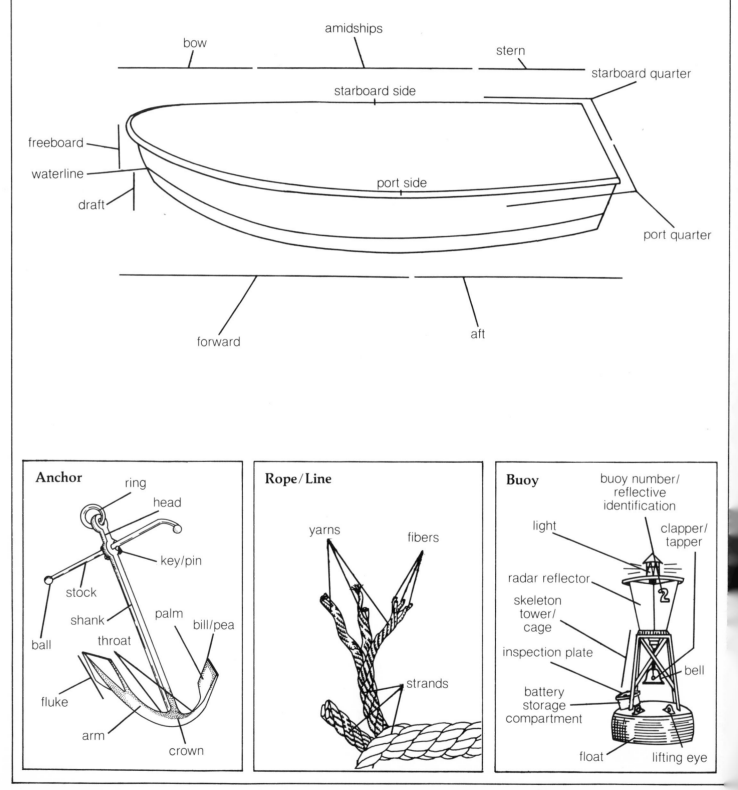

Anchor

ring
head
key/pin
stock
ball
shank
palm
throat
bill/pea
fluke
arm
crown

Rope/Line

yarns
fibers
strands

Buoy

buoy number/ reflective identification
light
clapper/ tapper
radar reflector
skeleton tower/ cage
inspection plate
battery storage compartment
bell
float
lifting eye

Rowboat

Any small *craft*, either *decked* or *open* and propelled by oars, is a rowboat, or *skiff*. If it is used to service a *yacht* or *motor cruiser*, it is called a *dinghy*, *dink* or *tender*.

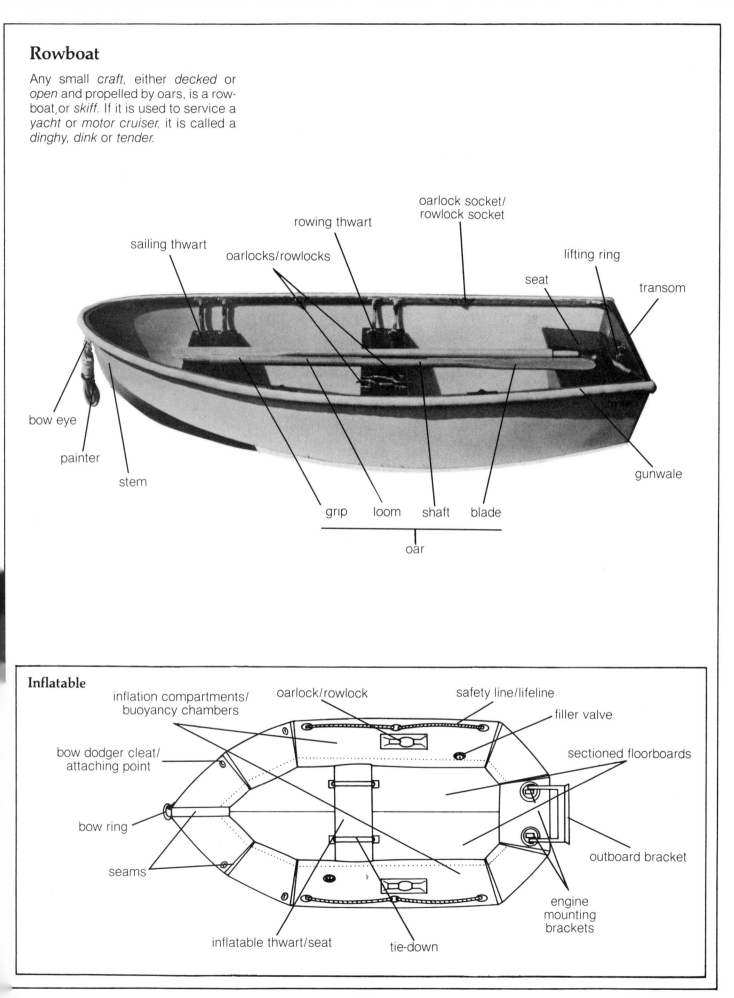

sailing thwart

rowing thwart

oarlock socket/
rowlock socket

oarlocks/rowlocks

lifting ring

seat

transom

bow eye

painter

stem

grip

loom

shaft

blade

oar

gunwale

Inflatable

inflation compartments/
buoyancy chambers

oarlock/rowlock

safety line/lifeline

filler valve

bow dodger cleat/
attaching point

sectioned floorboards

bow ring

seams

outboard bracket

engine
mounting
brackets

inflatable thwart/seat

tie-down

Sailboat

Standing rigging, shrouds and stays, keep a sailing vessel's mast, or *spar,* upright. *Halyards* are used to hoist sails and *running rigging,* lines and *sheets,* control them. On some boats a *tiller* is used instead of a wheel to steer.

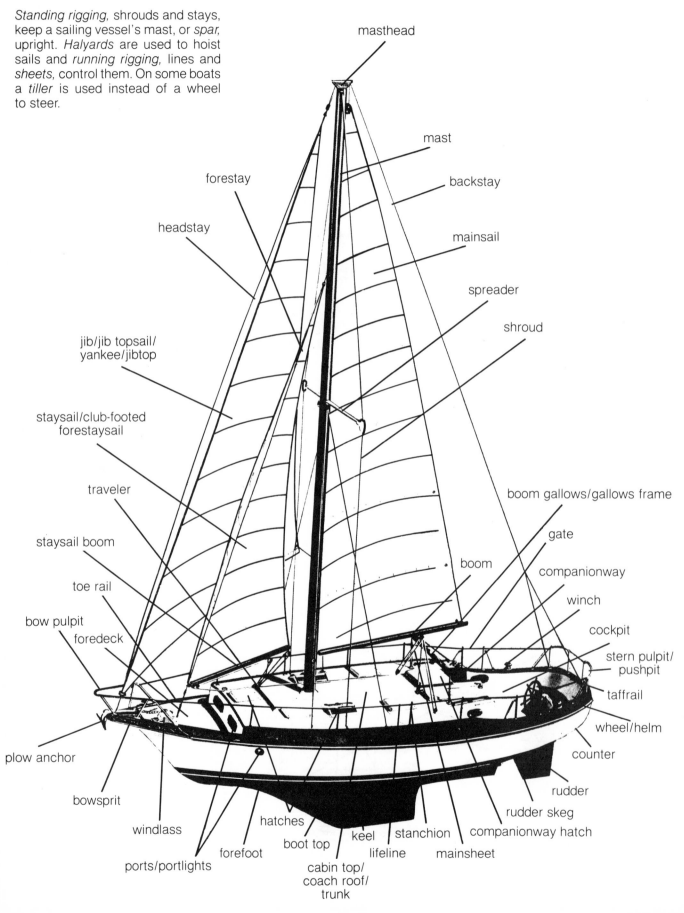

masthead

mast

backstay

mainsail

forestay

headstay

spreader

shroud

jib/jib topsail/ yankee/jibtop

staysail/club-footed forestaysail

boom gallows/gallows frame

traveler

gate

staysail boom

companionway

boom

winch

toe rail

cockpit

bow pulpit

stern pulpit/ pushpit

foredeck

taffrail

wheel/helm

plow anchor

counter

rudder

bowsprit

rudder skeg

windlass

companionway hatch

hatches

stanchion

keel

ports/portlights

boot top

lifeline

mainsheet

forefoot

cabin top/ coach roof/ trunk

Sailboat Accommodations

The area between a vessel's cabin sole and its hull is called the *bilge*. Boats with overnight accommodations usually have a *navigator's station*, featuring a *chart table*.

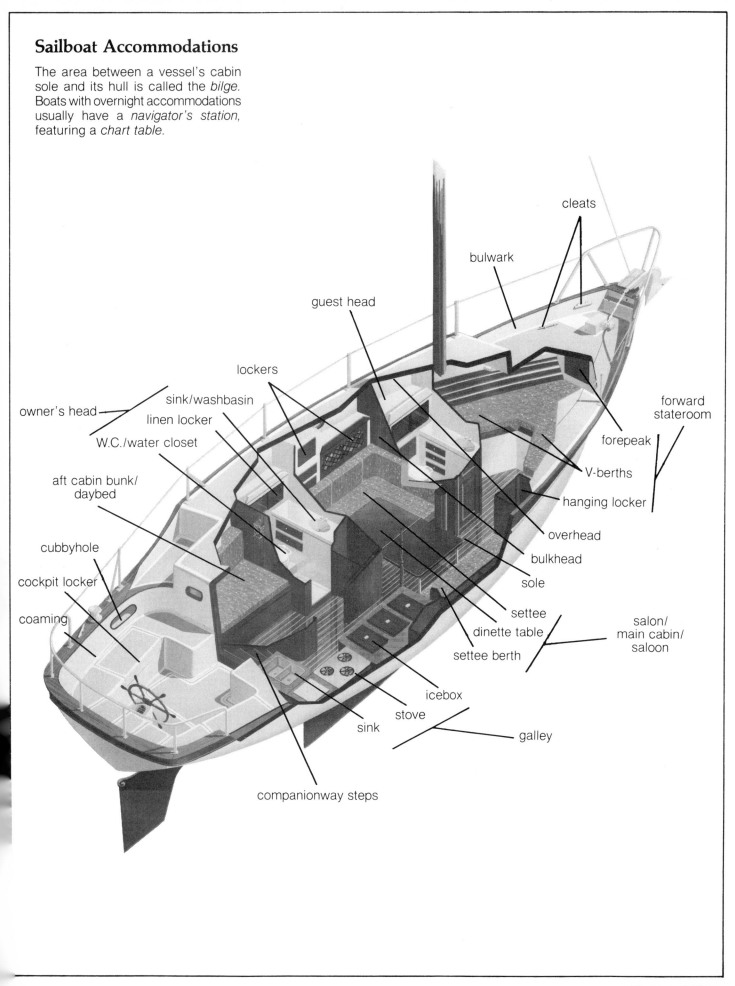

cleats

bulwark

guest head

lockers

sink/washbasin

owner's head

linen locker

W.C./water closet

forward stateroom

forepeak

V-berths

hanging locker

aft cabin bunk/ daybed

overhead

bulkhead

cubbyhole

sole

cockpit locker

settee

dinette table

coaming

salon/ main cabin/ saloon

settee berth

icebox

stove

sink

galley

companionway steps

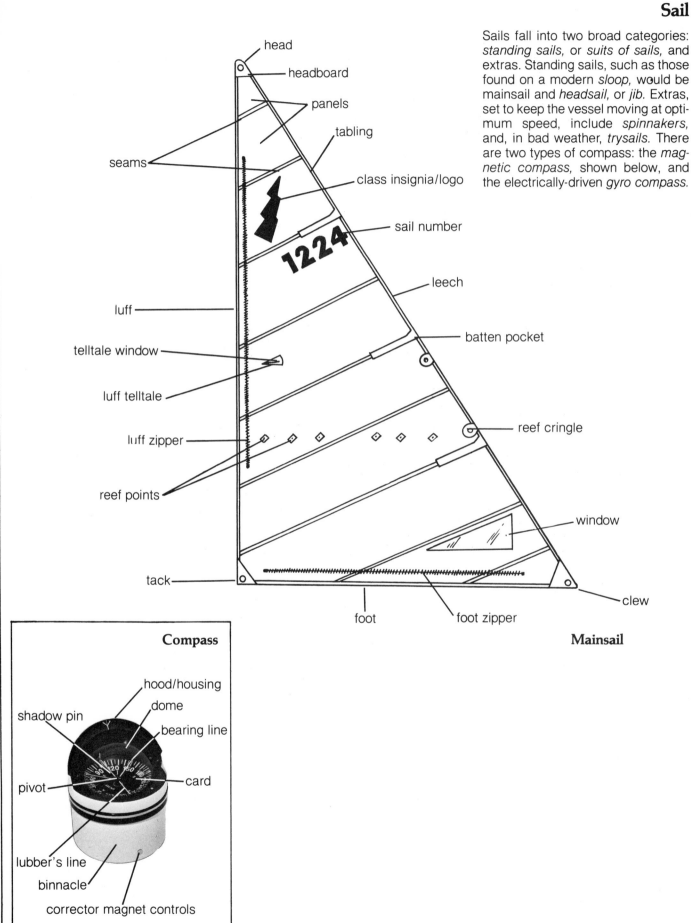

Sail

head

headboard

panels

tabling

seams

class insignia/logo

sail number

leech

luff

batten pocket

telltale window

luff telltale

reef cringle

luff zipper

reef points

window

tack

clew

foot

foot zipper

Mainsail

Sails fall into two broad categories: *standing sails,* or *suits of sails,* and extras. Standing sails, such as those found on a modern *sloop,* would be mainsail and *headsail,* or jib. Extras, set to keep the vessel moving at optimum speed, include *spinnakers,* and, in bad weather, *trysails.* There are two types of compass: the *magnetic compass,* shown below, and the electrically-driven *gyro compass.*

Compass

hood/housing

dome

shadow pin

bearing line

pivot

card

lubber's line

binnacle

corrector magnet controls

Outboard Engine

Three basic types of engines are used to power vessels: outboards, *inboard-outboards,* or *sterndrives,* and *inboards.* A marine sextant, a successor to the *octant* and *quadrant,* is used to measure the angle between a celestial body and the earth's horizon to help mariners determine their position at sea.

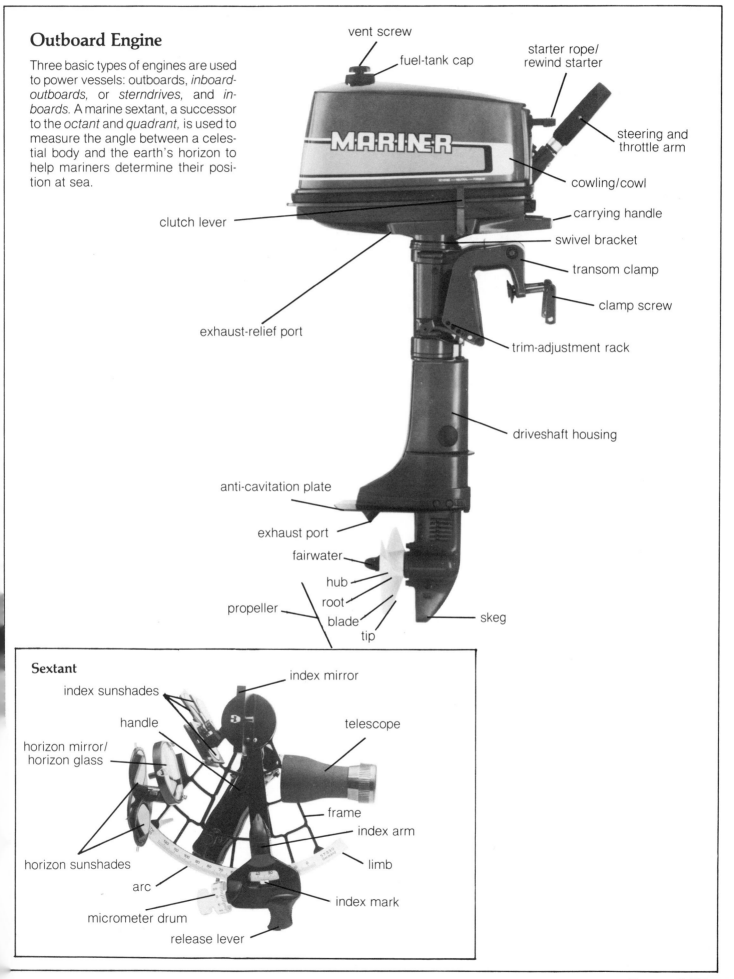

vent screw

fuel-tank cap

starter rope/ rewind starter

steering and throttle arm

cowling/cowl

carrying handle

swivel bracket

transom clamp

clamp screw

trim-adjustment rack

driveshaft housing

clutch lever

exhaust-relief port

anti-cavitation plate

exhaust port

fairwater

hub

root

propeller

blade

tip

skeg

Sextant

index sunshades

index mirror

handle

telescope

horizon mirror/ horizon glass

frame

index arm

limb

horizon sunshades

arc

index mark

micrometer drum

release lever

Powerboat

There are basically two kinds of powerboat *hull forms: displacement* and *planing.* Within these categories there are *V-bottom, cathedral, gull-wing, flat-bottom* and *round-bottom* hulls. *Houseboats* are boxlike vessels designed to provide maximum living space aboard. Projecting steel fittings used to hoist and carry a dinghy on a yacht are called *davits.*

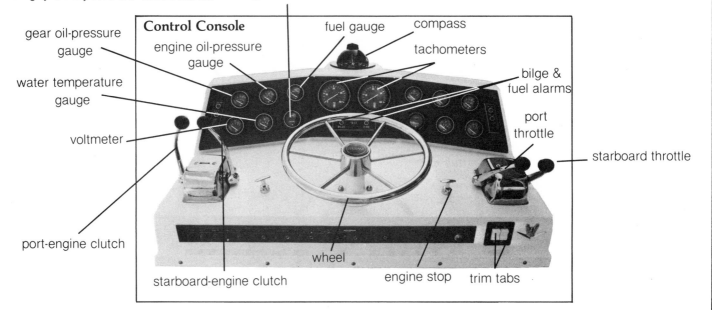

Control Console

- engine hour meter
- fuel gauge
- compass
- gear oil-pressure gauge
- engine oil-pressure gauge
- tachometers
- water temperature gauge
- bilge & fuel alarms
- voltmeter
- port throttle
- starboard throttle
- port-engine clutch
- starboard-engine clutch
- wheel
- engine stop
- trim tabs

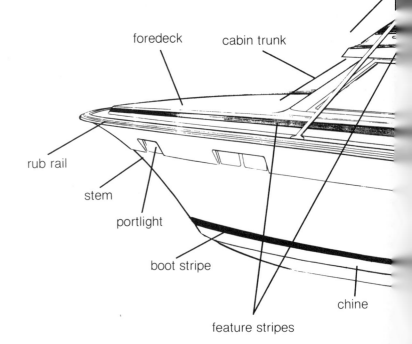

- flying bridge/flybridge
- foredeck
- cabin trunk
- rub rail
- stem
- portlight
- boot stripe
- chine
- feature stripes

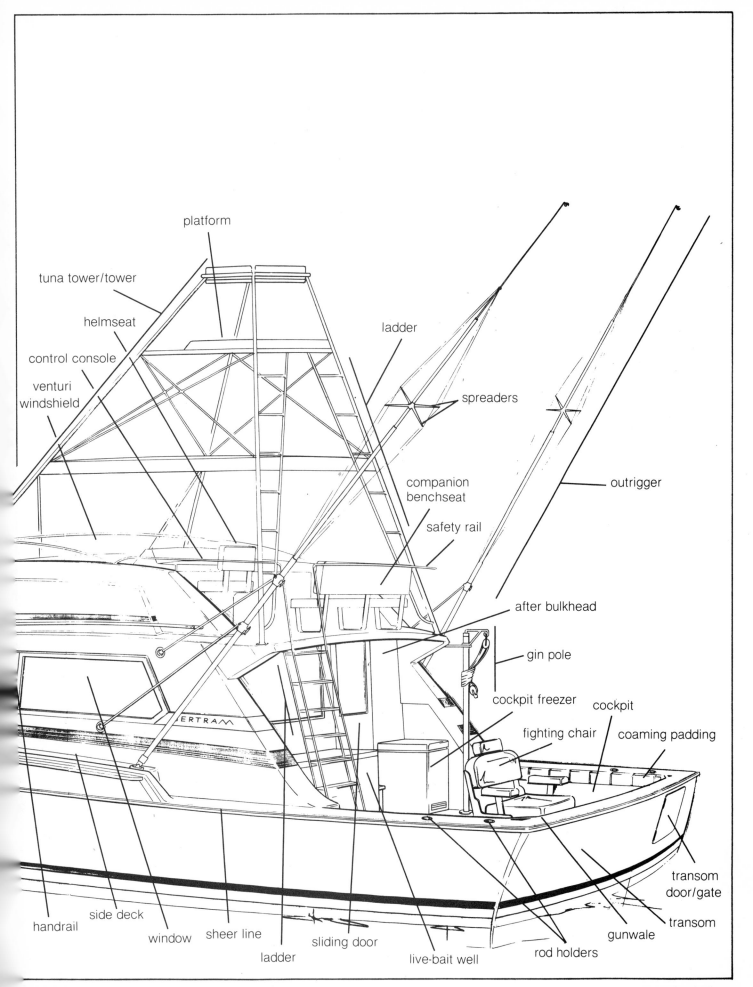

platform

tuna tower/tower

helmseat

control console

venturi
windshield

ladder

spreaders

companion
benchseat

safety rail

outrigger

after bulkhead

gin pole

cockpit freezer   cockpit

fighting chair   coaming padding

transom
door/gate

transom

handrail   side deck

window   sheer line

ladder

sliding door

live-bait well

rod holders

gunwale

Tanker

Cargo ships include *roll on-roll off ships; container ships; barge carriers; pallet ships; refrigerator ships,* or *reefers; dry-bulk carriers;* and *liquid-bulk carriers* such as the *super tanker* seen here. A *merchant ship* carrying *cargo* or *freight* is called a *liner* if it travels on scheduled routes at regular intervals, or a *tramp* if it does not have a fixed or scheduled route.

"catwalk" fore & aft gang

foremast

"crow's nest"/ lookout area

pressure & vacuum relief valves

belowdeck storage entrance

anchor windlass & mooring winch

anchor windlass & mooring winch

radar mast & radar antennas

bridge/wheelhouse

bridge wing

wireless, telegraph & navigation aerials

king post

lifeboat

hose-handling derrick

wed" derrick brackets

aft superstructure/ deckhouse

pressure & vacuum relief valves

deck manifold

tank hatches

rail

foam monitors & fire-fighting stations

vent lines

Passenger Ship/
Ocean Liner

Main bulkheads, steel walls running athwartships on a ship, are normally watertight. A *collision bulkhead* is a *watertight bulkhead* near the bow to prevent flooding in the event of collision. Circular windows aboard ship are called *ports* or *portholes*. A ship is boarded at the pier by a portable stairway, or *gangplank,* which fits in an opening in a ship's *rail* or *bulwark*. A metal shield on *berthing hawsers* to prevent rats from coming aboard is a *ratcatcher.*

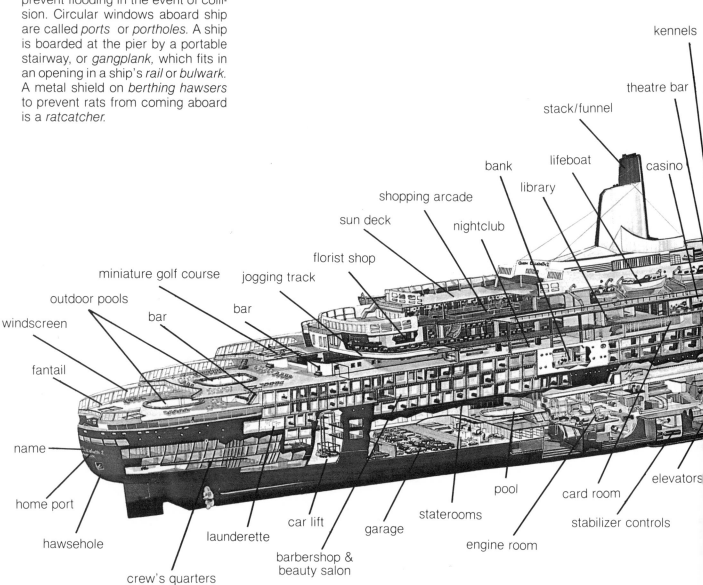

kennels

theatre bar

stack/funnel

bank

lifeboat

casino

shopping arcade

library

sun deck

nightclub

florist shop

miniature golf course

jogging track

outdoor pools

bar

bar

windscreen

fantail

name

elevators

home port

pool

card room

hawsehole

stabilizer controls

car lift

engine room

launderette

garage

staterooms

crew's quarters

barbershop & beauty salon

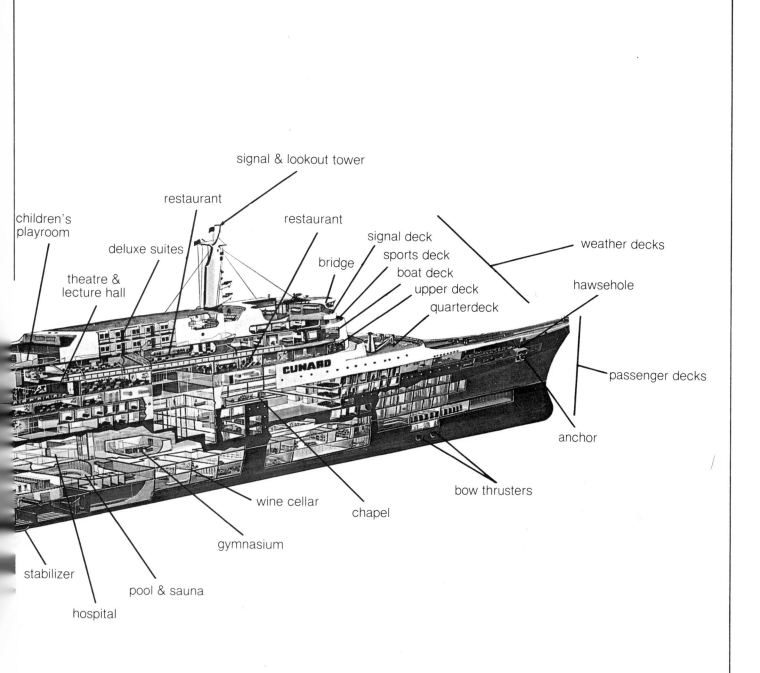

signal & lookout tower

restaurant

restaurant

children's playroom

deluxe suites

signal deck

bridge

sports deck

boat deck

upper deck

quarterdeck

weather decks

hawsehole

theatre & lecture hall

passenger decks

CUNARD

anchor

wine cellar

chapel

bow thrusters

gymnasium

stabilizer

pool & sauna

hospital

Boats and Ships

Surface Fighting Ship

Beginning with *dreadnoughts*, or *battleships*, modern surface *warships*, such as this *destroyer*, or *tin can*, have the capability to protect *shipping lanes*, deter invasions or support military operations on land. Today military vessels carry *surface-to-air missiles* and *surface-to-surface missiles*, as well as a range of *defensive guided weapons*. Many are *nuclear-powered*.

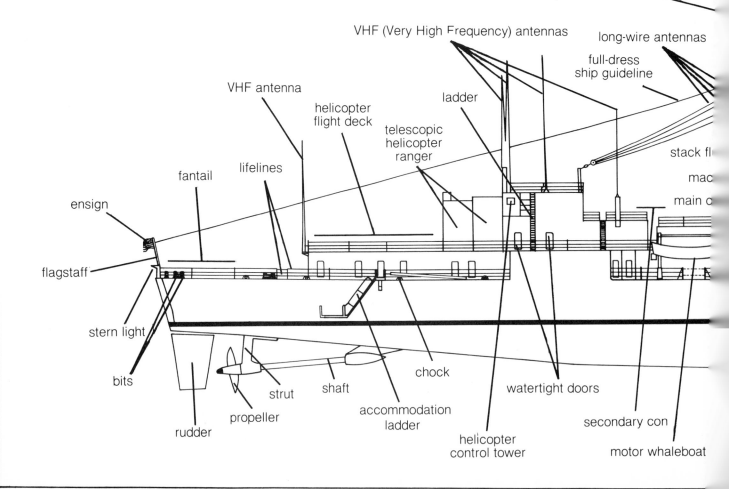

TACAN antenna

VHF (Very High Frequency) antennas

long-wire antennas

full-dress ship guideline

ladder

VHF antenna

helicopter flight deck

telescopic helicopter ranger

stack fl

mac

main c

lifelines

fantail

ensign

flagstaff

stern light

bits

rudder

propeller

strut

shaft

accommodation ladder

chock

watertight doors

helicopter control tower

secondary con

motor whaleboat

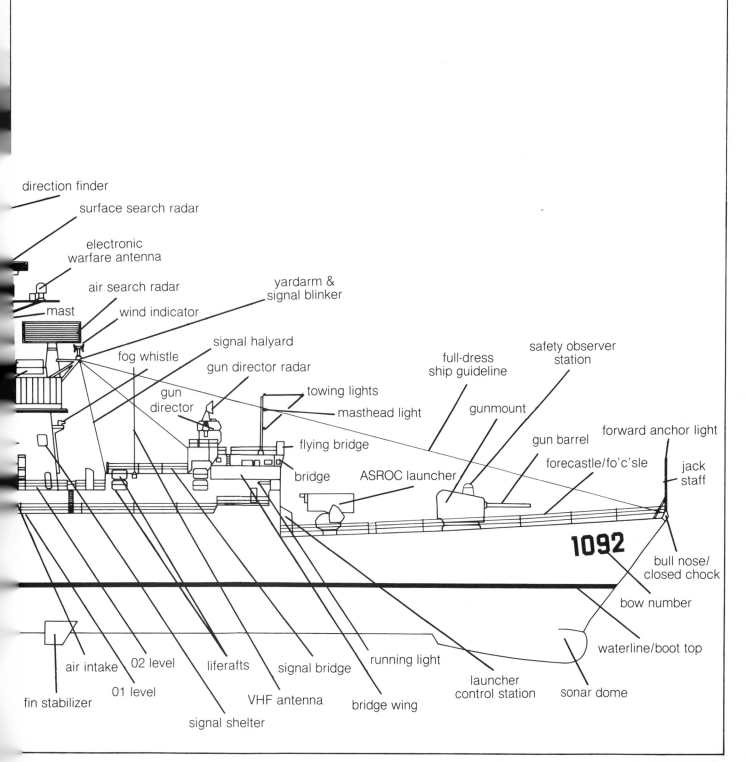

direction finder

surface search radar

electronic warfare antenna

air search radar

yardarm & signal blinker

mast

wind indicator

signal halyard

fog whistle

gun director radar

safety observer station

full-dress ship guideline

gun director

towing lights

gunmount

masthead light

gun barrel

forward anchor light

flying bridge

forecastle/fo'c'sle

jack staff

bridge

ASROC launcher

1092

bull nose/ closed chock

bow number

waterline/boot top

air intake

02 level

liferafts

signal bridge

running light

launcher control station

sonar dome

fin stabilizer

01 level

VHF antenna

bridge wing

signal shelter

Aircraft Carrier

The superstructure on an aircraft carrier, or *flattop*, is called the *island*. On take-off, aircraft are assisted by steam-driven catapults located on the *flight deck* or *angled deck*.

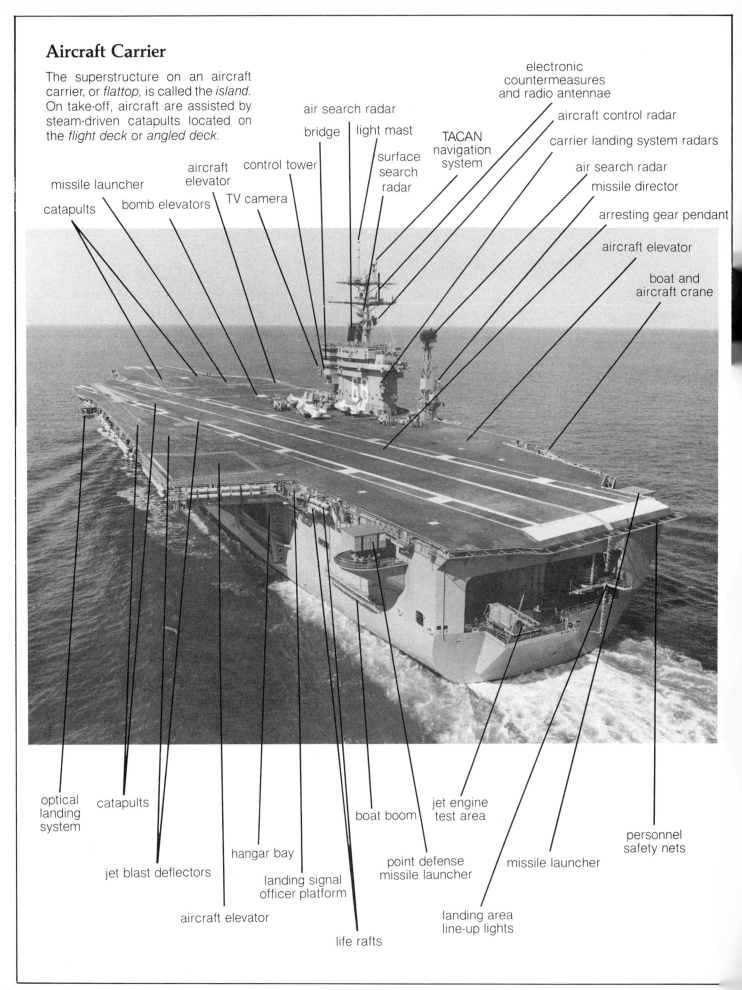

electronic
countermeasures
and radio antennae

air search radar

bridge   light mast

aircraft control radar

carrier landing system radars

TACAN
navigation
system

control tower

surface
search
radar

air search radar

missile launcher

aircraft
elevator

missile director

catapults

bomb elevators

TV camera

arresting gear pendant

aircraft elevator

boat and
aircraft crane

optical
landing
system

catapults

jet blast deflectors

hangar bay

landing signal
officer platform

aircraft elevator

boat boom

jet engine
test area

point defense
missile launcher

life rafts

landing area
line-up lights

missile launcher

personnel
safety nets

Submarine

Submarines, formerly called *U-boats* or *pigboats*, have thick inner *pressure hulls* and lighter *outer hulls*. The space between hulls is divided into several *ballast tanks*, used to control the vessel's buoyancy and trim. The conning tower contains *radio* and *radar antennas* and various *periscopes*, used for observation and navigation. In older submarines the sail also contained a *snorkel tube*. Navigation underwater is accomplished by means of an *inertial guidance system*. In addition to missiles, submarines can carry *torpedoes*.

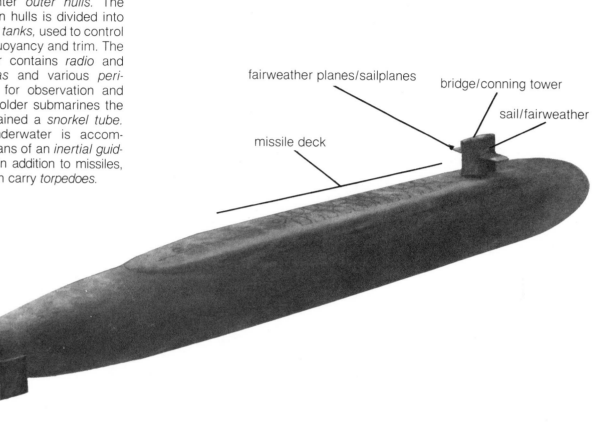

fairweather planes/sailplanes

bridge/conning tower

sail/fairweather

missile deck

rudder

propeller

Fleet Ballistic Missile Submarine

Nuclear-Powered Attack Submarine

safety-line track

hull number

turtleback

688

Tugboat and Fireboat

A *pudding fender* is a large fender made of old rope, formerly fitted to the bow of many *tugs,* or *towboats.* A *pusher tug,* also called a *pushboat,* is specially designed with a high flat bow for *barge cluster* push-towing. A fireboat is usually a tug fitted with such items as *high-pressure pumps, hoses* and *nozzles.*

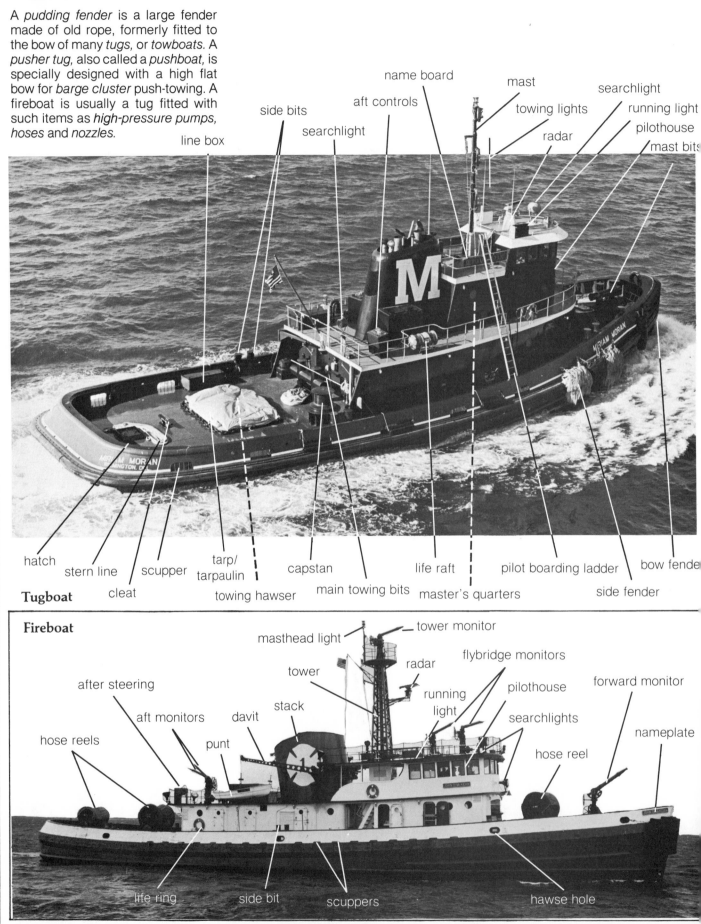

line box

side bits

searchlight

name board

aft controls

mast

towing lights

radar

searchlight

running light

pilothouse

mast bits

Tugboat

hatch

stern line

cleat

scupper

tarp/ tarpaulin

towing hawser

capstan

main towing bits

life raft

master's quarters

pilot boarding ladder

side fender

bow fender

Fireboat

masthead light

tower monitor

tower

radar

flybridge monitors

after steering

aft monitors

davit

stack

running light

pilothouse

forward monitor

hose reels

punt

searchlights

hose reel

nameplate

life ring

side bit

scuppers

hose hole

Boats and Ships

144

Hovercraft and Hydrofoil

Air Cushion Vehicles *(ACV)*, or *ground-effect machines*, are *amphibious vehicles* that ride on a cushion of air blown by *lift fans* through *slots* or *jets* around the underside of the hull. There are four classes of hydrofoils: *ladder, depth-effect, surface-piercing* and *submerged foils.*

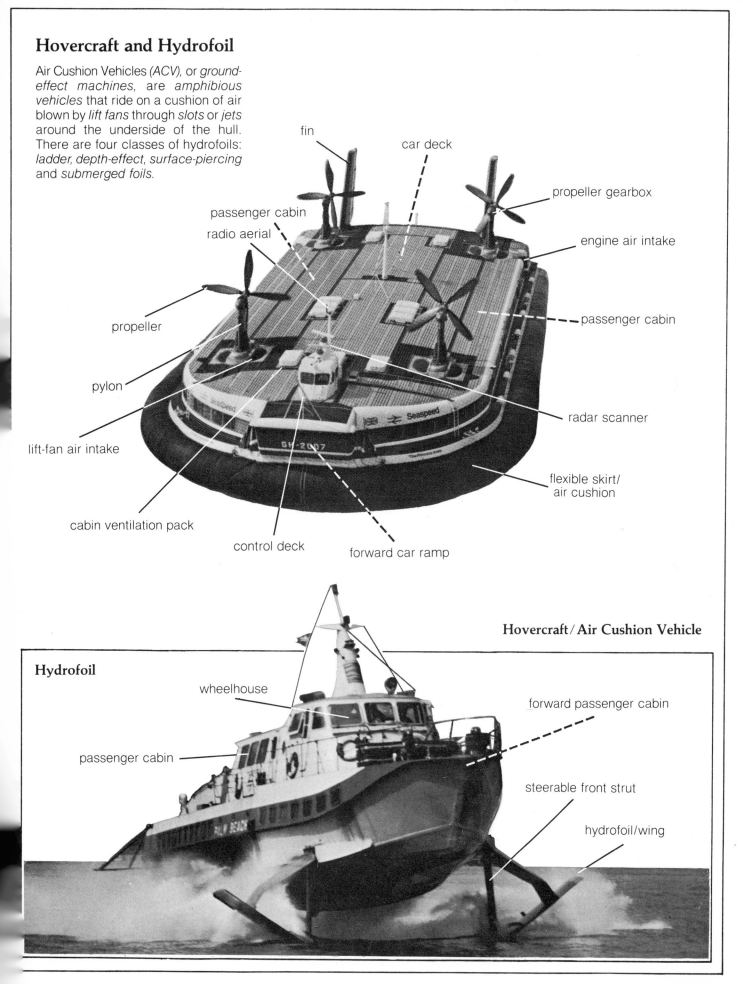

fin

car deck

propeller gearbox

passenger cabin

radio aerial

engine air intake

propeller

passenger cabin

pylon

radar scanner

lift-fan air intake

flexible skirt/
air cushion

cabin ventilation pack

control deck

forward car ramp

Hovercraft / Air Cushion Vehicle

Hydrofoil

wheelhouse

forward passenger cabin

passenger cabin

steerable front strut

hydrofoil/wing

Boats and Ships

Helicopter

The main body of a helicopter, *chopper, whirlybird,* or *eggbeater,* is called the *fuselage.* The rescue helicopter shown here has an *amphibious hull.* Armed military helicopters are called *gunships.*

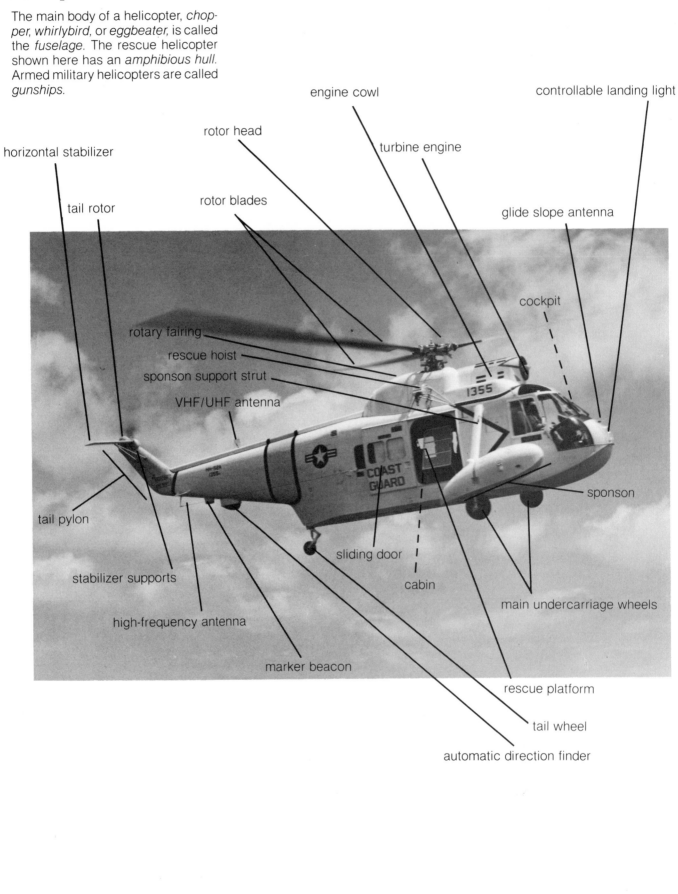

engine cowl

controllable landing light

rotor head

turbine engine

horizontal stabilizer

tail rotor

rotor blades

glide slope antenna

cockpit

rotary fairing

rescue hoist

sponson support strut

VHF/UHF antenna

tail pylon

sponson

stabilizer supports

high-frequency antenna

sliding door

cabin

main undercarriage wheels

marker beacon

rescue platform

tail wheel

automatic direction finder

Private Aircraft

A aircraft's central body portion is called the *fuselage*. To land on water, an airplane uses *pontoons*. To become airborne and begin *soaring*, a glider is pulled behind a motor-driven airplane or car by a cable attached to a *tow hook*. A glider lands on either a *landing wheel* or a *skid*.

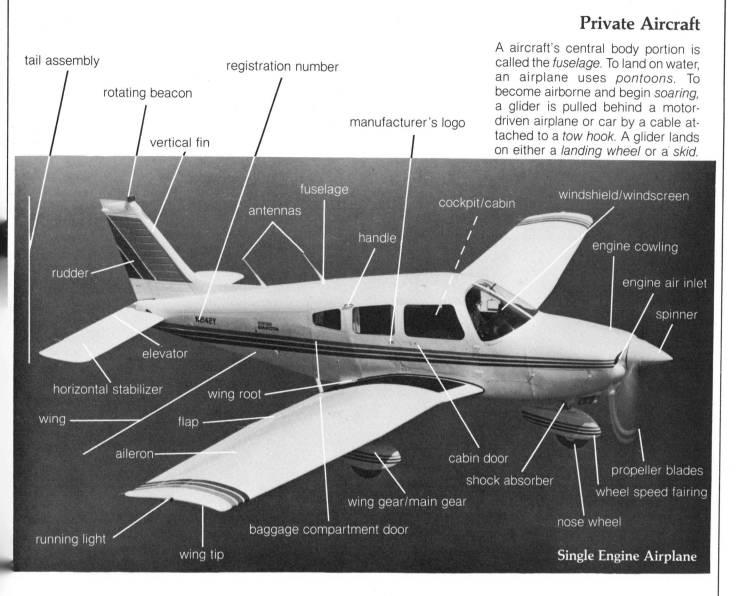

tail assembly

rotating beacon

vertical fin

registration number

manufacturer's logo

fuselage

antennas

cockpit/cabin

windshield/windscreen

handle

engine cowling

rudder

engine air inlet

spinner

elevator

horizontal stabilizer

wing root

wing

flap

aileron

cabin door

shock absorber

propeller blades

wing gear/main gear

wheel speed fairing

nose wheel

running light

baggage compartment door

wing tip

Single Engine Airplane

Glider / Sailplane

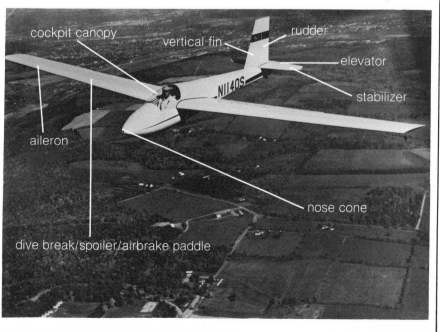

cockpit canopy

vertical fin

rudder

elevator

stabilizer

aileron

nose cone

dive break/spoiler/airbrake paddle

Civil Aircraft

The *trailing edge* of the wings on a *jumbo jet,* such as the one shown here, has small *static discharge wicks* to reduce electrical-charge buildup. Passengers store carry-on belongings in *overhead bins,* or *stowage compartments,* or in front *closets.* Aboard many aircraft, seat cushions double as *flotation devices. Life rafts* are stored in overhead ceiling compartments above the doors, and *emergency escape chutes* are folded inside the doors.

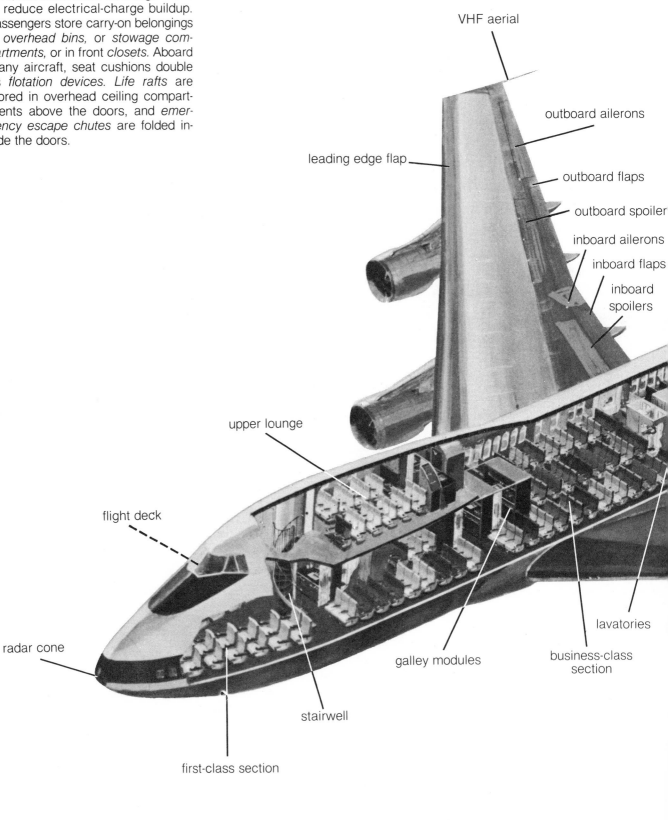

VHF aerial

outboard ailerons

outboard flaps

outboard spoiler

inboard ailerons

inboard flaps

inboard spoilers

leading edge flap

upper lounge

flight deck

radar cone

lavatories

business-class section

galley modules

stairwell

first-class section

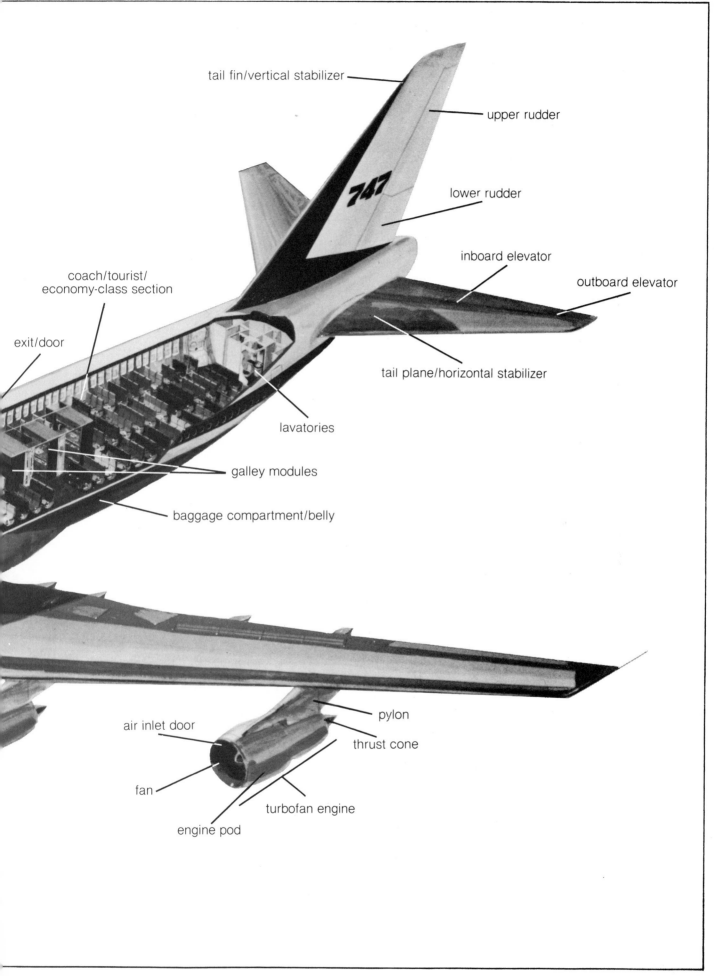

tail fin/vertical stabilizer

upper rudder

lower rudder

inboard elevator

outboard elevator

coach/tourist/
economy-class section

exit/door

tail plane/horizontal stabilizer

lavatories

galley modules

baggage compartment/belly

air inlet door

pylon

thrust cone

fan

turbofan engine

engine pod

747 Cockpit

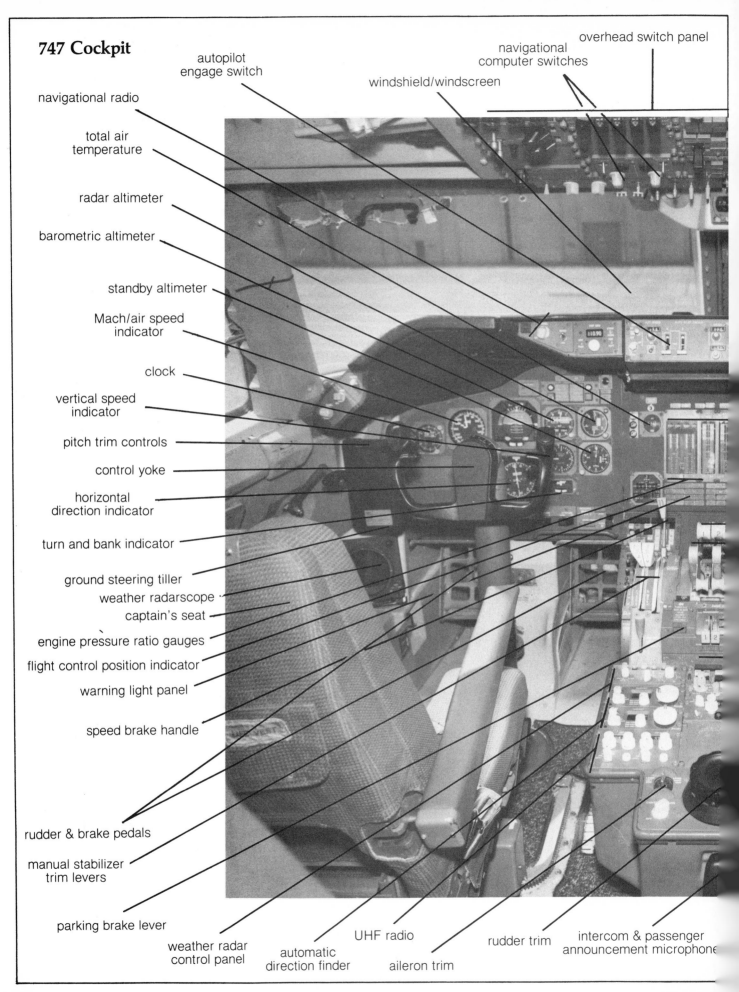

autopilot
engage switch

navigational radio

total air
temperature

radar altimeter

barometric altimeter

standby altimeter

Mach/air speed
indicator

clock

vertical speed
indicator

pitch trim controls

control yoke

horizontal
direction indicator

turn and bank indicator

ground steering tiller

weather radarscope

captain's seat

engine pressure ratio gauges

flight control position indicator

warning light panel

speed brake handle

rudder & brake pedals

manual stabilizer
trim levers

parking brake lever

navigational
computer switches

overhead switch panel

windshield/windscreen

weather radar
control panel

automatic
direction finder

UHF radio

aileron trim

rudder trim

intercom & passenger
announcement microphone

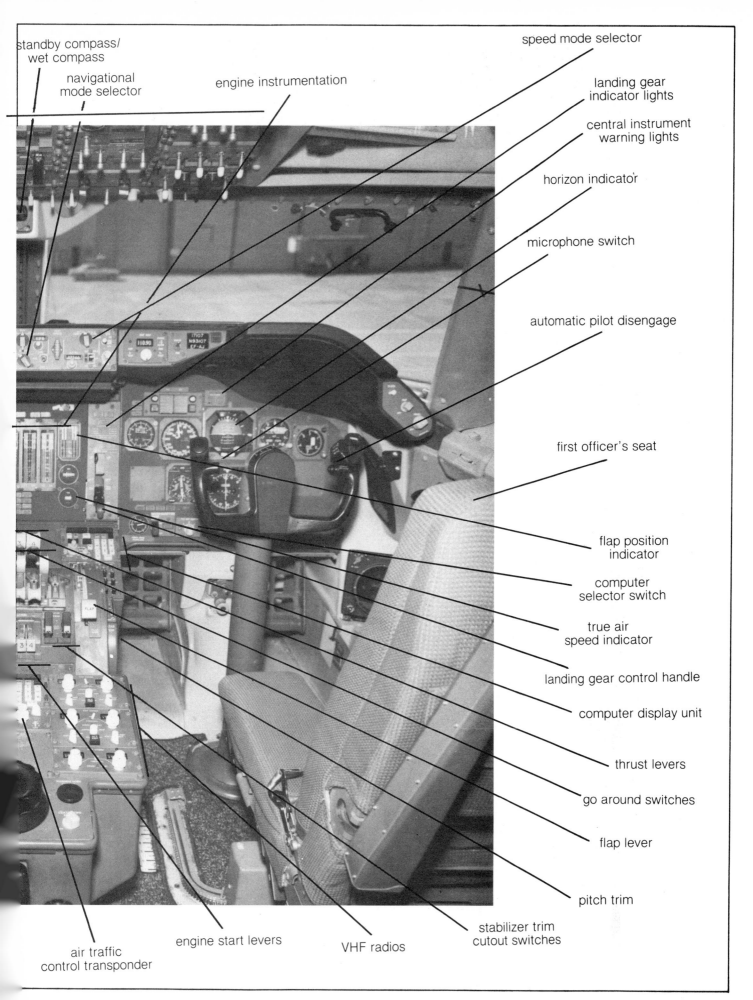

standby compass/
wet compass

speed mode selector

navigational
mode selector

engine instrumentation

landing gear
indicator lights

central instrument
warning lights

horizon indicator

microphone switch

automatic pilot disengage

first officer's seat

flap position
indicator

computer
selector switch

true air
speed indicator

landing gear control handle

computer display unit

thrust levers

go around switches

flap lever

pitch trim

stabilizer trim
cutout switches

air traffic
control transponder

engine start levers

VHF radios

Combat Aircraft

A fighter, such as the one shown here, has an advanced *airframe* with a *variable sweep wing* and a *long-range weapon system*. It is flown at speeds in excess of the speed of sound, or *mach speeds*.

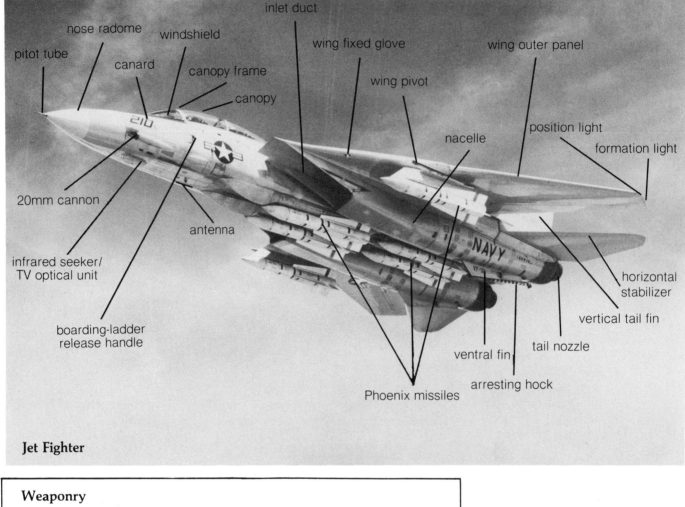

Jet Fighter

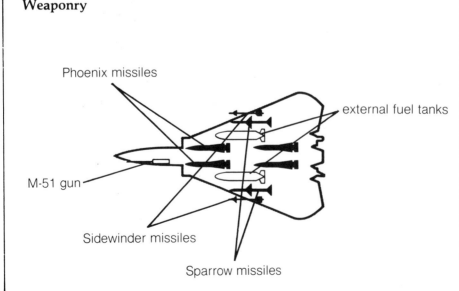

Weaponry

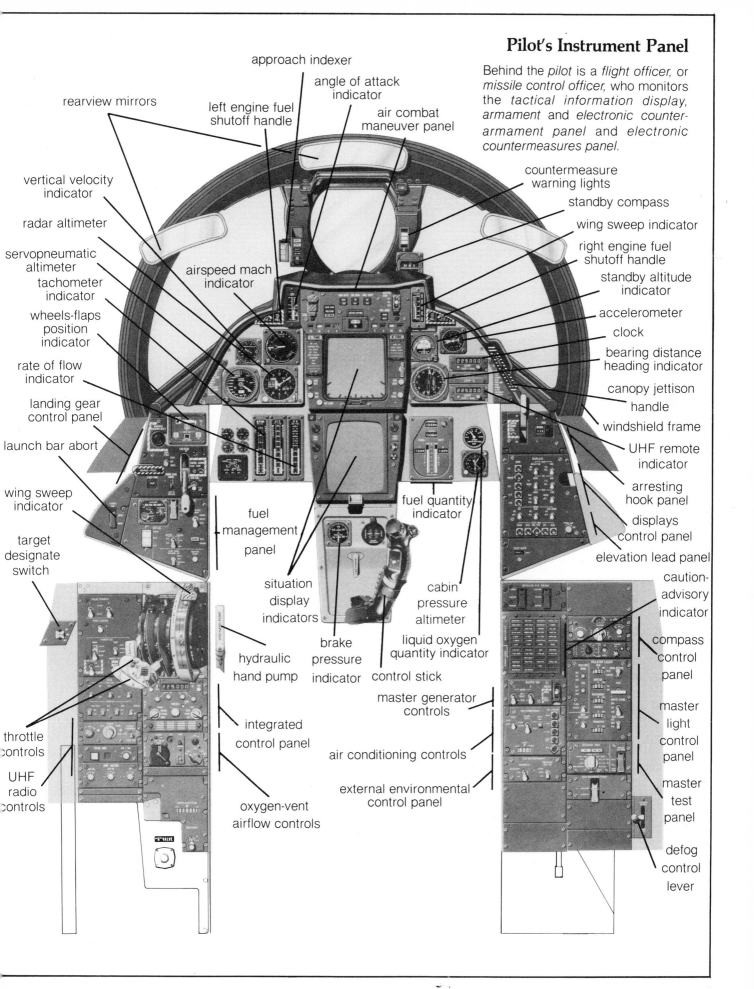

Pilot's Instrument Panel

Behind the *pilot* is a *flight officer*, or *missile control officer*, who monitors the *tactical information display, armament* and *electronic counter-armament panel* and *electronic countermeasures panel.*

rearview mirrors

approach indexer

angle of attack indicator

left engine fuel shutoff handle

air combat maneuver panel

vertical velocity indicator

radar altimeter

servopneumatic altimeter

tachometer indicator

airspeed mach indicator

wheels-flaps position indicator

rate of flow indicator

landing gear control panel

launch bar abort

wing sweep indicator

target designate switch

throttle controls

UHF radio controls

fuel management panel

situation display indicators

hydraulic hand pump

brake pressure indicator

integrated control panel

oxygen-vent airflow controls

cabin pressure altimeter

liquid oxygen quantity indicator

control stick

master generator controls

air conditioning controls

external environmental control panel

fuel quantity indicator

countermeasure warning lights

standby compass

wing sweep indicator

right engine fuel shutoff handle

standby altitude indicator

accelerometer

clock

bearing distance heading indicator

canopy jettison handle

windshield frame

UHF remote indicator

arresting hook panel

displays control panel

elevation lead panel

caution-advisory indicator

compass control panel

master light control panel

master test panel

defog control lever

Space Shuttle and Launch Pad

A shuttle has three main components: an orbiter, external tank and two solid-rocket boosters. Many launch pads have *flame buckets* designed to direct *fireballs* and steam away from the pad itself. A gantry is a movable structure used for erecting and servicing a rocket prior to launch.

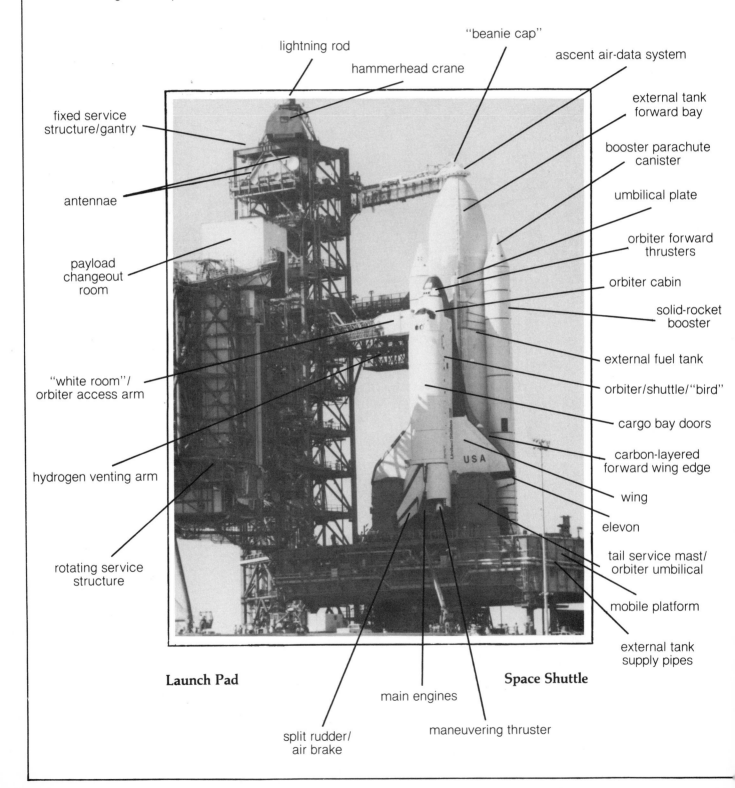

lightning rod

"beanie cap"

hammerhead crane

ascent air-data system

fixed service structure/gantry

external tank forward bay

booster parachute canister

antennae

umbilical plate

orbiter forward thrusters

payload changeout room

orbiter cabin

solid-rocket booster

external fuel tank

"white room"/ orbiter access arm

orbiter/shuttle/"bird"

cargo bay doors

hydrogen venting arm

carbon-layered forward wing edge

wing

elevon

tail service mast/ orbiter umbilical

rotating service structure

mobile platform

external tank supply pipes

Launch Pad

Space Shuttle

split rudder/ air brake

main engines

maneuvering thruster

Space Shuttle Flight Deck

Overhead controls include *circuit breakers, environmental monitors* and *fuel cell monitors*. The *orbiter* has work and living quarters for as many as seven people, including two pilots, *mission specialists* and *payload specialists*. It also features a *quad-redundant computer system*, including a fifth computer to arbitrate disputes among the first four.

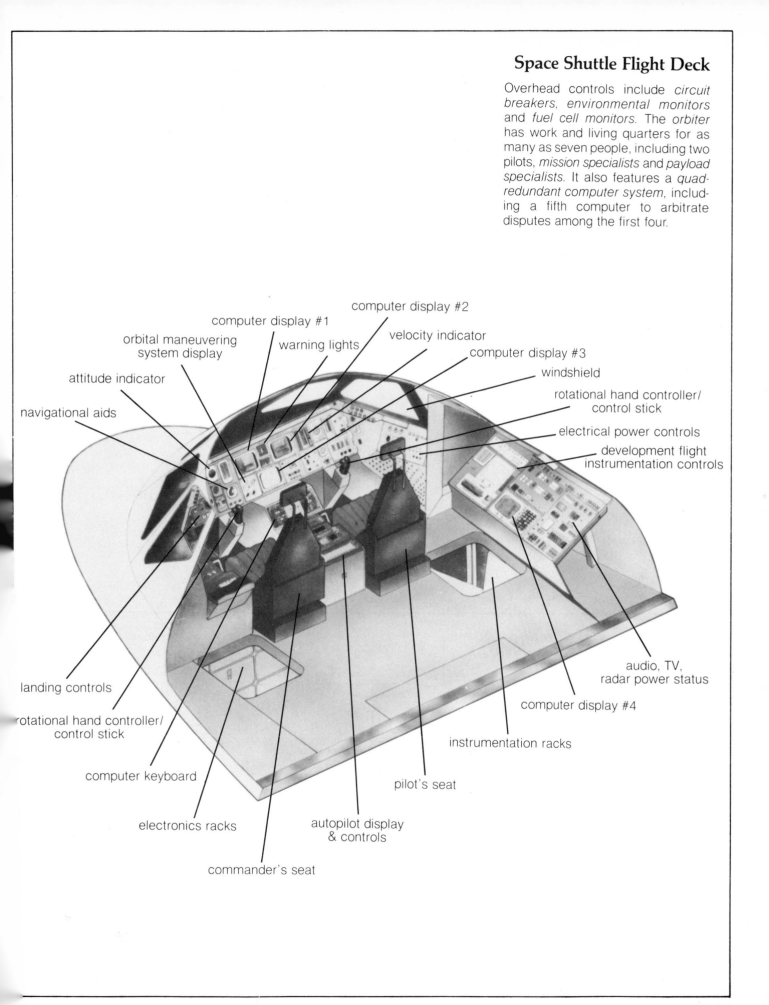

computer display #2
computer display #1
orbital maneuvering system display
warning lights
velocity indicator
computer display #3
attitude indicator
windshield
rotational hand controller/ control stick
navigational aids
electrical power controls
development flight instrumentation controls
audio, TV, radar power status
landing controls
rotational hand controller/ control stick
computer display #4
computer keyboard
instrumentation racks
electronics racks
autopilot display & controls
pilot's seat
commander's seat

Spacecraft

Lunar Lander

The *lunar module* consists of a lower *descent stage* which houses the *landing engine, exploration equipment, secondary tanks* and landing gear. The *ascent stage* contains *crew compartment* and *controls, equipment compartment, tanks* and *take-off engine,* used to rejoin the *command module.*

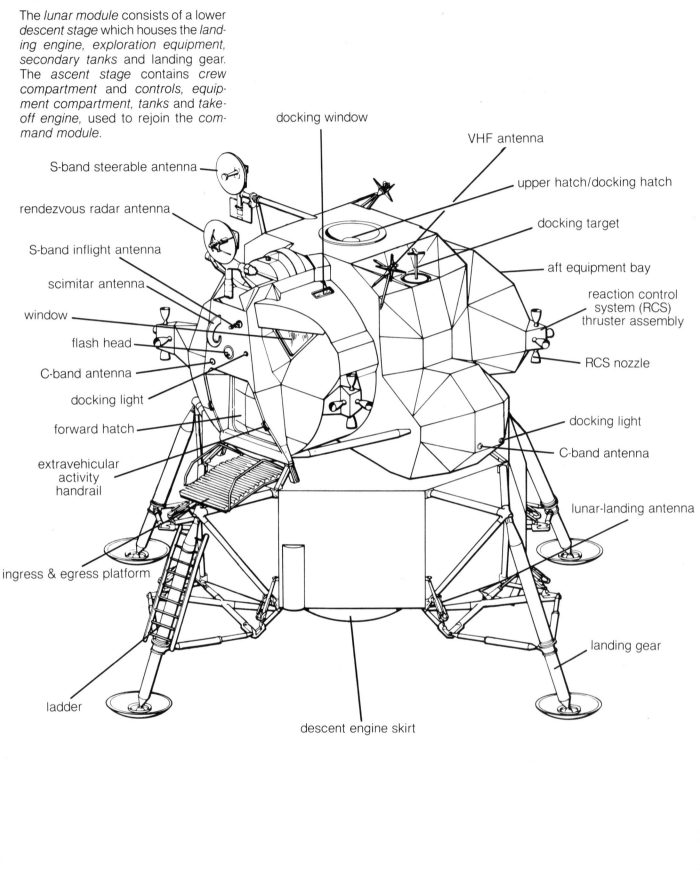

docking window

VHF antenna

upper hatch/docking hatch

docking target

aft equipment bay

reaction control system (RCS) thruster assembly

RCS nozzle

S-band steerable antenna

rendezvous radar antenna

S-band inflight antenna

scimitar antenna

window

flash head

C-band antenna

docking light

forward hatch

extravehicular activity handrail

ingress & egress platform

ladder

docking light

C-band antenna

lunar-landing antenna

landing gear

descent engine skirt

Lunar Rover

Officially called the *Lunar Roving Vehicle*, the *moon buggy* is folded in the Lunar Lander and deployed to transport astronauts and equipment on the lunar surface. The spacesuit, or *integrated thermal meteoroid garment*, is a many-layered structure laced to a *torso limb suit* which consists of an inner cloth *comfort lining*, a *bladder*, and a *restraint layer*.

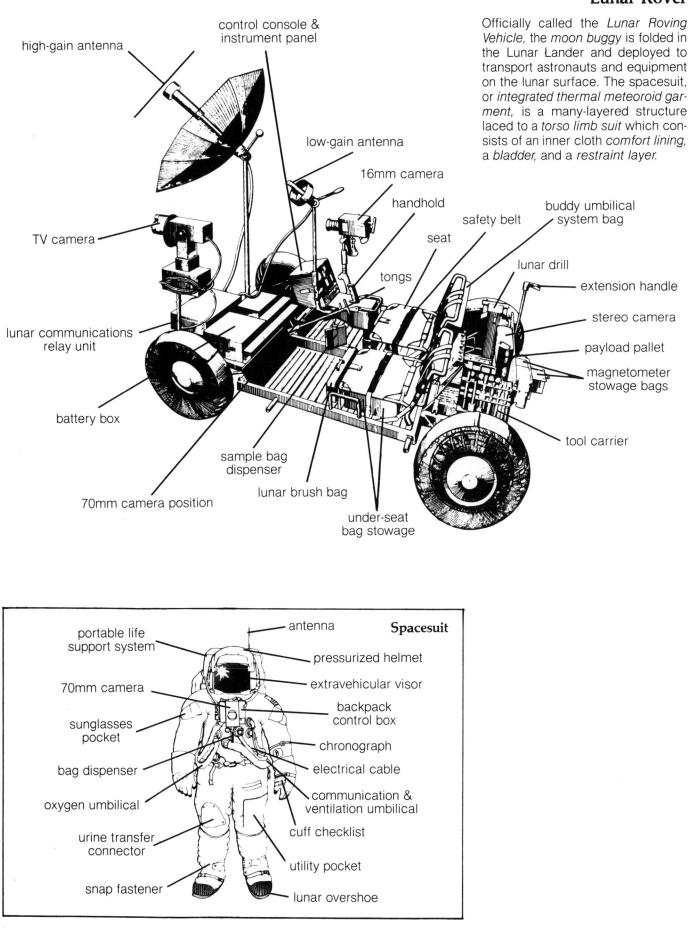

control console & instrument panel

high-gain antenna

low-gain antenna

16mm camera

handhold

safety belt

seat

buddy umbilical system bag

lunar drill

extension handle

stereo camera

payload pallet

magnetometer stowage bags

tool carrier

tongs

TV camera

lunar communications relay unit

battery box

sample bag dispenser

lunar brush bag

under-seat bag stowage

70mm camera position

Spacesuit

antenna

pressurized helmet

extravehicular visor

portable life support system

70mm camera

sunglasses pocket

backpack control box

chronograph

electrical cable

communication & ventilation umbilical

cuff checklist

bag dispenser

oxygen umbilical

urine transfer connector

utility pocket

snap fastener

lunar overshoe

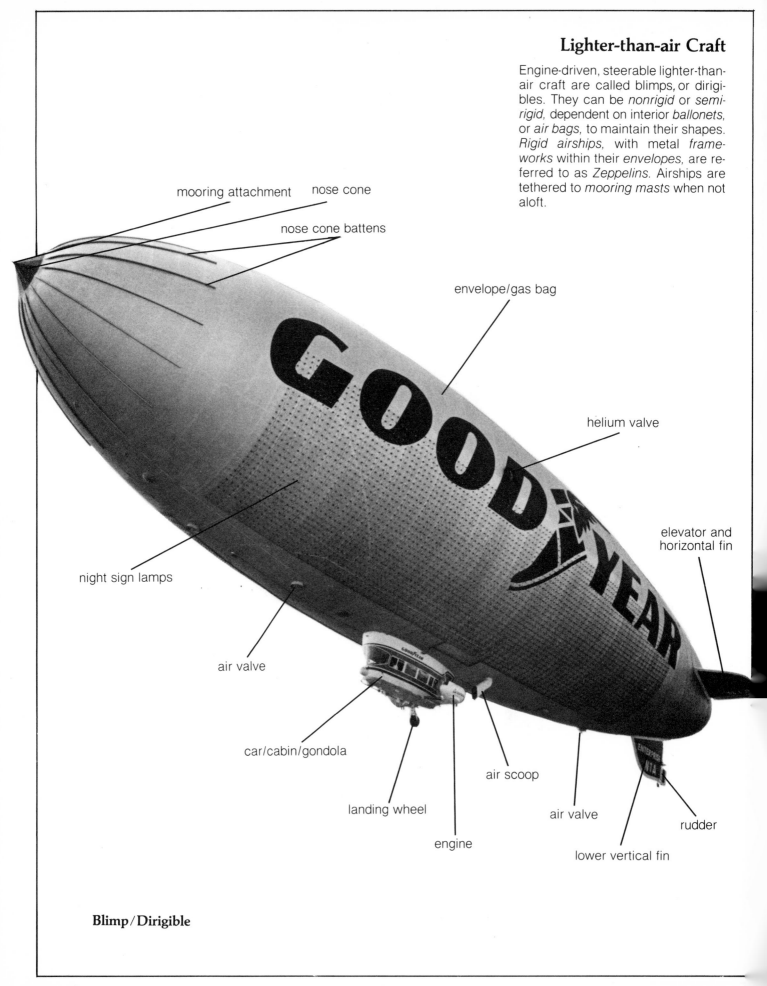

Lighter-than-air Craft

Engine-driven, steerable lighter-than-air craft are called blimps, or dirigibles. They can be *nonrigid* or *semi-rigid,* dependent on interior *ballonets,* or *air bags,* to maintain their shapes. *Rigid airships,* with metal *frameworks* within their *envelopes,* are referred to as *Zeppelins.* Airships are tethered to *mooring masts* when not aloft.

mooring attachment

nose cone

nose cone battens

envelope/gas bag

helium valve

elevator and horizontal fin

night sign lamps

air valve

car/cabin/gondola

landing wheel

engine

air scoop

air valve

rudder

lower vertical fin

Blimp/Dirigible

Communications

Communications ranks among the fastest-growing areas of modern life. Nevertheless, as this book is meant to demonstrate by providing visual access to language, print communications remains a vital part of the future. Print is therefore examined in some detail, up to and including a close look at the mailing label affixed to periodicals received every day by millions of subscribers.

Space limitations prevent presentation of industrial items such as transmitting stations and microwave towers, sound-recording and television studios and film-processing equipment.

But the devices used in all forms of communications—visual, aural and audiovisual—are represented by objects commonly used in most households. The single exception to this is the satellite which appears at the end of the section. It is included because of the vital role it plays in modern communications of all kinds.

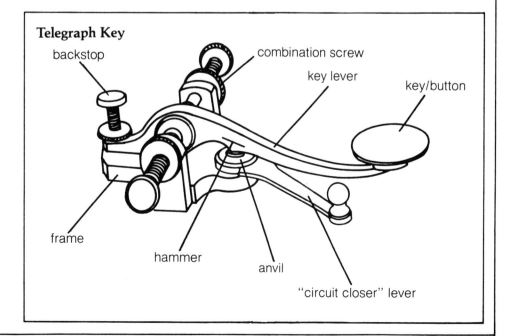

Telegraph Key

backstop

combination screw

key lever

key/button

frame

hammer

anvil

"circuit closer" lever

Pen and Pencil

In refillable *lead pencils* a *barrel cap* is turned in order to push new lead out the tip. Some fountain pens are *cartridge-loaded* but older models have a barrel, *ink reservoir* and *self-filling mechanism*. Quills, or *feather pens*, made from the horny, hollow barrel of bird feathers, were dipped in *ink wells*.

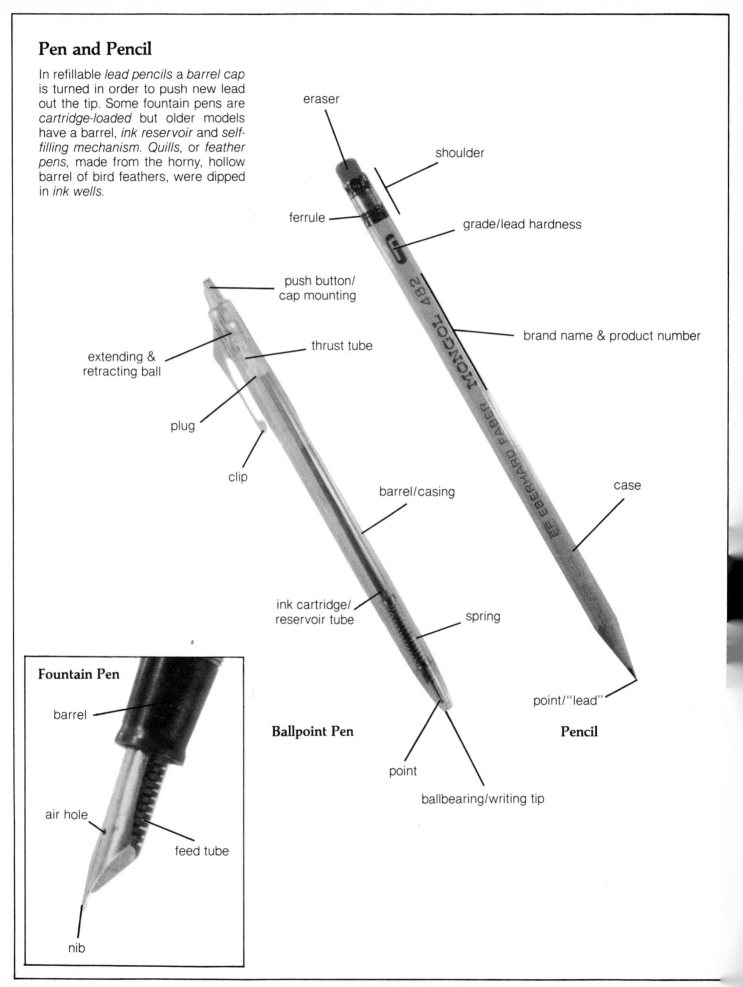

eraser

shoulder

ferrule

grade/lead hardness

push button/
cap mounting

brand name & product number

extending &
retracting ball

thrust tube

plug

clip

barrel/casing

case

ink cartridge/
reservoir tube

spring

point/"lead"

Ballpoint Pen

Pencil

point

ballbearing/writing tip

Fountain Pen

barrel

air hole

feed tube

nib

Correspondence

A note appended to a completed letter is called a *postscript*, abbreviated as *P.S.* When items are enclosed with a letter they are indicated by the word *enclosure(s)* or *encl.* The back portion of an envelope which is glued down after a letter has been inserted is the *flap.* Postage stamps can be purchased in *books, strips, blocks, coils* and *sheets,* or *panes.*

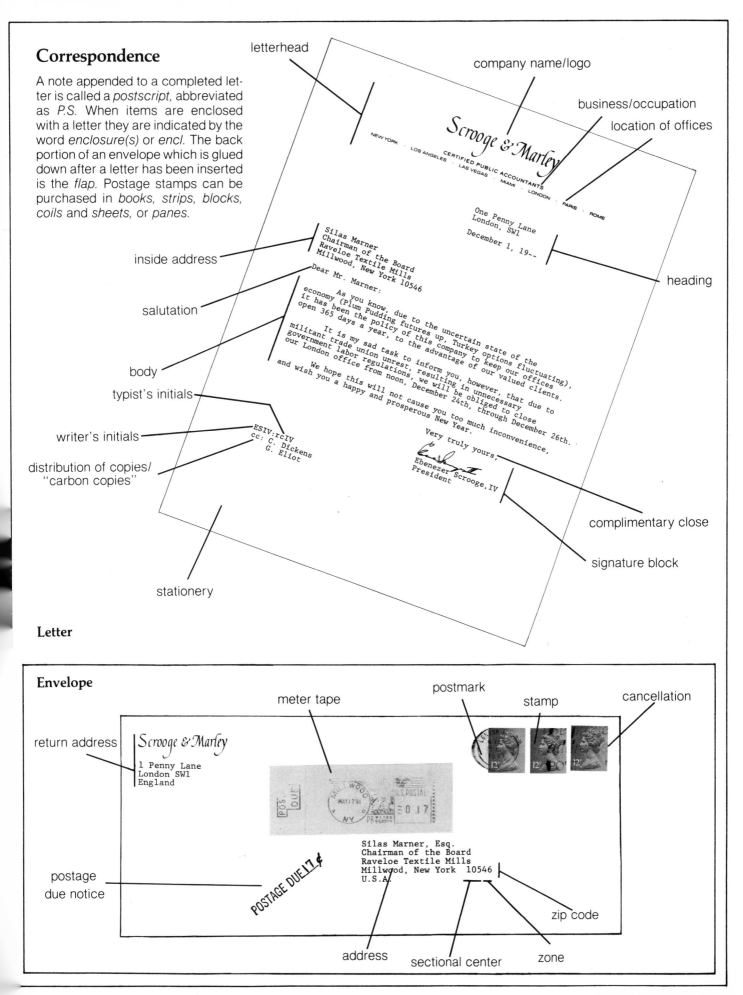

letterhead

company name/logo

business/occupation

location of offices

Scrooge & Marley

NEW YORK · LOS ANGELES · LAS VEGAS · MIAMI · LONDON · PARIS · ROME

CERTIFIED PUBLIC ACCOUNTANTS

One Penny Lane
London, SW1

December 1, 19--

heading

inside address

Silas Marner
Chairman of the Board
Raveloe Textile Mills
Millwood, New York 10546

salutation

Dear Mr. Marner:

body

As you know, due to the uncertain state of the economy (Plum Pudding futures up, Turkey options fluctuating), it has been the policy of this company to keep our offices open 365 days a year, to the advantage of our valued clients.

It is my sad task to inform you, however, that due to militant trade union unrest, resulting in unnecessary government labor regulations, we will be obliged to close our London office from noon, December 24th, through December 26th.

We hope this will not cause you too much inconvenience, and wish you a happy and prosperous New Year.

Very truly yours,

Ebenezer Scrooge, IV
President

typist's initials

writer's initials

distribution of copies/
"carbon copies"

ESIV:rcIV
cc: C. Dickens
     G. Eliot

complimentary close

signature block

stationery

Letter

Envelope

return address

Scrooge & Marley

1 Penny Lane
London SW1
England

meter tape

postmark

stamp

cancellation

MILLWOOD
MAY 17 '81
NY

U.S.POSTAGE
≈ 0.17

POS. DUE

postage
due notice

POSTAGE DUE 17¢

Silas Marner, Esq.
Chairman of the Board
Raveloe Textile Mills
Millwood, New York 10546
U.S.A.

zip code

address

sectional center

zone

Print Communications

Typewriter

On standard manual or *office type-writers*, lightweight *portables* and older *electrics*, when a key labeled with a *character* is struck, it sends the appropriate type bar toward an inked *ribbon*. On modern electric typewriters type bars in the *type basket* have been replaced with a ball.

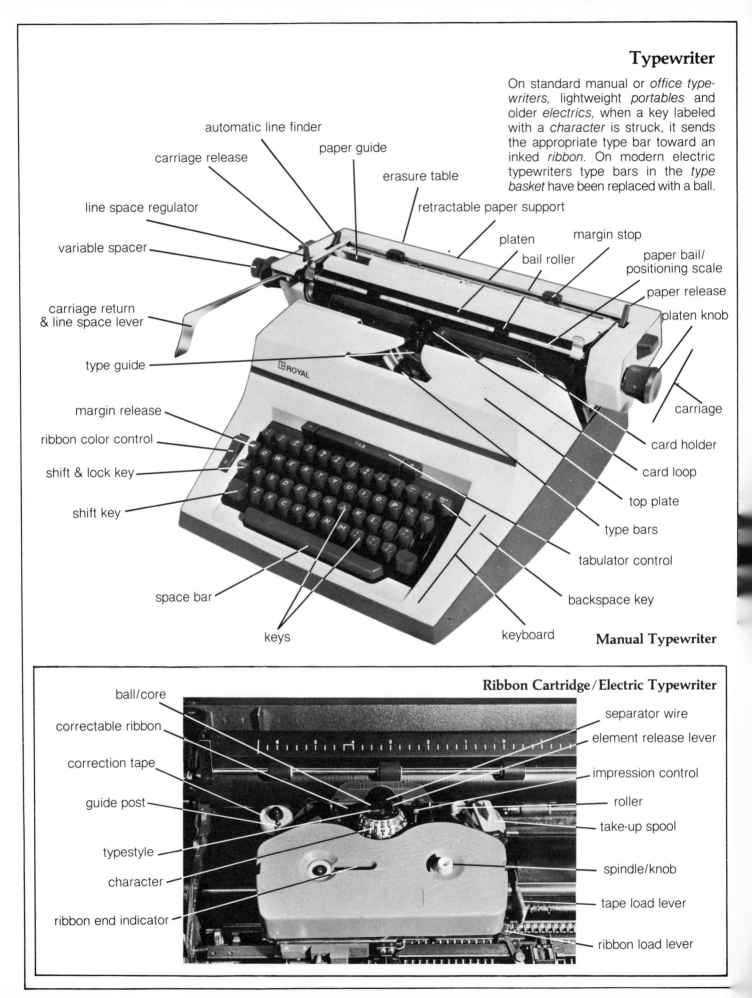

automatic line finder

carriage release

paper guide

erasure table

retractable paper support

line space regulator

variable spacer

platen

margin stop

bail roller

paper bail/ positioning scale

carriage return & line space lever

paper release

platen knob

type guide

ROYAL

carriage

margin release

ribbon color control

card holder

shift & lock key

card loop

shift key

top plate

type bars

tabulator control

space bar

backspace key

keys

keyboard

Manual Typewriter

Ribbon Cartridge / Electric Typewriter

ball/core

separator wire

correctable ribbon

element release lever

correction tape

impression control

guide post

roller

take-up spool

typestyle

character

spindle/knob

ribbon end indicator

tape load lever

ribbon load lever

Typography

Type with serifs is called *book type*.
Type without serifs is *sans serif*.

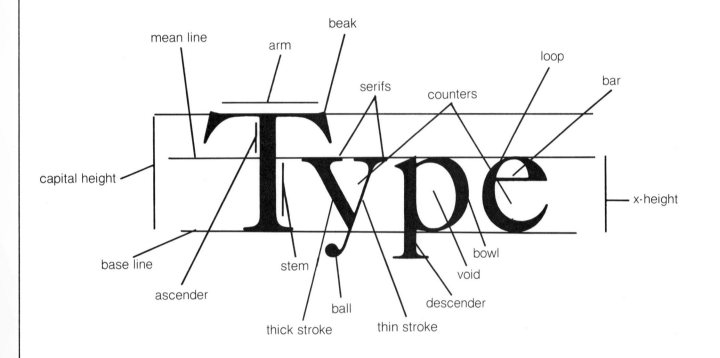

mean line · arm · beak · loop · bar

serifs · counters

capital height

x-height

base line · stem · bowl · void

ascender · ball · descender

thick stroke · thin stroke

Typeface Composition

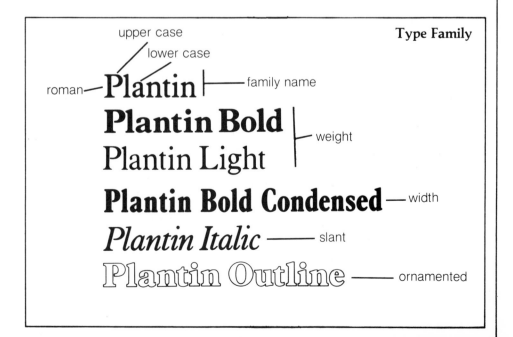

Type Family

upper case
lower case

roman — Plantin ⊢— family name

Plantin Bold

Plantin Light ⎤— weight

Plantin Bold Condensed — width

Plantin Italic — slant

Plantin Outline — ornamented

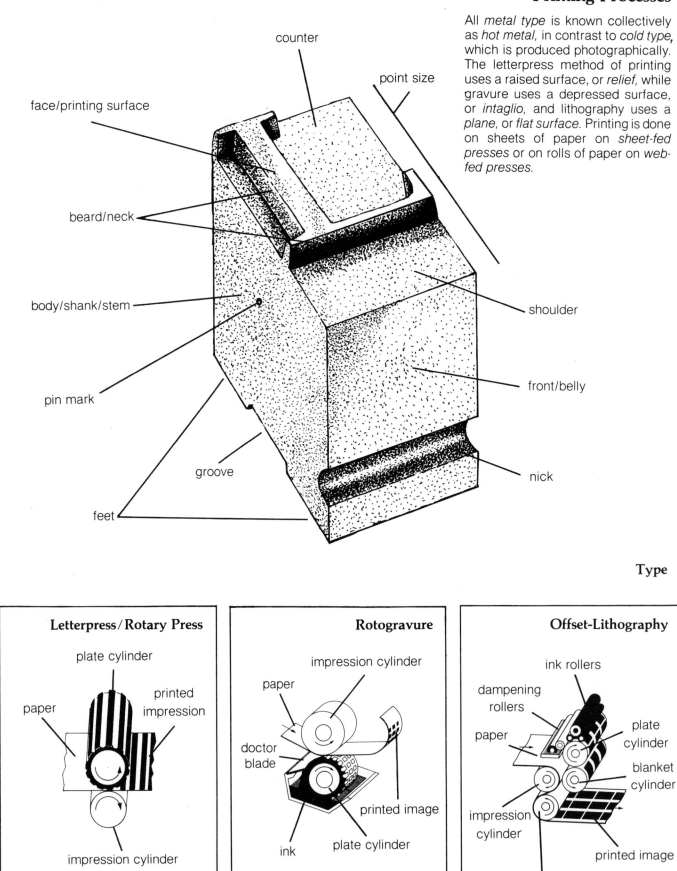

Printing Processes

All *metal type* is known collectively as *hot metal*, in contrast to *cold type*, which is produced photographically. The letterpress method of printing uses a raised surface, or *relief*, while gravure uses a depressed surface, or *intaglio*, and lithography uses a *plane*, or *flat surface*. Printing is done on sheets of paper on *sheet-fed presses* or on rolls of paper on *web-fed presses*.

counter

point size

face/printing surface

beard/neck

body/shank/stem

pin mark

shoulder

front/belly

groove

nick

feet

Type

Letterpress/Rotary Press

plate cylinder

printed impression

paper

impression cylinder

Rotogravure

impression cylinder

paper

doctor blade

printed image

ink

plate cylinder

Offset-Lithography

ink rollers

dampening rollers

plate cylinder

paper

blanket cylinder

impression cylinder

printed image

sheet-transfer cylinder

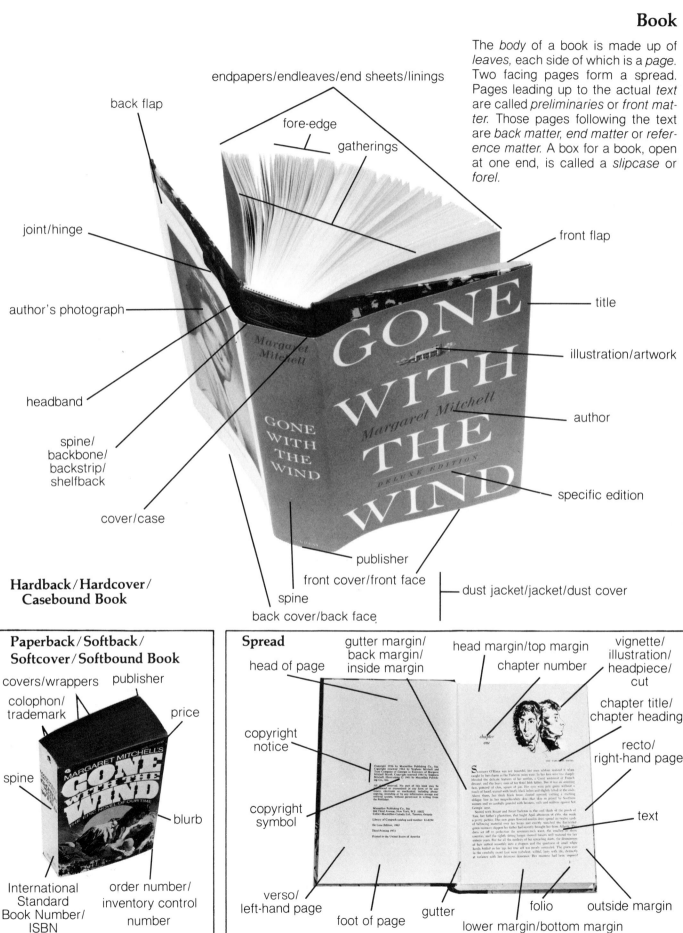

Book

The *body* of a book is made up of *leaves,* each side of which is a *page.* Two facing pages form a spread. Pages leading up to the actual *text* are called *preliminaries* or *front matter.* Those pages following the text are *back matter, end matter* or *reference matter.* A box for a book, open at one end, is called a *slipcase* or *forel.*

endpapers/endleaves/end sheets/linings

fore-edge

gatherings

back flap

joint/hinge

author's photograph

headband

spine/
backbone/
backstrip/
shelfback

cover/case

front flap

title

illustration/artwork

author

specific edition

publisher

front cover/front face

dust jacket/jacket/dust cover

spine

back cover/back face

**Hardback/Hardcover/
Casebound Book**

**Paperback/Softback/
Softcover/Softbound Book**

covers/wrappers

publisher

colophon/
trademark

price

spine

blurb

International
Standard
Book Number/
ISBN

order number/
inventory control
number

Spread

head of page

gutter margin/
back margin/
inside margin

head margin/top margin

chapter number

vignette/
illustration/
headpiece/
cut

chapter title/
chapter heading

recto/
right-hand page

copyright
notice

copyright
symbol

text

verso/
left-hand page

foot of page

gutter

folio

lower margin/bottom margin

outside margin

Print Communications

Newspaper

Terms vary from newspaper to newspaper. Those shown here are used at *The New York Times.* Small-size newspapers are called *tabloids.*

Labels pointing to the newspaper page:

- out-of-town prices
- skyline
- nameplate/flag/logo
- weather ear
- copyright
- issue date
- price
- left ear
- volume number
- folio line
- banner headline
- head
- deck/bank
- bar line
- byline
- dateline
- lead/lede
- italic refer
- body of story
- subhead
- jump line
- art
- hairline rule
- dingbat
- readout dash
- agate line
- twinned stories
- credit line
- caption/cut line
- index

Front page content (as shown in the image):

TODAY: SIX PAGES OF BICENTENNIAL ARTICLES AND PICTURES

"All the News That's Fit to Print"

The New York Times

LATE CITY EDITION
Weather: Partly cloudy and ion humid today through tomorrow. Temperature range: today 64-83; Sunday 63-82. Details on page 30.

VOL. CXXV...No. 43,262

NEW YORK, MONDAY, JULY 5, 1976

20 CENTS

Nation and Millions in City Joyously Hail Bicentennial

ISRAELIS RETURN WITH 103 RESCUED IN UGANDA RAID

Toll Is Put at 3 Hostages, 7 Hijackers, Army Officer and 20 of Amin's Men

FORD LAUDS OPERATION

Freed Captives Are Received Joyously at Airport After Their 7-Day Ordeal

By TERENCE SMITH

PRESIDENT TALKS | PANOPLY OF SAILS

Philadelphia Throngs Told U.S. Is Leader—Liberty Bell Rings

Harbor Armada Led by Tall Ships in Salute to Fourth

By JAMES T. WOOTEN | By RICHARD F. SHEPARD

Preceded by a fireboat, the Coast Guard training ship Eagle leads the armada of ships past the Battery up the Hudson for the naval review

French Officials See Signs Amin, Hijackers Colluded

By CHARLES MOHR

CARTER TO BEGIN TALKS ON TICKET

Will See Muskie Today and Other Possible Running Mates Soon After

A Day of Picnics, Pomp, Pageantry and Protest

By JOHN L. HESS

Ethnic Diversity Adds Spice to the Holiday

By FRED FERRETTI

City Hall is the scene of street dancing and music in July 4th in Old New York Festival

President Ford waves to the crowd at Valley Forge, Pa., where he signed a bill making it a national historical site. He stands on a covered wagon that represented Michigan, his home state, in the Bicentennial wagon train

O, Say, It Was a Glorious Patchwork-Quilt of a Fourth

By McCANDLISH PHILLIPS

NEWS INDEX

Magazine Cover and Contents Page

Periodicals may be consumer magazines, intended for the general public; *trade* or *technical magazines,* intended for particular industries and businesses; or *journals,* published for people engaged in professions. *House organs* are distributed within a specific company. Covers may have *cover blurbs* with *selling copy,* describing inside stories, and *cover captions.*

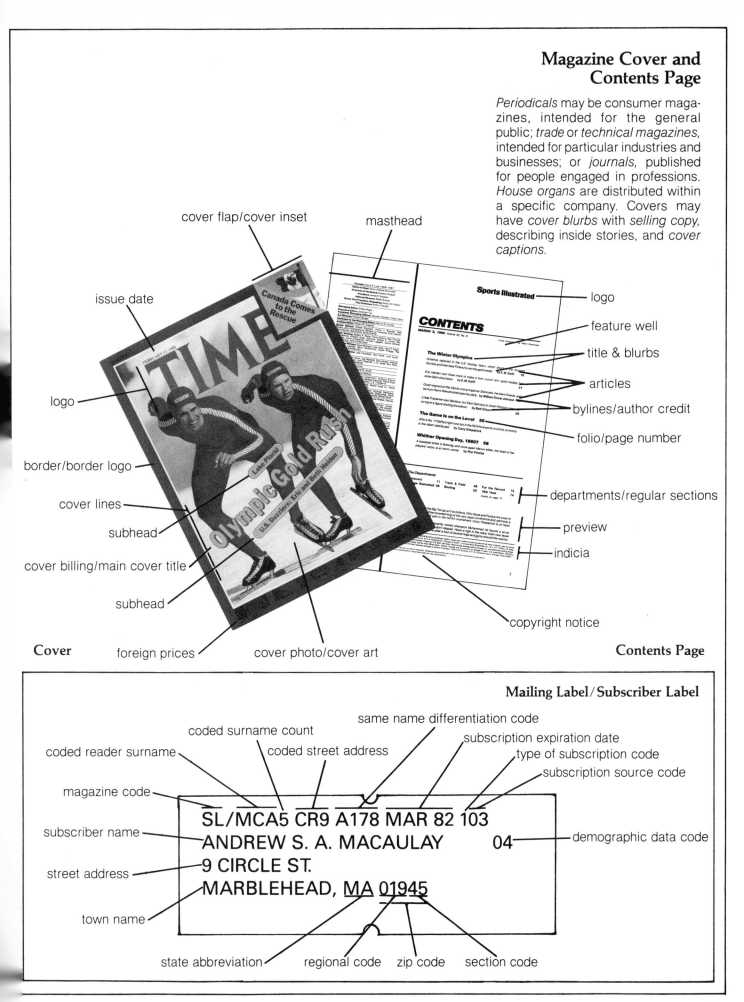

cover flap/cover inset

masthead

issue date

logo

border/border logo

cover lines

subhead

cover billing/main cover title

subhead

foreign prices

cover photo/cover art

Canada Comes to the Rescue

Lake Placid

Olympic Gold Rush

U.S. Dazzlers: Eric and Beth Heiden

Sports Illustrated — logo

CONTENTS
MARCH 3, 1980 Volume 52, No. 9

The Winter Olympics

The Game Is on the Level   30

Whither Opening Day, 1980?   56

feature well

title & blurbs

articles

bylines/author credit

folio/page number

departments/regular sections

preview

indicia

copyright notice

Cover

Contents Page

Mailing Label/Subscriber Label

coded surname count

same name differentiation code

coded reader surname

coded street address

subscription expiration date

type of subscription code

subscription source code

magazine code

subscriber name

street address

town name

SL/MCA5 CR9 A178 MAR 82 103
ANDREW S. A. MACAULAY   04
9 CIRCLE ST.
MARBLEHEAD, MA 01945

demographic data code

state abbreviation

regional code

zip code

section code

Magazine Feature

The design of a magazine page is called the *layout.* In the feature shown here *dummy type* has been substituted for *text* or *copy.* Two facing pages are called a spread, *double spread,* or *double-truck.* A *sidebar* is a self-contained, boxed *article* bearing on the main feature.

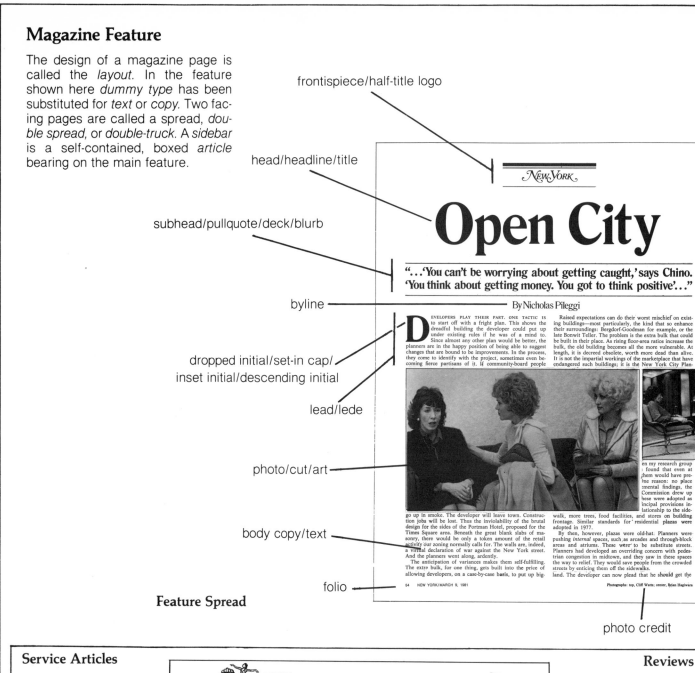

frontispiece/half-title logo

head/headline/title

subhead/pullquote/deck/blurb

byline

dropped initial/set-in cap/
inset initial/descending initial

lead/lede

photo/cut/art

body copy/text

folio

Feature Spread

photo credit

Service Articles

scotch rule

art/illustration

oxford rule

head

column rule

special-feature
photo treatment

sign-off

"nuts and bolts"

flush-left type

ragged-right type

Reviews

running title

subhead

decorated initial

introduction

breaker

boldface/highlight

column

A page that folds out to twice the size of a regular page is called a *gatefold*. A *jump line,* or *continued line,* at the end of a page refers the reader to the remaining text of a story appearing elsewhere in the magazine. A brief descriptive headline above the main head, designed to attract the reader's attention, is a *kicker, teaser, eyebrow,* or *highline.* Subscription cards bound into a magazine are called *inserts.* Those not physically connected are called *blow-ins.*

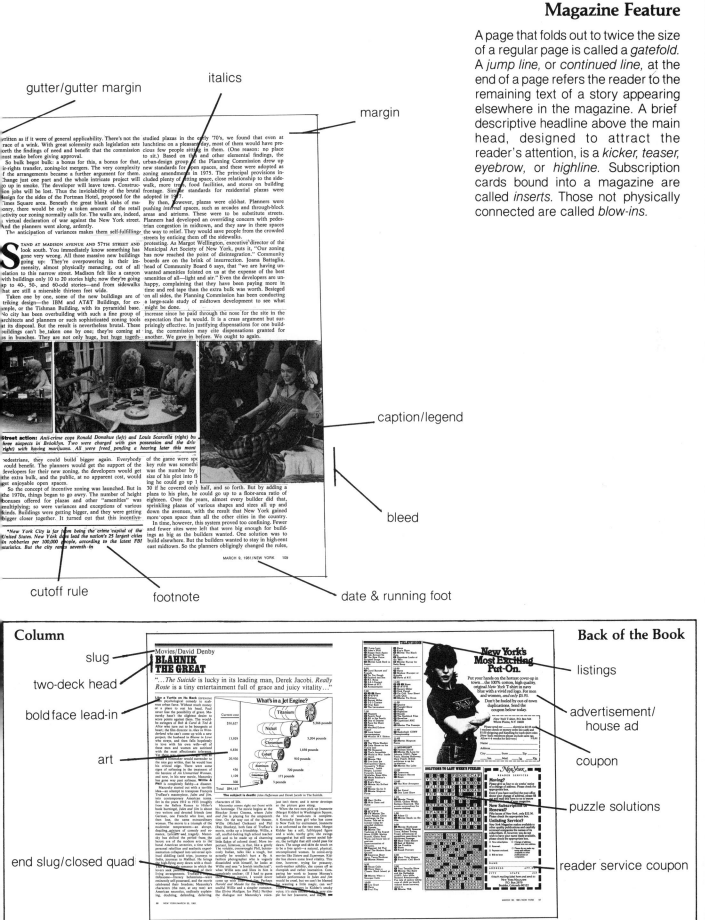

gutter/gutter margin

italics

margin

caption/legend

bleed

cutoff rule

footnote

date & running foot

Column

slug

two-deck head

bold face lead-in

art

end slug/closed quad

Back of the Book

listings

advertisement/house ad

coupon

puzzle solutions

reader service coupon

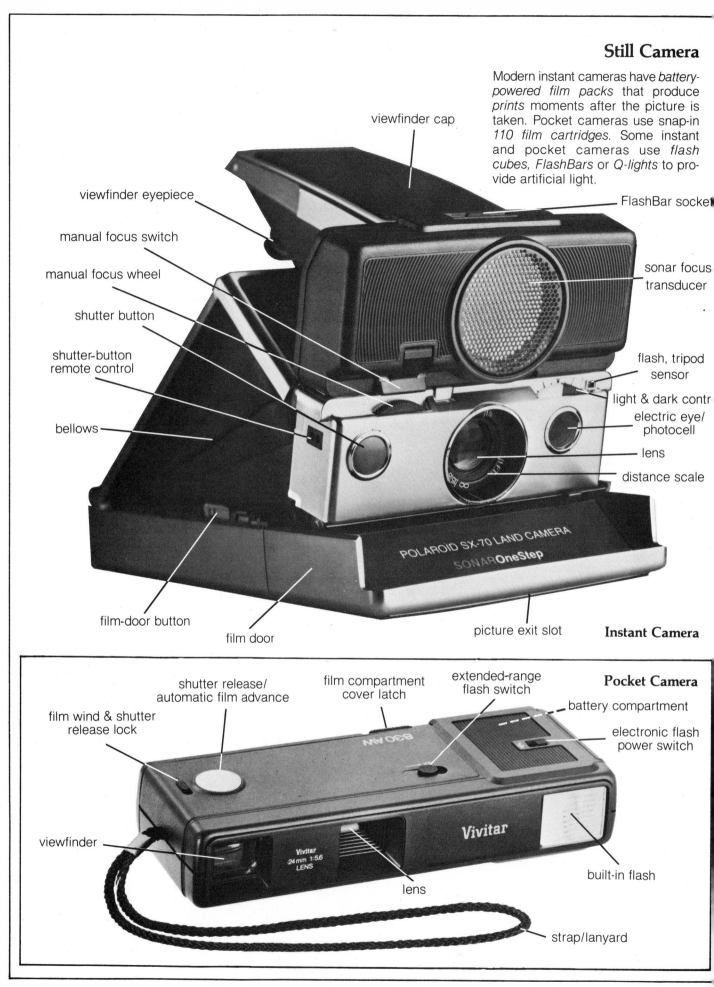

Still Camera

Modern instant cameras have *battery-powered film packs* that produce *prints* moments after the picture is taken. Pocket cameras use snap-in *110 film cartridges.* Some instant and pocket cameras use *flash cubes, FlashBars* or *Q-lights* to provide artificial light.

viewfinder cap

viewfinder eyepiece

manual focus switch

manual focus wheel

shutter button

shutter-button remote control

bellows

film-door button

film door

FlashBar socket

sonar focus transducer

flash, tripod sensor

light & dark contr

electric eye/ photocell

lens

distance scale

POLAROID SX-70 LAND CAMERA
SONAR**OneStep**

picture exit slot

Instant Camera

Pocket Camera

shutter release/ automatic film advance

film compartment cover latch

extended-range flash switch

battery compartment

film wind & shutter release lock

electronic flash power switch

viewfinder

lens

built-in flash

strap/lanyard

Still Camera and Film

To focus on an *image,* a *photographer* looks through the *viewfinder* on the back of the camera. In addition to the motor drive, or *power winder,* shown on this model, camera accessories include *interchangeable lenses— telephoto, wide-angle, zoom* and *special-purpose—lens caps* and *hoods, shutter-release cables, filters, focusing screens, eyecups, chest pods* and *action straps.*

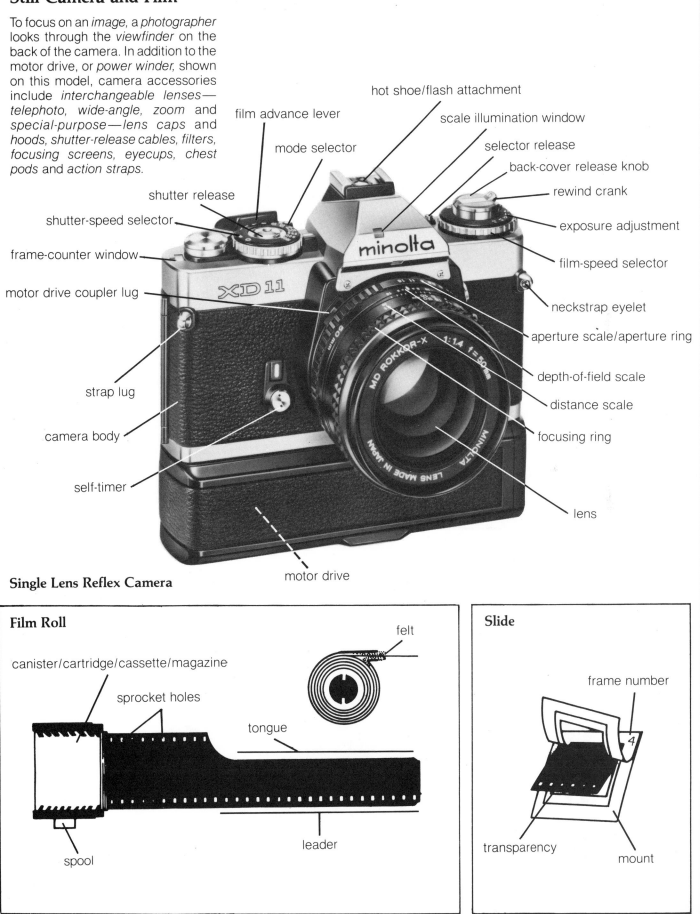

hot shoe/flash attachment

scale illumination window

film advance lever

mode selector

selector release

back-cover release knob

rewind crank

exposure adjustment

shutter release

shutter-speed selector

frame-counter window

film-speed selector

motor drive coupler lug

neckstrap eyelet

aperture scale/aperture ring

depth-of-field scale

distance scale

strap lug

focusing ring

camera body

self-timer

lens

motor drive

Single Lens Reflex Camera

Film Roll

felt

canister/cartridge/cassette/magazine

sprocket holes

tongue

leader

spool

Slide

frame number

4

transparency

mount

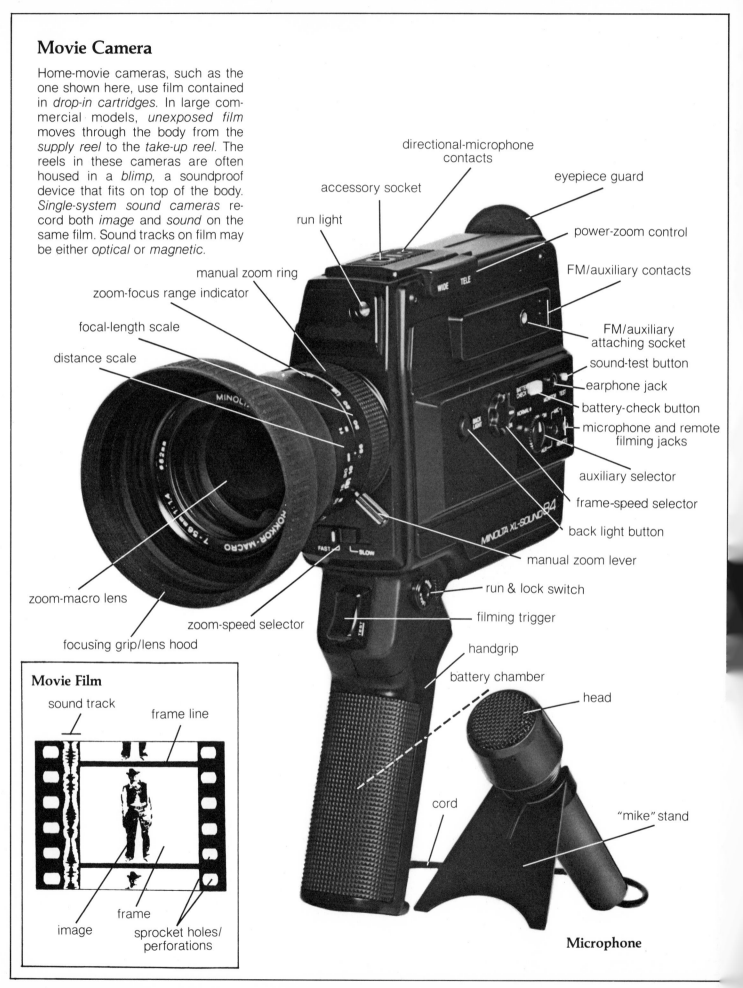

Movie Camera

Home-movie cameras, such as the one shown here, use film contained in *drop-in cartridges*. In large commercial models, *unexposed film* moves through the body from the *supply reel* to the *take-up reel*. The reels in these cameras are often housed in a *blimp,* a soundproof device that fits on top of the body. *Single-system sound cameras* record both *image* and *sound* on the same film. Sound tracks on film may be either *optical* or *magnetic*.

directional-microphone contacts

accessory socket

eyepiece guard

run light

power-zoom control

FM/auxiliary contacts

manual zoom ring

zoom-focus range indicator

FM/auxiliary attaching socket

focal-length scale

sound-test button

distance scale

earphone jack

battery-check button

microphone and remote filming jacks

auxiliary selector

frame-speed selector

back light button

zoom-macro lens

manual zoom lever

run & lock switch

zoom-speed selector

filming trigger

focusing grip/lens hood

handgrip

battery chamber

head

Movie Film

sound track

frame line

cord

"mike" stand

frame

image

sprocket holes/ perforations

Microphone

Projectors

The film projector shown here is a *self-threading, reel-to-reel model* with a built-in *speaker*. Slide projectors may have circular, or *carousel*, trays, *slide cubes* or *straight trays*.

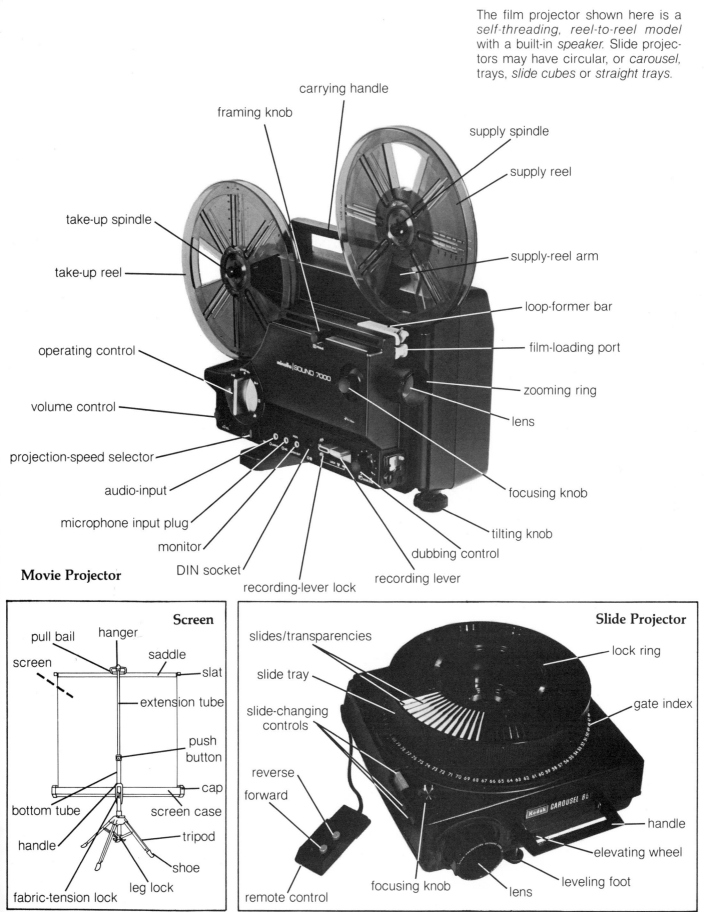

carrying handle

framing knob

supply spindle

supply reel

take-up spindle

supply-reel arm

take-up reel

loop-former bar

film-loading port

operating control

zooming ring

volume control

lens

projection-speed selector

audio-input

focusing knob

microphone input plug

monitor

tilting knob

DIN socket

dubbing control

recording-lever lock

recording lever

Movie Projector

Screen

pull bail

hanger

saddle

screen

slat

extension tube

push button

reverse

forward

cap

bottom tube

screen case

handle

tripod

shoe

leg lock

fabric-tension lock

remote control

focusing knob

lens

Slide Projector

slides/transparencies

lock ring

slide tray

slide-changing controls

gate index

handle

elevating wheel

leveling foot

173

Visual Communications

Photographic Accessories

In addition to the accessories shown here, *carrying straps, gadget bags,* and *cleaning supplies* such as *brushes, lens tissue* and *cleaning fluid* are used.

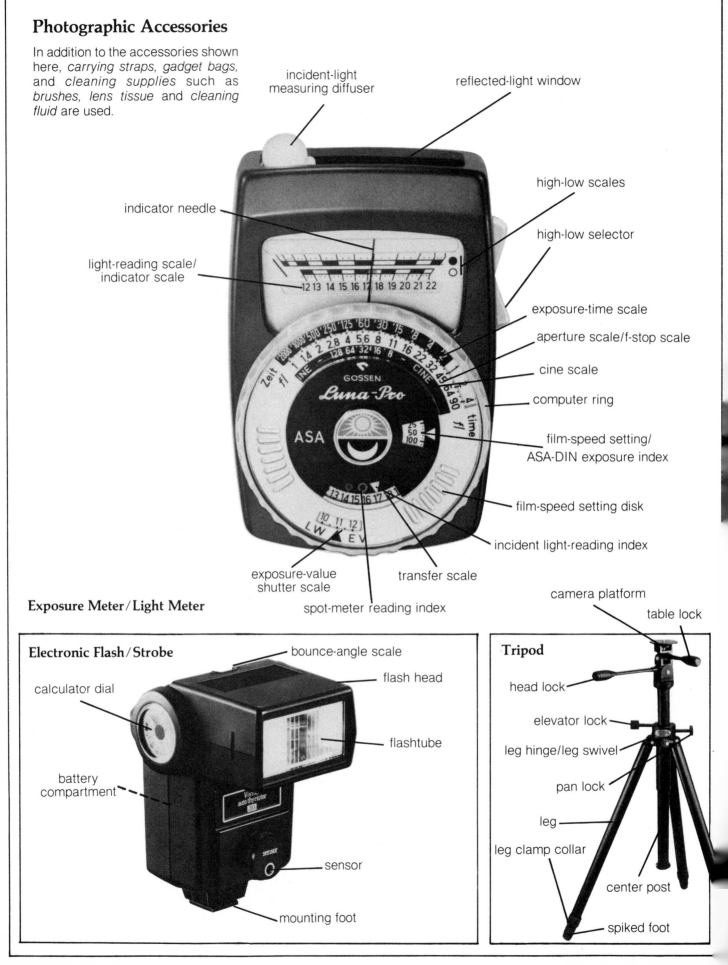

incident-light measuring diffuser

reflected-light window

indicator needle

high-low scales

high-low selector

light-reading scale/ indicator scale

exposure-time scale

aperture scale/f-stop scale

cine scale

computer ring

film-speed setting/ ASA-DIN exposure index

film-speed setting disk

incident light-reading index

exposure-value shutter scale

transfer scale

spot-meter reading index

Exposure Meter / Light Meter

Electronic Flash / Strobe

bounce-angle scale

flash head

calculator dial

flashtube

battery compartment

sensor

mounting foot

Tripod

camera platform

table lock

head lock

elevator lock

leg hinge/leg swivel

pan lock

leg

leg clamp collar

center post

spiked foot

Tape Recorders

Sound is recorded on *magnetic tape* by passing the tape over a *recording head.* Most cassette recorders have *built-in microphones* but are designed to work with *external mikes* as well. They are *battery-powered,* have *rechargeable battery packs* or *AC power cords.*

monitor switch

speed switch

equalizing switch

bias switch

power button

recording-mode buttons

supply reel

right-channel volume unit meter

front panel

reel lock/keeper

record indicator

take-up reel

left-channel volume unit meter

direction indicators

pause indicator

pause button

headphone jack

record button

microphone jacks

play button

stop button

microphone-recording level control

tape counter

fast-forward button

pinch roller

reset button

capstan

fast-rewind button

line-recording level control

repeat button

pinch roller

pitch-control dial

Reel-to-Reel Recorder and Playback Unit

Cassette Tape

safety lug

clamp

tape

locking screw

cover

hub

pressure pad

guide roller

Cassette Tape Recorder

speaker

cassette holder

telephone input jack

tape counter

line-in jack

tone control

speech & music selector

volume control

record & battery button

telephone indicator

microphone

eject button

telephone monitor

pause button

cue button

stop button

telephone-record button

review button

record button

175

Aural Communications

Phonographic Equipment

A *long-playing record*, or *LP*, contains several *recordings* on both the front and *flip sides*. A *stereo record* has *twin soundtracks* in a single groove, whereas a *monaural record* has one and a *quadraphonic record* has four. Records are protected by a *sleeve* which is slipped into an *album cover*, or *jacket*. A *jukebox* is a coin-operated phonograph that plays selected music.

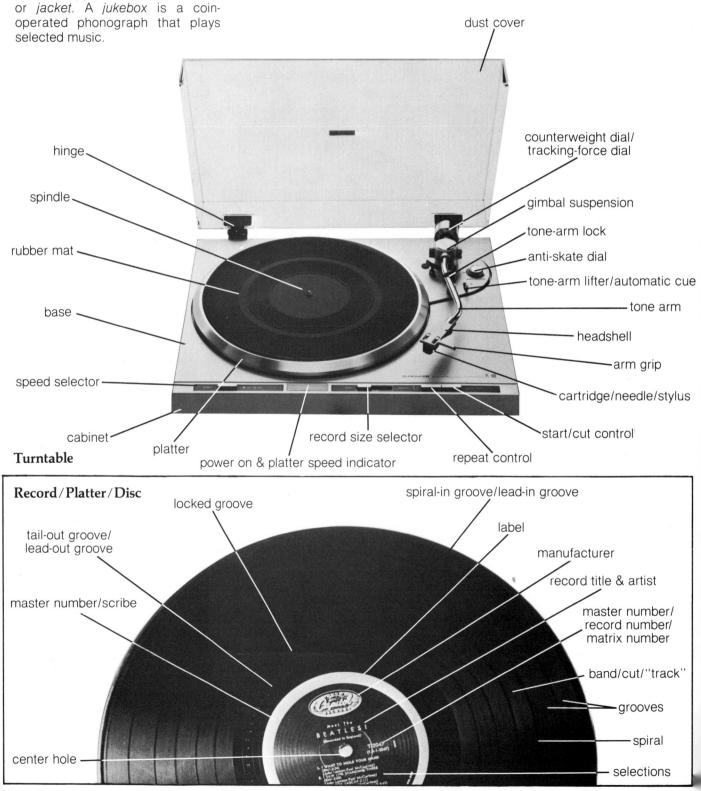

dust cover

hinge

spindle

rubber mat

base

speed selector

cabinet

platter

power on & platter speed indicator

record size selector

repeat control

counterweight dial/
tracking-force dial

gimbal suspension

tone-arm lock

anti-skate dial

tone-arm lifter/automatic cue

tone arm

headshell

arm grip

cartridge/needle/stylus

start/cut control

Turntable

Record/Platter/Disc

locked groove

spiral-in groove/lead-in groove

tail-out groove/
lead-out groove

label

manufacturer

record title & artist

master number/scribe

master number/
record number/
matrix number

band/cut/"track"

grooves

spiral

center hole

selections

Phonographic Equipment

A phonographic system produces minimally distorted sound, or *high fidelity*. It is usually comprised of a *tuner*, a *pre-amp*, an amplifier and speakers. Its power output is measured in *watts*.

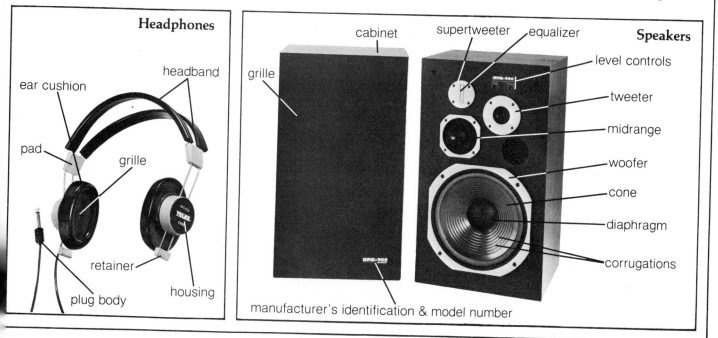

FM tuning/AM signal meter

power output meter

stereo indicator light

speaker indicator lights

tuning dial

AM/FM radio tuning dial

cabinet

power/on & off knob

volume dial

headphone jack

treble dial

function indicator lights

bass dial

speaker balance dial

mode & FM mute

loudness control

speaker selectors

function selector

tape-monitor switches

Receiver / Amplifier

Headphones

headband

ear cushion

pad

grille

retainer

plug body

housing

Speakers

cabinet

supertweeter

equalizer

grille

level controls

tweeter

midrange

woofer

cone

diaphragm

corrugations

manufacturer's identification & model number

Aural Communications

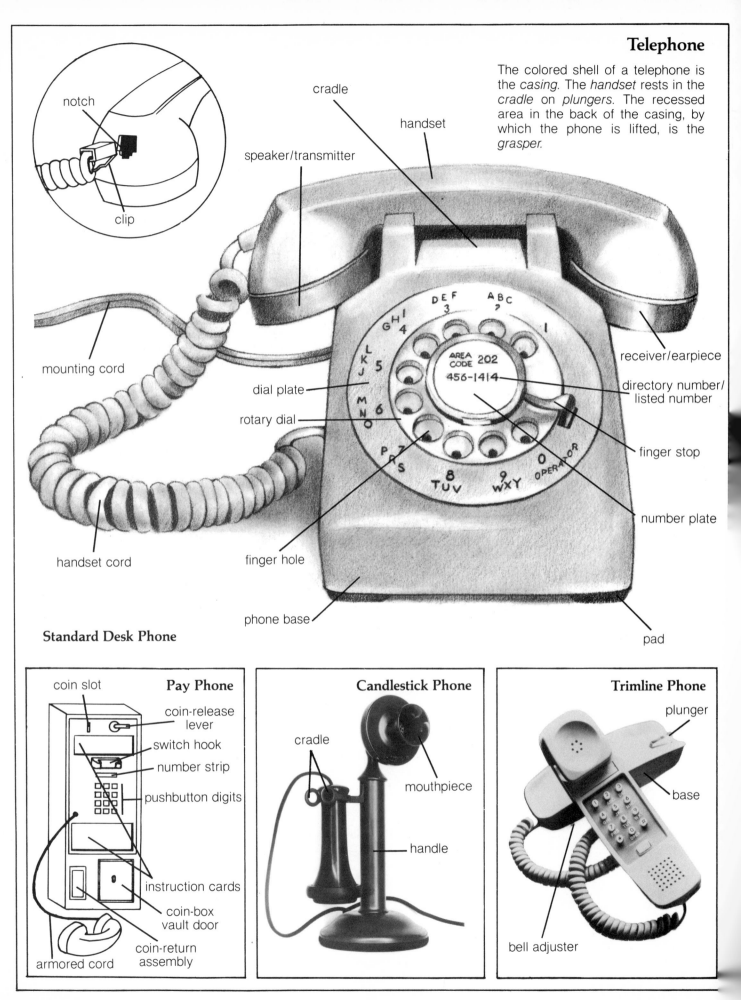

notch

clip

Telephone

The colored shell of a telephone is the *casing*. The *handset* rests in the *cradle* on *plungers*. The recessed area in the back of the casing, by which the phone is lifted, is the *grasper*.

cradle

handset

speaker/transmitter

mounting cord

AREA CODE 202
456-1414

receiver/earpiece

dial plate

directory number/ listed number

rotary dial

finger stop

handset cord

number plate

finger hole

phone base

pad

Standard Desk Phone

Pay Phone

coin slot

coin-release lever

switch hook

number strip

pushbutton digits

instruction cards

coin-box vault door

coin-return assembly

armored cord

Candlestick Phone

cradle

mouthpiece

handle

Trimline Phone

plunger

base

bell adjuster

Transceiver

A *walkie-talkie* is a hand-held transceiver used to transmit and receive over short distances. *CBs,* or Citizens Band radios, like the one shown here, have greater but still limited range. *Amateur radio operators,* or "hams," use transceivers capable of communicating over vast distances.

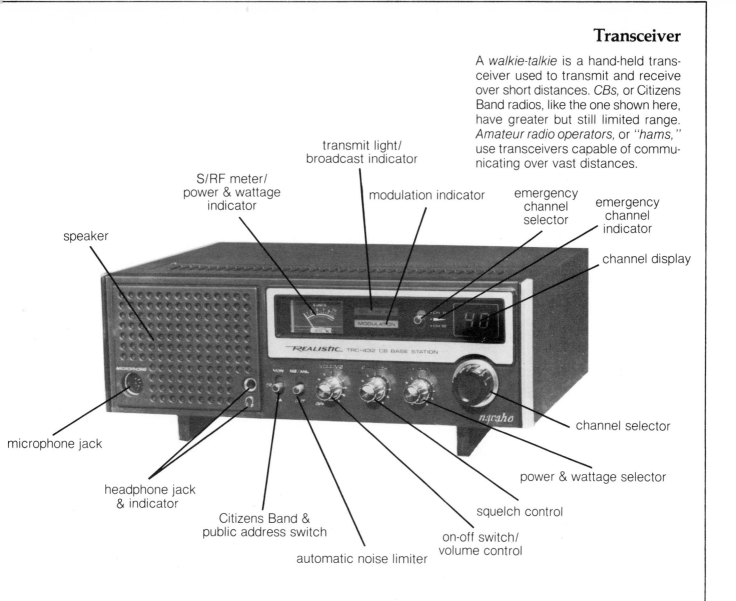

transmit light/
broadcast indicator

S/RF meter/
power & wattage
indicator

modulation indicator

emergency
channel
selector

emergency
channel
indicator

channel display

speaker

microphone jack

headphone jack
& indicator

Citizens Band &
public address switch

automatic noise limiter

on-off switch/
volume control

squelch control

power & wattage selector

channel selector

Base Station

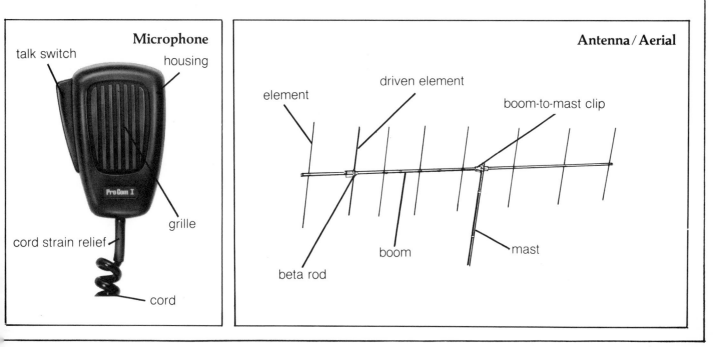

Microphone

talk switch

housing

grille

cord strain relief

cord

Antenna/Aerial

element

driven element

boom-to-mast clip

boom

mast

beta rod

Aural Communications

Video Recorder

Video recorders are used in conjunction with *television sets,* or *monitors.* They can be operated by hand-size *remote control units.* Some recorders use a grooveless *disc,* others use a *video cassette tape.*

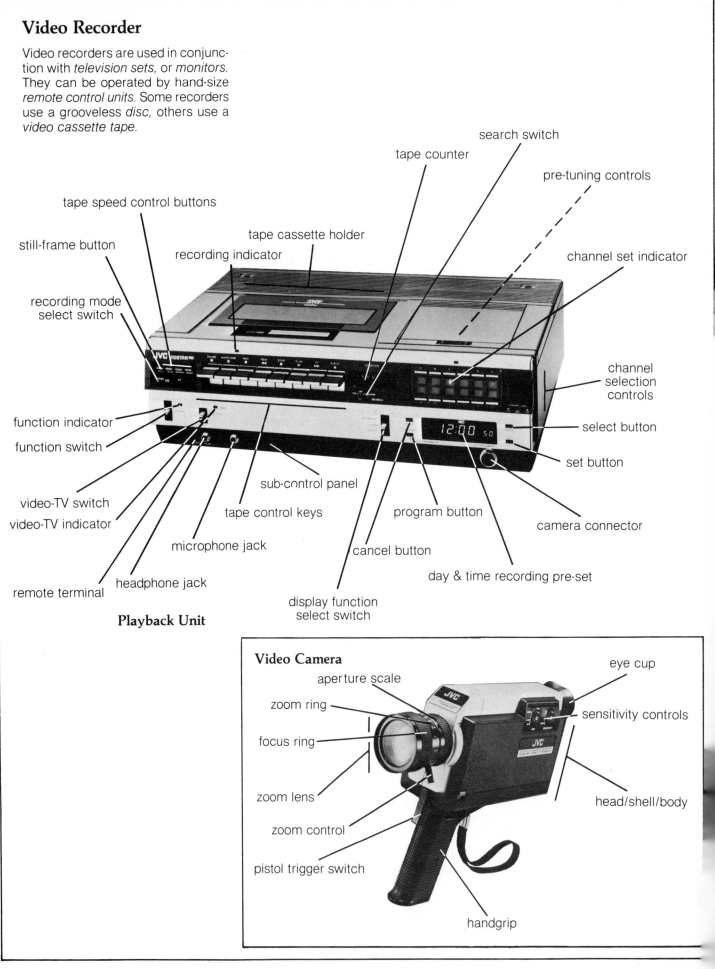

tape counter

search switch

pre-tuning controls

tape speed control buttons

tape cassette holder

channel set indicator

still-frame button

recording indicator

recording mode select switch

channel selection controls

function indicator

select button

function switch

set button

video-TV switch

sub-control panel

video-TV indicator

tape control keys

program button

camera connector

microphone jack

cancel button

day & time recording pre-set

remote terminal

headphone jack

display function select switch

Playback Unit

Video Camera

aperture scale

eye cup

zoom ring

sensitivity controls

focus ring

zoom lens

head/shell/body

zoom control

pistol trigger switch

handgrip

Television

The picture tube, or *"gun,"* is the largest single component in a television set's *chassis*. Today's sets are capable of receiving 105 channels, including *ultra-high frequency, very-high frequency, midband* and *super-band signals*. A low-power *laser beam* located in the player's *cabinet* translates 54,000 circular *tracks*, or *"frames,"* into pictures.

infrared remote-control command

power key

remote-control detector

response lamp

channel indicator

volume & contrast indicator

volume keys

channel number keys

channel keys

picture keys

cable television indicator

cable television controls

cabinet

screen/picture tube

mask

speaker

base/pedestal

SONY

speaker

Television Set/Monitor

LaserDisc ™ Player

viewer

spindle cover

spindle

disc/record/software

turntable

program setting, search & display buttons

freeze function

slow forward & reverse

scan button

fast forward and reverse

play button

pause button

reject button

power button

sound-track controls

Audiovisual Communications

Satellite

Active repeater satellites are communications satellites that amplify signals beamed to them for retransmission. *Passive* or *reflector satellites* mirror signals without amplifying them. Satellites used for space exploration, such as the one shown here, make scientific measurements and transmit the information back to earth.

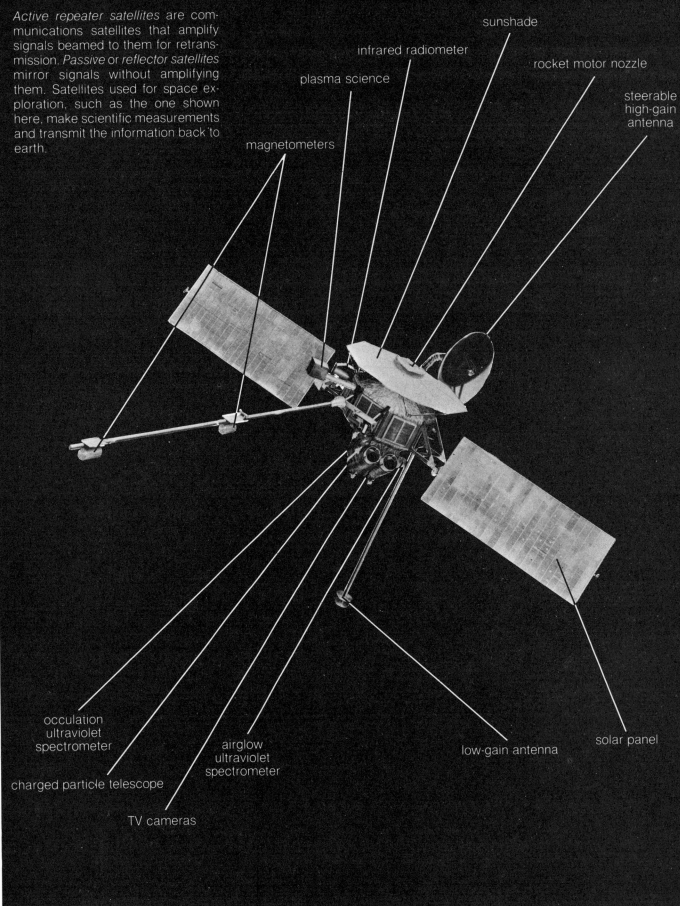

plasma science

infrared radiometer

sunshade

rocket motor nozzle

steerable high-gain antenna

magnetometers

occulation ultraviolet spectrometer

charged particle telescope

airglow ultraviolet spectrometer

TV cameras

low-gain antenna

solar panel

Personal Items

This section includes items people are likely to wear, carry or use in the course of their everyday lives. Thus, coverage includes clothing, hats, shoes, jewelry and money.

Wherever men's and women's apparel differ appreciably, items have been separated. But in the case of items such as sweaters and overcoats, articles worn by both sexes, only one version has been presented. Liberal use has been made to show the variations possible on single objects. However trendy clothing fashions or hairstyles may be, they share the same basic parts and details shown in the illustrations on the pages that follow.

Because cosmetics, grooming, hairstyles and jewelry are an important part of everyday life, they have been included in this section, as have such items as eyeglasses, handbags and wallets, timepieces and smoking materials. And because on rainy days an umbrella is essential to carry, it, too, appears here.

Identification Bracelet

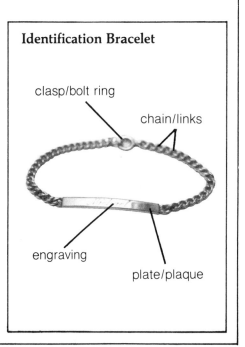

clasp/bolt ring

chain/links

engraving

plate/plaque

Jacket and Vest

A jacket, or *coat*, can be *single-* or *double-breasted*. A *handkerchief pocket* or *chest pocket* is usually found on the upper left front panel. The pouchlike attachment inside a side pocket is called a *change pocket*. Most jackets have a *vent* or *double vent* cut into the hem in the *back panel*. Vests have an adjustable *backstrap* in the back.

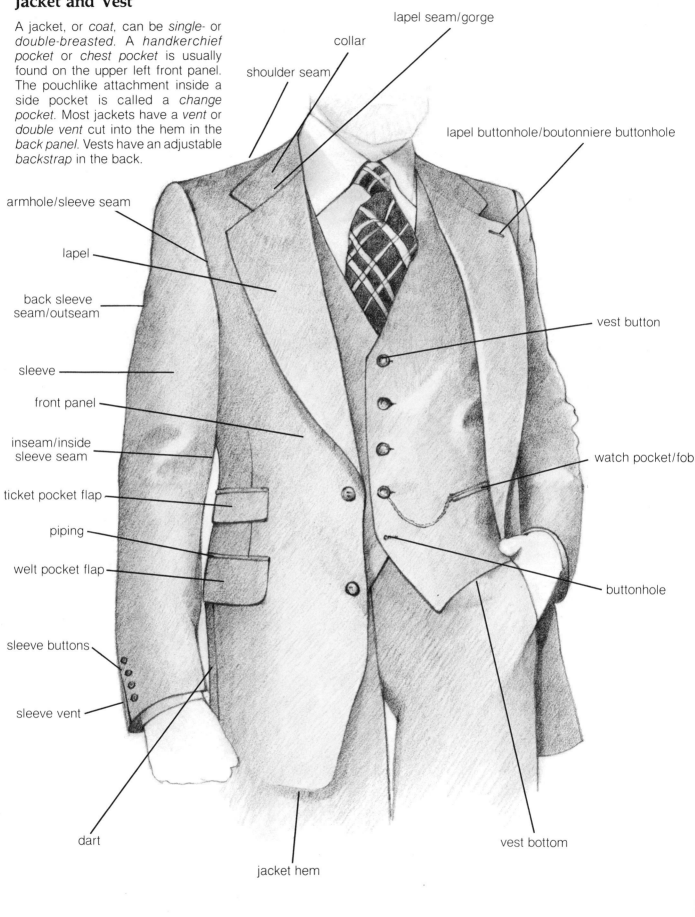

collar

lapel seam/gorge

shoulder seam

lapel buttonhole/boutonniere buttonhole

armhole/sleeve seam

lapel

back sleeve seam/outseam

sleeve

front panel

inseam/inside sleeve seam

ticket pocket flap

piping

welt pocket flap

sleeve buttons

sleeve vent

dart

jacket hem

vest button

watch pocket/fob

buttonhole

vest bottom

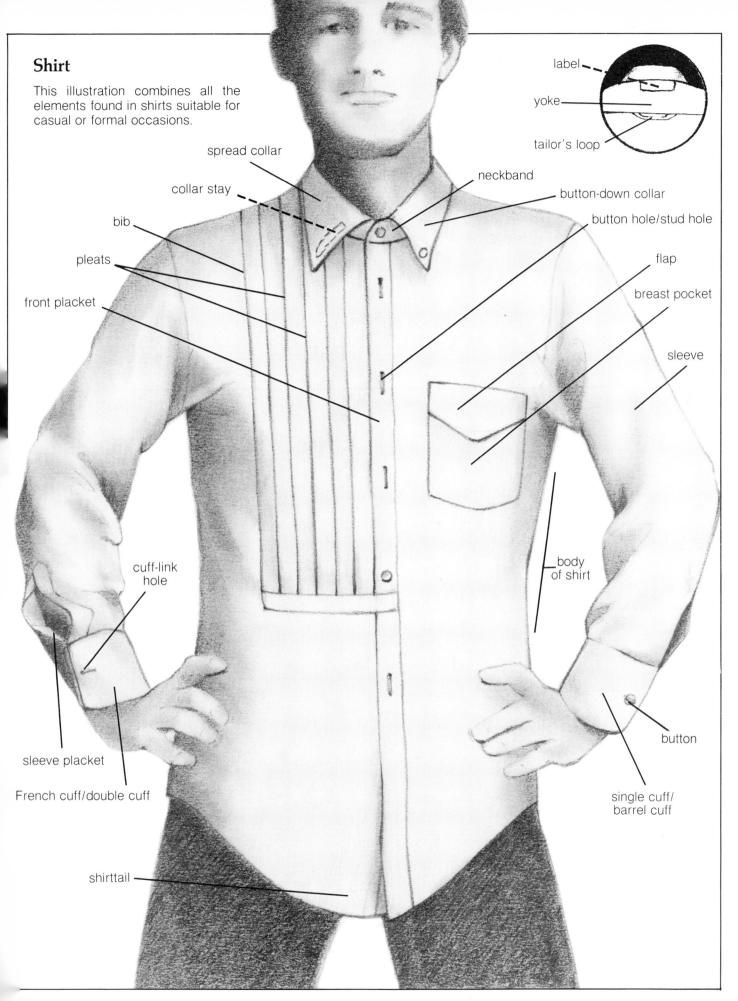

Shirt

This illustration combines all the elements found in shirts suitable for casual or formal occasions.

label

yoke

tailor's loop

spread collar

collar stay

bib

pleats

front placket

neckband

button-down collar

button hole/stud hole

flap

breast pocket

sleeve

cuff-link hole

body of shirt

sleeve placket

French cuff/double cuff

button

single cuff/ barrel cuff

shirttail

Belt and Suspenders

Large, often elaborately engraved buckles are called *plaque buckles.* *Military buckles,* or *ratchet buckles,* are adjusted by pushing a *tension rod* inside the *frame.* Some belts come with reinforcing *eyelets* in the punch holes. The composite pair of suspenders shown here are *fireman's, policeman's,* or *working man's suspenders.* They all have a single elastic band at the back, whereas *dress suspenders* have crossed bands.

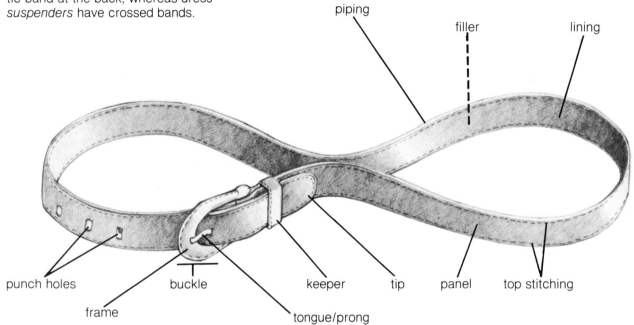

piping   filler   lining

punch holes   buckle   keeper   tip   panel   top stitching

frame   tongue/prong

Belt

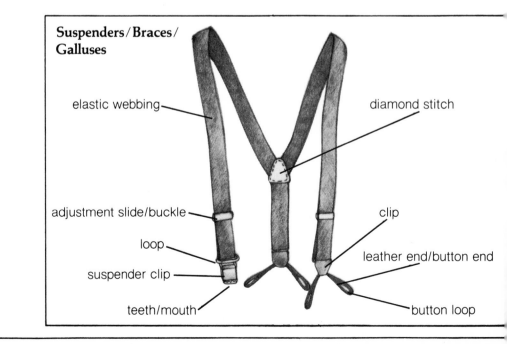

Suspenders/Braces/ Galluses

elastic webbing   diamond stitch

adjustment slide/buckle   clip

loop   leather end/button end

suspender clip

teeth/mouth   button loop

Pants

The back of a *pair of pants* is called the *seat*. Mid-thigh or knee length pants are *shorts*. *Jeans* often have pockets and seams reinforced with *rivets*. *Waistband closures* on pants are secured with *button tab closings* or metal *hook and eye closings*.

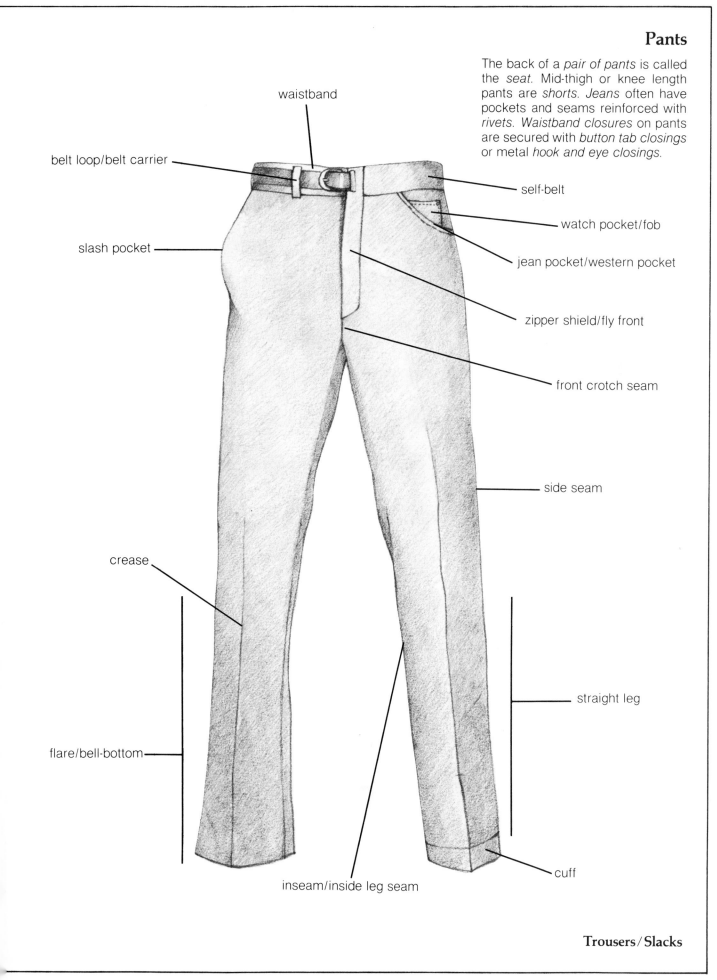

waistband

belt loop/belt carrier

self-belt

watch pocket/fob

jean pocket/western pocket

slash pocket

zipper shield/fly front

front crotch seam

side seam

crease

straight leg

flare/bell-bottom

cuff

inseam/inside leg seam

Trousers/Slacks

Men's Apparel

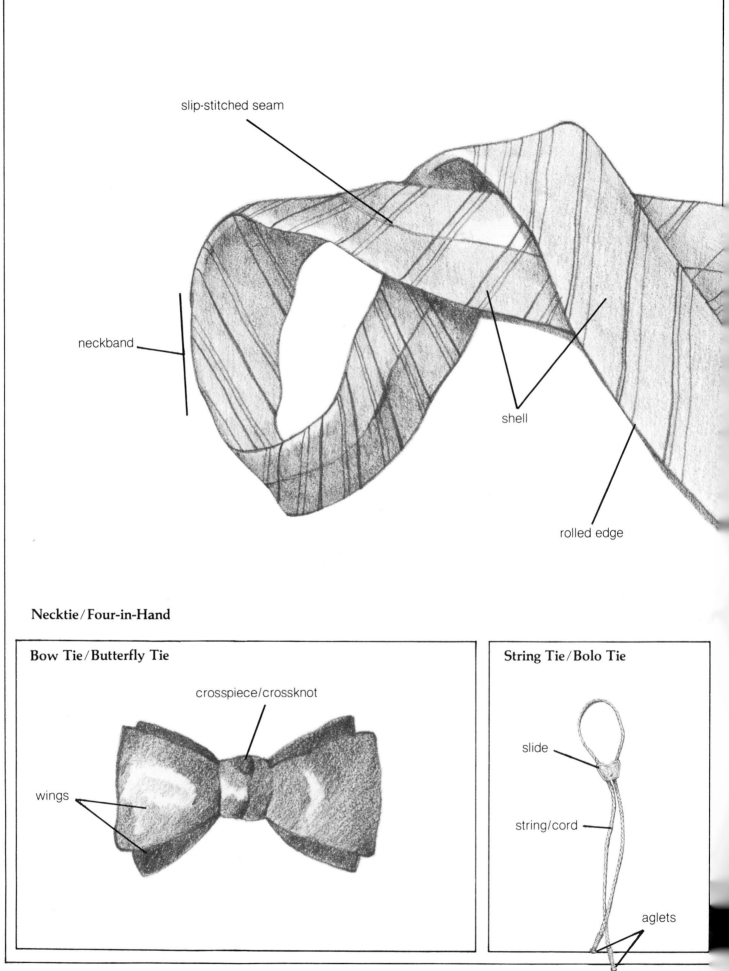

slip-stitched seam

neckband

shell

rolled edge

Necktie/Four-in-Hand

Bow Tie/Butterfly Tie

crosspiece/crossknot

wings

String Tie/Bolo Tie

slide

string/cord

aglets

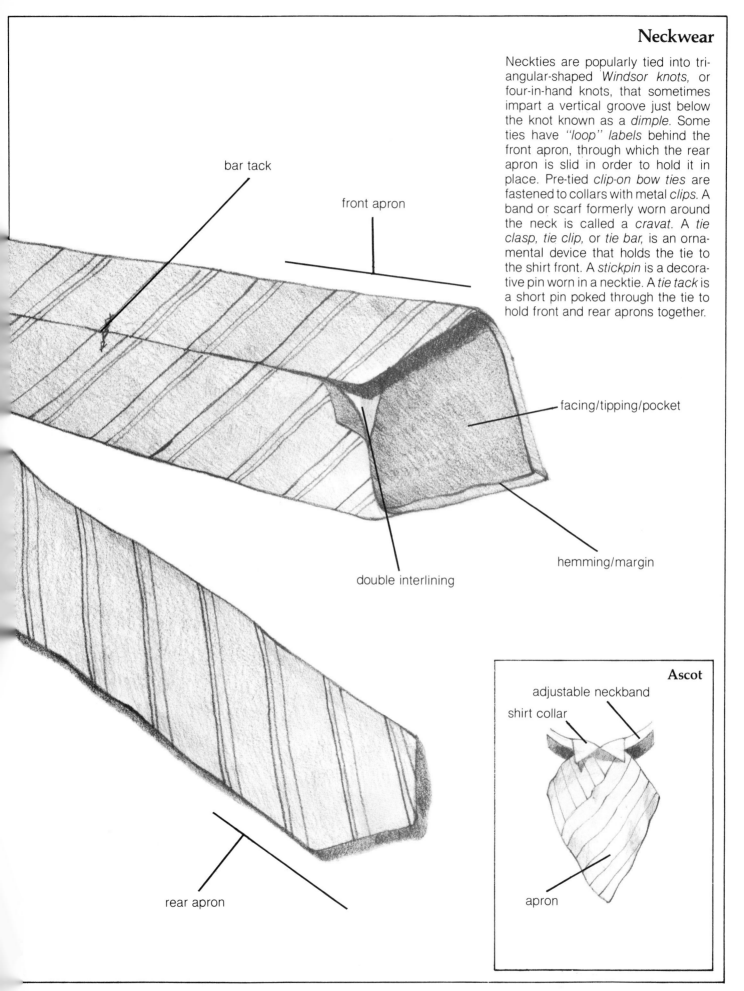

Neckties are popularly tied into tri-angular-shaped *Windsor knots*, or four-in-hand knots, that sometimes impart a vertical groove just below the knot known as a *dimple*. Some ties have *"loop" labels* behind the front apron, through which the rear apron is slid in order to hold it in place. Pre-tied *clip-on bow ties* are fastened to collars with metal *clips*. A band or scarf formerly worn around the neck is called a *cravat*. A *tie clasp*, *tie clip*, or *tie bar*, is an orna-mental device that holds the tie to the shirt front. A *stickpin* is a decora-tive pin worn in a necktie. A *tie tack* is a short pin poked through the tie to hold front and rear aprons together.

bar tack

front apron

facing/tipping/pocket

hemming/margin

double interlining

rear apron

Ascot

adjustable neckband

shirt collar

apron

Underwear

A *T-shirt* has short sleeves rather than shoulder straps. Loose-fitting *boxer shorts* have short, trouserlike legs rather than leg openings. Some athletic supporters, or *jockstraps*, have pockets in the pouch to accommodate rubber-lined *protective cups*.

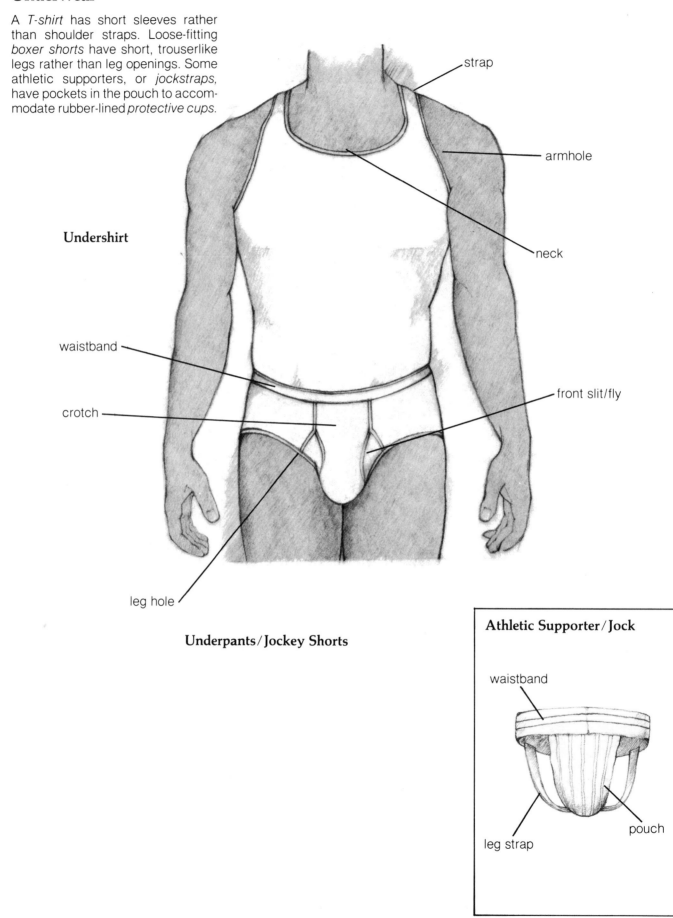

strap

armhole

neck

Undershirt

waistband

crotch

front slit/fly

leg hole

Underpants/Jockey Shorts

Athletic Supporter/Jock

waistband

leg strap

pouch

Foundation Garments

Most *bras* are secured with *hook-and-eye closures* either on a *back-strap* or in the front of the garment. Many have *underwiring* and/or *side-bones* for added support. *Cup padding* is another optional element. Girdles are sometimes stiffened with *spiral bones* or *stays*. *Corsets* are similar to girdles.

Brassiere

Girdle

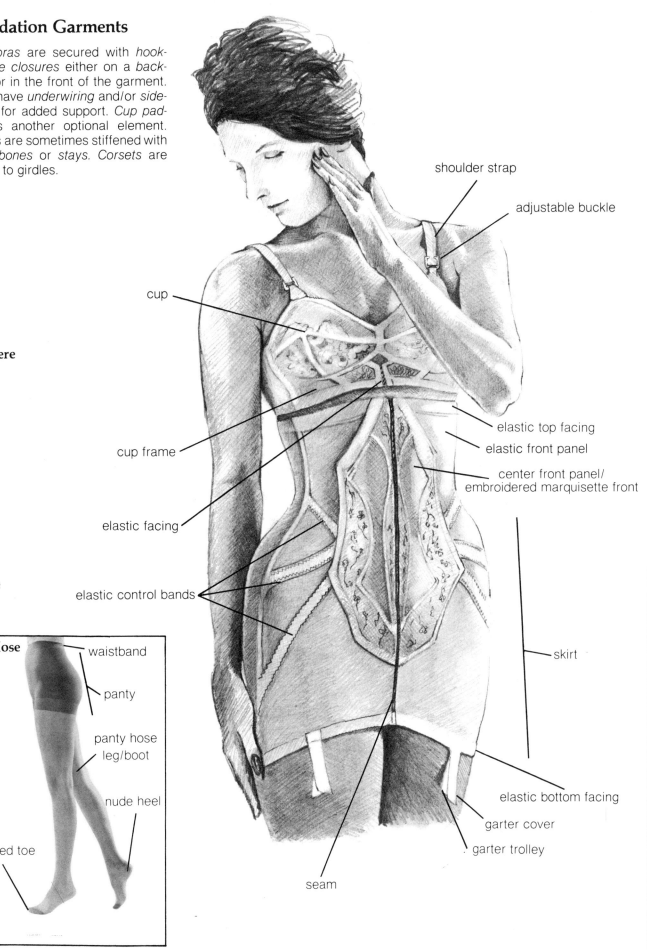

shoulder strap

adjustable buckle

cup

elastic top facing

elastic front panel

center front panel/
embroidered marquisette front

cup frame

elastic facing

elastic control bands

skirt

elastic bottom facing

garter cover

garter trolley

seam

Panty Hose

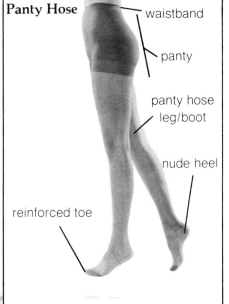

waistband

panty

panty hose
leg/boot

nude heel

reinforced toe

Jacket and Pants

Facing material is used on the underside of a lapel. *Lining* is used on the inside of a garment to cover up seamwork and provide body. A pair of lined pants has inside material from cuff to waist. In half-lined pants, the material stretches from waist to knee. In unlined garments, *seams* are clean finished with *bias tape,* or bias binding, sewn on a diagonal to provide stretch and support and to protect fabric from raveling.

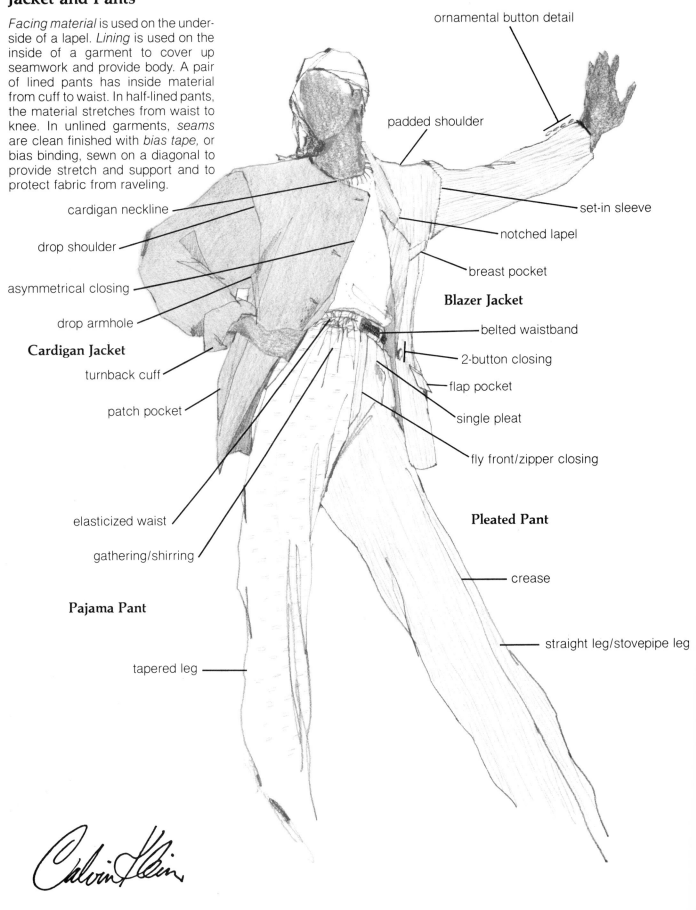

ornamental button detail

padded shoulder

set-in sleeve

cardigan neckline

notched lapel

drop shoulder

breast pocket

asymmetrical closing

Blazer Jacket

drop armhole

belted waistband

Cardigan Jacket

2-button closing

turnback cuff

flap pocket

patch pocket

single pleat

fly front/zipper closing

elasticized waist

Pleated Pant

gathering/shirring

crease

Pajama Pant

straight leg/stovepipe leg

tapered leg

Blouse and Skirt

The blouse and the skirt shown here are composites. Skirts can be secured at the waist with a *belt, tie, zipper, hook* and *eye,* or *buttons.*

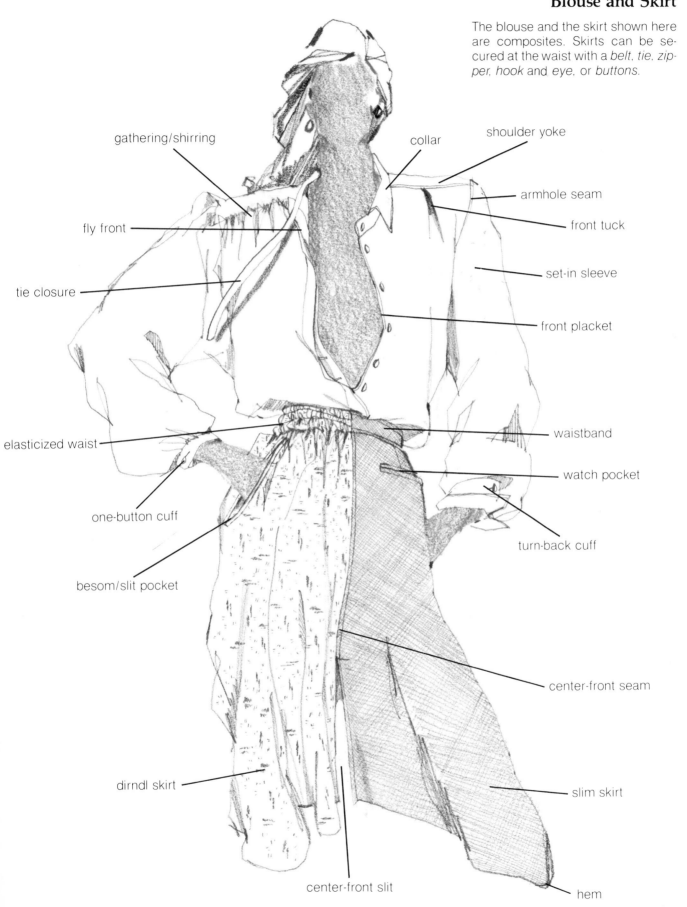

gathering/shirring

collar

shoulder yoke

armhole seam

front tuck

fly front

set-in sleeve

tie closure

front placket

elasticized waist

waistband

watch pocket

one-button cuff

turn-back cuff

besom/slit pocket

center-front seam

dirndl skirt

slim skirt

center-front slit

hem

Women's Apparel

Dress

This composite dress, or *gown,* has a *camisole top.* A dress hanging straight from the shoulders is a *chemise.* Some dresses have a fitted or shaped piece at the shoulder called a *yoke. Bratelles* are ornamental suspenderlike straps. Dresses are stored on hangers by means of *keepers, carriers, riders, loops* or *hangers.*

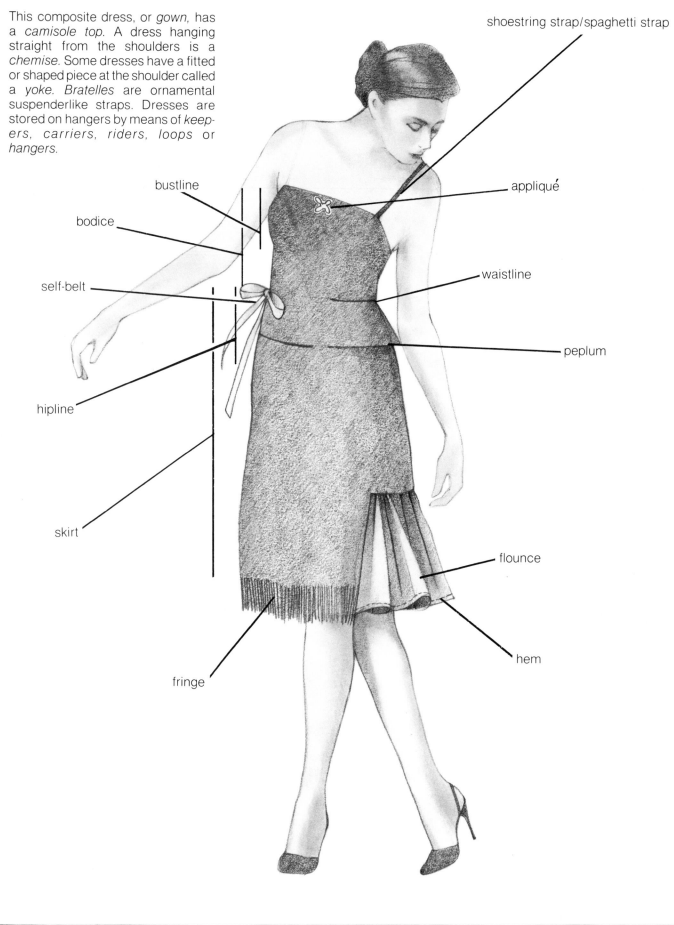

shoestring strap/spaghetti strap

appliqué

bustline

bodice

self-belt

hipline

skirt

fringe

waistline

peplum

flounce

hem

Sweater

A *crew neck sweater* is a pullover with a high, round neck. A *turtleneck* has a high neck that turns back over itself. A sweater with a neck opening that stretches from shoulder to shoulder is a *boat neck*, or *bateau neck*. A sweater without arms is a *vest*, or *knit vest*.

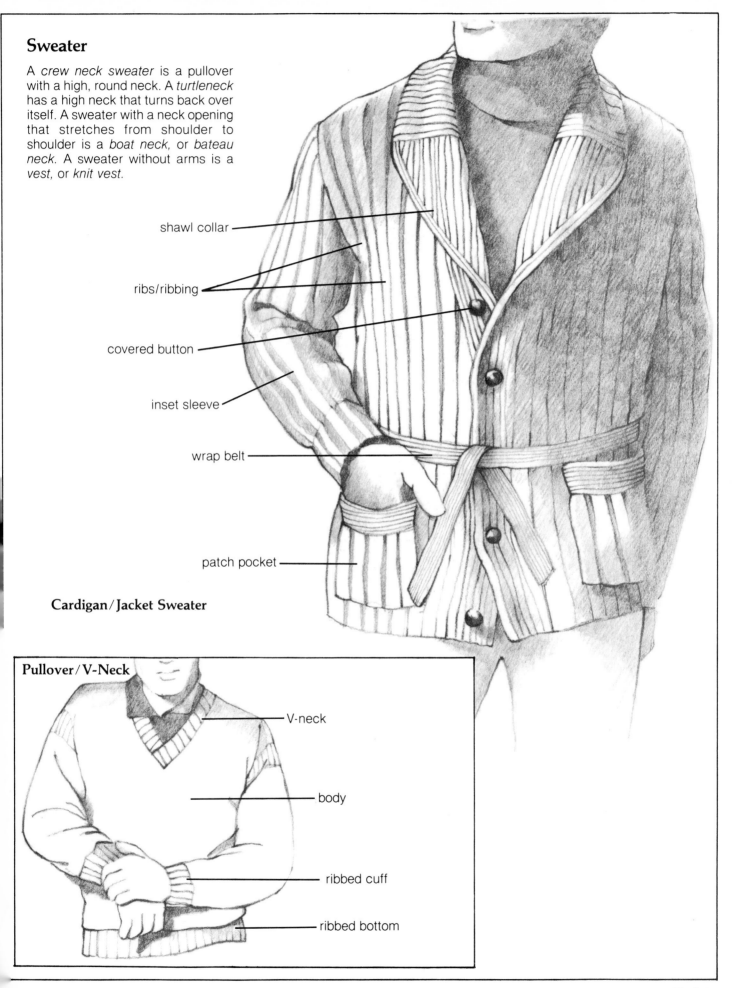

shawl collar

ribs/ribbing

covered button

inset sleeve

wrap belt

patch pocket

Cardigan/Jacket Sweater

Pullover/V-Neck

V-neck

body

ribbed cuff

ribbed bottom

Outerwear

The type of combination *overcoat* and *raincoat* shown here usually has a *button-out* or *zip-out robe lining* which provides warmth in cold weather. It also has a *storm shield* on the back, ornamental *'D' rings* hanging from the back of the belt and sometimes a *throat latch* strap around the collar.

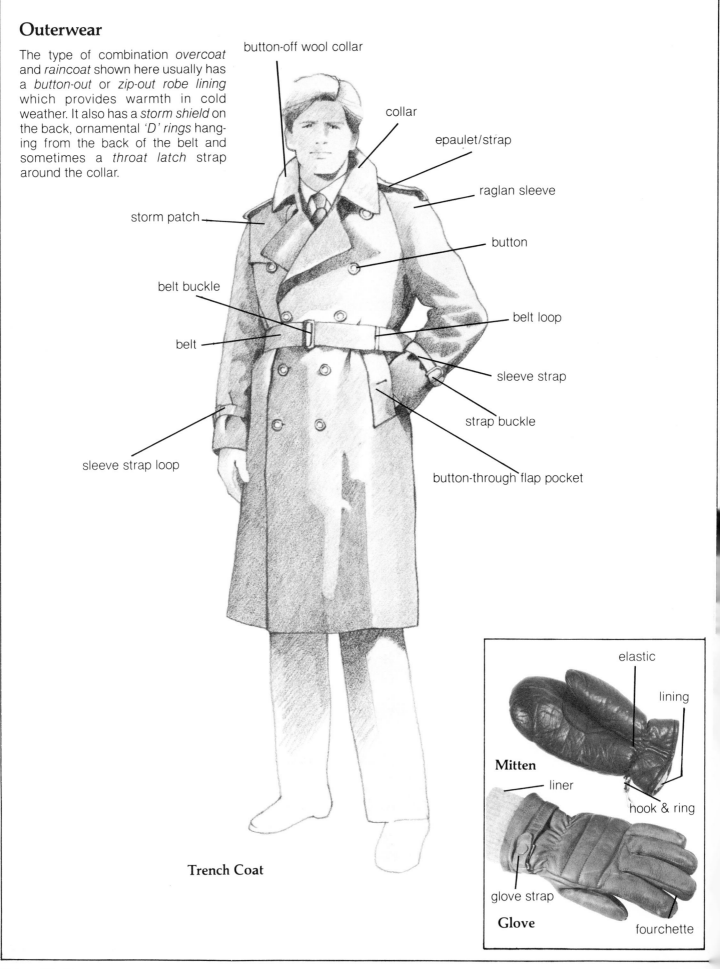

button-off wool collar

collar

epaulet/strap

raglan sleeve

button

storm patch

belt buckle

belt loop

belt

sleeve strap

strap buckle

sleeve strap loop

button-through flap pocket

Trench Coat

elastic

lining

Mitten

liner

hook & ring

glove strap

Glove

fourchette

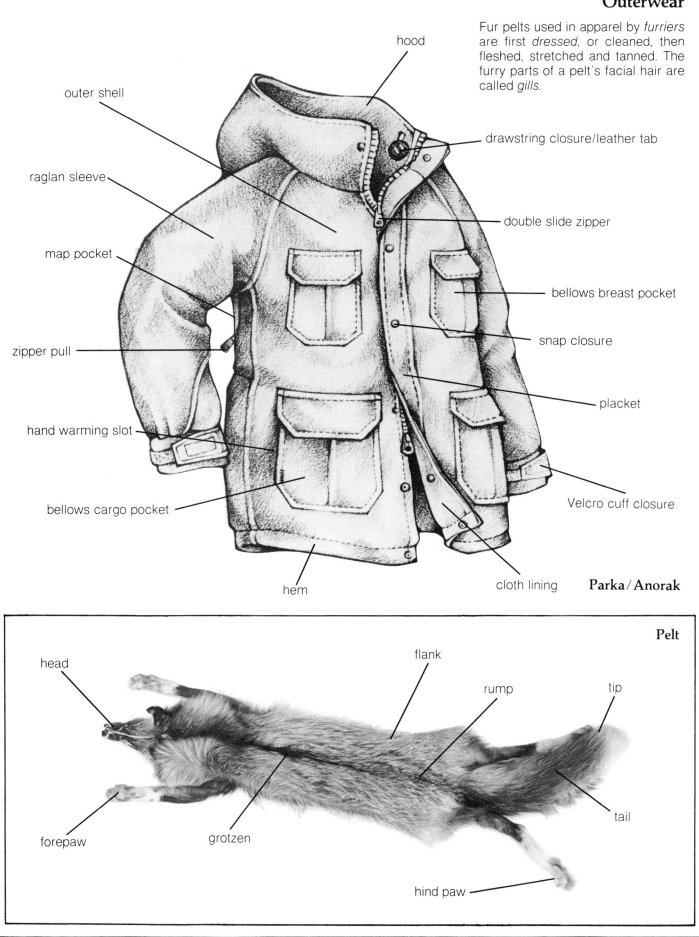

Outerwear

Fur pelts used in apparel by *furriers* are first *dressed,* or cleaned, then fleshed, stretched and tanned. The furry parts of a pelt's facial hair are called *gills.*

hood

outer shell

raglan sleeve

map pocket

zipper pull

hand warming slot

bellows cargo pocket

hem

drawstring closure/leather tab

double slide zipper

bellows breast pocket

snap closure

placket

Velcro cuff closure

cloth lining

Parka/Anorak

Pelt

head

flank

rump

tip

forepaw

grotzen

tail

hind paw

Unisex Clothing

Men's Hats

Hats are *styled,* or *blocked,* by a *hat-maker* or *hatter.* Hats that have not been creased have an *open crown.* Some hats have *plastic linings.*

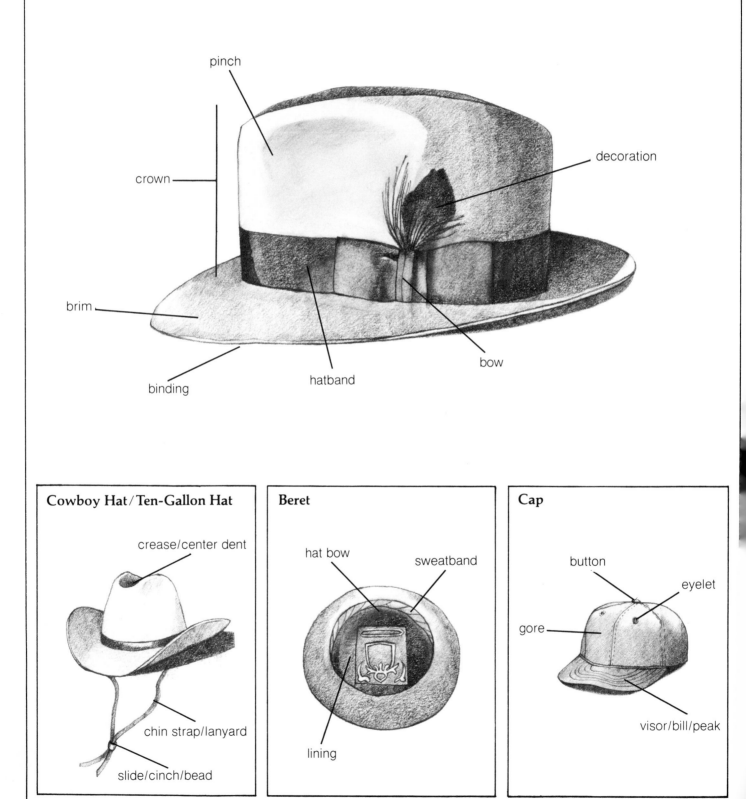

pinch

crown

brim

binding

hatband

bow

decoration

Cowboy Hat / Ten-Gallon Hat

crease/center dent

chin strap/lanyard

slide/cinch/bead

Beret

hat bow

sweatband

lining

Cap

button

eyelet

gore

visor/bill/peak

Women's Hats

Women's hats are designed, made and sold by *milliners*. *Malines*, or stiff, fine *netting*, is often used as a veil. *Buckles*, *sequins*, *plastic fruit*, *fabric flowers*, *buttons*, *tassels* and *braids* are among the many items used as decorative *trimming*. Brimless, close-fitting hats include a *toque*, a *cloche*, and a *turban*. A *picture hat* has a broad flexible brim and is often decorated with trimming. A shallow, round hat with vertical sides is a *pillbox*. A netlike hat or part of a hat or the fabric that holds or covers the back of a woman's hair is a *snood*.

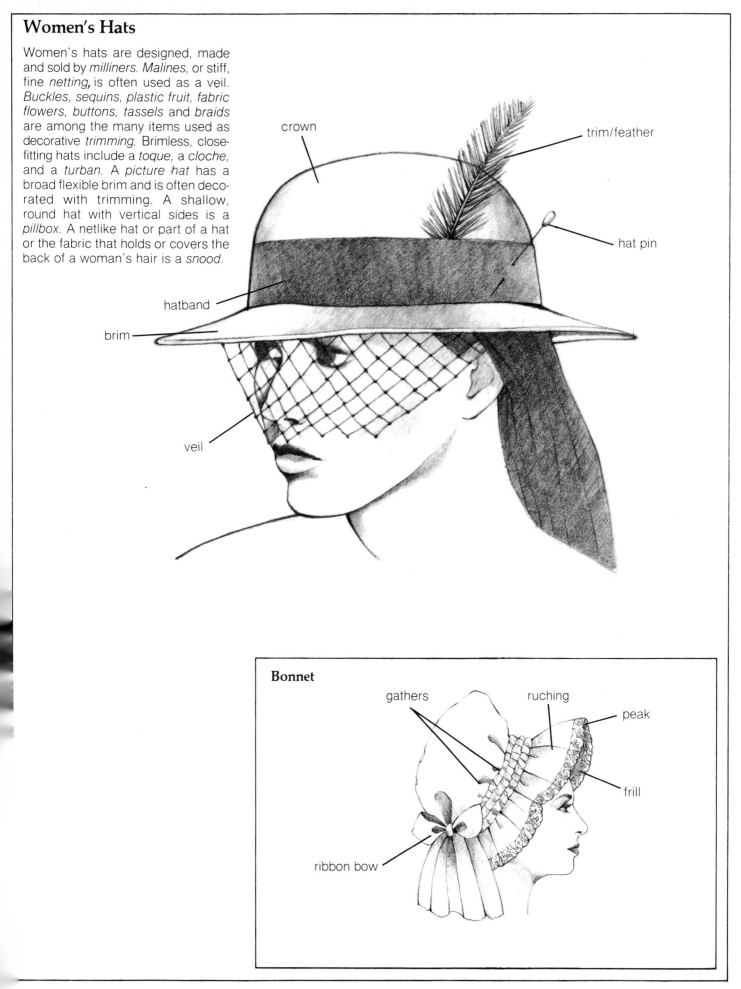

crown

trim/feather

hat pin

hatband

brim

veil

Bonnet

gathers

ruching

peak

frill

ribbon bow

Man's Shoe

A shoe consists of a *bottom,* or heel and sole, an *inner sole,* or *insole,* and an *upper.* Shoes like the one shown here, in which the flaps fold over the tongue or vamp, are *bluchers.* Shoes without this construction are *barrels.* A step-in shoe without laces is a *loafer,* whereas a *moccasin* has neither laces nor a heel. The fringed leather decoration on some shoes that covers the laces is the *kiltie.*

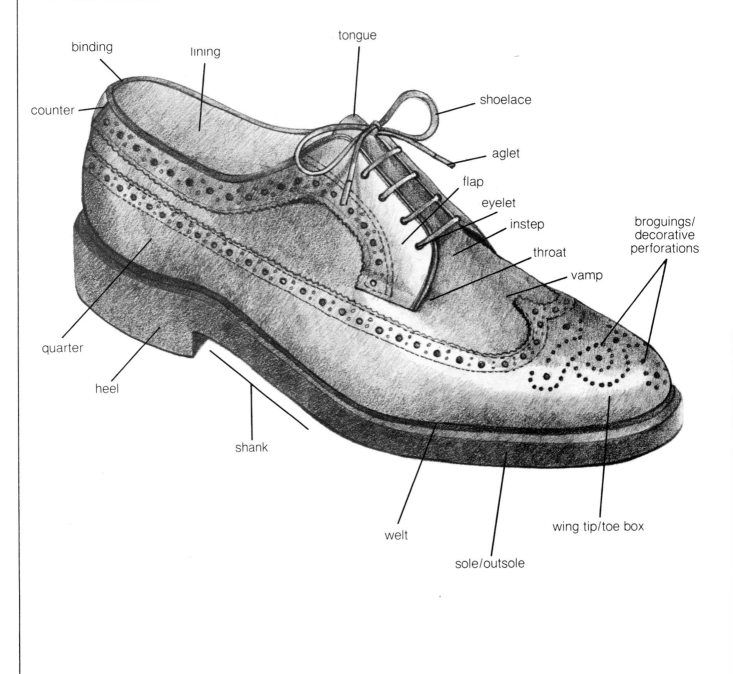

binding

lining

tongue

counter

shoelace

aglet

flap

eyelet

instep

throat

broguings/ decorative perforations

vamp

quarter

heel

shank

welt

sole/outsole

wing tip/toe box

Woman's Shoe

A shoe with an open front is an *open-toed shoe,* whereas a shoe with an open back, held on by a strap, is a *slingback,* or *sling shoe.* The *high-heel shoe* seen here is similar to a *pump* in that it grips both the toe and the heel. A high, thin heel is a *spiked,* or *stiletto, heel.* A shoe with a thick layer between the *inner sole* and the outsole is a *platform.*

piping/trim

instep strap

ankle strap

counter

throat

collar

vamp

heel seat

tip

heel

shank

outsole

heel breast

heel lift

andy Warhol

Boot and Sandal

The upper section of a boot, called the *shaft*, may extend from ankle to knee. The lower section is called the *foot*. Many boots have a contoured steel *shank*, located between outsole and *insole*, to provide support for the arch area. A *thong* is a type of sandal in which the strap comes up between the big toe and the toe next to it.

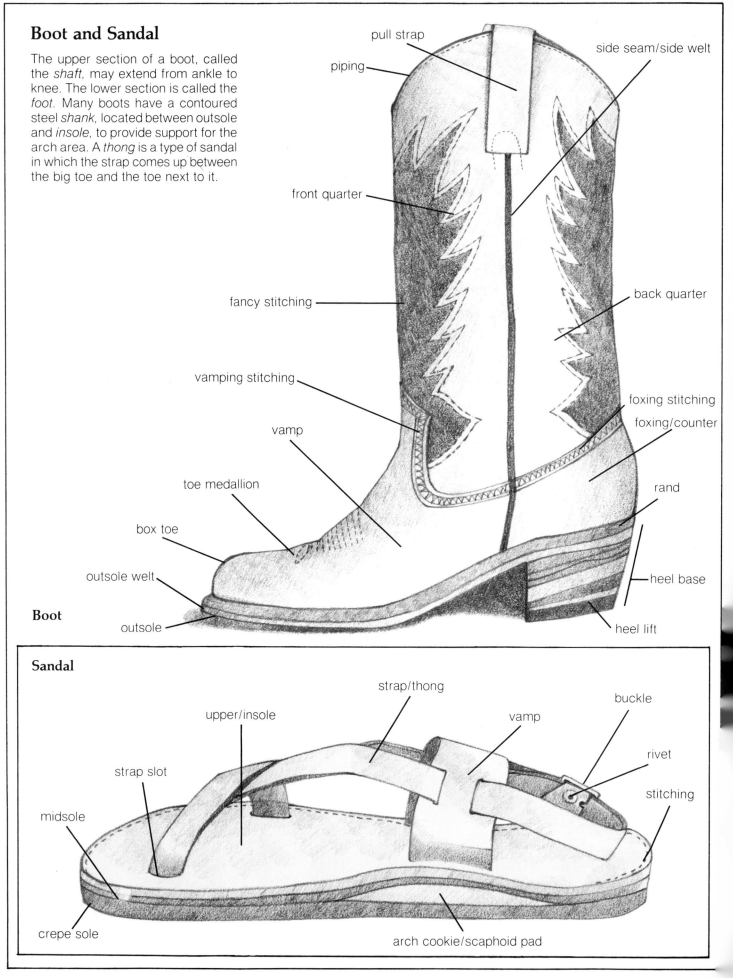

pull strap

piping

side seam/side welt

front quarter

fancy stitching

back quarter

vamping stitching

foxing stitching

foxing/counter

vamp

rand

toe medallion

box toe

heel base

outsole welt

heel lift

outsole

Boot

Sandal

strap/thong

buckle

upper/insole

vamp

strap slot

rivet

midsole

stitching

crepe sole

arch cookie/scaphoid pad

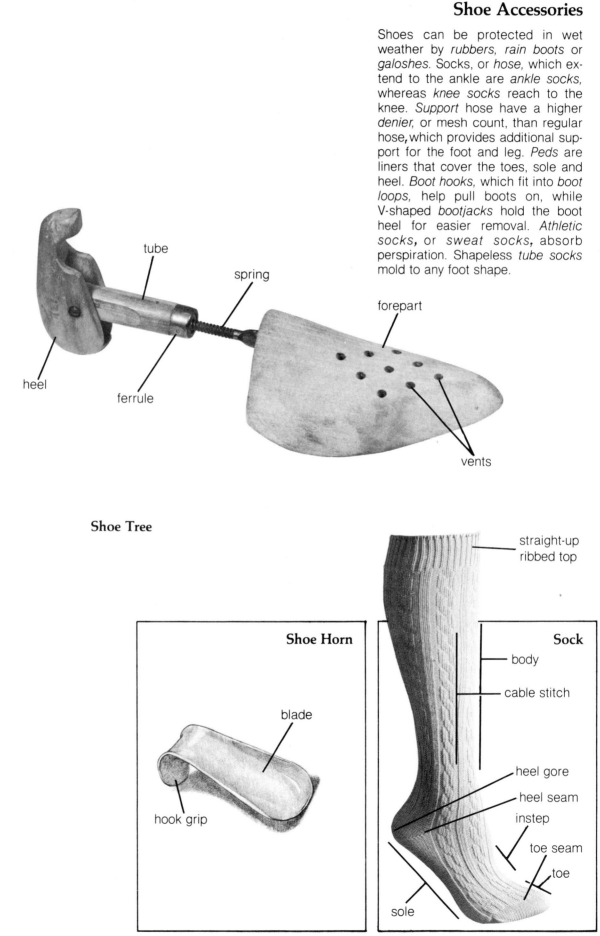

Shoe Accessories

Shoes can be protected in wet weather by *rubbers, rain boots* or *galoshes.* Socks, or *hose,* which extend to the ankle are *ankle socks,* whereas *knee socks* reach to the knee. *Support* hose have a higher *denier,* or mesh count, than regular hose, which provides additional support for the foot and leg. *Peds* are liners that cover the toes, sole and heel. *Boot hooks,* which fit into *boot loops,* help pull boots on, while V-shaped *bootjacks* hold the boot heel for easier removal. *Athletic socks,* or *sweat socks,* absorb perspiration. Shapeless *tube socks* mold to any foot shape.

tube

spring

forepart

heel

ferrule

vents

Shoe Tree

straight-up ribbed top

Shoe Horn

Sock

blade

body

cable stitch

hook grip

heel gore

heel seam

instep

toe seam

toe

sole

Fasteners

Heavy-duty hook-and-eye closures are called *hook and bars*. In a *cinch fastener*, a *strap* is pulled through two *rings* then back through the second ring to fasten. A *frog* consists of an intricately knotted *cord loop* through which a button is hooked.

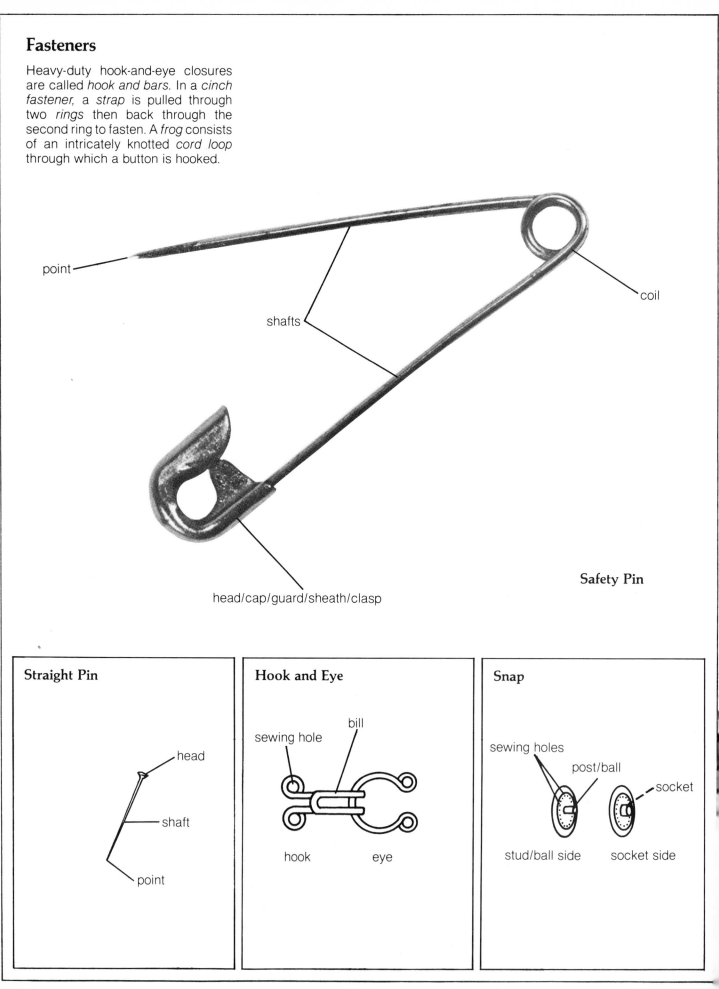

point

shafts

coil

head/cap/guard/sheath/clasp

Safety Pin

Straight Pin

head

shaft

point

Hook and Eye

sewing hole

bill

hook

eye

Snap

sewing holes

post/ball

socket

stud/ball side

socket side

A *divider* within the zipper slide separates teeth when it is moved downward. Some zippers have a *synthetic coil* rather than teeth. A *pull ring* is occasionally attached to the slide for decorative purposes. A *two-way zipper* can be opened from either end, while an *invisible zipper* is concealed when closed and appears to be a *seam*.

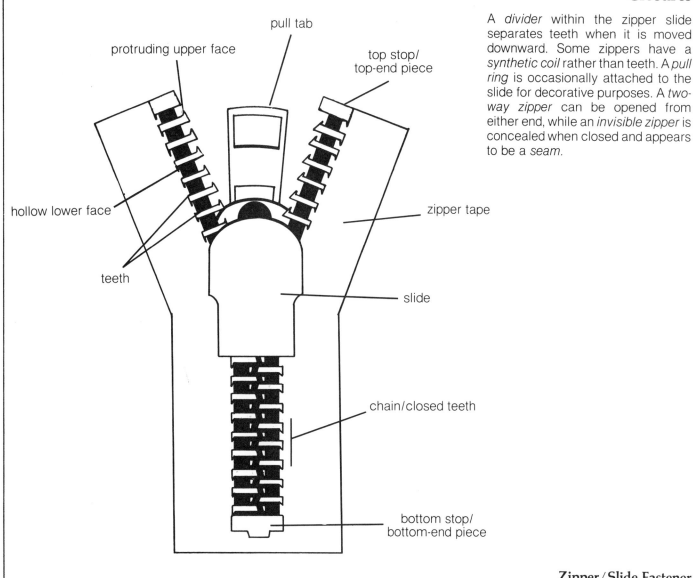

protruding upper face

pull tab

top stop/ top-end piece

hollow lower face

teeth

zipper tape

slide

chain/closed teeth

bottom stop/ bottom-end piece

Zipper / Slide Fastener

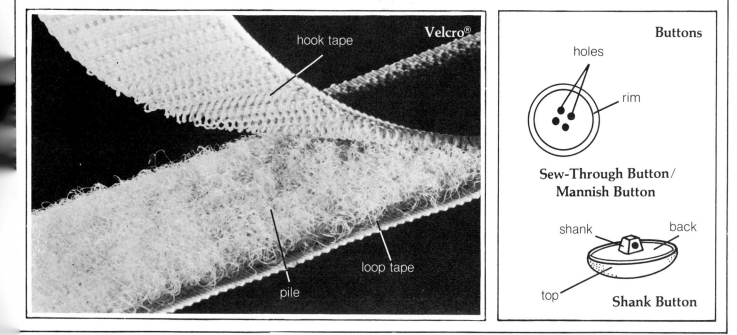

Velcro®

hook tape

pile

loop tape

Buttons

holes

rim

Sew-Through Button/ Mannish Button

shank

back

top

Shank Button

Shavers

A *straight razor* has a single, long blade which folds into a *handle*. It is sharpened on a long strip of leather called a *strop*. Other, older barbering equipment includes *shaving brushes* and *shaving mugs*. A *safety razor* has two *wings* on the *head* which are opened by a screw at the base of the handle. Bleeding from shaving cuts or nicks can be stopped with a *styptic pencil*.

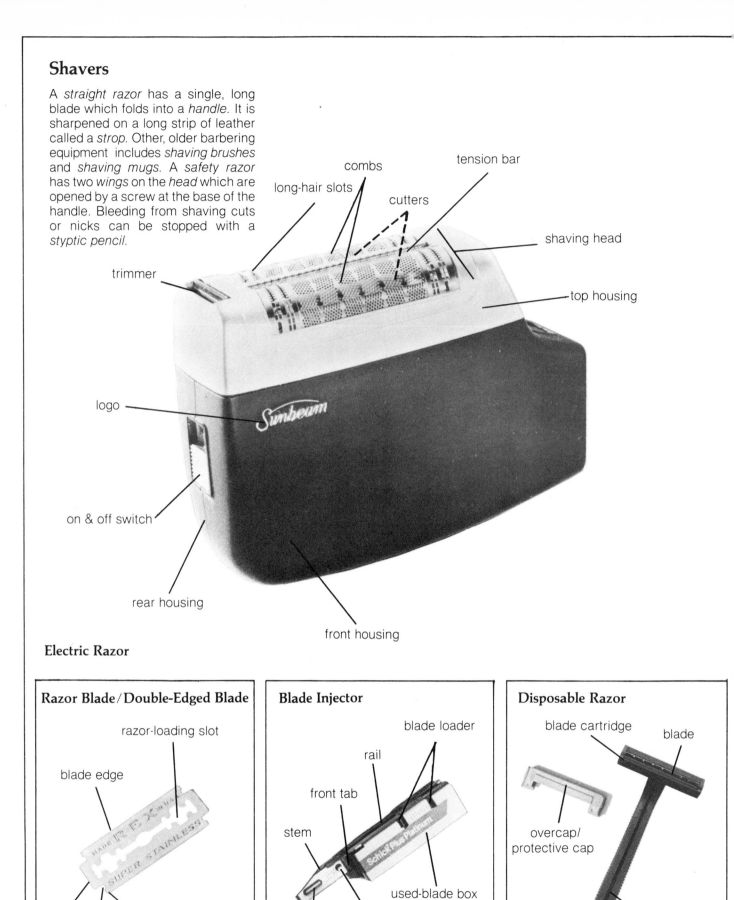

combs

long-hair slots

cutters

tension bar

shaving head

trimmer

top housing

logo

Sunbeam

on & off switch

rear housing

front housing

Electric Razor

Razor Blade/Double-Edged Blade

razor-loading slot

blade edge

tab

shoulder

undercut

Blade Injector

blade loader

rail

front tab

stem

gash

bump

used-blade box

Disposable Razor

blade cartridge

blade

overcap/ protective cap

handle

Men's Hair

Chevelure is a head of hair. A man without any hair on his *scalp* is said to be *bald*. *Wigs, hairpieces, toupees* or "rugs" can be used to conceal *bald spots*. *Pogonotrophy* is beard-growing and *pogonotomy* is beard-cutting. A partial growth is known as *stubble*. A small, tufted chin beard is a *goatee*. A trim, pointed one is a *Vandyke*. A mustache having long, curled ends is a *handlebar mustache*.

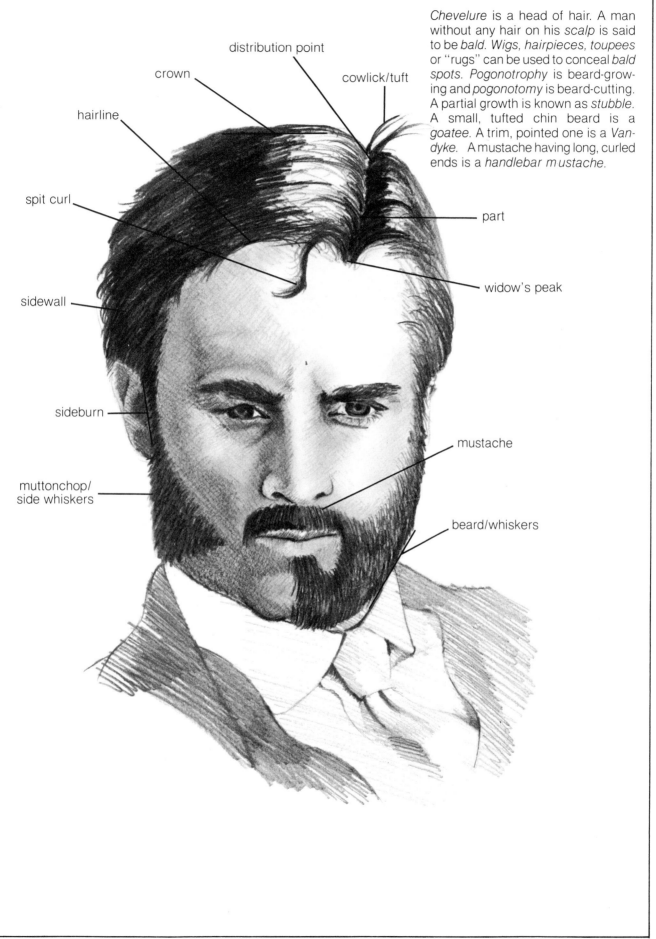

distribution point

crown

cowlick/tuft

hairline

spit curl

part

sidewall

widow's peak

sideburn

mustache

muttonchop/
side whiskers

beard/whiskers

207

Hair Grooming Implements

Among other attachments available for use with a *pro-style dryer* are combs, brush and an *air-flow nozzle*, to limit the amount of hot air.

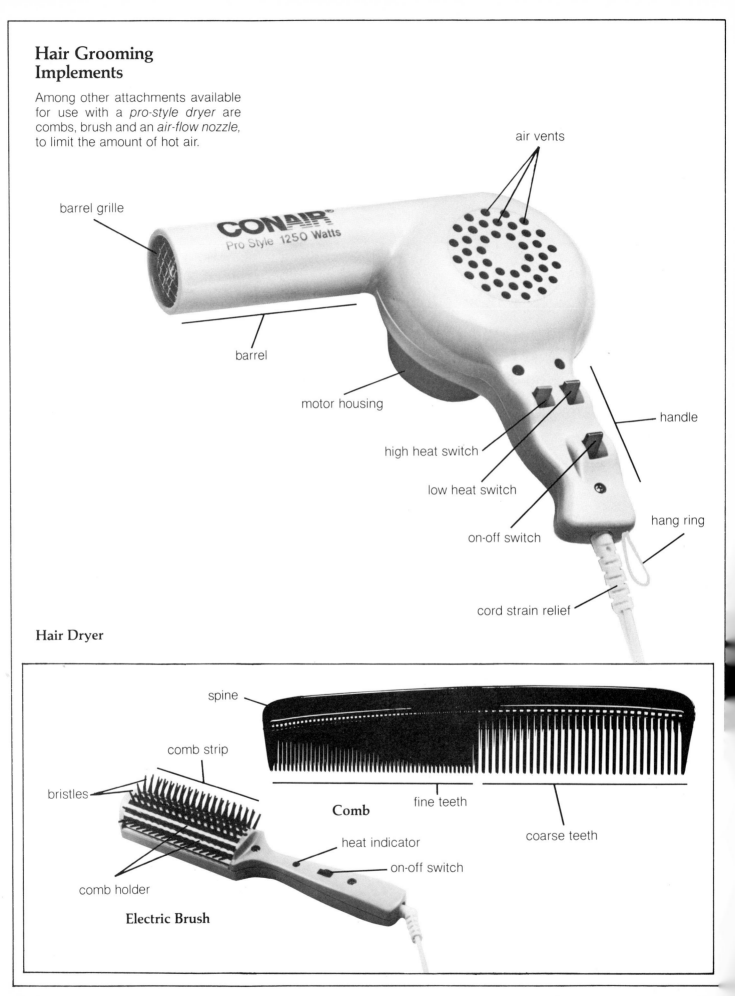

barrel grille

air vents

CONAIR®
Pro Style 1250 Watts

barrel

motor housing

high heat switch

low heat switch

on-off switch

handle

hang ring

cord strain relief

Hair Dryer

spine

comb strip

bristles

fine teeth

Comb

coarse teeth

heat indicator

on-off switch

comb holder

Electric Brush

Women's Hair

A small portion of hair in a woman's *hairdo,* or *coiffure,* is a *lock. Bouffant* is a puffed-out hairdo. *Teased,* or *back-combed, hair* is achieved by taking hold of a strand and pushing the short hairs toward the scalp with a comb. A braid on the back of the head is a *pigtail.* Hair that turns inward at the end, rather than outward, is a *pageboy.* A long piece of store-bought hair clipped to real hair is a *fall.*

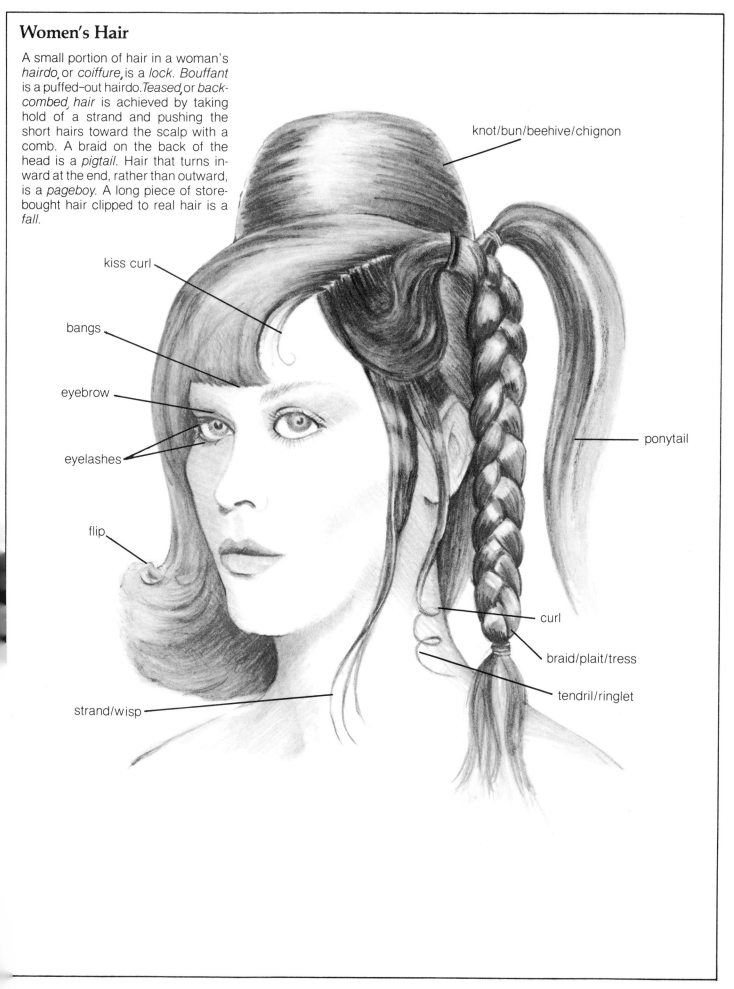

knot/bun/beehive/chignon

kiss curl

bangs

eyebrow

eyelashes

flip

ponytail

curl

braid/plait/tress

tendril/ringlet

strand/wisp

Hairstyles and Facial Hair

Hairstyling Implements

A curling iron is used to curl a *strand* of hair or to straighten it. Hair clips and bobby pins, which may be long or short, can be used to secure a roller while hair is being set. The roller shown here, however, is *self-clasping*. Barrettes, combs, hair ribbons, headbands and hair bands hold hair in place or serve as decorative *hair ornaments*. Professional *hairdressers* use *permanent rods* and *papers*, *applicator bottles* filled with *permanent lotion, setting lotion, rinse* or *dye*, plastic *caps, dryers* and *infrared lamps* to treat and style *hairdos*.

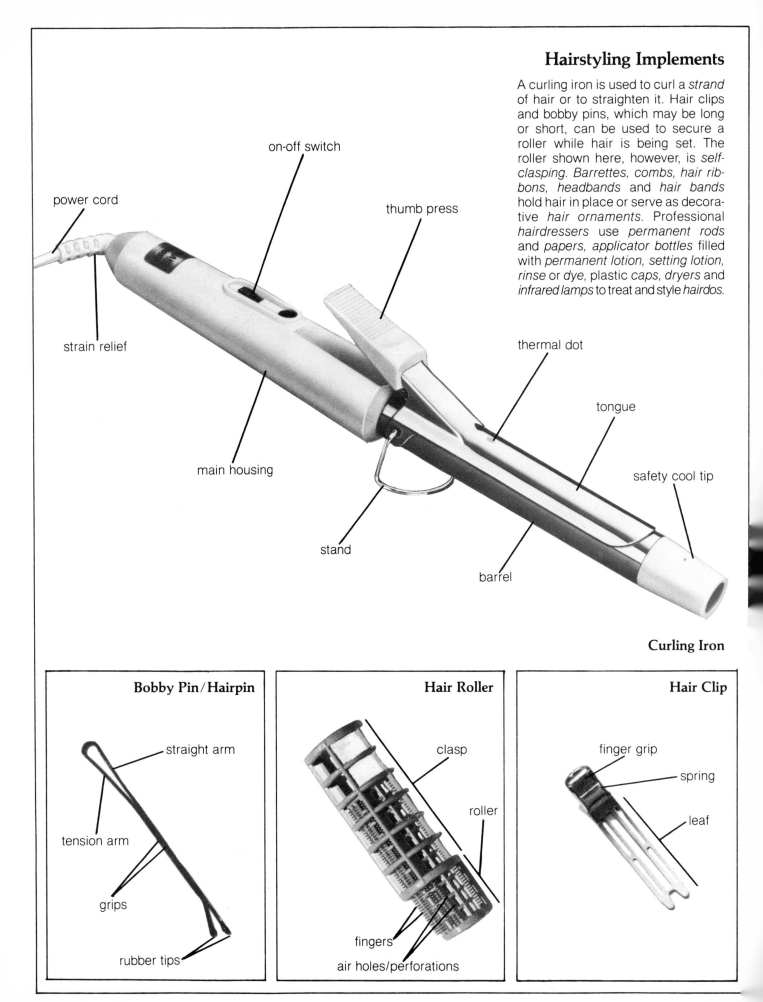

on-off switch

thumb press

power cord

strain relief

thermal dot

tongue

main housing

safety cool tip

stand

barrel

Curling Iron

Bobby Pin/Hairpin

straight arm

tension arm

grips

rubber tips

Hair Roller

clasp

roller

fingers

air holes/perforations

Hair Clip

finger grip

spring

leaf

Toothbrush

The stimulator tip on a toothbrush fits in what is called a *hang-up hole.* Teeth can also be cleaned with *dental floss,* a waxed string, and *high-pressure water-spray units.* Nails can be smoothed with an *emery board,* a cardboard strip covered with *powdered emery,* or a *nail file.*

bristles

stimulator tip

tuft hole

block head

block handle

Toothbrush

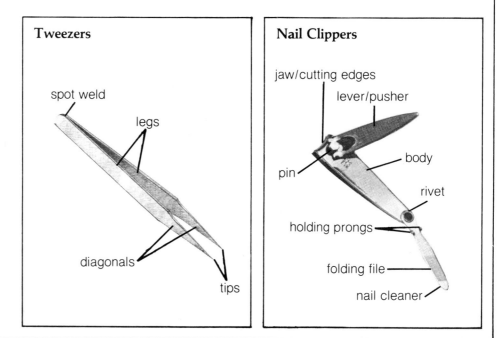

Tweezers

spot weld

legs

diagonals

tips

Nail Clippers

jaw/cutting edges

lever/pusher

body

pin

rivet

holding prongs

folding file

nail cleaner

Cosmetics

Makeup

A skin-colored *concealer,* or *coverup,* can be used to cover blemishes or undesirable shadows under the eyes. *Pancake makeup* is a thick face powder used by actors and actresses as a foundation. Makeup can be removed with a *cleansing cream* or *cold cream.*

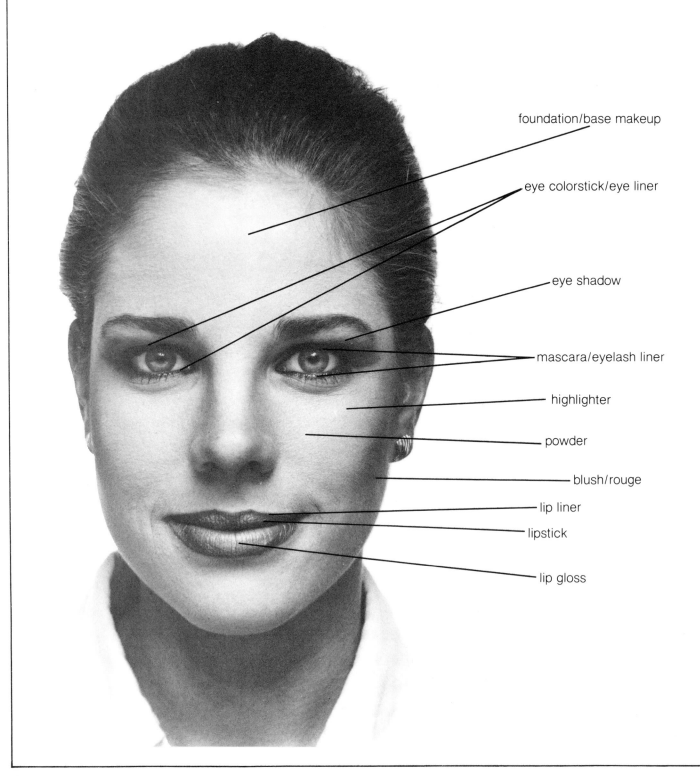

foundation/base makeup

eye colorstick/eye liner

eye shadow

mascara/eyelash liner

highlighter

powder

blush/rouge

lip liner

lipstick

lip gloss

Colored *nail polish* is often used to "paint" fingernails and toenails. In addition to those beauty products shown here, there are *scents,* such as *perfume,* applied by women to *pulse points; bath oils; body oils; moisturizers* and *lotions.* Men use *colognes* or *after-shave lotions.*

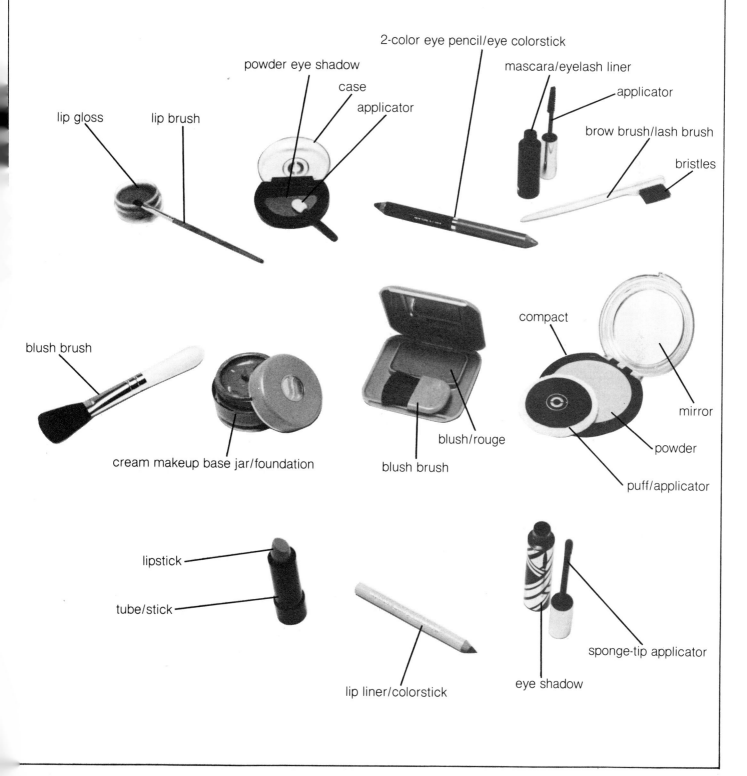

- lip gloss
- lip brush
- powder eye shadow
- case
- applicator
- 2-color eye pencil/eye colorstick
- mascara/eyelash liner
- applicator
- brow brush/lash brush
- bristles
- blush brush
- cream makeup base jar/foundation
- blush/rouge
- blush brush
- compact
- mirror
- powder
- puff/applicator
- lipstick
- tube/stick
- lip liner/colorstick
- sponge-tip applicator
- eye shadow

Cosmetics

Gemstone

The shades of color a gemstone gives off are called *fire*. A matched set of jewelry, or *parure,* often includes a necklace, earrings and a *brooch.* A *cameo* is a gem on which a relief carving has been made. Non-precious *costume jewelry* is made to simulate its precious counterparts. The end of a *cuff link* that is passed through the buttonhole and fastened is called a *wing-back,* or *airplane-back.*

table

star facet

bezel facet

upper-girdle facet

crown

girdle

lower-girdle facet

pavilion facet

pavilion

culet

Cut Gemstone

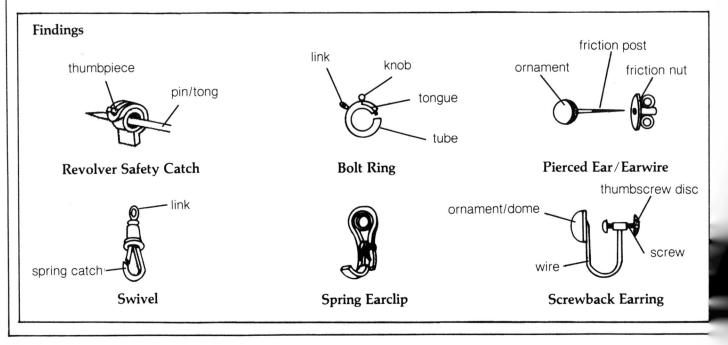

Findings

thumbpiece

pin/tong

Revolver Safety Catch

link

knob

tongue

tube

Bolt Ring

friction post

ornament

friction nut

Pierced Ear/Earwire

link

spring catch

Swivel

Spring Earclip

thumbscrew disc

ornament/dome

screw

wire

Screwback Earring

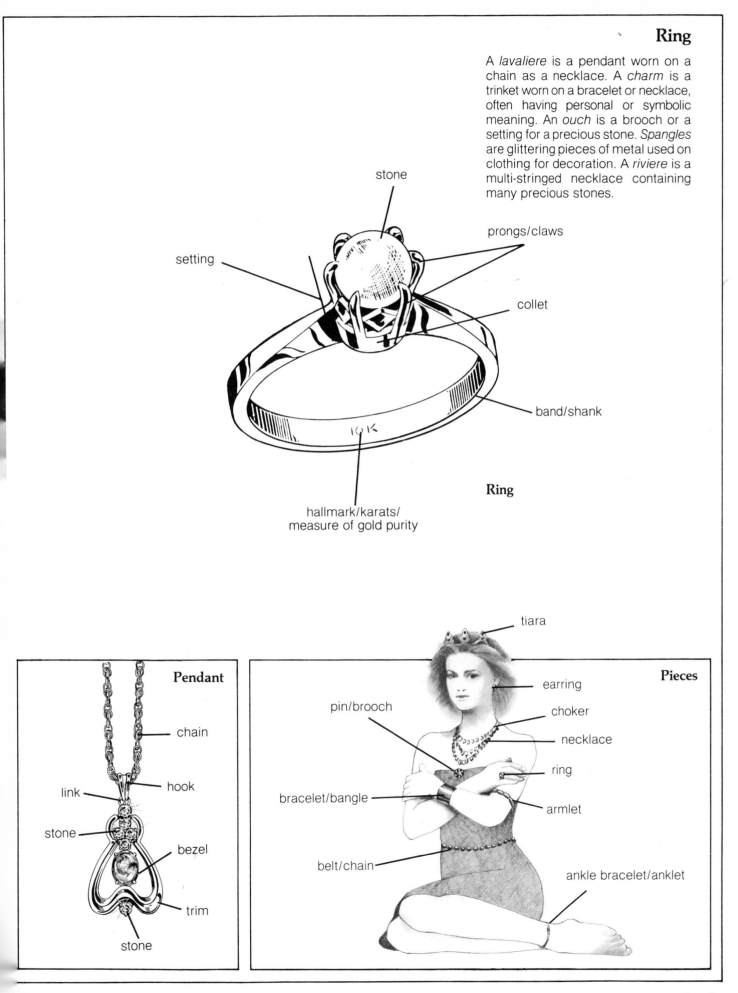

Ring

A *lavaliere* is a pendant worn on a chain as a necklace. A *charm* is a trinket worn on a bracelet or necklace, often having personal or symbolic meaning. An *ouch* is a brooch or a setting for a precious stone. *Spangles* are glittering pieces of metal used on clothing for decoration. A *riviere* is a multi-stringed necklace containing many precious stones.

stone

prongs/claws

setting

collet

band/shank

Ring

hallmark/karats/
measure of gold purity

Pendant

chain

hook

link

stone

bezel

trim

stone

Pieces

tiara

earring

pin/brooch

choker

necklace

ring

bracelet/bangle

armlet

belt/chain

ankle bracelet/anklet

Watches

The digital display on this watch can indicate date, seconds, time in a different time zone, and it can perform *stopwatch* functions. An extremely accurate timepiece is called a *chronometer*. A watchband, or *strap*, is attached to the case by *push-pins*, or *spring-bars*.

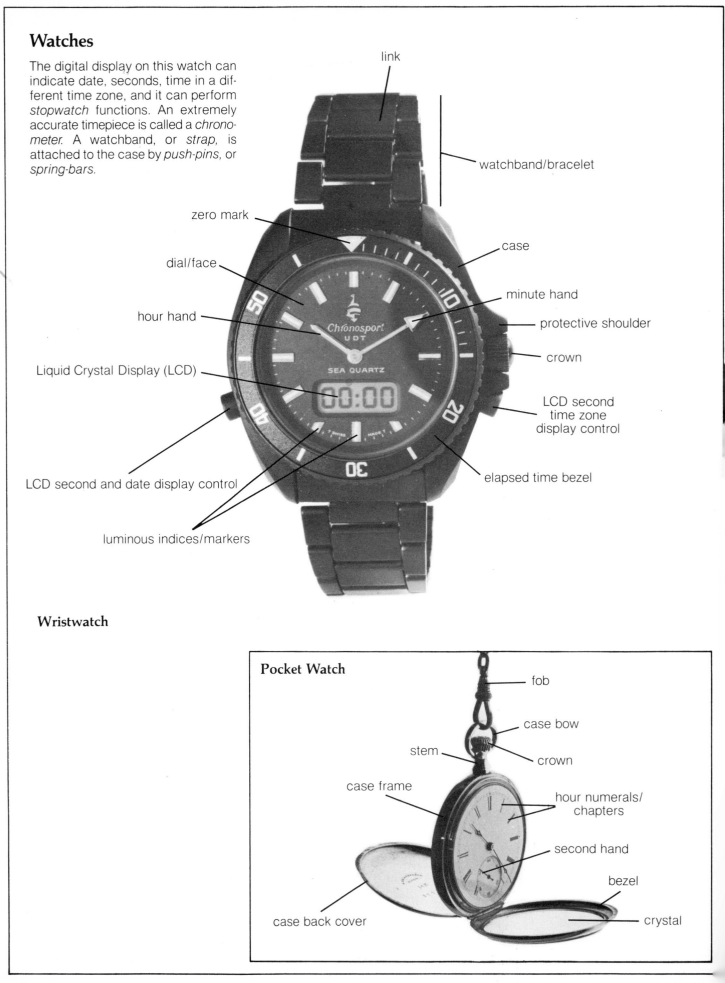

link

watchband/bracelet

zero mark

case

dial/face

minute hand

hour hand

protective shoulder

crown

Liquid Crystal Display (LCD)

LCD second time zone display control

LCD second and date display control

elapsed time bezel

luminous indices/markers

Wristwatch

Pocket Watch

fob

case bow

stem

crown

case frame

hour numerals/chapters

second hand

bezel

case back cover

crystal

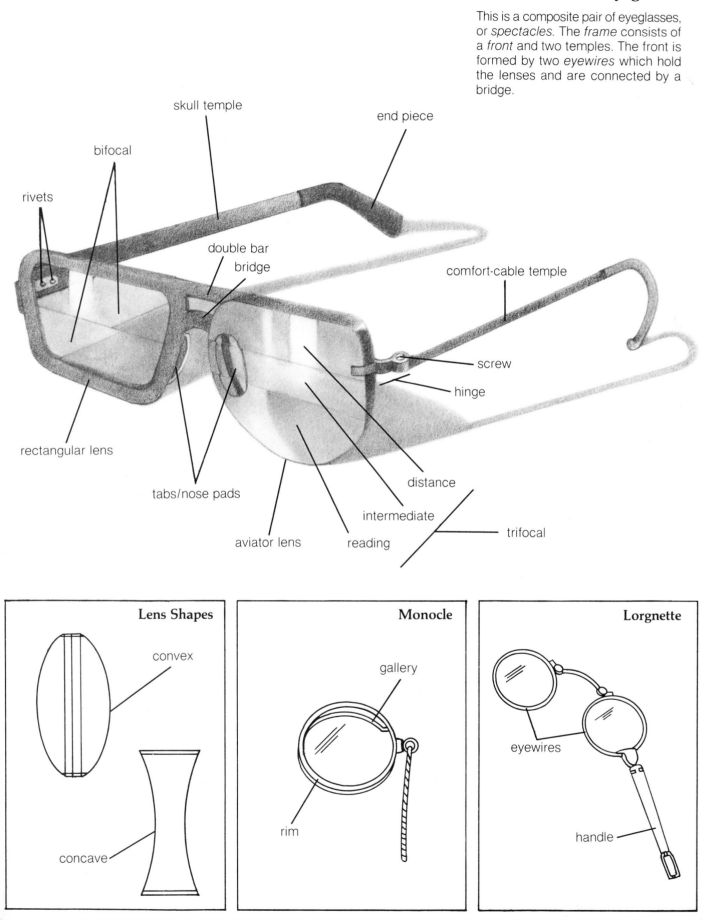

Eyeglasses

This is a composite pair of eyeglasses, or *spectacles*. The *frame* consists of a *front* and two temples. The front is formed by two *eyewires* which hold the lenses and are connected by a bridge.

skull temple

end piece

bifocal

rivets

double bar

bridge

comfort-cable temple

screw

hinge

rectangular lens

tabs/nose pads

distance

aviator lens

reading

intermediate

trifocal

Lens Shapes

convex

concave

Monocle

gallery

rim

Lorgnette

eyewires

handle

Handbag

A handbag can also be referred to as a *pocketbook* or *purse*. A bag with no handles is a *clutch*. *East-west* describes a handbag which is wider than it is long. A *north-south* bag has a long, narrow shape. The metal ornaments and closures on bags are collectively called *hardware* or *fittings*.

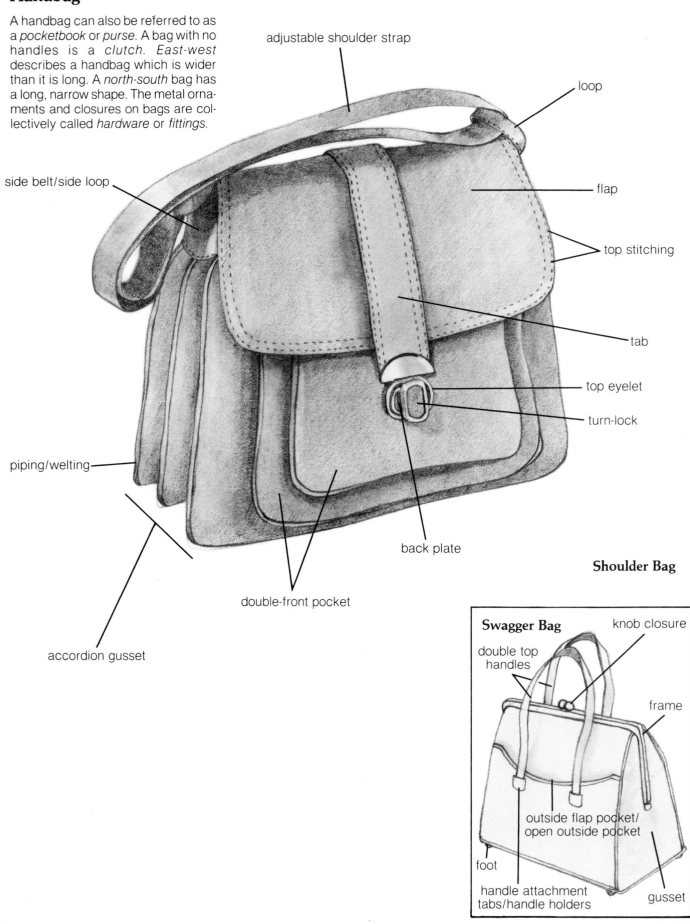

adjustable shoulder strap

loop

flap

top stitching

side belt/side loop

tab

top eyelet

turn-lock

piping/welting

back plate

double-front pocket

accordion gusset

Shoulder Bag

Swagger Bag

knob closure

double top handles

frame

outside flap pocket/ open outside pocket

foot

handle attachment tabs/handle holders

gusset

Wallet / Billfold

A wallet's exterior covering is called the *cover*. Women's wallets often have a *coin purse* within and a *tab closing* on the outside. *Photo holders* that unfold and become a long strip are called *accordion windows*.

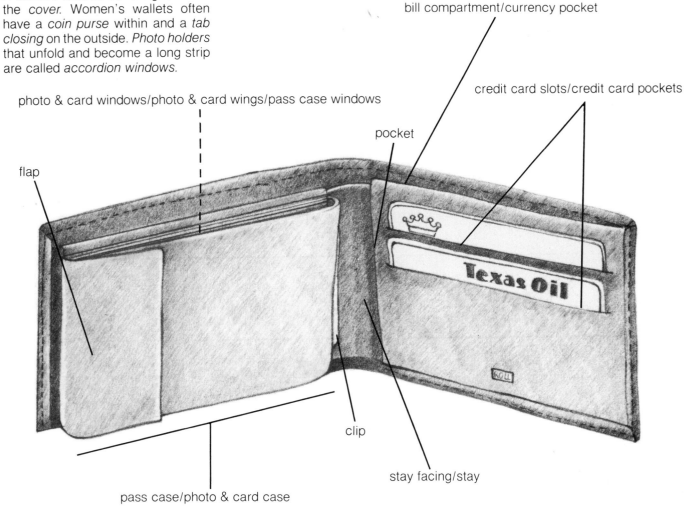

photo & card windows/photo & card wings/pass case windows

bill compartment/currency pocket

credit card slots/credit card pockets

pocket

flap

Texas Oil

flap

clip

stay facing/stay

pass case/photo & card case

Checkbook Clutch

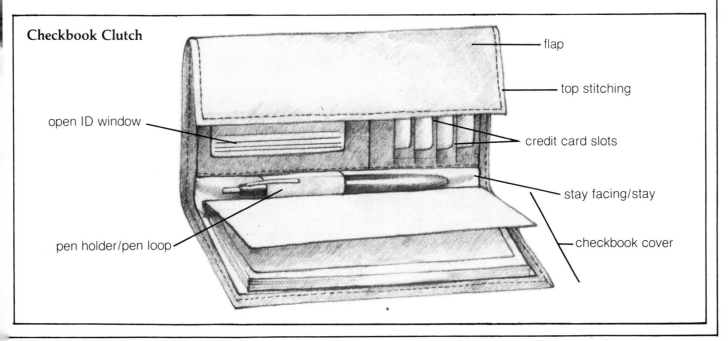

flap

top stitching

open ID window

credit card slots

stay facing/stay

pen holder/pen loop

checkbook cover

Money

There are three types of U.S. paper currency in circulation: green *Federal Reserve Notes,* or *"greenbacks,"* red *United States notes,* and blue *Silver Certificates. Bills* are printed from *engraved plates* on paper containing colored *fibers.* Notes damaged during printing are replaced with *star notes.* Money printed illegally and passed off as *legal tender* is called *counterfeit money.*

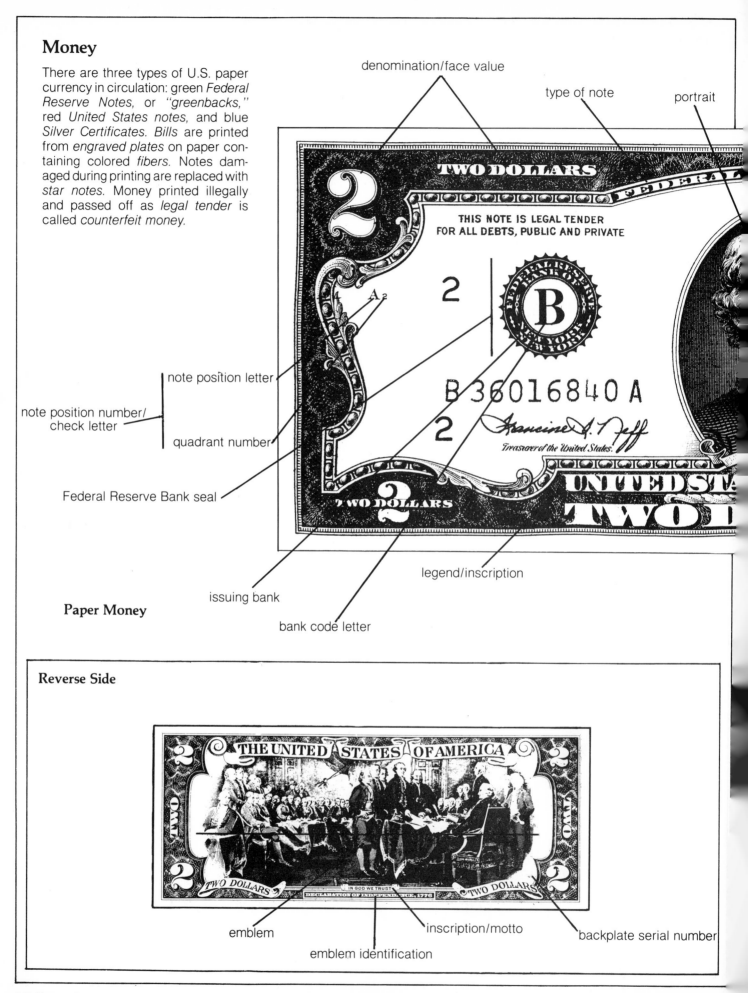

denomination/face value

type of note

portrait

note position letter

note position number/check letter

quadrant number

Federal Reserve Bank seal

issuing bank

bank code letter

legend/inscription

Paper Money

Reverse Side

emblem

emblem identification

inscription/motto

backplate serial number

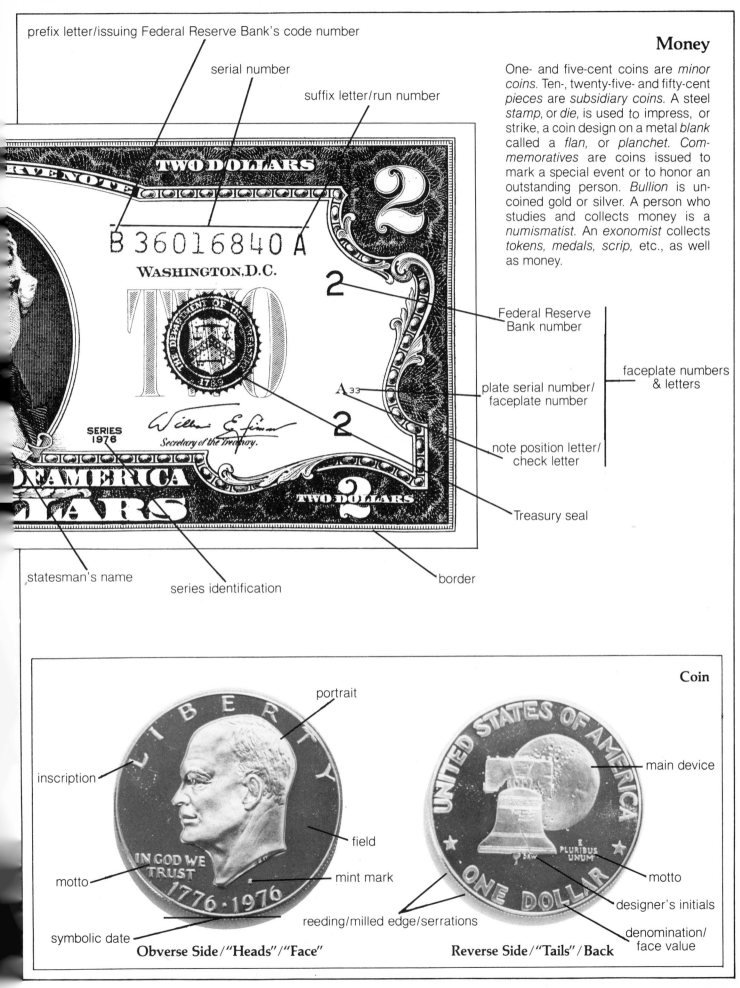

prefix letter/issuing Federal Reserve Bank's code number

serial number

suffix letter/run number

Money

One- and five-cent coins are *minor coins*. Ten-, twenty-five- and fifty-cent *pieces* are *subsidiary coins*. A steel *stamp*, or *die*, is used to impress, or strike, a coin design on a metal *blank* called a *flan*, or *planchet*. *Commemoratives* are coins issued to mark a special event or to honor an outstanding person. *Bullion* is uncoined gold or silver. A person who studies and collects money is a *numismatist*. An *exonomist* collects *tokens*, *medals*, *scrip*, etc., as well as money.

TWO DOLLARS

2

B 36016840 A

WASHINGTON, D.C.

TWO

Federal Reserve Bank number

A 33

plate serial number/ faceplate number

faceplate numbers & letters

note position letter/ check letter

SERIES 1976

Secretary of the Treasury.

OF AMERICA

LARS

TWO DOLLARS **2**

Treasury seal

statesman's name

series identification

border

Coin

portrait

inscription

main device

field

motto

mint mark

motto

designer's initials

reeding/milled edge/serrations

denomination/ face value

symbolic date

Obverse Side/"Heads"/"Face"

Reverse Side/"Tails"/Back

Check and Credit Card

A check must be signed by the payee, or *endorsed,* on the back to be valid. The back of a credit card contains a *signature panel* and a *magnetic strip* which contains account number, expiration date, name, address, personal identification number and *service code.* Some credit cards have a *card security number* hidden within the plastic to help prevent fraud.

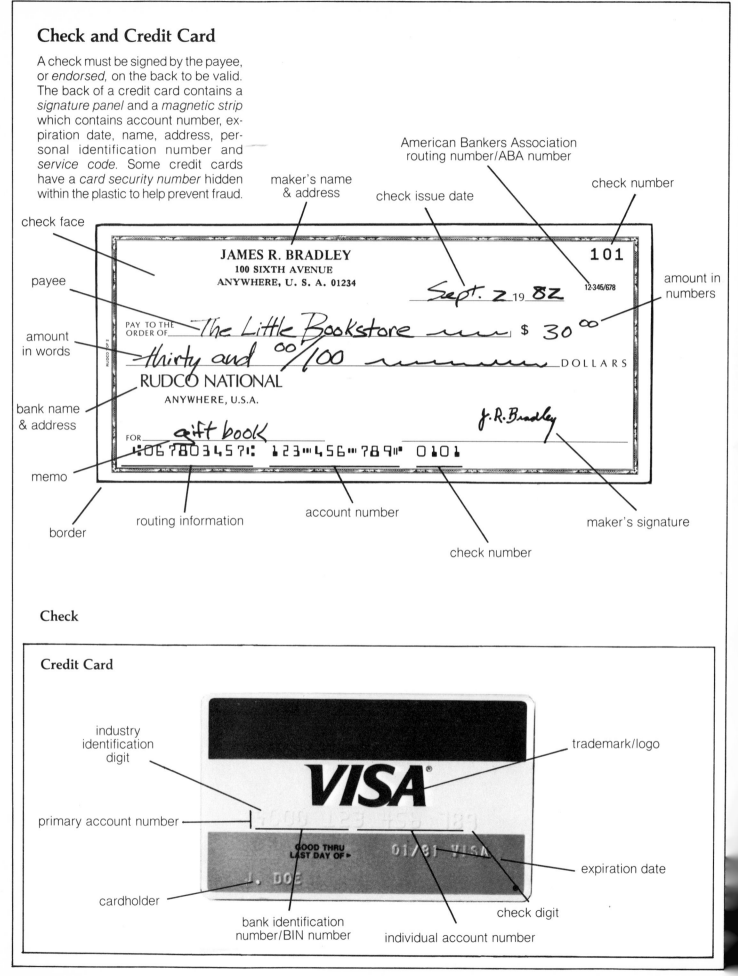

maker's name & address

American Bankers Association routing number/ABA number

check issue date

check number

check face

payee

amount in words

bank name & address

memo

border

routing information

account number

check number

maker's signature

amount in numbers

JAMES R. BRADLEY
100 SIXTH AVENUE
ANYWHERE, U. S. A. 01234

Sept. 2 19 82

PAY TO THE ORDER OF The Little Bookstore $ 30 00

thirty and 00/100 DOLLARS

RUDCO NATIONAL
ANYWHERE, U.S.A.

FOR gift book

J. R. Bradley

⑈06780345⑆: 123'''456'''789''' 0101

12-345/678

101

Check

Credit Card

industry identification digit

primary account number

cardholder

bank identification number/BIN number

individual account number

check digit

trademark/logo

expiration date

VISA

GOOD THRU
LAST DAY OF ▸

01/81 VISA

J. DOE

Money Order and Traveler's Check

A money order has a tear-off *customer's receipt* and *department voucher.* On the reverse side of the money order is an *endorsement block,* a *validation statement* and a *warning* to the cashing agency. Telegraph company money orders permit an individual to authorize payment to a specified individual at a distant location without the recipient having the original document.

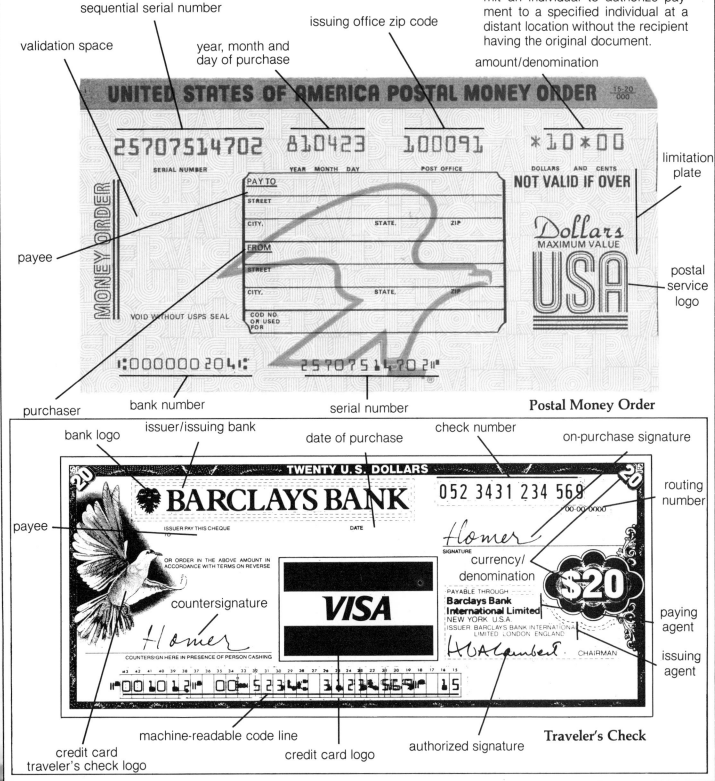

sequential serial number

validation space

year, month and day of purchase

issuing office zip code

amount/denomination

UNITED STATES OF AMERICA POSTAL MONEY ORDER 15-20/000

25707514702   810423   100091   *10*00

SERIAL NUMBER   YEAR MONTH DAY   POST OFFICE   DOLLARS AND CENTS

NOT VALID IF OVER

limitation plate

PAY TO
STREET
CITY,   STATE,   ZIP
FROM
STREET
CITY,   STATE,   ZIP
COD NO. OR USED FOR

MONEY ORDER

Dollars MAXIMUM VALUE
USA

postal service logo

payee

VOID WITHOUT USPS SEAL

1:000000204:   25707514702 11"

purchaser

bank number

serial number

Postal Money Order

bank logo   issuer/issuing bank   date of purchase   check number   on-purchase signature

TWENTY U.S. DOLLARS

BARCLAYS BANK   052 3431 234 569

ISSUER PAY THIS CHEQUE   DATE   00-00-0000

routing number

payee

OR ORDER IN THE ABOVE AMOUNT IN ACCORDANCE WITH TERMS ON REVERSE

Homer SIGNATURE

currency/ denomination   **$20**

VISA

countersignature

Homer
COUNTERSIGN HERE IN PRESENCE OF PERSON CASHING

PAYABLE THROUGH
Barclays Bank International Limited
NEW YORK U.S.A.
ISSUER BARCLAYS BANK INTERNATIONAL LIMITED LONDON ENGLAND

H.U.A.Lambert CHAIRMAN

paying agent

issuing agent

1"00 10 12"   00 5 2343   3 213 569"   15

machine-readable code line

credit card traveler's check logo

credit card logo

authorized signature

Traveler's Check

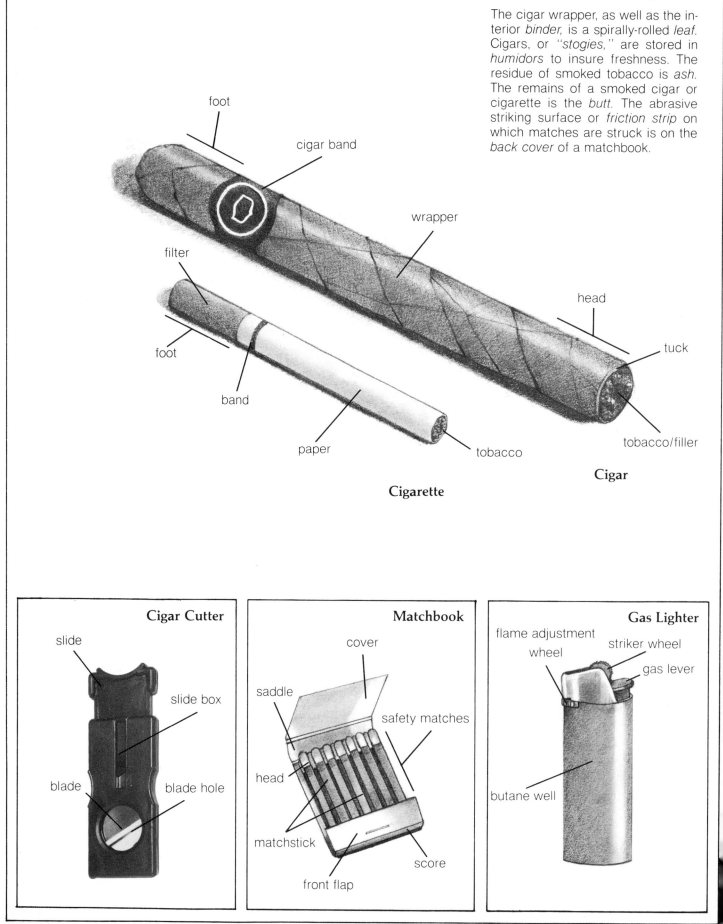

Cigar and Cigarette

The cigar wrapper, as well as the interior *binder,* is a spirally-rolled *leaf.* Cigars, or *"stogies,"* are stored in *humidors* to insure freshness. The residue of smoked tobacco is *ash.* The remains of a smoked cigar or cigarette is the *butt.* The abrasive striking surface or *friction strip* on which matches are struck is on the *back cover* of a matchbook.

foot

cigar band

wrapper

filter

head

foot

tuck

band

tobacco/filler

paper

tobacco

Cigar

Cigarette

Cigar Cutter

slide

slide box

blade

blade hole

Matchbook

cover

saddle

safety matches

head

matchstick

score

front flap

Gas Lighter

flame adjustment wheel

striker wheel

gas lever

butane well

Pipe

Pipe smoke is also called *lunt,* and unsmoked tobacco in the bottom of the bowl after smoking is called *dottle.* The pliable, tufted rod used to clean the inside of a pipe's stem is a *pipe cleaner.* Pipe tobacco is kept in a *pouch.* Some bowls are covered with a *pipe umbrella* or *bowl lid.* An Eastern pipe with a long, flexible tube by which the smoke is drawn through a jar of water and thus cooled is a *water pipe, hookah,* or *hubble-bubble.*

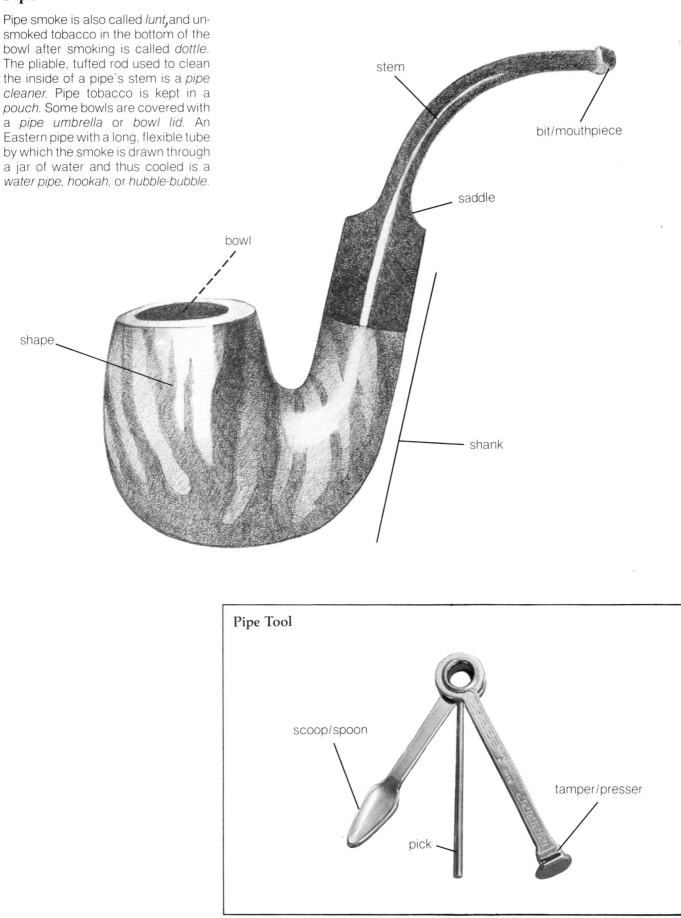

stem

bit/mouthpiece

saddle

bowl

shape

shank

Pipe Tool

scoop/spoon

pick

tamper/presser

Smoking Materials

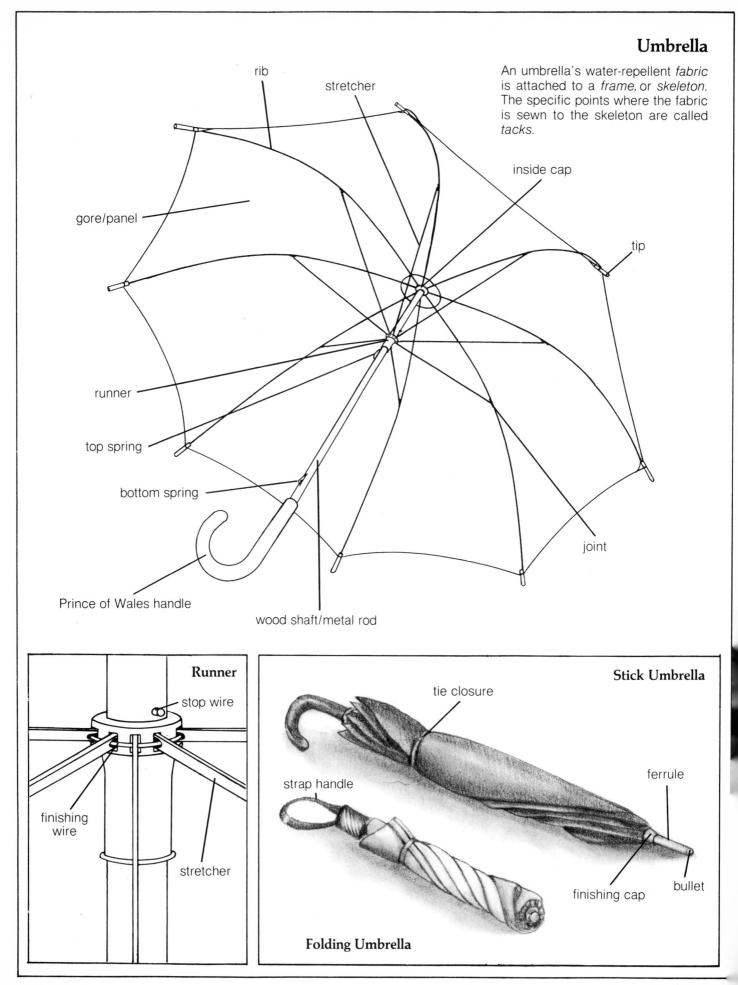

Umbrella

An umbrella's water-repellent *fabric* is attached to a *frame,* or *skeleton.* The specific points where the fabric is sewn to the skeleton are called *tacks.*

rib

stretcher

inside cap

gore/panel

tip

runner

top spring

bottom spring

joint

Prince of Wales handle

wood shaft/metal rod

Runner

stop wire

finishing wire

stretcher

Stick Umbrella

tie closure

strap handle

ferrule

finishing cap

bullet

Folding Umbrella

The Home

To facilitate locating items found in the home, the objects in this section have been grouped according to where they are most likely to be encountered: living room, dining room, kitchen, bedroom, bathroom, playroom, utility room or yard.

The kitchen subsection, for example, includes implements for preparing food as well as appliances that make food preparation easier. In addition to identifying the parts of containers used to bring groceries into the kitchen, coverage includes all the terms used in the designing and packaging of food and kitchenware. Knowing the names for these components will surely change how the reader views his or her cereal box at the breakfast table in the future.

The terms for details of desk equipment, found in the playroom/utility room subsection, apply as well to office furnishings. The seven parts of a paper clip, for example, are valid wherever this unique little device is used.

Although a nursery is not included as a subsection, objects used for or by children—stroller, car seat, playpen, and swings—have been incorporated in the subcategory of yard equipment.

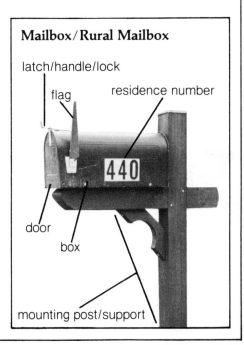

Mailbox/Rural Mailbox

latch/handle/lock

flag

residence number

440

door

box

mounting post/support

Fireplace

Many fireplaces have glass and metal *fire screens* to prevent heat loss and to keep sparks from flying into the room. Others have a low metal *fender* between the inner and outer hearth. A metal cover, used to shield a banked or dying fire, is called a *curfew*. Fireplace accessories include air-blowing *bellows, coal hods* and *wood carriers,* and *grates* or *heat exchangers* which can be used instead of andirons. A *firebrand* is a piece of burning wood.

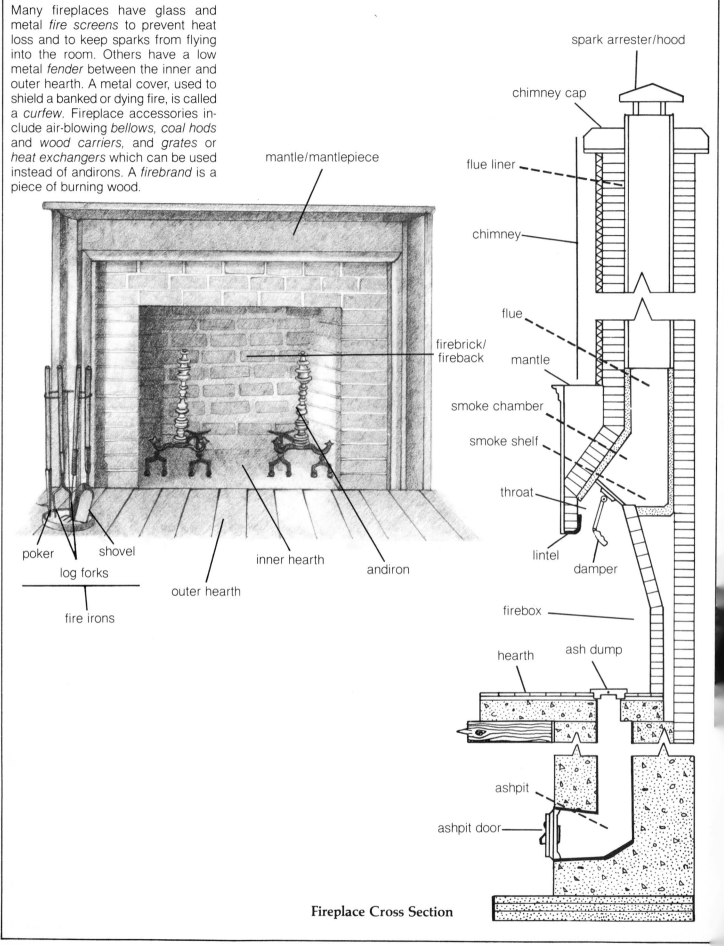

mantle/mantlepiece

firebrick/fireback

poker

shovel

log forks

inner hearth

andiron

fire irons

outer hearth

spark arrester/hood

chimney cap

flue liner

chimney

flue

mantle

smoke chamber

smoke shelf

throat

lintel

damper

firebox

hearth

ash dump

ashpit

ashpit door

Fireplace Cross Section

Clock

A *pendulum clock* tall enough to stand on the floor, either a grand-father or the shorter *grandmother clock,* is called a *tall-case clock.* The machinery or *movement* within is called the *clockworks.* A *rating,* the length of a pendulum swing, can be adjusted by a *rating nut,* usually found beneath the bob.

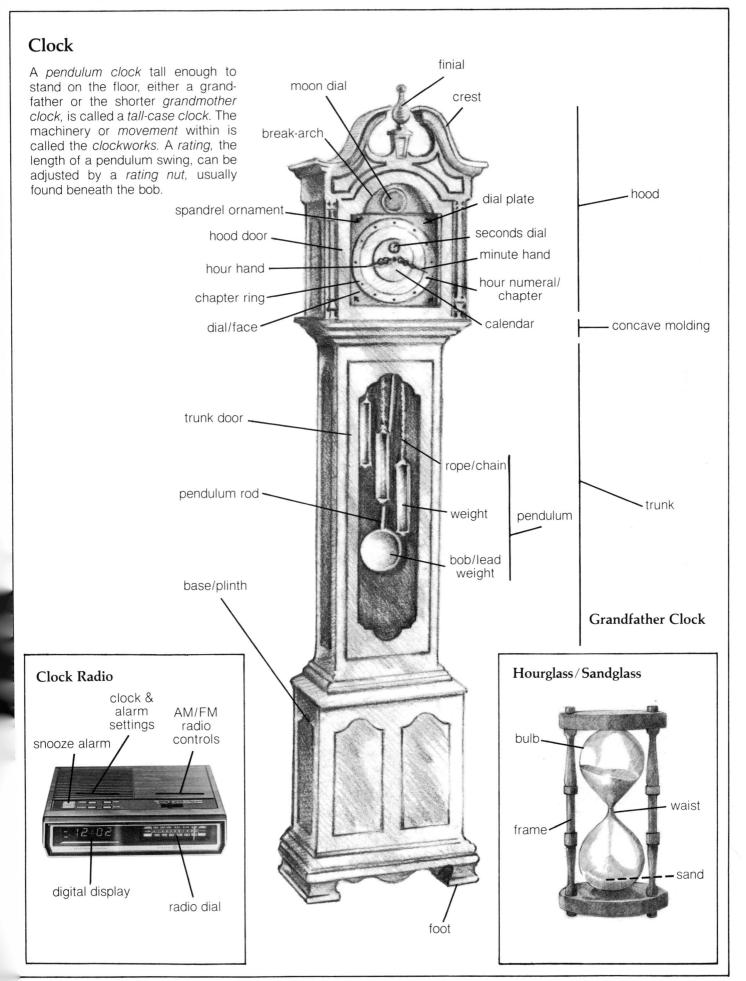

finial

moon dial

crest

break-arch

dial plate

hood

spandrel ornament

seconds dial

hood door

minute hand

hour hand

hour numeral/ chapter

chapter ring

dial/face

calendar

concave molding

trunk door

rope/chain

pendulum rod

weight

pendulum

trunk

base/plinth

bob/lead weight

Grandfather Clock

Clock Radio

clock & alarm settings

AM/FM radio controls

snooze alarm

digital display

radio dial

Hourglass/Sandglass

bulb

waist

frame

sand

foot

Chair

A single broad center upright used in place of spindles in a seat back is called a *splat*. Horizontal members across the seat back are called *slats*, or *crosspieces*. *Braces* are two spindles that form a "V" at the back of a chair seat. The crest of a chair may have a shape called a *handgrip, roll top* or *pillow*. A *slip seat* is a seat that is fitted into a molding and can be removed and covered with fabric, then replaced. An extended arm with a flat surface is called a *writing arm*.

headpiece/back rail

crest

ear

spindles

stile

seat back

arm/armrest

arm post/
arm stump/
arm support

spindle

seat

rear stretcher

rung/side stretcher

leg

rocker/curved slat

front stretcher

Rocking Chair / Rocker

Lounger

When the backrest of this *recliner,* or *Barcalounger,* is pushed back, the *footrest* rises to seat level. The term *ottoman,* or *pouf,* is often used to refer to an overstuffed *footstool.* An *arm pad* on an *easy chair* is also called a *manchette.*

padded backrest

button/tuft

welting

pleats

armrest

arm

seat cushion/pillow

side panel

foot

padded leg

reclining mechanism

hassock

Living Room

Sofa

A sofa is an upholstered *couch* with a back and two arms or raised ends. If it is composed of several independent sections that can be arranged individually or in various combinations, it is a *sectional*. A *davenport* or *convertible* can be converted into a bed for nighttime use, whereas a *divan* is a large couch without back or arms that is often used as a bed. A sofa for two is a *loveseat,* or *courting seat.* Cylindrical pillows, or *bolsters,* and *fitted* or *tailored pillows* or *cushions* are often used on sofas.

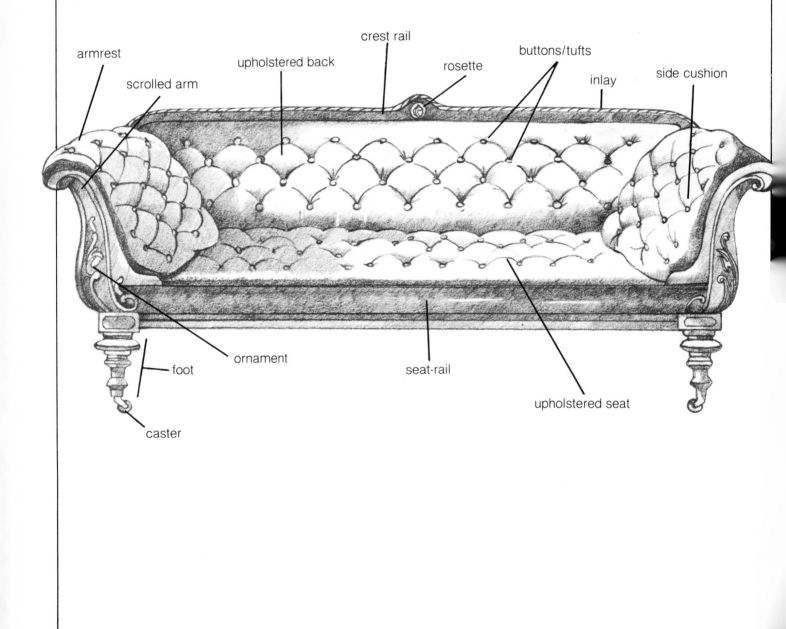

armrest

scrolled arm

upholstered back

crest rail

rosette

buttons/tufts

inlay

side cushion

ornament

foot

seat-rail

upholstered seat

caster

Candle and Candelabrum

Candles, or *tapers,* are made of *tallow, wax* or *paraffin.* Most are *dripless.* A collar placed at the top of a candle is a *burner.* The charred or partly consumed portion of a candlewick, or *snaste,* is the *snuff,* formerly referred to as the *snot.* The remains of a used candle is the *stub.* Many candlesticks have a pointed *pricket* on which a candle is impaled, rather than a socket. Small candles used for religious purposes are called *devotionals.*

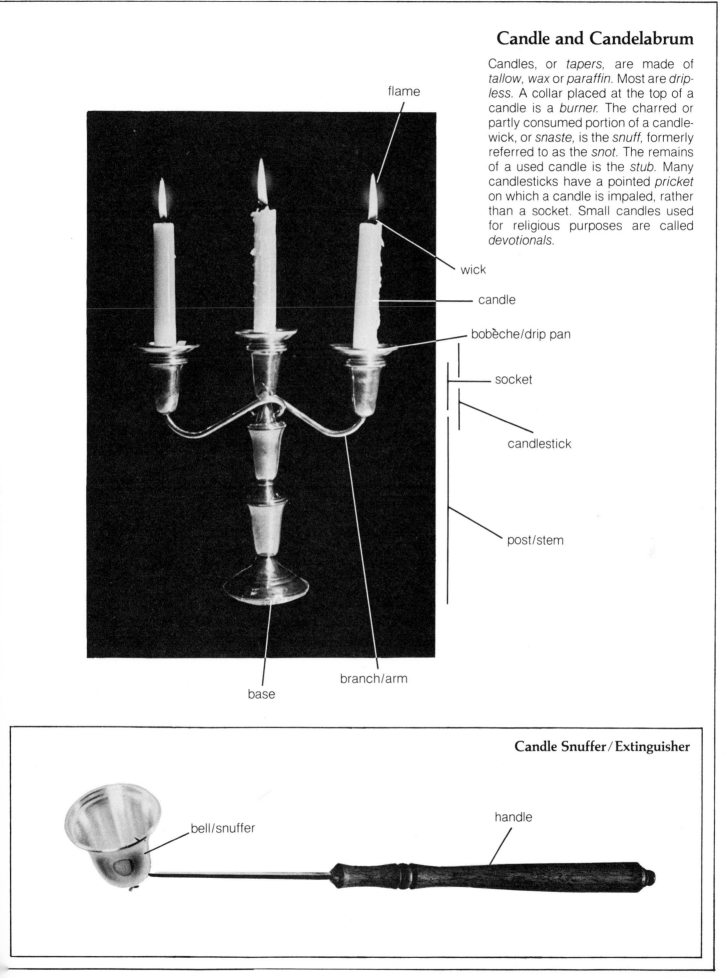

flame

wick

candle

bobèche/drip pan

socket

candlestick

post/stem

branch/arm

base

Candle Snuffer / Extinguisher

bell/snuffer

handle

Lamps and Lighting

Light output, measured in *lumens,* depends on the amount of electricity used by a bulb. *Long-life bulbs* have heavier filaments. *Three-way bulbs* have two filaments, used separately for two of the light levels and together for the third. Two general types of bulb glass are soft, or *lime glass,* and hard, or *heat-resistant glass.* Lamp shades come in *drum, empire* and *bell* shapes. Lighting fixtures suspended from the ceiling are called *chandeliers.* The ceiling cap that covers the *junction box* for hanging lighting fixtures is the *canopy.*

Lampshade

Table Lamp

Incandescent Bulb

Fluorescent Bulb

Lamps and Lighting

Adjustable lamps, such as the one seen here, have an *inner reflector* around the bulb to help ventilate the shade. *Gooseneck lamps* have flexible shafts which permit the shade to be turned in any direction. *High-intensity* lamps produce a strong beam of light that illuminates only a small area.

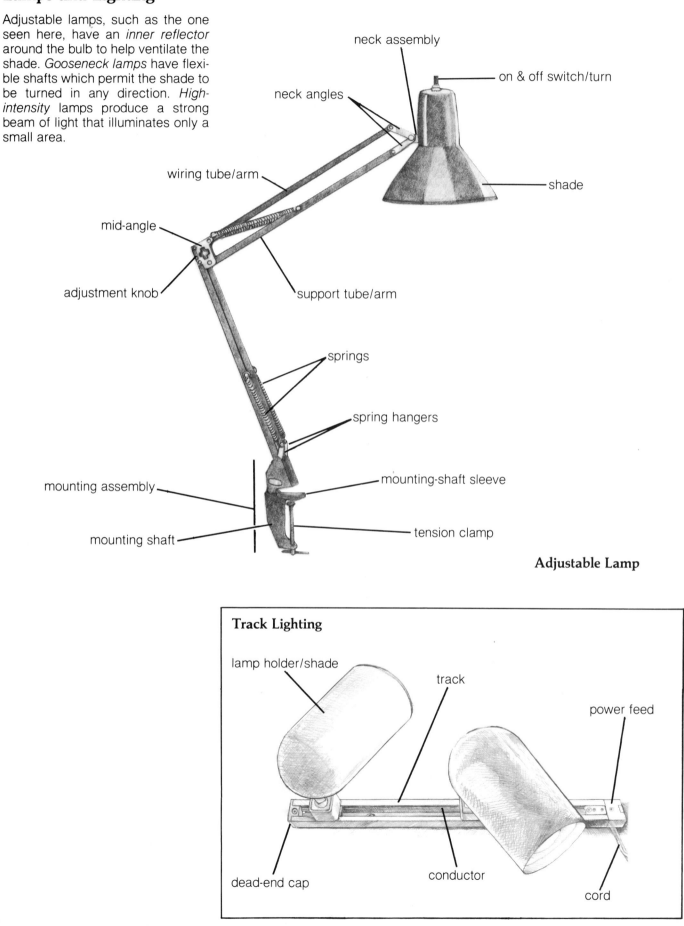

neck assembly

on & off switch/turn

neck angles

wiring tube/arm

shade

mid-angle

adjustment knob

support tube/arm

springs

spring hangers

mounting-shaft sleeve

mounting assembly

tension clamp

mounting shaft

Adjustable Lamp

Track Lighting

lamp holder/shade

track

power feed

dead-end cap

conductor

cord

Window Coverings

The gathering of material at the top of draperies, hidden by the valance in this illustration, is called the *heading*. A *curtain rod* is a simple metal or wooden rod on which curtains are hung and moved by hand, without aid of pulley mechanisms. A curtain *panel* is a vertical section of fabric. *Cafe curtains* are suspended from rings and cover only part of a window.

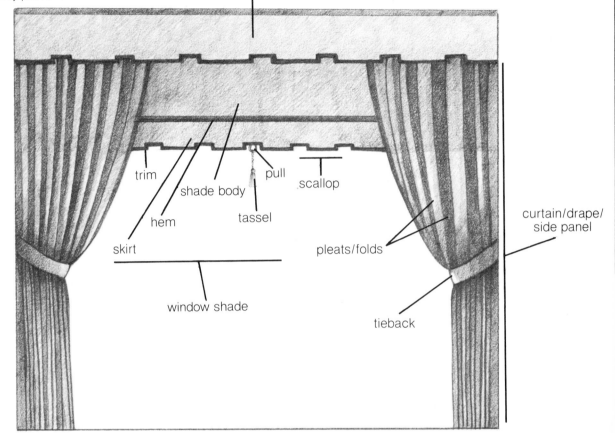

valance/cornice

trim

shade body

pull

scallop

hem

tassel

skirt

pleats/folds

curtain/drape/ side panel

window shade

tieback

Curtains/Draperies and Shade

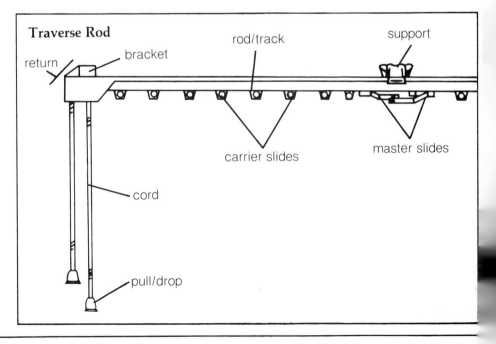

Traverse Rod

return

bracket

rod/track

support

carrier slides

master slides

cord

pull/drop

Window Coverings

Braided ladders are used in place of ladder tapes on some venetian blinds, and tubular *wands* are sometimes used instead of tilt cords. In *roll-up blinds*, slat tilt cannot be adjusted. A shutter consists of *panels*, each one of which contains louvers within a frame.

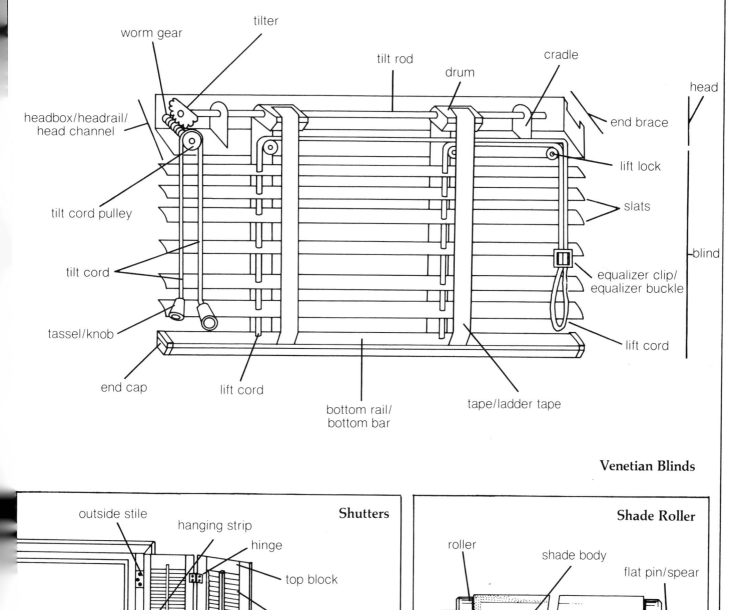

worm gear

tilter

tilt rod

drum

cradle

head

headbox/headrail/ head channel

end brace

lift lock

tilt cord pulley

slats

tilt cord

blind

equalizer clip/ equalizer buckle

tassel/knob

end cap

lift cord

lift cord

lift cord

bottom rail/ bottom bar

tape/ladder tape

Venetian Blinds

Shutters

outside stile

hanging strip

hinge

top block

louvers

tilt rod/control rod

bottom block

frame

Shade Roller

roller

shade body

flat pin/spear

slat

round pin/ gudgeon

hem/pocket

ring pull

Living Room

Table

A drop-leaf table is any table with a leaf that drops down to the side, such as a *gateleg* or a *butterfly table.* In a butterfly table, which has *splayed legs,* wooden wing-shaped *brackets* support the leaves. *Pedestal tables* rest on a single *base* rather than on legs. Some tables have an *apron,* wooden slats that run along the sides just beneath the top, to provide additional support. *Card tables,* or *bridge tables,* are lightweight, portable tables with folding *frames.*

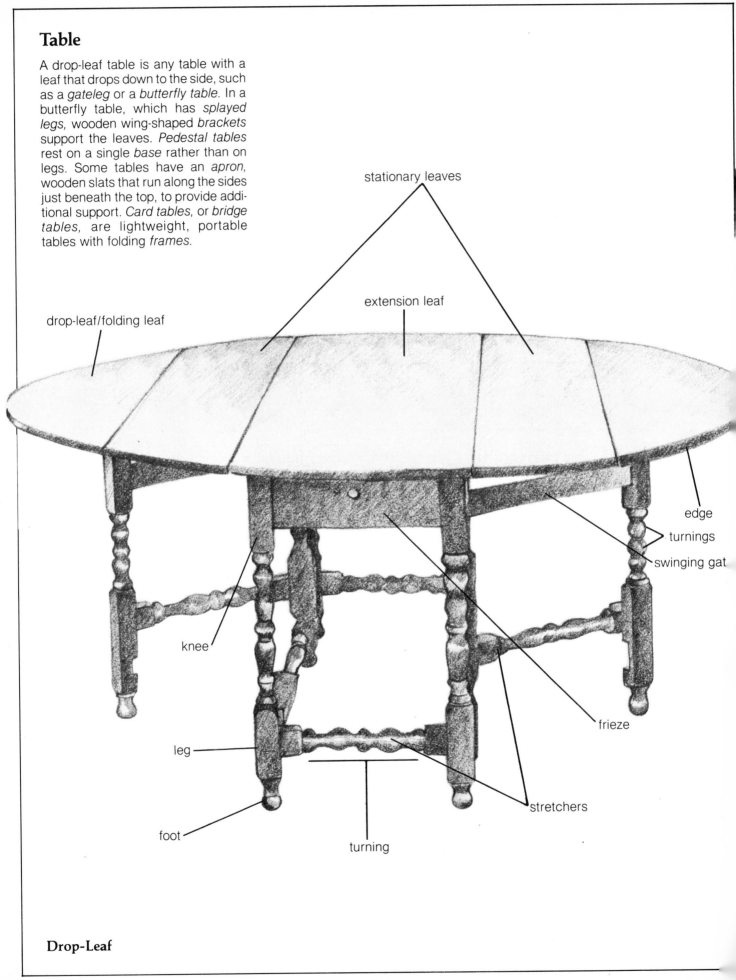

stationary leaves

extension leaf

drop-leaf/folding leaf

edge

turnings

swinging gat

knee

frieze

leg

stretchers

foot

turning

Drop-Leaf

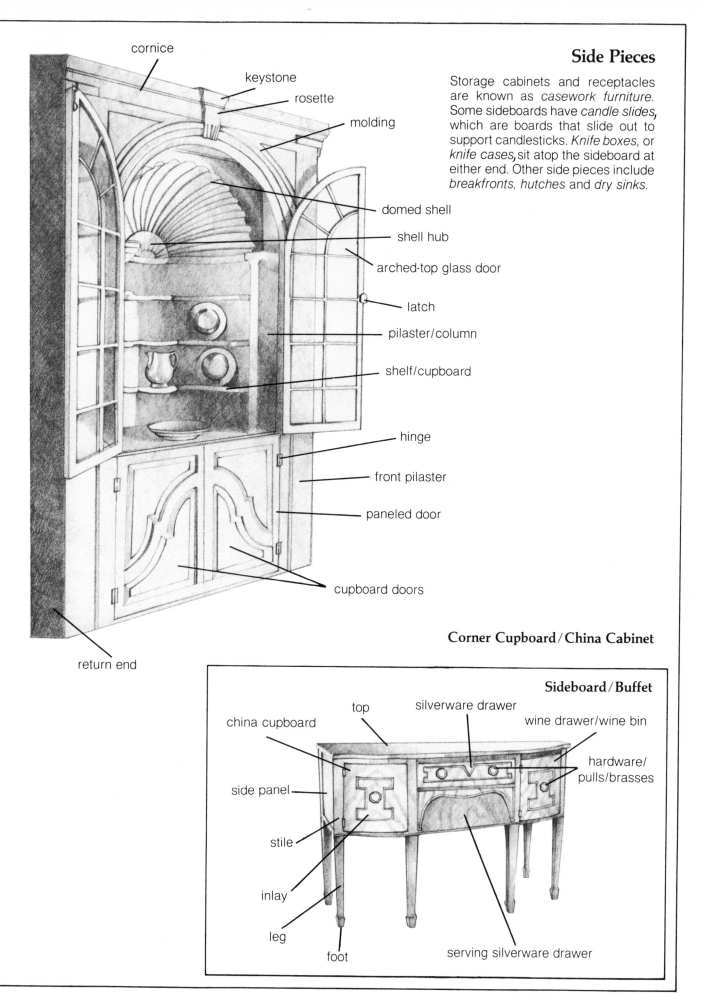

cornice

keystone

rosette

molding

Side Pieces

Storage cabinets and receptacles are known as *casework furniture.* Some sideboards have *candle slides,* which are boards that slide out to support candlesticks. *Knife boxes,* or *knife cases,* sit atop the sideboard at either end. Other side pieces include *breakfronts, hutches* and *dry sinks.*

domed shell

shell hub

arched-top glass door

latch

pilaster/column

shelf/cupboard

hinge

front pilaster

paneled door

cupboard doors

return end

Corner Cupboard/China Cabinet

Sideboard/Buffet

china cupboard

top

silverware drawer

wine drawer/wine bin

side panel

hardware/
pulls/brasses

stile

inlay

leg

foot

serving silverware drawer

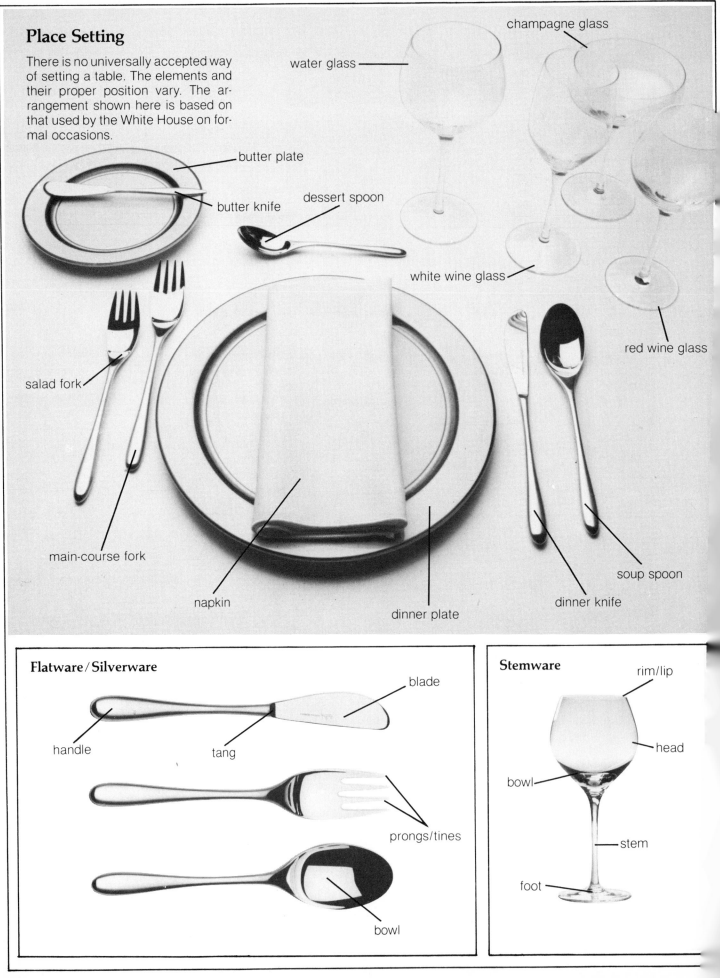

Place Setting

There is no universally accepted way of setting a table. The elements and their proper position vary. The arrangement shown here is based on that used by the White House on formal occasions.

water glass

champagne glass

butter plate

butter knife

dessert spoon

white wine glass

red wine glass

salad fork

main-course fork

napkin

dinner plate

dinner knife

soup spoon

Flatware/Silverware

blade

handle

tang

prongs/tines

bowl

Stemware

rim/lip

head

bowl

stem

foot

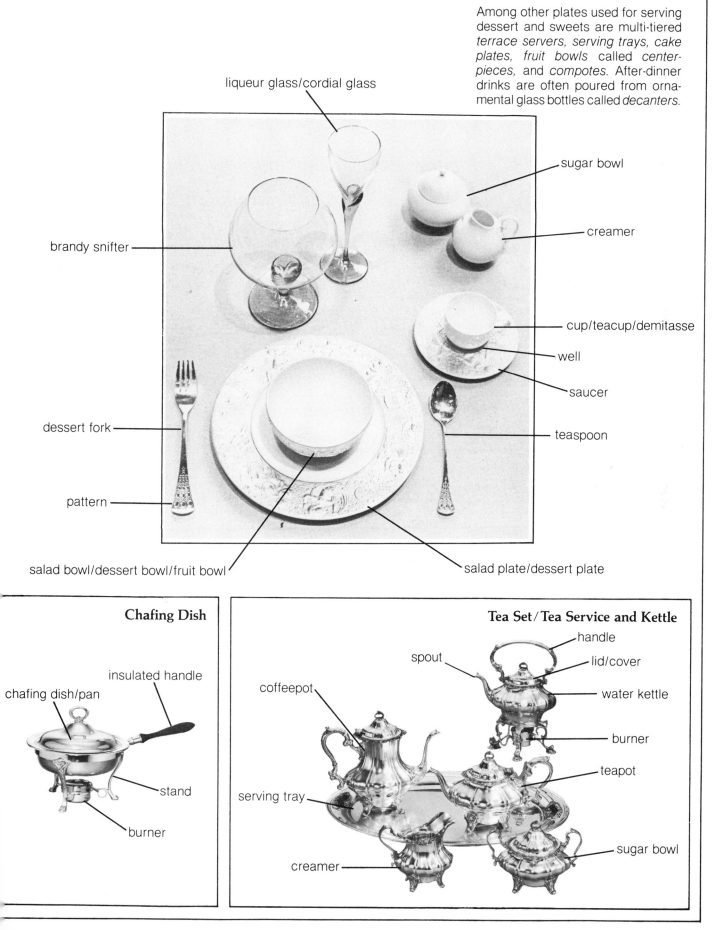

Dessert Setting

Among other plates used for serving dessert and sweets are multi-tiered *terrace servers*, *serving trays*, *cake plates*, *fruit bowls* called *centerpieces*, and *compotes*. After-dinner drinks are often poured from ornamental glass bottles called *decanters*.

liqueur glass/cordial glass

sugar bowl

brandy snifter

creamer

cup/teacup/demitasse

well

saucer

dessert fork

teaspoon

pattern

salad bowl/dessert bowl/fruit bowl

salad plate/dessert plate

Chafing Dish

insulated handle

chafing dish/pan

stand

burner

Tea Set / Tea Service and Kettle

handle

spout

lid/cover

coffeepot

water kettle

burner

teapot

serving tray

sugar bowl

creamer

Dining Room

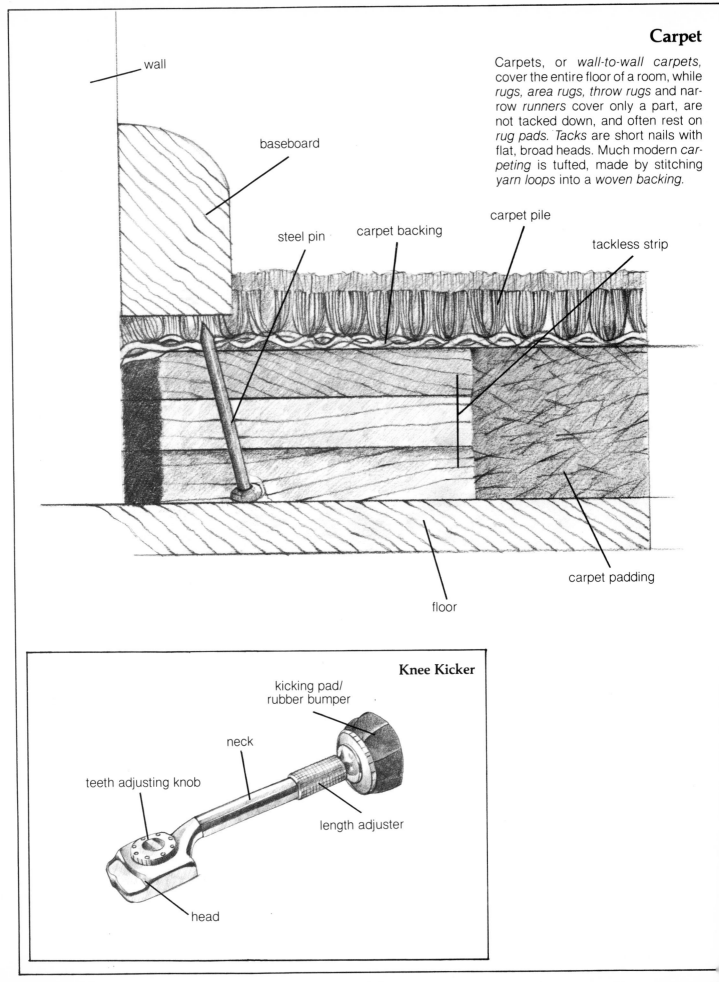

Carpet

wall

baseboard

steel pin

carpet backing

carpet pile

tackless strip

Carpets, or *wall-to-wall carpets*, cover the entire floor of a room, while *rugs, area rugs, throw rugs* and narrow *runners* cover only a part, are not tacked down, and often rest on *rug pads. Tacks* are short nails with flat, broad heads. Much modern *carpeting* is tufted, made by stitching *yarn loops* into a *woven backing*.

carpet padding

floor

Knee Kicker

kicking pad/ rubber bumper

neck

teeth adjusting knob

length adjuster

head

Sink and Compactor

The hardware in a sink, the faucet handles and spout, are known as *fixtures*. Sink drains usually have perforated *drain baskets* which trap debris but allow water to pass through. Many baskets are two-piece units that form a watertight seal when the *inner basket* is twisted. *Instant hot-water devices* mounted on the spout of some sinks have a constantly heated coil that produces small amounts of hot water on demand.

faucet handle/
hot-water handle/
spigot

spray hose

escutcheon plate

soap dispenser

spout/mixer

faucet handle/
cold-water handle/
spigot

splashboard

aerator

lotion dispenser

counter/worktop

deck

rim

garbage-disposal
compartment

bowl/basin compartment

Kitchen Sink

Garbage Disposal/Trash Compactor

control panel

litter bin

lock

cabinet

trash drawer

trash basket

storage
compartment
cover

bag-holding button

latch rod &
slide hook

basket-release handle

leveling foot

Kitchen

Stove/Range

On an *electric range, heating elements* connected to *terminal blocks* are used in place of burner grates on a gas model. The permanent flame, used to ignite individual burners on a gas stove, is called a *pilot light.* Some models have an *electric pilot.* The walls of a *self-cleaning oven* are covered with a heat-sensitive porcelain enamel finish.

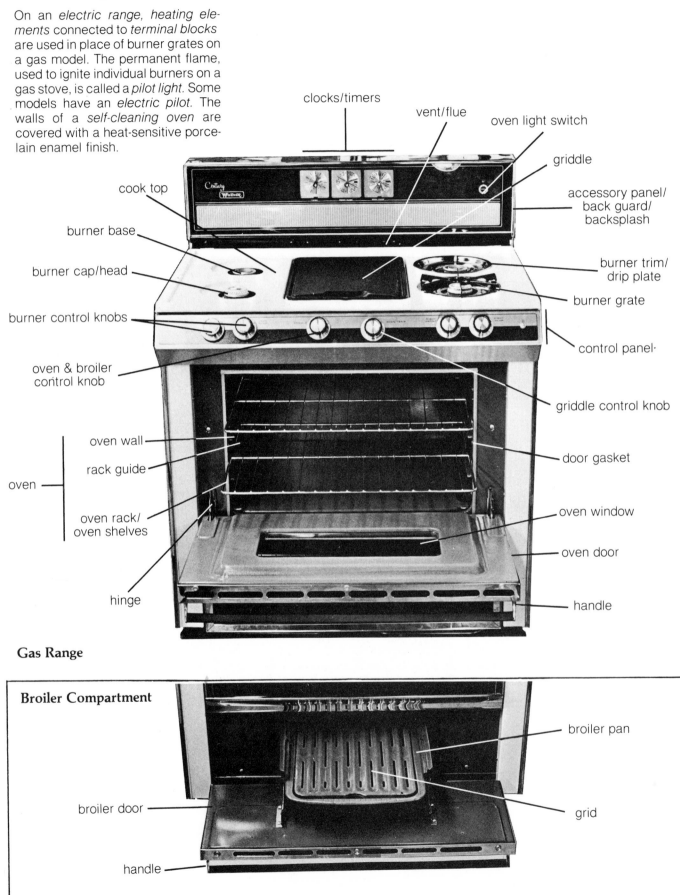

cook top

burner base

burner cap/head

burner control knobs

oven & broiler control knob

clocks/timers

vent/flue

oven light switch

griddle

accessory panel/ back guard/ backsplash

burner trim/ drip plate

burner grate

control panel

griddle control knob

oven wall

rack guide

oven

oven rack/ oven shelves

hinge

door gasket

oven window

oven door

handle

Gas Range

Broiler Compartment

broiler pan

broiler door

grid

handle

Refrigerator

Some refrigerators, or *iceboxes*, have an *ice dispenser* in the freezer section. Others have *ice trays*. A *frostfree*, or *no-frost*, model does not require defrosting.

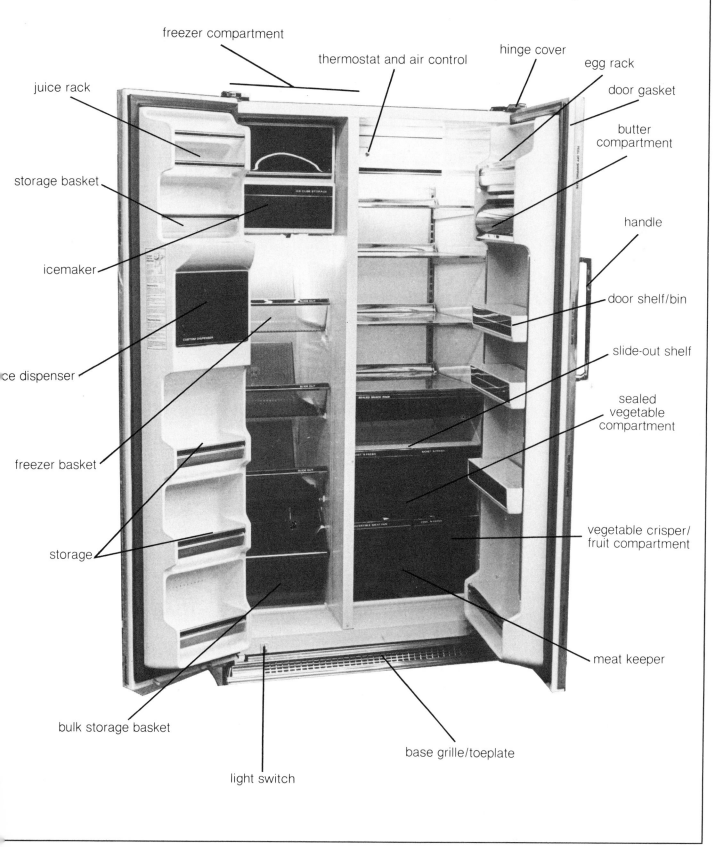

freezer compartment

thermostat and air control

hinge cover

egg rack

door gasket

juice rack

butter compartment

storage basket

handle

icemaker

door shelf/bin

ice dispenser

slide-out shelf

sealed vegetable compartment

freezer basket

storage

vegetable crisper/ fruit compartment

meat keeper

bulk storage basket

base grille/toeplate

light switch

Kitchen

Dishwasher

The *cycle-selector control panel* and *timer* are located on the outside of the door of this built-in dishwasher. The machine will operate only when the *external door switch*, or latch, is engaged.

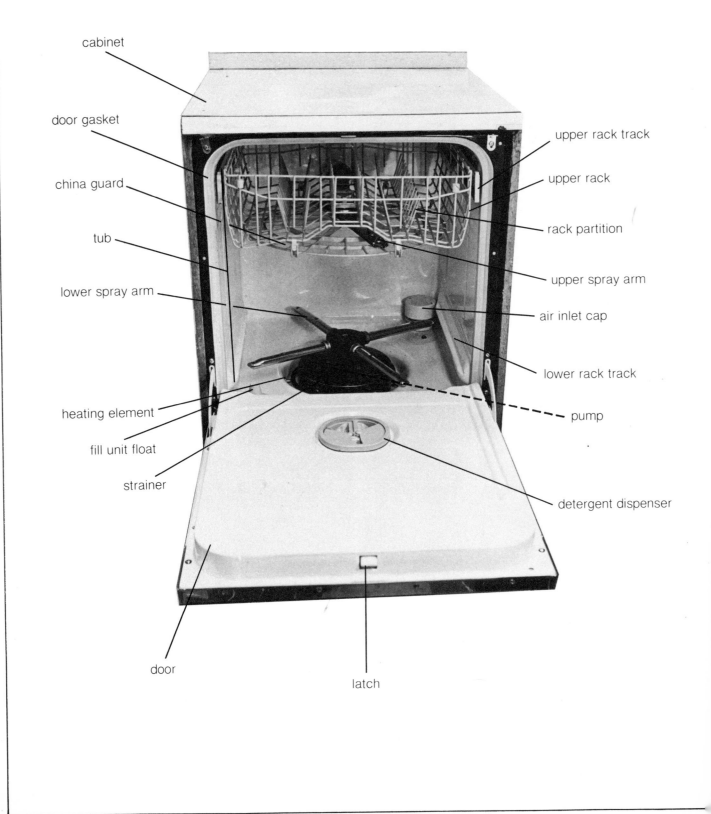

cabinet

door gasket

china guard

tub

lower spray arm

heating element

fill unit float

strainer

door

latch

upper rack track

upper rack

rack partition

upper spray arm

air inlet cap

lower rack track

pump

detergent dispenser

Openers

With manual openers, the can rim is held between a *cutting blade* and a *turning gear,* with pressure applied by squeezing two *handles* and the can rotated with a winged *key.* The blade and handle device used by military personnel to open food ration cans is called a *"John Wayne."* The corkscrew shown below is used by *sommeliers,* or *wine stewards.*

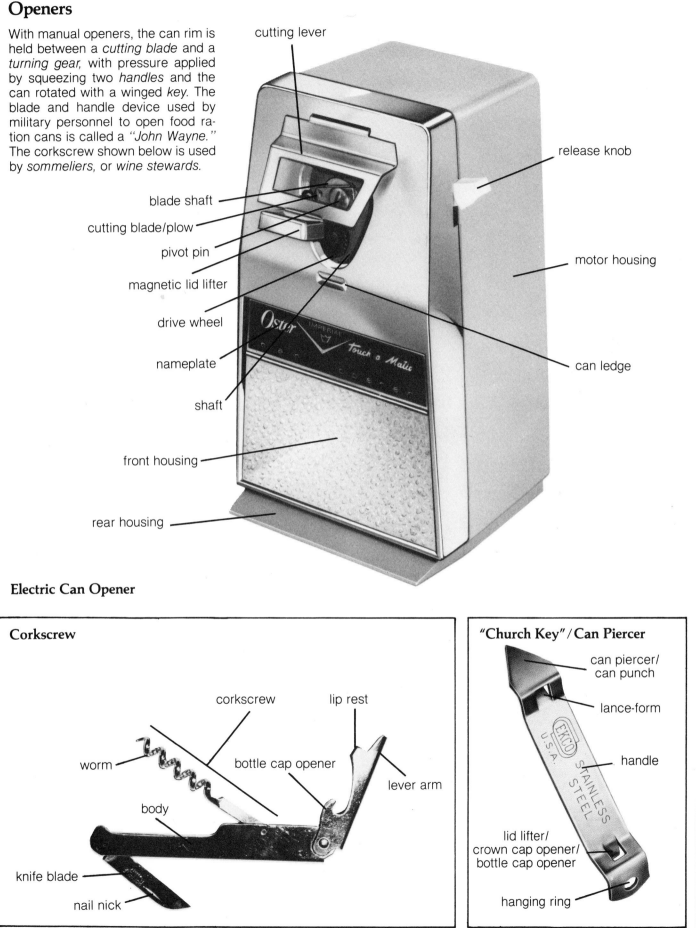

cutting lever

release knob

blade shaft

cutting blade/plow

pivot pin

magnetic lid lifter

drive wheel

nameplate

shaft

front housing

rear housing

motor housing

can ledge

Electric Can Opener

Corkscrew

corkscrew

lip rest

worm

bottle cap opener

lever arm

body

knife blade

nail nick

"Church Key" / Can Piercer

can piercer/ can punch

lance-form

handle

lid lifter/ crown cap opener/ bottle cap opener

hanging ring

Coffee Makers

Coffee is *brewed* by passing boiling water through *ground coffee* beans. *Espresso* is brewed by forcing steam through roasted beans. *Cappuccino* consists of espresso and steamed milk.

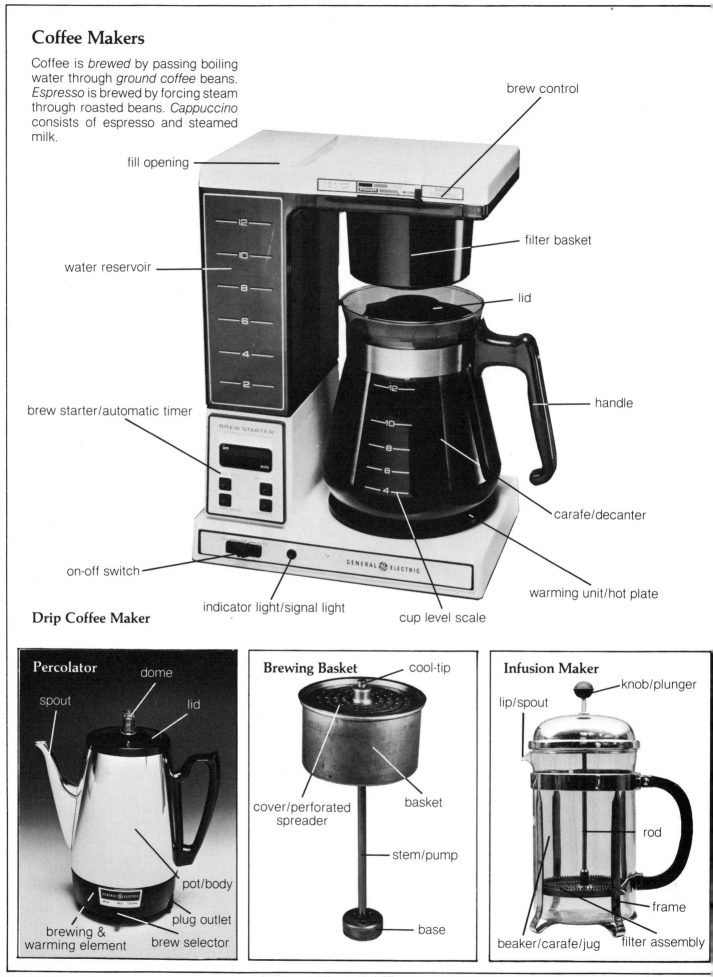

brew control

fill opening

filter basket

water reservoir

lid

handle

brew starter/automatic timer

carafe/decanter

on-off switch

indicator light/signal light

cup level scale

warming unit/hot plate

Drip Coffee Maker

Percolator

dome

spout

lid

pot/body

plug outlet

brewing & warming element

brew selector

Brewing Basket

cool-tip

cover/perforated spreader

basket

stem/pump

base

Infusion Maker

knob/plunger

lip/spout

rod

frame

beaker/carafe/jug

filter assembly

Toaster

Many toasters have removable *crumb trays*. The heating elements in toasters are flat *nichrome wires*. Toasters have either a spring-and-cylinder *dash-pot* or a simple spring device to pop toast up once it is browned. Toaster ovens have removable *baking trays*.

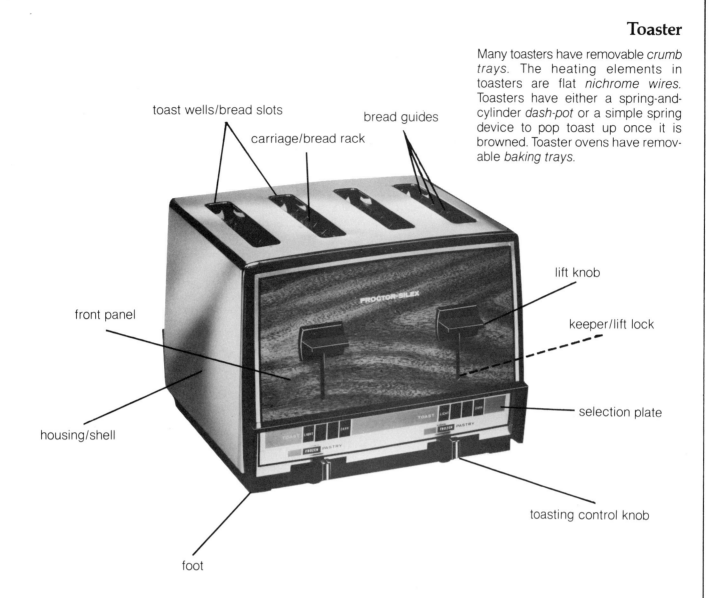

toast wells/bread slots

carriage/bread rack

bread guides

lift knob

front panel

keeper/lift lock

selection plate

housing/shell

toasting control knob

foot

Toaster

Toaster Oven

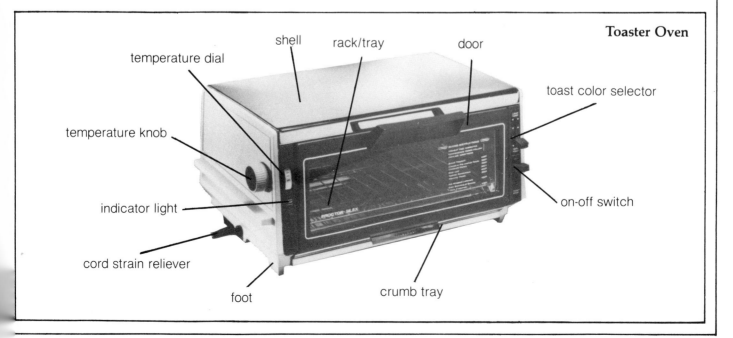

temperature dial

shell

rack/tray

door

toast color selector

temperature knob

indicator light

on-off switch

cord strain reliever

foot

crumb tray

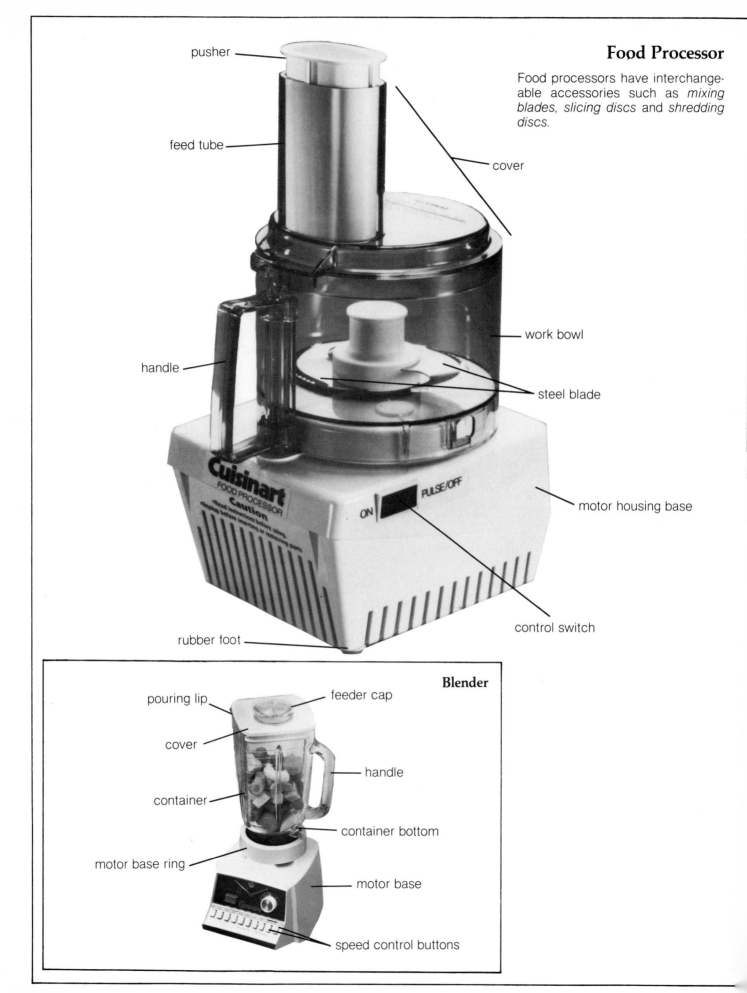

Food Processor

Food processors have interchangeable accessories such as *mixing blades, slicing discs* and *shredding discs.*

pusher

feed tube

cover

work bowl

handle

steel blade

motor housing base

control switch

rubber foot

Blender

pouring lip

feeder cap

cover

handle

container

container bottom

motor base ring

motor base

speed control buttons

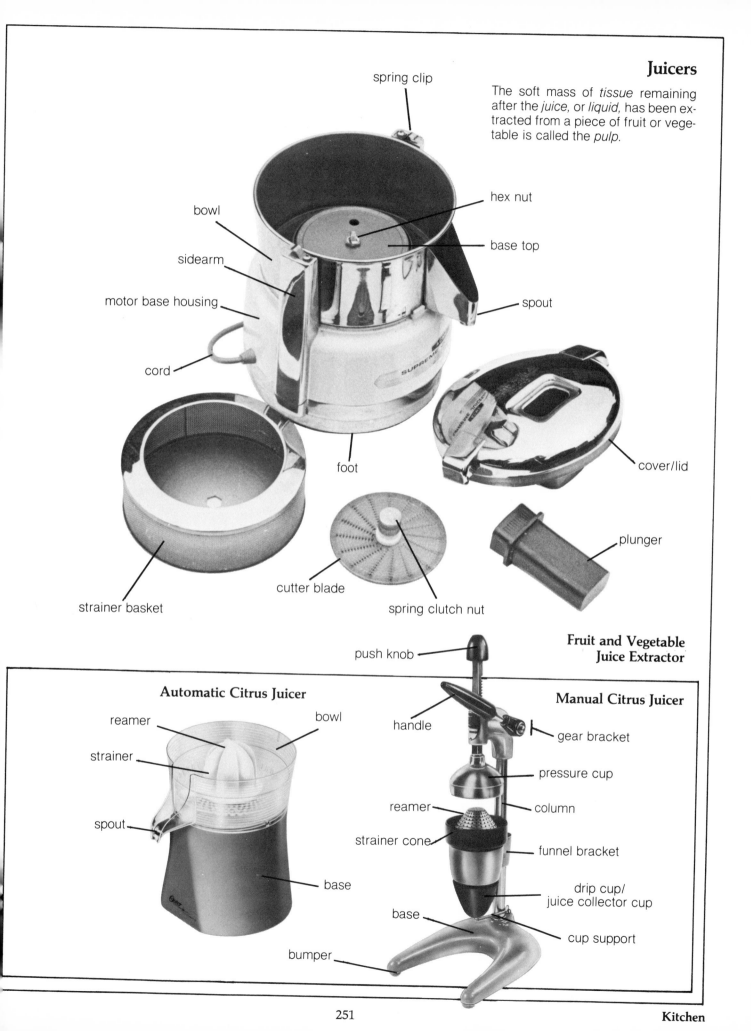

Juicers

The soft mass of *tissue* remaining after the *juice,* or *liquid,* has been extracted from a piece of fruit or vegetable is called the *pulp.*

spring clip

hex nut

bowl

base top

sidearm

motor base housing

spout

cord

cover/lid

foot

plunger

cutter blade

strainer basket

spring clutch nut

push knob

Fruit and Vegetable Juice Extractor

Automatic Citrus Juicer

Manual Citrus Juicer

reamer

bowl

handle

gear bracket

strainer

pressure cup

reamer

column

spout

strainer cone

funnel bracket

base

drip cup/
juice collector cup

base

cup support

bumper

Kitchen

Knife

The part of a knife blade that extends into the handle is called the *tang,* and the blade's formation is known as the *grind.* In a *flat grind,* the sides of the blade are smooth. In a *hollow grind* there is a marked curve or bevel along the length of the blade.

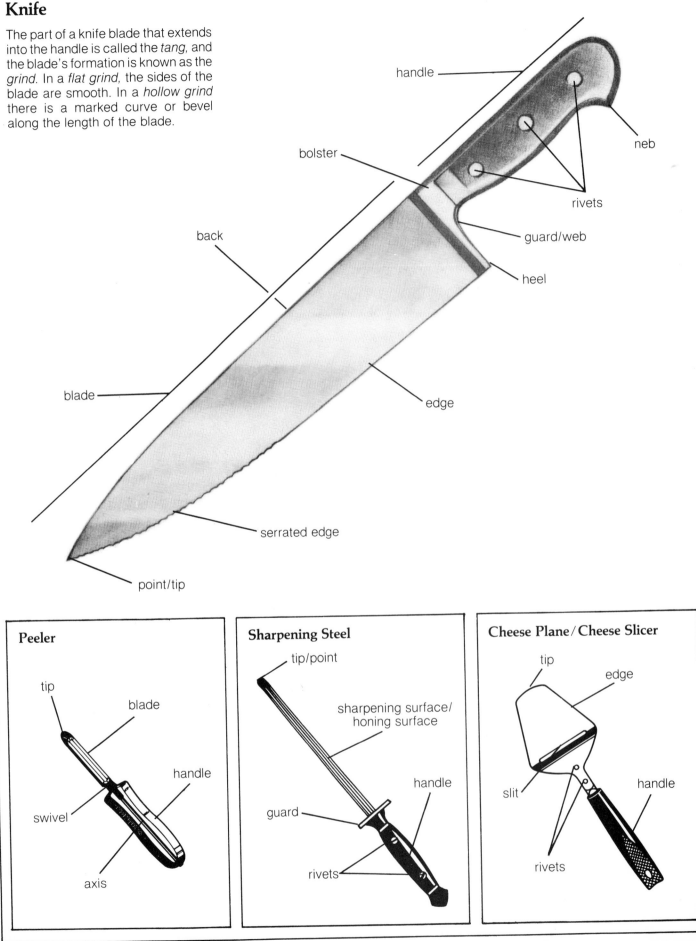

handle

neb

bolster

rivets

guard/web

back

heel

blade

edge

serrated edge

point/tip

Peeler

tip

blade

handle

swivel

axis

Sharpening Steel

tip/point

sharpening surface/honing surface

handle

guard

rivets

Cheese Plane / Cheese Slicer

tip

edge

slit

handle

rivets

Pots and Pans

Pots and pans are often described by their function—for example, a *boiler* or *steamer*. *Crockpots* are pots made of earthenware. *Casseroles* are earthenware, glass or cast-iron pots in which food can be both baked and served. A *pipkin* is a small saucepan with a long handle used to melt butter.

knob

cover/lid

handle

Stock Pot/Stew Pot

lift-out stem

perforated panel

rim

Steamer Basket

leg/foot

side

Saucepan

tang

bottom

hanging ring

handle

Skillet/Frying Pan

Electric Wok

knob

dome cover/lid

tempura rack

handle

bowl/wok

feet

heat-control dial

plug

cooking chopsticks

Pressure Cooker

pressure regulator

air vent/ cover lock

vent pipe

overpressure plug

body handle

cover handle

Kitchen

Mixing and Measuring Tools

In addition to the *meat,* or *rapid-response thermometer,* seen here, well-equipped kitchens have *oven* and *freezer thermometers, deep-frying thermometers, scales* and *funnels.*

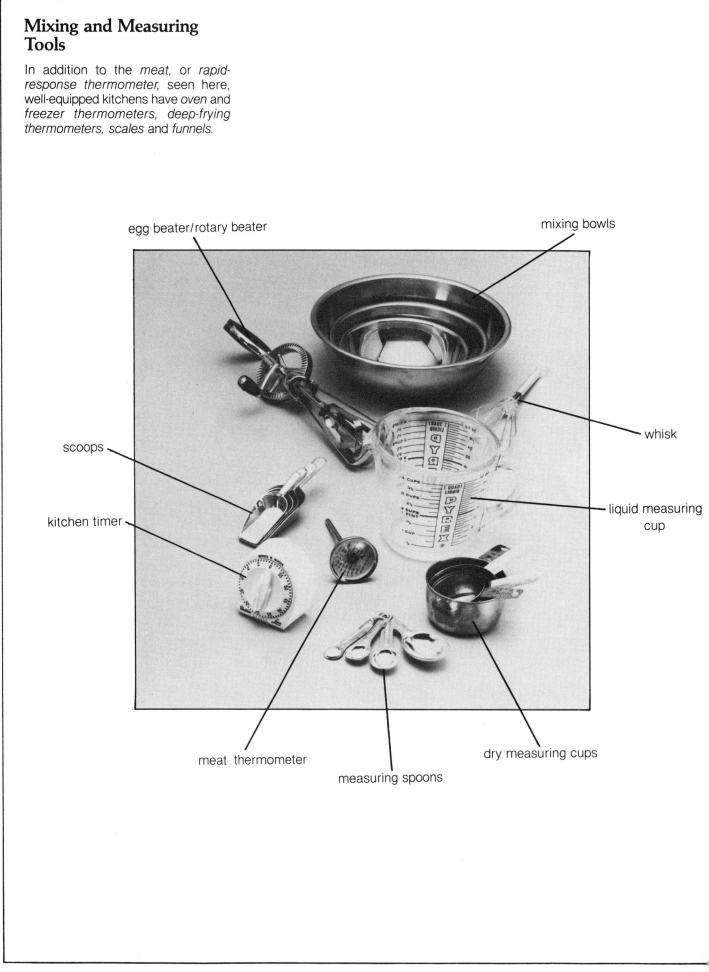

egg beater/rotary beater

mixing bowls

whisk

scoops

liquid measuring cup

kitchen timer

meat thermometer

measuring spoons

dry measuring cups

Preparation Utensils

Additional preparation implements include *molding scoops,* for soft foods, wooden *spaghetti spoons* with long *prongs* to wrap pasta and lift it from boiling water, *basting ladles* with an egg-shaped *bowl* for easy pouring, and cylindrical one-piece *pastry pins.*

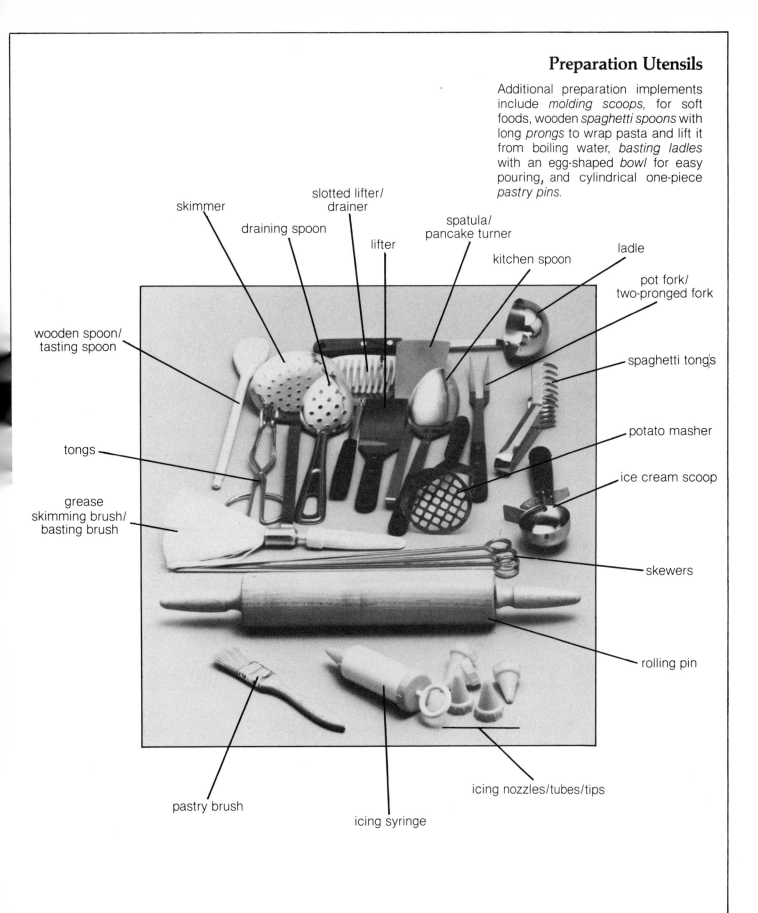

skimmer

slotted lifter/ drainer

draining spoon

lifter

spatula/ pancake turner

kitchen spoon

ladle

pot fork/ two-pronged fork

wooden spoon/ tasting spoon

spaghetti tongs

tongs

potato masher

grease skimming brush/ basting brush

ice cream scoop

skewers

rolling pin

pastry brush

icing syringe

icing nozzles/tubes/tips

Kitchen

Strainers and Drainers

Clean dishes, vegetables and fruits may be left on a *draining rack,* or *dish rack,* to dry. *Cooling racks* are used in conjunction with baked foods. A *sieve* has a mesh bottom for straining. A *food mill,* or *food foley,* is a heavy colander through which food is pressed by means of a flat *plate* attached to a *rotating handle.*

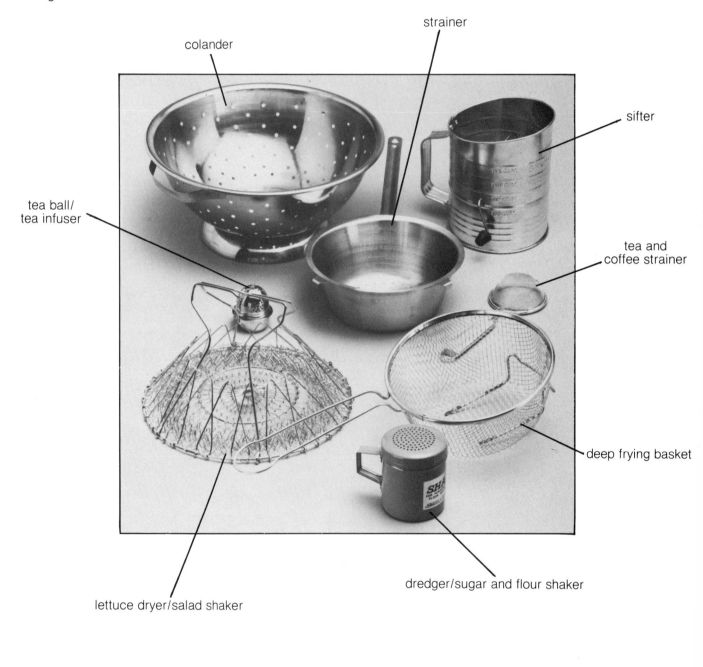

colander

strainer

sifter

tea ball/
tea infuser

tea and
coffee strainer

deep frying basket

lettuce dryer/salad shaker

dredger/sugar and flour shaker

A *potato peeler* has a swivel blade for following contours and a sharp tip for gouging. Hand-cranked *meat grinders* chop meats and other foods. A *zester* is a tool that shaves the thin surface off fruits.

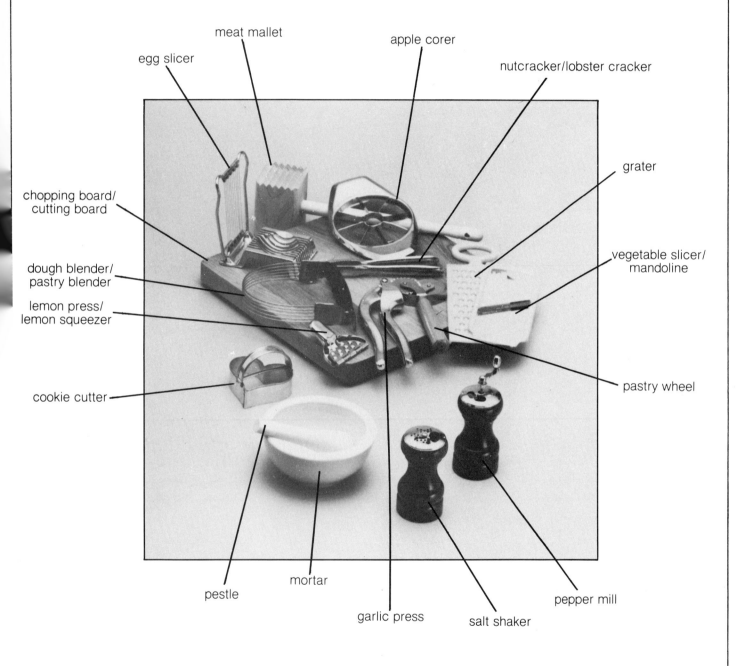

egg slicer

meat mallet

apple corer

nutcracker/lobster cracker

grater

chopping board/ cutting board

vegetable slicer/ mandoline

dough blender/ pastry blender

lemon press/ lemon squeezer

cookie cutter

pastry wheel

pestle

mortar

garlic press

salt shaker

pepper mill

Kitchen

Raw Ingredients

On *lettuce*, the entire mass of leaves is called the *head*, while the center leaves are the *heart*. A small slice of meat is a *collop*. A *peppercorn* is a dried berry of black pepper.

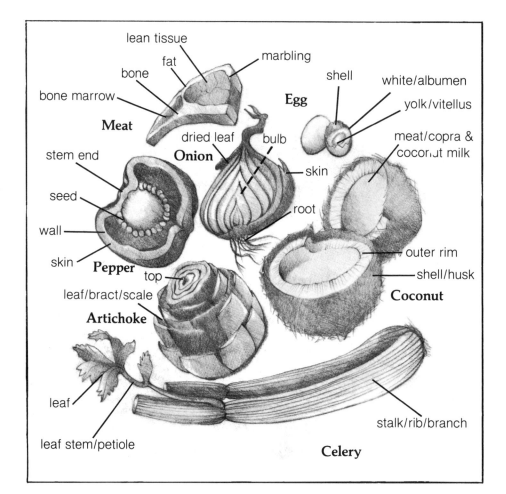

Prepared Foods

Appetizers, or *hors d'oeuvres,* are served before the main *course,* or *entree.* An ingredient, such as a *condiment, spice* or *herb,* added to food for the savor it imparts, is *seasoning.* Cheese is made by separating the *curd,* milk solids, from the *whey,* milk liquids. *Crumb* refers to both the soft inner portion of bread and any tiny piece that flakes off the loaf or a slice.

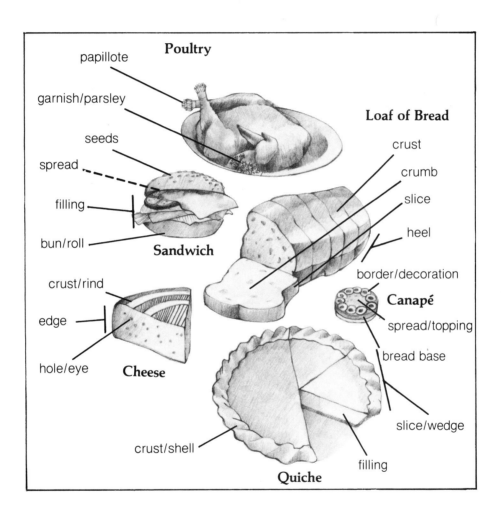

Poultry

papillote

garnish/parsley

seeds

spread

filling

bun/roll

Sandwich

Loaf of Bread

crust

crumb

slice

heel

border/decoration

Canapé

spread/topping

bread base

slice/wedge

crust/rind

edge

hole/eye

Cheese

crust/shell

filling

Quiche

Kitchen

Desserts

Baked desserts, or *sweet goods,* made of dough or having a crust made of enriched dough, such as *pies,* tarts and *turnovers,* are *pastries.* A *parfait* is similar to a sundae but may have layers of fruit and be frozen.

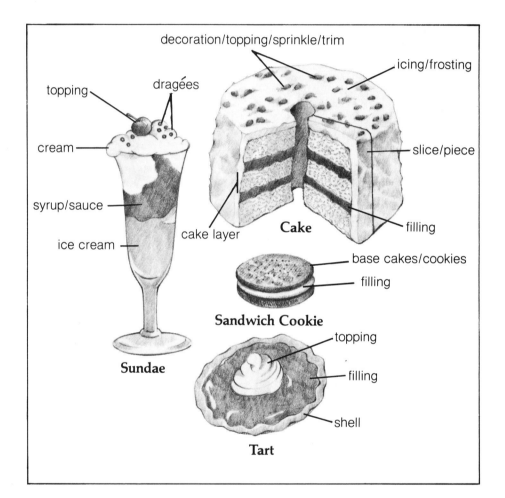

decoration/topping/sprinkle/trim

icing/frosting

topping

dragées

cream

syrup/sauce

ice cream

slice/piece

cake layer

Cake

filling

Sundae

base cakes/cookies

filling

Sandwich Cookie

topping

filling

shell

Tart

Snack Foods

Ice cream scoops are also put in flat-bottomed *wafer cones* and topped with other *fixings,* including *nuts* and *cherries.* When ice cream melts and drips down the cone, it forms *lickings.* The part of a hot dog roll that remains attached after the roll is sliced is the *hinge. Smoked sausages* are larger than franks and often include additional *seasonings.* Among other pizza toppings are *anchovies, extra cheese, pepperoni* and *onions.*

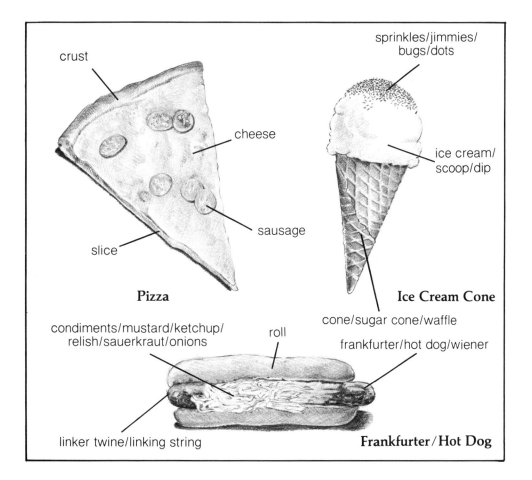

crust

cheese

sausage

slice

Pizza

sprinkles/jimmies/
bugs/dots

ice cream/
scoop/dip

Ice Cream Cone

cone/sugar cone/waffle

condiments/mustard/ketchup/
relish/sauerkraut/onions

roll

frankfurter/hot dog/wiener

linker twine/linking string

Frankfurter / Hot Dog

Containers

Most baskets are made by weaving individual *strands* or *rods* in front of one *stake* of the *frame* and behind the next. Some baskets have a border, or *foot,* on the bottom, just above the *base,* as well as a *cover,* or *lid,* which often rests on an inside *ledge.* A small, oblong veneer basket with rounded ends, the kind used for mushrooms, is a *climax basket,* and a little wooden paillike container with one stave extending up for a handle is a *piggin.*

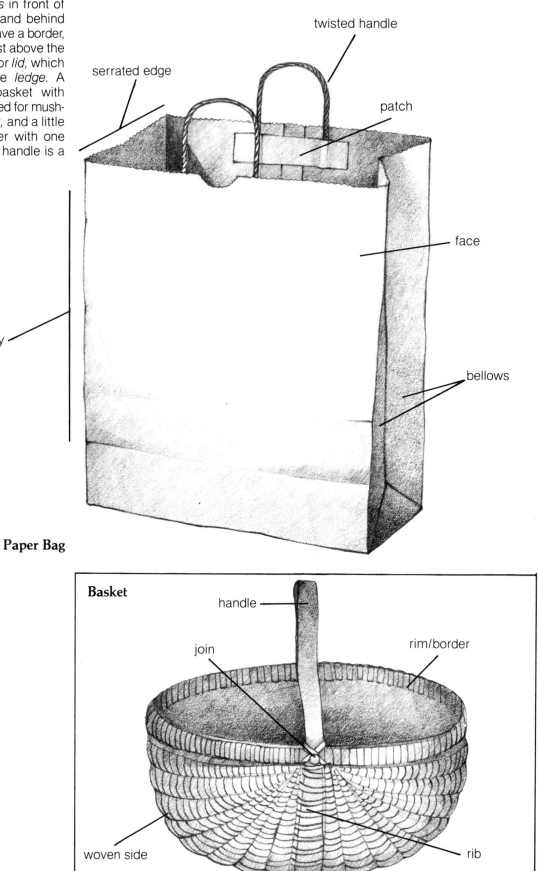

twisted handle

serrated edge

patch

face

body

bellows

Paper Bag

Basket

handle

join

rim/border

woven side

rib

Containers

The empty space inside a bottle, between the liquid and the top, is *ullage*. The wire arrangement covering the cork of a champagne bottle is called a *coiffe* if the bottle is from the Champagne region, a *wire hood* if it is domestic. Some barrels and *kegs* have a *taphole* in the top and a *bunghole* in the side. Large barrels are called *hogsheads* or *puncheons*.

mouth

cork

muzzle

lip

capsule

neck

shoulder

kick/punt

Bottle

saddle head

piston

container cap

accumulator

inductor/dip tube

Dispenser

Can

retained cap

double seam

top end

body/sidewall

Barrel/Cask

staves

chime

head

bottom

chime hoop

quarter hoop

Kitchen

Labeling and Packaging

Sketches or pictures on labels are called *vignettes*. When letters or vignettes on labels are raised, they are *embossed*. When they are recessed they are *debossed*. A seal of clear plastic that conforms to a product's shape is a *shrinkwrap*. A *promotional*, or *spot label*, often applied over the regular label, is a *tip-on*.

plastic squeeze bottle

threaded neck

hang-card hole

blister

squeeze spout

blister card

cap/closure

proof-of-purchase seal

die cut

PROOF OF PURCHASE

VINTAGE YEAR

for fun and knowledge

neck-band label

pull tab/zipper

pour spout

product label

side panel

directions for use

PULL TAB

Directions
soluta nobis eligend optio com
placeat facer possim omnis volu
aut tum rerum necessit atib
Itaque earud rerum hic tenetur
soluta nobis eligend optio com
placeat facer possim omnis volu
aut tum rerum necessit atib
Itaque earud rerum hic tenetur

die cut

NEW! easy-to-use

burst

trademark

Whatzit

BRAND

TM

®

brand designation

register mark

FOR FAST RELIEF OF MISNOMERS

Find any word you want-fast!

generic/ product name/ logo

Ingredients
soluta nobis eligend optio com
Itaque earud rerum hic tenetur
soluta nobis eligend optio com
placeat facer possim omnis volu
aut tum rerum necessit atib
Itaque earud rerum hic tenetur
soluta nobis eligend optio c
placeat facer possim
Itaque earud rerum hic te

ingredients

product blurb

interrupter

KILLS IMPRECISION ON CONTACT

graphic device

inner-liner pouch

precautionary statement

CAUTION: KEEP OUT OF REACH OF MUGWUMPS, KNOW-NOTHINGS, FUZZY THINKERS AND MUTTONHEADS. WHATZIT CONTAINS NO WHATCHAMACALLITS, THINGAMAJIGS, WHOOSIWHATSES, DOOHICKEYS, GIZMOS, DINGUSES, WIDGETS OR DOODADS.

net contents

576 FUN-FILLED PAGES

kosher symbol

Ⓤ

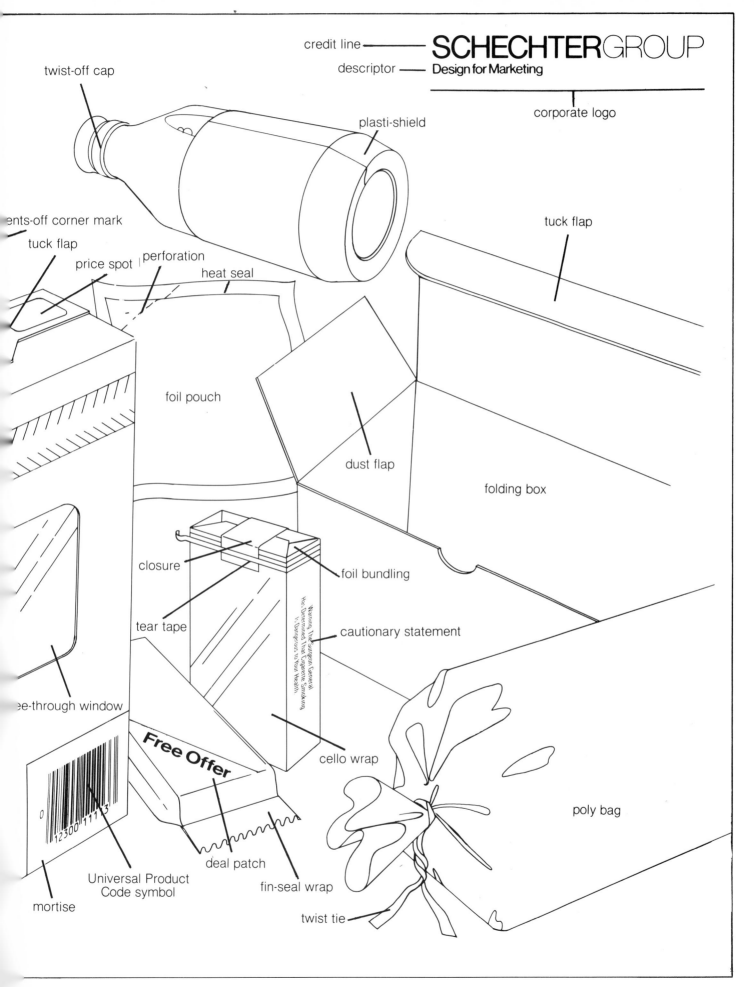

twist-off cap

credit line

SCHECHTERGROUP
Design for Marketing

descriptor

plasti-shield

corporate logo

ents-off corner mark

tuck flap

tuck flap

price spot | perforation

heat seal

foil pouch

dust flap

folding box

closure

foil bundling

tear tape

cautionary statement

Warning: The Surgeon General Has Determined That Cigarette Smoking Is Dangerous to Your Health

ee-through window

cello wrap

poly bag

Free Offer

0 12300 11113

deal patch

fin-seal wrap

mortise

Universal Product
Code symbol

twist tie

265

Kitchen

Bed and Bedding

A bedstead or *bed frame* consists of *side rails*, or *bedrails*, which connect the headboard to the *footboard*. A *twin bed* is a single bed, or one of a matching pair or beds, while a *double bed* is large enough to sleep two adults. A *comforter* is a small, thick quilt, while a *throw* is a bedspread with a short *side drop* rather than long *skirts*.

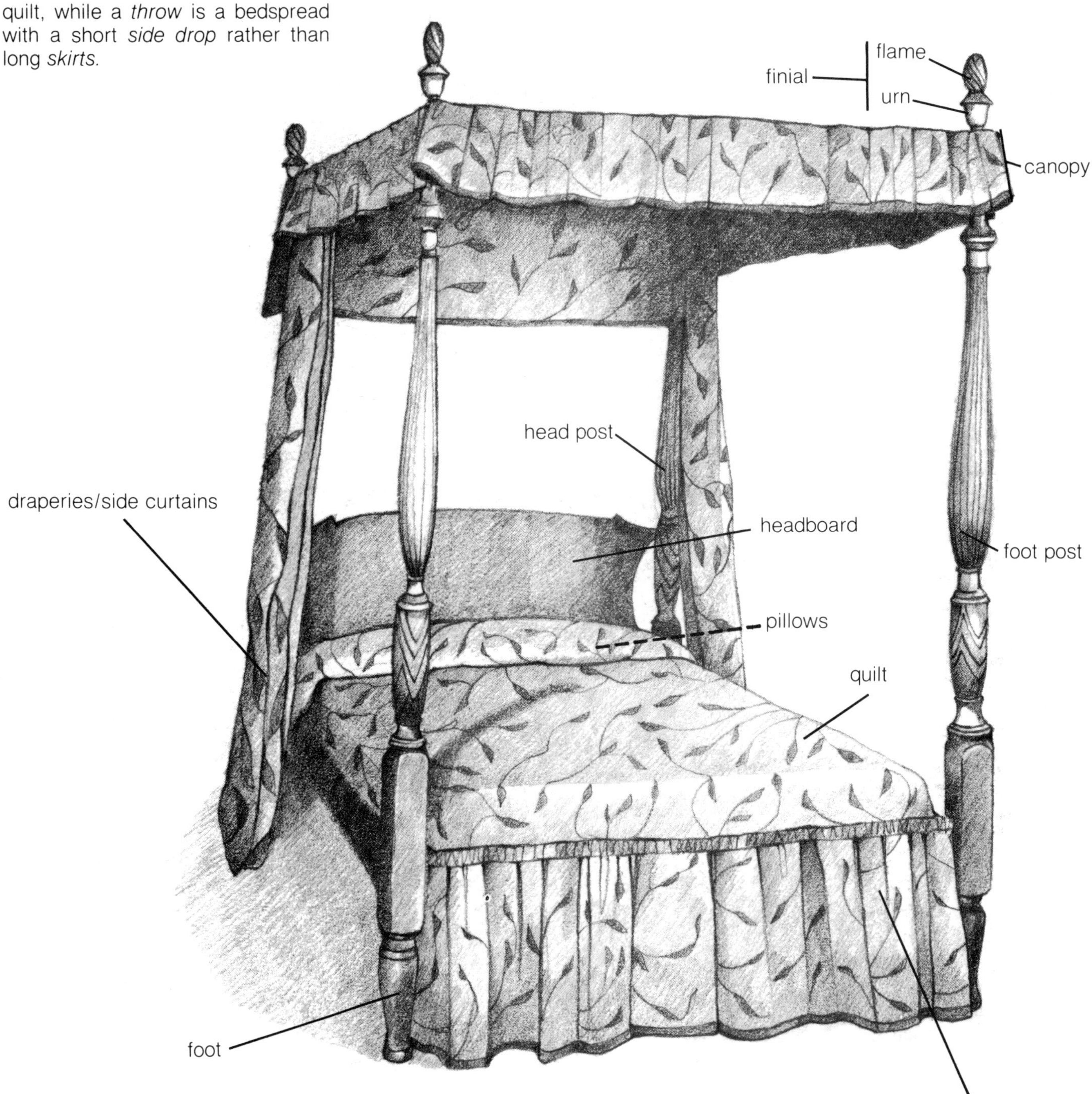

finial

flame

urn

canopy

head post

headboard

foot post

draperies/side curtains

pillows

quilt

foot

dust ruffle

Four-Poster/Canopy Bed

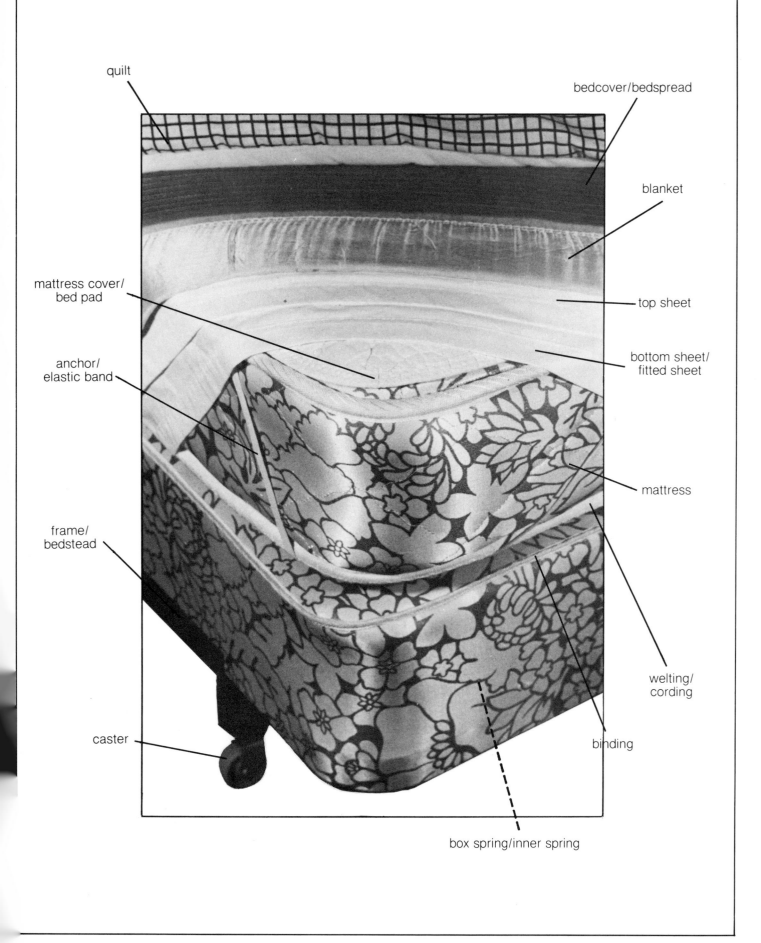

quilt

bedcover/bedspread

blanket

mattress cover/
bed pad

top sheet

bottom sheet/
fitted sheet

anchor/
elastic band

mattress

frame/
bedstead

welting/
cording

caster

binding

box spring/inner spring

Bedroom

Dressers

A dresser without the drawers in it is called the *main body,* or *carcass.* The thin plywood sheets between drawers, to keep *drawer cases* rigid, are *dust panels.* An *armoire,* or *wardrobe,* is a tall, movable closet in which to hang clothes. A *chiffonier* is a high, narrow chest of drawers.

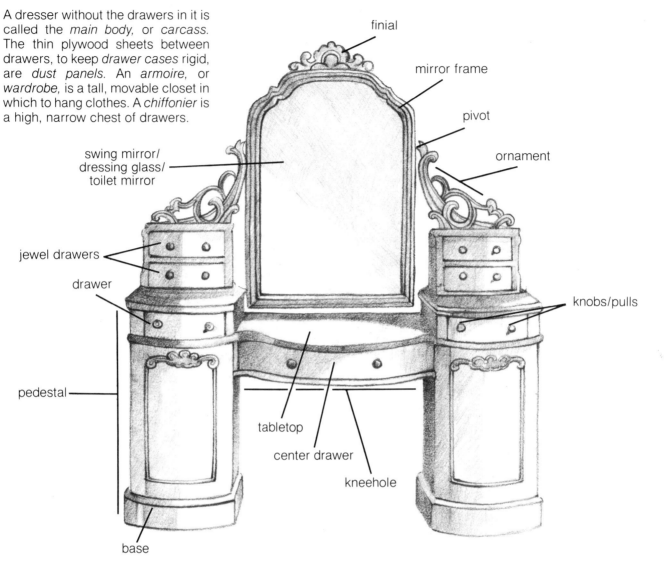

finial

mirror frame

pivot

ornament

swing mirror/
dressing glass/
toilet mirror

jewel drawers

drawer

knobs/pulls

pedestal

tabletop

center drawer

kneehole

base

Dressing Table / Vanity

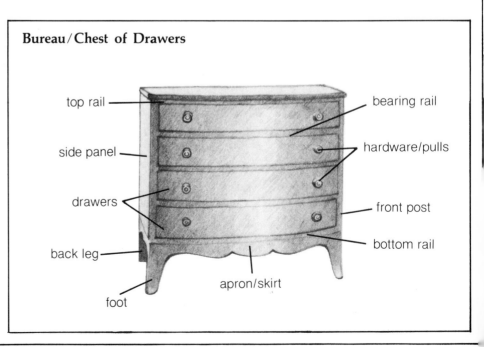

Bureau / Chest of Drawers

top rail

bearing rail

side panel

hardware/pulls

drawers

front post

back leg

bottom rail

foot

apron/skirt

Faucet and Sink

Some basins have *rubber plug* and *chain stoppers* to hold water, and *splash rims* or *lips* to prevent water from overflowing.

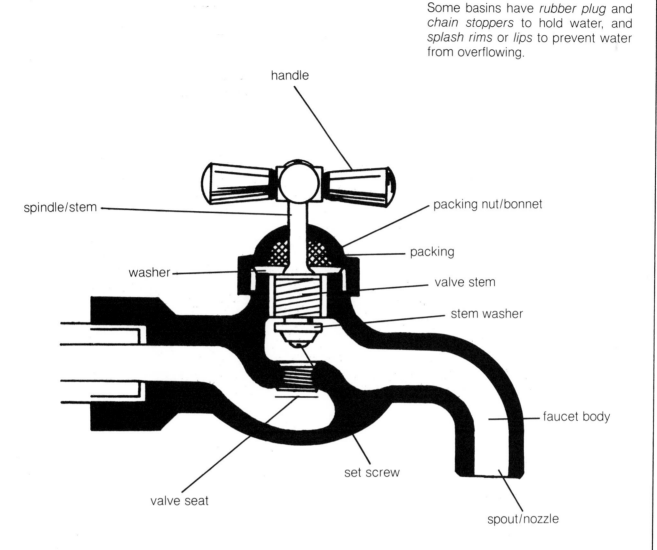

handle

spindle/stem

packing nut/bonnet

packing

washer

valve stem

stem washer

faucet body

set screw

spout/nozzle

valve seat

Faucet / Spigot / Tap / Bibcock

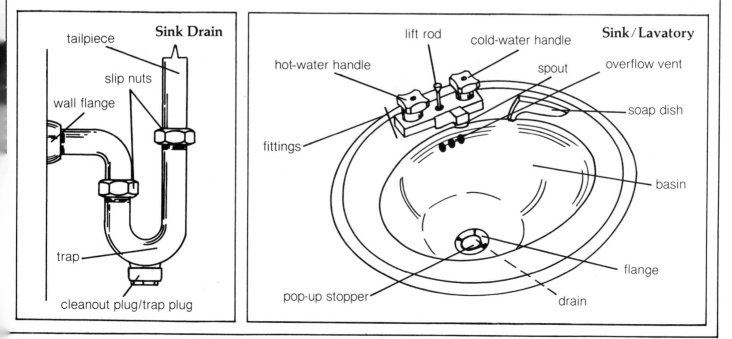

Sink Drain

tailpiece

slip nuts

wall flange

trap

cleanout plug/trap plug

Sink / Lavatory

lift rod

cold-water handle

hot-water handle

spout

overflow vent

soap dish

fittings

basin

flange

pop-up stopper

drain

Bathroom

Bath and Shower

Waterproof *shower curtains* or sliding glass *doors* enclose baths and showers and smaller *shower stalls*. Hand-held shower heads, *massagers,* or *spray heads* are popular shower accessories. Some *tubs* have *whirlpool jets* to circulate water. Floors of tubs and showers may have *non-skid,* or *non-slip,strips.*

curtain hooks

shower rod

Shower

shower arm

ball fitting

shower head

shower face

spray-adjustment knob

washcloth rack

shower curtain

towel rack

soap dish

safety rail/grab rail

ledge

spout

hot-water faucet

cold-water faucet

shower-diverter knob

overflow plate

drain-control lever

Bathtub

tub drain & stopper

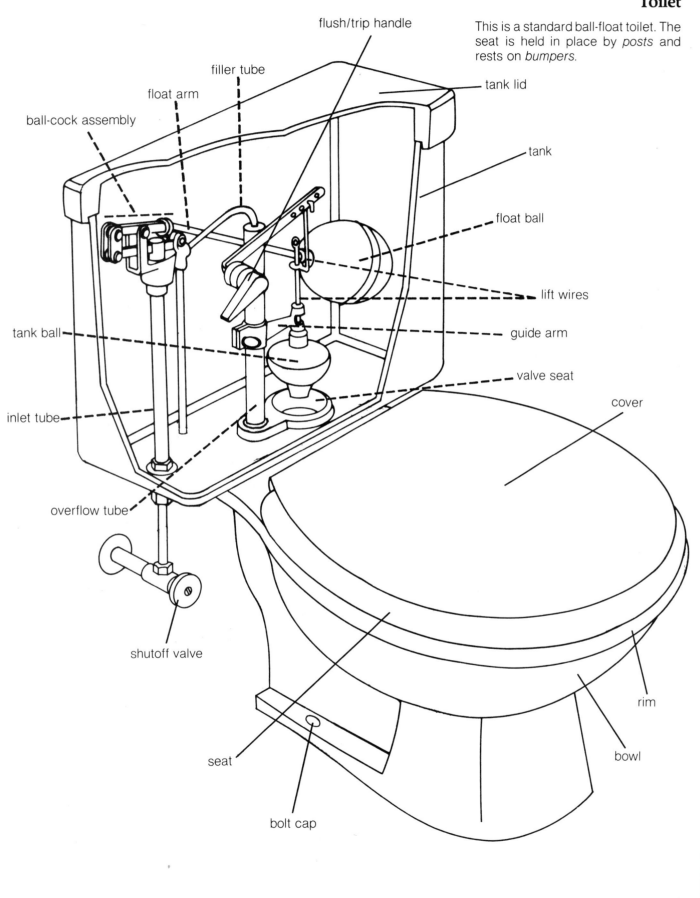

Toilet

This is a standard ball-float toilet. The seat is held in place by *posts* and rests on *bumpers*.

flush/trip handle

filler tube

float arm

ball-cock assembly

tank lid

tank

float ball

lift wires

tank ball

guide arm

valve seat

cover

inlet tube

overflow tube

shutoff valve

rim

bowl

seat

bolt cap

Bathroom

Desk

A *rolltop* or *cylinder desk* has a *sliding cover* that covers the desk's *writing area* when not in use. In *slant-front, falling-front* or *drop-lid desks*, the *front* flips down to offer a writing area which is supported by two *slide-out supports*. Some modern office desks have *elevator platforms* that can be raised and locked in place to hold a business machine, or lowered and closed behind a *cabinet door*.

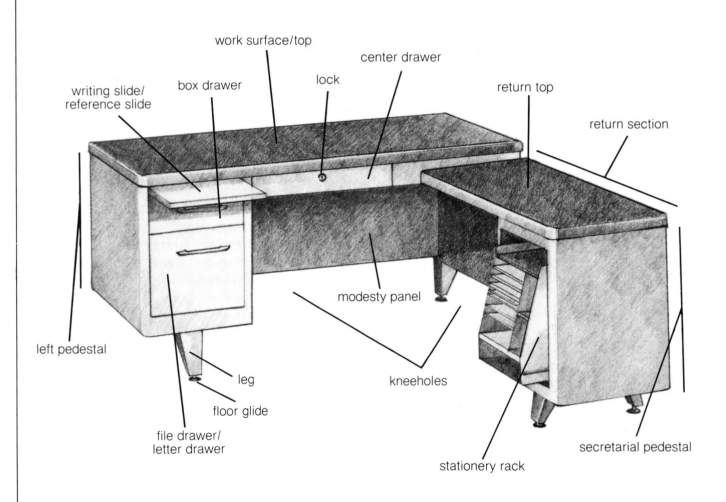

work surface/top

center drawer

box drawer   lock

writing slide/
reference slide

return top

return section

left pedestal

modesty panel

leg

floor glide

kneeholes

file drawer/
letter drawer

stationery rack

secretarial pedestal

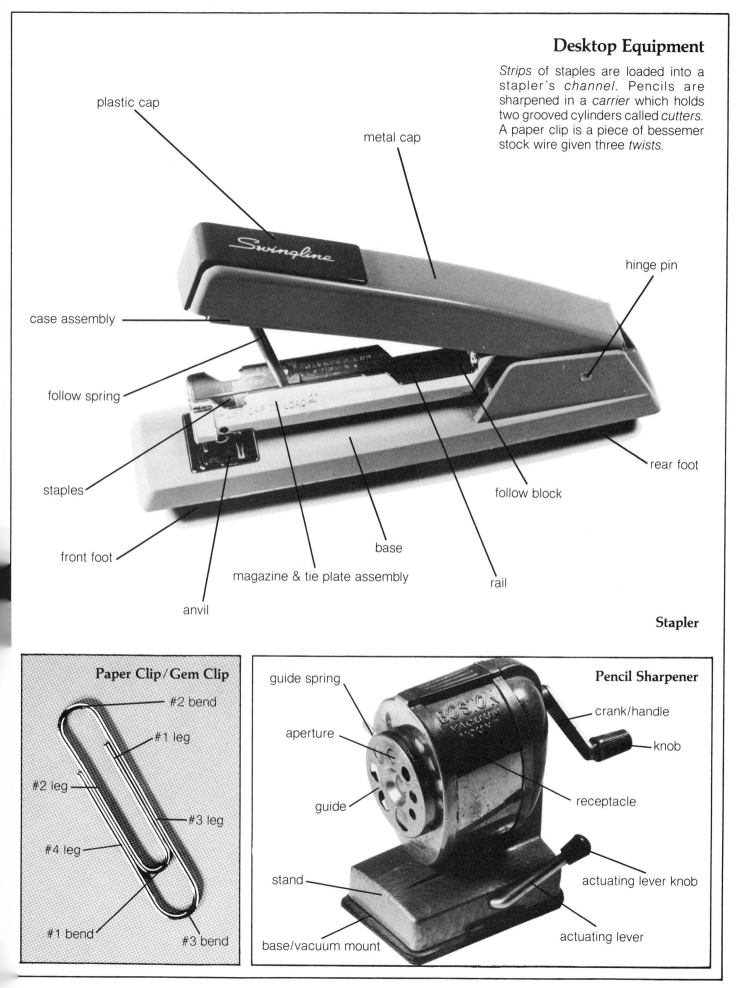

Desktop Equipment

Strips of staples are loaded into a stapler's *channel*. Pencils are sharpened in a *carrier* which holds two grooved cylinders called *cutters*. A paper clip is a piece of bessemer stock wire given three *twists*.

plastic cap

metal cap

hinge pin

case assembly

follow spring

staples

rear foot

follow block

front foot

base

magazine & tie plate assembly

rail

anvil

Stapler

Paper Clip/Gem Clip

#2 bend

#1 leg

#2 leg

#3 leg

#4 leg

#1 bend

#3 bend

Pencil Sharpener

guide spring

crank/handle

aperture

knob

guide

receptacle

stand

actuating lever knob

base/vacuum mount

actuating lever

Sewing Machine

The standard presser foot can be replaced by a variety of special attachments, including a *zipper foot, hemmer foot* and *roller foot*. Some machines have a *slide plate* as well as a needle plate that opens to provide access to the bobbin case.

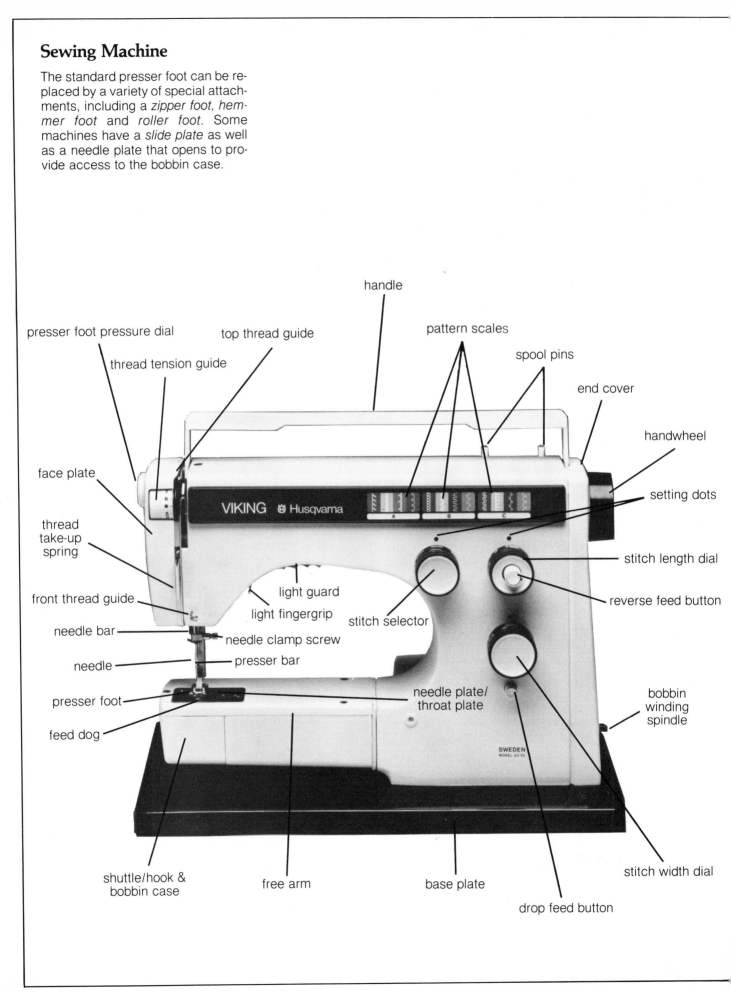

handle

pattern scales

presser foot pressure dial

top thread guide

thread tension guide

spool pins

end cover

handwheel

face plate

setting dots

thread take-up spring

stitch length dial

front thread guide

light guard

reverse feed button

light fingergrip

needle bar

needle clamp screw

stitch selector

needle

presser bar

presser foot

needle plate/ throat plate

bobbin winding spindle

feed dog

shuttle/hook & bobbin case

free arm

base plate

stitch width dial

drop feed button

VIKING ⚙ Husqvarna

SWEDEN MODEL 63 10

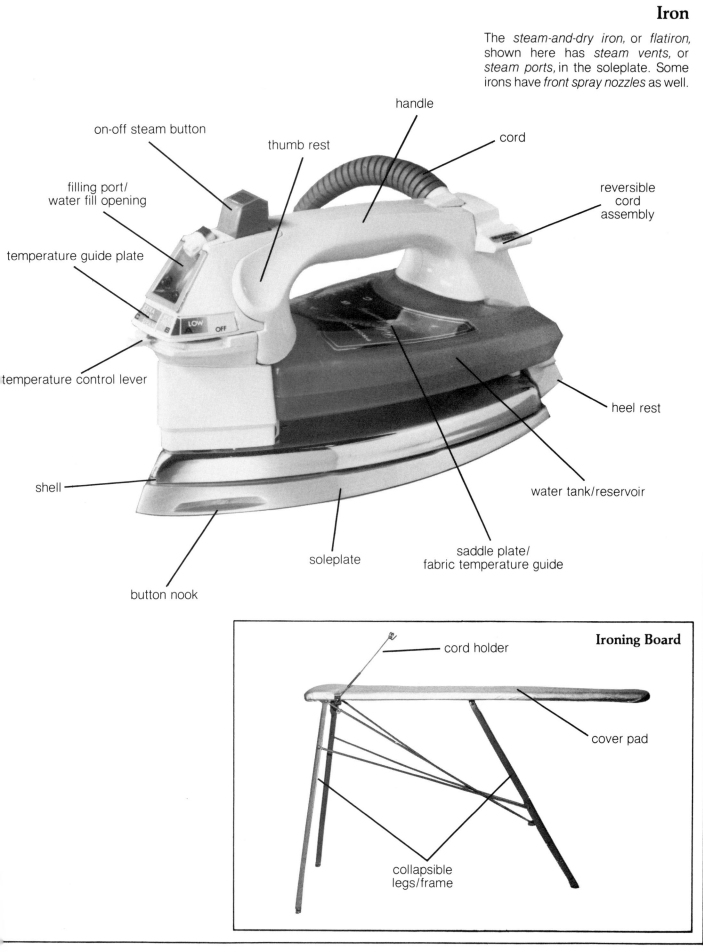

Iron

The *steam-and-dry iron*, or *flatiron*, shown here has *steam vents*, or *steam ports*, in the soleplate. Some irons have *front spray nozzles* as well.

handle

on-off steam button

thumb rest

cord

filling port/
water fill opening

reversible
cord
assembly

temperature guide plate

LOW   OFF

temperature control lever

heel rest

shell

water tank/reservoir

soleplate

saddle plate/
fabric temperature guide

button nook

Ironing Board

cord holder

cover pad

collapsible
legs/frame

Washing and Drying

Formerly, clothes were washed in a *washtub* with a *scrubboard* and *wringer* before being hung out to dry on *clotheslines,* or *washlines,* with clothespins. Wash-and-wear shirts are still air-dried on hangers. In automatic *top-loading washing machines* and *front-loading washers,* the basket, which has *drain holes* inside it, is contained within a metal *tub.* Some washers and dryers have a *window* in the *door* and a *tub light.*

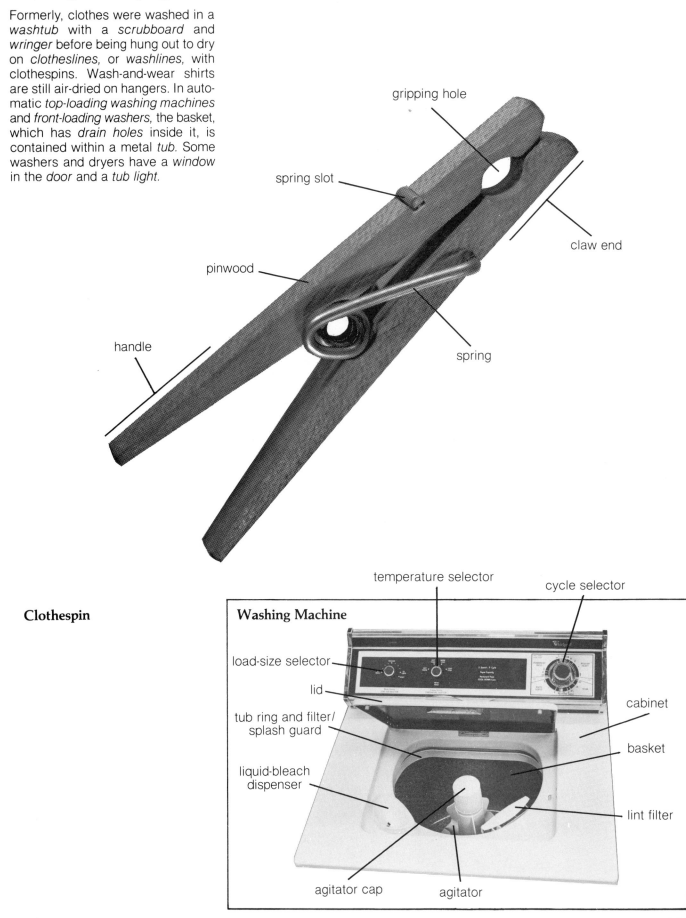

gripping hole

spring slot

claw end

pinwood

handle

spring

Clothespin

Washing Machine

temperature selector

cycle selector

load-size selector

lid

cabinet

tub ring and filter/ splash guard

basket

liquid-bleach dispenser

lint filter

agitator cap

agitator

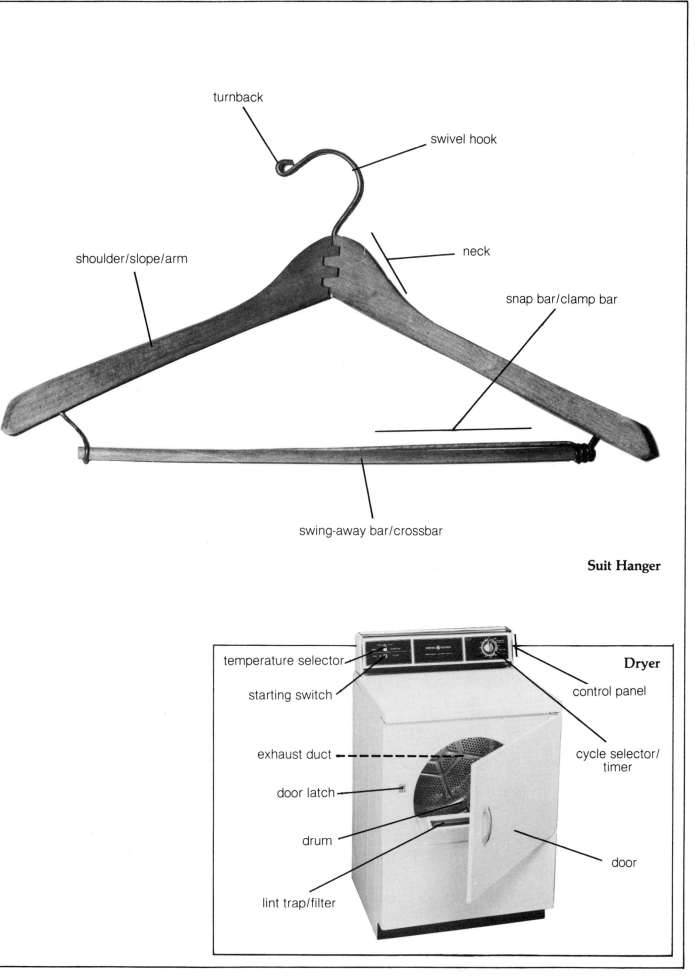

turnback

swivel hook

shoulder/slope/arm

neck

snap bar/clamp bar

swing-away bar/crossbar

Suit Hanger

temperature selector

starting switch

exhaust duct

door latch

drum

lint trap/filter

Dryer

control panel

cycle selector/
timer

door

Household Cleaning Equipment

A conventional mop has absorbent *strands* rather than a sponge. An *electric broom* is a lightweight vacuum cleaner on a handle. A *carpet sweeper* contains two revolving brushes in a box at the end of a pushing handle.

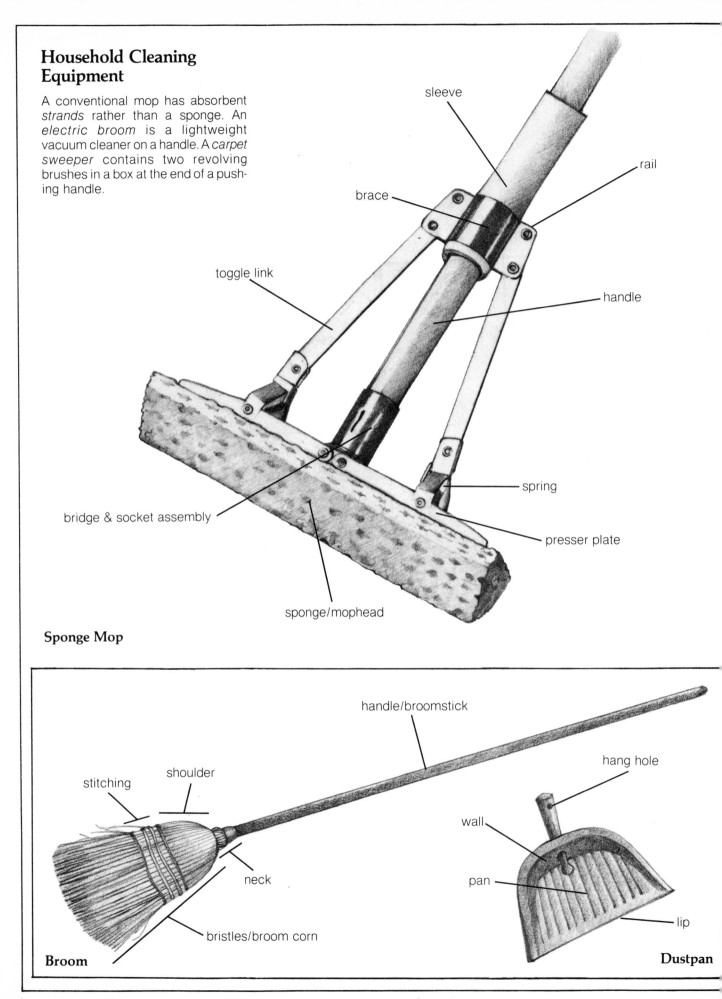

sleeve

rail

brace

toggle link

handle

spring

bridge & socket assembly

presser plate

sponge/mophead

Sponge Mop

handle/broomstick

hang hole

stitching

shoulder

wall

pan

neck

lip

bristles/broom corn

Broom

Dustpan

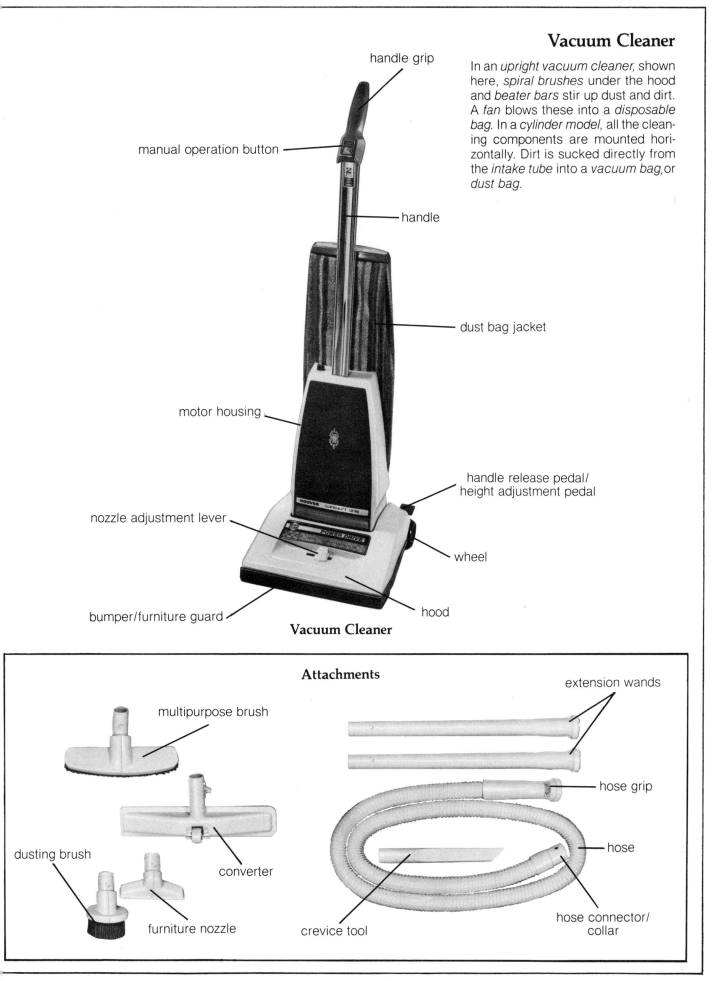

Vacuum Cleaner

handle grip

manual operation button

handle

dust bag jacket

motor housing

handle release pedal/
height adjustment pedal

nozzle adjustment lever

wheel

bumper/furniture guard

hood

Vacuum Cleaner

In an *upright vacuum cleaner,* shown here, *spiral brushes* under the hood and *beater bars* stir up dust and dirt. A *fan* blows these into a *disposable bag.* In a *cylinder model,* all the cleaning components are mounted horizontally. Dirt is sucked directly from the *intake tube* into a *vacuum bag,* or *dust bag.*

Attachments

multipurpose brush

extension wands

dusting brush

hose grip

converter

hose

furniture nozzle

crevice tool

hose connector/
collar

Firefighting Devices

Dry chemical extinguishers, containing chemicals and gas under pressure, are activated by squeezing or twisting the handle. *Soda-acid extinguishers*, inverted to mix the contents, produce a smothering *foam*.

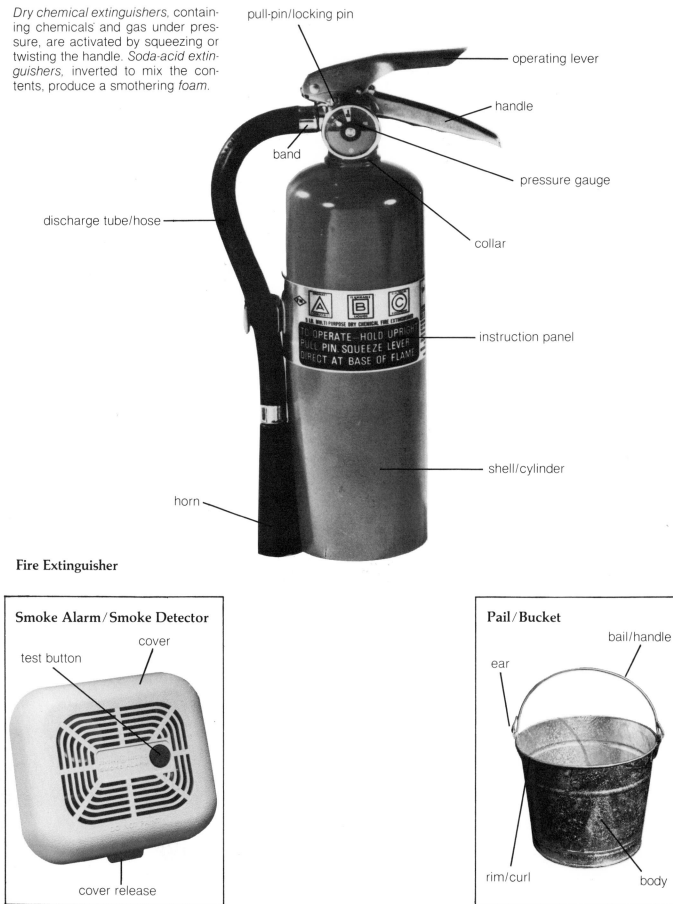

pull-pin/locking pin

operating lever

handle

pressure gauge

band

collar

discharge tube/hose

instruction panel

shell/cylinder

horn

Fire Extinguisher

Smoke Alarm/Smoke Detector

test button

cover

cover release

Pail/Bucket

bail/handle

ear

rim/curl

body

Luggage

The exterior parts of a *suitcase* or *bag* are identical to those of an *attaché* case. A suitcase that unfolds to be hung up is called a *garment bag*. Briefcases sometimes have zippered *file folders* or *portfolios* as well as paper storage *pockets*.

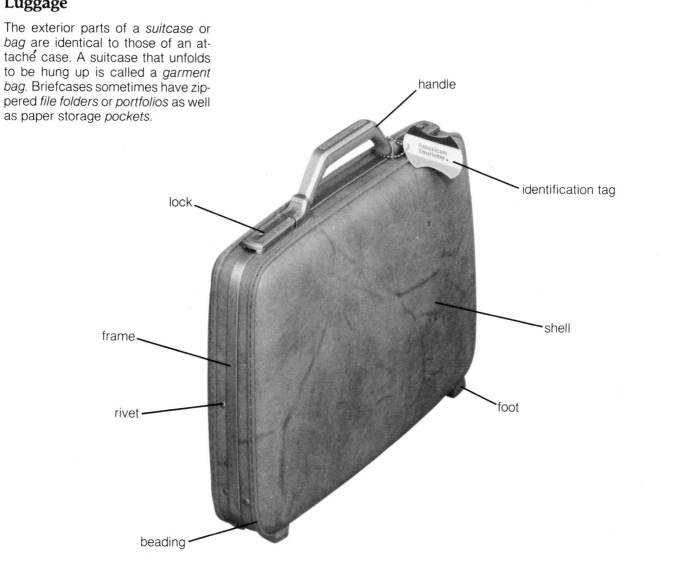

handle

identification tag

lock

shell

frame

foot

rivet

beading

Attaché Case/Briefcase

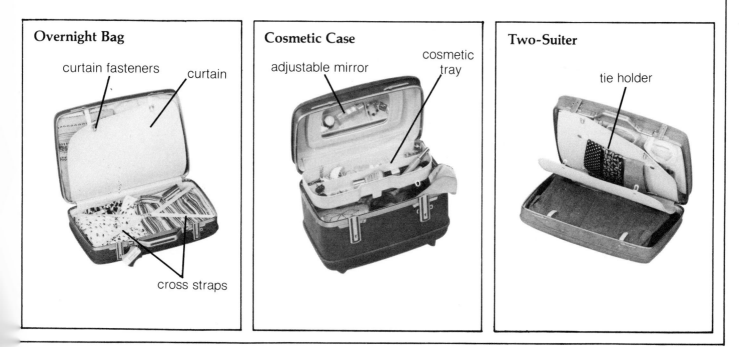

Overnight Bag

curtain fasteners

curtain

cross straps

Cosmetic Case

adjustable mirror

cosmetic tray

Two-Suiter

tie holder

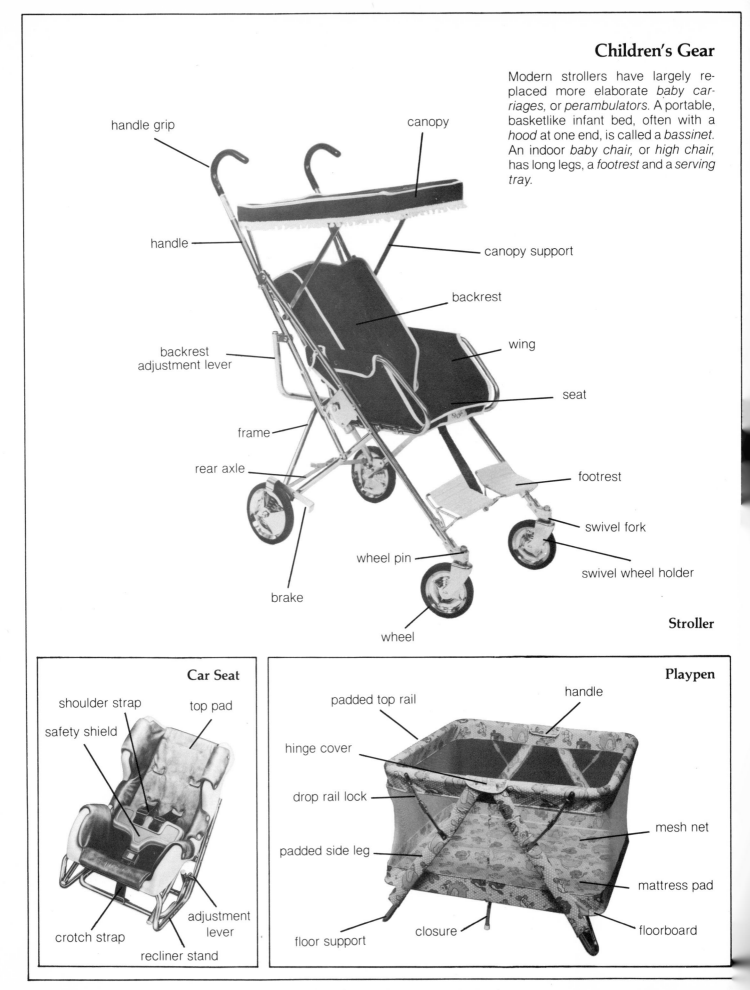

Children's Gear

Modern strollers have largely replaced more elaborate *baby carriages,* or *perambulators.* A portable, basketlike infant bed, often with a *hood* at one end, is called a *bassinet.* An indoor *baby chair,* or *high chair,* has long legs, a *footrest* and a *serving tray.*

handle grip

canopy

handle

canopy support

backrest

backrest adjustment lever

wing

seat

frame

rear axle

footrest

swivel fork

wheel pin

swivel wheel holder

brake

Stroller

wheel

Car Seat

shoulder strap

top pad

safety shield

crotch strap

adjustment lever

recliner stand

Playpen

padded top rail

handle

hinge cover

drop rail lock

padded side leg

mesh net

mattress pad

floor support

closure

floorboard

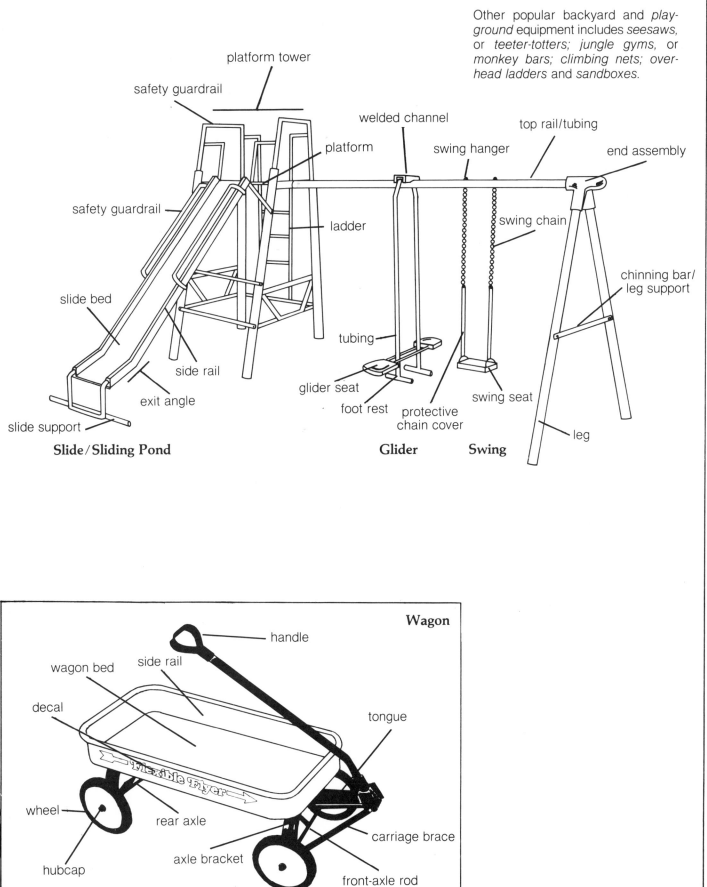

Backyard Equipment

Other popular backyard and *playground* equipment includes *seesaws*, or *teeter-totters*; *jungle gyms*, or *monkey bars*; *climbing nets*; *overhead ladders* and *sandboxes*.

platform tower

safety guardrail

platform

welded channel

top rail/tubing

swing hanger

end assembly

safety guardrail

ladder

swing chain

slide bed

chinning bar/ leg support

tubing

side rail

exit angle

glider seat

swing seat

slide support

foot rest

protective chain cover

leg

Slide/Sliding Pond

Glider   **Swing**

Wagon

handle

side rail

wagon bed

decal

tongue

Flexible Flyer

wheel

rear axle

carriage brace

hubcap

axle bracket

front-axle rod

Patio Accessories

On regular grills and *braziers,* food is cooked over *charcoal briquettes* resting in a *fire bowl,* whereas on gas and electric models food is grilled over *volcanic rock.* Other grills include *hibachis* and *kettle grills* featuring *damper controls, adjustable grills,* and *ash catchers.* On some outdoor lounges and *settees,* small springs, or *helicals,* connect the frame to metal supporting straps.

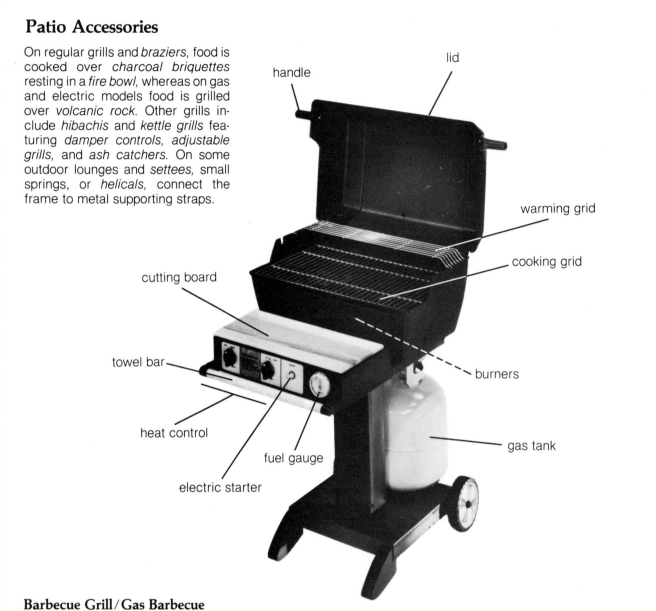

handle

lid

warming grid

cooking grid

cutting board

towel bar

heat control

fuel gauge

electric starter

burners

gas tank

Barbecue Grill/Gas Barbecue

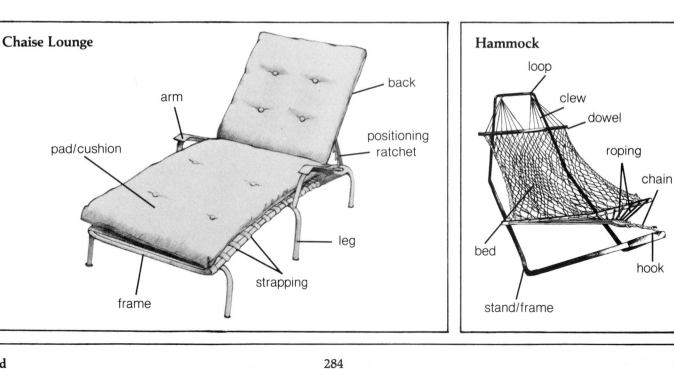

Chaise Lounge

arm

pad/cushion

back

positioning ratchet

leg

strapping

frame

Hammock

loop

clew

dowel

roping

chain

bed

hook

stand/frame

Sports and Recreation

Emphasis in this section is given to major sports and forms of recreational activity which involve gear and equipment. Word and picture games, for example, have been omitted, since the nomenclature involved is so limited.

In order to enable the reader to find particular items quickly, recreational activities have been grouped in the following way: team sports, competitive sports, individual sports, equestrian sports, automobile racing, outdoor sports, bodybuilding, board games, and casino games.

Because playing areas involved in team and competitive sports are an integral part of the activity, fields, courts and rinks have been diagramed with all the vital areas, lines and demarcations identified.

And to show the parts of clothing and equipment used by players, real athletes rather than models have been photographed: batter Rod Carew, football running back Bruce Harper, basketball guard Mike Glenn, hockey defenseman Ken Morrow and goalie Billy Smith.

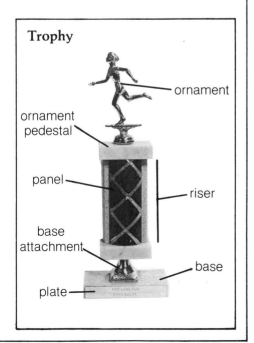

Trophy

ornament

ornament pedestal

panel

riser

base attachment

base

plate

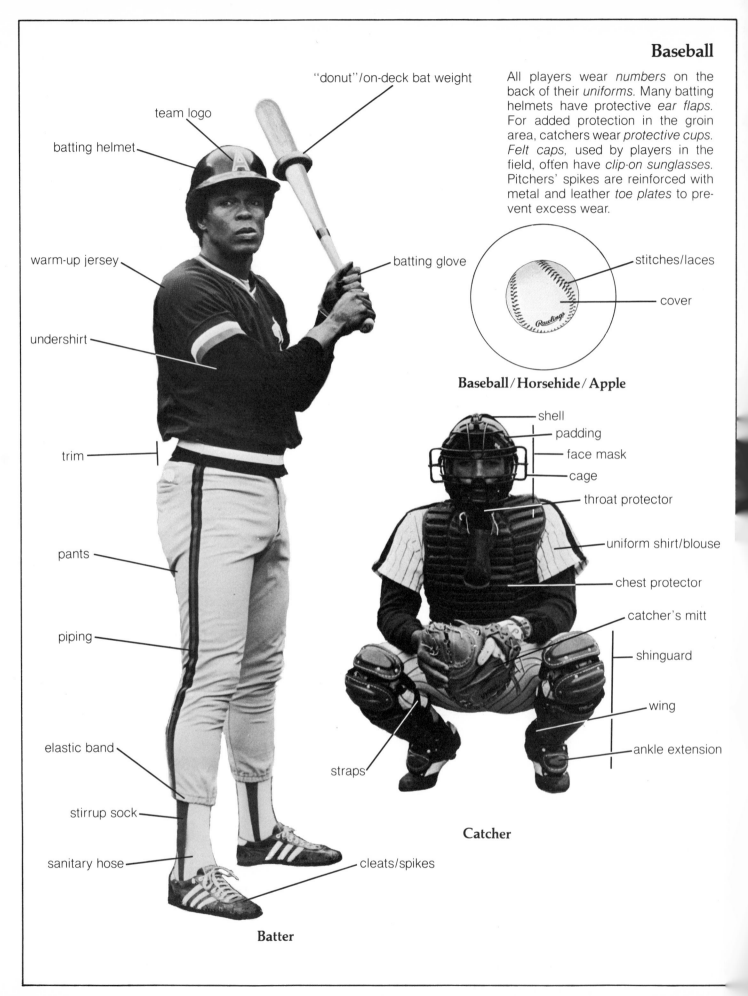

Baseball

"donut"/on-deck bat weight

team logo

batting helmet

warm-up jersey

undershirt

trim

pants

piping

elastic band

stirrup sock

sanitary hose

batting glove

cleats/spikes

Batter

All players wear *numbers* on the back of their *uniforms*. Many batting helmets have protective *ear flaps*. For added protection in the groin area, catchers wear *protective cups*. *Felt caps*, used by players in the field, often have *clip-on sunglasses*. Pitchers' spikes are reinforced with metal and leather *toe plates* to prevent excess wear.

stitches/laces

cover

Baseball/Horsehide/Apple

shell

padding

face mask

cage

throat protector

uniform shirt/blouse

chest protector

catcher's mitt

shinguard

wing

ankle extension

straps

Catcher

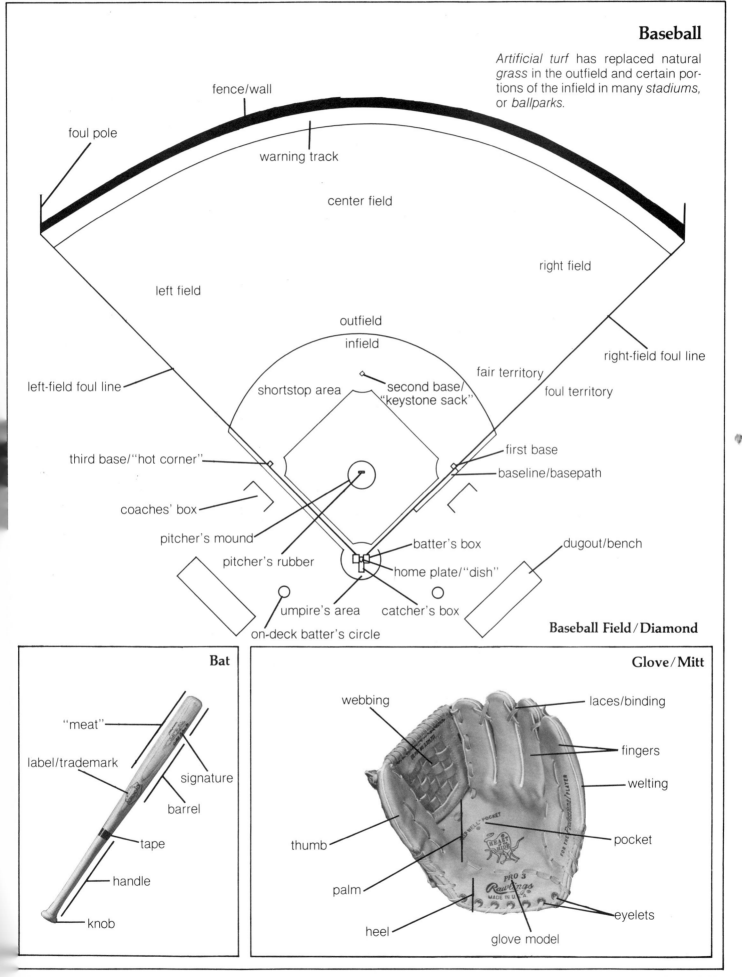

Baseball

Artificial turf has replaced natural *grass* in the outfield and certain portions of the infield in many *stadiums,* or *ballparks.*

fence/wall

foul pole

warning track

center field

right field

left field

outfield

infield

right-field foul line

left-field foul line

fair territory

shortstop area

second base/ "keystone sack"

foul territory

third base/"hot corner"

first base

baseline/basepath

coaches' box

pitcher's mound

batter's box

dugout/bench

pitcher's rubber

home plate/"dish"

umpire's area

catcher's box

on-deck batter's circle

Baseball Field/Diamond

Bat

"meat"

label/trademark

signature

barrel

tape

handle

knob

Glove/Mitt

webbing

laces/binding

fingers

welting

thumb

pocket

palm

heel

glove model

eyelets

Team Sports

Football

Protective equipment worn on the upper body is covered with a *numbered jersey*. A *tear-away jersey* is loosely sewn and meant to rip apart when grabbed by an opponent. Helmets are manufactured with different *suspension systems,* some of which are air-inflated. Football covers have a rough *pebble finish* and an air-retaining *bladder* which is filled by inserting an *inflation needle* in the valve.

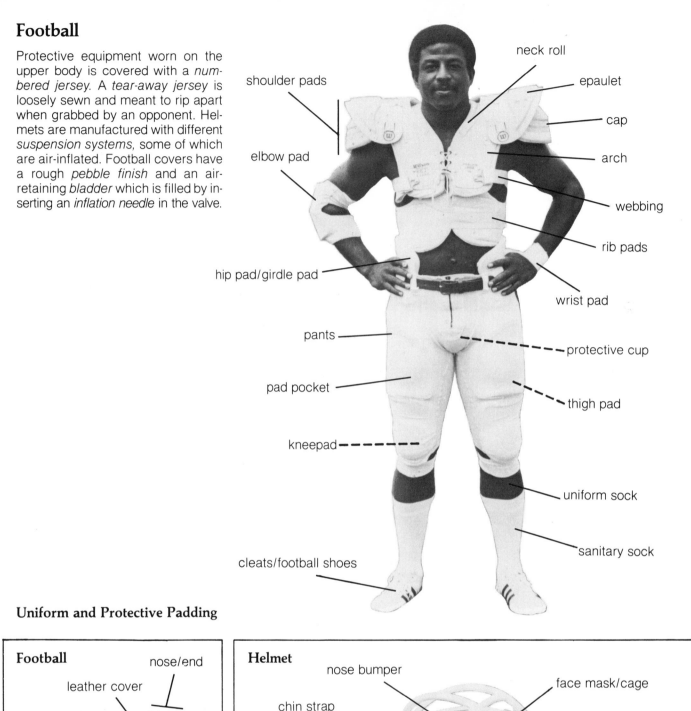

shoulder pads

neck roll

epaulet

cap

arch

webbing

rib pads

wrist pad

elbow pad

hip pad/girdle pad

pants

protective cup

pad pocket

thigh pad

kneepad

uniform sock

sanitary sock

cleats/football shoes

Uniform and Protective Padding

Football

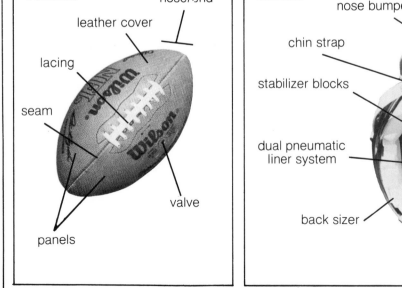

nose/end

leather cover

lacing

seam

valve

panels

Helmet

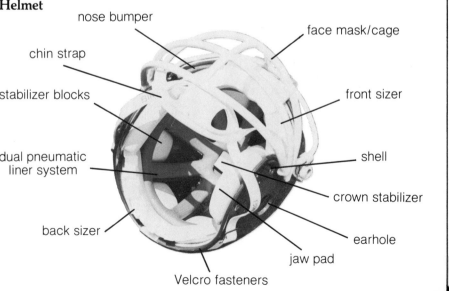

nose bumper

face mask/cage

chin strap

front sizer

stabilizer blocks

shell

dual pneumatic liner system

crown stabilizer

earhole

back sizer

jaw pad

Velcro fasteners

Football

A *down marker* is used to mark the exact location of the ball on the field between downs. The *flip chart* at the top of the down marker has *flip panels* to indicate what down is about to be played. The goalpost in college football has two support *standards* instead of a gooseneck, used in professional games. *Flags* are located at the junction of the goal line and sideline to mark in bounds. Small, rubber inverted V-shaped *yard markers* are placed at five-yard intervals along the sidelines.

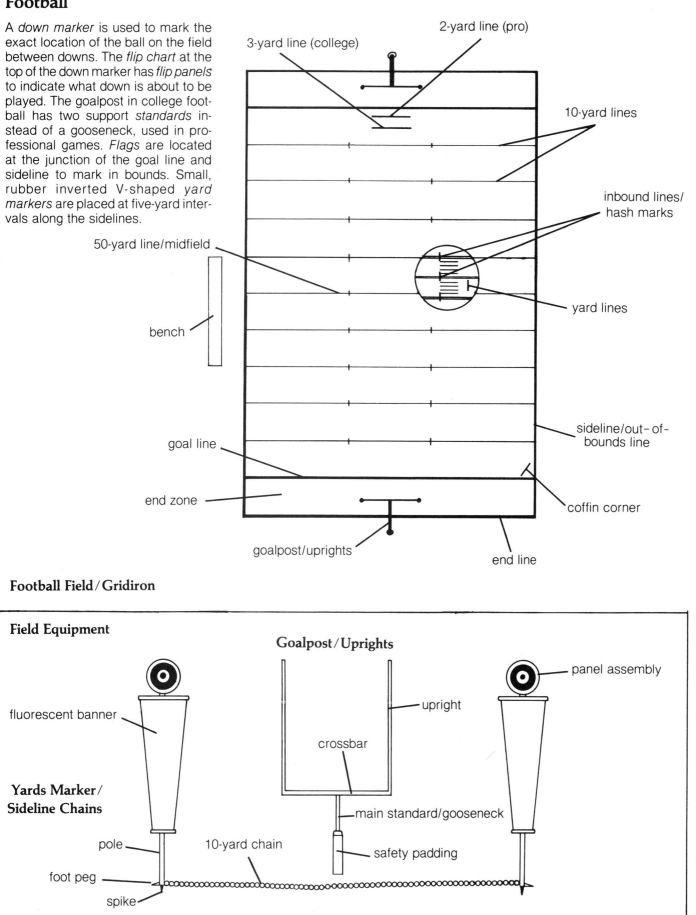

3-yard line (college)

2-yard line (pro)

10-yard lines

inbound lines/hash marks

50-yard line/midfield

yard lines

bench

sideline/out-of-bounds line

goal line

coffin corner

end zone

goalpost/uprights

end line

Football Field / Gridiron

Field Equipment

Goalpost / Uprights

fluorescent banner

panel assembly

upright

crossbar

Yards Marker / Sideline Chains

main standard/gooseneck

pole

10-yard chain

safety padding

foot peg

spike

Team Sports

Ice Hockey

Hockey players' pants are held up by *suspenders*. Socks are attached to a *garter belt*. The angle between the shaft of a hockey stick and the blade is called the *lie*. The game is played with a black vulcanized rubber *puck*. A blinking *red light* atop the goal judge's box indicates a goal.

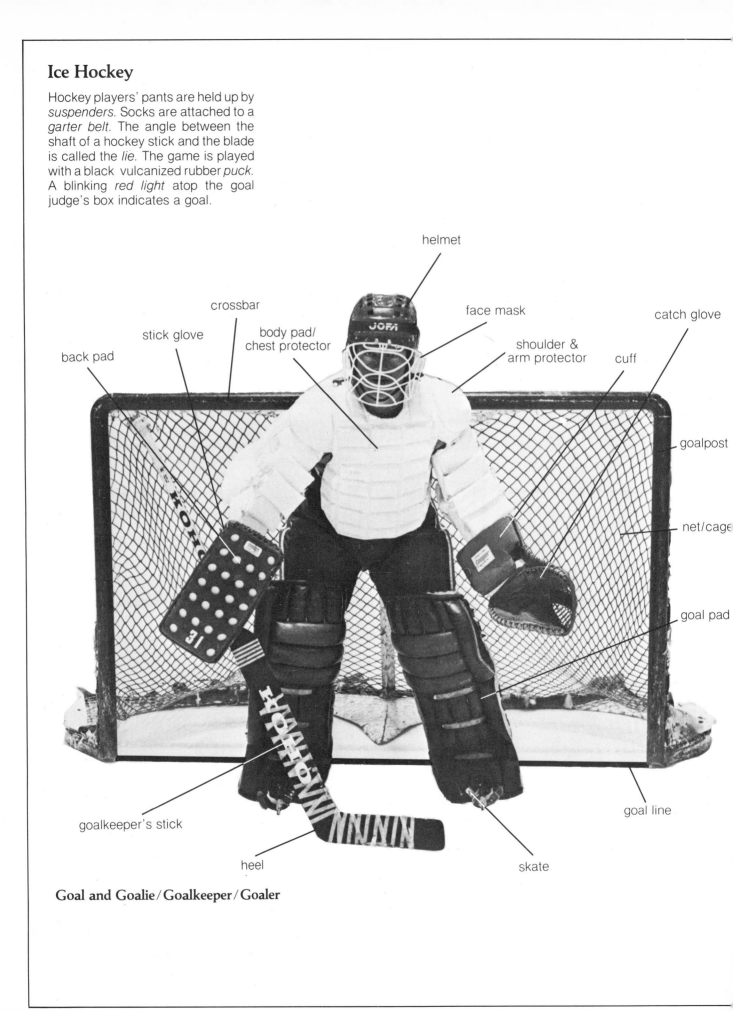

helmet

crossbar

stick glove

body pad/
chest protector

back pad

face mask

shoulder &
arm protector

catch glove

cuff

goalpost

net/cage

goal pad

goalkeeper's stick

heel

skate

goal line

Goal and Goalie / Goalkeeper / Goaler

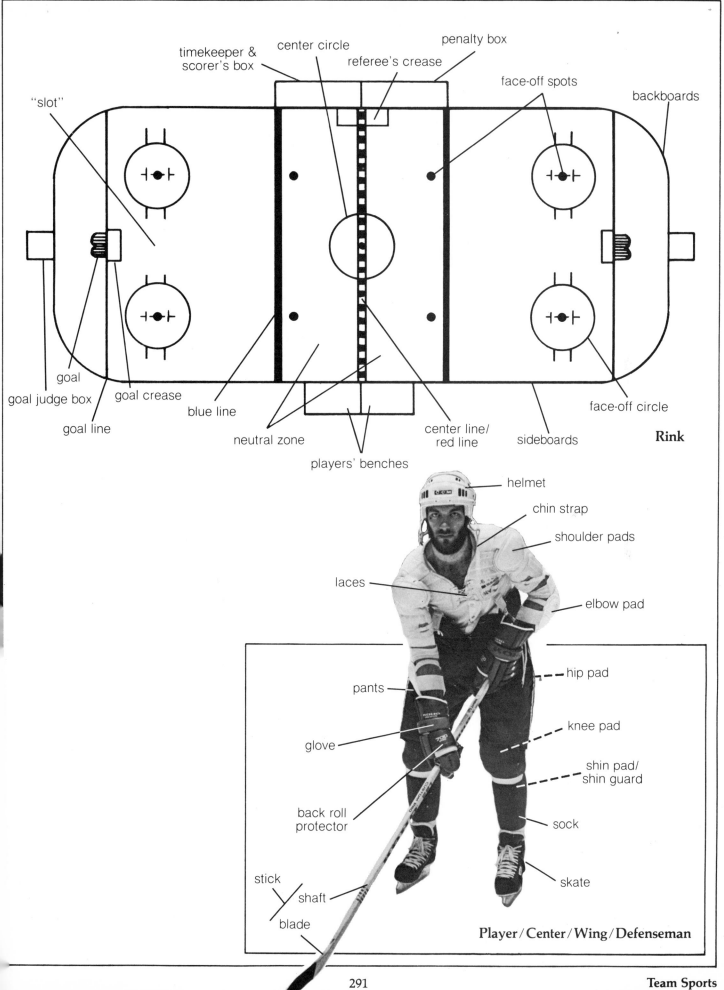

timekeeper & scorer's box

center circle

referee's crease

penalty box

face-off spots

backboards

"slot"

goal

goal judge box

goal crease

goal line

blue line

neutral zone

players' benches

center line/ red line

sideboards

face-off circle

Rink

helmet

chin strap

shoulder pads

laces

elbow pad

pants

hip pad

glove

knee pad

shin pad/ shin guard

back roll protector

sock

stick

shaft

blade

skate

Player / Center / Wing / Defenseman

Team Sports

Basketball

The offensive team advances from its own *backcourt* into the *forecourt*. The area at the top of the free-throw lane, usually patrolled by the *center* (as opposed to one of two *guards* or two *forwards*), is called the *pivot*. Many players wear *kneepads* and *elbow pads* for protection, and *warm-up suits* prior to games.

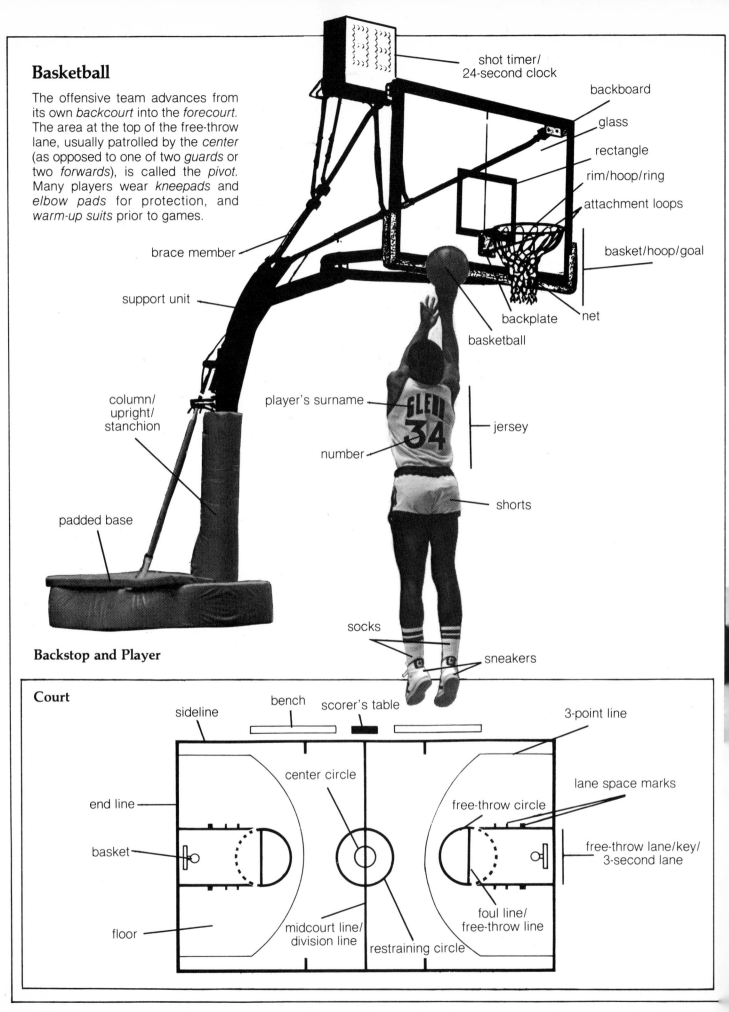

shot timer/
24-second clock

backboard

glass

rectangle

rim/hoop/ring

attachment loops

basket/hoop/goal

brace member

support unit

backplate

basketball

net

column/
upright/
stanchion

player's surname

jersey

number

shorts

padded base

GLEN
34

Backstop and Player

socks

sneakers

Court

sideline

bench

scorer's table

3-point line

end line

center circle

lane space marks

free-throw circle

basket

free-throw lane/key/
3-second lane

floor

midcourt line/
division line

restraining circle

foul line/
free-throw line

Soccer and Lacrosse

In soccer, or *association football,* players protect their legs with *shin-guards.* In lacrosse, players wear *helmets* and *face masks* for protection.

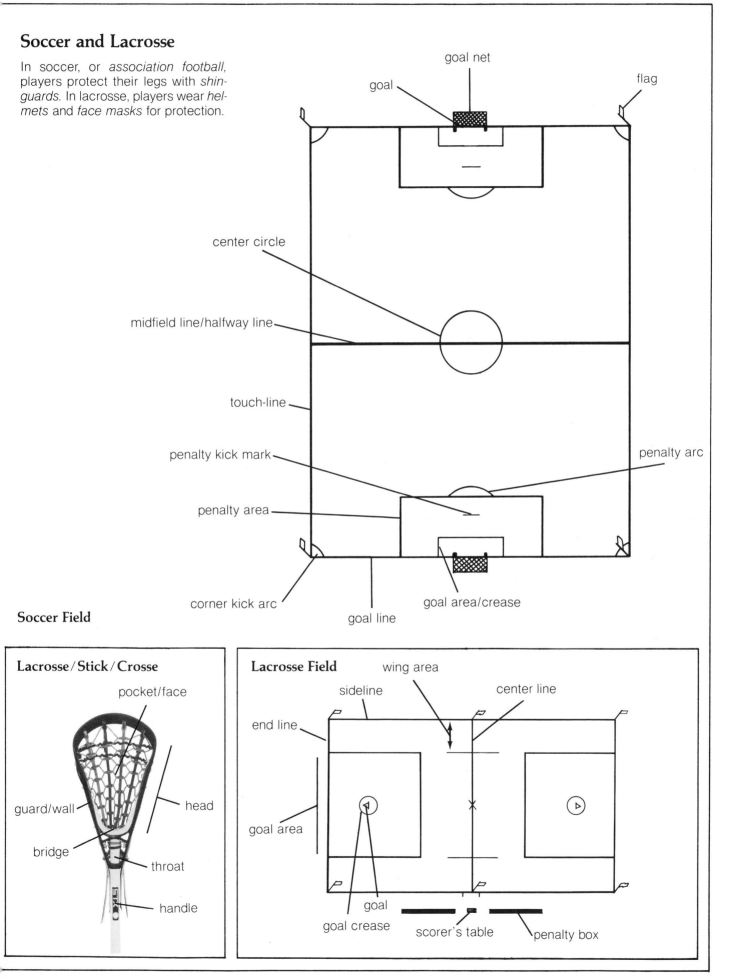

goal net

goal

flag

center circle

midfield line/halfway line

touch-line

penalty kick mark

penalty arc

penalty area

corner kick arc

goal line

goal area/crease

Soccer Field

Lacrosse/Stick/Crosse

pocket/face

guard/wall

head

bridge

throat

handle

Lacrosse Field

wing area

sideline

center line

end line

goal area

goal

goal crease

scorer's table

penalty box

Team Sports

Track and Field

Track-and-field events take place on a *running track* and the enclosed *field* within. Besides *jumping events* and *throwing events,* there are *footraces,* including *walking races, hurdle races, steeplechase, relay races, medley relays, runs* and the *marathon.* The *decathlon* is a ten-event contest, while the *pentathlon* consists of five events.

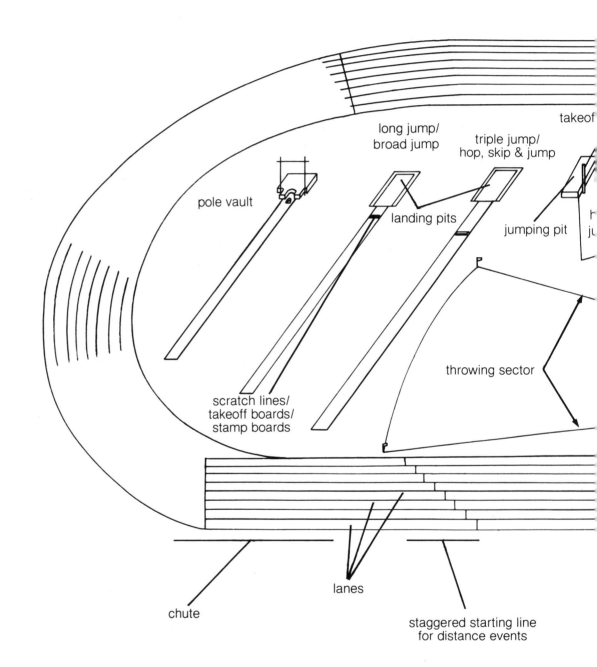

takeof

long jump/
broad jump

triple jump/
hop, skip & jump

pole vault

landing pits

jumping pit

h
ju

scratch lines/
takeoff boards/
stamp boards

throwing sector

lanes

chute

staggered starting line
for distance events

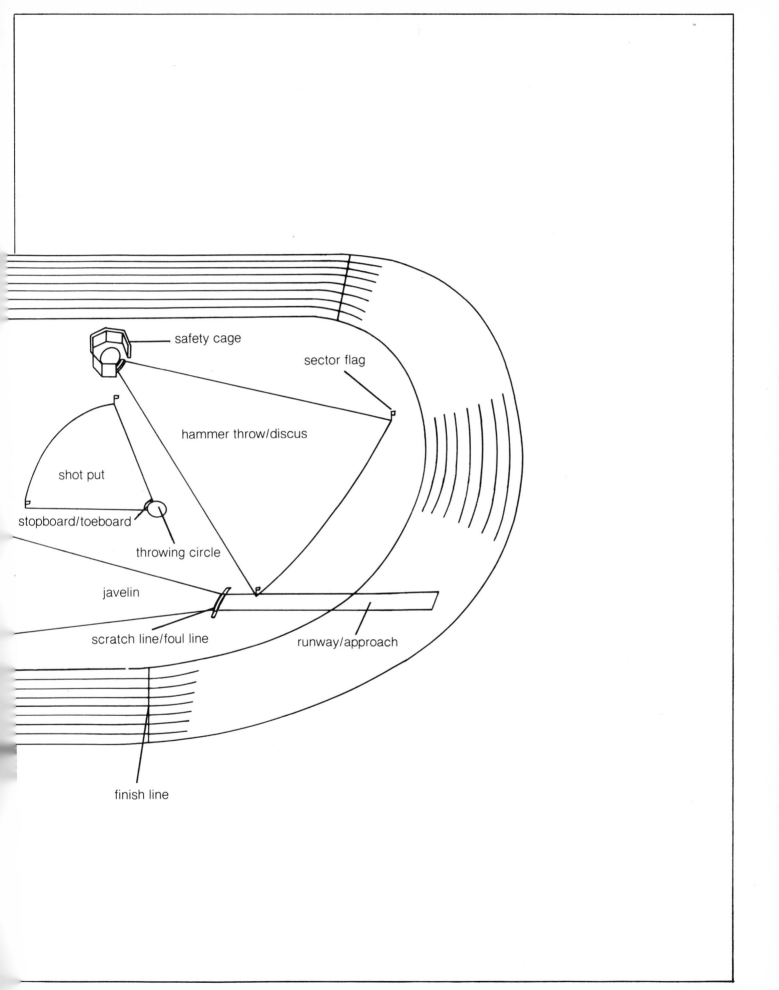

safety cage

sector flag

hammer throw/discus

shot put

stopboard/toeboard

throwing circle

javelin

scratch line/foul line

runway/approach

finish line

295

Competitive Sports

Running Shoe

These *training shoes*, or *trainers*, are more durable than lighter-weight *racing flats*. Lightweight running shoes are worn by *joggers* or *distance runners* in long races such as *marathons*. *Track shoes*, shoes with *spikes*, are used for most track-and-field events.

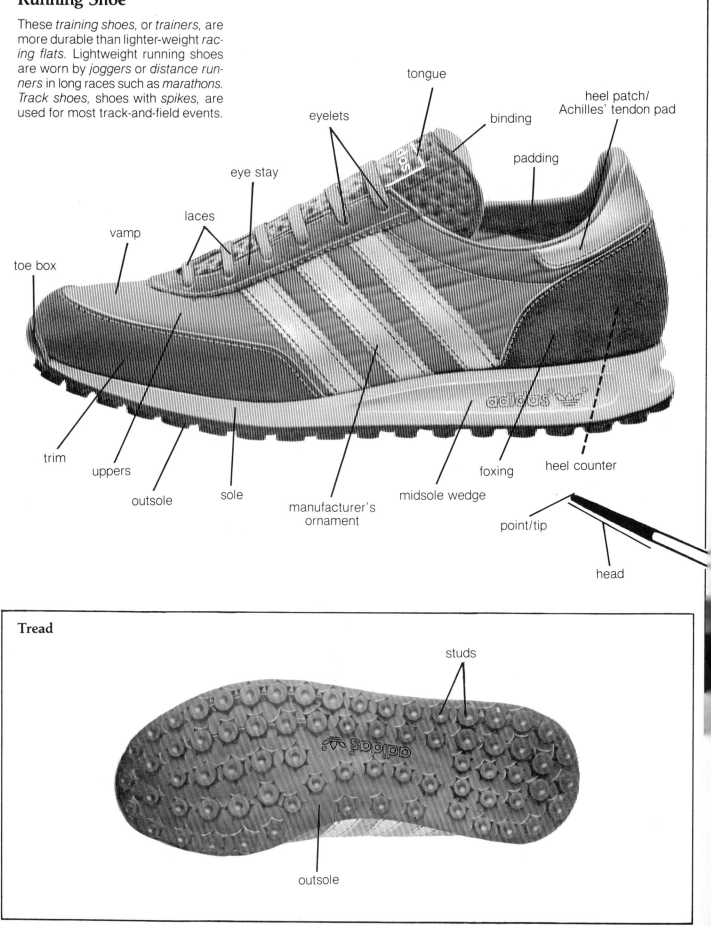

tongue

heel patch/
Achilles' tendon pad

binding

eyelets

padding

eye stay

laces

vamp

toe box

trim

uppers

outsole

sole

manufacturer's
ornament

midsole wedge

foxing

heel counter

point/tip

head

Tread

studs

outsole

Field Events Equipment

In addition to the equipment shown here, a round metal ball called a *shot put,* or *shot,* is also used in field events. Hammer throwers often wear *gloves* with padded palms.

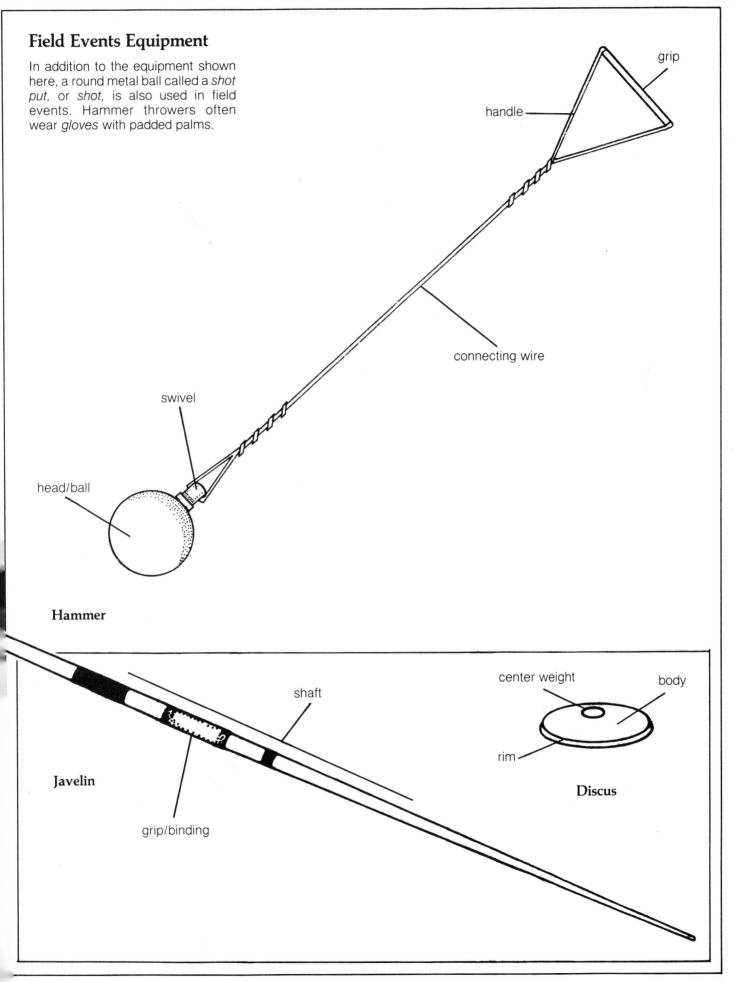

grip

handle

connecting wire

swivel

head/ball

Hammer

shaft

center weight

body

rim

Javelin

Discus

grip/binding

Hurdle

The height of hurdles can be adjusted for use in *high, intermediate* and *low hurdle* events. Base weights can also be adjusted to provide the proper *pull-over,* or *flipover,* the force required to knock them over. *Fixed hurdles* are used in a *steeplechase race,* an event that includes *water hazards.* Roller, or notched *lever locks* permit runners to adjust the slant on starting blocks, and a *plunger snap lock* allows them to position the blocks individually on the rail.

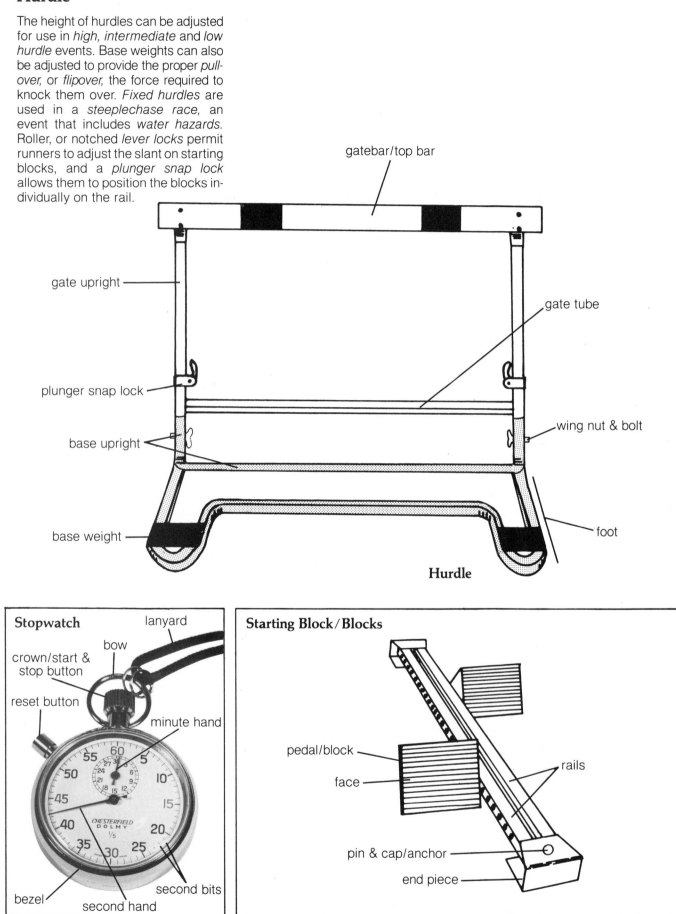

gatebar/top bar

gate upright

gate tube

plunger snap lock

wing nut & bolt

base upright

base weight

foot

Hurdle

Stopwatch

lanyard

bow

crown/start & stop button

reset button

minute hand

55 60 5
50 10
45 15
40 20
35 30 25

27 30
24 3
21 6
18 9
15 12

CHESTERFIELD
DOLMY
⅕

second bits

bezel

second hand

Starting Block / Blocks

pedal/block

face

rails

pin & cap/anchor

end piece

Pole Vault

The *fiberglass pole,* which replaced traditional *bamboo* and *metal poles,* enables a *vaulter* to catapult over the *bar.* A *high-jump pit* is similar to the pole vault, but the crossbar is considerably lower and there is no *box* in the *take-off area.*

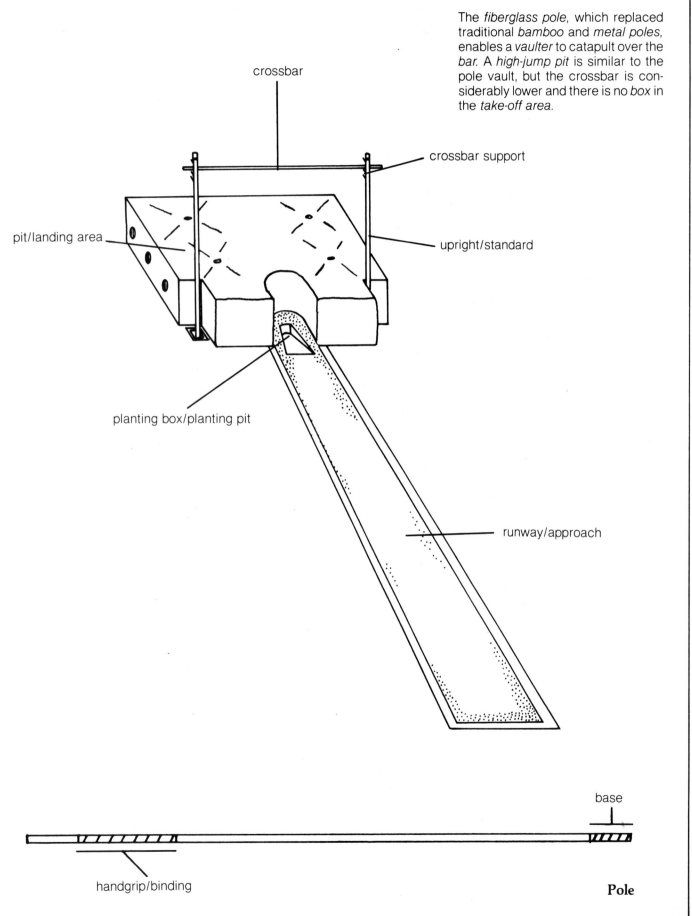

crossbar

crossbar support

pit/landing area

upright/standard

planting box/planting pit

runway/approach

base

handgrip/binding

Pole

Competitive Sports

Gymnastics

Protective *landing mats* are placed around each piece of gymnastic equipment when it is in use. In addition, during practice sessions, assistants called *spotters* stand by to aid the *gymnast.* Gymnastic competition called *floor exercises* takes place on lined *floor exercise mats.*

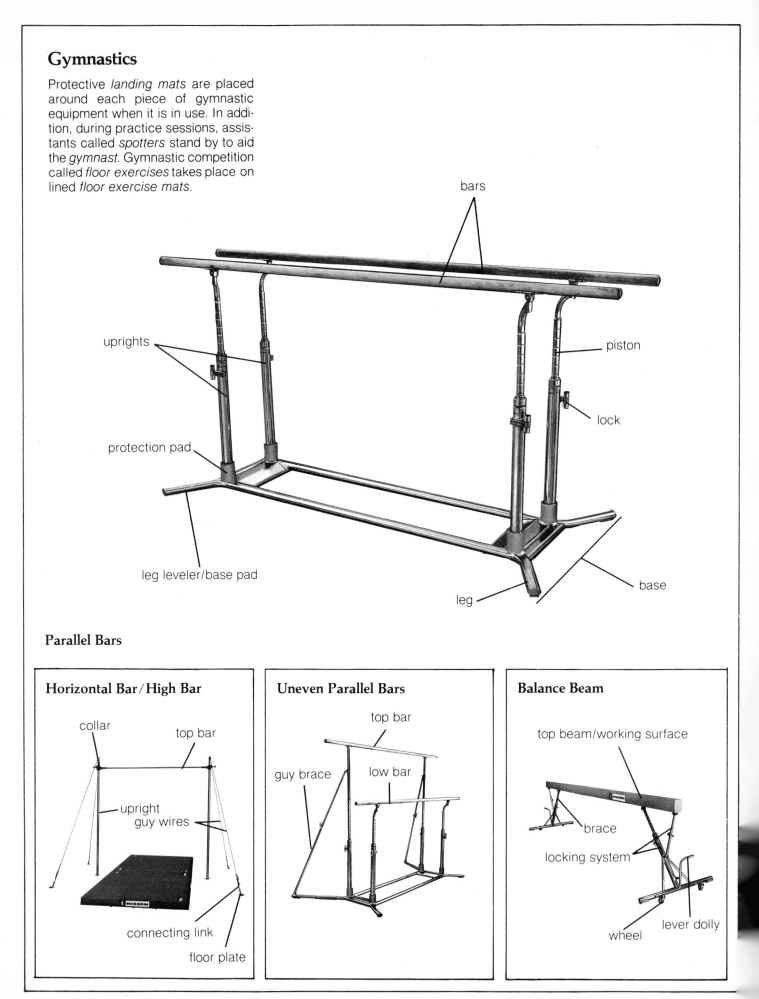

bars

uprights

piston

lock

protection pad

leg leveler/base pad

leg

base

Parallel Bars

Horizontal Bar/High Bar

collar

top bar

upright
guy wires

connecting link

floor plate

Uneven Parallel Bars

top bar

guy brace

low bar

Balance Beam

top beam/working surface

brace

locking system

wheel

lever dolly

Gymnastics

Some pommel horses, or *side horses*, can be converted into *vaulting*, or *long*, *horses* by removing the pommels and plugging the holes they fit in. *Vaulting boards*, or *springboards*, are used by *vaulters* to gain height when mounting the apparatus.

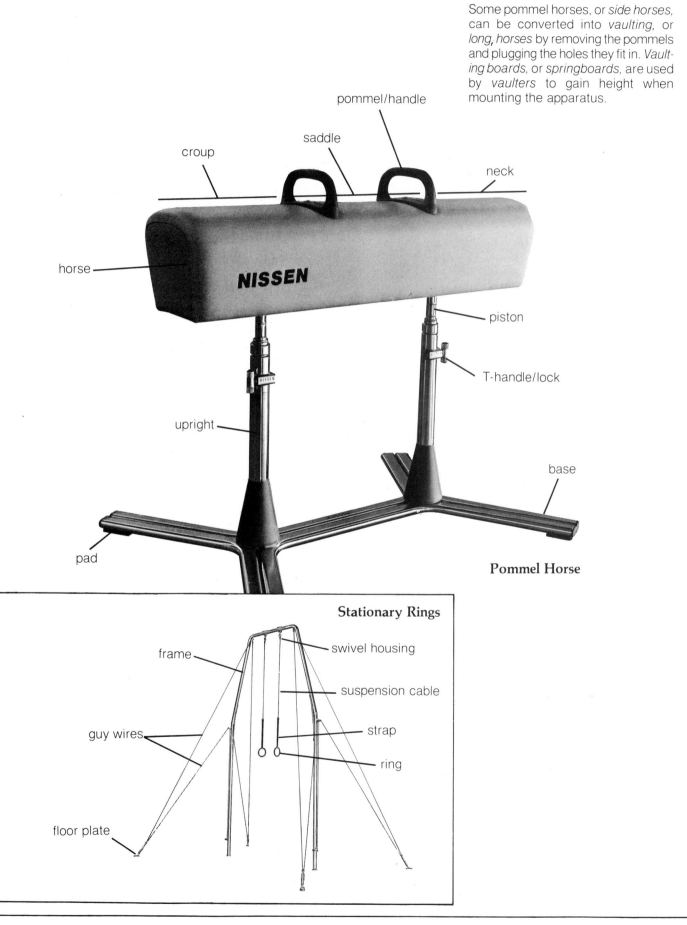

pommel/handle

saddle

croup

neck

horse

NISSEN

piston

upright

T-handle/lock

base

pad

Pommel Horse

Stationary Rings

frame

swivel housing

suspension cable

guy wires

strap

ring

floor plate

Competitive Sports

Trampoline

Trampolining, trampoline tumbling, or *rebound tumbling* is performed on the canvas or elastic-webbing bed. Smaller *trampolets* are often used as *springboards* for mounting gymnastic apparatus.

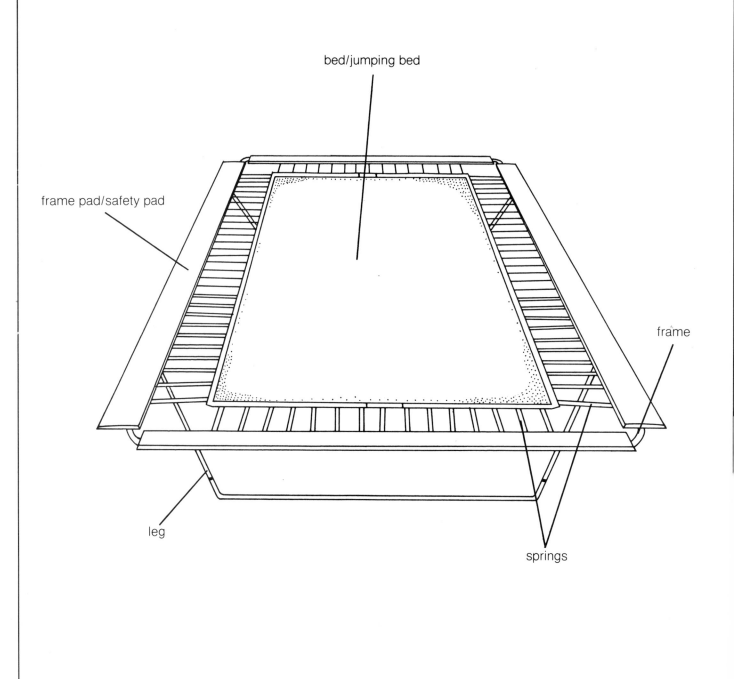

bed/jumping bed

frame pad/safety pad

frame

leg

springs

Boxing

In addition to the *sparring,* or practice, equipment shown here, *boxers* use a *mouthpiece* or *mouthguard* for protection of teeth. A *bell* at *ringside* is used to indicate the beginning and end of each *round.* Boxers rest on *stools* placed in their corners by assistants, or *handlers,* between rounds. Corners not used by fighters during these periods are called *neutral corners.*

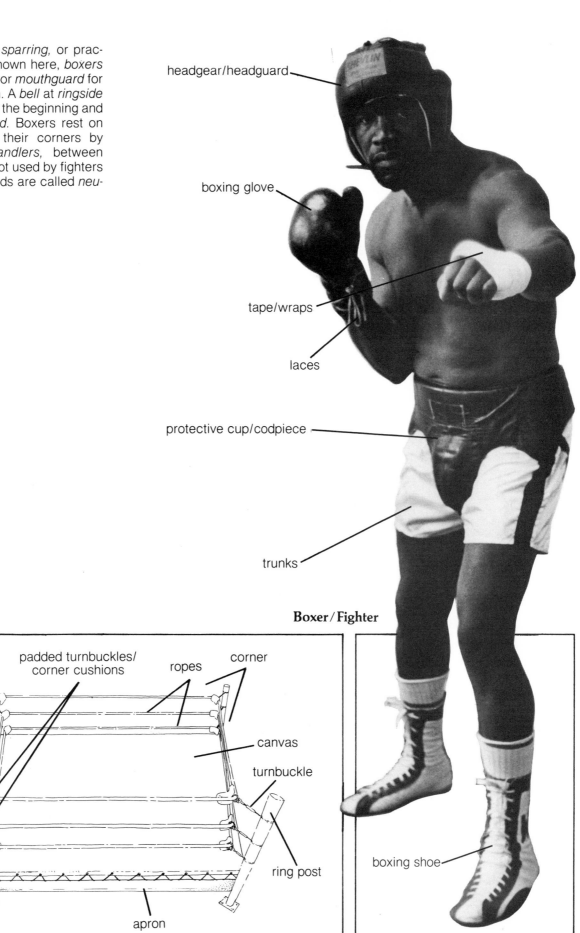

headgear/headguard

boxing glove

tape/wraps

laces

protective cup/codpiece

trunks

Boxer / Fighter

Boxing Ring

padded turnbuckles/
corner cushions

ropes

corner

canvas

turnbuckle

ring post

apron

boxing shoe

Golf

Clubs are numbered in order of increasing *loft*, the angle of the clubface from the vertical, with woods numbered from one to five and the irons numbered two through nine. A *golfer* may also carry a *pitching wedge*, a *sand wedge* and a putter. The spot where the ball lands after being hit is called the *lie*.

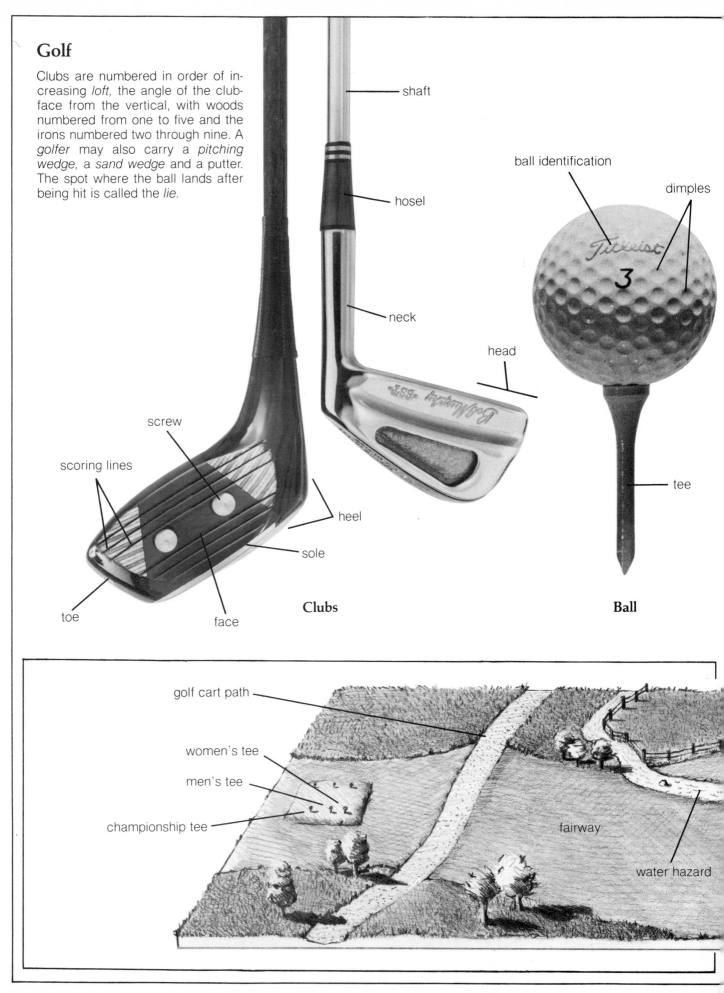

shaft

hosel

neck

head

ball identification

dimples

tee

screw

scoring lines

heel

sole

toe

face

Clubs

Ball

golf cart path

women's tee

men's tee

championship tee

fairway

water hazard

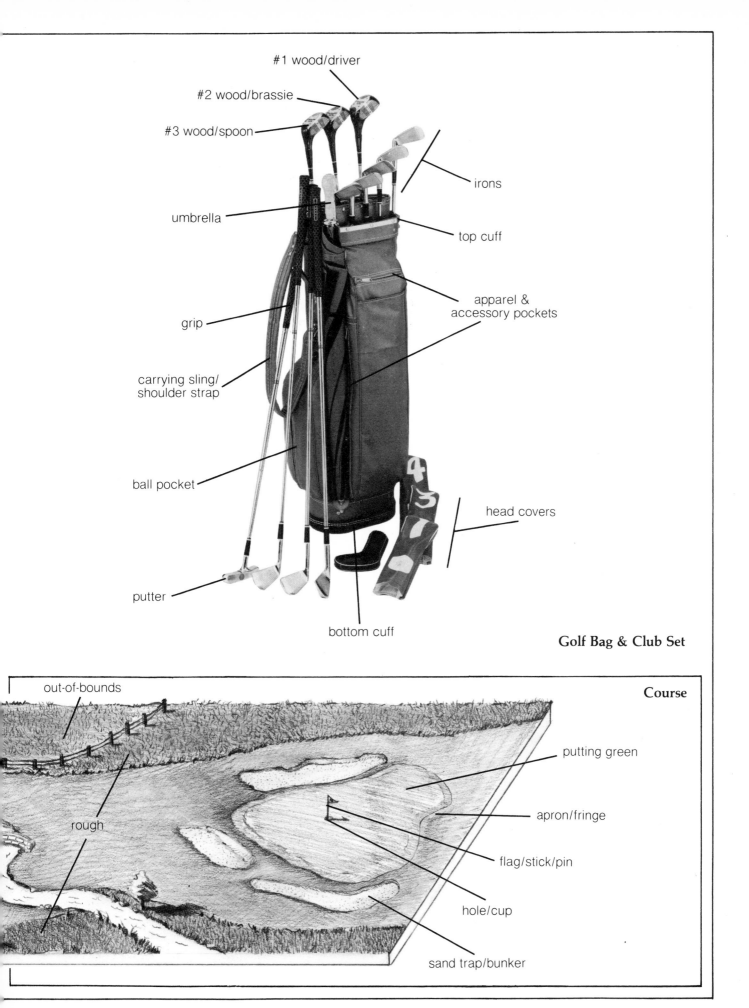

#1 wood/driver

#2 wood/brassie

#3 wood/spoon

irons

umbrella

top cuff

grip

apparel &
accessory pockets

carrying sling/
shoulder strap

ball pocket

head covers

putter

bottom cuff

Golf Bag & Club Set

Course

out-of-bounds

putting green

apron/fringe

rough

flag/stick/pin

hole/cup

sand trap/bunker

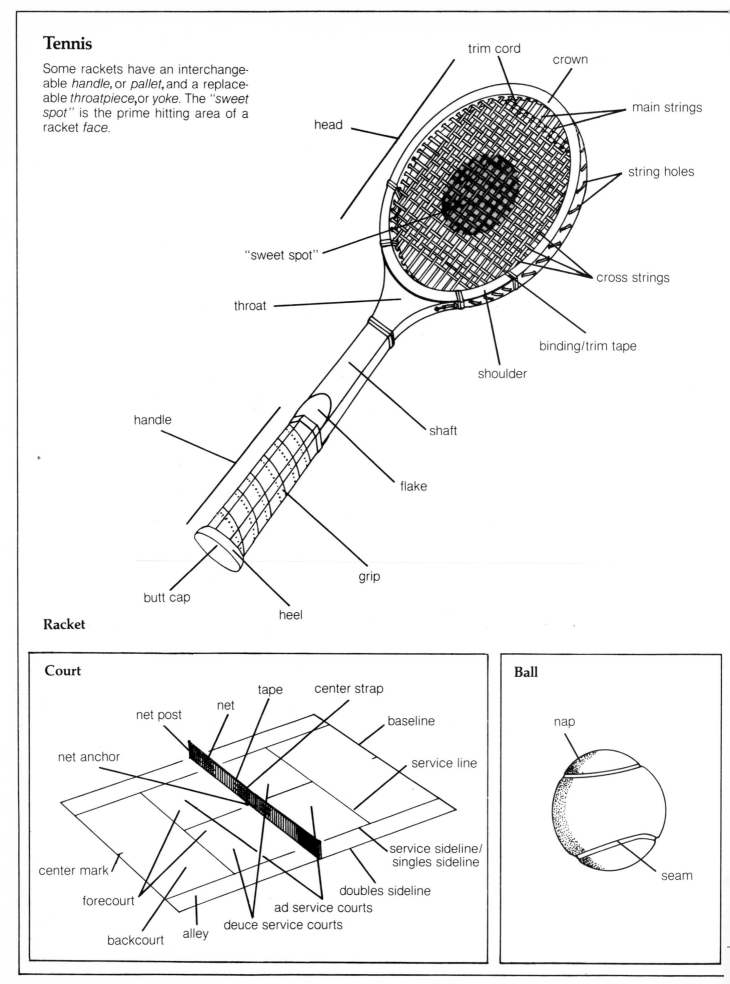

Tennis

Some rackets have an interchangeable *handle,* or *pallet,* and a replaceable *throatpiece,* or *yoke.* The *"sweet spot"* is the prime hitting area of a racket *face.*

trim cord

crown

main strings

head

string holes

"sweet spot"

cross strings

throat

binding/trim tape

shoulder

handle

shaft

flake

grip

butt cap

heel

Racket

Court

net post

net

tape

center strap

baseline

net anchor

service line

center mark

service sideline/
singles sideline

forecourt

doubles sideline

backcourt

alley

deuce service courts

ad service courts

Ball

nap

seam

Handball and Squash Courts

The composite court shown here includes both handball and squash rackets terms. In each case, the court is entered through a small *door* in the *back wall*. In handball, players alternately hit a hard black *ball* with their hands, whereas in squash a soft rubber ball is hit with a *racket*.

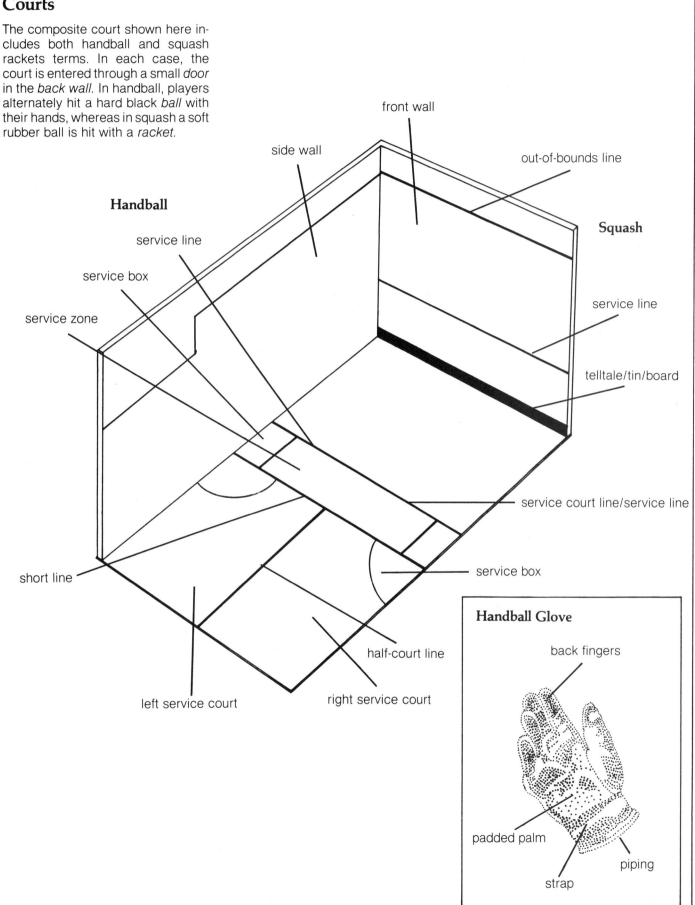

front wall

side wall

Handball

out-of-bounds line

service line

Squash

service box

service line

service zone

telltale/tin/board

service court line/service line

service box

short line

half-court line

left service court

right service court

Handball Glove

back fingers

padded palm

piping

strap

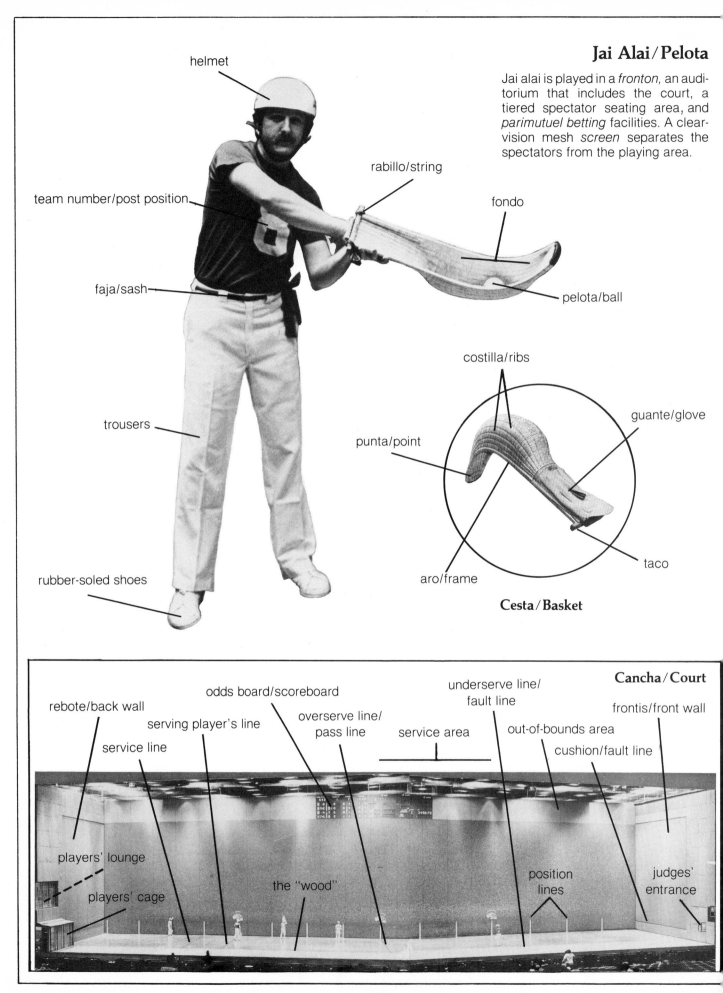

helmet

Jai Alai/Pelota

Jai alai is played in a *fronton,* an auditorium that includes the court, a tiered spectator seating area, and *parimutuel betting* facilities. A clear-vision mesh *screen* separates the spectators from the playing area.

rabillo/string

team number/post position

fondo

faja/sash

pelota/ball

trousers

costilla/ribs

punta/point

guante/glove

rubber-soled shoes

aro/frame

taco

Cesta/Basket

Cancha/Court

rebote/back wall

odds board/scoreboard

underserve line/
fault line

frontis/front wall

serving player's line

overserve line/
pass line

service area

out-of-bounds area

service line

cushion/fault line

players' lounge

the "wood"

position
lines

judges'
entrance

players' cage

Fencing

Foils, *sabres* or *épées,* which differ slightly in weight and design, are used in fencing *matches* or *bouts.* Each *fencer* must wear a chest-protecting *plastron* under his jacket, and women must also wear *breast protectors.* Four *judges* and a *director,* or *president,* referee *dry* or *non-electric* matches.

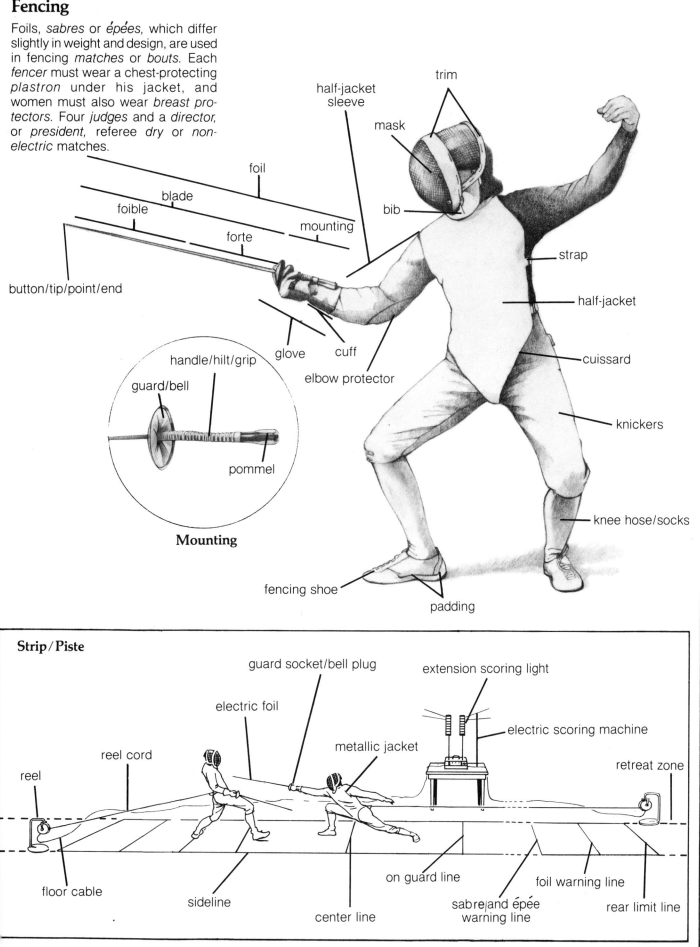

trim

half-jacket sleeve

mask

foil

blade

foible

mounting

forte

bib

button/tip/point/end

strap

half-jacket

glove

cuff

cuissard

elbow protector

handle/hilt/grip

guard/bell

knickers

pommel

knee hose/socks

Mounting

fencing shoe

padding

Strip/Piste

guard socket/bell plug

extension scoring light

electric foil

electric scoring machine

metallic jacket

reel cord

reel

retreat zone

floor cable

sideline

on guard line

foil warning line

center line

sabre and épée warning line

rear limit line

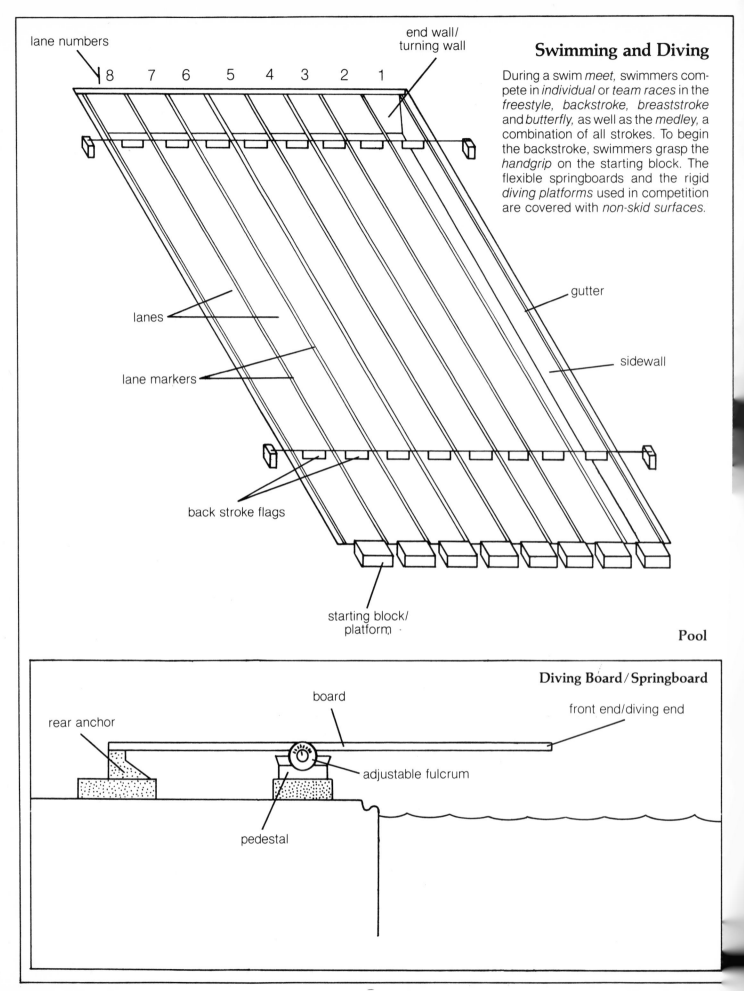

lane numbers

8 7 6 5 4 3 2 1

end wall/
turning wall

Swimming and Diving

During a swim *meet,* swimmers compete in *individual* or *team races* in the *freestyle, backstroke, breaststroke* and *butterfly,* as well as the *medley,* a combination of all strokes. To begin the backstroke, swimmers grasp the *handgrip* on the starting block. The flexible springboards and the rigid *diving platforms* used in competition are covered with *non-skid surfaces.*

lanes

lane markers

gutter

sidewall

back stroke flags

starting block/
platform

Pool

Diving Board / Springboard

rear anchor

board

front end/diving end

adjustable fulcrum

pedestal

Bowling

The strike pocket opposite to the hand delivering the ball is called the *Brooklyn pocket* or *Jersey pocket*. Pins are reset by a mechanical *pinsetter* or *pinspotter*. *Duckpins* and *candlepins* are forms of bowling in which differently shaped pins and lighter, smaller balls are used.

kingpin

mother-in-law

widow

headpin

weight

bridge

16

finger hole

span

thumb hole

left-handed strike pocket

right-handed strike pocket

Pins / Tenpins

Bowling Ball

Lane / Alley

pit

gutter/channel

spots/target arrows

foul line

approach/runway

cushion

setup/rack

ball return

12' markers

15' markers

Competitive Sports

Shuffleboard and Croquet

A shuffleboard game may begin at either end of a *court.* That end is designated the *head.* The opposite end is the *foot.* In croquet, *strikers* start at the *home stake* and return to it after going through wickets and hitting the *turning stake.*

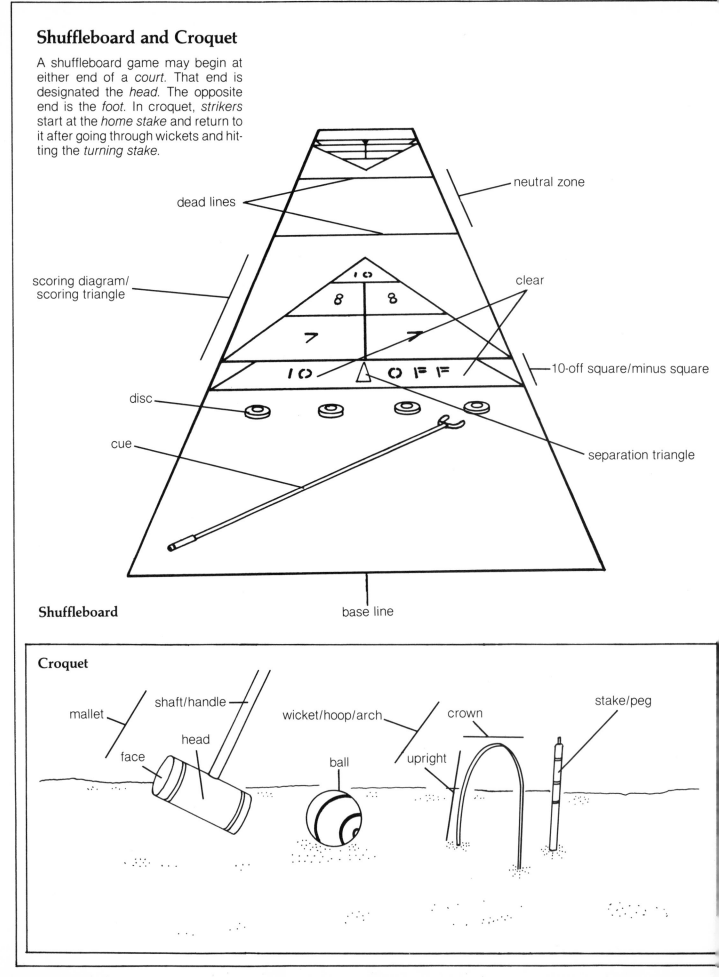

neutral zone

dead lines

scoring diagram/ scoring triangle

clear

10-off square/minus square

disc

separation triangle

cue

Shuffleboard

base line

Croquet

mallet

shaft/handle

wicket/hoop/arch

crown

stake/peg

head

face

ball

upright

Volleyball and Badminton

In volleyball, an inflated ball hit sharply is called a *spike* or *kill*. Badminton is played with a *racket* or *bat* whose parts are similar to those of a tennis racket. Some badminton shuttles have nylon *skirts* rather than feathers.

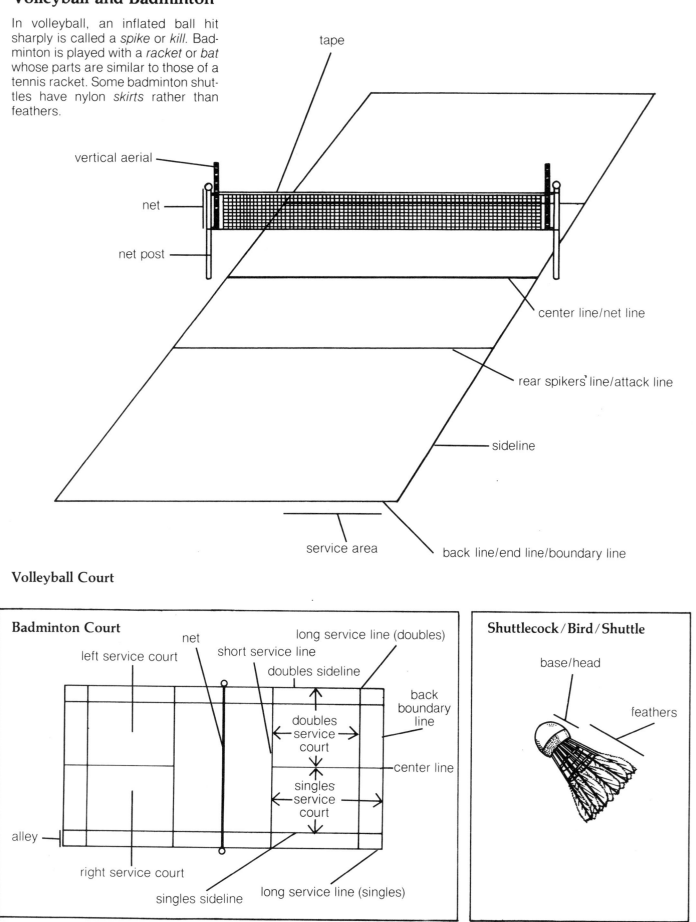

tape

vertical aerial

net

net post

center line/net line

rear spikers' line/attack line

sideline

service area

back line/end line/boundary line

Volleyball Court

Badminton Court

left service court

net

short service line

long service line (doubles)

doubles sideline

back boundary line

doubles service court

center line

singles service court

alley

right service court

singles sideline

long service line (singles)

Shuttlecock/Bird/Shuttle

base/head

feathers

Competitive Sports

Billiards and Pool

Billiard and pool tables are usually covered with a dark green cloth called *felt*, or *bed cloth*. A triangular *rack* is used to position object balls at the beginning of a pool or *snooker* game. *Chalk* is used on cue tips. A point scored in billiards is called a *carom*.

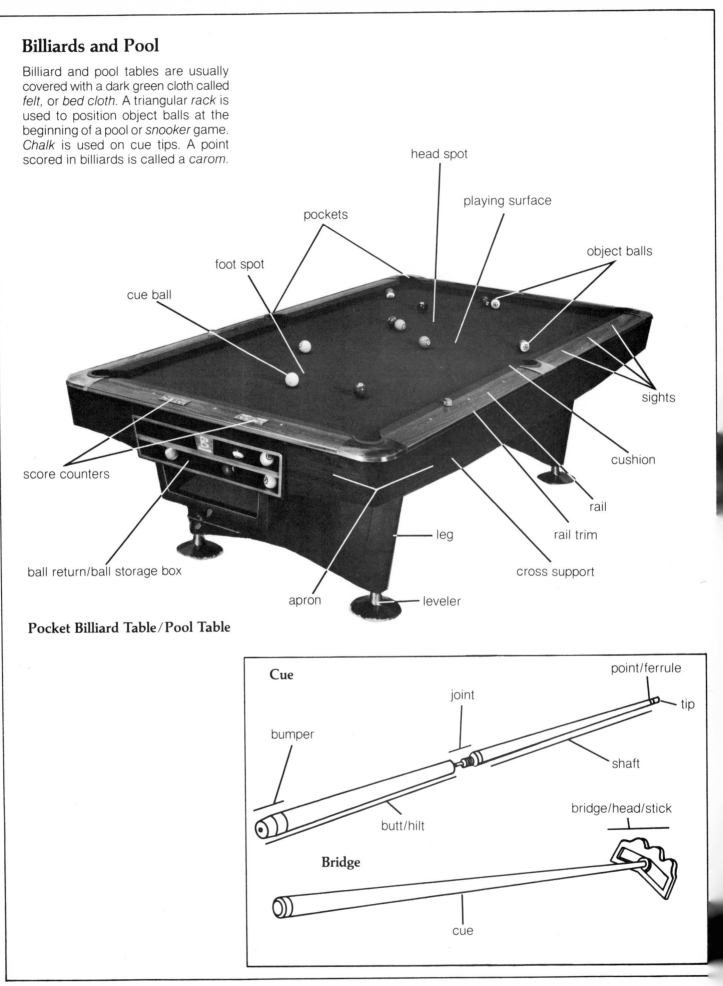

Pocket Billiard Table / Pool Table

Cue

Bridge

Ping-Pong/Table Tennis

Paddles have two types of grips, *shake-hands grips* and *penhold grips,* and two types of faces, *rubber* and *sponge.* The game is played with a ping-pong *ball.*

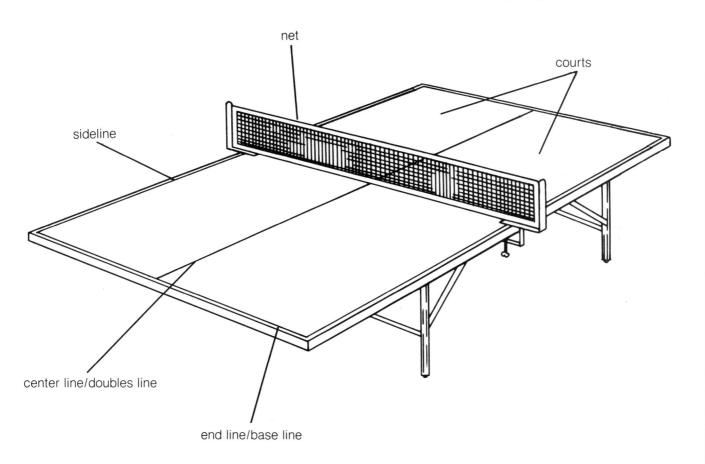

net

courts

sideline

center line/doubles line

end line/base line

Ping-Pong Table

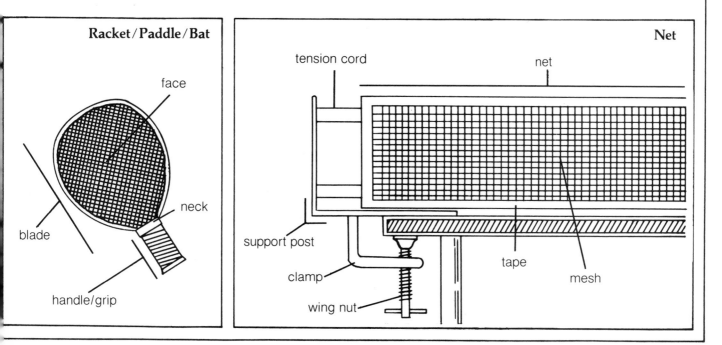

Racket/Paddle/Bat

face

neck

blade

handle/grip

Net

tension cord

net

support post

clamp

wing nut

tape

mesh

Table Games

Darts

Darts, or *darting*, is played by two *dartists* or teams of from two to eight. Darts are scored on *point of entry* on the board *face*. Of the *clock-face games, tournament darts* is the most popular. Other games include *round-the-clock, all-fives, baseball, high score, cricket, 51-in-5's, 14-stop, killer, Mulligan, 301, sudden death,* and *Shanghai.*

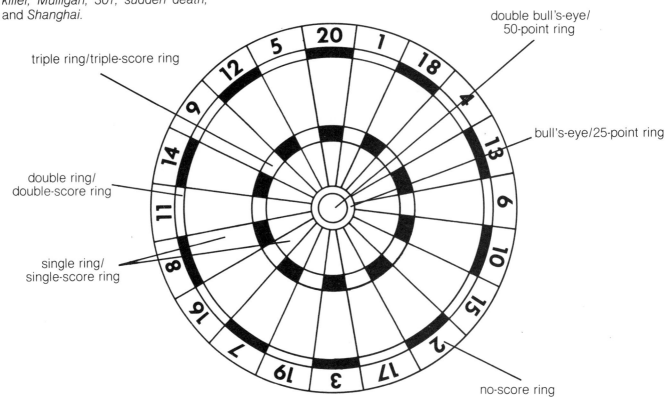

triple ring/triple-score ring

double bull's-eye/ 50-point ring

bull's-eye/25-point ring

double ring/ double-score ring

single ring/ single-score ring

no-score ring

Dart Board/English Clock

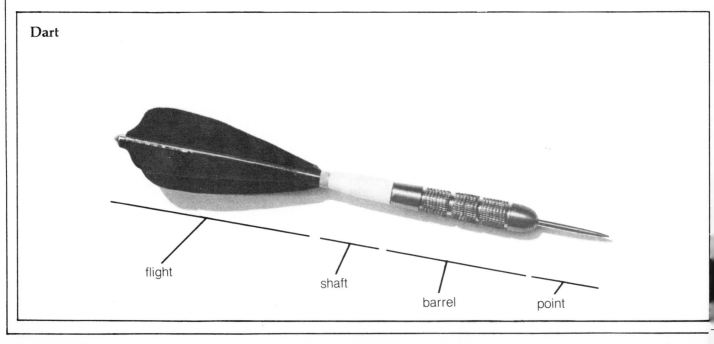

Dart

flight

shaft

barrel

point

Kites

Bridle lines are attached to the spine through holes in the front cover. They are shown here on the rear of the kite only for illustrative purposes. Among the limitless varieties of kites, there are six major categories: flat, *plane,* or *two-stick kites; bowed kites,* sometimes known by their classic example, the *Eddy;* box, or *cellular,* kites; *compound kites,* represented by the *Conyne kite; semiflexible kites,* such as *delta-keels;* and *Rogallos,* or *flexible,* kites. *Fighting kites* have two flying lines.

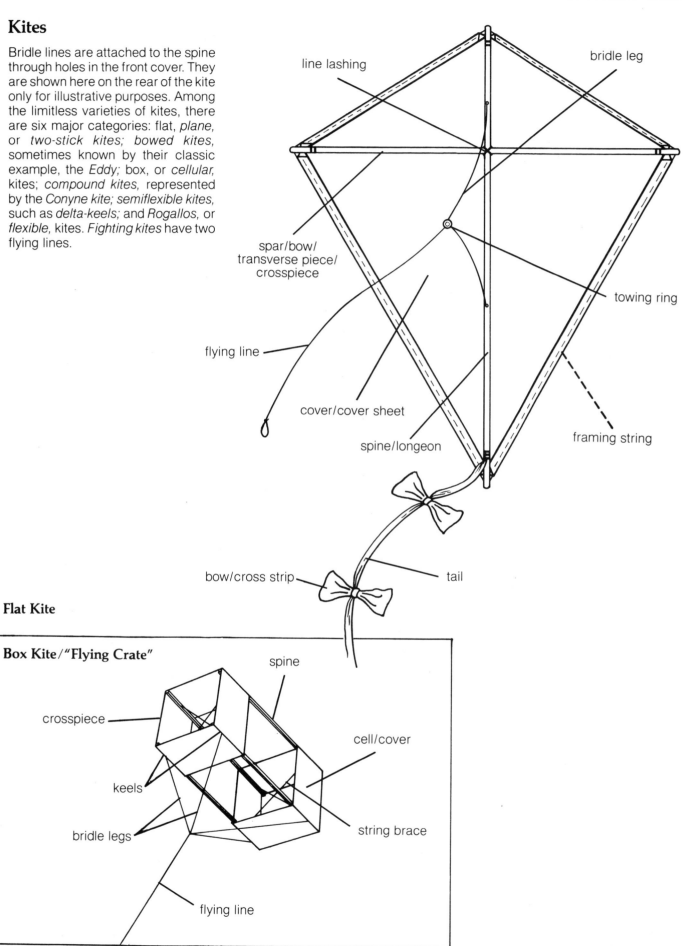

line lashing

bridle leg

spar/bow/ transverse piece/ crosspiece

towing ring

flying line

cover/cover sheet

spine/longeon

framing string

bow/cross strip

tail

Flat Kite

Box Kite/"Flying Crate"

spine

crosspiece

cell/cover

keels

string brace

bridle legs

flying line

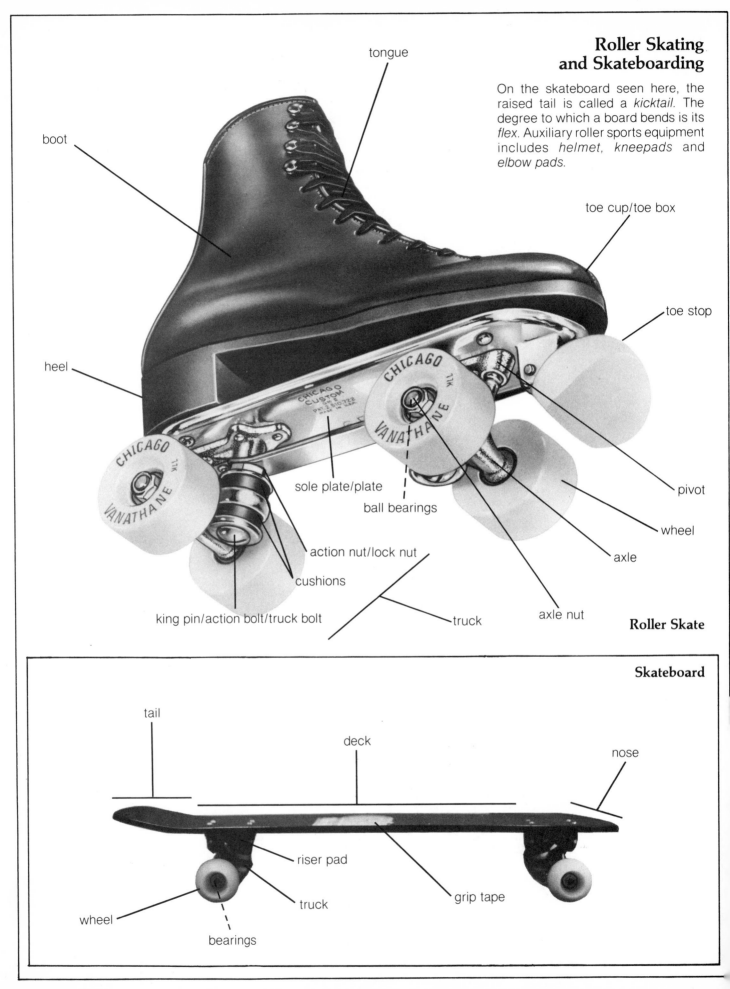

Roller Skating and Skateboarding

On the skateboard seen here, the raised tail is called a *kicktail*. The degree to which a board bends is its *flex*. Auxiliary roller sports equipment includes *helmet*, *kneepads* and *elbow pads*.

tongue

boot

toe cup/toe box

toe stop

heel

CHICAGO CUSTOM

CHICAGO VANATHANE 11k

CHICAGO VANATHANE 11k

sole plate/plate

ball bearings

pivot

action nut/lock nut

wheel

cushions

axle

king pin/action bolt/truck bolt

truck

axle nut

Roller Skate

Skateboard

tail

deck

nose

riser pad

truck

grip tape

wheel

bearings

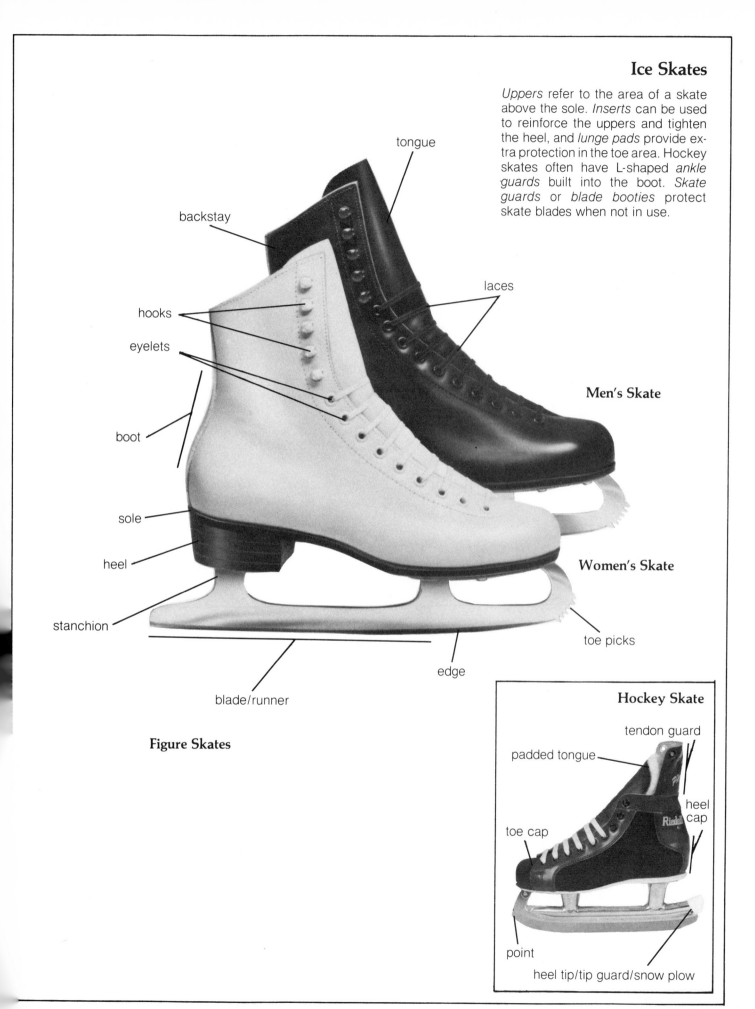

Ice Skates

Uppers refer to the area of a skate above the sole. *Inserts* can be used to reinforce the uppers and tighten the heel, and *lunge pads* provide extra protection in the toe area. Hockey skates often have L-shaped *ankle guards* built into the boot. *Skate guards* or *blade booties* protect skate blades when not in use.

tongue

backstay

laces

hooks

eyelets

Men's Skate

boot

sole

Women's Skate

heel

stanchion

toe picks

edge

blade/runner

Figure Skates

Hockey Skate

tendon guard

padded tongue

heel cap

toe cap

point

heel tip/tip guard/snow plow

Individual Sports

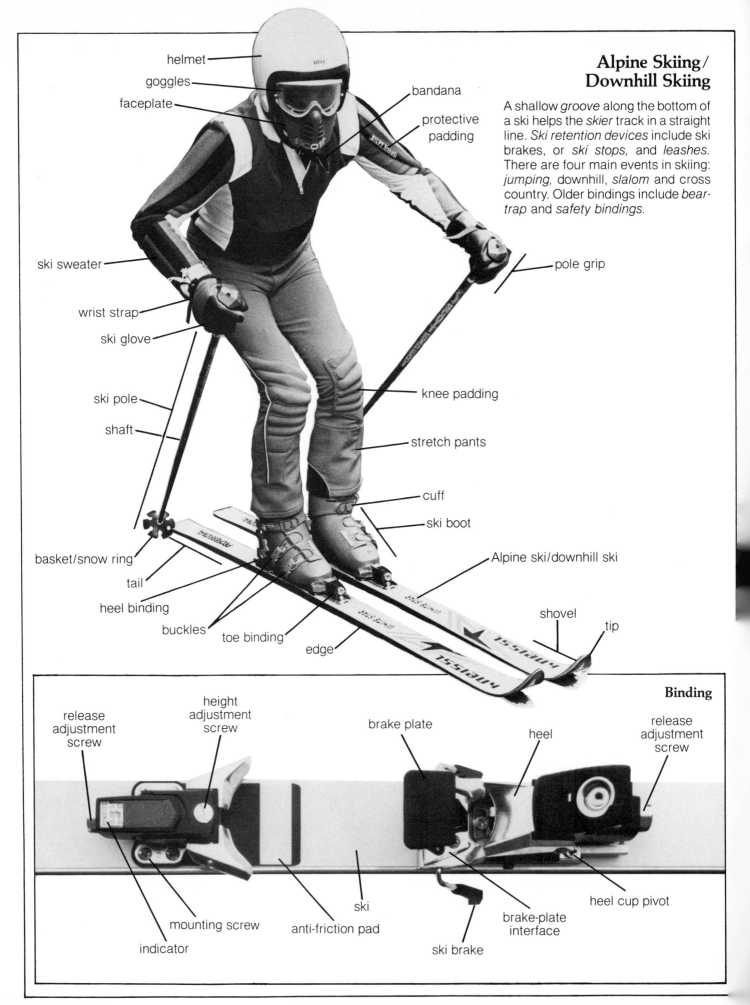

Alpine Skiing/ Downhill Skiing

A shallow *groove* along the bottom of a ski helps the *skier* track in a straight line. *Ski retention devices* include ski brakes, or *ski stops*, and *leashes*. There are four main events in skiing: *jumping*, downhill, *slalom* and cross country. Older bindings include *bear-trap* and *safety bindings*.

helmet

goggles

faceplate

bandana

protective padding

ski sweater

pole grip

wrist strap

ski glove

knee padding

ski pole

shaft

stretch pants

cuff

ski boot

Alpine ski/downhill ski

basket/snow ring

tail

heel binding

buckles

toe binding

edge

shovel

tip

Binding

release adjustment screw

height adjustment screw

brake plate

heel

release adjustment screw

mounting screw

indicator

anti-friction pad

ski

ski brake

brake-plate interface

heel cup pivot

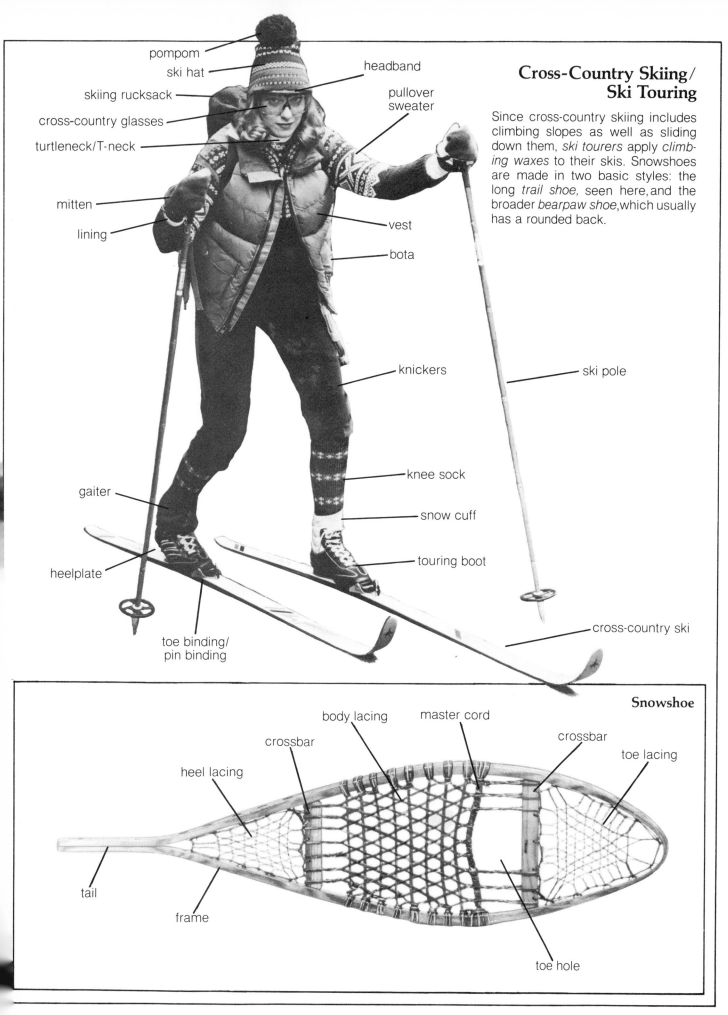

pompom

ski hat

skiing rucksack

cross-country glasses

turtleneck/T-neck

mitten

lining

gaiter

heelplate

toe binding/
pin binding

headband

pullover
sweater

vest

bota

knickers

knee sock

snow cuff

touring boot

ski pole

cross-country ski

Cross-Country Skiing/ Ski Touring

Since cross-country skiing includes climbing slopes as well as sliding down them, *ski tourers* apply *climbing waxes* to their skis. Snowshoes are made in two basic styles: the long *trail shoe,* seen here, and the broader *bearpaw shoe,* which usually has a rounded back.

Snowshoe

body lacing

master cord

crossbar

crossbar

heel lacing

toe lacing

tail

frame

toe hole

321

Individual Sports

Sledding and Tobogganing

Bobsleds, driven by two- or four-man crews, have a racing *cowl* and toothed metal *brake.* Small racing sleds called *luges* are controlled by reclining drivers using their feet and *hand ropes.*

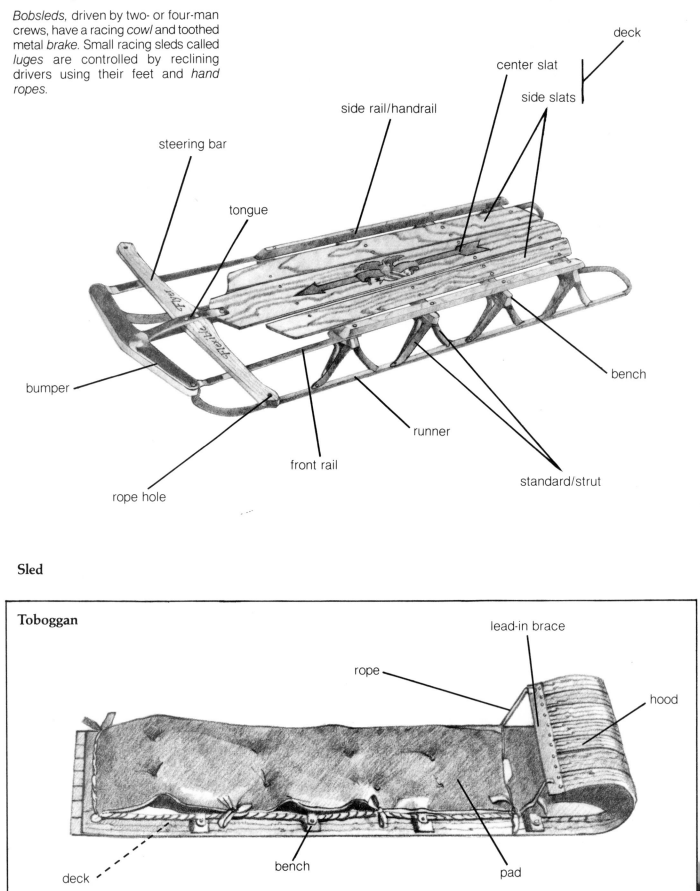

deck

center slat

side slats

side rail/handrail

steering bar

tongue

bumper

bench

runner

front rail

standard/strut

rope hole

Sled

Toboggan

lead-in brace

rope

hood

bench

pad

deck

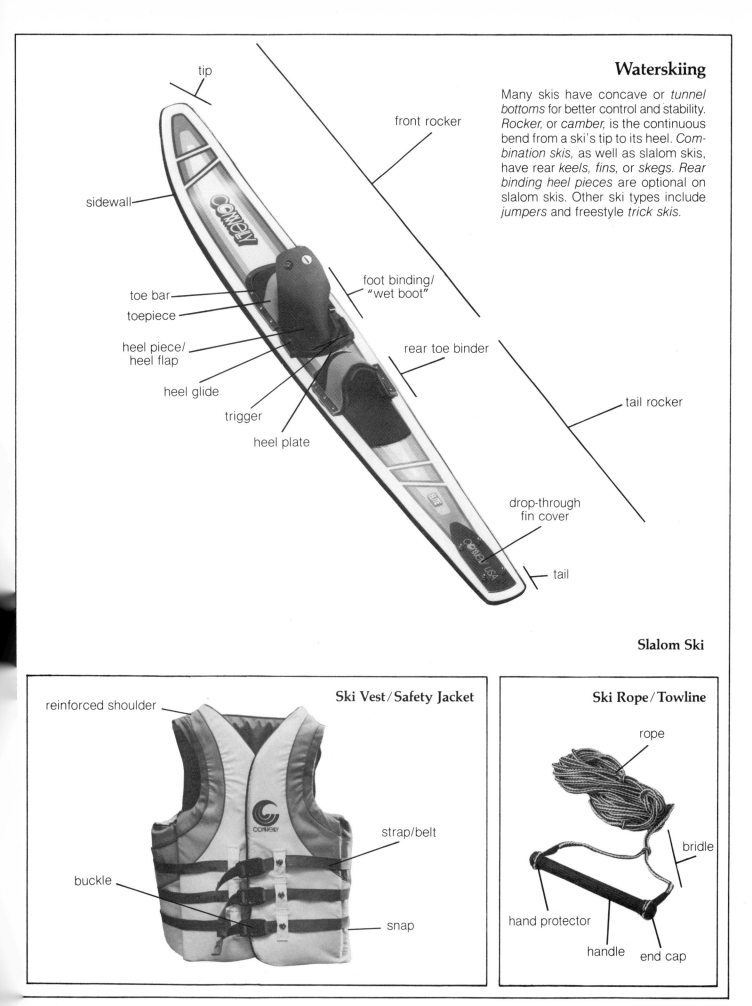

Waterskiing

Many skis have concave or *tunnel bottoms* for better control and stability. *Rocker,* or *camber,* is the continuous bend from a ski's tip to its heel. *Combination skis,* as well as slalom skis, have rear *keels, fins,* or *skegs. Rear binding heel pieces* are optional on slalom skis. Other ski types include *jumpers* and freestyle *trick skis.*

tip

front rocker

sidewall

foot binding/ "wet boot"

toe bar

toepiece

heel piece/ heel flap

rear toe binder

heel glide

tail rocker

trigger

heel plate

drop-through fin cover

tail

Slalom Ski

Ski Vest/Safety Jacket

reinforced shoulder

strap/belt

buckle

snap

Ski Rope/Towline

rope

bridle

hand protector

handle

end cap

Individual Sports

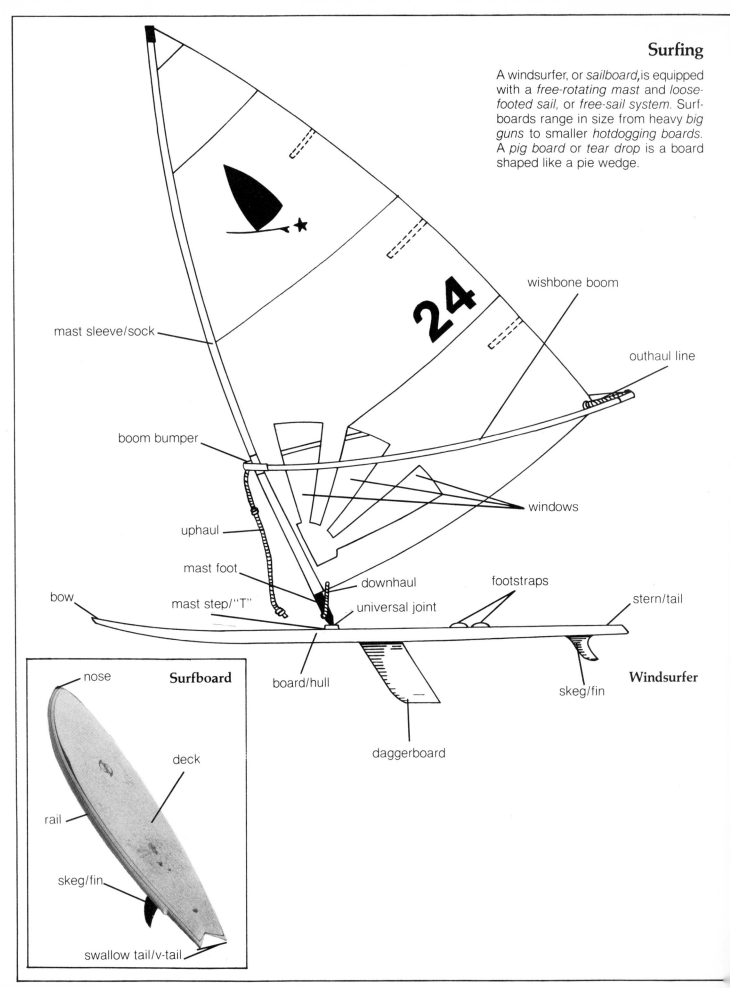

Surfing

A windsurfer, or *sailboard,* is equipped with a *free-rotating mast* and *loose-footed sail,* or *free-sail system.* Surfboards range in size from heavy *big guns* to smaller *hotdogging boards.* A *pig board* or *tear drop* is a board shaped like a pie wedge.

mast sleeve/sock

wishbone boom

outhaul line

boom bumper

windows

uphaul

mast foot

downhaul

footstraps

bow

stern/tail

mast step/"T"

universal joint

Windsurfer

skeg/fin

board/hull

daggerboard

Surfboard

nose

deck

rail

skeg/fin

swallow tail/v-tail

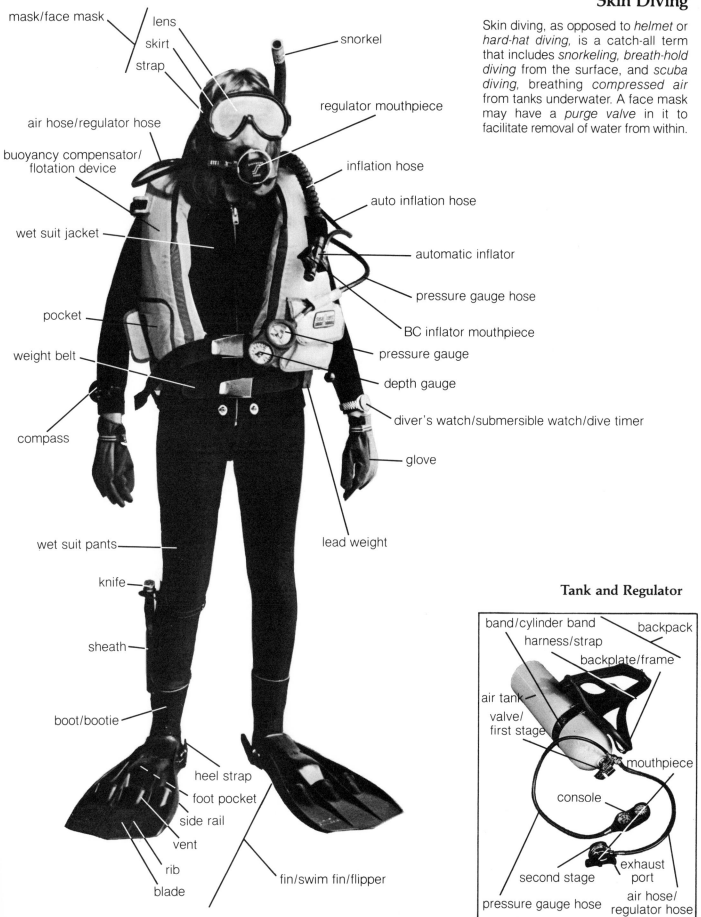

mask/face mask

lens

skirt

strap

snorkel

regulator mouthpiece

air hose/regulator hose

buoyancy compensator/
flotation device

inflation hose

auto inflation hose

automatic inflator

pressure gauge hose

wet suit jacket

BC inflator mouthpiece

pocket

pressure gauge

weight belt

depth gauge

diver's watch/submersible watch/dive timer

compass

glove

lead weight

wet suit pants

knife

sheath

boot/bootie

heel strap

foot pocket

side rail

vent

rib

blade

fin/swim fin/flipper

Skin Diving

Skin diving, as opposed to *helmet* or *hard-hat diving,* is a catch-all term that includes *snorkeling, breath-hold diving* from the surface, and *scuba diving,* breathing *compressed air* from tanks underwater. A face mask may have a *purge valve* in it to facilitate removal of water from within.

Tank and Regulator

band/cylinder band

backpack

harness/strap

backplate/frame

air tank

valve/
first stage

mouthpiece

console

second stage

exhaust
port

pressure gauge hose

air hose/
regulator hose

Hot Air Balloon

A balloon, or *montgolfier*, rises when *ballast*, usually water or *sandbags*, is jettisoned. A *drag* or *trail rope*, hangs from the balloon to give it stability in flight and slow it down upon landing. To deflate the balloon a *ripping panel*, or *rip panel*, near the top is opened.

parachute valve/
parachute vent

envelope/bag

registration number/
"N" number

envelope
graphic

panel seams

gore seams

load cords

panels

bottom girdle

skirt

skirt band

burner

suspension rope

load ring

padding

basket handle

mouth

valve line

burner support

basket/carriage

scuff leather

tether line

Parachuting and Hang Gliding

Unless attached to a *static line*, which automatically opens a *chute* once a *jumper* has cleared the *jump plane*, a *sky diver* can *free-fall* before pulling his *rip cord*.

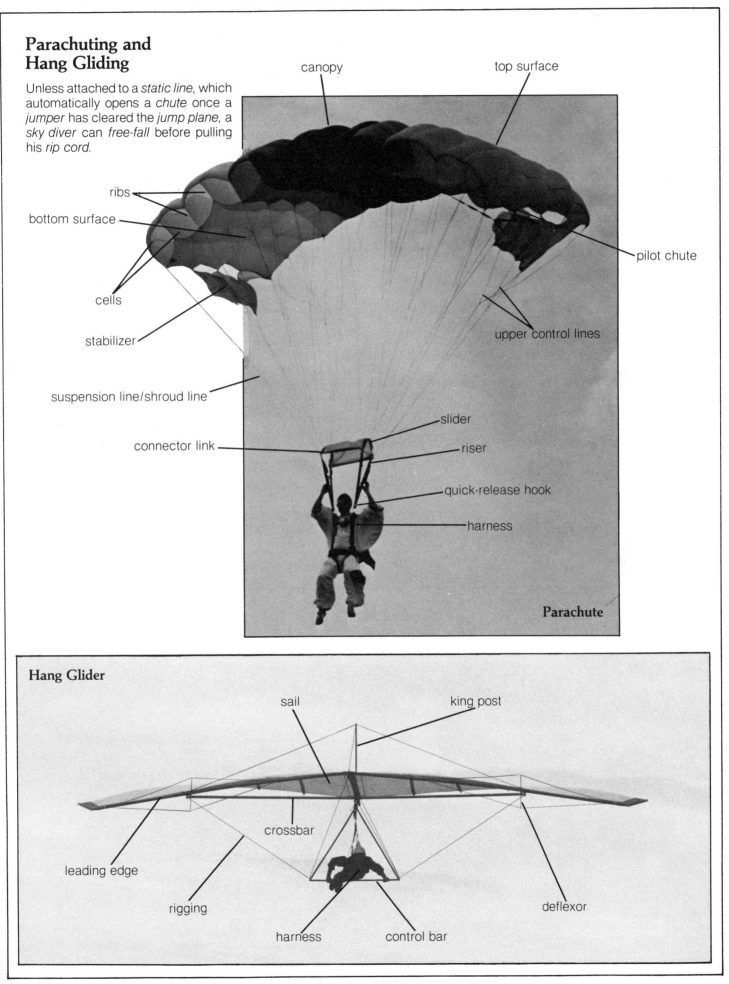

canopy

top surface

ribs

bottom surface

cells

stabilizer

pilot chute

upper control lines

suspension line/shroud line

slider

connector link

riser

quick-release hook

harness

Parachute

Hang Glider

sail

king post

crossbar

leading edge

rigging

harness

control bar

deflexor

Individual Sports

Mountain Climbing

Mountaineers use nylon webbing for *shoulder slings* and *swami belts.* Carabiners, either oval- or D-shaped, have spring-loaded *gates* for connecting various pieces of climbing equipment. Unlike *pitons,* which are hammered into cracks, nuts are wedged into cracks and easily removed. *Icescrews,* ring-topped threaded tubes, are actually screwed into the ice for protection.

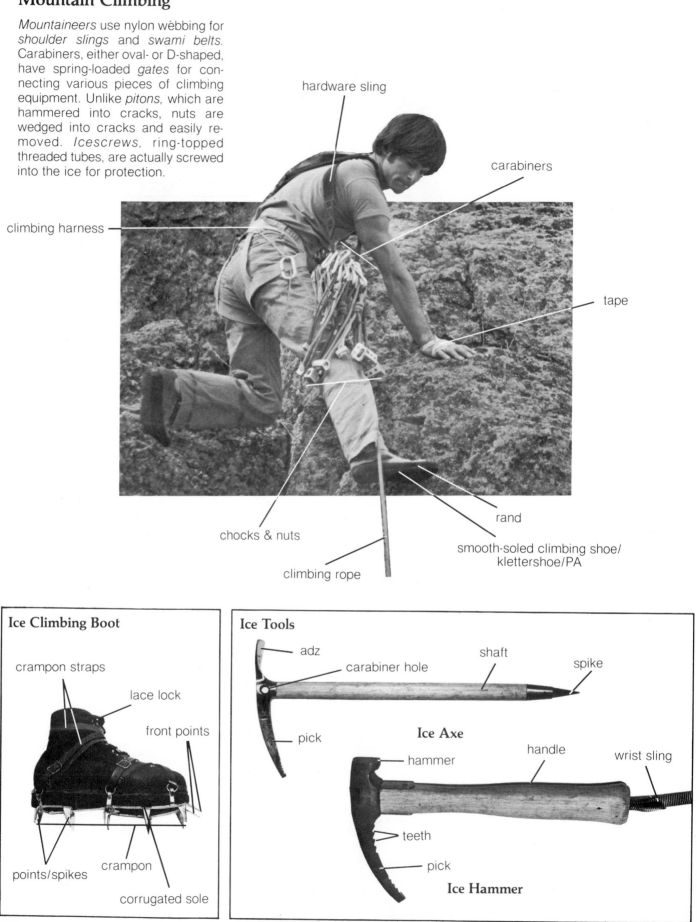

hardware sling

carabiners

climbing harness

tape

chocks & nuts

rand

climbing rope

smooth-soled climbing shoe/
klettershoe/PA

Ice Climbing Boot

crampon straps

lace lock

front points

points/spikes

crampon

corrugated sole

Ice Tools

adz

carabiner hole

shaft

spike

pick

Ice Axe

hammer

handle

wrist sling

teeth

pick

Ice Hammer

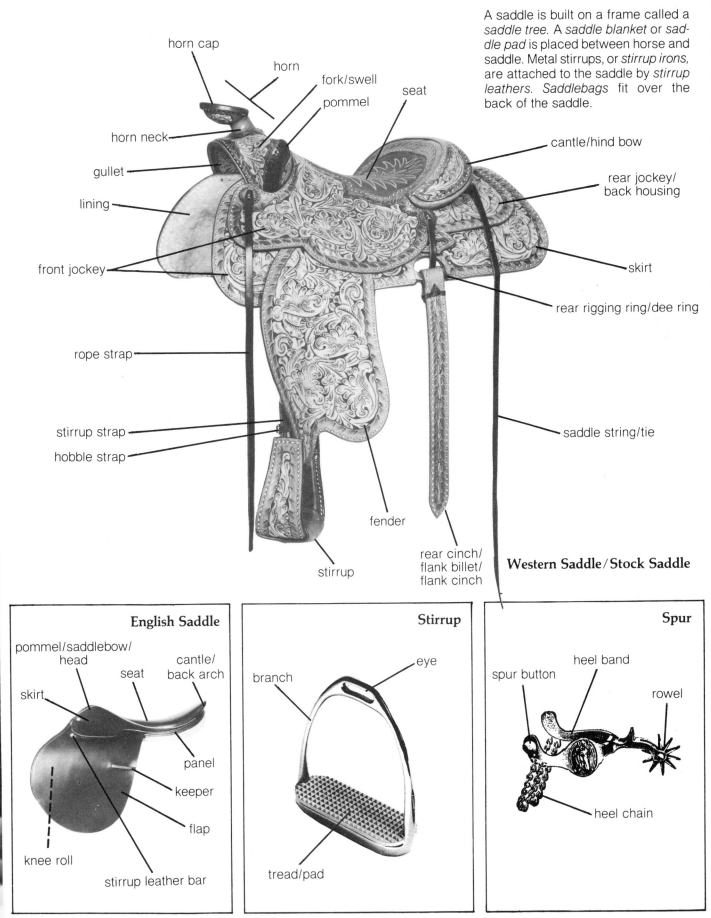

Riding Equipment

A saddle is built on a frame called a *saddle tree*. A *saddle blanket* or *saddle pad* is placed between horse and saddle. Metal stirrups, or *stirrup irons*, are attached to the saddle by *stirrup leathers*. *Saddlebags* fit over the back of the saddle.

horn cap

horn

fork/swell

seat

pommel

horn neck

cantle/hind bow

gullet

rear jockey/back housing

lining

front jockey

skirt

rear rigging ring/dee ring

rope strap

saddle string/tie

stirrup strap

hobble strap

fender

stirrup

rear cinch/flank billet/flank cinch

Western Saddle/Stock Saddle

English Saddle

pommel/saddlebow/head

cantle/back arch

seat

skirt

panel

keeper

flap

stirrup leather bar

knee roll

Stirrup

branch

eye

tread/pad

Spur

heel band

spur button

rowel

heel chain

Flat Racing

The equipment used on a racehorse is called the *tack*. *Thoroughbreds* start from a fixed *starting gate,* while harness racers start from a car-pulled *moving gate.* The most desirable *post position* in a race is gate number one, the *pole position* closest to the *rail.* Bettors pick horses to finish first, second and third, or *win, place* and *show.* Picking all three finishers in the right order is called a *trifecta.*

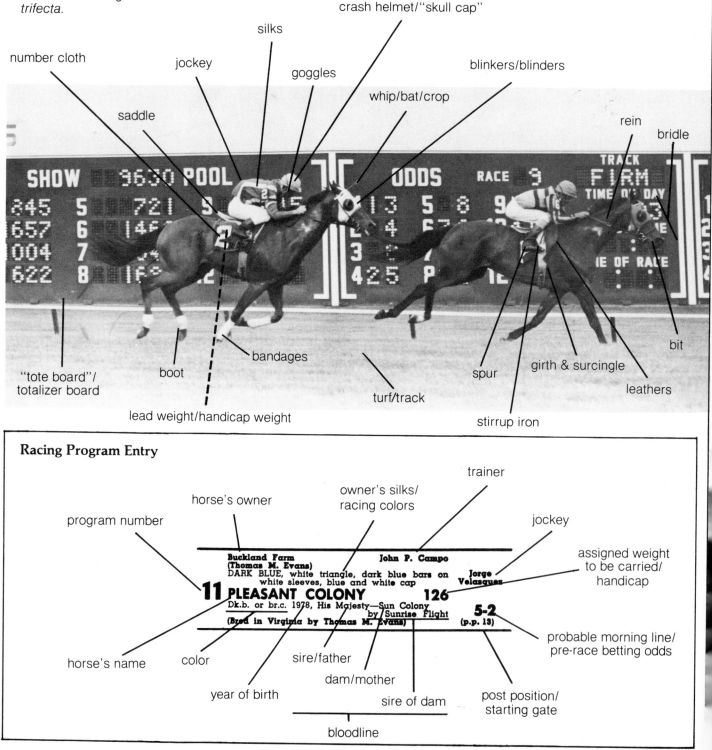

crash helmet/"skull cap"

silks

blinkers/blinders

number cloth

jockey

goggles

whip/bat/crop

rein

bridle

saddle

SHOW 9650 POOL ODDS RACE 9 TRACK FIRM
TIME OF DAY
845 5 721
657 6 146
004 7 16
622 8 16

bandages

boot

bit

"tote board"/ totalizer board

turf/track

spur

girth & surcingle

leathers

lead weight/handicap weight

stirrup iron

Racing Program Entry

horse's owner

owner's silks/ racing colors

trainer

program number

jockey

Buckland Farm
(Thomas M. Evans)   John P. Campo
DARK BLUE, white triangle, dark blue bars on   Jorge
white sleeves, blue and white cap   Velasquez

assigned weight to be carried/ handicap

11 PLEASANT COLONY   126

Dk.b. or br.c. 1978, His Majesty—Sun Colony
by Sunrise Flight   **5-2**
(Bred in Virginia by Thomas M. Evans)   (p.p. 13)

horse's name

color

sire/father

dam/mother

probable morning line/ pre-race betting odds

year of birth

sire of dam

post position/ starting gate

bloodline

Harness Racing

Trotters and pacers race in *harness.* Trotters move front and opposing rear legs in unison, *laterally gaited,* while pacers move front and rear legs on the same side in unison, *diagonally gaited.* Horses are assembled, saddled and paraded in the *paddock area.*

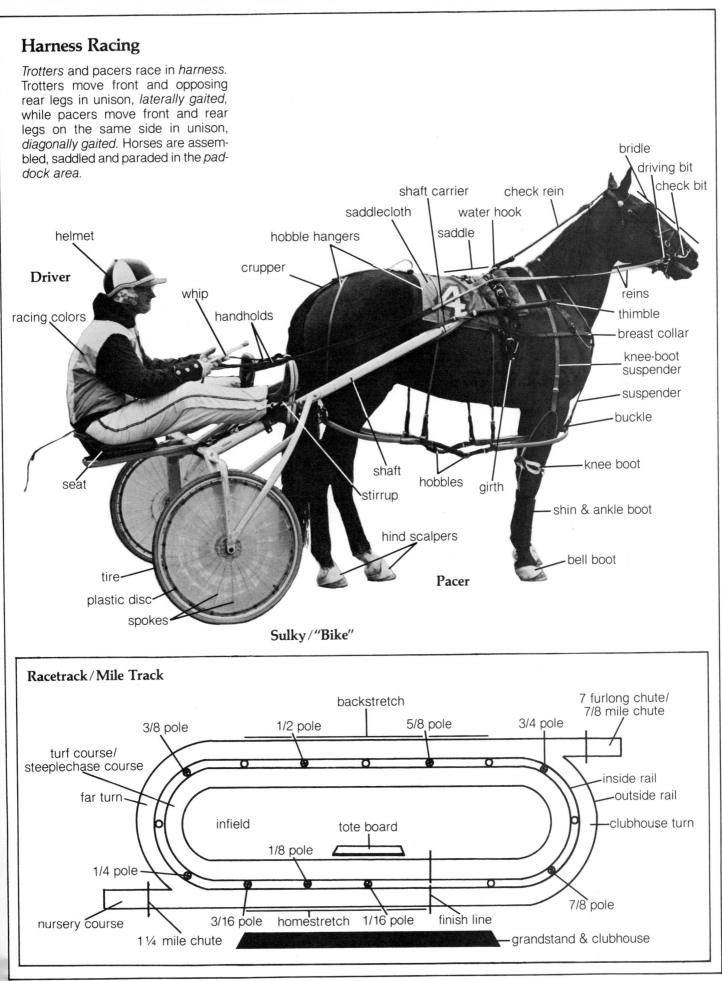

Driver

helmet

racing colors

whip

handholds

seat

tire

plastic disc

spokes

crupper

hobble hangers

saddlecloth

shaft carrier

saddle

water hook

shaft

stirrup

hobbles

girth

hind scalpers

bridle

driving bit

check bit

check rein

reins

thimble

breast collar

knee-boot suspender

suspender

buckle

knee boot

shin & ankle boot

bell boot

Pacer

Sulky/"Bike"

Racetrack/Mile Track

backstretch

7 furlong chute/ 7/8 mile chute

3/8 pole

1/2 pole

5/8 pole

3/4 pole

turf course/ steeplechase course

far turn

inside rail

outside rail

clubhouse turn

infield

tote board

1/8 pole

1/4 pole

nursery course

1¼ mile chute

3/16 pole

homestretch

1/16 pole

finish line

7/8 pole

grandstand & clubhouse

Equestrian Sports

Grand Prix Racing

International *road racing* takes place on *closed-circuit tracks* laid out through the countryside, as opposed to *speedway racing,* which takes place on banked, oval-shaped *race tracks. Formulas* primarily limit engine size and car weight, and range from *Super-Vee* to *Formula One,* used in Grand Prix racing.

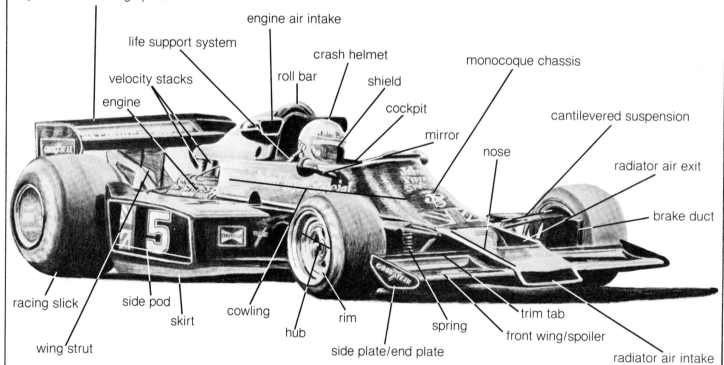

adjustable rear wing/spoiler

engine air intake

life support system

crash helmet

monocoque chassis

velocity stacks

roll bar

shield

engine

cockpit

cantilevered suspension

mirror

nose

radiator air exit

brake duct

racing slick

side pod

cowling

rim

trim tab

radiator air intake

wing strut

skirt

hub

spring

front wing/spoiler

side plate/end plate

Formula One Racing Car

Drag Racing

Each drag racing *event,* or *acceleration contest,* involves two-car *heats,* the winner of which is deemed the *eliminator.* Vehicles include *slingshot dragsters* and *funny cars* whose mismatched bodies, or *"hulls,"* and *chassis* give them an unusual appearance. The Christmas Tree is situated in the middle of a divided, two-lane *straight-line course, drag strip* or *dragway. Elapsed time,* or *"ET,"* is computed from the moment a car breaks a *light beam* at the *starting line* until it breaks a similar beam at the *finish.* A car leaving the starting line prematurely, in either *handicap* or *heads-up racing,* is said to be *"red-lighting."*

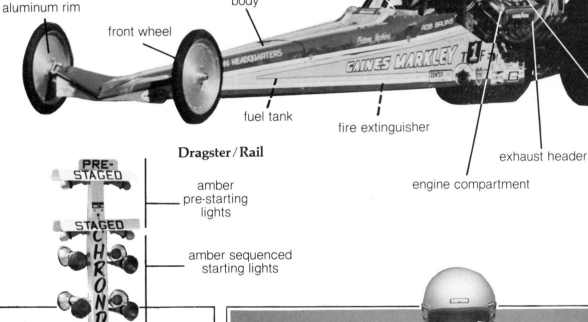

wing/air foil

intake valves

roll cage

support bar

cockpit

racing slick/tire

body

aluminum rim

front wheel

fuel tank

fire extinguisher

air blower

exhaust header

engine compartment

Dragster/Rail

amber pre-starting lights

amber sequenced starting lights

green GO light

base

red foul light

Starting Lights/Christmas Tree

eyeport shield

neck sock

vent port

helmet skirt

nose shroud & breathing filter

shoulder harness

driving glove

driving suit

lap belt

anti-submarine belt/crotch strap

racing shoe

Driver's Fire Suit

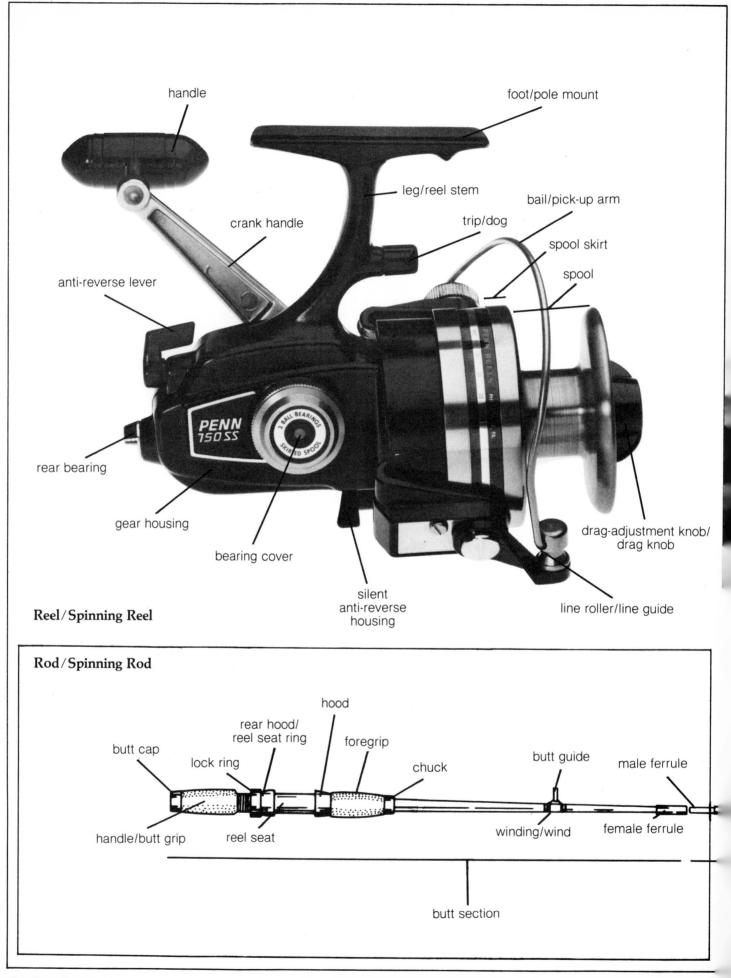

handle

foot/pole mount

leg/reel stem

crank handle

bail/pick-up arm

trip/dog

spool skirt

anti-reverse lever

spool

rear bearing

PENN
750 SS

3 BALL BEARINGS
SKIRTED SPOOL

gear housing

bearing cover

drag-adjustment knob/
drag knob

silent
anti-reverse
housing

line roller/line guide

Reel/Spinning Reel

Rod/Spinning Rod

hood

rear hood/
reel seat ring

foregrip

butt cap

lock ring

chuck

butt guide

male ferrule

handle/butt grip

reel seat

winding/wind

female ferrule

butt section

Fishing

Fishermen, or *anglers,* use a variety of *tackle,* from simple *cane rods,* or *bank rods,* to sophisticated *fly rods* and *trolling gear. Sinkers* hold bait underwater, while *floats,* or *bobbers,* keep it suspended from the surface. A *gaff* or *landing net* is used to land fish.

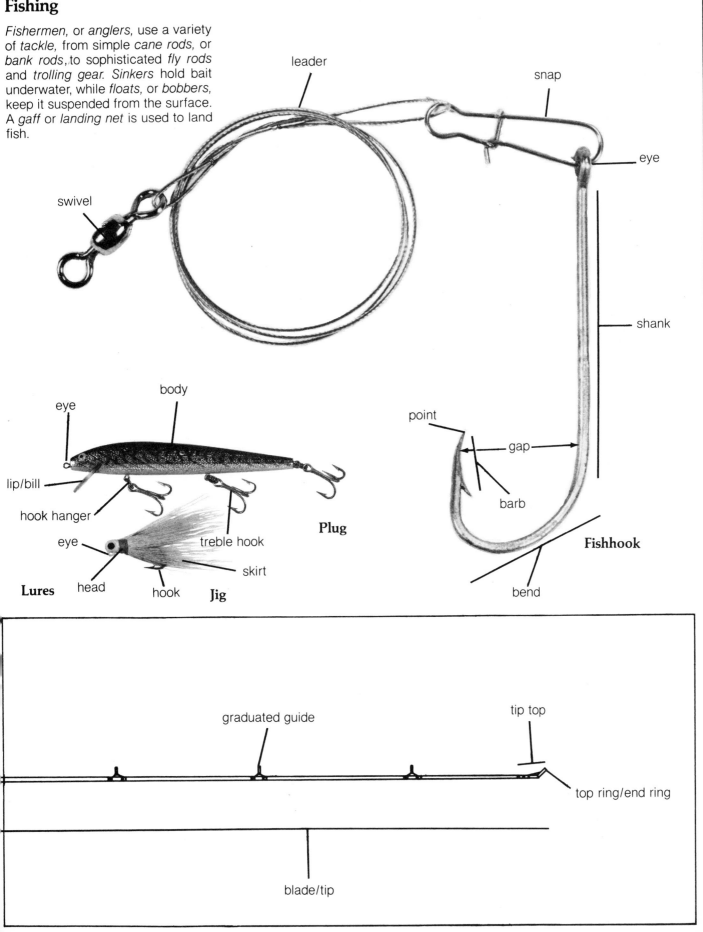

leader

snap

eye

swivel

shank

body

eye

point

gap

lip/bill

barb

hook hanger

Fishhook

treble hook

Plug

eye

bend

skirt

Lures   head   hook   **Jig**

graduated guide

tip top

top ring/end ring

blade/tip

Camping

Wall tents and pup tents are held up by tent poles. Many modern tents have *exterior frame* construction. Features in all the above-mentioned tents include *lap-felled* or *French seams*, which provide four layers for keeping out water, *webbed–tape backing* and pressed-on *grommets* or sewn-in *rings* for *ropes* secured to the ground with *pegs* or *stakes*, and sewn-in *flooring*. A lantern is primed by pumping the *pump valve* and lit by a match placed in the *lighting hole*.

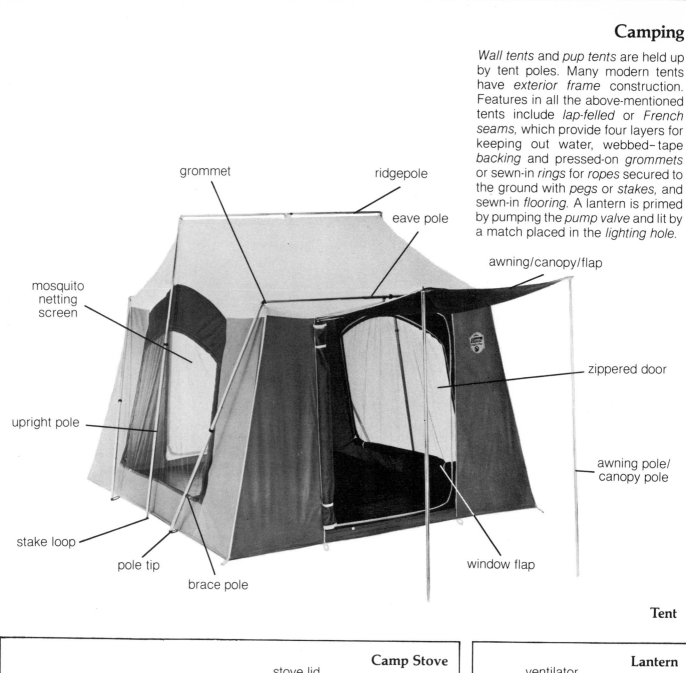

grommet

ridgepole

eave pole

mosquito netting screen

awning/canopy/flap

zippered door

upright pole

awning pole/ canopy pole

stake loop

pole tip

brace pole

window flap

Tent

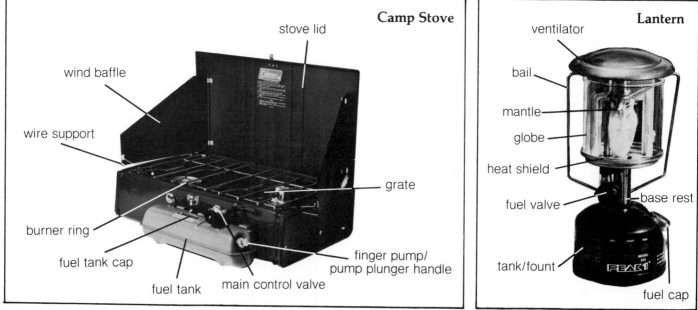

Camp Stove

stove lid

wind baffle

wire support

grate

burner ring

fuel tank cap

finger pump/ pump plunger handle

fuel tank

main control valve

Lantern

ventilator

bail

mantle

globe

heat shield

fuel valve

base rest

tank/fount

fuel cap

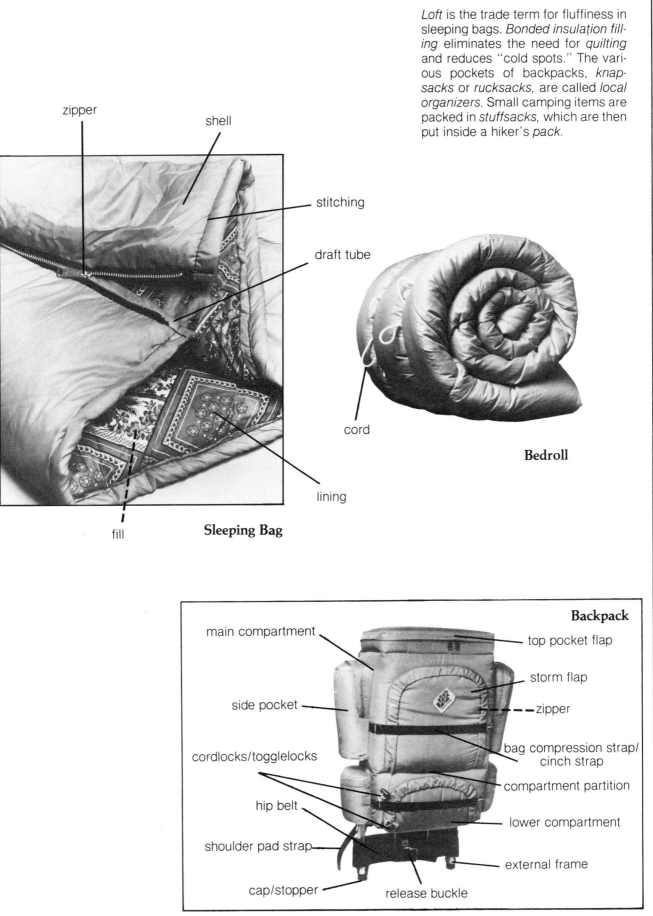

Backpacking

Loft is the trade term for fluffiness in sleeping bags. *Bonded insulation filling* eliminates the need for *quilting* and reduces "cold spots." The various pockets of backpacks, *knapsacks* or *rucksacks,* are called *local organizers.* Small camping items are packed in *stuffsacks,* which are then put inside a hiker's *pack.*

zipper

shell

stitching

draft tube

cord

Bedroll

lining

fill

Sleeping Bag

Backpack

main compartment

top pocket flap

storm flap

zipper

side pocket

bag compression strap/ cinch strap

cordlocks/togglelocks

compartment partition

hip belt

lower compartment

shoulder pad strap

external frame

cap/stopper

release buckle

Body Building

Among other *stations* in the universal gym, designed to improve muscle development through *isotonic exercises*, are *dead lift* and *low pulley*. Muscle-building and toning equipment includes *dumbbells, hand grips, or hand flexors, scissor grips, tone-up wheels, power twisters, exercise bikes, neck developers, ankle* and *wrist weights, triceps exercisers* and *waist trimmers*.

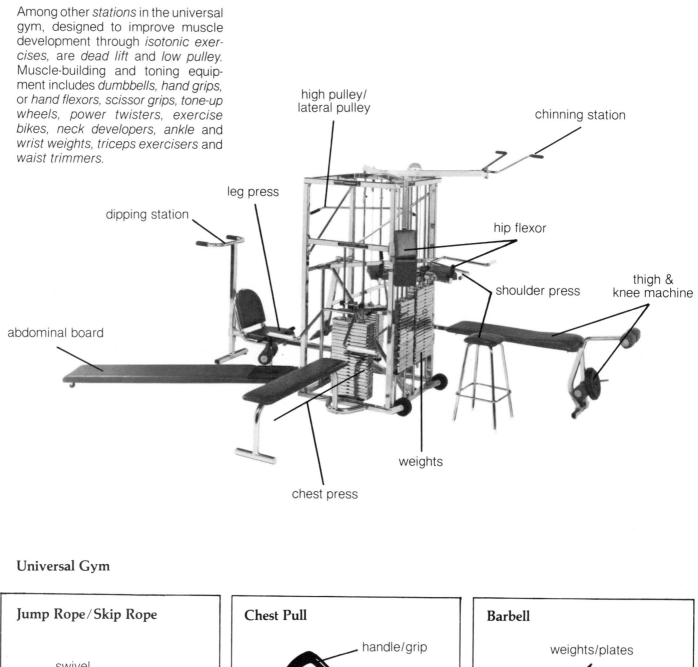

high pulley/
lateral pulley

chinning station

leg press

dipping station

hip flexor

shoulder press

thigh &
knee machine

abdominal board

weights

chest press

Universal Gym

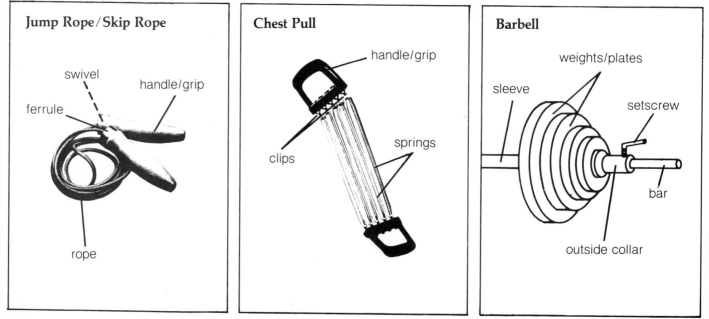

Jump Rope/Skip Rope

swivel

handle/grip

ferrule

rope

Chest Pull

handle/grip

clips

springs

Barbell

weights/plates

sleeve

setscrew

bar

outside collar

Chess, Checkers, Backgammon and Tile Games

When chessmen and checkers are arranged at the start of a game, they are positioned in a *setup*. A chessboard's horizontal rows are called *ranks*. Vertical rows are *files*. In backgammon, a player increases the stakes by turning a dicelike *doubling cube*. A single backgammon piece on a point is called a *blot*. Two or more on a point make a *block*. In dominos, pieces with identical numbers on both ends are called *doubles* or *spinners*. Dominos that have been played form a *layout*. In mah-jongg, tiles are arranged in a *wall* to begin a game.

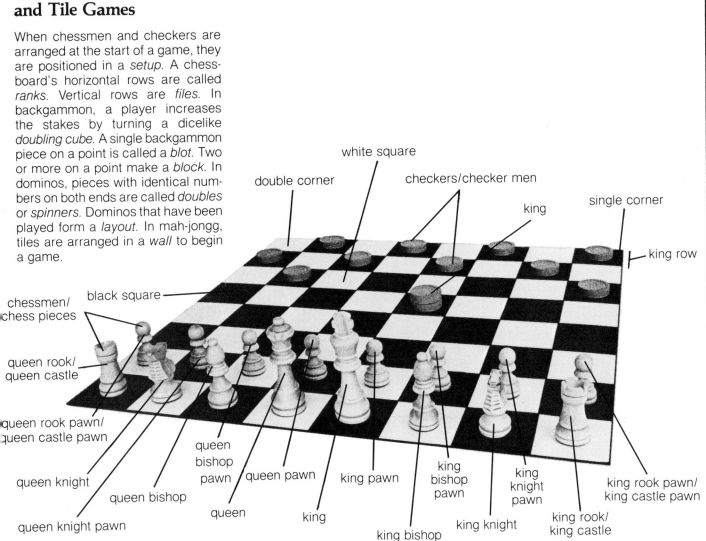

Chessboard / Checkerboard

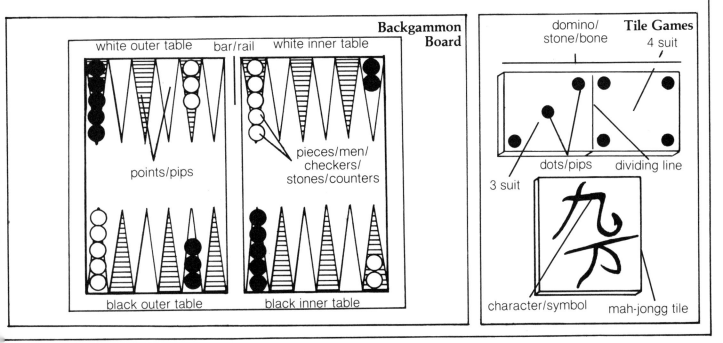

Board Games

Gambling Equipment

A roulette wheel is operated by a *croupier.* Bets are placed on a *layout.* Slots are divided into *red* and *black* for betting purposes. Dice players bet either with the person rolling the dice, the *shooter,* or with the casino, or *house.* The blackjack dealer pushes money won by the house into a double-locked *drop box* below the betting table. Other casino games include *baccarat, chemin de fer, wheel of fortune,* and *chuck-a-luck,* a game played with three dice.

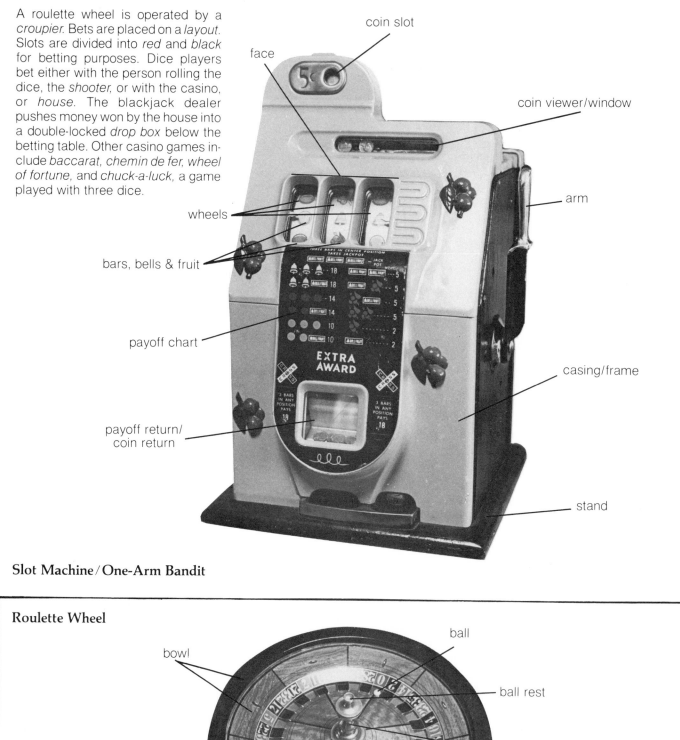

coin slot

face

coin viewer/window

arm

wheels

bars, bells & fruit

payoff chart

EXTRA AWARD

casing/frame

payoff return/ coin return

stand

Slot Machine / One-Arm Bandit

Roulette Wheel

bowl

ball

ball rest

pan/wheel

spindle

canoe/diamond

slot/groove

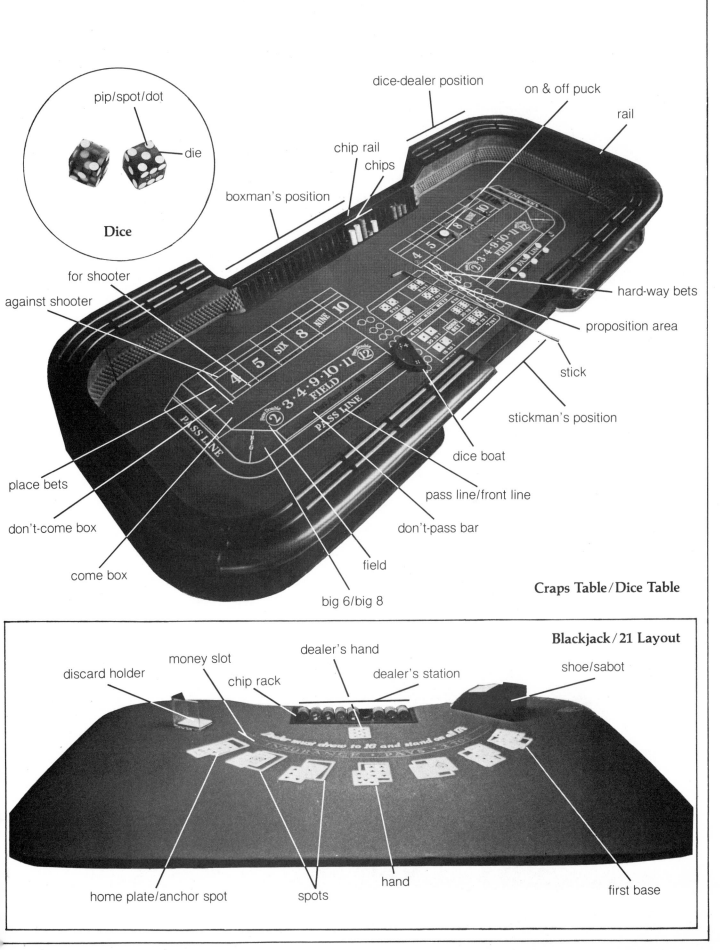

pip/spot/dot

die

Dice

dice-dealer position

on & off puck

rail

chip rail

chips

boxman's position

for shooter

against shooter

hard-way bets

proposition area

stick

stickman's position

place bets

don't-come box

dice boat

pass line/front line

don't-pass bar

come box

field

big 6/big 8

Craps Table/Dice Table

Blackjack/21 Layout

dealer's hand

money slot

dealer's station

shoe/sabot

discard holder

chip rack

home plate/anchor spot

spots

hand

first base

Playing Cards

There are 52 cards in a *deck* or *pack*. The *aces,* shown below, and cards numbered two through ten, are called *spot cards* or *pip cards.* An additional card, the *joker,* or *mistigris,* is used in *card games* requiring a *wild card.* A *marked deck* is one in which the card *backs* have been altered slightly to allow a player to read their *values* illegally.

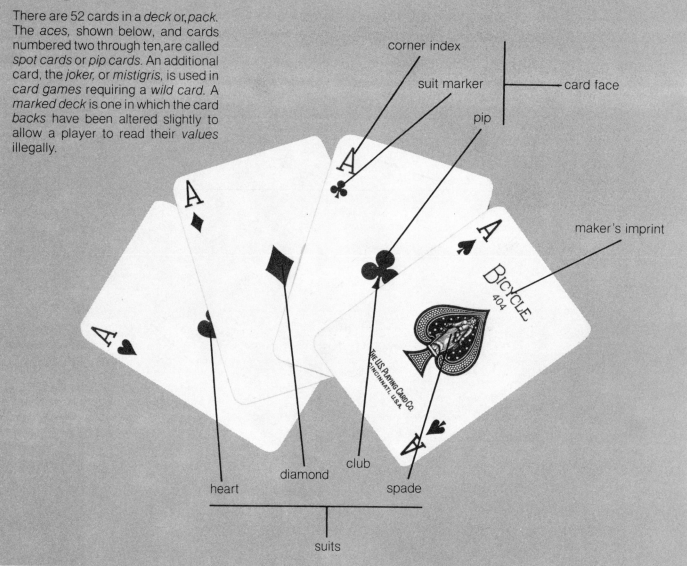

corner index

suit marker

pip

card face

maker's imprint

heart

diamond

club

spade

suits

Picture Cards/Court Cards/Face Cards

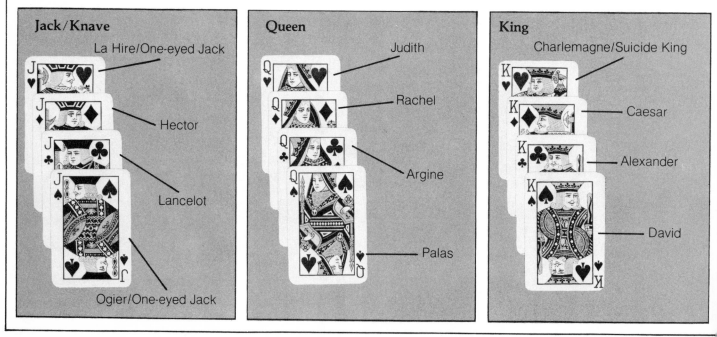

Jack/Knave

La Hire/One-eyed Jack

Hector

Lancelot

Ogier/One-eyed Jack

Queen

Judith

Rachel

Argine

Palas

King

Charlemagne/Suicide King

Caesar

Alexander

David

Arts and Crafts

The main subsections here include the platforms on which the performing arts take place; coverage of the music field, ranging from the symbols that appear on sheet music to the parts of various musical instruments; the fine arts and crafts.

In the fine arts subsection an effort has been made to identify the terms for elements of style, rather than to cover styles themselves. The equipment used in everything from painting and sculpting to relief arts and stained glass are also illustrated and their parts labeled. The crafts subsection covers decorative stitching, knitting and weaving, and also includes the terms used to identify a sewing pattern.

Cartooning has a subsection all to itself. Here, for the first time, the reader will be able to identify everything from the beads of fear on a comic character (plewds) to the meaning of double XX's on a cartoon bottle (boozex). In addition the reader will henceforth be able to recognize the difference between a thought balloon, a speech balloon and an idea balloon in a cartoon panel.

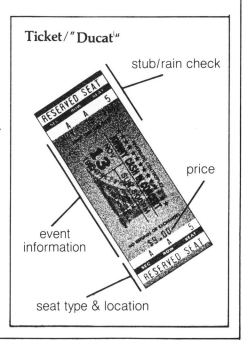

Ticket/"Ducat"

stub/rain check

price

event information

seat type & location

Stage

Also found on many stages are *tormentors*, or *legs,* which frame the stage to narrow the acting area, a *trapdoor,* or *scruto,* an *elevator,* and a fabric backdrop, or *scrim.* Everything used on stages, or *boards,* are *props,* or *properties.* The arrangement of *scenery,* properties and lighting is called a *set.*

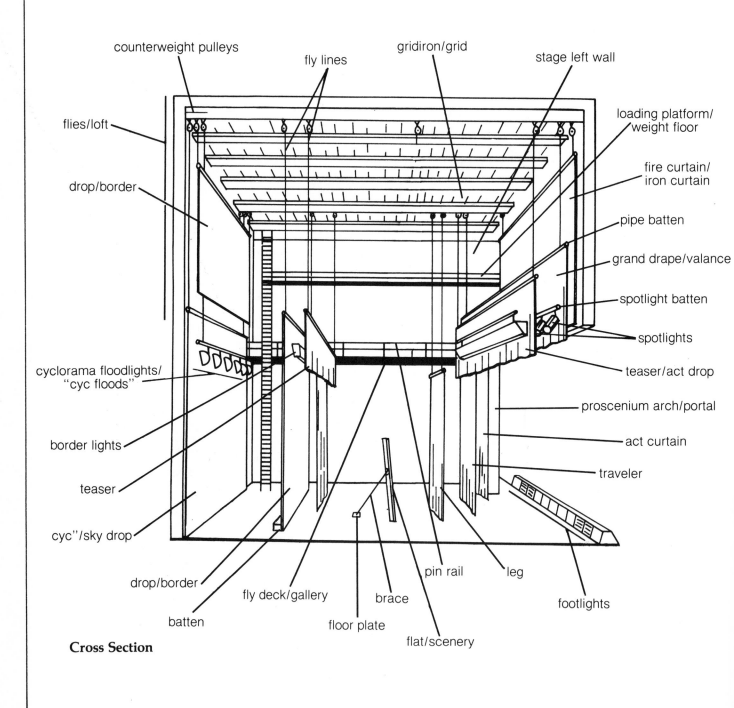

counterweight pulleys

fly lines

gridiron/grid

stage left wall

flies/loft

loading platform/weight floor

drop/border

fire curtain/iron curtain

pipe batten

grand drape/valance

spotlight batten

spotlights

teaser/act drop

cyclorama floodlights/"cyc floods"

proscenium arch/portal

act curtain

border lights

teaser

traveler

cyc"/sky drop

drop/border

fly deck/gallery

brace

pin rail

leg

footlights

batten

floor plate

flat/scenery

Cross Section

Theater

In a *performance hall,* the orchestra sits in a sunken *orchestra pit* between the audience and the stage. For some shows a *runway,* or *ramp,* extends from the stage into the *center aisle.* The seating area above the orchestra is the *balcony.* In theaters with more than one balcony, the lowest one is the *mezzanine,* the front section of which is the *loge.*

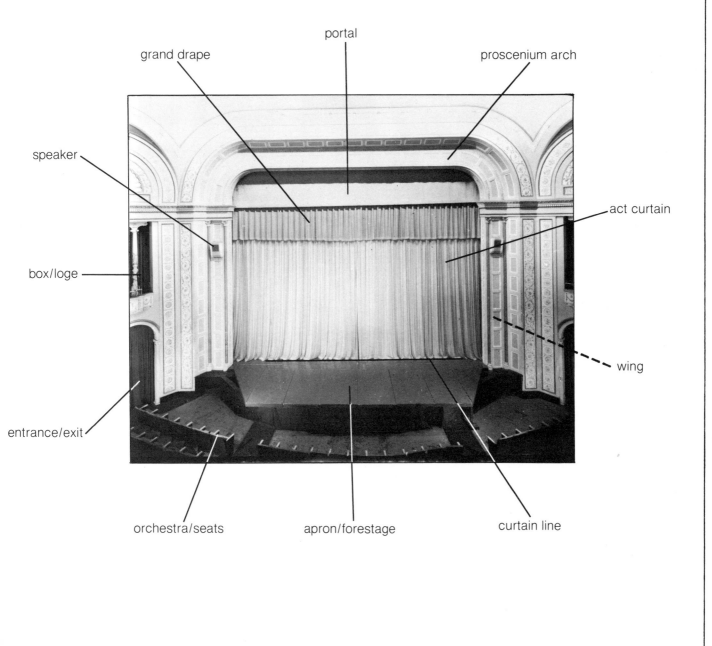

portal

grand drape

proscenium arch

speaker

act curtain

box/loge

wing

entrance/exit

orchestra/seats

apron/forestage

curtain line

Sheet Music Notations

Words to be sung, or *lyrics,* appear below the staff on sheet music. The notation ' is a *breath mark* indicating that the singer or musician should briefly pause. A combination of tones that blend harmoniously is a *chord.* Sharps, flats and naturals appearing directly in front of specific notes are called *accidentals.* A *quasihemi-demisemiquaver* is a 128th note.

Orchestra

In symphony orchestras, string, woodwind and brass parts are performed by many *musicians*. In *chamber music ensembles,* each part is usually played by a single *player. Bands* do not normally include stringed instruments. *Marching bands* generally use no oboes or bassoons, and flutes are replaced with piccolos or *fifes. Dance bands* and *jazz bands* are loosely structured.

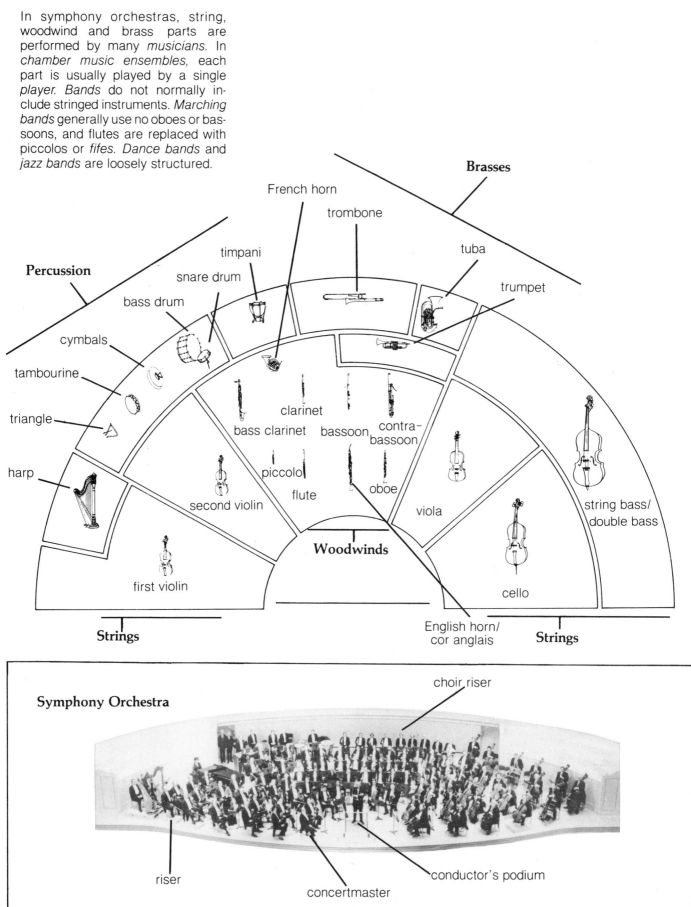

Brasses

French horn

trombone

tuba

Percussion

timpani

snare drum

trumpet

bass drum

cymbals

clarinet

tambourine

bass clarinet

bassoon

contra-bassoon

triangle

piccolo

oboe

harp

flute

viola

second violin

string bass/
double bass

Woodwinds

first violin

cello

Strings

English horn/
cor anglais

Strings

Symphony Orchestra

choir riser

conductor's podium

riser

concertmaster

Violin

Stringed instruments produce tones when a bow is drawn across the strings (*arco*) or they are finger-plucked (*pizzicato*). The sympathetic vibration produced between the instrument's belly and *back* adds *resonance* and *volume* to the sound.

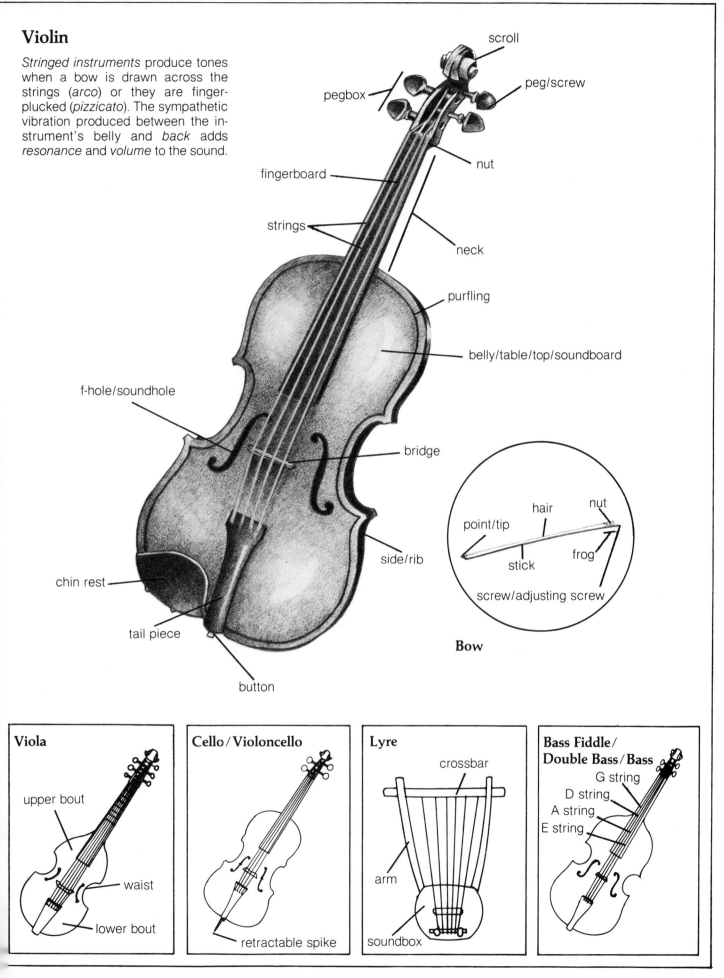

scroll

peg/screw

pegbox

nut

fingerboard

strings

neck

purfling

belly/table/top/soundboard

f-hole/soundhole

bridge

point/tip

hair

nut

stick

frog

screw/adjusting screw

side/rib

chin rest

Bow

tail piece

button

Viola

upper bout

waist

lower bout

Cello / Violoncello

retractable spike

Lyre

crossbar

arm

soundbox

Bass Fiddle / Double Bass / Bass

G string

D string

A string

E string

Music

Woodwinds

Woodwinds produce *tones* by the vibration of one or two reeds of pliant cane in the mouthpiece or by the passing of air across a blow hole.

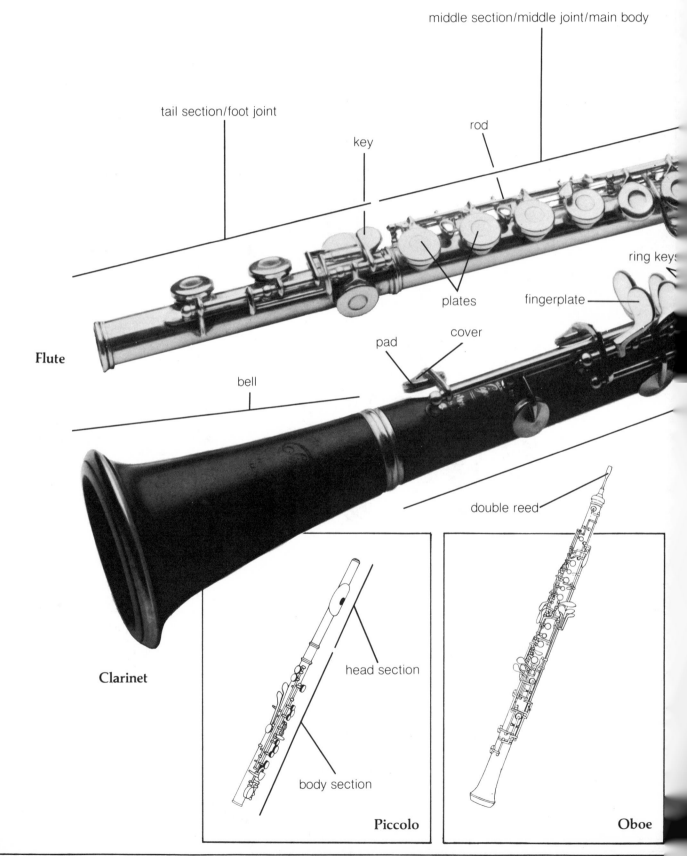

middle section/middle joint/main body

tail section/foot joint

rod

key

ring keys

plates

fingerplate

pad

cover

Flute

bell

double reed

Clarinet

head section

body section

Piccolo

Oboe

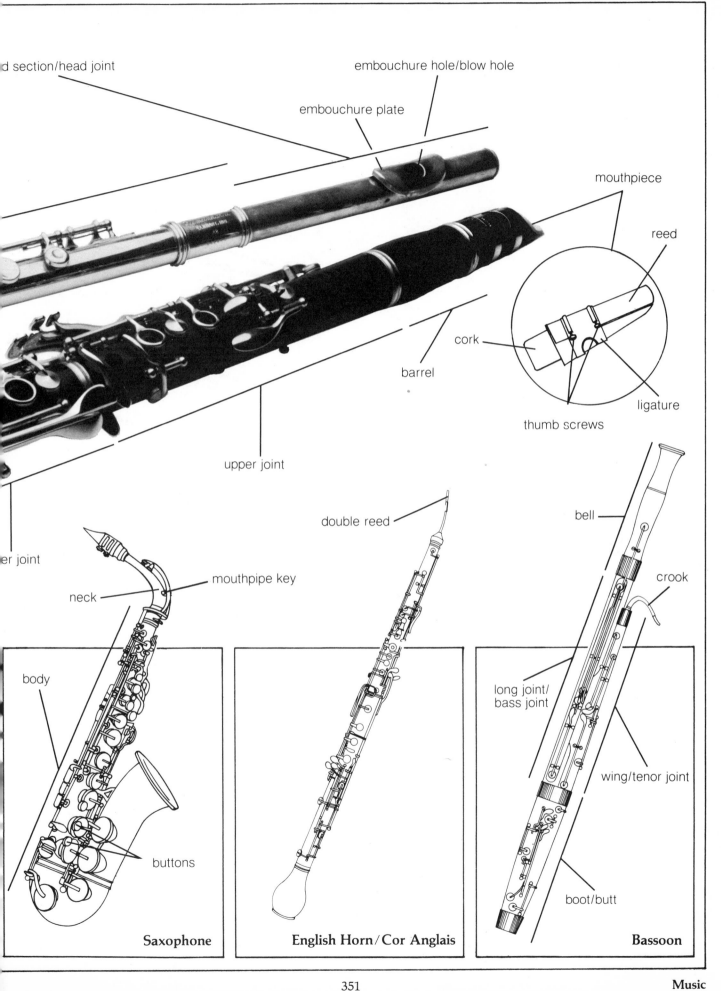

d section/head joint

embouchure hole/blow hole

embouchure plate

mouthpiece

reed

cork

barrel

ligature

thumb screws

upper joint

double reed

bell

crook

er joint

mouthpipe key

neck

long joint/
bass joint

body

wing/tenor joint

buttons

boot/butt

Saxophone

English Horn/Cor Anglais

Bassoon

Music

Brasses

Brasses are *wind instruments* that produce *tones* when lips are buzzed against the mouthpiece. The range of brass instruments is increased by added lengths of tubing called *crooks* or *shanks.*

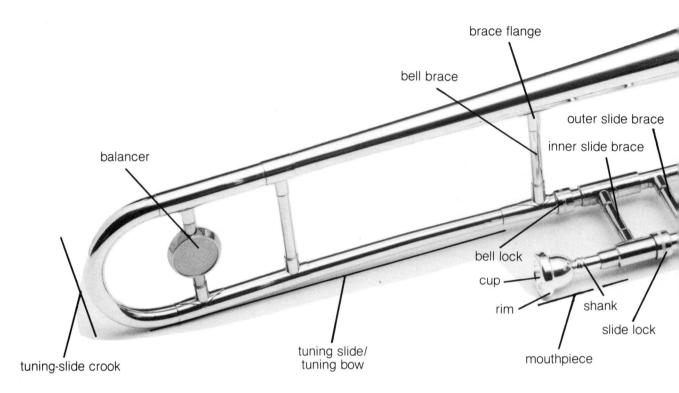

brace flange

bell brace

outer slide brace

inner slide brace

balancer

bell lock

cup

rim

shank

slide lock

mouthpiece

tuning slide/
tuning bow

tuning-slide crook

Trombone

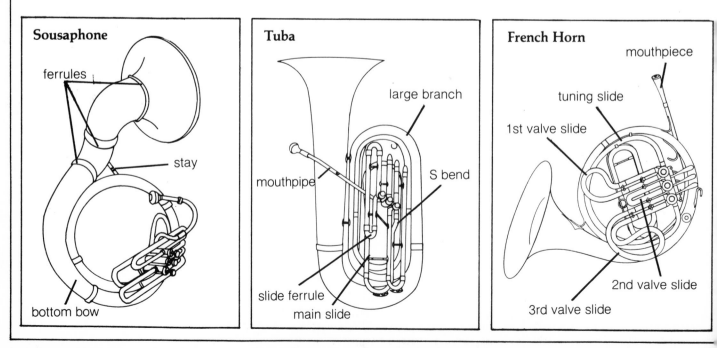

Sousaphone

ferrules

stay

bottom bow

Tuba

large branch

mouthpipe

S bend

slide ferrule

main slide

French Horn

mouthpiece

tuning slide

1st valve slide

2nd valve slide

3rd valve slide

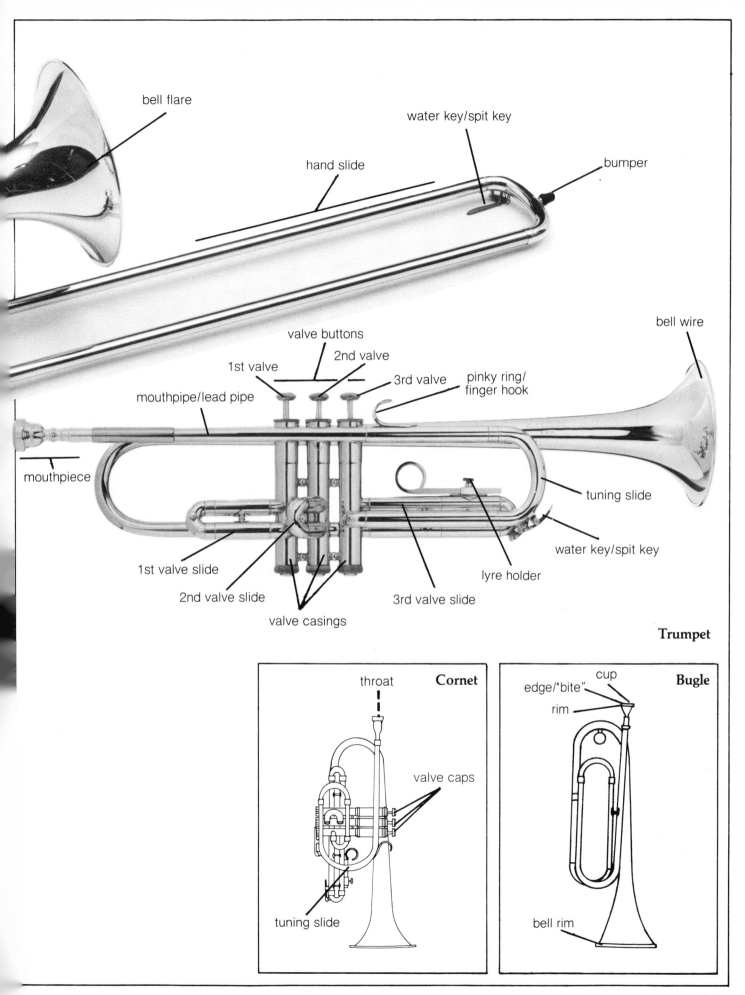

bell flare

water key/spit key

hand slide

bumper

bell wire

valve buttons

2nd valve

1st valve

3rd valve

pinky ring/
finger hook

mouthpipe/lead pipe

mouthpiece

tuning slide

1st valve slide

water key/spit key

2nd valve slide

3rd valve slide

lyre holder

valve casings

Trumpet

throat

Cornet

valve caps

cup

edge/"bite"

Bugle

rim

tuning slide

bell rim

Organ

The keyboards, or *manuals,* pedal board and *pipes* of a pipe organ, such as the one shown here, are contained in the body, or *console.* Music is produced when air, sent into a *wind chest* from an internal *bellows,* is directed into one of the organ's pipes. An *electric organ* produces tones mechanically. An *electronic organ* uses *transistors* and *tubes* to make sounds.

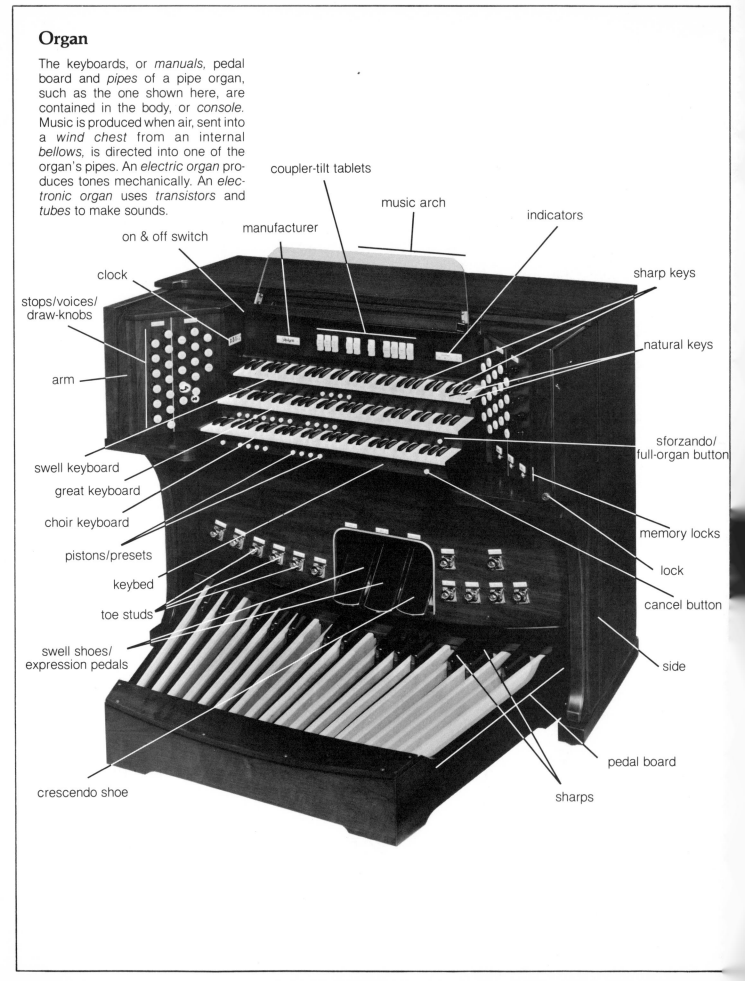

coupler-tilt tablets

music arch

indicators

manufacturer

on & off switch

clock

sharp keys

stops/voices/ draw-knobs

natural keys

arm

swell keyboard

great keyboard

choir keyboard

sforzando/ full-organ button

memory locks

pistons/presets

keybed

toe studs

lock

swell shoes/ expression pedals

cancel button

side

crescendo shoe

pedal board

sharps

Piano

A piano is made up of a *structural unit*, a *tone unit* and a *mechanical unit*. The keys activate a mechanism that throws felt-covered *hammers* against the strings in the piano *case*. A *digitorium* is a silent machine for piano practice.

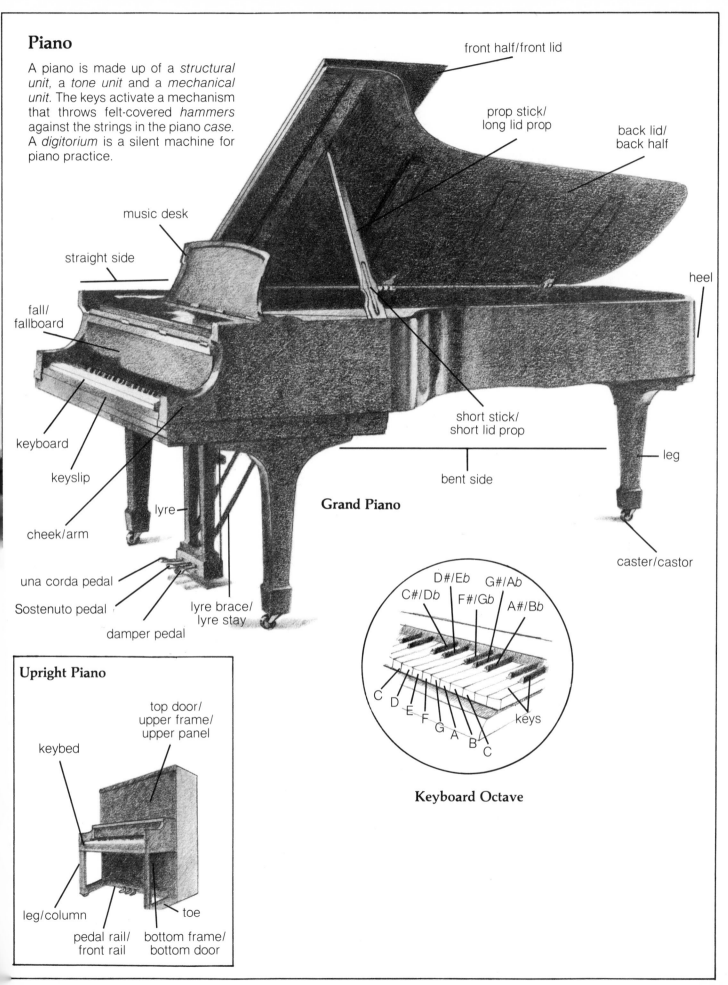

front half/front lid

prop stick/ long lid prop

back lid/ back half

music desk

straight side

heel

fall/ fallboard

short stick/ short lid prop

keyboard

leg

keyslip

bent side

lyre

Grand Piano

cheek/arm

caster/castor

una corda pedal

Sostenuto pedal

damper pedal

lyre brace/ lyre stay

C#/Db   D#/Eb   F#/Gb   G#/Ab   A#/Bb

C   D   E   F   G   A   B   C

keys

Keyboard Octave

Upright Piano

top door/ upper frame/ upper panel

keybed

leg/column

toe

pedal rail/ front rail

bottom frame/ bottom door

Guitar

These *chordophones*, or *stringed instruments*, are members of the lute family. They are played by plucking or strumming the strings with the fingers or with a stiff *plectrum* or *pick*. A movable device attached to a guitar neck, used to raise the pitch of the strings, is a *capo*. There are *sympathetic strings* inside the hollow neck of a sitar that vibrate in response to the drone or melody strings.

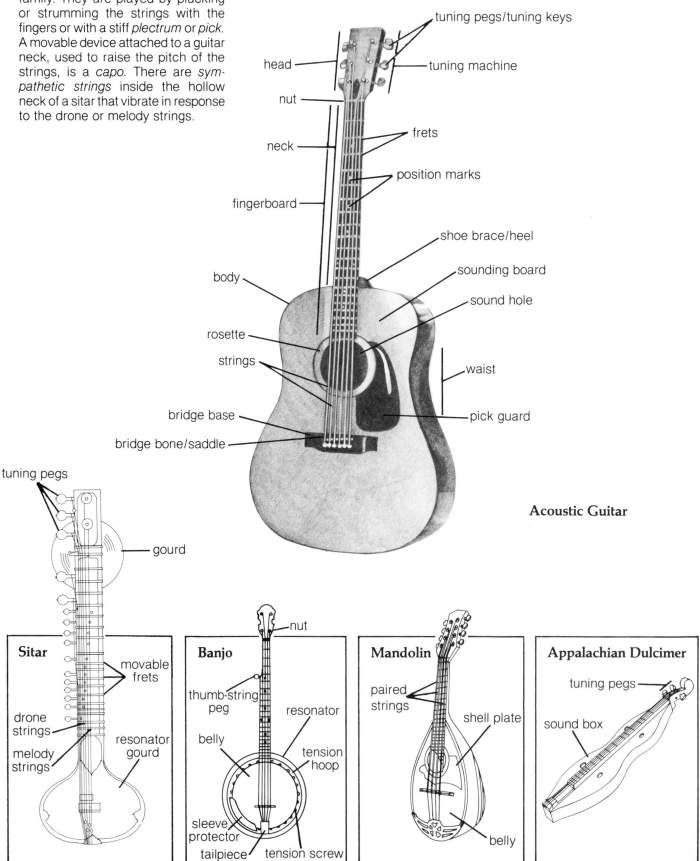

tuning pegs/tuning keys

head

tuning machine

nut

neck

frets

position marks

fingerboard

shoe brace/heel

body

sounding board

sound hole

rosette

strings

waist

bridge base

pick guard

bridge bone/saddle

Acoustic Guitar

tuning pegs

gourd

Sitar

movable frets

drone strings

melody strings

resonator gourd

Banjo

nut

thumb-string peg

resonator

belly

tension hoop

sleeve protector

tailpiece

tension screw

Mandolin

paired strings

shell plate

belly

Appalachian Dulcimer

tuning pegs

sound box

Electric Guitar

The electric guitar has a *solid body* rather than the *hollow* or *semi-hollow body* of an acoustic guitar. *Special-effects pedals*, among them *fuzz, fuzz-phaser, wah-wah* and *distortion,* can be linked to the amplifier. *Pre-amplifiers*, which serve to magnify weak signals, can also be hooked up to the amplifier.

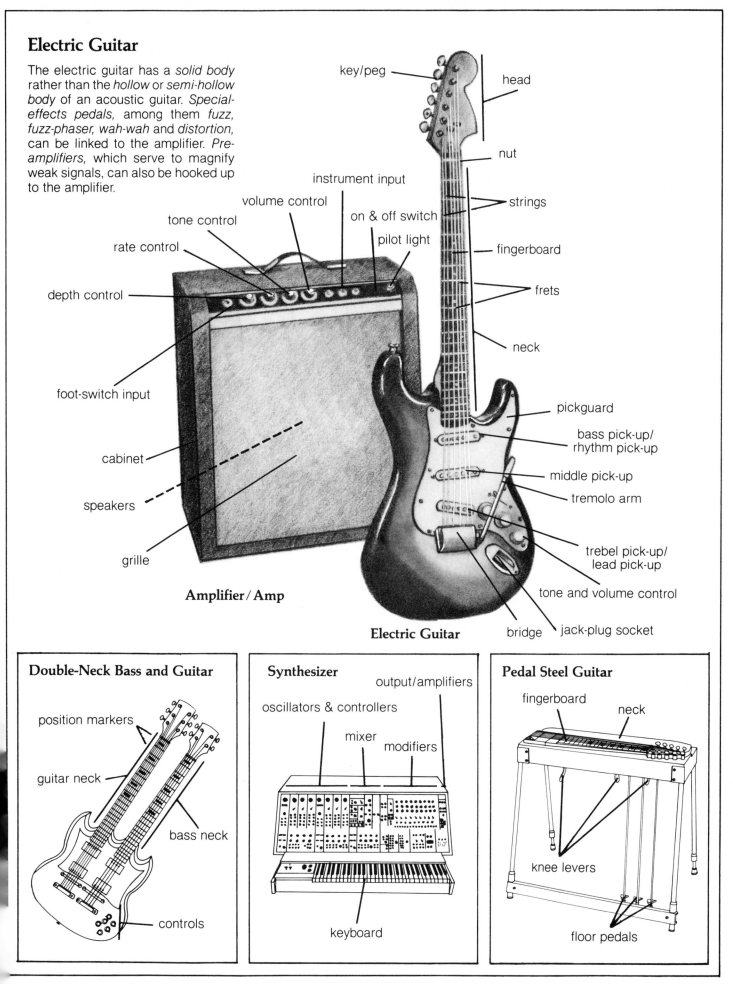

key/peg

head

nut

strings

fingerboard

frets

neck

instrument input

volume control

tone control

on & off switch

rate control

pilot light

depth control

foot-switch input

pickguard

bass pick-up/ rhythm pick-up

middle pick-up

tremolo arm

cabinet

trebel pick-up/ lead pick-up

speakers

tone and volume control

grille

bridge

jack-plug socket

Amplifier / Amp

Electric Guitar

Double-Neck Bass and Guitar

position markers

guitar neck

bass neck

controls

Synthesizer

output/amplifiers

oscillators & controllers

mixer

modifiers

keyboard

Pedal Steel Guitar

fingerboard

neck

knee levers

floor pedals

357

Music

Drums

Drums, or *membranophones,* in a *drum set* such as the one shown here, are played with *drumsticks, mallets* or *brushes.* A *gong* is struck with a *beater.* Adjustable metal, nylon or gut strings, called *snares,* are stretched across the bottom head, or *snare head,* of a snare drum. Timpani can be adjusted by screws or pedals to produce sounds of different pitches.

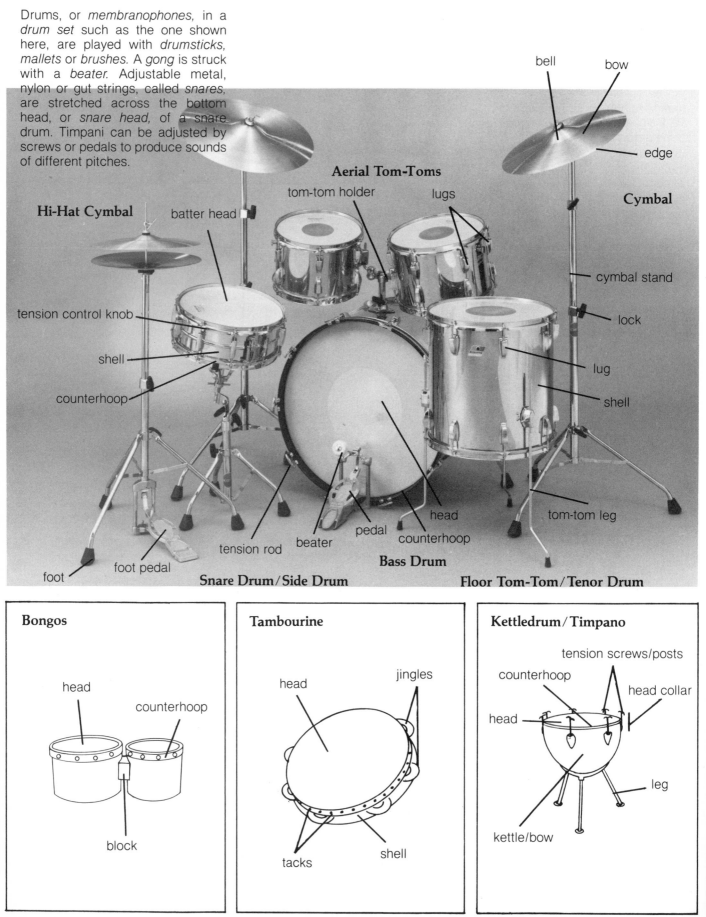

Hi-Hat Cymbal

Aerial Tom-Toms

Cymbal

bell

bow

edge

tom-tom holder

lugs

batter head

cymbal stand

lock

tension control knob

lug

shell

shell

counterhoop

head

tom-tom leg

counterhoop

pedal

tension rod

beater

foot

foot pedal

Snare Drum/Side Drum

Bass Drum

Floor Tom-Tom/Tenor Drum

Bongos

head

counterhoop

block

Tambourine

head

jingles

tacks

shell

Kettledrum/Timpano

tension screws/posts

counterhoop

head collar

head

leg

kettle/bow

Bagpipe

A *drone reed*, or *double-reed*, held inside the chanter by a *tenon*, creates music when air is blown into the *pipes* by a *bagpiper* or by pumping *bellows* strapped to the *piper's* body. The melody is played on the eight *open holes* in the chanter. The *leather bag* is usually covered with a decorative *bag cover*.

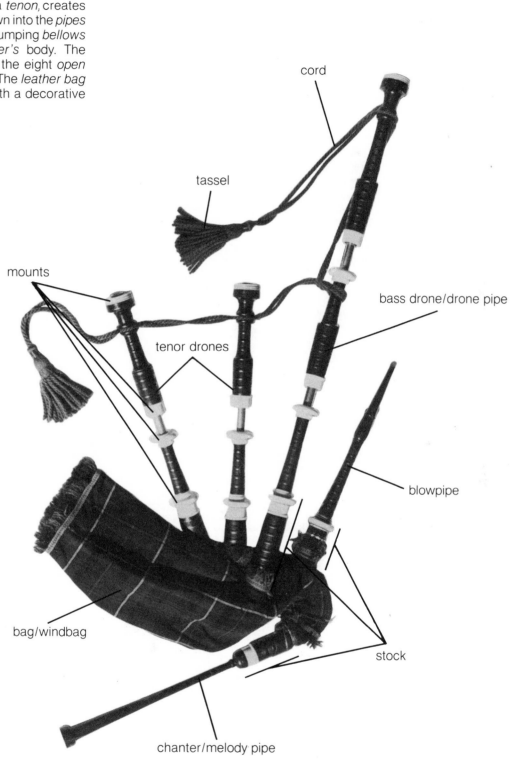

cord

tassel

mounts

tenor drones

bass drone/drone pipe

blowpipe

bag/windbag

stock

chanter/melody pipe

Folk Instruments

Like the harmonica, the accordion, or *piano-accordion,* is a *free-reed instrument.* Many accordions have *treble* and *bass register buttons* which allow the *accordionist* to change the tone of the instrument.

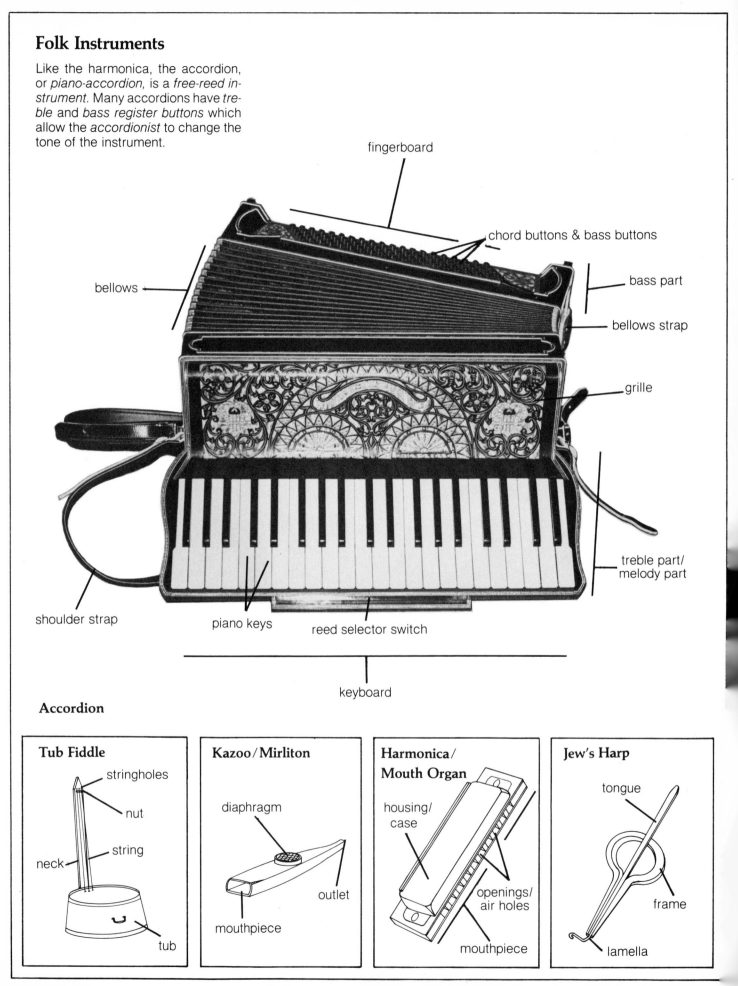

fingerboard

chord buttons & bass buttons

bass part

bellows

bellows strap

grille

shoulder strap

piano keys

reed selector switch

treble part/ melody part

keyboard

Accordion

Tub Fiddle

stringholes

nut

string

neck

tub

Kazoo/Mirliton

diaphragm

mouthpiece

outlet

Harmonica/ Mouth Organ

housing/ case

openings/ air holes

mouthpiece

Jew's Harp

tongue

frame

lamella

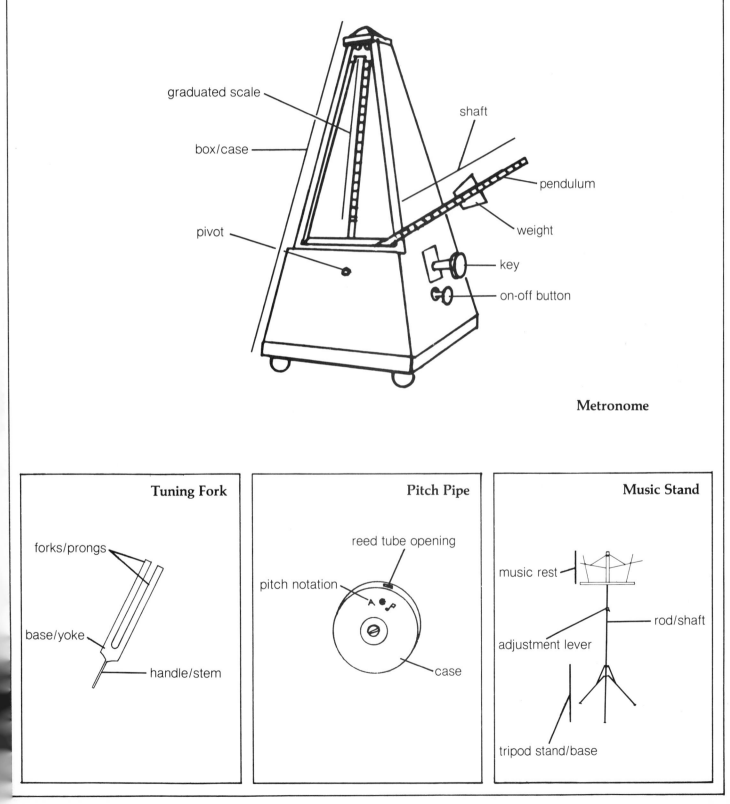

Musical Accessories

A metronome, used to find the correct speed for music in beats per minute, can be spring wound or electric. A tuning fork is constructed and tempered so as to give a pure *tone* when caused to vibrate. It can be used in conjunction with a *resonance box* to amplify its sound.

graduated scale

box/case

shaft

pendulum

pivot

weight

key

on-off button

Metronome

Tuning Fork

forks/prongs

base/yoke

handle/stem

Pitch Pipe

reed tube opening

pitch notation

case

Music Stand

music rest

rod/shaft

adjustment lever

tripod stand/base

Elements of Composition

The forms of *linear perspective* illustrated here allow an artist or illustrator to show *dimension – height, width* and *depth –* on a *flat surface*. The central focus of a work of art is the *subject.* The way an artist renders a subject, which ranges from *literal rendition* to forms of *abstraction,* is called *style.*

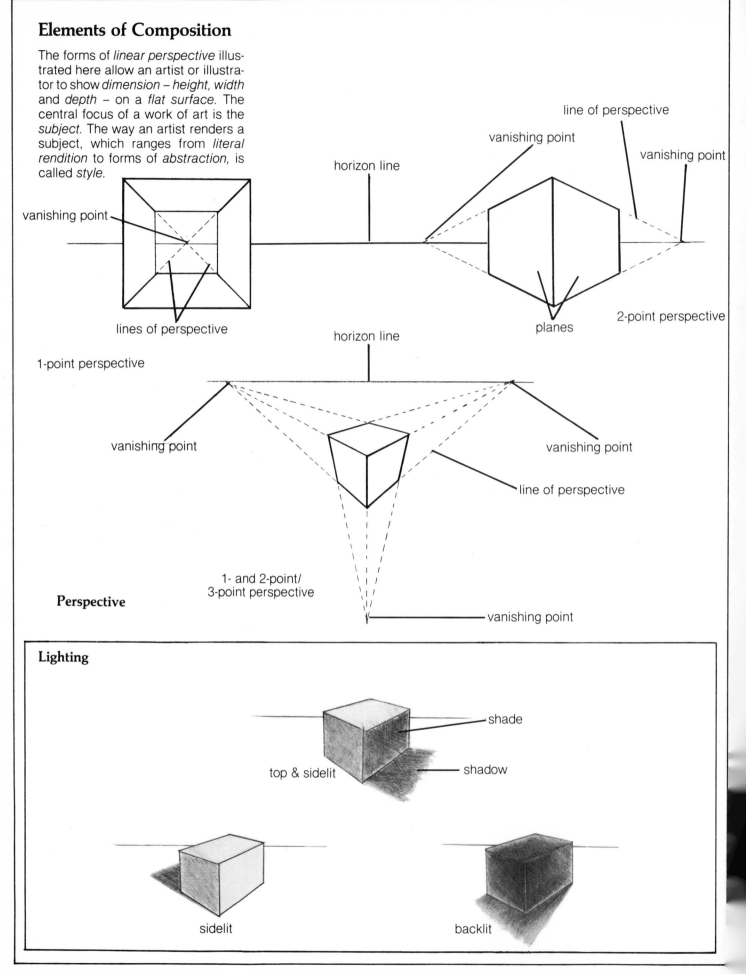

vanishing point

lines of perspective

1-point perspective

horizon line

line of perspective

vanishing point

vanishing point

planes

2-point perspective

horizon line

vanishing point

vanishing point

line of perspective

1- and 2-point/
3-point perspective

Perspective

vanishing point

Lighting

shade

shadow

top & sidelit

sidelit

backlit

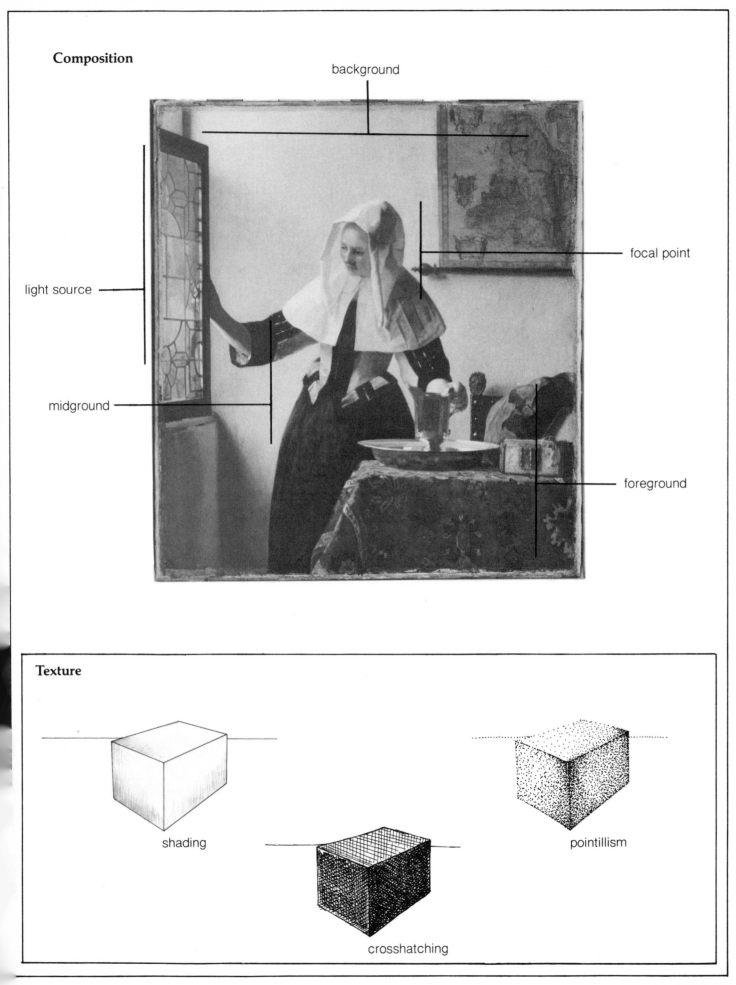

Composition

background

light source

midground

focal point

foreground

Texture

shading

crosshatching

pointillism

Fine Arts

Painting

Before paint is applied to a *canvas* it must be drawn taut on a *stretcher* and the surface coated with *primer,* usually a substance called *gesso.* The *artist,* or *painter,* chooses a type of paint, or *medium,* in which to work, the most common of which are *tempera, acrylic* and *oil.* A thin blade set in a handle, used for mixing colors or applying them to a canvas, is a palette knife.

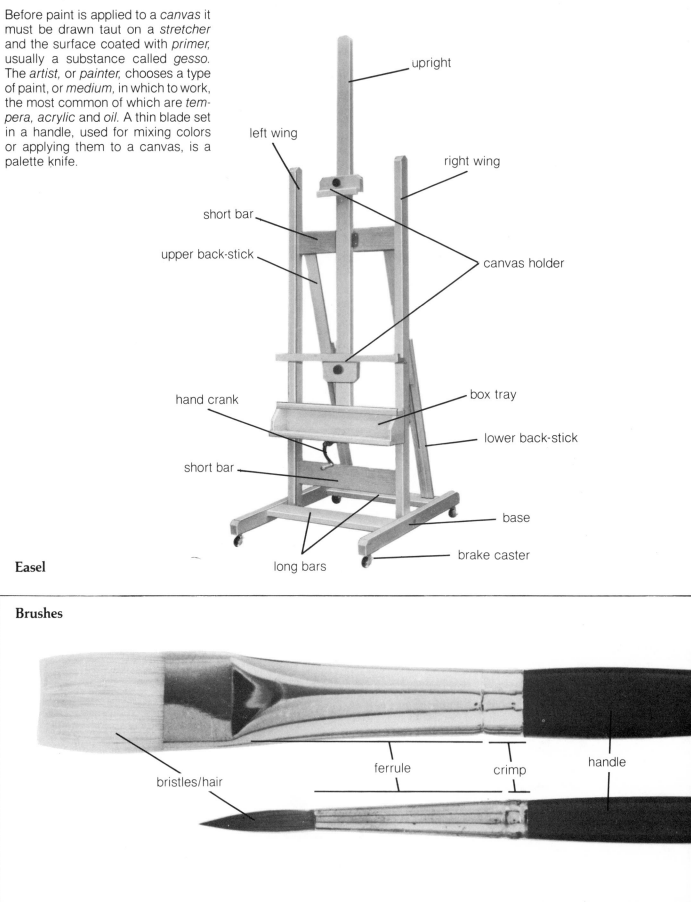

upright

left wing

right wing

short bar

upper back-stick

canvas holder

hand crank

box tray

lower back-stick

short bar

base

brake caster

long bars

Easel

Brushes

bristles/hair

ferrule

crimp

handle

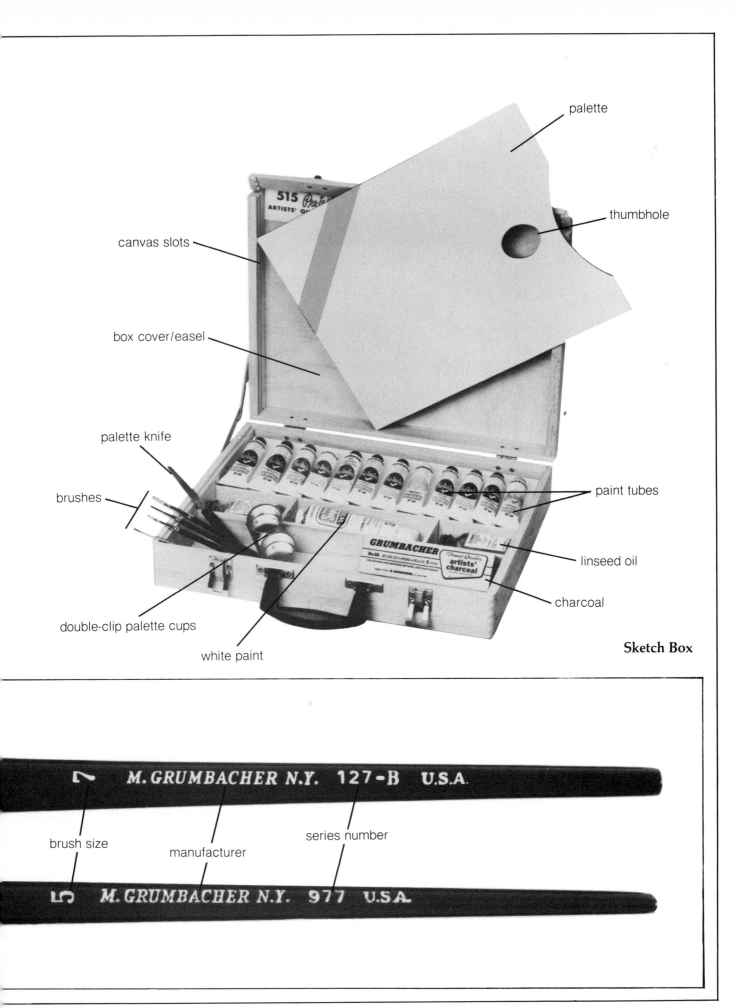

palette

thumbhole

canvas slots

box cover/easel

palette knife

brushes

paint tubes

linseed oil

GRUMBACHER
artists' charcoal

charcoal

double-clip palette cups

white paint

Sketch Box

7 M. GRUMBACHER N.Y. 127-B U.S.A.

brush size

manufacturer

series number

5 M. GRUMBACHER N.Y. 977 U.S.A.

Sculpting Tools

In stone sculpture, a *subtractive process,* forms or objects are created in *three dimensions* or in *relief.* Works may be carved or built up from some flexible material. Whenever a pliant material is used, it may be laid upon an inner skeleton, or *armature.* To make the finished product more durable, it may be fired or cast.

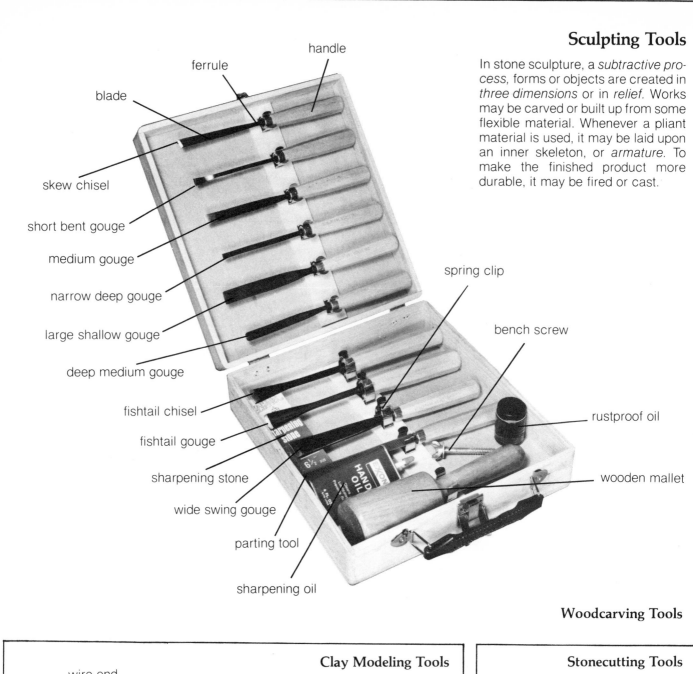

ferrule

handle

blade

skew chisel

short bent gouge

medium gouge

narrow deep gouge

large shallow gouge

deep medium gouge

fishtail chisel

fishtail gouge

sharpening stone

wide swing gouge

parting tool

sharpening oil

spring clip

bench screw

rustproof oil

wooden mallet

Woodcarving Tools

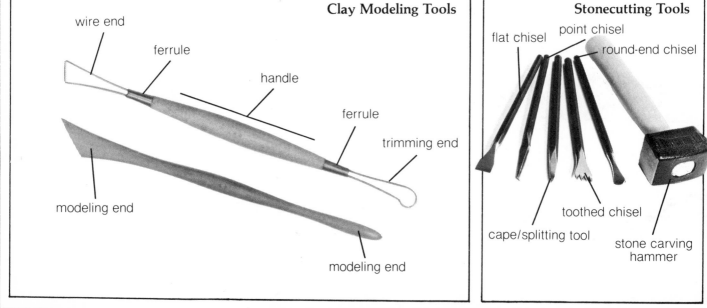

Clay Modeling Tools

wire end

ferrule

handle

ferrule

trimming end

modeling end

modeling end

Stonecutting Tools

flat chisel

point chisel

round-end chisel

toothed chisel

cape/splitting tool

stone carving hammer

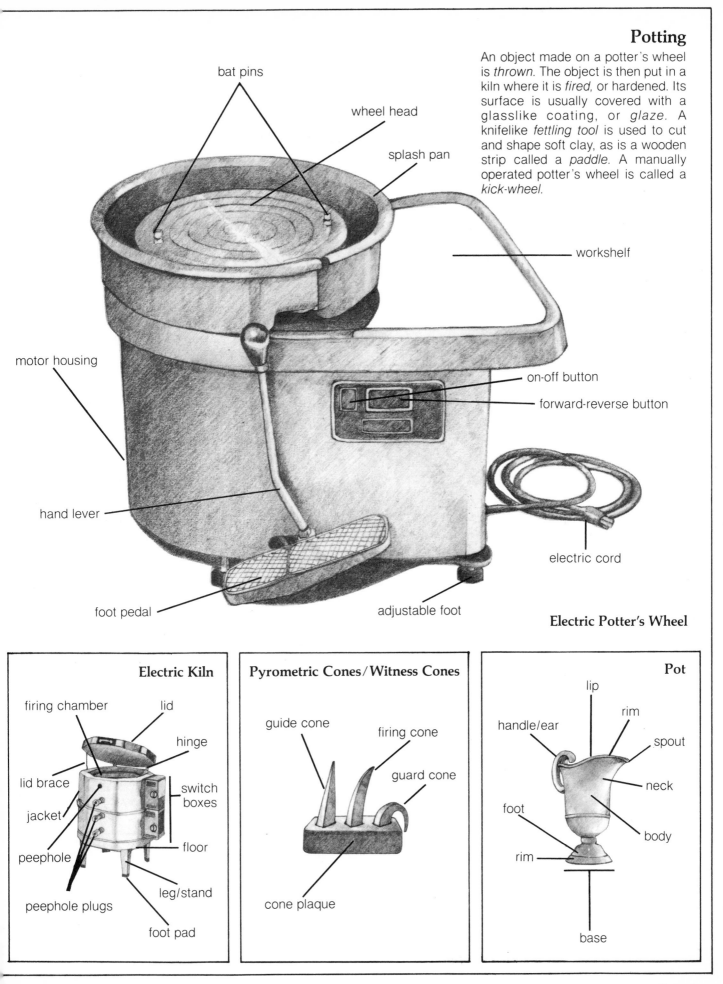

Potting

An object made on a potter's wheel is *thrown*. The object is then put in a kiln where it is *fired*, or hardened. Its surface is usually covered with a glasslike coating, or *glaze*. A knifelike *fettling tool* is used to cut and shape soft clay, as is a wooden strip called a *paddle*. A manually operated potter's wheel is called a *kick-wheel*.

bat pins

wheel head

splash pan

worfrom shelf

motor housing

on-off button

forward-reverse button

hand lever

electric cord

foot pedal

adjustable foot

Electric Potter's Wheel

Electric Kiln

firing chamber

lid

hinge

lid brace

switch boxes

jacket

peephole

floor

peephole plugs

leg/stand

foot pad

Pyrometric Cones / Witness Cones

guide cone

firing cone

guard cone

cone plaque

Pot

lip

rim

handle/ear

spout

neck

foot

body

rim

base

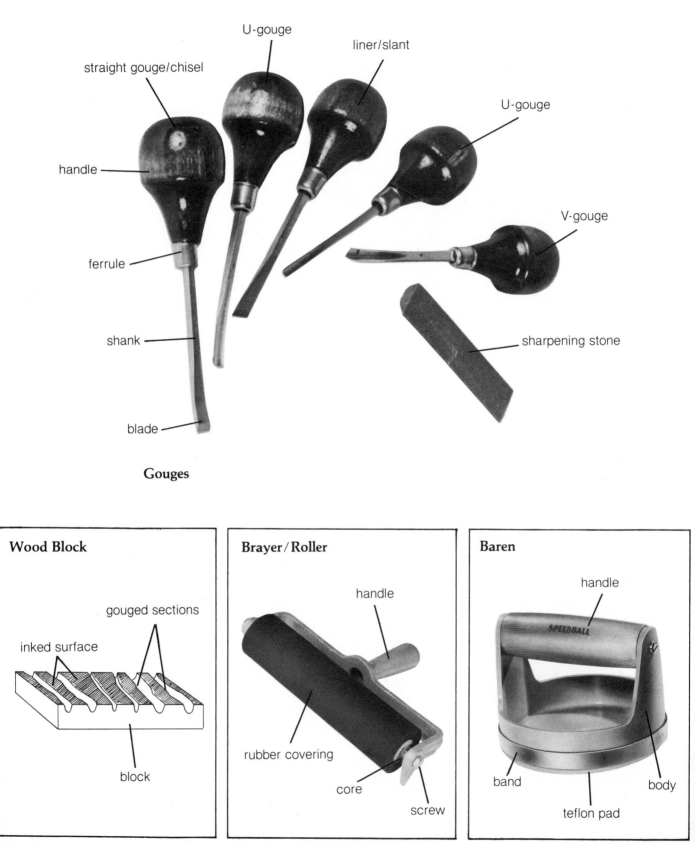

Woodcut Printing

The art of making *engravings* with wooden blocks is *xylography,* and the tools used to create the designs are called *gravers.*

straight gouge/chisel

U-gouge

liner/slant

U-gouge

handle

V-gouge

ferrule

sharpening stone

shank

blade

Gouges

Wood Block

gouged sections

inked surface

block

Brayer/Roller

handle

rubber covering

core

screw

Baren

handle

SPEEDBALL

band

teflon pad

body

Silk Screen and Scrimshaw

The *silk-screen printmaking process* is called *serigraphy*. A *stopping medium,* called a *resist,* blocks out or *masks* an area of the screen. Ink or paint passes through the unprotected areas of the screen to become the print. A person who does *decorative engravings* or *carvings* in *ivory* or *whalebone* is called a *scrimshander.*

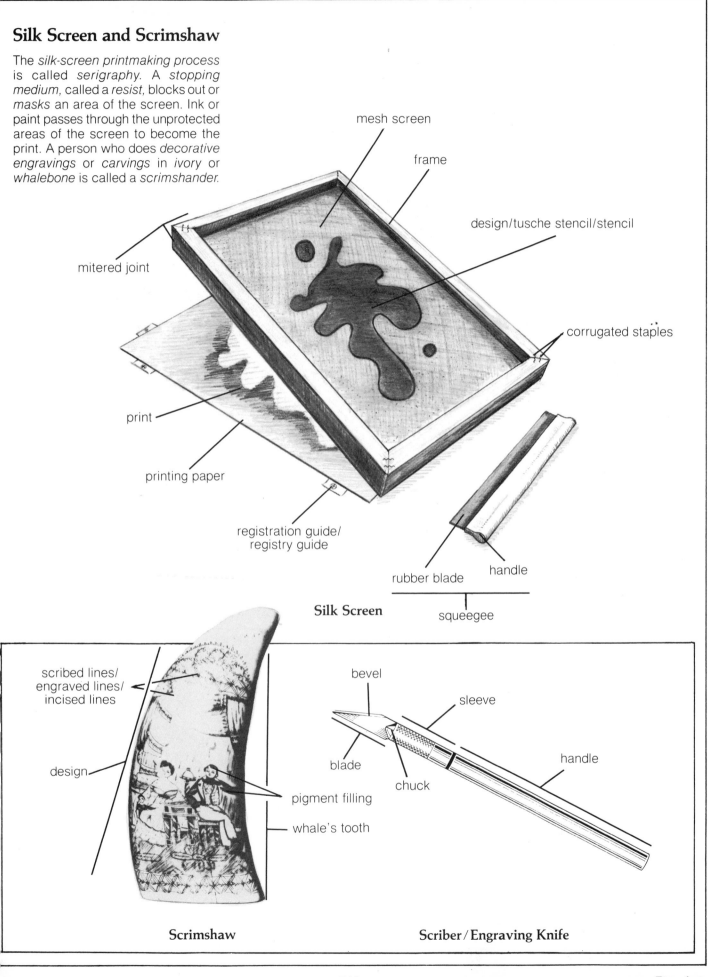

mesh screen

frame

design/tusche stencil/stencil

mitered joint

corrugated staples

print

printing paper

registration guide/
registry guide

rubber blade

handle

squeegee

Silk Screen

scribed lines/
engraved lines/
incised lines

bevel

sleeve

handle

design

blade

chuck

pigment filling

whale's tooth

Scrimshaw

Scriber/Engraving Knife

Fine Arts

Lithography

Lithography is a form of *planographic printing*. The design is made on a stone, prepared, or "grained," by spinning the levigator over its surface, or on a metal *plate* with a *lithographic crayon, lithographic pencil, rubbing ink* or *asphaltum*.

adjustment screw

manufacturer's identification

locknut

pressure bar

screws

cambox

cambox shaft

crank handle

uprights

scraper bar holder

lock screw

gear box

scraper

stone

printing surface

clutch

chain guard

stand

press body

press bed

bed handle

Lithographic Press

Levigator

head of bolt

washer

wooden pipe

detents

nut

body

Intaglio and Etching

Intaglio, or *incised printing,* is a type of *printmaking* in which a design is cut into a *plate* by techniques such as etching, *engraving, soft ground* or *aquatint.* A person who engraves metal is called a *chaser.*

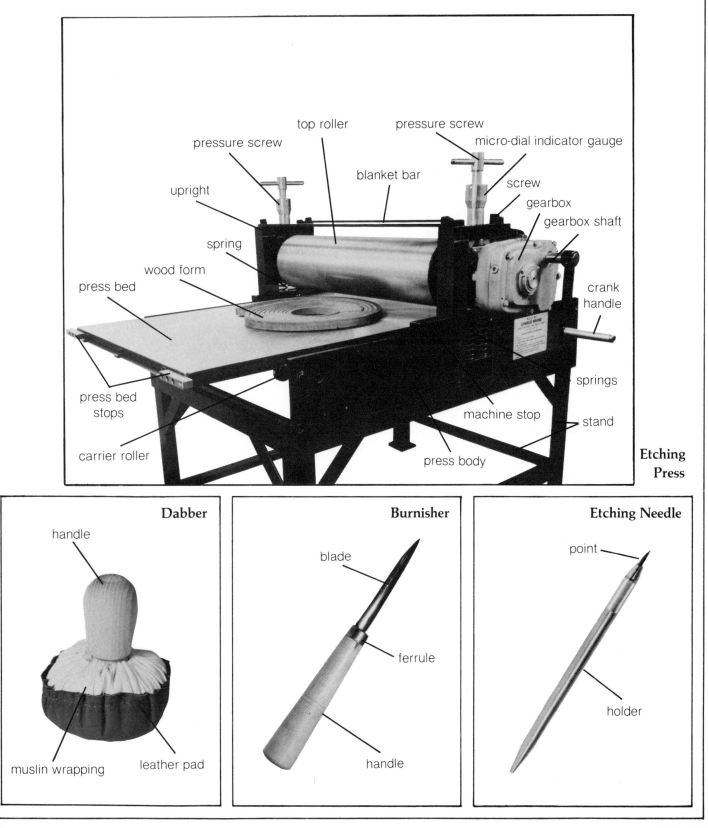

pressure screw
top roller
pressure screw
micro-dial indicator gauge
blanket bar
screw
upright
gearbox
gearbox shaft
spring
wood form
crank handle
press bed
press bed stops
springs
carrier roller
machine stop
stand
press body

Etching Press

Dabber
handle
muslin wrapping
leather pad

Burnisher
blade
ferrule
handle

Etching Needle
point
holder

Fine Arts

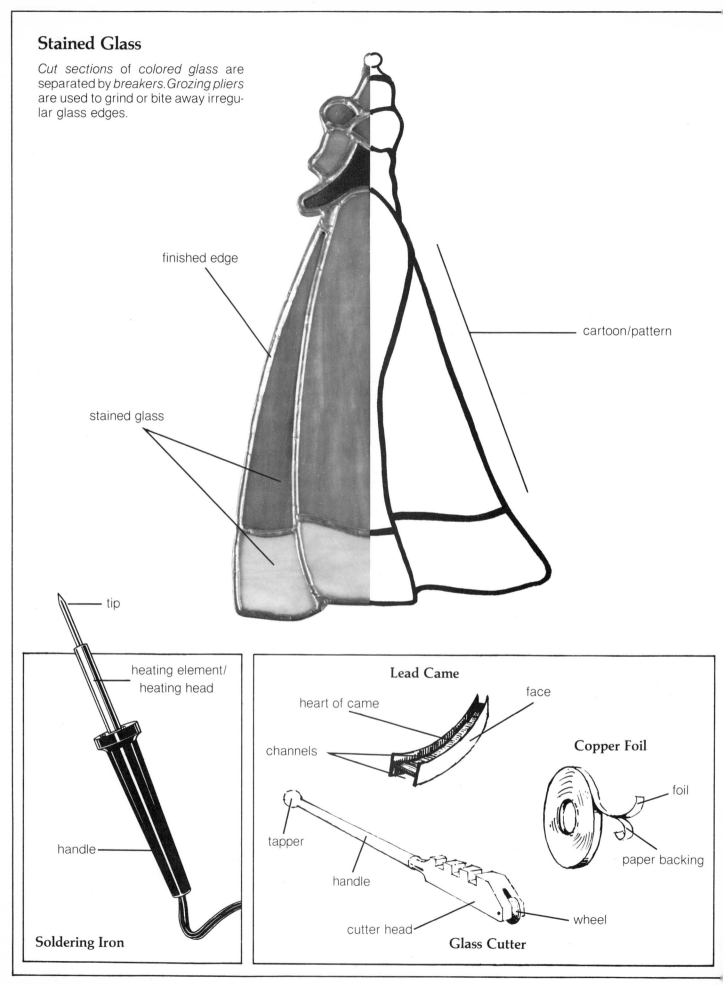

Stained Glass

Cut sections of *colored glass* are separated by *breakers.Grozing pliers* are used to grind or bite away irregular glass edges.

finished edge

stained glass

cartoon/pattern

tip

heating element/
heating head

handle

Soldering Iron

Lead Came

heart of came

face

channels

tapper

handle

cutter head

wheel

Glass Cutter

Copper Foil

foil

paper backing

Frame

The frame shown here is a long-lasting *archival frame*. The area cut out of the mat to reveal the artwork is the *mat window*. A wire hanger can be attached to L-shaped *shoulder hooks*, *picture hooks* or *nails* as well as to screw eyes. The process of permanently affixing artwork to a backing is called *mounting*. A *free-standing easel-back* or *piano frame* consists of an easel, backing and an angled support *stand*. In *passe-partout*, the framing elements are held together by strips of cloth or paper pasted over the edges.

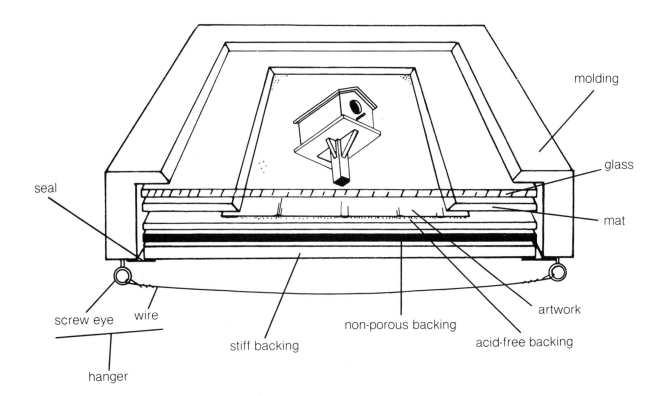

molding

glass

mat

seal

screw eye   wire

artwork

non-porous backing

acid-free backing

stiff backing

hanger

Cartooning

Many one-panel cartoons use *captions* or *labels* below the *illustration* for dialogue or explanation. Those appearing on the editorial pages of newspapers are called *editorial* or *political cartoons* and usually feature an exaggerated likeness, or *caricature*, of some well-known figure, as the main *character*. *Comics*, or *comic books*, use cartooning throughout. A complete *sphericasia*, or *swalloop*, is used by a *cartoonist* to depict a complete swing at an object, be it a golf ball or another person.

brick symbolia

thought balloon

agitrons

onomatopoeia

dites

ROWR!

lucaflect

staggeration

artist's signature

cross-hatching

vites

briffit

Comic Strip

strip title

cartoonist

cartoon panel/frame

speech balloon

border

beetle bailey®

by mort walker

DOES ANYONE KNOW WHERE I LEFT MY...MY, UH...

...WHERE I LEFT MY, UH...

...THINGAMAJIG?

Cartooning

Sewing

Each in-and-out movement of a threaded needle produces a *stitch*. A scissor's *bite* is the distance it cuts into a fabric on a single stroke. A small cushion into which pins or most-used needles are stuck until needed is called a *pincushion*.

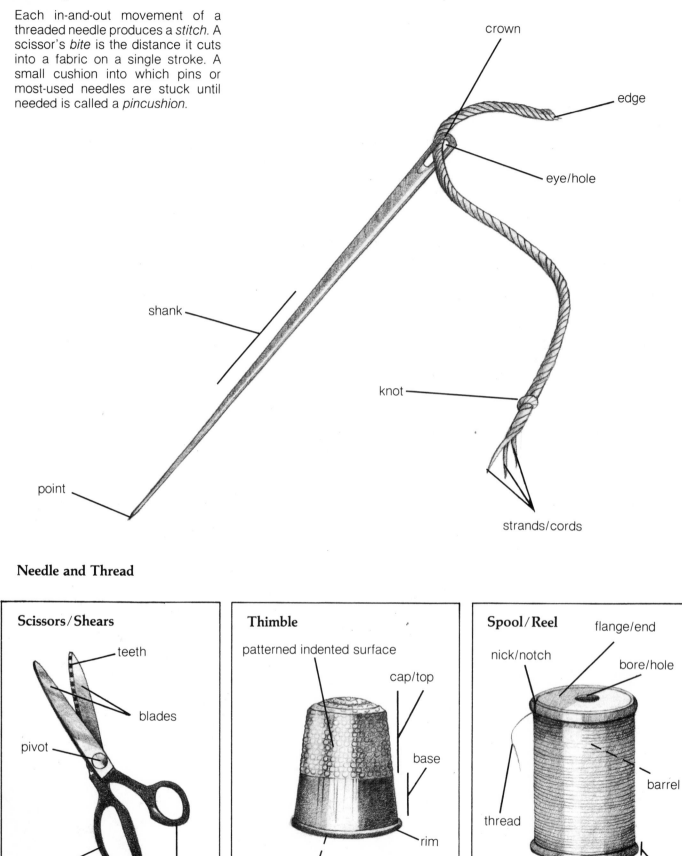

crown

edge

eye/hole

shank

knot

point

strands/cords

Needle and Thread

Scissors/Shears

teeth

blades

pivot

bow handle

ring handle

Thimble

patterned indented surface

cap/top

base

rim

cup

Spool/Reel

flange/end

nick/notch

bore/hole

barrel

thread

rim

Decorative Stitching

Stitchery, the art of decorating fabric with thread, includes embroidery, *crewel, needlepoint, petitpoint, grospoint* and *bargello.* Among quilting techniques are *appliqué,* sewing pieces of material to a background; *patchwork,* combining small geometric pieces of fabric; and *trapunto,* filling a small area with batting for a raised effect.

cross stitching/embroidery

fabric

fabric ridge

outer-ring lip

outer ring

Embroidery

inner ring

adjustable screw

Quilting

top fabric

batting/filler

backing

Crafts

Knitting

Knitting is the interlacing of *loops*. The main stitches are the *knit stitch*, or *stitch*, and the *purl stitch*, or *purl*. *Crocheting* is a form of *needlework* done by looping thread with a *crochet needle*. *Macrame* is knotting, and *tatting* is done by looping and knotting with a single cotton thread and a small shuttle.

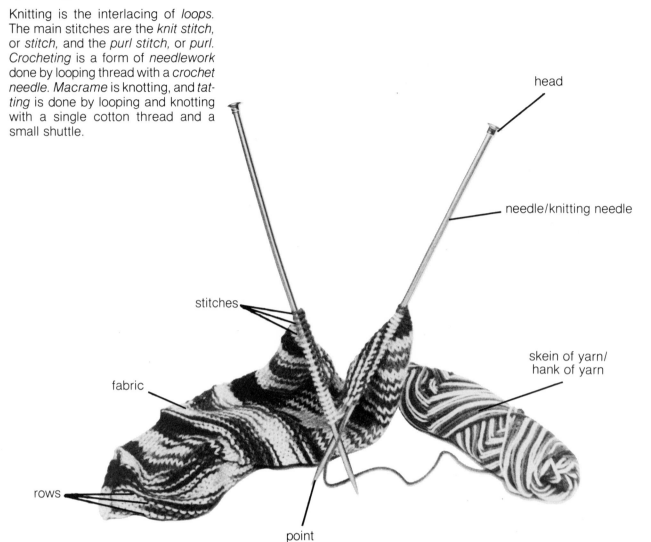

head

needle/knitting needle

stitches

skein of yarn/ hank of yarn

fabric

rows

point

Hand Knitting

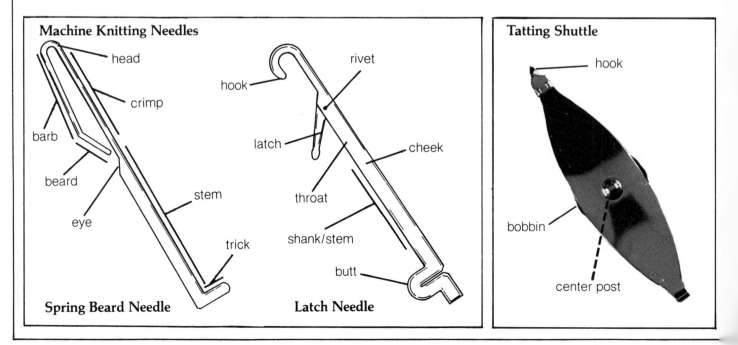

Machine Knitting Needles

head

crimp

hook

rivet

barb

latch

cheek

beard

throat

stem

eye

shank/stem

trick

butt

Spring Beard Needle

Latch Needle

Tatting Shuttle

hook

bobbin

center post

Weaving

The lengthwise (front to back) *yarn* or *threads* on a loom are called the warp. Threads taken together which run from side to side, or from *selvage* to selvage, are called the *weft*. The weft is also often called the *woof,* although more correctly, the woof is the same as the *web,* or finished *fabric.*

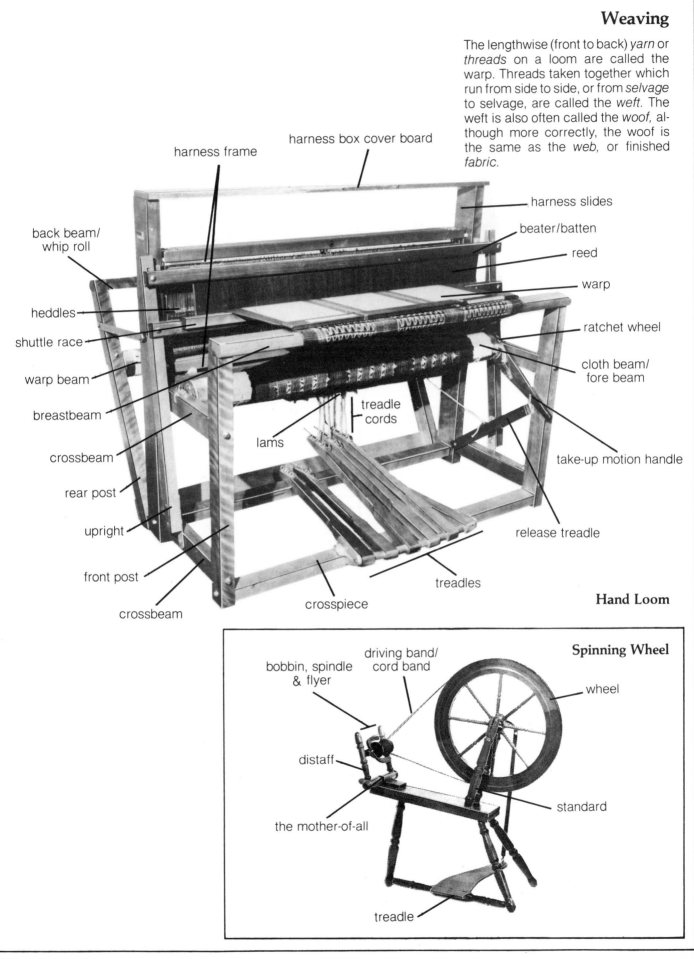

harness frame

harness box cover board

harness slides

beater/batten

reed

back beam/ whip roll

warp

heddles

ratchet wheel

shuttle race

cloth beam/ fore beam

warp beam

breastbeam

treadle cords

crossbeam

lams

rear post

take-up motion handle

upright

front post

release treadle

crossbeam

treadles

crosspiece

Hand Loom

Spinning Wheel

driving band/ cord band

bobbin, spindle & flyer

wheel

distaff

the mother-of-all

standard

treadle

Crafts

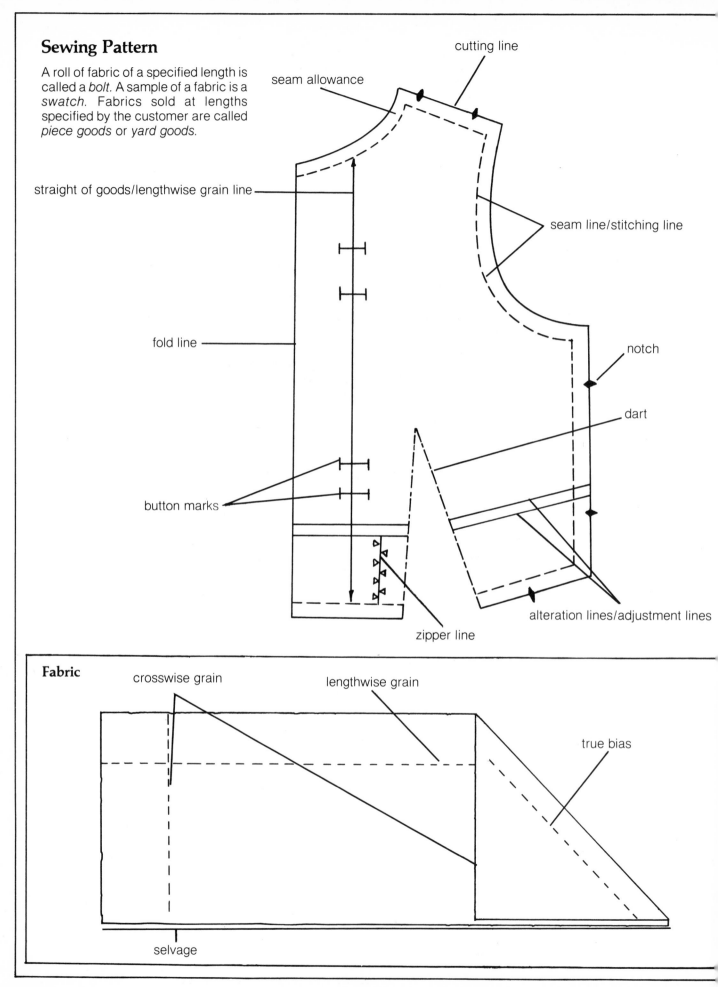

Sewing Pattern

A roll of fabric of a specified length is called a *bolt*. A sample of a fabric is a *swatch*. Fabrics sold at lengths specified by the customer are called *piece goods* or *yard goods*.

cutting line

seam allowance

straight of goods/lengthwise grain line

seam line/stitching line

fold line

notch

dart

button marks

alteration lines/adjustment lines

zipper line

Fabric

crosswise grain

lengthwise grain

true bias

selvage

Machinery, Tools and Weapons

Except for office and industrial equipment, which is outside the scope of this book, this section covers all the man-made equipment one is likely to encounter in everyday life, daily reading or classroom learning. It includes basic power systems and offshoots, everything from a nuclear power plant to an electrical plug, equipment used to control temperature in a house, and components of various engines.

Considerable space has been devoted to illustrating the parts of tools used around the home and in the yard while not ignoring the basic gear used by ranchers, trappers, farmers, scientists and doctors. Even penal equipment used for capital punishment has been included.

The weaponry subsection traces the names and parts of articles used in warfare from medieval times to objects used today. Thus, a student reading about King Arthur for the first time will be able to identify the parts of a sword as easily as a newspaper reader is able to identify the parts of a modern missile.

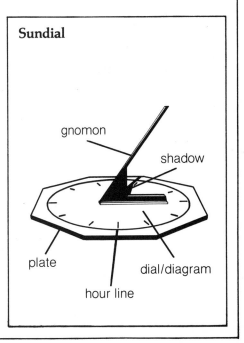

Sundial

gnomon

shadow

plate

hour line

dial/diagram

Wind Systems

The cloth sail on this *smock mill* is in a *first reef,* or *curled,* position, as opposed to *sword point, dagger point* or *full sail.* Sails or *shutters* on a fantail are called *vanes.* Some mills have *petticoats,* or vertical boards, below the cap, to provide protection where cap and tower meet, and *beards,* or decorated boards, behind the cannister.

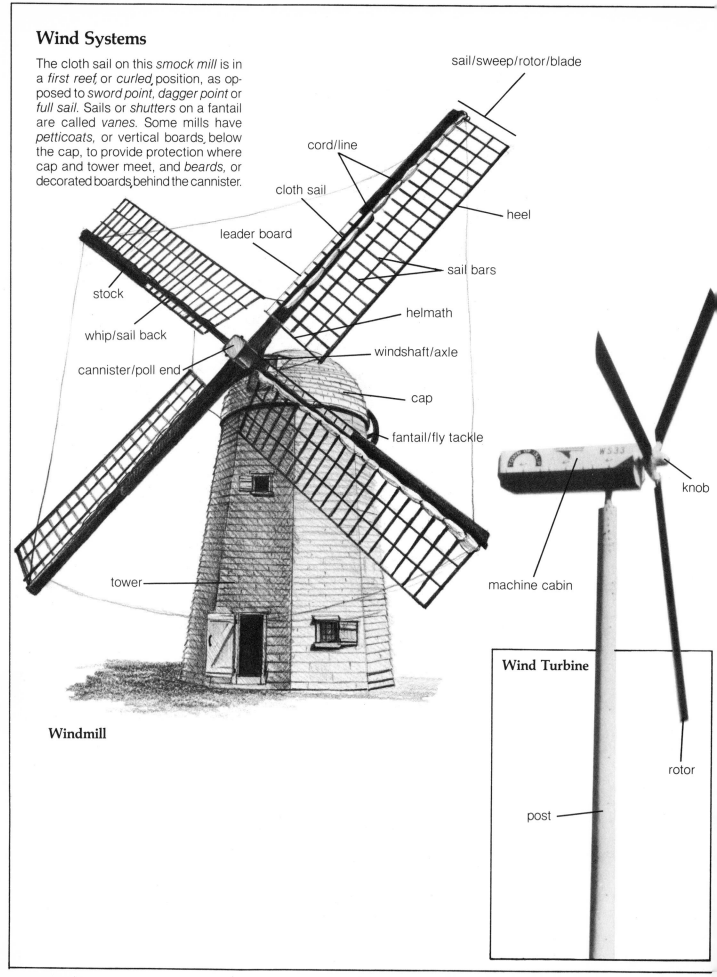

sail/sweep/rotor/blade

cord/line

cloth sail

leader board

heel

sail bars

stock

helmath

whip/sail back

windshaft/axle

cannister/poll end

cap

fantail/fly tackle

tower

Windmill

machine cabin

knob

rotor

Wind Turbine

post

Solar Power System

Solar energy can be collected by systems such as the one shown here, which operate like *radiators* working in reverse to produce hot water. The sun's energy can also be converted directly into *electricity* by *solar cells*. *Concentrating solar collectors* use *lenses* or *reflecting surfaces* to direct sunlight on a trough-type collector to produce large amounts of heat which can be converted into electricity.

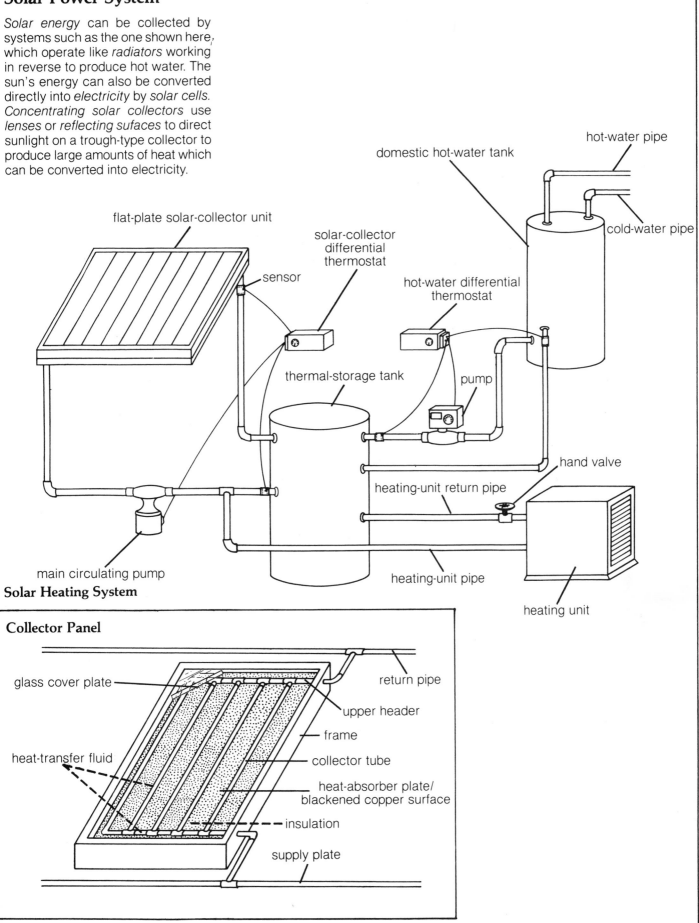

flat-plate solar-collector unit

solar-collector differential thermostat

sensor

hot-water differential thermostat

domestic hot-water tank

hot-water pipe

cold-water pipe

thermal-storage tank

pump

hand valve

heating-unit return pipe

main circulating pump

heating-unit pipe

heating unit

Solar Heating System

Collector Panel

glass cover plate

return pipe

upper header

frame

collector tube

heat-absorber plate/ blackened copper surface

insulation

heat-transfer fluid

supply plate

Nuclear Power Reactor

In order to generate *electricity* by using the heat produced by *fission,* the *chain reaction* must be slowed down and controlled. To control the reaction rate in a reactor, or *pile, rods* of neutron-absorbing material are moved in and out as required. The smallest amount of *fissionable material* in which fission is self-sustaining is called the *critical mass.* If more fissionable material is produced than consumed, the reactor is called a *breeder reactor.*

concrete shield & steel inner shell

relief valve

remote-operated block valve

steam generator

steam line

generator

turbine

condensate pump

pressurizer

emergency core-cooling system pump

control rods

reactor

borated-water storage tank

reactor core

condenser

radioactive-waste storage tank

sump pump

demineralizer

block valve

auxiliary feedwater pump

drain tank

reactor coolant pump

main feedwater pump

sump

Auxiliary Building

Turbine Building

Containment Building

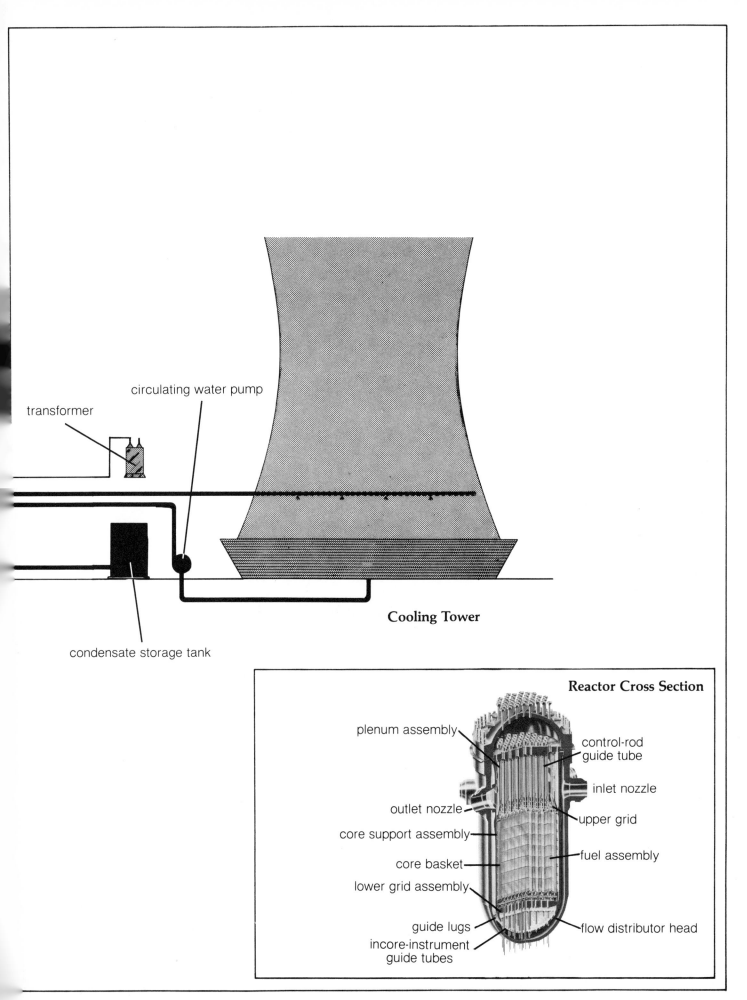

transformer

circulating water pump

condensate storage tank

Cooling Tower

Reactor Cross Section

plenum assembly

control-rod
guide tube

inlet nozzle

outlet nozzle

upper grid

core support assembly

core basket

fuel assembly

lower grid assembly

guide lugs

flow distributor head

incore-instrument
guide tubes

Power Line, Vacuum Tube and Transistor

An *overhead line support, lattice–work tower* or *double-circuit tower* transmits high-voltage electrical power from *generating plants* to various parts of a *power network*. A transistor consists of a small block of a *semiconductor* with at least three *electrodes*.

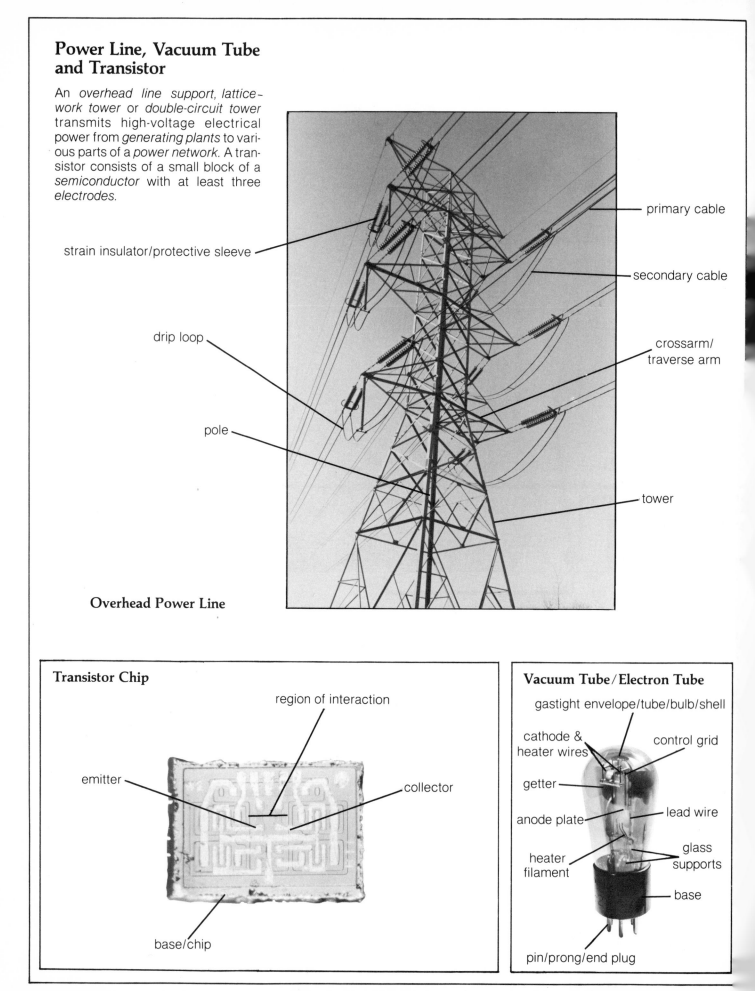

strain insulator/protective sleeve

drip loop

pole

primary cable

secondary cable

crossarm/ traverse arm

tower

Overhead Power Line

Transistor Chip

region of interaction

emitter

collector

base/chip

Vacuum Tube/Electron Tube

gastight envelope/tube/bulb/shell

cathode & heater wires

control grid

getter

anode plate

lead wire

heater filament

glass supports

base

pin/prong/end plug

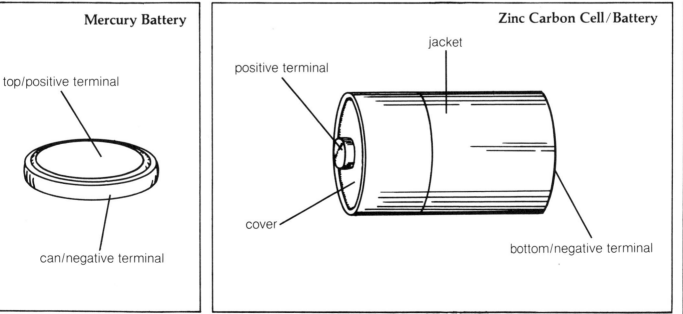

Battery

Batteries are marked with *polarity symbols*, + identifying the positive terminal, − the negative. *Secondary cells* can be recharged, while *primary cells* cannot.

positive terminal/post

vent cap

cell compartments

negative terminal/post

cover

case

Lead Acid Battery

Mercury Battery

top/positive terminal

can/negative terminal

Zinc Carbon Cell/Battery

jacket

positive terminal

cover

bottom/negative terminal

Switch, Receptacle and Plug

A wall switch conducts *electrical current* only when it is in the up, or *on position,* as opposed to the down, or *off position.* *Ground wires* are located inside the junction box. *Attachment plugs,* or *"dead front" plugs,* such as the one shown here, have no exposed current-carrying parts except prongs, blades or *pins.* A *male plug* is fitted into a *female receptacle.*

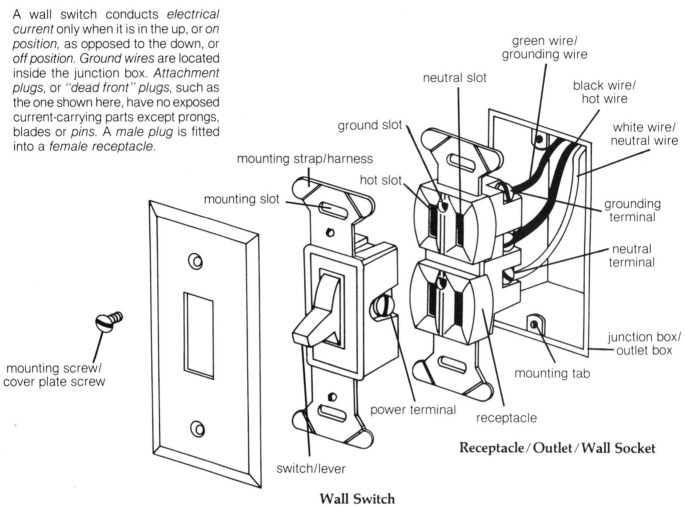

green wire/ grounding wire

black wire/ hot wire

neutral slot

white wire/ neutral wire

ground slot

mounting strap/harness

hot slot

grounding terminal

mounting slot

neutral terminal

junction box/ outlet box

mounting screw/ cover plate screw

mounting tab

power terminal

receptacle

Receptacle/Outlet/Wall Socket

switch/lever

Wall Switch

Cover Plate/Switch Plate

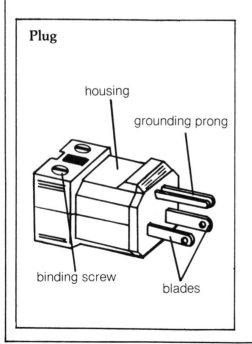

Plug

housing

grounding prong

binding screw

blades

Meter and Fuse Box

Fuses "blow" and circuit breakers "trip" when there is too much heat in the wires of a particular *circuit*. The fuse or circuit breaker acts as a safety device to keep fire from starting by heat caused by an *overload* or by a *short circuit*.

usage registers

shaft

KILOWATT HOURS

SINGLE-PHASE WATTHOUR METER TYPE I-30-A
15 AMPERES   115-120 VOLTS
K₈=1.5   60 CYCLES   3-WIRE
                MODEL AC10

18 690 382

primary cell

glass casing

specifications

electrical connection

LINE   LOAD

Electric Meter

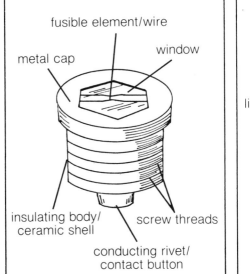

Plug Fuse

fusible element/wire

metal cap

window

primary cell

insulating body/
ceramic shell

screw threads

conducting rivet/
contact button

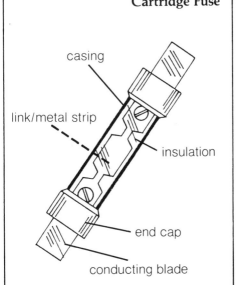

Cartridge Fuse

casing

link/metal strip

insulation

end cap

conducting blade

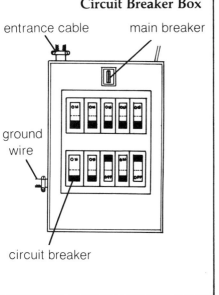

Circuit Breaker Box

entrance cable

main breaker

ground
wire

circuit breaker

Power Systems

Furnace

The furnace shown in this schematic illustration provides *steam heat* to radiators located in various parts of a building.

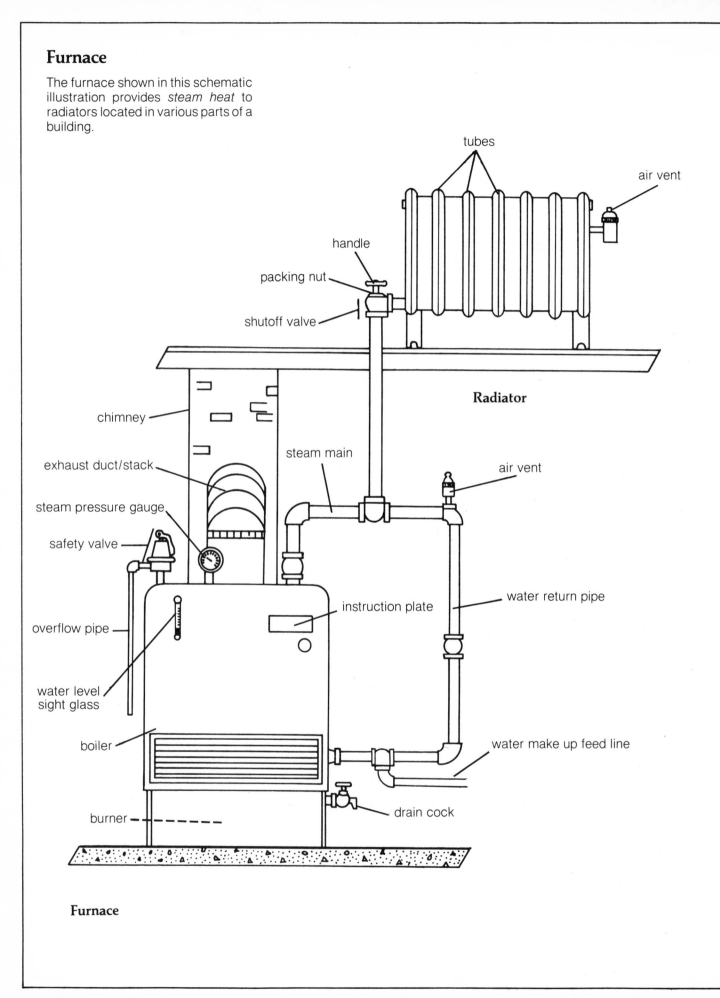

tubes

air vent

handle

packing nut

shutoff valve

Radiator

chimney

exhaust duct/stack

steam main

air vent

steam pressure gauge

safety valve

water return pipe

overflow pipe

instruction plate

water level sight glass

boiler

water make up feed line

burner

drain cock

Furnace

Hot Water Heater

The unit shown here is *gas-fired*. Other models include *electric water heaters* and *oil water heaters.*

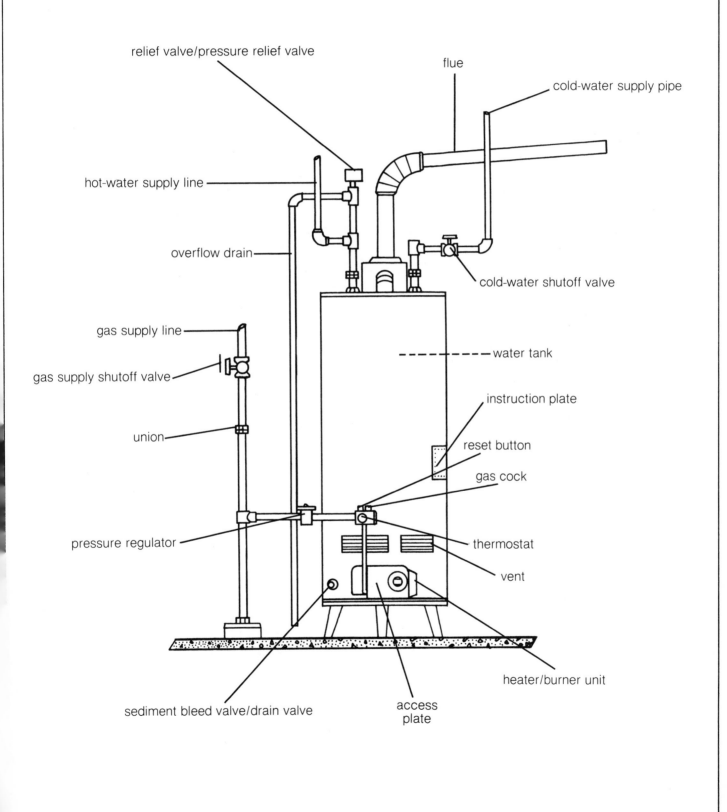

relief valve/pressure relief valve

flue

cold-water supply pipe

hot-water supply line

overflow drain

cold-water shutoff valve

gas supply line

water tank

gas supply shutoff valve

instruction plate

reset button

gas cock

union

pressure regulator

thermostat

vent

sediment bleed valve/drain valve

access plate

heater/burner unit

Climate Control Units

Air Conditioning

An air conditioner's *front grille* has *louvers* which allow cooled air to be directed to any part of a room. *Condenser coils* in the rear of the unit discharge heat outdoors. Hand-held *folding fans, overhead fans* and *rotary fans* circulate air without actually cooling it. A *dehumidifier* removes moisture from the air, whereas a humidifier adds moisture to it.

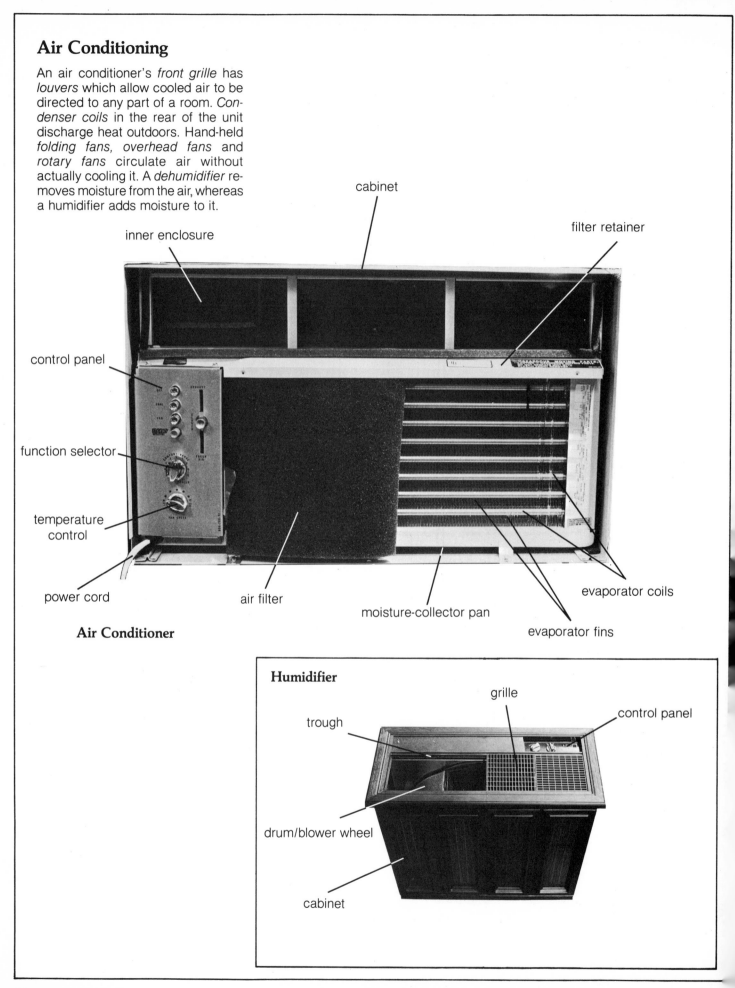

cabinet

filter retainer

inner enclosure

control panel

function selector

temperature control

power cord

air filter

moisture-collector pan

evaporator coils

evaporator fins

Air Conditioner

Humidifier

grille

trough

control panel

drum/blower wheel

cabinet

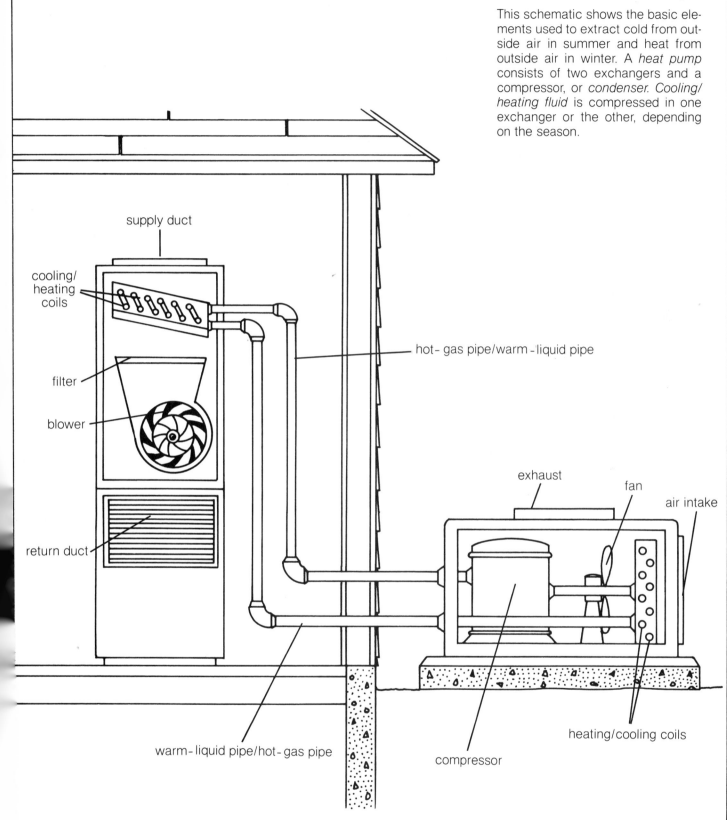

Heat Exchanger

This schematic shows the basic elements used to extract cold from outside air in summer and heat from outside air in winter. A *heat pump* consists of two exchangers and a compressor, or *condenser. Cooling/ heating fluid* is compressed in one exchanger or the other, depending on the season.

supply duct

cooling/ heating coils

filter

blower

return duct

hot-gas pipe/warm-liquid pipe

exhaust

fan

air intake

heating/cooling coils

compressor

warm-liquid pipe/hot-gas pipe

Climate Control Units

Woodburning Stove

When the *stove damper* is closed, interior *baffles* direct air into the *secondary combustion chamber,* then through the *smoke path* until it exits through the flue collar. A stovepipe led through a wall is attached to a *thimble.* The original *Franklin stove* was built into the wall, but three sides extended into the room to radiate heat.

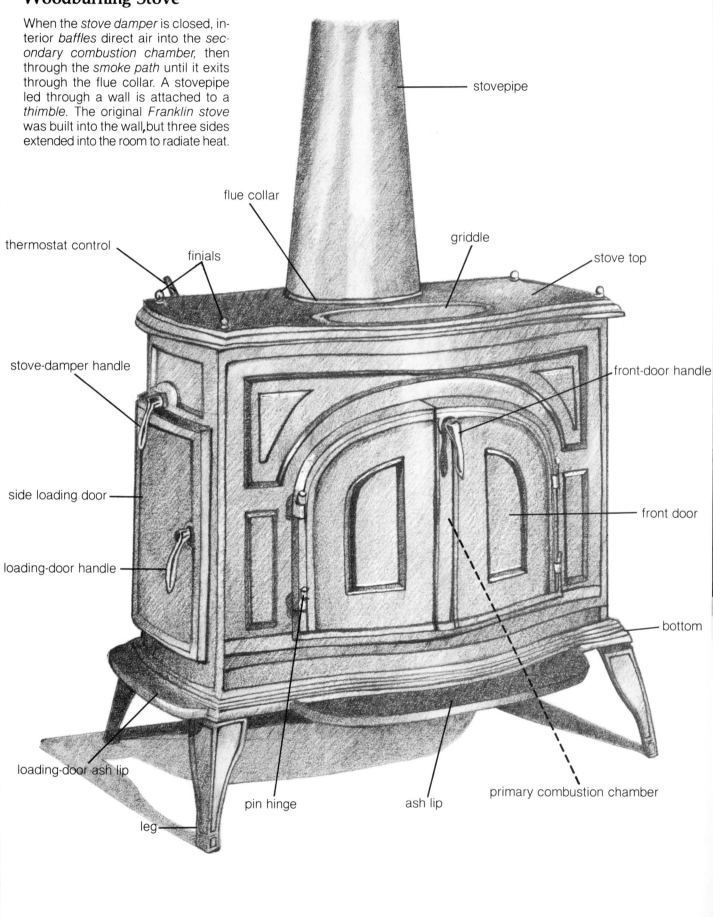

stovepipe

flue collar

griddle

thermostat control

finials

stove top

stove-damper handle

front-door handle

side loading door

front door

loading-door handle

bottom

loading-door ash lip

pin hinge

ash lip

primary combustion chamber

leg

Steam Engine

The steam engine was used to generate *mechanical power* from *thermal energy*. A *piston* inside the steam cylinder, or *engine cylinder*, was driven by *high-pressure steam*. It moved the crankshaft to provide *rotational motion*.

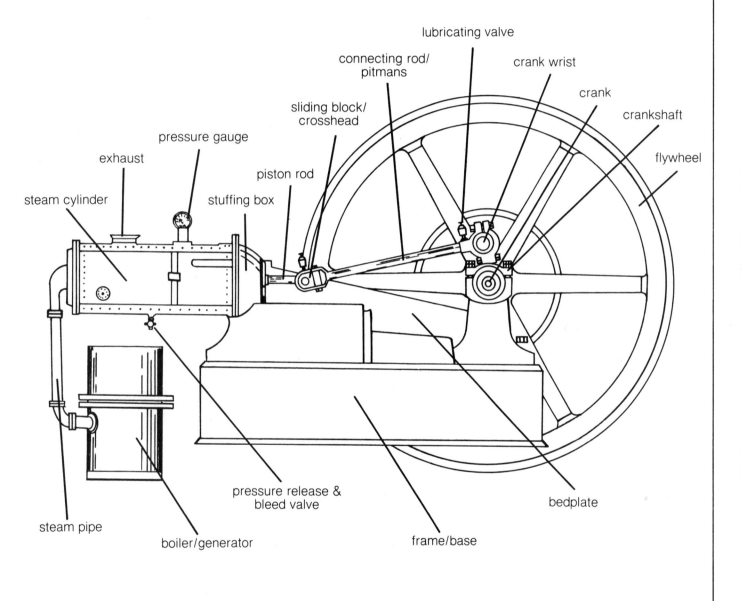

lubricating valve

connecting rod/ pitmans

crank wrist

crank

sliding block/ crosshead

crankshaft

pressure gauge

flywheel

exhaust

piston rod

steam cylinder

stuffing box

pressure release & bleed valve

bedplate

steam pipe

frame/base

boiler/generator

Internal Combustion Engine

The internal combustion engine is one in which combustion of fuel takes place within the *cylinder,* the product of which is measured in *horsepower.* Engines are *two-cycle, four-cycle,* or *Otto cycle; gas-* or *diesel-fueled; air-cooled* or *liquid-cooled.*

gas cap

gas tank

fuel cock

spark plug lead

throttle shaft

model, specification & serial number plate

air filter

WISCONSIN ROBIN

shroud

muffler

control lever

screen

stop plate

governor lever

oil filler dipstick

governor spring

recoil starter plate

oil-drain plug

exhaust

starter handle

crankcase/ cylinder body

Jet Engines

A *turboprop engine* is like a combustion jet engine or *turbofan jet*, except that its turbine wheel is attached to a *crankshaft* that turns a *propeller.* Unlike a rocket, a *ramjet,* or *flying stovepipe*, combines compressed incoming air with fuel injection and ignition for propulsion.

air inlets

exhaust cone

exhaust nozzle control

compressor fans

fuel nozzle

turbine

combustion chamber

Combustion Jet Engine

Rocket

liquid fuel

pump

exhaust port

liquid oxygen

combustion chamber

Engines

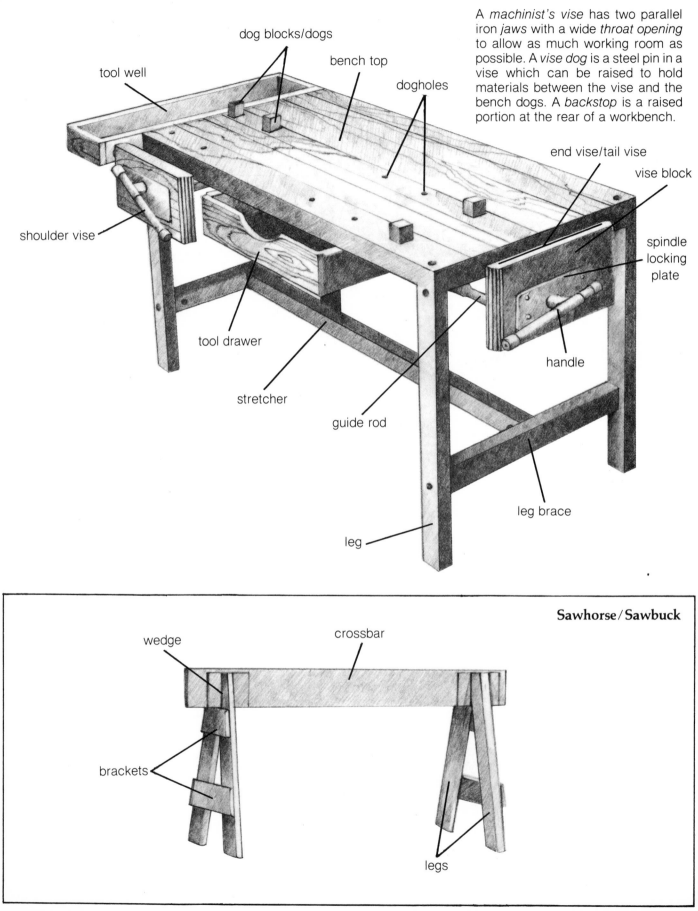

Workbench

A *machinist's vise* has two parallel iron *jaws* with a wide *throat opening* to allow as much working room as possible. A *vise dog* is a steel pin in a vise which can be raised to hold materials between the vise and the bench dogs. A *backstop* is a raised portion at the rear of a workbench.

dog blocks/dogs

bench top

tool well

dogholes

end vise/tail vise

vise block

shoulder vise

spindle locking plate

tool drawer

handle

stretcher

guide rod

leg brace

leg

Sawhorse / Sawbuck

wedge

crossbar

brackets

legs

Clamps

In addition to the *holding tools* shown here, there are *hand screws, bar clamps, miter clamps, band clamps* and *spring clamps.* A *woodworking vise* is similar to a *metalworking vise* except that its jaws are padded in order to hold lumber without marring it. In wood clamps, the steel screws operate through *pivots* so that the jaws can be set at any required angle. *Adjustable C-clamps,* also known as *short bar clamps,* have an adjustable jaw that slides along a flat metal bar to the desired position.

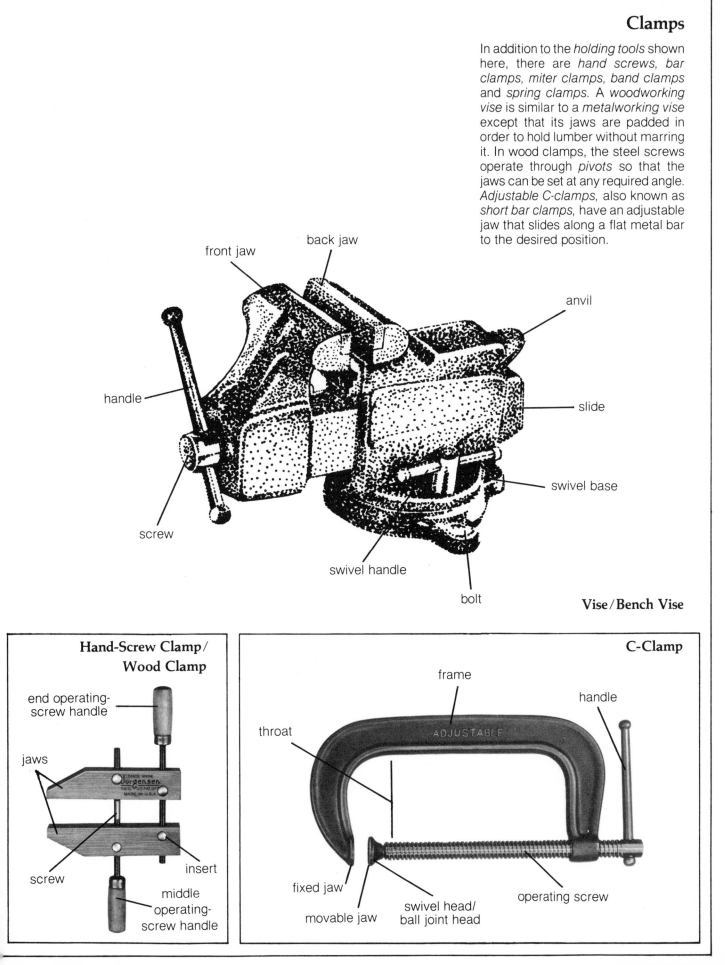

back jaw

front jaw

anvil

handle

slide

swivel base

screw

swivel handle

bolt

Vise / Bench Vise

Hand-Screw Clamp / Wood Clamp

end operating-screw handle

jaws

screw

insert

middle operating-screw handle

C-Clamp

frame

handle

throat

ADJUSTABLE

fixed jaw

movable jaw

swivel head/ ball joint head

operating screw

Household Tools

Nails and Screws

A nail is measured in *penny sizes*. A *brad* is a thin *finishing nail* with a tiny *nailhead* used mainly in cabinetwork. *Spikes* are large, heavy nails. The small hole drilled prior to driving a screw is called a *pilot hole*.

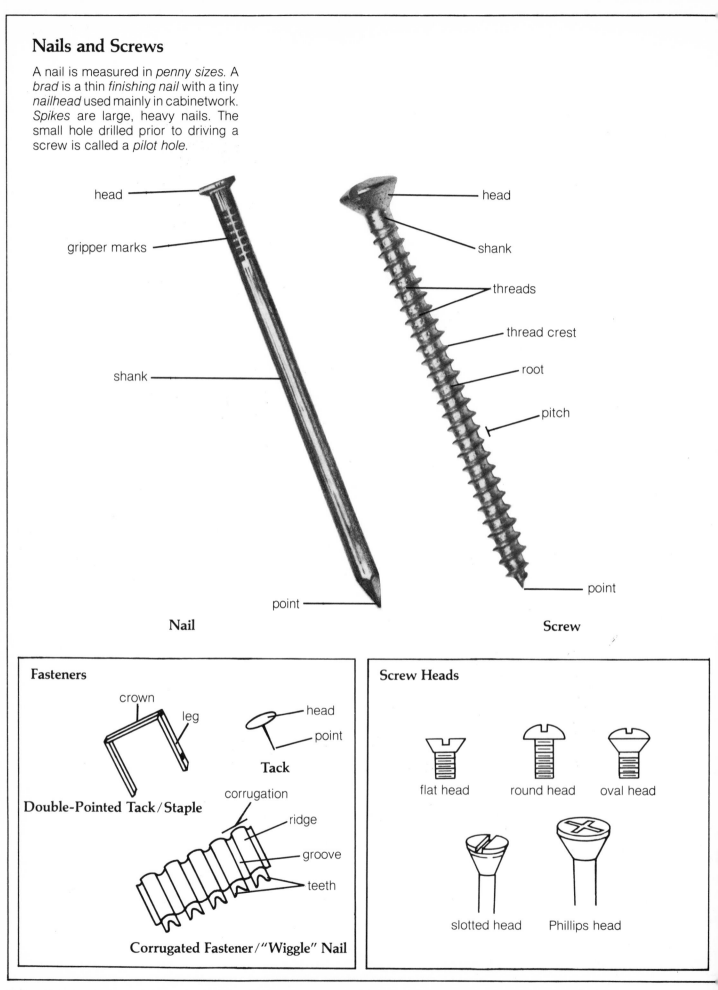

head

gripper marks

shank

point

Nail

head

shank

threads

thread crest

root

pitch

point

Screw

Fasteners

crown

leg

Double-Pointed Tack/Staple

head

point

Tack

corrugation

ridge

groove

teeth

Corrugated Fastener/"Wiggle" Nail

Screw Heads

flat head

round head

oval head

slotted head

Phillips head

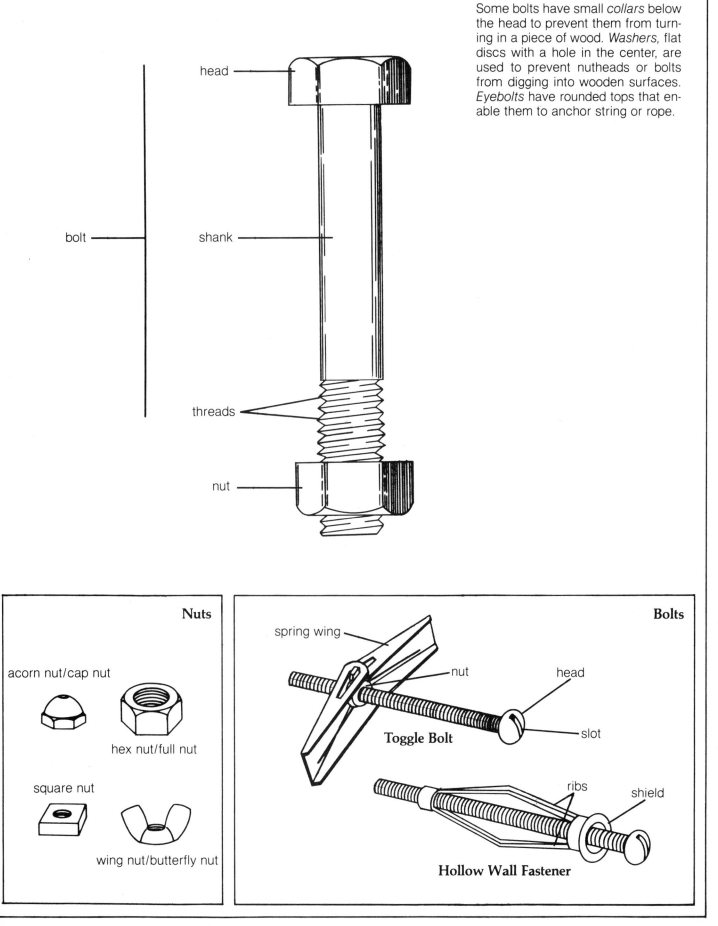

Nuts and Bolts

Some bolts have small *collars* below the head to prevent them from turning in a piece of wood. *Washers,* flat discs with a hole in the center, are used to prevent nutheads or bolts from digging into wooden surfaces. *Eyebolts* have rounded tops that enable them to anchor string or rope.

head

bolt

shank

threads

nut

Nuts

acorn nut/cap nut

hex nut/full nut

square nut

wing nut/butterfly nut

Bolts

spring wing

nut

head

slot

Toggle Bolt

ribs

shield

Hollow Wall Fastener

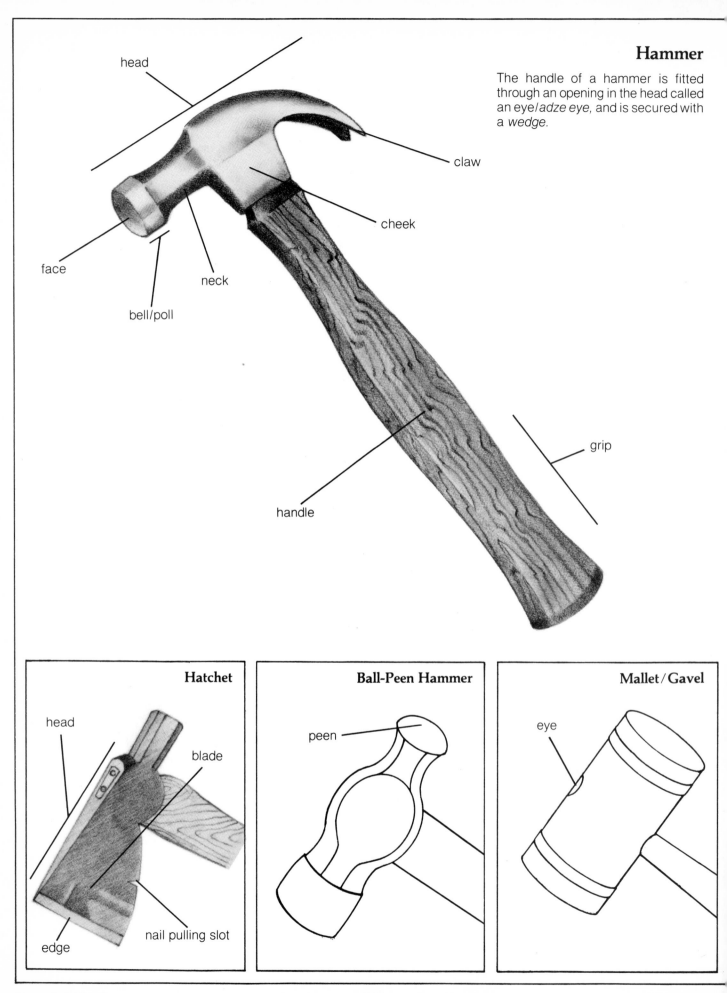

Hammer

The handle of a hammer is fitted through an opening in the head called an eye/*adze eye*, and is secured with a *wedge*.

head

claw

cheek

face

bell/poll

neck

grip

handle

Hatchet

head

blade

edge

nail pulling slot

Ball-Peen Hammer

peen

Mallet/Gavel

eye

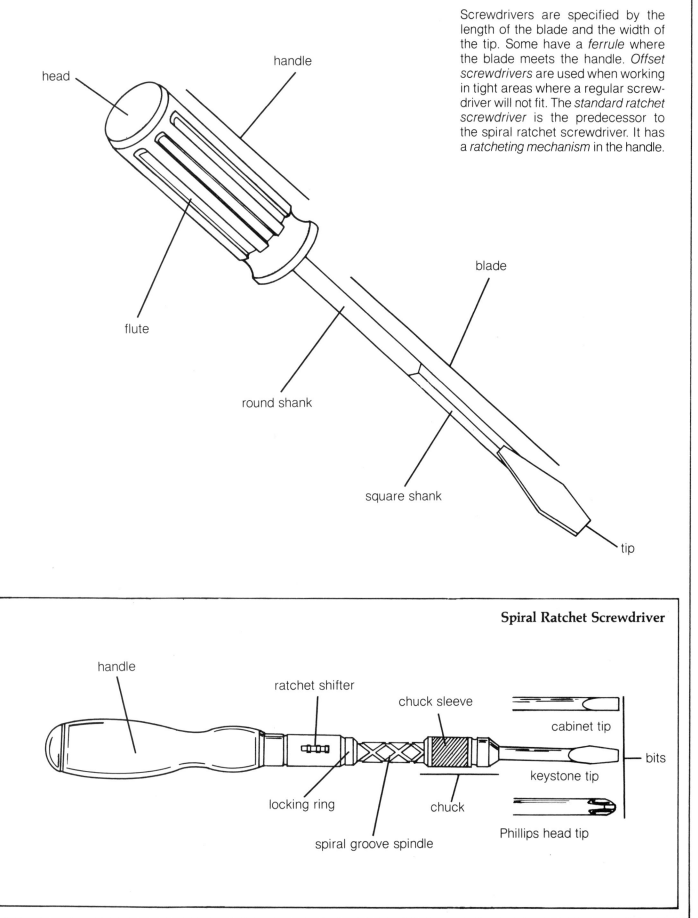

Screwdriver

Screwdrivers are specified by the length of the blade and the width of the tip. Some have a *ferrule* where the blade meets the handle. *Offset screwdrivers* are used when working in tight areas where a regular screwdriver will not fit. The *standard ratchet screwdriver* is the predecessor to the spiral ratchet screwdriver. It has a *ratcheting mechanism* in the handle.

head

handle

flute

round shank

blade

square shank

tip

Spiral Ratchet Screwdriver

handle

ratchet shifter

chuck sleeve

cabinet tip

bits

locking ring

keystone tip

chuck

spiral groove spindle

Phillips head tip

Pliers

In addition to the pliers seen here, there are heavy-duty *bolt cutters; midget pliers* and *needle-nose pliers,* often used for jewelry work or electrical jobs; *music wire pliers,* used for cutting piano wire; and *duckbill pliers,* used primarily by telephone workers and weavers.

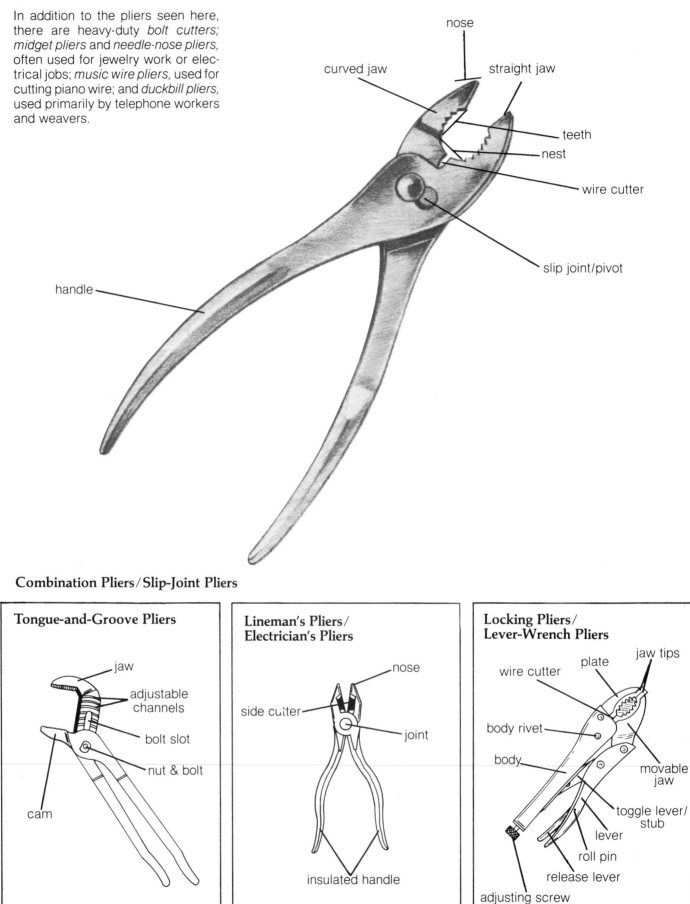

nose

curved jaw

straight jaw

teeth

nest

wire cutter

slip joint/pivot

handle

Combination Pliers/Slip-Joint Pliers

Tongue-and-Groove Pliers

jaw

adjustable channels

bolt slot

nut & bolt

cam

Lineman's Pliers/ Electrician's Pliers

nose

side cutter

joint

insulated handle

Locking Pliers/ Lever-Wrench Pliers

wire cutter

plate

jaw tips

body rivet

body

movable jaw

toggle lever/ stub

lever

roll pin

release lever

adjusting screw

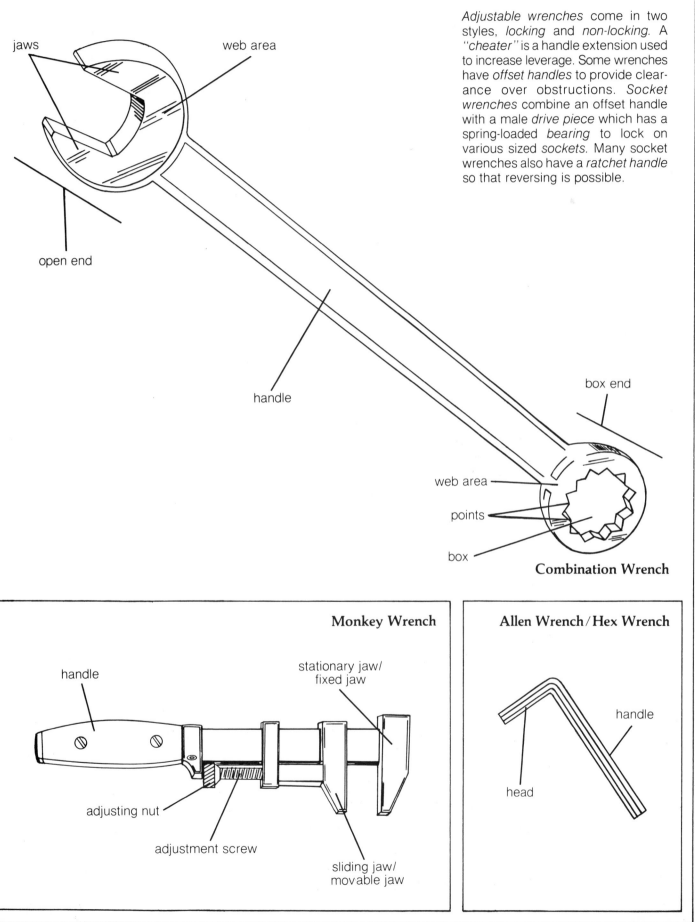

Wrench

jaws

web area

open end

handle

Adjustable wrenches come in two styles, *locking* and *non-locking*. A *"cheater"* is a handle extension used to increase leverage. Some wrenches have *offset handles* to provide clearance over obstructions. *Socket wrenches* combine an offset handle with a male *drive piece* which has a spring-loaded *bearing* to lock on various sized *sockets*. Many socket wrenches also have a *ratchet handle* so that reversing is possible.

box end

web area

points

box

Combination Wrench

Monkey Wrench

handle

stationary jaw/
fixed jaw

adjusting nut

adjustment screw

sliding jaw/
movable jaw

Allen Wrench/Hex Wrench

handle

head

Household Tools

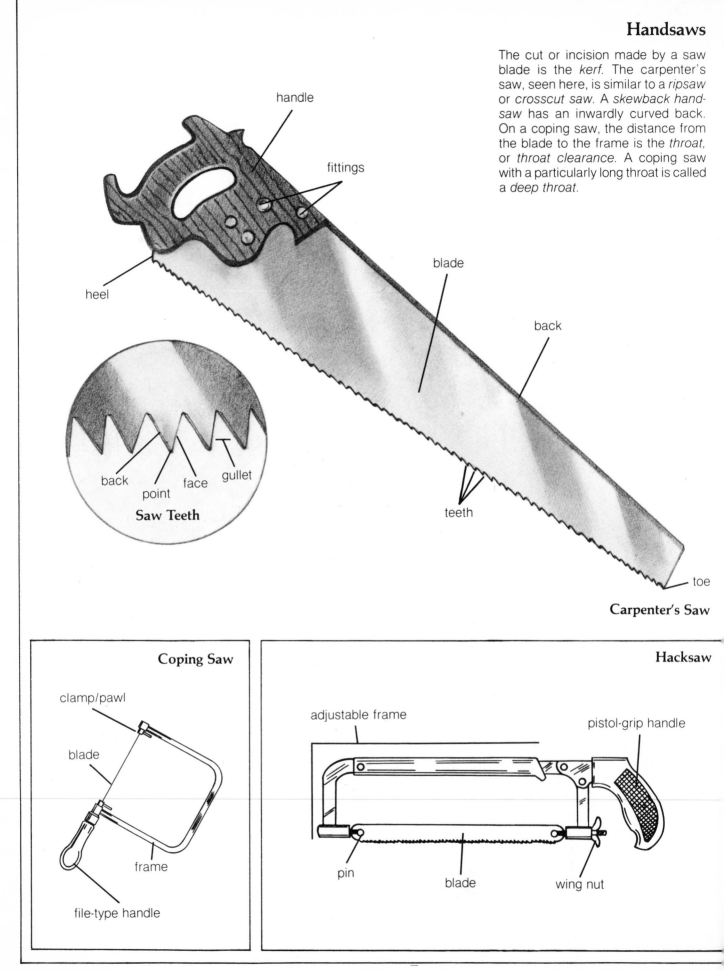

Handsaws

The cut or incision made by a saw blade is the *kerf*. The carpenter's saw, seen here, is similar to a *ripsaw* or *crosscut saw*. A *skewback handsaw* has an inwardly curved back. On a coping saw, the distance from the blade to the frame is the *throat*, or *throat clearance*. A coping saw with a particularly long throat is called a *deep throat*.

handle

fittings

heel

blade

back

back

point

face

gullet

Saw Teeth

teeth

toe

Carpenter's Saw

Coping Saw

clamp/pawl

blade

frame

file-type handle

Hacksaw

adjustable frame

pistol-grip handle

pin

blade

wing nut

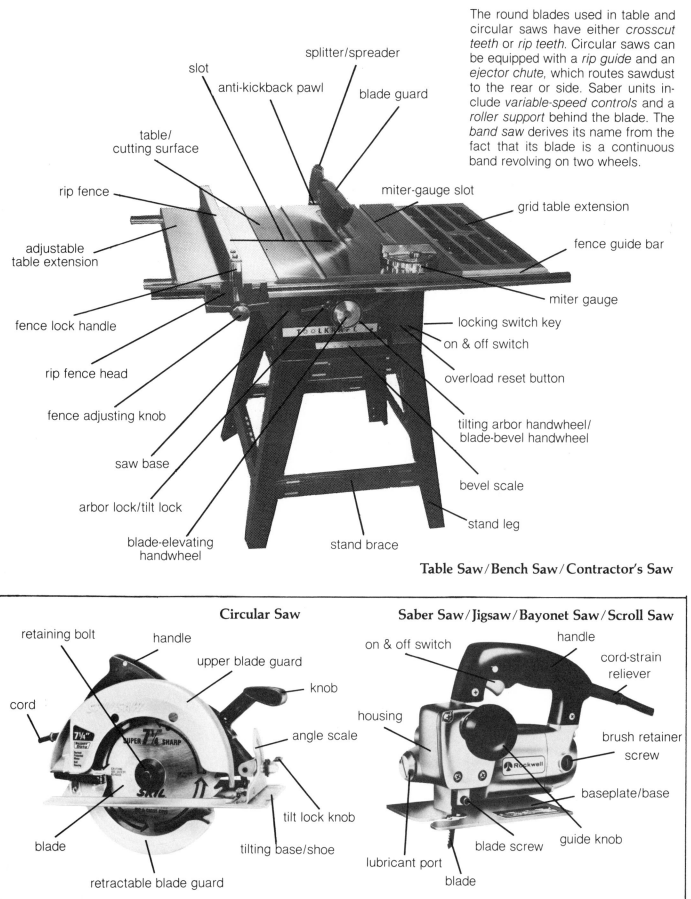

Power Saw

The round blades used in table and circular saws have either *crosscut teeth* or *rip teeth*. Circular saws can be equipped with a *rip guide* and an *ejector chute*, which routes sawdust to the rear or side. Saber units include *variable-speed controls* and a *roller support* behind the blade. The *band saw* derives its name from the fact that its blade is a continuous band revolving on two wheels.

splitter/spreader

slot

anti-kickback pawl

blade guard

table/ cutting surface

miter-gauge slot

rip fence

grid table extension

adjustable table extension

fence guide bar

fence lock handle

miter gauge

locking switch key

on & off switch

rip fence head

overload reset button

fence adjusting knob

tilting arbor handwheel/ blade-bevel handwheel

saw base

bevel scale

arbor lock/tilt lock

stand leg

blade-elevating handwheel

stand brace

Table Saw/Bench Saw/Contractor's Saw

Circular Saw

retaining bolt

handle

upper blade guard

cord

knob

angle scale

blade

tilt lock knob

tilting base/shoe

retractable blade guard

Saber Saw/Jigsaw/Bayonet Saw/Scroll Saw

on & off switch

handle

cord-strain reliever

housing

brush retainer screw

baseplate/base

guide knob

lubricant port

blade screw

blade

Household Tools

Manual Drill

Drilling accessories include a *bit gage, reamer, auger bits, dowel bits, expanding bits, screwdriver bits, countersink bits, twist drill bits, spade bits* and *power bore bits.* The circle described by turning the handle of a brace is called the *sweep.*

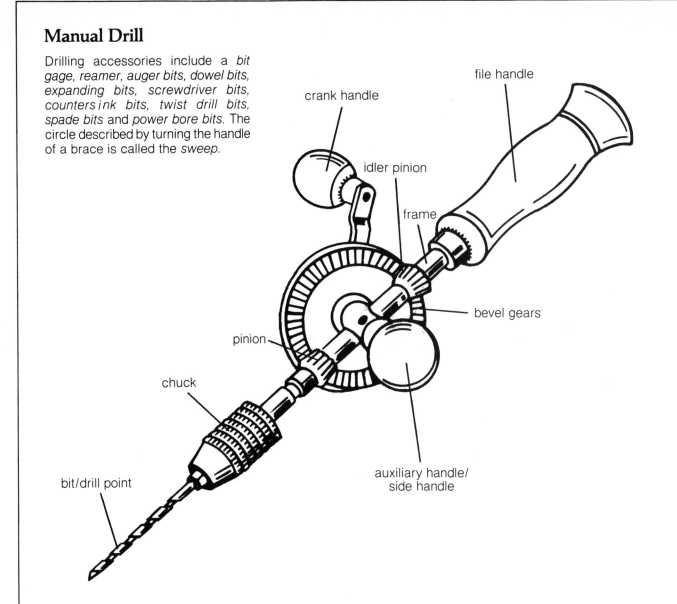

crank handle

file handle

idler pinion

frame

bevel gears

pinion

chuck

auxiliary handle/ side handle

bit/drill point

Hand Drill

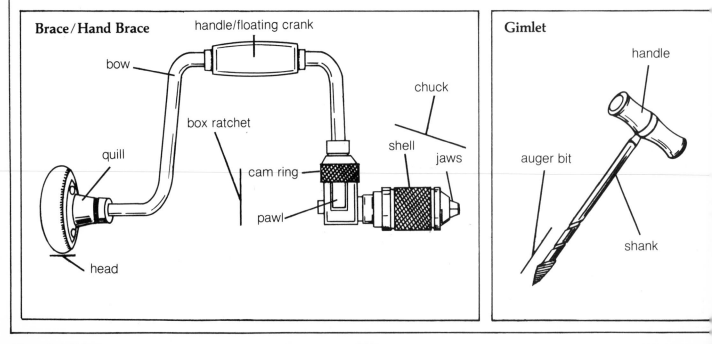

Brace / Hand Brace

handle/floating crank

bow

box ratchet

quill

cam ring

pawl

chuck

shell

jaws

head

Gimlet

handle

auger bit

shank

Power Drills

A regular bit, or *drill*, consists of a *point*, *body* and shank. Some bits have specially configured *tangs* at the end of the shank. If a drill has a *geared key chuck*, the bit is locked in place with a key. Holes can be drilled to predetermined depths by clamping an *adjustable bit gauge* to the bit shank. A drill is classified by the largest bit its chuck will accept. Some drills have *reversible motors*.

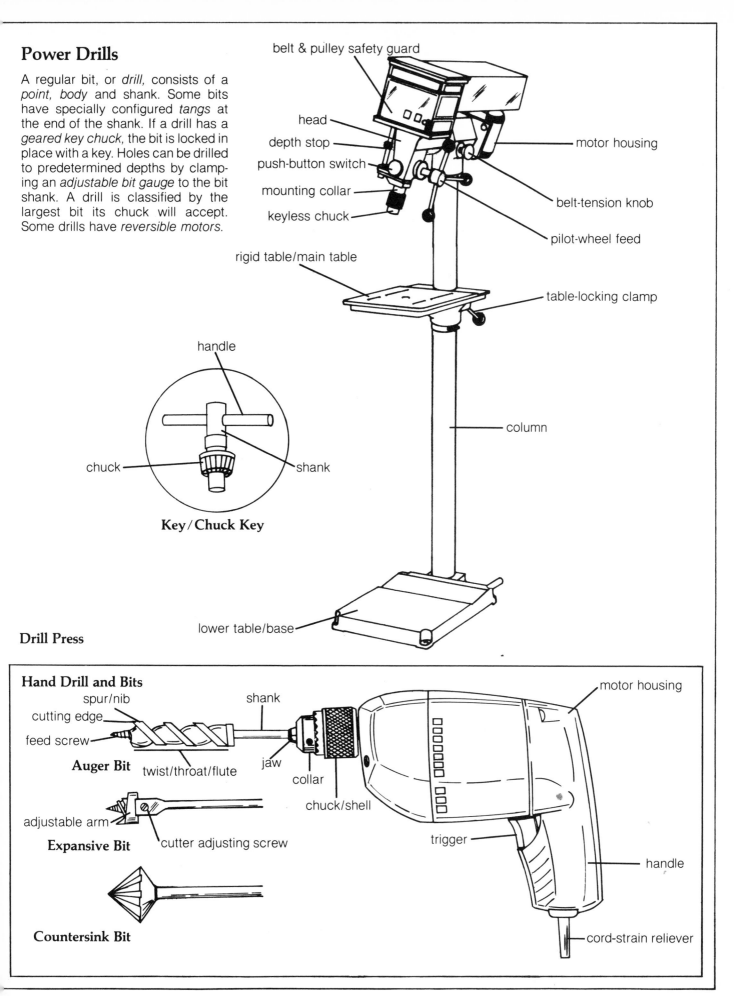

belt & pulley safety guard

head

depth stop

push-button switch

mounting collar

keyless chuck

motor housing

belt-tension knob

pilot-wheel feed

rigid table/main table

table-locking clamp

column

handle

chuck

shank

Key/Chuck Key

lower table/base

Drill Press

Hand Drill and Bits

spur/nib

cutting edge

feed screw

Auger Bit

twist/throat/flute

shank

jaw

collar

chuck/shell

motor housing

adjustable arm

Expansive Bit

cutter adjusting screw

Countersink Bit

trigger

handle

cord-strain reliever

Planing and Shaping Tools

The body of a plane is the *frame*. The angle of the blade is the *pitch*. The flat side of a chisel is its *back*. *Cold chisels* are designed to cut metal and have no handles. *Gouges* are either *in-cannel*, with the bevel ground on the inside of the curved blade, or *out-cannel*, with the bevel ground on the outside. The rough side of a rasp or file is the *face*. The smooth side is called the *"safe" side.*

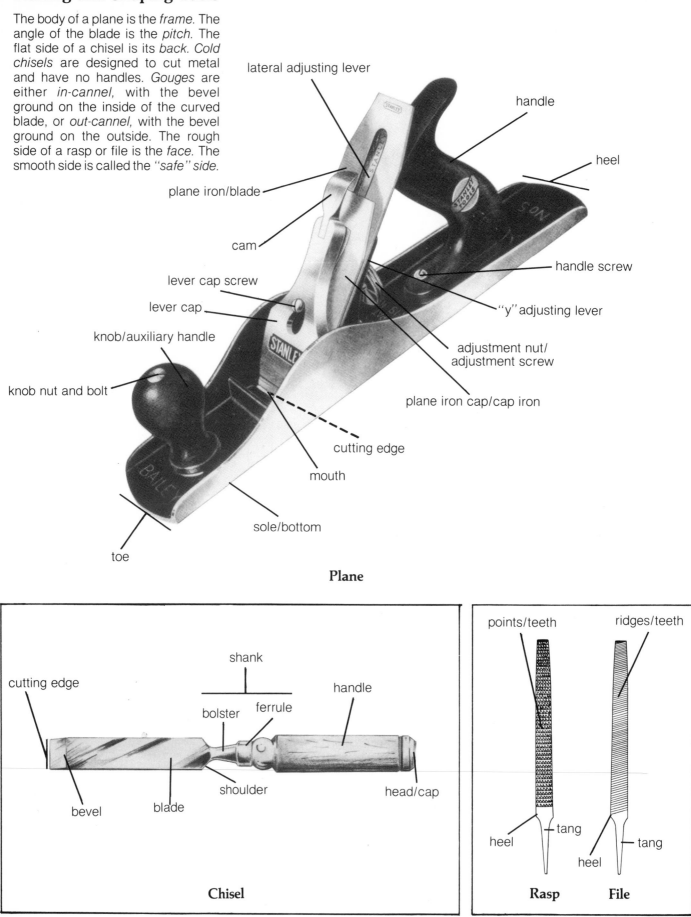

lateral adjusting lever

handle

heel

plane iron/blade

cam

handle screw

lever cap screw

lever cap

"y" adjusting lever

knob/auxiliary handle

adjustment nut/ adjustment screw

knob nut and bolt

plane iron cap/cap iron

cutting edge

mouth

sole/bottom

toe

Plane

cutting edge

shank

handle

bolster

ferrule

shoulder

head/cap

bevel

blade

Chisel

points/teeth

ridges/teeth

heel

tang

heel

tang

heel

Rasp

File

Sander

In a finishing, or *straight-line,* sander, the pad moves back and forth, whereas in the similar-looking *orbital sander,* the pad moves in a small orbital pattern. *Belt sanders* use a continuous *belt* of either *natural* or *artificial abrasive material,* and are available with or without *dust bags.* Sandpaper has either an *open* or *closed coat,* depending on spacing between *grains.*

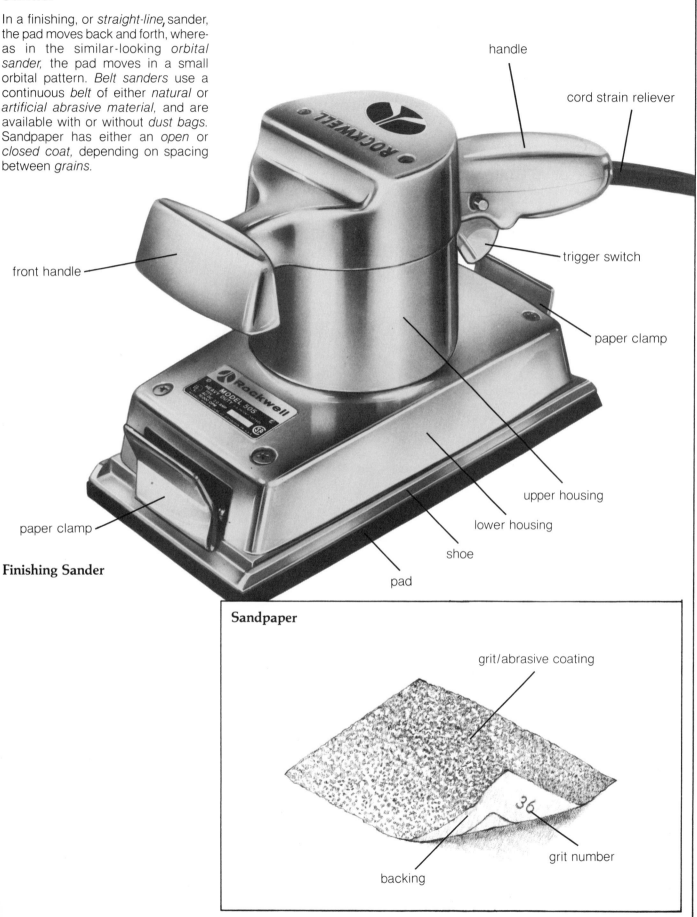

handle

cord strain reliever

trigger switch

paper clamp

front handle

upper housing

lower housing

shoe

pad

paper clamp

Finishing Sander

Sandpaper

grit/abrasive coating

36

grit number

backing

Household Tools

Plumbing Tools

In addition to the basic plumbing tools shown here, there are *tubing*, or *pipe cutters,* some of which have built-in *polishers; reamers* for removing *burrs* inside cut *pipe;* and *flaring tools,* used to spread the ends of copper *tubing* for *flare fittings.* In *sweat soldering, flux* and *solder* are used. When working with *threaded pipe,* a *pipe threader* (which consists of a *die, diestock* and *handles*) and *joint-sealing tape* or *compound* are used. Other basic plumbing tools are *hacksaws* and *pipe wrenches.*

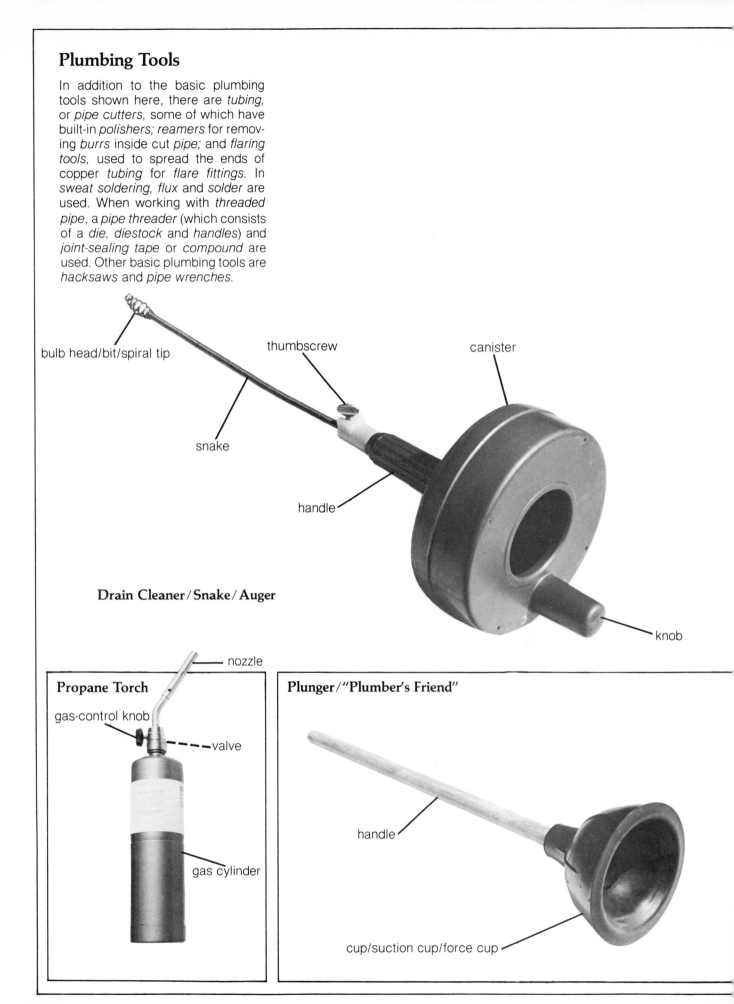

bulb head/bit/spiral tip

thumbscrew

canister

snake

handle

knob

Drain Cleaner / Snake / Auger

nozzle

Propane Torch

gas-control knob

valve

gas cylinder

Plunger / "Plumber's Friend"

handle

cup/suction cup/force cup

Electrician's Tools

A volt-ohm meter, also known as a *multimeter* or *volt-ohm-milliammeter,* is used with test *leads* and *jacks* attached to needle-type *probes* or *alligator clips.* The markings on the sheath of a wire describe *wire size,* number of *conductors,* the existence of a ground wire and cable type.

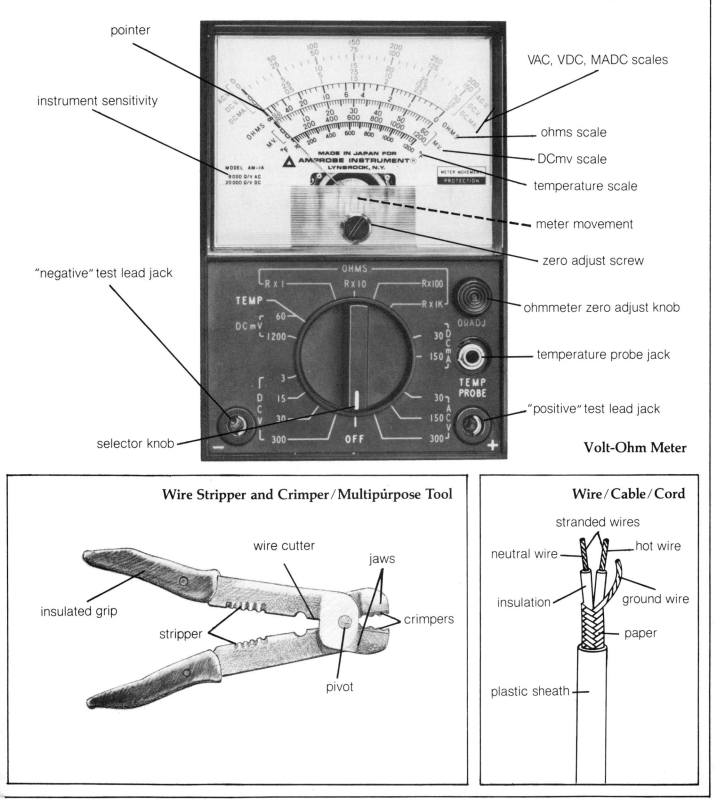

pointer

instrument sensitivity

VAC, VDC, MADC scales

ohms scale

DCmv scale

temperature scale

meter movement

zero adjust screw

"negative" test lead jack

ohmmeter zero adjust knob

temperature probe jack

"positive" test lead jack

selector knob

Volt-Ohm Meter

Wire Stripper and Crimper/Multipurpose Tool

wire cutter

jaws

insulated grip

crimpers

stripper

pivot

Wire/Cable/Cord

stranded wires

neutral wire

hot wire

insulation

ground wire

paper

plastic sheath

Measuring Tools

The basic measuring tool is the one-piece *bench rule,* or *ruler.* Tape measures also come in *reels* which can be manually rewound. An *L-shaped square* has two *arms* set at right angles. The longer arm is the *blade,* the shorter one is the *tongue.* They meet at the *heel.* A *combination square* substitutes for *try squares, depth gauges* and *marking gauges.* When the *air bubble* in a monovial stops between *marks,* the level is on the desired *plane.*

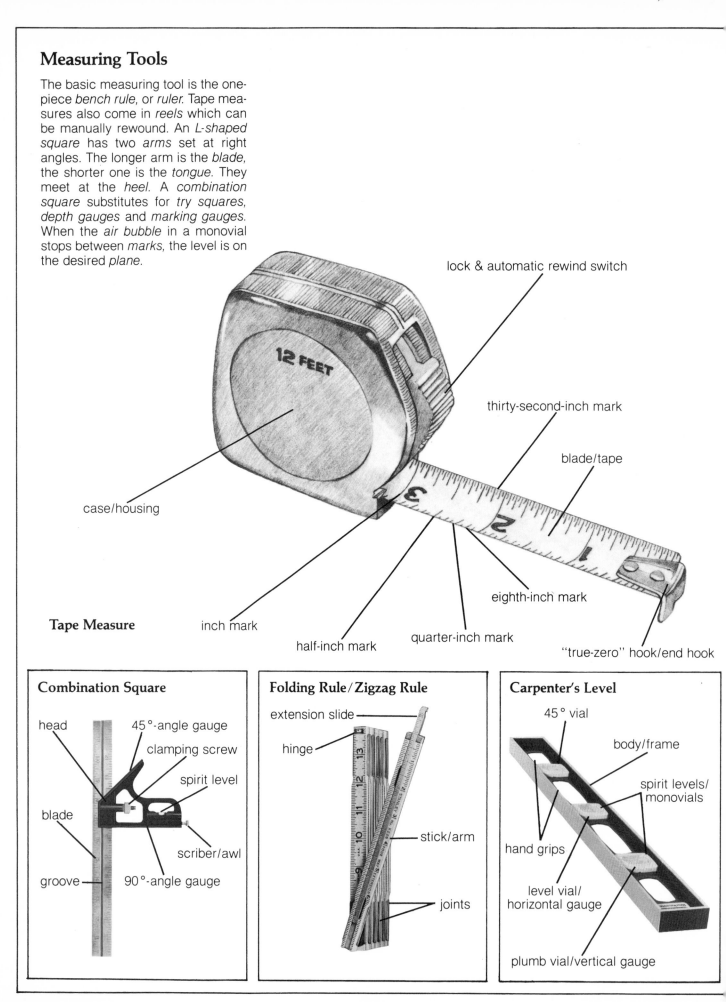

lock & automatic rewind switch

thirty-second-inch mark

blade/tape

case/housing

Tape Measure

inch mark

half-inch mark

quarter-inch mark

eighth-inch mark

"true-zero" hook/end hook

Combination Square

head

45°-angle gauge

clamping screw

spirit level

blade

scriber/awl

groove

90°-angle gauge

Folding Rule/Zigzag Rule

extension slide

hinge

stick/arm

joints

Carpenter's Level

45° vial

body/frame

spirit levels/ monovials

hand grips

level vial/ horizontal gauge

plumb vial/vertical gauge

Painting Tools

A regular *paint brush* has *bristles* with *split,* or *flagged, ends.* The *heel* section of a brush is where the *butt ends* of bristles fit into a *ferrule* attached to the handle. Other paint-application tools include *pressure brushes, foam brushes* and *pad applicators.* Accessories include *pot* and *brush holders* and *brush spinners.* Paint rollers may have *threaded handles* to accommodate *extenders. Tack cloth* is used to clean surfaces to be painted, and a *drop cloth* protects objects and areas against paint spills.

WAGNER

W350

housing

high-pressure pump

control knob

venthole

trigger

nozzle

safety guard

container cover

container

handle

plug

Paint Spray Gun

Tray and Roller

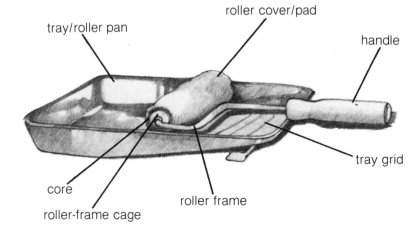

roller cover/pad

tray/roller pan

handle

core

roller-frame cage

roller frame

tray grid

Ladder/Stepladder

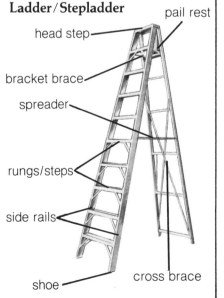

pail rest

head step

bracket brace

spreader

rungs/steps

side rails

shoe

cross brace

Household Tools

Swiss Army Knife

The *dividers* in the *handle* of a *jack-knife,* pocketknife or *camping knife* keep each blade or *tool* separate.

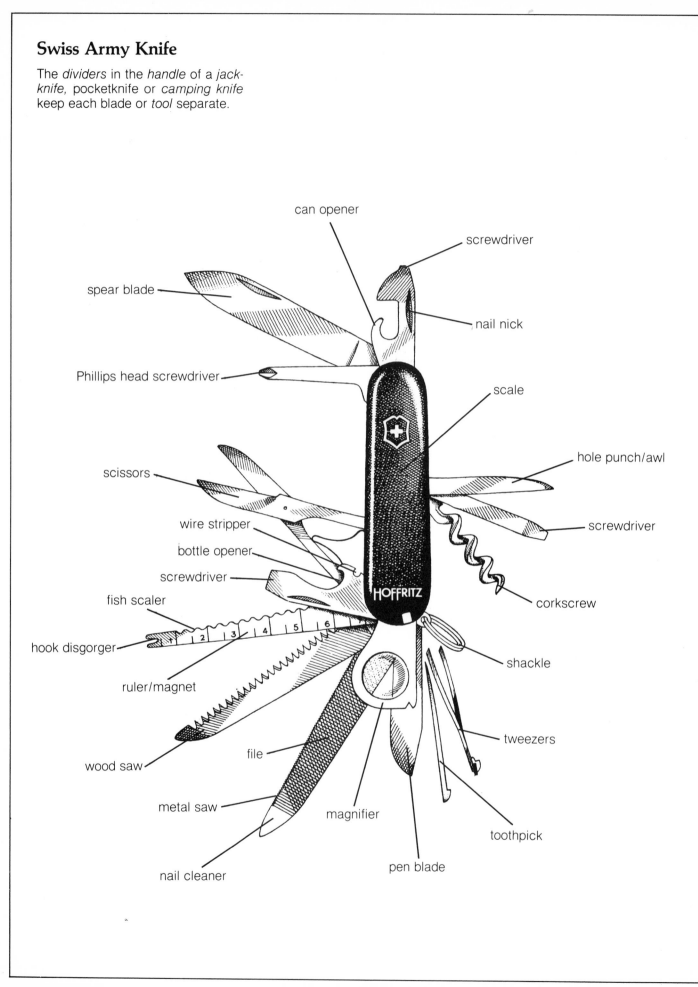

can opener

screwdriver

spear blade

nail nick

Phillips head screwdriver

scale

hole punch/awl

scissors

wire stripper

screwdriver

bottle opener

screwdriver

corkscrew

fish scaler

hook disgorger

shackle

ruler/magnet

tweezers

wood saw

file

metal saw

magnifier

toothpick

nail cleaner

pen blade

Gardening Implements

A hand tool with a small scooped blade used for potting and planting is a *trowel*. A *spading fork* is used for turning soil. Shears are generally of two types: *anvil,* in which a blade cuts through a branch and stops against an anvil, and *by-pass,* which uses a shearing action to cut.

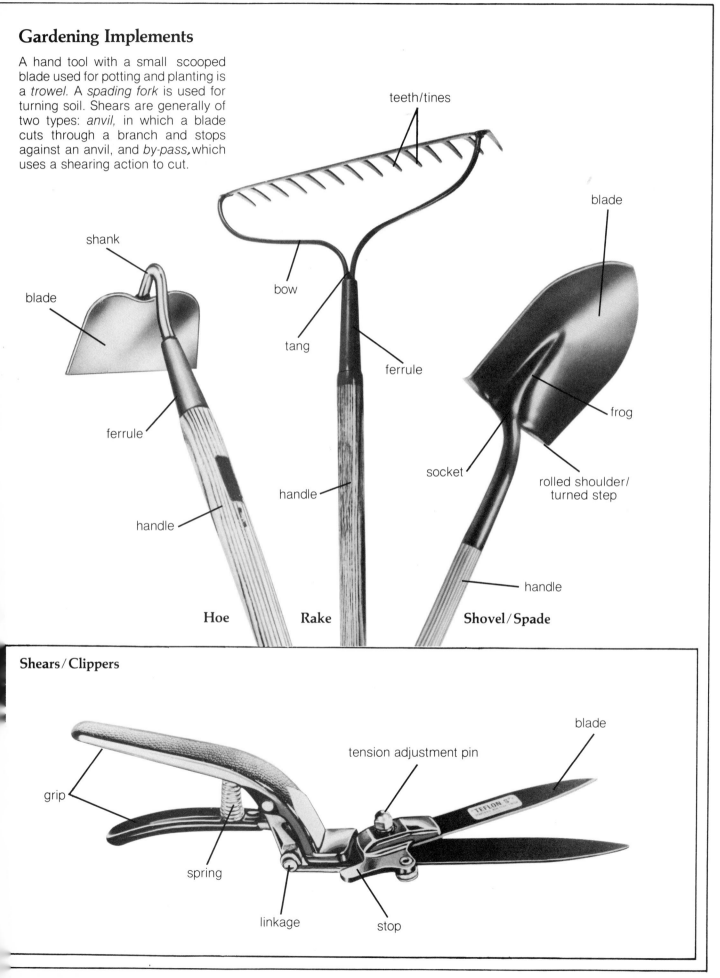

teeth/tines

blade

shank

blade

bow

tang

ferrule

ferrule

frog

socket

handle

rolled shoulder/ turned step

handle

handle

Hoe　　**Rake**　　**Shovel/Spade**

Shears/Clippers

blade

tension adjustment pin

grip

spring

linkage　　stop

Sprinkler and Nozzles

Revolving sprinklers have rotating *arms* that spray water through nozzles at each end. An inverted Y-shaped *coupling*, or *siamese*, makes it possible to connect two *hoses* to a single *faucet*. In making a *hose connection*, the larger *female coupling* is fitted over the *male coupling* and turned until the connection is made fast. *Washers* inside couplings make seals watertight.

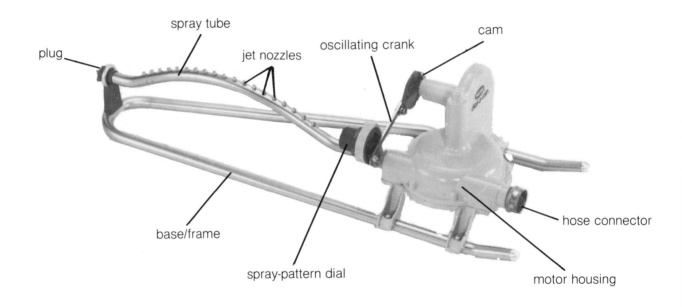

spray tube

plug

jet nozzles

oscillating crank

cam

base/frame

spray-pattern dial

hose connector

motor housing

Oscillating Lawn Sprinkler

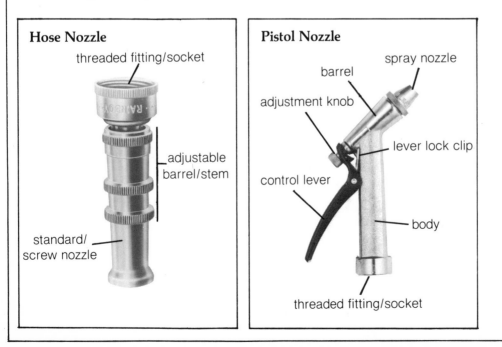

Hose Nozzle

threaded fitting/socket

adjustable barrel/stem

standard/ screw nozzle

Pistol Nozzle

barrel

spray nozzle

adjustment knob

lever lock clip

control lever

body

threaded fitting/socket

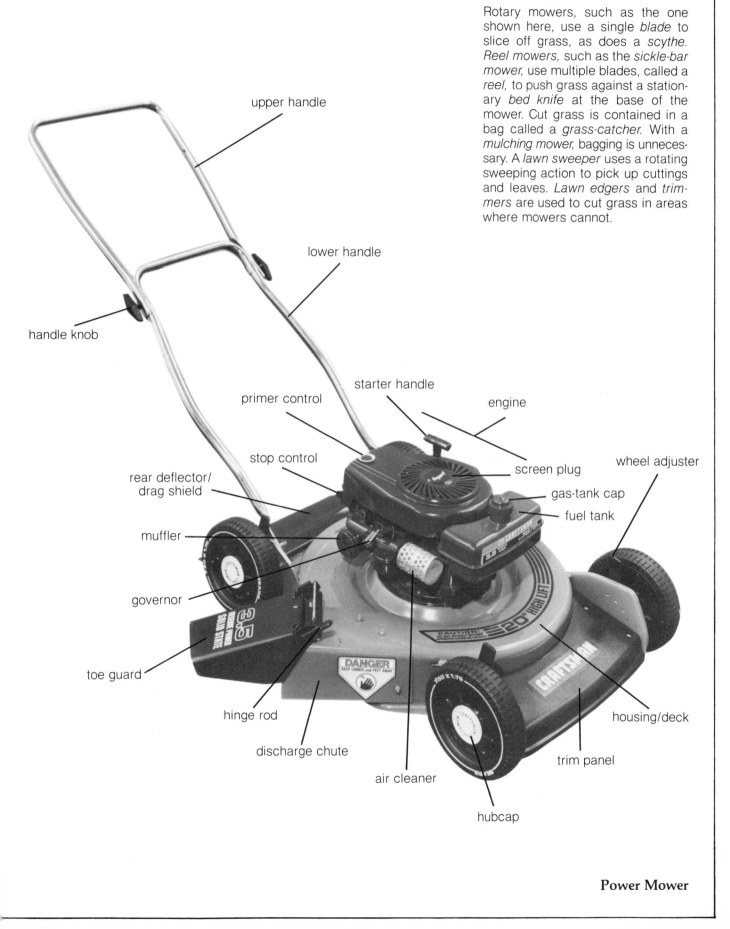

Lawn Mower

Rotary mowers, such as the one shown here, use a single *blade* to slice off grass, as does a *scythe*. *Reel mowers*, such as the *sickle-bar mower*, use multiple blades, called a *reel*, to push grass against a stationary *bed knife* at the base of the mower. Cut grass is contained in a bag called a *grass-catcher*. With a *mulching mower*, bagging is unnecessary. A *lawn sweeper* uses a rotating sweeping action to pick up cuttings and leaves. *Lawn edgers* and *trimmers* are used to cut grass in areas where mowers cannot.

upper handle

lower handle

handle knob

starter handle

primer control

engine

stop control

screen plug

wheel adjuster

rear deflector/ drag shield

gas-tank cap

muffler

fuel tank

governor

toe guard

hinge rod

housing/deck

discharge chute

trim panel

air cleaner

hubcap

DANGER
KEEP HANDS and FEET AWAY

Power Mower

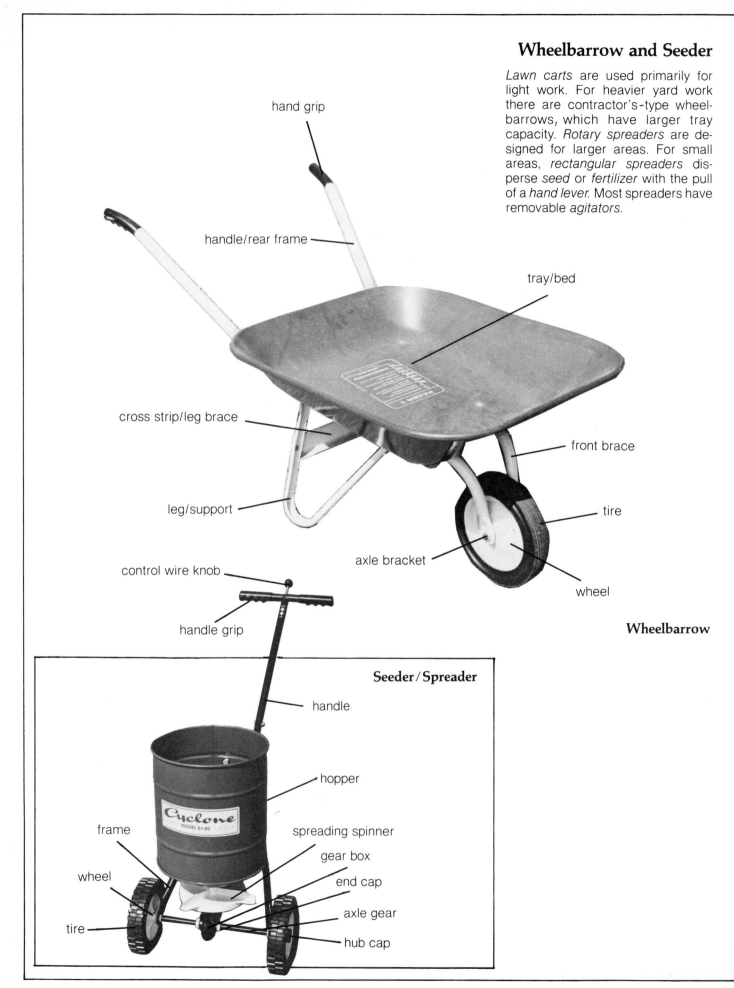

Wheelbarrow and Seeder

Lawn carts are used primarily for light work. For heavier yard work there are contractor's-type wheelbarrows, which have larger tray capacity. *Rotary spreaders* are designed for larger areas. For small areas, *rectangular spreaders* disperse *seed* or *fertilizer* with the pull of a *hand lever*. Most spreaders have removable *agitators*.

hand grip

handle/rear frame

tray/bed

cross strip/leg brace

front brace

leg/support

tire

axle bracket

wheel

Wheelbarrow

control wire knob

handle grip

Seeder / Spreader

handle

hopper

frame

spreading spinner

gear box

wheel

end cap

axle gear

tire

hub cap

Chain Saw

Chain saws are either gasoline- or electric-powered. Power output is measured in cubic inches of *piston displacement* in the *power head* rather than in horsepower. The *cutting head* may be *direct drive* or *gear drive*. A *sprocket-tip cutting bar* increases cutting speed because it eliminates most of the friction around the *bar tip*. Safety devices include a *chain brake* intended to stop the moving chain when the saw begins to kick back, *throttle latches* for safer starting, *safety triggers* to prevent accidental acceleration, *muffler shields*, and *chain catchers* designed to protect the operator from a broken or slipped chain.

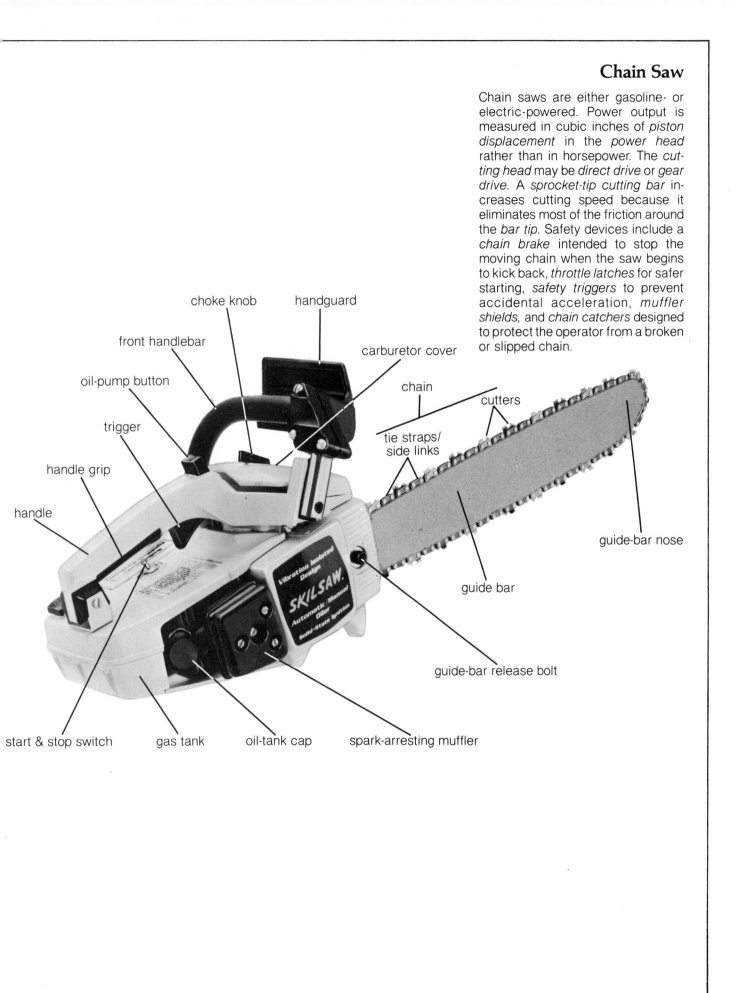

choke knob

handguard

front handlebar

carburetor cover

oil-pump button

chain

cutters

trigger

tie straps/
side links

handle grip

handle

guide-bar nose

guide bar

guide-bar release bolt

start & stop switch

gas tank

oil-tank cap

spark-arresting muffler

SKILSAW
Vibration Isolated Design
Automatic/Manual Oiler
Solid-State Ignition

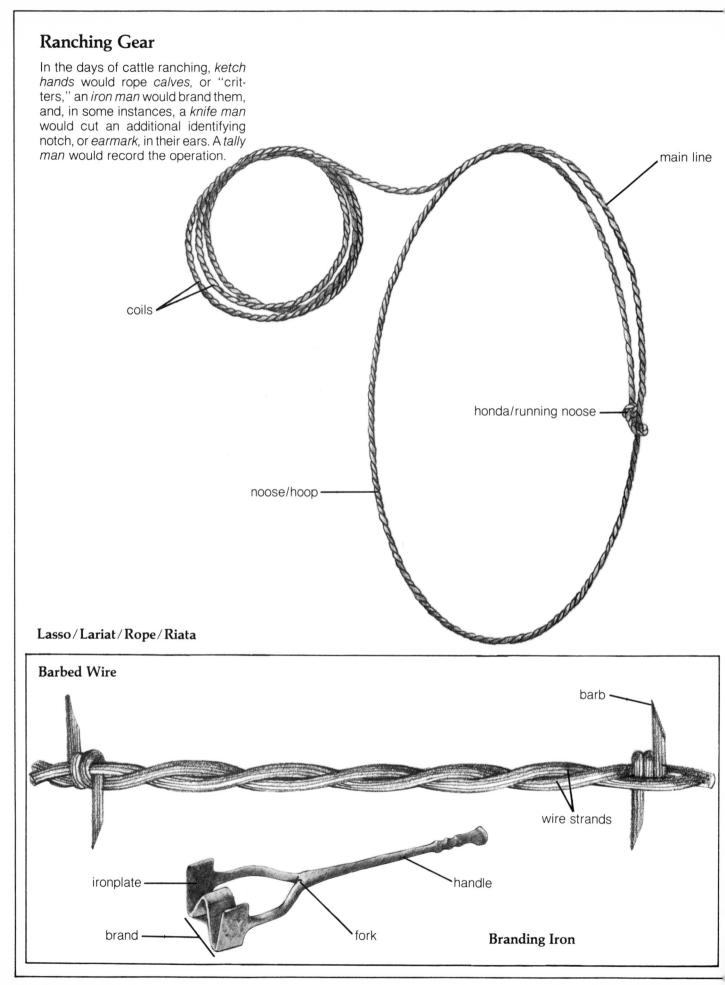

Ranching Gear

In the days of cattle ranching, *ketch hands* would rope *calves,* or "critters," an *iron man* would brand them, and, in some instances, a *knife man* would cut an additional identifying notch, or *earmark,* in their ears. A *tally man* would record the operation.

main line

coils

honda/running noose

noose/hoop

Lasso / Lariat / Rope / Riata

Barbed Wire

barb

wire strands

ironplate

handle

brand

fork

Branding Iron

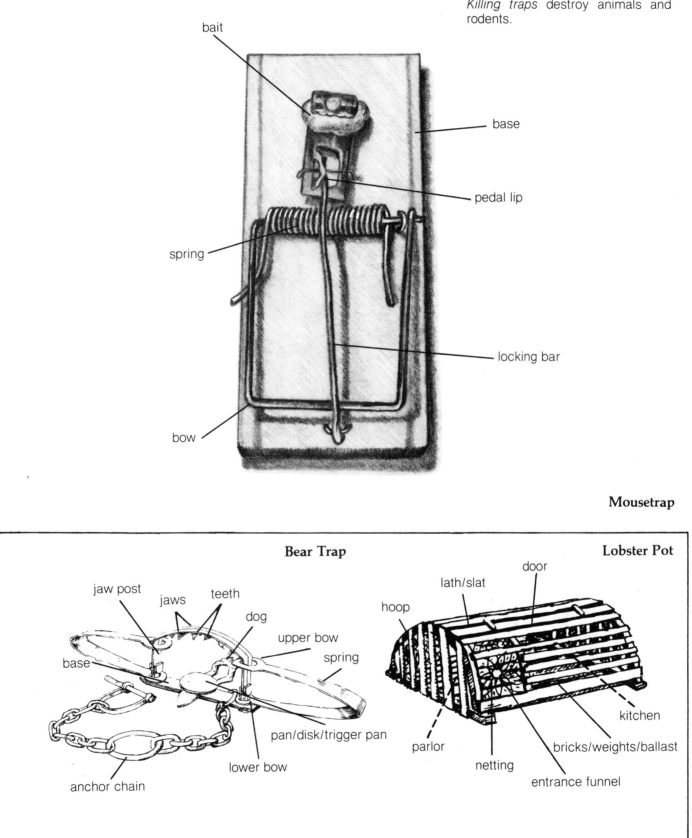

Traps

Enclosing traps catch animals without hurting them. *Arresting traps,* such as the bear trap shown here, catch and hold animals in their teeth. *Killing traps* destroy animals and rodents.

bait

base

pedal lip

spring

locking bar

bow

Mousetrap

Bear Trap

jaw post

jaws

teeth

dog

upper bow

spring

base

pan/disk/trigger pan

lower bow

anchor chain

Lobster Pot

door

lath/slat

hoop

kitchen

bricks/weights/ballast

entrance funnel

netting

parlor

Trapping Devices

Tractor

Plows, reapers, cultivators, like the harrow seen here, and various *planting machines* are coupled to a tractor to work the land. The operating speed of attachments is controlled by a *power takeoff.* Optional *outboard planetaries* with *adjustable wheel treads* and *add-on segment weights* help boost traction.

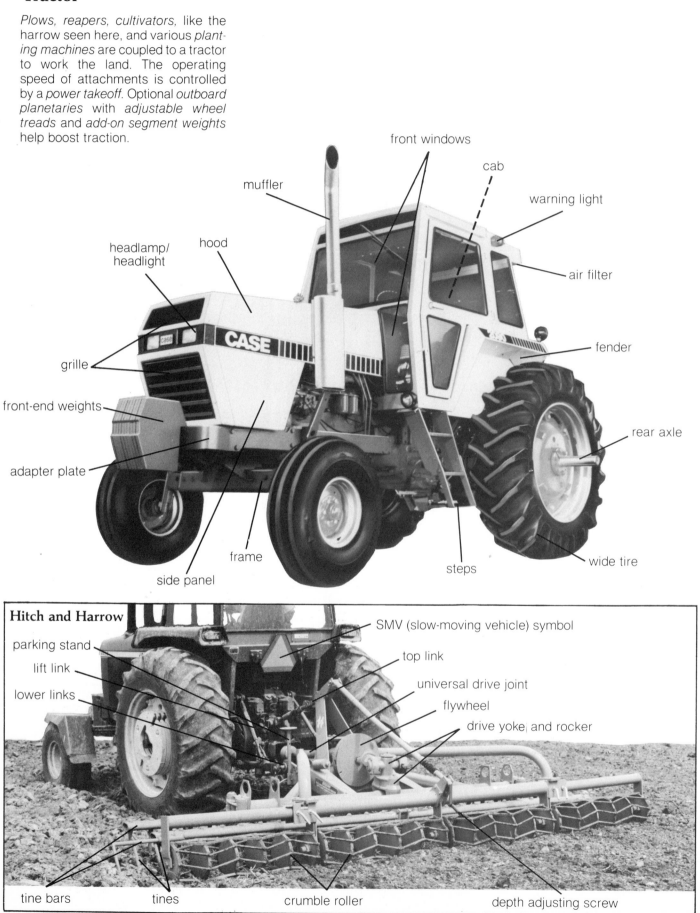

front windows

cab

muffler

warning light

hood

air filter

headlamp/ headlight

fender

grille

rear axle

front-end weights

adapter plate

wide tire

frame

steps

side panel

Hitch and Harrow

SMV (slow-moving vehicle) symbol

parking stand

top link

lift link

universal drive joint

lower links

flywheel

drive yoke and rocker

tine bars

tines

crumble roller

depth adjusting screw

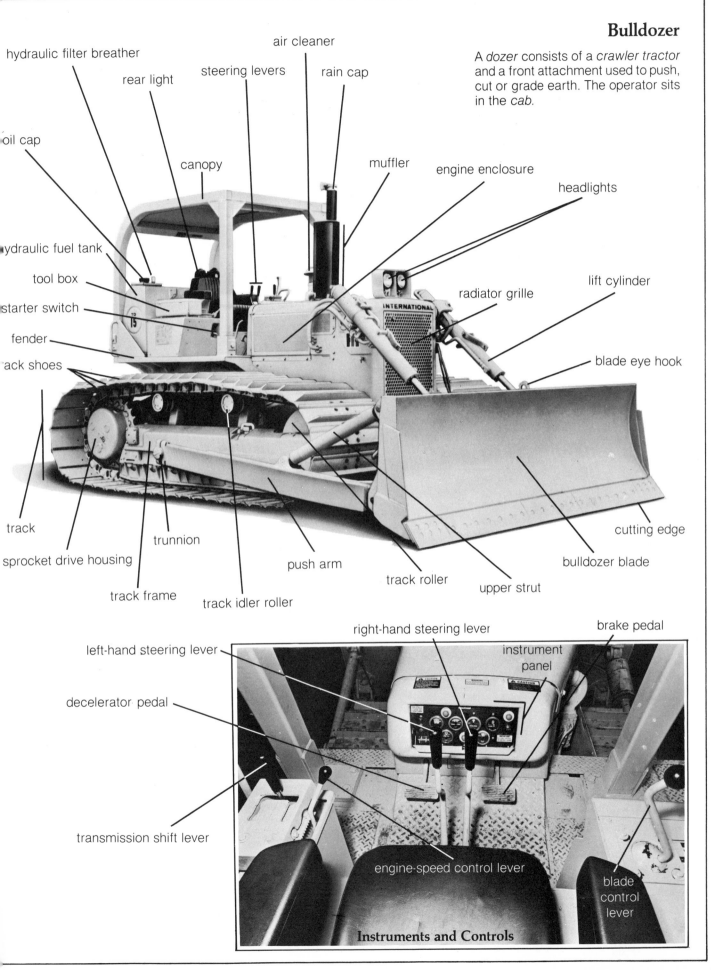

Bulldozer

A *dozer* consists of a *crawler tractor* and a front attachment used to push, cut or grade earth. The operator sits in the *cab*.

hydraulic filter breather

air cleaner

steering levers

rear light

rain cap

oil cap

canopy

muffler

engine enclosure

headlights

hydraulic fuel tank

lift cylinder

tool box

radiator grille

starter switch

fender

blade eye hook

track shoes

track

sprocket drive housing

trunnion

push arm

track roller

upper strut

cutting edge

bulldozer blade

track frame

track idler roller

right-hand steering lever

brake pedal

left-hand steering lever

instrument panel

decelerator pedal

transmission shift lever

engine-speed control lever

blade control lever

Instruments and Controls

Construction Equipment

Transit and Jackhammer

A transit is used by *engineers* and *surveyors* to determine *angles, bearings* and *levels*. It is mounted on a three-legged stand called a *tripod*. A weight, known as a *plumb* or *plumb bob,* is suspended directly below the telescope to determine *true vertical*.

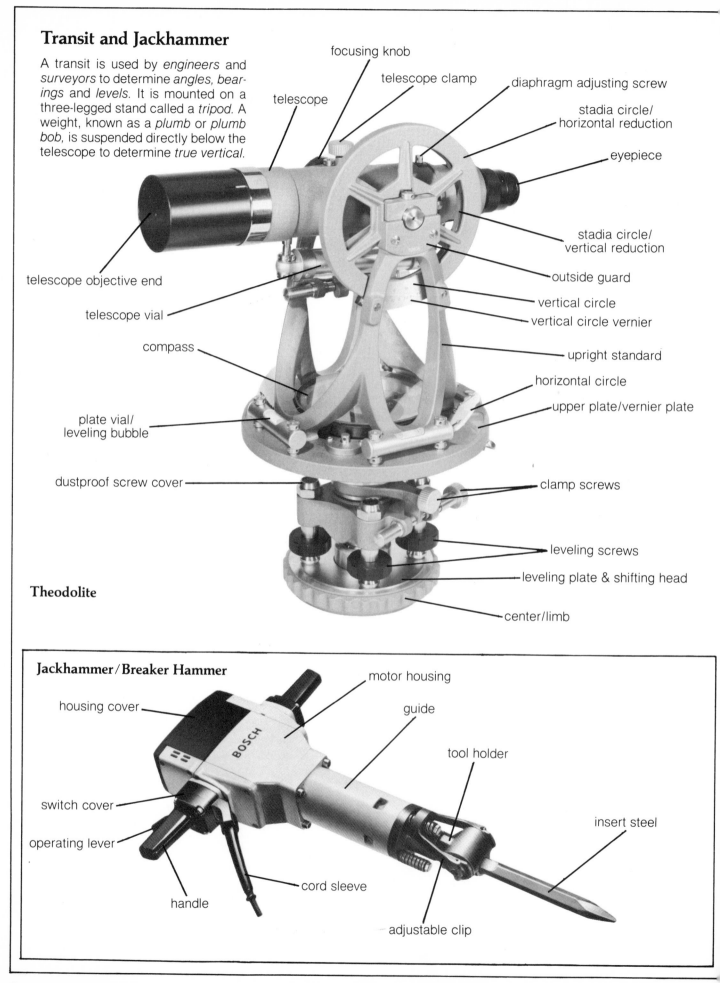

focusing knob

telescope clamp

telescope

diaphragm adjusting screw

stadia circle/ horizontal reduction

eyepiece

telescope objective end

stadia circle/ vertical reduction

telescope vial

outside guard

vertical circle

vertical circle vernier

compass

upright standard

horizontal circle

plate vial/ leveling bubble

upper plate/vernier plate

dustproof screw cover

clamp screws

leveling screws

leveling plate & shifting head

center/limb

Theodolite

Jackhammer/Breaker Hammer

housing cover

motor housing

guide

tool holder

switch cover

operating lever

cord sleeve

handle

adjustable clip

insert steel

BOSCH

Voting Booth

Voting booths, or *mechanized voting machines,* are located at *polling places,* or *polls.* An *x-indication* appears next to a candidate's name when a lever is pressed. When a *voter* presses levers for every candidate of a single political party, it is called voting a *straight ticket.* Any variation is a *split ballot.*

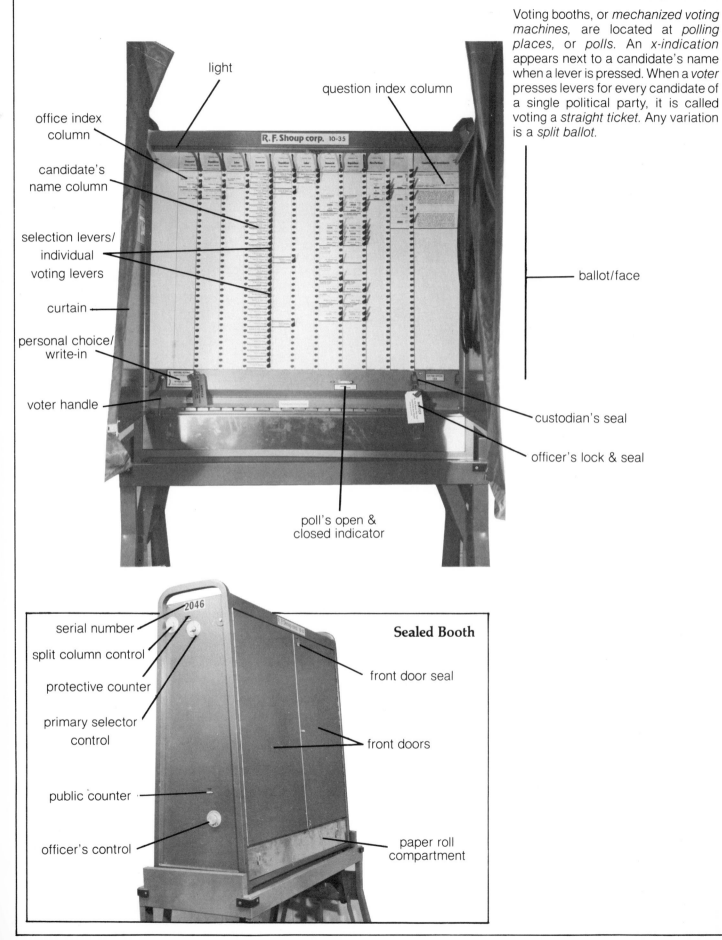

light

question index column

office index column

candidate's name column

R. F. Shoup corp. 10-35

selection levers/ individual voting levers

ballot/face

curtain

personal choice/ write-in

voter handle

custodian's seal

officer's lock & seal

poll's open & closed indicator

Sealed Booth

serial number

2046

split column control

front door seal

protective counter

primary selector control

front doors

public counter

officer's control

paper roll compartment

Computing Tools

Key Punch

A key punch or *card punch* codes data by punching holes in cards in a sequence of instructions designed by a *programmer.*

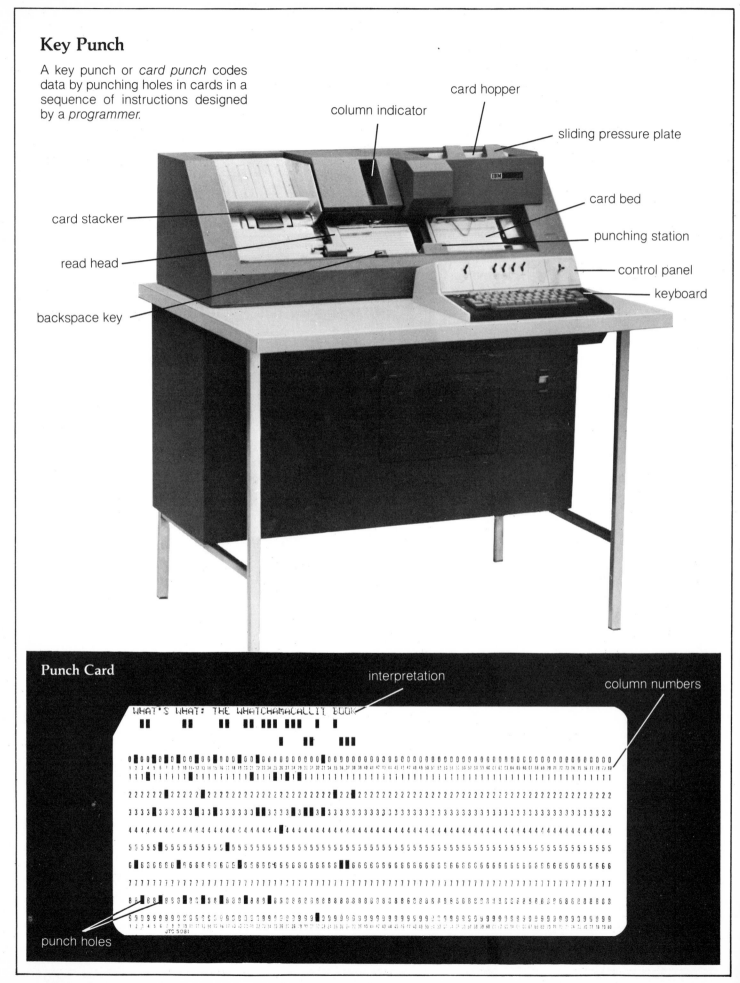

column indicator

card hopper

sliding pressure plate

card bed

punching station

control panel

keyboard

card stacker

read head

backspace key

Punch Card

interpretation

column numbers

WHAT'S WHAT: THE WHATCHAMACALLIT BOOK

punch holes

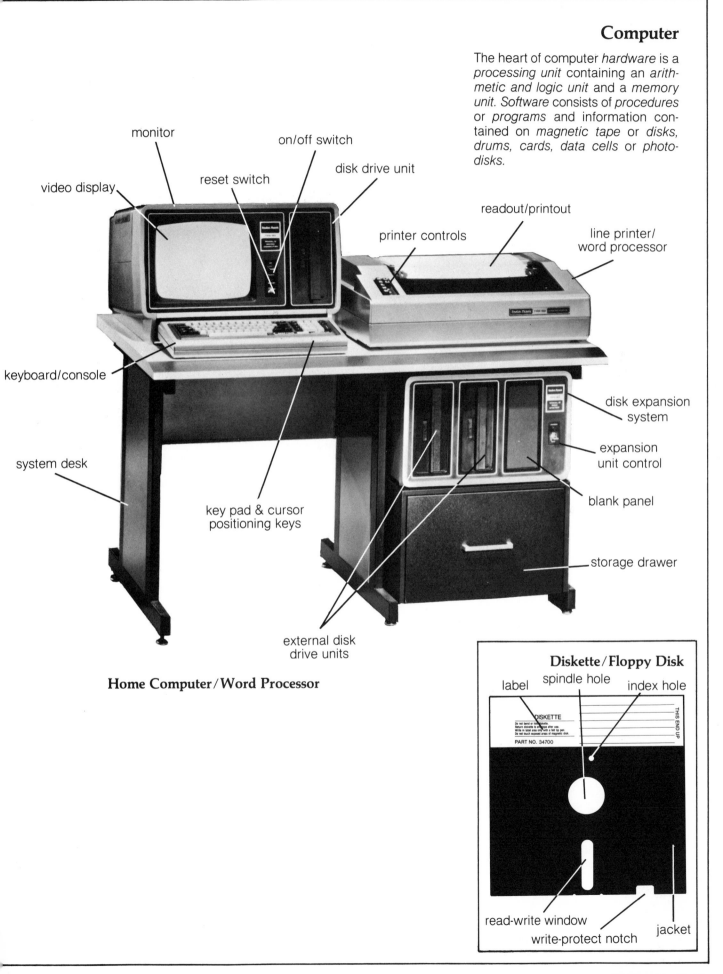

Computer

The heart of computer *hardware* is a *processing unit* containing an *arithmetic and logic unit* and a *memory unit*. *Software* consists of *procedures* or *programs* and information contained on *magnetic tape* or *disks, drums, cards, data cells* or *photodisks.*

monitor

on/off switch

reset switch

disk drive unit

video display

readout/printout

printer controls

line printer/ word processor

keyboard/console

disk expansion system

expansion unit control

system desk

blank panel

key pad & cursor positioning keys

storage drawer

external disk drive units

Home Computer/Word Processor

Diskette/Floppy Disk

label

spindle hole

index hole

DISKETTE

Do not bend or fold diskette.
Return diskette to envelope after use.
Write in label area only with a felt tip pen.
Do not touch exposed areas of magnetic disk.

PART NO. 34700

THIS END UP

read-write window

write-protect notch

jacket

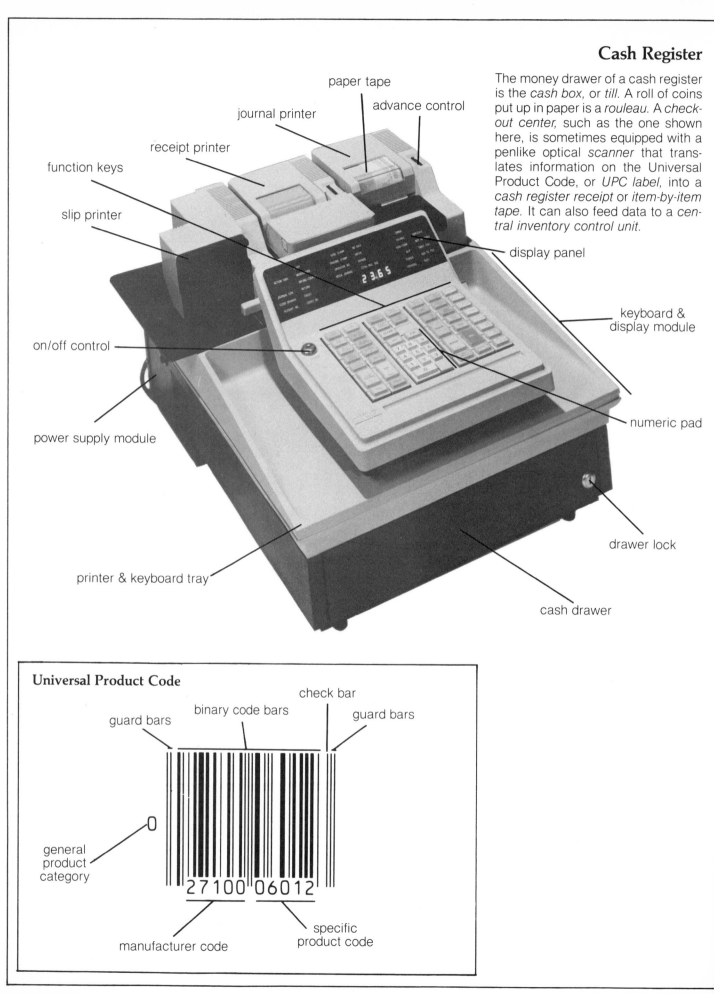

Cash Register

The money drawer of a cash register is the *cash box,* or *till.* A roll of coins put up in paper is a *rouleau.* A *check-out center,* such as the one shown here, is sometimes equipped with a penlike optical *scanner* that translates information on the Universal Product Code, or *UPC label,* into a *cash register receipt* or *item-by-item tape.* It can also feed data to a *central inventory control unit.*

paper tape

journal printer

advance control

receipt printer

function keys

slip printer

display panel

on/off control

keyboard & display module

power supply module

numeric pad

printer & keyboard tray

drawer lock

cash drawer

Universal Product Code

guard bars

binary code bars

check bar

guard bars

general product category

manufacturer code

specific product code

27100 06012

Calculators

The electronic calculator has generally replaced the *adding machine* today. The linear slide rule seen here often has scales on both sides. A *cylindrical slide rule* can only be used for *multiplication* and *division*. A *circular slide rule* is a series of long scales wound around a cylinder like a screw thread. The abacus is an ancient calculator used for solving problems of *addition* and *subtraction* by the movement of beads. Other early devices include *counting rods*, or *"bones."*

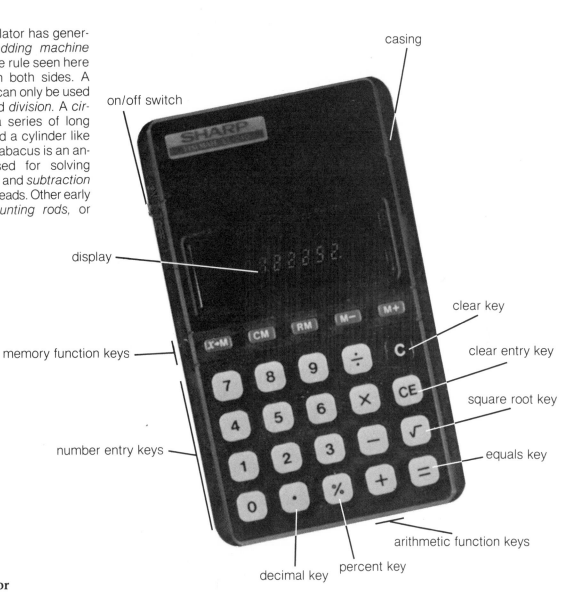

casing

on/off switch

display

memory function keys

number entry keys

clear key

clear entry key

square root key

equals key

arithmetic function keys

decimal key

percent key

Electronic Calculator

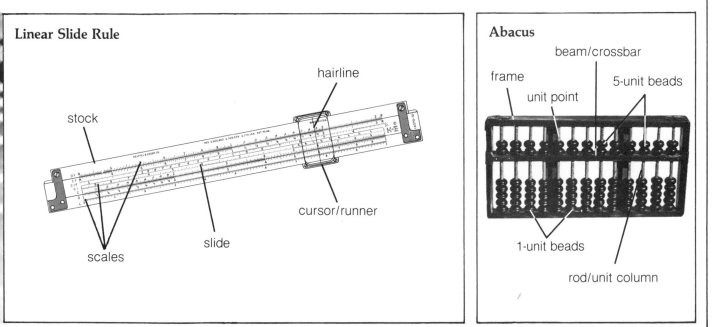

Linear Slide Rule

hairline

stock

cursor/runner

slide

scales

Abacus

beam/crossbar

frame

5-unit beads

unit point

1-unit beads

rod/unit column

Computing Tools

Microscope

The *magnifying power* of a microscope depends upon the relative *focal length* of objective and eyepiece. A *simple microscope* uses a single *lens* to magnify an image, while *compound microcopes* use two lenses or *lens systems*. The microscope seen here has a built-in *illuminator* in its base. Less sophisticated models use a *mirror* to direct existing light on *specimens*.

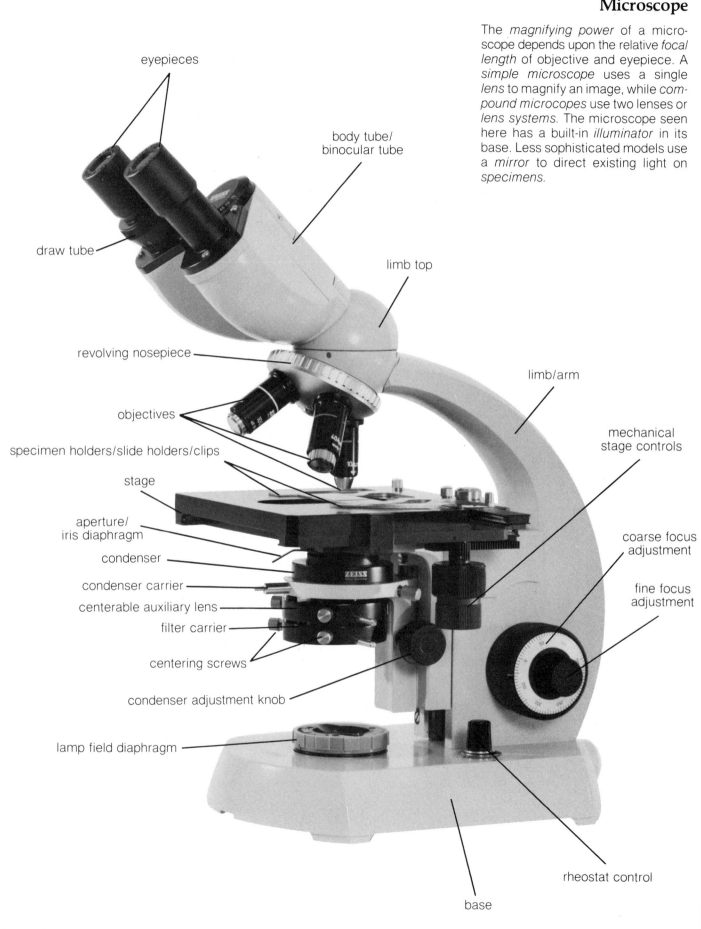

eyepieces

body tube/ binocular tube

draw tube

limb top

revolving nosepiece

limb/arm

objectives

specimen holders/slide holders/clips

mechanical stage controls

stage

aperture/ iris diaphragm

coarse focus adjustment

condenser

fine focus adjustment

condenser carrier

centerable auxiliary lens

filter carrier

centering screws

condenser adjustment knob

lamp field diaphragm

rheostat control

base

Telescope & Binoculars

A *refracting telescope,* such as the one seen here, relies on the objective lens to concentrate incoming light. A *reflecting telescope* employs a *concave mirror* to do the same task. Binoculars are composed of two similar telescopes, one for each eye. *Field glasses* are lightweight binoculars that employ *erecting telescopes* of the *spyglass* type, while *opera glasses,* designed for use inside, use *Galilean telescopes.*

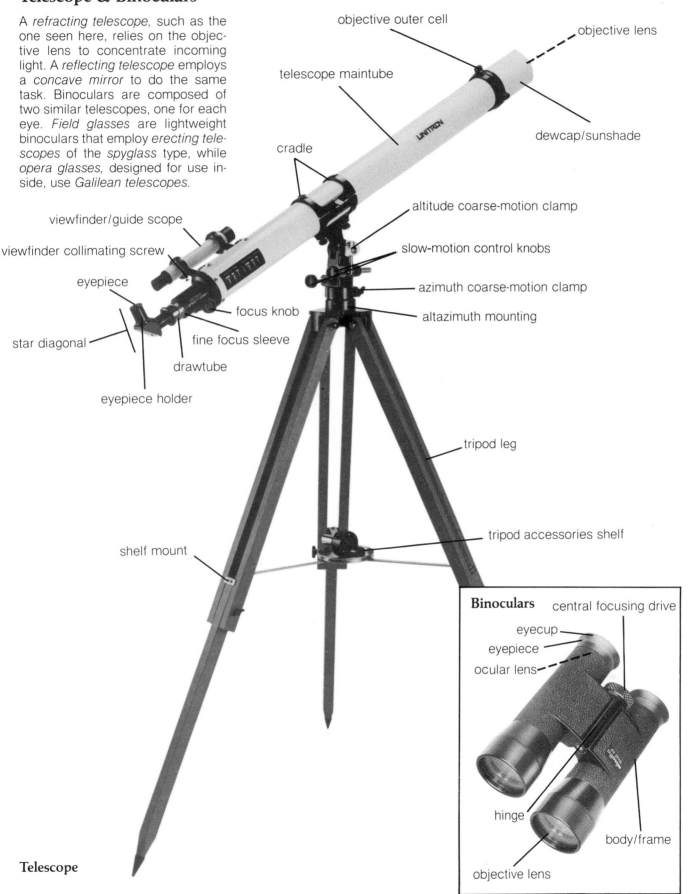

objective outer cell

objective lens

telescope maintube

dewcap/sunshade

cradle

altitude coarse-motion clamp

viewfinder/guide scope

slow-motion control knobs

viewfinder collimating screw

azimuth coarse-motion clamp

eyepiece

altazimuth mounting

focus knob

star diagonal

fine focus sleeve

drawtube

eyepiece holder

tripod leg

tripod accessories shelf

shelf mount

Binoculars   central focusing drive

eyecup

eyepiece

ocular lens

hinge

body/frame

objective lens

Telescope

Scientific Tools

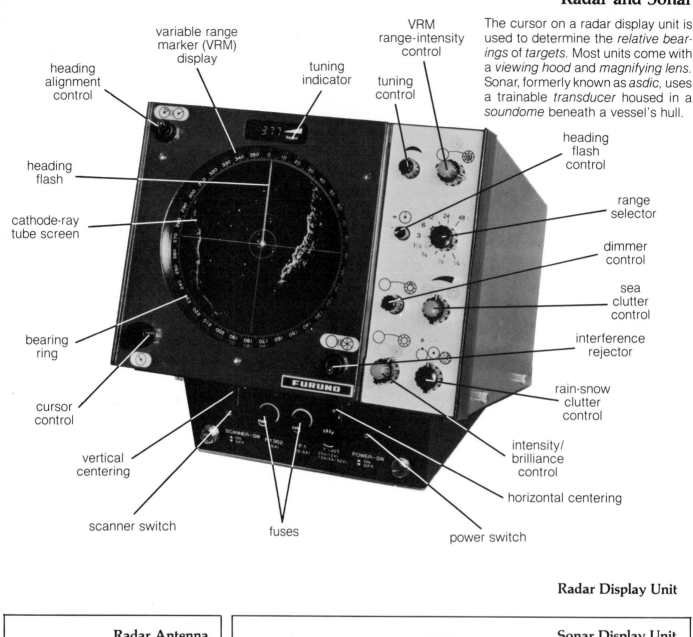

Radar and Sonar

The cursor on a radar display unit is used to determine the *relative bearings* of *targets*. Most units come with a *viewing hood* and *magnifying lens*. Sonar, formerly known as *asdic*, uses a trainable *transducer* housed in a *soundome* beneath a vessel's hull.

heading alignment control

variable range marker (VRM) display

tuning indicator

VRM range-intensity control

tuning control

heading flash control

heading flash

range selector

cathode-ray tube screen

dimmer control

sea clutter control

bearing ring

interference rejector

cursor control

rain-snow clutter control

vertical centering

intensity/ brilliance control

scanner switch

fuses

horizontal centering

power switch

Radar Display Unit

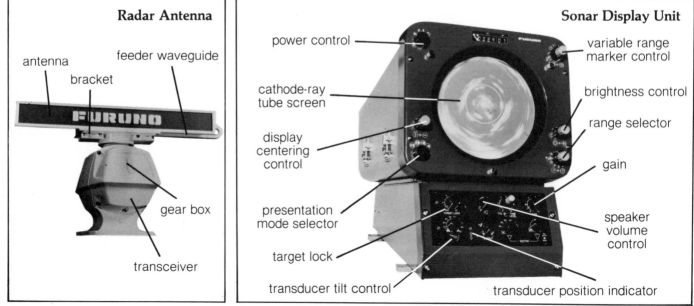

Radar Antenna

antenna

feeder waveguide

bracket

gear box

transceiver

Sonar Display Unit

power control

variable range marker control

cathode-ray tube screen

brightness control

display centering control

range selector

gain

presentation mode selector

speaker volume control

target lock

transducer tilt control

transducer position indicator

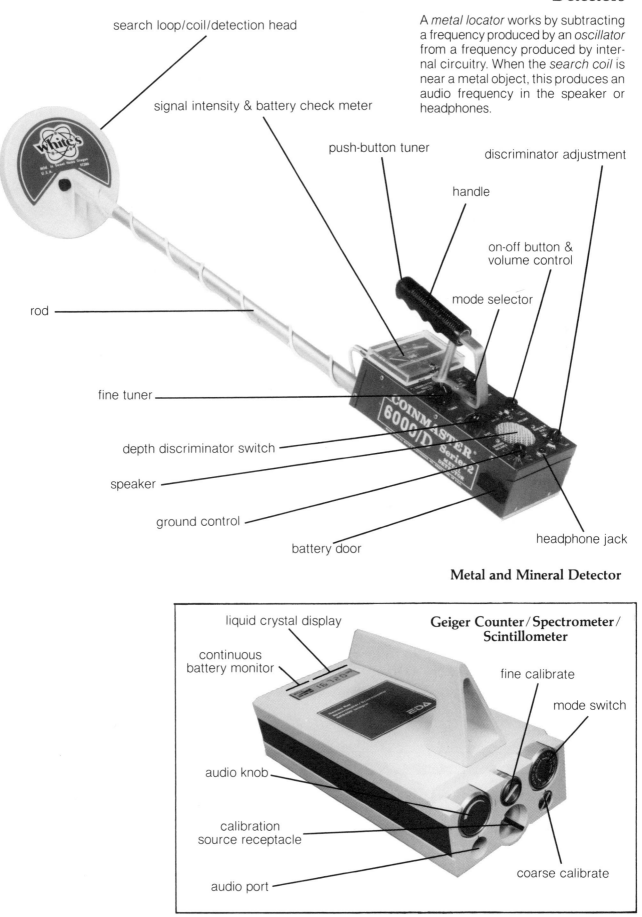

Detectors

A *metal locator* works by subtracting a frequency produced by an *oscillator* from a frequency produced by internal circuitry. When the *search coil* is near a metal object, this produces an audio frequency in the speaker or headphones.

search loop/coil/detection head

signal intensity & battery check meter

push-button tuner

discriminator adjustment

handle

on-off button & volume control

rod

mode selector

fine tuner

depth discriminator switch

speaker

ground control

battery door

headphone jack

Metal and Mineral Detector

liquid crystal display

Geiger Counter/Spectrometer/ Scintillometer

continuous battery monitor

fine calibrate

mode switch

audio knob

calibration source receptacle

coarse calibrate

audio port

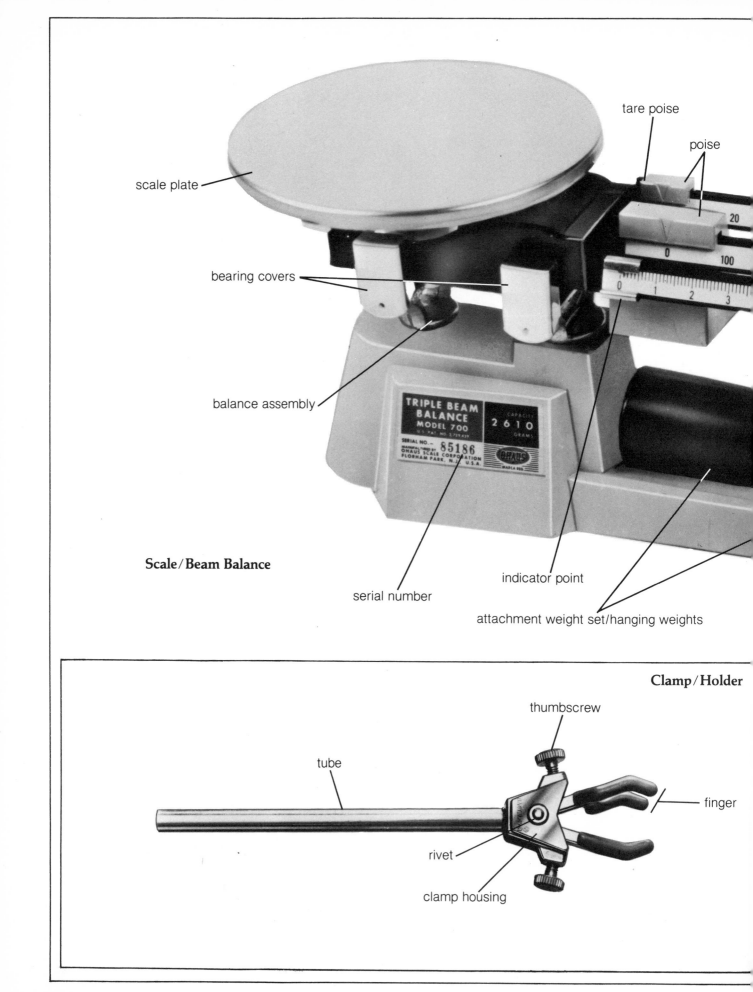

scale plate

tare poise

poise

20

0

100

0   1   2   3

bearing covers

balance assembly

TRIPLE BEAM
BALANCE
MODEL 700

CAPACITY
2610
GRAMS

SERIAL NO.— 85186
MANUFACTURED BY
OHAUS SCALE CORPORATION
FLORHAM PARK, N.J. U.S.A.

OHAUS
MARCA REG.

Scale/Beam Balance

indicator point

serial number

attachment weight set/hanging weights

Clamp/Holder

thumbscrew

tube

finger

rivet

clamp housing

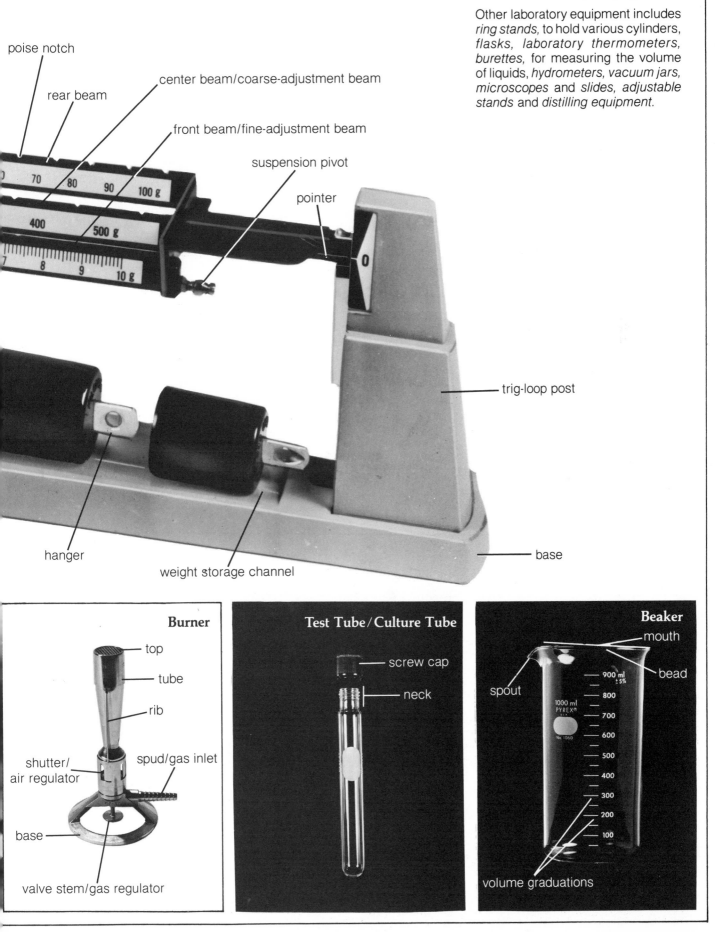

poise notch

rear beam

center beam/coarse-adjustment beam

front beam/fine-adjustment beam

suspension pivot

pointer

70 80 90 100 g

400 500 g

7 8 9 10 g

trig-loop post

hanger

weight storage channel

base

Laboratory Equipment

Other laboratory equipment includes *ring stands*, to hold various cylinders, *flasks*, *laboratory thermometers*, *burettes*, for measuring the volume of liquids, *hydrometers*, *vacuum jars*, *microscopes* and *slides*, *adjustable stands* and *distilling equipment*.

Burner

top

tube

rib

shutter/
air regulator

spud/gas inlet

base

valve stem/gas regulator

Test Tube/Culture Tube

screw cap

neck

Beaker

mouth

bead

spout

900 ml ±5%

1000 ml PYREX®

800

700

600

500

400

300

200

100

volume graduations

Sensing Devices

Examination Equipment

The scopes seen below are used by *Eye, Ear, Nose and Throat Doctors,* or *EENT specialists.* The speculum is used by *gynecologists* and *obstetricians.* *Headlights* mounted on headbands provide a light source for doctors.

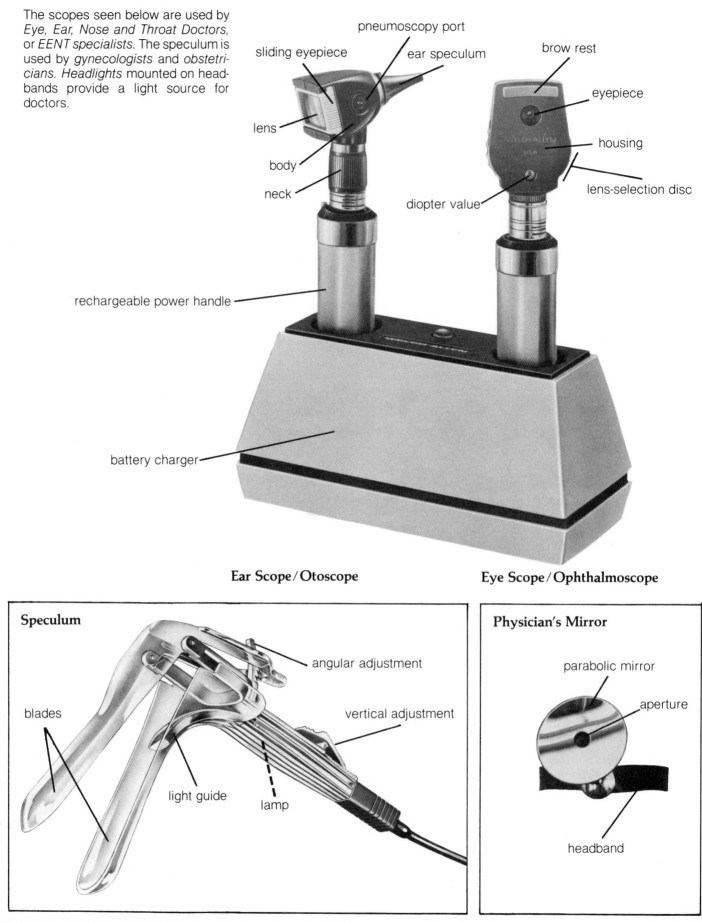

pneumoscopy port

sliding eyepiece

ear speculum

brow rest

eyepiece

lens

housing

body

diopter value

lens-selection disc

neck

rechargeable power handle

battery charger

Ear Scope/Otoscope

Eye Scope/Ophthalmoscope

Speculum

angular adjustment

blades

vertical adjustment

light guide

lamp

Physician's Mirror

parabolic mirror

aperture

headband

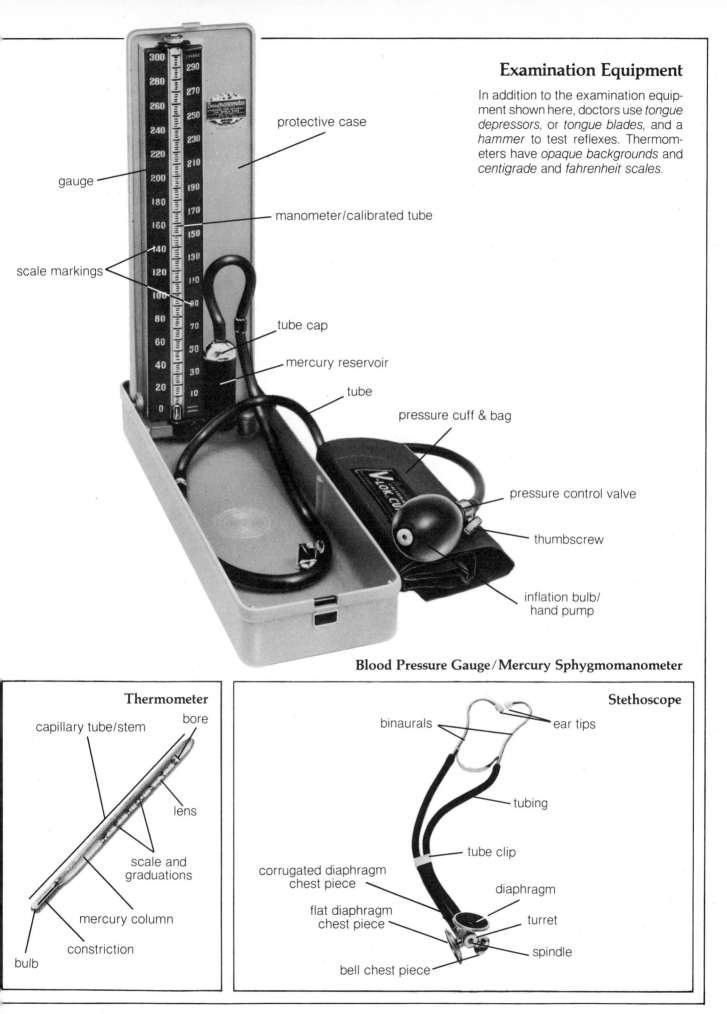

Examination Equipment

In addition to the examination equipment shown here, doctors use *tongue depressors,* or *tongue blades,* and a *hammer* to test reflexes. Thermometers have *opaque backgrounds* and *centigrade* and *fahrenheit scales.*

gauge

protective case

manometer/calibrated tube

scale markings

tube cap

mercury reservoir

tube

pressure cuff & bag

pressure control valve

thumbscrew

inflation bulb/ hand pump

Blood Pressure Gauge / Mercury Sphygmomanometer

Thermometer

capillary tube/stem

bore

lens

scale and graduations

mercury column

constriction

bulb

Stethoscope

binaurals

ear tips

tubing

tube clip

corrugated diaphragm chest piece

flat diaphragm chest piece

diaphragm

turret

spindle

bell chest piece

Medical Tools

Medical Tables

Surgical, or *operating room*, *tables*, have built-in *channels* for holding *x-ray cassettes*. Among the accessories that can be attached to them are *intravenous*, or *IV, equipment*, *arm-* and *footboard extensions*, *crutch sockets* for holding legs in position, and buckle-type *body-restraint straps*.

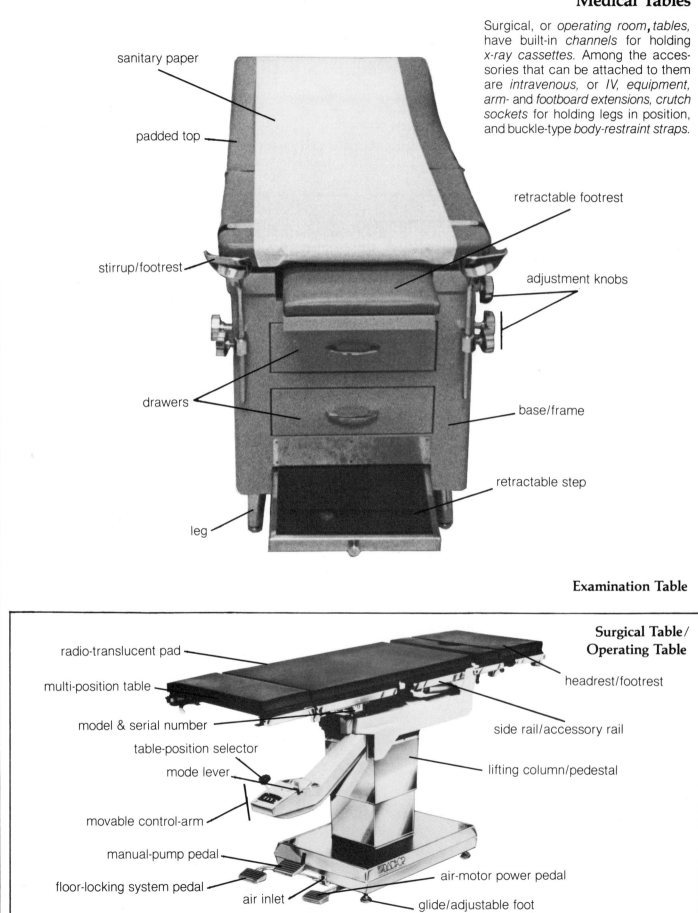

sanitary paper

padded top

retractable footrest

stirrup/footrest

adjustment knobs

drawers

base/frame

retractable step

leg

Examination Table

Surgical Table/ Operating Table

radio-translucent pad

multi-position table

headrest/footrest

model & serial number

side rail/accessory rail

table-position selector

mode lever

lifting column/pedestal

movable control-arm

manual-pump pedal

floor-locking system pedal

air-motor power pedal

air inlet

glide/adjustable foot

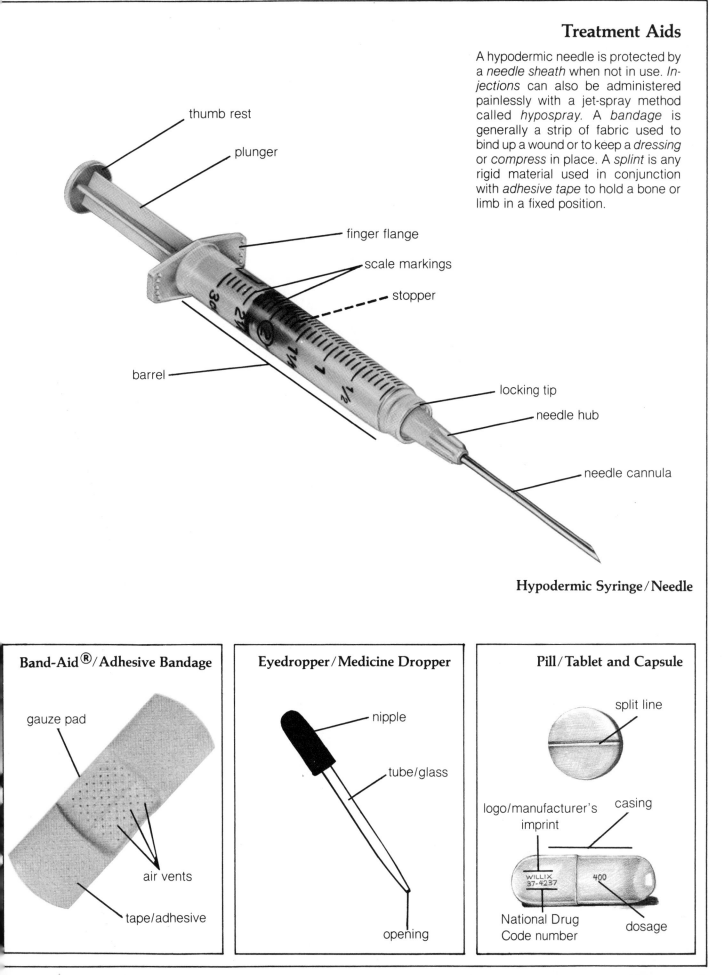

Treatment Aids

A hypodermic needle is protected by a *needle sheath* when not in use. *Injections* can also be administered painlessly with a jet-spray method called *hypospray*. A *bandage* is generally a strip of fabric used to bind up a wound or to keep a *dressing* or *compress* in place. A *splint* is any rigid material used in conjunction with *adhesive tape* to hold a bone or limb in a fixed position.

thumb rest

plunger

finger flange

scale markings

stopper

barrel

locking tip

needle hub

needle cannula

Hypodermic Syringe / Needle

Band-Aid®/ Adhesive Bandage

gauze pad

air vents

tape/adhesive

Eyedropper / Medicine Dropper

nipple

tube/glass

opening

Pill / Tablet and Capsule

split line

logo/manufacturer's imprint

casing

WILLIX 37-4237

400

National Drug Code number

dosage

Medical Tools

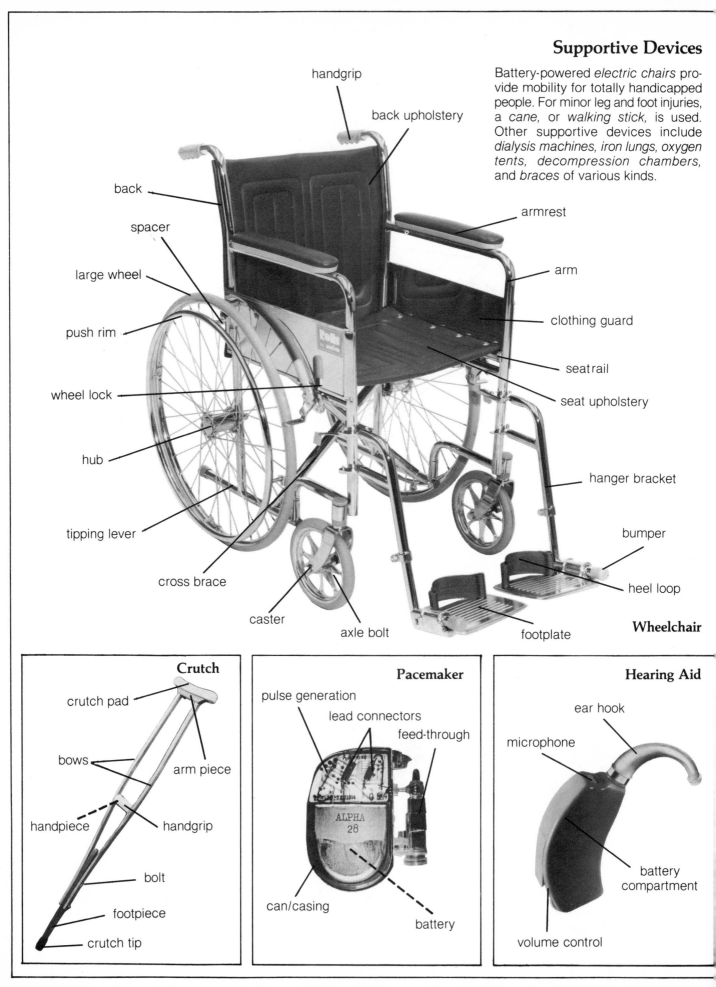

Supportive Devices

Battery-powered *electric chairs* provide mobility for totally handicapped people. For minor leg and foot injuries, a *cane*, or *walking stick*, is used. Other supportive devices include *dialysis machines*, *iron lungs*, *oxygen tents*, *decompression chambers*, and *braces* of various kinds.

handgrip

back upholstery

back

spacer

large wheel

push rim

wheel lock

hub

tipping lever

cross brace

caster

axle bolt

footplate

armrest

arm

clothing guard

seat rail

seat upholstery

hanger bracket

bumper

heel loop

Wheelchair

Crutch

crutch pad

bows

arm piece

handpiece

handgrip

bolt

footpiece

crutch tip

Pacemaker

pulse generation

lead connectors

feed-through

ALPHA 28

can/casing

battery

Hearing Aid

ear hook

microphone

battery compartment

volume control

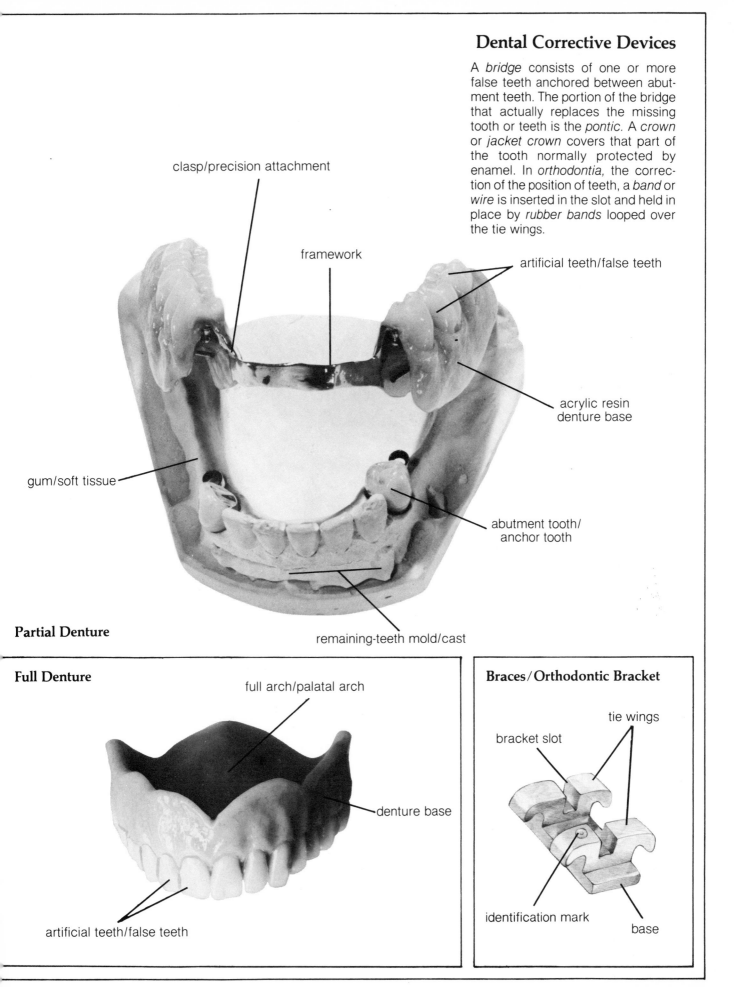

Dental Corrective Devices

A *bridge* consists of one or more false teeth anchored between abutment teeth. The portion of the bridge that actually replaces the missing tooth or teeth is the *pontic*. A *crown* or *jacket crown* covers that part of the tooth normally protected by enamel. In *orthodontia,* the correction of the position of teeth, a *band* or *wire* is inserted in the slot and held in place by *rubber bands* looped over the tie wings.

clasp/precision attachment

framework

artificial teeth/false teeth

acrylic resin denture base

gum/soft tissue

abutment tooth/ anchor tooth

Partial Denture

remaining-teeth mold/cast

Full Denture

full arch/palatal arch

denture base

artificial teeth/false teeth

Braces/Orthodontic Bracket

tie wings

bracket slot

identification mark

base

Dental Unit

A high-intensity *dental light* is usually attached to a dental unit, or *dental island.* Instrument trays may be attached to a *drift-free arm,* such as the one shown here, or to a *post-mounted arm.*

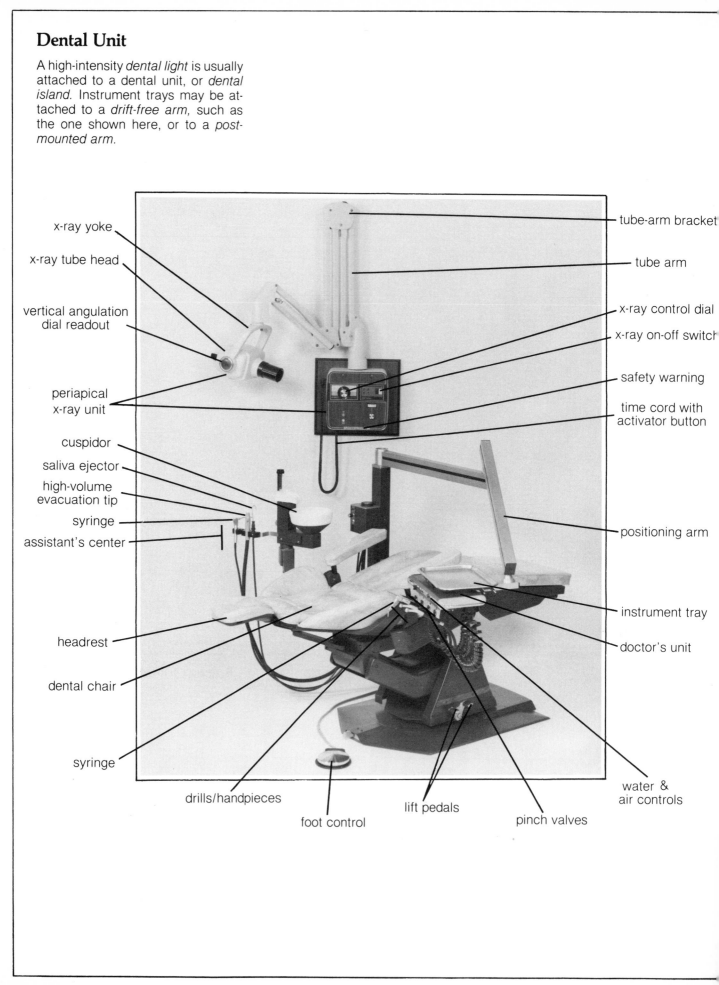

x-ray yoke

x-ray tube head

vertical angulation dial readout

periapical x-ray unit

cuspidor

saliva ejector

high-volume evacuation tip

syringe

assistant's center

headrest

dental chair

syringe

drills/handpieces

foot control

lift pedals

pinch valves

tube-arm bracket

tube arm

x-ray control dial

x-ray on-off switch

safety warning

time cord with activator button

positioning arm

instrument tray

doctor's unit

water & air controls

Dental Equipment

Fillings of *silver amalgam* or *inlays,* *cast restorations* of *gold, synthetic porcelain* or *acrylic resins,* are used to fill *cavities.* Teeth can also be fitted with *crowns* or *caps.*

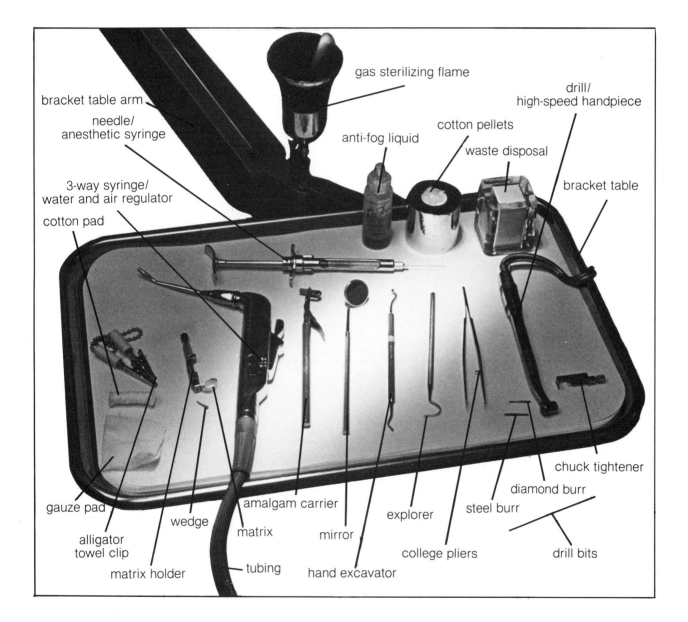

gas sterilizing flame

bracket table arm

needle/
anesthetic syringe

anti-fog liquid

cotton pellets

waste disposal

drill/
high-speed handpiece

3-way syringe/
water and air regulator

bracket table

cotton pad

gauze pad

alligator
towel clip

wedge

matrix holder

amalgam carrier

matrix

tubing

mirror

hand excavator

explorer

college pliers

steel burr

diamond burr

chuck tightener

drill bits

Medical Tools

Teeth

Each tooth has one or two *neighbors* and a biting *partner* in the opposite jaw. Teeth fit into *sockets*. The first set of teeth are *baby teeth,* or *milk teeth,* replaced in time by permanent teeth. A person with a fondness for sugary edibles is said to have a *sweet tooth.*

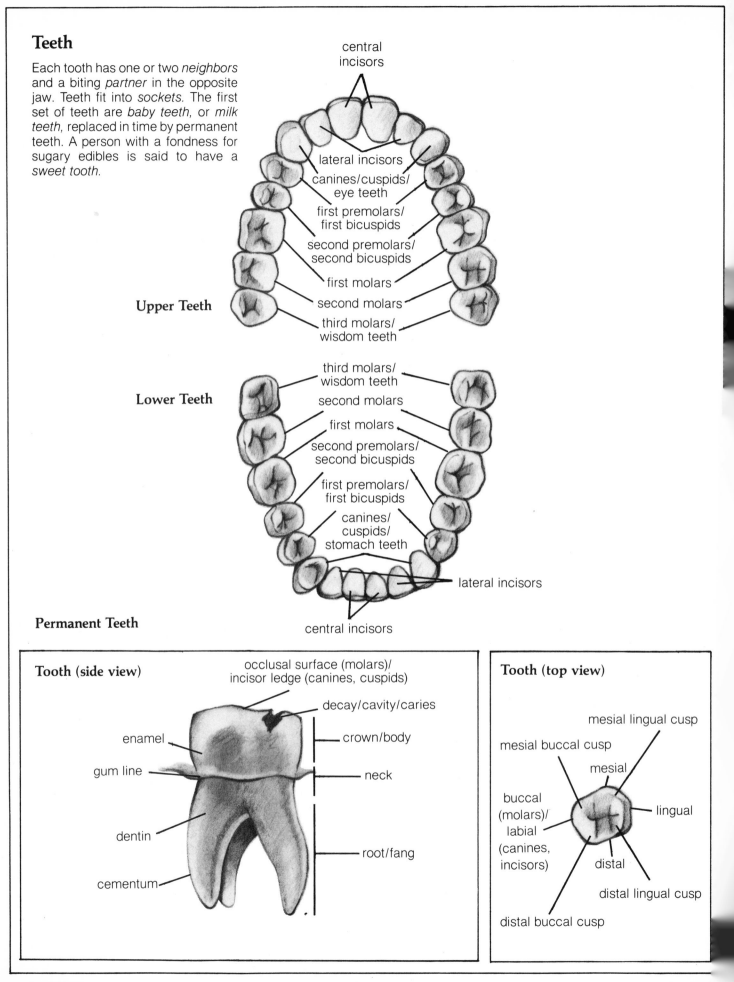

central incisors

lateral incisors

canines/cuspids/ eye teeth

first premolars/ first bicuspids

second premolars/ second bicuspids

first molars

second molars

Upper Teeth

third molars/ wisdom teeth

Lower Teeth

third molars/ wisdom teeth

second molars

first molars

second premolars/ second bicuspids

first premolars/ first bicuspids

canines/ cuspids/ stomach teeth

lateral incisors

central incisors

Permanent Teeth

Tooth (side view)

occlusal surface (molars)/ incisor ledge (canines, cuspids)

decay/cavity/caries

enamel

crown/body

gum line

neck

dentin

root/fang

cementum

Tooth (top view)

mesial lingual cusp

mesial buccal cusp

mesial

buccal (molars)/ labial (canines, incisors)

lingual

distal

distal lingual cusp

distal buccal cusp

Vault and Safe

Vaults are connected to *alarm systems*, which include *bells* and *silent alarms*. *Time locks* open safes or vaults at a predetermined time and prevent their being opened otherwise. A *strongbox* is a stoutly made box or chest for preserving valuable possessions. Most safes are insulated to protect against fire as well as theft. A home *money box, coin bank* or *piggy bank* is opened at the bottom or with a hammer.

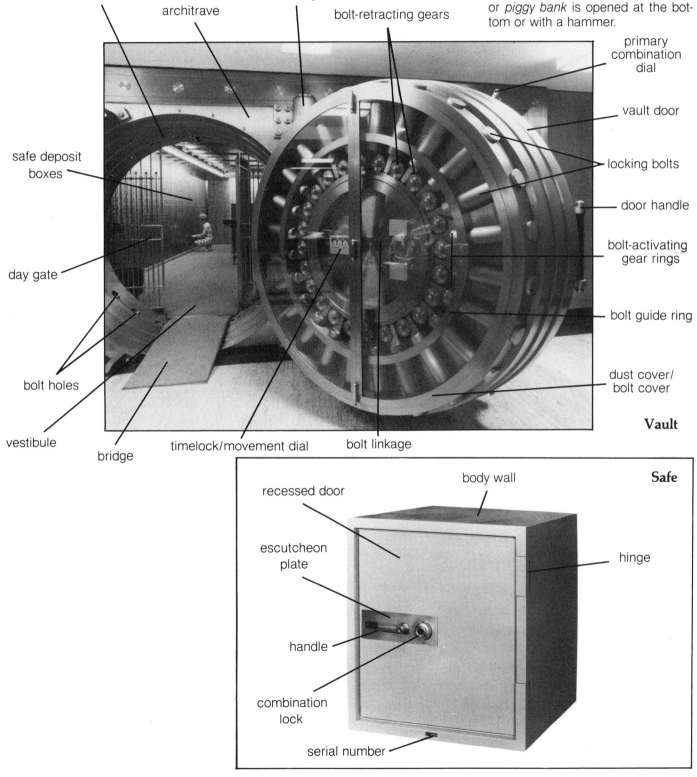

door jamb

architrave

door hinge

bolt-retracting gears

primary combination dial

vault door

locking bolts

door handle

bolt-activating gear rings

bolt guide ring

dust cover/ bolt cover

safe deposit boxes

day gate

bolt holes

vestibule

bridge

timelock/movement dial

bolt linkage

Vault

Safe

recessed door

body wall

escutcheon plate

hinge

handle

combination lock

serial number

Security Devices

Door Locks

Many mortise locks have two *buttons* below the latch bolt which allow the *outside knob* to be independently locked or unlocked. Bolts fit into a *striker plate,* attached to the door frame. A *latch* is a device which holds a door closed, but cannot be locked. A *catch* holds lightweight doors, such as cabinet doors, closed. A *lockset* has the features of a lock and a catch.

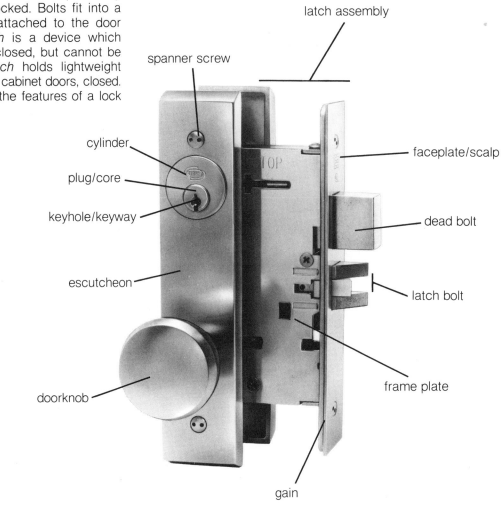

latch assembly

spanner screw

cylinder

plug/core

keyhole/keyway

escutcheon

doorknob

faceplate/scalp

dead bolt

latch bolt

frame plate

gain

Mortise Lock

Chain Lock / Door Bolt

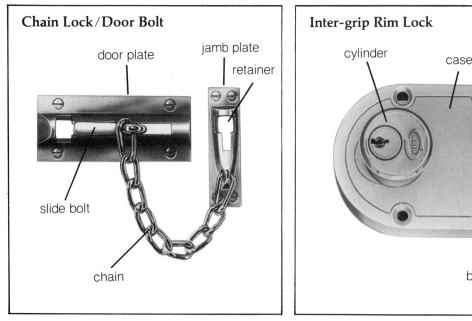

door plate

jamb plate

retainer

slide bolt

chain

Inter-grip Rim Lock

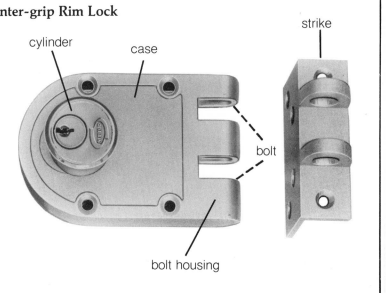

cylinder

case

strike

bolt

bolt housing

Key and Padlock

A key is inserted into a lock's cylinder via a *keyway*. The angled serrations, or *cuts*, on a key blade correspond to different sized *pin-tumblers*, or *pins*, within the lock cylinder. A key that has not yet been configured to any particular lock is a *blank*. A key used to open many common locks is a *skeleton key*.

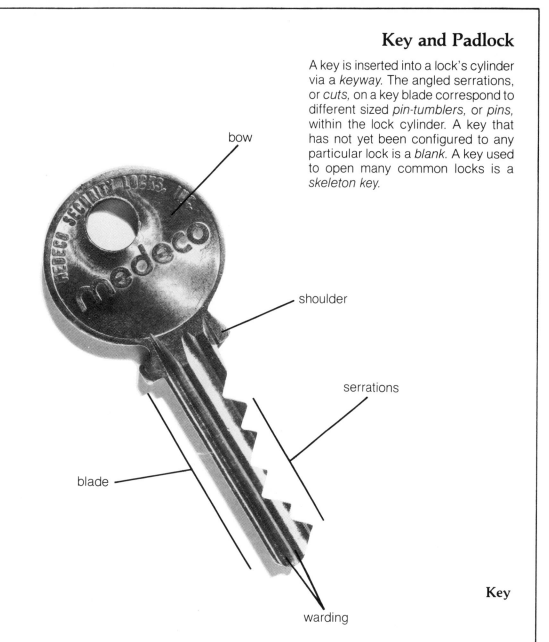

bow

shoulder

serrations

blade

warding

Key

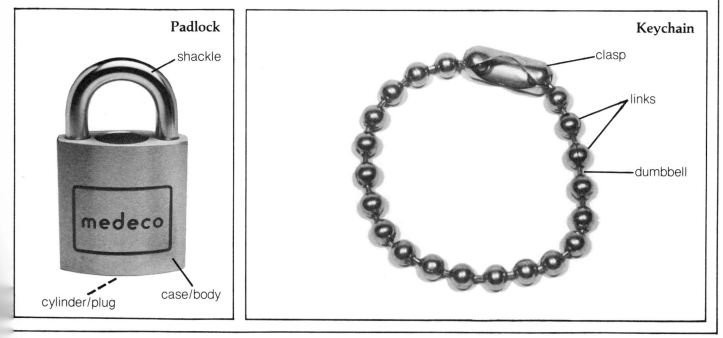

Padlock

shackle

medeco

cylinder/plug

case/body

Keychain

clasp

links

dumbbell

Security Devices

Hinge and Hasp

In addition to the *butt hinge,* seen here, there are *pivot hinges, full-surface hinges, half-surface hinges, spring hinges, strap hinges* and *continuous hinges.* Hinge pivot pins or *fixed pins,* used on smaller hinges, are available in a variety of ornamental *heads,* or *caps,* such as the ball tip seen here. A *safety hasp* is secured with a padlock or pin.

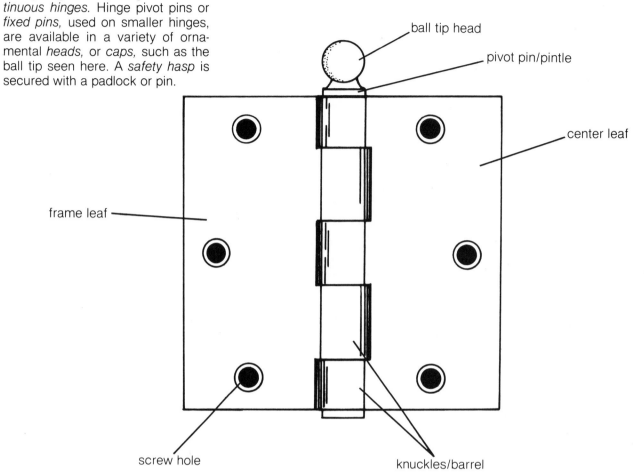

ball tip head

pivot pin/pintle

center leaf

frame leaf

screw hole

knuckles/barrel

Hinge

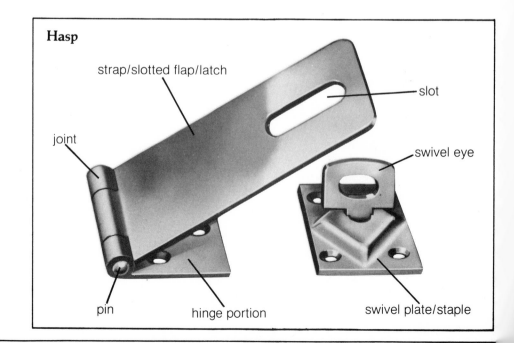

Hasp

strap/slotted flap/latch

slot

joint

swivel eye

pin

hinge portion

swivel plate/staple

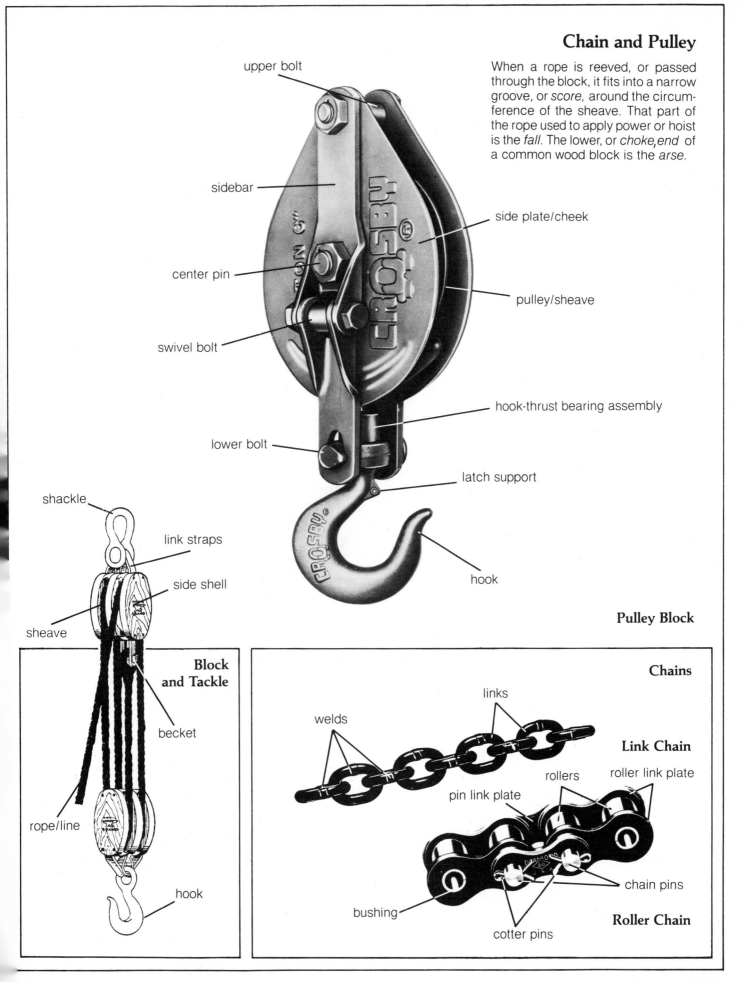

Chain and Pulley

When a rope is reeved, or passed through the block, it fits into a narrow groove, or *score,* around the circumference of the sheave. That part of the rope used to apply power or hoist is the *fall.* The lower, or *choke,end* of a common wood block is the *arse.*

upper bolt

sidebar

side plate/cheek

center pin

pulley/sheave

swivel bolt

hook-thrust bearing assembly

lower bolt

latch support

hook

Pulley Block

shackle

link straps

side shell

sheave

becket

Block and Tackle

rope/line

hook

Chains

links

welds

Link Chain

rollers

roller link plate

pin link plate

chain pins

bushing

cotter pins

Roller Chain

Execution Devices

The blade on the guillotine is released by a *release cord* or *release button*. The Italian *mannaia* and the Scottish *maiden* were variations of the French guillotine. A *gibbet,* similar to a gallows, has a single, horizontal arm from which the noose was hung. On an electric chair, electrodes are attached to the prisoner's head and leg to complete the circuit. A *tumbrel* is any vehicle used to bring condemned people to the place of execution.

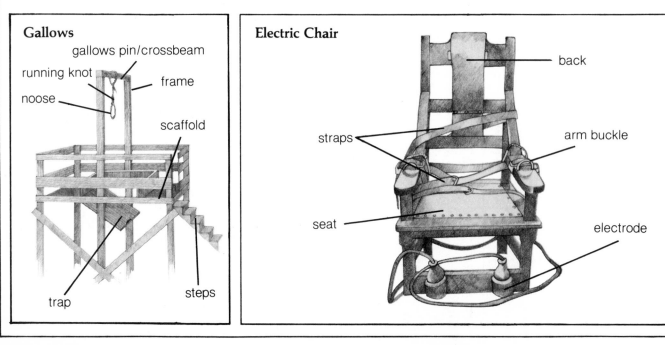

crossbeam

weight

blade/knife/ax

groove

post/upright

lunette

woven basket

trestle

ground beam

Guillotine

Gallows

gallows pin/crossbeam

running knot

noose

frame

scaffold

trap

steps

Electric Chair

back

straps

arm buckle

seat

electrode

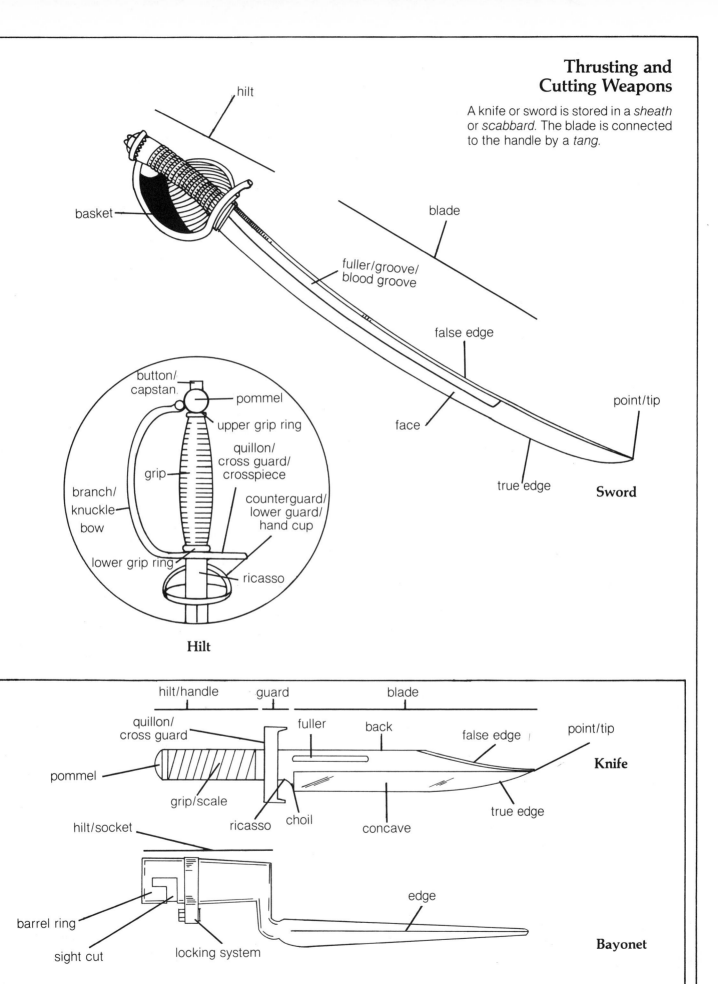

Thrusting and Cutting Weapons

A knife or sword is stored in a *sheath* or *scabbard.* The blade is connected to the handle by a *tang.*

hilt

basket

blade

fuller/groove/
blood groove

false edge

point/tip

face

true edge

Sword

button/
capstan

pommel

upper grip ring

grip

quillon/
cross guard/
crosspiece

branch/
knuckle
bow

counterguard/
lower guard/
hand cup

lower grip ring

ricasso

Hilt

hilt/handle   guard   blade

quillon/
cross guard

fuller   back   false edge   point/tip

pommel

Knife

grip/scale

ricasso   choil   concave   true edge

hilt/socket

barrel ring

edge

sight cut   locking system

Bayonet

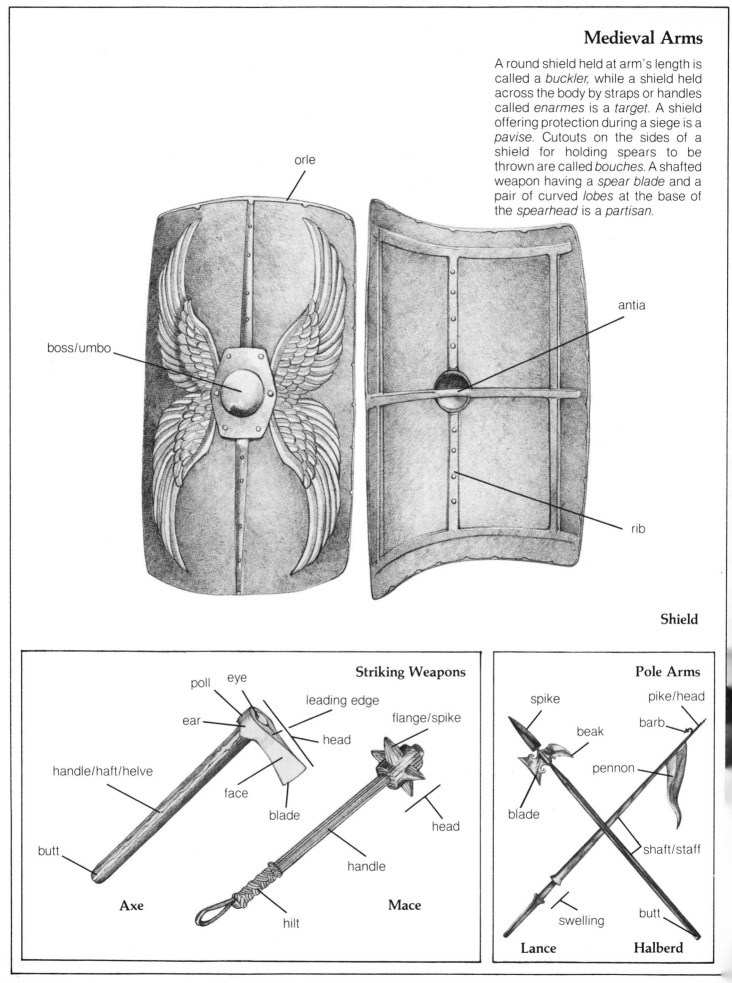

Medieval Arms

A round shield held at arm's length is called a *buckler*, while a shield held across the body by straps or handles called *enarmes* is a *target*. A shield offering protection during a siege is a *pavise*. Cutouts on the sides of a shield for holding spears to be thrown are called *bouches*. A shafted weapon having a *spear blade* and a pair of curved *lobes* at the base of the *spearhead* is a *partisan*.

orle

boss/umbo

antia

rib

Shield

Striking Weapons

poll · eye
ear
leading edge
flange/spike
head
handle/haft/helve
face
blade
butt
handle
hilt

Axe

Mace

Pole Arms

spike
pike/head
beak
barb
pennon
blade
shaft/staff
swelling
butt

Lance · **Halberd**

Armor

Body armor, *protective clothing* and *headgear*, was usually made of iron or thick leather. It was often adorned with *decorative inlays*.

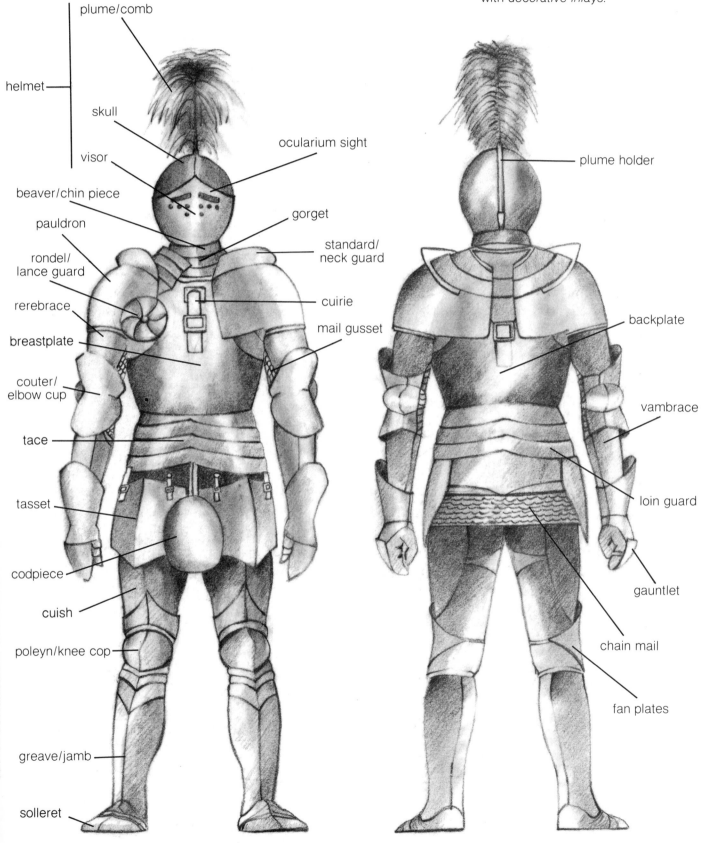

plume/comb

helmet

skull

visor

beaver/chin piece

pauldron

rondel/
lance guard

rerebrace

breastplate

couter/
elbow cup

tace

tasset

codpiece

cuish

poleyn/knee cop

greave/jamb

solleret

ocularium sight

gorget

standard/
neck guard

cuirie

mail gusset

plume holder

backplate

vambrace

loin guard

gauntlet

chain mail

fan plates

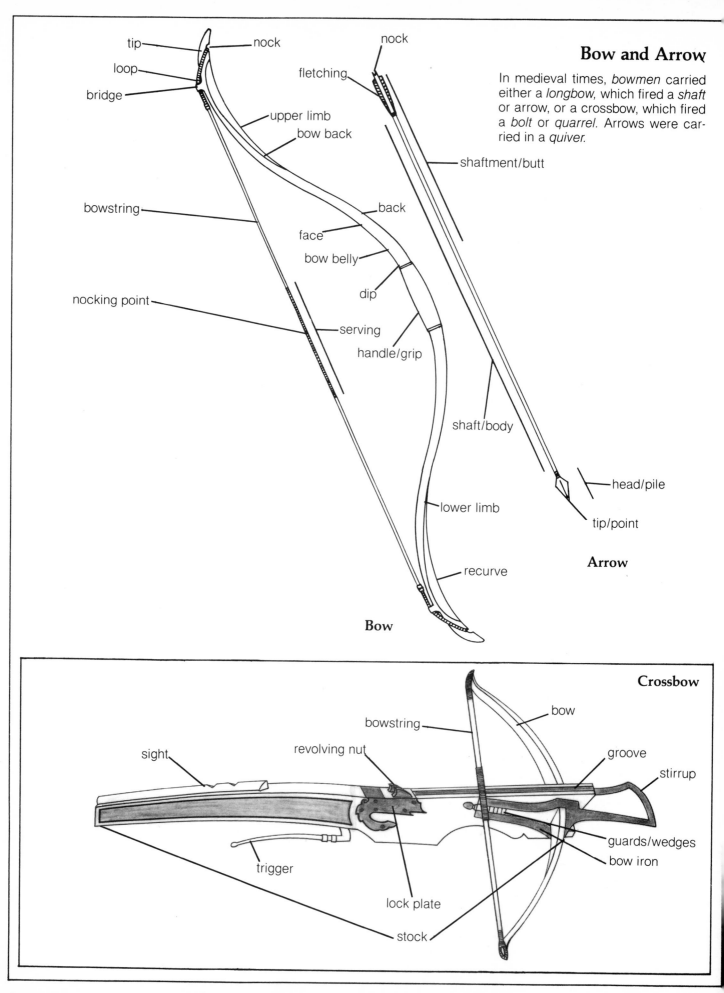

Bow and Arrow

In medieval times, *bowmen* carried either a *longbow,* which fired a *shaft* or arrow, or a crossbow, which fired a *bolt* or *quarrel.* Arrows were carried in a *quiver.*

tip

nock

loop

bridge

nock

fletching

upper limb

bow back

shaftment/butt

bowstring

back

face

bow belly

dip

nocking point

serving

handle/grip

shaft/body

head/pile

tip/point

lower limb

Arrow

recurve

Bow

Crossbow

bowstring

bow

sight

revolving nut

groove

stirrup

trigger

guards/wedges

bow iron

lock plate

stock

Cannon and Catapult

Cannonballs fired by *muzzle-loaders* were transported in *caissons* and stacked in trays called *monkeys*. *Loaders* used a *swab* or *sponge* to get rid of residue, a *worm* to remove obstructions, and a *rammer* to drive the *projectile* into the *bore* at the muzzle, or *mouth*, of the cannon. Catapults were used to fire javelinlike shafts a quarter of a mile or more. Ballistas, using the same system of hurling, were employed to heave heavy stones short distances.

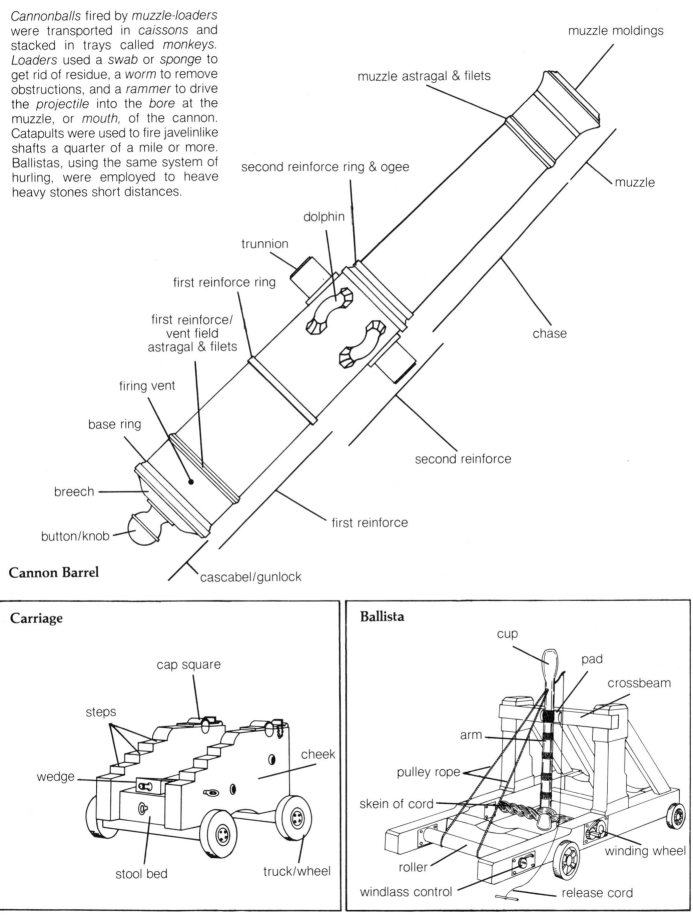

muzzle moldings

muzzle astragal & filets

second reinforce ring & ogee

dolphin

trunnion

first reinforce ring

first reinforce/ vent field astragal & filets

firing vent

base ring

breech

button/knob

muzzle

chase

second reinforce

first reinforce

cascabel/gunlock

Cannon Barrel

Carriage

cap square

steps

wedge

cheek

stool bed

truck/wheel

Ballista

cup

pad

crossbeam

arm

pulley rope

skein of cord

roller

windlass control

winding wheel

release cord

Weapons

Shotgun and Rifle

A shotgun fires small *pellets* through a *smooth bore,* while a rifle fires *bullets* through a *rifled barrel.* Shotgun barrels are usually tapered, or *choked,* to constrict the *shot pattern.* Rifles may be carried across the shoulder on a beltlike *sling* connected to the weapon by *sling swivels* and adjusted with bucklelike *claws.*

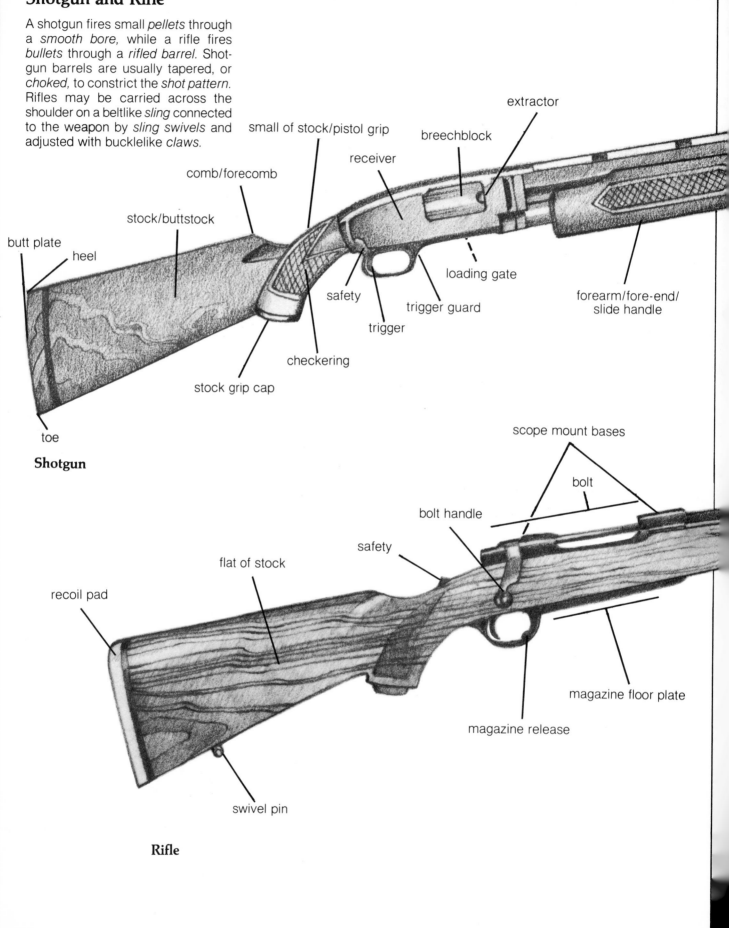

extractor

small of stock/pistol grip

breechblock

receiver

comb/forecomb

stock/buttstock

butt plate

heel

loading gate

safety

trigger guard

forearm/fore-end/ slide handle

trigger

checkering

stock grip cap

toe

Shotgun

scope mount bases

bolt

bolt handle

safety

flat of stock

recoil pad

magazine floor plate

magazine release

swivel pin

Rifle

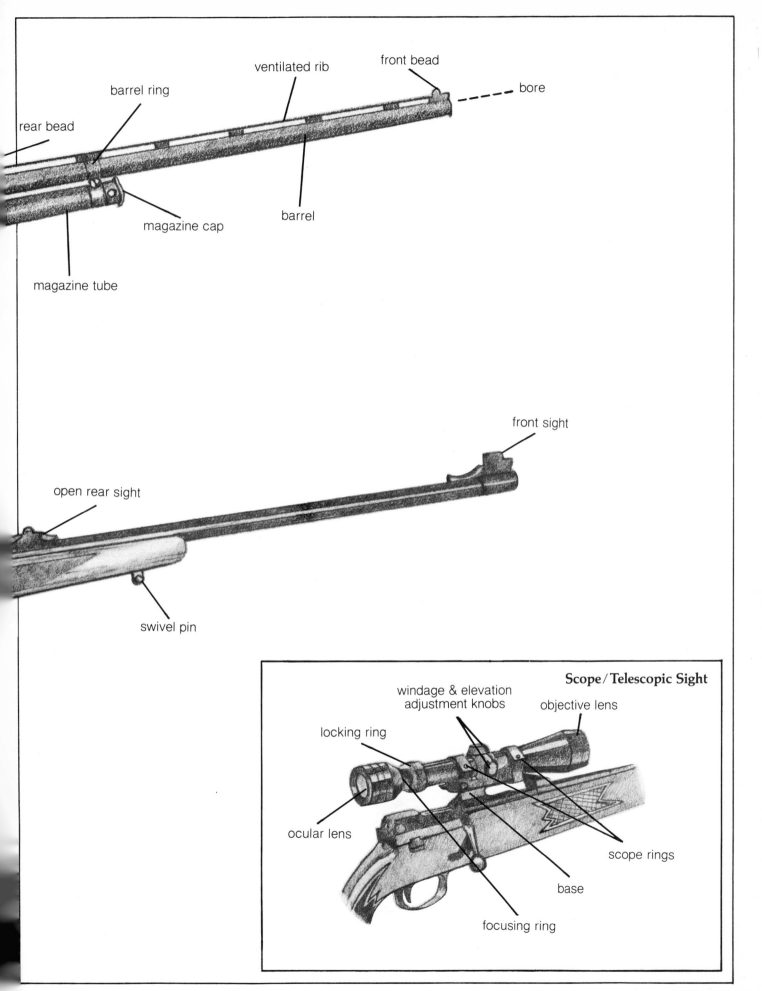

rear bead

barrel ring

ventilated rib

front bead

bore

magazine cap

barrel

magazine tube

open rear sight

front sight

swivel pin

Scope / Telescopic Sight

windage & elevation
adjustment knobs

objective lens

locking ring

ocular lens

scope rings

base

focusing ring

Handguns

A *gun,* or *side arm,* is *fired* when a *firing pin* in the *breech* strikes the cartridge primer. A *silencer* dampens the sound of a gun's *discharge.* Grooves in the barrel, called *rifling,* cause a fired bullet to spiral for stability in flight. Cartridges are measured in *calibers,* their diameters in hundredths or thousandths of an inch written in a decimal fraction, or in *millimeters.* Handguns are carried in *holsters.*

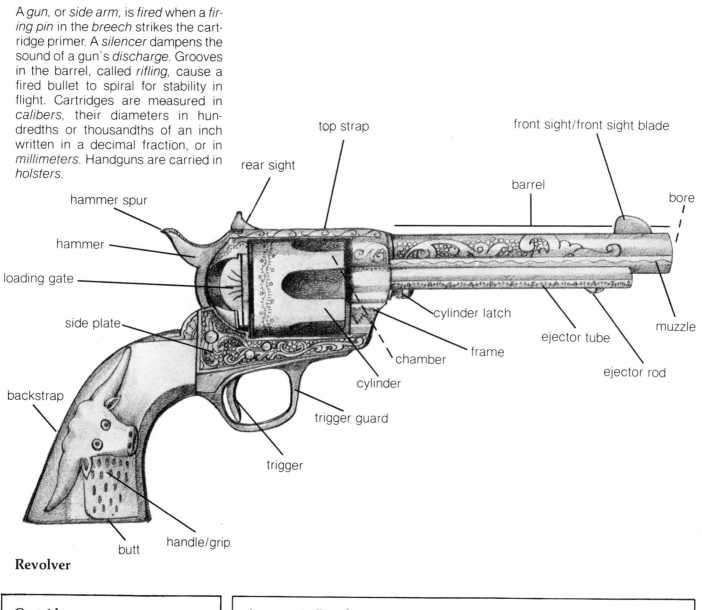

top strap

rear sight

front sight/front sight blade

barrel

bore

hammer spur

hammer

loading gate

side plate

backstrap

cylinder latch

ejector tube

muzzle

chamber

frame

ejector rod

cylinder

trigger guard

handle/grip

trigger

butt

Revolver

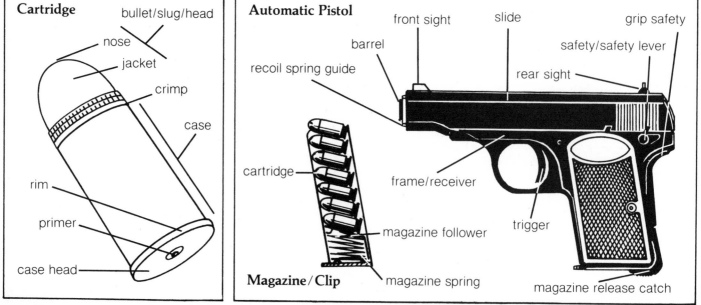

Cartridge

bullet/slug/head

nose

jacket

crimp

case

rim

primer

case head

Automatic Pistol

front sight

slide

grip safety

barrel

safety/safety lever

recoil spring guide

rear sight

cartridge

frame/receiver

trigger

magazine follower

Magazine/Clip

magazine spring

magazine release catch

Automatic Weapons

Multi-shot automatic weapons are grouped by weight: light, medium and heavy. The *air-cooled,* medium-weight machine gun shown here can be handled by one man on the ground or on a vehicle when mounted on *pintle mounts.* The light, hand-held automatic rifle is also able to deliver a rapid burst of continuous fire as long as the trigger is depressed. *Ammunition* is fed to it from *handle clips* or *banana clips.*

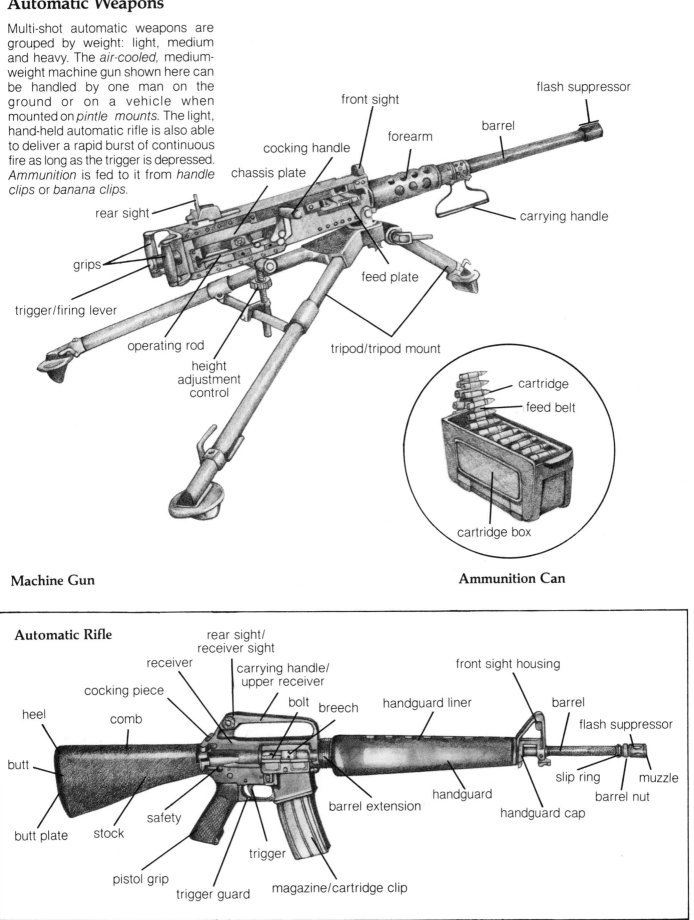

flash suppressor

front sight

forearm

barrel

cocking handle

chassis plate

carrying handle

rear sight

grips

feed plate

trigger/firing lever

operating rod

height adjustment control

tripod/tripod mount

cartridge

feed belt

cartridge box

Machine Gun

Ammunition Can

Automatic Rifle

rear sight/ receiver sight

receiver

carrying handle/ upper receiver

cocking piece

bolt

breech

front sight housing

heel

comb

handguard liner

barrel

flash suppressor

butt

slip ring

muzzle

safety

handguard

barrel nut

stock

barrel extension

handguard cap

butt plate

trigger

pistol grip

trigger guard

magazine/cartridge clip

461

Mortar and Bazooka

A mortar is a *muzzle-loading cannon,* or *midget howitzer,* used to throw *finned projectiles* at high angles. A bazooka is a portable shoulder weapon with an *open-breech smoothbore firing tube* that fires several types of *rockets.*

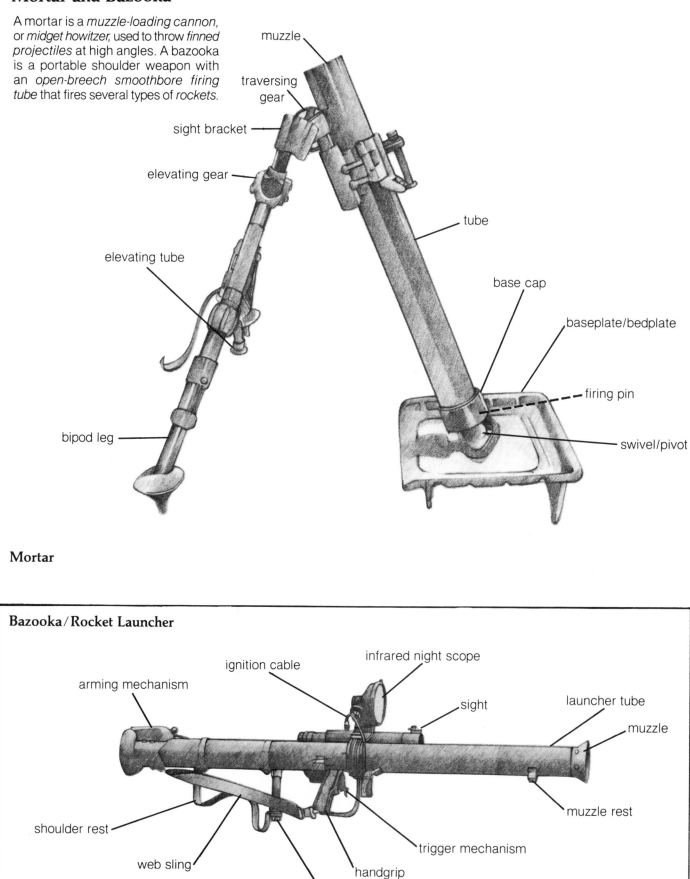

muzzle

traversing gear

sight bracket

elevating gear

elevating tube

bipod leg

tube

base cap

baseplate/bedplate

firing pin

swivel/pivot

Mortar

Bazooka/Rocket Launcher

ignition cable

infrared night scope

arming mechanism

sight

launcher tube

muzzle

shoulder rest

web sling

butt

handgrip

trigger mechanism

muzzle rest

Grenade and Mine

When the type of grenade shown here is detonated, it bursts into numerous metal fragments called *shrapnel.* Other types of grenades include *smoke grenades* and *concussion grenades.* Streamlined *rifle grenades* have rear *fins* to provide stability in flight. A *"Molotov cocktail,"* a crude grenade often thrown at tanks to set them on fire, consists of a gasoline-filled bottle with a lighted *wick* at the top.

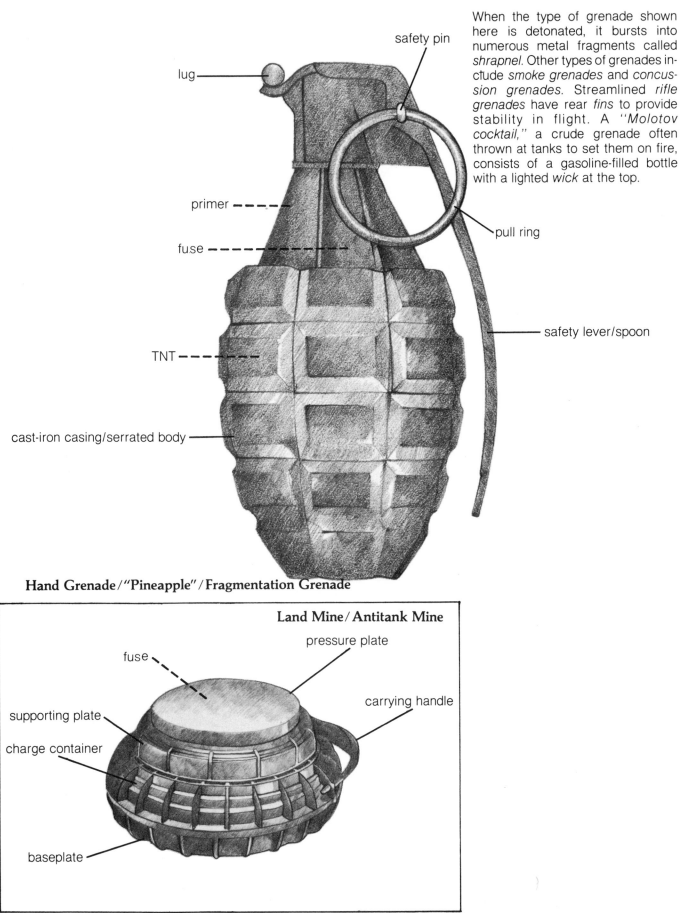

lug

safety pin

primer

fuse

TNT

cast-iron casing/serrated body

pull ring

safety lever/spoon

Hand Grenade/"Pineapple"/Fragmentation Grenade

Land Mine/Antitank Mine

pressure plate

fuse

carrying handle

supporting plate

charge container

baseplate

Weapons

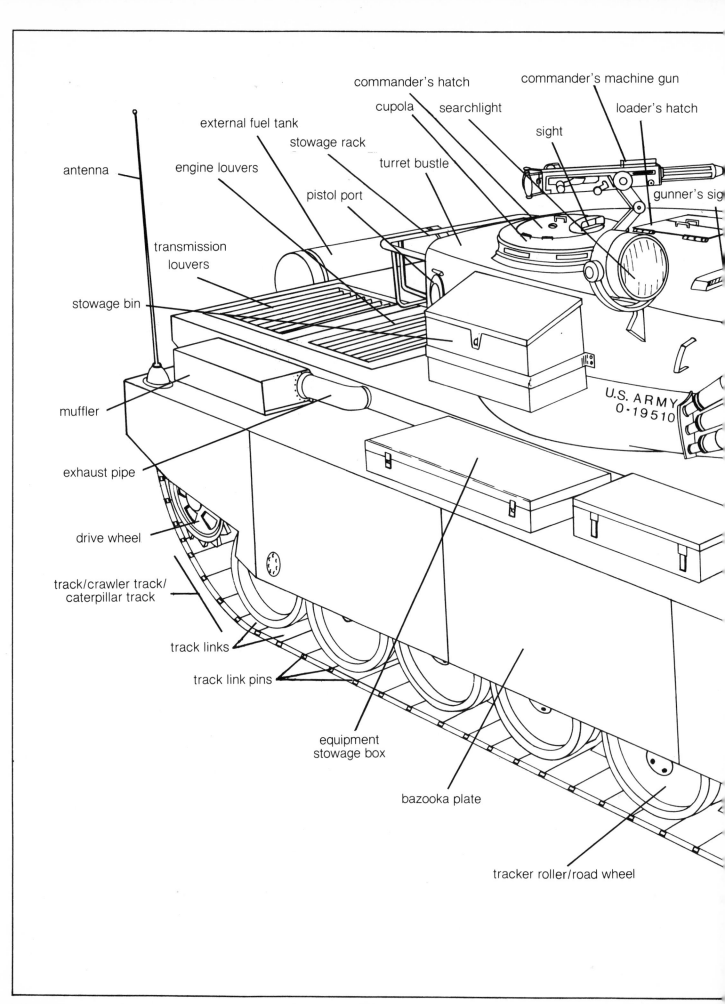

commander's hatch

commander's machine gun

cupola

searchlight

loader's hatch

sight

external fuel tank

stowage rack

turret bustle

gunner's sig

engine louvers

antenna

pistol port

transmission
louvers

stowage bin

muffler

U.S. ARMY
0-19510

exhaust pipe

drive wheel

track/crawler track/
caterpillar track

track links

track link pins

equipment
stowage box

bazooka plate

tracker roller/road wheel

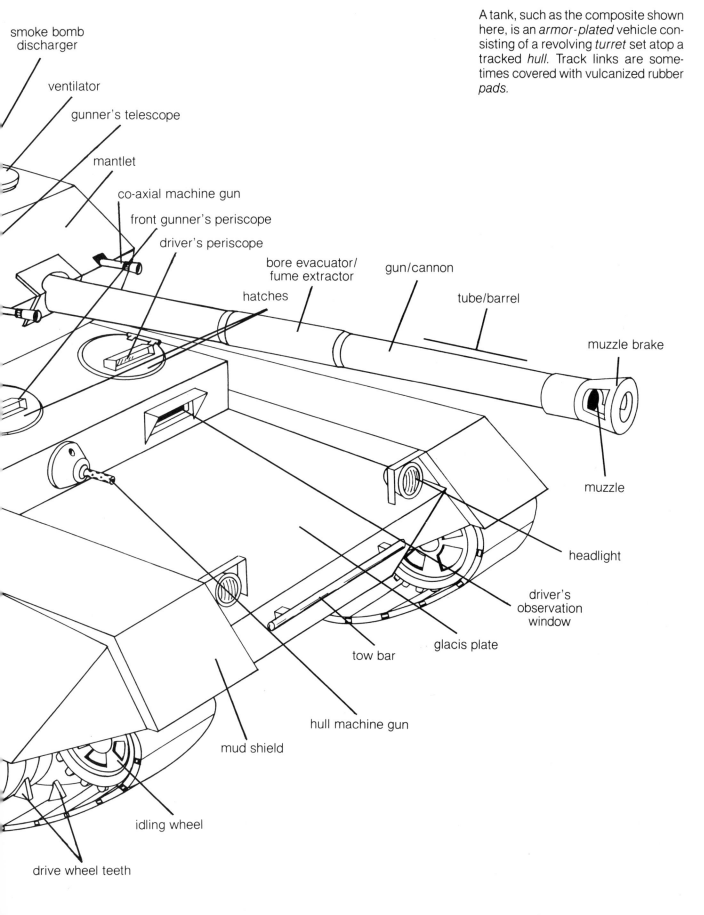

Tank

A tank, such as the composite shown here, is an *armor-plated* vehicle consisting of a revolving *turret* set atop a tracked *hull.* Track links are sometimes covered with vulcanized rubber *pads.*

smoke bomb discharger

ventilator

gunner's telescope

mantlet

co-axial machine gun

front gunner's periscope

driver's periscope

hatches

bore evacuator/ fume extractor

gun/cannon

tube/barrel

muzzle brake

muzzle

headlight

driver's observation window

glacis plate

tow bar

hull machine gun

mud shield

idling wheel

drive wheel teeth

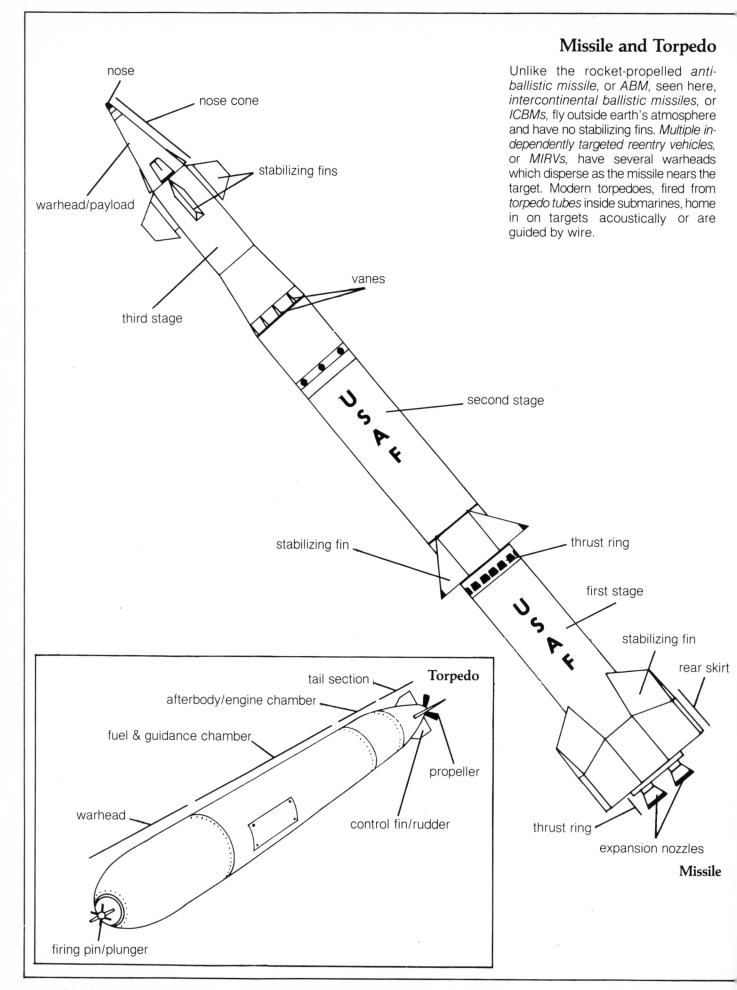

Missile and Torpedo

Unlike the rocket-propelled *anti-ballistic missile*, or *ABM*, seen here, *intercontinental ballistic missiles*, or *ICBMs*, fly outside earth's atmosphere and have no stabilizing fins. *Multiple independently targeted reentry vehicles*, or *MIRVs*, have several warheads which disperse as the missile nears the target. Modern torpedoes, fired from *torpedo tubes* inside submarines, home in on targets acoustically or are guided by wire.

nose

nose cone

stabilizing fins

warhead/payload

vanes

third stage

second stage

stabilizing fin

thrust ring

first stage

stabilizing fin

rear skirt

thrust ring

expansion nozzles

Missile

Torpedo

tail section

afterbody/engine chamber

fuel & guidance chamber

propeller

warhead

control fin/rudder

firing pin/plunger

Uniforms, Costumes and Ceremonial Attire

The attire presented in this section ranges from vestments and formal dress used on special occasions to dress of distinctive design or fashion worn by members of particular groups. The parts of military or municipal attire, for example, serve to identify not only branch of service but rank and distinction as well.

Garb can be highly stylized or informal. Manchu Court dress, for example, was worn only on formal occasions, whereas the clothes commonly worn by cowboys, dictated by the demands of the profession, was casual.

In addition to the trappings that have come to typify characters in history—a general, pirate, miser, magician—this section also includes clothing used by performers such as clowns, ballet dancers and drum majorettes.

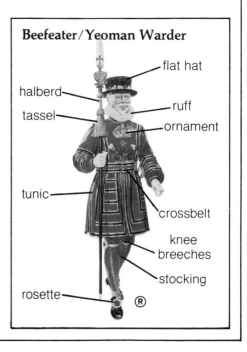

Beefeater / Yeoman Warder

halberd

tassel

flat hat

ruff

ornament

tunic

crossbelt

knee breeches

stocking

rosette

®

467

Royal Regalia

In coronations and investitures, a king wears a blunted sword called a *curtein* on his sash. Among a queen's foundation garments, or *underpinnings,* are a *corset, corselet, chemise* and *pantaloons.*

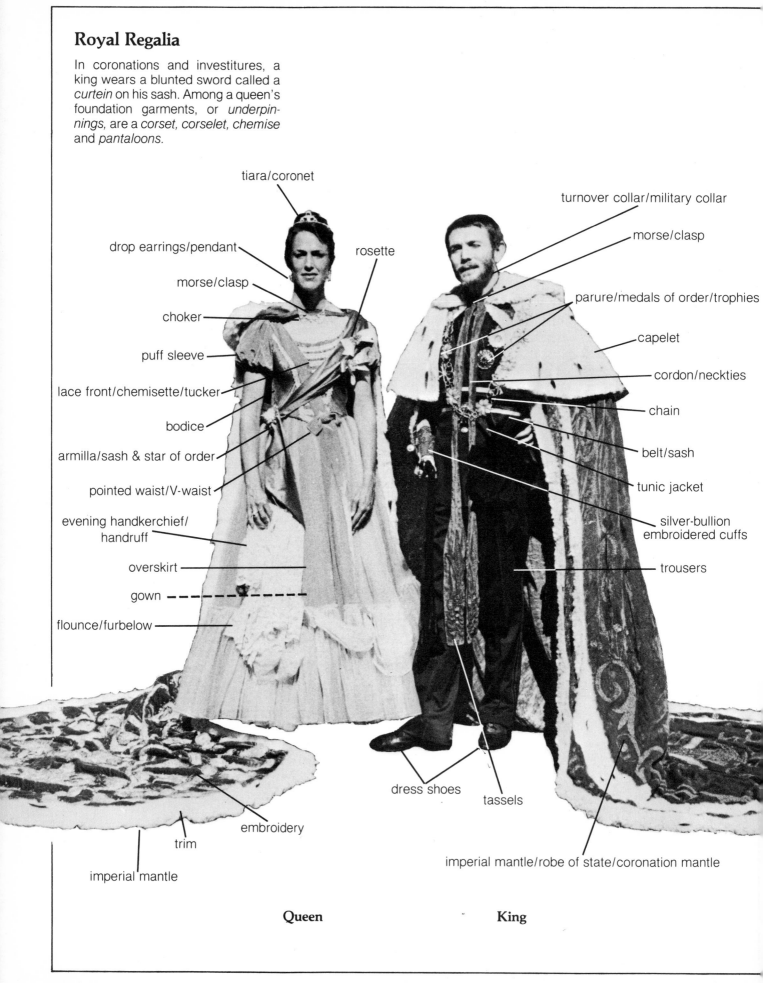

tiara/coronet

turnover collar/military collar

drop earrings/pendant

rosette

morse/clasp

morse/clasp

parure/medals of order/trophies

choker

capelet

puff sleeve

cordon/neckties

lace front/chemisette/tucker

chain

bodice

belt/sash

armilla/sash & star of order

tunic jacket

pointed waist/V-waist

silver-bullion embroidered cuffs

evening handkerchief/ handruff

trousers

overskirt

gown

flounce/furbelow

dress shoes

tassels

embroidery

trim

imperial mantle/robe of state/coronation mantle

imperial mantle

Queen

King

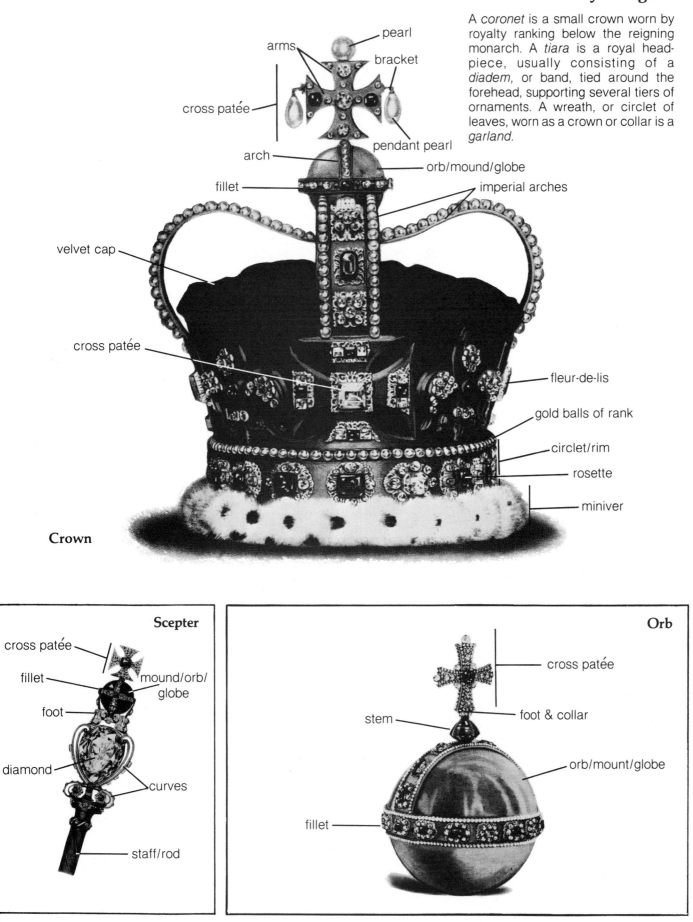

Royal Regalia

A *coronet* is a small crown worn by royalty ranking below the reigning monarch. A *tiara* is a royal headpiece, usually consisting of a *diadem,* or band, tied around the forehead, supporting several tiers of ornaments. A wreath, or circlet of leaves, worn as a crown or collar is a *garland.*

Crown

- pearl
- arms
- bracket
- cross patée
- arch
- pendant pearl
- fillet
- orb/mound/globe
- imperial arches
- velvet cap
- cross patée
- fleur-de-lis
- gold balls of rank
- circlet/rim
- rosette
- miniver

Scepter

- cross patée
- fillet
- mound/orb/globe
- foot
- diamond
- curves
- staff/rod

Orb

- cross patée
- stem
- foot & collar
- orb/mount/globe
- fillet

Royal Vestments

Jewish Ritual Items

During regular service in a *Temple,* or *Synagogue,* excerpts are read by the *Rabbi,* who is assisted in leading the service by a *Cantor,* who sings the liturgy. Their vestments are the same as the rest of the congregation. During morning prayer, a *shel rosh,* similar to the tefillin, is worn on the forehead. Some Jews hang a *mezuzah,* a decorative box containing passages from the Torah, on the doorpost of their homes.

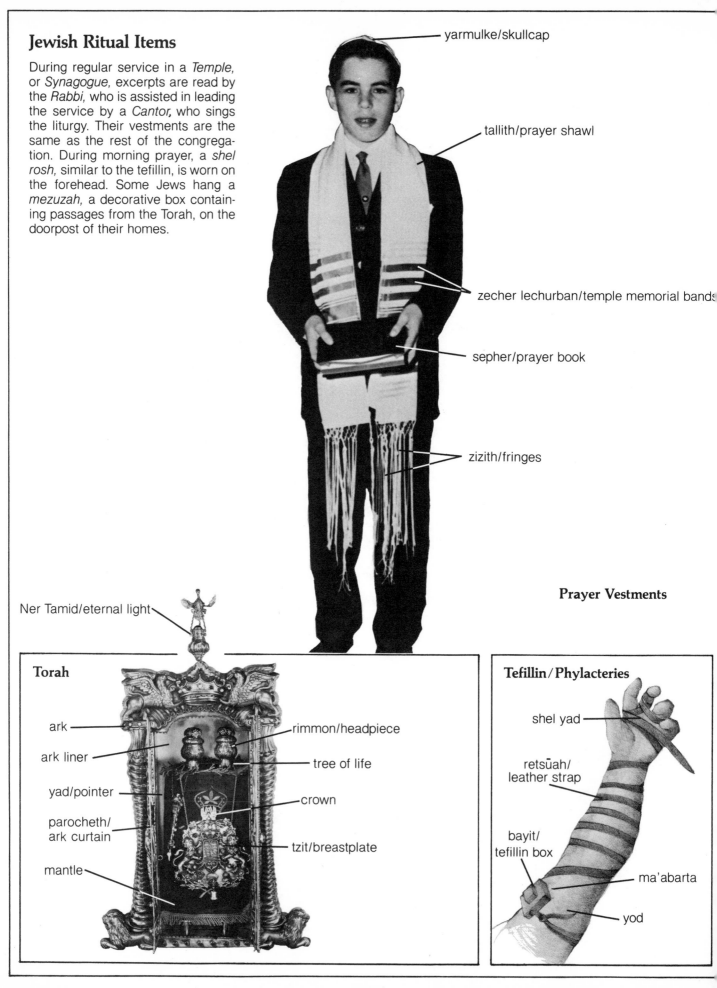

yarmulke/skullcap

tallith/prayer shawl

zecher lechurban/temple memorial bands

sepher/prayer book

zizith/fringes

Prayer Vestments

Ner Tamid/eternal light

Torah

ark

ark liner

yad/pointer

parocheth/ark curtain

mantle

rimmon/headpiece

tree of life

crown

tzit/breastplate

Tefillin/Phylacteries

shel yad

retsūah/leather strap

bayit/tefillin box

ma'abarta

yod

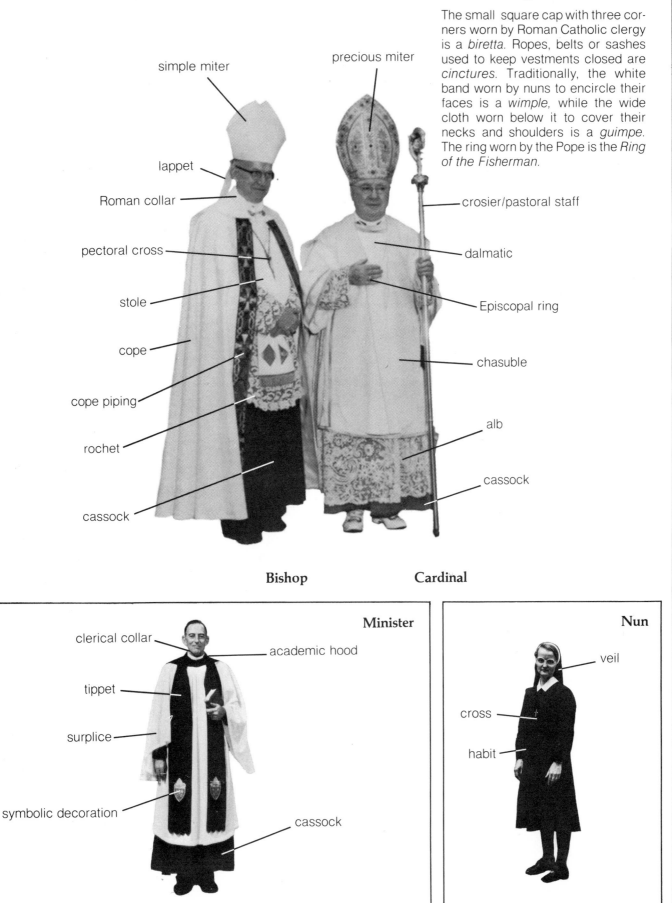

Religious Vestments

The small square cap with three corners worn by Roman Catholic clergy is a *biretta*. Ropes, belts or sashes used to keep vestments closed are *cinctures*. Traditionally, the white band worn by nuns to encircle their faces is a *wimple,* while the wide cloth worn below it to cover their necks and shoulders is a *guimpe.* The ring worn by the Pope is the *Ring of the Fisherman.*

simple miter

precious miter

lappet

Roman collar

pectoral cross

stole

cope

cope piping

rochet

cassock

crosier/pastoral staff

dalmatic

Episcopal ring

chasuble

alb

cassock

Bishop

Cardinal

Minister

clerical collar

academic hood

tippet

surplice

symbolic decoration

cassock

Nun

veil

cross

habit

Religious Attire

Bride and Groom

The bride, wearing white to symbolize purity, and a veil, symbol of modesty, is carrying a fan rather than the more traditional *wedding,* or *bridal, bouquet,* or *nosegay.* Some grooms wear semiformal evening dress at weddings: *tuxedos,* or *tuxes,* which are worn with *cummerbunds,* broad *waistbands, pleated* or *ruffled shirts* with *studs,* and *bow ties.*

picture hat/Gainsborough

veil

appliquéd lace/point d'appliqué

attached bertha/cascade collar/jabot

fan

princess waistline

modified leg-of-mutton sleeve/
modified bishop sleeve

fitted cuff

lace glove

train

scalloped hem

pumps

standing collar

white tie

boutonniere

formal shirt

cutaway coat/
morning coat

waistcoat/vest

French cuff

trousers

tail

Bridal Dress/Gown

Men's Formal Attire

Maid and Butler

Attire worn by male servants is called *livery.* Maids often wear a *bib,* an inverted triangular piece of white linen attached at the neck and descending to just above the waist, as well as a knee-length or ankle-length *apron.*

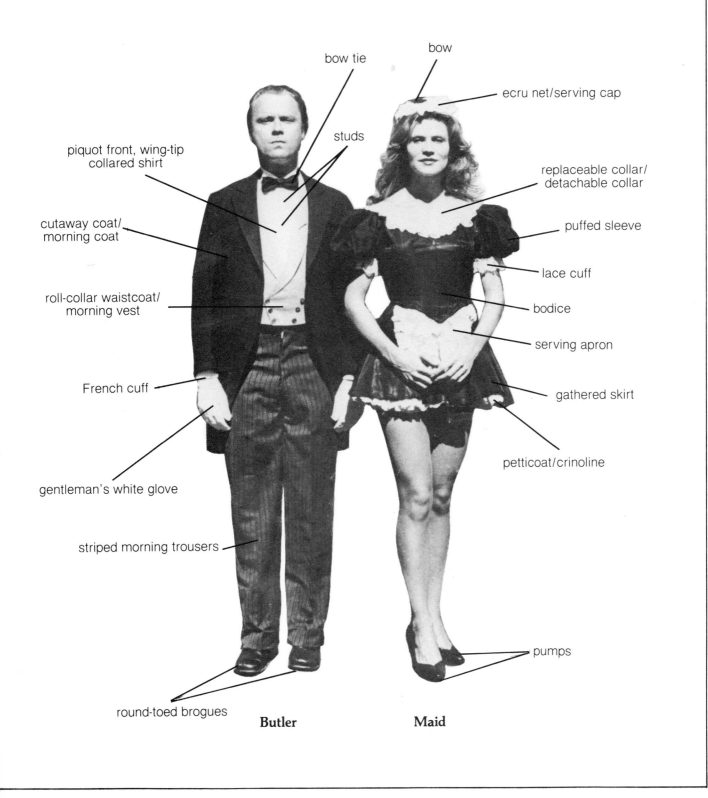

bow tie

bow

ecru net/serving cap

studs

piquot front, wing-tip collared shirt

replaceable collar/ detachable collar

puffed sleeve

cutaway coat/ morning coat

lace cuff

roll-collar waistcoat/ morning vest

bodice

serving apron

French cuff

gathered skirt

gentleman's white glove

petticoat/crinoline

striped morning trousers

pumps

round-toed brogues

Butler

Maid

Servants' Attire

Cowboy and Indian

On the range, cowboys, *cow punchers,* or *buckaroos,* carried *oilskin slickers,* a *tarp,* and heavy cotton or wool quilts to make up a *bedroll, crumb incubator, shakedown,* or *fleatrap.* Bullets, carried in *loops* on *cartridge belts,* were known as *blue whistlers* or *lead plums.* A cowboy's *ten-gallon hat* was held in place in a wind by buckskin thongs known as *bonnet strings.*

Members of most Indian tribes wore *leggings* and *moccasins.* Many decorated their faces with *war paint* prior to battle. Indians in the East shaved their heads except for a ridge of hair in the middle called a *roach.*

felt hat/stetson/John B.

neckerchief/wipe/bandanna

vest

western yoke shirt

belt

belt buckle

gun belt/holster/cartridge belt

bull denim trousers

utility pocket

gun/six-shooter/equalizer/
artillery/cutter/smoke-wagon/
hardware/lead-pusher/blue-lightnin'

chaps/shotgun chaps

fringe

holster/"hawg leg"

holster thong

cowboy boot

Cowboy

Indian

war bonnet

beaded browband

shirt strip

choker necklace

beaded shirt bib

fringe

ermine pendant

Native Dress

Romans wore full-length, loose-fitting robes called *togas*. East Indian women wear *sarongs*, but Indian (Hindu) women wear *saris*. An ankle-length Middle East garment with long sleeves and a waist sash is called a *caftan*. The loose-fitting, sleeveless robes worn by Arabs are called *abas*.

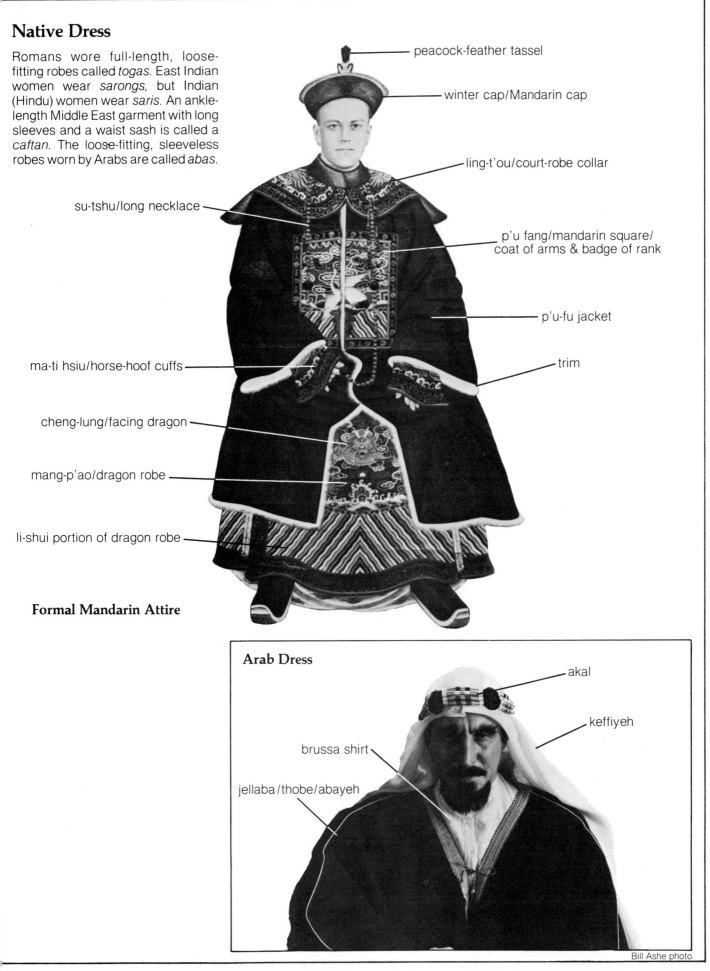

peacock-feather tassel

winter cap/Mandarin cap

ling-t'ou/court-robe collar

su-tshu/long necklace

p'u fang/mandarin square/ coat of arms & badge of rank

p'u-fu jacket

ma-ti hsiu/horse-hoof cuffs

trim

cheng-lung/facing dragon

mang-p'ao/dragon robe

li-shui portion of dragon robe

Formal Mandarin Attire

Arab Dress

akal

keffiyeh

brussa shirt

jellaba/thobe/abayeh

Historical Costumes

Many characters in popular lore and history have become identified or associated with the clothing they wear. Other military attire worn by *Revolutionary* officers included a tunic, a plain jacket with a stiff collar, and a particularly heavy overcoat called a *greatcoat*.

cockade
cocked hat
epaulette
infantry button
lapel
frock coat
button-down cuff
sword
scabbard
coat skirt

wig
crossbelt
embroidered buttonholes
waistcoat
gloves
knee britches
boot

Jim Leighton

Revolutionary War General

eyepatch
tricorne
crossbelt
scarf
petronel/revolver

Pirate

photo by BODI

top hat
Franklin glasses
muffler
fingerless glove
purse

Miser

Jim Vaum

steeple-crowned hat
magic wand
robe

Wizard

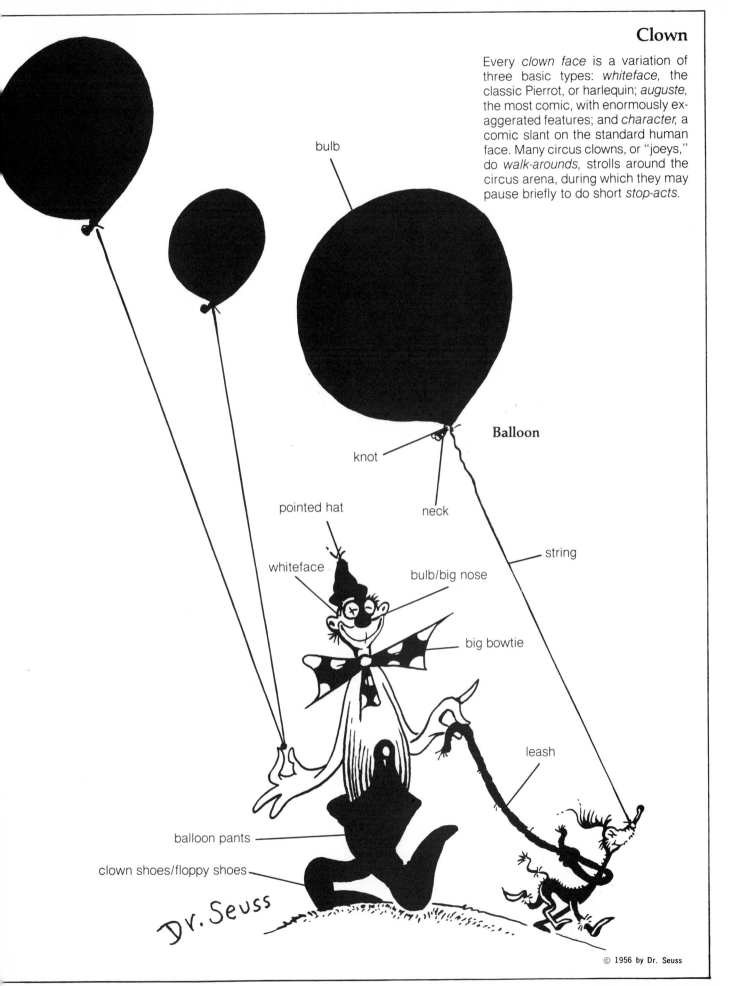

Clown

Every *clown face* is a variation of three basic types: *whiteface,* the classic Pierrot, or harlequin; *auguste,* the most comic, with enormously exaggerated features; and *character,* a comic slant on the standard human face. Many circus clowns, or "joeys," do *walk-arounds,* strolls around the circus arena, during which they may pause briefly to do short *stop-acts.*

bulb

Balloon

knot

neck

pointed hat

whiteface

bulb/big nose

string

big bowtie

leash

balloon pants

clown shoes/floppy shoes

Dr. Seuss

Performers' Costumes

Ballet Dancer

The toeshoes worn by this *ballerina* have thick, leather-covered wooden box toes. A short skirt of layered net often worn by female dancers is called a *tutu*.

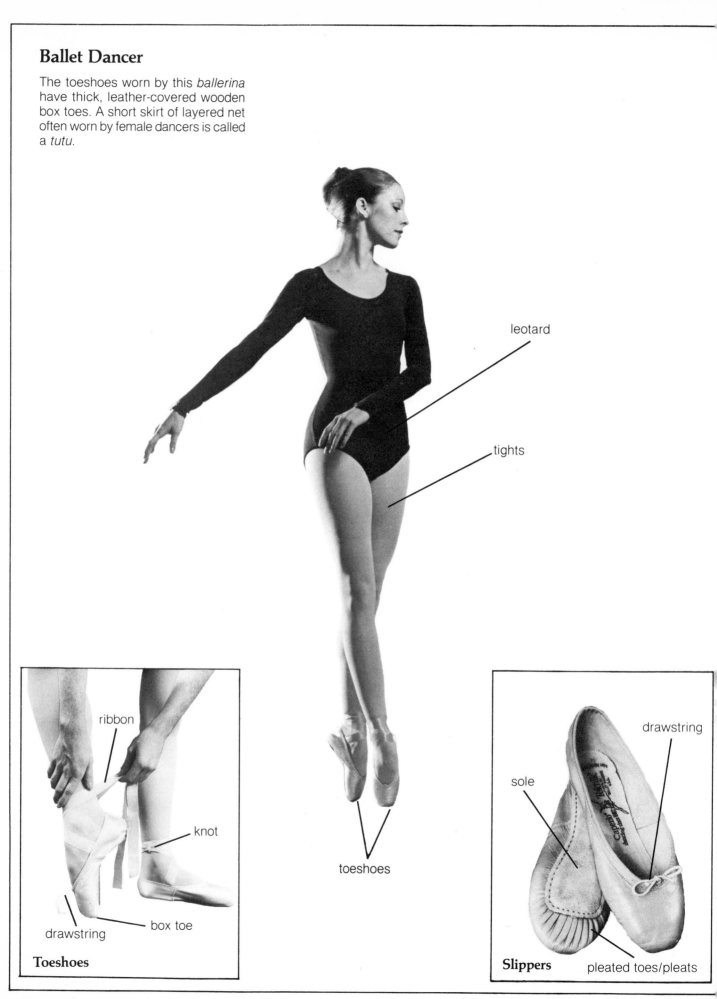

leotard

tights

ribbon

knot

box toe

drawstring

Toeshoes

toeshoes

sole

drawstring

pleated toes/pleats

Slippers

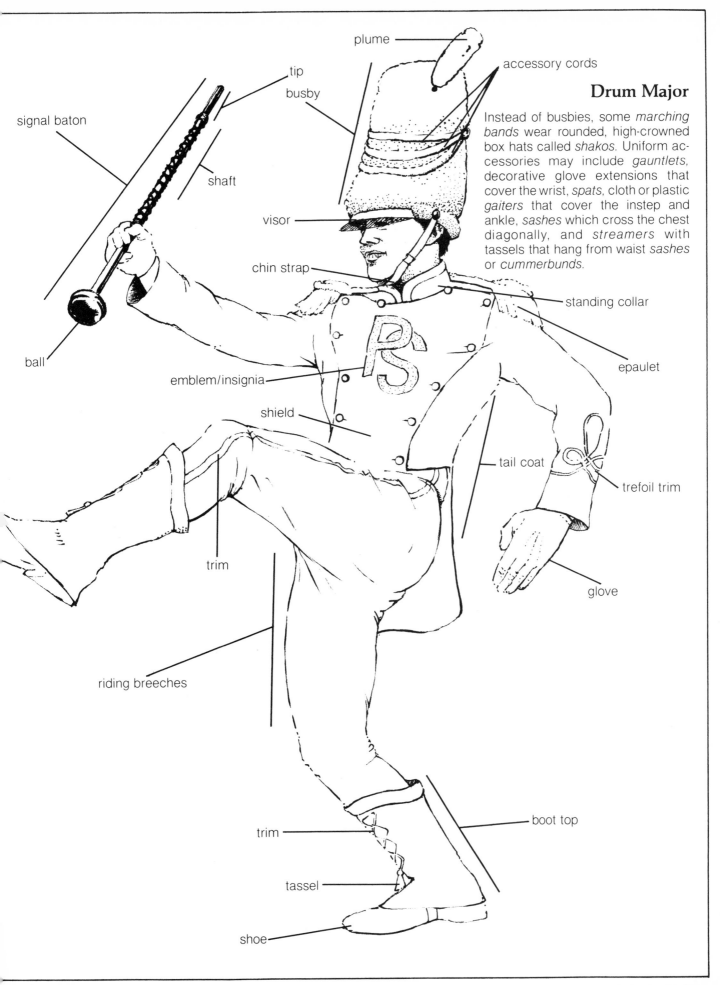

plume

accessory cords

tip

busby

signal baton

shaft

visor

chin strap

ball

emblem/insignia

shield

trim

riding breeches

Drum Major

Instead of busbies, some *marching bands* wear rounded, high-crowned box hats called *shakos*. Uniform accessories may include *gauntlets*, decorative glove extensions that cover the wrist, *spats*, cloth or plastic *gaiters* that cover the instep and ankle, *sashes* which cross the chest diagonally, and *streamers* with tassels that hang from waist *sashes* or *cummerbunds*.

standing collar

epaulet

tail coat

trefoil trim

glove

boot top

trim

tassel

shoe

Performers' Costumes

Military Uniforms

The *uniform of the day* is worn for the season, day or occasion. A cloth band worn around the arm above the elbow, such as the one worn by *Military Police*, or *MPs*, is a *brassard*. A leather belt for a dress uniform is a *Sam Browne, or garrison, belt*. Service ribbons are worn on a *ribbon bar*. The only *neck decoration* awarded to members of the armed services is the *Medal of Honor*.

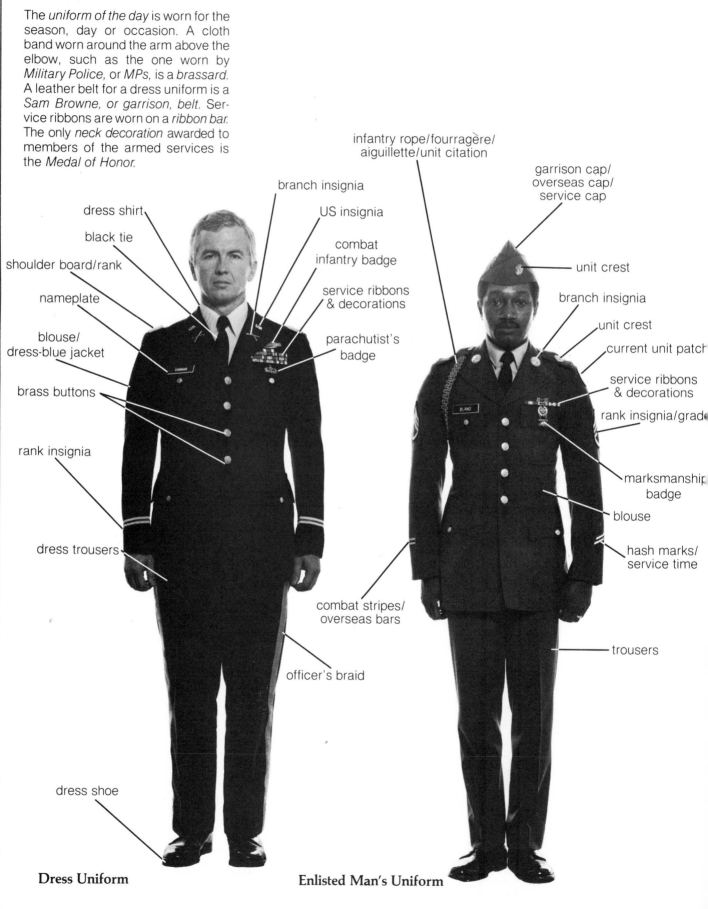

infantry rope/fourragère/ aiguillette/unit citation

branch insignia

US insignia

combat infantry badge

service ribbons & decorations

parachutist's badge

garrison cap/ overseas cap/ service cap

unit crest

branch insignia

unit crest

current unit patch

service ribbons & decorations

rank insignia/grade

marksmanship badge

blouse

hash marks/ service time

trousers

dress shirt

black tie

shoulder board/rank

nameplate

blouse/ dress-blue jacket

brass buttons

rank insignia

dress trousers

dress shoe

combat stripes/ overseas bars

officer's braid

Dress Uniform

Enlisted Man's Uniform

Military Uniforms

An *infantryman,* or "grunt," carries a *rain poncho* on his ammunition belt. A sailor, "swab," or "gob," may wear a *watch cap, leggings* and a *jersey* instead of a jumper. Sailors aboard ship keep their clothing in *seabags.*

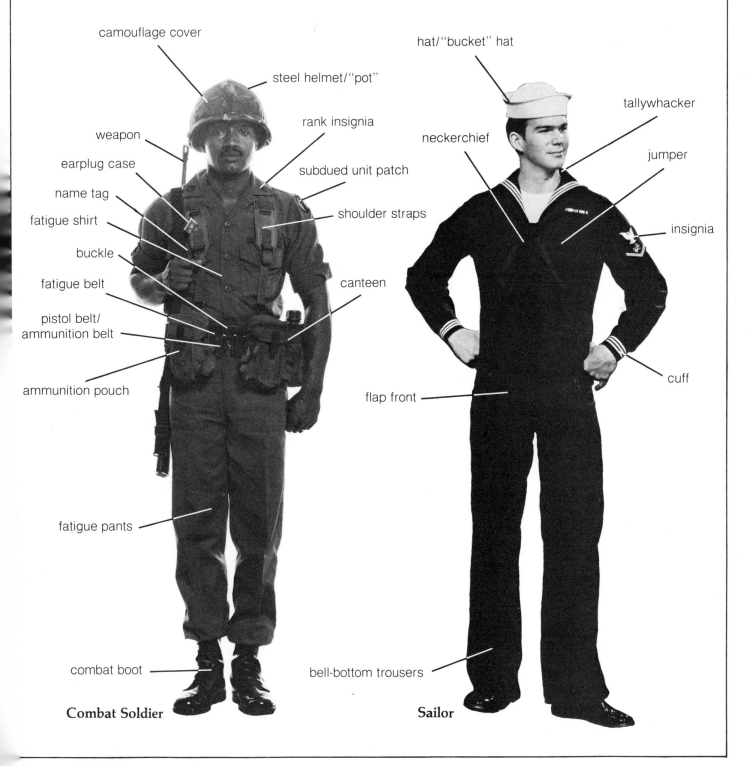

camouflage cover

steel helmet/"pot"

weapon

rank insignia

earplug case

subdued unit patch

name tag

shoulder straps

fatigue shirt

buckle

fatigue belt

canteen

pistol belt/
ammunition belt

ammunition pouch

fatigue pants

combat boot

hat/"bucket" hat

tallywhacker

neckerchief

jumper

insignia

cuff

flap front

bell-bottom trousers

Combat Soldier

Sailor

Military Attire

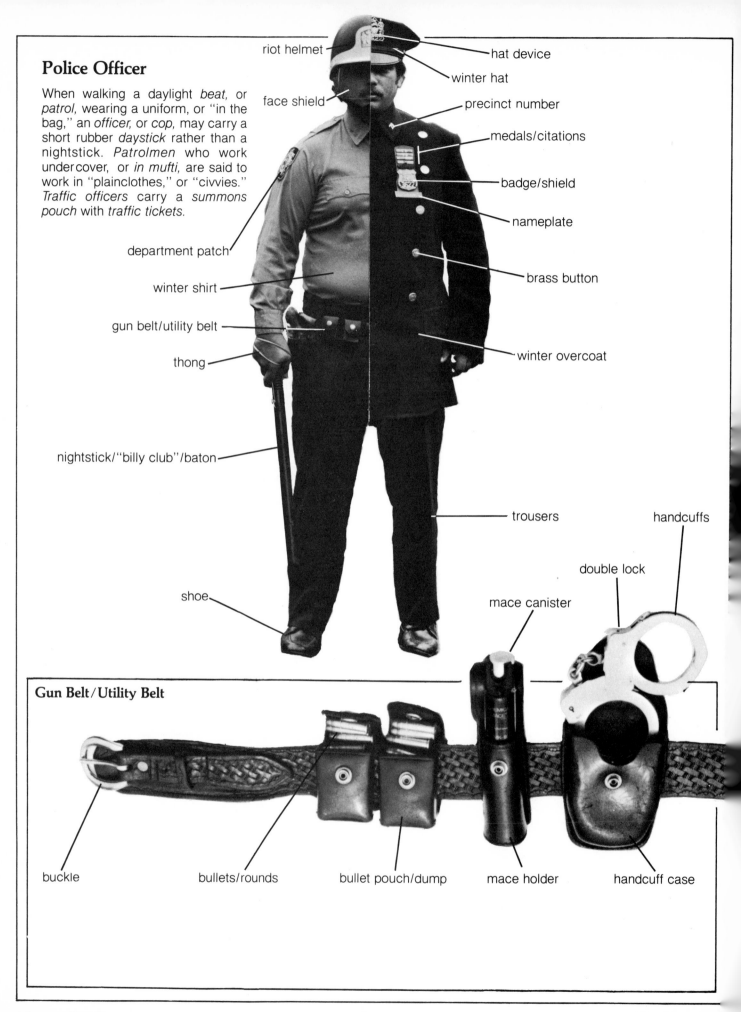

Police Officer

When walking a daylight *beat,* or *patrol,* wearing a uniform, or "in the bag," an *officer,* or *cop,* may carry a short rubber *daystick* rather than a nightstick. *Patrolmen* who work undercover, or *in mufti,* are said to work in "plainclothes," or "civvies." *Traffic officers* carry a *summons pouch* with *traffic tickets.*

riot helmet

face shield

hat device

winter hat

precinct number

medals/citations

badge/shield

nameplate

brass button

department patch

winter shirt

gun belt/utility belt

thong

winter overcoat

nightstick/"billy club"/baton

trousers

handcuffs

double lock

mace canister

shoe

Gun Belt/Utility Belt

buckle

bullets/rounds

bullet pouch/dump

mace holder

handcuff case

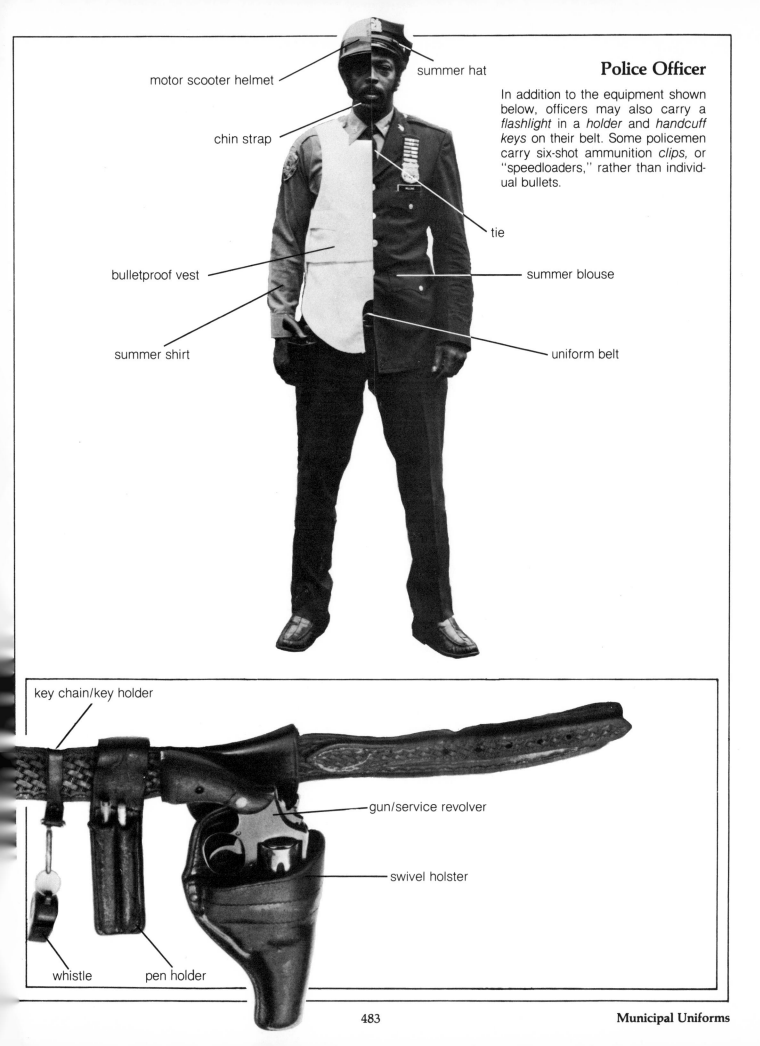

motor scooter helmet

summer hat

chin strap

Police Officer

In addition to the equipment shown below, officers may also carry a *flashlight* in a *holder* and *handcuff keys* on their belt. Some policemen carry six-shot ammunition *clips,* or "speedloaders," rather than individual bullets.

tie

bulletproof vest

summer blouse

summer shirt

uniform belt

key chain/key holder

gun/service revolver

swivel holster

whistle

pen holder

Municipal Uniforms

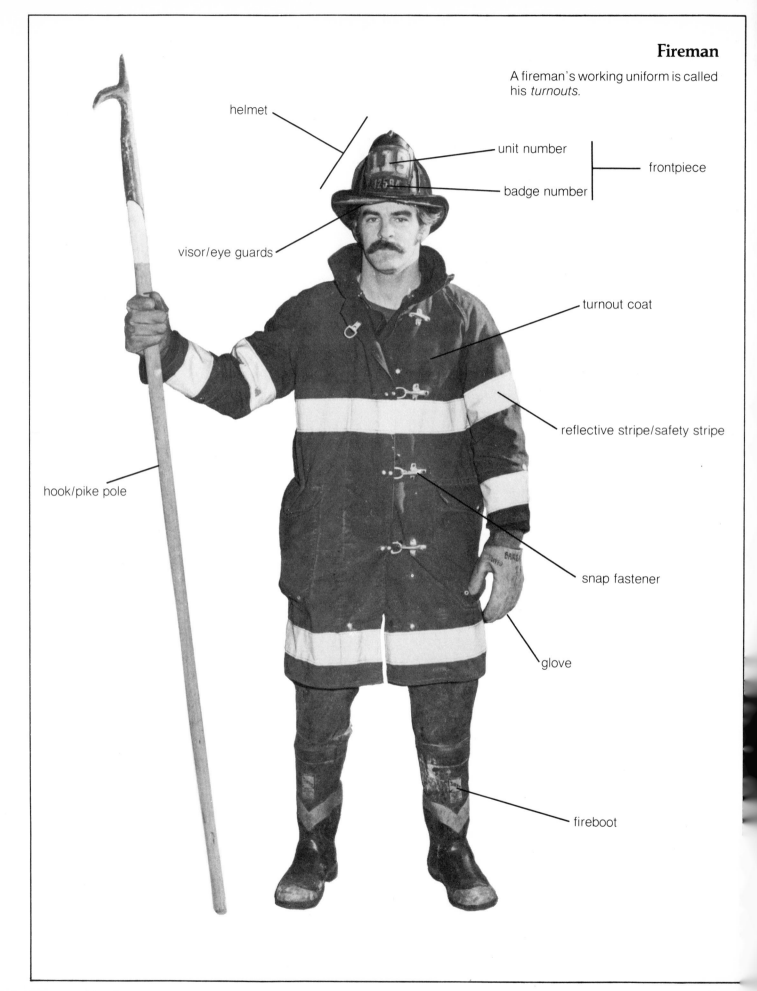

Fireman

A fireman's working uniform is called his *turnouts*.

helmet

unit number

badge number

frontpiece

visor/eye guards

turnout coat

reflective stripe/safety stripe

hook/pike pole

snap fastener

glove

fireboot

Signs and Symbols

While signs and symbols take the place of language or are used to represent meaning, either by suggestion, relationship or association, many have parts for which there are proper names. A flag is used as a sign of a nation, for example, or as a symbol of patriotism, yet it has distinctive components which are identifiable.

Other signs, such as editing and proofreading marks, also included in this section, are used to convey instructions, while sign language is a set of gestures used as a substitute for words or letters.

The fields of science, business and industry have all devised signs whose meanings have legal as well as instructional implications, and the world of transportation is largely controlled by traffic signs. Even hobos, whose pictographs appear here, use pictorial signs instead of written language to communicate messages.

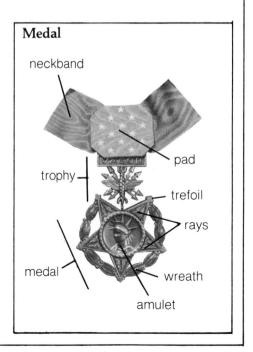

Medal

neckband

pad

trophy

trefoil

rays

medal

wreath

amulet

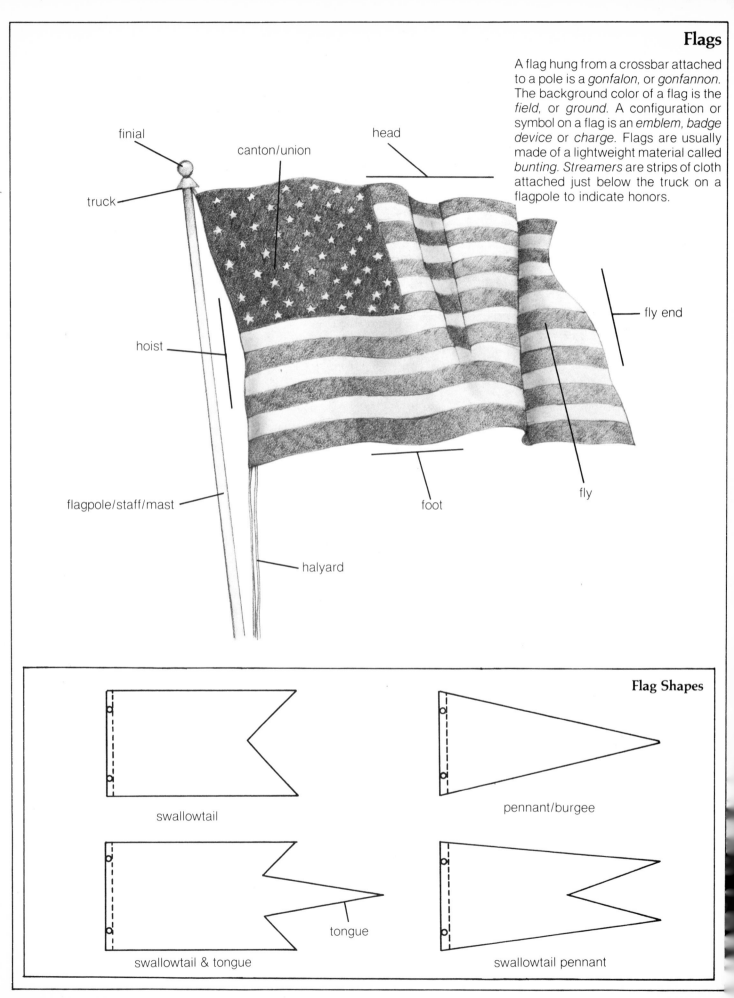

Flags

A flag hung from a crossbar attached to a pole is a *gonfalon,* or *gonfannon.* The background color of a flag is the *field,* or *ground.* A configuration or symbol on a flag is an *emblem, badge device* or *charge.* Flags are usually made of a lightweight material called *bunting. Streamers* are strips of cloth attached just below the truck on a flagpole to indicate honors.

finial

canton/union

head

truck

hoist

flagpole/staff/mast

halyard

fly end

fly

foot

Flag Shapes

swallowtail

pennant/burgee

swallowtail & tongue

tongue

swallowtail pennant

Coat of Arms

Technically, a coat of arms, or *achievement of arms,* consists only of a shield, the surface of which is called the *field.* Everything surrounding a shield is *exterior decoration.* The entire grouping is known as *armorial achievement.* To the wearer's left but the viewer's right is the *sinister side.* The opposite side is the *dexter side.*

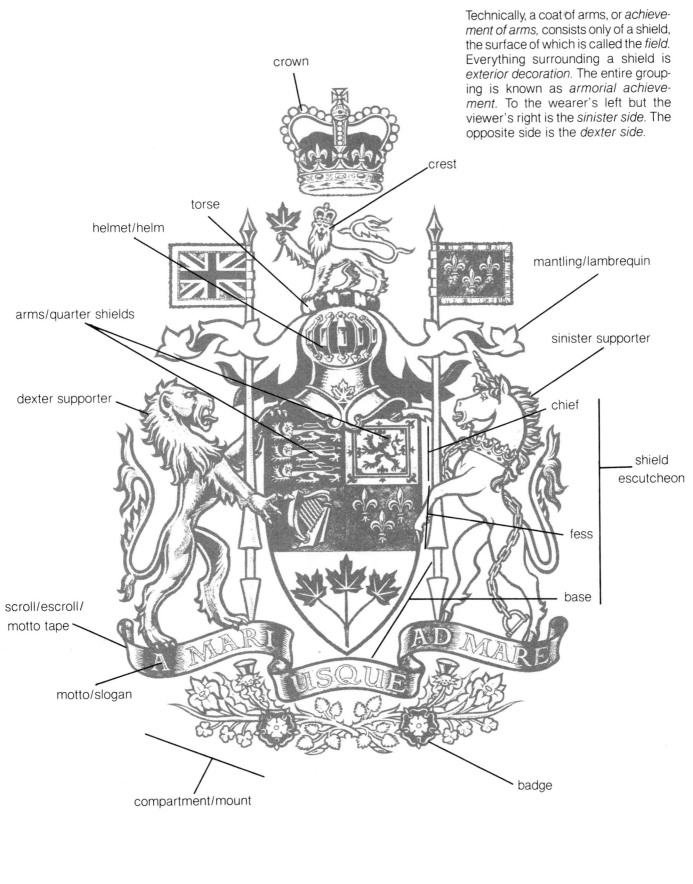

crown

crest

torse

helmet/helm

mantling/lambrequin

arms/quarter shields

sinister supporter

dexter supporter

chief

shield
escutcheon

fess

base

scroll/escroll/
motto tape

motto/slogan

badge

compartment/mount

A MARI AD MARE USQUE

Signs and Symbols

stop	yield	one way	one-way traffic/ do not enter	railroad crossing

no bicycles	no trucks	no U turn	no right turn	no left turn

interstate route	U.S. route	state route	trail	bike route

picnic area	camping	camping	hospital	telephone

Road Signs

With the exception of *route signs,* which are different shapes and colors, road signs are color-coded: red signs are *prohibit movement signs;* yellow are *warning signs;* white are *regulatory signs;* orange are *construction signs;* blue are *service signs;* green are *guide signs.* Octagonal red signs are used exclusively for *stop signs.* Rectangular signs with white letters on a green background are *destination signs.*

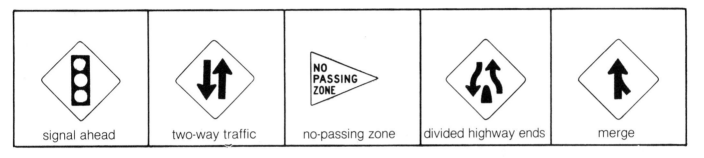

signal ahead	two-way traffic	no-passing zone	divided highway ends	merge

merge left	winding road	slippery when wet	hill	school crossing

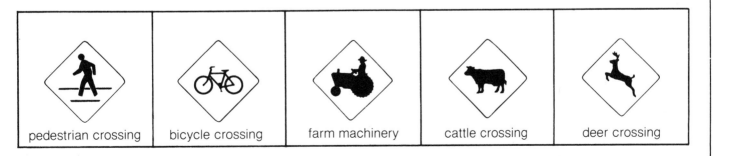

pedestrian crossing	bicycle crossing	farm machinery	cattle crossing	deer crossing

Signs and Symbols

Public Signs

Pasigraphy is a universal written language that uses signs and symbols rather than words, whereas *pictographs* can represent an object as well as a thought. A symbol or character that represents a word, syllable or phoneme is a *phonogram*. A symbolic representation of an idea rather than a word is an *ideogram* or *ideograph*.

gift shop	hotel information	restaurant	mail	first aid
baggage lockers	men's toilets	women's toilets	nursery	information
taxi stand	bus transportation	air transportation	car rental	rail transportation
coffee shop	bar	no smoking	no parking	parking

baggage check-in   baggage claim   customs   lost and found   currency exchange

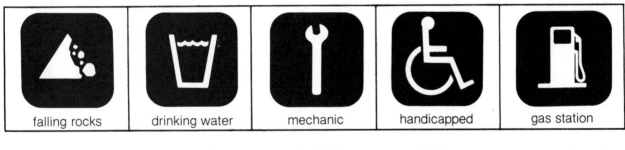

falling rocks   drinking water   mechanic   handicapped   gas station

viewing area   campfires   picnic area   launching ramp   horse trail

bicycle trail   hiking trail   playground   no entry   elevator

Signs and Symbols

Religious Symbols

The symbols shown here represent beliefs and religions such as Christianity, Judaism, Islam, Shinto, as well as Chinese philosophy. The ankh was an ancient Egyptian *symbol of life,* and the gammadion was an eon-old Oriental and Indian *good luck symbol.*

Latin cross

St. Anthony's cross/ tau cross

Celtic cross

Patriarchal cross

Papal cross

Russian cross

Jerusalem cross

Maltese cross

botonée

moline

Greek cross

torii

crescent and star

Star of David/Magen David/ Shield of David

menorah

ankh

Yin-Yang/female-male

gammadion/swastika

Signs of the Zodiac

The *zodiac* is an imaginary belt in the heavens divided into twelve parts named for constellations, called *houses*. A *horoscope*, drawn by an *astrologer*, foretells the influence of these heavenly bodies on human affairs.

Spring Signs

Aries

The Ram

Taurus

The Bull

Gemini

The Twins

Summer Signs

Cancer

The Crab

Leo

The Lion

Virgo

The Virgin

Autumn Signs

Libra

The Balance

Scorpio

The Scorpion

Sagittarius

The Archer

Winter Signs

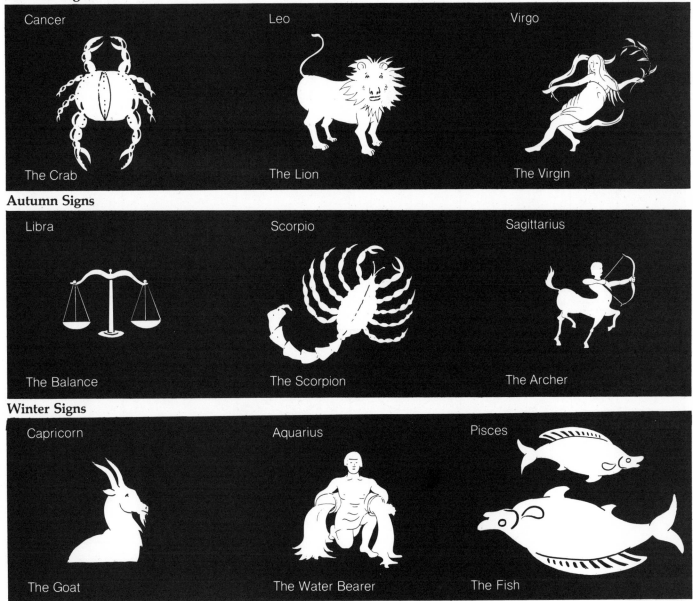

Capricorn

The Goat

Aquarius

The Water Bearer

Pisces

The Fish

Signs and Symbols

Symbols of Science, Business and Commerce

The symbols shown here are used in the medical and pharmaceutical fields, in chemistry, engineering and electronics, in mathematics and business, and by currency-exchange centers and banks. Also included are miscellaneous symbols used in other walks of life.

caduceus	**R** prescription	birth	death	male	female
Dx diagnosis	**Hx** history	**m** heart murmur	**Px** past history	**Rh +** blood factor positive	**Rh −** blood factor negative
scruple	dram	+ positive charge	— negative charge	center line	~ cycle
A ammeter	OHM ohmmeter	V voltmeter	W wattmeter	one-cell battery	ground
antenna	oscillator	+ add/plus	— subtract/minus	± add or subtract/ plus or minus	× multiply/times/by

÷	∶	=	≠	≈	>
divided by	equal/ratio	equals/is equal to	is not equal to	approximately equal to	greater than

<	≦	≧	✓	∞	∴
less than	equal or less	equal or greater	square root	infinity	therefore/hence

∵	m̲	π	°	′	″
since/because	measured by	pi/3.1416	degrees of arc	minutes of arc	seconds of arc

@	#	%	o\oo	$	¢
at/per/priced at	number	percent/per hundred	per thousand/ per mill	dollar	cents

£	F	DM	L	R	₨
pound	franc	deutsche mark	lira	ruble	rupee

Y	(skull and crossbones)	©	®	(Plimsoll mark)	(peace symbol)
yen	poison	copyright	registered	Plimsoll mark and load line	peace

Symbolic Language

Sign language, used by deaf-mutes, substitutes *gestures* for spoken words. Embossed *dots* are used by blind people to read by touch. *Semaphore* and *wigwag* are systems of signalling by hand-held flags.

Sign Language

Braille

a	b	c	d	e	f	g	h	i	j	k	l	m

n	o	p	q	r	s	t	u	v	w	x	y	z

In addition to these *punctuation*, *diacritic* and *pronunciation* symbols, there are *phonetic symbols*, *abbreviations* and *contractions*.

'a' single quotation marks	**"a"** quotation marks	**′** foot/minute/prime	**″** inch/second/ double prime	**a'** apostrophe
(a) parentheses	**[a]** brackets/crotchets	**a-a** hyphen	**a—a** dash	
a/a virgule/ slant/slash	**,** comma	**;** semicolon	**:** colon	**&** ampersand
* asterisk	**•** period/full point	**• • •** ellipsis/marks of omission	**!** exclamation point/ bang/ecphoneme	**?** question mark/ eroteme
a̲ underline/ underscore	**ﬀ** ligature	**é** acute accent	**à** grave accent	**â** circumflex accent/ doghouse
ñ tilde	**ç** cedilla	**ā** macron	**ă** breve	**äi** dieresis/umlaut

Proofreader's Marks

The marks illustrated below are used for the purpose of standardizing the transmittal of corrections and queries between *editors* and/or *proofreaders* and *typesetters* and/or *printers.* When the corrected *copy* is set in *type* it is *proved,* or *proofed,* and additional marks are then made on the *galley proofs.* The first *impressions* of the corrected galleys are called *page proofs.*

Mark

Enter HAMLET.

Ham. To be, or not to be: that is the question:

Whether 't is nobler in the mind to suffer

The slings and arrows of outrageous fortune

Or to take arms against a sea of troubles,

And end by opposing them? To die: to sleep:

No More; and by a sleep to say we end

The heart-ache and the 1000 natural shocks

That flesh is heir to 't is a consummation

Devoutly to be wish'd. To die, to sleep;

To sleep: perchance to dream: ay, there's

□ □ □ ⟵ the rub;

For in that sleep of death what dreams may come

When we have shuffled off this mortal coil,

Must give us pause. There's the res pect

That makes calamity of so long life;

For who would bear the whips and scorns of time,

The oppressor's wrong, the proud mans contumely,

The pangs of disprized love, the law's delay,

The ins olence of office, and the spurns

That patient merit of the unworthy takes,

When he himself might his quietus make

With a bare bodkin who would fardels bear,

to grunt and sweat under a weary life,

But that the dread of something death,

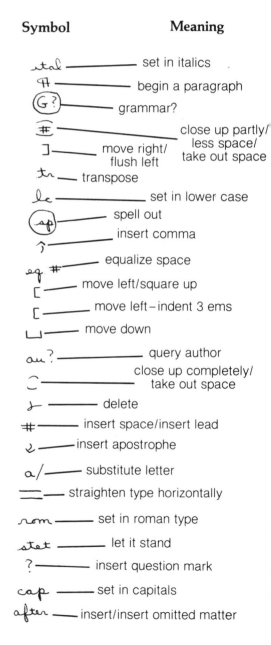

Symbol	Meaning
ital	set in italics
¶	begin a paragraph
G?	grammar?
#	close up partly/less space/take out space
]	move right/flush left
tr	transpose
lc	set in lower case
sp	spell out
⌃	insert comma
eq #	equalize space
[	move left/square up
[	move left—indent 3 ems
⊔	move down
au?	query author
⌒	close up completely/take out space
⟋	delete
#	insert space/insert lead
⌄	insert apostrophe
a/	substitute letter
＝	straighten type horizontally
rom	set in roman type
stet	let it stand
?	insert question mark
cap	set in capitals
after	insert/insert omitted matter

Hobo Signs

Symbols, inscriptions, phrases and signatures drawn in public places are collectively called graffiti. Those shown here are used among tramps and vagrants.

kindhearted lady	dishonest man	town asleep, cops inactive	town awake, cops active
housewife feeds for chores	tell pitiful story	town allows alcohol	town dislikes alcohol
dog	doctor	judge	chain gang
danger	man with gun	don't give up	be quiet
go	unsafe place	good for handout	officer

Signs and Symbols

Tombstone and Coffin

A stone placed at the foot of a grave is a *footstone.* *Crypts,* or *vaults,* are wholly or partly underground *burial chambers. Mausoleums* are large aboveground *tombs.*

ornament/carving

floral carving

inscription

year of birth

epitaph

base

tombstone/memorial/ monument/tablet/ gravestone/headstone

year of death

J.SMITH

1803 – 1875

I TOLD THE DOCTOR I WAS SICK

wreath

easel

grave/plot

MORT WALKER

Coffin / Casket

bridge

interior panel

overlay

lid panel   fishtail

pillow

drop

bed/ mattress

arm

handle

lug

end handle

Index

A

A: braille, 496; piano keyboard octave, 355; sheet music notation, 347; sign language, 496
aba, Arab robe, 475
abacus, 431; column, 71
ABA number, check, 222
abayeh, Arab dress, 475
abbreviation: grammatical symbol, 497; magazine mailing label, 167
abdomen: grasshopper, 39; horse, 36; human, 24; lobster, 45; spider, 38
abdominal board, universal gym, 338
ablation zone, glacier, 12
ABM, 466
abort, pilot's instrument panel, 153
abrasive material, sander, 411
abstraction, work of art, 362
abutment, arch, 70
abutment tooth, partial denture, 443
abyssal plain, continental margin, 15
academic hood, minister, 471
acceleration contest, drag racing, 333
accelerator pedal, car, 106
accelerometer, pilot's instrument panel, 153
accent, grammatical symbol, 497
access arm, launch pad, 154
access door, turbine locomotive coupler, 113
accessories: musical, 361; patio, 284; photographic, 174
accessories shelf, telescope, 433
accessory cords, drum major's busby, 479
accessory panel, stove, 244
accessory rail, surgical table, 440
accessory socket, movie camera, 172
access plate, water heater, 391
access road, highway cloverleaf, 110
accidental, music notation, 346
accommodation, sailboat, 131
accommodation ladder, destroyer, 140
accordion, 360
accordion gusset, shoulder bag, 218
accordion windows, wallet, 219
account number: check, 222; credit card, 222
accumulation zone, glacier, 12
accumulator, dispenser, 263

ace, playing card, 342
A cell block, prison, 74
achene, strawberry, 53
achievement of arms, 487
Achilles heel, 25
Achilles tendon, 29; pad, running shoe, 296
acid-free backing, frame, 373
acorn, seed, 49
acorn nut, 401
acoustic guitar, 350
AC power cord, tape recorder, 175
acroterion, masonry gate post, 65
acrylic, painting medium, 364
acrylic resin, dental, 443, 445
act, circus, 88
act curtain, stage, 344, 345
act drop, stage, 344
action bolt, roller skate, 318
action nut, roller skate, 318
action strap, still camera, 171
activating lever, pencil sharpener, 273
activator button, dental x-ray, 444
active pointer, aneroid barometer, 18
active repeater satellite, 182
acute accent, grammatical symbol, 497
ACV, 145
Adam's apple, human, 25
adapter plate, tractor, 424
add, symbol, 494
adding machine, 431
addition, with abacus, 431
add-on segment weight, tractor planetary, 424
add or subtract, symbol, 494
address: check, 222; envelope, 161; letter, 161; magazine mailing label, 167
adductor longus, human, 26
adductor muscle, scallop, 45
adductor policis, human, 26
adhesive: Band-Aid, 441; roofing shingle, 66
adhesive tape, 441
adipose fin, fish, 43
adjustable arm, expansive bit, 409
adjustable barrel, hose nozzle, 418
adjustable bit gauge, drill, 409
adjustable buckle, brassiere, 191
adjustable channel, pliers, 404
adjustable C-clamp, 399
adjustable clip, jackhammer, 426
adjustable foot: potter's wheel, 367; surgical table, 440
adjustable frame, hacksaw, 406

adjustable fulcrum, diving board, 310
adjustable grill, patio accessory, 284
adjustable lamp, 235
adjustable mirror, cosmetic case, 281
adjustable neckband, ascot, 189
adjustable rear wing, racing car, 332
adjustable reference pointer, barometer, 18
adjustable screw, embroidery ring, 377
adjustable shoulder strap, bag, 218
adjustable stand, laboratory, 437
adjustable table extension, saw, 407
adjustable wheel tread, tractor planetary, 424
adjustable wrench, 405
adjuster, power mower wheel, 419
adjusting knob: knee kicker, 242; saw, 407
adjusting lever, plane, 410
adjusting nut, monkey wrench, 405
adjusting screw: expansive bit, 409; hitch and harrow, 424; pliers, 404; theodolite, 426; violin bow, 349
adjust knob, volt-ohm meter, 413
adjustment: microscope focus, 432; reflex camera, 171; speculum, 438
adjustment control, machine gun, 461
adjustment knob: lamp, 235; medical examination table, 440; microscope, 432; nozzle, 418; rifle scope, 459
adjustment lever: child's car seat, 282; stroller, 282
adjustment lines, sewing pattern, 380
adjustment nut, plane, 410
adjustment screw: lithographic press, 370; monkey wrench, 405; plane, 410; ski binding, 320
adjustment screw, volt-ohm meter, 413
administration building, prison, 74
ad service courts, tennis, 306
adult, insect, 39
advance, pocket camera, 170
advance control, cash register, 430
advanced life-support unit, ambulance, 119
adventitious root, 49
advertisement, magazine, 169
advertising panel: bus, 114;

gas pump, 108; subway car, 115
adz, ice axe, 328
adze eye, hammer, 402
aerator, kitchen sink, 243
aerial: CB radio, 179; hovercraft, 145; jumbo jet, 148; tanker, 137
aerialist, circus, 88
aerial platform, tower ladder, 120
aerial tom-tom, 358
aeronautical light, nautical chart, 22
A flat, piano keyboard octave, 355
A-frame, ferris wheel, 91
aft, boat, 128
aft cabin bunk, sailboat, 131
aft controls, tugboat, 144
aft equipment bay, lunar lander, 156
afterbody, torpedo, 466
after bulkhead, powerboat, 135
after-shave lotion, 213
after steering, fireboat, 144
aft monitor, fireboat, 144
aft superstructure, tanker, 137
against shooter, craps table, 341
agate line, newspaper, 166
agent, traveler's check, 223
agitator: spreader, 420; washing machine, 276
agitron, cartoon, 374
aglet: shoelace, 200; stringtie, 188
Agulhas Current, ocean, 6
aid: hearing, 442; public sign, 490; space shuttle navigation, 155
aiguillette, enlisted man's uniform, 480
aileron: glider, 147; jumbo jet, 148; single engine airplane, 147
aileron trim, 747 cockpit, 150
air bags, blimp, 158
air bladder, seaweed, 55
air blower, drag racing dragster, 333
air brake, space shuttle, 154
airbrake hose, locomotive, 112
airbrake paddle, glider, 147
air bubble, monovial, 414
air cleaner: automobile engine, 107; bulldozer, 425; mechanical sweeper, 123; mower, 419; truck, 116
air combat maneuver panel, pilot's instrument panel, 153
air compressor, truck, 116
air conditioner, 392; camper, 126
air conditioner compressor, automobile engine, 107
air conditioning: control,

pilot's instrument panel, 153; intake, bus, 114
air connect lines, truck, 116
air control: dental unit, 444; refrigerator, 245
air-cooled engine, 396
air-cooled machine gun, 461
aircraft: airport, 93; civil, 148-149; combat, 152; instrument panel, 153; 747 cockpit, 150; single engine, 147
aircraft carrier, 142
aircraft tug, 93
air cushion vehicle (ACV), 145
air-data system, space shuttle, 154
air ducts, tunnel, 96
air filter: engine, 396; tractor, 424
airflow control, pilot's instrument panel, 153
airflow nozzle, hair dryer, 208
air foil, drag racing dragster, 333
airframe, jet fighter, 152
air gauge, subway motorman's cab, 115
airglow ultraviolet spectrometer, satellite, 182
air hole: fountain pen, 160; hair roller, 210; harmonica, 360; igloo, 83
air horn, truck, 116
air hose, skin diving, 325
air inlet: aircraft, 147, 149, 397; dishwasher, 246; surgical table, 440
air intake: destroyer, 141; heat exchanger, 393; hovercraft, 145; locomotive, 113; racing car, 332; truck, 116
airline identification location marker, airport, 92
air-motor power pedal, surgical table, 440
air movement, cloud, 16
airplane, see aircraft
airplane-back, cufflink, 214
air plate, standpipe, 57
airport, 92-93
air pump, bicycle, 124
air regulator: dental, 445; laboratory burner, 427
air reservoir, locomotive, 112
air scoop: automobile, 102; blimp, 158
air search radar: aircraft carrier, 142; destroyer, 141
airship, 158
air speed indicator, 747 cockpit, 150, 151
airspeed mach indicator, pilot's instrument panel, 153
airtank: fire engine, 120; skin diving, 325
air temperature, 747 cockpit, 150
air traffic control: operator facility, 93; tower, 92; transporter, 747 cockpit, 151
air transportation, public sign, 490
air valve: blimp, 158; motorcycle, 125; subway motorman's cab, 115
air vent: automobile, 103, 106; Band-Aid, 441; furnace, 390; hair dryer, 208; intercity bus, 114; pressure cooker, 253; radiator, 390
aisle: church, 85; courtroom, 87; House of Representatives, 72; theatre, 345
ait, river, 13
akal, Arab dress, 475

alarm: clock radio, 229; elevator car button, 76; powerboat, 134; prison, 74; vault, 447
alb, cardinal, 471
albedo, orange, 53
album cover, phonograph record, 176
albumen, egg, 258
alcohol, ambulance, 119
Alexander, playing card king, 342
algae, marine, 55
alignment control, radar, 434
alimentary canal, human, 27
Allen wrench, 405
alley: badminton court, 313; bowling, 311; tennis court, 306
alley light, police car, 118
all-fives, darts, 316
alligator, 41
alligator clip: dental towel, 445; and volt-ohm meter, 413
alluvial fan, river, 13
alp, mountain, 8
Alpine skiing, 320
altar, church, 85
altazimuth mounting, telescope, 443
alteration lines, sewing pattern, 380
alternator, automobile engine, 107
altimeter: pilot's instrument panel, 153; 747 cockpit, 150
altitude coarse-motion clamp, telescope, 433
altitude indicator, pilot's instrument panel, 153
altocumulus cloud, 16, 17
aluminum rim, drag racing dragster, 333
amalgam carrier, dental, 445
amateur radio operator, 179
amber starting light, drag racing, 333
ambu, ambulance, 119
ambulance, 119
ambulatory, church, 85
American Bankers Association routing number, check, 222
AM/FM controls, clock radio, 229
AM/FM radio tuning dial, phonograph receiver, 177
amidships, boat, 128
ammeter, symbol, 494
ammunition: automatic weapon, 461; combat soldier, 481; fort, 80
amount: check, 222; postal money order, 223
amp, electric guitar, 357
amperage rating, circuit breaker box, 389
ampersand, grammatical symbol, 497
amphibian, 42
amphibious hull, helicopter, 146
amphibious vehicle, 145
amplifier: guitar, 357; phonograph, 177; synthesizer, 357
AM signal meter, phonograph, 177
amulet, medal 485
amusement park, 90-91
anal fin, fish, 43
anal shield, snake, 41
anatomical snuffbox, human hand, 29
anatomy, literary, 25
anchor: boar, 128; diving board, 310; mattress cover, 267; passenger ship, 139; sailboat, 130; starting block, 298; tennis net, 306

anchorage, nautical chart, 22
anchor bolt, house, 58, 59
anchor chain: bear trap, 423; oil drilling platform, 99
anchor light, destroyer, 141
anchor spot, blackjack, 341
anchor spring, gas pump nozzle, 108
anchor tooth, denture, 443
anchor winch, oil drilling platform, 99
anchor windlass, tanker, 136
anchovies, pizza, 261
andiron, fireplace,, 228
anemometer, weather station, 18
aneroid barometer, 18
angle: fort, 81; incline track, 90; lamp, 235; slide, 283; transit, 426
angled deck, aircraft carrier, 142
angle of attack indicator, pilot's instrument panel, 153
angle of light, relief map, 21
angler, fishing, 335
angle scale, circular saw, 407
angular adjustment, speculum, 438
angulation dial readout, dental x-ray unit, 444
anima, human, 25
animal: cell, 23; circus, 88, 89; composite, 46-47
animal trainer, 88
animal skin, igloo, 83
ankh, symbol, 492
ankle, human, 24, 29
ankle boot, harness racing pacer, 331
ankle bracelet, 215
ankle extension, baseball catcher's shinguard, 286
ankle guard, hockey skate, 319
ankle sock, 203
ankle strap, woman's shoe, 201
anklet, 215
ankle weight, body building, 338
announcement microphone, 747; cockpit, 150
annual ring: lumber, 66; tree, 48
annulus, mushroom, 55
anode plate, vacuum tube, 386
anorak, 197
ant, 39
antenna: aircraft carrier, 142; airport control tower, 93; automobile, 102, 103; CB radio, 179; destroyer, 140, 141; helicopter, 146; house, 61; insect, 39; jet fighter, 152; launch pad, 154; lobster, 45; lunar lander, 156; lunar rover, 157; police car, 118; radar, 434; satellite, 182; single engine airplane, 147; spacesuit, 157; submarine, 143; symbol, 494; tank, 464; tanker, 137
antependium, church, 85
anther, flower stamen, 51
antia, shield, 454
anti-ballistic missile (ABM), 466
anti-cavitation plate, outboard engine, 133
anti-fog liquid,

dental, 445
anti-friction pad, ski binding, 320
antihelix, outer ear, 28
anti-kickback panel, saw, 407
antique, White House, 73
anti-reverse housing, fishing reel, 334
anti-rollback, incline track, 90
anti-shock trousers, paramedic equipment, 119
anti-skate dial, phonograph, 176
anti-submarine belt, drag racing driver, 333
antitank mine, 463
antitragus, outer ear, 28
antlers, ultimate beast, 46
anus, starfish, 44
anvil: stapler, 273; telegraph key, 159; vise, 399
anvil shears, gardening, 417
anvil toe, thundercloud, 17
aperture: microscope, 432; pencil sharpener, 273; physician's mirror, 438; univalve shell, 45
aperture ring, camera, 171
aperture scale: light meter, 174; still camera, 171; video camera, 180
apex: grass, 56; leaf, 50; pyramid, 69; univalve shell, 45
apostrophe: grammatical symbol, 497; proofreader's mark, 498
Appalachian dulcimer, 356
apparatus, animal cell, 23
apparel pocket, golf bag, 305
appendix, human, 27
appetizer, 259
apple, 53; baseball, 286; corer, 257
applicator, beauty product, 213
applicator bottle, hair styling lotion, 210
appliqué: dress, 194; quilting, 377
appliquéd lace, bridal gown, 472
approach: airport runway, 92; bowling lane, 311; javelin throw, 295; pole vault, 299
approach indexer, pilot's instrument panel, 153
approximately equal to, symbol, 495
apron: airport, 93; ascot, 189; barn, 100; boxing ring, 303; bureau, 268; circus aerialist, 88; golf course, 305; house driveway, 61; maid's uniform, 473; necktie, 189; pool table, 314; table, 238; theatre, 345; window, 63
apsidal chapel, church, 85
apterium, bird, 37
Aquarius, zodiac, 493
aquatint, printmaking, 371
Arab dress, 475
arbor lock, table saw, 407
arc: sextant, 133; soccer field, 293; Torah, 470
arcade, passenger ship, 138
arch, 70; church, 84; croquet, 312; denture, 443; dog, 34; football uniform, 288; house doorway, 60; human fingertip, 29; human foot, 29; kokoshniki, 68;

organ, 354; royal crown, 469; saddle, 329; stage, 344, 345
arch cookie, sandal, 202
arched-top glass door, corner cabinet, 239
archer, zodiac, 493
architect, house blueprint, 60
architecture, international, 68-69
architrave: column entablature, 71; vault, 447; White House, 73
archival frame, 373
arch-stones, arch, 70
arco, stringed instrument, 349
area rug, 242
A recreation yard, prison, 74
arena, circus, 88
areole, cactus,, 54
arête: glacier, 12; mountain, 9
Argine, playing card queen, 342
Aries, zodiac, 493
arithmetic unit, computer, 429
arithmetic function key calculator, 431
ark, synagogue, 86
arm: anchor, 128; automobile, 162, 164; ballista, 457; bobby pin, 210; cactus, 54; candelabrum, 233; chaise lounge, 284; clothes hanger, 277; coffin, 500; corkscrew, 247; dental, 444, 445; dishwasher, 246; dog, 34; drill bit, 409; fishing reel, 334; folding rule, 414; frog, 42; gas pump price-poster, 108; guitar, 357; human, 24, 25; jellyfish, 44; lamp, 235; launch pad, 154; lounger, 231; L-shaped square, 414; lyre, 349; microscope, 432; movie projector, 173; octopus, 44; outboard engine, 133; organ, 354; overhead power line, 386; phonograph turntable, 176; piano, 355; revolving sprinkler, 418; rocking chair, 230; sewing machine, 274; sextant, 133; shower, 270; slot machine, 340; sofa, 232; starfish, 44; toilet, 271; toll booth gate, 110; traffic light, 109; type, 163; wheelchair, 442; see also arms
armament countermeasure panel, 153
armament panel, pilot's, 153
armature, sculpture, 366
armboard extension, operating table, 440
arm buckle, electric chair, 452
armed guard, prison, 74
arm grip, phonograph turntable, 176
armhole: jacket, 184, 192; undershirt, 190
armhole seam, blouse, 193
armilla, queen's regalia, 468
arming mechanism, bazooka, 462
armlet, jewelry, 215
armoire, 268
armor, 455
armored cord, pay phone, 178

armorial achievement, coat of arms, 487
armor-plated vehicle, 464-465
armory, castle, 79
arm pad, lounger, 231
arm piece, crutch, 442
armpit: frog, 42; human, 24
arm post, rocking chair, 230
arm protector, ice hockey goalie, 290
armrail, commuter bus, 114
armrest: lounger, 231; rocking chair, 230; sofa, 232; wheelchair, 442
arms: church, 85; coat of, 487; Manchu coat dress, 475; medieval, 454; royal crown, 469; see also arm
aro, jai alai cesta, 308
arrester, fireplace sparks, 228
arresting gear pendant, aircraft carrier, 142
arresting hock, jet fighter, 152
arresting hook panel, pilot's instrument panel, 153
arresting trap, 423
arrow, 456; bowling lane, 311; road map, 20
arrowhead, weather vane, 19
arrow loop, castle, 78
arse, wood block, 451
art: book jacket, 165; composition, 362-363; in frame, 373; magazine, 167, 168, 169; newspaper, 166
artery, human, 27
article, magazine, 167, 168
artificial abrasive material, sander, 411
artificial teeth, denture, 443
artificial turf, baseball field, 287
artillery, cowboy, 474
artist: cartoon, 374; circus, 88; painting, 364; phonograph record, 176
ASA-DIN exposure index, light meter, 174
ascender, type, 163
ascent air-data system, space shuttle, 154
ascent stage, lunar lander, 156
ascot, 189
asdic, 434
ash: cigar and cigarrette, 224; volcano, 10
A sharp, piano keyboard octave, 355
ash catcher, grill, 284
ash dump, fireplace, 228
ash lip, woodburning stove, 394
ashpit, fireplace, 228
ashtray, car, 106
asparagus, 52
asphaltum, 370
ASROC launcher, destroyer, 141
assembly: backyard equipment, 283; lamp, 235; nuclear reactor, 385; pulley block, 451; scale, 436
assigned weight, flat racing entry, 330
assistant quartermaster, frontier fort, 80
assistant's center, dental unit, 444
assist handle, truck tractor, 116
association football, 293
asterisk, grammatical symbol, 497
asteroid, Milky Way, 2
astragal: cannon barrel, 457; column, 71
A string, double bass, 349
astrologer, 493
asymmetrical closing,

jacket, 192
at, symbol, 495
athletic sock, 203
athletic supporter, 190
athwartships, boat, 128
Atlantic Drift, ocean, 6
Atlantic North Equatorial Current, ocean, 6
Atlantic South Equatorial Current, ocean, 6
atmosphere, earth, 4
attaché case, 281
attached bertha, bridal gown, 472
attaching point, inflatable, 129
attaching socket, movie camera, 172
attachment: denture, 443; reflex camera, 171; vacuum cleaner, 279
attachment loop, basketball backstop, 292
attachment plug, electrical, 388
attachment weight set, scale, 436
attack indicator, pilot's instrument panel, 153
attack line, volleyball court, 313
attic, house, 60, 61
attitude indicator, space shuttle, 155
audience, circus, 89
audio control, police car, 118
audio-input, movie projector, 173
audio knob, Geiger counter, 435
audio port, Geiger counter, 435
audio power status, space shuttle, 155
auditorium, prison, 74
auditory canal, 28
auger, 412
auger bit, drill, 408, 409
auguste face, clown, 477
auricle, 28
auricular, bird, 37
author: book, 165; magazine, 167; music, 346
authorized signature, traveler's check, 223
auto gate, toll booth, 110
auto inflation, hose, skin diving, 325
automatic choke, automobile, 107
automatic citrus juicer, 251
automatic cue, phonograph turntable, 176
automatic direction finder: helicopter, 146; 747 cockpit, 150
automatic film advance, camera, 170
automatic inflator, skin diving, 325
automatic line finder, typewriter, 162
automatic noise limiter, CB radio, 179
automatic nozzle, gas pump, 108
automatic pilot disengage, 747 cockpit, 151
automatic pistol, 460
automatic rewind switch, tape measure, 414
automatic rifle, 461
automatic timer, coffee maker, 248
automatic weapons, 461
automobile: cutaway, 104-105; drag racing, 333; engine, 107; exterior, 102-103; Grand Prix racer, 332; interior, 106; police, 118; see also car

autopilot display, space shuttle, 155
autopilot engage switch, 747 cockpit, 150
auxiliary attaching socket, movie camera, 172
auxiliary building, nuclear reactor, 384
auxiliary car-station panel, elevator car, 76
auxiliary contact, movie camera, 172
auxiliary counterweight, lift bridge, 95
auxiliary feedwater pump, nuclear reactor, 384
auxiliary handle: hand drill, 408; plane, 410
auxiliary instruments arm, dental, 444
auxiliary lens, microscope, 432
auxiliary selector, movie camera, 172
auxiliary tank, truck, 117
avalanche area, mountain, 9
aven, cave, 11
aviation light, bridge, 95
aviation lens, eyeglasses, 217
awl: combination square, 414; knife, 416
awn, grass, 56
awning: barn, 100; tent, 336
ax: guillotine, 452; ice climbing, 328; medieval, 454
axilla, frog, 42
axillary bud, tree, 48
axis: fern, 55; peeler, 252
axle: automobile, 105; bicycle, 124; child's wagon, 283; ferris wheel, 91; Hansom cab, 127; roller skate, 318; stroller, 282; tractor, 424; wheelbarrow, 420; wheelchair, 442; windmill, 382
axle gear, seeder, 420
axle hole, tire, 101
azimuth coarse-motion clamp, telescope, 433

B

B: braille, 496; music notation, 347; piano keyboard octave, 355; sign language, 496
baby carriage, 282
baby chair, 282
baby teeth, 446
baccarat, 340
back: bird, 37; bow, 456; carpenter's saw, 406; cat, 35; chaise lounge, 284; chicken, 33; chisel, 410; coin, 221; dog 34; easel, 364; electric chair, 452; horse, 36; human, 24, 25; knife, 252, 453; playing card, 342; rocking chair, 230; saw tooth, 406; shank button, 205; sheep, 31; sofa, 232; stringed instrument, 349; wave, 14; wheelchair, 442
back arch, English saddle, 329
back beam, hand loom, 379
backboard: basketball backstop, 292; ice hockey rink, 291
backbone, hardback book, 165
back boundary line, badminton court, 313
backcombed hair, woman's, 209
backcourt: basketball, 292; tennis, 306
back cover: hardback book, 165;

matchbook, 224; reflex camera, 171
back face, hardback book, 165
backfill, underwater tunnel, 96
back finger, handball glove, 307
back flap, book jacket, 165
backgammon, 339
background, composition, 363
back guard, stove, 244
back half, piano, 355
back housing, saddle, 329
backing: carpet, 242; frame, 373; quilting, 377; sandpaper, 411; tent, 336
back jaw, vise, 399
back leg, bureau, 268
back lid, grand piano, 355
back light button, movie camera, 172
back line, volleyball court, 313
backlit composition, 362
back margin, book page, 165
back matter, book, 165
back of book, magazine, 169
back of hand, human, 29
backpack, 337; skin diving tank, 325
backpack control box, spacesuit, 157
backpacking, 337
back pad, ice hockey goalie, 290
back panel, man's jacket, 184
backplate: armor, 455; basketball backstop, 292; shoulder bag, 218; skin diving tank, 325
backplate serial number, paper money, 220
back quarter, boot, 202
back rail, rocking chair, 230
backrest: lounger, 231; stroller, 282
back roll protector, ice hockey player, 291
backshore, shoreline, 14
back sizer, football helmet, 288
back sleeve seam, jacket, 184
backspace key: key punch, 428; typewriter, 162
backsplash, stove, 244
backstay: ice skates, 319; sailboat, 130
backstep, pumper, 121
back-stick, easel, 364
backstop: basketball, 292; telegraph key, 159; workbench, 398
backstrap: brassiere, 191; revolver, 460; vest, 184
backstretch, harness racetrack, 331
backstrip, hardback book, 165
backstroke swimming race, 310
back upholstery, wheelchair, 442
back-up light, tow truck bed, 122
back wall: handball and squash courts, 307; jai alai cancha, 308
badge: coat of arms, 487; fireman's helmet, 484; flag, 486; military, 480; police, 482
badge of rank, Manchu court dress, 475
badminton, 313
baffle, stove, 336, 394
bag: backpacking, 337; bagpipe, 359; blood pressure gauge, 439; golf, 305; hot air balloon, 326;

luggage, 281; lunar rover, 157; packaging, 265; paper, 262; photographic, 174; vacuum cleaner, 279,
bag compression strap, backpack, 337
bag dispenser, spacesuit, 157
baggage car, passenger train, 112
baggage check-in, public sign, 491
baggage claim, public sign, 491
baggage compartment: bus, 114; jumbo jet, 149; single engine airplane, 147
baggage locker, public sign, 490
baggage rack, intercity bus, 114
bag-holding button, garbage disposal, 243
bagpipe, 359
bag resuscitator, ambulance, 119
bag stowage, lunar rover, 157
bail: fishing reel, 334; lantern, 336; pail, 280; screen, 173; typewriter, 162
bailey, castle, 78, 79
bail roller, typewriter, 162
bait, mousetrap, 423
baked dessert, 260
bakery: frontier fort, 80; prison, 74
baking tray, toaster oven, 249
balance: laboratory, 436-437; zodiac, 493
balance beam, gymnastics, 300
balance dial, phonograph, 177
balancer, trombone, 352
balance weight, tire, 101
balcony: minaret, 68; pagoda, 69; theatre, 345; White House, 73
bald spot, 207
balistraria, castle, 78
balk, lumber, 66
ball: anchor, 128; ballpoint pen, 160; baseball, 286; bowling, 311; croquet, 312; door, 62; drum major's baton, 479; field events hammer, 297; foot, 29; golf, 304; handball, 307; jai alai, 308; Ping-Pong, 315; pool table, 314; roulette wheel, 340; shower fitting, 270; snap fastener, 204; tea, 256; tennis, 306; thumb, 29; toilet tank, 271; type, 163; typewriter, 162
ballast: hot air balloon, 326; lobster pot, 423; railroad track, 111
ballast tank, submarine, 143
ball bearing: ballpoint pen, 160; roller skate, 318
ball-cock assembly, toilet, 271
ballet dancer, 478
ballista, 457
ballistic missile, 466; submarine, 143
ball joint, automobile, 104
ball joint head, C-clamp, 399
ball of rank royal crown, 469
ballonets, blimp, 158
balloon: cartoon, 374, 375; clown, 477; hot air, 326
balloon pants, clown, 477
balloon pointer, comic strip, 375
ballot, voting booth, 427

ballpark, 287
ball-peen hammer, 402
ball pocket, golf bag, 305
ballpoint pen, 160
ball rest, roulette wheel, 340
ball return: bowling lane, 311; pool table, 314
ball side, snap fastener, 204
ball storage box, pool table, 314
ball tip head, hinge, 450
baluster: column, 71; staircase, 64
balustrade: column, 71; escalator, 77; staircase, 64
bamboo pole, pole vault, 299
banana, 53
banana clip, automatic rifle, 461
band: baren, 368; baseball uniform, 286; cigar, 224; cigarette, 224; dance, 348; dental, 443; fire extinguisher, 280; frontier fort, 80; girdle, 191; horse's hoof, 36; hot air balloon, 326; Jewish prayer shawl, 470; marching; mattress cover, 267; phonograph record, 176; ring, 215; skin diving tank, 325; spinning wheel, 379; spur, 329; woman's hat, 199; wristwatch, 216
bandage, 441; paramedic equipment, 119; racehorse, 330
Band-Aid, 441
bandanna: cowboy, 474; skier's, 320
band clamp, 399
band organ, merry-go-round, 91
band saw, 407
bang: grammatical symbol, 497; woman's hair, 209
bangle, jewelry, 215
banister, staircase, 64
banjo, 356
bank: credit card identification number, 222; elevator, 75, 76; name and address, check, 222; newspaper, 166; number, postal money order, 223; paper money, 220; passenger ship, 138; river, 13; traveler's check, 223; vault, 447
bank indicator, 747 cockpit, 150
bank rod, fishing, 335
banner: circus tent, 89; football field, 289; newspaper headline, 166
banquette, permanent fort, 81
baptistery, church, 85
bar: backgammon board, 339; backyard equipment, 283; barbell, 338; barbecue grill, 284; bicycle, 124; chain saw, 421; commuter bus, 114; courtroom, 87; craps table, 341; drag racing dragster, 333; easel, 364; electric razor, 206; etching press, 371; fastener, 204; ferris wheel, 91; Grand Prix racer, 332; hang glider, 327; hurdle, 298; hitch and harrow, 424; horizontal bar, 300; horse's foot, 36; lithographic press, 370; military uniform, 480; mousetrap, 423; movie

projector, 173; music, 346, 347; necktie, 188; parallel bars, 300; passenger ship, 138; public sign, 490; railroad track, 111; saddle, 329; shoreline, 14; slalom water ski, 323; slot machine, 340; suit hanger, 277; table saw, 407; tank, 465; tow truck bed, 122; type, 163; typewriter, 162
barb: barbed wire, 422; bird, 37; fishhook, 335; lance, 454; spring beard needle, 378
barbed wire, 422
barbell, body building, 338
barbershop, passenger ship, 138
barbican, castle, 78, 79
Barcalounger, 231
bar clamp, 399
baren, woodcut printing, 368
bargeboard, house, 61
barge carrier, 136
barge cluster, pushboat, 144
bargello stitchery, 377
bark, wigwam, 82
barley, 56
bar line: music, 346; newspaper, 166
barn, 100
barnacle, 45
barometer, aneroid, 18
barometric altimeter, 747 cockpit, 150
barrack: castle, 79; frontier fort, 80
barred door, prison, 74
barrel, 263; automatic weapons, 458, 459, 460, 461; baseball bat, 287; cannon, 457; clarinet, 351; cow, 30; curling iron, 210; dart, 316; destroyer gun, 141; fire hydrant, 121; hair dryer, 208; hinge, 450; hypodermic syringe, 441; man's shoe, 200; pen, 160; shirt cuff, 185; spool, 376; tank gun, 465
barrel cap, lead pencil, 160
barrel grille, hair dryer, 208
barrel ring: bayonet, 453; shotgun, 459
barrel spiral galaxy, 2
barrette, 210
barrier, highway, 110
barrier beach, 15
barrier gate, toll booth, 110
barrier island, 15
bar scale, political map, 21
bar tack, necktie, 189
bar tip, chair saw, 421
bartizan, castle, 78
bascule bridge, 95
base: acoustic guitar, 356; badminton shuttlecock, 313; baseball field, 287; basket, 262; basketball backstop, 292; bear trap, 423; blackjack, 341; blender, 250; canapé, 259; candelabrum, 233; cannon barrel ring, 457; CB radio station, 179; citrus juicer, 251; coat of arms, 487; column, 71; dental brace, 443; denture, 443; drag racing

starting lights, 333; dressing table, 268; drill press, 409; easel, 364; elevator car, 76; food processor, 250; globe, 1; grandfather clock, 229; hurdle, 298; juice extractor, 251; laboratory burner, 437; laboratory scale, 437; lantern, 336; lawn sprinkler, 418; leaf, 50; light bulb, 234; makeup, 212; medical examination table, 440; microscope, 432; minaret, 68; mortar cap, 462; mousetrap, 423; music stand, 361; onion, 52; parallel bars, 300; pedestal table, 238; pencil sharpener, 273; percolator brewing basket, 248; phonograph turntable, 176; pole vault pole, 299; pommel horse, 301; pot, 367; power saw, 407; pyramid, 69; refrigerator grille, 245; rifle scope, 458, 459; sandwich cookie, 260; stapler, 273; steam engine, 395; stove burner, 244; telephone, 178; television set, 181; thimble, 376; tombstone, 500; transistor chip, 386; trimline phone, 178; trophy, 285; tuning fork, 361; vacuum tube, 386; vise, 399; White House, 73

baseball, 286-287; darts, 316
baseboard, and carpet, 242
baseline: baseball field, 287; Ping-Pong table, 315; shuffleboard court, 313; tennis court, 306; type, 163
basement, house, 58, 61
basepath, baseball field, 287
baseplate: land mine, 463; mortar, 462; railroad track, 111; saber saw, 407; sewing machine, 274
basin: ambulance, 119; dam, 98; river, 13; sink, 269
basin compartment, sink, 243
basket: basketball, 292; bee, 39; coffee maker, 248; container, 262; deep frying, 256; garbage disposal, 243; guillotine, 452; hot air balloon, 326; jai alai, 308; juice extractor, 251; nuclear reactor, 385; refrigerator, 245; sink, 243; ski pole, 320; sword, 453; toll booth, 110; typewriter type, 162; washing machine, 276
basketball, 292
basket-release handle, garbage disposal, 243
bass: accordion, 360; bagpipe drone, 359; bassoon joint, 351; fiddle, 348, 349; guitar, 357; music clef, 347; phonograph dial, 177
bas and guitar, double-neck, 357
bass clarinet, 348

bass drum, 348, 358
bass fiddle, 348, 349
bassinet, 282
bass neck, double-neck bass and guitar, 357
bassoon, 348, 351
basting brush, 255
basting ladle, 255
bastion: castle, 78, 79; permanent fort, 81
bat: badminton, 313; baseball, 287; brick wall, 67; flat racing, 330; Ping-Pong, 315
bateau neck, sweater, 195
bath, 270
bath oil, 213
batholith, volcano, 10
bathtub, 270
baton: drum major, 479; police, 482
bat pin, potter's wheel, 367
batten: hand loom, 379; stage, 344
batten pocket, mainsail, 132
batter, baseball, 286
batter head, snare drum, 358
batter's box, baseball, 287
batter's circle, baseball, 287
battery, 387; automobile, 104; buoy, 128; electronic flash, 174; Geiger counter, 435; hearing aid, 442; intercity bus, 114; lunar rover, 157; metal detector, 435; movie camera, 172; pacemaker, 442; pocket camera, 170; tape recorder, 175; truck, 116, 117
battery charger: medical examination equipment, 438; tow truck, 122
battery jumper cable, tow truck, 122
battery-powered film pack, camera, 170
battery-powered tape recorder, 175
batting, quilting, 377
batting glove, baseball, 286
batting helmet, baseball, 286
battlement, castle, 78
battleship, 140
bat weight, baseball, 286
bay: aircraft carrier, 142; barn, 100; coastline, 7, 15; space shuttle, 154
bay bar, 15
bay barrier, 15
baymouth, bar, 15
bayit, tefillin, 470
bayonet, 453
bayonet saw, 407
bay window, house, 60, 61
bazooka, 462
bazooka plate, tank, 464
B cell block, prison, 74
BC inflator mouthpiece, skin diving, 325
beach, 14, 15
beacon: helicopter, 146; police car, 118; single engine airplane, 147
bead: abacus, 431; beaker, 437; cowboy hat, 198; shotgun, 459
beading: attaché case, 281; Indian attire, 474
bead line, bell, III
beak: bird, 37; chicken, 33; clam, 45; dolphin, 43; halberd, 454; turtle, 40; type, 163
beaker: coffee maker, 248; laboratory, 437

beam: abacus, 431; automobile, 102; boat, 128; bus, 114; drag racing, 333; guillotine, 452; gymnastic, 300; hand loom, 379; house, 59; incline track, 90; laboratory scale, 437; lumber, 66; skyscraper, 75; subway car, 115; television, 181; tow truck bed, 122
beam balance, laboratory, 436-437
beanie cap, space shuttle, 154
beard: man's, 207; beard needle, 378; turkey, 33; type, 164; ultimate beast, 47; windmill, 382
bearing: airport runway, 92; fishing reel, 334; laboratory scale, 436; radar, 434; roller skate, 318; skateboard, 318; socket wrench, 405; transit, 426
bearing distance heading indicator, pilot's instrument panel, 153
bearing edge, horse's foot, 36
bearing line, compass, 132
bearing rail, bureau, 268
bearing ring, radar, 434
bearing surface, brick, 66
bearpaw shoe, snowshoe, 321
bear trap, 423
bear trap binding, ski, 320
beat, police, 482
beater: bass drum, 358; kitchen tool, 254; vacuum cleaner, 279
beauty products, 213
beauty salon, passenger ship, 138
beaver, armor, 455
because, symbol, 495
becket, block and tackle, 451
bed, 266-267; brick, 66; cannon carriage, 457; child's wagon, 283; coffin, 500; etching press, 371; hammock, 284; highway, 110; key punch, 428; lithographic press, 370; railroad track, 111; river, 13; slide, 283; tower ladder, 120; trampoline, 302; wheelbarrow, 420
bed cloth, pool table, 314
bedcover, 267
bedding, 266-267
bed handle, lithographic press, 370
bed joint, brick wall, 67
bed knife, sickle-bar mower, 419
bed mold, column entablature, 71
bedplate: mortar, 462; steam engine, 395
bedrail, 266
bedroll: backpacking, 337; cowboy, 474
bedspread, 267
bee, 39
beef, 30
Beefeater, 467
beehive, woman's hair, 209
begin paragraph, proofreader's mark, 498
belfry, church, 84
bell, III; bassoon, 351; boxing, 303; buoy, 128; candle snuffer, 233; clarinet, 350; cymbal, 358; fire engine, 120, 121; foil

mounting, 309
hammer, 402; jellyfish, 44; slot machine, 340; steam locomotive, 112; telephone, 178; trombone, 352, 353; vault, 447
bell boot, harness racing pacer 331
bell-bottom trousers, 187, 481
bell brace, trombone, 352
bell buoy, nautical chart, 22
bell chest piece, stethoscope, 439
bell cord, commuter bus, 114
bellows: accordion, 360; bagpipe, 359; camera, 170; fireplace, 228; organ, 354; paper bag, 262
bellows pocket, parka, 197
bellows strap, accordion, 360
bell plug, fencing foil, 309
bell rim, bugle, 353
bell shade, lamp, 234
bell wire, trumpet, 353
belly: baluster, 71; banjo, 356; cat, 35; horse, 36; human, 25; jumbo jet, 149; mandolin, 356; type, 164; violin, 349
bellybutton, 25
belowdeck storage entrance, tanker, 136
belt: automobile engine, 107; backpack, 337; cardigan sweater, 195; cowboy, 474; drag racing driver, 333; dress, 194; ice hockey player, 290; jewelry, 215; king's regalia, 468; machine gun ammunition, 461; man's, 186; military, 480, 481; Milky Way, 3; mountain climbing, 328; police, 482-483; sander, 411; shoulder bag, 218; skirt, 193; time, 5; trench coat, 196; trousers, 187; waterskiing vest, 323
belt carrier, trousers, 187
belted waistband, woman's pants, 192
belt safety guard, drill press, 409
belt sander, 411
belt-tension knob, drill press, 409
bench: baseball field, 287; basketball court, 292; courtroom, 87; football field, 289; ice hockey rink, 291; sled, 322; toboggan, 322
bench rule, 414
bench saw, 407
benchseat, powerboat, 135
bench screw, woodcarving, 366
bench top, workbench, 398
bench vise, 399
bend: fishhook, 335; paper clip, 273; tuba, 352
Benguela Current, ocean, 6
bent, roller coaster, 90
bent gouge, woodcarving, 366
bent side, grand piano 355
beret, 198
berg, glacier, 12
bergschrund, mountain, 9
bergy bit, glacier, 12
berm: permanent fort, 81; shoreline, 14
berry, tomato, 52
berth, sailboat, 131
berta, bridal gown, 472
berthing hawser, passenger ship, 138

besom, skirt, 193
beta rod, radio antenna, 179
betting: jai alai, 308; odds, flat racing, 330
bevel: chisel, 410; scriber, 369
bevel gear, hand drill, 408
bevel scale, table saw, 407
bezel: pendant, 215; watch, 216, 298
bezel facet, cut gemstone, 214
B flat, piano keyboard octave, 355
bias, fabric, 380
bias switch, tape recorder, 175
bias tape, garment seam, 192
bib: fencing mask, 309; Indian shirt, 474; maid's uniform, 473; man's shirt, 185
bibcock, 269
biceps, human 26
bicuspid, 446
bicycle, 124; body building, 338
bicycle crossing, road sign, 489
bicycle trail, public sign, 491
bifocal eyeglasses, 217
big bowtie, clown, 477
big cage, circus, 88
big 8, craps table, 341
big guns, surfboard, 324
big nose, clown, 477
bight, coastline, 15
big 6, craps table, 341
big toe, human foot, 29
big top, circus, 88
bike: body building, 338; harness racing, 331
bike route, road sign, 488
bilge, sailboat, 131
bilge alarm, powerboat, 134
bill: anchor, 128; bird, 37; duck, 33; fishing plug, 335; hook and eye, 204; man's cap, 198; paper money, 220
bill compartment, wallet, 219
billet, saddle, 329
billfold, 219
billiard table, 314
billing, magazine cover, 167
billy club, police, 482
bin: garbage disposal, 243; jumbo jet, 148; refrigerator, 245; sideboard, 239; silo, 100; tank, 464
binary code bars, Universal Product Code, 430
binary star, 3
binaural, stethoscope, 439
binder: cigar, 224; water ski, 323
binding: baseball glove, 287; hat, 198; javelin, 297; mattress, 267; pole vault pole, 299; shoe, 200, 296; ski, 320, 321, 323; tennis racket, 306
binding screw, electric plug, 388
binnacle, compass, 132
BIN number, credit card, 222
binoculars, 433
binocular tube, microscope, 432
bipod leg, mortar, 462
bird, 37; badminton, 313; space shuttle, 154
biretta, clergy, 471
birth: racing entry, 330; symbol, 494
bishop: chess, 339; vestments, 471
bishop pawn, chess, 339
bishop's arms, church, 85
bishop sleeve, bridal gown, 472
bishop's screen, church, 85
bit: dental, 445;

destroyer, 140; drain cleaner, 412; fireboat, 144; flat racing, 330; gimlet, 408; glacier, 12; hand drill, 408, 409; harness racing, 331; oil drilling, 99; pipe, 225; screwdriver, 403; stopwatch, 298; tugboat, 144
bite: bugle, 353; scissors, 376
bitee stick, ambulance, 119
bit gauge, drill, 408, 409
bitty berg, glacier, 12
bivalve shell, 45
blackened copper surface, solar collector panel, 383
black hole, 2
black inner table, backgammon, 339
blackjack, 341
black outer table, backgammon, 339
black slot, roulette, 370
black square, chessboard, 339
black tie, military uniform, 480
black wire, electrical receptacle, 388
bladder: football, 288; human, 27; seeweed, 55; spacesuit, 157
blade: airplane propeller, 147; ambulance, 119; ax, 454; bicycle, 124; booties, ice skates, 319; bulldozer, 425; burnisher, 371; can opener, 247; cartridge fuse, 389; chisel, 410; cigar cutter, 224; combination square, 414; corkscrew, 247; electric plug, 388; fencing foil, 309; fern, 55; fishing rod, 335; flower petal, 51; food processor, 250; gardening shears, 417; gouge, 368; grass, 56; guillotine, 452; halberd, 454; hatchet, 402; helicopter roter, 146; hoe, 417; ice hockey stick, 291; ice skates, 319; juice extractor, 251; key, 449; knife, 240, 252, 416, 453; lawn mower, 419; leaf, 50; L-shaped square, 414; outboard engine, 133; partisan, 454; peeler, 252; Ping-Pong racket, 315; plane, 410; razor, 206; rotogravure, 164; rowboat oar, 129; saw, 406, 407; scissors, 376; screwdriver, 403; scriber, 369; seaweed, 55; shoe horn, 203; shovel, 417; silk screen squeegee, 369; skin diving fin, 325; speculum, 438; sword, 453; tape measure, 414; windmill, 382; woodcarving tool, 366
blade-bevel handwheel, table saw, 407
blade cartridge, razor, 206
blade control lever, bulldozer, 425
blade-elevating handwheel, saw, 407
blade eye hook, bulldozer, 425
blade guard, power saw, 407
blade hole, cigar cutter, 224
blade injector, shaver, 206
blade screw, saw, 407

blade shaft, can opener, 247
blank: coin, 221; key, 449
blanket: bedding, 267; police car, 118; saddle, 329
blanket bar, etching press, 371
blanket cylinder, offset press, 164
blank panel, home computer, 429
blazer jacket, woman's, 192
bleach dispenser, washing machine, 276
bleed: magazine, 169; political map, 21
bleed valve, steam engine, 395
blender, 250; pastry, 257
blimp, 158; camera, 172
blind, window, 237
blinder, flat racing, 330
blinker: automobile, 102; destroyer, 141; flat racing, 330
blister: automobile fender, 103; packaging, 264
block: automobile engine, 107; backgammon, 339; bongo drum, 358; football helmet, 288; igloo, 83; letter, 161; money order, 223; postage stamps, 161; pulley, 451; racing, 298; stapler, 273; steam engine, swimming pool, 310; and tackle, 451; toothbrush, 211; window shutters, 237; woodcut printing, 368; workbench, 398
blocked man's hat, 198
block number, city plan, 20
block valve, nuclear reactor, 384
blood factor symbols, 494
blood groove, sword, 453
bloodline, flat racing entry, 330
blood-pressure cuff, 119
blood-pressure gauge, 439
blossom end, banana, 53
blot, backgammon, 339
blouse: baseball catcher, 286; military, 480; police, 483; woman's, 193
blower: drag racing dragster, 333; heat exchanger, 393
blow wheel, humidifier, 392
blowhole: dolphin, 43; flute, 351
blow-in, magazine, 169
blowpipe, bagpipe, 359
blowout preventor, oil drilling, 99
blucher, man's shoe, 200
blue lightnin', cowboy, 474
blue line, ice hockey rink, 291
blueprint, house, 60
Blue Room, White House, 73
blue whistler, cowboy, 474
bluff, nautical chart, 22
blurb: book, IV, 165; label, 264; magazine, 167, 168
blurgit, cartoon, 375
blush, makeup, 212, 213
boar, 32
board: backgammon, 339; barbecue grill, 284; darts, 316; diving, 310; guitar, 356; hand loom, 379; horseracing, 330, 331; jai alai cancha, 308; kitchen tool, 257; merry-go-round, 91; military uniform, 480; organ, 354; roller coaster, 90; squash

court, 307; stage, 344; track and field, 294; universal gym, 338; windsurfer, 324
boarding, barn, 100
boarding ladder: combat aircraft, 152; tugboat, 144
boat, 128; craps table, 341
boat boom, aircraft carrier, 142
boat deck, passenger ship, 139
boat neck, sweater, 195
bob, clock pendulum, 229
bobber, fishing, 335
bobbin: sewing machine, 274; spinning wheel, 379; tatting shuttle, 378
bobby pin, 210
bobeche, candelabrum, 233
bobsled, 322
bodice: dress, 194; maid's uniform, 473; queen's regalia, 468
body: arrow, 456; automobile, 102; baren, 368; binoculars, 433; book, 165; camera, 171, 180; can, 263; carpenter's level, 414; discus, 297; drag racing dragster, 333; drill bit, 409; ear scope, 438; faucet, 269; fishing plug, 335; garbage truck, 123; guitar, 356, 357; hand grenade, 463; human, 24-29; internal combustion engine, 396; letter, 161; levigator, 370; locking pliers, 404; locomotive, 113; nail clippers, 211; newspaper story, 166; padlock, 449; pail, 280; paper bag, 262; percolator, 248; pistol nozzle, 418; phonograph headphone, 177; piccolo, 350; pot, 367; printing press, 370, 371; saxophone, 351; shirt, 185; snake, 41; sock, 203; sweater, 195; tooth, 446; traffic light, 109; type, 164; window shade, 236, 237
body building, 338
body feather, chicken, 33
body handle, pressure cooker, 253
body lacing, snowshoe, 321
body lock handle, garbage truck, 123
body molding, automobile, 103
body oil, 213
body pad, ice hockey goalie, 290
body panel, stagecoach, 127
body-restraint strap, operating table, 440
body rivet, pliers, 404
body tube, microscope, 432
body wall, safe, 447
body whorl, univalve shell, 45
bogie, bus, 114
boiler: furnace, 390; locomotive, 112; pot, 253; steam engine, 395
bold face type, 163; magazine, 168, 169
bole, tree, 48
bollard, canal lock, 97
bolo tie, 188
bolster: chisel, 410; knife, 252; sofa, 232; stagecoach, 127
bolt, 401; bicycle, 124; saw, 407, 421;

crossbow, 456;
crutch, 442; door, 448;
fabric, 380; house, 59;
hurdle, 298;
levigator, 370; lock, 448;
plane knob, 410;
pliers, 404; pulley
block, 451; railroad
crossing signal, 111;
rifle, 458, 461; roller
skate, 318; ship's bell, III;
vault, 447; vise, 399;
wheelchair, 442
bolt-activating gear ring,
vault, 447
bolt cap, toilet, 271
bolt cutter, 404
bolt ring, 214;
identification bracelet, 183
bolt-retracting gear,
vault, 447
bomb elevators, aircraft
carrier, 142
bombproof, permanent
fort, 81
bond, wall, 67
bonded insulation filling,
sleeping bag, 337
bone: acoustic guitar, 356;
early calculator, 431;
girdle, 191;
human, 25, 26; meat, 258;
tile games, 339
bone marrow, meat, 258
bongos, 358
bonnet, 199; faucet, 269;
fire hydrant, 121;
Indian, 474
bonnet string,
cowboy, 474
book, 165; postage
stamps, 161; sample
page, IV; type, 163
boom: aircraft carrier, 142;
radio antenna, 179;
sailboat, 130; tower
ladder, 120; tow
truck, 122;
windsurfer, 324
boom bumper,
windsurfer, 324
boom gallows, sailboat, 130
boom light, truck bed, 122
boom-to-mast clip, CB radio
antenna, 179
booster, space shuttle, 154
booster fan, underwater
tunnel, 96
booster hose-reel,
pumper, 120
booster parachute canister,
space shuttle, 154
booster tank, pumper, 120
boot, 202; automobile, 102;
bassoon, 351;
cowboy, 474;
fireman, 484; harness
racing pacer, 331; ice
climbing, 328; ice
skate, 319; panty hose,
191; race horse, 330;
rain, 203; Revolutionary
War general, 476; roller
skate, 318; skin
diving, 325; skiing, 321,
323; soldier's, 481; spark
plug, 107; stagecoach, 127
booth, voting, 427
boot hook, 203
bootie, skin diving, 325
bootjack, 203
boot stripe, power boat, 134
boot top: destroyer, 141;
drum major's shoe, 479;
sailboat, 130
boozex, cartoon, 375
borated-water storage tank,
nuclear reactor, 384
border: basket, 262; book
page, IV; canape, 259;
check, 222; comic
strip, 374; magazine
cover, 167; paper

money, 221; stage, 344
bore: spool, 376;
thermometer, 439;
weapons, 457, 458, 459,
460
bore evacuator, tank
gun, 465
bosom, human, 25
boss, sheild, 454
bota, ski clothes, 321
botonée, symbol, 492
bottle, 263, 264; hair lotion
applicator, 210;
opener, 247, 416
bottle rack, oil drilling
platform, 99
bottom: barrel, 263; book
page, 165; girdle, 191;
golf bag, 305; man's
shoe, 200; parachute, 327;
piano, 355; plane, 410;
screen, 173; skillet, 253;
stove, 394; sweater, 195;
vest, 184; waterski, 323;
window shutter, 237; zinc
carbon cell, 387;
zipper, 205
bottom bow, sousaphone, 352
bottom girdle, hot air
balloon, 326
bottom pillow, stage
coach, 127
bottom plate, house, 59
bottom rail: bureau, 268;
door, 62; staircase, 64;
venetian blind 237;
window, 63
bottom sheet, bedding, 267
bottom spring, 226
bouffant hairdo,
woman's, 209
bounce-angle scale,
electronic flash, 174
bouche, shield, 454
boundaries, map, 5, 20
boundary line, volleyball
court, 313
bouquet, bridal, 472
bout: fencing, 309;
viola, 349
boutonniere, jacket, 184, 472
bow, 456; bear trap, 423;
bell, III; beret, 198;
boat, 128, 129, 144;
bonnet, 199; brace, 408;
crutch, 442; cymbal, 358;
kettledrum, 358; key, 449;
kite, 317; maid's
uniform, 473; man's
hat, 198; mousetrap, 423;
rake, 417; saddle, 329;
scissors, 376;
sousaphone, 352; sword
hilt, 453; trombone, 352;
violin, 349; watch, 216,
298; windsurfer, 324
bowel, human, 25
bowl: basting ladle, 255;
brazier, 284; dessert
setting, 241; electric
wok, 253; food
processor, 250; juice
extractor, 251; kitchen
sink, 243; mixing, 254;
pipe, 225; roulette
wheel, 340; spoon, 240;
stemware, 240; toilet, 271;
type, 163
bowling, 311
bowl track, railroad yard, 94
bowmen, 456
bow numbers, destroyer, 141
bow pulpit, sailboat, 130
bowsprit, sailboat, 130
bowstring, 456
bow thruster, passenger
ship, 139
bow tie, 188; butler, 473;
clown, 477; man's formal
attire, 472
bow window, house, 60
box: automobile steering
gear, 104; ballet

toeshoes, 478; barn, 100;
baseball field, 287;
blackjack table, 340; book
page, IV; boot, 202;
bus, 114; cigar
cutter, 224; circuit
breaker, 389;
courtroom, 87; craps
table, 341; dulcimer, 356;
easel, 364; electrical
receptacle, 388; handball
court, 307; ice hockey
rink, 291; lacrosse
field, 293; light
fixture, 234; lithographic
press, 370; machine gun
cartridge, 461; mail, 227;
map, 21; metronome, 361;
money, 447;
packaging, 265;
paramedic
equipment, 119; parking
meter, 109; pole
vault, 299; pool
table, 314; prison, 74;
radar antenna, 434;
railroad crossing
signal, 111; razor blade
injector, 206; running
shoe, 296; seeder, 420;
sideboard, 239;
sketch, 365;
stagecoach, 127; steam
engine, 395; subway
motorman's cab, 115;
tank, 464; tefillin, 470;
theatre, 345; tow
truck, 122; tugboat, 144;
vault, 447; wrench, 405
boxcar, train, 113
box drawer, desk, 272
boxer, pugilist, 303
boxer shorts, 190
boxing, 303
box kit, 317
boxman, craps table, 341
box ratchet, brace, 408
box spring, bed, 267
bra, 191
brace, 408; balance
beam, 300; basketball
backstop, 292; bridge, 95;
child's wagon, 283;
dental, 443; fence
gate, 67; guitar, 356;
house, 59; kiln, 367;
kite, 317; ladder, 415;
locomotive, 112;
man's, 186; oil drilling
platform, 99; parallel
bars, 300; rocking
chair, 230; sponge
mop, 279; stage, 344
stagecoach, 127;
supportive, 442; table
saw, 407; toboggan, 322;
trombone, 352; venetian
blind, 237;
wheelbarrow, 420;
wheelchair, 442;
workbench, 398
brace flange, trombone, 352
bracelet: human hand, 29;
identification, 183;
jewelry, 215;
wristwatch, 216
brace pole, tent, 336
brachioradialis, human, 26
bracket: butterfly table, 238;
child's wagon, 283; citrus
juicer, 251; dental
unit, 444; grammatical
symbol, 497; house, 60;
inflatable, 129;
ladder, 415; mortar, 462;
orthodontic, 443;
outboard engine, 133;
police car, 118; radar
antenna, 434; railroad
crossing signal, III; royal
crown, 469;
sawhorse, 398; ship's

bell, III; tanker, 137; tow
truck bed, 122; traverse
rod, 236;
wheelbarrow, 420;
wheelchair, 442
bracket slot, dental
braces, 443
bracket table, dental, 445
bract: grass, 56; lettuce, 258;
pineapple, 53
brad, 400
braid: military uniform, 480;
venetian blind, 237;
woman's hair, 209;
woman's hat, 199
braille, 496
brains, beef, 30
brake: bicycle, 124;
bobsled, 322;
bulldozer, 425;
car, 104, 106; chain
saw, 421;
locomotive, 112;
motorcycle, 125; 747
cockpit, 150; ski
binding, 320; space
shuttle, 154;
stagecoach, 127;
stroller, 282; subway
car, 115; tank gun
muzzle, 465
brake caliper:
automobile, 104;
bicycle, 124;
motorcycle, 125
brake caster, easel, 364
brake drum, automobile, 105
brake duct, racing car, 332
brake handle: 747
cockpit, 150; subway
motorman's cab, 115
brake plate, ski binding, 320
brake pressure indicator,
pilot's instrument
panel, 153
branch: cactus, 54;
candelabrum, 233;
celery, 258; hogan, 82;
horseshoe, 36; military
insignia, 480; river, 13;
stirrup, 329; sword
hilt, 453; tree, 48;
tuba, 352
brand: branding iron, 422;
gas pump, 108; label, 264;
pencil, 160
branding iron, 422
brandy snifter, 241
brass: musical
instruments, 348, 352-353;
sideboard, 239
brassard, military police, 480
brass button:
military, 480; police, 482
brassie, golf club, 305
brassiere, 191
bratelles, dress, 194
brayer, woodcut
printing, 368
brazier, patio, 284
Brazil Current, ocean, 6
bread: canapé base, 259;
Communion, 85; loaf, 159
breadbasket, human, 25
bread rack, toaster, 249
break, cat, 35
break-arch, grandfather
clock, 229
breaker: circuit, 389;
magazine, 168;
shoreline, 14; stained
glass, 372
breaker hammer, 426
breakfront, 239
breakout, political map, 21
breakpoint, continental
margin, 15
breast: chicken, 33;
horse, 36; human, 24;
lamb, 31; poultry, 33;
woman's shoe heel, 201
breastbeam, hand loom, 379
breast collar, harness

507

racing, 331
breastplate: armor, 455;
  Torah, 470
breast pocket: parka, 197;
  shirt, 185; woman's
  jacket, 192
breast protector, fencing, 309
breaststroke swimming
  race, 310
breastworks, permanent
  fort, 81
breath-hold diving, 325
breathing aid,
  paramedic, 119
breathing filter, drag racing
  fire suit, 333
breath mark, music, 346
B recreation yard, prison, 74
breech: human, 25;
  weapons, 457, 460, 461
breechblock, shotgun, 458
breeches, see trousers
breeder reactor, nuclear
  power, 384
breve, grammatical
  symbol, 497
brewed coffee, 248
brick: building material, 66;
  lobster pot, 423
brickmold, window, 63
brick symbolia, cartoon, 374
brick wall, 67
bridal dress, 472
bridge, 95; aircraft
  carrier, 142; airport, 92;
  billiards, 314; bow, 456;
  bowling ball, 311;
  castle, 78, 79; coffin, 500;
  dental, 443;
  destroyer, 141;
  eyeglasses, 217;
  guitar, 356, 357; highway
  cloverleaf, 110; lacrosse
  stick, 293; nose, 28;
  passenger ship, 139;
  railroad, 111; spider
  web, 38; submarine, 143;
  tanker, 137; vault, 447;
  violin, 349
bridge and socket assembly,
  sponge mop, 278
bridge table, 238
bridle: horseracing, 330, 331;
  kite leg, 317; waterskiing
  towline, 323
briefcase, 281
briffit, cartoon, 374
brightness control,
  sonar, 434
brilliance control, radar, 434
brim, hat, 198, 199
briquette, charcoal, 284
brisket: beef, 30; dog, 34;
  horse, 36; sheep, 31
bristle: broom, 278; brow
  brush, 213;
  hairbrush, 208; painting
  brush, 364; paint
  brush, 415;
  toothbrush, 211
broadcast indicator, CB
  radio, 179
broad jump, 294
brogues, butler's
  uniform, 473
broguings, man's shoe, 200
broiler, stove, 244
broken leader, book page, IV
brooch, 214, 215
brook, 13
Brooklyn pocket,
  bowling, 311
broom, 278; mechanical
  sweeper, 123
brow, human, 25
browband, Indian, 474
brow brush, beauty
  product, 213
brow rest, eye scope, 438
brush: beauty product, 213;
  cooking utensil, 225;
  dog, 34; drum, 358;
  electric, 208; house

painting, 415;
  painting, 364, 365;
  photographic
  supplies, 174;
  shaving, 206; ultimate
  beast's tail, 46; vacuum
  cleaner, 279
brush bag, lunar rover, 157
brush retainer screw, saber
  saw, 407
brushwood, wickiup, 82
brussa shirt, Arab dress, 475
bubble: monovial, 414;
  theodolite, 426
buccal, tooth, 446
buccal cusp, tooth, 446
buckaroo, 474
buckboard, 127
bucket, 280; launch
  pad, 154; tower
  ladder, 120
bucket hat, sailor, 481
bucket seat, car, 106
buckle: backpack, 337;
  brassiere, 191; combat
  soldier, 481; cowboy
  belt, 474; electric
  chair, 452; harness
  racing, 331; man's, 186;
  police gun belt, 482;
  sandal, 202; ski boot, 320;
  trench coat, 196; venetian
  blind, 237; waterskiing
  vest, 323; woman's
  hat, 199
buckler, medieval sheild, 454
bud: flower, 51; potato, 52;
  taste, 28; tree, 48
buddy umbilical system
  bag, lunar rover, 157
buffalo horn, ultimate
  beast, 47
buffer: elecator shaft, 76;
  train track, 112
buffet, 239
bug, ice cream cone, 261
buggy, horse-drawn, 127
bugle, 353
building, 75; city plan, 20;
  topographic map, 22;
  whole-timbered, 68
building material, 66
built-in microphone, tape
  recorder, 175
bulb: balloon, 477; blood
  pressure gauge, 439;
  clown, 477;
  hourglass, 229; light, 234;
  onion, 52, 258;
  thermometer, 18, 439;
  vacuum tube, 386
bulb head, drain cleaner, 412
bulb of heel, horse, 36
bulkhead: passenger
  ship, 138;
  powerboat, 135;
  sailboat, 131; truck
  platform, 117
bulkhead mounting flange,
  aneroid barometer, 18
bulk storage: oil drilling
  platform, 99;
  refrigerator, 245
bull, 30; zodiac, 493
bull denim trousers,
  cowboy, 474
bulldozer, 425
bullet: cartridge, 460; police
  gun belt, 482; stick
  umbrella, 226
bulletproof vest, 483
bullhorn, police car, 118
bullion, 221
bull nose, destroyer, 141
bull's-eye, dart board, 316
bulwark: castle, 78, 79;
  passenger ship, 138;
  sailboat, 131
bump, razor blade
  injector, 206
bumper: automobile, 102,
  103, 104; billiard cue, 314;
  bus, 114; citrus

juicer, 251; football
  helmet, 288; knee
  kicker, 242;
  locomotive, 113;
  mechanical sweeper, 123;
  sled, 322;
  snowmobile, 126;
  toilet, 271; train
  track, 112;
  trombone, 353; vacuum
  cleaner, 279;
  wheelchair, 442;
  windsurfer, 324
bumper car, amusement
  park, 90
bumper steps, truck
  tractor, 116
bun: sandwich, 259;
  woman's hair, 209
bundling, package, 265
bunghole, keg, 263
bunk, sailboat, 131
bunker, golf course, 395
bunting, flag, 486
buoy, 128; nautical chart, 22
buoyancy chamber,
  inflatable, 129
buoyancy compensator, skin
  diving, 325
bureau, dresser, 268
burette, laboratory, 437
burgee, flag, 486
burial chamber, 500
burner: barbecue grill, 284;
  camper stove, 336;
  candle, 233; chafing
  dish, 241; furnace, 390;
  hot air balloon, 326;
  laboratory, 437;
  stove, 244; tea kettle, 241;
  water heater, 391
burnisher, 371
burn sheet, ambulance, 119
burr: dental, 445; pipe, 412
burst, label, 264
bus, 114
busby, drum major, 479
bushing: automobile, 104;
  roller chain, 451
business, letter, 161
business-class section, jumbo
  jet, 148
bust, human, 25
bustle, tank, 464
bustline, dress, 194
bus transportation, public
  sign, 490
butane well, gas cigarette
  lighter, 224
butler, 473
butt: arrow, 456; ax, 454;
  bassoon, 351;
  bazooka, 462; billiard
  cue, 314; cigar, 224;
  cigarette, 224; fishing
  rod, 334; halberd, 454;
  latch needle, 378;
  pork, 32; revolver, 460;
  rifle, 461
butt cap: fishing rod, 334;
  tennis racket, 306
butte, mountain, 8
butt end, paint brush
  bristle, 415
butter compartment,
  refrigerator, 245
butterfly net, 401
butterfly swimming race, 310
butterfly table, 238
butterfly tie, 188
butter knife, 240
butter plate, 240
butte stile, door, 62
butt hinge, 450
buttock: horse, 36;
  human, 24
button, 205; accordion, 360;
  ballpoint pen, 160;
  blender, 250; camera, 170,
  172; cannon barrel, 457;
  cardigan sweater, 195;
  chain saw, 421; dental
  unit, 444; door lock, 448;

elevator car, 76;
  escalator, 77; fencing
  foil, 309; garbage
  disposal, 243;
  guillotine, 452;
  human, 25; incandescent
  bulb, 234; jacket, 184,
  192; lounger, 231; man's
  cap, 198;
  metronome, 361; military
  uniform, 480; organ, 354;
  plug fuse, 389; police
  car, 118; police
  uniform, 482; potter's
  wheel, 367; Revolutionary
  War general, 476;
  saxophone, 351;
  screen, 173; sewing
  machine, 274; skirt, 193;
  snake rattle, 40; sofa, 232;
  spur, 329; stopwatch, 298;
  suspenders, 186; sword
  hilt, 453; table saw, 407;
  tape recorder, 175;
  telegraph key, 159;
  television LaserDisc
  player, 181; trench
  coat, 196; trumpet, 353;
  vacuum cleaner, 279;
  vest, 184; video
  recorder, 180; violin, 349;
  woman's hat, 199
button-down collar,
  shirt, 185
button-down cuff,
  Revolutionary War
  general, 476
buttonhole: jacket, 184;
  Revolutionary War
  general, 476; shirt, 185;
  vest, 184
button mark, sewing
  pattern, 380
button nook, iron, 275
button-off collar, trench
  coat, 196
button-out robe
  lining, overcoat, 196
button rod, incandescent
  bulb, 234
button tab closings,
  pants, 187
button-through pocket,
  trench coat, 196
butt plate: rifle, 461;
  shotgun, 458
buttress, mountain, 8
butt section, fishing rod, 334
buttstock, shotgun, 458
by, symbol, 494
byline: magazine, 167, 168;
  newspaper, 166
by-pass shears,
  gardening, 417

C

C: braille, 496; piano
  keyboard octave, 355;
  music notation, 347; sign
  language, 496
cab: airport control
  tower, 93; bulldozer, 425;
  elevator, 76; fire
  engine, 120, 121; horse-
  drawn, 127;
  locomotive, 112;
  subway, 115; tractor, 424;
  truck, 116
cabin: aircraft, 146, 147, 158;
  hovercraft, 145;
  sailboat, 130, 131; space
  shuttle, 154
cabinet: air conditioner, 392;
  ambulance, 119;
  china, 239; desk, 272;
  dishwasher, 246;
  elevator, 76; garbage
  disposal, 243; guitar
  amplifier, 357;
  humidifier, 392;
  phonograph, 176, 177;
  television, 181; washing
  machine, 276

cabinet tip, screwdriver, 403
cabinetwork, house
    blueprint, 60
cabin pressure altimeter,
    pilot's instrument
    panel, 153
cabin trunk, powerboat, 134
cable: bazooka, 462;
    bicycle, 124; bridge, 95;
    camera, 171; circuit
    breaker box, 389;
    electrician's, 413; elevator
    shaft, 76; fencing
    strip, 309; gas pump, 108;
    motorcycle, 125; police
    car, 118; power line, 386;
    space suit, 157; stationary
    rings, 301; television, 181;
    tow truck, 122
cable stitch, sock, 203
caboose, train, 113
cabriolet, 127
cactus, 54
caduceus, symbol, 494
Caesar, playing card
    king, 342
cafe curtain, 236
caftan, 475
cage: baseball catcher's, 286;
    buoy, 128; circus, 89;
    drag racing dragster, 333;
    football helmet, 288;
    hammer throw, 295; ice
    hockey goal, 290; jai alai
    cancha, 308; police
    car, 118
caisson, cannon, 457
cake, 260
cake plate, 241
calamus, bird feather, 37
calcaneus, human, 26
calculator, 431
calculator dial, electronic
    flash, 174
calendar, grandfather
    clock, 229
calendar day, globe, 5
calf, 30, 422; frog, 42;
    human, 24
caliber, cartridge, 460
calibration: blood pressure
    gauge, 439; Geiger
    counter, 435
California Current, ocean, 6
caliper: automobile disc
    brake, 104; bicycle, 124;
    motorcycle, 125
calk, horseshoe, 36
calliope, merry-go-round, 91
callout, book page, IV
calm, hurricane, 17
calving, glacier, 12
calyx, coral polyp, 44
cam: lawn sprinkler, 418;
    motorcycle, 125;
    plane, 410; pliers, 404
camber, skiing, 323
cambium, tree, 48
cambox, lithographic
    press, 370
came, lead, 372
cameo, 214
camera: lunar rover, 157;
    satellite, 182;
    spacesuit, 157;
    still, 170, 171; video, 180
camera connector, video
    recorder, 180
camera platform, tripod, 174
camisole top, dress, 194
camouflage cover, soldier's
    helmet, 481
camper, 126
campfire, public sign, 491
camping, 336; road sign, 488
cam ring, brace, 408
can, 263; ammunition, 461;
    mercury battery, 387;
    nautical chart, 22;
    pacemaker, 442
canal lock, 97
canapé, 259
canard, jet fighter, 152

Canary Current, ocean, 6
cancel button: organ, 354;
    video recorder, 180
cancellation, envelope, 161
Cancer, zodiac, 493
cancha, jai alai, 308
candelabrum, 233
candidate's name column,
    voting booth, 427
candle, 233
candlepin, bowling, 311
candle slide, sideboard, 239
candlestick, 233; church, 85
candlestick phone, 178
cane, supportive device, 442
cane rod, fishing, 335
canine teeth, 446
canister: drain cleaner, 412;
    film roll, 171; police gun
    belt, 482; space
    shuttle, 154;
    windmill, 382
can ledge, can opener, 247
cannon, 457; horse, 36;
    jet fighter, 152; muzzle-
    loading, 462; tank, 465
cannonball, 457
cannula, hypodermic
    syringe, 441
canoe, roulette wheel, 340
can opener, 247; pocket
    knife, 416
canopy: bed, 266;
    bulldozer, 425;
    elevator, 76; glider
    cockpit, 147; jet
    fighter, 152; light
    fixture, 234;
    parachute, 327;
    stroller, 282; tent, 336;
    toll booth, 110
canopy jettison handle,
    pilot's instrument
    panel, 153
canteen, soldier's, 481
cantilevered suspension,
    racing car, 332
cantle, saddle, 329
canton, flag, 486
cantor, synagogue, 470
cantus, eye, 28
canvas: boxing ring, 303;
    painting, 364
canvas holder, easel, 364
canvas slot, sketch
    box, 365
canyon, 7, 13
cap: backpack, 337;
    baseball, 286;
    blender, 250; blood
    pressure gauge, 439;
    bottle, 264, 265;
    bulldozer, 425;
    camera, 170; can, 263;
    cartridge fuse, 389;
    chimney, 61, 228;
    chisel, 410; cornet, 353;
    dental, 445;
    dishwasher, 246;
    dispenser, 263;
    engine, 107, 133, 396;
    fence gate, 65; fire
    hydrant, 121; fishing
    rod, 334; football, 288;
    hair styling, 210; hinge
    pin, 450; hockey
    skate, 319; lamp, 234;
    lantern, 336;
    magazine, 168;
    maid's, 473; Manchu
    court dress, 475;
    man's, 198;
    military, 480, 481;
    mortar, 462;
    motorcycle, 125;
    mower, 419;
    mushroom, 55;
    pencil, 160; pin, 204;
    plane, 410; plug fuse, 389;
    racing, 330; razor, 206;
    railroad crossing
    signal, 111; rifle, 461;
    royal crown, 469;

saddle, 329; saw, 421;
    screen, 173; seeder, 420;
    shotgun, 458, 459; space
    shuttle, 154;
    standpipe, 57;
    stapler, 273; starting
    block, 298; stove, 244,
    336; tennis racket, 306;
    test tube, 437;
    thimble, 376; toilet, 271;
    track lighting, 235; traffic
    light, 109; umbrella, 226;
    venetian blind, 237;
    washing machine, 276;
    waterskiing towline, 323;
    windmill, 382
cape: land feature, 7;
    stonecutting, 336
capelet, king's, 468
capillary, human, 27
capillary tube,
    thermometer, 439
capital: column, 71; political
    map symbol, 20;
    proofreader's mark, 498;
    type height, 163; White
    House, 73
Capitol building, 72
cap mounting, ballpoint
    pen, 160
cap nut, 401
capo, guitar, 356
capon, 33
cappuccino, 248
Capricorn, zodiac, 493
cap opener, corkscrew, 247
cap square, carriage, 457
capstan: sword hilt, 453;
    tape recorder, 175;
    tugboat, 144
capstem, strawberry, 53
capstone, gate post, 65
capsule: bottle, 263;
    medicinal, 441
captain's seat, 747
    cockpit, 150
caption: book page, IV;
    cartoon, 374;
    magazine, 167, 169;
    newspaper, 166
car: amusement park
    ride, 90, 91; blimp, 158;
    drag racing, 333;
    elevator, 76; subway, 115;
    train, 94, 112, 113; see
    also automobile
carabiner, mountain
    climbing, 328
carbiner hole, ice ax, 238
carafe, coffee maker, 248
carapace: lobster, 45;
    turtle, 40
carbon copy, letter, 161
carbon-layered forward
    wing edge, space
    shuttle, 154
carburetor: automobile, 107;
    chain saw, 421;
    motorcycle, 125
carcass, furniture, 268
card: blister, 264;
    compass, 132;
    computer, 429;
    playing, 342
card bed, key punch, 428
card case, wallet, 219
car deck, hovercraft, 145
card holder: credit card, 222;
    elevator car, 76;
    typewriter, 162
card hopper, key punch, 428
cardigan: jacket, 192;
    sweater, 195
cardinal, religious
    vestments, 471
cardinal points, weather
    vane, 19
card loop, typewriter, 162
card punch, computer, 428
card room, passenger
    ship, 138
card stacker, key punch, 428
card table, 238

card window, wallet, 219
cargo, merchant ship, 136
cargo bay door, space
    shuttle, 154
cargo pocket, parka, 197
cargo ship, 136
cargo truck, airport, 93
caricature, cartooning, 374
caries, tooth, 446
carillon, III
car lift, passenger ship, 138
carom, billiards, 314
carousel, amusement
    park, 91
carousel tray, slide
    projector, 173
carpal, human, 26
carpels, samara, 50
carpenter's level, 414
carpenter's saw, 406
carpet, 242; sweeper, 278;
    tack, 242
carpus: dog, 34; human
    hand, 29
car ramp, hovercraft, 145
car rental, public sign, 490
carriage: baby, 282;
    cannon, 457; horse-
    drawn, 127; hot air
    balloon; toaster, 249;
    typewriter, 162
carriage bolster,
    stagecoach, 127
carriage brace, child's
    wagon, 283
carrier: aircraft, 142;
    dental, 445; dress, 194;
    etching press roller, 371;
    fireplace wood, 228;
    harness racing, 331;
    microscope, 432; pencil
    sharpener, 273; traverse
    rod, 236
carrot, 52
carrying chair,
    ambulance, 119
carrying handle: golf
    bag, 305; landmine, 463;
    machine gun, 461; movie
    projector, 173; outboard
    engine, 133; photographic
    bag, 174; rifle, 461
car seat, child's, 282
car service area, railroad
    yard, 94
car-station panel,
    elevator, 76
cart, lawn, 420
cartilage, human, 26
cartography, 5, 20
cartoon, stained glass, 372
cartooning, 374-375
cartridge: cowboy, belt, 474;
    film, 170, 171, 172;
    pen, 160; phonograph
    turntable, 176;
    weapons, 460, 461
cartridge fuse, 389
caruncle, turkey, 33
carving: scrimshaw, 369;
    tombstone, 500
carving hammer,
    stonecutting, 336
cascable, cannon, 457
cascade collar, bridal
    gown, 472
case: attaché, 281;
    battery, 387; beauty
    product, 213; blood
    pressure gauge, 439;
    cosmetic, 281; handgun
    cartridge, 460; hardback
    book, 165;
    harmonica, 360;
    lock, 448; luggage, 284;
    metronome, 361;
    padlock, 449; pencil, 160;
    pitch pipe, 361; police gun
    belt, 483; screen, 173;
    sideboard, 239;
    stapler, 273; tape
    measure, 414;
    thermometer, 18;

509

wallet, 219; watch, 216
casebound book, 165
casemate: castle, 78, 79;
  permanent fort, 87
casement window, 63
casework furniture, 239
cash register, 430
casing: calculator, 431;
  cartridge fuse, 389;
  door, 60, 62; electric
  meter, 389; hand
  grenade, 463;
  pacemaker, 442; pen, 160;
  pill, 441; pyramid, 69;
  slot machine, 340;
  telephone, 178; trumpet
  valve, 353; window, 63
casino, passenger ship, 138
cask, 263
casket, 500
casserole, 253
cassette: film, 171;
  operating table, 440;
  recorder, 175, 180;
  tape, 175
Cassini division, Saturn's
  rings, 3
cassock, 471
cast, denture, 443
caster; bed, 267; piano, 355;
  sofa, 232; wheelchair, 442
cast-iron casing, hand
  grenade, 463
castle, 78-79; chess, 339
castle pawn, chess, 339
castor, grand piano, 355
cast restoration, dental, 445
cat, 35; house, 59;
  circus, 88
catacomb, house, 60
catapult, 457; aircraft
  carrier, 142
cataract, river, 13
catch: door, 448; pistol, 460;
  swivel, 214
catcher: baseball, 286, 287;
  grill, 284; saw, 421
catch glove, ice hockey
  goalie, 290
catering truck, airport, 93
caterpillar track, tank, 464
cathedral, 84
cathedral hull,
  powerboat, 134
cathode-ray tube screen,
  radar and sonar, 434
cathode wire, vacuum
  tube, 386
catta, 35
cattle, 30
cattle crossing, road
  sign, 489
cat trainer, circus, 88
catwalk: canal lock, 97;
  prison, 74; tanker, 136;
  tunnel, 96
caudal fin, fish, 43
cadual peduncle, fish, 43
caution signal: pilot's
  instrument panel, 153; toll
  booth, 110; traffic
  light, 109
cautionary statement,
  label, 265
cavalry yard, frontier
  fort, 80
cave, 11
cavern, 11
cavity, tooth, 445, 446
C-band antenna, lunar
  lander, 156
CB radio, 179; police
  car, 118
C cell block, prison, 74
C-clamp, 399
cedilla, grammatical
  symbol, 497
ceiling: elevator car, 76;
  house, 59
celery, 258
cell: animal, 23;
  barometer, 18;
  battery, 387;

computer, 429; electric
  meter, 389; flower, 51;
  kite, 317; octopus, 44;
  parachute, 327;
  prison, 74; solar power
  system, 383;
  telescope, 433
cellar, passenger ship, 139
cello, 348, 349
cello wrap, packaging, 265
cellular kite, 317
Celsius scale,
  thermometer, 18
Celtic cross, symbol, 492
cementum, tooth, 446
cent, symbol, 495
center: basketball, 292;
  envelope, 161; ice
  hockey, 291; spider
  web, 38; theodolite, 426
centerable lens,
  microscope, 432
center aisle, theatre, 345
center beam, laboratory
  scale, 437
center bearing wall,
  house, 58
center circle: basketball
  court, 292; ice hockey
  rink, 291; soccer field, 293
center dent, cowboy hat, 198
center drawer: desk, 272;
  dressing table, 268
center field, baseball, 287
center front panel, girdle, 191
center-front seam, skirt, 193
center hole, phonograph
  record, 176
centering: radar, 434;
  sonar, 434
centering screw,
  microscope, 432
center leaf, hinge, 450
center line: airport
  runway, 92; badminton
  court, 313; fencing
  strip, 309; ice hockey
  rink, 291; lacrosse
  field, 293; Ping-Pong
  table, 315; symbol, 494;
  volleyball court, 313
center mark, tennis
  court, 306
centerpiece, dessert
  setting, 241
center pin, pulley block, 451
center post: camera
  tripod, 174; tatting
  shuttle, 378
center ring, circus, 88-89
center slat, sled, 322
center span, bridge, 95
center stand, motorcycle, 125
center stile, door, 62
center strap, tennis net, 306
center weight, discus, 297
centigrade scale,
  thermometer, 18, 439
central cleft, horse's foot, 36
central computer, prison, 74
central disc, starfish, 44
central focusing drive,
  binoculars, 433
central incisor, tooth, 446
central instrument warning
  light, 747 cockpit, 151
central inventory control
  unit, cash register, 430
central portal, church, 85
Central Standard Time, 5
central-vent volcano, 10
centriole, animal cell, 23
cents-off corner mark,
  label, 265
cephalothorax, spider, 38
ceramic shell, plug
  fuse, 389
cereal grass, 36
cercus, grasshopper, 39
certificate holder, elevator
  car, 76
certification, gas pump, 108
certification plate, truck

van, 117
cervical collar,
  ambulance, 119
cervical vertebrae,
  human, 26
cesta, jai alai, 308
chafing dish, 241
chain, 451; bear trap, 423;
  bicycle, 124; castle
  portcullis, 79; chain
  saw, 421; fire
  hydrant, 121; football
  sidelines, 289; gun
  belt, 483; grandfather
  clock, 229;
  hammock, 284;
  identification
  bracelet, 183; incline
  track, 90; jewelry, 215;
  king's regalia, 468;
  lock, 448; oil drilling
  platform, 99; spur, 329;
  swing, 283; tow truck
  bed, 122; zipper, 205
chain guard: bicycle, 124;
  lithographic press, 370;
  motorcycle, 125
chainlink fence, 65;
  prison, 74
chain lock, 448
chain mail, armor, 455
chain pin, roller chain, 451
chain reaction, nuclear
  reactor, 384
chain saw, 421
chain stopper, sink, 269
chair: ambulance, 119;
  dental, 444; electric, 452;
  powerboat, 135;
  reclining, 231;
  rocking, 230;
  wheeled, 442
chaise lounge, 284
chalice, 85
chalk, billiards, 314
chamber: burial, 500;
  camera, 172; cave, 11;
  Capitol, 72; combustion
  jet engine, 397;
  decompression, 442;
  fireplace, 228;
  revolver, 460; rocket, 397;
  stove, 394; torpedo, 466
chamber music
  ensemble, 348
champagne glass, 240
championship tee, golf
  course, 304
chancel, church, 85
chancellery, 84
chandelier: light
  fixture, 234; Senate, 72
changeout room, launch
  pad, 154
change pocket, jacket, 184
channel: backyard
  glider, 283; bowling
  lane, 311; canal lock, 97;
  CB radio, 179; laboratory
  scale, 437; lamp, 234; lead
  came, 372; nautical
  chart, 22; operating room
  table, 440; pliers, 404;
  police radio, 118;
  river, 13; stapler, 273;
  television set, 181;
  window, 63
channel selection controls,
  video recorder, 180
chanter, bagpipe, 359
chapel: castle, 79;
  church, 84, 85; frontier
  fort, 80; passenger
  ship, 139; prison, 74
chaps, cowboy, 474
chapter: book, 165;
  grandfather clock, 229;
  pocket watch, 216
character: cartooning, 374;
  clown face, 477; mah-
  jongg tile, 339;
  typewriter, 162
charcoal: briquette, 284;

sketch box, 365
charge, flag, 486
charge container, land
  mine, 463
charged particle telescope,
  satellite, 182
charger, tow truck, 122
chariot, merry-go-round, 91
Charlemagne, playing card
  king, 342
Charlie, stagecoach, 127
charm, jewelry, 215
chart: electronic weather
  station, 18; nautical, 22
chart table, sailboat, 131
chase: cannon barrel, 457;
  wall, 67
chaser, engraving, 371
chassis: automobile, 102;
  racing car, 332-333;
  machine gun, 461;
  television, 181
chasuble, cardinal, 471
chauffeur's cab, fire
  engine, 120, 121
cheater, wrench, 405
check: bank, 222;
  lumber, 66; ticket, 343;
  traveler's, 223
check bars, Universal
  Product Code, 430
check bit, harness
  racing, 331
checkbook clutch, 219
check digit, credit card, 222
checker, 339
checkerboard, 339
checkering, shotgun, 458
check-in, public sign, 491
check issue date, 222
check letter, paper
  money, 220, 221
checkout center, 430
checkpoint, prison, 74
check rein, harness
  racing, 331
cheek: cannon carriage, 457;
  dog, 34; horse, 36;
  hammer, 402; human, 24;
  latch needle, 378;
  piano, 355; pulley
  block, 451
cheese, 259; pizza, 261;
  slicer, 252
chelicera, spider, 38
chemin de fer, 340
chemise: dress, 194; queen's
  underpinnings, 468
cheng-lung, Manchu court
  dress, 475
cherry: ice cream cone, 261;
  police car, 118
cherry picker, tower
  ladder, 120
chess, 339
chest: dog, 34; horse, 36;
  human, 24; organ, 354
chest floor, cow, 30
chest of drawers, 268
chest piece, stethoscope, 439
chest pocket, jacket, 184
chest pod, still camera, 171
chest press, universal
  gym, 338
chest protector: baseball
  catcher, 286; ice
  hockey goalie, 290
chest pull, body
  building, 338
chevelure, 207
chevron, airport runway, 92
chicken, 33
chief, coat of arms, 487
chief clerk, Senate, 72
chiffonier, 268
chignon, woman's hair, 209
children: backyard
  equipment, 282-283;
  gear, 282; playroom,
  passenger ship, 139
chime: barrel, 263; bell, III
chimney: cave, 11;
  fireplace, 228;

furnace, 390; house, 60, 61; mountain, 8; volcano, 10
chin: bird, 37; human, 24
china cabinet, 239
china guard, dishwasher: 240
China Room, White House, 73
chine, powerboat, 134
chinning bar, backyard, 283
chinning station, universal gym, 338
chin piece, armor, 455
chin rest, violin, 349
chin strap: cowboy hat, 198; drum major's busby, 479; football helmet, 288; ice hockey player, 291; police helmet, 483
chip: blackjack, 341; craps table, 341; transistor, 386
chisel, 366, 368, 410
chitin, crustacean, 45
chock: destroyer, 140, 141; mountain climbing, 328
choil, knife, 453
choir, church, 85
choir keyboard, organ, 354
choir riser, orchestra, 348
choke, car, 106, 107
choked barrel, shotgun, 458
choke end, wood block, 451
choke knob, chain saw, 421
choker necklace, 215; Indian, 474; queen's, 468
chopper, helicopter, 257
chopping board, 257
chopsticks, electric wok, 253
chord: lift bridge, 95; music, 346
chord buttons, accordion, 360
chordophone, 356
choropleth map, 21
Christmas tree, drag racing starting lights, 333
chromatophore, octopus, 44
chrome, automobile, 103
chronograph, spacesuit, 157
chronometer, 216
chromosome, cell, 23
chuck: beef, 30; brace, 408; drill, 408, 409; fishing rod, 334; screwdriver, 403; scriber, 369
chuck-a-luck, 340
chuck tightener, dental, 445
church, 84-85
church key, can opener, 247
chute: dam, 98; jumbo jet, 148; mountain, 8; mower, 419; parachuting, 327; racetrack, 331; running track, 294; saw, 407; toll basket, 110
cigar, 224
cigarette, 224
cigarette lighter, 224; car, 106
cilia, eye, 28
cine scale, light meter, 174
cinch: backpack strap, 337; cowboy hat, 198; fastener, 204; saddle, 329
cincture: column, 71; religious vestments, 471
cinder, volcano, 10
cinquefoil, church, 84
circle: baseball field, 287; basketball court, 292; geodesic dome, 83; ice hockey rink, 291; shot put, 295; soccer field, 293; theodolite, 426
circlet, royal crown, 469
circuit, electric, 389
circuit breaker, 389; space shuttle, 155
circuit closer lever, telegraph key, 159
circular saw, 407

circular slide rule, 431
circulating pump: nuclear reactor, 385; solar heating system, 383
circulatory system, human, 27
circumflex accent, grammatical symbol, 497
circus, 88-89
cirque, mountain, 8
cirque glacier, 9, 12
cirrocumulus cloud, 16
cirrostratus cloud, 16, 17
cirrus cloud, 16, 17
citation: enlisted man, 480; police, 482
Citizen's Band radio, 179
citrus juicer, 251
city plan, map, 20
city symbol, political map, 20
civil aircraft, 148-149
cladophyll, asparagus, 52
clam, 45
clamp, 399; cassette tape, 175; drill press, 409; finishing sander, 411; laboratory, 436; lamp, 235; outboard engine, 133; Ping-Pong net, 315; paw, 406; telescope, 433; theodolite, 426
clamp bar, suit hanger, 277
clamp collar, camera tripod, 174
clamp holder, pumper, 121
clamp screw: combination square, 414; outboard engine, 133; sewing machine, 274; theodolite, 426
clapboard siding, house, 61
clapper: bell, III; buoy, 128
clarinet, 348, 350-351
clarstory, church, 84
clasp: denture, 443; hair roller, 210; identification bracelet, 183; keychain, 449; necktie, 188; pin, 204; royal regalia, 468
classification track, railroad yard, 94
class insignia, mainsail, 132
class interval, thematic map, 21
clavicle, human, 26
clavier, organ, 354
claw: bee, 39; bird, 37; cat, 35; clothespin, 276; flower petal, 51; grasshopper, 39; hammer, 402; lizard, 40; lobster, 45; rifle sling, 458; ring, 215; spider, 38; turkey, 33; turtle, 40; ultimate beast, 46
cleaner: automobile engine, 107; mower, 419; nail clippers, 211; pipe, 225
cleaning supplies, photographic, 174
cleanout plug, sink drain, 269
cleansing cream, 212
clear: shuffleboard court, 312; weather map, 19
clearance light: bus, 114; truck, 117
clear key, calculator, 431
cleat: baseball, 286; football, 288; sailboat, 131; snowmobile, 126; tugboat, 144
cleavage, human, 25
clef, music, 346, 347
cleft: horse's foot, 36; human, 25

clerical collar, minister, 471
clerestory, church, 84
clerk, Congress, 72
clerk's table, courtroom, 87
clew: hammock, 284; mainsail, 132
cliff, 7, 9
climax basket, 262
climbing, mountain, 328
climbing net, backyard, 283
climbing wax, ski, 321
clinch, horse's hoof, 36
clinic, White House, 73
clip: ammunition, 483; bicycle, 124; bow tie, 188; CB radio antenna, 179; chest pull, 338; dental, 445; hair, 210; jackhammer, 426; juice extractor, 251; microscope, 432; pen, 160; pistol, 460; pistol nozzle, 418; rifle, 461; stethoscope, 439; suspenders, 186; telephone, 178; venetian blinds, 237; and volt-ohm meter, 413; wallet, 219; woodcarving, 366
clip-on bow tie, 188
clip-on sunglasses, 286
clippers, gardening, 417
cloche, 199
clock, 229; basketball backstop, 292; car, 106; darts, 316; organ, 354; pilot's instrument panel, 153; 747 cockpit, 150; stove, 244
cloister, mosque, 68
close, letter, 161
closed chock, destroyer, 141
closed-circuit track, road racing, 332
closed coat, sandpaper, 411
closed quad, magazine, 169
closed teeth, zipper, 205
closer, brick wall, 67
closet, jumbo jet, 148
close up, proofreader's mark, 169
close way, permanent fort, 81
closure, 205; brassiere, 191; parka, 197; package, 264, 265; playpen, 282; swagger bag, 218; trousers, 187; woman's jacket and pants, 192
cloth: flat racing, 330; pool table, 314
cloth beam, hand loom, 379
clothes dryer, 277
clothesline, 276
clothespin, 276
clothing guard, wheelchair, 442
cloth lining, parka, 197
cloth said, windmill, 382
cloud, 2, 3, 16
cloudy, weather map, 19
cloven hoof, ultimate beast, 46
cloverleaf, highway, 110
clown, 477; circus act, 88
club: golf, 304, 305; playing cards, 342; police, 482
clubhouse, racetrack, 331
clubhouse turn, ractrack, 331
club-footed forestaysail, sailboat, 130
clutch: automobile, 104, 106, 107; checkbook, 219; handbag, 218; lithographic press, 370; powerboat, 134
clutch lever: motorcycle, 125; outboard engine, 133
clutch nut, juice extractor, 251
clutter control, radar, 434

coach: bus, 114; horse-drawn, 127; recreational vehicle, 126; train, 113
coaches' box, baseball field, 287
coach roof, sailboat, 130
coach section, jumbo jet, 149
coal hod, fireplace, 228
coal tender, steam locomotive, 112
coaming, sailboat, 131
coaming padding, powerboat, 135
coarse-adjustment beam, laboratory scale, 437
coarse calibrate, Geiger counter, 435
coarse focus adjustment, microscope, 432
coarse-motion clamp, telescope, 433
coarse teeth, hair comb, 208
coast, nautical chart, 22
coastal shield, turtle, 40
Coast Guard station, nautical chart, 22
coastline, 7, 15
coat: animal cell, 23; butler, 473; drum major, 479; fireman, 484; man, 184, 472; Revolutionary War general, 476; sandpaper, 411; ultimate beast, 46, 47
coating, sandpaper, 411
coat of arms, 487; Manchu court dress, 475
co-axial machine gun, tank, 465
cock: furnace, 390; internal combustion engine, 396; standpipe, 575
cockade, 476
cocked hat, 476
cocking handle, machine gun, 461
cocking piece, rifle, 461
cockpit: aircraft, 146, 147, 150-151; powerboat, 135; racing car, 332-333; sailboat, 130
coconut, 258; palm, 50
coda sign, music, 347
code: envelope, 161; magazine mailing label, 167; paper money, 220; traveler's check, 223
codpiece: armor, 455; boxing, 303
coffeepot, tea set, 241
coffe shop, public sign, 490
coffee strainer, 256
coffin, 500
coffin corner, football field, 289
coiffe, champagne cork, 263
coiffure, 209
coil: air conditioner, 392; automobile spring, 105; heat exchanger, 393; lasso, 422; metal detector, 435; postage stamps, 161; safety pin, 204; zipper, 205
coin, money, 221
coin bank, 447
coin box: parking meter, 109; pay phone, 178
coin chute, toll basket, 110
coin purse, wallet, 219
coin return: pay phone, 178; slot machine, 340
coin slot: parking meter, 109; pay phone, 178; slot machine, 340
col, mountain, 8
colander, 256
cold chisel, 410
cold cream, 212
cold front, 19
cold type, 164

cold-water faucet: bathtub, 270; sink, 243, 269
cold-water pipe: solar heating system, 383; water heater, 391
collapsible legs, ironing board, 275
collar: ambulance, 119; ascot, 189; barbell, 338; bishop, 471; blouse, 193; bolt, 401; bridal gown, 472; butler's, 473; camera tripod, 174; cardigan sweater, 195; drum major's coat, 479; fire extinguisher, 280; harness racing gear, 331; horizontal bar, 300; house beam, 59; jacket, 184, 472; kettledrum, 358; king's regalia, 468; maid's uniform, 473; Manchu court dress, 475; minaret, 68; minister, 471; power drill, 409; royal orb; 469; shirt, 185; shoe, 201; stove, 394; trench coat, 196; vacuum cleaner hose, 279
collarbone, human, 24
collection pan, air conditioner, 392
collector: solar panel, 383; transistor chip, 386
college pliers, dental, 445
collet, ring, 215
collimating screw, telescope, 433
collision bulkhead, passenger ship, 138
collop: human, 25; meat, 258
cologne, 213
colon: grammatical symbol, 497; human, 27
colophon, book, 165
color(s): horseracing, 330, 331; typewriter ribbon, 162
colored glass, 372
color selector, toaster oven, 249
colorstick, makeup, 212, 213
colt, 36
columbarium, church, 85
columella, nose, 28
column, 71; abacus, 431; basketball backstop, 292; cave, 11; citrus juicer, 251; cupboard, 239; drill press, 409; key punch indicator, 428; magazine, 168, 169; oil drilling platform, 99; piano, 355; punch card, 428; skycraper, 75; surgical table, 440; thermometer, 439; voting booth, 427
coma, comet, 3
comb: armor, 455; chicken, 33; escalator, 77; hair, 208; razor, 206; rifle, 461; shotgun, 458
combat aircraft, 152
combat infantry badge, 480
combat maneuver panel, pilot's instrument panel, 153
combat soldier's uniform, 481
comb holder, electric hairbrush, 208
combination dial, vault, 447
combination headlamp, automobile, 102
combination lock, safe, 447
combination pliers, 404
combination screw, telegraph key, 159
combination square, 414
combination water ski, 323
combination wrench, 405

comb strip, electric hairbrush, 208
combustion chamber: engine, 397; rocket, 397; stove, 394
combustion jet engine, 397
come box, craps table, 341
comet, 3
comfort-cable temple, eyeglasses, 217
comforter, bedding, 266
comfort lining, spacesuit, 157
comic book, 374
comic strip, 374-375
comma: grammatical symbol, 497; proofreader's mark, 498
command, television set, 181
commander's hatch, tank, 464
commander's seat, space shuttle, 155
command module, lunar lander, 156
command post, White House, 73
commemorative, coin, 211
commissary, prison, 74
commissure, horse's foot, 36
committee, room, Capitol, 72
common rafter, house, 59
common spiral galaxy, 2
communication umbilical, spacesuit, 157
Communion bread, 85
Communion cup, 85
commuter bus, 114
compact, beauty product, 213
compactor, trash, 243
companion benchseat, powerboat, 135
companionway, sailboat, 130, 131
company logo, pumper, 121
company name, letter, 161
company quarters, frontier fort, 80
compartment: backpack, 337; bus, 114; camera, 170; camper, 126; coat of arms, 487; drag racing dragster, 333; electronic flash, 174; garbage disposal, 243; hearing aid, 442; jumbo jet, 148, 149; refrigerator, 245; sealed voting booth, 427; sink, 243; wallet, 219
compass, 132; airplane, 151, 153; powerboat, 134; skin diving, 325; theodolite, 426
compass bearing, airport runway, 92
compass rose: nautical chart, 22; political map, 20
compensator sheave, elevator shaft, 76
complimentary close, letter, 161
composition: art, 362-363; typeface, 163
compote dish, 241
compound eye: bee, 39; grasshopper, 39
compound kite, 317
compound leaves, 50
compound microscope, 432
compress, medicinal, 441
compressed air: skin diving, 325; truck tractor, 116
compression member, geodesic dome, 83
compression strap, backpack, 337
compressor: automobile engine, 107; heat exchanger, 393

compressor fan, combustion engine, 397
computer, 429; key punch, 428; prison, 74; 747 cockpit, 150, 151; space shuttle, 155
computer ring, light meter, 174
concave knife, 453
concave lens, 217
concave mirror, telescope, 433
concave molding, grandfather clock, 229
concealer, makeup, 212
concentrating solar collector, 383
concentric sculpture, clam shell, 45
conceptacle, seaweed, 55
concertmaster, orchestra, 348
concha, outer ear, 28
conchology, 45
concourse, airport, 92
concrete block foundation, house, 58
concrete shield, nuclear reactor, 384
concussion grenade, 463
condensed type, 163
condenser: heat pump, 393; microscope, 432; nuclear reactor, 384
condenser coil, air conditioner, 392
condiment, 259, 261
conducting blade, cartridge fuse, 389
conducting rivet, plug fuse, 389
conductor: electrician's wire, 413; track lighting, 235
conductor's podium, orchestra, 348
conduit, 96; railroad crossing signal, 111; volcano, 10
cone: blimp, 158; citrus juicer, 251; combustion jet engine, 397; ice cream, 261; jumbo jet, 148, 149; missile, 466; phonograph receiver, 177; pine, 50; police car, 118; potting, 367; toll booth, 110; volcano, 10
Congress, 72
conical buoy, nautical chart, 22
connecting link, horizontal bar, 300
connecting rod: steam engine, 395; steam locomotive, 112
connecting wire, field events hammer, 297
connection: electric meter, 389; pacemaker, 442; parachute harness, 327; pumper, 121; sprinkler, 418; video recorder, 180
conning tower, submarine, 143
console: home computer, 429; lunar rover, 157; organ, 354; powerboat, 134, 135; skin diving tank, 325
constellation, 2
constriction, thermometer, 439
construction, road map, 20
construction sign, road, 489
contact: incandescent bulb, 234; movie camera, 172; plugfuse, 389
container, 262-263; blender, 250; land mine, 463; paint spray gun, 415

container ship, 136
containment building, nuclear reactor, 384
content, label, 264
content heading, book page, 12
contents page, magazine, 167
contest, drag racing, 333
continental margin, 15
continued line, magazine, 169
continuous battery monitor, Geiger counter, 435
continuous hinge, 450
contour: nautical chart, 22; topographic map, 22
contour feathers, bird, 37
contour line, map, 21, 22
contra-bassoon, 348
contraction, grammatical symbol, 497
contractor's saw, 407
contrast indicator, television set, 181
control, air conditioner, 392; aircraft, 150, 151, 153; automobile, 104, 106; ballista, 457; barbecue grill, 284; blender, 250; blood pressure gauge, 439; bulldozer, 425; camera, 170, 172, 180; canal lock, 97; cash register, 430; CB radio, 179; clock radio, 229; clothes dryer, 277; compass, 132; computer, 429; dam, 98; dental unit, 444; dishwasher, 246; drum, 358; engine, 396, 397; fire engine, 120, 121; food processor, 250; garbage disposal, 243; garbage truck, 123; girdle, 191; guitar, 357; hand glider, 327; hearing aid, 442; hovercraft, 145; humidifier, 392; iron, 275; key punch, 428; lunar lander, 156; lunar rover, 157; machine gun height, 461; metal detector, 435; microscope, 432; mower, 419; nozzle, 418; nuclear reactor, 384; paint spray gun, 415; parachute, 327; passenger ship, 138; phonograph, 176, 177; police car, 118; powerboat, 134, 135; projector, 173; radar, 434; railroad crossing signal, 111; saber saw, 407; sealed voting booth, 427; seeder, 420; sonar, 434; space shuttle, 155; spacesuit, 157; stove, 244, 336, 394; subway, 115; surgical table, 440; synthesizer, 357; telescope, 433; television set, 181; toaster, 249; toll booth, 110; torpedo, 466; tow truck, 122; tugboat, 144; typewriter, 162; vacuum tube, 386; video recorder, 180; wristwatch, 216
controllable landing light, helicopter, 146
control rod, window shutters, 237
control station, destroyer launcher, 141
control structure, dam 98
control tower: aircraft carrier, 142;

airport, 92, 93;
destroyer, 140
conversion scale, nautical
chart, 22
converter, vacuum cleaner, 279
convertible,
automobile, 102, 103
convertible sofa, 232
convex lens, 217
Conyne kite, 317
cookie, 260
cookie cutter, 257
cooking chopsticks, 253
cooking grid, barbecue
grill, 284
cooking unit, camper, 126
cook top, stove, 244
coolant pump, nuclear
reactor, 384
cooling fan clutch,
automobile engine, 107
cooling/heating coils, heat
exchanger, 393
cooling rack, kitchen, 256
cooling system: airport, 92;
automobile, 104
cooling tower, nuclear
reactor, 385
cool tip: curling iron, 210;
percolator basket, 248
cop, police, 482
cope, bishop, 471
coping, masonry gate
post, 65
coping saw, 406
copper foil, 372
copper surface, solar
collector panel, 383
copra, 258
copy: letter, 161; magazine
cover, 167
copyist, music, 347;
copyright: book, 165;
magazine, 167;
music, 347;
newspaper, 166;
symbol, 495
coral, cave, 11
coral polyp, 44
coral reef, 44
cor anglais, 348, 351
corbel, castle, 78
corbeled arch,
kokoshniki, 68
cord: air conditioner, 392;
bagpipe, 359;
ballista, 457; bedroll, 337;
bus, 114; CB radio, 179;
curling iron, 210; dental
X-ray unit, 444;
electrician's, 413;
fastener, 204; fencing
strip, 309; guillotine, 452;
hand loom, 379; hot air
balloon, 326; iron, 275;
jackhammer, 426; juice
extractor, 251; lamp, 234;
movie camera
microphone, 172;
parachute, 327; Ping Pong
net, 315; saw, 407;
snowshoe, 321; spinning
sheel, 379; string tie, 188;
tape recorder, 175;
telephone, 178;
thread, 376; track
lighting, 235; traverse
rod, 236; venetian
blind, 237; windmill, 382
cord holder, ironing
board, 275
cordial glass, 241
cording, mattress, 267
cordlock, backpack, 337
cordon, king's regalia, 468
cord strain relief: CB radio
microphone, 179;
finishing sander, 411; hair
dryer, 208; hand
drill, 409; saber saw, 407;
toaster oven, 249
core: apple, 53; brayer, 368;
earth, 4; human, 25;

mortise lock, 448; nuclear
reactor, 384, 385; paint
roller, 415; pineapple, 53;
skyscraper, 75;
typewriter, 162
corer, apple, 257
cork: bottle, 263; clarinet
mouthpiece, 351
corkscrew, 247; pocket
knife, 416
corn, 56
cornea, eye, 28
corner: boxing ring, 303;
brick wall, 67;
chessboard, 339; football
field, 289; house, 60, 61;
skyscraper, 75
corner cupboard, 239
corner cushion, boxing
ring, 303
corner index, playing
cards, 342
corner kick arc, soccer
field, 293
cornering lamp,
automobile, 102
corner mark, label, 265
corner post, house, 59
cornerstone, skyscraper, 75
cornet, 353
cornice: column
entablature, 71;
cupboard, 239;
curtain, 236; house, 59,
60; merry-go-round, 91;
minaret, 68; mosque, 68
cornsilk, 56
corolla, pea, 52
corona, column
entablature, 71
coronary band, horse's
hoof, 36
coronation mantle, king, 468
coronet: horse, 36;
queen, 468; royal
headpiece, 469
correctable ribbon,
typewriter, 162
correctional facility, 74
correction tape,
typewriter, 162
corrective device, dental, 443
corrector magnet control,
compass, 132
correspondence, 161
corridor, Capitol building, 72
corrugated diaphragm chest
piece, stethoscope, 439
corrugated fastener, 400
corrugated sole, ice climbing
boot, 328
corrugated staple, silk
screen, 369
corrugation: fastener, 400;
phonograph speaker, 177
corselet, queen's, 468
corset, 191; queen's, 468
cosmetic case, 281
cosmic mass, 2
cosmic rays, 3
costal fold, salamander, 42
costal groove, salamander, 42
costilla, jai alai cesta, 308
costume, historical, 476
costume jewelry, 214
cotter pin, roller chain, 451
cotton, dental, 445
couch, upholstered, 232
couloir, mountain, 8
count, magazine mailing
label, 167
counter: backgammon, 339;
footware, 200, 201, 202,
296; pool table, 314;
sink, 243; sailboat, 130;
sealed voting booth, 427;
tape recorder, 175;
type, 163, 164; video
recorder, 180
counterbalance, electronic
weather station, 18
counter current, ocean, 6
counterfeit money, 220

counterguard, sword
hilt, 453
counter hoop, drum, 358
countermeasures antenna,
aircraft carrier, 142
countermeasure warning,
pilot's instrument
panel, 153
counterscarp, permanent
fort, 81
countersignature, traveler's
check, 223
countersink bit,
drill, 408, 409
counterweight: elevator
shaft, 76; lift bridge, 95;
phonograph
turntable, 176; railroad
crossing signal, 111; stage
pulley, 344; window, 63
counting rod, 431
coupe, automobile, 102
coupled truck, 116
coupler, locomotive, 112, 113
coupler lug, camera, 171
coupler-tilt tablet, organ, 354
coupling: gas pump, 108;
hose, 418; train, 113
coupon, magazine, 169
course: brick wall, 67; drag
racing, 333; harness
racetrack, 331; meal, 259;
river, 13
court: badminton, 313;
barn, 100;
basketball, 292;
handball, 307; jai
alai, 308; Ping-Pong
table, 315;
shuffleboard, 312;
squash, 307; tennis, 306;
volleyball, 313
court cards, 342
court clerk's table,
courtroom, 87
court dress, Manchu, 475
courting seat, 232
courtroom, 87
couter, armor, 455
cove, 7
cove mold, staircase, 64
cover: automobile, 103, 107;
bagpipe, 359;
baseball, 286; basket, 262;
battery, 387; blender, 250;
book, 165; brayer, 368;
camera, 170; cassette
tape, 175; chain saw, 421;
clarinet pad, 350; combat
helmet, 481; desk, 272;
fishing reel, 334; food
processor, 250;
football, 288; garbage
disposal, 243; girdle, 191;
hand loom, 379; ironing
board, 275;
jackhammer, 426; juice
extractor, 251; kite, 317;
laboratory scale, 436;
magazine, 167;
matchbook, 224;
mattress, 267;
motorcycle, 125; paint
spray gun, 415; percolator
basket, 248; phonograph
record, 176; phonograph
turntable, 176;
playpen, 282; pocket
watch, 216; pots and
pans, 253; sewing
machine, 274; sketch
box, 365; skyscraper, 75;
smoke alarm, 280;
swing, 283; tea
kettle, 241; television
LaserDisc player, 181;
tepee, 82; theodolite, 426;
toilet, 271; vault, 447;
wallet, 219; water
ski, 323; window, 237
covered button cardigan
sweater, 195
covered way, permanent

fort, 81
cover plate: electrical, 338;
solar panel, 383
cover sheet, kite, 317
covert: bird, 37; permanent
fort, 81; turkey, 33
coverup, makeup, 212
cow, 30
cowboy, 474; hat, 198
cowcatcher, locomotive, 112
cow hoof, ultimate beast, 46
cowl: bobsled, 322;
helicopter, 146; outboard
engine, 133
cowlick, 207
cowling: airplane, 147;
outboard engine, 133;
racing car, 332
cow puncher, 474
coxa: grasshopper, 39;
spider, 38
crab, 45; zodiac, 493
cracker, nut, 257
cradle: telephone, 178;
telescope, 433; venetian
blind, 237
craft, 128, 129
cramp, wall, 67
crampon, ice climbing, 328
crane: aircraft carrier, 142
launch pad, 154; oil
drilling platform, 99;
skyscraper, 75
cranial crest, toad, 42
cranium, human, 26
crank: brace, 408;
camera, 171; drill, 408;
easel, 364;
engine, 395, 396, 397;
fishing reel, 334; lawn
sprinkler, 418; pencil
sharpener, 273; printing
press, 370, 371; truck
platform, 117
crank arm, bicycle, 124
cranked axle, Hansom
cab, 127
crankset, bicycle, 124
craps table, 341
crash helmet, 330, 332
crater, volcano, 10
cravat, 188
crawler track, tank, 464
crawler tractor,
bulldozer, 425
crawl space, house, 58
crayfish, 45
crayon, lithographic, 370
cream: makeup, 212, 213;
sundae, 260
creamer, tea set, 241
crease: cowboy hat, 198;
human hand, 29; ice
hockey rink, 291; lacrosse
field, 293; soccer
field, 293; trousers, 187;
woman's pants, 192
C recreation yard, prison, 74
credit, magazine, 167, 169
credit card, 222
credit card logo, traveler's
check, 223
credit card slots, wallet, 219
credit line, newspaper, 166
creek: frontier fort, 80;
river, 13
crenel, castle, 78
crepe sole, sandal, 202
crescendo, music, 346
crescendo, shoe, organ, 354
crescent, fingernail, 29
crescent and star, symbol,
492
crescent moon, 4
crest: coat of arms, 487;
dam, 98; dog, 34; enlisted
men's uniform, 480;
grandfather clock, 229;
horse, 36; human, 25;
iceberg, 12; lizard, 40;
mountain, 9; rocking
chair, 230; screw
thread, 400; wave, 14

crest rail, sofa, 232
crevasse, mountain, 9
crevice, mountain, 9
crevice tool, vacuum
　cleaner, 279
crew compartment, lunar
　lander, 156
crewel, stitchery, 377
crew neck sweater, 195
crew's quarters, passenger
　ship, 138
cricket, darts, 316
crier, and minaret, 68
crimp: cartridge, 460;
　painting brush, 364;
　spring board needle, 378
crimper, electrician's wire
　stripper, 413
cringle, mainsail, 132
crinoline, maid's
　uniform, 473
cripples, house, 59
crisper, refrigerator, 245
critical mass, nuclear
　power, 384
crocheting, 378
crocket, church, 84
crockpot, 253
crocodile, 41
crook: of arm, 25;
　bassoon, 351; brasses,
　352,353
crop: cow, 30; flat
　racing, 330; masonry gate
　post, 65
croquet, 312
crosier, cardinal, 471
cross, 84, 471; symbol, 492
crossarm: power line, 386;
　railroad crossing
　signal, 111; weather
　station, 18
crossbar: abacus, 431;
　bicycle, 124; football
　goalpost, 289; hand
　glider, 327; ice hockey
　goal, 290; lyre, 349; pole
　vault, 299; sawhorse, 398;
　snowshoe, 321; suit
　hanger, 277; weather
　vane, 19
crossbeam: ballista, 457
　gallows, 452;
　guillotine, 452; hand
　loom, 379
crossbelt, 467, 476
crossbow, 456
cross brace: ladder, 45;
　wheelchair, 442
crossbuck, railroad crossing
　signal, 111
cross-country skiing, 321
crosscut saw, 406, 407
crosse, lacrosse stick, 293
cross guard, knife, 453
crosshatching: cartoon, 374;
　and texture,
　composition, 363
crosshead, steam engine, 395
crossing: church, 85;
　railroad, 111
cross joint, brick wall, 67
crossknot, bow tie, 188
Cross of Christ, church, 85
crossover, railroad yard, 94
cross patée, royal
　regalia, 469
crosspiece: bow tie, 188;
　hand loom, 379; kite, 317;
　rocking chair, 230; sword
　hilt, 453; torii, 69
cross section: cave, 11;
　coral polyp, 44;
　fireplace, 228; frame, 373;
　hurricane, 17; insulated
　window, 63; lumber, 66;
　nuclear reactor, 385;
　permanent fort, 81;
　river, 13; stage, 344; tree
　trunk, 48; tunnel, 96;
　volcano, 10
cross stitching, 377
cross straps, overnight
　bag, 281

cross strings, tennis
　racket, 306
cross strip: kite, 317;
　wheelbarrow, 420
cross support, pool
　table, 314
crosstie, railroad track, 111
crosswise grain, fabric, 380
crotch: underpants, 190;
　trousers, 187
crotchet: grammatical
　symbol, 497; music, 346
crotch strap: child's car
　seat, 282; drag racing
　driver's belt, 333
croup: dog, 34; horse, 36;
　pommel horse, 301
croupier, roulette, 340
crown: anchor, 128; arch,
　70; bell, III; bird, 37;
　cactus, 54; coat of
　arms, 487; croquet
　wicket, 312; cut
　gemstone, 214; incline
　track, 90; man's hair, 207;
　man's hat, 198;
　needle, 376; palm, 50;
　pineapple, 53; royal, 469;
　staple, 400; tennis
　racket, 306; tooth, 443,
　445, 446; Torah, 470;
　tree, 48; watch, 216, 298;
　woman's hat, 199
crown cap opener, 247
crowning pavilion,
　minaret, 68
crown stabilizer, football
　, helmet, 288
crow's nest: tanker, 136;
　train caboose, 113
crucifix, church, 85
crumb, bread, 259
crumb incubator,
　cowboy's, 474
crumble roller, hitch
　and harrow, 424
crumb tray, toaster, 249
crupper, harness racing, 331
crusher claw, lobster, 45
crust: earth, 4; prepared
　food, 259, 261
crustacean, 45
crutch, 442
crutch socket, operating
　table, 440
crypt: burial chamber, 500;
　Capitol, 72
crystal, watch, 216
crystal pool, cave, 11
C sharp, piano keyboard
　octave, 355
C-strap, motorcycle, 125
cubbyhole, sailboat, 131
cube: backgammon, 339;
　camera, 170; slide
　projector, 173
cucumber, 52
cue: billiards, 314; cassette
　tape recorder,
　button, 175; phonograph
　turntable, 176;
　shuffleboard, 312
cuff: blood pressure gauge,
　439; blouse, 193; bridal
　gown, 472; butler, 473;
　fencing glove, 309; golf
　bag, 305; ice hockey
　goalie's glove, 290;
　jacket, 192; king's
　regalia, 468; maid, 473;
　Manchu court dress, 475;
　paramedic, 119;
　parka, 197; Revolutionary
　War general, 476;
　sailor, 481; shirt, 185,
　472; ski boot, 320, 321;
　sweater, 195;
　trousers, 187
cuff checklist, spacesuit, 157
cuff link, 214
cuirie, armor, 455
cuish, armor, 455
cuissard, fencing, 309

culet, cut gemstone, 214
cull, lobster, 45
culm, grass, 56
cultivator, 424
culture tube, laboratory, 437
cummerbund, 472, 479
cumulonimbus cloud, 16, 17
cumulus congestus cloud, 16
cup: armor, 455; athletic
　supporter, 190;
　ballista, 457; baseball
　catcher, 286;
　brassiere, 191; bugle, 353;
　citrus juicer, 251;
　Communion, 85; coral
　polyp, 44; football
　uniform, 288; golf
　course, 305;
　measuring, 254; plumber's
　plunger, 412; seed, 49;
　sketch box, 365; table
　setting, 241; thimble, 376;
　trombone, 352; video
　camera, 180; weather
　station, 18
cupboard, 239
cup level scale, coffee
　maker, 248
cupola: barn, 100;
　Capitol, 72;
　kokoshniki, 68;
　mosque, 68,69; tank, 464;
　train caboose, 113
curbside sidewall, truck
　van, 117
curb window, bus, 114
curd, cheese, 259
curfew, fireplace, 228
curl: pail, 280; wave, 14;
　woman's hair, 209
curled position,
　windmill, 382
curling iron, 210
currency exchange,
　public sign, 491
currency pocket, wallet, 219
current: electrical, 388;
　ocean, 6
current temperature,
　thermometer, 18
current unit patch, enlisted
　man's uniform, 480
cursor: linear slide rule,
　431; radar, 434
cursor positioning key, home
　computer, 429
curtain: cave, 11; four-
　poster bed, 266; living
　room, 236; overnight
　bag, 281; permanent
　fort, 81; shower, 270;
　stage, 344;
　stagecoach, 127;
　theatre, 345; Torah, 470;
　voting booth, 427
curtain rod, 236
curtain wall: castle, 79;
　skyscraper, 75
curtein, king's regalia, 468
curve, royal scepter, 469
curved jaw, combination
　pliers, 404
curved slat, rocking
　chair, 230
cushion: bowling lane, 311;
　boxing ring, 303; chaise
　lounge, 284; dog, 34; jai
　alai cancha, 308;
　lounger, 231; phonograph
　headphone, 177; pool
　table, 314; roller
　skate, 318; sofa, 232
cusp, tooth, 446
cuspid, 446
cuspidor, dental unit, 444
custodian's seal, voting
　booth, 427
customer's receipt, money
　order, 223
customized
　automobile, 102-103
customs, public sign, 491
cut: book, 165; key
　blade, 449; label, 264;

　magazine, 168;
　phonograph record, 176
cutaway coat: butler's, 473;
　man's formal attire, 472
cut gemstone, 214
cuticle: human fingernail,
　29; leaf, 50
cut line, newspaper, 166
cutoff rule, magazine, 169
cutout switch, 747 cockpit, 151
cut section, stained glass, 372
cutter: can opener, 247;
　chain saw chain, 421;
　cigar, 224; cowboy, 474;
　electric razor, 206;
　glass, 372; juice
　extractor, 251; kitchen
　tool, 257; pencil
　sharpener, 273;
　pliers, 404;
　wirestripper, 413
cutter adjusting-screw,
　expansive bit, 409
cutting board, 257;
　barbecue grill, 284
cutting edge: auger bit, 409;
　bulldozer, 425;
　chisel, 410; nail
　clippers, 211; plane, 410
cutting line, sewing
　pattern, 380
cutting surface, table
　saw, 407
cutting teeth, lobster, 45
cwm, mountain, 8
cyc, stage, 344
cyc hood, stage, 344
cycle: internal combustion
　engine, 396; symbol, 494
cycle selector: clothes
　dryer, 277;
　dishwasher, 246; washing
　machine, 276
cyclorama floodlight,
　stage, 344
cylinder: ambulance, 119;
　automobile, 104, 107; fire
　extinguisher, 280; internal
　combustion engine, 396;
　letterpress, 164; lock 448;
　locomotive, 112; offset-
　lithography, 164;
　padlock, 449; propane
　torch, 412; revolver, 460;
　rotogravure, 164; skin
　diving, 325; steam
　engine, 395
cylinder desk, 272
cylinder model, vacuum
　cleaner, 279
cylindrical buoy, nautical
　chart, 22
cylindrical slide rule, 431
cymatium, column
　entablature, 71
cymbal, 348, 358
cytoplasm, animal cell, 23

D

D: braille, 496; music
　notation, 347: piano
　keyboard octave, 335;
　sign language, 496
dabber, 371
dado, column pedastal, 71
daggerboard, windsurfer,
　324
dagger point position,
　windmill, 382
daiwa, torii, 69
dalmatic, cardinal, 471
dal segno sign, music, 347
dam, 98; cave, 11;
　horse, 36, 330
dampening roller, offset-
　lithography, 164
damper: fireplace, 228
　grill, 284; woodburning
　stove, 394
damper pedal, grand
　piano, 355
dance band, 348
dark control, camera, 170
dart: jacket, 184;

514

sewing pattern, 380
dart board, 316
darts, 316
dash: book page, IV;
car, 106; grammatical
symbol, 497
dashboard: car, 106; Hansom
cab, 127
dash-pot, toaster, 249
data cell, computer, 429
data code, magazine mailing
label, 167
date: check, 222; coin, 221
credit card, 222;
magazine, 167, 169;
money order, 223;
newspaper, 166; traveler's
check, 223
date display control,
wristwatch, 216
dateline: map, 5;
newspaper, 166
davenport, 232
David, playing card king,
342
davit: fireboat, 144;
powerboat, 134
day, globe, 5
day and time pre-set,
video reader, 180
daybed, sailboat, 131
day gate, vault, 447
daystick, police, 482
D cell block, prison, 74
DCmv scale, volt-ohm
meter, 413
dead bolt, mortise lock, 448
dead-end cap, track
lighting, 235
dead front plug,
electrical, 388
dead lift, universal
gym, 338
dead line, shuffle board
court, 312
dead man's stick, subway
motorman's cab, 115
dealer, blackjack, 341
deal patch, label, 265
death, darts, 316;
symbol, 494
debossed label, 264
decal, child's wagon, 283
decanter, 241; coffee
maker, 248
decathlon, 294
decay, tooth, 446
decelerator pedal,
bulldozer, 425
decimal key, electronic
calculator, 431
deck: aircraft carrier, 142;
destroyer, 140;
escalator, 77; fleet ballistic
missile submarine, 143;
house, 61;
hovercraft, 145; jumbo
jet, 148; kitchen sink, 243;
magazine, 168;
newspaper, 166; passenger
ship, 138, 139; playing
cards, 342; power
mower, 419;
powerboat, 134, 135;
skateboard, 318;
skyscraper, 75; sled, 322;
stage, 344;
surfboard, 324;
tobaggan, 322; truck
platform, 117
deck brace, steam
locomotive, 112
decked craft, 129
deckhouse, tanker, 137
deck manifold, tanker, 137
decompression chamber, 442
decorated initial,
magazine, 168
decoration: cake, 260;
canape, 259; man's
hat, 198; military
uniform, 480;
minister, 471

decorative engravings,
scrimshaw, 369
decorative inlays,
armor, 455
decorative perforations,
man's shoe, 200
decorative stitching, 377
deep, continental margin, 15
deep-frying basket, 256
deep-frying thermometer, 254
deep gouge, woodcarving,
366
deep medium gouge,
woodcarving, 366
deep throat, coping paw, 406
deer crossing, road sign, 489
deer ear, ultimate beast, 46
dee ring, Western
saddle, 329
defendant's table,
courtroom, 87
defenseman, ice hockey, 291
defensive guided weapons, 140
defibrillator, paramedic
equipment, 119
deflector: aircraft carrier,
142; power mower, 419
deflexor, hang glider, 327
defog control lever,
pilot's instrument
panel, 153
defroster, car windshield, 106
degree: longitude, 5; music
notation, 347; political
map, 20
degrees of arc, symbol, 495
dehumidifier, 392
delete, proofreader's
mark, 498
delta, 7, 13
delta-keel, kite, 317
deltoid, human 26
deluge gun, pumper, 121
deluxe suite, passenger
ship, 139
demarcation groove,
escalator, 77
demineralizer, nuclear
reactor, 384
demisemiquaver, music, 347
demitasse cup, 241
Democrat, Congress, 72
demographic data code,
magazine mailing
label, 167
denier, support base, 203
denim trousers, cowboy, 474
denomination: money, 221;
postal money order, 223;
traveler's check, 223
dental corrective devices, 443
dental equipment, 445
dental floss, 211
dental unit, 444
dentin, tooth, 446
denture, 443
department, magazine, 167
department patch,
police, 482
department voucher, money
order, 223
deposit box, vault, 447
depository, ambulance, 119
depression contour,
topographic map, 22
depth adjusting screw, hitch
and harrow, 424
depth: nautical chart, 22;
and perspective, 362
depth control, guitar
amplifier, 357
depth discriminator switch,
metal detector, 435
depth-effect hydrofoil, 145
depth gauge: 414; skin
diving, 325
depth-of-field scale,
camera, 171
depth stop, drill press, 409
derailleur, bicycle, 124
derrick: oil drilling
platform, 99; tanker, 137
derrière, human, 25

descender, type, 163
descending initial,
magazine, 168
descent stage, lunar
lander, 156
design: scrimshaw, 369;
silk screen, 369
designation: label, 264;
topographic map, 22
designer's initials, coin, 221
desk, 272; grand piano, 355
home computer, 429
desk phone, 178
dessert, 260
dessert setting, 240, 241
destination sign:
bus, 114; road, 489;
subway car, 115
destroyer, 140, 141
detachable collar,
maid's, 473
detail: house blueprint, 60;
political map, 21;
woman's jacket, 192
detection head, metal
detector, 435
detector: elevator
shaft, 76; metal, 435;
television set, 181
detent, levigator, 370
detergent dispenser,
dishwasher, 246
deuce service courts,
tennis, 306
deutsche mark,
symbol, 495
development flight
instrumentation control,
space shuttle, 155;
device: coin, 221;
execution, 452; flag, 486;
label, 264; police
uniform, 482;
supportive, 442
devilfish, 44
devotional candle, 233
dewbill, turkey, 33
dewcap, telescope, 433
dewclaw: cat, 35; cow, 30;
dog, 34; ultimate beast, 46
dewlap: cow, 30; dog, 34;
lizard, 40
dew point sensor, weather
station, 18
dexter supporter, coat of
arms, 487
D flat, piano keyboard
octave, 355
diacritic grammatical
symbol, 497
diadem, tiara, 469
diagnosis, symbol, 494
diagonal: telescope, 433;
tweezers, 211
diagonally gaited pacer, 331
diagram: political map, 21;
shuffleboard, 312;
sundial, 381
dial: aneroid
barometer, 18; clock
radio, 229; dental
unit, 444; electronic
flash, 174; electric
wok, 253; gas pump, 108;
globe, 1; grandfather
clock, 229; lawn
sprinkler, 418; parking
meter, 109;
phonograph, 176, 177;
sewing machine, 274;
sundial, 381; tape
recorder, 175;
telephone, 178; toaster
oven, 249; vault, 447;
wristwatch, 216
dialogue, comic strip, 375
dialysis machine, 442
diamond: baseball, 287;
dental burr, 445; playing
card, 342; roulette
wheel, 340; royal
scepter, 469
diamond stitch,

suspenders, 186
diaphragm: aneroid
barometer, 18;
kazoo, 360;
microscope, 432;
phonograph speaker, 177;
stethoscope, 439
diaphragm adjusting screw,
theodolite, 426
dice, 341
dice boat, craps table, 341
dice table, 341
dickey, Hansom cab, 127
die: 341; coin, 221; pipe
threader, 412
die cut, label, 264
dieresis, grammatical
symbol, 497
diesel-fueled internal
combustion engine, 396
diesel locomotive, 112
diestock, pipe threader, 412
differential, automobile, 105
differential thermostat, solar
heating system, 383
differentiation code,
magazine mailing
label, 167
diffuser, light meter, 174
digestive system, human, 27
digit: credit card, 222;
human, 25, 29; pay
phone, 178
digital display, clock
radio, 229
digital speed readout, police
car, 118
digiton, cartoon, 375
digitorium, piano, 355
dike, 98; volcano, 10
dimension: house
blueprint, 60; and
perspective, 362
diminuendo, music, 346
dimmer control, radar, 434
dimple: golf ball, 304;
human, 25; necktie, 188
dinette table, sailboat, 131
dingbat, newspaper, 166
dinghy, 129
dining car, passenger
train, 112
dining room, White
House, 73
DIN socket, movie
projector, 173
dink, 129
dinner knife, 240
dinner plate, 240
dinosaur, 40
diopter value, eye
scope, 438
dip: bow, 456; ice
cream cone, 261
dipping station,
universal gym, 338
diplomatic reception room,
White House, 73
dipstick, 107, 396
dip tube, dispenser, 263
direct drive, chain saw, 421
directional arrow, road
map, 20
directional letter,
weather vane, 19
directional light,
automobile, 102
directional-microphone
contact, movie
camera, 172
directional signal,
automobile, 102, 106
direction finder:
destroyer, 141;
helicopter, 146; 747
cockpit, 150
direction indicator: tape
recorder, 175; 747
cockpit, 150
directions for use,
package, 264
director, fencing match, 309
directory, elevator car, 76

directory number, desk phone, 178
dirigible, 158
dirigible mooring mast, skyscraper, 75
dirndl skirt, 193
dirt bike, 125
dirt shoe, mechanical sweeper, 123
disc, *see* disk
discard holder, blackjack, 341
disc brake: automobile, 104; motorcycle, 125
discharge chute, power mower, 419
discharge tube, fire extinguisher, 280
discriminator adjustment, metal detector, 435
discus, 295, 297
dish: bathtub, 270; chafing, 241; table setting, 240-241
dish rack, 256
dishwasher, 246
disk: bear trap, 423; computer, 429; eye scope, 438; harness racing sulky, 331; incandescent bulb, 234; light meter, 174; phonograph, 176; screwback earring, 214; shuffleboard, 312; starfish, 44; stingray, 43; television LaserDisc player, 181; video recorder, 180
dispenser: dishwasher, 246; kitchen sink, 243; washing machine, 276
displacement, chain saw, 421
displacement hull, powerboat, 134
display: calculator, 431; cash register, 430; CB radio, 179; home computer, 429; radar, 434; space shuttle, 155
display button, television LaserDisc player, 181
display control: pilot's instrument panel, 153; sonar, 434; wristwatch, 216
display function select switch, video recorder, 180
disposable bag, vacuum cleaner, 279
disposable razor, 206
distaff, spinning wheel, 379
distal, tooth, 446
distal transverse, human hand, 29
distance event, track and field, 294
distance heading indicator, pilot's instrument panel, 153
distance lens, eyeglasses, 217
distance runner, shoe, 296
distance scale, camera, 170, 171, 172
distilling equipment, laboratory, 437
distortion pedal, guitar, 357
distributary, river, 13
distribution map, 21
distribution of copies, letter, 161
distribution point, man's hair, 207
distributor, automobile engine, 107
distributor head, nuclear reactor, 385
district, thematic map, 21
ditch: castle, 79; permanent fort, 81
dite, cartoon, 374
divan, 232

dive break, glider, 147
divers' oxygen bottle rack, oil drilling platform, 99
diver's watch, skin diving, 325
dive timer, skin diving, 325
divided by, symbol, 495
divided highway, 110
divided highway ends, road sign, 489
divider: highway, 110; pocket knife, 416; zipper, 205
dividing line, domino, 339
diving board, 310
diving platform, 310
division: thematic map, 21; with slide rule, 431
division line, basketball court, 292
dock: horse, 36; sheep, 31
doctor blade, rotogravure, 164
doctor's unit, dental, 144
dodger cleat, inflatable, 129
dog, 34; bear trap, 423; fishing reel, 334; snack food, 261; workbench, 398
doghouse: grammatical symbol, 497; oil drilling platform, 99
dog's tooth, brick wall, 67
doldrums, wind, 6
dollar, symbol, 495
dolly, balance beam, 300
dome: Capitol, 72; compass, 132; destroyer, 141; dog, 34; locomotive, 112; mosque, 68, 69; percolator, 248; screwback earring, 214; silo, 100
dome cover, wok, 253
domed shell, cupboard, 239
domed structures, 83
domestic hot-water tank, solar heating system, 383
domino, 339
donjon, castle, 78
do not enter, road sign, 488
don't-come box, craps table, 341
don't-pass bar, craps table, 341
donut, baseball bat, 286
door: 62; automobile, 102, 103; barn, 100; bath and shower, 270; bolt, 448; bus, 114; camera, 170; church, 85; clothes dryer, 277; cupboard, 239; destroyer, 140; dishwasher, 246; elevator car, 76; fireplace ashpit, 288; garage, 61; garbage truck, 123; grandfather clock, 229; handball and squash courts, 307; helicopter, 146; house, 59, 60, 61; jumbo jet, 149; lobster pot, 423; lock, 448; locomotive, 113; mailbox, 227; mechanical sweeper, 123; piano, 355; powerboat, 135; prison, 74; refrigerator, 245; safe, 447; sealed voting booth, 427; single engine airplane, 147; space shuttle, 154; stove, 244, 394; subway car, 115; synagogue ark, 86; tent, 336; tepee, 82; toaster

oven, 249; vault, 447; washing machine, 276
doorknob, 62, 448
doormat, 62
door mirror, bus, 114
doppler shift, 2
dormer: barn, 100; house, 60, 61
dorsal fin, fish, 43
dorsal scale, snake, 41
dorso-lateral fold, frog, 42
dosage, pill, 441
dot: braille, 496; curling iron, 210; dice, 341; domino, 339; ice cream cone, 261; music notation, 347; sewing machine, 274
dotted half note, music, 346
dottle, pipe, 225
double, dominos, 339
double bar, music, 347
double bar bridge, eyeglasses, 217
double bass, 348, 349
double bed, 266
double-breasted jacket, 184
double bull's eye, dart board, 316
double-circuit tower, power network, 386
double-clip palette cup, sketch box, 365
double corner, chessboard, 339
double cuff shirt, 185
double-edged blade, shaver, 206
double-front pocket, shoulder bag, 218
double-hung window, 61, 65
double interlining, necktie, 189
double lancet window, church, 84
double lock, police gun belt, 482
double-neck bass and guitar, 357
double-pointed tack, 400
double prime, grammatical symbol, 497
double reed: bagpipe, 359; English horn, 351; oboe, 350
double ring, dart board, 316
double-score ring, dart board, 316
double seam, can, 263
double slide zipper, parka, 197
doubles line, Ping-Pong table, 315
double spread, magazine, 168
doubles service court, badminton, 313
doubles sideline: badminton court, 313; tennis court, 306
double star, 3
double top handles, swagger bag, 218
double-truck, magazine, 168
double vent, jacket, 184
doubling, house, 59
doubling cube, backgammon, 339
dough blender, 257
dowel, hammock, 284
dowel bit, manual drill, 408
down, bird, 37
down haul, windsurfer, 324
downhill skiing, 320
down marker, football field, 289
downpipe, house, 61
downspout, house, 61
downstream, river, 13
downstream gate, canal lock, 97
downstream stop log hoist, dam, 98

downtube, bicycle, 124
dozer, 425
draft, boat, 128
draftsman, house blueprint, 60
draft tube, sleeping bag, 337
drag, hot air ballon, 326
dragee, sundae, 260
drag knob, fishing reel, 334
dragon, 46; Manchu court dress, 475
drag racing, 333
drag shield, power mower, 419
dragster, drag racing, 333
drain: bathtub, 270; cleaner, 412; sink, 243, 269; washing machine basket, 276; water heater, 391
drain cock, furnace, 390
drainer, kitchen tool, 255, 256
draining rack, kitchen, 256
draining spoon, kitchen utensil, 255
drainpipe, house, 61
drain tank, nuclear reactor, 384
dram, symbol, 494
drape: curtain, 236; stage, 344, 345
drapery, 236; cave, 4; four-poster bed, 266
drawbridge, 95; castle, 78; permanent fort, 81
drawer: bureau, 268; cash register, 430; desk, 272; dressing table, 268; garbage disposal, 243; home computer, 429; medical examination table, 440; sideboard, 239; workbench, 398
drawer case, furniture, 268
drawing, house, 60
draw-knob, organ, 354
drawstring: ballet slippers, 478; parka, 197
drawtube: microscope, 432; telescope, 433
draw-works, oil drilling platform, 99
dreadnought, 140
D recreation yard, prison, 74
dredger, kitchen tool, 256
dress, 194; native, 475
dress-blue jacket, military, 480
dressed pelt, 197
dresser, 268
dressing medicinal, 441
dressing table, 268
dress shoe: king's, 468; military, 480
dress suspenders, 186
dress uniform, military, 480
dried leaf, onion, 258
drift, ocean, 6
drift-free arm, dental unit, 444
drill: dental, 444, 445; hand, 408, 409; oil drilling platform, 99
drilling platform, oil, 99
drill press, 409
D-ring, trenchcoat, 196
drinking water, public sign, 491
drip coffee maker, 248
drip cup, citrus juicer, 251
drip edge, house, 60
drip hoop, overhead power line, 386
drip molding, automobile, 103
dripless candle, 233
drip pan, candelabrum, 233
drip plate, stove, 244
dripstone, cave, 11; church, 84

drive: camera, 171
  chain saw, 421;
  merry-go-round, 91
drive axle tire, bus, 114
drive chain: bicycle, 124;
  motorcycle, 125
drive joint, hitch and
  harrow, 424
driven element, CB radio
  antenna, 179
drive piece, socket
  wrench, 405
driver: golf club, 305;
  harness racing, 331;
  stagecoach, 127
driver's box, stagecoach, 127
driver's fire suit, drag
  racing, 333
driver sideview mirror,
  automobile, 102
driver's observation window,
  tank, 465
driver's seat: bus, 114;
  Hansom cab, 127
driveshaft: automobile, 105;
  outboard engine, 133
drive unit, computer, 429
driveway apron, house, 61
drive wheel: can opener, 247;
  locomotive, 112;
  tank, 464, 465
drive yoke, hitch and
  harrow, 424
driving band, spinning
  wheel, 379
driving bit, harness
  racing, 331
driving glove, drag
  racing, 333
driving light, truck
  tractor, 116
driving suit, drag
  racing, 333
drone, bagpipe, 359
drone string, sitar, 356
drop: coffin, 500; roller
  coaster, 90; stage, 344;
  traverse rod, 236
drop armhole, woman's
  jacket, 192
drop box, blackjack, 340
drop cloth, painting, 415
drop earrings, queen's
  regalia, 468
drop feed button, sewing
  machine, 274
drop-in cartridge, movie
  film, 172
drop-leaf table, 238
drop-lid desk, 272
drop-out, bicycle, 124
dropped handlebar,
  bicycle, 124
dropped initial,
  magazine, 168
drop rail lock, playpen, 282
drop shoulder, woman's
  jacket, 192
drop-through fin cover,
  slalom water ski, 323
drug box, paramedic, 119
drum, 348, 358; automobile
  brake, 105; clothes
  dryer, 277;
  computer, 429;
  humidifier, 392; sextant, 133; venetian
  blind, 237
drum brake, motocycle, 125
drumlin, glacier, 12
drum major, 479
drum set, 358
drum shade, lamp, 234
drumstick: drum, 358;
  poultry, 33
drupe, peach, 53
dry-bulk carrier, 136
dry chemical fire
  extinguisher, 280
dryer: clothes, 277;
  hair, 210; lettuce, 256
dry fencing match, 309
drying, laundry, 276

dry measuring cup, 254
dry sink, 239
d.s., music notation, 347
D sharp, piano keyboard
  octave, 355
D string, double bass, 349
dual pneumatic liner system,
  football helmet, 288
dual rear wheel, tow
  truck, 122
dual scale thermometer, 18
dual wheel hub, tow
  truck 122
dubbing control, movie
  projector, 173
ducat, 343
duck, 33
duckbill pliers, 404
duckpin, 311
duct: clothes dryer, 277;
  eye, 28; furnace, 390; heat
  exchanger, 393; jet
  fighter, 152; racing
  car, 332
dugout, baseball field, 287
dulcimer, Appalachian, 356
dumbbell: body
  building, 338;
  keychain, 449
dummy type, magazine, 168
dump: fireplace ashes, 228;
  police gun belt, 482
dune: nautical chart, 22;
  shoreline, 14; topographic
  map, 22
dune buggy, 126
dust bag: sander, 411;
  vacuum cleaner, 279
dust cover: hardback
  book, 165; phonograph
  turntable, 176; vault, 447
dust flap, folding box, 265
dustproof screw cover,
  theodolite, 426
dusting brush, vacuum
  cleaner, 279
dust jacket, hardback
  book, 165
dustpan, 278
dust panel, furniture, 268
dust ruffle, bedding, 266
Dutch door, 62
dwarf star, 3
dye, hair, 210
dynamic marking, music, 346
dynamic positioning equipment,
  oil drilling platform, 99

E

E: braille, 496; music
  notation, 347; piano
  keyboard octave, 355;
  sign language, 496
ear: ax, 454; cat, 35;
  corn, 56; dog, 34;
  grasshopper, 39;
  horse, 36; human, 24, 28;
  lizard, 40; pail, 280;
  pig, 32; pot, 367; rocking
  chair, 230; scallop, 45;
  sheep, 31; tepee, 82;
  turkey, 33; turtle, 40;
  ultimate beast, 46
earclip, spring, 214
ear covert, bird, 37
ear cushion, phonograph
  headphone, 177
ear doctor, examination
  equipment, 438
eardrum, frog, 42
ear flap, baseball batting
  helmet, 286
earhole, football helmet, 288
ear hook, hearing aid, 442
earlobe, chicken, 33
earmark, cattle, 422
earphone jack, movie
  camera, 172
earpiece, desk, 178
earplug case, combat
  soldier's uniform, 481
earring, 215; findings, 214;
  queen's regalia, 468

ear scope, 438
earth, 3; core, 4; hogan, 82
earth dam section, dam, 98
earthen breastwork,
  permanent fort, 81
ear tip, stethoscope, 439
ear wire, findings, 214
easel: painting, 364, 365;
  tombstone, 500
East Australia Current,
  ocean, 6
Eastern Standard Time, 5
east longitude, 5
East Room, White House, 73
east-west handbag, 218
easy chair, 231
eave: barn, 100;
  house, 59, 61
eave pole, tent, 336
E cell block, prison, 74
eachinus, column, 71
ecphoneme, grammatical
  symbol, 497
economy-class section,
  jumbo jet, 149
ecru net, maid's uniform, 473
Eddy, kite, 317
edge: auger bit, 409; ax, 454;
  bayonet, 453; bugle, 353;
  cheese, 259; cheese
  plane, 252; coin, 221;
  cymbal, 358; drop-leaf
  table, 238; hang
  glider, 327; hatchet, 402;
  horse's foot, 36; ice
  skates, 319; knife, 252,
  453; necktie, 188;
  paper bag, 262; razor
  blade, 206; ski, 320;
  space shuttle wing, 154;
  sword, 453
edge flap, jumbo jet, 148
edge marking, airport
  runway, 92
edger, lawn, 419
edition, book, 165
editorial cartoon, 374
EENT specialist, 438
E flat, piano keyboard
  octave, 355
egg, 258; insect, 39
eggbeater: helicopter, 146;
  kitchen tool, 254
egg cell, flower, 51
egg rack, refrigerator, 245
egg slicer, 257
eighth-inch mark, tape
  measure, 414
eighth-mile pole, harness
  racetrack, 331
eighth note, music, 346
eighth rest, music, 346
eight pin, bowling, 311
eject button, cassette tape
  recorder, 175
ejector, dental unit, 444
ejector chute, circular
  saw, 407
ejector rod, revolver, 460
elapsed time, drag
  racing, 333
elapsed time bezel,
  wristwatch, 216
elastic, mitten, 196
elastic band: baseball
  uniform, 286; mattress
  cover, 267
elastic facing: brassiere, 191;
  girdle, 191
elasticized waist: shirt, 193;
  woman's pants, 192
elastic webbing,
  suspenders, 186
elbow: cat, 35; dog, 34;
  fence gate, 65; horse, 36;
  human, 24
elbow cup, armor, 455
elbow pad: basketball, 292;
  football, 288; ice
  hockey, 291;
  rollerskating, 318
elbow protector, fencing, 309
electrical cable, spacesuit, 157

electrical conduit, railroad
  crossing signal, 111
electrical connection:
  meter, 389;
  truck, 116, 117
electrical current, switch, 388
electrical power control,
  space shuttle, 155
electrical system,
  automobile, 104
electric broom, 278
electric can opener, 247
electric chair, 452
electric cord, potter's
  wheel, 367
electric eye, camera, 170
electric foil, fencing
  strip, 309
electric guitar, 357
electric hair brush, 208
electrician's pliers, 404
electrician's tools, 413
electricity: nuclear
  reactor, 384; solar power
  system, 383
electric kiln, 367
electric locomotive, 112;
  canal lock, 97
electric meter, 389; house, 61
electric organ, 354
electric pilot, stove, 244
electric potter's wheel, 367
electric range, 244
electric razor, 206
electric scoring machine,
  fencing strip, 309
electric starter, barbecue
  grill, 284
electric typewriter, 162
electric water heater, 391
electric wheelchair, 422
electric wire, railroad
  crossing signal, 111
electric wok, 253
electrocardiogram, 119
electrode: electric chair, 452;
  transistor, 386
electronic calculator, 431
eclectronic organ, 354
electronic countermeasures
  antenna, aircraft
  carrier, 142
electronic countermeasure
  warning light, pilot's
  instrument panel, 153
electronic flash,
  photographic, 170, 174
electronics rack, space
  shuttle, 155
electronic warfare antenna,
  destroyer, 141
electronic weather
  station, 18
electron tube, 386
electropneumatic retarder,
  railroad yard, 94
element, CB radio
  antenna, 179;
  dishwasher, 246
element release lever,
  typewriter, 162
elephant, ultimate beast, 47
elevated track, subway, 115
elevating tube, mortar, 462
elevating wheel, slide
  projector, 173
elevation: house, 60;
  topographic map, 22
elevation adjustment knob,
  rifle scope, 459
elevation lead panel, pilot's
  instrument panel, 153
elevator, 76; aircraft
  carrier, 142; airplane, 147;
  blimp, 158; glider, 147;
  jumbo jet, 149; passenger
  ship, 138; public
  sign, 491; skycraper, 75;
  stage, 344
elevator lock, camera
  tripod, 174
elevator platforms, desk, 272
elevator shaft, lift

bridge, 95
elevon, space shuttle, 154
eliminator, drag racing, 333
ellipsis, grammatical
    symbol, 497
elliptical galaxy, 2
embankment, railroad, 111
embattled parapet, castle, 78
emblem: drum major's
    coat, 479; flag, 486; paper
    money, 220
embossed label, 264
embouchure hole, flute, 351
embrasure, castle, 78
embroidered buttonhole,
    Revolutionary War
    general, 476
embroider cuff, king, 468
embroidered marquisette
    front, girdle, 191
embroidery, 377;
    queen's regalia, 468
emergency air vent, bus, 114
emergency brake: car, 106;
    subway car, 115
emergency channel: CB
    radio, 179; police
    radio, 118
emergency core-cooling
    system pump, nuclear
    reactor, 384
emergency escape chute,
    jumbo jet, 148
emergency exit, elevator
    shaft, 76
emergency light selector,
    police car, 118
emergency stop: elevator
    car, 76; escalator, 77
emery board, 211
emesis basin,
    ambulance, 119
emitter, transistor
    chip, 386
empire shade, lamp, 234
EMT, fire engine, 120
enamel, tooth, 446
enarme, shield, 454
enclosing trap, 423
enclosure: air
    conditioner, 392;
    letter, 161
end: banana, 53; can, 263;
    clay modeling tool, 366;
    clothespin, 276;
    cupboard, 239; diving
    board, 310; domino, 339;
    fencing foil, 309;
    flag, 486; football, 288;
    music, 347; spool, 376;
    suspenders, 186;
    theodolite, 426;
    tomato, 52; wrench, 405
end assembly, backyard
    equipment, 283
end cap: cartridge fuse, 389;
    seeder, 420; venetian
    blind, 237; waterskiing
    towline, 323
end cover, sewing
    machine, 274
end grain, lumber, 66
end handle, coffin, 500
end hook, tape measure, 414
endleaves, hardback
    book, 165
end line: basketball
    court, 292; football
    field, 289; lacrosse
    field, 293; Ping Pong
    table, 315; volleyball
    court, 313
end matter, book, 165
endocarp, peach, 53
end operating-screw
    handle, hand-screw
    clamp, 399
endoplasmic reticulum,
    animal cell, 23
endorsed check, 222
endorsement block, money
    order, 223
endpapers, hardback

book, 165
end piece: eyeglasses, 217;
    starting block, 298;
    zipper, 205
end plate, racing car, 332
end plug, vacuum tube, 386
endpost, fence gate, 65
end ring, fishing rod, 335
end slug, magazine, 169
end vise, workbench, 398
end wall, swimming
    pool, 310
end zone, football field, 289
energy: solar, 383; steam
    engine, 395
energy absorber: automobile
    bumper, 104; highway
    barrier, 110
engage switch, 747
    cockpit, 150
engine:
    automobile, 104, 106, 107;
    blimp, 158;
    bulldozer, 425; fire
    fighter, 121;
    helicopter, 146;
    hovercraft, 145; internal
    combustion, 396;
    jet, 149, 397; lunar
    lander, 156; mechanical
    sweeper, 123;
    motorcycle, 125;
    outboard, 133; power
    mower, 419; racing
    car, 332, 333; single
    engine airplane, 147;
    space shuttle, 154;
    steam, 395; train, 112;
    truck tractor, 116
engine chamber,
    torpedo, 466
engine company number,
    pumper, 121
engineer, and transit, 426
engine fuel shutoff
    handle, pilot's instrument
    panel, 153
engine hour meter,
    powerboat, 134
engine instrumentation, 747
    cockpit, 150, 151
engine louvers, tank, 464
engine mounting brackets
    inflatable, 129
engine oil-pressure gauge,
    powerboat, 134
engine room, passenger
    ship, 138
engine terminal, railroad
    yard, 94
engine test area, aircraft
    carrier, 142
English clock, darts, 316
English horn, 348, 351
English saddle, 329
engraved line,
    scrimshaw, 369
engraved plate, paper
    money, 220
engraving: identification
    bracelet, 183; knife, 369;
    and printing, 368, 371
enlarged scale detail inset,
    political map, 21
enlisted man's uniform, 480
ensemble, chamber
    music, 348
ensign, destroyer, 140
entablature, column, 71
entrails, fowl, 33
entrance: airport, 92;
    bus, 114; circuit breaker
    box, 389; highway
    cloverleaf, 110; igloo, 83;
    jai alai cancha, 308;
    lobster pot, 423; tanker
    belowdeck storage, 136;
    theatre, 345; White
    House, 73
entrée, meal, 259
entry, darts, 316
entry word, book page, IV
enumerating district,

thematic map, 21
envelope, 161; animal
    cell, 23; hot air
    balloon, 326; vacuum
    tube, 386; Zeppelin, 158
environmental control,
    pilot's instrument
    panel, 153
environmental monitor,
    space shuttle, 155
epaulet: drum major's
    coat, 479; football
    uniform, 288;
    Revolutionary War
    general, 476; trench
    coat, 196
epée, 309
epiglottis, tongue, 28
Episcopal ring, cardinal, 471
epitaph, tombstone, 500
equal, symbol, 495
equalizer; cowboy, 474;
    phonograph speaker, 177
equalizer buckle, venetian
    blind, 237
equalize space, proofreader's
    mark, 498
equalizing switch, tape
    recorder, 175
equal or greater, symbol, 495
equal or less, symbol, 495
equals: calculator key, 431;
    symbol, 495
equator, 5, 6
equatorial counter current,
    ocean, 6
equatorial current, ocean, 6
equipment bay, lunar
    lander, 156
equipment stowage box,
    tank, 464
eraser, pencil, 160
erasure table, typewriter, 162
erecting telescope, field
    glasses, 433
ermine pendant, Indian, 474
eroteme, grammatical
    symbol, 497
escalator, 77
escape chute, jumbo jet, 148
escarp, permanent fort, 81
escarpment, continental
    margin, 15
escroll, coat of arms, 487
escutcheon: coat of
    arms, 487; mortise
    lock, 448
escutcheon plate: kitchen
    sink, 243; safe, 447
espresso coffee, 248
E string, double bass, 349
ET, drag racing, 333
etching, 371
eternal light: synagogue, 86;
    Torah, 470
evacuation tip, dental
    unit, 444
evaporator coil, air
    conditioner, 392
evening handkerchief,
    queen's regalia, 468
event: drag racing, 333;
    information, ticket, 343;
    track and field, 294
ewe, 31
examination equipment,
    medical, 439
examination table,
    medical, 440
excavator, dental, 445
exchanger, fireplace
    heat, 228
exclamation point,
    grammatical symbol, 491
execution device, 452
executive office, White
    House, 73
exercise, body building, 338
exercise yard, prison, 74
exhaust: automobile
    engine, 107; combustion
    jet engine, 397; drag
    racing dragster, 333; heat

exchanger, 393; internal
    combustion engine, 396;
    locomotive, 113;
    motorcycle, 125; steam
    engine, 395; tank, 464;
    truck tractor, 116
exhaust duct: clothes
    dryer, 277; furnace, 390;
    tunnel, 96
exhaust port, outboard
    engine, 133; rocket, 397;
    skin diving tank, 325
exhaust tube, incandescent
    bulb, 234
exhibit hall, church, 85
exit: elevator, 76; jumbo
    jet, 149; theatre, 345
exit angle, slide, 283
exit bar, bus, 114
exit door, bus, 114
exit ramp, highway
    cloverleaf, 110
exit slot, instant camera, 170
exocarp: orange, 53;
    pineapple, 53
exonomist, 221
exoskeleton, insect, 39
exosphere, earth, 4
expanding bit, drill, 408
expansion chamber,
    thermometer, 18
expansion nozzle,
    missile, 466
expansion system, home
    computer, 429
expansion tank,
    automobile, 104
expansive bit, drill, 409
expiration date: credit
    card, 222; magazine
    mailing label, 167
exploration equipment, lunar
    lander, 156
explorer, dental, 445
exposure adjustment,
    camera, 171
exposure index, light
    meter, 174
exposure meter, 174
expression pedal, organ 354
expressway, 110
extended bay, barn, 100
extended-range flash switch,
    pocket camera, 170
extender, paint roller, 415
extending ball, pen, 160
extension: automatic rifle
    barrel, 461; baseball
    catcher's shinguard, 286;
    drop-leaf table, 238;
    folding rule, 414;
    operating table, 440;
    political map, 21; table
    saw, 407; vacuum
    cleaner, 279
extension handle, lunar
    rover, 157
extension ladder, pumper 120
extension scoring light,
    fencing strip, 309
extension tube:
    ambulance, 119;
    screen, 173
exterior, window, 63
exterior decoration, coat
    of arms, 487
exterior frame, tent, 336
exterior panagraph gate,
    subway motorman's
    cab, 115
exterior slope, permanent
    fort, 87
external auditory canal,
    ear, 28
external bud, potato, 52
external disk drive unit,
    home computer, 429
external door switch,
    dishwasher, 246
external environmental
    control, pilot's instrument
    panel, 153
external frame, 337

external fuel tank: jet fighter, 152; space shuttle, 154; tank, 464
external galaxy, 2
external microphone, cassette tape recorder, 175
external tank forward bay, space shuttle, 154
extinguisher: candle, 233; drag racing dragster, 333
extra cheese, pizza, 261
extractor: juice, 251; shotgun, 458
extrados, arch, 70
extravehicular activity handrail, lunar lander, 156
extravehicular visor, spacesuit, 157
extremities, human, 29
eye: ant, 39; ax, 454; bee, 39; cat, 35; cheese, 259; fish, 43; fishhook, 335; fishing jig, 335; frame, 373; frog, 42; grasshopper, 39; hammer, 402; hasp, 450; hook and eye, 204; human, 24, 28; hurricane, 17; instant camera, 170; lobster, 45; mallet, 402; needle, 376; octopus, 44; pineapple, 53; potato, 52; reptile, 40; sheep, 31; snake, 41; spider, 38; spring beard needle, 378; stirrup, 329; tadpole, 42; toad, 42
eyeball, 28
eyebolt, 401
eyebrow, 28; magazine, 169; woman's, 209
eye colorstick, 212, 213
eyecup: binoculars, 433; camera, 171, 180
eye doctor, examination equipment, 438
eyedropper, 441
eyeglasses, 217
eye guards, fireman's helmet, 484
eyelashes, 28, 209; liner, 212, 213
eyelet: baseball glove, 287; camera, 171; ice skates, 319; man's belt, 186; cap, 198; man's shoe, 200; running shoe, 296; shoulder bag, 218
eyelid: frog, 42; human, 28
eyeliner, makeup, 212
eyepatch, pirate, 476
eye pencil, 213
eyepiece: binoculars, 433; camera, 170, 172; ear scope, 438; eye scope, 438; microscope, 432; telescope, 433; theodolite, 426
eyeport shield, drag racing driver, 333
eye scope, 438
eye shadow, 213
eye socket, 28
eyespot, starfish, 44
eyestay, running shoe, 296
eye teeth, 446
eyewires, eyeglasses, 217

F

F: braille, 496; music notation, 347; piano keyboard octave, 355; sign language, 496
fabric, 380; embroidery, 377; hand knitting,

quilting, 377; umbrella, 226; weaving, 379
fabric flowers, woman's hat, 199
fabric ridge, embroidery ring, 377
fabric temperature guide, iron, 275
fabric-tension lock, screen, 173
face: ax, 454; bow, 456; brick, 66; check, 222; clown, 477; coin, 221; croquet mallet, 312; dart board, 316; elliptical galaxy, 2; file, 410; gas pump, 108; geodesic dome, 83; golf club, 304; grandfather clock, 229; hammer, 402; lacrosse stick, 293; lead came, 372; lumber, 66; mountain, 8, 9; obelisk, 69; paper bag, 262; Ping-Pong racket, 315; playing cards, 342; rasp, 410; saw tooth, 406; sheep, 31; shower, 270; slot machine, 340; spider, 38; starting block, 298; sword, 453; tennis racket, 306; traffic light, 109; type, 164; voting booth, 427; wall, 67; wristwatch, 216; zipper, 205
face cards, 342
face mask: baseball catcher, 286; football helmet, 288; ice hockey goalie, 290; lacrosse, 293; skin diving, 325
face-off circle, ice hockey rink, 291
faceplate: mortise lock, 448; paper money, 221; sewing machine, 274; ski helmet, 320
face shield, police, 482
facet, cut gemstone, 214
face value, money, 220, 221
facing: brassiere, 191; girdle, 191; necktie, 189; skyscraper, 75; woman's jacket, 192
facing dragon, Manchu court dress, 475
Fahrenheit scale, thermometer, 18, 439
fairing, helicopter, 146
fair territory, baseball field, 287
fairwater, outboard engine, 133
fairway, golf course, 304
fairweather, submarine, 143
faja, jai alai player, 308
fall: grand piano, 355; pulley block rope, 451; woman's hair, 209
falling front desk, 272
falling rock, public sign, 491
false edge, knife, 453
false teeth, 443
family name, typeface, 163
fan: air circulating, 392; automobile, 104, 107; bridal costume, 472; combustion jet engine, 397; heat exchanger, 393; high jump, 294; hovercraft, 145; jumbo jet, 149; lizard throat, 40; lobster tail, 45; subway car, 115; underwater tunnel, 96; vacuum cleaner, 279
fan belt, 107
fan clutch, 107
fancy stitching, boot, 202
fang: snake, 40, 41;

spider, 38; tooth, 446
fanlight, door, 62
fan plate, armor, 455
fan switch, elevator, 76
fantail: destroyer, 140; passenger ship, 138; windmill, 382
fare box, commuter bus, 114
faring, motorcycle, 125
farm machinery, road sign, 489
far turn, harness racetrack, 331
fascia, house, 58, 59
fastener, 204; corrugated, 400; football helmet, 288; hollow wall, 401; overnight bag, 281; spacesuit, 157
fastening, bell, III
fast forward: tape recorder, 175; television LaserDisc player, 181
fastigiated top, skyscraper, 75
fast-rewind button, tape recorder, 175
fat, meat, 258
fat back, pork, 32
father, flat racing entry, 330
fathom, nautical chart, 22
fatigue belt, 481
fatigue pants, 481
fatigue shirt, 481
fauces, tongue, 28
faucet, 269; bathtub, 270; hose coupling, 418; kitchen sink, 243
fault line, jai alai cancha, 308
F clef, music, 347
feather: badminton shuttlecock, 313; bird, 37; chicken, 33; turkey, 33; weather vane, 19; woman's hat, 199
feather pen, 160
feature spread, magazine, 168-169
feature stripes, powerboat, 134
feature well, magazine, 167
Federal Reserve Bank seal, paper money, 220
Federal Reserve note, 220
federal route number, road map, 20
feed: drill press, 409; machine gun ammunition, 461; track lighting, 235
feed dog, sewing machine, 274
feeder cap, blender, 250
feeder waveguide, radar antenna, 434
feeding pen, barnyard, 100
feed line, furnace, 390
feed passage, barn, 100
feed plate, machine gun, 461
feed screw, auger bit, 409
feed-through, pacemaker, 442
feed tube: food processor, 250; fountain pen, 160
feedwater pump, nuclear reactor, 384
fee indicator, toll booth, 110
feeler: cat, 35; lobster, 45
feet: nautical chart, 22; type, 164
felloe, stagecoach, 127
felt: film roll, 171; pool table, 314
felt cap, baseball gear; 286
felt hat, cowboy, 474
female, symbol, 494
female coupling, hose connection, 418
female ferrule, fishing rod, 334
female flower, corn, 56
female-male, symbol, 492

female receptacle, electrical, 388
femur: frog, 42; grasshopper, 39; human, 26; spider, 38
fence, 65; baseball field, 287; house, 61; prison, 74; table saw, 407
fence posts, 65
fencing, 309; barnyard, 100
fencing shoe, 309
fencing strip, wood fence, 65
fender: automobile, 102, 103; bicycle, 124; bulldozer, 425; fireplace, 228; lift bridge, 95; motorcycle, 125; saddle, 329; tractor, 424; tugboat, 144
fender guard, gas pump automatic nozzle, 108
fermata, music, 346
fern, 55
ferris wheel, 91
ferrule: billiard cue, 314; burnisher, 371; clay modeling tool, 366; chisel, 410; fishing rod, 334; gouge, 368; hoe, 417; jump rope, 338; paint brush, 415; painting brush, 364; pencil, 160; rake, 417; screwdriver, 403; shoe tree, 203; sousaphone, 352; stick umbrella, 226; tuba, 352; woodcarving tool, 366
fertilizer, 420
fess, coat of arms, 487
fetlock, horse, 36
fettling tool, potter's wheel, 367
F-hole, violin, 349
fiber: paper money, 220; rope, 128
fiberglass pole, pole vaulting, 299
fibula, human, 26
fiddle: bass, 349; tub, 360
field: baseball, 287; coat of arms, 487; coin, 221; craps table, 341; flag, 486; football, 289; lacrosse, 293; mountain, 9; soccer, 293; track and field, 294-295
field events equipment, 297
field fortification, 80
fieldglasses, 433
fife, marching band, 348
15' marker, bowling lane, 311
fifth wheel, truck trailer, 116
50-yard line, football field, 289
51-in-5's, darts, 316
50-point ring, dart board, 316
fighter, jet aircraft, 152
fighting chair, powerboat, 135
fighting kite, 317
fighting ship, surface, 140-141
figure skates, 319
filament: coral polyp, 44; flower stamen, 51; incandescent bulb, 234; vacuum tube, 386
file, 410; briefcase, 281; chessboard, 339; desk, 272; nail, 211; pocket knife, 416
file handle, drill, 408
filet, cannon barrel, 457
file-type handle, coping saw, 406
fill, sleeping bag, 337
filler: cigar, 224; inflatable, 129; locomotive, 113; man's

belt, 186; quilting, 377
filler neck, automobile gas
    tank, 105
filler tube: automobile engine
    power steering, 107;
    toilet, 271
fillet, royal regalia, 469
filling, dental, 445;
    dessert, 260; quiche, 259;
    sandwich, 259;
    scrimshaw, 369; sleeping
    bag, 337
filling port, iron, 275
fill opening, coffee
    maker, 248
fill unit float,
    dishwasher, 246
filly, horse, 36
film, camera, 170, 171, 172
filming trigger, movie
    camera, 172
film-loading port, movie
    projector, 173
film projector, 173
film speed: camera, 171;
    lightmeter, 174
filter: air conditioner, 392;
    camera, 171;
    cigarette, 224; dryer, 277;
    coffee maker, 248; drag
    racing driver's fire
    suit, 333; engine, 107,
    396; heat exchanger, 393;
    tractor, 424; washing
    machine, 276
filter carrier, microscope, 432
fin: air conditioner, 392;
    automobile, 103;
    blimp, 158; fish, 43;
    glider, 147;
    hovercraft, 145; jet
    fighter, 152; jumbo
    jet, 149; missile, 466; rifle
    grenade, 463; single
    engine airplane, 147; skin
    diving, 325; stingray, 43;
    surfboard, 324;
    torpedo, 466;
    waterskiing, 323;
    windsurfer, 324
fin cover, slalom water
    ski, 323
findings, jewelry, 214
fine-adjustment beam,
    laboratory scale, 437
fine calibrate, Geiger
    counter, 435
fine focus: microscope, 432;
    telescope, 433
fine tooth, hair comb, 208
fine tuner, metal
    detector, 435
finger: baseball glove, 287;
    frog, 42; hair roller, 210;
    handball glove, 307;
    human, 24, 29; laboratory
    clamp, 436; ultimate
    beast, 47
fingerboard: accordion, 360;
    guitar, 356, 357;
    violin, 349
finger flange, hypodermic
    syringe, 441
fingerless glove, miser, 476
finger grip: hair clip, 210;
    sewing machine, 274
finger hole: bowling
    ball, 311; desk phone, 178
finger hook, trumpet, 353
fingernail, 29
finger pad, 29
fingerplate, clarinet, 350
fingerprint, human, 29
finger pump, camp
    stove, 336
finger stop, desk phone, 178
fingertip: dog, 34; human, 29
finial: church, 84; dressing
    table, 268; flagpole, 486;
    four-poster bed, 266; gate
    post, 65; grandfather
    clock, 229; lamp, 234;
    pagoda, 69; woodburning

stove, 394
finish: drag racing, 333;
    football, 288; stained
    glass, 372
finishing cap, umbrella, 226
finishing nail, 400
finishing sander, 411
finishing wire, umbrella
    runner, 226
finish line: harness
    racetrack, 331; running
    track, 295
finned projectile, mortar, 462
fin-seal wrap, package, 265
fin stabilizer, destroyer, 141
fire, gemstone, 214
fireback, fireplace, 228
fireball, launch pad, 154
fireboat, 144
fireboot, 484
fire bowl, brazier, 284
firebox, fireplace, 228
fire curtain, stage, 344
fired handguns, 460
fired pot, 367
fire-eater, circus, 88
fire engine, 120-121
fire extinguisher, 280; drag
    racing dragster, 333;
    police car, 118; tow
    truck, 122
fire-fighting station,
    tanker, 137
fire hydrant, 121
fire irons, fireplace, 228
fireman, 484;
    suspenders, 186
fire pit, tepee, 82
fireplace, 228
fire plug, 121
fire screen, fireplace, 228
fire stop, house, 58
fire suit, drag racing
    driver's, 333
firing chamber, kiln, 367
firing cone, potting, 367
firing lever, machine
    gun, 461
firing pin: gun, 460;
    mortar, 462; torpedo, 466
firing tube, bazooka, 462
firing vent, cannon
    barrel, 457
firn, mountain, 9
first aid, public sign, 490
first-aid box, fire engine, 120
first-aid kit, police car, 118
first base: baseball field, 287;
    blackjack, 341
first baseman's mitt, 287
first bicuspid, 446
first-class section, jumbo
    jet, 148
first floor, White House, 73
First Lady's office, White
    House, 73
first meridian, globe, 5
first molar, 446
first officer's seat,
    747 cockpit, 151
first premolar, 446
first quarter moon, 4
first reef position, windmill,
    382
first reinforce, cannon
    barrel, 457
first stage: missile, 466; skin
    diving tank, 325
first valve, trumpet, 353
first valve slide: French
    horn, 352; trumpet, 353
first violin, 348
fish, 43; zodiac, 493
fishing, 334-335
fish ladder, dam, 98
fishplate, railroad track, 111
fish scaler, pocket knife, 416
fish tail, coffin, 500
fishtail chisel,
    woodcarving, 366
fishtail gouge,
    woodcarving, 366
fishway, dam, 98

fission, nuclear reactor, 384
fissure volcano, 10
fist, human, 25
fitted cuff, bridal gown, 472
fitted pillow, sofa, 232
fitted sheet, bedding, 267
fitting: nozzle, 418;
    pumper, 121; saw, 406;
    shoulder bag, 218;
    shower, 270; sink, 269
five pin, bowling, 311
5/8 pole, harness
    racetrack, 331
five-unit beads, abacus, 431
fixed bridge, 95
fixed glove, jet fighter, 152
fixed hurdle, 298
fixed jaw: C-clamp, 399;
    monkey wrench, 405
fixed pin, hinge, 450
fixed service structure,
    launch pad, 154
fixed window, 63
fixings, ice cream, 261
fixture, sink, 243
flag, 486; courtroom, 87;
    football field, 289; golf
    course, 305; mailbox, 227;
    music note, 347;
    newspaper, 166; parking
    meter, 109; soccer
    field, 293; swimming
    pool, 310; track and
    field, 295
flagged end, paint brush
    bristle, 415
flagpole, 486
flagstaff, destroyer, 140
flake, tennis racket, 306
flame: candle, 233;
    dental, 445; four-poster
    bed finial, 266
flame bucket, launch
    pad, 154
flame adjustment wheel, gas
    cigarette lighter, 224
flan, coin, 221
flange: barometer, 18;
    hypodermic syringe, 441;
    mace, 454; sink, 269;
    spool, 376; trombone, 352
flank: beef, 30; cat, 35;
    dog, 34; horse, 36;
    human, 25; lamb, 31;
    pelt, 197; permanent
    fort, 81; pork, 32
flank billet, Western
    saddle, 329
flap, 486; backpack, 337; baseball
    helmet, 286; checkbook
    clutch, 219;
    envelope, 161; hasp, 450;
    jumbo jet, 148; magazine
    cover, 167; man's
    shoe, 200; matchbook, 224;
    package, 265;
    pocket, 184, 185, 192,
    196; saddle, 329; sailor's
    uniform, 481; shoulder
    bag, 218; single engine
    airplane, 147; slalom
    water ski, 323; tent, 336;
    tepee, 82; tow truck, 122;
    wallet, 219
flap lever, 747 cockpit, 151
flare: police car, 118;
    solar, 3; trombone, 353;
    trousers, 187
flare fitting, plumbing, 412
flaring tool, plumbing, 412
flash: camera, 170, 171;
    electronic, 174; radar, 434
flasher, locomotive, 113
flash head: electronic
    flash, 174; lunar lander, 156
flashlight, police, 483
flash suppressor, automatic
    weapon, 461
flask, laboratory, 437
flat: music, 346; stage, 344
flat bed, truck, 117
flat-bottom hull,

powerboat, 134
flatcar, train, 113
flat chisel, stonecutting, 366
flat coast, nautical chart, 22
flat diaphragm chest piece,
    stethoscope, 439
flat four-cylinder automobile
    engine, 107
flat grind, knife, 252
flat hat, Beefeater, 467
flat head, screw, 400
flatiron, 275
flat kite, 317
flat of stock, rifle, 458
flat pin, window shade
    roller, 237
flat plate, solar heating
    system collector unit, 383
flat racing, 330
flat surface: perspective, 362;
    printing, 164
flattop, 142
flatware, 240
flavedo, orange, 53
fleatrap, cowboy, 474
fleet ballistic missile
    submarine, 143
flesh, banana, 53
fleshy root, carrot, 52
fleshy tissue, succulent, 54
fletching, arrow, 456
fleur-de-lis, royal crown, 469
flews, dog, 34
flex, skateboard, 318
flexible kite, 317
flexible skirt, hovercraft, 145
flexor, universal gym, 338
flexor carpi radialis,
    human, 26
flier, staircase, 64
flies, stage, 344
flight: dart, 316; of steps, 64
flight control position
    indicator, 747 cockpit, 150
flight deck: aircraft
    carrier, 142;
    destroyer, 140; jumbo
    jet, 148
flight feather, bird, 37
flight instrumentation
    control, space shuttle, 155
flight officer, airplane, 153
flip, woman's hair, 209
flip chart, football down
    marker, 289
flipover, hurdle, 298
flip panel, football down
    marker, 289
flipper: dolphin, 43; skin
    diving, 325; turtle, 40
flip side, phonograph
    record, 176
float: buoy, 128;
    dishwasher, 246;
    fishing, 335; toilet, 271
floating crank, brace, 408
floating pier, pontoon
    bridge, 95
floating position, oil drilling
    platform, 99
floe, glacier, 12
floeberg, glacier, 12
flood: river, 13; stage, 344
flood plain, 13, 15
floodlight, stage, 344
floor: barn, 100; basketball
    court, 292; canal lock, 97;
    and carpet, 242; cave, 11;
    church, 114; elevator
    car, 76; house, 58, 59, 60;
    kiln, 367; oil drilling
    platform, 99;
    skyscraper, 75; stage, 344;
    White House, 73
floorboards: inflatable, 129;
    playpen, 282
floor cable, fencing strip, 309
floor exercise,
    gymnastics, 300
floor glide, desk, 272
flooring, tent, 336
floor leader, House of
    Representatives, 72

floor-locking system pedal, surgical table, 440
floor pan, automobile, 105
floor pedal, pedal steel guitar, 357
floor plate: escalator, 77; horizontal bar, 300; rifle, 458; stage, 344; stationary rings, 301
floor selector, elevator car, 76
floor support, playpen, 282
floor tom-tom, 358
floppy disk, computer, 429
floppy shoe, clown, 477
floral carving, tombstone, 500
floral organs, grass, 56
floral tube, apple, 53
floret, grass, 56
florist shop, passenger ship, 138
flotation device: skin diving, 325; jumbo jet, 148
flounce: dress, 194; queen's regalie, 468
flour shaker, 256
flow, volcano, 10
flow distributor head, nuclear reactor, 385
flower, 51; cactus, 54; corn, 56; grass, 56; woman's hat, 199
flow indicator, pilot's instrument panel, 153
flowstone, cave, 11
flue: destroyer, 140; fireplace, 228; house, 60; stove, 244, 394; water heater, 391
fluff, chicken, 33
fluid, solar collector panel, 383
fluke: anchor, 128; dolphin, 43
fluorescent banner, football field, 289
fluorescent bulb, lighting, 234
flush, toilet, 271
flusher, sanitation vehicle, 123
flush left, proofreader's mark, 498
flush-left type, 168
flute, 348, 350-351; auger bit, 409; screwdriver, 403
fluted spire, kokoshniki, 68
fluting, column, 71
flux, plumbing, 412
fly: flag, 486; man's underpants, 190
flybridge: powerboat, 134
flybridge monitor, fireboat, 144
fly deck, stage, 344
fly end, flag, 486
flyer: circus, 88; spinning wheel, 379
fly front: blouse, 193; trousers, 187; woman's pants, 192
flying bridge: destroyer, 141; powerboat, 134
flying crate, kite, 317
flying horse, merry-go-round, 91
flying line, kite, 317
flying stovepipe, jet engine, 397
fly line, stage, 344
fly rod, fishing, 335
fly tackle, windmill, 382
flywheel: automobile engine, 107; hitch and harrow, 424; steam engine, 395
FM: movie camera, 172; phonograph receiver, 177
foal, horse, 36

foam, fire extinguisher, 280
foam brush, house painting, 415
foam monitor, tanker, 137
fob: pocket watch, 216; trousers, 187; vest, 184
focal length: microscope, 432; movie camera, 172
focal point, composition, 363
fo'c'sle, destroyer, 141
focus: binoculars, 433; camera, 170, 171, 172, 180; microscope, 432; projector, 173; rifle scope, 459; telescope, 433; theodolite, 426
fog, weather map, 19
fog whistle, destroyer, 141
foible, fencing foil, 309
foil: copper, 372; drag racing dragster, 333; electric, 309; fencing, 309; package, 265
fold: curtain, 236; frog, 42; salamander, 42
fold-down seat, automobile, 102
folder, briefcase, 281
folding box, package, 265
folding fan, 392
folding file, nail clippers, 211
folding leaf, drop-leaf table, 238
folding rule, 414
folding umbrella, 226
fold line, sewing pattern, 380
foley, 256
foliage, 50; carrot, 52
folio: book page, IV, 165; magazine, 167, 168; newspaper, 166
folk instruments, 360
follow block, stapler, 273
follower, magazine, 460
follow spring, stapler, 273
fondo, jai alai cesta, 308
food: desserts, 260; prepared, 259; raw, 258
food mill, 256
food processor, 250
foot: attaché case, 281; basket, 262; bed, 266; bird, 37; book page, 165; boot, 202; bureau, 268; camera tripod, 174; cat, 35; cigar, 224; cigarette, 224; clam, 45; cymbal, 358; drop-leaf table, 238; electronic flash, 174; fishing reel, 334; flag, 486; food processor, 250; frog, 42; garbage disposal, 243; grammatical symbol, 491; grandfather clock, 229; horse, 36; human, 24, 29; hurdle, 298; juice extractor; lounger, 231; mainsail, 132; pig, 32; pot; potter's wheel, 367; rail, 111; royal regalia, 469; sewing machine, 274; shoulder bag, 218; shuffleboard court, 312; sideboard, 239; slide projector, 173; sofa, 232; stapler, 273; steamer basket, 253; stemware, 240; surgical table, 440; toaster, 249; ultimate beast, 47; windsurfer mast, 324; wok, 253
football, 288-289; association, 293
foot binding, slalom water ski, 323
footboard: bed, 266; stagecoach, 127; operating table, 440

foot control, dental unit, 444
foothills, 7
footing: elevator shaft, 76; house, 58
foot joint, flute, 350
footline, book page, IV
footlight: circus, 88; stage, 344
footnote, magazine, 169
foot pad, kiln, 367
footpath, bridge, 95
foot peg: football field, 289; motorcycle, 125
footpiece, crutch, 442
footplate, wheelchair, 442
foot pocket, skin diving fin, 325
foot pump, paramedic equipment, 119
footrace, 294
footrest: baby's high chair, 282; car, 106; glider, 283; lounger, 231; medical examination table, 440; stroller, 282
foot spot, pool table, 314
footstool, 231
foot-switch input, guitar amplifier, 357
footstraps, windsurfer, 324
foot zipper, mainsail, 132
force cup, plumber's plunger, 412
fore and aft gangway, tanker, 136
forearm: dog, 34; frog, 42; horse, 36; human, 24; machine gun, 461; shotgun, 458
forebay, canal lock, 97
fore beam, hand loom, 379
forecast, weather, 18
forecastle, destroyer, 141
forecomb, shotgun, 458
forecourt: basketball, 292; tennis, 306
foredeck: powerboat, 134; sailboat, 130
fore-edge, book, 165
forefinger, hand, 29
forefoot: cat, 35; pig, 32; sailboat, 130
foregrip, fishing rod, 334
forehead: bird, 37; cat, 35; cow, 30; dog, 34; horse, 36; human, 24; sheep, 31
foreign price, magazine, 167
forel, book, 165
foreleg: bee, 39; cat, 35; sheep, 31
forelock, horse, 36
foremast, tanker, 136
forepart, shoe tree, 203
forepaw, pelt, 197
forepeak, sailboat, 131
foreshank: beef, 30; lamb, 31
foreslope, shoreline, 14
forestage, theatre, 345
forestay, sailboat, 130
forestaysail, sailboat, 130
forewing, grasshopper, 39
fork: bicycle, 124; branding iron, 422; fireplace logs, 422; kitchen utensil, 255; motorcycle, 125; river, 13; saddle, 329; spading, 417; stroller, 282; table setting, 240, 241; tuning, 361
form, etching press, 371
formal Mandarin attire, 475
formal shirt, man's, 472
formation light, jet fighter, 152
Formula One racing car, 332
for shooter, craps table, 341
fort, frontier, 80
forte: fencing foil, 309; music notation, 346
fortification, 80, 81
fortress, castle, 78

45°-angle gauge, combination square, 414
45° vial, carpenter's level, 414
forward: basketball, 292; boat, 128; destroyer, 141; fireboat, 144; hovercraft, 145; lunar lander, 156; sailboat, 131; slide projector, 173; space shuttle, 154; television LaserDisc player, 181
forward-reverse button, potter's wheel, 367
foul light, drag racing, 333
foul line: baseball field, 287; basketball court, 292; bowling lane, 311; javelin throw, 295
foundation: beauty product, 212, 213; house, 58; skyscraper, 75; undergarment, 191
foundation lines, spider web, 38
foundation plan, house, 60
fount, lantern, 336
fountain pen, 160
fourchette, glove, 196
four-cycle internal combustion engine, 396
four-cylinder automobile engine, 107
four-face traffic signals, 109
four-in-hand tie, 188-189
four-poster bed, 266
fourragere, enlisted man's uniform, 480
four suit, domino, 339
14-stop, darts, 316
fourth toe, human foot, 29
fourth tooth, crocodile, 41
four-wheel drive jeep, 126
fowl, 33
foxing: boot, 202; running shoe, 296
foyer, skyscraper, 75
fraction, political map, 21
fracture, volcano, 10
fragmentation grenade, 463
frame, 373; abacus, 431; attaché case, 281; automobile, 102, 105; automatic pistol, 460; backpack, 337; basket, 262; bed, 266, 267; bicycle, 124; binoculars, 433; brassiere, 191; card table, 238; carpenter's level, 414; C-clamp, 399; chaise lounge, 284; circus, 88; coffee maker, 248; comic strip, 374; drill, 408; dressing table mirror, 268; eyeglasses, 217; film, 171, 172; gallows, 452; garbage truck, 123; hammock, 284; hand loom, 379; hourglass, 229; house, 59; ironing board, 275; jai alai cesta, 308; jet fighter canopy, 152; Jew's harp, 360; lawn sprinkler, 418; man's belt buckle, 186; medical examination table, 440; paint roller, 415; piano, 355; pilot's instrument panel, 153; plane, 410; pocket watch, 216; revolver, 460; sailboat, 130; saw, 406; seeder, 420; sextant, 133; shutters, 237; silk screen, 369; skin diving tank, 325; skyscraper, 75; slot machine, 340; snowshoe, 321; solar collector panel, 383;

stationary rings, 301; steam engine, 395; stroller, 282; swagger bag, 218; telegraph key, 159; television LaserDisc player, 181; tent, 336; tepee, 82; tractor, 424; trampoline, 302; umbrella, 226; wheelbarrow, 420; window, 63
frame-counter window, camera, 171
frame cover, motorcycle, 125
frame leaf, hinge, 450
frame plate, mortise lock, 448
frame rail, truck tractor, 116
framework: denture, 443; yurt, 68; Zeppelin, 158
framing string, kite, 317
framing knob, movie projector, 173
franc, symbol, 495
frankfurter, 261
Franklin glasses, miser, 476
Franklin stove, 394
free arm, sewing machine, 274
freeboard, boat, 128
free-fall, parachuting, 327
free-reed instrument, 360
free-rotating mast, windsurfer, 324
free-sail system, windsurfer, 324
free-standing easel-back frame, 373
freestyle swimming race, 310
free-throw circle, basketball court, 292
freeway, 110
freewheel, bicycle, 124
freeze function, television LaserDisc player, 181
freezer: powerboat, 135; refrigerator, 245; thermometer, 254
freezing rain, weather map, 19
freight, merchant ship, 136
freight car: railroad yard, 94; train, 112-113
French cuff, shirt, 185, 472, 473
French door, 60, 62
French horn, 348, 352
French seam, tent, 336
frequency, television, 181
frequency selector, police car, 118
fresh air plate, standpipe, 57
fresh-air supply duct, tunnel, 96
fret: guitar, 356, 357; sitar, 356
friction post, jewelry findings, 214
frieze: column entablature, 71; drop-leaf table, 238; house, 60; White House, 73
frill, bonnet, 199
fringe: cowboy, 474; dress, 194; golf course, 305; Indian, 474; Jewish prayer shawl, 470; lizard crest, 40
frock coat, Revolutionary War general, 476
frog, 42; fastener, 204; horse's foot, 36; shovel, 417; violin bow, 349
from the sign, music notation, 347
frond: fern, 55; palm, 50; seaweed, 55
front: butler's shirt, 473; church, 85; desk, 272; eyeglasses, 217; glacier, 12; queen's

regalia, 468; sailor's uniform, 481; steam locomotive boiler, 112; type, 164; weather map, 19; woman's pants, 192
frontal, church high altar, 85
frontal bone, human, 26
front apron, 189
front-axle rod, child's wagon, 283
front bead, shotgun, 459
front beam, laboratory scale, 437
front boot, stagecoach, 127
front brace, wheelbarrow, 420
front brake, bicycle, 124
front bumper: automobile, 102; bus, 114
front cover, book, 165
front crotch seam, trousers, 187
front derailleur, bicycle, 124
front disc brake, motorcycle, 125
front door: automobile, 102; bus, 114; sealed voting booth, 427; woodburning stove, 394
front end, diving board, 310
front end weight, tractor, 424
front face, book, 165
front fender, motorcycle, 125
front flap: book jacket, 165; matchbook, 224
front foot, stapler, 273
front gate, prison; 74
front grille, air conditioner, 392
front gunner's periscope, tank, 465
front half, grand piano, 355
front handle, sander, 411
front handlebar, chain saw, 421
front housing: can opener, 247; electric razor, 206
front hub: automobile, 104; bicycle, 124
front hydraulic fork, motorcycle, 125
frontier fort, 80
frontis, jai alai cancha, 308
frontispiece, magazine, 168
front jaw, vise, 399
front jockey, saddle, 329
front leg, bee, 39
front lid, grand piano, 355
front line, craps table, 341
front-loading washing machine, 276
front matter, book, 165
fronton, jai alai, 308
front panel: jacket, 184; tape recorder, 175; toaster, 249
frontpiece, fireman's helmet, 484
front pilaster, cupboard, 239
front placket: blouse, 193; shirt, 185
front point, ice climbing boot, 328
front post: bureau, 268; hand loom, 379
front-push plate, tow truck, 122
front quarter: automobile, 102; boot, 202
front rail: piano, 355; sled, 322
front rocker, slalom water ski, 323
front service door, gas pump, 108
front sight, weapon, 459, 460, 461
front sizer, football helmet, 288
front slit, man's

underpants, 190
front spray nozzle, iron, 275
front stretcher, rocking chair, 230
front strut, hydrofoil, 145
front tab, razor blade injector, 206
front thread guide, sewing machine, 274
front tire, bus, 114
front tuck, blouse, 193
front walk, house, 61
front wall: jai alai cancha, 308; squash, 307; truck van, 117
front wheel: bicycle, 124; drag racing dragster, 333
front window: automobile, 102; camper, 126; tractor, 424
front wing: grasshopper, 39; racing car, 332
front yard, house, 60
frosting, cake, 260
frostfree refrigerator, 245
fruit, 53; grass, 56; palm, 50; slot machine, 340; woman's hat, 199
fruit bowl, 241
fruit compartment, refrigerator, 245
fruit juice extractor, 251
fruitlet, pineapple, 53
fruit wall, pea, 52
fry, fish, 43
frying basket, 256
frying pan, 253
F sharp, piano keyboard octave, 355
f-stop scale, light meter, 174
fuel, rocket, 397
fuel alarm, powerboat, 134
fuel assembly, nuclear reactor, 385
fuel cap, lantern, 336
fuel cell monitor, space shuttle, 155
fuel chamber, torpedo, 466
fuel cock, internal combustion engine, 306
fuel filler, locomotive, 113
fuel gauge: barbecue grill, 284; powerboat, 134
fuel indicator, car, 106
fuel-line hose, automobile engine, 107
fuel management panel, pilot's instrument panel, 153
fuel nozzle, combustion jet engine, 397
fuel tank: bulldozer, 425; camper, 126; camp stove, 336; drag racing dragster, 333; garbage truck, 123; jet fighter, 152; motorcycle, 125; mower, 419; outboard engine, 133; space shuttle, 154; tank, 464; truck tractor, 116
fuel truck, airport, 93
fuel valve, lantern, 336
fulcrum, diving board, 310
full denture, 443
full-dress ship guideline, destroyer, 140, 141
fuller: horseshoe, 36; knife, 453; sword, 453
full face, elliptical galaxy, 2
full moon, 4
full nut, 401
full-organ button, organ, 354
full point, grammatical symbol, 497
full sail position, windmill, 382
full-service island, service station, 108
full-surface hinge, 450
fumarole, volcano, 10

fume extractor, tank gun, 465
function indicator: phonograph receiver, 177; video recorder, 180
function key, cash register, 430
function selector: air conditioner, 392; phonograph receiver, 177; video recorder, 180
funerary structure, pyramid, 68
fungi, 55
funnel: citrus juicer, 251; kitchen, 254; lobster pot, 423; passenger ship, 138; tornado, 17
funny bone, 25
funny car, drag racing, 333
furbelow, queen's regalia, 468
furnace, 390;
furniture guard, vacuum cleaner, 279
furniture nozzle, vacuum cleaner, 279
furrier, 197
furrow, horse's foot, 36
fuse: cartridge, 389; hand grenade, 463; land mine, 463; plug, 389; radar, 434
fuselage: helicopter, 146; single engine airplane, 147
fusible element, plug fuse, 389
fuzz pedal, electric guitar, 357

G

G: braille, 496; music notation, 347; piano keyboard octave, 355; sign language, 496
gable: barn, 100; church, 84; house, 61
gadget bag, photographic, 174
gaff, fishing, 335
gage, drill, 408
gain: mortise lock, 448; sonar, 434
Gainsborough, bride's hat, 472
gaited horse, 331
gaiter: drum major, 479; ski clothes, 321
gakuzuka, torii, 68, 69
galaxy, Milky Way, 2, 3
Galilean telescopes, opera glasses, 433
gall bladder, human, 27
gallery: cave, 11; church, 84; Congress, 72; house, 61; monocle, 217; stage, 344
galley, sailboat, 131
galley module, jumbo jet, 148, 149
gallon totalizer, gas pump, 108
galloper, merry-go-round, 91
gallows, 454; sailboat, 130
galluses, man's, 186
galoshes, 203
gam, human, 25
gambling equipment, 340, 341
gammadion, symbol, 492
gangplank; passenger ship, 138; tanker, 136
gantry, launch pad, 154
gap, fishhook, 335
garage; house, 61; passenger ship, 138; prison, 74
garbage disposal, 243
garbage truck, 123
gardening implement, 417
garlic press, 257
garment bag, 281
garnish, poultry, 259

garland, royal regalia, 469
garret, house, 60
garrison belt, 480
garrison cap, 480
garter belt, ice hockey
 player, 290
garter trolley, girdle, 191
gas bag, blimp, 158
gas barbeque, 284
gas cap, internal combustion
 engine, 396
gas cigarette lighter, 224
gas cloud, 3
gas cock, water heater, 391
gas cylinder, plumber's
 torch, 412
gas-fired water heater, 391
gas-fueled internal
 combustion engine, 396
gas gauge, car, 106
gas inlet, laboratory
 burner, 437
gash, razor blade
 injector, 206
gasket: dishwasher, 246;
 refrigerator, 245; stove
 oven, 244
gaskin, horse, 36
gasoline pump, 108
gas range, 244
gas regulator, laboratory
 burner, 437
gas shutoff valve,
 standpipe, 57
gas station, public sign, 491
gas sterilizing flame,
 dental, 145
gas supply line, water
 heater, 391
gas tank: automobile, 103,
 105; barbeque grill, 284;
 chain saw, 421; internal
 combustion engine, 396;
 mower, 419
gaster, ant, 39
gastight envelope, vacuum
 tube, 386
gastrocnemius, human, 26
gas-vent line, tanker, 137
gate: airport, 92; canal
 lock, 97; dam, 98; drop-
 leaf table, 238; flat
 racing, 330; frontier
 fort, 80; hurdle, 298;
 mountain climbing
 carabiner, 328;
 powerboat, 135;
 prison, 74; railroad
 crossing signal, 111;
 sailboat, 130;
 shotgun, 458; subway
 motorman's cab, 115; toll
 booth, 110; vault, 447
gatebar, hurdle, 298
gated spillway, dam, 98
gatefold, magazine, 169
gatehouse: castle, 78, 79;
 lift bridge, 95
gate index, slide
 projector, 173
gateleg table, 238
gate pier, fence, 65
gatepost, steel chain
 fence, 65
gateway: castle, 79; Shinto
 temple, 68, 69
gather, bonnet, 199
gathered skirt, maid's
 uniform, 473
gathering: blouse, 193;
 hardback book, 165;
 woman's pants, 192
gauge: barbecue grill, 284;
 blood pressure, 439;
 car, 106; carpenter's
 level, 414; combination
 square, 414; drill, 409;
 etching press, 371; fire
 extinguisher, 280;
 furnace, 380;
 powerboat, 134;
 pumper, 121;
 railroad, 111;

747 cockpit, 150; skin
 diving, 325; steam
 engine, 395; subway
 motorman's cab, 115;
 table saw, 407; weather
 station, 18
gauge needle, paramedic
 equipment, 119
gauntlet: armor, 455; drum
 major, 479
gauze, 119, 441, 445
gavel, 87, 402
G clef, music, 346, 347
gear: can opener, 247;
 fishing, 335; hand
 drill, 408; mortar, 462;
 seeder, 420; single engine
 airplane, 147; vault, 447;
 venetian blinds, 237
gearbox, automobile, 104;
 etching press, 371;
 hovercraft propeller, 145;
 lithographic press, 370;
 radar antenna, 434;
 seeder, 420
gear bracket, citrus
 juicer, 251
gear cluster, bicycle, 124
gear drive, chain saw, 421
geared key chuck, power
 drill, 409
gear housing, fishing
 reel, 334
gear oil-pressure gauge,
 powerboat, 134
gear ring, vault, 447
gearshift; car, 106;
 motorcycle, 125
Geiger counter, 435
gelatin casing, pill, 441
gelding, horse, 36
gem clip, 273
Gemini, zodiac, 493
gemstone, 214
gendarme, mountain, 9
general, Revolutionary
 War, 476
general product category,
 Universal Product
 Code, 430
generating plant, power
 network, 386
generation, pacemaker, 442
generator: nuclear
 reactor, 384; steam
 engine, 395
generator control, pilot's
 instrument panel, 153
generic name, label, 264
genitalia, human, 24
gentleman's white glove,
 butler's uniform, 473
geodesic dome, 83
geographical boundaries,
 world, 5
geologist, 4
gesso, 364
gestures, sign language, 496
getter, vacuum tube, 386
geyser, volcano, 10
G flat, piano keyboard
 octave, 355
giant, circus, 88
gibbet, 452
gibbous moon, 4
giblets, fowl, 33
gift shop, public sign, 490
gig, horse-drawn carriage, 127
gill: fish, 43; mushroom, 55;
 pelt, 197
gimbal suspension,
 phonograph
 turntable, 176
gimlet, 408
gin pole, powerboat, 135
giraffe, ultimate beast, 46
girder: house, 58;
 skyscraper, 75; suspension
 bridge, 95
girdle, 191; cut
 gemstone, 214; hot air
 balloon, 326
girdle pad, football

uniform, 288
girth, racing, 330, 331
gizzard, fowl, 33
glacial plain, mountain, 8
glacier, 8, 9, 12
glacis, permanent fort, 81
glacis plate, tank, 465
gladhand, truck van, 117
gland, octopus, 44
glass: basketball
 backboard, 292; cupboard
 door, 239; dressing
 table, 268; eye
 dropper, 441; electric
 meter casing, 389;
 fluorescent bulb
 tube, 234; frame, 373;
 light bulb, 234;
 sextant, 133; solar panel
 cover plate, 383;
 stained, 372; table
 setting, 240, 241
glass cutter, 372
glasses: field, 433;
 miser, 476; ski
 touring, 321
glass support, vacuum
 tube, 386
glaze, pot, 367
glazing, window, 65
glide: desk, 272; slalom
 water ski, 323; surgical
 table, 440
glider, 147; backyard, 283;
 hang, 327
glide slope antenna,
 helicopter, 146
glide slope indicator, airport
 runway, 92
globe, 1, 5; lantern, 336;
 royal regalia, 469
glochidia, cactus, 54
gloss, makeup, 212
glove, 196; baseball, 286,
 287; boxing, 303; bridal
 costume, 472; butler's
 uniform, 473; drag racing
 driver's, 333; drum
 major, 479; fencing, 309;
 fireman, 484; hammer
 thrower, 297; ice hockey
 handball, 307;
 player, 290, 291; jai alai
 cesta, 308; jet fighter, 152;
 miser, 476; Revolutionary
 War general, 476;
 skiing, 320; skin
 diving, 325
glove compartment, car, 106
glume, grass, 56
gluteus medius, human, 26
gnomon, sundial, 381
gnu beard, ultimate beast, 47
goal: basketball, 292;
 football, 289; ice
 hockey, 290, 291;
 lacrosse, 293; soccer, 293
go around switch, 747
 cockpit, 151
goat, zodiac, 493
goat beard, ultimate
 beast, 47
goatee, men's beard, 207
goggles: flat racing, 330; ski
 helmet, 320
gold: dental, 445; ring, 215
gold ball of rank, royal
 crown, 469
golf ball, 304;
golf club, 304, 305
golf course, 304, 305;
 passenger ship, 138
golgi apparatus, animal cell;
 23
GO light, drag racing, 333
gondola: blimp, 158; ferris
 wheel, 91; merry-go-
 round, 91
gonfalon, 486
gonfannon, 486
gong, drums, 358
good luck symbol, 492
goose, 33

gooseneck: football
 goalpost, 289; lamp, 235
gore: hot air balloon, 326;
 man's cap, 198; sock, 203;
 umbrella, 226
gore area, highway
 cloverleaf, 110
gorge: human, 25;
 jacket, 184; permanent
 fort, 81; river, 13
gorget, armor, 455
gouge, 368, 410;
 woodcarving, 366
gouged sections, wood
 block, 368
gourd, sitar, 356
gour dam, cave, 11
governor: internal
 combustion engine, 396;
 power mower, 419
governor-rope tension
 sheave, elevator shaft, 76
gown, 194; queen's
 regalia, 468
grab iron, locomotive, 113
grab rail, bathtub, 270
grab strap, motorcycle, 125
gracilis, human, 26
grade: enlisted man's
 uniform, 480;
 gasoline, 108; pencil, 160;
 railroad crossing, 111
graduated guide, fishing
 rod, 335
graduated scale,
 metronome, 361
graduation: beaker, 437;
 thermometer, 18, 439
grain: fabric, 380;
 lumber, 66;
 sandpaper, 411
grain pit, barnyard, 100
grammar, proofreader's
 mark, 498
grammatical symbol, 497
grand drape, stage, 344, 345
grandfather clock, 229
grandmother clock, 229
grand piano, 355
Grand Prix racing, 332
grandstand, harness
 racetrack, 331
granule, roofing
 shingle, 66
graphic, hot air balloon, 326
graphic device, label, 264
graphic scale, house
 blueprint, 60
grasper, desk phone, 178
grasping foot, bird, 37
grass, 56; baseball field, 287
grass-catcher, lawn
 mower, 419
grasshopper, 39
grate: fireplace, 228;
 stove, 244, 336
grater, kitchen tool, 257
graticule, political map, 21
grating, castle portcullis, 79
grave, 500
grave accent, grammatical
 symbol, 497
gravure, printing, 164, 368
grawlix, cartoon, 375
grease skimming brush, 255
great choir, church, 85
great circle, geodesic
 dome, 83
greatcoat, Revolutionary
 officer, 476
great door, barn, 100
greater than, symbol, 495
great keyboard, organ, 354
greave, armor, 455
Greek cross, symbol, 492
green, golf course, 305
greenback, paper money, 220
green light: drag racing, 333;
 traffic, 109
Green Room, White
 House, 73
Greenwich Mean Time, 5
green wire, electrical

receptacle, 388
grenade, 463
grid: barbecue grill, 284; earth, 5; geodesic dome, 83; nuclear reactor, 385; paint tray, 415; political map, 21; stage, 344; stove broiler, 244; vacuum tube, 386
griddle, stove, 244, 394
gridiron, 289; stage, 344
grid marking, topographic map, 22
grid table extension, saw, 407
grill, barbecue, 284
grille: accordion, 360; air conditioner, 392; automobile, 102; CB radio antenna, 179; guitar amplifier, 357; hair dryer, 208; humidifier, 392; phonograph, 177; refrigerator, 245; tractor, 424; truck, 116
grind, knife, 252
grinder, kitchen tool, 257
grip: automatic weapon, 461; bobby pin, 210; bow, 456; carpenter's level, 414; chain saw, 421; chest pull, 338; field events hammer, 297; fishing rod, 334; foil mounting, 309; gardening shears, 417; golf club, 305; hair clip, 210; hammer, 402; javelin, 297; jump rope, 338; knife, 453; movie camera, 172; Ping-Pong racket, 315; revolver, 460; rowboat car, 129; seeder, 420; shoe horn, 203; shotgun, 458; ski pole, 320; stroller, 282; sword hilt, 453; tennis racket, 306; wheelbarrow, 420; wire stripper, 413
grip cap, shotgun, 458
gripper mark, nail, 400
gripping hole, clothespin, 276
grip safety, pistol, 460
grip tape, skateboard, 318
gristle, human, 26
grit, sandpaper, 411
groin, human, 25
grommet, tent, 336
groove: combination square, 414; corrugated fastener, 400; crossbow, 456; escalator, 77; guillotine, 452; horse, 36; phonograph record, 176; roulette wheel, 340; salamander, 42; ski, 320; sword, 453; type, 164
grospoint, stitchery, 377
grotto, 11
grotzen, pelt, 197
ground: flag, 486; symbol, 494
ground beam, guillotine, 452
ground coffee, 248
ground control, metal detector, 435
ground-effect machine, amphibious, 145
ground floor, White House, 73
grounding prong, electric plug, 338
grounding terminal, electrical receptacle, 388
ground steering tiller 747 cockpit, 150
ground wire: circuit

breaker box, 389; electrician's, 413; electrical receptacle junction box, 388
grout, tunnel, 96
growler, glacier, 12
growthline, clam shell, 45
growth ring, lumber, 66
grozing pliers, for stained glass, 372
grunting, 32
G sharp, piano keyboard octave, 355
G string, double bass, 349
guante, jai alai cesta, 308
guard: armor, 455; basketball, 292; crossbow, 456; dishwasher, 246; drill press, 409; elevator shaft, 76; foil mounting, 309; gas pump automatic nozzle, 108; guitar, 356, 357; ice hockey player, 291; knife, 252, 453; lacrosse stick, 293; lithographic press, 370; movie camera eyepiece, 172; mower, 419; prison, 74; revolver, 460; rifle, 461; safety pin, 204; saw, 407; sharpening steel, 252; shotgun trigger, 458; stagecoach, 127; sword hilt, 453; theodolite, 426; tow truck, 122; washing machine, 276; wheelchair, 442
guard bars, Universal Product Code, 430
guard cone, potting, 367
guard house, frontier fort, 80
guardrail, highway, 110; slide, 283; tow truck, 122
guard socket, fencing foil, 309
guard tower, frontier fort, 80; prison, 74
gudgeon, window shade roller, 237
guest head, sailboat, 131
guidance chamber, torpedo, 466
guidance system, submarine, 143
guide: fishing reel, 334; fishing rod, 334, 335; Hansom cab rein, 127; incline track, 90; jackhammer, 426; pencil sharpener, 273; power saw, 407; silk screen, 369; speculum, 438; toaster, 249
guide arm, toilet, 271
guide bar, saw, 407, 421
guide cone, potting, 367
guided weapons, defensive, 140
guideline, destroyer, 140, 141
guide lug, nuclear reactor, 385
guide post, typewriter, 162
guide rail, elevator shaft, 76
guide ring, vault, 447
guide rod, workbench, 398
guide roller, cassette tape, 175
guide scope, telescope, 433
guide shoe, elevator shaft, 76
guide sign, road, 489
guide spring, pencil sharpener, 273
guide tube, nuclear reactor, 385
guide wall, dam, 98
guide wheel, roller coaster, 90
guillotine, 452

guimpe, nun, 471
guitar, 356, 357
gular region, salamander, 42
gulf, 7
Gulf Stream, ocean, 6
gullet, 25, 28; saddle, 329; saw teeth, 406
gull-wing hull, powerboat, 134
gully, mountain, 8
gum, and denture, 443
gum line, tooth, 446
gun, 460; cowboy, 474; jet fighter, 152; machine, 461; police, 483; police car, 118; pumper, 121; tank, 464, 465; television, 181
gun barrel, destroyer, 141
gun belt: cowboy, 474; police, 482-483
gun director, destroyer, 141
gunlock, cannon barrel, 457
gunmount, destroyer, 141
gunner's periscope, tank, 465
gunship, helicopter, 146
gunwale: powerboat, 135; rowboat, 129
gusset: armor, 455; handbag, 218; house, 59
gut, human, 25
gutter: barn, 100; book, 165; bowling lane, 311; house, 61; magazine, 169; swimming pool, 310; gutter broom, mechanical sweeper, 123
gutter margin, book page, 165
guy brace, uneven parallel bars, 300
guy rope, circus tent, 89
guy wire: horizontal bar, 300; stationary rings, 301
gym, universal, 338
gymnasium, passenger ship, 139
gymnastics, 300-301
gynecologist, examination equipment, 438
gyro compass, 132

H

H: braille, 496; sign language, 496
habit, nun, 471
hackle, chicken, 33
hackney carriage, 127
hacksaw, 406, 412
haft, ax, 454
hailstone, 17
hair: human, 24, 207, 209; painting brush, 364; violin bow, 349
hair band, 210
hairbrush, electric, 208
hair clip, 210
hairdo, 210
hair dryer, 208
hairline: linear slide rule, 431; man's, 207; newspaper, 166
hairpiece, man's, 207
hairpin, 210
halberd: Beefeater, 467; medieval, 454
half-court line, handball, 307
half-door, Hansom cab, 127
half-inch mark, tape measure, 414
half-jacket, fencing, 309
half-mile pole, harness racetrack, 331
half-moon, 4
half note, music, 346
half-surface hinge, 450
half-title logo, magazine, 168
halfway line, soccer field, 293
haligan tool, police

car, 118
hall: church, 85; mosque, 68-69; theatre, 345; White House, 73
hallmark, ring, 215
Hall of Columns, Capitol, 72
hallux, human foot, 20
halyard: destroyer, 141; flag, 486; sailboat, 130
ham, 32; human, 24; radio operator, 179
hammer: ball-peen, 402; carillon, III; field events, 297; ice climbing, 328; jackhammer, 426; piano, 355; revolver, 460; stonecutting, 366; for testing reflexes, 439; telegraph key, 159
hammerhead crane, launch pad; 154
hammer throw, track and field, 295
hammock, 284
hance, arch, 70
hand: blackjack, 341; cattle ranch, 422; frog, 42; grandfather clock, 229; human, 24, 29; pocket watch, 216; stopwatch, 298; wristwatch, 216
handbag, 218
handball court, 307
hand brace, 408
hand controller, space shuttle, 155
hand crank, easel, 364
handcuff, police gun belt, 482
hand cup, sword hilt, 453
hand drill, 408, 409
hand excavator, dental, 445
hand flexor, body building, 338
hand grenade, 463
handgrip: bazooka, 462; body building, 338; carpenter's level, 414; crutch, 442; motorcycle, 125; movie camera, 172; pole vault pole, 299; rocking chair, 230; swimming pool, 310; video camera, 180; wheelbarrow, 420; wheelchair, 442
handguard, automatic rifle, 461; chain saw, 421
handgun, 460
handhold: harness racing driver, 331; lunar rover, 157
handicap: drag racing, 333; flat racing entry, 330
handicapped, public sign, 491
handkerchief, queen's regalia, 468
handkerchief pocket, jacket, 184
hand knitting, 378
handle: attaché case, 281; automobile door, 103; ax, 454; barbecue grill, 284; baren, 368; baseball bat, 287; basket, 262; blender, 250; bow, 456; brace, 408; branding iron, 422; brayer, 368; broom, 278; burnisher, 371; candle snuffer, 233; can opener, 247; C-clamp, 399; chafing dish, 241; cheese plane, 252; chest pull, 338; child's wagon, 283; chisel, 410; citrus juicer, 251; clay

modeling tool, 366; clothespin, 276; coffee maker, 248; coffin, 500; croquet mallet, 312; dabber, 371; drain cleaner, 412; drill, 408, 409; ear scope, 438; etching press, 371; faucet, 269; field events hammer, 297; finishing sander, 411; fire engine, 121; fire extinguisher, 280; fishing reel, 334; fishing rod, 334; foil mounting, 309; food mill, 256; food processor, 250; garbage disposal, 243; garbage truck, 123; gimlet, 408; glass cutter, 372; gouge, 368; hair dryer, 208; hammer, 402; handbag, 218; hand loom, 379; hoe, 417; hot air balloon, 326; ice hammer, 328; internal combustion engine, 396; iron, 275; jackhammer, 426; jet fighter, 152; jump rope, 338; knife, 240, 252, 453; land mine, 463; lacrosse stick, 293; lithographic press, 370; lorgnette, 217; mace, 454; mailbox, 227; metal detector, 435; mower, 419; outboard engine, 133; pail, 280; painting brush, 364; paint roller, 415; paint spray gun, 415; paper bag, 262; parking meter, 109; peeler, 252; pencil sharpener, 273; pilot's instrument panel, 153; Ping-Pong racket, 315; plane, 410; playpen, 282; pliers, 404; plumber's plunger, 412; pocket knife, 416; pommel horse, 301; pots and pans, 253; projector, 173; radiator, 390; rake, 417; razor, 206; refrigerator door, 245; revolver, 460; rifle, 461; safe, 447; scissors, 376; saw, 406, 407, 421; screen, 173; screwdriver, 403; scriber, 369; seeder, 420; 747 cockpit, 150, 151; sewing machine, 274; sextant, 133; sharpening steel, 252; shaver, 206; shotgun, 458; shovel, 417; silk screen squeegee, 369; single engine airplane, 147; sink, 243, 269; soldering iron, 372; sponge mop, 278; stove, 336, 244, 394; stroller, 282; tea kettle, 241; telephone, 178; tennis racket, 306; thrown pot, 367; toilet, 271; toothbrush, 211; tuning fork, 361; umbrella, 226; vacuum cleaner, 279; vault, 447; vise, 398, 399; voting booth, 427; waterskiing towline, 323; wheelbarrow, 420; woodcarving tool, 366; wrench, 405
handlebar: bicycle, 124; chain saw, 421; snowmobile, 126
handlebar mustache, 207
handle grip: chain saw, 421; seeder, 420; stroller, 282;

vacuum cleaner, 279
handler, boxing, 303
handle release pedal, vacuum cleaner, 279
handle screw, plane, 410
hand lever: potter's wheel, 367; spreader, 420
hand loom, 379
handpiece: crutch, 442; dental, 444, 445
hand protector, waterskiing towline, 323
hand pump: blood pressure gauge, 439; pilot's instrument panel, 153
handrail: bus, 114; elevator car, 76; escalator, 77; locomotive, 112, 113; lunar lander, 156; powerboat, 135; roller coaster, 90; sled, 322; staircase, 64; subway car, 115
hand rope, racing sled, 322
handruff, queen's regalia, 468
handsaw, 406
hand screw, 399
handset, desk phone, 178
hand slide, trombone, 353
handstrap: bus, 114; subway car, 115
hand throttle, car, 106
hand valve, solar heating system, 383
hand warming slot, parka, 197
handwheel: sewing machine, 274; table saw, 407
hangar, airport, 93
hangar bay, aircraft carrier, 142
hanger: dress, 194; fishing plug, 335; frame, 373; harness racing, 331; laboratory scale weight, 437; lamp, 235; screen, 173; swing, 283
hanger bracket, wheelchair, 442
hang glider, 327
hang hole: blister card, 264; dustpan, 278
hanging glacier, mountain, 8
hanging locker, sailboat, 131
hanging ring: can opener, 247; skillet, 353
hanging strip, window shutters, 237
hanging weight, laboratory scale, 436
hang ring, hair dryer, 208
hang-up hole, toothbrush, 211
hank, knitting yarn, 378
Hansom cab, 127
hardback book, 165
hardcover book, 165
hard-hat diving, 325
hardness, pencil lead, 160
hard suction connection hose, pumper, 121
hardware: bureau, 268; computer, 429; cowboy, 474; shoulder bag, 218; sideboard, 239
hardware sling, mountain climbing, 328
hard-way bets, craps table, 341
hare traction splint, paramedic equipment, 119
harmonica, 360
harness: drag racing driver, 333; electrical wall switch, 388; hang glider, 327; harness racing, 331; mountain climbing, 328; parachute, 327; skin diving tank, 325
harness frame, hand

loom, 379
harness racing, 330, 331
harp: orchestra, 348; table lamp, 234
harrow, tractor, 424
hash mark: enlisted man's uniform, 480; football field, 289
hassock, lounger, 231
hasp, 450
hat: automobile engine, 107; Beefeater, 467; circus ringmaster, 88; clown, 477; cowboy, 474; miser, 476; pirate, 476; police, 482, 483; Revolutionary War general, 476; sailor, 481; skiing, 321; wizard, 476; woman's, 199
hatband, 198, 199
hat bow, beret, 198
hatch: bus, 114; fireboat, 144; lunar lander, 156; sailboat, 130; tank, 464, 465; tanker, 137; tugboat, 144
hatchet, 402
hatmaker, 198
hat pin, woman's hat, 199
hatter, men's hats, 198
haunch: arch, 70; human, 25
hawg leg, cowboy, 474
hawsehole: fireboat, 144; passenger ship, 138, 139
hawser: and canal lock, 97; passenger ship, 138; tugboat, 144
hay door, barn, 100
hay scale, frontier fort, 80
hay yard, frontier fort, 80
hazard, golf course, 304-305
head: Allen wrench, 405; anchor, 128; arrow, 456; automobile engine, 107; ax, 454; badminton shuttlecock, 313; barrel, 263; bell, III; billiard bridge, 314; bolt, 401; book page, IV, 165; bowling lane, 311; brace, 408; cartridge, 460; C-clamp, 399; chain saw, 421; chisel, 410; cigar, 224; coin, 221; combination square, 414; comet, 3; croquet mallet, 312; dental x-ray tube, 444; dispenser, 263; drain cleaner, 412; drill press, 409; drum, 358; electric razor, 206; electronic flash, 174; field events hammer, 297; fish, 49; fishing jig, 335; flag, 486; golf club, 304; grasshopper, 39; guitar, 356, 357; hammer, 402; hatchet, 402; helicopter rotor, 146; hinge fixed pin, 450; human, 24; javelin, 296; key punch, 428; knee kicker, 242; knitting needle, 378; lacrosse stick, 293; lance, 454; lettuce, 258; levigator bolt, 370; mace, 454; magazine, 168, 169; mainsail, 132; match, 224; mechanical sweeper gutter broom, 123; movie camera microphone, 172; music note, 347; nail, 400; newspaper, 166; octopus, 44; pelt, 197; pin, 204; saddle, 329; sailboat, 131; screw, 400; screwdriver, 403; shower, 270; shuffleboard court, 312; soldering iron, 372; spring beard

loom, 379
harness racing, 330, 331
needle, 378; stemware, 240; stove burner, 244; tambourine, 358; table saw, 407; tack, 400; tape recorder, 175; tennis racket, 306; theodolite, 426; toothbrush, 211; venetian blinds, 237; video camera, 180
headband: hair ornament, 210; hardback book, 165; phonograph headphone, 177; physician's mirror, 438; ski bat, 321
headboard: four-poster bed, 266; mainsail, 132
head box, venetian blind, 237
head channel, venetian blind, 237
head collar, kettledrum, 358
head cover, golf club, 305
header: brick wall, 67; drag racing dragster, 333; house, 58, 59; solar collector panel, 383
headgear: armor, 455; boxing, 303
headguard, boxing, 303
heading: book page, IV; draperies, 236; letter, 161; radar, 434
heading alignment control, radar, 434
head jamb, window, 63
head joint: brick wall, 67; flute, 351
headlight: automobile, 102; bulldozer, 425; bus, 114; locomotive, 112, 113; medical examination equipment, 438; motorcycle, 125; snowmobile, 126; tank, 465; tractor, 424; truck, 116
headlight controls, car, 106
headline: human hand, 29; magazine, 168; newspaper, 166
head lock, camera tripod, 174
head lug, bicycle, 124
head margin, book page, 165
head mold, church, 84
head piece: book, 165; rocking chair, 230
headphone, phonograph, 177
headphone jack: CB radio, 179; metal detector, 435; phonograph receiver, 177; tape recorder, 175; video recorder, 186
headpiece, Torah, 470
headpin, bowling, 311
head post, four-poster bed, 266
headquarters, frontier fort, 80
headrail, venetian blind, 237
headrest: bumper car, 90; dental unit, 444; surgical table, 440
headsail, 132
head section: flute, 351; piccolo, 350
headset, bicycle, 124
headshell, phonograph turntable, 176
head spot, pool table, 314
headstay, sailboat, 130
head step, ladder, 415
headstone, grave, 500
heads-up, drag racing, 333
head tube, bicycle, 124
headwall, mountain, 9

hearing aid, 442
heart: fowl, 33;
    human, 25, 27;
    lettuce, 258; playing
    cards, 342
hearth, fireplace, 228
heart line, human hand, 29
heart murmur, symbol, 494
heart of came, lead
    came, 372
heartwood, tree, 48
heat, drag racing, 333
heat-absorber plate, solar
    collector panel, 383
heat control: barbecue
    grill, 284; electric
    wok, 253
heater: camper, 126;
    water, 391
heater filament, vacuum
    tube, 386
heater wire, vacuum tube, 386
heat exchanger: 393;
    fireplace, 228; oil drilling
    platform, 99
heat indicator, electric hair
    brush, 208
heating controls, car, 106
heating/cooling coils, heat
    exchanger, 393
heating element:
    dishwasher, 246; soldering
    iron, 372; stove, 244
heating system, airport, 92
heating unit: camper, 126;
    solar heating system, 383
heat pump, 393
heat-resistant glass, light
    bulb, 234
heat-riser valve, automobile
    engine, 107
heat seal, foil pouch, 265
heat shield, lantern, 336
heat switch, hair dryer, 208
heat-transfer fluid, solar
    collector panel, 383
Hector, playing card
    jack, 342
heddle, hand loom, 379
heel: Achilles, 25;
    automatic rifle, 461;
    baseball glove, 287;
    boot, 202; bread, 259;
    carpenter's saw, 406;
    cat, 35; file, 410; frog, 42;
    golf club, 304; grand
    piano, 355; guitar, 356;
    horse, 36; horseshoe, 36;
    human foot, 24, 29;
    human hand, 29; ice
    hockey goalkeeper's
    stick, 290; ice skate, 319;
    knife, 252; L-shaped
    square, 414; man's
    shoe, 200; paint
    brush, 415; panty
    hose, 191; plane, 410;
    rasp, 410; roller
    skate, 318; shoe tree, 203;
    shotgun, 458; ski
    binding, 320; tennis
    racket, 306;
    windmill, 382; woman's
    shoe, 201
heel band, spur, 329
heel binding, ski, 320
heel breast, woman's
    shoe, 201
heel cap, hockey skate, 319
heel chain, spur, 329
heel counter, running
    shoe, 296
heel cup pivot, ski
    binding, 320
heel glide, slalom water
    ski, 323
heel gore, sock, 203
heelknob, dog, 34
heel lacing, snowshoe, 321
heel lift: boot, 202;
    woman's shoe, 201
heel loop, wheelchair, 442
heel patch, running shoe, 296

heel piece, slalom water
    ski, 323
heelplate, ski, 321, 323
heel rest, iron, 275
heel seam, sock, 203
heel seat, woman's shoe, 201
heel strap, skin diving
    fin, 325
heel tip, hockey skate, 319
heifer, 30
height: and perspective, 362;
    wave, 14
height adjustment: machine
    gun, 461; ski binding, 320;
    vacuum cleaner, 279
helical, settee, 284
helicopter, 146
helicopter flight deck,
    destroyer, 140
helictite, cave, 11
helipad, White House, 73
heliport, oil drilling
    platform, 99
helium valve, blimp, 158
helix, outer ear, 28
helm: coat of arms, 487;
    sailboat, 130
helmath, windmill, 382
helmet: armor, 455;
    baseball batter, 286; coat
    of arms, 487; combat
    soldier, 481; downhill
    skiing, 320; drag racing
    driver's fire suit, 333;
    fireman, 484; flat
    racing, 330; football
    uniform, 288; Grand Prix
    racing, 332; harness
    racing, 331; ice
    hockey, 291; jai alai, 308;
    lacrosse, 293;
    police, 482, 483; roller
    skating, 318;
    spacesuit, 157
helmet diving, 325
helmet skirt, drag racing
    driver's fire suit, 333
helmseat, powerboat, 135
helve, axe, 454
hem: bridal gown, 472;
    dress, 194; jacket, 184;
    parka, 197; skirt, 193;
    window shade, 236, 237
hemmer foot, sewing
    machine, 274
hemming, necktie, 189
hen, 33
hence, symbol, 495
herb, prepared foods, 259
hex nut, 401; juice
    extractor, 251; table
    lamp, 234
hex wrench, 405
hibachi, 284
hide, ultimate beast, 47
hide rope, tepee, 82
hieroglyph, obelisk, 69
high altar, church, 85
high bar, gymanastics, 300
high beam, automobile, 102
high chair, 282
high fidelity
    phonograph, 177
high-frequency antenna,
    helicopter, 146
high-gain antenna, lunar
    rover, 157
high heat switch, hair
    dryer, 208
high-heel woman's shoe, 201
high hurdle, 298
high intensity lamp, 235
high jump, 294, 299
highlight, magazine, 168
highlighter, makeup, 212
highline, magazine, 169
high-low combination
    headlamp,
    automobile, 102
high-low scale, light
    meter, 174
high pressure, weather
    map, 19

high-pressure pump:
    fireboat, 144;
    paint spray gun, 415
high-pressure steam,
    steam engine, 395
high pressure water spray,
    tooth cleaner, 211
high pulley, universal
    gym, 338
high score, darts, 316
high-speed handpiece,
    dental, 445
high tide, 15
high-volume evacuation tip,
    dental, 444
high water mark,
    topographic map, 22
highway, 110; map, 20, 22
high-wire act, circus, 88
hi-hat cymbal, 358
hiking trail, public
    sign, 491
hill, 7; road sign, 489;
    roller coaster, 90
hilt: bayonet, 453;
    billiard cue, 314; foil
    mounting, 309; knife, 453;
    mace, 454; sword, 453
hind bow, saddle, 329
hind foot: cat, 35; pig, 32;
    sheep, 31
hind paw, pelt, 197
hindquarters, 35
hind scalper, harness racing
    pacer, 331
hind shank, beef, 30
hind toe: cat, 35;
    chicken, 33
hind wing, grasshopper, 39
hinge, 450; binoculars, 433;
    book, 165; camera
    tripod, 174;
    cupboard, 239;
    eyeglasses, 217; folding
    rule, 414; hot dog
    roll, 261; kiln, 367;
    locomotive, 112;
    phonograph
    turntable, 176; railroad
    signal, III; safe, 447;
    scallop shell, 45;
    stapler, 273; stove oven
    door, 244; vault, 447;
    window shutters, 37;
    woodburning stove, 394
hinge cover: playpen, 282;
    refrigerator, 245
hinge portion, hasp, 450
hinge rod, power
    mower, 419
hip: barn, 100; bell, III;
    horse, 36; human, 24
hip belt, backpack, 37
hip flexor, universal
    gym, 338
hipline, dress, 194
hip pad: football, 288;
    ice hockey, 291
hippodrome track, circus, 88
historical costumes, 476
history, symbol, 494
hitch, tractor, 424
hite, cartoon, 374
hobble, harness racing
    gear, 331
hobble strap, saddle, 329
hock: chicken, 3; cow, 30;
    dog, 34; horse, 36; jet
    fighter, 152; pork, 32
hockey, ice, 290, 291
hockey skate, 319
hod, fireplace coal, 228
hoe, 417
hog, 32
hogan, 82
hogshead, 263
hoist: dam, 98; flag, 486;
    helicopter, 146
hoist cable, elevator shaft, 76
hoisting equipment, oil
    drilling platform, 99
hold, music notation, 346
holder: blackjack, 341;

casette tape recorder, 175;
    dental, 445; easel, 364;
    elevator car, 76; etching
    needle, 371;
    jackhammer, 426;
    laboratory, 436;
    lithographic press, 370;
    microscope slide, 432;
    police uniform, 482, 483;
    stroller, 282;
    telescope, 433;
    tom-tom, 358; track
    lighting, 235;
    two-suiter, 281
holdfast, seaweed, 55
holding prong, nail
    clippers, 211
holding tools, 399
hole: bagpipe, 359; blister
    card, 264; bowling
    ball, 311; button, 205;
    cheese, 259; cigar cutter
    blade, 224;
    clothespin, 276; computer
    diskette, 429; film, 171,
    172; fireboat, 144;
    fountain pen, 160; golf
    course, 305; guitar, 356;
    hair roller, 210;
    hinge, 450; hook and
    eye, 204; horsehoe, 36; ice
    axe, 328; igloo, 83;
    lantern, 336; man's
    belt, 186; man's
    underwear, 190; Milky
    Way, 2; needle, 376; oil
    drilling platform, 99;
    phonograph record, 176;
    punch card, 428; snap
    fastener, 204;
    snowshoe, 321;
    spool, 376;
    stagecoach, 127;
    telephone, 178; tire, 101;
    tow truck bed, 122;
    vault, 447
hole punch, pocket knife, 416
hollow body, acoustic
    guitar, 357
hollow grind, knife, 252
hollow lower face,
    zipper, 205
hollow of throat,
    human, 25
hollow wall fastener, 401
holster, 460, 474, 483
home, White House, 73
home computer, 429
home plate: baseball
    field, 287; blackjack, 341
home port, passenger
    ship, 138
home stake, croquet, 312
homestretch, harness
    racetrack, 331
honda, lasso, 422
honing surface, sharpening
    steel, 252
hood: automobile, 102;
    barn, 100; basinet, 282;
    bus, 114; camera
    lens, 171, 172; cobra, 40;
    compass, 132;
    fireplace, 228; fishing
    rod, 334; grandfather
    clock, 229; minister, 471;
    parka, 197; radar, 434;
    toboggan, 322;
    tractor, 424; truck, 116;
    vacuum cleaner, 279
hood door, grandfather
    clock, 229
hood release, car, 106
hoof: cow, 30; horse, 36;
    ultimate beast, 46
hook: block and tackle, 451;
    boot, 203; bulldozer, 425;
    fire engine, 120, 121;
    fireman, 484; fishing
    jig, 335; fishing plug, 335;
    frame, 373; garbage
    disposal, 243;

hammock, 284; harness racing gear, 331; hearing aid, 442; ice skates, 319; latch needle, 378; parachute, 327; pendant, 215; pulley block, 451; shower curtain, 270; suit hanger, 277; tape measure, 414; tatting shuttle, 378; tow truck bed, 122; trumpet, 353; *see also* hook and eye
hookah, 225
hook and bar, fastener, 204
hook and bobbin case, sewing machine, 274
hook and eye: brassiere, 191; fastener, 204; pants, 187; skirt, 193; *see also* hook
hook and ring, mitten, 196
hook disgorger, pocket knife, 416
hooked-up truck, 116
hook grip, shoe horn, 203
hook panel, pilot's instrument panel, 153
hook tape, Velcro, 205
hook-thrust bearing assembly, pulley block, 451
hoop: banjo, 356; barrel, 263; basketball backstop, 292; croquet, 312; lasso, 422; lobster pot, 423
hopper: garbage truck, 123; key punch, 428; mechanical sweeper, 123; seeder, 420
hopper car, train, 112
hop, skip, and jump, track and field, 294
horizontal bar, gymnastics, 300
horizontal centering, radar, 434
horizontal circle, theodolite, 426
horizontal direction indicator, 747 cockpit, 150
horizontal fin, blimp, 158
horizontal gauge, carpenter's level, 414
horizontally opposed automobile engine, 107
horizontal reduction, theodolite, 426
horizontal stabilizer: helicopter, 146; jet fighter, 152; jumbo jet, 149; single engine airplane, 147
horizon glass, sextant, 133
horizon indicator, 747 cockpit, 151
horizon line, perspective, 362
horizon mirror, sextant, 133
horizon sunshade, sextant, 133
horn: car, 106; cow, 30; fire engine, 120, 121; fire extinguisher, 280; French, 352; glacier, 12; motorcycle, 125; orchestra, 348; saddle, 329; shoe, 203; subway motorman's cab, 115; truck tractor, 116; ultimate beast, 46
horny scales, crocodilians, 41
horoscope, 493
hors d'oeuvre, 259
horse, 36; flat racing entry, 330; merry-go-round, 91; pommel, 301
horse-drawn carriage, 127
horsehide, baseball, 286
horse-hoof cuff, Manchu court dress, 475
horse latitudes, wind, 6
horsepower, internal combustion engine, 396

horseracing, 330-331
horse rod, merry-go-round, 91
horse shoe, 36
horse trail, public sign, 491
hose, 203; automobile engine, 107; baseball batter, 286; fireboat, 144; fire extinguisher, 280; gas pump, 108; kitchen sink, 243; lawn sprinkler, 418; locomotive, 112; panty, 191; pumper, 121; skin diving, 325; vacuum cleaner, 279
hose-handling derrick, tanker, 137
hosel, golf club, 304
hose nozzle, 418; fire hydrant, 121
hose reel: fireboat, 144; tower ladder, 120
hospital: frontier fort, 80; passenger ship, 139; prison, 74; road sign, 488
hot air balloon, 326
hot corner, baseball field, 287
hot dog, 261
hotdogging board, surfboard, 324
hotel, airport, 92
hotel information, public sign, 490
hot gas pipe, heat exchanger, 393
hot metal, printing, 164
hot plate, coffee maker, 248
hot shoe, camera, 171
hot slot, electrical receptacle, 388
hot springs, volcano, 10
hot type, printing, 164
hot-water differential thermostat, solar heating system, 383
hot-water device, sink, 243
hot-water faucet, bathtub, 270
hot water handle, sink, 243, 269
hot-water heater, 391; camper, 126
hot-water tank, solar heating system, 383
hot wire: electrical receptacle, 388; electrician's, 413
hourglass, 229
hour hand: clock, 229; watch, 216
hour line, sundial, 381
hour meter, powerboat engine, 134
house, craps, 340; foundation, 58; exterior, 60-61; frame, 59; roof truss, 59; zodiac, 493
house ad, magazine, 169
houseboat, 134
house car, train, 113
House corridor, Capitol, 72
housekeeper's room, White House, 73
House of Representatives chamber, Capitol, 72
house organ magazine, 167
house plan, White House, 73
housing: automatic rifle, 461; automobile license plate, 102; can opener, 247; CB radio microphone, 179; compass, 132; curling iron, 210; drill, 409; electric plug, 388; eye scope, 438; finishing sander, 411; fishing reel, 334; hair dryer, 208; harmonica, 360; jackhammer, 426; juice extractor, 251; laboratory

clamp, 436; lawn sprinkler, 418; mechanical sweeper, 123; outboard engine, 133; paint spray gun, 415; phonograph headphone, 177; potter's wheel, 367; power mower, 419; razor, 206; saber saw, 407; saddle, 329; stationary rings, 301; tape measure, 414; toaster, 249
hovercraft, 145
howitzer, midget, 462
hub: automobile, 104; bicycle, 124; cassette tape, 175; cupboard, 239; geodesic dome, 83; hypodermic syringe, 441; outboard engine, 133; racing car, 332; spider web, 38; stagecoach, 127; tow truck, 122; wheelchair, 442
hubble-bubble, 225
hubcap: automobile, 103
hubcap: child's wagon, 283; power mower, 419; seeder, 420
hull: boat, 128; drag racing, 333; helicopter, 146; submarine, 143; tank, 465; windsurfer, 324
hull column, oil drilling platform, 99
hull form, powerboat, 134
hull machine gun, tank, 465
hull number: mainsail, 132; submarine, 143
human body, 24-29
Humboldt Current, ocean, 6
humerus, human, 26
humidifier, 392
humidity sensor, weather station, 18
humidor, cigar, 224
hump: crocodile, 41; frog, 42; railroad yard, 94; ultimate beast, 47
hump yard, railroad, 94
hung ceiling, elevator car, 76
hurdle, 298
hurdle race, track and field, 294
hurricane, 17; weather map, 19
hurst tool, police car, 118
husk: coconut, 258; corn, 56
hutch, side piece, 239
hydrant intake, pumper, 121
hydraulic filter breather, bulldozer, 425
hydraulic fork, motorcycle, 125
hydraulic fuel tank, bulldozer, 425
hydraulic hand pump, pilot's instrument panel, 153
hydraulic lifter, tower ladder, 120
hydraulic line, garbage truck, 123
hydraulic-pneumatic device, oil drilling platform, 99
hydraulic tank, garbage truck, 123
hydroelectric powerhouse, dam, 98
hydrofoil, 145
hydrogen venting arm, launch pad, 154
hydrometer, laboratory, 437
hyphen, grammatical symbol, 497
hypodermic fang, snake, 40
hypodermic needle, 441
hypodermic syringe, 441
hydrosphere, earth, 4
hypospray, 441
hypothenar, human hand, 29

I

I: braille, 496; sign language, 496
ICBM, 466
ICC bumper, truck platform, 117
ice, thundercloud, 17
ice ax, mountain climbing, 328
iceberg, glacier, 12
icebox, 245; sailboat, 131
ice cliff, mountain, 9
ice climbing boot, 328
ice cream: cone, 261; scoop, 255; sundae, 260
ice crystal, clouds, 16
ice dispenser, refrigerator, 245
ice face, mountain, 8
icefall, mountain, 9
ice field, mountain, 9
ice hammer, mountain climbing, 328
ice hockey, 290-291
icemaker, refrigerator, 245
ice pack, 12
ice screw, mountain climbing, 328
ice sheet, 8
ice skates, 319
ice tray, refrigerator, 245
ice window, igloo, 83
icing, cake, 260
icing nozzle, 255
icing syringe, 255
idea balloon, cartoon, 375
identification: golf ball, 304; paper money, 220, 221; political map, 21
identification bracelet, 183
identification digit, credit card, 222
identification mark, dental braces, 443
identification number: credit card, 222; phonograph speaker, 117
identification tags, attaché case, 281
ideogram, public sign, 490
ideograph, public sign, 490
idler pinion, hand drill, 408
idle-speed, solenoid, automobile engine, 107
idling wheel, tank, 465
ID window, checkbook clutch, 219
igloo, 83
ignition, car, 106
ignition cable, bazooka, 462
ignition wire, automobile engine, 107
iguana, 40
ilial crest, human, 25
ilium, human, 26
illuminator, microscope, 432
illustration: book jacket, 165; book page IV, 165; cartooning, 374; magazine, 168
image: church, 84; movie film, 172; offset-lithography, 164; rotogravure, 164; still camera, 171
immature fruit, cucumber, 52
impact attenuation device, highway, 110
imperial arch, royal crown, 469
imperial mantle, royal regalia, 468
impost, arch, 70
impression, letterpress, 164
impression control, typewriter, 162
impression cylinder, printing press, 164
inboard aileron, jumbo jet, 148
inboard elevator, jumbo jet, 149
inboard engine, 133

inboard-outboard engine, **133**
inboard spoiler, jumbo jet, **148**
inbound line, football field, **289**
incandescent bulb, lighting, **234**
in-cannel, gouge, **410**
inch, grammatical symbol, **497**
inches of mercury, aneroid barometer, **18**
inch mark, tape measure, **414**
incident-light index, light meter, **174**
incised line, scrimshaw, **369**
incised printing, **371**
incisor, tooth, **446**
incline, roller coaster, **90**
incline track, amusement park, **9**
incore-instrument guide tube, nuclear reactor, **385**
indent, proofreader's mark, **498**
indented surface, thimble, **376**
index: light meter, **174**; newspaper, **166**; playing card, **342**; political map, **20**; slide projector, **173**; wristwatch, **216**
index arm, sextant, **133**
index column, voting booth, **427**
index contour, topographic map, **22**
indexer, pilot's instrument panel, **155**
index finger, human hand, **29**
index hole, computer diskette, **429**
index mark, sextant, **133**
index mirror, sextant, **133**
index reference key, political map, **20**
index sunshade, sextant, **133**
Indian, **474**
indicator: CB radio, **179**; destroyer, **141**; key punch, **428**; laboratory scale, **436**; light meter, **174**; organ, **354**; phonograph turntable, **176**; pilot's instrument panel, **153**; roadmap, **20**; 747 cockpit, **150**, **151**; ski binding, **320**; space shuttle, **155**; tape recorder, **175**; television set, **181**; toll booth fee, **110**; voting booth, **427**
indicator light: airport runway, **92**; coffee maker, **248**; phonograph receiver, **177**; 747 cockpit, **151**; subway motorman's cab, **115**; toaster oven, **249**
indicia, magazine, **167**
individual account number, credit card, **222**
individual race, swimming pool, **310**
individual lever, voting booth, **427**
inductor: dispenser, **263**; elevator shaft, **76**
industry indentification digit, credit card, **222**
inertial guidance system, submarine, **143**
infantry badge, military uniform, **480**
infantry banquette, permanent fort, **81**
infantry button, Revolutionary War general, **476**
infantryman, uniform, **480**, **481**
infantry rope, uniform, **480**
infield: baseball, **287**; harness racetrack, **331**

infinity, symbol, **495**
inflatable anti-shock trousers, paramedic equipment, **119**
inflation bulb, blood pressure gauge, **439**
inflation needle, football, **288**
infill, fence, **65**
inflatable, **129**
inflation hose, skin diving, **325**
inflation valve, tire, **101**
inflator, skin diving, **325**
inflorescence, grass, **56**
information: check routing, **222**; public sign, **490**; ticket, **343**; toll booth, **110**
information display, pilot's instrument panel, **153**
infrared lamp, hair styling, **210**
infrared night scope, bazooka, **462**
infrared radiometer, satellite, **182**
infrared remote-control command, television set, **181**
infrared seeker, jet fighter, **152**
infuster, tea, **256**
infusion coffee maker, **248**
ingredient, package, **264**
ingress and egress platform, lunar lander, **156**
initial: letter, **161**; magazine, **168**
injection, hypodermic syringe, **441**
injector, razor blade, **206**
injector pipe, locomotive, **112**
ink: octopus, **44**; pen, **160**; rotogravure, **164**; rubbing, **370**; well, **160**
inked surface, wood block, **368**
ink roller, offset-lithography, **164**
inlay: armor, **455**; dental, **445**; sideboard, **239**; sofa, **232**
inlet: coastline, **15**; combustion jet engine, **397**; jet fighter, **152**; laboratory burner, **437**; nuclear reactor, **385**; surgical table, **440**; toilet, **271**
in-line six automobile engine, **107**
inmate, prison, **74**
in mufti, police, **482**
innards, human, **25**
inner bailey, castle, **78**, **79**
inner basket, sink, **243**
inner cantus, eye, **28**
inner core, earth, **4**
inner cornice, merry-go-round, **91**
inner deck, escalator, **77**
inner enclosure, air conditioner, **392**
inner hearth, fireplace, **228**
inner-liner pouch, package, **264**
inner lip, univalve shell, **45**
inner reflector, adjustable lamp, **235**
inner ring, embroidery, **377**
inner sash, window, **63**
inner shell, nuclear reactor, **384**
inner slide brace, trombone, **352-353**
inner sole, shoe, **200**, **201**
inner spring, bed, **267**
inner table, backgammon board, **339**
inner ward, castle, **78**, **79**
inner wheel, ferris wheel, **91**
input, guitar amplifier, **357**
input jack, cassette tape recorder, **175**
input plug, movie

projector, **173**
inscription: money, **220**; tombstone, **500**
inseam: jacket, **184**; trousers, **187**
insect, **39**
insert: clamp, **399**; ice skates, **319**; magazine, **169**; proofreader's mark, **498**
insert steel, jackhammer, **426**
inset: magazine, **167**, **168**; political map, **21**
inset sleeve, cardigan sweater, **195**
inside address, letter, **161**
inside cap, umbrella, **226**
inside drive, merry-go-round, **91**
inside leg seam, trousers, **187**
inside margin, book page, **165**
inside rail, harness racetrack, **331**
inside sleeve seam, jacket, **184**
insignia: drum major's coat, **479**; mainsail, **132**; military uniform, **480**, **481**
insole: boot, **202**; man's shoe, **200**; sandal, **202**
inspection plate, buoy, **128**
instant camera, **170**
instant hot-water device, sink, **243**
instep: human foot, **29**; shoe, **200**, **201**; sock, **203**
instruction: fire extinguisher, **280**; furnace, **390**; parking meter, **109**; pay telephone, **178**; sheet music, **346**; water heater, **391**
instrument, musical, **348-360**
instrument approach, airport runway, **92**
instrumentation, 747 engine, **151**
instrumentation control, space shuttle, **155**
instrument input, guitar amplifier, **357**
instrument panel: airplane, **153**; bulldozer, **425**; lunar rover, **157**; snowmobile, **126**
instrument sensitivity, volt-ohm meter, **413**
instrument tray, dental unit, **444**
instrument warning light, 747 cockpit, **151**
insulated grip, wire stripper, **413**
insulated handle: chafing dish, **241**; lineman's pliers, **404**
insulated window, **63**
insulating body, plug fuse, **389**
insulating glass, window, **63**
insulation: cartridge fuse, **389**; electrician's wire **413**; solar collector panel, **383**
insulator, overhead power line, **386**
intaglio: and etching, **371**; printing, **164**
intake: bus, **114**; destroyer, **141**; racing car, **332**, **333**; silo, **100**; turbine locomotive, **113**; vacuum cleaner, **279**
integrated control panel, pilot's instrument panel, **153**
integrated thermal meteoroid garment, **157**
intensity control, radar, **434**
interaction region, transistor chip, **386**
intercarpal, human, **26**
interchange, highway, **110**
interchangeable lens,

camera, **171**
interchange symbol number, road map, **20**
intercity bus, **114**
intercolumniation, **71**
intercom: prison, **74**; 747 cockpit, **150**
intercontinental ballistic missile (ICBM), **466**
interdigital pad, human hand, **29**
interface, ski binding, **320**
interference rejector, radar, **434**
inter-grip rim lock, **448**
interlining, necktie, **189**
interlocking timbered joint, Japanese architecture, **68**
interior: Hansom cab, **127**; window, **63**
interior panel, coffin, **500**
interior slope, permanent fort, **81**
intermediate hurdle, **298**
intermediate lens, eyeglasses, **217**
intermediate pipe, automobile, **104**
internal combustion engine, **396**
internal organs, human, **27**
internal wave, **14**
international architecture, **68-69**
International Date Line, **5**
International Standard Book Number, **165**
interpretation, punch card, **428**
interrupter, label, **264**
intersection, highway, **110**
interstate route: road map, **20**; road sign, **488**
interstellar cloud, **2**
interval, thematic map, **21**
intestine, human, **27**
intrados, arch, **70**
intravenous equipment, operating room table, **440**
introduction, magazine, **168**
intubation box, paramedic equipment, **119**
inventory control number, paperback book, **165**
inverted hub, two truck, **122**
invisible zipper, **205**
involuntary muscle, human, **26**
ion particle cloud, **3**
iris, eye, **28**
iris diaphragm, microscope, **432**
iron, **275**; branding, **422**; crossbow, **456**; fireplace, **228**; flat racing, **330**; golf club, **305**; hair styling, **210**; plane, **410**
iron curtain, stage, **344**
ironing board, **275**
iron lung, **442**
iron man, cattle ranch, **422**
irregular galaxy, **2**
isarithmic map, **21**
ISBN, book, **165**
ischium, human, **26**
is equal to, symbol, **495**
island, **7**, **15**; aircraft carrier, **142**; dental, **444**; highway, **110**; river, **13**; service station, **108**; toll booth, **110**
isle, **7**
islet, **7**
is not equal to, symbol, **495**
isobar, weather map, **19**
isopleth line, thematic map, **21**
isotonic exercises, body building, **338**
issue date: check, **222**; magazine, **167**; newspaper, **166**
issuer: paper money, **220**; postal money order, **223**; traveler's check, **223**

issuing Federal Reserve Bank's code number, paper money, 221
isthmus, 7
italic: proofreader's mark, 498; type, 163
italic refer, newspaper, 166
item-by-item tape, cash register, 430
IV equipment, operating room table, 440
ivory carving, scrimshaw, 369

J

J: braille, 496; sign language, 496
jabot, bridal gown, 472
jack: CB radio, 179; garbage truck, 123; metal detector, 435; movie camera, 172; phonograph receiver, 177; playing cards, 342; tape recorder, 175; video recorder, 180; volt-ohm meter, 413
jacket: cartridge, 460; computer diskette, 429; fencing, 309; hardback book, 165; kiln, 367; king's regalia, 468; locomotive, 112; Manchu court dress, 475; man's, 184; military uniform, 480; phonograph record, 176; skin diving, 325; sweater, 195; vacuum cleaner dust bag, 279; waterskiing, 323; woman's, 192; zinc carbon cell, 387
jacket crown, dental, 443
jackhammer, 426
jack knife, 416
jack-plug socket, electric guitar, 357
jack staff, destroyer, 141
jack stud, house, 59
jaguar coat, ultimate beast, 46
jail, 74
jai alai, 308
jalousie window, 63
jamb: arrow, 455; castle portcullis, 79; door, 62; vault, 447; window, 63
jamb plate, chain lock, 448
Japan Current, ocean, 7
jar: beauty product, 213; laboratory, 437
jarn, cartoon, 375
javelin, 295, 297
jaw: bear trap, 423; brace chuck, 408; cat, 35; clamp, 399; drill, 409; fish, 43; human, 24; nail clippers, 211; pliers, 404; snake, 41; vise, 398, 399; wire stripper, 413; wrench, 405
jaw pad, football helmet, 288
jaws of life, police car, 118
jazz band, 348
jean pocket, trousers, 187
jeans, 187
jeep, 126
Jehu, stagecoach, 127
jellaba, Arab dress, 475
jellyfish, 44
jersey: basketball, 292; football, 288; sailor, 481
Jersey pocket, bowling, 311
Jerusalem cross, symbol, 492
jet: bath, 270; engine, 397; fighter, 152; hovercraft, 145; jumbo, 148
jet blast deflector, aircraft carrier, 142
jet bridge, airport, 92
jet engine test area, aircraft carrier, 142
jet nozzle, lawn sprinkler, 418
jettison handle, pilot's instrument panel, 153
jetty, nautical chart, 22

jewel drawer, dressing table, 268
Jewish ritual items, 470
Jew's harp, 360
j-hook, tow truck bed, 122
jib: sail, 132; sailboat, 130
jibtop, 130
jib topsail, 130
jig, fishing, 335
jigsaw, 407
jingle, tambourine, 358
jock, 190
jockey: flat racing, 330; saddle, 329
jockey shorts, 190
jockstrap, 190
jockey wheel, bicycle, 124
jogger, running shoe, 296
jogging track, passenger ship, 138
John B., cowboy hat, 474
"John Wayne," can opener, 247
join, basket, 262
joint: automobile, 105; billiard cue, 314; brick wall, 67; folding rule, 414; hardback book, 165; hasp, 450; hitch and harrow, 424; human, 26, 29; oil drilling platform, 99; pliers, 404; silkscreen, 369; timbered, 68; umbrella, 226; windsurfer, 324
joint bar, railroad track, 111
joint-sealing compound, plumbing, 412
joist, house, 58, 59
joker, playing cards, 342
journal, 167
journal clerk, Congress, 12
journal printer, cash register, 430
jowl, pork, 32
judge, 87; fencing match, 309
judge's box, ice hockey rink, 291
judge's chambers, 87
judge's entrance, jai alai cancha, 308
judge's seat, courtroom, 87
judge's secretary's table, courtroom, 87
Judith, playing card queen, 342
jug, infusion coffee maker, 248
juggler, circus, 88
jugular groove, horse, 36
juice extractor, 251
juicer, 251
juice rack, refrigerator, 245
jukebox, 176
jumbo jet, 148-149
jump, track and field, 294
jumper: merry-go-round, 91; parachuting, 327; sailor's uniform, 481; waterskiing, 323
jumper cable, tow truck, 122
jumping: ski, 320; track and field, 294
jumping bed, trampoline, 302
jumping pit, high jump, 294
jump line: magazine, 169; newspaper, 166
jump plane, parachuting, 327
jump rope, body building, 338
junction, highway, 110
junction box: electrical receptacle, 388; light fixture, 234
jungle gym, backyard, 283
Jupiter, planet, 3
jury box, courtroom, 87
juryroom, 87

K

K: braille, 496; sign language, 496
kame, mountain, 8
kangaroo crane, skyscraper, 75

kangaroo pouch, ultimate beast, 46
karat, ring, 215
kasagi, torii, 68-69
kazoo, 360
keel: box kite, 317; sailboard, 130; turkey, 33; waterskiing, 323
keep, castle, 78
keeper: dress, 194; man's belt, 186; saddle, 329; tape recorder, 175; toaster, 249
keffiyah, 475
keg, 263
kennel, passenger ship, 138
kerf, saw, 406
kernel, grass, 56
ketch hand, cattle ranch, 422
ketchup, and frankfurter, 261
kettle, tea service, 241
kettledrum, 348, 358
kettle grill, 284
key, 449; accordion, 360; anchor, 128; basketball court, 292; calculator, 431; can opener, 247; cash register, 430; clarinet, 350; computer, 429; drill press, 409; flute, 350; fruit, 50; globe, 1; guitar, 356, 357; key punch, 428; metronome, 361; organ, 354; piano, 355; political map, 20; saw, 401; saxophone, 351; telegraph key, 159; television set, 181; trombone, 353; trumpet, 353; typewriter, 162; video recorder, 180
keyboard: accordion, 360; carillon, III; cash register, 430; computer, 429; key punch, 428; organ, 354; piano, 355; space shuttle computer, 155; synthesizer, 357; typewriter, 162
keychain, 449; police gun belt, 483
key chuck, power drill, 409
keyed point of interest, city plan, 20
keyhold, mortise lock, 448
key holder, police gun belt, 482
keyhole, door, 62
keyless chuck, drill press, 409
key lever, telegraph, 159
key pad, computer, 429
key punch, computer, 428
key signature, music, 346
keyslip, grand piano, 355
keystone: arch, 70; arched window, 60; cupboard, 239; door, 62
keystone tip, screwdriver, 403
keyway, lock, 448, 449
kick, bottle, 263
kick arc, soccer field, 293
kicker, magazine, 169
kick mark, soccer field, 293
kicking pad, knee kicker, 242
kickstand, motorcycle, 125
kicktail, skateboard, 318
kick-wheel, potter's wheel, 367
kidney, human, 27
kill, volleyball, 313
killer, darts, 316
killing trap, 423
kiln, 367
kiltie, man's shoe, 200
king: checkers, 339; chess, 339; playing cards, 342; royal regalia, 468
king block, igloo, 83
kingpin: bowling, 311; roller skate, 318; truck van, 117
king post: hang glider, 327; house, 59; tanker, 137
king row, checkers, 339
kingside men, chess, 339

kiss curl, woman's hair, 209
kitchen: lobster pot, 423; prison, 74
kitchen range, house blueprint, 60
kitchen sink, 243
kitchen spoon, 255
kitchen timer, 254
kite, 317
kitten, 35
klettershoe, mountain climbing, 328
knapsack, 337
knave, playing cards, 342
knee: cat, 35; cow, 30; dog, 34; drop-leaf table, 238; frog, 42; horse, 36; human, 24
knee boot, harness racing, 331
knee breeches: Beefeater, 467; Revolutionary War general, 476
knee cup, armor, 455
kneehole: desk, 272; dressing table, 268
knee hose, fencing, 309
knee kicker, for carpet laying, 242
knee lever, guitar 357
knee machine, universal gym, 338
kneepad: basketball, 292; football, 288; ice hockey, 291; rollerskating, 318; ski pants, 320
knee roll, saddle, 329
knee sock, 203; ski clothes, 321
knickers: fencing, 309; ski clothes, 321
knife: corkscrew, 247; engraving, 369; guillotine, 452; kitchen, 252; mower, 419; painting, 364; pocket, 416; skin diving, 325; Swiss army, 416; table, 240; thrusting and cutting weapon, 453
knife box, sideboard, 239
knife case, sideboard, 239
knife man, cattle ranch, 422
knight, chess, 339
knight pawn, chess, 339
knitting needle, 378
knit vest, 195
knob: baseball bat, 287; bathtub, 270; bolt ring, 214; camera, 171; cannon barrel, 457; can opener, 247; chain saw, 421; citrus juicer, 251; coffee maker, 248; door, 62, 448; drain cleaner, 412; dressing table, 268; drill press, 409; drum, 358; fishing reel, 334; handbag, 218; knee kicker, 242; lamp, 235; medical examination table, 440; microscope, 432; mower, 419; paint spray gun, 415; pencil sharpener, 273; phonograph receiver, 177; plane, 410; pots and pans, 253; projector, 173; propane torch, 412; rifle scope, 459; saw, 407; seeder, 420; telescope, 433; theodolite, 426; toaster, 249; typewriter, 162; venetian blind, 237; volt-ohm meter, 413; wind turbine, 382
knob nut and bolt, plane, 410
knocker, door, 62
knot: ballet toeshoes, 478; balloon, 477; gallows, 452; lumber, 66; thread, 376; woman's hair, 209
knothole, lumber, 6
knuckle: dog, 34; hinge, 450; human hand, 29
knuckle bow, sword hilt, 453

kokoshniki, architecture, 68
kosher symbol, label, 264
kudu horn, ultimate beast, 46
Kuroshio Current, ocean, 6
kusabi, torii, 69

L

L: braille, 496; sign
  language, 496
label: baseball bat, 287;
  cartooning, 374;
  church, 84; computer
  diskette, 429; gas
  pump, 108;
  magazine, 167;
  necktie, 188;
  package, 264-265;
  phonograph record, 176;
  shirt, 185
labeling, 264-265
labial, tooth, 446
laboratory
  equipment, 436-437
labrum, grasshopper, 39
laccolith, volcano, 10
lace: baseball, 286; baseball
  glove, 287; boxing
  glove, 303; bridal
  gown, 472; ice
  hockey, 291; ice
  skates, 319; maid's
  uniform, 473; man's
  shoe, 200; queen's
  regalia, 468; running
  shoe, 296
lace lock, ice climbing
  boot, 328
lacing: football, 288;
  snowshoe, 321
lacrosse, 293
ladder, 415; circus
  aerialist, 88;
  destroyer, 140; ferris
  wheel, 91; hydrofoil, 145;
  lunar lander, 156;
  powerboat, 135; silo, 100;
  slide, 283; tower
  ladder, 120; tugboat, 144;
  venetian blind, 237
ladle, 255
lagoon, 7, 15
La Hire, playing card
  jack, 342
lake, 7, 13; dam, 98;
  mountain, 8
lam, hand loom, 379
lamb, 31
lambrequin, coat of
  arms, 487
lamella, Jew's harp, 360
lamina, leaf, 50
lamp, 234; adjustable, 235;
  automobile, 102;
  blimp, 158; hair
  styling, 210; Hansom
  cab, 127; house, 61;
  locomotive, 112;
  speculum, 438;
  stagecoach, 127; television
  set, 181; track
  lighting, 235
lamp field diaphragm,
  microscope, 432
lampshade, 234
lance, medieval, 454
lance guard, armor, 455
Lancelot, playing card
  jack, 342
lancet window, church, 84
land feature, 7
landing, staircase, 64
landing area: aircraft
  carrier, 142; pole
  vault, 299
landing control, space
  shuttle, 155
landing gear, lunar
  lander, 156
landing gear controls: pilot's
  instrument panel, 153; 747
  cockpit, 151
landing light, helicopter, 146

landing mat, gymnastics, 300
landing net, fishing, 335
landing pit, track and
  field, 294
landing system, aircraft
  carrier, 142
landing threshold, airport
  runway, 92
landing wheel: blimp, 158;
  glider, 147
landing-zone detector,
  elevator shaft, 76
landmark object, topographic
  map, 22
landmass, and continental
  shelf, 5
land mine, 463
landscaping, house, 61
lane: basketball court, 292;
  bowling, 311;
  highway, 110; running
  track, 294; swimming
  pool, 310; toll booth, 110
language, symbolic, 496
lantern, camping, 336
lanyard: cowboy hat, 198;
  camera, 170;
  stopwatch, 298
lap belt, drag racing
  driver, 333
lapel: jacket, 184, 192;
  Revolutionary War
  general, 476
lap-felled seam, tent, 336
lappet, bishop, 471
large branch, tuba, 352
large intestine, human, 27
large shallow gouge,
  woodcarving, 366
large wheel, wheelchair, 442
lariat, ranching gear, 422
larva, insect, 39
LaserDisc player,
  television, 181
lash brush, beauty
  product, 213
lashing, flat kite, 317
lasso, 422
latch: camera, 170; chain
  saw, 421; clothes
  dryer, 277;
  cupboard, 239;
  dishwasher, 246;
  door, 448; garbage
  disposal, 243; hasp, 450;
  mailbox, 227; mortise
  lock, 448; needle, 378;
  revolver, 460;
  trenchcoat, 196
latch needle, 378
latch support, pulley
  block, 451
lateral adjusting lever,
  plane, 410
lateral furrow, horse's
  foot, 36
lateral incisor, tooth, 446
lateral line, fish, 43
laterally gaited trotter, 331
lateral moraine, 8, 9, 12
lateral pulley, universal
  gym, 338
lath, lobster pot, 423
Latin cross, symbol, 492
latissimus dorsi, human, 26
latitude, parallel of, 5, 20
latticework tower, power
  network, 386
launch bar abort, pilot's
  instrument panel, 153
launcher: aircraft
  carrier, 142;
  destroyer, 141;
  rocket, 462
launcher tube, bazooka, 462
launching ramp, public
  sign, 491
launch pad, space
  shuttle, 154
laundry: frontier fort, 80;
  passenger ship, 138;
  prison, 74
lava flow, volcano, 10

lavaliere, 215
lavatory, 269; bus, 114;
  jumbo jet, 148, 149
lawn cart, 420
lawn mower, 419
lawn sprinkler, 418
layout: dominos, 339;
  magazine, 168;
  roulette, 370
LCD, wristwatch, 216
lead: internal combustion
  engine, 396;
  magazine, 168;
  newspaper, 166;
  pencil, 160; proofreader's
  mark, 498; and volt-ohm
  meter, 413
lead acid battery, 387
lead came, 372
lead connector,
  pacemaker, 442
leader: book page, IV; film
  roll, 171; fishhook, 335;
  house, 61; House of
  Representatives, 72
leader board, windmill, 382
leader-pusher, cowboy, 474
lead-in, magazine, 169
lead-in brace, toboggan, 322
leading edge: ax, 454; hang
  glider, 327; jumbo jet, 148
lead-in groove, phonograph
  record, 176
lead-in wire, bulb, 235
lead-out groove, phonograph
  record, 176
lead pencil, 160
lead pick-up, guitar, 357
lead pipe, trumpet, 353
lead plum, cowboy, 474
lead track, railroad yard, 94
lead weight: flat
  racing, 330; grandfather
  clock pendulum, 229; skin
  diving, 325
lead wire, vacuum tube, 386
leaf, 50; book, 165; canal
  lock, 97; carrot, 52;
  celery, 258; cigar, 224;
  corn, 56; fern, 55;
  grass, 56; hair clip, 210;
  hinge, 450; lettuce, 258;
  onion, 52, 258;
  pineapple, 53; table, 238;
  tree, 48
leaf springs, truck
  tractor, 116
lean tissue, meat, 258
leash: clown, 477; ski, 320
leather: bagpipe bag, 359;
  dabber pad, 371; dog, 34;
  flat racing, 330;
  football, 288; hot air
  balloon, 326; parka
  tab, 197; saddle bar, 329;
  stirrup, 329;
  suspenders, 186; tefillin
  strap, 470
lechurban, Jewish prayer
  shawl, 470
lecture hall, passenger
  ship, 139
lede: magazine, 168;
  newspaper, 166
ledge: basket, 262;
  bathtub, 270; can
  opener, 247; mountain, 9
ledger, incline track, 90
ledger line, music, 347
leech, mainsail, 132
leeward side, boat, 128
left bank, river, 13
left-channel volume unit
  meter, tape recorder, 175
left ear, newspaper, 166
left engine fuel shutoff
  handle, pilot's instrument
  panel, 153
left field, baseball, 287
left-handed strike pocket,
  bowling, 311
left-hand page, book, 165
left-hand steering lever,

bulldozer, 425
left pedestal, desk, 272
left service court:
  badminton, 313;
  handball, 307
left wing, easel, 364
leg: backyard
  equipment, 283; bee, 39;
  bridge, 95; bureau, 268;
  camera tripod, 174;
  cat, 35; chaise
  lounge, 284; dog, 34;
  desk, 272; ferris
  wheel, 91; fishing
  reel, 334; human, 24;
  ironing board, 275;
  kettledrum, 358;
  kiln, 367; kite, 317;
  lamb, 31; lobster, 45;
  lounger, 231; medical
  examination table, 440;
  mortar, 462; panty
  hose, 191; paper clip, 273;
  parallel bars, 300;
  piano, 355; playpen, 282;
  pool table, 314;
  poultry, 33; rocking
  chair, 230; sawhorse, 398;
  sheep, 31; sideboard, 239;
  stage, 344; staple, 400;
  steamer basket, 253;
  stove, 394; table, 238;
  table saw, 407;
  telescope, 433;
  tom-tom, 358;
  trampoline, 302;
  trousers, 187;
  tweezers, 211;
  wheelbarrow, 420;
  woman's pants, 192;
  workbench, 398; see also
  limb
legal tender, paper
  money, 220
leg brace: wheelbarrow, 420;
  workbench, 398
legend: magazine, 169;
  money, 220; political
  map, 21
legging: Indian, 474;
  sailor, 481
leg hole, man's
  underpants, 190
legislative clerk, Senate, 72
leg leveler, parallel bars, 300
leg lock, screen, 173
leg-of-mutton sleeve, bridal
  gown, 472
leg press, universal gym, 338
leg strap, athletic
  supporter, 190
leg support, backyard
  equipment, 283
legume, pea, 52
lemon press, 257
lemon squeezer, 257
length adjuster, knee
  kicker, 242
lengthwise grain, fabric, 380
lengthwise grain line, sewing
  pattern, 380
lens: automobile, 102;
  binoculars, 433;
  camera, 170, 171, 172,
  180; ear scope, 438;
  eye, 28; eyeglasses, 217;
  microscope, 432;
  projector, 173; radar, 434;
  rifle scope, 459;
  shapes, 217; skin diving
  mask, 325; solar power
  system, 383;
  telescope, 433;
  thermometer, 439; traffic
  light, 109
lens-selection disc, eye
  scope, 438
lens tissue, photographic, 174
lenticel, tree, 48
Leo, zodiac, 493
leopard coat, ultimate
  beast, 46
leotard, ballet dancer, 478

less space, proofreader's mark, **498**
less than, symbol, **495**
let it stand, proofreader's mark, **498**
letter, **161**; paper money, 220, **221**; weather vane, **19**
letter drawer, desk, **272**
letterhead, **161**
letterpress printing, **164**
lettuce, **52, 258**
lettuce dryer, **256**
levee, **98**; river, **13**
level: carpenter's, **414**; combination square, **414**; transit, **426**
level control, phonograph speaker, **177**
leveler: parallel bars, **300**; pool table, **314**
leveling bubble, theodolite, **426**
leveling foot: garbage disposal, **243**; slide projector, **173**
lever: bathtub, **270**; bicycle, **124**; bulldozer, **425**; camera, **171**; can opener, **247**; child's car seat, **282**; guitar, **357**; electrical wall switch, **388**; fire extinguisher, **280**; fishing reel, **334**; gas cigarette lighter, **224**; gas pump, **108**; hand grenade, **463**; internal combustion engine, **396**; iron, **275**; jackhammer, **426**; machine gun, **461**; motorcycle, **125**; movie projector, **173**; nail clippers, **211**; outboard engine, **133**; pay phone, **178**; pencil sharpener, **273**; pilot's instrument panel, **153**; pistol nozzle, **418**; plane, **410**; pliers, **404**; potter's wheel, **367**; 747 cockpit, **150, 151**; sextant, **133**; spreader, **420**; stagecoach, **127**; stroller, **282**; surgical table, **440**; telegraph key, **159**; typewriter, **162**; voting booth, **427**; wheelchair, **442**
lever arm, corkscrew, **247**
lever cap, plane, **410**
lever dolly, balance beam, **300**
lever knob, pencil sharpener, **273**
lever lock: pistol nozzle, **418**; starting block, **298**
lever-wrench pliers, **404**
levigator, lithography, **370**
Libra, zodiac, **493**
library: passenger ship, **138**; White House, **73**
license plate: automobile, **102, 103**; tow truck bed, **122**
lickings, ice cream cone, **261**
lid: automobile trunk, **103**; barbecue grill, **284**; basket, **262**; camp stove, **336**; can opener, **247**; coffee maker, **248**; coffin, **500**; juice extractor, **251**; kiln, **367**; percolator, **248**; piano, **355**; pipe bowl, **225**; pots and pans, **253**; tea kettle, **241**; toilet, **271**; washing machine, **276**
lie: golf, **304**; ice hockey stick, **290**

life, symbol of, **492**
lifeboat: destroyer, **141**; oil drilling platform, **99**; passenger ship, **138**; tanker, **137**
life jacket, waterskiing, **323**
lifeline: destroyer, **140**; human hand, **29**; inflatable, **129**; sailboat, **130**
lifepack, paramedic equipment, **119**
life raft: aircraft carrier, **142**; jumbo jet, **148**; tugboat, **144**
life ring, fireboat, **144**
life-support system: ambulance, **119**; racing car, **332**; spacesuit, **157**
lift: body building, **338**; boot, **202**; passenger ship, **138**
lift bridge, **95**
lift cord, venetian blind, **237**
lift cylinder, bulldozer, **425**
lifter: can opener, **247**; kitchen utensil, **255**; phonograph, **176**; tower ladder, **120**
lift fan, hovercraft, **145**
lifting column, surgical table, **440**
lifting eye, buoy, **128**
lifting ring, rowboat, **129**
lift knob, toaster, **249**
lift link, hitch and harrow, **424**
lift lock: toaster, **249**; venetian blind, **237**
lift-net, tower ladder, **120**
lift pedal, dental unit, **444**
lift-out stem, steamer basket, **253**
lift rod, sink, **269**
lift span, bridge, **95**
lift wires, toilet, **271**
ligature: clarinet mouthpiece, **351**; grammatical symbol, **497**
light: aircraft carrier, **142**; airport runway, **92**; automobile, **102, 103**; bulldozer, **425**; buoy, **128**; bus, **114**; camera, **172**; camper, **126**; CB radio, **179**; church, **85**; coffee maker, **248**; dental unit, **444**; destroyer, **140, 141**; door, **62**; drag racing, **333**; fencing strip, **309**; fireboat, **144**; fire engine, **120, 121**; guitar amplifier, **357**; helicopter, **146**; house, **61**; ice hockey, **290**; jet fighter, **152**; lift bridge, **95**; locomotive, **113**; lunar lander, **156**; mechanical sweeper, **123**; motorcycle, **125**; nautical chart, **22**; phonograph receiver, **177**; pilot's instrument panel, **153**; police car, **118**; powerboat, **134**; railroad crossing signal, **111**; relief map, **21**; sailboat, **130**; 747 cockpit, **150, 151**; sewing machine, **274**; single engine airplane, **147**; space shuttle, **155**; speculum, **438**; stage, **344**; subway car, **115**; synagogue, **86**; taxi roof, **115**; toaster oven, **249**; toll booth, **110**; Torah, **470**; tow truck, **122**; tractor, **424**; traffic, **109**; truck, **116, 117**; tugboat, **144**; voting

booth, **427**; washing machine, **276**
light control: camera, **170**; pilot's instrument panel, **153**
light-diffuser panel, elevator car, **76**
light-duty road, topographic map, **22**
lighter, cigarette, **224**
light-horn, nautical chart, **22**
lighthouse, nautical chart, **22**
lighting: and composition, **362**; track, **235**
lighting hole, lantern, **336**
light mast, aircraft carrier, **142**
light meter, photographic, **174**
lightning, **17**
lightning rod, launch pad, **154**
light-reading index, light meter, **174**
light selector, police car, **118**
light source, composition, **363**
light switch: elevator, **76**; refrigerator, **245**; stove oven, **244**
light type, **167**
ligule, grass, **56**
limb: bow, **456**; human, **24, 25**; microscope, **432**; sextant, **133**; theodolite, **426**; tree, **48**; *see also* leg
limb top, microscope, **432**
lime, crustacean chitin, **45**
lime glass, light bulb, **234**
limestone cup, coral polyp, **44**
limitation plate, postal money order, **223**
limited access highway, road map, **20**
limiter, CB radio noise, **179**
limit line, fencing strip, **309**
limit switch, elevator shaft, **76**
Lincoln Suite, White House, **73**
line: badminton court, **313**; basketball court, **292**; bell, **III**; block and tackle, **451**; boat, **128**; book page, **IV**; bowling lane, **311**; compass, **132**; craps table, **341**; drag racing, **333**; fencing strip, **309**; flat racing entry, **330**; football field, **289**; garbage truck, **123**; globe, **5**; handball court, **307**; harness racetrack, **331**; horse's foot, **36**; hot air balloon, **326**; ice hockey, **290, 291**; jai alai cancha, **308**; kite, **317**; lacrosse field, **293**; lasso, **422**; magazine, 167, **169**; map, 20, **21**; movie film, **172**; music notation, 346, **347**; newspaper, **166**; nuclear reactor, **384**; parachute, **327**; perspective, **362**; power, **386**; powerboat, **135**; scrimshaw, **369**; shuffleboard court, **312**; soccer field, **293**; squash court, **307**; spider web, **38**; stage, **344**; sundial, **381**; tanker, **137**; theatre, **345**; track and field, **294, 295**; tugboat, **144**; volleyball court, **313**; windmill, **382**;

windsurfer, **324**
linear perspective, and composition, **362**
linear slide rule, **431**
line box, tugboat, **144**
line finder, typewriter, **162**
line guide, fishing reel, **334**
line-in jack, tape recorder, **175**
line lashing, kite, **317**
lineman's pliers, **404**
linen, ambulance, **119**
linen locker, sailboat, **131**
line of perspective, **362**
line printer, computer, **429**
liner: automatic rifle handguard, **461**; fireplace flue, **228**; football helmet, **288**; glove, **196**; gouge, **368**; makeup, **212**; ship, 136, **138**; Torah, **470**
line-recording level control, tape recorder, **175**
line roller, fishing rod, **334**
line space lever, typewriter, **162**
line support, power network, **386**
line symbol, political map, **20**
line-up light, aircraft carrier, **142**
linework, map, **20**
ling-t'ou, Manchu court dress, **475**
lingual, tooth, **446**
lingual cusp, tooth, **446**
lining: beret, **198**; garment, **192**; hardback book, **165**; man's belt, **186**; man's shoe, **200**; mitten, **196**; parka, **197**; saddle, **329**; ski clothes, **321**; sleeping bag, **337**; trenchcoat, **196**; tunnel, **96**
link: bolt ring, **214** cartridge fuse, **389**; chain, **451**; chain saw chain, **421**; hitch and harrow, **424**; horizontal bar, **300**; identification bracelet, **183**; keychain, **449**; parachute harness, **327**; pendant, **215**; sponge mop, **278**; swivel, **214**; tank track, **464**; wristwatch band, **216**
linkage: gardening shears, **417**; vault, **447**
link chain, **451**
linking string, frankfurter, **261**
link strap, block and tackle, **451**
linseed oil, sketch, **365**
lintel: church, **84**; door, **62**; fireplace, **228**; house, **59**; torii, **68-69**
lint filter, washing machine, **276**
lint trap, clothes dryer, **277**
lion: ultimate beast, **46**; zodiac, **493**
lip: bell, **III**; blender, **250**; bottle, **263**; cat, **35**; coffee maker, **248**; dustpan, **278**; embroidery ring, **377**; fishing plug, **335**; human, **24**; mousetrap, **423**; mouth, **28**; pot, **367**; sink, **269**; stemware, **240**; stove, **394**; univalve shell, **45**
lip brush, **213**
lip gloss, **212, 213**
lip liner, **212, 213**
lip rest, corkscrew, **247**
lipstick, **212, 213**
liqueur glass, **241**

liquid: dental, 445; fruit, 251
liquid-bleach dispenser, washing machine, 276
liquid-bulk carrier, 136
liquid column, dual scale thermometer, 18
liquid-cooled internal combustion engine, 396
liquid crystal display: Geiger counter, 435; wristwatch, 216
liquid fuel, rocket, 397
liquid measuring cup, 254
liquid oxygen: pilot's instrument panel indicator, 153; rocket, 397
lira, symbol, 495
li-shui portion of dragon robe, Manchu court attire, 475
listed number, telephone, 178
listing, magazine, 169
literal rendition, work of art, 362
literary anatomy, 25
lithographic crayon, 370
lithographic pencil, 370
lithographic press, 370
lithography, 164, 370
lithosphere, 4
litter bin, 243
little finger, human hand, 29
little toe, human foot, 29
littoral zone, coastline, 15
live-bait well, powerboat, 135
liver: fowl, 33; human, 27
livery, servant, 473
living quarters: oil drilling platform, 99; White House, 73
liwan, mosque, 68-69
lizard, 40
load bearing wall, house, 58
load cord, hot air balloon, 326
loader: cannon, 457; razor blade, 206
loader's hatch, tank, 464
loading bridge, airport, 92
loading door, stove, 394
loading gate: revolver, 460; shotgun, 458
loading platform, stage, 344
loading slot, razor blade, 206
load lever, typewriter, 162
load line, symbol, 495
load ring, hot air balloon, 326
load-size selector, washing machine, 276
loaf, bread, 259
loafer, man's shoe, 200
lobby, skyscraper, 75
lobe: leaf, 50; outer ear, 28; partisan, 454; ultimate beast, 47
lobster, 45
lobster cracker, 257
lobster pot, 423
local elevator, skyscraper, 75
local galaxy, 2
local organizer, backpack, 337
local political boundary, road map, 20
local route number, road map, 20
local street, city plan, 20
location marker, airport, 92
location of office, letter, 161
locator diagram, political map, 21
lock: attache case, 281; bus, 114; camera, 170; canal lock, 97; cash register, 430; cymbal stand, 358; desk, 272; garbage disposal, 243; garbage truck, 123; handbag, 218; human, 25; hurdle, 298; ice climbing boot lace, 328; lift

bridge, 95; mailbox, 227; movie projector, 173; organ, 354; parallel bars, 300; parking meter, 109; phonograph tone arm, 176; playpen, 282; police gun belt, 482; pommel horse, 301; pressure cooker, 253; safe, 447; screen, 173; sonar, 434; starting block, 298; tape recorder, 175; table saw, 407; toaster, 249; tripod, 174; trombone, 352; vault, 447; venetian blinds, 237; voting booth, 427; wheelchair, 442; window, 63
locked groove, phonograph record, 176
locker: public sign, 490; sailboat, 131
locking bar, mousetrap, 423
locking bolt, vault, 447
locking pin, fire extinguisher, 280
locking plate, workbench vise, 398
locking pliers, 404
locking ring: rifle scope, 459; screwdriver, 403
locking screw, cassette tape, 174
locking system: balance beam, 300; bayonet, 453
locking tip, hypodermic syringe, 441
locking adjustable wrench, 405
lock key, typewriter shift, 162
locknut: lamp, 234; lithographic press, 370; roller skate, 318
lockout tool, tow truck, 122
lock plate, crossbow, 456
lock ring: fishing rod, 334; slide projector, 173
lock screw, lithographic press, 370
lock set, door, 448
lockside, canal lock, 97
lock stile, door, 62
lock switch: movie camera, 172; tape measure, 414
lock wall, canal lock, 97
lock washer, lamp, 234
locomotive: canal lock, 97; railroad yard, 94; train, 112-113
lodge pole, tepee, 82
loft: barn, 100; golf clubs, 304; sleeping bag, 337; stage, 344
log chute, dam, 98
loge, theatre, 345
log fork, fire iron, 228
log hoist, dam, 98
logo: baseball team, 286; bus, 114; credit card, 222; electric razor, 206; fire engine, 121; label, 264; letter, 161; locomotive, 113; magazine, 167, 168; mainsail, 132; newspaper, 166; pill, 441; postal money order, 223; single engine airplane, 147; traveler's check, 223
loin: beef, 30; lamb, 31; pork, 32
loin guard, armor, 455
loins: cat, 35; dog, 34; horse, 36; human, 25
long bar, easel, 364
longbow, 456

longeon, flat kite, 317
long-hair slot, electric razor, 206
long horse, gymnastics, 301
longitude, meridian of, 5, 20, 22
long joint, bassoon, 351
long jump, track and field, 294
long lid prop, grand piano, 355
long-life light bulb, 234
long necklace, Manchu court dress, 475
long-playing phonograph record, 176
long-range weapon system, jet fighter, 152
long service line, badminton court, 313
longshore bar, 14
longshore trough, 14
long-term parking lot, airport, 92
long-wire antenna, destroyer, 140
lookout area, tanker, 136
lookout tower, passenger ship, 139
loom: rowboat oar, 129; weaving, 379
loop: basketball backstop, 292; bell, III; book, 203; bow, 456; carpet, 242; checkbook clutch, 219; circus aerialist, 88; cowboy cartridge belt, 474; dress, 194; fastener, 204; hammock, 284; handbag, 218; human fingertip, 29; knitting, 378; overhead power line, 386; roller coaster, 90; suspenders, 186; tent, 336; trench coat, 196; type, 163; wheelchair, 442
loop-former bar, movie projector, 173
loophole, castle, 78
loop label, necktie, 188
loop ramp, highway cloverleaf, 110
loop tape, Velcro, 205
loosefooted sail, windsurfer, 324
lore, bird, 37
lorgnette, 217
lost and found, public sign, 491
lotion, beauty product, 210, 213
lotion dispenser, kitchen sink, 243
loud, music notation, 346
loudness control, phonograph receiver, 177
loudspeaker, fire engine, 120, 121
lounge: jai alai cancha, 308; jumbo jet, 148; passenger train, 112
lounger, 231
louver: air conditioner, 392; church window, 84; tank, 464; window shutters, 237
loveseat, 232
low bar, uneven parallel bars, 300
low beam, automobile, 102
lower back-stick, easel, 364
lower bolt, pulley block, 451
lower bout, viola, 349
lower bow, bear trap, 423
lower case: proofreader's mark, 498; type, 163
lower chord, lift bridge, 95
lower compartment, backpack, 337

lower control arm, automobile, 104
lower eyelid, 28
lower face, zipper, 205
lower gate, canal lock, 97
lower-girdle facet, cut gemstone, 214
lower grid assembly, nuclear reactor, 385
lower grip ring, sword hilt, 453
lower guard, sword hilt, 453
lower handle, power mower, 419
lower housing, finishing sander, 411
lower jaw, snake, 41
lower joint, clarinet, 351
lower limb, bow, 456
lower link, hitch and harrow, 424
lower mandible, bird, 37
lower margin, book page, 165
lower pool, canal lock, 97
lower rack track, dishwasher, 246
lower rail, balustrade, 71
lower rudder, jumbo jet, 149
lower sash, window, 63
lower shell, turtle, 40
lower side-rail, truck van, 117
lower spray arm, dishwasher, 246
lower table, drill press, 409
lower tail crest, tadpole, 42
lower teeth, 446
lower thigh, dog, 34
lower vertical fin, blimp, 158
low-gain antenna: lunar rover, 157; satellite, 182
low heat switch, hair dryer, 208
low hurdle, 298
low-level outlet, dam, 98
low pressure, weather map, 19
low pulley, universal gym, 338
low tide, 15
low-tide terrace, 14
lozenge, church, 84
LP phonograph record, 176
L-shaped square, 414
lubber's line, compass, 132
lubricant port, saber saw, 407
lubricating valve, steam engine, 395
lucaflect, cartoon, 374
luff, mainsail, 132
lug: bicycle, 124; camera, 171; cassette tape, 175; coffin, 500; drum, 358; hand grenade, 463; nuclear reactor, 385; truck tractor, 116
luge, 322
luggage, 284
luggage rack: camper, 126; stagecoach, 127
lug hole, tire, 101
lug nuts, automobile, 102
lumber, building material, 66
lumber girder, 58
lumber post, 58
lumen, light, 234
luminous indices, wristwatch, 216
lunar lander, 156
lunar module, 156
lunar month, 4
lunar overshoe, spacesuit, 157
lunar rover, 157
lunette, guillotine, 452
lung: human, 27; iron, 442
lunge pads, ice skates, 319
lunt, pipe, 225
lunula, human fingernail, 29

lure, fishing, 335
lyre, 349; grand piano, 355
lyre holder, trumpet
    lyrics, music, 346
lysosome, animal cell, 23

M

M: braille, 496; sign
    language, 496
ma'abarta, tefellin, 470
mace: House of
    Representatives, 72;
    medieval, 454
mace canister, police gun
    belt, 482
machicolations, castle, 78
mach indicator: pilot's
    instrument panel, 153; 747
    cockpit, 150
machine: acoustic
    guitar, 356;
    ambulance, 119;
    dialysis, 442;
    planting, 424; toll
    basket, 110; voting, 427
machine cabin, wind
    turbine, 382
machine gun, 461; tank, 464,
    465
machine knitting needle, 378
machine-readable code line,
    traveler's check, 223
machinery tower, lift
    bridge, 95
machine stop, etching
    press, 371
machinist's vise,
    workbench, 398
mach speed, jet fighter, 152
mack, destroyer, 140
macrame, 378
macron, grammatical
    symbol, 497
MADC scale, volt-ohm
    meter, 413
madreporite, starfish, 44
magazine: cover and
    contents page, 167;
    feature spread, 168, 169;
    film roll, 171; fort, 80;
    pistol, 460; rifle, 458, 461;
    shotgun, 459; stapler, 273
Magen David, 86, 492
magic wand, wizard, 476
magma reservoir,
    volcano, 10
magnet, pocket knife, 416
magnetic compass, 132
magnetic lid lifter, can
    opener, 247
magnetic north, compass
    rose, 22
magnetic sound track, movie
    film, 172
magnetic strip, credit
    card, 222
magnetic tape, 175;
    computer, 429
magnetometer, satellite, 182
magnetometer stowage bags,
    lunar rover, 157
magnifier, pocket knife, 416
magnifying lens, radar, 434
magnifying power,
    microscope, 432
mag wheel: automobile, 102;
    motorcycle, 125
mah-jongg tile, 339
maid, 473
maiden, execution
    device, 452
mail: armor, 455; public
    sign, 490
mailbox, 227
mail drop, door, 62
mailing label, magazine, 167
main, furnace, 390
main body: flute, 350;
    furniture, 268
main breaker, circuit breaker
    box, 389
main bulkhead, passenger

ship, 138
main cabin, sailboat, 131
main cable, suspension
    bridge, 95
main channel, river, 13
main circulating pump,
    solar heating system, 383
main compartment,
    backpack, 337
main control valve,
    camp stove, 336
main counterweight, lift
    bridge, 95
main-course table fork, 240
main cover title,
    magazine, 167
main deck, destroyer, 140
main device, coin, 221
main engine, space
    shuttle, 154
main-engine heat exchanger,
    oil drilling platform, 99
main feedwater pump,
    nuclear reactor, 384
main gate, frontier fort, 80
main gear, single engine
    airplane, 147
main housing, curling
    iron, 210
main illustration, book
    page, IV
mainland, 7
mainland beach, 15
main line: lasso, 422;
    railroad yard, 94
main rod, steam
    locomotive, 112
mainsail, 132; sailboat, 130
main sanctuary, mosque, 68,
    69
mainsheet, sailboat, 130
main slide, tuba, 352
main standard, football
    goalpost, 289
main strings, tennis
    racket, 306
main table, drill press, 409
maintenance safety rope,
    roller coaster, 90
main towing bit,
    tugboat, 144
maintube, telescope, 433
main undercarriage wheel,
    helicopter, 146
main vein, leaf, 50
majority secretary,
    Senate, 72
major road, 110
maker's imprint, playing
    cards, 342
maker's signature, check, 222
makeup, 212, 213
malacology, 45
maladicta balloon,
    cartoon, 375
malar, human, 24, 26
male, symbol, 94
male coupling, hose
    connection, 418
male ferrule, fishing rod, 334
male flower, corn, 56
male plug, electrical, 388
maline, woman's hat, 199
malleolus, human foot, 29
mallet, 402; croquet, 312;
    drums, 358; kitchen
    tool, 257;
    woodcarving, 366
Maltese cross, symbol, 492
man: backgammon, 339;
    chess, 339; ranching, 422
manara, architecture, 68
manchette, lounger, 231
Manchu court dress, 475
mandible: ant, 39; bird, 37;
    fish, 43; grasshopper, 39;
    human, 26
mandolin, 356
mandoline, kitchen
    cutter, 257
mane: horse, 36; human, 25;
    ultimate beast, 46
maneuvering system, space

shuttle, 154, 155
manger, barn, 100
mang-p'ao, Manchu court
    dress, 475
manifold: automobile
    engine, 107; tanker, 137
mannaia, execution
    device, 452
mannish button, 205
manometer, blood pressure
    gauge, 439
man's formal attire, 472
man's hair, 207
man's hat, 198
mansion, White House, 73
man's shirt, 185
man's shoe, 200
man's skate, 319
man's underwear, 90
manticore, legendary
    beast, 46
mantle: earth, 4;
    fireplace, 228;
    lantern, 336; octopus, 44;
    pyramid, 69; royal
    regalia, 468; Torah, 470
mantlepiece, fireplace, 228
mantlet, tank, 465
mantling, coat of arms, 487
manual, organ, 354
manual citrus juicer, 251
manual drill, 408
manual focus switch,
    camera, 170
manual operation button,
    vacuum cleaner, 279
manual-pump pedal, surgical
    table, 440
manual stabilizer trim lever,
    747 cockpit, 150
manual typewriter, 162
manual zoom lever, movie
    camera, 172
manubrium, jellyfish, 44
manufacturer: gas
    pump, 108; lithographic
    press, 370; organ, 354;
    painting brush, 365;
    phonograph record, 176;
    phonograph speaker, 177;
    running shoe, 296; single
    engine airplane, 147;
    Universal Product
    Code, 430
manure gutter, barn, 100
manure pit, barnyard, 100
map, 5, 20-22; subway
    car, 115
map pocket, parka, 197
marathon, 294; running
    shoe, 296
marbling, meat, 258
marching band, 348, 479
mare, 36
margin: book page, 165;
    jellyfish, 44; leaf, 50;
    magazine page, 169;
    map, 22; necktie, 189
marginal shield, turtle, 40
margin stop, typewriter, 162
marine algae, 55
marine life, 44
mark: basketball court, 292;
    coin, 221; dental
    braces, 443; grammatical
    symbol, 497; guitar, 356;
    label, 264, 265; military
    uniform, 480;
    monovial, 414; music
    notation, 346; nail, 400;
    proofreader's, 498;
    sextant, 133; soccer
    field, 293; tape
    measure, 414; topographic
    map, 22; type, 164
marked deck, playing
    card, 342
marker: airport, 82; bowling
    lane, 311; football
    field, 289; swimming pool
    lane, 310; tow truck, 122;
    wristwatch, 216
marker beacon,

helicopter, 146
marker control, sonar, 434
marker lamp,
    locomotive, 112
marker light: bus, 114; fire
    engine, 120;
    locomotive, 113; truck
    van, 117
marking: airport runway, 92;
    blood pressure
    gauge, 439; hypodermic
    syringe, 441; music, 346;
    topographic map, 22
marking gauge, measuring
    tool, 414
mark of omission,
    grammatical symbol, 497
marksmanship badge,
    military uniform, 480
marrow, meat bone, 258
Mars, planet, 3
marsh: coastline, 15;
    river, 13; topographic
    map, 22
marshalling yard,
    railroad, 94
mars light, fire
    engine, 120,121
mascara, 212, 213
masher kitchen utensil, 255
mask: baseball catcher, 286;
    fencing, 309; football
    helmet, 288; ice hockey
    goalie, 290; lacrosse, 293;
    silk screen, 369; skin
    diving, 325; television
    set, 181
masonry: building
    material, 66; permanent
    fort, 81; wall, 67
masonry gate post, fence, 65
mass: cosmic, 2; nuclear
    reactor, 384
massager shower, 270
mast: aircraft carrier, 142;
    CB radio antenna, 179;
    destroyer, 141; flag, 486;
    sailboat, 130; skyscraper,
    75; space shuttle, 154;
    tanker, 136, 137; tugboat,
    144; windsurfer, 324
mastabe, pyramid, 68
master control, pilot's
    instrument panel, 153
master cord, snowshoe, 321
master cylinder,
    automobile, 104
master number, phonograph
    record, 176
master slide, traverse
    rod, 236
master's quarters,
    tugboat, 144
masthead: magazine, 167;
    sailboat, 130
masthead light:
    destroyer, 141;
    fireboat, 144
mat: in frame, 373;
    gymnastics, 300;
    phonograph
    turntable, 176;
    wigwam, 82
match, 224; fencing, 309
matchbook, 224
material identification, house
    blueprint, 60
ma-ti hsiu, Manchu court
    dress, 475
matrix, dental, 445
matrix number, phonograph
    record, 176
mattress, 267; coffin, 500;
    playpen pad, 282
mature fruit, tomato, 52
mat window, frame, 373
mausoleum, 500
maw human, 25
maxilla: fish, 43; human, 26
maximum security prison, 74
meadow, mountain, 8
mear high water mark,
    topographic map, 22

mean line, type, 163
mean time, 5
measure, music, 346;
tape, 414
measured by, symbol, 495
measure of gold purity,
ring, 215
measuring cup, 254
measuring diffuser, light
meter, 174
measuring spoon, 254
measuring tool, 414;
kitchen, 254; oil drilling
platform, 99
meat: baseball bat, 287;
beef, 30; coconut, 258;
lamb, 31; pork, 32;
poultry, 33; raw, 258
meat grinder, 257
meat keeper, refrigerator, 245
meat mallet, 257
meat thermometer, 254
mechanic, public sign, 491
Mechanical floor;
skyscraper, 75
mechanical power, steam
engine, 395
mechanical stage control,
microscope, 432
mechanical sweeper, 123
mechanical unit, piano, 355
mechanic's shops, frontier
fort, 80
mechanism: bazooka, 462;
fountain pen, 160;
recliner, 231
mechanized voting
machine, 427
medal, 485; collector, 221;
military, 480; police, 482
medallion, boat, 202
medallion number, taxi, 115
Medal of Honor, 480
medal of order, king's
regalia, 468
medial malleolus, human
foot, 29
medial moraine, 9, 12
median, highway, 110
median furrow, horse, 36
medical examination
equipment, 438
medical table, 440
medical treatment aids, 441
medication, 441
medicine dropper, 441
medieval arms, 454
medium, painting, 364
medium gouge,
woodcarving, 366
medley relay, track and
field, 294
medley swimming race, 310
meeting rails, window, 63
melody part, accordion, 360
melody pipe, bagpipe, 359
melody string, sitar, 356
melon, silo, 100
member: basketball
backstop, 292; geodesic
dome, 83; house, 59
membrane, animal cell, 23
membranophone, 358
memo, check, 222
memorabilia, White
House, 73
memorial, tombstone, 500
memorial band, Jewish
prayer vestment, 470
memory function key,
electronic calculator, 431
memory lock, organ, 354
memory unit, computer, 429
menorah: symbol, 492;
synagogue, 86
men's tee, golf course, 304
men's toilet, public sign, 490
mentum, human, 24
Mercator grid, map, 22
merchant ship, 136
mercury: barometer, 18;
battery, 387; blood
pressure gauge, 439;
planet, 3;

thermometer, 439
mercury
sphygmomanometer, 439
merge, road sign, 489
merge left, road sign, 489
meridian of longitude, 1, 5
merlon, castle, 78
merry-go-round, 91
mesentery, coral polyp, 44
mesh: Ping-Pong net, 315;
playpen net, 282; silk
screen, 369
mesial, tooth, 446
mesial buccal cusp, 446
mesial lingual cusp, 446
mesocarp: orange, 53;
peach, 53
mesosphere, earth, 4
mess, frontier fort, 80
mess hall, prison, 74
metacarpopalangeal crease,
human hand, 29
metacarpus, cat, 35
metal: fuse cap, 389;
vaulting pole, 299;
printing type, 164; stapler
cap, 273; umbrella
rod, 226
metal detector, 435
metallic jacket, fencing, 309
metal locator, 435
metal saw, pocket knife, 416
metal shop, prison, 74
metalworking vise, 399
metamorphosis, insect, 39
metatarsals, human, 26
metatarsus: cat, 35;
spider, 38
meteor, 2
meteorologist, weather
monitoring equipment, 18
meter: CB radio, 179; and
fuse box, 389; house, 61;
nautical chart, 22;
parking, 109; phonograph
receiver, 177;
powerboat, 134; tape
recorder, 175;
volt-ohm, 413
meter tape, envelope, 161
metronome, 361
mezuzah, Jewish ritual
item, 470
mezzanine, theatre, 345
mezzo forte, music
notation, 346
M-51 gun, jet fighter, 152
mica disc, incandescent
bulb, 234
Michigan marker light,
bus, 114
micro-dial indicator gauge,
etching press, 371
micrometer drum,
sextant, 133
microphone: CB radio, 179;
hearing aid, 442; movie
camera, 172; police
car, 118; 747 cockpit, 150;
tape recorder, 175;
microphone input plug,
movie projector, 173
microphone jack: CB
radio, 179; movie
camera, 172; tape
recorder, 175; video
recorder, 180
microscope, 432, 437
mid-angle, lamp, 235
midband signal,
television, 181
midchannel nautical
chart, 22
midcount line, basketball
court, 292
middle finger, human
hand, 29
middle joint, flute, 350
middle leg, bee, 39
middle operating-screw
handle, clamp, 399
middle pick-up, guitar, 357
middle section, flute, 350
midfield: football, 289;

soccer, 293
midget, circus, 88
midget howitzer, 462
midget pliers, 404
midground, composition, 363
midnight, globe, 5
midrange phonograph
speaker, 177
midrib: fern, 55; leaf, 50
midriff, human, 25
midsole: running shoe, 296;
sandal, 202
mike stand, movie
camera, 172
mileage indicator, road
map, 20
milestone, highway, 110
mile track, harness
racing, 331
military buckle, man's
belt, 186
military collar, king's
regalia, 468
military uniform, 480-481
milk, coconut, 258
milk teeth, 446
milk well, cow, 30
Milky Way galaxy, 2-3
mill, pepper grinder, 257
milled edge, coin, 221
millimeters, cartridge, 460
milliner, 199
minaret: architecture, 68;
iceberg, 12
mind, human, 25
mine, 463
mineral detector, 435
miniature golf course,
passenger ship, 138
minim, music notation, 346
minimum security prison, 74
minimus: foot, 29; hand, 29
minister, religious
vestments, 471
miniver, royal crown, 469
minor coin, 221
minor road, highway, 110
minority secretary,
Senate, 72
mint mark, coin, 221
minus, symbol, 494
minus square, shuffleboard
court, 312
minute, grammatical
symbol, 497
minute hand: grandfather
clock, 229; stopwatch, 298;
wristwatch, 216
minutes of arc, symbol, 495
mirliton, 360
mirror, 213; automobile, 102,
106; bus, 114; cosmetic
case, 284; dental, 445;
dressing table, 268; fire
engine, 121;
locomotive, 113;
mechanical sweeper, 123;
microscope, 432;
physician's, 438; pilot's
instrument panel, 153;
racing car, 332;
sextant, 133;
telescope, 433; truck
tractor, 116
MIRV, 466
miser, costume, 476
missile, 466; jet fighter, 152;
surface-to-air, 140;
surface-to-surface, 140
missile control officer, and
pilot's instrument
panel, 153
missile deck, submarine, 143
missile launcher, aircraft
carrier, 142
mission specialist, space
shuttle, 155
mistigris, playing cards, 342
miter: bishop, 471;
cardinal, 471
miter clamp, 399
mitered joint, silk
screen, 369

miter gauge, table
saw, 407
mitochondrion, animal
cell, 23
mitt, baseball, 286, 287
mitten, 196; ski clothes, 321
mixer: kitchen sink, 243;
synthesizer, 357
mixing blades, food
processor, 250
mixing bowl, 254
mixing tools, kitchen, 254
moat: castle, 78, 79;
mountain, 9; permanent
fort, 81
moccasin: Indian, 474; man's
shoe, 200
model: baseball
glove, 287; internal
combustion engine, 396
modeling end, clay modeling
tool, 366
mode lever, surgical
table, 440
model number: phonograph
speaker, 177; surgical
table, 440
mode mute, phonograph
receiver, 177
moderately loud, music, 346
mode selection control,
police car, 118
mode selector: camera, 171;
metal detector, 435; 747
cockpit, 151; sonar, 434
modesty panel, desk, 272
mode switch, Geiger
counter, 435
modified bishop sleeve,
bridal gown, 472
modified leg-of-mutton
sleeve, bridal gown, 472
modifier, synthesizer, 357
modulation indicator, CB
radio, 179
module, jumbo jet
gallery, 148, 149
moisture collector pan, air
conditioner, 392
moisturizer, beauty
product, 213
molar, tooth, 446
mold: church, 84;
denture, 443
molding: automobile, 102,
103; church, 84;
cupboard, 239;
escalator, 77; frame, 373;
grandfather clock, 229;
minaret, 68
molding scoop, cooking
utensil, 255
moline, symbol, 492
Molotov cocktail, 463
molten material, volcano, 10
monaural record,
phonograph, 176
money, 220-221
money box, 447
money order, 223
money slot, blackjack, 341
money totalizer, gas pump;
108
monitor: computer, 429;
fireboat, 144; movie
projector, 173; prison, 74;
space shuttle, 155;
tanker, 137; tape
recorder, 175;
television, 181; and video
recorder, 180
monkey, caisson, 457
monkey bars, backyard
equipment, 283
monkey board, oil drilling
platform, 99
monkey ear, ultimate
beast, 46
monkey wrench, 405
monocle, 217

monocoque chassis, racing car, 332
monorial, carpenter's level, 414
Monroe Room, White House, 73
monsoon, 6
montgolfier hot air balloon, 326
month, lunar, 4
month of purchase, postal money order, 223
monticule, 7
monument, tombstone, 500
moon, 3; phases, 4
moon buggy, 157
moon dial, grandfather clock, 229
moon roof, automobile, 102
mooring mast: airship, 158; skyscraper,, 75
mooring winch, tanker, 136
moose antler, ultimate beast, 46
mop, 278
moraine, 8, 9, 12
morning coat: butler's uniform, 473; man's formal attire, 472
morning line, flat racing entry, 330
morse, royal regalia, 468
mortar, 462; kitchen tool, 257
mortar joint, brick wall, 67
mortice hole, stagecoach, 127
mortise, label, 265
mortise lock, 448
mosque, 68
mosquito, 39
mosquito netting screen, tent, 336
mother, flat racing entry, 330
mother-in-law, bowling pin, 311
mother-of-all, spinning wheel, 379
motion, steam engine, 395
motion compensator, oil drilling platform, 99
motor: automobile, 104; automobile engine starter, 107; power drill, 409
motor cruiser, 129
motorcycle, 125
motor drive, camera, 171
motor home, 126
motor housing: blender, 250; can opener, 247; food processor, 250; hair dryer, 208; jackhammer, 426; juice extractor, 251; lawn sprinkler, 418; potter's wheel, 367; power drill, 409; vacuum cleaner, 279
motorman's cab, subway, 115
motor mount, automobile engine, 107
motor scooter helmet, police, 482
motor whaleboat, destroyer, 140
motto: coat of arms, 487; money, 220
mound: baseball field, 287; royal regalia, 469
mount: automobile engine, 107; bagpipe, 359; castle, 78, 79; coat of arms, 487; film slide, 171; fire engine, 120; fishing reel, 334; machine gun tripod, 461; pencil sharpener, 273
mountain, 8-9; peak, 7
mountain climbing, 328
Mountain Standard Time, 5
mount base, rifle scope, 458

mounting: ballpoint pen, 160; bicycle caliper brake, 124; drill press, 409; electrical receptacle, 388; electrical wall switch, 388; electronic flash, 174; fencing foil, 309; frame, 373; lamp, 235; mailbox, 227; ski binding, 320; telephone, 178; telescope, 433
mousetrap, 423
mouth: beaker, 437; bell, III; bottle, 263; cannon, 457; coral polyp, 44; fish, 43; frog, 42; hot air balloon, 326; human, 24, 28; jellyfish, 44; plane, 410; river, 7, 13; starfish, 44; suspenders, 186; tadpole, 42
mouth organ, 360
mouthpiece: boxing, 303; clarinet, 351; French horn, 352; harmonica, 360; kazoo, 360; pipe, 225; skin diving, 325; telephone, 178; trombone, 352; trumpet, 353; tuba, 352
mouthpiece key, saxophone, 351
movable bridge, 95
movable control-arm, surgical table, 440
movable fret, sitar, 356
movable jaw: C-clamp, 399; locking pliers, 404; monkey wrench, 405
move down, proofreader's mark, 498
move left, proofreader's mark, 498
movement, clock, 229
movement dial, vault, 447
move right, proofreader's mark, 498
movie camera, 172
movie projector, 172
movie film, 172
moving gate, racing, 330
moving sidewalk, 77
mower, lawn, 419
MP, uniform, 480
mucoprotein coat, animal cell, 23
mud: hogan, 82; nautical chart, 22
mud flap, truck, 116, 117, 122
mud shield, tank, 465
muezzin, and minaret, 68
muffler: automobile, 105; bulldozer, 425; internal combustion engine, 396; miser, 476; motorcycle, 125; power mower, 419; tank, 464; tractor, 424
muffler shield, chain saw, 421
mufti, police, 482
mug, shaving, 206
mulching lawn mowe, 419
mule, canal lock, 97
Mulligan, darts, 316
mullion, church, 84
multifoil window, church, 84
multimeter, 413
multiple fruit, 53
multiple independently targeted reentry vehicle (MIRV), 466
multiplication, with slide rule, 431
multiply, symbol, 494
multi-position surgical table, 440
multipurpose electrician's tool, 413

multipurpose vacuum cleaner brush, 279
muntins, window, 63
muscle: human, 26; scallop, 45
mushroom, 55
music: accessories, 361; notation, 346
music arch, organ, 354
music desk, grand piano, 355
music ensemble, 348
musician, orchestra, 348
music selector, tape recorder, 175
music stand, 361
music wire pliers, 404
Muslim temple, 68-69
muslin wrapping, dabber, 371
mussel, 45
mustache, 207
mustard, and frankfurter, 261
mute, phonograph receiver, 177
mutton, 31
muttonchop whiskers, 207
muzzle: automatic rifle, 461; bazooka, 462; cannon barrel, 457; cat, 35; cow, 30; dog, 34; horse, 36; mortar, 462; neck, 263; revolver, 460; sheep, 31; tank gun, 465
muzzle-loading cannon, 462
mycelium, mushroom, 55
mystery gas cloud, Milky Way, 3

N

N: braille, 496; sign language, 496
nacelle, jet fighter, 152
nail, 400; bird, 37; frame, 373; human hand, 29
nail cleaner: clippers, 211; pocket knife, 416
nail clippers, 211
nail crease, horseshoe, 36
nail file, 211
nail hole, horseshoe, 36
nail nick: corkscrew, 247; pocket knife, 416
nail polish, 213
nail pulling slot, hatchet, 402
name: flat racing entry, 330; label, 264; letter, 161; magazine mailing label, 167; paper money, 221; passenger ship, 138; pencil brand, 20; political map, 160; tugboat, 144
name column, voting booth, 427
nameplate: automobile, 103; can opener, 247; fireboat, 144; military uniform, 480; newspaper, 166; police uniform, 482
name tag, soldier's uniform, 481
nap, tennis ball, 306
nape: bird, 37; cat, 35; human, 25
napkin, 240
nare, nose, 28
narrow deep gouge, woodcarving, 366
narthex, church, 85
naso-labial groove, salamander, 42
native dress, 475
natural, music notation, 346
natural abrasive material, sander, 411
natural key, organ, 354
natural lever, river, 13
nautical chart, 22
nautical terminology, 128
nave, church, 85
navel, human, 24
navigation aerial, tanker, 137
navigational aid, space shuttle, 155

navigational instruments, 747 cockpit, 150, 151
navigation system, aircraft carrier, 142
navigator's station, sailboat, 131
neb: bird, 37; knife, 252
nebula, Milky Way, 2
neck: balloon, 477; bottle, 263, 264; broom, 278; cat, 35; column, 71; ear scope, 438; golf club, 304; guitar, 356; hammer, 402; horse, 36; human, 24, 25; knee kicker, 242; kokoshniki, 68; lamb, 31; lamp, 234; Ping-Pong racket, 315; pommel horse, 301; pot, 367; poultry, 33; saddle, 329; saxophone, 351; suit hangar, 277; sweater, 195; test tube, 437; tooth, 446; tub fiddle, 360; type, 164; undershirt, 190; violin, 349
neckband: ascot, 189; medal, 485; necktie, 188; shirt, 185
neckband label, 264
neck decoration, military uniform, 480
neck developer, body building, 338
neckerchief: cowboy, 474; sailor, 481
neck guard, armor, 455
necklace: Indian, 474; jewelry, 215; Manchu court dress, 475
neckline, woman's sweater, 192
neck roll: ambulance, 119; football uniform, 288
neck sock, drag racing driver, 333
neckstrap eyelet, camera, 171
necktie, 188-189, king's regalia, 468
needle: crochet, 378; dental, 445; etching, 371; football, 288; hypodermic, 441; knitting, 378; latch, 378; light meter, 174; mountain, 9; paramedic, 119; phonograph, 176; sewing, 376; sewing machine, 274; spring board, 378
needle-nose pliers, 404
needlepoint, 377
needlework, 378
negative charge, symbol, 494
negative terminal, battery, 387
negative test lead jack, volt-ohm meter, 413
neighbor, teeth, 446
Neptune, planet, 2
Ner Tamid, 86, 470
nest: pliers, 404; spider, 38
net: carrier, 142; backyard equipment, 283; badminton court, 313; basketball backstop, 292; circus aerialist, 88; fishing, 335; ice hockey goal, 290; maid's uniform, 473; Ping-Pong, 315; playpen, 282; tennis, 306; soccer field, volleyball court, 313
net contents, label, 264
netting: lobster pot, 423; woman's hat, 199
netting screen, tent, 336
network, power, 386
neutral corner, boxing ring, 303
neutral terminal, electrical receptacle, 388
neutral wire: electrical receptacle, 388; electrician's, 413
neutral zone: ice hockey rink, 291; shuffleboard court, 312
neve, mountain, 9

new crescent moon, 4
newel post, staircase, 64
newel skirt, escalator, 77
new gibbous moon, 4
new moon, 4
newspaper, 166
nib: auger bit, 409; bird, 37; fountain pen, 160
nichrome wire, toaster, 249
nick: corkscrew, 247; spool, 376; type, 164
nightclub, passenger ship, 138
night scope, bazooka, 462
night sign lamps, blimp, 158
nightstick, police, 482
nimbostratus cloud, 17
90 degree gauge, combination square, 414
nine pin, bowling, 311;
nipple: eyedropper, 441; human, 24; lamp, 234
nittle, cartoon, 375
N number, hot air balloon, 326
no bicycles, road sign, 488
nock, bow and arrow, 456
node, grass, 56
no entry, public sign, 491
no-frost refrigerator, 245
noggin, human, 25
noise limiter, CB radio, 179
no left turn, road sign, 488
nonelectric fencing match, 309
non-glacial stream, mountain, 8
non-glaciated valley, 12
non-locking adjustable wrench, 405
non-overflow section, dam, 98
non-porous backing, frame, 373
nonprecision approach marking, airport runway, 92
nonrigid lighter-than-air craft, 158
non-skid strip, bath and shower, 270
non-skid surface, diving platform, 310
noon, 5
noose: gallows, 452; lasso, 422
no parking, public sign, 490
no-passing zone, road sign, 489
no right turn, road sign, 488
north, compass rose, 22
North Atlantic Drift, ocean, 6
North Equatorial Current, ocean, 6
north fork, river, 13
north latitude, globe, 5
North Pacific Drift, ocean, 6
North Pole pin, globe, 1
north porch, church, 85
north portal, church, 85
north portico, White House, 73
north-south handbag, 218
north tower, church, 85
north transept, church, 85
north wing, Capitol, 72
no-score ring, dart board, 316
nose: cartridge, 460; cat, 35; chain saw guide bar, 421; clown, 477; destroyer, 141; dog, 34; football, 288; human, 24, 28; missile, 466; pliers, 404; racing car, 332; skateboard, 318; surfboard, 324
nose bridge, airport, 92
nose bumper, football helmet, 288
nose cone: blimp, 158; glider, 147; missile, 466; snowmobile, 126
nose doctor, examination equipment, 438

nosegay, bride, 472
nose leather, cat, 35
nose pads, eyeglasses, 217
nosepiece, microscope, 432
nose radome, jet fighter, 152
nose shroud, drag racing driver's fire suit, 333
nose wheel, single engine airplane, 147
nosing, staircase, 64
no smoking, public sign, 490
nostril: alligator, 41; bird, 37; fish, 43; frog, 42; horse, 36; human, 28; tadpole, 42; toad, 42
notation: music, 346; pitch pipe, 361
notch: computer diskette, 429; laboratory scale, 437; mountain, 8; sewing pattern, 380; spool, 376; telephone, 178; woman's jacket lapel, 192
note, music, 346, 347
note position letter and number, paper money, 220, 221
notice: envelope, 161; magazine, 167; sheet music, 347
no trucks, road sign, 488
no U turn, road sign, 488
nozzle: combustion jet engine, 397; faucet, 269; fireboat, 144; fire engine, 120, 121; gas pump, 108; icing syringe, 255; iron, 275; jet fighter, 152; lawn sprinkler, 418; lunar lander, 156; missile, 466; nuclear reactor, 385; paint spray gun, 415; propane plumber's torch, 412; satellite, 182; sprinkler, 418; vacuum cleaner, 279
nuchal shield, turtle, 40
nuclear envelope, animal cell, 23
nuclear membrane, animal cell, 23
nuclear-powered attack submarine, 143
nuclear-powered ship, 140-141
nuclear power reactor, 384-385
nucleolus, animal cell, 23
nucleus, animal cell, 23
nude heel, panty hose, 191
number: airport runway, 92; baseball uniform, 286; basketball player, 292; bus, 114; check, 222; credit card, 222; destroyer, 141; envelope, 161; film slide frame, 171; football jersey, 288; hot air balloon, 326; laboratory scale, 436; magazine page, 167; mailbox, 227; mainsail, 132; map, 20; painting brush, 365; paper money, 220, 221; pencil, 160; phonograph record, 176; phonograph speaker, 177; police uniform, 482; postal money order, 223; punch card column, 428; racing program entry, 330; safe, 447; sealed voting booth, 427; submarine, 143; surgical table, 440; swimming pool lane, 310; symbol, 495; taxi, 115; telephone, 178; traveler's check, 223
number cloth, flat racing, 330
number entry keys, electronic calculator, 431
number key, television set, 181
number plate: internal combustion engine, 396;

telephone, 178
one bend, paper clip, 273
one leg, paper clip, 273
#1 wood, golf club, 305
two bend, paper clip, 273
two leg, paper clip, 273
#2 wood, golf club, 305
three bend, paper clip, 273
three leg, paper clip, 273
#3 wood, golf club, 305
four leg, paper clip, 273
numerals, pocket watch, 216
numeric pad, cash register, 430
numismatist, 221
nun, religious vestments, 471
nun buoy, nautical chart, 22
nursery, public sign, 490
nursery course, harness racetrack, 331
nut: automobile, 102; banjo, 356; crossbow, 456; faucet, 269; fire hydrant, 121; food, 53; guitar, 356, 357; hacksaw, 406; hurdle, 298; ice cream cone, 261; jewelry findings, 214; juice extractor, 251; lamp, 234; levigator, 370; monkey wrench, 405; mountain climbing, 328; nuts and bolts, 401; pendulum clock, 229; Ping-Pong net, 315; plane, 410; pliers, 404; radiator, 390; rifle, 461; roller skate, 318; sink drain, 269; tub fiddle, 360; violin and bow, 349
nutcracker, 257
nuts and bolts, 401; magazine article, 168
nyki, torii, 69

O

O: braille, 496; sign language, 496
oar, rowboat, 129
oarlock: inflatable, 129; rowboat, 129
oat, 56
obelisk, 69
object ball, pool table, 314
objective, microscope, 432
objective end, theodolite, 426
objective lens: binoculars, 433; rifle scope, 459; telescope, 433
objective outer cell, telescope, 433
oboe, 348, 350
observation car, passenger train, 112
observation deck, skyscraper, 75
observation window, tank, 465
observer station, destroyer, 141
obstetrician, examination equipment, 438
obverse side, coin, 221
occiput, dog, 34
occluded front, weather map, 19
occlusal surface, tooth, 446
occulation ultraviolet spectrometer, satellite, 182
occupation, letter, 161
ocean, 7; basin, 15; currents, 6
oceanic crust, 15
ocean liner, 138-139
ocellus, grasshopper, 39
octane number, gasoline, 108
octant, 133
octave, piano, 355
octopus, 44
oculama, cartoon, 375
ocularium sight, armor, 455
ocular lens: binoculars, 433; rifle scope, 459
oculus window, house, 60
odds, flat racing entry, 330

odds board, jai alai cancha, 308
odometer, car, 106
off-duty sign, taxi, 115
office: frontier fort, 80; White House, 73
office index column, voting booth, 427
office location, letter, 161
officer: airplane, 153; police, 482
officer's braid, military uniform, 480
officer's lock and seal, voting booth, 427
officers' quarters, frontier fort, 80
office typewriter, 162
office window, airport control tower, 93
office zip code, postal money order, 223
official reporter, Congress, 72
off position, electrical wall switch, 388
offset handle, wrench, 405
offset-lithography, printing, 164
offshore rig, oil drilling, 99
off-the-road vehicle, 126
offset screwdriver, 403
ogee, cannon barrel, 457
ogee section, dam, 98
Ogier, playing card jack, 342
ohmmeter, symbol, 494
ohms scale, volt-ohm meter, 413
oil: beauty product, 213; painting medium, 364; sketch box, 365; woodcarving, 366
oil buffer, elevator shaft, 76
oil cap: automobile, engine, 107; bulldozer, 425
oil dipstick, engine, 107, 396
oil-drain plug, engine, 396
oil drilling platform, 99
oil filter, 107
oil pan, 107
oil pressure gauge: car, 106; powerboat, 134
oil-pump button, chain saw, 421
oilskin slicker, cowboy, 474
oil-tank cap, chain saw, 421
oil water heater, 391
old crescent moon, 4
old gibbous moon, 4
old lava flow, volcano, 10
old Senate chamber, Capitol, 72
omission, grammatical symbol, 497
on and off lever, gas pump, 108
on and off puck, craps table, 341
on and off switch: guitar amplifier, 357; lamp, 235; organ, 354; phonograph receiver, 177; razor, 206; power saw, 407
on-deck batter's circle, baseball field, 287
on-deck bat weight, baseball bat, 286
1¼ mile chute, harness racetrack, 331
one-arm bandit, 340
one-button cuff, blouse, 193
one-cell battery, symbol, 494
1/8 pole, harness racetrack, 331
one-eyed jack, playing card, 342
½ pole, harness racetrack, 331
100-fathom curve, continental shelf, 15
110 film cartridge, camera, 170
one pin, bowling, 311
one-point perspective, 362

¼ pole, harness racetrack, 331
1/16 pole, harness racetrack, 331
one-unit beads, abacus, 431
one way, road sign, 488
one-way traffic, road sign, 488
on guard line, fencing strip, 309
onion, 258, 261
on-off button: iron, 275; metal detector, 435; metronome, 361; police car, 118; potter's wheel, 367
on-off control, cash register, 430
on-off switch: CB radio, 179; coffee maker, 248; computer, 429; curling iron, 210; dental unit, 444; electric hairbrush, 208; electronic calculator, 431; hair dryer, 208; toaster oven, 249
onomatopoeia, cartoon, 374
on position, electrical wall switch, 388
on-purchase signature, traveler's check, 233
01 level, destroyer, 141
opaque background, thermometer, 439
opaque balustrade, escalator, 77
open and close: elevator car, 76; voting booth, 427
open-breech smoothbore firing tube, bazooka, 462
open coat, sandpaper, 411
open craft, 129
open crown, man's hat, 198
open end, wrench, 405
opener, kitchen tool, 247
open hole, bagpipe, 359
open ID window, checkbook clutch, 219
opening: eyedropper, 441; harmonica, 360; machinist's vise, 398; pitch pipe, 361
open outside pocket, shoulder bag, 218
open rear sight, rifle, 459
open-toed woman's shoe, 201
open-top freight car, 112
opera glasses, 433
operating control, movie projector, 173
operating lever: fire extinguisher, 280; jackhammer, 426
operating nut, fire hydrant, 121
operating rod, machine gun, 461
operating room table, 440
operating screw, clamp, 399
operating table, 440
operator, radio, 179
operators facility, airport control tower, 93
operculum, fish, 43
ophthalmoscope, 438
opisthenar, human hand, 29
optical landing system, aircraft carrier, 142
optical sound track, movie film, 172
optical unit, jet fighter, 152
oral arm, jellyfish, 44
oral surface, starfish, 44
orange, 53
orb: human, 25; royal regalia, 469; spider web, 38
orbit, eye, 28
orbital sander, 411
orbiter, space shuttle, 154, 155
orchestra, 348; theatre, 345
orchestra pit, theatre, 345
order number, paperback book, 165

organ, 354; church, 85; merry-go-round, 91
organizer, backpack, 337
orle, shield, 454
ornament: automobile hood, 102; Beefeater, 467; church, 84; dressing table, 268; earring, 214; grandfather clock, 229; running shoe, 296; scallop shell, 45; sofa, 232; tombstone, 500; trophy, 285; woman's jacket, 192
ornamented type, 163
ornament pedestal, trophy, 285
Ortez bar, tow truck bed, 122
orthodontia, 443
orthodontic bracket, 443
oscillating lawn sprinkler, 418
oscillator: metal detector, 435; symbol, 494; synthesizer, 357
otoscope, 438
Otto cycle internal combustion engine, 396
ottoman, 231
02 level, destroyer, 141
ouch, jewelry, 215
outboard aileron, jumbo jet, 148
outboard bracket, inflatable, 129
outboard elevator, jumbo jet, 149
outboard engine, 133
outboard flap, jumbo jet, 148
outboard planetaries, tractor, 424
outboard spoiler, jumbo jet, 148
out-cannel, gouge, 410
outdoor pool, passenger ship, 138
outer bailey, castle, 78, 79
outer cantus, eye, 28
outer cell, telescope, 433
outer core, earth, 4
outer curtain wall, castle, 79
outer ear, 28
outer hearth, fireplace, 228
outer hull, submarine, 143
outer lip, univalve shell, 45
outer panel, jet fighter, 152
outer rim: coconut, 258; ferris wheel, 91
outer ring, embroidery, 377
outer sash, window, 63
outer shell, parka, 197
outer slide brace, trombone, 352
outer table, backgammon, 339
outer ward, castle, 78, 79
outerwear, 196
outer wheel, ferris wheel, 91
outfield, baseball, 287
outhaul line, windsurfer, 324
outlet: dam, 98; electrical, 388; fire engine, 121; kazoo, 360
outlet nozzle, nuclear reactor, 385
outline type, 163
out of bounds: football field, 289; golf course, 304-305; jai alai cancha, 308; squash, 307
out-of-town prices, newspaper, 166
output, synthesizer, 357
output meter, phonograph, 177
outrigger: fire engine, 120; house, 59; powerboat, 135
outseam, jacket, 184
outside collar, barbell, 338
outside flap pocket, shoulder bag, 218
outside guard, theodolite, 426
outside knob, door, 448
outside load bearing wall, house, 58

outside margin, book page, 165
outside pole, tepee, 82
outside rail, harness racetrack, 331
outside stile, window shutters, 237
outside speaker selector, police car, 118
outsole: boot, 202; man's shoe, 200; running shoe, 296; woman's shoe, 201
outwash mountain, 8
outwork, castle, 78
oval head, screw, 400
ovary: cucumber, 52; flower pistil, 51
ovary wall, tomato, 52
oven: stove, 244; toaster, 249
oven thermometer, 254
overcap, disposable razor, 206
overcoat, 196; police uniform, 482
overflow drain, water heater, 391
overflow pipe, furnace, 390
overflow plate, bathtub, 270
overflow section, dam, 98
overflow tube, toilet, 271
overflow vent, sink, 269
overhang: house, 61; mountain, 9
overhead, sailboat, 131
overhead baggage rack, bus, 114
overhead bin, jumbo jet, 148
overhead fan, 392
overhead ladder, backyard equipment, 283
overhead power line, 386
overhead switch panel, 747 cockpit, 150
overlay, coffin, 500
overload, fuse box, 389
overload reset button, table saw, 407
overlook highway, 110
overnight bag, 181
overpass, highway cloverleaf, 110
overpressure plug, pressure cooker, 253
overrun area, airport runway, 92
overseas bars, military uniform, 480
overseas cap, military uniform, 480
overserve line, jai alai cancha, 308
overshoe, spacesuit, 157
overskirt, queen's regalia, 468
ovipositer, grasshopper, 39
ovule, flower, 51
owner, racing entry, 330
owner's head, sailboat, 131
owner's silks, racing entry, 330
oxbow lake, river, 13
oxen, 30
oxford rule, magazine, 168
oxter, human, 24
oxygen, rocket, 397
oxygen bottle rack, oil drilling platform, 99
oxygen cylinder, ambulance, 119
oxygen quantity indicator, pilot's instrument panel, 153
oxygen tank, ambulance, 119
oxygen tent, 442
oxygen umbilical, spacesuit, 157
oxygen unit, police car, 118
oyster, 45

P

P: braille, 496; sign language, 496
PA, mountain climbing, 328

pacemaker, 442
pacer, harness racing, 331
Pacific Drift, ocean, 6
Pacific Standard Time, 5
pack: backpacking, 337; camera, 170; glacier, 12; playing cards, 342
packaging, 264-265
packer controls, garbage truck, 123
packing, faucet, 269
packing nut: faucet, 269; radiator, 390
pad: ballista, 457; Band-Aid, 441; baren, 368; basketball, 292; bed, 267; cassette tape, 175; cat, 35; chaise lounge, 284; child's car seat, 282; clarinet, 350; crutch, 442; dabber, 371; dental, 445; dog, 34; fire engine, 120; football uniform, 288; handball glove, 307; human hand, 29; ice hockey player, 290, 291; kiln, 367; knee kicker, 242; launch, 154; lounger, 231; medal, 485; medical examination table, 440; paint roller, 415; parallel bars, 300; phonograph headphone, 177; playpen, 282; pommel horse, 301; rifle, 458; roller skate, 318; rug, 242; running shoe, 296; saddle, 329; sandal, 202; sander, 411; ski binding, 320; stirrup, 329; surgical table, 440; tank, 465; telephone, 178; toboggan, 322; trampoline, 302
pad applicators, house painting, 415
padded turnbuckles, boxing ring, 303
padding: baseball catcher's mask, 286; brassiere, 191; carpet, 242; fencing shoe, 309; football goalpost, 289; hockey skate, 319; hot air balloon, 326; playpen, 282; powerboat, 135; running shoe, 296; ski clothes, 320; woman's jacket, 192
paddle: glider airbrake, 147; for potting, 367; Ping-Pong, 315
paddock area, harness racetrack, 331
padlock, 449
pad pocket, football uniform, 288
page: book, IV, 165; magazine, 167
pageboy, woman's hair, 209
pagoda, 69
pail, 280
pail rest, ladder, 415
pain-killer, paramedic equipment, 119
paint: Indian, 474; sketch box, 365
paint brush, 415
painter, 364; rowboat, 129
painting, 364-365; merry-go-round, 91; tools, 415
paired string, mandolin, 356
pair of pants, 187
pajama pants, woman's, 192
Palas, playing card queen, 342
palatal arch, denture, 443
palate, mouth, 28
pale, wood fence, 65
palette, sketch box, 365
palette knife, 364, 365
palisade, frontier fort, 80
pallet, tennis racket, 306
pallet ship, 136

palm anchor, **128**; baseball glove, **387**; handball glove, **307**; human hand, **29**; tree, **50**
palpus, grasshopper, **39**
pan: air conditioner, **392**; automobile, 105, 107; bear trap, **423**; candelabrum, **233**; chafing dish, **241**; dustpan, **278**; kitchen, **253**; potter's wheel, **367**; roulette wheel, **340**; stove broiler, **244**
panagraph gate, subway motorman's cab, **115**
pancake makeup, **212**
pancake turner, **255**
pancreas, human, **27**
pane: postage stamps, **161**; window, **63**
panel: air conditioner, **392**; automobile, 102, 103, 105; book page, **IV**; bureau, **268**; bus, **114**; cartoon, **37**; clothes dryer, **277**; coffin, **500**; computer, **429**; cupboard door, **239**; curtain, **236**; desk, **272**; dishwasher, **246**; door, **62**; elevator car, **76**; football, **288**; football down marker, **289**; garbage disposal, **243**; girdle, **191**; hot air balloon, **326**; humidifier, **392**; jacket, **184**; jet fighter, **152**; key punch, **428**; lounger, **231**; mainsail, **132**; man's belt, **186**; mower, **419**; package, **264**; piano, **355**; pilot's instruments, **153**; satellite, **182**; saddle, **329**; 747 cockpit, **150**; sideboard, **239**; snowmobile, **126**; solar collector, **383**; stagecoach, **127**; steamer basket, **253**; subway car, **115**; tape recorder, **175**; toaster, **249**; tractor, **424**; trophy, **285**; umbrella, **226**; video recorder, **180**; window shutter, **237**
panel assembly, football field, **289**
panel painting, merry-go-round, **91**
panier cases, motorcycle, **125**
pan lock, camera tripod, **174**
pantaloons, queen's underpinnings, **468**
pants, **187**; baseball batter, **286**; clown, **477**; combat soldier, **481**; football, **288**; ice hockey, **291**; skiing, **320**; skin diving, **325**; woman's, **192**; *see also* trousers
panty hose, **191**
Papal cross, symbol, **492**
paper: cigarette, **224**; copper foil backing, **372**; electrician's wire, **413**; hair styling, **210**; medical examination table, **440**; printing, **164**; silkscreen, **369**
paper money, **220–221**
paper roll compartment, sealed voting booth, **427**
paperback book, **165**
paper bag, **262**
paper bail, typewriter, **162**
paper clamp, finishing sander, **411**
paper clip, **273**
paper guide, typewriter, **162**
paper tape, cash register, **430**
papillote, poultry, **259**
parabolic mirror, physician's, **438**
parachute, **327**; silo, **100**; spider, **38**
parachute canister, space shuttle, **154**

parachute vent, hot air balloon, **326**
parachutist's badge, military uniform, **480**
parade: circus, **88**; fort, **81**
parade ground, fort, 80, 81
paraffin, candle, **233**
paragraph, proofreader's mark, **498**
parallel bars, **300**
parallel of latitude, **5**
parallel tracks, railroad yard, **94**
parallel-veined leaves, grass, **56**
paramedic equipment, **119**
parapet: castle, 78, 79; fort, 80, 81; house, **60**
parenthesis, grammatical symbol, **497**
parfait, dessert, **260**
parimutuel betting, jai alai, **308**
park: amusement, **90–91**; road map, **20**
parka, **197**
parking, public sign, **490**
parking brake lever, 747; cockpit, **150**
parking light, truck tractor, **116**
parking lot, airport, 92, 93
parking meter, **109**
parking stand, hitch and harrow, **424**
parliamentarian, Congress, **72**
parlor, lobster pot, **423**
parocheth, Torah, **470**
parotoid gland, toad, **42**
parsley, and poultry, **259**
part: man's hair, **207**; poultry, **33**
partial denture, **443**
parting strip, window, **63**
parting tool, woodcarving, **366**
partisan, medieval weapon, **454**
partition: backpack, **337**; dishwasher, **246**; house, **58**
partly cloudy, weather map, **19**
partner, teeth, **446**
parure: jewelry, **214**; king's regalia, **468**
pash, human, **25**
pasigraphy, **490**
pas, mountain, **8**
passage, barn, **100**
pass case, wallet, **219**
passenger cabin: hovercraft, **145**; hydrofoil, **145**
passenger car, train, **113**
passenger concourse, airport, **92**
passenger deck, ship, **139**
passenger grab strap, motorcycle, **125**
passenger loading bridge, airport, **92**
passenger ship, **138–139**
passenger sideview mirror, automobile, **102**
passenger steps, Hansom cab, **127**
passenger terminal building, airport, **93**
passenger train, **112**
passe-partout, **373**
passive satellite, **182**
pass line: craps table, **341**; jai alai cancha, **308**
pastern: cow, **30**; dog, **34**; horse, **36**; sheep, **31**
past history, symbol, **494**
pastoral staff, cardinal, **471**
pastry, **260**
pastry blender, **257**
pastry brush, **255**
pastry pin, **255**
pastry wheel, **257**
patch: label, **265**; military uniform, 480, 481; paper

bag, **262**; police uniform, **482**; running shoe, **296**
patch pocket: cardigan, **195**; woman's jacket, **192**
patchwork quilting, **377**
pate, human, **25**
patella: human, **26**; spider, **38**
paten, for Communion bread, **85**
path, golf course, **304**
patio, **61**; accessories, **284**
Patriarchal cross, symbol, **492**
patrol, police, **482**
patrolman, police, **482**
pattern: sewing, **390**; stained glass, **372**; table setting, **241**; wind, **6**
patterned indented surface, thimble, **376**
pattern scale, sewing machine, **272**
pauldron, armor, **455**
pause button: tape recorder, **175**; television LaserDisc player, **181**
pavement light, church, **85**
pavilion: cut gemstone, **214**; minaret, **68**
pavise, medieval shield, **454**
paw: cat **35**; dog, **34**; human, **25**; ultimate beast, **46**
pawl: brace, **408**; saw, 406, 407
pawn, chess, **339**
payee: check, **222**; postal money order, **223**; traveler's check, **223**
paying agent, traveler's check, **223**
payload, missile, **466**
payload changeout room, launch pad, **154**
payload pallet, lunar rover, **157**
payload specialist, space shuttle, **155**
payoff chart, slot machine, **340**
payoff return, slot machine, **340**
pay phone, **178**
pea, **52**, anchor, **128**
peace, symbol, **495**
peach, **53**
peacock-feather tassel, Manchu court dress, **475**
peak: bonnet, **199**; glacier, **12**; house, 59, 61; man's cap, **198**; mountain, **7**
pearl: cave, **11**; royal crown, **469**
pebble finish, football, **288**
pectoral cross, bishop, **471**
pectoral fin: fish, **43**; stingray, **43**
pectoralis major, human, **26**
ped, **206**
pedal: brass drum, **358**; bicycle, **124**; bulldozer, **425**; car, **106**; cymbal, **385**; dental unit, **444**; guitar, **357**; organ, **354**; piano, **355**; potter's wheel, **367**; 747 cockpit, **150**; starting block, **298**; surgical table, **440**; vacuum cleaner, **279**
petal lip, mousetrap, **423**
pedal steel guitar, **357**
pedestal: animal tamer, **88**; column, **71**; desk, **272**; diving board, **310**; dressing table, **268**; House of Representatives, **72**; obelisk, **69**; surgical table, **440**; television set, **181**; trophy, **285**
pedestal table, **238**
pedestrian crossing, road sign, **489**
pedestrian safety mirror, mechanical sweeper, **123**

pedicel: flower, **51**; grass, **56**; spider, **38**
pedipalpi, spider, **38**
peduncle, flower, **51**
peel, fruit, **53**
peeler, 252, 257
peen, hammer, **402**
peephole: door, **62**; kiln, **367**
peg: banjo, **356**; croquet, **312**; dulcimer, **356**; guitar, **356**, **357**; sitar, **356**; tent, **336**; tepee, **82**; violin, **349**
pegbox, violin, **349**
pellet: dental, **445**; shotgun, **458**
pelota, jai alai, **308**
pelt, **197**
pelvic fin, fish, **43**
pelvic region, salamander, **42**
pen: barnyard, **100**; writing tool, **160**
penalty arc, soccer field, **293**
penalty area, soccer field, **293**
penalty box: ice hockey rink, **291**; lacrosse field, **293**
penalty kick mark, soccer field, **293**
pen blade, pocket knife, **416**
pencil: beauty product, **213**; lithographic, **370**; styptic, **206**; writing tool, **160**
pencil sharpener, **273**
pendant: aircraft carrier, **142**; Indian, **474**; jewelry, **215**; queen's regalia, **468**
pendant pearl, royal crown, **469**
pendentive, mosque, **69**
pendulum: clock, **229**; metronome, **361**
pen holder: checkbook clutch, **219**; police gun belt, **483**
penhold grip, Ping-Pong
pen loop, checkbook clutch, **219**
pennant, **486**; circus tent, **89**
pennon, lance, **454**
penny size, nail, **400**
penstock control, dam, **98**
Pentateuch, Torah, **86**
pentathlon, track and field, **294**
penthouse, barn, **100**
pent roof, pagoda, **69**
people-mover, **77**
peplum, dress, **194**
pepper, raw, **258**
peppercorn, **258**
pepper mill, **257**
pepperoni, pizza, **261**
per, symbol, **495**
perambulator, **282**
percent key, electronic calculator, **431**
percolator, **248**
percussion, orchestra, **348**
perforated panel, steamer basket, **253**
perforated spreader, percolator brewing basket, **248**
perforation: envelope, **161**; foil pouch, **265**; hair roller, **210**; man's shoe, **200**; movie film, **172**
performance hall, theatre, **345**
performance instruction, music, **346**
performing rights organization, music, **347**
perfume, **213**
per hundred, symbol, **495**
periapical dental x-ray unit, **444**
pericarp, pea, **52**
period: grammatical symbol, **497**; wave, **14**
periodical, **167**
periople, horse's hoof, **36**
periscope: submarine, **143**; tank, **465**

538

permanent current, ocean 6
permanent fort, 81
permanent lotion, hair styling, 210
permanent rod, hair styling, 210
permanent teeth, 446
per mill, symbol, 495
peroxide, ambulance, 119
personal choice, voting booth, 427
personnel safety net, aircraft carrier, 142
perspective, and composition, 362
per thousand, symbol, 495
Peru Current, ocean, 6
pestle, kitchen tool, 257
petal, flower, 51
petiole: celery, 258; fern, 55; leaf, 50
petitpoint, stitchery, 377
petronel, pirate, 476
petticoat: maid's uniform, 473; windmill, 382
pew, synagogue, 86
phalanges, human, 26, 29
pharynx, mouth, 28
phase of moon, 4
pheasant, 33
Phillips head, screw, 400
Phillips head screwdriver, pocket knife, 416
Phillips head tip, screwdriver, 403
philtrum, face, 28
phloem, tree, 48
Phoenix missile, jet fighter, 152
phone, 178
phonetic symbol, grammatical, 497
phonograph equipment, 176, 177
phonogram, public sign, 490
photo, magazine, 167, 168
photo and card case, wallet, 219
photocell, camera, 170
photo-disk, computer, 429
photograph, book jacket, 165
photographer, 171
photographic accessories, 174
photo holder, wallet, 219
phyllacteries, Jewish ritual items, 470
physician's mirror, 438
physician's room, White House, 73
pi, symbol, 495
pianissimo, music notation, 347
piano, 355; music notation, 346
piano-accordion, 360
piano frame, 373
piccolo, 348, 350
pick: figure skates, 319; ice ax, 328; ice hammer, 328; pipe tool, 225; stringed instrument, 356
picket fence, 61, 65
pick guard, guitar, 356, 357
pick-up, guitar, 357
pick-up arm, fishing reel, 334
pick-up broom, mechanical sweeper, 123
pick-up selector, guitar, 357
picnic area: public sign, 491; road sign, 488
picnic shoulder, pork, 32
pictograph, public sign, 490
picture card, 342
picture exit slot, instant camera, 170
picture frame, 373
picture hat, 199; bride's, 472
picture hook, 373
picture key, television set, 181
picture tube, television set, 181
pie, 260

piece: backgammon, 339; cake, 260; chess, 339; coin, 221; crutch, 442; jewelry, 215; kite, 317; rifle, 461; slalom water ski, 323
piece goods, fabric, 380
pier: arch, 70 bridge, 95; dam, 98; house, 58; nautical chart, 22; skyscraper, 75
pierced ear findings, 214
piercer, can opener, 247
pig, 32
pig board, windsurfer, 324
pigboat, 143
piggin, container, 262
piggy bank, 447
pigment cell, octopus, 44
pigment filling, scrimshaw, 369
pigpen, 100
pigtail, woman's hair, 209
pike, lance, 454
pike pole, fireman, 484
pilaster: cupboard, 239; house, 60
pile: arrow, 468; carpet, 242; nuclear, 384; skyscraper, 75; Velcro, 205
pileus, mushroom, 55
pill, medicinal, 441
pillar: arch, 70; automobile windshield, 105; house, 60; mountain, 9; and obelisk, 68; torii, 69
pillbox, woman's hat, 199
pillow: bedding, 266; coffin, 500; lounger, 231; police car, 118; rocking chair, 230; sofa, 232; stagecoach, 127
pilot: airplane, 153; locomotive, 112
pilot boarding ladder, tugboat, 144
pilot chute, 327
pilot hole, screw, 400
pilothouse: fireboat, 144; tugboat, 144
pilot light: guitar amplifier, 357; stove, 244
pilot's seat, space shuttle, 155
pilot-wheel feed, drill press, 409
pin: anchor, 128; attachment plug, 388; bowling, 311; can opener, 247; and carpet, 242; compass, 132; fastener, 204; fire extinguisher, 280; fluorescent bulb, 234; gallows, 452; gardening shears, 417; globe, 1; golf course, 305; hacksaw, 406; hair, 210; hand grenade, 463; hasp, 450; jewelry, 215; kitchen utensil, 255; lock cylinder, 449; mortar, 462; nail clippers, 211; pliers, 404; potter's wheel, 367; pulley block, 451; revolver safety catch, 214; rifle, 458, 459; roller chain, 451; roller skate, 318; sewing machine, 274; stapler, 273; starting block, 298; stroller, 282; tepee, 82; torpedo, 466; track link, 464; vacuum tube, 386; window shade roller, 237; woman's hat, 199
pin binding, ski, 321
pinbone, cow, 30
pincer, lobster, 45
pinch, man's hat, 198
pinch roller, tape recorder, 175
pinch valve, dental unit, 444
pincushion, 376
pineapple, 53; grenade, 463
pine cone, 50
Ping-Pong, 315
pin hinge, stove, 394

pinion, hand drill, 408
pinkie, human hand, 29
pinky ring, trumpet, 353
pin link plate, roller chain, 451
pin mark, type, 164
pinna, 28; fern, 55
pinnacle: church, 84; mountain, 9
pinnule, fern, 55
pin rail, stage, 344
pinsetter, bowling, 311
pinspotter, bowling, 311
pintle, hinge, 450
pintle mount, machine gun, 461
pin-tumbler, lock cylinder, 449
pinwood, clothespin, 276
pip: apple, 53; backgammon board, 339; dice, 341; domino, 339; pineapple, 53; playing card, 342
pip card, 342
pipe: automobile, 104; bagpipe, 359; furnace, 390; heat exchanger, 393; lamp, 234; levigator, 370; locomotive, 112; motorcycle, 125; oil drilling platform, 99; organ, 354; pitch, 361; plumbing, 412; pressure cooker, 253; silo, 100; smoking, 225; solar heating system, 383; space shuttle, 154; standpipe, 57; steam engine, 395; steel chain fence gate, 65; tank, 464; trumpet, 353; water heater, 391
pipe batten, stage, 344
pipe cleaner, 225
pipe cutter, plumbing, 412
pipe-holding jaw, vise, 399
pipeline, wave, 14
pipe nozzle, fire engine, 120
piper, bagpipe, 359
pipe standard, parking meter, 109
pipe threader, 412
pipe tool, 225
pipe umbrella, 225
pipe wrench, plumbing, 412
piping: baseball uniform, 286; bishop's cope, 471; boot, 202; handball glove, 307; jacket, 184; man's belt, 186; shoulder bag, 218; woman's shoe, 201
pipkin, 253
pipquot front, butler's shirt, 473
pirate, costume, 476
Pisces, zodiac, 493
piste, fencing, 309
pistil, flower, 51
pistol, 460; lobster, 45
pistol belt, soldier, 481
pistol grip: hacksaw, 406; rifle, 461; shotgun, 458
pistol nozzle, 418
pistol port, tank, 464
pistol trigger switch, video camera, 180
piston: garbage truck, 123; dispenser, 263; organ, 354; parallel bars, 300; pommel horse, 310; steam engine, 395
piston displacement, chain saw, 421
piston rod, steam engine, 395
pit: barnyard, 100; bowling lane, 311; high jump, 299; peach, 53; pole vault, 299; snake, 41; theatre, 345
pitch: plane blade, 410; screw, 400
pitch-control dial, tape recorder, 175
pitcher's mound, baseball field, 287
pitcher's rubber, baseball field, 287

pitching wedge, golf club, 304
pitch pipe, 361
pitch trim, 747 cockpit, 151
pitmans, steam engine, 395
piton, mountain climbing, 328
pitot tube, jet fighter, 152
pivot: basketball, 292; clamp, 399; compass, 132; dressing table mirror, 268; jet fighter wing, 152; laboratory, scale, 437; metronome, 361; mortar, 462; pliers, 404; roller skate, 418; scissors, 376; ski binding, 320; wire stripper, 413
pivot bolt, bicycle caliper brake, 124
pivot gear housing, mechanical sweeper, 123
pivot hinge, 450
pivot pin: can opener, 247; hinge, 450
pivot point, bicycle caliper brake, 124
pix, church, 85
pizza, 261
pizzicato, stringed instruments, 349
place, flat racing, 330
place bets, craps table, 341
placenta, tomato, 52
place setting, 240
placket: blouse, 193; parka, 197; shirt, 185
plain, 7, 8, 15
plaintiff's table, courtroom, 87
plait, woman's hair, 209
plan: church, 85; White House, 73
planchet, coin, 221
plane, 410; monorail, 414; perspective, 362
plane iron, 410
plane kite, 317
plane surface, printing, 164
planet, 2, 3
planetary, tractor, 424
planetoid, 2
planing hull, powerboat, 134
plank, lumber, 66
planographic printing, 370
plant, power network, 386
plantar arch, human foot, 29
Plantin typeface, 163
planting box, pole vault, 299
planting machine, 424
planting pit, pole vault, 299
plague: identification bracelet, 183; man's belt buckle, 186; pyrometric cone, 367
plasma membrane, animal cell, 23
plasma science, satellite, 182
plastic cap, stapler, 273
plastic disc, harness racing sulky, 331
plastic fruit, woman's hat, 199
plastic lining, man's hat, 198
plastic sheath, electrician's wire, 413
plastic squeeze bottle, 264
plasti-shield, bottle, 265
plastron: fencing, 309; turtle, 40;
plate: armor, 455; automatic weapon, 461; barbell, 338; baseball field, 287; baseball pitcher's spikes, 286; bathtub, 270; blackjack, 341; beef, 30; bicycle, 241; chain lock, 448; crossbow, 456; escalator, 77; flute, 350; food mill, 256; furnace, 390; hasp, 450; horizontal bar, 300; house, 59; identification bracelet, 183; intaglio, 371; internal combustion engine, 396;

iron, 275; keypunch, 428, kitchen sink, 243; laboratory scale, 436; land mine, 463; lithographic, 370; locomotive, 112; mandolin, 356; mortise lock, 448; onion, 52; outboard engine, 133; paper money, 220; parking meter, 109; pliers, 404; postal money order, 223; pulley block, 451; racing car, 332; railroad track, 111; rifle, 458; roller chain, 451; roller skate, 318; safe, 447; sewing machine, 274; shotgun butt, 458; ski binding, 320; slalom water ski, 323; solar collector panel, 383; space shuttle, 154; sponge mop, 278; stage, 344; standpipe, 57; stationary rings, 301; sundial, 381; table setting, 240, 241; tank, 464, 465; telephone, 178; theodolite, 426; toaster, 249; tow truck, 122; tractor, 424; trophy, 285; typewriter, 162; vacuum tube, 386; vise, 398
plate number: envelope, 161; paper money, 221
plate vial, theodolite, 426
plateau, 7
plate cylinder, printing, 164
platen, typewriter, 162
platform: aircraft carrier, 142; camera tripod, 174; circus aerialist, 88; diving, 310; elevator shaft, 76; fire engine, 120; helicopter, 146; iceberg, 12; lunar lander, 156; merry-go-round, 91; powerboat, 135; slide, 283; space shuttle, 154; stage, 344; swimming pool, 310; truck, 117
platform car, train, 113
platform shoe, woman's, 210
platform tower, slide, 283
platter, phonograph, 176
playback unit: tape recorder, 175; video recorder, 180
play button: tape recorder, 175; television LaserDisc player, 181
player: basketball, 292; ice hockey, 291; jai alai cancha, 308; orchestra, 348
playground: equipment, 283; public signs, 491
playing cards, 342
playing surface, pool table, 314
playpen, child's, 282
playroom, passenger ship, 139
plaza, skyscraper, 75
pleat: ballet slippers, 478; curtain, 236; lounger, 231; shirt, 185; woman's pants, 192
pleated pants, woman's, 192
pleated ruffled shirt, man's, 472
plectrum, stringed instrument, 356
plenum assembly, nuclear reactor, 395
plewd, cartoon, 375
plexus, human, 25
pliers, 404; dental, 445; stained glass, 372
Plimsoll mark, symbol, 495
plinth: column, 71; grandfather clock, 229
plot, grave, 500
plow, 424; can opener, 247
plow anchor, sailboat, 130
plug: ballpoint pen, 160; electric, 388; fishing, 335; internal combustion engine, 396; kiln, 367;

lawn sprinkler, 418; locomotive boiler, 112; mortise lock, 448; movie projector, 173; mower, 419; padlock, 449; paint spray gun, 415; percolator, 248; pots and pans, 253; vacuum tube, 386
plug body, phonograph headphone, 177
plug fuse, 389
plum, cowboy bullet, 474
plumb, transit, 426
plumber's friend, 412
plumbing tool, 412
plumb vial, carpenter's level, 414
plume: armor, 455; drum major's busby, 479
plunge pool, dam, 98
plunger: coffee maker, 248; hypodermic syringe, 441; juice extractor, 251; plumbing tool, 412; telephone, 178; torpedo, 466
plunger handle, camp stove, 336
plunger snap lock, starting block, 298
plunge step, shoreline, 14
plus, symbol, 494
plus or minus, symbol, 494
Pluto, planet, 2
pneumatic liner system, football helmet, 288
pneumoscopy port, ear scope, 438
pocket: backpack, 337; baseball glove, 287; bowling, 331; briefcase, 281; cardigan sweater, 195; cowboy, 474; football uniform, 288; golf bag, 305; handbag, 218; jacket, 184; lacrosse stick, 293; mainsail, 132; necktie, 189; parka, 197; pool table, 314; shirt, 185; skin diving gear, 325; skirt, 193; spacesuit, 157; trench coat, 196; trousers, 187; wallet, 219; woman's jacket and pants, 192; window shade, 237
pocket billiard table, 314
pocketbook, 218
pocket camera, 170
pocket flap, backpack, 337
pocketknife, 416
pocket watch, 216
pod: camera, 171; jumbo jet engine, 149; pea, 52; racing car, 332
podium, symphony orchestra, 348
pogonotomy, 207
pogonotrophy, 207
point: arrow, 456; backgammon board, 339; ballpoint pen, 160; billiard cue, 314; chicken comb, 33; clown's hat, 477; dart, 316; drill bit, 409; etching needle, 371; fencing foil, 309; fish hook, 335; grammatical symbol, 497; hockey skate, 319; ice climbing boot, 328; jai alai cesta, 308; javelin, 296; knife, 252, 453; knitting needle, 378; laboratory scale, 436; land, 7; mainsail, 132; nail, 400; needle, 376; pencil, 160; pin, 204; rasp, 410; river, 13; saw tooth, 406; screw, 400; sharpening steel, 252; star fort, 81; sword, 453; tack, 400; violin bow, 349; weather vane, 19; wrench, 405; wrought iron fence, 65
point chisel, stonecutting, 366

point d'appliqué, bridal gown, 472
point defense missile launcher, aircraft carrier, 142
pointed waist, queen's regalia, 468
pointer: barometer, 18; comic strip, 375; laboratory scale, 437; Torah, 470; volt-ohm meter, 413; weather vane, 19
pointillism and texture, composition, 363
point of entry, darts, 316
point of hip, horse, 36
point of hock, horse, 36
point of interest, city plan, 20
point of shoulder, horse, 36
point ring, darts, 316
point size, type, 164
point symbol, political map, 21
poise, laboratory scale, 436
poison, symbol, 495
poisonous snake, 40
poker, fire iron, 228
polarity symbol, battery, 387
pole: baseball field, 287; bumper car, 90; circus tent, 89; football field, 289; globe, 5, harness racetrack, 331; overhead power line, 386; pole vaulting, 299; powerboat, 135; skiing, 320, 321; stagecoach, 127; tent, 336; tepee, 82
pole arms, medieval, 454
pole grip, ski pole, 320
pole mount, fishing reel, 334
pole position, flat racing, 330
pole vault, 294, 299
poleyn, armor, 455
police car, 118
police officer, 482-483
polish, beauty product, 213
polisher, pipe cutter, 412
political boundary, map, 5, 20
political capital symbol, map, 20
political cartoon, 374
political map, 20-21
poll(s): ax, 454; cow, 30; hammer, 402; horse, 36; pig, 32; voting, 427
pollen, flower, 51
pollen basket, bee, 39
poll end, windmill, 382
pollen sac, flower stamen, 51
polling place, 427
polliwog, 42
pollution control valve, automobile engine, 107
poly bag, packaging, 265
polygonal base, minaret, 68
polygonal tower, architecture, 69
polyp, coral, 44
pommel: foil mounting, 309; knife, 453; pommel horse, 301; saddle, 329; sword hilt, 453
pommel horse, 301
pompon, ski hat, 321
poncho, infantryman's uniform, 481
pond, topographic map, 22
pontic, dental bridge, 443
pontoon, single engine airplane, 147
pontoon bridge, 95
ponytail, woman's hair, 209
pool, 314; canal lock, 97; cave, 11; dam, 98; passenger ship, 138, 139; swimming, 310
pool table, 314
popcorn, cave, 11
pop-up stopper, sink, 269
porcelain, dental, 445
porch: church, 85; house, 61
porcupine, ultimate beast, 46
pork, 32

port: drag racing driver's fire suit, 333; ear scope, 438; movie projector, 173; outboard, engine, 133; passenger ship, 138; rocket, 397; saber saw, 407; sailboat, 130; tank, 464
portable electrocardiogram, paramedic equipment, 119
portable life support system, spacesuit, 157
portable telemetry radio, paramedic equipment, 119
portable typewriter, 162
portal: church, 84-85; stage, 344, 345; underwater tunnel, 96
portcullis, castle, 79
port-engine clutch, powerboat, 134
portfolio, briefcase, 281
porthole, passenger ship, 138
portico: Capitol, 72; White House, 73
portlight: powerboat, 134; sailboat, 130
port quarter, boat, 128
portrait: money, 221; White House, 73
port side, boat, 128
port throttle, powerboat, 134
position: flat racing, 330; globe, 5
position indicator: elevator car, 76, 747; cockpit, 150; sonar, 434
positioning arm, dental unit, 444
positioning key, computer, 429
positioning ratchet, chaise lounge, 284
positioning scale, typewriter, 162
position letter, paper money, 220, 221
position light, jet fighter, 152
position lines, jai alai cancha, 308
position mark, guitar, 356, 357
position number, paper money, 220
positive charge, symbol, 494
positive terminal, battery, 387
positive test lead jack, volt-ohm meter, 413
post: battery, 387; bear trap, 423; bed, 266; bicycle, 124; boxing ring, 303; bureau, 268; camera tripod, 174; candelabrum, 233; fence, 65; guillotine, 452; hand loom, 379; hang glider, 327; house, 58, 59; jewelry findings, 214; kettledrum, 358; laboratory scale, 437; mailbox, 227; Ping-Pong net, 315; railroad crossing signal, 111, rocking chair, 230; snap fastener, 204; tanker, 137; tatting shuttle, 378; toilet, 271; typewriter guide, 162; wind turbine, 382
postage due notice, envelope, 161
postal money order, 223
post cap, railroad crossing signal, 111
poster arm, gas pump, 108
poster frame, garbage truck, 123
post footing, house, 58
posthole, fence, 65
post lamp, house, 61
postmark, envelope, 161
post-mounted arm, dental unit, 444
post office, Capitol, 72
post position: flat racing, 330; jai alai player, 308

postscript, letter, 161
pot, 367; combat soldier's helmet, 481; kitchen, 253; percolator, 248; tea set, 241
potato, 52; masher, 255; peeler, 257
pot fork, 255
pot holder, house painting, 415
potter's wheel, 367
pouch: athletic supporter, 190; combat soldier's uniform, 481; package, 264, 265; police gun belt, 482; tobacco, 255; ultimate beast, 46
pouf, footstool, 231
poult, turkey, 33
poultry, 33, 259
pound, symbol, 495
pound lock, 97
pouring lip, blender, 250
pour spout, package, 264
powder: fortification, 80; makeup, 212, 213
powdered emery, nail file, 211
powder eye shadow, 213
power, steam engine 395
powerboat, 134-135
power bore bit, drill, 408
power button: tape recorder, 175; television LaserDisc player, 181
power cable, police car, 118
power control: sonar, 434; space shuttle, 155
power cord: air conditioner, 392; camper, 126; curling iron, 210; lamp, 234; tape recorder, 175
power drill, 409
power feed, track lighting, 235
power handle, ear scope, 438
power head, chain saw, 421
powerhouse: dam, 98; prison, 74
power, indicator, CB radio, 179
power key, television set, 181
power knob, phonograph receiver, 177
power lawn mower, 419
power line, overhead, 386
power network, 386
power on indicator, phonograph turntable, 176
power output meter, phonograph receiver, 177
power pedal, surgical table, 440
power saw, 407
power station, dam, 98
power status, space shuttle, 155
power steering, automobile engine, 107
power supply module, cash register, 430
power switch: camera, 170; radar, 434
power takeoff, tractor, 424
power terminal, electrical wall switch, 338
power train, automobile, 104
power twister, body building, 338
power winder, camera, 171
power window control, car, 106
power-zoom control, camera, 172
prayer book, Jewish, 470
prayer hall, mosque, 68-69
prayer shawl, Jewish, 470
prayer vestment, Jewish, 470
pre-amp, phonograph, 177
preamplifier, guitar, 357
precautionary statement, label, 264
precinct number, police uniform, 482

precious miter, cardinal, 471
precipitation gauge, weather station, 18
precision approach marking, runway, 92
precision attachment, denture, 443
prediction, weather map, 19
prefix letter, paper money, 221
preheater hose, automobile engine, 107
prehensile lobe, ultimate beast, 47
preliminaries, book, 165
premolar, 446
preparation utensils, cooking, 255
prepared foods, 259
prepercle, fish, 43
pre-race betting odds, flat racing entry, 330
presbytery, church, 85
prescription, symbol, 494
presentation mode selector, sonar, 434
preset: organ, 354; video recorder, 180
president: fencing match, 309; Senate, 72
President's executive office, White House, 73
President's living quarters, White House, 73
press: curling iron, 21; etching, 371; incandescent bulb, 234; kitchen tool, 257; lithographic, 370; printing, 164; universal gym, 338
presser, pipe tool, 225
presser foot, sewing machine, 274
presser plate, sponge mop, 278
pressure, weather map, 19
pressure altimeter, pilot's instument panel, 153
pressure brush, house painting, 415
pressure cooker, 253
pressure cup, citrus juicer, 251
pressure cuff, blood pressure gauge, 439
pressure dial, sewing machine presser foot, 274
pressure gauge: fire extinguisher, 280; furnace, 390; skin diving, 325; steam engine, 395
pressure hull, submarine, 143
pressure indicator, pilot's instrument panel, 153
pressure pad, cassette tape, 175
pressure plate: key punch, 420; land mine, 463
pressure ratio gauge, 747; cockpit, 150
pressure regulator: pressure cooker, 253; steam engine, 395; water heater, 391
pressure relief valve: tanker, 136, 137; water heater, 391
pressure screw, etching press, 371
pressure sensor, weather station, 18
pressurized helmet, spacesuit, 157
pressurizer, nuclear reactor, 384
pre-starting light, drag racing, 333
pre-tuning controls, video recorder, 180
preview, magazine, 167
price: book, 165; gas pump, 108; magazine, 167; newspaper, 166; ticket, 343
priced at, symbol, 495
price spot, label, 265
pricket, candlestick, 233

primary, bird, 37
primary account number, credit card, 222
primary cable, overhead power line, 386
primary cell: battery, 387; electric meter, 389
primary combination dial, vault, 447
primary combustion chamber, woodburning stove, 394
primary root, 49
primary selector control, sealed voting booth, 427
prime, grammatical symbol, 497
prime meridian, 5
primer: cartridge, 460; hand grenade, 463; painting, 364
primer control, mower, 419
prime ribs, beef, 30
Prince of Wales handle, umbrella, 226
princess waistline, bridal gown, 472
principal doorway, church, 85
principal rafter, house, 59
principal street, city plan, 20
print: camera, 170; silk screen, 369
printed image, 164
printed impression, 164
printer: cash register, 430; computer, 429
printing: incised, 371; planographic, 370; processes, 164; silk screen, 269; woodcut, 368
printing surface: lithographic press, 370; type, 164
printmaking, 371; silk screen, 369
printout, computer, 429
prison, 74
probable morning line, flat racing, 330
probe jack, volt-ohm meter, 413
proboscis: mosquito, 39; ultimate beast, 47
procedures, computer, 429
proceed signal, traffic light, 109
processing unit, computer, 429
product label, 264
product number, pencil, 160
profile, shoreline, 14, 15
program, computer, 429
program button, video recorder, 180
programmer, computer, 428
program number, flat racing entry, 330
program setting button, television LaserDisc player, 181
prohibit movement sign, road, 489
projectile: cannon, 457; mortar, 462
projection, map, 20, 21
projection speed selector, movie projector, 173
project name, house blueprint, 60
projector, 173
prominence, solar, 2-3
promotional label, 264
prong: electric plug, 388; fork, 240, 255; man's belt, 186; nail clippers, 211; ring, 215; tuning fork, 361; vacuum tube, 386
pronunciation symbol, 497
proof-of-purchase seal, package, 264
proofreader's marks, 498
prop: grand piano, 355; stage, 344
propane gas, camper, 126
propane plumber's torch, 412

propeller: destroyer, 140; hovercraft, 145; outboard, engine, 133; single engine airplane, 147; submarine, 143; torpedo, 466; turboprop jet engine, 397
property, stage, 344
proposed road, road map, 20
proposition area, craps table, 341
prop root, corn, 56
prop stick, grand piano, 355
proscenium arch, stage, 344, 345
prosecutor's table, courtroom, 87
pro-style hair dryer, 208
protection pad, parallel bars, 300
protective cap, razor, 206
protective case, blood pressure gauge, 439
protective chain cover, swing, 283
protective clothing, armor, 455
protective counter, sealed voting booth, 427
protective cup: athletic supporter, 190; baseball catcher, 286; boxing, 303; football player, 288
protective padding, ski clothes, 320
protective shoulder, wristwatch, 216
protective sleeve, overhead power line, 386
protector: banjo, 356; baseball catcher, 286; ice hockey player, 290, 291; tow truck bed, 122; waterskiing towline, 323
protruding upper face, zipper, 205
proximal transverse, human hand, 29
pubes, human, 25
pubis, human, 26
public address switch, CB radio, 179
public counter, sealed voting booth, 427
public sign, 490-491
publisher, book, 165
puck: craps table, 341; ice hockey, 290
pudding fender, tugboat, 144
p'u fang, Manchu court dress, 475
puff, beauty product, 213
puff sleeve: maid's uniform, 473; queen's regalia, 468
p'u-fu, Manchu court dress, 475
pull: bureau, 268; dressing table, 268; sideboard, 239; traverse rod, 236; window shade, 236, 237
pull bail, screen, 173
pulley, 451; automobile engine, 107; block and tackle, 451; stage, 344; tow truck, 122; universal gym, 338; venetian blind, 237
pulley block, 451
pulley chain, castle portcullis, 79
pulley rope, ballista, 457
pulley safety guard, drill press, 409
pullover: hurdle, 298; sweater, 195, 321
pull-pin, fire extinguisher, 280
pullquote, magazine, 168
pull ring: hand grenade, 463; zipper slide, 205
pull strap, boot, 202
pull tab: package, 264; zipper, 205
pulp, fruit, 53, 251
pulpit: church, 85; sailboat, 130; synagogue, 86

pulsar, **3**
pulse generation, pacemaker, **442**
pulse point, and perfume, **213**
pump: automobile engine, **107**; bicycle, **124**; blood pressure gauge, **439**; dishwasher, **246**; fireboat, **144**; gas, **108**; nuclear reactor, **384, 385**; paint spray gun, **415**; paramedic equipment, **119**; percolator brewing basket, **248**; pilot's instrument panel, **153**; rocket, **397**; solar heating system, **383**; woman's shoe, **201, 472, 473**
pumper, fire engine, **121**
pumpkin, silo, **100**
pump plunger handle, camp stove, **336**
pump valve, lantern, **336**
punch card, key punch, **428**
puncheon, **263**
punch hole: man's belt, **186**; punch card, **428**
punching station, key punch, **428**
punch line, comic strip, **375**
punctuation, grammatical symbol, **497**
punt: bottle, **263**; fireboat, **144**
punta, jai alai cesta, **308**
pupa, insect, **39**
pupil, eye, **28**
pup tent, **336**
purchaser: postal money order, **223**; traveler's check, **223**
purfling, violin, **349**
purge valve, skin diving face mask, **325**
purl, knitting, **378**
purlicue, human hand, **29**
purlin, house, **59**
purl stitch, knitting, **378**
purse, **218**; miser, **476**
push arm, bulldozer, **425**
push axle tire, bus, **114**
pushboat, **144**
pushbutton: ballpoint pen, **160**; drill press, **409**; metal detector, **435**; screen, **173**; telephone, **178**
pusher: food processor, **250**; nail clippers, **211**
pusher tug, **144**
push knob, citrus juicer, **25**
push-pin, wristwatch, **216**
pushpit, sailboat, **130**
push plate, tow truck bed, **122**
push rim, wheelchair, **422**
putter, golf club, **305**
putting green, **305**
puzzle solution, magazine, **169**
pylon: helicopter, **146**; hovercraft, **145**; jumbo jet, **149**
pyramid, **69**
pyramidion, obelisk, **69**
pyrometric cones, potting, **367**

Q

Q: braille, **496**; sign language, **496**
Q-light, camera, **170**
quad, magazine column, **169**
quadrant, **133**
quadrant number, paper money, **220**
quadraphonic record, phonograph, **176**
quadredundant computer system, space shuttle, **155**
quadrilateral structure, pyramid, **68**
quantity indicator, pilot's instrument panel, **153**
quark, **3**
quarrel, crossbow, **456**
quarter: boat, **202**; horse's

hoof, **36**; man's shoe, **200**
quarterdeck, passenger ship, **139**
quarter glass, automobile, **103**
quarter hoop, barrel, **263**
quarter-inch mark, tape measure, **414**
quartermaster, frontier fort, **80**
quarter-mile pole, harness racetrack, **331**
quarter moon, **4**
quarter note, music, **346**
quarter panel, automobile, **102, 103**
quarter rest, music, **347**
quarters: frontier fort, **80**; oil drilling platform, **99**; passenger ship, **138**; tugboat, **144**; White House, **73**
quarter shield, coat of arms, **487**
quasar, **3**
quasihemidemisemiquaver, music, **346**
quatrefoil, church, **84**
quaver, music, **346**
queen: chess, **339**; playing cards, **342**; royal regalia, **468**
queen post, house, **59**
queenside men, chess, **339**
query author, proofreader's mark, **498**
question index column, voting booth, **427**
question mark: grammatical symbol, **497**; proofreader's mark, **498**
quiche, **259**
quick claw, lobster, **45**
quick-release hook, parachute, **327**
quill: bird feather, **37**; brace, **408**; pen, **160**; ultimate beast, **46**
quillon: knife, **453**; sword hilt, **453**
quilt, **266, 267**
quilting, sleeping bag, **337**
quimp, cartoon, **375**
quiver, arrow, **456**
quoin: brick wall, **67**; masonry gate post, **65**
quotation mark, **497**

R

R: braille, **496**; sign language, **496**
rabbi, **470**
rabbit ear, ultimate beast, **47**
rabillo, jai alai cesta, **308**
race: hand loom, **379**; swimming, **310**; track and field, **294**
race track: Grand Prix, **332**; harness, **331**
Rachel, playing card queen, **342**
rachis: bird feather, **37**; fern, **55**
racing: drag, **333**; flat, **330**; Grand Prix, **332**; harness, **331**; starting block, **298**
racing colors, flat racing entry, **330**
racing flat, **296**
racing handlebar, bicycle, **124**
racing slick, **332, 333**
rack: automobile, **105**; bathtub, **270**; bicycle, **124**; billiards, **314**; blackjack, **314**; bowling lane, **311**; bus, **114**; camper, **126**; desk, **272**; dishwasher, **246**; kitchen tool, **256**; lamb, **31**; oil drilling platform, **99**; outboard engine, **133**; space shuttle, **155**; stagecoach, **127**; stove oven, **244**; tank, **464**; toaster,

249; wok, **253**
racket: badminton, **313**; Ping-Pong, **315**; squash, **307**; tennis, **306**
radar, **434**; aircraft carrier, **142**; buoy, **128**; destroyer, **141**; fireboat, **144**; hovercraft, **145**; jumbo jet, **148**; pilot's instrument panel, **153**; police car, **118**; 747: cockpit, **150**; space shuttle, **155**; submarine, **143**; tanker, **137**; tugboat, **144**
radial: lumber, **66**; scallop shell, **45**; spider web, **38**
radiation belt, Milky Way, **3**
radiator, **390**; automobile, **104**; bulldozer, **425**; racing car, **332**; solar power system, **383**
radicle, root system, **49**
radii, spider web, **38**
radio: aircraft carrier, **142**; ambulance, **119**; Citizens Band, **179**; clock, **229**; hovercraft, **145**; pilot's instrument panel, **153**; police car, **118**; 747 cockpit, **150**; submarine, **143**
radioactive-waste storage tank, nuclear reactor, **384**
radio mast, skyscraper, **75**
radiometer, satellite, **182**
radio operator, **179**
radio-translucent pad, surgical table, **440**
radio tuning dial, phonograph receiver, **177**
radio wave, **2-3**
radius, human, **26**
radome, jet fighter, **152**
raft: aircraft carrier, **142**; jumbo jet, **148**; tugboat, **144**
rafter: house, **59**; lumber, **66**
ragged-right type, magazine, **168**
raglan sleeve: parka, **197**; trench coat, **196**
rail: backgammon board, **339**; backyard equipment, **283**;
rail: backgammon board, **339**; backyard equipment, **283**; balustrade, **71**; bathtub, **270**; bed, **266**; bridge, **95**; bureau, **268**; child's wagon, **283**; church, **85**; craps table, **341**; door, **62**; drag racing, **333**; escalator, **77**; fence, **65**; flat racing, **330**; harness racetrack, **331**; ladder, **415**; passenger ship, **138**; **355**; playpen, **282**; pool table, **314**; powerboat, **134, 135**; railroad, **111**; rocking chair, **130**; sailboat, **130**; skin diving fin, **325**; sled, **322**; slide, **283**; snowmobile, **126**; sofa, **232**; sponge mop **278**; stage, **344**; staircase, **64**; stapler, **273**; starting block, **298**; subway, **115**; surfboard, **324**; surgical table, **440**; tanker, **137**; truck, **116, 117**; venetian blind, **237**; wheelchair, **442**; window, **63**
railing: highway, **110**; tunnel, **96**
railroad, **112-113**
railroad crossing, **111**; road sign, **488**
railroad track, **111**
railroad yard, **94**
rail transportation, public sign, **490**
rain, **17, 19**
rain boot, **203**
rain cap, bulldozer, **425**

rain check, ticket, **343**
raincoat, **196**
rain gauge, weather station, **18**
rain poncho, infantryman's uniform, **481**
rain-snow clutter control, radar, **434**
rake, **417**
ram, **31**; iceberg, **11**; zodiac, **493**
ram control, garbage truck, **123**
ramjet, **397**
rammer, cannon, **457**
ramp: airport, **92**; highway cloverleaf, **110**; hovercraft, **145**; theatre stage, **345**
rampart: castle, **78, 79**; fort, **81**
ranching gear, **422**
rand: boot, **202**; mountain climbing, **328**
range: kitchen, **233**; mountain, **7, 8**; thematic map, **21**
range control: police car, **118**; radar, **434**; sonar, **434**
range indicator, movie camera, **172**
rank: chessboard, **339**; military uniform, **480, 481**
rank badge, Manchu court dress, **475**
rapid-response thermometer, **254**
rapids, river, **13**
rapid transit system, **115**
rasp, **410**
ratcatcher, passenger ship, **138**
ratchet: brace, **408**; chaise lounge, **284**; screwdriver, **403**
ratchet angle, incline track, **90**
ratchet buckle, man's belt, **186**
ratchet handle, socket wrench, **405**
ratchet wheel, hand loom, **379**
rate control, guitar amplifier, **357**
rate of flow indicator, pilot's instrument panel, **153**
rate plate, parking meter, **109**
rating, clock, **229**
ratio: political map, **21**; symbol, **495**
rattlesnake, **40-41**
ravine, mountain, **8**
raw ingredients, food, **258**
ray: fish, **43**; medal, **485**; Milky Way, **3**
razor, **206**
razor blade, **206**
RCS nozzle, lunar lander, **156**
reaction, nuclear power, **384**
reaction control system (RCS) thruster assembly, lunar lander, **156**
reactor, nuclear, **384**
reader service coupon, magazine, **169**
reader surname, magazine mailing label, **167**
read head, key punch, **428**
reading clerk, House of Representatives, **72**
reading lens, eyeglasses, **217**
reading light, bus, **114**
readout: computer, **429**; dental unit, **444**
readout dash, newspaper, **166**
read-write window, computer diskette, **429**
reamer: citrus juicer, **251**; drill, **408**; plumbing, **412**
reaper, **424**
rear anchor, diving board, **310**
rear apron, necktie, **189**

rear axle: automobile, **105;**
   stroller, **282;** tractor, **424;**
   truck, **116;** wagon, **283**
rear bead, shotgun, **459**
rear beam, laboratory
   scale, **437**
rear bearing, fishing reel, **334**
rear binding heel piece,
   slalom water ski, **323**
rear boot, stagecoach, **127**
rear brake, bicycle, **124**
rear bumper,
   automobile, **103**
rear cinch, saddle, **309**
rear coil spring,
   automobile, **105**
rear deflector, mower, **419**
rear derailleur, bicycle, **124**
rear door, automobile, **103**
rear drive sprocket,
   motorcycle, **125**
rear drop-out, bicycle, **124**
rear drum brake,
   motorcycle, **125**
rear end, automobile, **105**
rear fender, motorcycle, **125**
rear foot, stapler, **273**
rear frame,
   wheelbarrow, **420**
rear hood, fishing rod, **334**
rear housing: can opener,
   247; razor, **206**
rear jockey, saddle, **329**
rear leg, bee, **39**
rear light, bulldozer, **425**
rear limit line, fencing
   strip, **309**
rear post, hand
   loom, **379**
rear quarter panel,
   automobile, **103**
rear push plate, tow truck
   bed, **122**
rear rigging ring, saddle, **329**
rear section, bicycle, **124**
rear shock absorber:
   automobile, **105;**
   motorcycle, **125**
rear sight, weapon, **459,
   460, 461**
rear skirt, missile, **466**
rear spikers' line, volleyball
   court, **313**
rear stretcher, rocking
   chair, **230**
rear tire, bus, **114**
rear wing, racing car, **332**
rear toe binder, slalom water
   ski, **323**
rearview mirror: bus, **114;**
   car, **106;** locomotive, **113;**
   pilot's instrument panel,
   153; truck, **116**
rear wheel, tow truck, **122**
rear window,
   automobile, **103**
rear windshield,
   automobile, **103**
rebote, jai alai cancha, **308**
rebound tumbling,
   trampoline, **302**
receipt: cash register, **430;**
   money order, **223;** toll
   booth, **110**
receiver: automatic weapon,
   460, 461; phonograph,
   177; shotgun, **458;**
   telephone, **178**
receiving track, railroad
   yard, **94**
receptacle: electrical, **388;**
   flower, **51;** pencil
   sharpener, **273;**
   strawberry, **53**
reception center, prison, **74**
reception room, White
   House, **73**
recessed back-up light, tow
   truck bed, **122**
recessed door, safe, **447**
recessed taillight, tow truck
   bed, **122**
rechargeable battery pack,
   tape recorder, **175**
rechargeable power handle,

ear scope, **438**
recirculating valve,
   automobile engine, **107**
recliner, **231**
recliner stand, child's car
   seat, **282**
reclining seat, bus, **114**
recoil pad, rifle, **458**
recoil spring guide,
   automatic pistol, **460**
recoil starter plate, internal
   combustion engine, **396**
record: phonograph, **176;**
   television LaserDisc
   player, **181**
record button, tape
   recorder, **175**
recorder: tape, **175;** weather
   station, **18**
recording phonograph, **176**
recording lever, movie
   projector, **173**
red light, ice hockey, **290**
red line, ice hockey, **291**
recording mode select
   switch, video recorder, **180**
recording pre-set, video
   recorder, **180**
record meter, tape
   recorder, **175**
record size selector,
   phonograph turntable, **176**
recreational vehicle, **126**
recreation area, road map, **20**
recreation yard, prison, **74**
rectangle, basketball
   backstop, **292**
rectangular lens,
   eyeglasses, **217**
rectangular spreader, **420**
recto, book page, **165**
rectory, **84**
rectus, human, **26**
recurve, bow, **456**
red foul light, drag
   racing, **333**
red light, traffic
   light, **109**
red lighting, drag
   racing, **333**
red marker light,
   truck van, **117**
Red Room, White House, **73**
red slot, roulette, **370**
red supergiant star, **2**
reduction, theodolite, **426**
red wine glass, **240**
reed: bagpipe, **359;**
   clarinet, **351;** English
   horn, **351;** hand loom, **379;**
   oboe, **350**
reeding, coin, **221**
reed selector switch,
   accordion, **360**
reed tube opening, pitch
   pipe, **361**
reef, coral, **44**
reef cringle, mainsail, **132**
reefer: refrigerator ship, **136;**
   truck, **116**
reef point, mainsail, **132**
reel: fencing strip, **309;**
   fireboat, **144;** fishing, **334;**
   movie camera, **172;** movie
   projector, **173;** mower,
   419; tape measure, **414;**
   tape recorder, **175;**
   thread, **376**
reel lawn mower, **419**
reel seat, fishing rod, **334**
referee's crease, ice hockey
   rink, **291**
reference key, political
   map, **20**
reference matter, book, **165**
reference slide, desk, **272**
reflected-light window, light
   meter, **174**
reflecting surface, solar
   power system, **383**
reflecting telescope, **433**
reflective identification,
   buoy, **128**
reflective stripe, fireman's
   coat, **484**

reflector: bicycle, **124;** bus,
   114; lamp, **235;** mechanical
   sweeper, **123;** railroad
   crossing signal, **111;** truck
   van, **117**
reflector satellite, **182**
reflex camera, **171**
refracting telescope, **433**
refrigeration van,
   truck, **116, 117**
refrigerator, **245**
refrigerator ship, **136**
regalia, royal, **469**
regional code, magazine
   mailing label, **167**
regional name, political
   map, **20**
regional temperature
   prediction, weather
   map, **19**
region of interaction,
   transistor chip, **386**
register, electric meter, **389**
register buttons, accordion, **360**
registered, symbol, **495**
registered architect seal,
   house blueprint, **60**
register mark, label, **264**
registration guide, silk
   screen, **369**
registration number, hot air
   balloon. **326**
registration number,
   single engine airplane, **147**
registry guide, silk
   screen, **369**
regular section,
   magazine, **167**
regulator: dental, **445;** gas
   pump automatic nozzle,
   108; laboratory burner,
   437; pressure cooker, **253;**
   skin diving, **325**
regulatory sign, road, **489**
rehabilitation, prison, **74**
rehearsal marking,
   music, **346**
rein, horseracing, **330, 331**
reinforce, cannon barrel, **457**
reinforced shoulder,
   waterskiing vest, **323**
reinforced toe, panty
   hose, **191**
reinforce ring, cannon
   barrel, **457**
rein guide, Hansom cab, **127**
reject button, television
   LaserDisc player, **181**
relative bearing, radar, **434**
relay race, track and
   field, **294**
relay unit, lunar rover, **157**
release: backpack, **337;**
   ballista, **457;** camera, **170,
   171;** can opener, **247;** chain
   saw, **421;** guillotine, **452;**
   hand loom, **379;** jet fighter,
   152; pistol, **460;** pliers, **404;**
   rifle, **458;** sextant, **133;** ski
   binding, **320;** steam
   engine, **395;**
   typewriter, **162**
relief: printing, **164;** stone
   sculpture, **366**
relief map, **21**
relief shading key, globe, **1**
relief valve: nuclear reactor,
   384; tanker, **136, 137;**
   water heater, **391**
reliever, saber saw, **407**
religious symbol, **492**
religious vestment, **471**
relish, and frankfurter, **261**
remaining-teeth mold,
   denture, **443**
remnants of universal veil,
   mushroom, **55**
remote control: camera, **170;**
   slide projector, **173;**
   television set, **181;** video
   recorder, **180**
remote filming jack, movie
   camera, **172**
remote-operated block valve,
   nuclear reactor, **384**

remote terminal, video
   recorder, **180**
rendezvous radar antenna,
   lunar lander, **156**
rendition, work of art, **362**
repeat button, tape
   recorder, **175**
repeat control, phonograph
   turntable, **176**
repeat sign, music, **346**
replaceable collar, maid's
   uniform, **473**
reporter, Congress, **72**
reptiles, **40-41**
representative fraction,
   political map, **21**
Republican, Congress, **72**
rerebrace, armor, **455**
rescue, hoist, helicopter, **146**
rescue platform,
   helicopter, **146**
reservoir: blood pressure
   gauge, **439;** dam, **98;** iron
   275; locomotive, **112;**
   pen, **160**
reset: computer, **429;** gas
   pump, **108;** stopwatch,
   298; table saw, **407;** tape
   recorder, **175;** water
   heater, **391**
residence number,
   mailbox, **227**
resin, dental, **443, 445**
resist, silk screen, **369**
resonance, stringed
   instruments, **349**
resonance box, tuning
   fork, **361**
resonator: banjo, **356;**
   sitar, **356**
respiratory system,
   human, **27**
response lamp, television
   set, **181**
rest: bazooka, **462;** child's
   glider, **283;** corkscrew, **247;**
   eye scope, **483;** hypodermic
   syringe, **441;** lantern, **336;**
   music notation, **346, 347;**
   music stand, **361**
rest area, highway, **110**
restaurant: Capitol, **72;**
   passenger ship, **139;** public
   sign, **490**
restoration, dental, **445**
restraining circle, basketball
   court, **292**
restraint layer, spacesuit, **157**
resuscitator, ambulance, **119**
retained cap, can, **263**
retainer: air conditioner, **392;**
   chain lock, **448;**
   phonograph headphone,
   177; saw, **407**
retaining wall fence, **65**
retarder, railroad yard, **94**
retention device, ski, **320**
reticulum, animal cell, **23**
retractable blade guard,
   circular saw, **407**
retractable footrest, medical
   examination table, **440**
retractable paper support,
   typewriter, **162**
retractable spike, cello, **349**
retractable step, medical
   examination table, **440**
retracting ball, pen, **160**
retreat zone, fencing
   strip, **309**
retrieving cable, gas
   pump, **108**
retsuah, tefillin, **470**
return: bowling lane, **311;**
   traverse rod, **236**
return address,
   envelope, **161**
return duct, heat
   exchanger, **393**
return end, cupboard, **239**
return panel, elevator car, **76**
return pipe: furnace, **390;**
   solar heating system, **383**
return section, desk, **272**
return top, desk, **272**

reverse: locomotive, 112; money, 221; sewing machine, 274; slide projector, 173
reverse light, automobile, 103
reversible cord assembly, iron, 275
reversible motor, power drill, 409
revetment, canal lock, 97
review, magazine, 168
review button, tape recorder, 175
Revolutionary War general, costume, 476
revolver, 460; pirate, 476; police gun belt, 483
revolver safety catch, jewelry findings, 214
revolving nosepiece, microscope, 432
revolving nut, crossbow, 456
revolving sprinkler, 418
rewind button, tape recorder, 175
rewind crank, camera, 171
rewind starter, outboard engine, 133
rewind switch, tape measure, 414
rheostat control, microscope, 432
rhinoceros horn, ultimate beast, 47
rhizome, grass, 56
rhumb line, globe, 5
rhythm pick-up, guitar, 357
riata, 422
rib: basket, 262; beef, 30; cactus, 54; celery, 258; dog, 34; hollow wall fastener, 401; horse, 36; human, 26; jai alai cesta, 308; laboratory burner, 437; lamb, 31; lampshade, 234; mountain, 9; parachute, 327; scallop shell, 45; shield, 454; shotgun, 459; skin diving fin, 325; sock, 203; sweater, 195; umbrella, 226; violin, 349
ribbon: ballet toeshoe, 378; bonnet, 199; hair ornament, 210; military uniform, 480
ribbon cartridge typewriter, 162
rib cage, human, 24
ribosome, animal cell, 23
rib pad, football uniform, 288
ricasso: knife, 453; sword hilt, 453
rider, dress, 194
ridge: barn, 100; corrugated fastener, 400; embroidery ring, 377; file, 410; mountain, 8, 9
ridgeboard, house, 59
ridgeline, house, 61
ridgepole, house, 59; tent, 336
riding breeches, drum major, 479
riding compartment, pumper, 121
riding equipment, 329
riding instructions, escalator, 77
rifle, 458-459; automatic, 461
rifle grenade, 463
rifle, gun, 460
rig, 116; oil drilling, 99; wrecker, 122
rigging: circus, 88; hang glider, 327; sailboat, 130
rigging ring, saddle, 329
right bank, river, 13
right-channel volume unit meter, tape recorder, 175
right engine fuel shutoff handle, pilot's instrument panel, 153
right field, baseball, 287
right-handed strike pocket, bowling, 311

right-hand page, book, 165
right-hand steering lever, bulldozer, 425
right of way, railroad, 111
right service court: badminton, 313; handball, 307
right wing, easel, 364
rigid airships, 158
rigid table, dull press, 409
rim: basket, 262; basketball backstop, 292; bicycle wheel, 124; bugle, 353; button, 205; cartridge, 460; coconut, 258; discus, 297; ferris wheel, 91; merry-go-round, 91; monocle, 217; pail, 280; pot, 367; racing car, 332, 333; royal crown, 469; saucepan, 353; sink, 243; spool, 376; stagecoach wheel, 127; stemware, 240; thimble, 376; tire, 101; toilet, 271; trombone, 352; wheelchair, 442
rimmon, Torah, 470
rimstone, cave, 11
rind: cheese, 259; orange, 53
ring: anchor, 128; basketball backstop, 292; bayonet, 453; bicycle, 124; blender, 250; boxing, 303; brace, 408; camera, 171; cannon barrel, 457; can opener, 247; cardinal, 471; cinch fastener, 204; circus, 88, 89; clock, 229; dart board, 316; domed structure, 83; embroidery, 377; fire engine, 120, 121; fishing rod, 334, 335; grenade, 463 hair dryer, 208; hot air balloon, 326; jewelry, 215; kite, 317; lampshade, 234; light meter, 174; lumber, 66; missile, 466; mitten, 196; mushroom, 55; projector 173; radar, 434; rifle, 459, 461; rowboat, 129; saddle, 329; Saturn, 3; screwdriver, 403; shotgun barrel, 459; skillet, 353; ski pole, 320; stationary rings, 301; stove, 336; sword hilt, 453; tent, 336; tree, 48; trumpet, 353; vault, 447; video camera, 180; window shade pull, 237
ring contact, incandescent bulb, 243
ring finger, human hand, 29
ring handle, scissors, 376
ring key, clarinet, 350
ringlet, woman's hair, 209
ringmaster, circus, 88
ring molding, minaret, 68
Ring of the Fisherman, Pope, 471
ringside, boxing, 303
ring stand, laboratory, 437
rink, ice hockey, 291
riot gun, police car, 118
riot helmet, police, 482
rip cord, parachute, 327
rip fence, saw, 407
rip guide, saw 407
rip panel, hot air balloon, 326
rip teeth, saw, 407
ripper claw, lobster, 45
ripping panel, hot air balloon, 326
ripsaw, 406
rise: arch 70; continental, 15
riser: orchestra, 348; parachute, 327; staircase, 64; trophy, 285
riser pad, skateboard, 318
ritard, music notation, 346
ritual item, Jewish, 470
river, 7, 13; and underwater tunnel, 96
rivet: attaché case, 281;

cheese plane, 252; eyeglasses, 217; jeans, 187; knife, 252; latch needle, 378; laboratory clamp, 436; nail clippers, 211; pliers, 404; plug fuse, 389; sandal, 202; sharpening steel, 252
rivière, jewelry, 215
rivulet, 13
riwaq, mosque, 68
roach, Indian, 474
road: airport, 92; highway, 110; topographic map, 22
roadbed: highway, 110; railroad, 111
road light, camper, 126
road map, 20
road racing, 332
roadside sidewall, truck 117
road sign, 488-489
road under construction, map, 20
roadway: bridge, 95; dam, 98; highway, 110; railroad, 111; tunnel, 96
road wheel: roller coaster, 90 tank, 464
roaring forties, wind, 6
robe: judge, 87; Manchu court dress, 475; wizard, 476
robe of state, king's regalia, 468
rochet, bishop, 471
rock: brazier, 284; nautical chart, 22
rocker: rocking chair, 230; hitch and harrow, 424; waterski, 323
rocker panel, automobile, 102, 105
rocket, 397; bazooka, 462
rocket, launcher, 462
rocket motor nozzle, satellite, 182
rockfill section, dam, 98
rocking chair, 230
rod: abacus, 431; basket, 262; belt buckle, 186; CB radio antenna, 179; child's wagon, 283; coffee maker, 248; drum, 358; fishing, 334-335; flute, 350; garbage disposal, 243; grandfather clock, 229; hair styling 210; Hansom cab, 127; incandescent bulb, 234; launch pad, 154; locomotive, 112; machine gun, 461; merry-go-round, 91; metal detector, 435; mower, 419; music stand, 361; nuclear reactor, 384; powerboat, 135; royal scepter, 469; shower, 270; stagecoach, 127; steam engine, 395; traverse, 236; umbrella, 226; window shutter, 273; workbench, 398
Rogallo kite, 317
roll: ambulance, 119; football uniform, 288; frankfurter, 261; hand loom, 379; saddle, 329; sandwich, 259
roll bag, racing car, 332
roll cage, drag racer, 333
roll-collar waistcoat, butler's uniform, 473
rolled edge, necktie, 188
rolled shoulder, shovel, 417
roller: ballista, 457; bulldozer, 425; cassette tape, 175; chain, 451; etching press, 371; fishing reel, 334; hair, 210; hitch and harrow, 424; offset-lithography, 164; painting, 415; tank, 464; tape recorder, 175; typewriter, 162; window shade, 237; roller, woodcut

printing, 368
roller-coaster, 90
roller guide shoe, elevator shaft, 76
roller link plate, chain, 451
roller foot, sewing machine, 274
roller skate, 318
roller support, saw, 407
rolling pin, 255
rolling stock, railroad, 94, 112-113
roll on-roll off ship, 136
roll pin, pliers, 404
roll top, rocking chair, 230
rolltop desk, 272
roll-up blind, window, 237
Roman collar, bishop, 471
roman type, 163; proofreader's mark, 498
rondel, armor, 455
rood screen, church, 85
roof: automobile, 102, 103, 105; bus, 114; church, 84; house, 58, 59, 60, 61; mountain, 8; pagoda, 69; skyscraper, 75
roof air conditioner, camper, 126
roofing shingle, 66
roof light, subway, 115
roof seam, tent, 336
rook, chess, 339
rook pawn, chess, 339
room: cave, 11; house blueprint, 60; launch pad, 154; White House, 73
rooster, 33
root: carrot, 52; corn, 56; grass, 56; onion, 258; outboard engine, 133; screw, 400; tertiary, 49; tooth, 446; tree, 48
rope, 128; ballista, 457; block and tackle, 451; boxing ring, 303; bridge, 95; circus tent, 89; elevator shaft, 76; military uniform, 480; grandfather clock, 229; hot air balloon, 326; jump rope, 338; mountain climbing, 328; outboard engine, 133; ranching gear, 422; roller coaster, 90; tent, 336; tepee, 82; toboggan, 322; waterskiing towline, 323
rope hole, sled, 322
rope ladder, circus aerialist, 88
rope strap, saddle, 329
roping, hammock, 284
Rose Room, White House, 73
rosette: Beefeater, 467; cupboard, 239; guitar, 356; queen's regalia, 468; royal crown, 469; sofa, 232
rosette cap, traffic light, 109
rose window, church, 84
rotary beater, kitchen, 254
rotary dial, telephone, 178
rotary fairing, helicopter, 146
rotary fan, 392
rotary lawn mower, 419
rotary press, printing, 164
rotary spreader, 420
rotating beacon: police car, 118; single engine airplane, 147
rotating frame, merry-go-round, 91
rotating handle, food mill, 256
rotating mast, windsurfer, 324
rotating service structure, launch pad, 154
rotational hand controller, space shuttle, 155
rotational motion, steam engine, 395
rotogravure, printing, 164
rotor: automobile disc brake, 104; helicopter, 146; windmill, 382; wind

turbine, 382
rotunda, Capitol, 72
rouge, 212, 213
rough, golf course, 304-305
roughneck, oil drilling, 99
rough sill, house, 59
rouleau, 430
roulette wheel, 340
round: beef, 30; boxing, 303;
    police ammunition, 482
round-bottom hull,
    powerboat, 134
round-end chisel,
    stonecutting, 366
round head, screw, 400
roundhouse, railroad yard, 94
rounding board,
    merry-go-round, 91
round pin, window shade
    roller, 237
round shank,
    screwdriver, 403
round-the-clock, darts, 316
round-toed brogues, butler's
    uniform, 473
roustabout, circus, 88
route: bus, 114; road map, 20;
    subway, 115
route sign, road, 489
routing number: check, 222;
    traveler's check, 223
row, hand knitting, 378
rowboat, 129
rowel, spur, 329
royal regalia, 468-469
rubber: baseball pitcher, 287;
    shoe accessory, 203
rubber band, dental, 443
rubber blade, silkscreen
    squeegee, 369
rubber bumper, knee
    kicker, 242
rubber covering, brayer, 368
rubber face, Ping-Pong
    racket, 315
rubber foot, food
    processor, 250
rubber mat, phonograph
    turntable, 176
rubber plug, sink, 269
rubber-soled shoe, jai alai
    player, 308
rubber tip, bobby pin, 210
rubbing ink, 370
ruble, symbol, 495
rub rail: powerboat, 134;
    truck platform, 117
ruching, bonnet, 199
rucksack: backpacking, 337;
    ski touring, 321
rudder: blimp, 158; destroyer,
    140, glider, 147; jumbo jet,
    149; sailboat, 130; single
    engine airplane, 147; space
    shuttle, 154; submarine,
    143; torpedo, 466
rudder pedal, 747 cockpit, 150
rudimentary root, 49
ruff, Beefeater, 467
ruffled shirt, man's, 472
rug, 242; hairpiece, 207
rule: magazine, 168, 169;
    measuring, 414
ruler, 414; pocket knife, 416
rumble seat, automobile, 102
rump: beef, 130; bird, 37; cat,
    35; dog, 34; horse, 36; pelt,
    197; sheep, 31
run: step tread, 64; track and
    field, 294
run and lock switch, movie
    camera, 172
rung: ladder, 415; rocking
    chair, 230
run light, movie camera, 172
runner: grass, 56; ice skates,
    319; rug, 242; running
    shoe, 296; sled, 322; slide
    rule, 431; umbrella, 226
running board,
    automobile, 103
running foot: book page, IV;
    magazine, 169
running knot, gallows, 452
running light: camper, 126;
    destroyer, 141; fireboat,

144; single engine airplane,
    147; tow truck, 122;
    tugboat, 144
running mold, church, 84
running noose, lasso, 422
running ornament,
    church, 84
running rigging, sailboat, 130
running shoe, 296
running title, magazine, 168
running track, 294
run number: bus, 114; paper
    money, 221
runway: airport, 92; bowling
    lane, 311; javelin throw,
    295; pole vault, 299;
    stage, 345
rupee, symbol, 495
rural mailbox, 227
Russian Cross, symbol, 492
rustproof oil,
    woodcarving, 366

S

S: braille, 496; sign
    language, 496
saber saw, 407
sabot, blackjack, 341
sabre, 309
sabre and épée warning
    line, fencing strip, 309
sac: flower stamen, 51;
    octopus, 44
sacral hump, frog, 42
sacristy, church, 85
sacrum, human, 26
saddle: bicycle, 124;
    door, 62; guitar, 356;
    horse, 329, 330, 331;
    matchbook, 224;
    motorcycle, 125;
    mountain, 8; pipe, 225;
    pommel horse, 301;
    screen, 173
saddlebag: 329;
    motorcycle, 125
saddle feather,
    chicken, 33
saddle head, dispenser, 263
saddle plate, iron, 275
safe, 447
safe deposit box, 447
safe side, file, 410
safety: elevator
    shaft, 76; weapon, 458,
    460, 461
safety bar, ferris
    wheel, 91
safety belt: car, 106;
    lunar rover, 157
safety binding, ski, 320
safety cage, hammer
    throw, 295
safety catch, revolver, 214
safety-chain hole, tow
    truck bed, 122
safety cool tip, curling
    iron, 210
safety dome, train tank
    car, 112
safety edge, elevator
    door, 76
safety guard: drill press, 409;
    paint spray gun, 415
safety guardrail, slide, 283
safety hasp, 450
safety jacket,
    waterskiing, 323
safety ladder, ferris
    wheel, 91
safety lever: hand
    grenade, 463; pistol, 460
safety line, inflatable, 129
safety-line track,
    submarine, 143
safety loop, circus
    aerialist, 88
safety lug, cassette
    tape, 175
safety matches, 224
safety mirror, mechanical
    sweeper, 123
safety net: aircraft

carrier, 142; circus
    aerialist, 88
safety observer station,
    destroyer, 141
safety pad, trampoline, 302
safety padding, football
    goalpost, 289
safety pin, 204; hand
    grenade, 463
safety rail: bathtub, 270;
    bridge, 95;
    powerboat, 135
safety razor, 206
safety rope, roller
    coaster, 90
safety shield, child's
    car seat, 282
safety stripe, fireman's
    coat, 484
safety trigger, chain
    saw, 421
safety valve, furnace, 390
safety warning, dental
    x-ray unit, 444
Sagittarius, zodiac, 493
sail, 130, 132; hang
    glider, 327;
    submarine, 143;
    windmill, 382;
    windsurfer, 324
sailboard, 324
sailboat, 130-131
sailing thwart,
    rowboat, 129
sailor, uniform, 481
sailplane, 147;
    submarine, 143
St. Anthony's cross,
    symbol, 492
salad bowl, 241
salad fork, 240
salad plate, 241
salad shaker, 256
salamander, 42
salient angle, 81
saline, paramedic
    equipment, 119
saliva ejector, dental
    unit, 444
sally port, frontier fort, 80
salon, sailboat, 131
salt shaker, 257
salutation, letter, 161
samara, 50
Sam Browne belt, 480
same name differentiation
    code, magazine mailing
    label, 167
same scale extension inset,
    political map, 21
sample bag dispenser, lunar
    rover, 157
sanctuary: church, 85;
    mosque, 68-69
sand, hourglass, 229
sandal, 202
sand area, topographic
    map, 22
sandbag: ambulance, 119;
    hot air balloon, 326
sandbar: coastline, 14, 15;
    river, 13
sandbox: backyard, 283;
    locomotive, 112, 113
sander, 411
sandglass, 229
sandhill, nautical chart, 22
sandpaper, 411
sand shoe, truck van, 117
sand tower, railroad
    yard, 94
sand trap, golf course, 305
sand wedge, golf club, 304
sandwich, 259
sandwich cookie, 260
sanitary hose, baseball, 286
sanitary paper, medical
    examination table, 440
sanitary sock, football, 288
sanitation vehicle, 123
sanman, 123
sans serif type, 163
sapwood, tree, 48
sari, 475

sarong, 475
sartorius, human, 26
sash: drum major, 479; jai
    alai player, 308; royal
    regalia, 468; window, 63
satellite, 3, 182
Saturn, planet, 3
sauce, sundae, 260
saucepan, 253
saucer, 241
sauerkraut, and
    frankfurter, 261
sauna, passenger ship, 139
sausage, pizza, 261
saw, 406, 407; pocket
    knife, 416
sawbuck, 398
sawhorse, 398
saxophone, 351
S-band antenna, lunar
    lander, 156
S bend, tuba, 352
scabbard: knife, 453;
    Revolutionary War
    general, 476
scaffold, gallows, 452
scaffolding web, spider, 38
scale: bird foot, 37; blood
    pressure gauge, 439;
    camera, 170, 171, 172,
    180; coffee maker, 248;
    crocodilian, 41; electronic
    flash, 174; fish, 43;
    frontier fort, 80; house
    blueprint, 60; hypodermic
    syringe, 441; kitchen, 254;
    knife, 416, 453;
    laboratory, 436-437;
    lettuce, 258; light
    meter, 174; metronome, 361; nautical
    chart, 22; pine cone, 50;
    political map, 21;
    saw, 407; sewing
    machine, 274; slide
    rule, 431; snake, 41;
    thermometer, 18, 439;
    typewriter, 162; volt-ohm
    meter, 413
scallop, 45; bridal gown
    hem, 472; curtain, 236
scalp, 207; mortise lock, 448
scalper, harness racing
    pacer, 331
scan button, television
    LaserDisc player, 181
scanner: cash register, 430;
    hovercraft, 145;
    radar, 434
scapha, outer ear, 28
scaphoid pad, sandal, 202
scapula, human, 26
scapular, bird, 37
scapular region,
    salamander, 42
scarf, pirate, 476
scarp, fort, 81
scend, wave, 14
scenery, stage, 344
scenic overlook,
    highway, 110
scent, 213
scepter, royal, 469
school: fish, 43; prison, 74
school crossing, road
    sign, 489
scimitar antenna, lunar
    lander, 156
scintillometer, 435
scissor grip, body
    building, 338
scissors, 376; pocket
    knife, 416
scoop: ice cream cone, 261;
    kitchen tool, 254, 255;
    pipe tool, 225
scoop stretcher,
    ambulance, 119
scooter car, amusement
    park, 90
scooter helmet, police, 483
scope: bazooka, 462;
    rifle, 459; telescope, 433
scopula, spider, 38

score: matchbook, 224; pulley block, 451
scoreboard, jai alai cancha, 308
score counter, pool table, 314
score ring, darts, 316
scorer's box, ice hockey rink, 291
scorer's table: basketball court, 292; lacrosse field, 293
scoring diagram, shuffleboard court, 312
scoring lines, golf club, 304
scoring machine, fencing strip, 309
scoring triangle, shuffleboard court, 312
Scorpio, zodiac, 493
scorpion, 46; zodiac, 493
scotch rule, magazine, 168
scotia, column, 71
scraper, lithographic press, 370
scratch line, track and field, 294, 295
screen: camera, 171; case, 173; church, 85; fireplace, 228; internal combustion engine, 396; jai alai cancha, 308; projector, 173; radar, 434; silk, 369; sonar, 434; television set, 181; tent, 336
screendoor, 62
screen fence, 65
screen plug, mower, 419
scree slope, mountain, 8
screw, 400; banjo, 356; brayer, 368; cassette tape, 175; clamp, 399; combination square, 414; drill bit, 409; earring, 214; electric plug, 388; embroidery ring, 377; etching press, 371; eyeglasses, 217; faucet, 269; golf club, 304; hitch and harrow, 424; kettledrum, 358; lithographic press, 370; lock, 448; microscope, 432; outboard engine, 133; paramedic equipment, 119; plane, 410; pliers, 404; saw, 407; sewing machine, 274; ski binding, 320; telegraph key, 159; telescope, 433; theodolite, 426; violin, 349; violin bow, 349; vise, 399; volt-ohm meter, 413; woodcarving, 366; wrench, 405
screwback earring findings, 214
screw cap, test tube, 437
screwdriver, 403; pocket knife, 416
screwdriver bit, drill, 408
screw eye, frame, 373
screw hole, hinge, 450
screw nozzle, 418
screw thread, plug fuse, 389
scribe, phonograph record, 176
scribed line, scrimshaw, 369
scriber, 369; combination square, 414
scrim, stage, 344
scrimshander, 369
scrimshaw, 369
scrip, collector, 221
Scripture, Torah, 86
scroll: coat of arms, 487; fence, 65; Torah, 86; violin, 349
scrolled arm, sofa, 232

scroll saw, 407
scrubboard, 276
scruff, human, 25
scruple, symbol, 494
scruto, stage, 344
scuba diving, 325
scuff leather, hot air balloon, 326
sculpting tools, 366
scupper: fireboat, 144; tugboat, 144
scythe, 419
sea, 7
seabag, 481
sea clutter control, radar, 434
seal: frame, 373; house architect, 60; package, 264-265; paper money, 220; voting booth, 427
sealant strip, roofing shingle, 66
sealed voting booth, 427
sealed vegetable compartment, refrigerator, 245
seam: blouse, 193; boot, 202; can, 263; football, 288; garment, 192; girdle, 191; hot air balloon, 326; inflatable, 129; jacket, 184; mainsail, 132; necktie, 188; sewing pattern, 380; skirt, 193; sock, 203; tennis ball, 306; tent, 336; trousers, 187; and zipper, 205
search button, television LaserDisc player, 181
search coil, metal detector, 435
searchlight: fireboat, 144; tank, 464; tugboat, 144
search loop, metal detector, 435
search switch, video recorder, 180
seasonal current, ocean, 6
seasoning: frankfurter, 261; prepared food, 259
seasoning check, lumber, 66
sea star, 44
seat: ambulance, 119; automobile, 102, 103, 106, 282; backyard glider, 283; bicycle, 124; bumper car, 90; bus, 114; courtroom, 87; electric chair, 452; ferris wheel, 91; fishing rod, 334; harness racing sulky, 331; inflatable, 129; lounger, 231; lunar rover, 157; motorcycle, 125; pants, 187; rocking chair, 230; rowboat, 129; saddle, 329; 747 cockpit, 150, 151; snowmobile, 126; sofa, 232; space shuttle, 155; stagecoach, 127; stroller, 282; subway car, 115; swing, 283; theatre, 345; toilet, 271; wheelchair, 442; woman's shoe heel, 201
seat belt, car, 106
seat location, ticket, 343
seaweed, 55
second, grammatical symbol, 497
secondary cable, overhead power line, 386
secondary cell, battery, 387
secondary combustion chamber, stove, 394
secondary con, destroyer, 140

secondary feather, 33, 37
secondary highway, 22
secondary root, 49
secondary tank, lunar lander, 156
secondary vein, leaf, 50
second base, baseball, 287
second bicuspid, 446
second bow, bell, III
second floor, White House, 73
second hand, watch, 216, 298
second molar, 446
second premolar, 446
second reinforce, cannon barrel, 457
seconds bit, stopwatch, 298
seconds dial, grandfather clock, 229
seconds of arc, symbol, 495
second stage: missile, 466; skin diving tank, 325
second thigh: dog, 34; horse, 36
second toe, human foot, 29
second valve slide: French horn, 352; trumpet, 353
second violin, orchestra, 348
secretarial pedestal, desk, 272
secretary, Senate, 72
secretary's table, courtroom, 87
section: dam, 98; fishing rod, 334; jumbo jet, 148, 149; lumber, 66; magazine, 167; orange, 53; theatre, 345; torpedo, 466
sectional center, envelope, 161
sectional sofa, 232
section code, magazine mailing label, 167
sectioned floorboard, inflatable, 129
sector, track and field, 294
sector flag, hammer throw, 295
security number, credit card, 222
security system, prison, 74
sedan, automobile, 102
sediment bleed valve, water heater, 391
seed, 49; apple, 53; flower, 51; gardening, 420; grass, 56; pea, 52; peach, 53; pepper, 258; sandwich, 259; tomato, 52
seeder, gardening, 420
seeker, jet fighter, 152
seesaw, 283
see-through window, package, 265
segment: orange, 53; snake rattle, 40
seiche, 14
select button, video recorder, 180
selection, phonograph record, 176
selection lever, voting booth, 427
selection plate, toaster, 249
selector: accordion, 360; air conditioner, 392; camera, 171, 172; CB radio, 179; clothes dryer, 277; light meter, 174; movie projector, 173; phonograph, 176, 177; radar, 434; surgical table, 440; toaster oven, 249; video recorder, 180; volt-ohm meter, 413; washing machine, 276
selector control, sealed voting booth, 427
self-belt: dress, 194; trousers, 187
self-clasping hair roller, 210

self-cleaning oven, 244
self-filling mechanism, pen, 160
self-service gas station island, 108
self-starting timer, parking meter, 109
self-threading projector, 173
self-timer, camera, 171
selling copy, magazine cover, 167
selvage: fabric, 380; weaving, 379
semaphore, 496
semibreve, music, 346
semicolon, grammatical symbol, 497
semiconductor, transistor, 386
semiflexible kite, 317
semi-hollow body, guitar, 357
semiquaver, music, 346
semirigid lighter-than-air craft, 158
semisubmersible design, oil drilling platform, 99
semitrailer, truck, 117
Senate side, Capitol, 72
sense organs, 28
sensitivity, volt-ohm meter, 413
sensitivity control, video camera, 180
sensor: electronic flash, 174; solar heating system, 383; weather station, 18
sepals, flower, 51
separation triangle, shuffleboard court, 312
separator wire, typewriter, 162
sepher, Jewish prayer book, 470
septum, nose, 28
septum linguae, tongue, 28
sequential serial number, postal money order, 223
sequenced starting light, drag racing, 333
sequins, woman's hat, 199
serac, mountain, 9
sergeant at arms, Senate, 72
serial number: internal combustion engine, 396; laboratory scale, 436; paper money, 220, 221; postal money order, 223; safe, 447; sealed voting booth, 427; surgical table, 440
series identification, paper money, 221
series number, painting brush, 365
serif, type, 163
serigraphy, 369
serrated body, hand grenade, 463
serrated edge: knife, 252; paper bag, 262
serration: coin, 221; key, 449
server, dessert, 241
service, tea, 241
service area: highway, 110; jai alai cancha, 308; railroad yard, 94; volleyball court, 313
service article, magazine, 168
service box, handball, 307
service cabinet, elevator, 76
service cap, military uniform, 480
service code, credit card, 222
service coupon, magazine, 169
service court: badminton, 313; barn, 100; handball, 307
service door, gas pump, 108

service line: handball, 307; jai alai, 308; squash, 307; tennis, 306
service mast, space shuttle, 154
service revolver, police gun belt, 483
service ribbon, military uniform, 480
service road, highway, 110
service sideline, tennis court, 306
service sign, road, 489
service station island, 108
service structure, launch pad, 154
service time, military, 480
service vehicle, airport, 93
service zone, handball, 307
serving, bow, 456
serving apron, maid, 473
serving cap, maid, 473
serving player's line, jai alai, 308
serving silverware drawer, sideboard, 239
serving tray, 241; baby's high chair, 282
servopneumatic altimeter, pilot's instrument panel, 153
set: scale weights, 436; stage, 344; tea, 241; television, 181
setback, skyscraper, 75
set button, video recorder, 180
set-in cap, magazine, 168
set-in sleeve: blouse, 193; jacket, 192
set of tail, dog, 34
setscrew: barbell, 338; faucet, 269
settee: patio, 284; sailboat, 131
setting: clock radio, 229; light meter, 174; ring, 215
setting dots, sewing machine, 274
setting lotion, hair, 210
setup: bowling lane, 311; chess, 339
7/8 mile chute, harness racetrack, 331
7/8 pole, harness racetrack, 331
747 cockpit, 150-151
seven furlong chute, harness racetrack, 331
seven pin, bowling, 311
70mm camera: lunar rover, 157; spacesuit, 157
sewer valve, camper, 126
sewing hole: hook and eye, 204; snap fastener, 204
sewing machine, 274
sewing pattern, 380
sew-through button, 205
sextant, 133
sforzando, organ, 354
shackle: block and tackle, 451; padlock, 449; pocket knife, 416
shade: and composition, 362; lamp, 234, 235; stagecoach, 127; track lighting 235; window covering, 236
shading: relief map, 21; and texture, compostion, 363
shading key, globe, 1
shadow: and composition, 362; makeup, 212, 213; sundial, 381
shadow pin, compass, 132
shaft: arrow, 456; billiard cue, 314; bird feather, 37; boot, 202; bridge, 95; can opener, 247; cave, 11; column, 71; croquet mallet, 312; dart, 316;

destroyer, 140; drum major's baton, 479; electric meter, 389; elevator, 76; golf club, 304; Hansom cab, 127; halberd, 454; harness racing, 331; ice ax, 328; ice hockey stick, 291; internal combustion engine, 396; javelin, 297; lamp, 235; lance, 454; longbow, 456; metronome, 361; music stand, 361; oar, 129; obelisk, 69; pin, 204; printing press, 370, 371; ski pole, 320; stagecoach 127; tennis racket, 306; umbrella, 226; underwater tunnel, 96; White House, 73
shaftment, arrow, 456
shake, wooden roofing shingle, 66
shakedown, cowboy, 474
shake-hands grip, Ping-Pong racket, 315
shaker: kitchen tool, 256; salt, 257
shako, drum major, 479
shallow gouge, woodcarving, 366
Shanghai, darts, 316
shank: anchor, 128; bolt, 401; boot, 202; brasses, 352; button, 205; cat, 35; chicken, 33; chisel, 410; shank, drill, 409; fishhook, 335; gimlet, 408; gouge, 368; hoe, 417; human, 25; lamb, 31; latch needle, 378; nail, 400; needle, 376; pipe, 225; ring, 215; screw, 400; screwdriver, 403; shoe, 200, 201; trombone, 352; type, 164
shape, pipe, 225
sharp: music, 346; organ, 354
sharpening oil, woodcarving, 366
sharpening steel, 252
sharpening stone: gouge, 368; woodcarving, 366
shaver, 206
shaving brush, 206
shawl, Jewish prayer vestment, 470
shawl collar, sweater, 195
shears, 376; gardening, 417
sheath: cat, 35; grass, 56; knife, 453; safety pin, 204; skin diving, 325; snake fang, 41; wire, 413
sheathing, house, 58
sheave: block and tackle, 451; elevator shaft, 76
shed, oil drilling platform, 99
sheep, 31
sheer line, powerboat, 135
sheet: ambulance, 119; bedding, 267; kite, 317; postage stamps, 161
sheet-fed press, printing, 164
sheet music notation, 346-347
sheet-transfer cylinder, offset-lithography, 164
shelf: cupboard, 239; fireplace, 228; igloo, 83; refrigerator, 245; stove oven, 244; telescope, 433
shelfback, book, 165
shelf break, continental margin, 15
shelf mount, telescope, 433
shell: attaché case, 281; baseball catcher's

mask, 286; bivalve, 45; block and tackle, 451; brace chuck, 408; coconut, 258; cupboard, 239; drill, 409; drum, 350; egg, 258; fire extinguisher, 280; football helmet, 288; iron, 275; lamp, 234; lobster, 45; necktie, 188; nuclear reactor, 384; parka, 197; pea, 52; plug fuse, 389; quiche, 259; sleeping bag, 337; tambourine, 358; tart, 260; toaster, 249; turtle, 40; univalve, 45; vacuum tube, 386; video camera, 180
shellfish, 45
shell plate, mandolin, 356
shel rosh, Jewish ritual item, 470
shelter, destroyer, 141
shel yad, tefillin, 470
shield: car seat, 282; chain saw muffler, 421; coat of arms, 487; drag racing driver's fire suit, 333; drum major's coat, 479; hollow wall fastener, 401; lantern, 336; medieval, 454; merry-go-round, 91; mower 419; nuclear, 384; police, 482; racing car, 332; tank, 465; toll basket, 110; tunnel, 96; turtle, 40
Shield of David, 86, 492
shift, doppler, 2
shifter, bicycle, 124
shifting head, theodolite, 426
shift key, typewriter, 162
shift lever, bulldozer, 425
shimagi, torii, 68-69
shin, human, 24
shin boot, harness racing pacer, 331
shiner, brick wall, 67
shingle, roofing, 66
shinguard: baseball, 286; ice hockey, 291; soccer, 293
shin pad, ice hockey, 291
Shinto temple gateway, 68-69
ship: aircraft carrier, 142; cargo, 136-137; passenger, 138-139; submarine, 143; surface fighting, 140-141
shipboard lines, canal lock, 97
shipping lane, 140
shirring: blouse, 193; woman's pants, 192
shirt, 185; Arab dress, 475; baseball, 286; butler, 473; cowboy, 474; Indian, 474; man's formal attire, 472; military, 480, 481; police, 483
shoaling wave, shoreline, 14
shoat, 32
shock absorber: automobile, 105; motorcycle, 125; single engine airplane, 147; snowmobile, 126
shoe: accessories, 203; blackjack, 341; boxing, 303; bridge, 95; bulldozer track, 425; camera, 171; clown, 477; drag racing driver, 333; drum major, 479; elevator shaft, 76; fencing, 309; football, 288; horse, 36; jai alai, 308; king's regalia, 468; ladder, 415; man's, 200; mechanical sweeper, 123; military, 480; mountain climbing,

328; organ, 354; police, 482; running, 296; sander, 411; saw, 407; screen, 173; snowshoe, 321; stagecoach, 127; woman's, 201
shoe brace, guitar, 356
shoe horn, 203
shoelace, 200
shoe house, prison, 74
shoestring strap, dress, 194
shoe tree, 203
shoot: asparagus, 52; grass, 56
shooter: dice, 340; craps table, 341
shooting star, 2
shop: frontier fort, 80; passenger ship, 138; prison, 74; railroad yard, 94
shore, 14
shoreline, 14; iceberg, 12; nautical chart, 22
short bar, easel, 364
short bar clamp, 399
short bent gouge, woodcarving, 366
short circuit, fuse box, 389
short lid prop, grand piano, 355
short line, handball, 307
short loin, beef, 30
short ribs, beef, 30
shorts, 187; basketball, 292; man's underwear, 190
short service line, badminton court, 313
short stick, grand piano, 355
shortstop area, baseball, 287
short-term parking lot, airport, 93
shot, field events equipment, 297
shotgun, 458-459; stagecoach, 127
shotgun chaps, cowboy, 474
shot put, 295, 297
shot timer, basketball backstop, 292
shoulder: bell, iii; bottle, 263; broom, 278; cat, 35; chisel, 410; dog, 34; highway, 110; horse, 36; human, 24; key, 449; lamb, 31; mountain, 8; pencil, 160; pork, 32; razor blade, 206; shovel, 417; suit hanger, 277; tennis racket, 306; type, 164; waterskiing vest, 323; wave, 14; woman's jacket, 192; wristwatch, 216
shoulder bag, 218
shoulder blade, human, 24
shoulderboard, military uniform, 480
shoulder butt, pork, 32
shoulder harness, drag racing driver, 333
shoulder hook, frame, 373
shoulder pad: football, 288; ice hockey, 291
shoulder pad strap, backpack, 337
shoulder press, universal gym, 338
shoulder protector, ice hockey goalie, 290
shoulder rest, bazooka, 462
shoulder seam, jacket, 184
shoulder sling, mountain climbing, 328
shoulder strap: accordion, 360; brassiere, 191; child's car seat, 282; combat soldier, 481; golf

bag, 305; handbag, 218
shoulder vise,
    workbench, 398
shoulder yoke blouse, 193
shovel, 417; fire iron, 228;
    ski, 320
show, flat racing, 330
shower: bath, 270;
    thunderstorm, 17; weather
    map, 19
shrapnel, grenade, 463
shredding disc, food
    processor, 250
shrimp, 45
shrine, pyramid, 68
shrinkwrap, packaging, 264
shroud: internal combustion
    engine, 396; parachute
    line, 327; sailboat, 130
shuffleboard, 312
shutoff handle, pilot's
    instrument panel, 153
shutoff valve: radiator, 390;
    standpipe, 57; toilet, 271;
    water heater, 391
shutter: camera, 170, 171;
    house, 60, 61; laboratory
    burner, 437;
    windmill, 382;
    window, 237
shutter scale, light
    meter, 174
shuttle: badminton, 313;
    sewing machine, 274;
    space, 154; tatting, 378
shuttlecock, badminton, 313
shuttle race, hand loom, 379
siamese: hose, 418;
    standpipe, 57
sickle, chicken, 33
sickle-bar lawn mower, 419
side: accordion, 360;
    basket, 262; elliptical
    galaxy, 2; lumber, 66;
    organ, 354; phonograph
    record, 176; piano, 355;
    skillet, 253; snap
    fastener, 204; violin, 349
sidearm, 460; juice
    extractor, 251
sidebar: courtroom, 87;
    magazine, 168; pulley
    block, 451
side belt, handbag, 218
side bit: fireboat, 144;
    tugboat, 144
sideboard, 239; ice hockey
    rink, 291
side body molding,
    automobile, 103
sidebones, brassiere, 191
side broom balance
    assembly, mechanical
    sweeper, 123
sideburns, 207
side cleft, horse's
    foot, 36
side curtains, four-poster
    bed, 266
side cushion, sofa, 232
side cutter, pliers, 404
side deck, powerboat, 135
side drop, bedding, 266
side drum, 358
side fender, tugboat, 144
side handle, drill, 408
side handrail, subway
    car, 115
side horse, gymnastics, 301
side jamb, window, 63
side leg, playpen, 282
sidelight: door, 62: Hansom
    cab, 127; house, 60;
    stagecoach, 127
sideline, basketball, 292;
    fencing strip, 309;
    football, 289;
    lacrosse, 293;
    Ping-Pong, 315;
    volleyball, 313
side link, chain saw
    chain, 421
sidelit composition, 362

side-loading collection
    truck, 123
side loading door, stove, 394
side loop, handbag, 218
side marker:
    automobile, 102;
    bus, 114; tow truck, 122
side panel: bureau, 268;
    bus, 114; curtain, 236;
    lounger, 231;
    package, 264;
    sideboard, 239;
    tractor, 424
side pieces, furniture, 239
side plate: pulley block, 451;
    racing car, 332;
    revolver, 460
side pocket, backpack, 337
side pod, racing car, 332
side rail: bed, 266; child's
    wagon, 283; ladder, 45;
    skin diving fin, 325;
    sled, 322; slide, 283;
    surgical table, 440; truck
    van, 117
side seam: boot, 202;
    trousers, 187
side shell, block and
    tackle, 451
sideshow, circus, 88
side sign: bus, 114;
    subway car, 115
side slats, sled, 322
side span, bridge, 95
sidestand, motorcycle, 125
side stretcher, rocking
    chair, 230
side vent, volcano, 10
sideview mirror:
    automobile, 102;
    mechanical sweeper, 123
sidewalk, moving, 77
sidewall: can, 263; circus
    tent, 89; horse's hoof, 36;
    man's hair, 207; slalom
    water ski, 323;
    squash, 307; swimming
    pool, 310; tire, 101; truck
    van, 117
side welt, boot, 202
side whiskers, 207
Sidewinder missile, 152
side window: bus, 114;
    camper, 126
siding: house, 60, 61;
    railroad yard, 94
sieve, 256
sifter, 256
sight: armor, 455; automatic
    weapons, 460, 461;
    bazooka, 462;
    crossbow, 456; pool
    table, 314; rifle, 459;
    tank, 464
sight bracket, mortar, 462
sight cut, bayonet, 453
sight glass, furnace, 390
sightseeing bus, 114
sign: bus, 114;
    music, 346, 347;
    public, 490-491;
    road, 488-489; subway
    car, 115
signal: automobile, 102;
    bus, 114; railroad
    crossing, 111;
    television, 181; traffic
    light, 109
signal ahead, road sign, 489
signal baton, drum
    major, 479
signal bridge, destroyer, 141
signal deck, passenger
    ship, 139
signal halyard, destroyer, 141
signal intensity meter,
    metal detector, 435
signal light:
    automobile, 102;
    bus, 114; coffee
    maker, 248; mechanical
    sweeper, 123;
    motorcycle, 125; taxi, 115

signal meter,
    phonograph, 177
signal shelter, destroyer, 141
signal tower, passenger
    ship, 139
signature: baseball bat, 287;
    cartoon, 374; check, 222;
    letter, 161; music, 346;
    traveler's check, 223
sign: taxi roof light, 115;
    toll booth, 110; zodiac, 493
signature panel, credit
    card, 222
sign language, 496
sign-off, magazine article, 168
silencer, 460
silent alarm, vault, 447
silent anti-reverse housing,
    fishing reel, 334
silk: corn, 56;
    flat racing, 330
silk screen, 369
silk threads, spider, 38
sill: dam, 98; door, 62;
    house, 58, 59, 60;
    volcano, 10
sill cock, standpipe, 57
silo, 100
silver amalgam, dental, 445
silver-bullion embroidered
    cuff, king's regalia, 468
silver certificate, paper
    money, 220
silverware, 240
silverware drawer,
    sideboard, 239
simple eye, grasshopper, 39
simple microscope, 432
simple miter, bishop, 471
since, symbol, 495
single-breasted jacket, 184
single corner,
    checkerboard, 339
single cuff, shirt, 185
single engine airplane, 147
single lens reflex camera, 171
single-membered foot,
    ultimate beast, 47
single pleat, woman's
    pants, 192
single quotation mark, 497
single ring, dart board, 316
single-score ring, dart
    board, 316
single service court,
    badminton, 313
singles sideline: badminton,
    313; tennis, 306
single system movie sound
    camera, 172
sinister side, coat of
    arms, 487
sinister supporter, coat of
    arms, 487
sink, 60, 243, 269;
    sailboat, 131;
    sidepiece, 239
sinker, fishing, 335
sinus, leaf, 50
siphon: clam, 45; octopus, 44
sire, horse, 36, 330
siren: fire engine, 120, 121;
    police car, 118
sirloin, beef, 30
sissy bar, motorcycle, 125
sitar, 356
situation display indicator,
    pilot's instrument
    panel, 153
six pin, bowling, 311
six-shooter, cowboy, 474
16mm camera, lunar
    rover, 157
sixteenth note, music, 346
sixteenth-of-a-mile pole,
    harness racetrack, 331
sixty-fourth note, music, 347
size: electrician's wire, 413;
    nail, 400; painting
    brush, 365; tire, 101;
    type, 164
sizer, football helmet, 288

size selector, phonograph
    turntable, 176
skate: ice, 319; ice
    hockey, 291
skateboard, 318
skeg: outboard engine, 133;
    sailboat, 130;
    surfboard, 324;
    waterskiing, 323;
    windsurfer, 324
skein: ballista cord, 457;
    knitting yarn, 378
skeleton: coral polyp, 44;
    human, 26;
    skyscraper, 75;
    umbrella, 226
skeleton key, 449
skeleton tower, buoy, 128
sketch box, painting, 365
skewback: arch, 70;
    handsaw, 406
skew chisel, woodcarving, 366
skewer, 255
ski, 320, 321, 323;
    snowmobile, 126
skid, glider, 147
skiff, 129
skiing: cross-country, 321;
    downhill, 320; water, 323
skillet, 253
skimmer, 255
skimming brush, 255
skin: fruit, 53; geodesic
    dome, 83; igloo, 83;
    skyscraper, 75; tepee, 82;
    vegetables, 52, 258;
    yurt, 68
skin diving, 325
skink, 40
skip rope, body building, 338
skirt: badminton shuttlecock,
    313; bedding, 266;
    bureau, 268; drag racing
    driver's helmet, 333;
    dress, 194; escalator, 77;
    fishing jig, 335; fishing
    reel, 334; gas pump, 108;
    girdle, 191; hot air
    balloon, 326; hovercraft,
    145; maid's, 473;
    missile, 466; octopus, 44;
    palm, 50; racing car, 332;
    Revolutionary War
    general's coat, 476;
    saddle, 329; skin diving
    mask, 328; window, 63;
    window shade, 236;
    woman's, 193
skull: armor, 455; human, 26
skull cap: flat racing, 330;
    Jewish prayer
    vestment, 470
skull temple, eyeglasses, 217
sky, 2
skydiver, 327
sky drop, stage, 344
skyline, newspaper, 166
skyscraper, 75
slab: house, 58; lumber, 66
slacks, 187
slalom skiing, 320, 323
slant: gouge, 368;
    grammatical symbol, 497;
    type, 163
slant-front desk, 272
slash, grammatical
    symbol, 497
slash pocket, trousers, 187
slat: fence, 65; lobster
    pot, 423; rocking
    chair, 230; screen, 173;
    sled, 322; train stock
    car, 113; venetian
    blind, 237; window, 63;
    window shade, 237
sled, 322
sleeper, railroad track, 111
sleeping bag, backpacking, 337
sleeping box, truck cab, 116
sleeping car, passenger
    train, 112
sleeping shelf, igloo, 83
sleet, 17

sleeve: baluster, 71; barbell 338; blouse, 193; bridal gown, 472; cardigan, 195; fencing, 309; jacket, 184, 192; jackhammer, 426; lamp, 234, 235; maid's uniform, 473; overhead power line, 386; parka, 197; phonograph record, 176; queen's regalia, 468; scriber, 369; shirt, 185; sponge mop, 278; telescope, 433; trenchcoat, 196; windsurfer mast, 324
sleeve protector, banjo, 356
slice: bread, 259; cake, 260; pizza, 261; quiche, 259
slicer, vegetable, 257
slicing disc, food processor, 250
slick, racing, 332, 333
slicker, cowboy, 474
slide: backyard equipment, 283; cigar cutter, 224; cornet, 353; cowboy hat, 198; desk, 272; film, 171; French horn, 325; hand loom, 379; laboratory, 437; pistol, 460; projector, 173; rule, 414, 431; string tie, 188; suspenders, 186; traverse rod, 236; trombone, 352, 353; trumpet, 353; tuba, 352; vise, 399; zipper, 205
slide bed, 283
slide bolt, chain lock, 448
slide fastener, 205
slide handle, shotgun, 458
slide holder, microscope, 432
slide hook, garbage disposal, 243
slide-out shelf, refrigerator, 245
slide plate, sewing machine, 274
slide projector, 173
slider, parachute, 327
slide rail, snowmobile, 126
slide rule, 431
slide support, 282
sliding block, steam engine, 395
sliding cover, desk, 272
sliding door: barn, 100; helicopter, 146; powerboat, 135
sliding eyepiece, ear scope, 438
sliding jaw, monkey wrench, 405
sliding pond, backyard, 283
sliding pressure plate, key punch, 428
sliding tandem wheels, truck, 117
slim fin, skin diving, 325
slim skirt, 193
sling: bazooka, 462; elevator shaft, 76; golf bag, 305; ice hammer, 328; mountain climbing, 328; rifle, 458
sling shoe, woman's, 201
slingshot dragster, 333
sling swivel, rifle, 458
slipcase, book, 165
slip-joint pliers, 404
slip nut, sink drain, 269
slipper, ballet, 478
slippery when wet, road sign, 489
slip printer, cash register, 430
slip ring, automatic rifle, 461
slip seat, rocking chair, 230
slip stitched seam, necktie, 188-189
slit: cheese plane, 252; man's underpants, 190;

tepee, 82
slit pocket, skirt, 193
slogan, coat of arms, 487
sloop, sail, 132
slope: continental, 15; mountain, 8; permanent fort, 81; suit hanger, 277
slope indicator, runway, 92
sloping dormer, house, 60
slot: blackjack, 341; camera, 170; checkbook clutch, 219; clothespin, 276; dental brace, 443; electrical receptacle, 388; electrical switch, 388; hasp, 450; hovercraft, 145; ice hockey rink, 291; parking meter, 109; pliers, 404; razor, 206; roulette wheel, 340; sandal, 202; screw head, 400; sketch box, 365; slot machine, 340; table saw, 407; telephone, 178; toaster, 249; toggle bolt, 401; toll basket, 110; wallet, 219
slot machine, 340
slotted lifter, kitchen tool, 255
slow down, music notation, 346
slow forward and reverse, television LaserDisc player, 181
slow-motion control knobs, telescope, 433
slow-moving vehicle symbol, hitch and harrow, 424
slug: book page, IV; cartridge, 460; magazine, 169; and parking meter, 109
sluice gate: canal lock, 97; dam, 98
softnose, canal lock, 97
slur, music notation, 346
small intestine, human, 27
small of back, human, 25
small of stock, shotgun, 458
smock mill, 382
smoke alarm, 280
smoke bomb discharger, tank, 465
smoke chamber, fireplace, 228
smoke detector, 280
smoked sausage, 261
smoke ejector, fire engine, 120
smoke flap, tepee 82
smoke grenade, 463
smokehouse, 100
smoke path, stove, 394
smoke shelf, fireplace, 228
smokestack, locomotive, 112
smoke-wagon, cowboy, 474
smooth bore, shotgun, 458
smoothbore firing tube, bazooka, 462
smooth-soled climbing shoe, 328
SMV symbol, hitch and harrow, 424
snack food, 261
snail, 45
snake, 40-41; plumbing tool, 412
snap, fishhook, 317
snap bar, suit hanger, 277
snap fastener, 204; fireman's coat, 484; parka, 197; spacesuit, 157; waterskiing vest, 323
snap lock, starting block, 298
snare drum, 358
snaste, candlewick, 233
sneaker, basketball, 292
snifter, 241
snood, 199; turkey, 33
snooker, billiards, 314
snooze alarm, clock radio, 229
snorkel, skin diving, 325
snorkel tube, submarine, 143
snot, candlewick, 233

snout: crocodilian, 41; fish, 43; glacier, 12; pig, 32; stingray, 43
snow, 19
snow block, igloo, 83
snow couloir, 8
snow cuff, ski boot, 321
snowfield, 9, 12
snow gully, 8
snowmobile, 126
snow plow, garbage truck, 123; hockey skate, 319
snow spoiler, snowmobile, 126
snow ring, ski pole, 320
snowshoe, 321
snuff, candlewick, 233
snuffbox, anatomical, 29
snuffer, candle, 233
soap dish: bathtub, 270; sink, 269
soap dispenser, 243
soaring, glider, 147
soccer field, 293
sock, 203; baseball, 286; basketball, 292; drag racing driver, 333; fencing, 309; football, 288; ice hockey, 291; skiing, 321; windsurfer, 324
socket: bayonet, 453; camera, 172; candlestick, 233; eye, 28; guitar, 357; lamp, 234; movie projector, 173; nozzle, 418; operating table, 440; rowboat, 129; shovel, 417; snap fastener, 204; teeth, 446
socket wrench, 405
sod, hogan, 82
soda-acid fire extinguisher, 280
soda straw, cave, 11
sofa, 232
soft, music notation, 346, 347
softback book, 165
softbound book, 165
softcover book, 165
soft dorsal fin, fish, 43
soft ground, printmaking, 371
softnose, canal lock, 97
soft ray, fish, 43
soft suction connection hose, pumper, 121
soft tissue, and denture, 443
software: computer, 429; television LaserDisc player, 181
solar flare, 3
solar heating system, 383
solar panel: satellite, 182; weather station, 18
solar plexus, 25
solar power system, 383
solar prominence, 3
solar radiation sensor, weather station, 18
solar time, 5
solar system, 2-3
solder, plumbing, 412
soldering iron, 372
soldier: brick wall, 67; uniform, 480, 481
sole: ballet slippers, 478; boot, 202; golf club, 304; horse's foot, 36; human foot, 29; ice climbing boot, 328; ice skates, 319; man's shoe, 200; plane, 410; running shoe, 296; sailboat, 131; sandal, 202; sock, 203; woman's shoe, 201
solenoid, automobile engine, 107
soleplate: house, 59; iron, 275; rollerskate, 318
soleus, human, 26
solid body, guitar, 357
solid-rocket booster, space shuttle, 154

solid spoke wheel, motorcycle, 125
solitary confinement, prison, 74
solleret, armor, 455
solrad, cartoon, 375
solution, magazine puzzle, 169
sommelier, corkscrew, 247
sonar, 434
sonar dome, destroyer, 141
sonar focus transducer, camera, 170
sostenuto pedal, piano, 355
soul, human, 25
sound, movie film, 172
soundboard, violin, 349
sound box: dulcimer, 356; lyre, 349
sound hole: guitar, 256; violin, 349
sounding, nautical chart, 22
sounding board, guitar, 356
sounding datum reference, nautical chart, 22
soundome, sonar, 434
sound-test button, movie camera, 172
soundtrack: movie film, 172; phonograph record, 176
soundtrack control, television LaserDisc player, 181
soup spoon, 240
source, composition lighting, 363
source code, magazine mailing label, 167
source lake, river, 13
sousaphone, 352
South Equatorial Current, ocean, 6
south fork, river, 13
south latitude, globe, 5
South Pole pin, globe, 1
south wing, Capitol, 72
sow, 32
space: music clef, 347; proofreader's mark, 498
space bar, typewriter, 162
space mark, basketball court, 292
spacer: typewriter, 162; wheelchair, 442
space shuttle, 154-155
spacesuit, 157
spade, 417; playing cards, 342
spade bit, drill, 408
spading fork, 417
spaghetti spoon, 255
spaghetti strap, dress, 194
spaghetti tongs, 255
spall, brick, 66
span: arch, 70; bowling ball, 311; bridge, 95
spandrel: arch, 70; mosque, 69
spandrel ornament, grandfather clock, 229
spangle, 215
spanner screw, mortise lock, 448
span wire, traffic light, 109
spar: kite, 317; sailboat, 130
spareribs, 32
spare tire, automobile, 102
spare wheel, truck, 116
spark-arrester: chain saw, 421; fireplace, 228
spark plug: automobile engine, 107; internal combustion engine, 396
sparring, 303
Sparrow missile, jet fighter, 152
spats, drum major, 479
spatula, 255
spawning, fish, 43
speaker: CB radio, 179; guitar amplifier, 357; House of Representatives, 72; metal detector, 435; phonograph, 177;

projector, 173; sonar, 434;
tape recorder, 175;
telephone, 178; television
set, 181; theatre, 345
speaker selector:
phonograph, 177; police
car, 118
spear: asparagus, 52;
window shade roller, 237
spear blade: partisan, 454;
pocket knife, 416
spearhead, partisan, 454
spear point, fence, 65
special-effect pedal,
guitar, 357
special-feature photo
treatment, magazine, 168
special instructions card
holder, elevator car, 76
specialist, space shuttle, 155
special-purpose lens,
camera, 171
specification: electric
motor, 389; internal
combustion engine, 396
specific edition, book, 165
specific product code,
Universal Product
Code, 430
specimen holder,
microscope, 432
spectacles, 217
spectator seating,
courtroom, 87
spectrometer, 435;
satellite, 182
speculum, 438
speech balloon, comic
strip, 374
speech selector, tape
recorder, 175
speed, jet fighter, 152
speed controls: blender, 250;
car, 106; motorcycle, 125;
phonograph turntable, 176;
police car, 118;
747 cockpit, 150;
tape recorder, 175
speedway racing, 332
spell out, proofreader's
mark, 498
spelunking, 11
sphericasia, cartooning, 374
sphygmomanometer, 439
spice, 259
spider, 38; lampshade, 234
spigot, 243, 269
spike, 400; baseball
batter, 286; castle
portcullis, 79; cello, 349;
fence, 65; football
field, 289; halberd, 454;
ice climbing, 328;
mace, 454; pineapple, 53;
railroad track, 111; track
shoe, 296; volleyball, 313
spiked foot, camera
tripod, 174
spiked heel, woman's
shoe, 201
spikelet, grass, 56
spillway, dam, 98
spindle: faucet, 269; movie
projector, 173; phonograph
turntable, 176; rocking
chair, 230; roulette
wheel, 340; screwdriver,
403; sewing machine, 274;
spinning wheel, 379;
stethoscope, 439;
television LaserDisc
player, 181; typewriter,
162; weather vane, 19
spindle hole, computer
diskette, 429
spindle locking plate,
workbench vise, 398
spindrift, wave, 14
spine: book, 165; cactus, 54;
dust jacket, 165; hair
comb, 308; kite, 317;
starfish, 44; stingray, 43
spinnaker, sail, 132

spinner: dominos, 339;
seeder, 420; single engine
airplane, 147
spinneret, spider, 38
spinning reel, 334
spinning rod, 334-335
spinning wheel, 379
spiny dorsal fin, fish, 43
spiny ray, fish, 43
spiracle: grasshopper, 39;
tadpole, 42
spiral: phonograph
record, 176; spider
web, 38
spiral bone, girdle, 191
spiral brush, vacuum
cleaner, 279
spiral galaxy, 2
spiral ratchet screwdriver, 403
spiral tip, drain cleaner, 412
spire: church, 84;
kokoshniki, 68;
mountain, 9; univalve
shell, 45
spirit level, 414
spit, of land, 7, 15, 22
spit curl, 207
spit key: trombone, 353;
trumpet, 353
spitter, toll basket, 110
spitz, glacier, 12
splashboard: Hansom
cab, 127; sink, 243
splash guard:
truck, 116, 117, 122;
washing machine, 276
splash pan, potter's
wheel, 367
splash rim, sink, 269
splat, rocking chair, 230
splayed leg, butterfly
table, 238
spleen, human, 25, 27
splint, 119, 441
split ballot, voting, 427
split end, paint brush
bristle, 415
split line, pill, 441
split-rail fencing,
barnyard, 100
split-rim wheel, tow
truck, 122
split rudder, space
shuttle, 154
splitter, table saw, 407
splitting tool,
stonecutting, 366
spoiler: glider, 147;
jumbo jet, 148; racing
car, 332; snowmobile, 126
spoke: bicycle, 124;
ferris wheel, 91; geodesic
dome, 83; harness racing
sulky, 331; spider
web, 38; stagecoach, 127
sponge: cannon, 457;
mop, 278
sponge face, Ping-Pong
racket, 315
sponge mop, 278
sponge-tip applicator, 213
sponson, helicopter, 146
spool, 376; film roll, 171;
fishing reel, 334;
typewriter, 162
spool pin, sewing
machine, 274
spoon: golf club, 305;
hand grenade, 463;
kitchen, 254, 255; pipe
tool, 255; table setting, 240
spore, fern, 55
sports car, 102
sports deck, passenger
ship, 139
spot: billiard table, 314;
blackjack, 341; bowling
lane, 311; dice, 341; ice
hockey rink, 291;
label, 265; playing
card, 342; sun, 3
spot label, 264
spotlight: circus, 89;

pumper, 121; stage, 344;
truck bed, 122
spot-meter reading index,
light meter, 174
spotter, gymnastics, 300
spot weld, tweezers, 211
spout: bathtub, 270;
beaker, 437; faucet, 269;
gas pump automatic
nozzle, 108; coffee maker,
248; juice extractor, 251;
package, 264; pot, 367;
sink, 243, 269; tea
kettle, 241
spray: bathtub, 270;
dishwasher, 246;
iron, 275; lawn
sprinkler, 418; paint, 415;
pistol nozzle, 418;
shower, 270; sink, 243
spread: book, 165;
canape, 259; magazine,
168-169; sandwich, 259;
shirt collar, 185
spreader: gardening tool, 420;
ladder, 415; powerboat,
135; sailboat, 130;
saw, 407
spreading spinner, seeder, 420
spring: automobile, 105;
ballpoint pen, 160; bear
trap, 423; bed, 267; chest
pull, 338; clothespin, 276;
etching press, 371;
gardening shears, 417;
gas pump nozzle, 108;
hair clip, 210; internal
combustion engine, 396;
lamp, 235; mousetrap,
423; pencil sharpener, 273;
pistol magazine, 460;
racing car, 332; sewing
machine, 274; shoe tree,
203; sponge mop, 278;
stapler, 273;
trampoline, 302;
truck, 116; umbrella, 226
spring-bar, wristwatch, 216
spring beard needle, 378
springboard: diving, 310;
gymnastics, 301;
trampoline, 302
spring catch, swivel, 214
spring clamp, 399
spring clip: juice
extractor, 251;
woodcarving, 366
spring earclip, 214
springer, arch, 70
spring guide, pistol, 460
spring hanger, lamp, 235
spring hinge, 450
springhouse, barnyard, 100
spring slot, clothespin, 276
spring wing, toggle bolt, 401
sprinkle: cake, 260;
ice cream cone, 261
sprinkler, 418
sprocket, motorcycle, 125
sprocket drive housing,
bulldozer, 425
sprocket hole, film, 171, 172
sprocket-tip cutting bar,
chain saw, 421
spud, laboratory burner, 437
spur: auger hit, 409;
chicken, 33; flat
racing, 330; revolver
hammer, 460; riding
equipment, 329
spurl, cartoon, 375
spyglass, 433
squall cloud, 17
square: cannon carriage, 457;
chessboard, 339;
combination, 414;
Manchu court dress, 475;
shuffleboard court, 312
square nut, 401
square up, proofreader's
mark, 498
square root: calculator
key, 431; symbol, 495

square shank, screwdriver, 403
squash, vegetable, 52
squash court, 307
squean, cartoon, 375
squeegee, silk screen, 369
squeeze bottle, 264
squeezer, kitchen tool, 257
squelch control, CB radio, 179
squid, 44
S/RF meter, CB radio, 179
stabilizer: destroyer, 141;
fire engine, 120;
glider, 147;
helicopter, 146; jet
fighter, 152; jumbo
jet, 149; missile, 466;
parachute, 327; passenger
ship, 139; single engine
airplane, 147
stabilizer block, football
helmet, 288
stabilizer trim,
747 cockpit, 150
stable, frontier fort, 80
stack: destroyer, 140;
fireboat, 144;
furnace, 390; passenger
ship, 138; racing car, 332
stacker, keypunch, 428
stadia circle, theodolite, 426
stadium, baseball, 287
staff: cardinal, 471;
destroyer, 140, 141;
flag, 486; halberd, 454;
lance, 454; music, 346-347;
royal scepter, 469;
weather vane, 19
stage, 344-345;
microscope, 432;
missile, 466
stagecoach, 127
staggeration, cartoon, 374
staggered starting line for
distance events, track and
field, 294
stained glass, 372
stairs: 64; house
blueprint, 60; jumbo
jet, 148; White House, 73
stake: basket frame, 262;
croquet, 312; tent, 89, 336
stake pockets, truck
platform, 117
stalactite, 11
stalagmite, 11
stalk: asparagus, 52;
celery, 258; corn, 56;
flower, 51;
mushroom, 55;
seaweed, 55
stalk end, tomato, 52
stall: railroad yard, 94;
shower, 270
stallion, 36
stamen, flower, 51
stamp: coin, 221;
envelope, 161;
house blueprint, 60
stamp board, track and
field, 294
stamp plate number,
envelope, 161
stanchion: barn, 100;
basketball backstop, 292;
ice skates, 319;
sailboat, 130;
tow truck, 122
stand: chafing dish, 241;
child's car seat, 282;
courtroom, 87; curling
iron, 210; cymbal, 358;
etching press, 371;
frame, 373; hammock,
284; kiln, 367;
laboratory, 437;
lithographic press, 370;
movie camera
microphone, 172;
music, 361; pencil
sharpener, 273; slot
machine, 340
standard: armor, 455;
football goalpost, 289;

hose nozzle, 418; pole vault, 299; sled, 322; spinning wheel, 379; theodolite, 426
standard desk phone, 178
standard ratchet screwdriver, 403
standard time, 5
stand brace, table saw, 407
standby altimeter, 747 cockpit, 150
standby altitude indicator, pilot's instrument panel, 153
standby compass: pilot's instrument panel, 153; 747 cockpit, 151
standee window, bus, 114
standing collar: drum major's coat, 479; man's formal attire, 472
standing rigging, sailboat, 130
standing sail, 132
stand leg, table saw, 407
standpipe, fire hydrant, 121
stang, fire engine, 120-121
staple, 400; hasp, 450; silk screen frame, 369
stapler, 273
star: Milky Way, 2-3; sea, 44
starboard: boat, 128; powerboat, 134
star diagonal, telescope, 433
star facet, cut gemstone, 214
starfish, 44
star fort, 81
star note, paper money, 220
Star of David, 86, 492
star of order, queen's regalia, 468
starter: automobile, 104, 107; barbecue, 284; bulldozer, 425; chain saw, 421; clothes dryer, 277; elevator, 76; internal combustion engine, 396; mower, 419; outboard engine, 133; phonograph, 176; 747 cockpit, 151; stopwatch, 298
starting block: racing, 298; swimming pool, 310
starting gate, flat racing, 330
starting light, drag racing, 333
starting line: drag racing, 333; running track, 294
state abbreviation, magazine mailing label, 167
state dining room, White House, 73
state political division, thematic map, 21
stateroom: passenger ship, 138; sailboat, 131
state route: road map, 20; road sign, 488
statesman's name, paper money, 221
static discharge wick, jumbo jet, 148
static line, parachuting, 327
station: dam, 98; keypunch, 428; nautical chart, 22; subway, 115; universal gym, 338
stationary front, weather map, 19
stationary jaw, wrench, 405
stationary leaf, table, 238
stationary rings, gymnastics, 301
stationery, 161
stationery rack, desk, 272
station model, weather map, 19
station wagon, 102
Statue of Freedom, Capitol, 72
stave, barrel, 263
stay: bicycle, 124;

checkbook clutch, 219; girdle, 191; running shoe, 296; shirt collar, 185; sousaphone, 352; wallet, 219
stay rope, bridge, 95
staysail, sailboat, 130
steam-and-dry iron, 275
steam engine, 395
steamer, pot, 253
steamer cap, fire hydrant, 121
steam generator, nuclear reactor, 384
steam heat, furnace, 390
steam line, nuclear reactor, 384
steam locomotive, 112
steam main, furnace, 390
steel: jackhammer, 426; sharpening, 252
steel blade, food processor, 250
steel burr, dental, 445
steel cage, circus, 88
steel guitar, 357
steel helmet, combat soldier, 481
steel inner shell, nuclear reactor, 384
steel pin, and carpet, 242
steel shield, tunnel, 96
steeplechase: harness racetrack, 331; hurdle, 298; track and field, 294
steeple-crowned hat, wizard, 476
steer, 30
steerable front strut, hydrofoil, 145
steerable high-gain antenna, satellite, 182
steering: automobile, 104, 106; bulldozer, 425; bumper car, 90; fireboat, 144; fire engine, 121; outboard engine, 133; 747 cockpit, 150; sled, 322; snowmobile, 126
stela, architecture, 69
stem: apple, 53; bicycle, 124; cactus, 54; candelabrum, 233; carrot, 52; celery, 258; faucet, 269; fern, 55; fishing reel, 334; flower, 51; grass, 56; hose nozzle, 418; laboratory burner, 437; latch needle, 378; leaf, 50; lettuce, 52; mushroom, 55; onion, 52; pepper, 258; percolator brewing basket, 248; pipe, 225; potato, 52; powerboat, 134; razor blade injector, 206; rowboat, 129; royal orb, 469; steamer basket, 253; glassware, 240; spring beard needle, 378; thermometer, 439; tuning fork, 361; type, 163-164; watch, 216
stem press, incandescent bulb, 234
stemware, 240
stencil, silk screen, 369
stenographer's table, courtroom, 87
step: cannon carriage, 457; church, 85; escalator, 77; fire engine, 120; gallows, 452; Hansom cab, 127; house, 61; ladder, 415; locomotive, 112-113; medical examination table, 440; sailboat, 131; shoreline, 14; shovel, 417;

staircase, 64; tractor, 424; truck, 116, 122; windsurfer mast, 324
stepladder, 415
step well, bus, 114
stereo camera, lunar rover, 157
stereo indicator light, phonograph receiver, 177
stereo record, phonograph, 176
sterilizing flame, dental, 445
stern: boat, 128; destroyer, 140; dog, 34; sailboat, 130; tugboat, 144; windsurfer, 324
sterndrive engine, 133
sternocleidomastoid, human, 26
sternum, human, 26
stet, proofreader's mark, 498
stethoscope, 439
stetson, cowboy hat, 474
steward, corkscrew, 247
stew pot, 253
stick: ambulance, 119; beauty product, 213; billiard bridge, 314; car shift, 106; craps table, 341; folding rule, 414; golf course, 305; ice hockey, 291; internal combustion engine, 396; lacrosse, 293; piano, 355; pilot's instrument panel, 153; space shuttle, 155; subway motorman's cab, 115; violin bow, 349; walking, 442
stick glove, ice hockey goalie, 290
stickman, craps table, 341
stick pin, 188
stick umbrella, 226
stiff backing, frame, 373
stiffening truss, bridge, 95
stifle: cow, 30; dog, 34; horse, 36
stigma, flower pistil, 51
stile: door, 62; rocking chair, 230; shutters, 237; sideboard, 239; window, 63
stiletto heel, 201
still camera, 170, 171
still-frame button, video recorder, 180
stilling basin, dam, 98
stimulator tip, toothbrush, 211
sting, bee, 39
stingray, 43
stipe: fern, 55; mushroom, 55
stipule, leaf, 50
stirrup: crossbow, 456; medical examination table, 440; saddle, 329-331
stirrup sock, baseball batter, 286
stitch and stitching, 376: baseball, 286; boot, 202; broom, 278; checkbook clutch, 219; decorative, 377; handbag, 218; knitting, 378; man's belt, 186; sandal, 202; sewing machine, 247; sleeping bag, 337; sock, 203; suspenders, 186
stitching line, sewing pattern, 380
stock: anchor, 128; bagpipe, 359; bell, iii; crossbow, 456; rifle, 458, 461; shotgun, 458; slide rule, 431; windmill, 382
stockade, frontier fort, 80
stockcar, train, 113
stock grip cap, shotgun, 458
stocking, Beefeater, 467
stock pot, 253

stock saddle, 329
stogies, 224
stole, bishop, 471
stolon, grass, 56
stomach: human, 27, 29; jellyfish, 44
stomach teeth, 446
stone: backgammon, 339; dominos, 339; lithographic press, 370; peach, 53; pendant, 215; ring, 215; wall, 67; woodcarving, 366
stonecutting, 366
stool: boxing, 303; window, 63
stool bed, cannon carriage, 457
stoop, 64; door, 62; house, 61
stop: dam, 98; dog, 34; drill press, 409; elevator car, 76; etching press, 371; gardening shears, 417; mower, 419; organ, 354; road sign, 488; subway, 115; tape recorder, 175; typewriter, 162; window, 63; zipper, 205
stop-act, clown, 477
stopboard, shot put, 295
stoplight, truck, 117, 122
stopper: backpack, 337; bathtub, 270; hypodermic syringe, 441; sink, 269
stopping medium, silk screen, 369
stop plate, internal combustion engine, 396
stop sign, road, 489
stop signal, traffic light, 109
stopwatch, 216, 298
stop wire, umbrella runner, 226
storage: ambulance, 119; buoy, 128; camper, 126; car, 106; computer, 429; fire engine, 120, 121; garbage disposal, 243; gasoline pump, 108; laboratory scale, 437; nuclear reactor, 384; oil drilling platform, 99; pool table, 314; refrigerator, 245; stagecoach, 127; tanker, 136
storm, 19
storm door: house, 61; subway car, 115
storm flap, backpack, 337
storm igloo, 83
storm patch, trench coat, 196
storm surge, 14
story: minaret, 68; newspaper, 166; skyscraper, 75
stove: camping, 336; kitchen, 244; sailboat, 131; woodburning, 394
stovepipe leg, woman's pants, 192
stowage: jumbo jet, 148; lunar rover, 157; tank, 464
stowed derrick bracket, tanker, 137
straight arm, bobby pin, 210
straightaway, roller coaster, 90
straighten type horizontally, proofreader's mark, 498
straight gouge, 368
straight jaw, pliers, 404
straight leg: trousers, 187; woman's pants, 192
straight-line course, drag racing, 333
straight-line sander, 411
straight of goods, sewing pattern, 380
straight pin, 204
straight razor, 206
straight side, grand piano, 355

straight ticket, voting, 427
straight tray, slide
     projector, 173
straight-up ribbed top,
     sock, 203
strainer: dishwasher, 246;
     juice extractor, 251;
     kitchen tool, 256
strain insulator, overhead
     power line, 386
strain reliever: curling iron
     cord, 210; hand drill
     cord, 409; toaster oven
     cord, 249
strait, 7
strand: barbed wire, 422;
     basket, 262; electrician's
     wire, 413; hair, 209, 210;
     land feature, 7; mop, 278;
     rope, 128; thread, 376
strap: accordion, 360;
     athletic supporter, 190;
     backpack, 337; baseball
     catcher, 286; bicycle, 124;
     block and tackle, 451;
     boot, 202; brassiere, 191;
     camera, 170, 171; chain
     saw chain, 421; child's car
     seat, 282; cinch fastener,
     204; cowboy hat, 198;
     drag racing driver, 333;
     dress, 194; electrical wall
     switch, 388; electric
     chair, 452; fencing half-
     jacket, 309; football
     helmet, 288; glove, 196,
     307; golf bag, 305;
     hasp, 450; ice climbing
     boot, 328; ice hockey
     player, 291; man's
     undershirt, 190;
     motorcycle, 125;
     operating table, 440;
     overnight bag, 281;
     photographic, 174; police
     uniform, 483; sandal, 202;
     handbag, 218; saddle, 329;
     sandal, 202; skin diving
     gear, 325; ski pole, 320;
     stationary rings, 301;
     subway car, 115; tefillin,
     470; trench coat, 196;
     umbrella, 226; waterskiing
     vest, 323; woman's shoe,
     201; wristwatch, 216
strap hinge, 450
strapping, chaise lounge, 284
stratocumulus cloud, 16, 17
stratosphere, 4
stratus cloud, 16
straw, cave, 11
strawberry, 53
stream: mountain, 8;
     ocean, 6; river, 13;
     topographic map, 22
streamer: drum major's waist
     sash, 479; flagpole, 486
streamway, cave, 11
street, city plan, 20
street address, magazine
     mailing label, 167
street cleaner, 123
stretcher: ambulance, 119;
     brick wall, 67; drop-leaf
     table, 238; fire
     engine, 120; painting
     canvas, 364; rocking
     chair, 230; umbrella, 226;
     workbench, 398
stretch pants, skiing, 320
strike: bell, iii;
     lock, 448
strike pocket, bowling, 311
striker, croquet, 312
striker plate, door lock, 448
striker wheel, cigarette
     lighter, 224
striking weapons,
     medieval, 454
string: balloon, 477;
     cowboy hat, 474; double
     bass, 349; frankfurter,
     261; guitar, 356, 357;

jai alai cesta, 308;
     kite, 317; mandolin, 356;
     orchestra section, 348;
     saddle, 329; sitar, 356;
     tennis racket, 306;
     tie, 188; tub fiddle, 360;
     violin, 349
string bass, 348
string brace, kite, 317
stringed instruments, 349, 356
string hole: tennis racket, 306;
     tub fiddle, 360
string tie, 188
strip: bath, 270;
     cartridge fuse, 389;
     fence, 65; fencing, 309;
     Indian shirt, 474;
     kite, 317; matchbook,
     224; postage stamps, 161;
     roofing shingle, 66;
     staples, 273; tackless,
     carpet, 242; wheelbarrow,
     420; window shutters, 237
stripe: enlisted man's
     uniform, 480;
     powerboat, 134;
     runway, 92; toll booth, 110
striped morning trousers,
     butler, 473
stripper, wire, 413
strip title, comic strip, 374
strobe, photographic, 174
strobe flasher, locomotive, 113
stroller, child's, 282
strongbox, 447
strongbox storage,
     stagecoach, 127
strop, razor, 206
structural unit, piano, 355
structure: domed, 83;
     launch pad, 154;
     pyramids, 68
strut: bulldozer, 425;
     destroyer, 140; geodesic
     dome, 83; helicopter, 146;
     house, 59; hydrofoil, 145;
     racing car, 332; sled, 322
stub: candle, 233;
     pliers, 404; ticket, 343
stubble, beard, 207
stud: butler's uniform, 473;
     house, 59; man's formal
     attire, 472; organ, 354;
     running shoe tread, 296
stud hole, shirt, 185
stud side, snap fastener, 204
stuffing box, steam engine, 395
stuffsack, backpacking, 337
stump: rocking chair, 230;
     tree, 48
stupa, pagoda, 69
style: art, 362;
     flower pistil, 51; pea, 52
styled man's hat, 198
stylet, mosquito, 39
stylus, phonograph
     turntable, 176
styptic pencil, 206
subcategory, book page, iv
sub-control panel, video
     recorder, 180
subdued unit patch,
     combat soldier, 481
subflooring, house, 58
subhead: book page, iv;
     magazine, 167-168;
     newspaper, 166
subject, work of art, 362
subleaflet, fern, 55
submarine, 143
submerged foil hydrofoil, 145
submerged rock, nautical
     chart, 22
submersible watch, skin
     diving, 325
subordinate illustration,
     book page, iv
subscriber, magazine, 167
subsidiary coin, 221
subsidiary road, 110
substitute letter, proofreader's
     mark, 498
subtract, symbol, 494

subtraction, with abacus, 431
subtractive process, stone
     sculpture, 366
subway, 115;
     city plan, 20
succulent, 54
sucker, octopus, 44
suction cup, plumber's
     plunger, 412
suction machine,
     ambulance, 119
suction unit, paramedic
     equipment, 119
sudden death, darts, 316
suffix letter, paper money, 221
sugar bowl, 241
sugar cone, ice cream, 261
sugar shaker, 256
suicide king, playing
     cards, 342
suit: basketball, 292;
     drag racing driver, 333;
     playing cards, 342;
     sails, 132
suitcase, 281
suit hanger, 277
suite, passenger ship, 139
sulky, harness racing, 331
summer berm, shoreline, 14
summer squash, 52
summer uniform, police, 483
summit, mountain, 8
summons pouch, police, 482
sump, nuclear reactor, 384
sun, 3
sundae, 260
sun deck, passenger
     ship, 138
sundial, 381
sunglasses, baseball gear, 286
sunglasses pocket,
     spacesuit, 157
sun roof, automobile, 102
sunshade: satellite, 182;
     sextant, 133;
     telescope, 433
sun spot, 3
sun visor, car, 106
superband signal,
     television, 181
supercooled water,
     thundercloud, 17
supergiant star, 2
superior slope,
     permanent fort, 81
supernova, 3
superstructure, tanker, 137
super tanker, 136-137
supertweeter, phonograph
     speaker, 177
Super-Vee racing car, 332
supply duct, heat
     exchanger, 393
supply line, water
     heater, 391
supply pipe: space
     shuttle, 154; water
     heater, 391
supply plate, solar collector
     panel, 383
supply reel: movie
     camera, 172;
     projector, 173;
     tape recorder, 175
support: backyard
     equipment, 283; camp
     stove, 336; citrus
     juicer, 251; desk, 272;
     ferris wheel, 91;
     helicopter, 146;
     hot air balloon, 326;
     mailbox, 227;
     playpen, 282; pole
     vault, 299; pool
     table, 314; power
     line, 386; power saw, 407;
     pulley block, 451; rocking
     chair arm, 230;
     stroller, 282; traverse
     rod, 236;
     vacuum tube, 386;
     wheelbarrow, 420;
support assembly, nuclear

reactor, 385
support bar, drag racing
     dragster, 333
support beam: bus, 114;
     subway car, 115
supporter: athletic, 190; coat
     of arms, 487
support hose, 203
supporting members,
     fence, 65
supporting plate, land
     mine, 463
supportive devices, 442
support leg, truck, 117
support post, Ping-Pong
     net, 315
support system, racing
     car, 332
support tube, lamp, 235
support unit, basketball
     backstop, 292
support wire, incandescent
     bulb, 234
suppressor, automatic
     weapon flash, 461
surbase, column pedestal, 71
surcingle, flat racing, 330
surf, 14
surface: brick, 66; desk, 272;
     diving platform, 310;
     lithographic press, 370;
     parachute, 327; and
     perspective, 362; pool
     table, 314; printing, 164;
     solar power system, 383;
     starfish, 44; table
     saw, 407; type, 164
surface fighting ship, 140-141
surface-piercing
     hydrofoil, 145
surface search radar: aircraft
     carrier, 142;
     destroyer, 141
surface-to-air missiles, 140
surface-to-surface
     missiles, 140
surface wave, 14
surfboard, 325
surfing, 324
surgical table, 440
surname: basketball
     player, 292; magazine
     mailing label, 167
surplice, minister, 471
surveyor, and transit, 426
suspended ceiling, elevator
     car, 76
suspender, harness
     racing gear, 331
suspender cable, bridge, 95
suspenders, 186;
     ice hockey player, 290
suspension: phonograph
     turntable, 176; racing
     car, 332
suspension bridge, 95
suspension cable,
     stationary rings, 301
suspension line,
     parachute, 327
suspension pivot,
     laboratory scale, 437
suspension rope, hot
     air balloon, 326
suspension system:
     automobile, 104; football
     helmet, 288
suspension wheel,
     snowmobile, 126
sutler, frontier fort, 80
su-tshu, Manchu court
     dress, 475
suture, univalve shell, 45
swab, cannon, 457
swagger bag, 218
swalloop, cartoon, 374
swallowtail: flag, 486;
     surfboard, 324
swallowtail pennant, 486
swami belt, mountain
     climbing, 328

swamp: coastline, 15;
river, 13
swan neck, house, 61
swash, wave, 14
swatch, fabric, 380
swastika, symbol, 492
sweatband, beret, 198
sweater, 195;
skiing, 320, 321
sweat sock, 203
sweat soldering,
plumbing, 412
sweep: brace, 408;
windmill, 382
sweeper: carpet, 278;
lawn, 419
sweep indicator, pilot's
instrument panel, 153
sweet goods, 260
sweet spot, tennis
racket, 306
sweet tooth, 446
swell, 14; saddle, 329
swelling, lance, 454
swell keyboard, organ, 354
swell shoe, organ, 354
swim fin, skin diving, 325
swimming, 310
swimming foot, bird, 37
swine, 32
swing, backyard, 283
swing-away bar,
suit hanger, 277
swing chain, 283
swing gouge,
woodcarving, 366
swing hanger, 283
swinging gate,
drop-leaf table, 238
swing mirror,
dressing table, 268
swing seat, 283
Swiss army knife, 416
switch: accordion, 360
calculator, 431;
camera, 170, 172, 180; car
directional signal, 106; CB
radio, 179; clothes
dryer, 277;
computer, 429; cow, 30;
curling iron, 210; dental
unit, 444;
dishwasher, 246; drill
press, 409; electric, 388;
electric hairbrush, 208;
electric razor, 206;
elevator, 76; finishing
sander, 411; food
processor, 250; guitar
amplifier, 357; hair
dryer, 208;
jackhammer, 426;
kiln, 367; lamp, 234, 235;
microphone, 179;
organ, 354; outboard
engine, 133; phonograph
receiver, 177; pilot's
instrument panel, 153;
radar, 434; railroad
yard, 94; saw, 407, 421;
747 cockpit, 150, 151;
tape recorder, 175; tape
measure, 414;
telephone, 178; toaster
oven, 249; video
recorder, 180
swivel: camera tripod, 174;
C-clamp, 399; field events
hammer, 297;
fishhook, 335; hasp, 450;
jewelry findings, 214;
jump rope, 338;
mortar, 462; peeler, 252;
pulley block, 451;
rifle, 458, 459; stationary
rings, 301; stroller, 282;
suit hanger, 277; vise, 399
swivel holster,
police gun belt, 483
sword, 453, 476
sword point position,
windmill, 382
sword-swallower,
circus, 88

symbol: grammatical, 497;
label, 264, 265; of
life, 492; mah-jongg
tile, 339; map, 20;
religious, 492; science,
business, and
commerce, 494-495
symbolia, cartoon, 375
symbolic date, coin, 221
symbolic decoration,
minister, 471
symbolic language, 496
sympathetic string,
sitar, 356
symphony orchestra, 348
synagogue, 86, 470
synodic period, moon, 4
synoptic chart, weather, 19
synthesizer, 357
synthetic coil, zipper, 205
synthetic porcelain,
dental, 445
syringe: dental, 444, 445;
hypodermic, 441;
kitchen, 255;
paramedic, 119
syrup, sundae, 260

T

T: braille, 496; sign
language, 496;
windsurfer, 324
tab: electrical receptacle, 388;
eyeglasses, 217;
handbag, 218;
package, 264; parka, 197;
powerboat, 134; racing
car, 332; razor, 206;
roofing shingle, 66;
wallet, 219; zipper, 205
tabernacle, church, 85
table, 238; basketball
court, 292; courtroom, 87;
cut gemstone, 214;
dental, 445; drill press, 409;
lacrosse field, 293;
medical, 440; Ping-
Pong, 315; pocket
billiards, 314; sailboat, 131;
saw, 407; violin, 349
table arm, dental, 445
table lamp, 234
table lock, camera tripod, 174
table-locking clamp, drill
press, 409
table position selector,
surgical table, 440
table saw, 407
table setting, 240-241
tablet: medicinal, 441;
organ, 354;
tombstone, 500
table tennis, 315
tabletop, dressing table, 268
tabling, mainsail, 132
tabloid newspaper, 166
tabulator control,
typewriter, 162
TACAN antenna,
destroyer, 140
Tacan navigation system,
aircraft carrier, 142
tace, armor, 455
tach, car, 106
tachometer: car, 106;
motorcycle, 125; pilot's
instrument panel, 153;
powerboat, 134
tack, 400; carpet, 242;
mainsail, 132; necktie, 189;
racehorse, 330;
tambourine, 358;
umbrella, 226
tack cloth, painting, 415
tackle, fishing, 335
tackless strip, carpet, 242
taco, jai alai cesta, 308
tactical information display,
pilot's instrument
panel, 153
tadpole, 42
taenia, column
entablature, 71
taffrail, sailboat, 130

tag: attaché case, 281; combat
soldier's uniform, 451
tail: cat, 35; coffin, 500;
coin, 221; comet, 3; cow,
30; dog, 34; fish, 43; horse,
36; house, 59; kite, 317;
lobster, 45; pelt, 197; pig,
32; single engine airplane,
147; skateboard, 318; ski,
320, 323; snowshoe, 321;
stingray, 43; surfboard,
324; ultimate beast, 46;
weather station vane, 18;
windsurfer, 324
tail coat: butler's uniform,
473; circus ringmaster, 88;
drum major, 479; man's
formal attire, 472
tail crest, tadpole, 42
tail fan, lobster, 45
tail feather, 33, 37
tail fin: automobile, 103;
fish, 43; jet fighter, 152;
jumbo jet, 149
tailgate, garbage
truck, 123
tailhead, cow, 30
taillight: automobile, 103;
locomotive, 113;
motorcycle, 125;
truck, 117, 122
tail nozzle, jet fighter, 152
tailored pillow, sofa, 232
tailor shop, prison, 74
tailor's loop, shirt, 185
tail-out groove, phonograph
record, 176
tailpiece: banjo, 356; sink
drain, 269; violin, 349
tailpipe, tow truck, 122
tail plane, jumbo jet, 149
tail pylon, helicopter, 146
tail rocker, slalom water
ski, 323
tail rotor, helicopter, 146
tail section: flute, 350;
snowmobile, 126;
torpedo, 466
tail service mast, space
shuttle, 154
tail vise, workbench, 398
tail water, dam, 98
tail wheel, helicopter, 146
taintor gate, dam, 98
takeoff area, high jump, 299
takeoff board, track and
field, 294
takeoff engine, lunar
lander, 156
takeoff fan, high jump, 294
take out space, proofreader's
mark, 498
take-up motion handle, hand
loom, 379
take-up reel: movie
camera, 172; movie
projector, 173; tape
recorder, 175
take-up spool,
typewriter, 162
talk switch, CB radio
microphone, 179
tall-case clock, 229
tallith, Jewish prayer
vestment, 470
tallow, candle, 233
tally clerk, House of
Representatives, 72
tally man, cattle ranch, 422
tallywhacker, sailor's
uniform, 481
talon, bird, 37
talus slope, mountain, 8
tambourine, 348, 358
tamer, circus, 88
Tamid, 86, 470
tamper, pipe tool, 225
tandem wheels, truck, 117
tang: drill bit, 409; file, 410;
knife, 240, 252, 453;
rake, 417; rasp, 410;
skillet, 253
tangential section,
lumber, 66
tank, 464-465;

ambulance, 119;
automobile, 103, 104, 105;
barbecue grill, 284;
camper, 126; camp
stove, 336; chain saw, 421;
drag racing dragster, 333;
fire engine, 120; garbage
truck, 123; gasoline
storage, 108; internal
combustion engine, 396;
iron, 275; jet fighter, 152;
lantern, 336; lunar
lander, 156; mower, 419;
nuclear reactor, 384; oil
drilling platform, 99;
railroad yard, 94; skin
diving, 325; solar heating
system, 383; space shuttle,
154; submarine ballast,
143; toilet, 271;
truck, 116, 117; water
heater, 391
tank car, train, 112
tanker, ocean-going, 136-137
tank forward bay, space
shuttle, 154
tap, 269
tape: Band-Aid, 441; baseball
bat, 287; boxing, 303; cash
register, 430; cassette, 175;
coat of arms, 487;
computer, 429;
envelope, 161; garment
seam, 192; measuring, 414;
mountain climbing, 328;
package, 265; Ping-Pong
net, 315; skateboard, 318;
tennis net, 306;
typewriter, 162; Velcro,
205; venetian blind, 237;
video recorder, 180;
volleyball net, 313;
zipper, 205
tape measure, 414
tape-monitor switch,
phonograph receiver, 177
taper, 233
tape recorder, 175
tapered leg, woman's
pants, 192
taphole, keg, 263
tapper: buoy, 128; glass
cutter, 372
taproot, 49; carrot, 52
tare poise, laboratory
scale, 436
target: medieval shield, 454;
radar, 434; railroad
crossing signal, 111
target arrow, bowling
lane, 311
target designate switch,
pilot's instrument
panel, 153
target lock, sonar, 434
tassel: drum major's boot top,
479; king's regalia, 468;
Manchu court dress, 475;
venetian blind, 237;
window shade, 236;
woman's hat, 199
tasset, armor, 455
taste buds, tongue, 28
tasting spoon, 255
tatting shuttle, 378
tattooed lady, circus, 88
tau cross, symbol, 492
Taurus, zodiac, 493
taxi roof light, 115
taxi stand, public sign, 490
taxiway, airport, 93
t-bar, truck bed, 122
tea ball, 256
teacup, 241
tea infuser, 256
team logo, baseball, 286
team number, jai alai, 308
team race, swimming
pool, 310
teamsters' mess, frontier
fort, 80
teamsters' quarters, frontier
fort, 80

teapot, 241
tear-away jersey, football uniform, 288
tear drop, surfboard, 324
tear duct, eye, 28
tear tape, package, 265
teased hair, woman's, 209
teaser: magazine, 169; stage, 344
tea set, 241
tea spoon, 241
tea strainer, 256
teat: cow, 30; pig, 32
technical magazine, 167
technician's set, ambulance, 119
tee: golf, 304; pagoda, 69
teepee, 82
teeterboard, circus, 88
teeter-totter, backyard, 283
teeth, *see* tooth
tefillin, Jewish ritual items, 470
teflon pad, baren, 368
telegraph aerial, tanker, 137
telegraph key, 159
telemetry radio, ambulance, 119
telephone, 178; road sign, 488
telephone monitor, tape recorder, 175
telephoto lens, camera, 171
telescope, 433; satellite, 182; sextant, 133; tank, 465; theodolite, 426
telescopic helicopter ranger, destroyer, 140
telescopic sight, rifle, 459
television, 180-181; antenna, house, 61; mast, skyscraper, 75
telltale: mainsail, 132; squash court, 307
telson, lobster, 45
tempera, painting medium, 364
temperature: 747 cockpit, 150; thermometer, 18; weather map, 19
temperature control: air conditioner, 393; dryer, 277; iron, 275; toaster oven, 249; washing machine, 276
temperature gauge, car engine, 106
temperature prediction, weather map, 19
temperature scale, volt-ohm meter, 413
temperature sensor, weather station, 18
temple: eyeglasses, 217; human, 24; Jewish, 86, 470; Muslim, 68-69
temple gateway, Shinto, 68
temple memorial band, Jewish prayer shawl, 470
temporary traffic-control device, toll booth, 110
tempura rack, wok, 253
tenant floor, skyscraper, 75
tender, 129; locomotive, 112
tenderloin, pork, 32
tender truck, locomotive, 112
tendon, human foot, 29
tendon guard, hockey skate, 319
tendril, hair, 209
ten-gallon hat, 198, 474
tennis, 306
10-off square, shuffleboard court, 312
tenon, bagpipe, 359
tenor drone, bagpipe, 359
tenor drum, 358
tenor joint, bassoon, 35
tenpins, bowling, 311
tension adjustment pin, gardening shears, 417
tension arm, bobby pin, 210
tension bar: razor, 206; steel

chain fence gate, 65
tension clamp, lamp, 235
tension control knob, snare drum, 358
tension cord, Ping-Pong net, 315
tension guide, sewing machine, 274
tension hoop, banjo, 356
tension ring, dome, 83
tension rod: bass drum, 358; man's buckle, 186
tension screw: banjo, 356; kettledrum, 358; paramedic equipment, 119
tension sheave, elevator shaft, 76
tension wheel, bicycle, 124
tent, 336; circus, 88; oxygen, 442; yurt, 68
tentacle: coral polyp, 44; jellyfish, 44; octopus, 44; starfish, 44
10-yard chain, football, 289
10-yard line, football field, 289
tepal, flower, 51
tepee, 82
terminal: airport, 93; electrical wall switch, 388; fence gate, 65; railroad yard, 94; video recorder, 180
terminal block, stove, 244
terminal bud, tree, 48
terminal moraine, 8, 12
terminology, nautical, 128
terminus, glacier, 12
terrace: house, 61; shoreline, 14
terrace server, 241
terreplein, permanent fort, 81
territory, baseball field, 287
tertiary root, 49
test area, aircraft carrier, 142
test button: police car, 118; smoke alarm, 280
test lead jack, volt-ohm meter, 413
test panel, pilot's instrument, 153
test tube, 437
tether line, hot air balloon, 326
text: book, 165; magazine, 168
textblock, book page, IV
texture, and composition, 363
T-handle, pommel horse, 301
theatre, 345; passenger ship, 39
thematic map, 21
thenar, human hand, 29
theodolite, 426
therefore, symbol, 495
thermal dot, curling iron, 210
thermal energy, steam engine, 395
thermal-storage tank, solar heating system, 383
thermistor, weather station, 18
thermometer, 439; dual scale, 18; kitchen, 254; laboratory, 437
thermosphere, earth, 4
thermostat: refrigerator, 245; solar heating system, 383; stove, 394; water heater, 391
thick stroke, type, 163
thigh: bird, 37; cat, 35; chicken, 33; cow, 30; dog, 34; frog, 42; horse, 36; human, 24; poultry, 33
thigh pad, football uniform, 288
thigh machine, universal gym, 338
thimble, 376; harness racing, 331; stove, 394
thin stroke, type, 163
third base, baseball field, 287

third eye, tuatara, 40
third molar, 446
third quarter moon, 4
third rail, subway, 115
third stage, missile, 466
third toe, human foot, 29
third valve, trumpet, 353
third valve slide: French horn, 352; trumpet, 353
thirty-second-inch mark, tape measure, 414
thirty-second note, music, 347
thobe, Arab dress, 475
thong: cowboy holster, 474; police nightstick, 482; sandal, 202
thorax, grasshopper, 39
thorn, ultimate beast, 46
thoroughbrace, stagecoach, 127
thoroughbred, flat racing, 330
thought balloon, cartoon, 374
thread, bolt, 401; plug fuse, 389; screw, 400; sewing, 376; spider, 38; weaving, 379
threaded fitting, nozzle, 418
threaded handle, paint roller, 415
threaded neck, bottle, 264
threaded pipe, 412
thread guide, sewing machine, 274
three dimensions, stone sculpture, 366
3/8 pole, harness racetrack, 331
301, darts, 316
three pin, bowling, 311
three-point line, basketball court, 292
three-point perspective, 362
3/4 pole, harness racetrack, 331
three-ring circus, 88
three-second lane, basketball court, 292
3/16 pole, harness racetrack, 331
three suit, domino, 339
three-way light bulb, 234
three-way syringe, dental, 445
three-yard line, football, 289
threshold: airport runway, 92; door, 62; house, 60
throat: anchor, 128; auger bit, 409; bird, 37; clamp, 399; cornet, 353; fireplace, 228; human, 24, 25, 28; lacrosse stick, 293; latch needle, 378; salamander, 42; saw, 406; shoe, 200, 201; tennis racket, 306
throat doctor, examination equipment, 438
throat fan, lizard, 40
throating, church, 84
throat latch strap, trenchcoat, 196
throat opening, vise, 398
throatpiece, tennis racket, 306
throat plate, sewing machine, 274
throat protector, baseball catcher, 286
throat pump, paramedic equipment, 119
throttle: car, 106; horse, 36; internal combustion engine, 396; motorcycle, 125; outboard engine, 133; pilot's instrument panel, 153; powerboat, 134
throttle latch, chain saw, 421
throw: bedding, 266; track and field, 295
throwing circle, shot put, 295
throwing sector, javelin, 294
thrown pot, 367

throw rug, 242
thrust cone, jumbo jet, 149
thruster: lunar lander, 156; passenger ship, 139; space shuttle, 154
thrusting and cutting weapon, 453
thrust lever, 747 cockpit, 151
thrust ring, missile, 466
thrust tube, ballpoint pen, 160
thruway, 110
thumb: baseball glove, 287; dog, 34; frog, 42; human hand, 29
thumbhole: bowling ball, 311; painter's palette, 365
thumbpiece, revolver safety catch, 214
thumb press, curling iron, 210
thumb rest: hypodermic syringe, 441; iron, 275
thumbscrew: blood pressure gauge, 439; clarinet mouthpiece, 351; drain cleaner, 412; earring, 214; laboratory clamp, 436
thumb-string peg, banjo, 356
thunder, 17
thundercloud, 17
thunderhead, 16, 17
thunderstorm, 17, 19
thurl, cow, 30
thwart, rowboat, 129
tiara, 215, 468, 469
tibia: frog, 42; grasshopper, 39; human, 26; spider, 38
tibialis anterior, 26
tibialis posterior, 26
ticket, 343; police, 482; voting, 427
ticket pocket flap, jacket, 184
ticket spitter, toll basket, 110
tidal inlet, 15
tidal marsh, 15
tidal wave, 14
tide, 15
tie: butler, 473; man, 188-189, 472; military, 480; music notation, 347; package, 265; police, 483; railroad track, 111; saddle, 329; skirt, 193; wall, 67
tieback, curtain, 236
tie bar, 188
tie beam: house, 59; incline track, 90
tie brace, bridge, 95
tie clasp, 188
tie closure: blouse, 193; umbrella, 226
tie-down, inflatable, 129
tie holder, suitcase, 281
tie plate: railroad track, 111; stapler, 273
tie rod end, automobile, 104
tie strap, chain saw chain, 421
tie wing, dental brace, 443
tiger, circus, 88
tightener, dental, 445
tightrope act, circus, 88
tights, ballet dancer, 478
tilde, grammatical symbol, 497
tile: domino, 339; mah-jongg, 339
till, cash register, 430
tiller: boat, 130; grass, 56; 747 cockpit, 150
tilt control, sonar, 434
tilt cord, venetian blind, 237
tilting arbor handwheel, saw, 407
tilting base, saw, 407
tilting knob, movie projector, 173
tilt lock, saw, 407
tilt rod, window shutters, 237
timber, 66; castle portcullis, 79

timbered joint, Japanese building, **68**

timberline, **8**

time: drag racing, **333**; map, **5**; parking meter, **109**

time belt, **5**

time cord, dental x-ray unit, **444**

time dial, globe, **1**

time dot, music, **347**

timekeeper: House of Representatives, **72**; ice hockey, **291**

time lock, vault, **447**

timer: basketball, **292**; clothes dryer, **277**; dishwasher, **246**; kitchen, **254**; parking meter, **109**; skin diving, **325**; stove, **244**; traffic light, **109**

times, symbol, **494**

time signature, music, **346**

Times Square, prison, **74**

time zone, map, **5**

time zone display control, wristwatch, **216**

timing case cover, automobile engine, **107**

timpani, **348**, **358**

tin, squash court, **307**

tin can, surface fighting ship, **140**

tine: fork, **240**; hitch and harrow, **424**; rake, **417**

tip: arrow, **456**; asparagus, **52**; ballpoint pen, **160**; bicycle, **124**; billiard cue, **314**; bobby pin, **210**; bow, **456**; cheese plane, **252**; crutch, **442**; curling iron, **210**; dental unit, **444**; drain cleaner, **412**; drum major's baton, **479**; fencing foil, **309**; fishing rod, **335**; grass, **56**; hypodermic syringe, **441**; iceberg, **12**; icing nozzle, **255**; javelin, **296**; knife, **252**, **453**; leaf, **50**; man's belt, **186**; nose, **28**; outboard engine, **133**; peeler, **252**; pelt, **197**; pliers, **404**; saw, **421**; screwdriver, **403**; sharpening steel, **252**; ski, **320**, **323**; soldering iron **372**; sword, **453**; tent pole, **336**; toothbrush, **211**; tweezers, **211**; umbrella, **226**; univalve shell, **45**; violin bow, **349**; woman's shoe, **201**

tip contact, incandescent bulb, **234**

tip guard, hockey skate, **319**

tipi, **82**

tip-in, magazine, **169**

tip-on label, **264**

tippet, minister, **471**

tipping, necktie, **189**

tipping lever, wheelchair, **442**

tip top, fishing rod, **335**

tire, **101**; automobile, **102**, **103**; bicycle, **124**; bus, **114**; drag racing dragster, **333**; harness racing sulky, **331**; motorcycle, **125**; seeder, **420**; stagecoach, **127**; tractor, **424**; truck, **116**; wheelbarrow, **420**

tissue: and denture, **443**; fruit, **251**; meat, **258**; photographic supplies, **174**; succulent, **54**

Titan, **3**

title: book, **165**; comic strip, **374**; magazine, **167**, **168**, **169**; map, **21**; music, **346**; nautical chart, **22**; phonograph record, **176**

title block, house blueprint, **60**

T-neck, ski clothes, **321**

TNT, hand grenade, **463**

toad, **42**

toadstool, **55**

toaster, **249**

toaster oven, **249**

tobacco, **224**

tobacco pouch, **225**

toboggan, **322**

toe: bird, **37**; boot, **202**; cat, **35**; chicken, **33**; dog, **34**; frog, **42**; hockey skate, **319**; golf club, **304**; horseshoe, **36**; horse's hoof, **36**; human, **24**, **29**; ice skate, **319**; man's shoe, **200**; panty hose, **191**; piano, **355**; plane, **410**; roller skate, **318**; running shoe, **296**; saw, **406**; shotgun, **458**; ski, **320**, **321**, **323**; snowshoe, **321**; sock, **203**

toeboard, shot put, **295**

toe clip: bicycle, **124**; horse's hoof, **36**

toe disc, toad, **42**

toe guard: elevator shaft, **76**; mower, **419**

toenail: cat, **35**; human, **29**; turkey, **33**; ultimate beast, **47**

toe plate: baseball pitcher, **286**; refrigerator, **245**

toe rail, sailboat, **130**

toeshoe, ballet dancer, **478**

toe strap, bicycle, **124**

toe stud, organ, **354**

toga, **475**

toggle bolt, **401**

toggle lever, pliers, **404**

toggle link, sponge mop, **278**

togglelock, backpack, **337**

toilet, **271**; public sign, **490**

toilet mirror, dressing table, **268**

token, collector, **221**

toll basket, **110**

toll booth, highway, **110**

tom, turkey, **33**

tomato, **52**

tomb, **500**

tombolo, **7**

tombstone, **500**

tomcat, **35**

tom-tom, **358**

tone: tuning fork, **361**; woodwind, **350**, **352**, **353**

tone arm, phonograph turntable, **176**

tone control: guitar, **357**; tape recorder, **175**

tone unit, piano, **355**

tone-up wheel, body building, **338**

tong(s): kitchen, **255**; lunar rover, **157**; oil drilling platform, **99**; revolver safety catch, **214**

tongue: bolt ring, **214**; child's wagon, **283**; cow, **30**; curling iron, **210**; film roll, **171**; flag, **486**; human, **28**; Jew's harp, **360**; L-shaped square, **414**; man's belt, **186**; man's shoe, **200**; running shoe, **296**; skate, **318**, **319**; sled, **322**; snake, **41**

tongue-and-groove pliers, **404**

tongue blade, **119**, **439**

tongue depressor, **439**

tonsil, **28**

tool: ice climbing, **328**; pipe, **225**; pocket knife, **416**; police car, **118**; sculpting, **366**

tool stowage: bulldozer, **425**; jackhammer, **426**; lunar rover, **157**; motorcycle, **125**; tow truck, **122**; workbench, **398**

tooth, **446**; bear trap, **423**; corrugated fastener, **400**; crocodile, **41**; denture, **443**; duck bill, **33**; fern, **55**; file, **410**; hair comb, **208**; ice hammer, **328**; knee kicker, **242**; lobster, **45**; pliers, **404**; rake, **417**; rasp, **410**; saw, **406**, **407**; scissors, **376**; scrimshaw, **369**; snake, **41**; suspenders, **186**; tank drive wheel, **465**; zipper, **205**

toothbrush, **211**

toothed chisel, **366**

toothpick, pocket knife, **416**

top: automobile, **103**; balance beam, **300**; battery, **387**; button, **205**; can, **263**; circus, **88**; desk, **272**; fishing rod, **335**; golf bag, **305**; handbag, **218**; horizontal bar, **300**; hurdle, **298**; juice extractor, **251**; laboratory burner, **437**; lettuce, **258**; medical examination table, **440**; microscope limb, **432**; mountain, **8**; parachute, **327**; parallel bars, **300**; piano, **355**; rocking chair, **230**; sideboard, **239**; skyscraper, **75**; sock, **203**; stove, **394**; thimble, **376**; violin, **349**; workbench, **398**; zipper, **205**

top block, window shutters, **237**

top exit, elevator, **76**

top fabric, quilting, **377**

top hat: circus ringmaster, **88**; miser, **476**

top housing, electric razor, **206**

top link, hitch and harrow, **424**

toplit composition, **362**

top-loading washing machine, **276**

top margin, book page, **165**

topographic map, **22**

top pad, child's car seat, **282**

top pillow, stagecoach, **127**

topping: canapé, **259**; dessert, **260**

top plate: house, **59**; typewriter, **162**

top pocket flap, backpack, **337**

top rail: backyard equipment, **283**; bureau, **268**; door, **62**; fence gate, **65**; playpen, **282**; staircase, **64**; window, **63**

top ring, fishing rod, **335**

top roller, etching press, **371**

topsail, sailboat, **130**

top sheet, bedding, **267**

top spring, umbrella, **226**

top stitching: checkbook clutch, **219**; handbag, **218**; man's belt, **186**

top strap, revolver, **460**

top thread guide, sewing machine, **274**

top tube, bicycle, **124**

toque, **199**

Torah, **86**, **470**

torch, propane, **412**

torii, **68-69**, **492**

tormentor: fire engine, **120**; stage, **344**

tornado, **17**

torpedo, **466**; submarine, **143**

torsade, wrought iron fence, **65**

torse, coat of arms, **487**

torso: cow, **30**; human, **24**; space suit, **157**

tortoise, **40**

torus, column, **71**

tossut, igloo, **83**

total air temperature, 747 cockpit, **150**

totalizer, gas pump, **108**

totalizer board, flat racing, **330**

tote board, horseracing, **330**, **331**

touchdown area, airport runway, **93**

touch-line, soccer field, **293**

toupee, **207**

touring, ski, **321**

tourist section, jumbo jet, **149**

tournament darts, **316**

towboat, **144**

tow-cable pulley, tow truck, **122**

towel bar, barbecue grill, **284**

towel clip, dental, **445**

towel rack, bathtub, **270**

tower: aircraft carrier, **142**; bridge, **95**; castle, **78**, **79**; church, **84**, **85**; destroyer, **140**; ferris wheel, **91**; fireboat, **144**; frontier fort, **80**; globe, **1**; mountain, **9**; nautical chart, **22**; passenger ship, **139**; polygonal, **69**; powerboat, **135**; power network, **386**; prison, **74**; railroad yard, **94**; slide, **283**; windmill, **382**

tower bin, silo, **100**

tower control, airport, **93**

tower ladder, **120**

towing gear: glider, **147**; fire engine, **120**, **121**; tank, **465**; tow truck, **122**; tugboat, **144**

towing light: destroyer, **141**; tugboat, **144**

towing ring, kite, **317**

towline, waterskiing, **323**

town: magazine mailing label, **167**; map, **20**; nautical chart, **22**

towpath, canal lock, **97**

tow ring, fire engine, **120**, **121**

tow truck, **122**

tracery, church, **84**

track: baseball field, **287**; bulldozer, **425**; canal lock, **97**; circus, **88-89**; dishwasher, **246**;

Grand Prix, 332; horseracing, 330, 331; incline, 90; lighting, 235; movie film, 172; passenger ship, 138; phonograph record, 176; railroad, 94, 111; roller coaster, 90; snowmobile, 126; submarine, 143; subway, 115; tank, 464; television LaserDisc player, 181; traverse rod, 236

track and field, 294-295

tracking-force dial, phonograph turntable, 176

track lighting, 235

track shoe, 296; bulldozer, 425

traction splint, 119

tractor, 424; bulldozer, 425; truck, 116

tractor wheel, roller coaster, 90

trade magazine, 167

trademark: baseball bat, 282; book, 165; credit card, 222; label, 264

trade winds, 6

trading post, 80

traffic control, 109; airport, 92, 93; toll booth, 110

traffic light, 109

traffic police officer, 482

traffic signals, 109

traffic ticket, 482

tragus, outer ear, 28

trail: public sign, 491; road sign, 488

trail bike, 125

trailer, 126

trailer connecter, truck, 116

trailing edge, jumbo jet, 148

trailing truck, locomotive, 112

trail rope, hot air balloon, 326

trail shoe, snowshoe, 321

train: bridal gown, 472; railroad, 94, 112-113; roller coaster, 90; subway, 115

trainer: circus, 88; flat racing entry, 330; running shoe, 296

training shoe, 296

tramp, merchant ship, 136

trampolets, 302

trampoline, 302

tranquilizer, 119

transceiver: CB radio, 179; radar antenna, 434

transducer: camera, 170; sonar, 434

transept, church, 85

transfer scale, light meter, 174

transfer to local elevator, skyscraper, 75

transformer, nuclear reactor, 385

transistor, electronic organ, 354

transistor chip, 386

transit, 426

transit system, 115

transmission: automobile, 105; bulldozer, 425; tank, 464

transmit light, CB radio, 179

transmitter, telephone, 178

transom: door, 62; elevator car, 76; powerboat, 135; rowboat, 129

transom clamp, outboard engine, 133

transparency: film slide, 171; projector, 173

transparent balustrade, escalator, 77

transparent roof, bus, 114

transponder, 747 cockpit, 151

transportation, public sign, 490

transportation office, Capitol building, 72

transpose, proofreader's mark, 498

transverse arch, human foot, 29

transverse piece, kite, 317

trap, 423; clothes dryer, 277; gallows, 452; sink drain, 269

trapdoor: Hansom cab, 127; stage, 344

trapeze artist, circus, 88

trapezius, human, 26

trap plug, sink drain, 269

trapunto, quilting, 377

trash basket, 243

trash compactor, 243

trauma box, paramedic equipment, 119

traveler: sailboat, 130; stage, 344

traveler's check, 223

traverse arm, overhead power line, 386

traverse rod, 236

traversing gear, mortar, 462

tray: baby's high chair, 282; cosmetic case, 281; dental unit, 444; easel, 364; house painting, 415; slide projector, 173; tea set, 241; toaster, 249

tread: planetary wheel, 424; running shoe, 296; staircase, 64; stirrup, 329; tire, 101

treadboard, escalator, 77

treadle: hand loom, 379; spinning wheel, 379

treasure box, stagecoach, 127

Treasury seal, paper money, 221

treatment, magazine photo, 168

treatment aids, medical, 441

treble clef, music, 346

treble dial, phonograph receiver, 177

treble hook, fishing plug, 335

treble part, accordion, 360

treble pick-up, guitar, 357

tree, 48; saddle, 329; shoe, 203

tree of life, Torah, 470

trefoil: church, 84; drum major's coat, 479;

medal, 485

tremolo arm, guitar, 357

trench: continental margin, 15; underwater funnel, 96

trench coat, 196

tress, 25, 209

trestle, guillotine, 452

triangle: orchestra, 348; shuffleboard court, 312

tributary, river, 13

triceps, human, 26

triceps exerciser, body building, 338

trick, spring beard needle, 378

trick ski, waterskiing, 323

tricorne, pirate, 476

tricycle, 124

trifecta, flat racing, 330

trifocal lenses, eyeglasses, 217

triforium, church, 84

trigger: bear trap, 423; chain saw, 421; crossbow, 456; drill, 409; gas pump automatic nozzle, 108; movie camera, 172; paint spray gun, 415; sander, 411; slalom water ski, 323; weapon, 458, 460, 461, 462

trig-loop post, laboratory scale, 437

trim: automobile, 103; baseball uniform, 286; cake, 260; door, 62; drum major's uniform, 479; fencing mask, 309; Manchu court dress, 475; pendant, 215; pool table, 314; queen's regalia, 468; running shoe, 296; 747 cockpit, 150; stove, 244; tennis racket, 306; window shade, 236; woman's hat, 199; woman's shoe, 201

trim-adjustment rack, outboard engine, 133

trimline phone, 178

trimmer: body building, 338; lawn, 419; razor, 206

trimming, woman's hat, 199

trimming end, clay modeling tool, 366

trim tab: powerboat, 134; racing car, 332

trip, fishing reel, 334

trip handle, toilet, 271

triple jump, track and field, 294

triple ring, dart board, 316

triple-score ring, dart board, 316

triplet, music notation, 346

tripod: machine gun, 461; music stand, 361; photographic, 174; screen, 173; telescope, 433; transit, 426

trip odometer, car, 106

tripod sensor, camera, 170

trochanter: grasshopper, 39; spider, 38

trolley, girdle, 191

trolley pole, bumper car, 90

trolling gear, fishing, 338

trombone, 348, 352-353

trophy, 285; king's

regalia, 468; medal, 485

tropical storm, 19

troposphere, earth, 4

trotter, harness racing, 33

trough: barn, 100; humidifier, 392; longshore, 14; wave, 14

trousers, 187; bull denim, 474; butler's uniform, 474; cowboy, 474; jai alai player, 308; king's regalia, 468; man's formal attire, 472; military uniform, 480, 481; paramedic equipment, 119; police uniform, 482

trowel, 417

truck, 116-117; airport, 93; cannon carriage, 457; fire engine, 120; flagpole, 486; garbage, 123; locomotive, 112, 113; platform, 117; roller skate, 318; semitrailer, 117; skateboard, 318; tractor, 116

truck bed, tow truck, 122

true air speed indicator, 747 cockpit, 150

true bias, fabric, 380

true edge: knife, 453; sword, 453

true north, 22

true vertical, transit, 426

true-zero hook, tape measure, 414

trumpet, 348, 353

trunk: automobile, 103; cactus, 54; fish, 43; grandfather clock, 229; human, 24; octopus, 44; palm, 50; police car, 118; powerboat, 134; and root, 49; sailboat, 130; tree, 48; ultimate beast, 47

trunks, boxing, 303

trunnion: bulldozer, 425; cannon barrel, 457

truss: bridge, 95; roof, 59

trysail, 132

try square, 414

T-shirt, man's, 190

tsunami, 14

tuatara, 40

tub: bath, 270; dishwasher, 246; tub fiddle, 360; washing machine, 276

tuba, 348, 352

tube: ambulance, 119; automobile engine, 107; bazooka, 462; beauty product, 213; bicycle, 124; blood pressure gauge, 439; bolt ring, 214; dental unit, 444; dispenser, 263; electronic organ, 354; eyedropper, 441; fire extinguisher, 280; food processor, 250; hurdle, 298; icing nozzle, 255; jet fighter, 152; laboratory burner, 437; laboratory clamp, 436; lamp, 234, 235; lawn sprinkler, 418; light bulb, 234; microscope, 432; mortar, 462; nuclear reactor, 385; pen, 160; pitch pipe, 361; radiator, 390; screen, 173; shoe tree, 203; shotgun, 459; sketch box, 365;

sleeping bag, 337;
solar collector panel, 383;
stethoscope, 439;
submarine, 143;
subway, 115; tank gun,
465; telescope, 433;
television set, 181;
test, 437; thermometer,
439; toilet, 271; torpedo,
466; vacuum, 386;
wave, 14
tuber, potato, 52
tubercles, stingray, 43
tube sock, 203
tub fiddle, 360
tubing: backyard
glider, 283; dental,
445; plumbing, 412;
stethoscope, 439
tub ring and filter,
washing
machine, 276
tuck: blouse, 193;
cigar, 224
tucker, queen's
regalia, 468
tuck flap,
package, 265
tuft: lounger, 231; man's
hair, 207; sofa, 232;
toothbrush, 211
tug, 144; airport, 93
tugboat, 144
tumbling,
trampoline, 302
tumbrel, execution
vehicle, 452
tummy, human, 25
tuna tower,
powerboat, 135
tuner, phonograph, 177
tunic: Beefeater, 467;
king's regalia, 468
tuning fork, 361
tuning gear: cornet,
353; dulcimer, 356;
French horn, 352;
guitar, 356;
phonograph
receiver, 177;
radar, 434; sitar,
356; trombone, 352-353;
trumpet, 353
tunnel, 96; igloo, 83;
prison, 74; railroad,
111; subway, 115;
wave, 14
tunnel bottom,
waterski, 323
tunnel visor, traffic
light, 109
turban, woman's, 199
turbine: combustion jet
engine, 397; nuclear
reactor, 384
turbine engine,
helicopter, 146
turbine locomotive, 112
turbofan jet engine,
149, 397
turboprop jet engine, 397
turf: baseball field, 287;
racetrack, 330, 331
turkey, 33
turn: lamp, 235;
racetrack, 331
turnback, suit
hanger, 277
turnback cuff: blouse,
193; jacket, 192
turnbuckle, boxing
ring, 303
turned step, shovel, 417
turner, kitchen
utensil, 255
turn indicator,
747 cockpit, 152
turning, drop-leaf
table, 238
turning gear, can
opener, 247
turning signal,
automobile, 102
turning stake,
croquet, 312

turning wall, swimming
pool, 310
turn-lock,
handbag, 218
turnouts, fireman, 484
turnover, 260
turnover collar,
king's regalia, 468
turn signal light: bus,
114; truck, 116, 117
turntable: fire engine,
120; phonograph, 176;
railroad yard, 94;
television
LaserDisc, 181
turret: castle, 78;
stethoscope, 439;
tank, 465
turtle, 40
turtleback,
submarine, 143
turtleneck: clothes,
321; sweater, 195
tusche stencil, silk
screen, 369
tush, ultimate beast, 47
tusk, ultimate beast, 47
tutu, ballerina, 478
tuxedo, man's formal
attire, 472
TV camera:
aircraft carrier,
142; lunar rover, 157;
satellite, 182
TV monitor, prison, 74
TV optical unit, jet
fighter, 152
TV power status, space
shuttle, 155
tweeter, phonograph
speaker, 177
tweezers, 211; pocket
knife, 416
twelve foot marker,
bowling lane, 311
21, layout, 341
25-point ring, dart
board, 316
20mm cannon, jet
fighter, 152
24-second clock,
basketball, 292
twig, tree, 48
twilight zone, cave, 11
twin bed, 266
twine, frankfurter, 261
twinned stories,
newspaper, 166
twins, zodiac, 493
twin soundtrack,
stereo phonograph
record, 176
twist: drill bit, 408,
409; paper clip, 273
twisted handle, paper
bag, 262
twister, 17; body
building, 338
twist-off cap, bottle, 265
twist tie, package, 265
two-button closing,
woman's jacket, 192
two-color eye
pencil, 213
two-cycle internal
combustion
engine, 396
two-deck head,
magazine, 169
two-pronged fork, 255
two-suiter, 281
two-point
perspective, 362
two-stick kite, 317
two-way traffic, road
sign, 489
two-way zipper, 205
two-yard line,
football, 289
typanum: church, 84;
frog, 42; grasshopper,
39; toad, 42
type, 163; magazine,
168, 169; printing, 164;
typewriter, 162

type of subscription
code, magazine
mailing label, 167
typewriter, 162
typhoon, 17
typist's initials,
letter, 161
typography, 163
tzit, Torah, 470

U

U: braille, 496; sign
language, 496
U-boat, 143
udder, cow, 30
U-gouge, 368
UHF radio, pilot's
instrument panel, 153;
747 cockpit, 150
ullage, bottle, 263
ulna, human, 26
ultimate beast, 46-47
ultra-high frequency
signal,
television, 181
ultraviolet
spectrometer,
satellite, 182
umbilical:
spaceshuttle, 154;
spacesuit, 157
umbilical system bag,
lunar rover, 157
umbilicus, human, 24
umbo, shield, 454
umbone, clam, 45
umbrella, 226; golf, 305;
pipe, 225: silo, 100
umlaut, grammatical
symbol, 497
umpire's area,
baseball field, 287
una corda pedal,
piano, 355
undercarriage,
stagecoach, 127
undercarriage
protector, tow
truck bed, 122
undercarriage
wheels,
helicopter, 146
undercoat, bird, 37
undercut, razor
blade, 206
underline,
grammatical
symbol, 497
underpants, 190
underpass, 110
underpinnings,
queen's
regalia, 468
underscore,
grammatical
symbol, 497
under-seat bag
stowage, lunar
rover, 157
underserve line, jai
alai cancha, 308
undershirt, 190, 286
underwater tunnel, 96
underwear, man's, 190
underwiring,
brassiere, 191
uneven parallel
bars, 300
unexposed film, movie
camera, 172
unicycle, 124
uniform: baseball, 286;
basketball, 292;
boxer, 303; butler, 473;
drag racing
driver, 333; fencing,
309; football, 288; ice
hockey, 290, 291; jai
alai, 308; jockey,
330, 331; maid, 473;
military, 480-481;
police, 482-483;
Revolutionary War
general, 476;
skiing, 320, 321;

skin diving, 325
unimproved road,
topographic map, 22
union: flag, 486; water
heater, 391
unistrut, ferris wheel, 91
unit: ambulance, 191;
computer, 429;
masonry, 66
unit citation,
military uniform, 480
unit column,
abacus, 431
unit crest, military
cap, 480
US insignia,
military uniform, 480
United States notes,
paper money, 220
U.S. interstate route
number, road map, 20
U.S. route, road
sign, 488
unit number, fireman's
helmet, 484
unit patch, military
uniform, 480, 481
unit point,
abacus, 431
unit value, thematic
map, 21
univalve shell, 45
universal cross
connection,
traffic light, 109
universal drive joint,
hitch and
harrow, 424
universal gym, 338
universal joint:
automobile, 105;
windsurfer, 324
Universal Product Code,
430; symbol, label, 265
Universal Transverse
Mercator grid
marking,
topographic map, 22
universal veil,
remnants, mushroom, 55
universe, 2-3
UPC label, 430
updraft, tornado, 17
uphaul, windsurfer, 324
upholstery: sofa, 232;
wheelchair, 442
upper: ice skate, 319;
man's shoe, 200;
running shoe, 296;
sandal, 202
upper arm: dog, 34; frog,
42; human, 24; traffic
light, 109
upper back-stick,
easel, 364
upper ball joint,
automobile, 104
upper blade guard,
saw, 407
upper bolt, pulley
block, 451
upper bout, viola, 349
upper bow, bear trap, 423
upper case, type, 163
upper chord, bridge, 95
upper control arm,
automobile, 104
upper control line,
parachute, 327
upper deck, passenger
ship, 139
upper eyelid, frog, 42
upper face, zipper, 205
upper frame, piano, 355
upper gate, canal
lock, 97
upper-girdle facet,
cut gemstone, 214
upper grid, nuclear
reactor, 385
upper grip ring, sword
hilt, 453
upper handle, mower, 419
upper hatch, lunar
lander, 156

upper header, solar
collector panel, 383
upper housing,
sander, 411
upper jaw, fish, 43
upper joint,
clarinet, 351
upper limb, bow, 456
upper lounge, jumbo
jet, 148
upper mandible, bird, 37
upper panel, piano, 355
upper plate,
theodolite, 426
upper spray arm,
dishwasher, 246
upper tail crest,
tadpole, 42
upper teeth, 446
upper thigh, dog, 34
upper pool, canal
lock, 97
upper rack,
dishwasher, 246
upper rail,
balustrade, 71
upper receiver,
rifle, 461
upper rudder, jumbo jet, 149
upper sash, window, 63
upper shell, turtle, 40
upper side-rail,
truck van, 117
upper windshield,
bus, 114
upright: basketball
backstop, 292;
croquet wicket, 312;
easel, 364; etching
press, 371; football, 289;
guillotine, 452; hand
loom, 379; horizontal
bar, 300; hurdle, 298;
lithographic press,
370; parallel bars,
300; pole vault, 299;
pommel horse, 301; roller
coaster, 90; tow
truck, 122
upright handlebar,
bicycle, 124
upright piano, 355
upright pole, tent, 336
upright standard,
theodolite, 426
upright vacuum
cleaner, 279
uprush, wave, 14
upstop wheel, roller
coaster, 90
upstream, river, 13
upstream gate, canal
lock, 97
Uranus, planet, 3
urine transfer
connector,
spacesuit, 157
urn, bed finial, 266
uropod, lobster, 45
usage register,
electric meter, 389
use, label, 264
used-blade box, razor
blade injector, 206
utility belt, police,
482-483
utility pocket: cowboy,
474; spacesuit, 157
uvula, 28

V

V: braille, 496; sign
language, 496
VAC scale, volt-ohm
meter, 413
vacuum cleaner, 279
vacuum hose,
automobile
engine, 107
vacuum jar,
laboratory, 437

vacuum mount, pencil
sharpener, 273
vacuum relief valve,
tanker, 136, 137
vacuum tube, 386
valance: curtain,
236; stage, 344
validation, postal
money order, 223
valley, 7; house roof, 61;
non-glaciated, 12;
river, 13
valley glacier, 12
value: coin, 221;
thematic map, 21
value range,
isarithmic map, 21
valve: automobile
engine, 107;
bicycle, 124; blood
pressure gauge, 439;
camper, 126; camp
stove, 336; clam, 45;
cornet, 353; drag
racing dragster,
333; dental unit, 444;
faucet, 269; football,
288; French horn, 352;
furnace, 390; hot air
balloon, 326;
inflatable, 129;
laboratory burner, 437;
lantern, 336;
motorcycle, 125;
nuclear reactor,
384; playing cards,
342; plumber's torch,
412; radiator, 390;
scallop, 45; skin
diving, 325; solar
heating system, 383;
standpipe, 57; steam
engine, 395; subway
motorman's cab, 115;
tanker, 136, 137;
toilet, 271; trumpet, 353;
water heater, 391
vambrace, armor, 455
vamp: boot, 202; man's
shoe, 200; running
shoe, 296; sandal, 202;
woman's shoe, 201
van, truck, 117
Vandyke beard, 207
vane: barn, 100; bird
feather, 37; missile,
466; weather, 18, 19;
windmill, 382
vanishing point,
perspective, 362
vanity, dresser, 268
varashield, truck
cab, 116
variable range
marker, radar and
sonar, 434
variable spacer,
typewriter, 162
variable-speed
control, saw, 407
variable sweep wing,
jet fighter, 152
vase, church, 85
VASI, airport runway, 92
vastus medialis,
human, 26
vault: bank, 447;
burial chamber, 500;
dome, 83; parking
meter, 109; pay
telephone, 178; pole,
294, 299
vaulter: gymnastics,
301; pole vault, 299
vaulting board, 301
vaulting horse, 301
V-berth, sailboat, 131
V-bottom hull,
powerboat, 134
VDC scale, volt-ohm
meter, 413
vegetable, 52, 53, 258;

juice extractor,
251; refrigerator
compartment, 245
vegetable organ,
grass, 56
vegetable slicer, 257
vehicle: airport, 93;
armor-plated, 464-465
V-8 automobile
engine, 107
veil: bride's, 472; nun's,
471; remnants of
universal, mushroom,
55; woman's hat, 199
Velcro closure, 205;
football helmet, 288;
parka cuff, 197
velocity indicator:
pilot's instrument
panel, 153; space
shuttle, 155
velocity stack,
racing car, 332
velvet cap, royal
crown, 469
venetian blind, 237
venom, snake, 40
vent: automobile, 103;
Band-Aid, 441;
battery, 387; bus, 114;
cannon barrel, 457;
furnace, 390; hair dryer,
208; hot air balloon,
326; house gable, 61;
jacket, 184; paint
spray gun, 415;
radiator, 390; shoe
tree, 203; skin
diving fin, 325;
stove, 244; truck van,
117; volcano, 10; water
heater, 391
vent field astragal
and filets, cannon
barrel, 457
ventilated rib,
shotgun, 459
ventilation
building, underwater
tunnel, 96
ventilation hatch,
bus, 114
ventilation-heating
controls, car, 106
ventilation pack,
hovercraft, 145
ventilation
umbilical,
spacesuit, 157
ventilator: barn, 100;
lantern, 336;
locomotive, 113;
subway car, 115;
tank, 465
venting arm, launch
pad, 154
vent pipe: house, 60;
pressure cooker, 253
vent port, drag
racing driver's
fire suit, 333
ventral fin: fish, 43; jet
fighter, 152
ventral scale,
snake, 41
vent screw, outboard
engine, 133
venturi windshield,
powerboat, 135
Venus, planet, 3
veranda, house, 61
verge, barn, 100
vergeboard, house, 61
Vermeil Room, White
House, 73
vernier, theodolite, 426
verso, book page, 165
vertebral column,
human, 26
vertebral shield,
turtle, 40
vertex, pyramid, 69
vertical, transit, 426

vertical adjustment,
speculum, 438
vertical aerial,
volleyball net, 313
vertical angulation
dial readout, dental
x-ray unit, 444
vertical brace:
bridge, 95; oil
drilling platform, 99
vertical centering,
radar, 434
vertical circle,
theodolite, 426
vertical exhaust,
truck tractor, 116
vertical fin: blimp,
158; glider, 147;
single engine
airplane, 147
vertical gauge,
carpenter's level, 414
vertical reduction,
theodolite, 426
vertical speed
indicator,
747 cockpit, 150
vertical stabilizer,
jumbo jet, 149
vertical tail fin, jet
fighter, 152
vertical updraft,
tornado, 17
vertical velocity
indicator, pilot's
instrument panel, 153
very high frequency
antenna,
destroyer, 140
very high frequency
signal,
television, 181
very soft, music
notation, 347
vessel, 128
vest, 184; butler, 473;
cowboy, 474; man's
formal attire, 472;
police, 483; ski
clothes, 321, 323;
sweater, 195
vestibule, vault, 447
vestment, Jewish
ritual, 470
vestry, church, 85
V-gouge, 368
VHF aerial, jumbo
jet, 148
VHF antenna:
destroyer, 140, 141;
helicopter, 146; lunar
lander, 156
VHF radio,
747 cockpit, 151
vial: carpenter's
level, 414;
theodolite, 426
vibration damper
pulley, automobile
engine, 107
vibrissa: cat, 35;
ultimate beast, 46
vice president,
Senate, 72
video camera, 180
video cassette
tape, 180
video display,
computer, 429
video recorder, 180
viewer, television
LaserDisc
player, 181
viewfinder: camera,
170, 171; telescope, 433
viewing area,
public sign, 491
viewing hood,
radar, 434
vignette: book, 165;
label, 264
viola, 348, 349
violation flag,
parking meter, 109

558

violin, 348, 349
violoncello, 349
virgule, grammatical
symbol, 497
virgin, zodiac, 493
Virgo, zodiac, 493
viscid spiral,
spider web, 38
vise, 399;
workbench, 398
visor: armor, 455; drum
major's busby, 479;
fireman's helmet, 484;
man's cap, 198;
spacesuit, 157;
traffic light, 109
visual-approach
slope indicator
light, airport
runway, 92
vite, cartoon, 374
vitellus, egg, 258
V-neck, sweater, 195
vocational
rehabilitation,
prison, 74
voice, organ, 354
void, type, 163
volcanic rock,
brazier, 284
volcano, 7, 10
volleyball court, 313
voltmeter: powerboat, 134;
symbol, 494
volt-ohm meter, 413
volt-ohm milliameter, 413
volume, stringed
instruments, 349
volume control: CB
radio, 179; guitar,
357; hearing aid,
442; metal detector,
435; movie projector,
173; police radio,
118; sonar, 434; tape
recorder, 175
volume dial,
phonograph
receiver, 177
volume graduation,
beaker, 437
volume key, television
set, 181
volume number,
newspaper, 166
volume unit meter, tape
recorder, 175
voluntary muscle,
human, 26
volva, mushroom, 55
voting booth, 427
voting machines,
mechanized, 427
voucher, postal money
order, 223
voussoir, arch, 70
VRM range-intensity
control, radar, 434
V-tail, surfboard, 324
V-waist, queen's
regalia, 468

W

W: braille, 496; sign
language, 496
wafer, Communion, 85
wafer ice cream
cone, 261
waffle ice cream
cone, 261
waftarom, cartoon, 375
wagon, child's toy, 283
wagon masters'
quarters, frontier
fort, 80
wagon pole,
stagecoach, 127
wah-wah pedal,
guitar, 357
waist: ant, 39; bell, III;
guitar, 356;
hourglass, 229; human,
24; queen's regalia,

468; skirt, 193; viola, 349;
woman's pants, 192
waistband: athletic
supporter, 190; man's
formal attire, 472;
man's underpants,
190; panty hose, 191;
skirt, 193; trousers,
287; woman's pants, 192
waistcoat: butler, 473;
man's formal attire,
472; Revolutionary
War general, 476
waistline: bridal
gown, 472; dress, 194
waist trimmer, body
building, 338
walk, house, 61
walk-around, clown, 477
walk board, roller
coaster, 90
walkie-talkie
radio, 179
walking leg, lobster, 45
walking race, 294
walking stick, 442
wall: barn, 100;
baseball field, 287;
brick, 67; canal
lock, 97; and
carpet, 242; cave,
11; circus tent, 89;
dam, 98; dustpan, 278;
elevator car, 76; fort,
81; handball court,
307; horse's hoof, 36;
house, 58, 60; jai
alai cancha, 308;
lacrosse stick, 293;
mah-jongg, 339;
mountain, 9; oil
drilling platform, 99;
pea, 52; pepper, 258;
prison, 74; safe, 447;
squash court, 307;
stage, 344; stove
oven, 244; swimming
pool, 310; tomato, 52;
truck, 117; wave, 14
wallaby pouch,
ultimate beast, 46
wallet, 219
wall fastener, 401
wall flange: aneroid
barometer, 18; sink
drain, 269
wall socket,
electrical, 388
wall switch,
electrical, 388
wall tent, 336
wall-to-wall carpet, 242
wand: venetian blind,
237; wizard, 476
waning moon, 4
war bonnet, Indian, 474
ward, castle, 78, 79
warding, key, 449
wardrobe, 268
warhead: missile, 466;
torpedo, 466
warm front, weather
map, 19
warming element,
percolator, 248
warming grid,
barbecue grill, 284
warming unit, coffee
maker, 248
warm liquid pipe, heat
exchanger, 393
warm-up jersey,
baseball batter, 286
warm-up suit,
basketball, 292
warning: dental x-ray
unit, 444; postal money
order, 223
warning light: car, 106;
fire engine, 120, 121;
pilot's instrument
panel, 153; railroad
crossing signal, 111;
747 cockpit, 150, 151;

space shuttle, 155;
tractor, 424
warning lines,
fencing strip, 309
warning sign,
road, 489
warning track,
baseball field, 287
warp, hand loom, 379
war paint, Indian, 474
warship, 140
warts, toad, 42
washbasin,
sailboat, 131
washcloth rack,
bathtub, 270
washer, 401; faucet, 269;
hose coupling, 418;
lamp, 234; levigator,
370; and parking
meter, 109
washing machine, 276
washline, 276
washout plug,
locomotive boiler, 112
washtub, 276
waste disposal,
dental, 445
watch, 216; skin
diving, 325
watchband, 216
watch cap,
sailor's, 481
watch pocket: skirt,
193; trousers, 187;
vest, 184
watchtower, train
caboose, 113
water: dam, 98; public
sign, 491;
thundercloud, 17
water bearer,
zodiac, 493
water buffalo horn,
ultimate beast, 47
water closet,
sailboat, 131
watercolor, painting
medium, 364
water control, dental
unit, 444
watercourse, river, 13
water droplet, cave, 11
waterfalls, 13
water fill: camper, 126;
iron, 275
watergate: castle, 79;
frontier fort, 80
water glass, 240
water hazard: golf
course, 304-305;
steeplechase
race, 298
water heater, 391;
camper, 126
water hook, harness
racing, 331
water kettle, tea
set, 241
water key: trombone, 353;
trumpet, 353
water level sight glass,
furnace, 390
waterline: boat, 128;
destroyer, 141
water pipe, 225
water pressure gauge,
pumper, 121
water pump: automobile
engine, 107; nuclear
reactor, 385
water regulator,
dental, 445
water reservoir, coffee
maker, 248
water return pipe,
furnace, 390
waterskiing, 323
water spray:
mechanical
sweeper, 123; tooth
cleaner, 211
water tank: iron, 275;
railroad yard, 94;

water heater, 391
water temperature
gauge,
powerboat, 134
watertight bulkhead,
passenger ship, 138
watertight door,
destroyer, 140
water tower, nautical
chart, 22
wattage selector, CB
radio, 179
wattle: chicken, 33;
turkey, 33
wattmeter, symbol, 494
watts, phonograph, 177
wave, 14; radio, 3
wave-cut platform,
iceberg, 12
waveguide, radar
antenna, 434
wave height, 14
wavelength, 14
wax: candle, 233;
ski, 321
waxing moon, 4
way, permanent fort, 81
W.C., sailboat, 131
weaponry, 453-466;
combat soldier, 481;
defensive guided,
140; jet fighter, 152
weather boarding,
barn, 100
weather deck,
passenger ship, 139
weather ear,
newspaper, 166
weather forecast, 18
weather map, 19
weather radarscope,
747 cockpit, 150
weather stripping,
window, 63
weather vane, 19;
barn, 100
weaving, 379
web: bird foot, 33, 37;
circus aerialist, 88;
horseshoe, 36; knife,
252; spider, 38; toad,
42; weaving, 379
web area, wrench, 405
webbing: baseball
glove, 287; football
uniform, 288;
suspenders, 186
web-fed press,
printing, 164
web sling, bazooka, 462
wedding bouquet,
bride, 472
wedge: cannon
carriage, 457;
crossbow, 456; dental,
445; hammer, 402;
quiche, 259; running
shoe, 296; sawhorse,
398; snowmobile, 126
weep hole: brick wall,
67; fence, 65
weft, weaving, 379
weight: barbell, 338;
baseball bat, 286;
bowling ball, 311;
discus, 297; flat
racing, 330;
grandfather clock,
229; guillotine, 452;
hurdle, 298; laboratory
scale, 436, 437;
lobster, 423; metronome,
361; skin diving,
325; tractor, 424; type,
163; universal
gym, 338
weight floor, stage, 344
weights and measures
certification,
gas pump, 108
weight to be carried,
flat racing
entry, 330
weiner, 261

weld: link chain, **451**; tweezers, **211**
welded channel, backyard glider, **283**
well: automobile, **102, 105**; bus steps, **114**; cigarette lighter, **224**; ink, **160**; magazine, **167**; powerboat, **135**; saucer, **241**; toaster, **249**; workbench, **398**
well-contents measuring tool, oil drilling platform, **99**
welt: boot, **202**; shoe, **200**
welting: baseball glove, **287**; lounger, **231**; handbag, **218**; mattress, **267**
welt pocket flap, jacket, **184**
West Australia Current, ocean, **6**
West Coast mirror, truck, **116**
westerlies, wind, **6**
western pocket, trousers, **187**
western saddle, **329**
western yoke shirt, cowboy, **474**
west front, church, **85**
west longitude, **5**
west portico, Capital, **72**
west wind drift, ocean, **6**
wet boot, slalom water ski, **323**
wet compass, 747 cockpit, **151**
wet suit, skin diving, **325**
whaleboat, destroyer, **140**
whalebone carving, scrimshaw, **369**
whale's tooth, scrimshaw, **369**
wharf, castle, **78, 79**
wheat, **56**
wheel: automobile, **102, 103**; balance beam, **300**; ballista, **457**; bicycle, **124**; blimp, **158**; body building, **338**; bumper car, **90**; camera, **170**; cannon carriage, **457**; can opener, **247**; child's wagon, **283**; cigarette lighter, **224**; drag racing dragster, **333**; ferris, **91**; glass cutter, **372**; hand loom, **379**; helicopter, **146**; humidifier, **392**; locomotive, **112**; motorcycle, **125**; mower, **419**; pastry cutter, **257**; potter's, **367**; powerboat **134**; roller coaster, **90**; roller skate, **318**; roulette, **340**; sailboat, **130**; seeder, **420**; single engine airplane, **147**; skateboard, **318**; slide projector, **173**; slot machine, **340**; snowmobile, **126**; spinning, **379**; stagecoach, **127**; stroller, **282**; tank, **464, 465**; tire, **101**; tractor, **424**; truck, **116, 117, 122**; vacuum cleaner, **279**; wheelbarrow, **420**; wheelchair, **442**
wheelbarrow, **420**
wheelchair, **442**

wheelhouse: hydrofoil, **145**; tanker, **137**
wheel of fortune, **340**
wheels-flaps position indicator, pilot's instrument panel, **153**
wheel speed fairing, single engine airplane, **147**
wheel window, church, **84**
whey, and cheese, **259**
whip: flat racing, **330**; harness racing, **331**; stagecoach, **127**; windmill, **382**
whip roll, hand loom, **379**
whirlpool jet, bath, **270**
whirlybird, **146**
whisk, kitchen tool, **254**
whiskers: cat, **35**; man, **207**; ulimate beast, **46**
whistle: destroyer, **141**; locomotive, **112**; police gun belt, **483**; subway motorman's cab, **115**
white, egg, **258**
whitecap, wave, **14**
white dwarf star, **3**
whiteface, clown, **477**
white glove, butler, **473**
White House, **73**
white inner table, backgammon board, **339**
white line, horse's foot, **36**
white outer table, backgammon board, **339**
white paint, sketch box, **365**
white room, launch pad, **154**
white square, chessboard, **339**
white tie, man's, **472**
whitewall tire, automobile, **103**
white wine glass, **240**
white wire, electrical receptacle, **388**
whole note, music, **346**
whole note rest, music, **346**
whole-timbered building, **68**
whorl: human fingertip, **29**; univalve shell, **45**
wick: candle, **233**; jumbo jet, **148**; Molotov cocktail, **463**
wicket, croquet, **312**
wickiup, **82**
wide-angle lens, camera, **171**
wide swing gouge, woodcarving, **366**
wide tire, tractor, **424**
width, and perspective, **362**
widow, bowling pin, **311**
widow's peak, hair, **207**
widow's walk, house, **60**
width, type, **163**
wig, **207, 476**
wiggle nail, **400**
wigwag, symbolic language, **496**
wigwam, **82**
wild card, **342**
wimple, nun, **471**
win, flat racing, **330**
winch: oil drilling platform, **99**; sailboat, **130**; tanker, **136**; tow truck, **122**
wind: fishing rod, **334**; thunderstorm, **17**
windage adjustment knob, rifle scope, **459**

wind baffle, camp stove, **336**
windbag, bagpipe, **359**
windbreaker, automobile, **103**
wind chest, organ, **354**
wind direction sensor, weather station, **18**
wind-door, garbage truck, **123**
wind drift, ocean, **6**
winder, camera, **171**
wind indicator, destroyer, **141**
winding, fishing rod, **334**
winding road, road sign, **489**
wind instruments: brass, **352-353**; wood, **350-351**
windlass: ballista, **457**; sailboat, **130**; tanker, **136**
windmill, **382**
window, **63**; airport control tower, **93**; automobile, **102, 103**; bridge, **95**; bus, **114**; camera, **171**; camper, **126**; checkbook clutch, **219**; church, **84**; computer diskette, **429**; house, **60, 61**; igloo, **83**; light meter, **174**; lunar lander, **156**; mainsail, **132**; mat, **373**; package, **265**; parking meter, **109**; plug fuse, **389**; powerboat, **135**; slot machine, **340**; stove oven door, **244**; subway car, **115**; tank, **465**; tractor, **424**; wallet, **219**; washing machine door, **276**; windsurfer, **324**
window control, car, **106**
window coverings, **236, 237**
window flap, tent, **336**
window shade, **236, 237**
wind patterns, **6**
windscreen: passenger ship, **138**; 747 cockpit, **150**; single engine airplane, **147**
windshaft, windmill, **382**
windshield: automobile, **102, 103**; bus, **114**; jet fighter, **152**; powerboat, **135**; 747 cockpit, **150**; single engine airplane, **147**; snowmobile, **126**; space shuttle, **155**; truck, **116**
windshield defroster, **106**
windshield frame, pilot's instrument panel, **153**
windshield wiper: bus, **114**; car, **102, 106**; locomotive, **113**; subway motorman's cab, **115**
Windsor knot, necktie, **188**
wind speed sensor, weather station, **18**
windsurfer, **324**
wind system, **382**
wind turbine, **382**
wind vane, **18, 19**
wind wall, oil drilling platform, **99**
windward side, boat, **128**
wine, consecrated, **85**
wine bin, sideboard, **239**
wine cellar, passenger ship, **139**

wine drawer, sideboard, **239**
wine glass, **240**
wine steward's corkscrew, **247**
wing: baseball catcher's shinguard, **286**; bassoon, **351**; bird, **37**; bow tie, **188**; Capitol, **72**; dental braces, **443**; destroyer bridge, **141**; easel, **364**; grasshopper, **39**; house, **61**; hydrofoil, **145**; ice hockey, **291**; jet fighter, **152**; lamp, **234**; poultry, **33**; racing car, **332, 333**; safety razor, **206**; scallop, **45**; single engine airplane, **147**; space shuttle, **154**; stroller, **282**; tanker, **137**; theatre, **345**; toggle bolt, **401**; turkey, **33**; wallet, **219**
wing area, lacrosse field, **293**
wing-back cuff link, **214**
wing fixed glove, jet fighter, **152**
wing nut, **401**; hacksaw, **406**; hurdle, **298**; Ping-Pong net, **315**
wing strut, racing car, **332**
wing sweep indicator, pilot's instrument panel, **153**
wing tip: butler's shirt, **473**; man's shoe, **200**; single engine airplane, **147**
winter berm, shoreline, **14**
winter cap, Manchu court dress, **475**
winter squash, **52**
winter uniform, police, **482**
wipe, cowboy, **474**
wiper: bus windshield, **114**; car windshield, **102, 106**; locomotive windshield, **113**
wire: automobile engine, **107**; barbed, **422**; circuit breaker box, **389**; dental, **443**; earring, **214**; electrical receptacle, **388**; electrician's, **413**; field events hammer, **297**; fire engine, **120**; frame, **373**; horizontal bar, **300**; incandescent bulb, **234**; plug fuse, **389**; railroad crossing signal, **111**; size, **413**; stationary rings, **301**; toaster, **249**; traffic light, **109**; trumpet, **353**; typewriter **162**; vacuum tube, **386**
wire cutter: electrician's wire stripper, **413**; pliers, **404**
wire end, clay modeling tool, **366**
wire hood, champagne cork, **263**
wire knob, seeder, **420**
wireless aerial, tanker, **137**
wireline-logging unit, oil drilling platform, **99**
wire stripper: electrician's, **413**; pocket knife, **416**

wire support, camp
  stove, 336
wiring tube, lamp, 235
wisdom teeth, 446
wishbone, poultry, 33
wishbone boom,
  windsurfer, 324
wisp, woman's hair, 209
withers: cow, 30; dog, 34;
  sheep, 31
witness cone,
  potting, 367
witness stand,
  courtroom, 87
wizard, costume, 476
wok, 253
woman's hair, 209
woman's hat, 199
woman's jacket, 192
woman's pants, 192
woman's shoe, 201
woman's skate, 319
women's tee, golf
  course, 304
women's toilet, public
  sign, 490
wood, jai alai
  cancha, 308
wood block, 368, 451
woodburning stove, 394
wood carrier,
  fireplace, 228
woodcarving tool, 366
wood clamp, 399
woodcut printing, 368
wooded marsh,
  topographic map, 22
wooden beam, tow truck
  bed, 122
wooden mallet,
  woodcarving, 366
wooden pipe,
  levigator, 370
wooden roofing
  shingle, 66
wooden siding, house, 60
wooden spoon, 255
wood fence, 65
woofer, phonograph
  speaker, 177
wood form, etching
  press, 371
wood saw, pocket
  knife, 416
wood shaft, umbrella, 226
wood splice, house, 59
woodwind, 348, 350-351
woodworking vise, 399
woodyard, frontier
  fort, 80
woof, weaving, 379
wool collar, trench
  coat, 196
word, book page, IV

word processor,
  computer, 429
workbench, 398
work bowl, food
  processor, 250
working drawing,
  house, 60
workingman,
  circus, 88
workingman's
  suspenders, 186
working surface,
  balance beam, 300
workshelf, potter's
  wheel, 367
work spotlight, tow truck
  bed, 122
work surface, desk, 272
worktop, kitchen
  sink, 243
worm: cannon, 457;
  corkscrew, 247
worm gear, venetian
  blind, 237
woven backing,
  carpet, 242
woven basket,
  guillotine, 452
woven side, basket, 262
woven wire fabric,
  steel chain
  fence, 65
wrap: boxing, 303;
  packaging, 265
wrap belt,
  cardigan, 195
wrapper: cigar, 224;
  paperback book,
  165; Torah, 86
wrapping, dabber, 371
wreath: medal, 485;
  tombstone, 500
wreck, nautical
  chart, 22
wrecker, 122
wrench, 405
wringer, 276
wrist: cat, 35; human,
  24, 29; steam engine
  crank, 395
wrist pad, football
  uniform, 288
wrist sling, ice
  hammer, 328
wrist strap, ski
  pole, 320
wristwatch, 216
wrist weight, body
  building, 338
write-in, voting, 427
write-protect notch,
  computer
  diskette, 429
writer's initials,
  letter, 161

writing area,
  desk, 272
writing arm, rocking
  chair, 230
writing slide, desk, 272
writing tip, pen, 160
wrought iron fence, 65

X
X: braille, 496; sign
  language, 496
x-height, type, 163
x-indication,
  voting booth, 427
x-ray cassette,
  operating room
  table, 440
x-ray dental unit, 444
xylem, tree, 48
xylography, 368

Y
Y: braille, 496; sign
  language, 496
yacht, 129
yad, Torah, 470
y adjusting lever,
  plane, 410
yankee, sailboat, 130
yard: barn, 100;
  frontier fort, 80;
  house, 60; prison, 74
yardarm, destroyer, 141
yard goods,
  fabric, 380
yard line, football
  field, 289
yardmaster, railroad
  yard, 94
yarmulke, Jewish
  prayer vestment, 470
yarn: knitting, 378;
  rope, 128; weaving, 379
yarn loop, 242
year of birth: flat
  racing entry, 330;
  tombstone, 500
year of death,
  tombstone, 500
year of puchase,
  postal money order, 223
yellow traffic light, 109
yen, symbol, 495
Yeoman warder, 467
yield, road sign, 488
Yin-Yang, symbol, 492
yod, tefillin, 470
yoke: blouse, 193; dental
  x-ray unit, 444;
  dress, 194; 747
  cockpit, 150;
  shirt, 185; tennis
  racket, 306; tuning
  fork, 361; window, 63
yoke cable, bicycle

caliper brake, 124
yoke shirt, cowboy, 474
yolk, egg, 258
yurt, 68

Z
Z: braille, 496; sign
  language, 496
zebra coat, ultimate
  beast, 47
zecher lechurban,
  Jewish prayer
  vestment, 470
Zeppelin, 158
zero adjust knob, volt-ohm
  meter, 413
zero mark,
  wristwatch, 216
zester, kitchen
  tool, 257
ziggurat, pyramid, 68
zigzag rule, 414
zinc carbon cell, 387
zip code: envelope, 161;
  magazine
  mailing label, 167;
  postal money order, 223
zip-out robe lining,
  overcoat, 196
zipper, 205;
  backpack, 337;
  mainsail, 132;
  package, 264;
  parka, 197;
  skirt, 193; sleeping
  bag, 337; trousers, 187;
  woman's pants, 192
zippered door, tent, 336
zipper foot, sewing
  machine, 274
zipper foot, sewing
  machine, 274
zipper line, sewing
  pattern, 380
zizith, Jewish prayer
  shawl, 470
zonal pattern, wind, 6
zone: envelope, 161;
  football field, 289;
  glacier, 12;
  handball court, 307;
  ice hockey
  rink, 291;
  shuffleboard
  court, 312; time, 5
zoom control, video
  camera, 180
zooming ring, movie
  projector, 173
zoom lens, 171, 172, 180
zoom ring: movie
  camera, 172; video
  camera, 180

Credits

pages 2-3, illustration by Neal Adams; **5**, Time Zone map courtesy of Hammond Incorporated, Maplewood, NJ; **8-9**, illustration by Dee Molenaar; **18**, photo courtesy of Science Associates Inc.; **21**, thematic map of "Number of Irish Foreign Born 1930" courtesy of Carnegie Institution of Washington; **22**, photography by Color Lab, Hawthorne, NY; **58-59**, illustrations courtesy of American Plywood Association; **60**, illustration by Charles Addams, blueprint by Carl Hribar; **72-73**, photos by David Burnett, courtesy of Contact Press Images, Inc.; **74**, photo courtesy of State of N.Y. Department of Correctional Services; **75**, top photo courtesy of The Port Authority of New York & New Jersey, lower photo courtesy of Empire State Building; **76**, elevator shaft illustration courtesy of Westinghouse Elevator, elevator car illustration courtesy of Williamsburg Steel Products, Co.; **78**, photograph courtesy of British Information Service; **84-85**, illustrations courtesy of Cathedral Church of St. John the Divine, New York, NY; **86**, courtesy of Temple Emanuel, New York, NY; **88-89**, courtesy of Ringling Brothers and Barnum & Bailey; **90-91**, roller coaster courtesy of Magic Mountain Amusement Park, ferris wheel and merry-go-round courtesy of Rye Playland; **92-93**, airport photo courtesy of American Airlines; **94**, photo courtesy of Association of American Railroads; **95**, photos courtesy of Triborough Bridge and Tunnel Authority; **99**, photograph by Carroll S. Grevemberg, Grevy Photography, New Orleans, LA; **102-103**, AnyCar photos courtesy of Manufacturers Hanover Trust, New York, NY; **104-105**, photo courtesy of Buick Division, General Motors Corp.; **106**, photo courtesy of Alfa Romeo; **107**, photo courtesy of Bradford La Riviera Inc.; **110**, courtesy of Triborough Bridge & Tunnel Authority; **112-113**, steam locomotive photo courtesy of Association of American Railroads, turbine engine photo courtesy of National Railroad Passenger Corporation, panels courtesy of The Train Shop, Ltd.; **114**, coach courtesy of American Eagle, commuter bus interior courtesy of NY Metropolitan Transit Authority; **115**, courtesy of NY Metropolitan Transit Authority Museum; **116-117**, photos courtesy of Mack Trucks Corporation; **120-121**, photos courtesy of New York City Fire Department; **122**, tow truck courtesy of LST Towing, New York, NY; **123**, courtesy of NYC Department of Sanitation; **125**, photo courtesy of Kawasaki Motorcycles; **126**, camper photo courtesy of Winnebago Industries, Inc., snowmobile photo courtesy of Yamaha Motor Corporation; **127**, stagecoach courtesy of Wells Fargo Bank History Department, hansom cab courtesy of The New York Historic Society; **129**, photo courtesy of Dyer Jones, Warren, RI; **130-131**, illustrations courtesy of CSY Yacht Corporation, Tampa, FL; **132**, compass photo courtesy of Aqua Meter Instrument Corporation, Roseland, NJ; **133**, sextant photo courtesy of Weems & Plath, Annapolis, MD, outboard photo courtesy of Mariner Outboards, Fond du Lac, WI; **134-135**, illustration courtesy of Bertram Yachts, Miami, FL; **138-139**, illustration courtesy of Cunard Line Limited, New York, NY; **140-141**, courtesy of the officers and men of *USS Thomas C. Hart* (DE 1092); **142-143**, photos courtesy of US Navy Department; **144**, tugboat courtesy of Moran, fireboat courtesy of NYC Fire Department; **145**, hovercraft photo courtesy of British Hovercraft Corp. Ltd.; **146**, photo courtesy of Sikorsky; **147**, airplane photo courtesy of Piper Aircraft Corp.; **148-149**, illustration courtesy of Boeing; **150-151**, photo courtesy of Boeing; **152-153**, photo and illustrations courtesy of Grumman; **154-155**, photograph and illustration courtesy of NASA; **156-157**, illustrations courtesy of NASA; **158**, photo courtesy of Goodyear; **161**, caligraphy by Melissa, text by Sean Kelly; **162**, manual typewriter photo courtesy of Royal Business Machines, Inc.; **164**, illustrations courtesy of International Paper Company; **167**, *TIME* cover reprinted by permission from *TIME*, The Weekly Newsmagazine, copyright Time Inc., 1980, contents page reprinted courtesy of *SPORTS ILLUSTRATED*, from the March 3, 1980 issue. Copyright (c) 1980, Time, Inc.; **166**, courtesy of *The New York Times*, New York, NY; **168-169**, prepared by *New York Magazine*, New York, NY; **170**, top photo courtesy of Poloroid Corp., panel photo courtesy of Vivitar; **171**, camera photo courtesy of Minolta Camera Co., Ltd.; **172**, photo courtesy of Minolta Camera Co., Ltd.; **173**, movie photo projector courtesy of Minolta, slide projector photo courtesy of Kodak, screen courtesy of Da-Lite Screen Company; **174**, light meter courtesy of Gossen-Luna Pro, electronic flash courtesy of Vivitar Corp., tripod courtesy of E. Leitz Inc.; **175**, reel-to-reel recorder photo courtesy of Pioneer Electronics, cassette tape photo courtesy of Sony; **176-177**, photographs courtesy of Pioneer Electronics Corp., NJ, and Executive Recording Limited, N.Y.; **179**, photo courtesy of Radio Shack; **180**, video recorder courtesy of U.S. JVC Corp.; **181**, television photo courtesy of Sony, LasarDisc courtesy of Pioneer; **182**, illustration courtesy of NASA; **191**, panty hose photo courtesy of Hanes Corp.; **192-193**, illustrations by Calvin Klein; **197**, fur photo courtesy of Rosette, NY; **201**, courtesy of Andy Warhol; **203**, sock photo courtesy of Alexander Lee Wallan Inc.; **205**, photo courtesy of Velcro USA; **206**, electric razor photo courtesy of Sunbeam Corp.; **208**, hair dryer photo courtesy of Conair; **210**, curling iron photo courtesy of Conair; **212-213**, products courtesy of Avon Products, Inc., make-up by Tom Gearhard; **214-215**, ring and pendant illustrations courtesy of Jane Evans; **216**, wristwatch courtesy of Chronosport Inc., Rowayton, CT; **222**, check courtesy of Rudco Corp., credit card courtesy of Visa; **223**, traveler's check courtesy of Barclay's Bank, New York, NY, money order courtesy of U.S. Postal Service; **233**, candle snuffer courtesy of Fortunoff Department Store, New York, NY; **240**, place setting courtesy of Rosenthal China Co.; **241**, desert setting courtesy of Rosenthal China, panels courtesy of Gorham Division of Textron Inc.; **243**, sink courtesy of Elkay Manufacturing Company, disposal unit courtesy of Hobart Corporation; **247**, electric opener courtesy of Oster Corp., can piercer courtesy of Ekco Industries; **251**, vegetable juicer courtesy of Hamilton Beach, automatic juicer courtesy of Oster Corp., manual juicer courtesy of Acme Juicer Manufacture Corp.; **253**, pressure cooker courtesy of National Presto Industries, electric wok courtesy of Faberware; **254-257**, courtesy of H&P Mayer Corp.; **263**, pump dispenser courtesy of Calmar Division/Diamond International; **264-265**, illustration by The Schecter Group; **274**, courtesy of Viking Sewing Machine Co.; **275**, courtesy Proctor-Silex; **277**, dryer courtesy of General Electric; **279**, vacuum cleaner courtesy of Hoover Co.; **280**, fire extinguisher courtesy of Amerex Corp., smoke alarm courtesy of General Electric; **282**, stroller courtesy of Perego/Pines, Milan, Italy, playpen

and car seat courtesy of Century Products, Los Angeles, CA; **283**, wagon illustration courtesy of Flexible Flyer; **284**, barbecue courtesy of King Seeley Company; **287**, glove courtesy of Rawlings Sporting Goods, models: Rod Carew, California Angels (batter), Ossie Virgil Jr., Philadelphia Phillies (catcher); **288**, helmet courtesy of Bike Athletic Company, model: Bruce Harper, New York Jets; **290-291**, models: Ken Morrow (defenseman) and Billy Smith (goalie), New York Islanders; **292**, model: Mike Glenn, New York Knickerbockers; **296**, running show courtesy of Adidas; **300**, photos courtesy of Nissen/Walter Kidde & Company; **301**, photos courtesy of Nissen/Walter Kidde & Company; **303**, model: Wendal Newton; **304-305**, equipment photos courtesy of Northwestern Golf Company; **308**, courtesy of Bridgeport, Conn. Jai Alai, model: Donald Mazza; **309**, piste courtesy of George Santelli Fencing School, NYC; **314**, photo courtesy of Brunswick Corp.; **318**, photo courtesy of Chicago Roller Skates Inc.; **316**, courtesy of Darts Unlimited, New York, NY; **320**, equipment courtesy of Scandinavian Ski Shop; **321**, cross-country equipment courtesy of Scandinavian Ski Shop, snowshoe courtesy of The Snowcraft Corp.; **323**, ski courtesy of Connelly Skis, Inc.; **325**, equipment courtesy of Atlantic Divers World, NY; **326**, photo courtesy of The Balloon Works, Statesville, NC; **327**, parachute courtesy of Para-Flite Inc., US Parachuting Assoc., hang glider courtesy of United States Hang Gliding Assoc.; **328**, photos courtesy of George Willig, Topanga, CA; **329**, Western saddle courtesy of H. Kauffman and Sons, Inc., English saddle by Crosby, courtesy of Millers, NY; **330**, program entry courtesy of Pimlico Race Track; **331**, Meadowlands Racetrack, East Rutherford, NJ, model: Courtney Foos; **332**, illustration by Jack Lane, courtesy of L'Art et L'Automobile Gallery, 354 E. 66 Street, New York, NY, Jacques Vaucher; **333**, photos courtesy of National Hot Rod Association; **334-335**, fishing reel photo courtesy of Penn Reels, rod photo courtesy of Shakespeare Fishing Rods; **336**, photos courtesy of Coleman Co.; **337**, backpack photo courtesy of Johnson/Camp Trails; **338**, universal gym photo courtesy of Nissen; **340-341**, courtesy of Mr. Lucky Equipment, Rosedale, NY; **343**, ticket courtesy of Globe Ticket Company **345**, photo of the Bardavon Theatre courtesy of Robert Paul Molay; **346**, *Theme From What's What Book* written by John Hill, John Hill Music Inc.; **348**, illustration and photo courtesy of Chicago Symphony Orchestra; **354**, photo courtesy of Rodgers Organ, New York, NY; **359**, bagpipes courtesy of Larry Cole; **360**, accordion courtesy Stuyvesant Music; **363**, painting courtesy of the Metropolitan Museum of Art, New York, NY; **364-365**, painting equipment courtesy of Grumbacher; **366**, Sculpture House, New York, NY; **368**, equipment courtesy of Rembrant Graphic Arts, NJ; **370**, courtesy of Rembrant Graphic Arts, NJ and Charles Brand Machinery Inc., NY; **371**, Rembrant Graphic Arts, NJ and Charles Brand Machinery, Inc., NY; **372**, equipment courtesy of Glassmaster Guild; **374-375**, cartoon by Mike Witte, comic strip by Mort Walker, copyright 1978 King Features Syndicate, Inc.; **377**, quilt courtesy of Fairfield Processing; **378**, shuttle courtesy of C.J. Bates & Son, Inc.; **379**, loom courtesy of LaClerc Weaving Looms; **382**, wind turbine photo courtesy of Grumman Corp.; **386**, transistor photo courtesy Bell Laboratories; **392**, courtesy of Hampton Sales; **396**, courtesy of Teledyne Wisconsin Motor; **399**, photos courtesy of Adjustable Clamp Company; **407**, table saw photo courtesy of ToolKraft, circular saw photo courtesy of Skil, saber saw photo courtesy of Rockwell International; **411**, sander photo courtesy of Rockwell International; **413**, voltmeter courtesy of Amprobe Instruments; **414**, folding rule courtesy of Stanley Tools, carpenter's level courtesy of Toolkraft; **415**, spray painter courtesy of Spray Tech Corp.; **416**, photo courtesy of Hoffritz; **417**, courtesy of Douglas Products; **418**, photos courtesy of L.R. Nelson Corp.; **419**, photo courtesy of Sears, Roebuck & Company; **420**, wheelbarrow courtesy of Jackson Manufacturing Company, seeder courtesy of Cyclone Seeder Company, Inc.; **421**, chainsaw photo courtesy of Skil Corporation; **424**, tractor photo courtesy of J.I. Case; **426**, theodolite courtesy of Dietzgen Corp., jackhammer courtesy of Bosch Power Tools; **427**, photos courtesy of R.F. Shoup Corp., Bryn Mawr, PA; **428**, courtesy of International Business Machine; **429**, computer photo courtesy of Radio Shack; **430**, courtesy of NCR Corporation; **432**, photo courtesy of Carl Zeiss Inc.; **433**, telescope photo courtesy of Unitron Instruments Inc., binoculars photo courtesy of Minolta Camera Co., Ltd.; **434**, photos courtesy of Furuno U.S.A., Inc.; **435**, metal detector photo courtesy of White Electronics Inc., geiger counter photo courtesy of EDA Instruments; **436-437**, burner courtesy of Fisher Scientific Company, scale courtesy of Ohaus Scale Corporation; **438**, photos courtesy of Welch Allyn, Skaneateles Falls, NY; **439**, photos courtesy of Sybron Corp.; **440**, courtesy of Affiliated Hospital Products; **442**, wheelchair photo courtesy of Invacare Corporation, hearing aid photo courtesy of Dahlberg Electronics, pacemaker photo courtesy of Medtronic, Inc.; **443**, denture photo courtesy of Sterndent Corporation, braces bracket photo courtesy of 'A' Company, Inc.; **444**, courtesy of Ritter Dental Corp.; **445**, courtesy of Dr. Herbert Spasser; **447**, photographs courtesy of Mosler Safe Company; **448**, Safe Hardware Corporation, Emhart Industries Inc.; **449**, lock photo courtesy of Medico Security Locks Inc.; **450**, hasp photo courtesy of Lawrence Brothers, Inc.; **451**, chains courtesy of Diamond Chain Co., block and pulley courtesy of The Crosby Group; **467**, illustration courtesy of James Burrough Limited, New York, NY; **468**, costumes courtesy of Eaves-Brooks Costume Company; **470**, photograph courtesy of Irving Fisher; **471**, minister photo courtesy of The Very Reverend Francis B. Sayre; **472**, photo courtesy of After Six Formal Wear; **473**, costumes courtesy of Eaves-Brooks Costume Company; **474**, costume courtesy of Eaves-Brookes Costume Company, Indian courtesy of the Museum of the American Indian, Bronx, NY; **475**, Manchu Court Dress courtesy of Reginald Bragonier, Arab courtesy of Bill Ashe, model: Jan Leighton; **476**, model: Jan Leighton, pirate photograph by BODI, mizer photograph by Michael Weiss; **477**, illustration by Ted Geisel; **478**, photo courtesy of Lois Greenfield/Capezio Ballet Makers; **480-481**, photographs courtesy of Phil Koenig, soldiers courtesy of US Army, sailor courtesy of US Navy; **487**, courtesy of Government of Canada; **484**, photo courtesy of New York Fire Department; **490-491**, symbols courtesy of Handbook of Pictorial Symbols, Rudolph Modley, Dover Publications, Inc., New York, NY; **498**, courtesy of Mary Grace and Maria Maggi; **500**, casket courtesy of Simmons Casket Company/Gulf and Western Casket Co.

Acknowledgements

Harold Adler, Adler Monument and Granite Works; Roslyn Alexander, librarian Charles Evans Hughes High School; `
Jack Arnoff; Dave Lipsky, Juana Torres and Frank Coppinger, Army Corps of Engineers; Martin Bacheller, Hammond,
Inc.; Sandy Bartram; Susan Bates Inc.; Roberta Baker, LIFE Magazine; Barney's Clothing Store; David Baxley,
Triborough Bridge & Tunnel Authority; Mitch Becker, Globe Ticket Corp.; Paul Berkovitz, Algoma Net Company;
Randy Black, Bike Athletic Corp.; Mitchell and George Tepper, Bond Street Suspender Inc.; Bonny Products;
Carol Boswell and Gina Frantz, Boswell-Frantz Public Relations; Jerry Boxer, Abraham Boxer and Sons; Lee Bracy,
Westinghouse Elevator Inc.; Benjamin Bragonier; Dana Bragonier; queen model Penelope Bragonier; Bill and Betty
Brennan; Andreas Brown, Gotham Book Store; Cadillac Meat Company; Camrod Motorcycles; Carez Health Care
Corp.; Zack Carr, Calvin Klein Ltd.; cross-country skiing model Catherine Carlen; Robert E. Lewis and
William S. DeArment, Channellock Corp.; Betty Charak, Personality Hanger Inc.; Jerry Charles, Hollco Tools;
Coats and Clark, Inc.; accordion supplied by Larry Cole; Phil Colicchio, Oreo Cookies; Dita Comacho;
Nancy Conforti, H & P-Mayer Inc.; H.C. Cook, Inc., Division of Gem Products; Ron Coplon, Rubin Gloves Inc.;
Richard Curtis, Richard Curtis Associates; Elmer Danch and Elaine Harr, DaLite Movie Screen Company; Frank Davis;
John and Jessica Dorfman; Rose Dreger; Alfred Dunhill Inc.; Ernest DuPuy, Hammond Inc.; Ken Durst, Rawlings Inc.;
John Edelmann; EKCO Housewares Corp.; Lt. Juan Torres and Ray Florida, NYC Emergency Medical Service;
Lee Entwhistle, Eves-Brooks Costumes Inc.; Herbert Eskelson, Para-Flite Inc.; Eye Center Inc.; Penny Farber,
Foxmore Inc.; staff of Fashion Institute of Technology library; Arthur Ferguson, Metropolian Transit Authority;
Steve Fineberg, Feinberg Associates; Ira Finke, Ira Finke Photography; Nini Finkelstein, Ringling Brothers &
Barnum and Bailey Circus; Irving and Sylvia Fisher; butler model Jim Fitzgerald; Anthony Forgione,
Consolidated Wafer and Cone Corp.; Joann Forster, International School of Harness Racing at Roosevelt Raceway;
William Free Advertising Agency; Bill Freeman, The Gill Track and Field Equipment Company; Steve Friedman;
Lois Fry, Shakespeare Fishing Equipment; Fuller Brush Corp.; Louise Gaither, Executive Services Advertising;
Gary Galante, Museum of American Indian; cosmetic model make-up by Tom Gerhart; Irv Goldfinger, Forsyth
Monument Works; Matthew Goldman, M & F Hanger; Brian Goodman; Mary Grace: Kathy Graham,
Bridgeport, Conn, Jai Alai; J.F. Grgula, Structo Division, King-Seeley Thermos Comp.; John Growth, School of Visual
Arts; Mike Gue, Ethics Automobile Racing; Walter Guslawski, Williamsberg Steel Products; Stephen A. Hallis, Jr.,
Digital Equipment Corp.; Dana Hammond, Hammond Inc.; Dean Hammond, Hammond Inc.; Stuart Hammond,
President, Hammond Inc.; management and staff of Hampton Sales; Harvey Sound Corp.; Irving Heiberger,
Marshall Clark Inc.; Joyce Heiberger, JBH Advertising; Kenneth Heinz, Welch-Allyn Corporation; Paul Heller,
International Creative Management; Katharine Hill; Hoffritz Inc.; Edward Irrizarry; PO Ken Kaufman, NYPD
co-author of *The Incredible Scooter Cops*; Scrooge's letter by Sean Kelly, former editor of THE NATIONAL
LAMPOON; Chris Kelly; cowboy model by William Ketchum Jr., author of *Western Memorabilia*; George Klauber,
George Klauber Graphic Arts Studio; Morris and Ruth Kleinman; Drew Kuber, Hammond Inc.; Richard and Elyse
Langsam; Larry Letizia, Joyson Motors; Leaf Tent and Sail Inc.; Charles Leib; Leland-Penn; Patricia Lewis; Robert
Lewis, Chrysler Corporation; Teresa Longhitano; Mel and Cheryl London, authors of *Bread Winners*; Lionel V. Lorona,
New York Public Library; Candace Lovell; Donald A. Macaulay; Joseph W. Maresca, Jr., SRI Institute; Daniel
Mazzarella, Science Associates Inc.; Ken McAdams; Kay McDowell, US Postal Data Center; Frank 'Tug' McGraw,
Philadelphia Phillies; Dave McNamara, Wilson Sporting Goods, Inc.; The Meadowlands Racetrack management; John
Meyers, Fisher Scientific Company; Ray Miller, VISA; Mr. Lucky School of Gambling; Macmillan Publishing Corp.;
Captain Don Mitchell, Eastern Airlines; Jenny Moradfar; Ruth Grevey and Larry Osterman, Mosler Safe Corp.; Edward
J. Murphy, Edward J. Murphy Corp.; Neckwear Association of America; Steve Nesbitt, Mark Hess, Tom Jacqua,
NASA; New York Jets; New York Knickerbockers; New York Yankess; Don Morris and Suzanne Eagle, NEW YORK
Magazine; PO George Legas and Steve Berenhaus, NYPD; John Nicholson; C. Michael Oldenberg, Centennial
Management Corp.; Joan Rubin and Christine Martorana, Omega Fashions Ltd.; John Pace, National Cash Register;
Rolando Pena; Arthur and Lois Perschetz; LTC Gerald Perschetz U.S. Army (Ret.); Clarence Peskac, Dietzgen Corp.;
Allen Petersen, Petersen Manufacturing Co., Inc.; Robert Pledge, Contact Press Images; Brigit Polk, The Factory;
Marian Powers, TIME Magazine; Donald Quest, Southwest Texas Drilling Co.; Jim Ramsey, Rodgers Organ Corp.;
Mark Resnick, Hammond Inc.; Rock of Ages Corp.; Rosemary Rodgers, John Hill Music, Inc.; Linda Rosenblatt,
R.D.H.; Joan Evanish, Judith Johnson and Canon West, St. John the Divine; Teddi Sann, Avon Products, Inc.; Gene
Sayet, Executive Recording Ltd.; Frank and Harriet Sayre; Rosette Schecter, Furs by Rosette; Deputy Police
Commissioner 'Mickey' Schwartz, NYPD; Ann Scott, SPORTS ILLUSTRATED; Elizabeth Scott, Chicago Symphony
Orchestra; Ray Scroggins, Wisconsin-Teledyne; Dr. John H. Seward, MD EENT; Joel Shaffer, Hammond Inc.; J. Ronald
Shumate, Association of American Railroads; Craig Siebert; Harold Silver, Caldwell Button Corp.; Robert Simon,
Wallin, Simon and Black; Robert Smith; NY-NJ Port Authority; Dr. Herbert Spasser, D.D.S.; cosmetics model Tina
Stahle; Stappers Equipment Corp.; Stuyvesant Music; Tom Szobe, Paragon Sporting Goods; Bob Taylor, Hedstrom
Baby Furniture; Technigraph Studio; Marilyn Tempkins, Vivitar Inc.; caligraphy lettered on Scrooge's letter by
Melissa Topping; Tower Manufacturing; Paul Schulhaus, Russ Levin, Train Shop Ltd.; Bobbie Tupper, Park West
Chapel; Helen Turi, General Motors Corp.; Helen Tutt, American Eagle; Universal Fastenings Inc.; Anna Urband, US
Navy Public Relations; officers and men of the *USS Thomas C. Hart* (DE 1092); Jaques Vaucher, L'Art et L'Automobile
Gallery; Ossie Virgil Jr., Philadelphia Phillies; Dan Walden, Consolidated Edison Corp.; John Wanamaker; Sam
Weinstein, Color Group; Western Union Corp.; George Willig; king model Robert Wills; PO 'Scooter' Joe Willins,
NYPD, co-author of *The Incredible Scooter Cops*; John Wisdom; Laurie Wolford; Janet Wygall; Will Yolin, author of
The Complete Book of Kites and Kite Flying; Richard Ziskin, American Umbrella Co.; Roger Zissu, Cowan, Liebowitz
& Latman; Nell Znamierowski, Fashion Institute of Technology; and special thanks to the Hammond staff, both in
Maplewood, NJ, and New York City, for their numerous contributions and assistance in producing this book.

Afterword

Creating and executing an imaginative new concept is a
rewarding task. In that respect, WHAT'S WHAT has
been no exception. We have been inordinately lucky in
having been able to attract like-minded people with
vision and imagination who have helped make this book
what it is. They, like us, have made every effort to make
the information and its presentation as useful and
accurate as possible. But, as with any major new
undertaking, errors are bound to creep in. If you found
the book engaging and informative, if it has given
you some of the pleasure it has given us, we ask that
you help make future editions of WHAT'S WHAT even
more complete and accurate by sharing your special
knowledge and observations with us in writing.

David Fisher
Reginald Bragonier Jr.
Post Office Box 1
Chappaqua, NY 10514

The reader is advised that the objects pictured in this book (some of which show brand-name labels) are representative only of similar objects of that class. Moreover, these representations in no way constitute endorsements of those products, nor does the accompanying text necessarily follow the manufacturer's instructions as to their use.